ST/CTC/76
Vol. II

United Nations Centre on Transnational Corporations

Centre des Nations Unies sur les sociétés transnationales

Transnational Corporations

A Selective Bibliography, 1983-1987

Volume II

Subject index

Les sociétés transnationales

Bibliographie sélective, 1983-1987

Volume II

Index des matières

United Nations

Nations Unies

New York, 1988

This work is dedicated to Edith Ward   Cette oeuvre est dédiée á Edith Ward

NOTE

The designations employed and the presentation of the material in this publication do not imply the expression of any opinion whatsoever on the part of the Secretariat of the United Nations concerning the legal status of any country or territory or of its authorities, or concerning the delimitation of its frontiers.

Les appellations employées dans la présente publication et la présentation des données qui y figurent n'impliquent de la part du Secrétariat de l'Organisation des Nations Unies aucune prise de position quant au statut juridique des pays, territoires, villes ou zones, ou de leurs autorités, ni quant au tracé de leurs frontières ou limites.

ST/CTC/76(Vol.II)

UNIV. OF MD COLLEGE PARK

3 1430 03250834 5

UNITED NATIONS PUBLICATION

Sales No. E.88.II.A.10

04900

ISBN 92-1-004031-7

TABLE OF CONTENTS / TABLE DES MATIERES

VOLUME ONE / VOLUME UN

INTRODUCTORY NOTE / NOTE D'INTRODUCTION . . . .

MAIN LIST BY CATEGORY / LISTE PRINCIPALE PAR CATEGORIE . . . . . .

0100   GENERAL STUDIES, CONCEPTUAL QUESTIONS / ETUDES GENERALES,
        QUESTIONS THEORIQUES . . . .

0200   FOREIGN DIRECT INVESTMENT AND OTHER EXTERNAL FINANCIAL FLOWS /
        INVESTISSEMENT DIRECT A L'ETRANGER ET AUTRES FLUX FINANCIERS
        EXTERIEURS . . . .

0210   Inward and outward investment / Investissement interne et
        investissement à l'extérieur . . . .

0220   International bank loans, other flows, debt / Prêts des
        banques internationales, autres flux, dette . . . .

0300   ENTERPRISES / ENTREPRISES . . . .

0310   Profiles / Profils . . . .
0320   Enterprises from specific home countries and regions /
        Entreprises de certains pays et régions d'origine . . . . .
0330   Management and organization / Gestion et organisation . . . .
0340   Corporate strategies / Stratégies des sociétés . . . .
0350   Factors affecting foreign direct investment and
        industrial location decisions / Facteurs qui
        influencent l'investissement direct à l'étranger et les
        décisions d'implantation industrielle . . . .

0400   TRANSNATIONAL CORPORATIONS IN SPECIFIC ECONOMIC SECTORS /
        ROLE DES SOCIETES TRANSNATIONALES DANS CERTAINS SECTEURS
        ECONOMIQUES . . . .

0410   Agriculture, forestry, fishing / Agriculture,
        sylviculture, pêche . . . .
0420   Mining and petroleum / Industries extractives et
        production de pétrole . . . .
0430   Manufacturing industries / Industries manufacturières . . . .
0440   Electricity, gas, water / Electricité, gaz, eau . . . .
0450   Construction / Bâtiment et travaux publics . . . .
0460   Wholesale and retail trade / Commerce de gros et de
        détail . . . .
0470   Transport, communications / Transports, communications . . . .
0480   Business services / Services fournis aux entreprises . . . . .
0490   Community, social and personal services / Services
        fournis à la collectivité, services sociaux et
        services personnels . . . .

0500   TRANSNATIONAL CORPORATIONS IN SPECIFIC COUNTRIES AND REGIONS /
          ROLE DES SOCIETES TRANSNATIONALES DANS CERTAINS PAYS ET
          REGIONS . . . .

    0510   Developing Countries / Pays en développement . . . .
    0511   Africa / Afrique . . . .
    0512   Asia and the Pacific / Asie et Pacifique . . . .
    0513   Latin America and the Caribbean / Amérique latine et
            Caraïbes . . . .
    0514   Western Asia / Asie occidentale . . . .
    0520   Developed market economies / Pays développés à économie de
            marché . . . .
    0530   Centrally planned economies of Eastern Europe / Pays à
            économie planifiée d'Europe orientale . . . .
    0540   Southern Africa / Afrique australe . . . .

0600   ECONOMIC ISSUES / QUESTIONS ECONOMIQUES . . . .

    0610   International economic system / Système économique
            international . . . .
    0620   Industrial and economic development / Développement
            industriel et économique . . . .
    0630   Trade and balance of trade / Commerce et balance
            commerciale . . . .
    0640   Transfer of technology and know-how, Research and
            Development / Transfert de technologie et de
            savoir-faire, recherche-développement . . . .
    0650   Ownership and control / Participation et contrôle . . . .
    0660   Market structure and restrictive business practices /
            Structure du marché et pratiques commerciales
            restrictives . . . .
    0670   Transfer pricing and taxation / Prix de cession interne et
            régime fiscal . . . .

0700   POLITICAL, SOCIAL AND ENVIRONMENTAL ISSUES / QUESTIONS
          POLITIQUES, SOCIALES ET ENVIRONNEMENTALES . . . .

    0710   Investment climate / Climat pour les investissements . . . . .
    0720   Social issues / Questions sociales . . . .
    0730   Employment / Emploi . . . .
    0740   Environmental issues / Questions relatives à
            l'environnement . . . .

0800   INTERNATIONAL LEGAL AND POLICY FRAMEWORK / CADRE JURIDIQUE
          ET DIRECTEUR INTERNATIONAL . . . .

    0810   Multilateral arrangements and agreements, codes of
            conduct / Mécanismes et accords multilatéraux, codes de
            conduite . . . .
    0820   Bilateral arrangements: promotion and protection of
            foreign direct investment, tax and trade agreements /
            Mécanismes bilatéraux : promotion et protection de
            l'investissement direct à l'étranger, accords fiscaux
            et commerciaux . . . .

0830   Standards of accounting and reporting / Normes de
        comptabilité et d'établissement des rapports . . . .

0840   Other international arrangements / Autres mécanismes
        internationaux . . . .

0900   NATIONAL LEGAL AND POLICY FRAMEWORK / CADRE JURIDIQUE ET
        DIRECTEUR NATIONAL . . . .

0910   Texts, analyses of national legislation / Textes et
        analyses concernant la législation nationale . . . .

0920   Incentives, performance requirements / Incitations,
        résultats exigés . . . .

0930   Nationalization and compensation / Nationalisation et
        indemnisation . . . .

0940   Extraterritorial application of laws and regulations,
        anti-trust / Application extraterritoriale des lois et
        des règlements, législation antitrust . . . .

0950   Institutional mechanisms / Mécanismes institutionnels . . . . .

0960   Export processing zones / Zones franches industrielles . . . .

1000   CONTRACTS AND AGREEMENTS BETWEEN TRANSNATIONAL CORPORATIONS
        AND HOST COUNTRY ORGANIZATIONS / CONTRATS ET ACCORDS ENTRE
        LES SOCIETES TRANSNATIONALES ET LES ORGANISMES DU PAYS HOTE . .

1010   Texts, analyses of contractual arrangements / Textes et
        analyses concernant les mécanismes contractuels . . . . . .

1020   Negotiating capabilities and bargaining power / Capacités
        et pouvoir de négociation . . . .

1030   Dispute settlement / Règlements des différends . . . .

1100   TRANSNATIONAL CORPORATIONS AND OTHER ACTORS / SOCIETES
        INTERNATIONALES ET AUTRES AGENTS . . . .

1110   International, regional and religious organizations /
        Organisations internationales, régionales et
        religieuses . . . .

1120   Trade unions / Syndicats . . . .

1200   TECHNICAL ASSISTANCE / ASSISTANCE TECHNIQUE . . . .

1210   Advisory services, aid programmes / Services consultatifs,
        programmes d'assistance . . . .

1300   REFERENCE SOURCES / REFERENCES . . . .

1310   Directories and lists of companies / Répertoires et listes
        de sociétés . . . .

1320   Bibliographies / Bibliographies . . . .

1330   Other reference sources / Autres références . . . .

AUTHOR INDEX / INDEX DES AUTEURS . . . .

TITLE INDEX / INDEX DES TITRES . . . .

SUBJECT INDEX

INDEX DES MATIERES

Subject Index - Index des matières

ABSTRACTS.
----Vneshneekonomicheskaia ekspansiia
imperialisticheskikh stran. - 1984.
(002680)

ACCOUNTING.
----Accounting analysis of the efficiency of
public enterprises. - 1984.
(002114)
----Advanced accounting. - 1988.
(002089)
----Consolidation policies in OECD
countries. - 1987.
(002101)
----Coping with worldwide accounting
changes. - 1984.
(002067)
----Glossary of terms for state auditors. -
1983.
(002711)
----International accounting. - 1983.
(002106)
----International accounting. - 1985.
(002062)
----International accounting. - 1984.
(002085)
----The international accounting and tax
researches' publication guide. - 1982.
(002066)
----International accounting standards. -
1986.
(002087)
----Management accounting terminology. -
1983.
(002092) (002717)
----Managerial accounting. - 1984.
(002093)
----Municipal accounting for developing
countries. - 1984.
(002090)
----The relationship between taxation and
financial reporting. - 1987.
(002103)
----Statements of international accounting
standards. - 1985-   .
(002112)
----Who audits the world. - 1983.
(002061)
----Working documents. - 1986-   .
(002123)

ACCOUNTING--ASIA AND THE PACIFIC.
----Proceedings : Asia and Pacific
Conference on Accounting Education for
Development, Manila, Philippines,
November 12-16, 1984. - 1985.
(002060)

ACCOUNTING--EUROPE.
----The seventh directive. - 1984.
(002094)

ACCOUNTING--GERMANY, FEDERAL REPUBLIC OF.
----Die finanzielle Führung und Kontrolle
von Auslandsgesellschaften. - 1983.
(000447)

ACCOUNTING--INDIA.
----Compendium of statements and standards.
- 1986.
(002074)

ACCOUNTING--SINGAPORE.
----Accounting technology transfer to less
developed countries and the Singapore
experience. - 1986.
(001498)

ACCOUNTING--UNITED STATES.
----Accounting and law in a nutshell. - 1984.
(002208)

ACCOUNTING--WESTERN EUROPE.
----Zur Angleichung des Bilanzrechts in der
Europäischen Gemeinschaft. - 1984.
(002097)

ACCOUNTING AND REPORTING.
----Accounting and reporting policies and
practices of transnational corporations.
- 1983.
(002120)
----Accounting in developing countries. -
1986.
(002057)
----Accounting reports and performance
measurement of multinational enterprises
in less developed countries. - 1987.
(002107)
----Appropriate measures to give effect to
the work of the Group. - 1986.
(002121)
----Auditing non-U.S. operations. - 1984.
(002113)
----Availability of financial statements. -
1987.
(002100)
----Clarification of the accounting terms in
the OECD Guidelines. - 1983.
(002071)
----Comparative international auditing
standards. - 1985.
(002073)
----Consolidation policies in OECD
countries. - 1987.
(002101)
----Coping with worldwide accounting
changes. - 1984.
(002067)
----Disclosure of information by
multinational enterprises. - 1983.
(002075)
----Financial reporting by private
companies. - 1983.
(002056)
----Foreign currency translation. - 1986.
(002102)
----Frontiers of international accounting. -
1985.
(002069)
----Harmonization of accounting standards. -
1986.
(002082)
----Information disclosure and the
multinational corporation. - 1984.
(002078)
----International accounting. - 1985.
(002111)
----International accounting. - 1984.
(002070)
----International accounting. - 1984.
(002083)
----International accounting and
multinational enterprises. - 1985.
(002058)

ACCOUNTING AND REPORTING (continued)
----International accounting and reporting.
  - 1985.
    (002076)
----International accounting and reporting
  issues : 1984 review. - 1985.
    (002115)
----International accounting and reporting
  issues, 1985 review. - 1985.
    (002116)
----International accounting and reporting
  issues, 1986 review. - 1986.
    (002117)
----International accounting and reporting
  issues, 1987 review. - 1988.
    (002118)
----International accounting and
  transnational decisions. - 1983.
    (002086)
----International accounting standards. -
  1986.
    (002087)
----International dimensions of accounting.
  - 1984.
    (002059)
----International financial reporting. -
  1984.
    (002079)
----International financial reporting and
  auditing. - 1984.
    (002088)
----International standards of accounting
  and reporting. - 1984.
    (002119)
----Inventories and foreign currency
  translation requirements. - 1983.
    (002064)
----Issues in international accounting. -
  1986.
    (002098)
----Managerial accounting and analysis in
  multinational enterprises. - 1986.
    (002084)
----MNE disclosure alternatives and their
  consequences. - 1984.
    (002065)
----Multinational accounting. - 1986.
    (002105)
----Multinational enterprises and the OECD
  industrial relations guidelines. - 1983.
    (001963)
----The new environment in international
  accounting. - 1988.
    (002063)
----Planungs- und Kontrollrechnung im
  internationalen Konzern. - 1984.
    (002068)
----Principles of international accounting.
  - 1986.
    (002077)
----Le risque de change et la consolidation
  des comptes de groupes multinationaux. -
  1983.
    (002104)
----Statements of international accounting
  standards. - 1985-   .
    (002112)
----Die Umrechnung der Jahresabschlusse
  auslandischer Konzernunternehmen und die
  Verrechnung der daraus resultierenden
  Umrechnungsdifferenzen. - 1986.
    (002095)
----UNCTC bibliography, 1974-1987. - 1988.
    (002695)

----Die Wahrungsumrechnung im Rahmen der
  internationalen Konzernrechnungslegung.
  - 1985.
    (002096)
----Working documents. - 1986-   .
    (002123)
----World business reports. - 1982-   .
    (001863)

ACCOUNTING AND REPORTING--EUROPE.
----The seventh directive. - 1984.
    (002094)

ACCOUNTING AND REPORTING--GERMANY, FEDERAL
REPUBLIC OF.
----Der konsolidierte Abschluss. - 1983.
    (002091)

ACCOUNTING AND REPORTING--MIDDLE EAST.
----The recent accounting and economic
  developments in the Middle East. - 1985.
    (002109)

ACCOUNTING AND REPORTING--SOUTHEAST ASIA.
----Comparative accounting practices in
  ASEAN. - 1984.
    (002072)

ACCOUNTING AND REPORTING--UNITED KINGDOM.
----Accounting for overseas operations. -
  1986.
    (002122)
----Inflation accounting. - 1975.
    (002156)
----International segment disclosures by
  U.S. and U.K. multinational enterprises:
  a descriptive study. - 1984.
    (002080)

ACCOUNTING AND REPORTING--UNITED STATES.
----Internal accountability. - 1984.
    (002055)
----International segment disclosures by
  U.S. and U.K. multinational enterprises:
  a descriptive study. - 1984.
    (002080)
----Joint ventures. - 1987.
    (001613)

ACCOUNTING AND REPORTING--WESTERN EUROPE.
----The recent accounting and economic
  developments in Western Europe. - 1985.
    (002110)

ACCOUNTING STANDARDS.
----International accounting standards and
  transnational corporations. - 1986.
    (002108)

ACCULTURATION.
----Managing cultural differences. - 1983.
    (001871)

ACP STATES.
----Agro-industrial co-operation between the
  European Community and the ACP
  countries. - 1986.
    (002605)
----Codes des investissements des Etats
  A.C.P. - 1978.
    (002162)
----Industrialization and the ACPs. - 1984.
    (002608)

ACP STATES (continued)
----Investment in ACP states. - 1987.
(001004)
----Le système conjoint de garantie des
investissements CEE/ACP de la Convention
de Lomé III. - 1987.
(002147)

ACP-EEC.
----Commercial arbitration and the European
Economic Community. - 1985.
(002481)
----Industrialization and the ACPs. - 1984.
(002608)
----Infratechnologies, technologies de
pointe, investissements dans et pour les
pays en développement. - 1985.
(001444)
----Le système conjoint de garantie des
investissements CEE/ACP de la Convention
de Lomé III. - 1987.
(002147)
----Toward Lomé III. - 1984.
(002606)

ACP-EEC CONVENTION (1975).
----Toward Lomé III. - 1984.
(002606)

ACP-EEC CONVENTION (1979).
----Toward Lomé III. - 1984.
(002606)

ACP-EEC CONVENTION (1984).
----L'Afrique, l'Europe et la crise. - 1986.
(001287)
----Agro-industrial co-operation between the
European Community and the ACP
countries. - 1986.
(002605)
----Bilateral investment promotion
protection and treaties : a model for
Community promotion of mining
investment? - 1986.
(002052)
----Promotion of mining and energy
investment under the Lomé Convention. -
1986.
(002607)
----Le système conjoint de garantie des
investissements CEE/ACP de la Convention
de Lomé III. - 1987.
(002147)

ACUERDO DE CARTAGENA.
----Las empresas transnacionales y la
inversión extranjera directa en la
primera mitad de los años ochenta. -
1987.
(000194)
----Foreign debt, direct investment, and
economic development in the Andean Pact.
- 1987.
(001110)
----Industrial cooperation in regional
economic groupings among developing
countries and lessons for SAARC. - 1987.
(001009)
----La inversión estadounidense en el Grupo
Andino. - 1985.
(000112)

----Los regímenes de garantía a la inversión
extranjera y su aplicabilidad en los
países de la ALADI. - 1985.
(002126)
----The role of transnational enterprises in
Latin American economic integration
efforts. - 1983.
(001126)

ACUERDO DE CARTAGENA--ANDEAN REGION.
----La empresa multinacional andina. - 1983.
(002246)

ACUERDO DE CARTAGENA (1969).
----Empresas multinacionales y Pacto andino.
- 1983.
(001102)
----Legislación de inversiones extranjeras y
Pacto Andino. - 1984.
(002234)

ADJUSTMENT ASSISTANCE MEASURES.
----Trade [and] structural change. - 1984.
(001391)

ADJUSTMENT ASSISTANCE MEASURES--CANADA.
----An automotive strategy for Canada. -
1983.
(000686)

ADJUSTMENT PROCESS.
----Compendium of selected studies on
international monetary and financial
issues for the developing countries. -
1987.
(001243)

ADMINISTRATIVE FEES.
----Arrangements between joint venture
partners in developing countries. - 1987.
(002450)

ADVANCE TECHNOLOGY ALERT SYSTEM.
----Microelectronics-based automation
technologies and development. - 1985.
(000753)

ADVERTISING.
----Consumer choice in the Third World. -
1983.
(000878)
----The economic aspects of a new
international information-communication
order. - 1984.
(000917)
----Medicine advertising regulation and
self-regulation in 54 countries. - 1985.
(000815)
----Publicidad. - 1987.
(000937)

ADVERTISING--EUROPE.
----Market share strategy in Europe. - 1985.
(000493)

ADVERTISING AGENCIES--ASIA.
----Madison Avenue in Asia. - 1984.
(000801)

ADVERTISING AGENCIES--UNITED STATES.
----Madison Avenue in Asia. - 1984.
(000801)

ADVISORY SERVICES.
----Technical co-operation programme of the
    United Nations Centre on Transnational
    Corporations. - 1988.
        (002610)
----Technical co-operation programme,
    1976-1987 : United Nations Centre on
    Transnational Corporations. - 1988.
        (002611)

AFFILIATE CORPORATIONS.
----Corporate performance: America's
    international winners. - 1986.
        (000344)
----Cross-border transactions between
    related companies. - 1985.
        (001735)
----Decision-making regarding restructuring
    in multinational enterprises. - 1986.
        (000411)
----Host countries and the R [and] D of
    multinationals. - 1987.
        (001479)
----Joint venture instability: is it a
    problem? - 1987.
        (001581)
----Managing the multinational subsidiary. -
    1986.
        (000405)
----Multinationale Unternehmen und
    Mitbestimmung. - 1986.
        (000406)
----On the theory of an exhaustible resource
    extractive multinational firm. - 1986.
        (000610)

AFFILIATE CORPORATIONS--AUSTRALIA.
----The Australian multinational -- parent
    and subsidiary relationships. - 1986.
        (000390)

AFFILIATE CORPORATIONS--CANADA.
----Taxation of income of foreign
    affiliates. - 1983.
        (001765)

AFFILIATE CORPORATIONS--EASTERN EUROPE.
----Eastern bloc international enterprises
    -- still in statu nascendi. - 1985.
        (000332)

AFFILIATE CORPORATIONS--GERMANY, FEDERAL
REPUBLIC OF.
----Gewinne verbundener Unternehmen,
    Verrechnungspreise. - 1984.
        (001749)
----Die Steuerung auslandischer
    Tochtergesellschaften. - 1983.
        (000400)

AFFILIATE CORPORATIONS--JAPAN.
----Directory of foreign capital affiliated
    enterprises in Japan. - 198?-   .
        (002632)
----US and Japanese manufacturing affiliates
    in the UK. - 1985.
        (001149)

AFFILIATE CORPORATIONS--LATIN AMERICA.
----The debt crisis and bank lending to
    subsidiaries of transnational
    corporations in Latin America. - 1984.
        (000219)

AFFILIATE CORPORATIONS--SWEDEN.
----Underskott vid joint venture- och annan
    verksamhet i utlandet, m.m. - 1985.
        (001760)

AFFILIATE CORPORATIONS--UNITED KINGDOM.
----Decision-making in foreign-owned
    multinational subsidiaries in the United
    Kingdom. - 1985.
        (000521)
----Foundations of foreign success. - 1987.
        (000421)
----US and Japanese manufacturing affiliates
    in the UK. - 1985.
        (001149)

AFFILIATE CORPORATIONS--UNITED STATES.
----Capital expenditures by majority-owned
    foreign affiliates of U.S. companies,
    1986 and 1987. - 1986.
        (000479)
----Foreign direct investment in the United
    States. - 1985.
        (000197)
----Die Steuerung auslandischer
    Tochtergesellschaften. - 1983.
        (000400)
----US and Japanese manufacturing affiliates
    in the UK. - 1985.
        (001149)

AFRICA--AGRIBUSINESS.
----Agribusiness in Africa. - 1984.
        (001025)
----Agro-industrial co-operation between the
    European Community and the ACP
    countries. - 1986.
        (002605)

AFRICA--AGRICULTURE.
----Limite des alternatives capitalistes
    d'état ou privées à la crise agricole
    africaine. - 1985.
        (001575)

AFRICA--APPROPRIATE TECHNOLOGY.
----Directory of African technology
    institutions. - 1985.
        (002706)
----Gaspillages technologiques. - 1985.
        (001435)

AFRICA--BANKING LAW.
----The role of transnational banks and
    financial institutions in Africa's
    development process. - 1986.
        (000935)

AFRICA--BUSINESS ENTERPRISES.
----Owen's Worldtrade Africa business
    directory. - 1986-   .
        (002657)

AFRICA--CAPITAL MOVEMENTS.
----Nezavisimye strany Afriki. - 1986.
        (001280)

AFRICA--COMMERCIAL BANKS.
----The role of transnational banks and
    financial institutions in Africa's
    development process. - 1986.
        (000935)

AFRICA--COMMERCIAL LAW.
----International marketing to Black Africa
    and the Third World. - 1988.
    (001001)

AFRICA--COST EFFECTIVENESS.
----Gaspillages technologiques. - 1985.
    (001435)

AFRICA--CREDIT POLICY.
----Nezavisimye strany Afriki. - 1986.
    (001280)

AFRICA--DEVELOPMENT ASSISTANCE.
----Foreign powers and Africa. - 1983.
    (001031)

AFRICA--DEVELOPMENT FINANCE INSTITUTIONS.
----The role of transnational banks and
    financial institutions in Africa's
    development process. - 1986.
    (000935)

AFRICA--DIRECTORIES.
----African trade unions. - 1983-   .
    (002592) (002593) (002698)

----Asia-Pacific/Africa-Middle East
    petroleum directory. - 1984-   .
    (000579) (002618)
----Directory of African technology
    institutions. - 1985.
    (002706)
----Owen's Worldtrade Africa business
    directory. - 1986-   .
    (002657)
----Répertoire de la législation relative
    aux investissements étrangers dans les
    pays membres de L'OCI. - 1984.
    (002264)

AFRICA--ECONOMIC CO-OPERATION.
----Current problems of economic
    integration. - 1986.
    (001312)

AFRICA--ECONOMIC DEVELOPMENT.
----The role of transnational banks and
    financial institutions in Africa's
    development process. - 1986.
    (000935)

AFRICA--ECONOMIC INTEGRATION.
----Current problems of economic
    integration. - 1986.
    (001312)

AFRICA--ECONOMIC RELATIONS.
----Les sociétés transnationales en Afrique.
    - 1986.
    (001028)
----Toward Lomé III. - 1984.
    (002606)

AFRICA--EXPORT MARKETING.
----International marketing to Black Africa
    and the Third World. - 1988.
    (001001)

AFRICA--FINANCIAL INSTITUTIONS.
----The role of transnational banks and
    financial institutions in Africa's
    development process. - 1986.
    (000935)

AFRICA--FINANCIAL STATISTICS.
----The role of transnational banks and
    financial institutions in Africa's
    development process. - 1986.
    (000935)

AFRICA--FINANCING.
----Nezavisimye strany Afriki. - 1986.
    (001280)

AFRICA--FOOD INDUSTRY.
----Agribusiness in Africa. - 1984.
    (001025)

AFRICA--FOREIGN DIRECT INVESTMENT.
----Investment in ACP states. - 1987.
    (001004)

AFRICA--FOREIGN INVESTMENTS.
----L'Afrique, l'Europe et la crise. - 1986.
    (001287)
----Répertoire de la législation relative
    aux investissements étrangers dans les
    pays membres de L'OCI. - 1984.
    (002264)

AFRICA--INDUSTRIAL CO-OPERATION.
----Agro-industrial co-operation between the
    European Community and the ACP
    countries. - 1986.
    (002605)
----Current problems of economic
    integration. - 1986.
    (001312)

AFRICA--INDUSTRY.
----Investment in ACP states. - 1987.
    (001004)
----Owen's Worldtrade Africa business
    directory. - 1986-   .
    (002657)

AFRICA--INSURANCE COMPANIES.
----The role of transnational banks and
    financial institutions in Africa's
    development process. - 1986.
    (000935)

AFRICA--INSURANCE LAW.
----The role of transnational banks and
    financial institutions in Africa's
    development process. - 1986.
    (000935)

AFRICA--INVESTMENT INSURANCE.
----Investment in ACP states. - 1987.
    (001004)

AFRICA--JOINT VENTURES.
----Investment in ACP states. - 1987.
    (001004)

AFRICA--LEGISLATION.
----Répertoire de la législation relative
    aux investissements étrangers dans les
    pays membres de L'OCI. - 1984.
    (002264)

AFRICA--MINERAL INDUSTRY.
----Mineral industries of Africa. -
    1976-   .
    (000620)

AFRICA--MONETARY POLICY.
----Nezavisimye strany Afriki. - 1986.
   (001280)

AFRICA--MULTINATIONAL INDUSTRIAL PROJECTS.
----Current problems of economic
   integration. - 1986.
   (001312)

AFRICA--PETROLEUM INDUSTRY.
----Asia-Pacific/Africa-Middle East
   petroleum directory. - 1984-   .
   (000579) (002618)

AFRICA--PRIVATE ENTERPRISES.
----Limite des alternatives capitalistes
   d'état ou privées à la crise agricole
   africaine. - 1985.
   (001575)

AFRICA--PUBLIC ENTERPRISES.
----Limite des alternatives capitalistes
   d'état ou privées à la crise agricole
   africaine. - 1985.
   (001575)

AFRICA--REGIONAL CO-OPERATION.
----Current problems of economic
   integration. - 1986.
   (001312)

AFRICA--REGIONAL DEVELOPMENT BANKS.
----Current problems of economic
   integration. - 1986.
   (001312)

AFRICA--STATISTICAL DATA.
----The role of transnational banks and
   financial institutions in Africa's
   development process. - 1986.
   (000935)

AFRICA--TECHNOLOGY.
----Directory of African technology
   institutions. - 1985.
   (002706)

AFRICA--TECHNOLOGY TRANSFER.
----Gaspillages technologiques. - 1985.
   (001435)
----Les techniques de negociation en matière
   de transfert de technologie. - 1987.
   (001511)

AFRICA--TRADE AGREEMENTS.
----Toward Lomé III. - 1984.
   (002606)

AFRICA--TRADE UNIONS.
----African trade unions. - 1983-   .
   (002592) (002593) (002698)

AFRICA--TRAINING AND RESEARCH INSTITUTIONS.
----Directory of African technology
   institutions. - 1985.
   (002706)

AFRICA--TRANSNATIONAL BANKS.
----The role of transnational banks and
   financial institutions in Africa's
   development process. - 1986.
   (000935)

AFRICA--TRANSNATIONAL CORPORATIONS.
----Agribusiness in Africa. - 1984.
   (001025)
----Les finances des multinationales en
   Afrique. - 1983.
   (001024)
----Foreign powers and Africa. - 1983.
   (001031)
----International marketing to Black Africa
   and the Third World. - 1988.
   (001001)
----Les techniques de negociation en matière
   de transfert de technologie. - 1987.
   (001511)
----The political economy of regulation. -
   1985.
   (001959)
----Les sociétés transnationales en Afrique.
   - 1986.
   (001028)
----The transnational focus. - 1982-   .
   (001033)

AFRICA SOUTH OF SAHARA--AGRICULTURE.
----The differentiation process in the
   economies of black Africa. - 1984.
   (001694)

AFRICA SOUTH OF SAHARA--ECONOMIC CONDITIONS.
----La privatisation des entreprises
   publiques en Afrique au sud du Sahara,
   (2). - 1986.
   (001564)

AFRICA SOUTH OF SAHARA--ECONOMIC DEVELOPMENT.
----The differentiation process in the
   economies of black Africa. - 1984.
   (001694)

AFRICA SOUTH OF SAHARA--ECONOMIC STRUCTURE.
----The differentiation process in the
   economies of black Africa. - 1984.
   (001694)

AFRICA SOUTH OF SAHARA--INDUSTRIAL
DEVELOPMENT.
----The differentiation process in the
   economies of black Africa. - 1984.
   (001694)

AFRICA SOUTH OF SAHARA--INDUSTRIALIZATION.
----Industrialization and the ACPs. - 1984.
   (002608)

AFRICA SOUTH OF SAHARA--INTERNATIONAL
ECONOMIC RELATIONS.
----Uoll-strit protiv Afriki. - 1985.
   (001030)

AFRICA SOUTH OF SAHARA--PRIVATE ENTERPRISES.
----La privatisation des entreprises
   publiques en Afrique au sud du Sahara,
   (2). - 1986.
   (001564)

AFRICA SOUTH OF SAHARA--PUBLIC ENTERPRISES.
----La privatisation des entreprises
   publiques en Afrique au sud du Sahara,
   (2). - 1986.
   (001564)

AFRICA SOUTH OF SAHARA--TRANSNATIONAL
CORPORATIONS.
----Transnatsional'nye korporatsii v
    Tropicheskoi Afrike. - 1986.
    (001020)
----Uoll-strit protiv Afriki. - 1985.
    (001030)

AFRICAN DEVELOPMENT BANK.
----Current problems of economic
    integration. - 1986.
    (001312)
----State intervention, foreign economic
    aid, savings and growth in LDCs. - 1985.
    (001337)

AGRARIAN REFORM--HONDURAS.
----Guanchias Limitada. - 1985.
    (001094)

AGRIBUSINESS.
----The private sector and rural
    development: can agribusiness help the
    small farmer? - 1985.
    (000566)

AGRIBUSINESS--AFRICA.
----Agribusiness in Africa. - 1984.
    (001025)
----Agro-industrial co-operation between the
    European Community and the ACP
    countries. - 1986.
    (002605)

AGRIBUSINESS--ARGENTINA.
----Empresas transnacionales en la industria
    de alimentos. - 1983.
    (000573)

AGRIBUSINESS--CAMEROON.
----Agro-industrial co-operation between the
    European Community and the ACP
    countries. - 1986.
    (002605)

AGRIBUSINESS--CANADA.
----Public and private returns from joint
    venture research: an example from
    agriculture. - 1986.
    (001650)

AGRIBUSINESS--CARIBBEAN REGION.
----Agro-industrial co-operation between the
    European Community and the ACP
    countries. - 1986.
    (002605)

AGRIBUSINESS--LATIN AMERICA.
----Agricultura y alimentos en América
    Latina. - 1985.
    (000562)
----Transnacionalizacion y desarrollo
    agropecuario en America Latina. - 1984.
    (000574)

AGRIBUSINESS--PACIFIC OCEAN REGION.
----Agro-industrial co-operation between the
    European Community and the ACP
    countries. - 1986.
    (002605)

AGRIBUSINESS--RWANDA.
----Agro-industrial co-operation between the
    European Community and the ACP
    countries. - 1986.
    (002605)

AGRIBUSINESS--SRI LANKA.
----Agribusiness TNCs in Sri Lanka. - 1986.
    (000560)

AGRIBUSINESS--UNITED STATES.
----U.S.-EEC confrontation in the
    international trade of agricultural
    products: consequences for third
    parties. - 1985.
    (001380)

AGRIBUSINESS--WESTERN EUROPE.
----Agro-industrial co-operation between the
    European Community and the ACP
    countries. - 1986.
    (002605)

AGRICULTURAL CO-OPERATIVES--HONDURAS.
----Guanchias Limitada. - 1985.
    (001094)

AGRICULTURAL DEVELOPMENT.
----Economics of change in less developed
    countries. - 1986.
    (001000)

AGRICULTURAL DEVELOPMENT--HONDURAS.
----Guanchias Limitada. - 1985.
    (001094)

AGRICULTURAL INNOVATIONS.
----Technology choice and change in
    developing countries. - 1983.
    (001505)

AGRICULTURAL MACHINERY.
----Transnational corporations in the
    agricultural machinery and equipment
    industry. - 1983.
    (000746)

AGRICULTURAL POLICY--CHINA.
----Agriculture in China. - 1985.
    (000561)

AGRICULTURAL PRODUCTION--CHINA.
----Agriculture in China. - 1985.
    (000561)

AGRICULTURAL PRODUCTS--CHINA.
----Agriculture in China. - 1985.
    (000561)

AGRICULTURAL PRODUCTS--PARAGUAY.
----Las empresas transnacionales en la
    economía del Paraguay. - 1987.
    (001124)

AGRICULTURE--AFRICA.
----Limite des alternatives capitalistes
    d'état ou privées à la crise agricole
    africaine. - 1985.
    (001575)

AGRICULTURE--AFRICA SOUTH OF SAHARA.
----The differentiation process in the
    economies of black Africa. - 1984.
    (001694)

AGRICULTURE--NAMIBIA.
----Transnational corporations in South
    Africa and Namibia : United Nations
    public hearings. Volume 1, Reports of
    the Panel of Eminent Persons and of the
    Secretary-General. - 1986.
      (001216)

AGROINDUSTRY.
----Les cent premiers groupes
    agro-industriels mondiaux. - 1983.
      (000563)
----Industry in the 1980s. - 1985.
      (001341)

AGROINDUSTRY--BURKINA FASO.
----Une enclave industrielle : la Société
    sucrière de Haute-Volta. - 1984.
      (001032)

AGROINDUSTRY--EASTERN EUROPE.
----Technological cooperation and
    specialization. - 1986.
      (001500)

AGROINDUSTRY--FRANCE.
----L'internationalisation de l'agriculture
    francaise. - 1984.
      (000567)

AGROINDUSTRY--LATIN AMERICA.
----Las nuevas formas de inversión
    internacional en la agroindustria
    latinoamericana. - 1986.
      (000569)

AGROINDUSTRY--PERU.
----Agroindustria y transnacionales en el
    Perú. - 1983.
      (000565)

AID FINANCING.
----Does concessionary aid lead to higher
    investment rates in low-income
    countries? - 1987.
      (002311)

AID PROGRAMMES.
----Corporate aid programs in twelve
    less-developed countries. - 1983.
      (002609)

AIR TRANSPORT.
----International income taxation and
    developing countries. - 1988.
      (001759)
----Négociations internationales. - 1984.
      (002463)

AIR TRANSPORT--KENYA.
----The role of transnational corporations
    in hotel and tourism industry in
    selected PTA member countries. - 1986.
      (000782) (000936)

AIR TRANSPORT--MAURITIUS.
----The role of transnational corporations
    in hotel and tourism industry in
    selected PTA member countries. - 1986.
      (000782) (000936)

AIR TRANSPORT--WESTERN EUROPE.
----Air and maritime transport and the EEC
    competition rules : Ministère Publique
    v. Asjes, Nouvelles Frontières et al. -
    1987.
      (000794)
----Attempt to regulate restrictive
    commercial practices in the field of air
    transportation within a transnational
    antitrust legal and institutional
    framework. - 1984.
      (000788) (001659)

AIR TRANSPORT--ZIMBABWE.
----The role of transnational corporations
    in hotel and tourism industry in
    selected PTA member countries. - 1986.
      (000782) (000936)

AIRCRAFT INDUSTRY.
----Multinational ventures in the commercial
    aircraft industry. - 1985.
      (000721)

AIRCRAFT INDUSTRY--UNITED STATES.
----Alliance politics and economics. - 1987.
      (000719)

ALCOA (PITTSBURGH, PA.).
----The American take-over. - 1983.
      (000287)

ALCOHOL FUELS--UNITED STATES.
----A competitive assessment of the U.S.
    methanol industry. - 1985.
      (000671)

ALGERIA--ECONOMIC POLICY.
----Aperçu sur le statut de la société mixte
    en Algérie. - 1984.
      (002283)

ALGERIA--FOREIGN INVESTMENTS.
----Aperçu sur le statut de la société mixte
    en Algérie. - 1984.
      (002283)

ALGERIA--LAWS AND REGULATIONS.
----National legislation and regulations
    relating to transnational corporations.
    Volume 3. - 1983.
      (002252)

ALGERIA--TRANSNATIONAL CORPORATIONS.
----National legislation and regulations
    relating to transnational corporations.
    Volume 3. - 1983.
      (002252)

ALIEN PROPERTY.
----Eigentum, Enteignung und Entschädigung
    im geltenden Völkerrecht. - 1985.
      (002321)
----The international law of expropriation
    of foreign-owned property. - 1983.
      (002330)
----An international standard of partial
    compensation upon the expropriation of
    an alien's property. - 1987.
      (002317)

ALLOYS--LATIN AMERICA.
----La industria siderúrgica
     latinoamericana. - 1984.
       (000601)

ALUMINA--GOVE PENINSULA (AUSTRALIA).
----The history and contractual arrangements
     of the Gove bauxite/alumina project in
     the Northern Territory of Australia. -
     1985.
       (000596)

ALUMINA--NORTHERN TERRITORY (AUSTRALIA).
----The history and contractual arrangements
     of the Gove bauxite/alumina project in
     the Northern Territory of Australia. -
     1985.
       (000596)

ALUMINIUM INDUSTRY.
----The aluminum multinationals and the
     bauxite cartel. - 1987.
       (000599)
----Assessing industry concentration: the
     case of aluminum. - 1984.
       (000611)
----Les enjeux de la bauxite. - 1983.
       (000585)
----The transnational politics of the
     aluminum multinationals. - 1984.
       (000598)
----Vertical integration and joint ventures
     in the aluminum industry. - 1983.
       (000636)

ALUMINIUM INDUSTRY--CARIBBEAN REGION.
----Multinational corporations and regional
     revenue retention in a vertically
     integrated industry: bauxite/aluminium
     in the Caribbean. - 1983.
       (000582)

ALUMINIUM INDUSTRY--GHANA.
----The price and availability of energy for
     an aluminium smelter : recent
     renegotiations in Ghana. - 1987.
       (002467)

ALUMINIUM INDUSTRY--GUYANA.
----The American take-over. - 1983.
       (000287)

ALUMINIUM INDUSTRY--SURINAME.
----The American take-over. - 1983.
       (000287)

ALUMINIUM INDUSTRY--UNITED STATES.
----The RJR story. - 1983.
       (000296)
----Vertical integration and joint ventures
     in the aluminum industry. - 1983.
       (001642)

AMERICAS--ARBITRAL AWARDS.
----Les conventions interaméricaines sur
     l'arbitrage commercial et la Commission
     interaméricaine d'arbitrage commercial.
     - 1983.
       (002535)

AMERICAS--INTERNATIONAL COMMERCIAL
ARBITRATION.
----Les conventions interaméricaines sur
     l'arbitrage commercial et la Commission
     interaméricaine d'arbitrage commercial.
     - 1983.
       (002535)

AMERICAS--TREATIES.
----Les conventions interaméricaines sur
     l'arbitrage commercial et la Commission
     interaméricaine d'arbitrage commercial.
     - 1983.
       (002535)

ANDEAN REGION--ACUERDO DE CARTAGENA.
----La empresa multinacional andina. - 1983.
       (002246)

ANDEAN REGION--ECONOMIC INTEGRATION.
----Andean multinational enterprises: a new
     approach to multinational investment in
     the Andean Group. - 1983.
       (000313)

ANDEAN REGION--FOREIGN DIRECT INVESTMENT.
----The Andean foreign investment code's
     impact on multinational enterprises. -
     1983.
       (001977)
----Empresas multinacionales y Pacto andino.
     - 1983.
       (001102)
----Legislación de inversiones extranjeras y
     Pacto Andino. - 1984.
       (002234)

ANDEAN REGION--GUIDELINES.
----The Andean foreign investment code's
     impact on multinational enterprises. -
     1983.
       (001977)

ANDEAN REGION--INVESTMENT POLICY.
----The Andean foreign investment code's
     impact on multinational enterprises. -
     1983.
       (001977)

ANDEAN REGION--LAWS AND REGULATIONS.
----La empresa multinacional andina. - 1983.
       (002246)
----Legislación de inversiones extranjeras y
     Pacto Andino. - 1984.
       (002234)

ANDEAN REGION--TRANSNATIONAL CORPORATIONS.
----The Andean foreign investment code's
     impact on multinational enterprises. -
     1983.
       (001977)
----Andean multinational enterprises: a new
     approach to multinational investment in
     the Andean Group. - 1983.
       (000313)
----La empresa multinacional andina. - 1983.
       (002246)
----Empresas multinacionales y Pacto andino.
     - 1983.
       (001102)
----Estudios jurídicos sobre la Empresa
     Multinacional Andina, E.M.A. - 1986.
       (000314)

ANGLO AMERICAN CORPORATION
(MARSHALLTOWN,SOUTH AFTRICA)--UNITED STATES.
----Anglo in America. - 1986.
    (000292)

ANTI-APARTHEID MOVEMENTS--SOUTH AFRICA.
----Trade unions against apartheid. - 1984.
    (002601)

ANTIDUMPING DUTIES--JAPAN.
----Antitrust aspects of U.S.-Japanese
    trade. - 1983.
    (002345)

ANTIDUMPING DUTIES--UNITED STATES.
----Antitrust aspects of U.S.-Japanese
    trade. - 1983.
    (002345)
----Competition and world markets. - 1983.
    (001665)

ANTITRUST LAW.
----Antitrust and direct regulation of
    international transfer of technology
    transactions. - 1984.
    (001411)
----Anti-trust and restrictive business
    practices. - 1983-   .
    (001957)
----Antitrust for high-technology
    industries: assessing research joint
    ventures and mergers. - 1985.
    (001621)
----Gemeinschaftsunternehmen im EGKS- und
    EWG-Kartellrecht. - 1986.
    (001978)
----The implementation of international
    antitrust principles. - 1983.
    (002344)
----International business and national
    jurisdiction. - 1988.
    (002351)
----Joint ventures : do they restrict
    competition? - 1986.
    (001596)
----Merger policies and recent trends in
    mergers. - 1984.
    (001618)
----Le società multinazionali nel diritto
    comunitario. - 1984.
    (002011)

ANTITRUST LAW--AUSTRALIA.
----Extraterritorial effects of United
    States commercial and antitrust
    legislation. - 1983.
    (002352)

ANTITRUST LAW--GERMANY, FEDERAL REPUBLIC OF.
----Fakultatives Kollisonsrecht im
    internationalen Wettbewerbsrecht? - 1984.
    (002247)

ANTITRUST LAW--JAPAN.
----Antitrust aspects of U.S.-Japanese
    trade. - 1983.
    (002345)

ANTITRUST LAW--UNITED KINGDOM.
----Corporate acquisitions and mergers. -
    1985.
    (001544)

ANTITRUST LAW--UNITED STATES.
----Antitrust aspects of U.S.-Japanese
    trade. - 1983.
    (002345)
----Antitrust law developments (second). -
    1984.
    (002339)
----Antitrust policy and joint research and
    development ventures. - 1984.
    (002356)
----Arbitration of private antitrust claims
    in international trade. - 1986.
    (002471)
----Competition and world markets. - 1983.
    (001665)
----Cooperative research and development. -
    1984.
    (001630)
----Exclusive licenses as restraints of
    trade under US and Common Market
    antitrust law. - 1984.
    (002414)
----The extraterritorial effects of
    antitrust laws. - 1984.
    (002342)
----Extraterritorial effects of United
    States commercial and antitrust
    legislation. - 1983.
    (002352)
----International antitrust law. - 1985.
    (002539)
----Joint research and development
    legislation. - 1987.
    (002286)
----Mitsubishi and the arbitrability of
    antitrust claims. - 1986.
    (002486)

ANTITRUST LAW--WESTERN EUROPE.
----The antitrust law of the European
    Community and the UNCTAD code on
    restrictive business practices. - 1984.
    (001992)
----Attempt to regulate restrictive
    commercial practices in the field of air
    transportation within a transnational
    antitrust legal and institutional
    framework. - 1984.
    (000788) (001659)
----Corporate acquisitions and mergers. -
    1985.
    (001544)
----The EEC patent licencing regulation :
    practical guidelines. - 1986.
    (001966)
----Exclusive licenses as restraints of
    trade under US and Common Market
    antitrust law. - 1984.
    (002414)

APARTHEID.
----Business in the shadow of apartheid :
    U.S. firms in South Africa. - 1985.
    (001194)
----A code for misconduct? - 1980.
    (002009)
----The costs of disinvestment. - 1986.
    (001207)
----Disinvestment and black workers
    attitudes in South Africa. - 1985.
    (001210)

APARTHEID (continued)
----Measures regarding the activities of
    transnational corporations in South
    Africa and Namibia. - 1985.
       (001220)
----The political economy of U.S. policy
    toward South Africa. - 1985.
       (001196)
----Trade unions against apartheid. - 1984.
       (002601)
----Transnational corporations : follow-up
    to the recommendations of the Panel of
    Eminent Persons Established to Conduct
    the Public Hearings on the Activities of
    Transnational Corporations in South
    Africa and Namibia. - 1988.
       (001221)
----Transnational corporations in South
    Africa and Namibia : United Nations
    public hearings. Volume 1, Reports of
    the Panel of Eminent Persons and of the
    Secretary-General. - 1986.
       (001216)
----Transnational corporations in South
    Africa and Namibia. - 1986.
       (001217)
----Transnational corporations in South
    Africa and Namibia : United Nations
    public hearings. Volume 3, Statements
    and submissions. - 1987.
       (001215)
----Transnational corporations in South
    Africa and Namibia : United Nations
    Public Hearings. Volume 4, Policy
    instruments and statements. - 1987.
       (001218)
----U.S. corporate activities in South
    Africa. - 1983.
       (001222)

APARTHEID--SOUTH AFRICA.
----Leaving South Africa/Kellogg's
    private war against apartheid/Black
    unions. - 1985.
       (001200)

APPROPRIATE TECHNOLOGY.
----Appropriate or underdeveloped
    technology? - 1982.
       (001428)
----Bibliography of appropriate technology
    information for developing countries. -
    1983.
       (002683)
----Employment and technological choice of
    multinational enterprises in developing
    countries. - 1983.
       (001909)
----Infratechnologies, technologies de
    pointe, investissements dans et pour les
    pays en développement. - 1985.
       (001444)
----Research and technology for the Third
    World. - 1985.
       (001489)
----Technological inconsistencies in
    promoting development. - 1984.
       (001516)
----Technology : management and acquisition.
    - 1984-   .
       (001501)
----Technology and employment in industry. -
    1985.
       (001503)

----Technology choice and change in
    developing countries. - 1983.
       (001505)
----The world of appropriate technology. -
    1983.
       (001447)

APPROPRIATE TECHNOLOGY--AFRICA.
----Directory of African technology
    institutions. - 1985.
       (002706)
----Gaspillages technologiques. - 1985.
       (001435)

APPROPRIATE TECHNOLOGY--GHANA.
----Technology and development :
    socio-economic implications for Ghana. -
    1987.
       (001478)

ARAB COUNTRIES--ARBITRATION.
----Arab comparative and commercial law. -
    1987.
       (002223)

ARAB COUNTRIES--COMMERCIAL ARBITRATION.
----Particularités et problèmes de
    l'arbitrage dans les droits des pays
    arabes. - 1986.
       (002530)

ARAB COUNTRIES--ECONOMIC CO-OPERATION.
----Arab joint ventures. - 1986.
       (001137)
----Current problems of economic
    integration. - 1986.
       (001312)

ARAB COUNTRIES--ECONOMIC INTEGRATION.
----Current problems of economic
    integration. - 1986.
       (001312)

ARAB COUNTRIES--ECONOMIC RELATIONS.
----The Arab world is still importing. -
    1987.
       (001134)

ARAB COUNTRIES--ENERGY LEGISLATION.
----Arab comparative and commercial law. -
    1987.
       (002223)

ARAB COUNTRIES--FINANCIAL INSTITUTIONS.
----The development of Arab international
    banking. - 1983.
       (000803)

ARAB COUNTRIES--FOREIGN TRADE.
----The Arab world is still importing. -
    1987.
       (001134)

ARAB COUNTRIES--IMPORTS.
----The Arab world is still importing. -
    1987.
       (001134)

ARAB COUNTRIES--INDUSTRIAL CO-OPERATION.
----Current problems of economic
    integration. - 1986.
       (001312)

ARAB COUNTRIES--INTERNATIONAL BANKING.
----The development of Arab international
    banking. - 1983.
        (000803)
----The problems of developing-country debt
    and a strategy for Arab banking
    institutions. - 1983.
        (000256)

ARAB COUNTRIES--JOINT VENTURES.
----Arab comparative and commercial law. -
    1987.
        (002223)
----Arab joint ventures. - 1986.
        (001137)
----The Arab world is still importing. -
    1987.
        (001134)

ARAB COUNTRIES--MULTINATIONAL INDUSTRIAL
PROJECTS.
----Current problems of economic
    integration. - 1986.
        (001312)

ARAB COUNTRIES--PETROLEUM INDUSTRY.
----The oil companies and the Arab world. -
    1984.
        (000613)

ARAB COUNTRIES--REGIONAL CO-OPERATION.
----Current problems of economic
    integration. - 1986.
        (001312)

ARAB COUNTRIES--REGIONAL DEVELOPMENT BANKS.
----Current problems of economic
    integration. - 1986.
        (001312)

ARAB COUNTRIES--TRANSNATIONAL CORPORATIONS.
----The oil companies and the Arab world. -
    1984.
        (000613)

ARBITRAL AWARDS.
----Arbitration clauses in international
    loans. - 1987.
        (002569)
----Arbitration with governments. - 1983.
        (002493)
----The arbitrator's power to award punitive
    damages in international contract
    actions. - 1986.
        (002534)
----Drafting the international arbitration
    clause. -. 1986.
        (002581)
----International commercial arbitration. -
    1974-   .
        (002523)
----International commercial arbitration. -
    1983.
        (002520)
----La reconnaissance et l'exécution des
    sentences arbitrales étrangères. - 1985.
        (002564)

ARBITRAL AWARDS--AMERICAS.
----Les conventions interaméricaines sur
    l'arbitrage commercial et la Commission
    interaméricaine d'arbitrage commercial.
    - 1983.
        (002535)

ARBITRAL AWARDS--CUBA.
----Cuba's system of international
    commercial arbitration. - 1984.
        (002490)

ARBITRAL AWARDS--LATIN AMERICA.
----International commercial arbitration. -
    1983.
        (002538)
----International commercial arbitration in
    Latin America. - 1986.
        (002546)

ARBITRAL AWARDS--SWEDEN.
----Das anzuwendende Recht beim
    internationalen Schiedsverfahren in
    Schweden. - 1986.
        (002515)

ARBITRAL AWARDS--UNITED STATES.
----Enforcement of arbitral awards issued by
    the Additional Facility of the
    International Centre of Settlement of
    Investment Disputes (ICSID). - 1985.
        (002536)
----International commercial arbitration : a
    comparative analysis of the United
    States system and the UNCITRAL model
    law. - 1986.
        (002487)
----International commercial arbitration. -
    1983.
        (002538)
----Jurisdiction over foreign sovereigns. -
    1983.
        (002480)

ARBITRAL AWARDS--WESTERN EUROPE.
----Commercial arbitration and the European
    Economic Community. - 1985.
        (002481)

ARBITRAL AWARDS--YUGOSLAVIA.
----Les développements nouveaux concernant
    la reconnaissance et l'exécution des
    sentences arbitrales étrangères en
    Yougoslavie. - 1983.
        (002582)

ARBITRATION.
----Arbitration and the courts. - 1985.
        (002532)
----Multilateral negotiations and
    third-party roles. - 1986.
        (002689)
----Problèmes de base de l'arbitrage. -
    1987-   .
        (002531)

ARBITRATION--ARAB COUNTRIES.
----Arab comparative and commercial law. -
    1987.
        (002223)

ARBITRATION--KUWAIT.
----State contracts and oil expropriations.
    - 1984.
        (002577)

ARBITRATION--UNITED STATES.
----State contracts and oil expropriations.
    - 1984.
        (002577)

ARBITRATION RULES.
----L'Arbitrage transnational et les
     tribunaux nationaux. - 1984.
       (002492)
----A code of ethics for arbitrators in
     international commercial arbitration? -
     1985.
       (002519)
----La conciliation, nouvelle méthode de
     règlement des différends. - 1985.
       (002512)
----The future of international commercial
     arbitration. - 1987.
       (002573)
----How international arbitration can always
     prevail over litigation. - 1987.
       (002497)
----ICSID's emerging jurisprudence. - 1986.
       (002562)
----La loi-type de la C.N.U.D.C.I. sur
     l'arbitrage commercial international. -
     1986.
       (002527)
----The nature and extent of an arbitrator's
     powers in international commercial
     arbitration. - 1987.
       (002559)
----Sanctions to control party misbehavior
     in international arbitration. - 1986.
       (002537)
----The status of the UNCITRAL Model Law on
     International Commercial Arbitration
     vis-à-vis the ICC, LCIA and UNCITRAL
     arbitration rules. - 1986.
       (002583)

ARBITRATION RULES--HONG KONG.
----Arbitration in Hong Kong. - 1986.
       (002578)

ARBITRATION RULES--UNITED STATES.
----International commercial arbitration : a
     comparative analysis of the United
     States system and the UNCITRAL model
     law. - 1986.
       (002487)

ARBITRATION RULES--USSR.
----The Soviet position on international
     arbitration. - 1986.
       (002571)

AREA STUDIES.
----World business reports. - 1982-   .
       (001863)

ARGENTINA--AGRIBUSINESS.
----Empresas transnacionales en la industria
     de alimentos. - 1983.
       (000573)

ARGENTINA--BUSINESS ENTERPRISES.
----Cooperación empresarial entre países
     semiindutrializados. - 1984.
       (000202)
----Sociedades y grupos multinacionales. -
     1985.
       (000004)

ARGENTINA--COMMERCIAL LAW.
----Sociedades y grupos multinacionales. -
     1985.
       (000004)

ARGENTINA--COMPUTER INDUSTRY.
----L'informatique en Argentine. - 1986.
       (000772)

ARGENTINA--COMPUTER SCIENCE.
----L'informatique en Argentine. - 1986.
       (000772)

ARGENTINA--CONTRACTS.
----Petroleum service contracts in
     Argentina, Brazil and Colombia : issues
     arising from their legal nature. - 1987.
       (002422)

ARGENTINA--CORPORATE PLANNING.
----The new Argentina. - 1984.
       (001777)

ARGENTINA--DEBT MANAGEMENT.
----Los bancos transnacionales y el
     endeudamiento externo en la Argentina. -
     1987.
       (000819)

ARGENTINA--DEBT RENEGOTIATION.
----Los bancos transnacionales y el
     endeudamiento externo en la Argentina. -
     1987.
       (000819)

ARGENTINA--DEBT REORGANIZATION.
----Los bancos transnacionales y el
     endeudamiento externo en la Argentina. -
     1987.
       (000819)

ARGENTINA--DIFFUSION OF INNOVATIONS.
----Exportaciones de tecnología de Brasil y
     Argentina. - 1986.
       (001491)

ARGENTINA--ECONOMIC CONDITIONS.
----The new Argentina. - 1984.
       (001777)
----Transnacionalización y política
     económica en la Argentina. - 1985.
       (001115)

ARGENTINA--ECONOMIC CO-OPERATION.
----Cooperación empresarial entre países
     semiindutrializados. - 1984.
       (000202)

ARGENTINA--ECONOMIC DEVELOPMENT.
----Multinationals and maldevelopment. -
     1987.
       (000995)

ARGENTINA--ECONOMIC POLICY.
----Multinationals and maldevelopment. -
     1987.
       (000995)
----The new Argentina. - 1984.
       (001777)
----Transnacionalización y política
     económica en la Argentina. - 1985.
       (001115)

ARGENTINA--ECONOMIC STATISTICS.
----Las empresas transnacionales en la
     Argentina. - 1986.
       (001122)

ARGENTINA--ELECTRONICS INDUSTRY.
----La industria electrónica argentina :
apertura comercial y
desindustrialización. - 1987.
(000654)
----Telecomunicaciones. - 1987.
(000792)

ARGENTINA--EXPORTS.
----Internacionalización de empresas y
tecnología de origen argentino. - 1985.
(000301)

ARGENTINA--EXTERNAL DEBT.
----Los bancos transnacionales y el
endeudamiento externo en la Argentina. -
1987.
(000819)

ARGENTINA--FINANCIAL STATISTICS.
----Las empresas transnacionales en la
Argentina. - 1986.
(001122)

ARGENTINA--FOREIGN DIRECT INVESTMENT.
----Las empresas transnacionales en la
Argentina. - 1986.
(001122)
----Las empresas transnacionales y la
inversión extranjera directa en la
primera mitad de los años ochenta. -
1987.
(000194)

ARGENTINA--FOREIGN INVESTMENTS.
----The new Argentina. - 1984.
(001777)

ARGENTINA--FOREIGN LOANS.
----Los bancos transnacionales y el
endeudamiento externo en la Argentina. -
1987.
(000819)

ARGENTINA--FOREIGN TRADE.
----La industria electrónica argentina :
apertura comercial y
desindustrialización. - 1987.
(000654)

ARGENTINA--GRAINS.
----Empresas transnacionales en la industria
de alimentos. - 1983.
(000573)

ARGENTINA--IMPORTS.
----La industria electrónica argentina :
apertura comercial y
desindustrialización. - 1987.
(000654)

ARGENTINA--INDUSTRIAL CO-OPERATION.
----La cooperación empresarial
argentino-brasileña. - 1983.
(001097)
----Joint venture y sociedad. - 1984.
(001602)

ARGENTINA--INDUSTRIAL POLICY.
----La estructura de los mercados y la
desindustrialización en la Argentina
1976-1981. - 1983.
(001321)

ARGENTINA--INDUSTRIAL PRODUCTION.
----Las empresas transnacionales en la
Argentina. - 1986.
(001122)

ARGENTINA--INDUSTRIAL STATISTICS.
----Las empresas transnacionales en la
Argentina. - 1986.
(001122)

ARGENTINA--INDUSTRIAL TECHNOLOGY.
----Exportaciones de tecnología de Brasil y
Argentina. - 1986.
(001491)

ARGENTINA--INDUSTRIALIZATION.
----Exports of technology by newly
industrializing countries: Argentina. -
1984.
(001494)

ARGENTINA--INDUSTRY.
----La estructura de los mercados y la
desindustrialización en la Argentina
1976-1981. - 1983.
(001321)
----The new Argentina. - 1984.
(001777)

ARGENTINA--IRON AND STEEL INDUSTRY.
----La industria siderúrgica
latinoamericana. - 1984.
(000601)

ARGENTINA--JOINT VENTURES.
----Joint venture y sociedad. - 1984.
(001602)
----Joint ventures of public enterprises in
Argentina with other developing
countries. - 1984.
(001657)

ARGENTINA--MANUFACTURES.
----Internacionalización de empresas y
tecnología de origen argentino. - 1985.
(000301)

ARGENTINA--MANUFACTURING.
----Las empresas transnacionales en la
Argentina. - 1986.
(001122)

ARGENTINA--MANUFACTURING ENTERPRISES.
----Internacionalización de empresas y
tecnología de origen argentino. - 1985.
(000301)

ARGENTINA--MEAT INDUSTRY.
----Empresas transnacionales en la industria
de alimentos. - 1983.
(000573)

ARGENTINA--METALLURGICAL INDUSTRY.
----La industria siderúrgica
latinoamericana. - 1984.
(000601)

ARGENTINA--MINING LAW.
----Petroleum service contracts in
Argentina, Brazil and Colombia : issues
arising from their legal nature. - 1987.
(002422)

ARGENTINA--NATURAL RESOURCES.
----Petroleum service contracts in
Argentina, Brazil and Colombia : issues
arising from their legal nature. - 1987.
(002422)

ARGENTINA--PETROLEUM LAW.
----Petroleum service contracts in
Argentina, Brazil and Colombia : issues
arising from their legal nature. - 1987.
(002422)

ARGENTINA--PHARMACEUTICAL INDUSTRY.
----Transnational corporations in the
pharmaceutical industry of developing
countries. - 1984.
(000749)

ARGENTINA--POLITICAL CONDITIONS.
----The new Argentina. - 1984.
(001777)
----Transnacionalización y política
económica en la Argentina. - 1985.
(001115)

ARGENTINA--PUBLIC ENTERPRISES.
----Las empresas públicas en la Argentina. -
1984.
(001119)
----Joint ventures of public enterprises in
Argentina with other developing
countries. - 1984.
(001657)

ARGENTINA--PUBLIC SECTOR.
----Las empresas públicas en la Argentina. -
1984.
(001119)

ARGENTINA--STATISTICAL DATA.
----Las empresas transnacionales en la
Argentina. - 1986.
(001122)

ARGENTINA--TECHNOLOGICAL CHANGE.
----Telecomunicaciones. - 1987.
(000792)

ARGENTINA--TECHNOLOGICAL INNOVATIONS.
----Internacionalización de empresas y
tecnología de origen argentino. - 1985.
(000301)

ARGENTINA--TECHNOLOGY TRANSFER.
----La cooperación empresarial
argentino-brasileña. - 1983.
(001097)
----Exportaciones de tecnología de Brasil y
Argentina. - 1986.
(001491)
----Exports of technology by newly
industrializing countries: Argentina. -
1984.
(001494)

ARGENTINA--TELECOMMUNICATION INDUSTRY.
----Telecomunicaciones. - 1987.
(000792)

ARGENTINA--TRANSNATIONAL BANKS.
----Los bancos transnacionales y el
endeudamiento externo en la Argentina. -
1987.
(000819)

ARGENTINA--TRANSNATIONAL CORPORATIONS.
----Las empresas transnacionales en la
Argentina. - 1986.
(001122)
----Empresas transnacionales en la industria
de alimentos. - 1983.
(000573)
----Multinationals and maldevelopment. -
1987.
(000995)
----Multinationals from Argentina. - 1983.
(000340)
----Transnacionalización y política
económica en la Argentina. - 1985.
(001115)
----Transnational corporations in Argentina,
1976-1983. - 1986.
(001081)

ARMAMENTS.
----Mezhdunarodnyi voenno-promyshlennyi
biznes. - 1985.
(000993)
----Zloveshchii molokh. - 1987.
(000385) (000994)

ARMAMENTS--SOUTH AFRICA.
----Transnational corporations in South
Africa and Namibia : United Nations
public hearings. Volume 1, Reports of
the Panel of Eminent Persons and of the
Secretary-General. - 1986.
(001216)

ARMAMENTS--UNITED STATES.
----The nuclear weapons industry. - 1984.
(000659)

ARMS EMBARGO--SOUTH AFRICA.
----Activities of transnational corporations
in South Africa and Namibia and the
responsibilities of home countries with
respect to their operations in this
area. - 1986.
(001192)
----Transnational corporations in South
Africa and Namibia : United Nations
public hearings. Volume 1, Reports of
the Panel of Eminent Persons and of the
Secretary-General. - 1986.
(001216)
----Transnational corporations in South
Africa and Namibia. - 1986.
(001217)

ARMS INDUSTRY.
----Transnational corporations and
militarism. - 1985.
(000663)

ARMS INDUSTRY--PACIFIC OCEAN REGION.
----Technology transfer in the Pacific
Basin. - 1985.
(001413)

ARMS INDUSTRY--UNITED STATES.
----Stocking the arsenal. - 1985.
(000738)

ARRANGEMENT REGARDING INTERNATIONAL TRADE IN
TEXTILES (1973).
----The fourth multifibre arrangement and
the new legal regime for international
trade in textiles. - 1987.
(001401)
----International Colloquium on the Proposed
New Round of Multilateral Trade
Negotiations and Developing Countries :
proceedings and papers. - 1986.
(001365)

ARRANGEMENT REGARDING INTERNATIONAL TRADE IN
TEXTILES (1973). PROTOCOLS, ETC. 1981 DEC.
22.
----The fourth multifibre arrangement and
the new legal regime for international
trade in textiles. - 1987.
(001401)

ASAHI GLASS CO. (TOKYO).
----The process of internationalization at
Asahi Glass Co. - 1986.
(000360)

ASEAN.
----ASEAN economic co-operation. - 1985.
(001039)
----Aspects of ASEAN. - 1984.
(001406)
----Australian direct investment in the
ASEAN countries. - 1983.
(000110)
----Basic framework for ASEAN industrial
co-operation. - 1986.
(002149)
----Comparative accounting practices in
ASEAN. - 1984.
(002072)
----Foreign direct investment and
industrialization in ASEAN countries. -
1987.
(000144)
----Foreign direct investment in ASEAN. -
1987.
(000139)
----Industrial cooperation in regional
economic groupings among developing
countries and lessons for SAARC. - 1987.
(001009)
----Investitionsbedingungen in der
ASEAN-region. - 1986.
(001814)
----Japanese direct investment in ASEAN. -
1983.
(000171)
----The Japanese economic strategy. - 1983.
(000366)
----Kulturelle und wirtschaftliche
Interdependenz der ASEAN-Staaten. - 1986.
(001067)
----Legal development and the promotion of
intra-ASEAN trade and investment. - 1986.
(002307)
----Neue Wachstumsmärkte in Fernost. - 1983.
(001800)
----Small-and medium-scale industries in the
ASEAN countries. - 1984.
(001036)
----Subsidy to capital through tax
incentives in the ASEAN countries. -
1983.
(002300)

----Transnational corporations and the
electronics industries of ASEAN
economies. - 1987.
(000754)
----Wachstumsmarkt Südostasien. - 1984.
(001785)

ASIA--ADVERTISING AGENCIES.
----Madison Avenue in Asia. - 1984.
(000801)

ASIA--BANKS.
----Bankers handbook for Asia. - 1976-   .
(002621)

ASIA--BUSINESS.
----Critical issues for business in Asia. -
1984.
(001787)
----New business strategies for developing
Asia, 1983-1990. - 1984.
(000498)

ASIA--BUSINESS ENTERPRISES.
----Asia's 7500 largest companies. -
1985-   .
(002619)
----Major companies of the Far East. -
1983-   .
(002651)

ASIA--CAPITAL INVESTMENTS.
----Effects of foreign capital inflows on
developing countries of Asia. - 1986.
(001059)

ASIA--CAPITAL MOVEMENTS.
----The impact of foreign capital inflow on
investment and economic growth in
developing Asia. - 1985.
(001048)

ASIA--CORPORATE MERGERS.
----International law of take-overs and
mergers. - 1986.
(001572)

ASIA--CORPORATION LAW.
----International law of take-overs and
mergers. - 1986.
(001572)

ASIA--DEVELOPING COUNTRIES.
----Japanese direct foreign investment in
Asian developing countries. - 1983.
(000155)

ASIA--DEVELOPMENT FINANCE.
----The impact of foreign capital inflow on
investment and economic growth in
developing Asia. - 1985.
(001048)

ASIA--DIRECTORIES.
----Asia-Pacific/Africa-Middle East
petroleum directory. - 1984-   .
(000579) (002618)
----Asia's 7500 largest companies. -
1985-   .
(002619)
----Bankers handbook for Asia. - 1976-   .
(002621)

ASIA--DIRECTORIES (continued)
----Major companies of the Far East. -
    1983-   .
        (002651)

ASIA--ECONOMIC CONDITIONS.
----Asia yearbook. - 1973-   .
        (002699)

ASIA--ECONOMIC CO-OPERATION.
----Current problems of economic
    integration. - 1986.
        (001312)

ASIA--ECONOMIC DEVELOPMENT.
----Foreign trade and investment. - 1985.
        (001047)

ASIA--ECONOMIC GROWTH.
----Effects of foreign capital inflows on
    developing countries of Asia. - 1986.
        (001059)
----The impact of foreign capital inflow on
    investment and economic growth in
    developing Asia. - 1985.
        (001048)

ASIA--ECONOMIC INTEGRATION.
----Current problems of economic
    integration. - 1986.
        (001312)

ASIA--ECONOMIC POLICY.
----Export processing zones and economic
    development in Asia. - 1987.
        (002389)

ASIA--ELECTRONICS INDUSTRY.
----Kisvállatok Azsia fejlodo országainak
    elektronikai iparban. - 1987.
        (000630)

ASIA--FINANCIAL FLOWS.
----The impact of foreign capital inflow on
    investment and economic growth in
    developing Asia. - 1985.
        (001048)

ASIA--FINANCIAL INSTITUTIONS.
----Bankers handbook for Asia. - 1976-   .
        (002621)

ASIA--FOREIGN DIRECT INVESTMENT.
----The allocation of Japanese direct
    foreign investment and its evolution in
    Asia. - 1985.
        (000153)
----Effects of foreign capital inflows on
    developing countries of Asia. - 1986.
        (001059)
----Foreign trade and investment. - 1985.
        (001047)
----Japanese and American direct investment
    in Asia. - 1985.
        (000154)

ASIA--FOREIGN INVESTMENTS.
----Effects of foreign capital inflows on
    developing countries of Asia. - 1986.
        (001059)
----The impact of foreign capital inflow on
    investment and economic growth in
    developing Asia. - 1985.
        (001048)

----New business strategies for developing
    Asia, 1983-1990. - 1984.
        (000498)
----The special economic zones of China. -
    1985.
        (002392)

ASIA--FOREIGN TRADE.
----Export processing zones and economic
    development in Asia. - 1987.
        (002389)
----Foreign trade and investment. - 1985.
        (001047)

ASIA--FREE EXPORT ZONES.
----Economic and social impacts of export
    processing zones in Asia. - 1983.
        (002387)
----Export processing zones and economic
    development in Asia. - 1987.
        (002389)
----The special economic zones of China. -
    1985.
        (002392)
----TWARO (ITGLWF-ARO) Asian Seminar on Free
    Trade Zones, Tokyo, 6th-13th March 1983.
    - 1983.
        (002396)
----Wages, hours and working conditions in
    Asian free trade zones. - 1984.
        (001897)

ASIA--FREE TRADE AREAS.
----Export processing zones and economic
    development in Asia. - 1987.
        (002389)
----TWARO (ITGLWF-ARO) Asian Seminar on Free
    Trade Zones, Tokyo, 6th-13th March 1983.
    - 1983.
        (002396)

ASIA--HOURS OF WORK.
----Wages, hours and working conditions in
    Asian free trade zones. - 1984.
        (001897)

ASIA--INDUSTRIAL CO-OPERATION.
----Current problems of economic
    integration. - 1986.
        (001312)
----Joint ventures in Asien. - 1983.
        (001597)

ASIA--INDUSTRIAL POLLUTION.
----Asia's struggle to affirm wholeness of
    life : report of a consultation on TNC's
    in Asia. - 1985.
        (001935)

ASIA--INDUSTRY.
----Major companies of the Far East. -
    1983-   .
        (002651)

ASIA--INVESTMENTS.
----The impact of foreign capital inflow on
    investment and economic growth in
    developing Asia. - 1985.
        (001048)

ASIA--JOINT VENTURES.
----Joint ventures in Asien. - 1983.
        (001597)

ASIA--JOINT VENTURES (continued)
----New business strategies for developing
    Asia, 1983-1990. - 1984.
    (000498)

ASIA--MANAGEMENT.
----Critical issues for business in Asia. -
    1984.
    (001787)

ASIA--MARKETING.
----New business strategies for developing
    Asia, 1983-1990. - 1984.
    (000498)

ASIA--MULTINATIONAL INDUSTRIAL PROJECTS.
----Current problems of economic
    integration. - 1986.
    (001312)

ASIA--PETROLEUM INDUSTRY.
----Asia-Pacific/Africa-Middle East
    petroleum directory. - 1984-   .
    (000579) (002618)

ASIA--POLITICAL CONDITIONS.
----Asia yearbook. - 1973-   .
    (002699)

ASIA--PRIVATE ENTERPRISES.
----Private enterprise wins in Asia. - 1985.
    (001078)

ASIA--REGIONAL CO-OPERATION.
----Current problems of economic
    integration. - 1986.
    (001312)

ASIA--REGIONAL DEVELOPMENT BANKS.
----Current problems of economic
    integration. - 1986.
    (001312)

ASIA--RISK ASSESSMENT.
----Critical issues for business in Asia. -
    1984.
    (001787)
----New business strategies for developing
    Asia, 1983-1990. - 1984.
    (000498)

ASIA--SAVINGS.
----Effects of foreign capital inflows on
    developing countries of Asia. - 1986.
    (001059)

ASIA--TRANSNATIONAL CORPORATIONS.
----Asia's struggle to affirm wholeness of
    life : report of a consultation on TNC's
    in Asia. - 1985.
    (001935)
----Critical issues for business in Asia. -
    1984.
    (001787)
----Ekspansiia mezhdunarodnykh monopolii v
    razvivaiushchiesia strany Azii. - 1987.
    (001068)
----International law of take-overs and
    mergers. - 1986.
    (001572)
----Joint ventures in Asien. - 1983.
    (001597)
----Madison Avenue in Asia. - 1984.
    (000801)

----New business strategies for developing
    Asia, 1983-1990. - 1984.
    (000498)

ASIA--WAGE SURVEYS.
----Wages, hours and working conditions in
    Asian free trade zones. - 1984.
    (001897)

ASIA--WORKING CONDITIONS.
----TWARO (ITGLWF-ARO) Asian Seminar on Free
    Trade Zones, Tokyo, 6th-13th March 1983.
    - 1983.
    (002396)
----Wages, hours and working conditions in
    Asian free trade zones. - 1984.
    (001897)

ASIA AND THE PACIFIC--ACCOUNTING.
----Proceedings : Asia and Pacific
    Conference on Accounting Education for
    Development, Manila, Philippines,
    November 12-16, 1984. - 1985.
    (002060)

ASIA AND THE PACIFIC--ECONOMIC GROWTH.
----Foreign direct investment and economic
    growth in the Asian and Pacific region.
    - 1987.
    (000175)
----The great continental divide : Asian and
    Latin American countries in the world
    economic crisis. - 1986.
    (001299)

ASIA AND THE PACIFIC--ECONOMIC INTEGRATION.
----Japanese transnational corporations and
    the economic integration of Australian
    and the Asian-Pacific region. - 1983.
    (000323)

ASIA AND THE PACIFIC--ECONOMIC POLICY.
----The great continental divide : Asian and
    Latin American countries in the world
    economic crisis. - 1986.
    (001299)
----Transnational corporations and external
    financial flows of developing economies
    in Asia and the Pacific. - 1986.
    (000196)

ASIA AND THE PACIFIC--ECONOMIC STRUCTURE.
----The great continental divide : Asian and
    Latin American countries in the world
    economic crisis. - 1986.
    (001299)

ASIA AND THE PACIFIC--EDUCATION.
----Proceedings : Asia and Pacific
    Conference on Accounting Education for
    Development, Manila, Philippines,
    November 12-16, 1984. - 1985.
    (002060)

ASIA AND THE PACIFIC--EXTERNAL DEBT.
----The great continental divide : Asian and
    Latin American countries in the world
    economic crisis. - 1986.
    (001299)

ASIA AND THE PACIFIC--FINANCIAL FLOWS.
----Transnational corporations and external
financial flows of developing economies
in Asia and the Pacific. - 1986.
(000196)

ASIA AND THE PACIFIC--FINANCIAL STATISTICS.
----Transnational corporations and external
financial flows of developing economies
in Asia and the Pacific. - 1986.
(000196)

ASIA AND THE PACIFIC--FOREIGN DIRECT
INVESTMENT.
----Foreign direct investment and economic
growth in the Asian and Pacific region.
- 1987.
(000175)
----Technology transfer under alternative
arrangements with transnational
corporations. - 1987.
(001513)
----Transnational corporations and external
financial flows of developing economies
in Asia and the Pacific. - 1986.
(000196)

ASIA AND THE PACIFIC--HUMAN RESOURCES.
----Technology transfer under alternative
arrangements with transnational
corporations. - 1987.
(001513)

ASIA AND THE PACIFIC--LICENCE AGREEMENT.
----Technology transfer under alternative
arrangements with transnational
corporations. - 1987.
(001513)

ASIA AND THE PACIFIC--NATURAL GAS INDUSTRY.
----Natural gas clauses in petroleum
arrangements. - 1987.
(002452)

ASIA AND THE PACIFIC--STATISTICAL DATA.
----Transnational corporations and external
financial flows of developing economies
in Asia and the Pacific. - 1986.
(000196)

ASIA AND THE PACIFIC--TECHNOLOGY TRANSFER.
----Technology transfer under alternative
arrangements with transnational
corporations. - 1987.
(001513)

ASIA AND THE PACIFIC--TRANSNATIONAL
CORPORATIONS.
----Asia-Pacific TNC review. - 1984-   .
(001076)
----Japanese transnational corporations and
the economic integration of Australian
and the Asian-Pacific region. - 1983.
(000323)
----Natural gas clauses in petroleum
arrangements. - 1987.
(002452)
----Technology transfer under alternative
arrangements with transnational
corporations. - 1987.
(001513)

----Transnational corporations and external
financial flows of developing economies
in Asia and the Pacific. - 1986.
(000196)

ASIAN DEVELOPMENT BANK.
----Current problems of economic
integration. - 1986.
(001312)

ASIAN DOLLAR MARKET.
----Japanese offshore banking. - 1984.
(000933)

ASIAN LEASING ASSOCIATION.
----Analysis of equipment leasing contracts.
- 1984.
(002407)

ASIA-PACIFIC TRAINING WORKSHOP ON REGULATING
AND NEGOTIATING TECHNOLOGY TRANSFER THROUGH
TRANSNATIONAL CORPORATIONS (1985 : FUZHOU,
CHINA)--PARTICIPANTS.
----Proceedings of the SSTCC/UNCTC/ESCAP
Asia-Pacific Training Workshop on
Regulating and Negotiating Technology
Transfer through Transnational
Corporations, 14-25 October 1985,
Fuzhou, Fujian, China. - 1986.
(001405) (002169)

ASOCIACION LATINOAMERICANA DE INTEGRACION.
----Measures strengthening the negotiating
capacity of Governments in their
relations with transnational
corporations. - 1983.
(002461)
----El proceso de revisión de los mecanismos
financieros de la ALADI. - 1983.
(001248)
----Régimen jurídico de las inversiones
extranjeras en los países de la ALADI. -
1985.
(002262)
----Los regímenes de garantía a la inversión
extranjera y su aplicabilidad en los
países de la ALADI. - 1985.
(002126)

ASSEMBLY-LINE WORK--MEXICO.
----Restructuring industry offshore. - 1983.
(000692)

ASSEMBLY-LINE WORK--UNITED STATES.
----Restructuring industry offshore. - 1983.
(000692)

AUDIOVISUAL MATERIALS.
----Third World resource directory. - 1984.
(002719)

AUDITING.
----Auditing non-U.S. operations. - 1984.
(002113)
----Availability of financial statements. -
1987.
(002100)
----Comparative international auditing
standards. - 1985.
(002073)
----Glossary of terms for state auditors. -
1983.
(002711)

AUDITING (continued)
----International accounting and
     multinational enterprises. - 1985.
       (002058)
----International accounting and reporting.
     - 1985.
       (002076)
----International accounting and reporting
     issues, 1986 review. - 1986.
       (002117)
----International financial reporting and
     auditing. - 1984.
       (002088)
----Who audits the world. - 1983.
       (002061)

AUDITING--INDIA.
----Compendium of statements and standards.
     - 1986.
       (002074)

AUDITING--WESTERN EUROPE.
----The recent accounting and economic
     developments in Western Europe. - 1985.
       (002110)

AUSTRALIA--AFFILIATE CORPORATIONS.
----The Australian multinational -- parent
     and subsidiary relationships. - 1986.
       (000390)

AUSTRALIA--ANTITRUST LAW.
----Extraterritorial effects of United
     States commercial and antitrust
     legislation. - 1983.
       (002352)

AUSTRALIA--AUSTRALIAN ABORIGINES.
----Aborigines and mining companies in
     Northern Australia. - 1983.
       (001874)

AUSTRALIA--BUSINESS ENTERPRISES.
----Kompass Australia. - 1970-
       (002649)

AUSTRALIA--CAPITAL MARKETS.
----Financial institutions and markets in
     the Southwest Pacific. - 1985.
       (000854)

AUSTRALIA--COMMERCIAL LAW.
----Extraterritorial effects of United
     States commercial and antitrust
     legislation. - 1983.
       (002352)

AUSTRALIA--COMMODITIES.
----Kompass Australia. - 1970-
       (002649)

AUSTRALIA--COMPARATIVE ANALYSIS.
----Foreign investment control in the mining
     sector. - 1983.
       (000577)

AUSTRALIA--CONCILIATION.
----Mediation, conciliation and arbitration
     : an international comparison of
     Australia, Great Britain and the United
     States. - 1987.
       (002476)

AUSTRALIA--CORPORATE MERGERS.
----International law of take-overs and
     mergers. - 1986.
       (001572)
----Private agreements for takeovers of
     public companies. - 1984.
       (001626)

AUSTRALIA--CORPORATION LAW.
----International law of take-overs and
     mergers. - 1986.
       (001572)

AUSTRALIA--DIRECTORIES.
----Kompass Australia. - 1970-
       (002649)

AUSTRALIA--DISPUTE SETTLEMENT.
----Dispute resolution in the Asia/Pacific
     region. - 1987.
       (002556)

AUSTRALIA--DOMESTIC TRADE.
----Multinational enterprise behaviour and
     domestic industry adjustment under
     import threat. - 1986.
       (000518)

AUSTRALIA--ECONOMIC DEPENDENCE.
----Beyond dependence. - 1986.
       (000640)

AUSTRALIA--ECONOMIC INTEGRATION.
----Japanese transnational corporations and
     the economic integration of Australian
     and the Asian-Pacific region. - 1983.
       (000323)

AUSTRALIA--FINANCIAL INSTITUTIONS.
----Financial institutions and markets in
     the Southwest Pacific. - 1985.
       (000854)

AUSTRALIA--FOREIGN DIRECT INVESTMENT.
----Australia deregulated : new freedoms for
     multinational investment. - 1987.
       (001797)
----Australian direct investment abroad. -
     1984.
       (000108)
----Australian direct investment in New
     Zealand. - 1983.
       (000109)
----Australian direct investment in the
     ASEAN countries. - 1983.
       (000110)
----The Australian multinational -- parent
     and subsidiary relationships. - 1986.
       (000390)
----Capital xenophobia. - 1984.
       (002228)
----Fiji : client State of Australasia? -
     1984.
       (001046) (002358)
----Foreign investment control in the mining
     sector. - 1983.
       (000577)
----Foreign investment in Australia,
     1960-1981. - 1983.
       (000141)
----Foreign investment law in Australia. -
     1985.
       (002210)

AUSTRALIA--FOREIGN DIRECT INVESTMENT
(continued)
----New Zealand business. - 1985.
    (000352)
----Some aspects of Japanese manufacturing
    investment in Australia. - 1984.
    (001044)

AUSTRALIA--FOREIGN INVESTMENTS.
----Australia's foreign investment policy. -
    198?-   .
    (002170)
----Investment protection agreements. - 1987.
    (002135)
----United States investment in Australia. -
    1987.
    (002180)

AUSTRALIA--HOST COUNTRY RELATIONS.
----MNCs and the Australian government: some
    emerging policy issues. - 1983.
    (002289)

AUSTRALIA--HOTEL INDUSTRY.
----Characteristics of major industries
    supplying tourist services in Australia.
    - 1983.
    (000824)

AUSTRALIA--IMPORT RESTRICTIONS.
----Multinational enterprise behaviour and
    domestic industry adjustment under
    import threat. - 1986.
    (000518)

AUSTRALIA--INDUSTRIAL ARBITRATION.
----Mediation, conciliation and arbitration
    : an international comparison of
    Australia, Great Britain and the United
    States. - 1987.
    (002476)

AUSTRALIA--INDUSTRIAL DEVELOPMENT.
----The public interest IR & D program. -
    1985.
    (001485)

AUSTRALIA--INDUSTRIAL LOCATION.
----The geography of Australian corporate
    power. - 1984.
    (001166)

AUSTRALIA--INDUSTRIAL RESEARCH.
----The public interest IR & D program. -
    1985.
    (001485)

AUSTRALIA--INDUSTRY.
----Australia deregulated : new freedoms for
    multinational investment. - 1987.
    (001797)
----Kompass Australia. - 1970-   .
    (002649)

AUSTRALIA--INVESTMENT POLICY.
----Australia deregulated : new freedoms for
    multinational investment. - 1987.
    (001797)
----Australia's foreign investment policy. -
    198?-   .
    (002170)

----Capital xenophobia. - 1984.
    (002228)
----Foreign investment control in the mining
    sector. - 1983.
    (000577)
----Foreign investment in Australia,
    1960-1981. - 1983.
    (000141)
----MNCs and the Australian government: some
    emerging policy issues. - 1983.
    (002289)
----New Zealand business. - 1985.
    (000352)
----United States investment in Australia. -
    1987.
    (002180)

AUSTRALIA--INVESTMENT PROMOTION.
----The effectiveness of investment
    incentives. - 1985.
    (002304)

AUSTRALIA--INVESTMENTS.
----The effectiveness of investment
    incentives. - 1985.
    (002304)

AUSTRALIA--JOINT VENTURES.
----The mineral and petroleum joint venture
    in Australia. - 1986.
    (000588)

AUSTRALIA--LABOUR DISPUTES.
----Mediation, conciliation and arbitration
    : an international comparison of
    Australia, Great Britain and the United
    States. - 1987.
    (002476)

AUSTRALIA--LAND RIGHTS.
----Indigenous resource rights and mining
    companies in North America and
    Australia. - 1986.
    (000616)

AUSTRALIA--LAND TENURE.
----Aborigines and mining companies in
    Northern Australia. - 1983.
    (001874)

AUSTRALIA--LAWS AND REGULATIONS.
----Foreign investment law in Australia. -
    1985.
    (002210)
----National legislation and regulations
    relating to transnational corporations.
    Volume 3. - 1983.
    (002252)
----New Zealand business. - 1985.
    (000352)
----United States investment in Australia. -
    1987.
    (002180)

AUSTRALIA--MANUFACTURING.
----Some aspects of Japanese manufacturing
    investment in Australia. - 1984.
    (001044)

AUSTRALIA--MEDIATION.
----Mediation, conciliation and arbitration
    : an international comparison of
    Australia, Great Britain and the United
    States. - 1987.
      (002476)

AUSTRALIA--MINERAL INDUSTRY.
----Beyond dependence. - 1986.
      (000640)
----Foreign investment control in the mining
    sector. - 1983.
      (000577)
----The mineral and petroleum joint venture
    in Australia. - 1986.
      (000588)
----Mineral industries of Australia, Canada,
    and Oceania. - 1985.
      (000603)

AUSTRALIA--MINERAL RESOURCES.
----Indigenous resource rights and mining
    companies in North America and
    Australia. - 1986.
      (000616)

AUSTRALIA--MINING INDUSTRY.
----Aborigines and mining companies in
    Northern Australia. - 1983.
      (001874)
----Beyond dependence. - 1986.
      (000640)
----Indigenous resource rights and mining
    companies in North America and
    Australia. - 1986.
      (000616)

AUSTRALIA--PASSENGER TRANSPORT.
----Characteristics of major industries
    supplying tourist services in Australia.
    - 1983.
      (000824)

AUSTRALIA--PETROLEUM INDUSTRY.
----The mineral and petroleum joint venture
    in Australia. - 1986.
      (000588)

AUSTRALIA--PROGRAMME EVALUATION.
----The public interest IR & D program. -
    1985.
      (001485)

AUSTRALIA--PUBLIC ENTERPRISES.
----Private agreements for takeovers of
    public companies. - 1984.
      (001626)

AUSTRALIA--RELOCATION OF INDUSTRY.
----The geography of Australian corporate
    power. - 1984.
      (001166)

AUSTRALIA--STATISTICAL DATA.
----Australian direct investment in New
    Zealand. - 1983.
      (000109)
----Australian direct investment in the
    ASEAN countries. - 1983.
      (000110)
----Characteristics of major industries
    supplying tourist services in Australia.
    - 1983.
      (000824)

AUSTRALIA--TAX INCENTIVES.
----The effectiveness of investment
    incentives. - 1985.
      (002304)

AUSTRALIA--TAXATION.
----New Zealand business. - 1985.
      (000352)

AUSTRALIA--TOURISM.
----Characteristics of major industries
    supplying tourist services in Australia.
    - 1983.
      (000824)

AUSTRALIA--TRANSNATIONAL CORPORATIONS.
----Aborigines and mining companies in
    Northern Australia. - 1983.
      (001874)
----Australia deregulated : new freedoms for
    multinational investment. - 1987.
      (001797)
----The Australian multinational -- parent
    and subsidiary relationships. - 1986.
      (000390)
----Beyond dependence. - 1986.
      (000640)
----Fiji : client State of Australasia? -
    1984.
      (001046) (002358)
----Foreign investment in Australia,
    1960-1981. - 1983.
      (000141)
----The geography of Australian corporate
    power. - 1984.
      (001166)
----Indigenous resource rights and mining
    companies in North America and
    Australia. - 1986.
      (000616)
----International law of take-overs and
    mergers. - 1986.
      (001572)
----Japanese transnational corporations and
    the economic integration of Australian
    and the Asian-Pacific region. - 1983.
      (000323)
----MNCs and the Australian government: some
    emerging policy issues. - 1983.
      (002289)
----Multinational enterprise behaviour and
    domestic industry adjustment under
    import threat. - 1986.
      (000518)
----National legislation and regulations
    relating to transnational corporations.
    Volume 3. - 1983.
      (002252)

AUSTRALIA--TRAVEL AGENTS.
----Characteristics of major industries
    supplying tourist services in Australia.
    - 1983.
      (000824)

AUSTRALIA--URANIUM INDUSTRY.
----Extraterritorial effects of United
    States commercial and antitrust
    legislation. - 1983.
      (002352)

AUSTRALIA. FOREIGN INVESTMENT REVIEW BOARD.
----Foreign investment in Australia,
    1960-1981. - 1983.
      (000141)

AUSTRALIAN ABORIGINES.
----Indigenous resource rights and mining
    companies in North America and
    Australia. - 1986.
      (000616)

AUSTRALIAN ABORIGINES--AUSTRALIA.
----Aborigines and mining companies in
    Northern Australia. - 1983.
      (001874)

AUSTRIA--DEVELOPING COUNTRIES.
----Investitionsschutzabkommen. - 1986.
      (002041)

AUSTRIA--ECONOMIC AGREEMENTS.
----Investitionsschutzabkommen. - 1986.
      (002041)

AUSTRIA--FOREIGN INVESTMENTS.
----Investitionsschutzabkommen. - 1986.
      (002041)

AUTOMATION.
----Automation and the worldwide
    restructuring of the electronics
    industry: strategic implications for
    developing countries. - 1985.
      (000683)
----Foreign investment and the restructuring
    of technology. - 1987.
      (000702)
----Microelectronics-based automation
    technologies and development. - 1985.
      (000753)
----Recent developments in operations and
    behaviour of transnational corporations.
    - 1987.
      (000103)
----Technological change. - 1985.
      (001499)

AUTOMATION--CHINA.
----Microelectronics-based automation
    technologies and development. - 1985.
      (000753)

AUTOMATION--CUBA.
----Microelectronics-based automation
    technologies and development. - 1985.
      (000753)

AUTOMATION--GERMAN DEMOCRATIC REPUBLIC.
----Microelectronics-based automation
    technologies and development. - 1985.
      (000753)

AUTOMATION--JAPAN.
----Microelectronics-based automation
    technologies and development. - 1985.
      (000753)
----Postindustrial manufacturing. - 1986.
      (000698)

AUTOMATION--SWEDEN.
----Microelectronics-based automation
    technologies and development. - 1985.
      (000753)

AUTOMATION--UNITED STATES.
----A competitive assessment of the U.S.
    manufacturing automation equipment
    industries. - 1984.
      (000756)
----Postindustrial manufacturing. - 1986.
      (000698)

AUTOMOBILE INDUSTRY.
----Creating the GM-Toyota joint venture: a
    case in complex negotiation. - 1987.
      (001656)
----Foreign investment and the restructuring
    of technology. - 1987.
      (000702)
----Latinskaja Amerika. - 1984.
      (001089)
----La notion de produit-système et la
    décomposition internationale des
    processus productifs dans l'industrie
    automobile. (With English summary.). -
    1984.
      (000687)
----Prospects for automotive transnationals
    in the Third World. - 1983.
      (000708)
----Techno-economic aspects of the
    international division of labour in the
    automotive industry. - 1983.
      (000752)
----Transnational corporations in the
    international auto industry. - 1983.
      (000747)

AUTOMOBILE INDUSTRY--FRANCE.
----Labour, production and the state :
    decentralization of the French
    automobile industry. - 1987.
      (000724)

AUTOMOBILE INDUSTRY--INDIA.
----Technology transfer under alternative
    arrangements with transnational
    corporations. - 1987.
      (001513)

AUTOMOBILE INDUSTRY--JAPAN.
----America's new no. 4 automaker -- Honda.
    - 1985.
      (000294)
----Automotive parts industry and the U.S.
    aftermarket for Japanese cars and light
    trucks. - 1985.
      (000759)
----The Japanese automobile industry. - 1985.
      (000278)

AUTOMOBILE INDUSTRY--LATIN AMERICA.
----Transnational corporations and the Latin
    American automobile industry. - 1987.
      (000701)

AUTOMOBILE INDUSTRY--MEXICO.
----Transnational corporations versus the
    state. - 1985.
      (000657)

AUTOMOBILE INDUSTRY--NIGERIA.
----Vertical corporate linkages. - 1986.
      (000709)

AUTOMOBILE INDUSTRY--REPUBLIC OF KOREA.
----Technology transfer under alternative
arrangements with transnational
corporations. - 1987.
(001513)

AUTOMOBILE INDUSTRY--THAILAND.
----Technology acquisition under alternative
arrangements with transnational
corporations. - 1987.
(001512)
----Technology transfer under alternative
arrangements with transnational
corporations. - 1987.
(001513)

AUTOMOBILE INDUSTRY--UNITED STATES.
----America's new no. 4 automaker -- Honda.
- 1985.
(000294)
----Automotive parts industry and the U.S.
aftermarket for Japanese cars and light
trucks. - 1985.
(000759)
----Blind intersection? policy and the
automobile industry. - 1987.
(000660)
----Industrial renaissance : producing a
competitive future for America. - 1983.
(000300)
----Oil industry mergers. - 1984.
(001652)

AUTOMOBILE INDUSTY.
----Les investissements des multinationales
de l'automobile dans le Tiers-Monde.
(With English summary.). - 1984.
(000729)

BAHLSEN (FIRM : HANNOVER, FEDERAL REPUBLIC
OF GERMANY).
----Importance et implantations comparées
des quatre plus grands biscuitiers
mondiaux, Nabisco Brands, United
Biscuits, Générale Biscuit, Bahlsen. -
1984.
(000273)

BAKERY PRODUCTS.
----Importance et implantations comparées
des quatre plus grands biscuitiers
mondiaux, Nabisco Brands, United
Biscuits, Générale Biscuit, Bahlsen. -
1984.
(000273)

BALANCE OF PAYMENTS.
----Balance of payments statistics. - 1983.
(000111)
----Debt-equity swaps and the heavily
indebted countries. - 1987.
(000263)
----Les désajustements mondiaux de balances
des paiements. - 1984.
(001284)
----La dette du Tiers monde. - 1984.
(000223)
----Dette du Tiers monde. - 1984.
(000260)
----International capital movements and
developing countries. - 1985.
(001282)
----International debt quagmire. - 1983.
(000262)

----The international payments crisis and
the development of East-West trade. -
1977.
(000242)
----Multinational corporation and national
regulation: an economic audit. - 1987.
(002270)
----Les services : enjeux pour l'emploi et
le commerce international. - 1986.
(000960)
----Die Stabilisierungspolitik des
Internationalen Währungsfonds. - 1986.
(001234)

BALANCE OF PAYMENTS--EASTERN EUROPE.
----Les mécanismes de l'endettement des pays
de l'Europe de l'Est envers les
économies de marché. - 1984.
(000221)

BALANCE OF PAYMENTS--GERMANY, FEDERAL
REPUBLIC OF.
----Technological balance of payments and
international competitiveness. - 1983.
(001442)

BALANCE OF PAYMENTS--JAPAN.
----Japan as capital exporter and the world
economy. - 1985.
(000384)
----Japon : du commerce à la finance. - 1987.
(000374)

BALANCE OF PAYMENTS--KUWAIT.
----Impact of the operations of
transnational corporations on
development in Kuwait. - 1987.
(001143)

BALANCE OF PAYMENTS--LATIN AMERICA.
----Banco de datos sobre inversión
extranjera directa en América Latina y
el Caribe : información de los países
receptores y de organismos regionales y
subregionales, t. 2. - 1987.
(000193)
----Las empresas transnacionales y la
inversión extranjera directa en la
primera mitad de los años ochenta. -
1987.
(000194)

BALANCE OF PAYMENTS--OMAN.
----Impact of the operations of
transnational corporations on
development in the Sultanate of Oman. -
1988.
(001144)

BALANCE OF PAYMENTS--PERU.
----Transnational banks and the external
finance of Latin America : the
experience of Peru. - 1983.
(000840)
----Transnational banks and the external
finance of Latin America : the
experience of Peru. - 1985.
(000975)

BALANCE OF PAYMENTS--UNITED KINGDOM.
----Assessing the consequences of overseas
investment. - 1986.
(001296)

BALANCE OF PAYMENTS--UNITED STATES.
----The external deficit. - 1987.
    (000216)

BALANCE OF PAYMENTS--WESTERN ASIA.
----Trade in services : growth and balance
    of payments implications for countries
    of Western Asia. - 1987.
    (000968)

BALANCE OF TRADE.
----East-West trade and CMEA indebtedness in
    the seventies and eighties. - 1979.
    (000209)
----L'internazionalizzazione dell'industria.
    - 1984.
    (000080)

BALANCE OF TRADE--UNITED STATES.
----International countertrade. - 1984.
    (001396)

BALL BEARINGS--UNITED STATES.
----A competitive assessment of the U.S.
    ball and roller bearings industry. -
    1985.
    (000760)

BANANAS--CENTRAL AMERICA.
----Las transnacionales del banano en
    Centroamérica. - 1983.
    (000564)

BANGLADESH--CAPITAL MOVEMENTS.
----Domestic saving and foreign capital
    inflow : the case of Bangladesh. - 1986.
    (001034)

BANGLADESH--ECONOMIC POLICY.
----Courting private foreign investment :
    the Bangladesh experience. - 1986.
    (001854)

BANGLADESH--FOREIGN INVESTMENTS.
----Courting private foreign investment :
    the Bangladesh experience. - 1986.
    (001854)
----Domestic saving and foreign capital
    inflow : the case of Bangladesh. - 1986.
    (001034)

BANGLADESH--FOREIGN TRADE.
----Trade and investment possibilities in
    Bangladesh, Nepal and Sri Lanka. - 1983.
    (001840)

BANGLADESH--INVESTMENT POLICY.
----Trade and investment possibilities in
    Bangladesh, Nepal and Sri Lanka. - 1983.
    (001840)

BANGLADESH--SAVINGS.
----Domestic saving and foreign capital
    inflow : the case of Bangladesh. - 1986.
    (001034)

BANGLADESH--TRADE POLICY.
----Trade and investment possibilities in
    Bangladesh, Nepal and Sri Lanka. - 1983.
    (001840)

BANK LOANS.
----Changes in the international financial
    market and implications for
    transnational banks, transnational
    corporations and developing countries. -
    1986.
    (000976)
----The growth of international bank
    lending, 1972-1982: concepts,
    measurement and causes. - 1983.
    (000222)
----Issues in negotiating international loan
    agreements with transnational banks. -
    1983.
    (002459)
----Market competition, conflict and
    collusion. - 1987.
    (001680)

BANK LOANS--LATIN AMERICA.
----The debt crisis and bank lending to
    subsidiaries of transnational
    corporations in Latin America. - 1984.
    (000219)
----Foreign direct investment in Latin
    America. - 1986.
    (000190)

BANK LOANS--PERU.
----Transnational banks and the external
    finance of Latin America : the
    experience of Peru. - 1983.
    (000840)
----Transnational banks and the external
    finance of Latin America : the
    experience of Peru. - 1985.
    (000975)

BANK LOANS--SOUTH AFRICA.
----Activities of transnational corporations
    in South Africa and Namibia and the
    responsibilities of home countries with
    respect to their operations in this
    area. - 1986.
    (001192)
----Foreign investment in South Africa and
    Namibia. - 1984.
    (001198) (002641)
----U.S. and Canadian investment in South
    Africa and Namibia. - 1986.
    (001212) (002671) (002672)

BANK LOANS--UNITED STATES.
----Foreign investment in South Africa and
    Namibia. - 1984.
    (001198) (002641)
----Rehearing granted : Allied Bank
    International v. Banco Agricola Credito
    de Cartago and the current international
    debt crisis. - 1984.
    (000233)

BANK SECRECY.
----International co-operation in tax
    matters : guidelines for international
    co-operation against the evasion and
    avoidance of taxes (with special
    reference to taxes on income, profits,
    capital and capital gains). - 1984.
    (001724)

BANKERS' COMMERCIAL CREDITS.
----UNCITRAL, the United Nations Commission
    on International Trade Law. - 1986.
    (002155)

BANKING.
----Banking deregulation and the new
    competition in financial services. -
    1984.
    (000833)
----International co-operation in tax
    matters : guidelines for international
    co-operation against the evasion and
    avoidance of taxes (with special
    reference to taxes on income, profits,
    capital and capital gains). - 1984.
    (001724)
----The multinational bank. - 1987.
    (000950)

BANKING--BRAZIL.
----La internacionalización financiera en
    Brasil. - 1983.
    (001082)

BANKING--CHINA.
----The People's Republic of China. - 1986.
    (001841)

BANKING--GULF STATES.
----A historical perspective of U.S.-GCC
    economic and financial interdependence.
    - 1987.
    (000143)

BANKING--JAPAN.
----Japanese offshore banking. - 1984.
    (000933)

BANKING--MEXICO.
----La internacionalización financiera
    mexicana. - 1983.
    (001288)

BANKING--NAMIBIA.
----Transnational corporations in South
    Africa and Namibia. - 1986.
    (001217)

BANKING--OMAN.
----Impact of the operations of
    transnational corporations on
    development in the Sultanate of Oman. -
    1988.
    (001144)

BANKING--PERU.
----Transnational banks and the external
    finance of Latin America : the
    experience of Peru. - 1985.
    (000975)

BANKING--SOUTH AFRICA.
----Transnational corporations in South
    Africa and Namibia. - 1986.
    (001217)

BANKING--UNITED KINGDOM.
----Tax havens and offshore finance. - 1983.
    (001729)

BANKING--UNITED STATES.
----Banking deregulation and the new
    competition in financial services. -
    1984.
    (000833)
----A historical perspective of U.S.-GCC
    economic and financial interdependence.
    - 1987.
    (000143)

BANKING LAW.
----Banking deregulation and the new
    competition in financial services. -
    1984.
    (000833)
----International trade in services. - 1984.
    (000876)
----Kin'yu torihiki to kokusai sosho. - 1983.
    (002525)

BANKING LAW--AFRICA.
----The role of transnational banks and
    financial institutions in Africa's
    development process. - 1986.
    (000935)

BANKING LAW--HONG KONG.
----A survey of banking laws and policies in
    Hong Kong and Singapore. - 1986.
    (001829)

BANKING LAW--SINGAPORE.
----A survey of banking laws and policies in
    Hong Kong and Singapore. - 1986.
    (001829)

BANKING LAW--UNITED STATES.
----Banking deregulation and the new
    competition in financial services. -
    1984.
    (000833)

BANKING SYSTEMS--CHINA.
----Ouverture et dynamique interne du
    capital en Chine. - 1987.
    (001064)

BANKING SYSTEMS--MEXICO.
----Doing business in Mexico. - 1984.
    (001791)

BANKRUPTCY.
----Die Haftungsproblematik bei Konkurs
    einer Gesellschaft innerhalb eines
    transnationalen Unternehmens. - 1984.
    (002233)
----The international void in the law of
    multinational bankruptcies. - 1987.
    (002214)

BANKRUPTCY--GERMANY, FEDERAL REPUBLIC OF.
----Die Haftungsproblematik bei Konkurs
    einer Gesellschaft innerhalb eines
    transnationalen Unternehmens. - 1984.
    (002233)

BANKRUPTCY--UNITED STATES.
----Structuring natural resources
    development agreements between foreign
    governments and United States companies
    to prevent transfer of rights under the
    agreement should the company enter
    bankruptcy. - 1984.
    (002411)

BANKS.
----Determinants of multinational banks. -
    1986.
    (000825)
----The multinational bank. - 1987.
    (000950)
----Size, growth, and transnationality among
    the world's largest banks. - 1983.
    (000969)

BANKS--ASIA.
----Bankers handbook for Asia. - 1976-   .
    (002621)

BANKS--FRANCE.
----Nationalisation of the banks in France.
    - 1983.
    (001568)
----Die Nationalisierungen in Frankreich
    1981/82. - 1983.
    (002337)

BANKS--LIBERIA.
----The impact of the transnational
    corporations in the banking and other
    financial institutions on the economy of
    Liberia. - 1986.
    (000873)

BANKS--MEXICO.
----Expropriation and aftermath : the
    prospects for foreign enterprise in the
    Mexico of Miguel de la Madrid. - 1983.
    (002328)
----La nacionalización de la banca. - 1983.
    (001529)

BANKS--TURKEY.
----Turkish banking and finance : the
    markets mature. - 1986.
    (000970)

BANKS--UNITED KINGDOM.
----The bankers' almanac and year book. -
    1886-   .
    (002620)

BANKS--UNITED STATES.
----American banks in the international
    interbank market. - 1983.
    (000829)
----Foreign government and foreign investor
    control of U.S. banks. - 1983.
    (001654)
----Foreign ownership of U.S. banks: trends
    and effects. - 1983.
    (001591)

BANTUSTANS.
----Lagging behind the bantustans. - 1985.
    (001223)

BARBADOS--TOURISM.
----Reassessing Third World tourism. - 1984.
    (000802)

BARTER.
----Countertrade contracts in international
    business. - 1986.
    (002429)
----Guide to countertrade and international
    barter. - 1985.
    (001368)

----Negotiating and drafting contracts in
    international barter and countertrade
    transactions. - 1984.
    (002428)

BAUXITE--GOVE PENINSULA (AUSTRALIA).
----The history and contractual arrangements
    of the Gove bauxite/alumina project in
    the Northern Territory of Australia. -
    1985.
    (000596)

BAUXITE--GUINEA.
----Les enjeux de la bauxite. - 1983.
    (000585)

BAUXITE--NORTHERN TERRITORY (AUSTRALIA).
----The history and contractual arrangements
    of the Gove bauxite/alumina project in
    the Northern Territory of Australia. -
    1985.
    (000596)

BAUXITE INDUSTRY.
----The aluminum multinationals and the
    bauxite cartel. - 1987.
    (000599)

BAUXITE INDUSTRY--CARIBBEAN REGION.
----Multinational corporations and regional
    revenue retention in a vertically
    integrated industry: bauxite/aluminium
    in the Caribbean. - 1983.
    (000582)

BEECHAM GROUP (BRENTFORD, MIDDLESEX).
----From national to multinational
    enterprise. - 1983.
    (000277)

BELGIUM--DECISION-MAKING.
----Employment decision-making in
    multinational enterprises. - 1984.
    (001888)

BELGIUM--DEVELOPMENT ASSISTANCE.
----Infratechnologies, technologies de
    pointe, investissements dans et pour les
    pays en développement. - 1985.
    (001444)

BELGIUM--DIVESTMENT.
----Recent trends in foreign direct
    investment and disinvestment in Belgium.
    - 1985.
    (000185)

BELGIUM--ECONOMETRIC MODELS.
----Location and investment decisions by
    multinational enterprises. - 1984.
    (000552)

BELGIUM--ECONOMIC CONDITIONS.
----Note sur la transnationalisation de
    l'économie belge. - 1985.
    (000123)

BELGIUM--EMPLOYMENT POLICY.
----Employment decision-making in
    multinational enterprises. - 1984.
    (001888)

BELGIUM--FOREIGN DIRECT INVESTMENT.
----Recent trends in foreign direct
    investment and disinvestment in Belgium.
    - 1985.
        (000185)

BELGIUM--INDUSTRIAL SECTOR.
----La structure professionnelle des
    secteurs secondaire et tertiaire. - 1987.
        (000823)

BELGIUM--PERSONNEL MANAGEMENT.
----Employment decision-making in
    multinational enterprises. - 1984.
        (001888)

BELGIUM--PROFESSIONAL WORKERS.
----La structure professionnelle des
    secteurs secondaire et tertiaire. - 1987.
        (000823)

BELGIUM--SERVICE INDUSTRIES.
----La structure professionnelle des
    secteurs secondaire et tertiaire. - 1987.
        (000823)

BELGIUM--TRANSNATIONAL CORPORATIONS.
----Employment decision-making in
    multinational enterprises. - 1984.
        (001888)
----European headquarters of American
    multinational enterprises in Brussels
    and Belgium. - 1984.
        (000381)
----Location and investment decisions by
    multinational enterprises. - 1984.
        (000552)
----Note sur la transnationalisation de
    l'économie belge. - 1985.
        (000123)

BETA LTD.(ONTARIO).
----Beyond borders. - 1986.
        (000280)

BHOPAL (INDIA)--CHEMICAL INDUSTRY.
----The lessons of Bhopal. - 1985.
        (001933)
----Mass disasters and multinational
    liability : the Bhopal case. - 1986.
        (001936)

BHOPAL (INDIA)--EMPLOYERS' LIABILITY
INSURANCE.
----Mass disasters and multinational
    liability : the Bhopal case. - 1986.
        (001936)

BHOPAL (INDIA)--ENVIRONMENTAL DEGRADATION.
----Mass disasters and multinational
    liability : the Bhopal case. - 1986.
        (001936)

BHOPAL (INDIA)--ENVIRONMENTAL IMPACT
ASSESSMENT.
----Mass disasters and multinational
    liability : the Bhopal case. - 1986.
        (001936)

BHOPAL (INDIA)--INDUSTRIAL ACCIDENTS.
----For whom the bell tolls in the aftermath
    of the Bhopal tragedy. - 1987.
        (001950)

----The lessons of Bhopal. - 1985.
        (001933)
----Mass disasters and multinational
    liability : the Bhopal case. - 1986.
        (001936)

BHOPAL (INDIA)--LIABILITY INSURANCE.
----Mass disasters and multinational
    liability : the Bhopal case. - 1986.
        (001936)

BHOPAL (INDIA)--MAN-MADE DISASTERS.
----Asia's struggle to affirm wholeness of
    life : report of a consultation on TNC's
    in Asia. - 1985.
        (001935)
----For whom the bell tolls in the aftermath
    of the Bhopal tragedy. - 1987.
        (001950)

BHOPAL (INDIA)--MULTINATIONAL INDUSTRIAL
PROJECTS.
----Mass disasters and multinational
    liability : the Bhopal case. - 1986.
        (001936)

BHOPAL (INDIA)--TRANSNATIONAL CORPORATIONS.
----The lessons of Bhopal. - 1985.
        (001933)

BIBLIOGRAPHIES.
----Bibliografía sobre inversiones
    extranjeras y empresas multinacionales.
    - 1986.
        (002681)
----Bibliographic guide to studies on the
    status of women. - 1983.
        (002682)
----Bibliography of appropriate technology
    information for developing countries. -
    1983.
        (002683)
----Business information sources. - 1985.
        (002701)
----The economic theory of the multinational
    enterprise. - 1985.
        (000009)
----The export of hazard. - 1985.
        (001941)
----Financial institutions and markets in
    the Southwest Pacific. - 1985.
        (000854)
----Foreign direct investment and the
    multinational enterprise. - 1988.
        (002696)
----Foreign investment in the American and
    Canadian West, 1870-1914. - 1986.
        (002690)
----Industrial structure and policy in less
    developed countries. - 1984.
        (001322)
----The international accounting and tax
    researches' publication guide. - 1982.
        (002066)
----International business reference
    sources. - 1983.
        (002691)
----International financial markets and
    capital movements. - 1985.
        (001267)
----The literature of international business
    finance. - 1984.
        (002687)

BIBLIOGRAPHIES (continued)
----Managing cultural differences. - 1983.
     (001871)
----The military origins of
     industrialisation and international
     trade rivalry. - 1984.
     (001335)
----Multilateral negotiations and
     third-party roles. - 1986.
     (002689)
----Multi-national corporations and Third
     World development. - 1984.
     (000074)
----Political risk assessment. - 1985.
     (001842) (002659)
----Sales publications of the United Nations
     Centre on Transnational Corporations,
     1973-1987. - 1987.
     (002693)
----Service-led growth. - 1986.
     (000931)
----Third World resource directory. - 1984.
     (002719)
----Trade [and] structural change. - 1984.
     (001391)
----Transnational corporations and uneven
     development : the internationalization
     of capital and the Third World. - 1987.
     (001270)
----UNCTC bibliography, 1974-1987. - 1988.
     (002695)
----Work by the United Nations Centre on
     Transnational Corporations on the Code
     of Conduct on Transnational
     Corporations, other international
     arrangements and agreements, and
     national laws and regulations relating
     to transnational corporations. - 1986.
     (002694)
----World-traded services : the challenge
     for the eighties. - 1984.
     (000889)

BIBLIOGRAPHIES--LATIN AMERICA.
----Transnational corporations and
     industrial transformation in Latin
     America. - 1984.
     (001099)

BIBLIOGRAPHIES--UNITED STATES.
----Fundamentals of international taxation.
     - 1985.
     (001700)

BIG BUSINESS.
----Big business blunders. - 1983.
     (000507)
----Export-processing zones and
     industrialization: some considerations
     from the economics of large
     organizations. - 1983.
     (002364)
----Growth patterns of the world's largest
     firms, 1962-82. - 1984.
     (000041)
----A review of capital investment trends in
     larger companies. - 1987.
     (000503)
----The world's largest industrial
     enterprises, 1962-1983. - 1985.
     (000298)

BIG BUSINESS--INDIA.
----Multinationals in Indian big business:
     industrial characteristics of foreign
     investments in a heavily regulated
     economy. - 1983.
     (001058)

BIG BUSINESS--LATIN AMERICA.
----Small nations, giant firms. - 1987.
     (001091)

BIG BUSINESS--SWEDEN.
----De Svenska storforetagen. - 1985.
     (000324)

BIG BUSINESS--TAIWAN (CHINA).
----Networks of Taiwanese big business. -
     1986.
     (001063)

BILATERAL TRADE AGREEMENTS--CANADA.
----The legal markets of international
     trade. - 1987.
     (002038)

BILATERAL TRADE AGREEMENTS--UNITED STATES.
----The legal markets of international
     trade. - 1987.
     (002038)

BIOGRAPHY.
----The blue book of Canadian business. -
     1976-   .
     (002622)

BIOMASS ENERGY.
----Economic aspects of biotechnology. -
     1986.
     (000693)

BIOTECHNOLOGY.
----Analyse de l'activité de 95 firmes
     industrielles étrangères dans la
     bio-industrie. - 1983.
     (000652)
----Economic aspects of biotechnology. -
     1986.
     (000693)
----Genetic engineering and biotechnology
     firms worldwide directory. - 1981-   .
     (000688) (002642)
----High technology industries. - 1983-   .
     (000695)

BIOTECHNOLOGY--JAPAN.
----Commercial biotechnology. - 1984.
     (000643)

BIOTECHNOLOGY--UNITED STATES.
----Commercial biotechnology. - 1984.
     (000643)
----Double dividends? - 1986.
     (000682)

BIOTECHNOLOGY--WESTERN EUROPE.
----Commercial biotechnology. - 1984.
     (000643)

BLACKS--SOUTH AFRICA.
----Business in the shadow of apartheid :
     U.S. firms in South Africa. - 1985.
     (001194)

BLACKS--SOUTH AFRICA (continued)
----A code for misconduct? - 1980.
  (002009)
----Disinvestment and black workers
    attitudes in South Africa. - 1985.
  (001210)
----Leaving South Africa/Kellogg's
    private war against apartheid/Black
    unions. - 1985.
  (001200)
----Political change in South Africa. - 1986.
  (001205)
----Trade unions against apartheid. - 1984.
  (002601)
----U.S. firms and black labor in South
    Africa: creating a structure for change.
    - 1986.
  (001195)

BLACKS--UNITED STATES.
----U.S. firms and black labor in South
    Africa: creating a structure for change.
    - 1986.
  (001195)

BLOOMFIELD, ARTHUR I.
----International financial markets and
    capital movements. - 1985.
  (001267)

BOLIVIA--FOREIGN INVESTMENTS.
----National legislation and regulations
    relating to transnational corporations.
    Volume 4. - 1986.
  (002253)

BOLIVIA--IRON AND STEEL INDUSTRY.
----La industria siderúrgica
    latinoamericana. - 1984.
  (000601)

BOLIVIA--LAWS AND REGULATIONS.
----National legislation and regulations
    relating to transnational corporations.
    Volume 4. - 1986.
  (002253)

BOLIVIA--METALLURGICAL INDUSTRY.
----La industria siderúrgica
    latinoamericana. - 1984.
  (000601)

BOLIVIA--PETROLEUM INDUSTRY.
----Transnacionales y nación. - 1986.
  (000594)

BOLIVIA--TRANSNATIONAL CORPORATIONS.
----National legislation and regulations
    relating to transnational corporations.
    Volume 4. - 1986.
  (002253)
----Transnacionales y nación. - 1986.
  (000594)

BOOK INDUSTRY--INDIA.
----Nation-building media and TNCs. - 1984.
  (000941)

BOTSWANA--FOREIGN INVESTMENTS.
----National legislation and regulations
    relating to transnational corporations.
    Volume 4. - 1986.
  (002253)

BOTSWANA--LAWS AND REGULATIONS.
----National legislation and regulations
    relating to transnational corporations.
    Volume 4. - 1986.
  (002253)

BOTSWANA--TRANSNATIONAL CORPORATIONS.
----National legislation and regulations
    relating to transnational corporations.
    Volume 4. - 1986.
  (002253)

BRANDED MERCHANDISE.
----Multinational production: effect on
    brand value. - 1986.
  (000540)

BRAZIL--BANKING.
----La internacionalización financiera en
    Brasil. - 1983.
  (001082)

BRAZIL--BUSINESS ENTERPRISES.
----Cooperación empresarial entre países
    semiindutrializados. - 1984.
  (000202)

BRAZIL--CAPITAL INVESTMENTS.
----Capital intensity and export propensity
    in some Latin American countries. - 1987.
  (001389)

BRAZIL--CHOICE OF TECHNOLOGY.
----Capital intensity and export propensity
    in some Latin American countries. - 1987.
  (001389)

BRAZIL--COMMUNICATION INDUSTRY.
----La industria nacional de informática. -
    1987.
  (000818)

BRAZIL--COMPARATIVE ANALYSIS.
----Technological spill-overs and manpower
    training: a comparative analysis of
    multinational and national enterprises
    in Brazilian manufacturing. - 1986.
  (001899)

BRAZIL--COMPUTER INDUSTRY.
----Brazilian informatics policy. - 1985.
  (000880)
----L'informatique brésilienne dans la
    nouvelle république. - 1986.
  (000765)
----Politische Gestaltungsspielräume von
    Schwellenländern in der
    Mikroelektronik-Industrie. - 1987.
  (000617)
----Technology and competition in the
    Brazilian computer industry. - 1983.
  (000741)

BRAZIL--CONTRACTS.
----Petroleum service contracts in
    Argentina, Brazil and Colombia : issues
    arising from their legal nature. - 1987.
  (002422)

BRAZIL--CORPORATION LAW.
----Capitais estrangeiros. - 1984.
  (002275)

BRAZIL--DIFFUSION OF INNOVATIONS.
----Exportaciones de tecnología de Brasil y
    Argentina. - 1986.
    (001491)

BRAZIL--DOMESTIC TRADE.
----Technological spill-overs and manpower
    training: a comparative analysis of
    multinational and national enterprises
    in Brazilian manufacturing. - 1986.
    (001899)

BRAZIL--ECONOMIC CO-OPERATION.
----Cooperación empresarial entre países
    semiindutrializados. - 1984.
    (000202)

BRAZIL--ECONOMIC POLICY.
----Business in a democratic Brazil. - 1985.
    (001776)

BRAZIL--EMPLOYMENT POLICY.
----Employment effects of exports by
    multinationals and of export processing
    zones in Brazil. - 1987.
    (001915)

BRAZIL--EXPORT FINANCING.
----O sistema brasileiro de financiamento às
    exportaçoes. - 1985.
    (001349)

BRAZIL--EXPORT ORIENTED INDUSTRIES.
----Capital intensity and export propensity
    in some Latin American countries. - 1987.
    (001389)

BRAZIL--EXPORT PROMOTION.
----Política industrial, joint ventures e
    exportaçoes. - 1986.
    (001658)

BRAZIL--EXTERNAL DEBT.
----La internacionalización financiera en
    Brasil. - 1983.
    (001082)

BRAZIL--FOREIGN DIRECT INVESTMENT.
----Las empresas transnacionales y la
    inversión extranjera directa en la
    primera mitad de los años ochenta. -
    1987.
    (000194)
----Investimentos estrangeiros no Brasil. -
    1985.
    (000177)
----New forms of overseas investment by
    developing countries : the case of
    India, Korea and Brazil. - 1986.
    (001616)
----Regulation of foreign investment in
    Brazil. - 1983.
    (002266)

BRAZIL--FOREIGN INVESTMENTS.
----Business in a democratic Brazil. - 1985.
    (001776)
----Capitais estrangeiros. - 1984.
    (002275)
----The comparative performance of foreign
    and domestic firms in Brazil. - 1986.
    (001130)

----La internacionalización financiera en
    Brasil. - 1983.
    (001082)
----Investments in Brazil. - 1981.
    (002165)
----Mining investment in Brazil, Peru, and
    Mexico. - 1984.
    (002443)
----National legislation and regulations
    relating to transnational corporations.
    Volume 4. - 1986.
    (002253)

BRAZIL--FOREIGN RELATIONS.
----Brazilian imports of technology from
    Sweden, 1965-1980. - 1985.
    (001408)

BRAZIL--FREE EXPORT ZONES.
----Employment effects of exports by
    multinationals and of export processing
    zones in Brazil. - 1987.
    (001915)

BRAZIL--IMPORT CHARGES AND SUBCHARGES.
----Market imperfections and import pricing
    behavior by multinational enterprises. -
    1986.
    (001681)

BRAZIL--INDUSTRIAL CO-OPERATION.
----La cooperación empresarial
    argentino-brasileña. - 1983.
    (001097)

BRAZIL--INDUSTRIAL EQUIPMENT LEASES.
----Analysis of equipment leasing contracts.
    - 1984.
    (002407)

BRAZIL--INDUSTRIAL MANAGEMENT.
----Como enfrentar as multinacionais. - 1983.
    (001092)

BRAZIL--INDUSTRIAL POLICY.
----Política industrial, joint ventures e
    exportaçoes. - 1986.
    (001658)

BRAZIL--INDUSTRIAL TECHNOLOGY.
----Exportaciones de tecnología de Brasil y
    Argentina. - 1986.
    (001491)

BRAZIL--INDUSTRIALIZATION.
----Exports of technology by newly
    industrializing countries: Brazil. -
    1984.
    (001492)

BRAZIL--INFORMATION POLICY.
----Brazilian informatics policy. - 1985.
    (000880)

BRAZIL--INFORMATION TECHNOLOGY.
----Brazilian informatics policy. - 1985.
    (000880)
----La industria nacional de informática. -
    1987.
    (000818)

BRAZIL--INTERNATIONAL TRADE.
----Dos estudios sobre empresas
transnacionales en Brasil. - 1983.
   (001120)

BRAZIL--IRON AND STEEL INDUSTRY.
----La industria siderúrgica
latinoamericana. - 1984.
   (000601)

BRAZIL--JOINT VENTURES.
----New forms of overseas investment by
developing countries : the case of
India, Korea and Brazil. - 1986.
   (001616)
----Política industrial, joint ventures e
exportaçoes. - 1986.
   (001658)

BRAZIL--LABOUR SUPPLY.
----Technological spill-overs and manpower
training: a comparative analysis of
multinational and national enterprises
in Brazilian manufacturing. - 1986.
   (001899)

BRAZIL--LAWS AND REGULATIONS.
----O codigo de conduta das empresas
transnacionais. - 1984.
   (001968)
----Multinacionais. - 1984.
   (002183)
----National legislation and regulations
relating to transnational corporations.
Volume 4. - 1986.
   (002253)
----Regulation of foreign investment in
Brazil. - 1983.
   (002266)

BRAZIL--MANAGEMENT.
----Multinacionais. - 1984.
   (002183)

BRAZIL--MANPOWER NEEDS.
----Technological spill-overs and manpower
training: a comparative analysis of
multinational and national enterprises
in Brazilian manufacturing. - 1986.
   (001899)

BRAZIL--MANUFACTURING ENTERPRISES.
----The comparative performance of foreign
and domestic firms in Brazil. - 1986.
   (001130)
----The determinants of manufacturing
ownership in less developed countries. -
1986.
   (000712)
----Technological spill-overs and manpower
training: a comparative analysis of
multinational and national enterprises
in Brazilian manufacturing. - 1986.
   (001899)

BRAZIL--MARKET DISRUPTION.
----Market imperfections and import pricing
behavior by multinational enterprises. -
1986.
   (001681)

BRAZIL--MEAT INDUSTRY.
----Empresas transnacionales y ganadería de
carnes en Brasil. - 1983.
   (000568)

BRAZIL--METALLURGICAL INDUSTRY.
----La industria siderúrgica
latinoamericana. - 1984.
   (000601)

BRAZIL--MICROELECTRONICS.
----Microelectronics-based automation
technologies and development. - 1985.
   (000753)
----Politische Gestaltungsspielräume von
Schwellenländern in der
Mikroelektronik-Industrie. - 1987.
   (000617)

BRAZIL--MINING INDUSTRY.
----Mining investment in Brazil, Peru, and
Mexico. - 1984.
   (002443)

BRAZIL--MINING LAW.
----Mining investment in Brazil, Peru, and
Mexico. - 1984.
   (002443)
----Petroleum service contracts in
Argentina, Brazil and Colombia : issues
arising from their legal nature. - 1987.
   (002422)

BRAZIL--MIXED ENTERPRISES.
----Las empresas transnacionales y la
inversión extranjera directa en la
primera mitad de los años ochenta. -
1987.
   (000194)

BRAZIL--MONETARY SYSTEMS.
----La internacionalización financiera en
Brasil. - 1983.
   (001082)

BRAZIL--MULTINATIONAL MARKETING ENTERPRISES.
----Market imperfections and import pricing
behavior by multinational enterprises. -
1986.
   (001681)

BRAZIL--NATURAL RESOURCES.
----Petroleum service contracts in
Argentina, Brazil and Colombia : issues
arising from their legal nature. - 1987.
   (002422)

BRAZIL--PETROLEUM EXPLORATION.
----Social and economic effects of petroleum
development. - 1987.
   (000633)

BRAZIL--PETROLEUM INDUSTRY.
----Natural gas clauses in petroleum
arrangements. - 1987.
   (002452)
----PETROBRAS : eines der grössten
Industrieunternehmen der
kapitalistischen Welt. - 1984.
   (000282)
----Petroleum development in Brazil. - 1987.
   (000638)

BRAZIL--PETROLEUM INDUSTRY (continued)
----Social and economic effects of petroleum
development. - 1987.
(000633)

BRAZIL--PETROLEUM LAW.
----Petroleum service contracts in
Argentina, Brazil and Colombia : issues
arising from their legal nature. - 1987.
(002422)

BRAZIL--PETROLEUM POLICY.
----Petroleum development in Brazil. - 1987.
(000638)

BRAZIL--PHARMACEUTICAL INDUSTRY.
----Transnational corporations in the
pharmaceutical industry of developing
countries. - 1984.
(000749)

BRAZIL--POLITICAL CONDITIONS.
----Business in a democratic Brazil. - 1985.
(001776)

BRAZIL--PRIVATE ENTERPRISES.
----The determinants of manufacturing
ownership in less developed countries. -
1986.
(000712)

BRAZIL--PUBLIC ENTERPRISES.
----The determinants of manufacturing
ownership in less developed countries. -
1986.
(000712)
----PETROBRAS : eines der grössten
Industrieunternehmen der
kapitalistischen Welt. - 1984.
(000282)

BRAZIL--RISK ASSESSMENT.
----Business in a democratic Brazil. - 1985.
(001776)

BRAZIL--STATISTICAL DATA.
----Brazilian imports of technology from
Sweden, 1965-1980. - 1985.
(001408)
----O sistema brasileiro de financiamento às
exportaçoes. - 1985.
(001349)

BRAZIL--TAX LAW.
----Investimentos estrangeiros no Brasil. -
1985.
(000177)

BRAZIL--TECHNOLOGY TRANSFER.
----Brazilian imports of technology from
Sweden, 1965-1980. - 1985.
(001408)
----La cooperación empresarial
argentino-brasileña. - 1983.
(001097)
----Exportaciones de tecnología de Brasil y
Argentina. - 1986.
(001491)
----Exports of technology by newly
industrializing countries: Brazil. -
1984.
(001492)

----Politische Gestaltungsspielräume von
Schwellenländern in der
Mikroelektronik-Industrie. - 1987.
(000617)
----Technological spill-overs and manpower
training: a comparative analysis of
multinational and national enterprises
in Brazilian manufacturing. - 1986.
(001899)
----Technology and competition in the
Brazilian computer industry. - 1983.
(000741)

BRAZIL--TRADE UNIONS.
----Brazil, the new militancy. - 1984.
(002596)

BRAZIL--TRANSNATIONAL CORPORATIONS.
----Business in a democratic Brazil. - 1985.
(001776)
----Capitais estrangeiros. - 1984.
(002275)
----O codigo de conduta das empresas
transnacionais. - 1984.
(001968)
----Como enfrentar as multinacionais. - 1983.
(001092)
----The comparative performance of foreign
and domestic firms in Brazil. - 1986.
(001130)
----The determinants of manufacturing
ownership in less developed countries. -
1986.
(000712)
----Dos estudios sobre empresas
transnacionales en Brasil. - 1983.
(001120)
----Employment effects of exports by
multinationals and of export processing
zones in Brazil. - 1987.
(001915)
----Empresas transnacionales y ganadería de
carnes en Brasil. - 1983.
(000568)
----Multinacionais. - 1984.
(002183)
----Multinationals from Brazil. - 1983.
(000382)
----National legislation and regulations
relating to transnational corporations.
Volume 4. - 1986.
(002253)
----Natural gas clauses in petroleum
arrangements. - 1987.
(002452)
----New forms of overseas investment by
developing countries : the case of
India, Korea and Brazil. - 1986.
(001616)
----Technological spill-overs and manpower
training: a comparative analysis of
multinational and national enterprises
in Brazilian manufacturing. - 1986.
(001899)
----Transnational corporations in peripheral
societies. - 1983.
(001016)

BRITISH COLUMBIA (CANADA)--FOREIGN DIRECT
INVESTMENT.
----Foreign investment in the American and
Canadian West, 1870-1914. - 1986.
(002690)

BUDGET DEFICITS--UNITED STATES.
----What's causing America's capital
    imports? - 1987.
      (000539)

BUDGETARY POLICY--WESTERN EUROPE.
----Mélanges 2 : harmonisation fiscale,
    marché commun des services, perspectives
    budgétaires 1988, fonds structurels. -
    1987.
      (000897)

BULGARIA--JOINT VENTURES.
----East-West joint ventures. - 1988.
      (001570)

BULGARIA--LAWS AND REGULATIONS.
----East-West joint ventures. - 1988.
      (001570)

BULGARIA--STATISTICAL DATA.
----East-West joint ventures. - 1988.
      (001570)

BURKINA FASO--AGROINDUSTRY.
----Une enclave industrielle : la Société
    sucrière de Haute-Volta. - 1984.
      (001032)

BURKINA FASO--SUGAR INDUSTRY.
----Une enclave industrielle : la Société
    sucrière de Haute-Volta. - 1984.
      (001032)

BURKINA FASO--TRANSNATIONAL CORPORATIONS.
----Une enclave industrielle : la Société
    sucrière de Haute-Volta. - 1984.
      (001032)

BURMA--NATIONALIZATION.
----Les nationalisations dans quelques pays
    d'Asie de tradition britannique : Inde,
    Sri Lanca, Birmanie. - 1984.
      (002329)

BURUNDI--ECONOMIC CONDITIONS.
----Guide des investisseurs. - 1983-   .
      (001805)

BURUNDI--FINANCIAL REGULATIONS.
----Guide des investisseurs. - 1983-   .
      (001805)

BURUNDI--FOREIGN DIRECT INVESTMENT.
----Manuel de procedures contractuelles
    susceptibles d'être mise en oeuvre par
    les contrats internationaux concernant
    la realisation de projets industriels. -
    1984.
      (002417)

BURUNDI--INDUSTRIAL DEVELOPMENT.
----Guide des investisseurs. - 1983-   .
      (001805)

BURUNDI--INDUSTRIAL POLICY.
----Guide des investisseurs. - 1983-   .
      (001805)

BURUNDI--JOINT VENTURES.
----Manuel de procedures contractuelles
    susceptibles d'être mise en oeuvre par
    les contrats internationaux concernant
    la realisation de projets industriels. -
    1984.
      (002417)

BURUNDI--LAWS AND REGULATIONS.
----Manuel de procedures contractuelles
    susceptibles d'être mise en oeuvre par
    les contrats internationaux concernant
    la realisation de projets industriels. -
    1984.
      (002417)

BURUNDI--MULTINATIONAL INDUSTRIAL PROJECTS.
----Manuel de procedures contractuelles
    susceptibles d'être mise en oeuvre par
    les contrats internationaux concernant
    la realisation de projets industriels. -
    1984.
      (002417)

BURUNDI--RESEARCH AND DEVELOPMENT CONTRACTS.
----Manuel de procedures contractuelles
    susceptibles d'être mise en oeuvre par
    les contrats internationaux concernant
    la realisation de projets industriels. -
    1984.
      (002417)

BUSINESS.
----Business information sources. - 1985.
      (002701)
----Business International index. -
    1983-
      (002684)

BUSINESS--ASIA.
----Critical issues for business in Asia. -
    1984.
      (001787)
----New business strategies for developing
    Asia, 1983-1990. - 1984.
      (000498)

BUSINESS--CANADA.
----Operating strategies for a Canada in
    transition. - 1984.
      (001778)

BUSINESS--CHINA.
----The People's Republic of China. - 1986.
      (001841)

BUSINESS--INDONESIA.
----The Indonesian business. - 1986.
      (001839)

BUSINESS--MIDDLE EAST.
----International business in the Middle
    East. - 1986.
      (001135)

BUSINESS--OMAN.
----The commercial legal system of the
    Sultanate of Oman. - 1983.
      (002218)

BUSINESS CYCLES.
----International business, the recession
    and economic restructuring. - 1985.
      (000025)

BUSINESS ENTERPRISE BRANCHES--CANADA.
----Operating foreign subsidiaries. - 1983.
    (000388)

BUSINESS ENTERPRISE BRANCHES--UNITED STATES.
----Operating foreign subsidiaries. - 1983.
    (000388)

BUSINESS ENTERPRISE BRANCHES--WESTERN EUROPE.
----Operating foreign subsidiaries. - 1983.
    (000388)

BUSINESS ENTERPRISES.
----Coping with worldwide accounting
    changes. - 1984.
    (002067)
----Financial directories of the world. -
    1982-
    (002685)
----La fiscalité internationale des
    entreprises. - 1985.
    (001743)
----How to find information about companies.
    - 1983.
    (002714)
----Internationale Wettbewerbsfähigkeit. -
    1984.
    (000005)
----List of company directories and summary
    of their contents. - 1983.
    (002686)
----Strategic planning for international
    corporations. - 1979.
    (000461)
----World business reports. - 1982-   .
    (001863)
----Worldscope : industrial company
    profiles. - 1987.
    (000299)

BUSINESS ENTERPRISES--AFRICA.
----Owen's Worldtrade Africa business
    directory. - 1986-   .
    (002657)

BUSINESS ENTERPRISES--ARGENTINA.
----Cooperación empresarial entre países
    semiindutrializados. - 1984.
    (000202)
----Sociedades y grupos multinacionales. -
    1985.
    (000004)

BUSINESS ENTERPRISES--ASIA.
----Asia's 7500 largest companies. -
    1985-   .
    (002619)
----Major companies of the Far East. -
    1983-
    (002651)

BUSINESS ENTERPRISES--AUSTRALIA.
----Kompass Australia. - 1970-   .
    (002649)

BUSINESS ENTERPRISES--BRAZIL.
----Cooperación empresarial entre países
    semiindutrializados. - 1984.
    (000202)

BUSINESS ENTERPRISES--CANADA.
----The blue book of Canadian business. -
    1976-   .
    (002622)

----Canadian standard industrial
    classification for companies and
    enterprises, 1980. - 1986-   .
    (002718)
----Concentration and foreign control in
    retail and wholesale trade in Canada,
    1979. - 1983.
    (000783)

BUSINESS ENTERPRISES--CHINA.
----China adopts law on foreign enterprises.
    - 1986.
    (002294)
----Tax aspects of doing business with the
    People's Republic of China. - 1984.
    (001713)

BUSINESS ENTERPRISES--COLOMBIA.
----Directorio de empresas y ejecutivos. -
    1979-   .
    (002628)

BUSINESS ENTERPRISES--EL SALVADOR.
----Directorió comercial e industrial de El
    Salvador. - 1986-   .
    (002627)

BUSINESS ENTERPRISES--EQUATORIAL GUINEA.
----Directorio nacional de empresas y
    establecimientos. - 1985-   .
    (002629)

BUSINESS ENTERPRISES--FRANCE.
----Ces patrons qui gagnent. - 1986.
    (001146)

BUSINESS ENTERPRISES--GERMANY, FEDERAL
REPUBLIC OF.
----Handbuch der Grossunternehmen. -
    1940-   .
    (002644)

BUSINESS ENTERPRISES--HUNGARY.
----Hungarian Chamber of Commerce handbook.
    - 1984-   .
    (001811)
----Hungarian foreign trade reform. - 1986.
    (002250)

BUSINESS ENTERPRISES--JAPAN.
----The economic analysis of the Japanese
    firm. - 1984.
    (000322)

BUSINESS ENTERPRISES--KUWAIT.
----Impact of the operations of
    transnational corporations on
    development in Kuwait. - 1987.
    (001143)

BUSINESS ENTERPRISES--LATIN AMERICA.
----Dun's Latin America's top 25,000. -
    1984-
    (002636)

BUSINESS ENTERPRISES--LUXEMBOURG.
----Répertoire des entreprises
    luxembourgeoises. - 1979-   .
    (002662)

BUSINESS ENTERPRISES--MALAWI.
----Malawi buyers' guide. - 1983-   .
    (002653)

BUSINESS ENTERPRISES--MEXICO.
----Inversión extranjera directa. - 1985.
     (000138)

BUSINESS ENTERPRISES--NETHERLANDS.
----Statistiek van het ondernemingen- en
     vestigingenbestand. - 1983-   .
     (002666)

BUSINESS ENTERPRISES--NORWAY.
----Kompass. - 1970-   .
     (002647)

BUSINESS ENTERPRISES--SAUDI ARABIA.
----Impact of the operations of
     transnational corporations on
     development in Saudi Arabia. - 1987.
     (001140)

BUSINESS ENTERPRISES--SWEDEN.
----Sveriges största företag. - 1968-   .
     (002667)

BUSINESS ENTERPRISES--TAIWAN (CHINA).
----Networks of Taiwanese big business. -
     1986.
     (001063)

BUSINESS ENTERPRISES--UNITED ARAB EMIRATES.
----Impact of operations of transnational
     corporations on development in United
     Arab Emirates. - 1987.
     (001136)

BUSINESS ENTERPRISES--UNITED KINGDOM.
----A code for misconduct? - 1980.
     (002009)
----Kompass. - 196?-   .
     (002648)
----Sell's British exporters. - 1916-   .
     (002663)
----The United Kingdom merger boom in
     perspective. - 1987.
     (001638)

BUSINESS ENTERPRISES--UNITED STATES.
----Democratic development. - 1986.
     (001334)
----Directory of American firms operating in
     foreign countries. - 1955-   .
     (002630)
----Forbes annual directory. - 1969-   .
     (002640)
----Foreign direct investment in the United
     States. - 1985-   .
     (000131)
----The knowledge industry 200. - 1983.
     (000884) (002646)
----Major companies of the USA. - 1986-   .
     (002652)
----Million dollar directory. - 1959-   .
     (002655)
----Performance requirements for foreign
     business. - 1983.
     (002314)
----United States jurisdiction over foreign
     subsidiaries. - 1983.
     (002355)
----US corporate interests and the political
     economy of trade policy. - 1984.
     (000505)

BUSINESS ENTERPRISES--URUGUAY.
----La transformación de sociedad irregular
     en sociedad regular. - 1984.
     (001545)

BUSINESS ENTERPRISES--USSR.
----Businessman's Moscow. - 1984-   .
     (002625)
----La nouvelle législation soviétique sur
     les entreprises mixtes. - 1987.
     (002181)

BUSINESS ENTERPRISES--WESTERN EUROPE.
----Abhängige Unternehmen und Konzerne im
     europäischen Gemeinschaftsrecht. - 1984.
     (002133)

BUSINESS ENTERPRISES--YUGOSLAVIA.
----Doing business with Yugoslavia. - 1986.
     (001793)
----Privredni adresar SFRJ. - 1965-   .
     (002660)

BUSINESS ETHICS.
----Codes of conduct of multinationals. -
     1984.
     (001974)
----Corporations and the common good. - 1986.
     (000022)
----Ethics and the multinational enterprise.
     - 1986.
     (001873)
----Going international. - 1985.
     (001786)
----The implementation of international
     antitrust principles. - 1983.
     (002344)
----A transnacionalizacao da America Latina
     e a missao das igrejas. - 1983.
     (002591)

BUSINESS ETHICS--PAPUA NEW GUINEA.
----Economic policies pertaining to foreign
     enterprises in PNG. - 1986.
     (002287)
----Reconciling ethical behaviour. - 1986.
     (001719)

BUSINESS ETHICS--SOUTH AFRICA.
----The politics of sentiment. - 1984.
     (002588)
----South Africa: the churches vs. the
     corporations. - 1983.
     (002589)

BUSINESS ETHICS--UNITED STATES.
----South Africa: the churches vs. the
     corporations. - 1983.
     (002589)

BUSINESS LIBRARIES.
----International business reference
     sources. - 1983.
     (002691)

BUSINESSMEN.
----International business and cultures. -
     1987.
     (001872)

CAMEROON--AGRIBUSINESS.
----Agro-industrial co-operation between the
    European Community and the ACP
    countries. - 1986.
        (002605)

CAMEROON--CAPITAL INVESTMENTS.
----The political economy of development in
    Cameroon. - 1986.
        (001834)

CAMEROON--DEVELOPMENT ASSISTANCE.
----The private sector, the public sector,
    and donor assistance in economic
    development. - 1983.
        (000268)

CAMEROON--DEVELOPMENT POLICY.
----The political economy of development in
    Cameroon. - 1985.
        (001833)
----The political economy of development in
    Cameroon. - 1986.
        (001834)

CAMEROON--ECONOMIC CONDITIONS.
----The political economy of development in
    Cameroon. - 1986.
        (001834)

CAMEROON--ECONOMIC DEVELOPMENT.
----The ICSID Klöckner v. Cameroon award. -
    1984.
        (002553)
----The private sector, the public sector,
    and donor assistance in economic
    development. - 1983.
        (000268)

CAMEROON--ECONOMIC POLICY.
----The private sector, the public sector,
    and donor assistance in economic
    development. - 1983.
        (000268)

CAMEROON--FOREIGN DIRECT INVESTMENT.
----L'investissement dans les pays en
    développement. - 1985.
        (000135)

CAMEROON--FOREIGN INVESTMENTS.
----The political economy of development in
    Cameroon. - 1985.
        (001833)
----The political economy of development in
    Cameroon. - 1986.
        (001834)

CAMEROON--INDUSTRIAL CO-OPERATION.
----Agro-industrial co-operation between the
    European Community and the ACP
    countries. - 1986.
        (002605)

CAMEROON--INVESTMENT DISPUTES.
----The ICSID Klöckner v. Cameroon award. -
    1984.
        (002553)

CAMEROON--INVESTMENT POLICY.
----The political economy of development in
    Cameroon. - 1986.
        (001834)

CAMEROON--PRIVATE ENTERPRISES.
----The private sector, the public sector,
    and donor assistance in economic
    development. - 1983.
        (000268)

CAMEROJN--PUBLIC SECTOR.
----The private sector, the public sector,
    and donor assistance in economic
    development. - 1983.
        (000268)

CANADA--ADJUSTMENT ASSISTANCE MEASURES.
----An automotive strategy for Canada. -
    1983.
        (000686)

CANADA--AFFILIATE CORPORATIONS.
----Taxation of income of foreign
    affiliates. - 1983.
        (001765)

CANADA--AGRIBUSINESS.
----Public and private returns from joint
    venture research: an example from
    agriculture. - 1986.
        (001650)

CANADA--BILATERAL TRADE AGREEMENTS.
----The legal markets of international
    trade. - 1987.
        (002038)

CANADA--BUSINESS.
----Operating strategies for a Canada in
    transition. - 1984.
        (001778)

CANADA--BUSINESS ENTERPRISE BRANCHES.
----Operating foreign subsidiaries. - 1983.
        (000388)

CANADA--BUSINESS ENTERPRISES.
----The blue book of Canadian business. -
    1976-   .
        (002622)
----Canadian standard industrial
    classification for companies and
    enterprises, 1980. - 1986-   .
        (002718)
----Concentration and foreign control in
    retail and wholesale trade in Canada,
    1979. - 1983.
        (000783)

CANADA--CAPITAL MOVEMENTS.
----Canada's reversal from importer to
    exporter of foreign direct investment. -
    1987.
        (000181)

CANADA--CLASSIFICATION.
----Canadian standard industrial
    classification for companies and
    enterprises, 1980. - 1986-   .
        (002718)

CANADA--COMPARATIVE ANALYSIS.
----Foreign investment control in the mining
    sector. - 1983.
        (000577)

CANADA--COMPETITION.
----Industrial organization paradigms,
    empirical evidence, and the economic
    case for competition policy. - 1987.
      (001670)

CANADA--COMPUTER INDUSTRY.
----High technology plant location
    decisions. - 1983.
      (000528)

CANADA--CORPORATE MERGERS.
----A cross sectional study of relative
    take-over activity. - 1983.
      (001633)
----International law of take-overs and
    mergers. - 1986.
      (001573)
----Private agreements for takeovers of
    public companies. - 1984.
      (001626)

CANADA--CORPORATE PLANNING.
----Operating strategies for a Canada in
    transition. - 1984.
      (001778)

CANADA--CORPORATION LAW.
----International law of take-overs and
    mergers. - 1986.
      (001573)

CANADA--CORPORATION TAX.
----The corporate income tax system. - 1985.
      (001767)
----The taxation of controlled foreign
    corporations. - 1986.
      (001699)

CANADA--CORPORATIONS.
----Canadian standard industrial
    classification for companies and
    enterprises, 1980. - 1986-   .
      (002718)

CANADA--DECISION-MAKING.
----Operating foreign subsidiaries. - 1983.
      (000388)

CANADA--DIRECTORIES.
----Business directory of Canadian trade
    representation abroad. - 1984-   .
      (002700)
----Foreign investment in South Africa and
    Namibia. - 1984.
      (001198) (002641)

CANADA--DISTRIBUTIVE AND SERVICE TRADE
STATISTICS.
----Canada's international trade in
    services. - 1986-   .
      (000821)

CANADA--DOMESTIC ECONOMIC ASSISTANCE.
----An automotive strategy for Canada. -
    1983.
      (000686)

CANADA--DOMESTIC TRADE.
----Concentration and foreign control in
    retail and wholesale trade in Canada,
    1979. - 1983.
      (000783)

CANADA--ECONOMIC POLICY.
----Industrial organization paradigms,
    empirical evidence, and the economic
    case for competition policy. - 1987.
      (001670)

CANADA--ECONOMIC RELATIONS.
----The role of multinational enterprises in
    US-Canadian economic relations. - 1986.
      (001159)

CANADA--EXCLUSIVE ECONOMIC ZONE.
----U.S. fishery negotiations with Canada
    and Mexico. - 1985.
      (002462)

CANADA--FISHERY EXPLOITATION.
----U.S. fishery negotiations with Canada
    and Mexico. - 1985.
      (002462)

CANADA--FOREIGN DIRECT INVESTMENT.
----Advising nonresidents on taking care of
    Canadian business. - 1986.
      (001789)
----Beyond borders. - 1986.
      (000280)
----Canada in the USA : foreign direct
    investment flows reversed. - 1987.
      (000180)
----Canada's reversal from importer to
    exporter of foreign direct investment. -
    1987.
      (000181)
----Foreign direct investment. - 1985.
      (001160)
----Foreign investment control in the mining
    sector. - 1983.
      (000577)
----Foreign investment in South Africa and
    Namibia. - 1984.
      (001198) (002641)
----Foreign investment law in Canada. - 1983.
      (002222)
----Operating foreign subsidiaries. - 1983.
      (000388)
----Regulation of foreign direct investment
    in Canada and the United States. - 1983.
      (002263)
----Taxation in Canada. - 1985.
      (001701)
----Taxation of income of foreign
    affiliates. - 1983.
      (001765)
----U.S. and Canadian investment in South
    Africa and Namibia. - 1986.
      (001212) (002671) (002672)

CANADA--FOREIGN INVESTMENTS.
----Canada's Foreign Investment Review
    Agency and the direct investment process
    in Canada. - 1984.
      (002359)
----An examination of the legality of the
    use of the Foreign Investment Review Act
    by the government of Canada to control
    intra- and extraterritorial commercial
    activity by aliens. - 1984.
      (002257)
----Operating strategies for a Canada in
    transition. - 1984.
      (001778)

CANADA--FOREIGN INVESTMENTS (continued)
----U.S. and Canadian business in South
    Africa. - 1987-   .
      (001211)

CANADA--FOREIGN TRADE.
----Business directory of Canadian trade
    representation abroad. - 1984-   .
      (002700)

CANADA--FREE TRADE.
----The legal markets of international
    trade. - 1987.
      (002038)
----Multinationals and free trade: the
    implications of a US-Canadian
    agreement. - 1986.
      (002029)

CANADA--HOST COUNTRY RELATIONS.
----Performance of the multinational drug
    industry in home and host countries: a
    Canadian case study. - 1983.
      (000690)

CANADA--INDUSTRIAL LOCATION.
----High technology plant location
    decisions. - 1983.
      (000528)

CANADA--INDUSTRIAL ORGANIZATION.
----Industrial organization paradigms,
    empirical evidence, and the economic
    case for competition policy. - 1987.
      (001670)

CANADA--INDUSTRIAL POLICY.
----Transnational corporations and the
    state. - 1985.
      (001860)

CANADA--INDUSTRIAL RESEARCH.
----Multinationals and technology transfer.
    - 1983.
      (001636)

CANADA--INDUSTRY.
----Canadian standard industrial
    classification for companies and
    enterprises, 1980. - 1986-   .
      (002718)

CANADA--INTERNATIONAL COMPETITION.
----Trade among multinationals. - 1987.
      (001678)

CANADA--INTERNATIONAL TRADE.
----The strategic management of
    multinationals and world product
    mandating. - 1986.
      (000511)

CANADA--INTRA-INDUSTRY TRADE.
----Le commerce interregional des services:
    le role des relations intra-firme et des
    facteurs organisationnels. - 1983.
      (000921)
----Trade among multinationals. - 1987.
      (001678)

CANADA--INVESTMENT POLICY.
----Foreign investment control in the mining
    sector. - 1983.
      (000577)

CANADA--INVESTMENT TAX CREDIT.
----International income taxation and
    developing countries. - 1988.
      (001759)

CANADA--JOINT VENTURES.
----Public and private returns from joint
    venture research: an example from
    agriculture. - 1986.
      (001650)

CANADA--LAWS AND REGULATIONS.
----An examination of the legality of the
    use of the Foreign Investment Review Act
    by the government of Canada to control
    intra- and extraterritorial commercial
    activity by aliens. - 1984.
      (002257)
----Foreign investment law in Canada. - 1983.
      (002222)
----International income taxation and
    developing countries. - 1988.
      (001759)
----National legislation and regulations
    relating to transnational corporations.
    Volume 3. - 1983.
      (002252)
----Regulation of foreign direct investment
    in Canada and the United States. - 1983.
      (002263)
----Taxation in Canada. - 1985.
      (001701)
----Taxation of income of foreign
    affiliates. - 1983.
      (001765)

CANADA--LICENCES.
----Comparative licensing aspects of
    Canadian and United Kingdom petroleum
    law. - 1986.
      (002176)

CANADA--MACHINERY INDUSTRY.
----An automotive strategy for Canada. -
    1983.
      (000686)

CANADA--MANAGEMENT.
----A cross sectional study of relative
    take-over activity. - 1983.
      (001633)
----Entry, exit, and the theory of the
    multinational corporation. - 1983.
      (000092)
----The strategic management of
    multinationals and world product
    mandating. - 1986.
      (000511)

CANADA--MANAGERS.
----The blue book of Canadian business. -
    1976-   .
      (002622)

CANADA--MANDATES.
----The strategic management of
    multinationals and world product
    mandating. - 1986.
      (000511)

CANADA--MINERAL INDUSTRY.
----Foreign investment control in the mining
    sector. - 1983.
    (000577)
----Mineral industries of Australia, Canada,
    and Oceania. - 1985.
    (000603)

CANADA--MOTOR VEHICLE INDUSTRY.
----An automotive strategy for Canada. -
    1983.
    (000686)

CANADA--NEGOTIATION.
----U.S. fishery negotiations with Canada
    and Mexico. - 1985.
    (002462)

CANADA--OIL AND GAS LEASES.
----Comparative licensing aspects of
    Canadian and United Kingdom petroleum
    law. - 1986.
    (002176)

CANADA--PETROLEUM INDUSTRY.
----Multinational Oil Limited: issues in
    transfer pricing and foreign ownership.
    - 1985.
    (001750)
----La multinationalisation des pétrolières
    canadiennes. - 1984.
    (000627)

CANADA--PETROLEUM LAW.
----Comparative licensing aspects of
    Canadian and United Kingdom petroleum
    law. - 1986.
    (002176)

CANADA--PHARMACEUTICAL INDUSTRY.
----Performance of the multinational drug
    industry in home and host countries: a
    Canadian case study. - 1983.
    (000690)

CANADA--PRIVATE ENTERPRISES.
----Public and private returns from joint
    venture research: an example from
    agriculture. - 1986.
    (001650)

CANADA--PUBLIC ENTERPRISES.
----Private agreements for takeovers of
    public companies. - 1984.
    (001626)
----Public and private returns from joint
    venture research: an example from
    agriculture. - 1986.
    (001650)

CANADA--REGIONAL DEVELOPMENT.
----Multinational corporations and regional
    development. - 1983.
    (001326)

CANADA--SERVICE INDUSTRIES.
----Canada's international trade in
    services. - 1986-   .
    (000821)
----Le commerce interregional des services:
    le role des relations intra-firme et des
    facteurs organisationnels. - 1983.
    (000921)

----The service sector: engine of growth? -
    1985.
    (000965)

CANADA--SHOE INDUSTRY.
----Beyond borders. - 1986.
    (000280)

CANADA--STANDARDS.
----Canadian standard industrial
    classification for companies and
    enterprises, 1980. - 1986-   .
    (002718)

CANADA--STATISTICAL DATA.
----Concentration and foreign control in
    retail and wholesale trade in Canada,
    1979. - 1983.
    (000783)

CANADA--SUBSIDIARY BODIES.
----Operating foreign subsidiaries. - 1983.
    (000388)

CANADA--TAX INCENTIVES.
----International income taxation and
    developing countries. - 1988.
    (001759)

CANADA--TAX REVENUES.
----Transfer pricing issues: a critical
    discussion of the Revenue Draft
    Information Circular. - 1984.
    (001702)

CANADA--TAX SYSTEMS.
----The corporate income tax system. - 1985.
    (001767)

CANADA--TAX TREATIES.
----Advising nonresidents on taking care of
    Canadian business. - 1986.
    (001789)

CANADA--TAXATION.
----Advising nonresidents on taking care of
    Canadian business. - 1986.
    (001789)
----Draft guidelines on international
    transfer pricing: Canada. - 1986.
    (001734)
----International income taxation and
    developing countries. - 1988.
    (001759)
----Multinational Oil Limited: issues in
    transfer pricing and foreign ownership.
    - 1985.
    (001750)
----Taxation in Canada. - 1985.
    (001701)
----The taxation of controlled foreign
    corporations. - 1986.
    (001699)
----Taxation of income of foreign
    affiliates. - 1983.
    (001765)

CANADA--TECHNOLOGY TRANSFER.
----Canada's reversal from importer to
    exporter of foreign direct investment. -
    1987.
    (000181)

CANADA--TECHNOLOGY TRANSFER (continued)
----Multinationals and technology transfer.
   - 1983.
      (001636)

CANADA--TOURISM.
----Business directory of Canadian trade
   representation abroad. - 1984-   .
      (002700)

CANADA--TRADE AGREEMENTS.
----Multinationals and free trade: the
   implications of a US-Canadian
   agreement. - 1986.
      (002029)

CANADA--TRADE POLICY.
----Trade among multinationals. - 1987.
      (001678)

CANADA--TRADE RESTRICTIONS.
----Transfer pricing policies under tariff
   barriers. - 1983.
      (001709)

CANADA--TRANSFER PRICING.
----Draft guidelines on international
   transfer pricing: Canada. - 1986.
      (001734)
----Multinational Oil Limited: issues in
   transfer pricing and foreign ownership.
   - 1985.
      (001750)
----Transfer pricing issues: a critical
   discussion of the Revenue Draft
   Information Circular. - 1984.
      (001702)
----Transfer pricing policies under tariff
   barriers. - 1983.
      (001709)

CANADA--TRANSNATIONAL CORPORATIONS.
----Advising nonresidents on taking care of
   Canadian business. - 1986.
      (001789)
----Canada in the USA : foreign direct
   investment flows reversed. - 1987.
      (000180)
----Canadian multinationals. - 1985.
      (000373)
----Canadian multinationals. - 1985.
      (000362)
----Concentration and foreign control in
   retail and wholesale trade in Canada,
   1979. - 1983.
      (000783)
----A cross sectional study of relative
   take-over activity. - 1983.
      (001633)
----Draft guidelines on international
   transfer pricing: Canada. - 1986.
      (001734)
----Entry, exit, and the theory of the
   multinational corporation. - 1983.
      (000092)
----Foreign direct investment. - 1985.
      (001160)
----Foreign investment in South Africa and
   Namibia. - 1984.
      (001198) (002641)
----High technology plant location
   decisions. - 1983.
      (000528)

----International law of take-overs and
   mergers. - 1986.
      (001573)
----Multinational Oil Limited: issues in
   transfer pricing and foreign ownership.
   - 1985.
      (001750)
----Les multinationales canadiennes. - 1982.
      (000363)
----La multinationalisation des pétrolières
   canadiennes. - 1984.
      (000627)
----Multinationals and free trade: the
   implications of a US-Canadian
   agreement. - 1986.
      (002029)
----Multinationals and technology transfer.
   - 1983.
      (001636)
----National legislation and regulations
   relating to transnational corporations.
   Volume 3. - 1983.
      (002252)
----Operating foreign subsidiaries. - 1983.
      (000388)
----Operating strategies for a Canada in
   transition. - 1984.
      (001778)
----Performance of the multinational drug
   industry in home and host countries: a
   Canadian case study. - 1983.
      (000690)
----Reference book on major transnational
   corporations operating in Namibia. -
   1985.
      (002674)
----The role of multinational enterprises in
   US-Canadian economic relations. - 1986.
      (001159)
----The strategic management of
   multinationals and world product
   mandating. - 1986.
      (000511)
----Taxation in Canada. - 1985.
      (001701)
----The taxation of controlled foreign
   corporations. - 1986.
      (001699)
----Taxation of income of foreign
   affiliates. - 1983.
      (001765)
----Trade among multinationals. - 1987.
      (001678)
----Transnational corporations and the
   state. - 1985.
      (001860)
----U.S. and Canadian business in South
   Africa. - 1987-   .
      (001211)
----U.S. and Canadian investment in South
   Africa and Namibia. - 1986.
      (001212) (002671) (002672)

CANADA. FOREIGN INVESTMENT REVIEW AGENCY.
----Canada's Foreign Investment Review
   Agency and the direct investment process
   in Canada. - 1984.
      (002359)

CAPITAL.
----La structure financière du capitalisme
multinational. - 1983.
(001259)

CAPITAL--ECUADOR.
----Ecuador. - 1984.
(001831)

CAPITAL ASSETS.
----A country risk appraisal model of
foreign asset expropriation in
developing countries. - 1987.
(001553) (001775)

CAPITAL BUDGET.
----A review of capital investment trends in
larger companies. - 1987.
(000503)

CAPITAL FORMATION--UNITED STATES.
----Corporate capital structures in the
United States. - 1985.
(000315)

CAPITAL GAINS TAX.
----International co-operation in tax
matters : guidelines for international
co-operation against the evasion and
avoidance of taxes (with special
reference to taxes on income, profits,
capital and capital gains). - 1984.
(001724)
----International income taxation and
developing countries. - 1988.
(001759)

CAPITAL GOODS.
----The capital goods sector in developing
countries. - 1985.
(001651)
----International accounting and reporting
issues, 1986 review. - 1986.
(002117)
----Towards a theory of innovation in
services. - 1986.
(000808)
----Transnational corporations in world
development. - 1983.
(000102)

CAPITAL INVESTMENTS.
----Capital allowance schemes for mining
projects in LDCs. - 1983.
(000607)
----Capital inflows to LDC's and their
impact on imports. - 1986.
(001010)
----Contract efficiency and natural resource
investment in developing countries. -
1984.
(002409)
----Developing country access to capital
markets in transition. - 1987.
(001609)
----Le développement de la protection
conventionnelle des investissements
étrangers. - 1986.
(002048)
----Energy sector investment in LDCs. - 1986.
(000773)
----Finance and protection of investments in
developing countries. - 1987.
(002128)

----A review of capital investment trends in
larger companies. - 1987.
(000503)

CAPITAL INVESTMENTS--ASIA.
----Effects of foreign capital inflows on
developing countries of Asia. - 1986.
(001059)

CAPITAL INVESTMENTS--BRAZIL.
----Capital intensity and export propensity
in some Latin American countries. - 1987.
(001389)

CAPITAL INVESTMENTS--CAMEROON.
----The political economy of development in
Cameroon. - 1986.
(001834)

CAPITAL INVESTMENTS--CARIBBEAN REGION.
----Regulación de la inversión extranjera en
América Latina y el Caribe. - 1984.
(002194)

CAPITAL INVESTMENTS--CENTRAL AMERICA.
----Capital intensity and export propensity
in some Latin American countries. - 1987.
(001389)

CAPITAL INVESTMENTS--CHINA.
----China experiments with modernisation. -
1983.
(002384)
----Ouverture et dynamique interne du
capital en Chine. - 1987.
(001064)

CAPITAL INVESTMENTS--COLOMBIA.
----Capital intensity and export propensity
in some Latin American countries. - 1987.
(001389)

CAPITAL INVESTMENTS--LATIN AMERICA.
----Regulación de la inversión extranjera en
América Latina y el Caribe. - 1984.
(002194)

CAPITAL INVESTMENTS--MEXICO.
----Capital intensity and export propensity
in some Latin American countries. - 1987.
(001389)
----Industrialización, capital extranjero y
transferencia de tecnología. - 1986.
(001524)

CAPITAL INVESTMENTS--QATAR.
----Petro-industrialization in Qatar. - 1985.
(000600)

CAPITAL INVESTMENTS--SIBERIA (USSR).
----Investment and reindustrialization in
the Soviet economy. - 1984.
(001333)

CAPITAL INVESTMENTS--UNITED STATES.
----Applying uniform margin requirements to
foreign entities attempting to acquire
U.S. corporations. - 1984.
(002173)

CAPITAL INVESTMENTS--USSR.
----Investment and reindustrialization in
the Soviet economy. - 1984.
(001333)

CAPITAL MARKETS.
----Changes in the international financial
    market and implications for
    transnational banks, transnational
    corporations and developing countries. -
    1986.
    (000976)
----Developing country access to capital
    markets in transition. - 1987.
    (001609)
----Globalisation of financial flows and
    trends in international capital market.
    - 1986.
    (001281)
----The GT guide to world equity markets. -
    1986-   .
    (002712)
----The importance of international monetary
    markets and the international crisis of
    indebtedness. - 1987.
    (000244)
----International banks and financial
    markets in developing countries. - 1984.
    (000859)
----International capital markets :
    developments and prospects. - 1986.
    (001266)
----International financial markets and
    capital movements. - 1985.
    (001267)
----International trade in services :
    securities. - 1987.
    (000915)
----The literature of international business
    finance. - 1984.
    (002687)
----Recent developments in operations and
    behaviour of transnational corporations.
    - 1987.
    (000103)
----Stratégies des entreprises et marché
    international des capitaux. - 1984.
    (001273)
----The use of international finance
    subsidiaries in the Netherlands
    Antilles. - 1983.
    (000871)
----Wisselkoersinstabiliteit en
    schuldproblematiek. - 1984.
    (001310)

CAPITAL MARKETS--AUSTRALIA.
----Financial institutions and markets in
    the Southwest Pacific. - 1985.
    (000854)

CAPITAL MARKETS--FIJI.
----Financial institutions and markets in
    the Southwest Pacific. - 1985.
    (000854)

CAPITAL MARKETS--HONG KONG.
----Hong Kong and Singapore. - 1985.
    (000879)

CAPITAL MARKETS--JAPAN.
----The European investments of Japanese
    financial institutions. - 1986.
    (000118)
----Japan as capital exporter and the world
    economy. - 1985.
    (000384)

CAPITAL MARKETS--NEW ZEALAND.
----Financial institutions and markets in
    the Southwest Pacific. - 1985.
    (000854)

CAPITAL MARKETS--PAPUA NEW GUINEA.
----Financial institutions and markets in
    the Southwest Pacific. - 1985.
    (000854)

CAPITAL MARKETS--REPUBLIC OF KOREA.
----Riding a tiger : joint ventures under
    South Korea's new Foreign Capital
    Inducement Act. - 1985.
    (002290)

CAPITAL MARKETS--SINGAPORE.
----Hong Kong and Singapore. - 1985.
    (000879)

CAPITAL MARKETS--TURKEY.
----Turkish banking and finance : the
    markets mature. - 1986.
    (000970)

CAPITAL MARKETS--UNITED STATES.
----Die Aussenexpansion des Kapitals. - 1984.
    (000037)

CAPITAL MOVEMENTS.
----American banks in the international
    interbank market. - 1983.
    (000829)
----Capital inflows to LDC's and their
    impact on imports. - 1986.
    (001010)
----Capital movements within the CMEA. -
    1986.
    (001256)
----Circuits des capitaux, balances
    extérieures et flux majeurs
    d'investissement.= Capital circuits,
    foreign balances and major flows of
    investment). - 1985.
    (001308)
----Controls and impediments affecting
    inward direct investment in OECD member
    countries. - 1987.
    (000122) (002193)
----Debt problems. - 1986.
    (000229)
----Les désajustements mondiaux de balances
    des paiements. - 1984.
    (001284)
----Dette du Tiers-Monde. - 1987.
    (000224)
----Effets de la mobilité internationale du
    capital sur les pays membres d'une union
    douanière. - 1987.
    (001250)
----Endettement international et théorie des
    transferts. - 1987.
    (000213)
----Les flux d'investissement direct entre
    la France et l'extérieur, 1965-1978. -
    1981.
    (000119)
----A general equilibrium model of
    multinational corporations in developing
    economies. - 1986.
    (000003)

CAPITAL MOVEMENTS (continued)
----The importance of international monetary
    markets and the international crisis of
    indebtedness. - 1987.
        (000244)
----Increasing private capital flows to
    LDCs. - 1984.
        (001297)
----Inostrannyi kapital v ekonomike
    kapitalisticheskikh gosudarstv. - 1984.
        (001225)
----International capital flows and economic
    development. - 1985.
        (001241)
----International capital markets :
    developments and prospects. - 1986.
        (001266)
----International capital movements. - 1984.
        (001224)
----International capital movements and
    developing countries. - 1985.
        (001282)
----The international debt crisis. - 1985.
        (000240)
----International financial markets and
    capital movements. - 1985.
        (001267)
----International money flows and currency
    crises. - 1984.
        (001261)
----International movements and crises in
    resource oriented companies: the case of
    INCO in the nickel sector. - 1985.
        (000271)
----Internationalization of capital and the
    semi-industrialized countries: the case
    of the motor industry. - 1985.
        (000700)
----The intertemporal effects of
    international transfers. - 1986.
        (001262)
----Intra-industry foreign direct
    investment. - 1984.
        (001375)
----Introduction to the OECD codes of
    liberalisation. - 1987.
        (001984)
----Issues in capital flows to developing
    countries. - 1987.
        (001276)
----Mezinárodni financni a kapitálové vztahy
    rozvojovych zemí. - 1985.
        (000230)
----Modelling foreign aid, capital inflows
    and economic development. - 1987.
        (001313)
----Les mouvements de capital au sein du
    Comecon. - 1984.
        (001257)
----Muködotoke-beruházások a fejlodo
    országokban. - 1986.
        (001275)
----A negotiating strategy for trade in
    services. - 1983.
        (000865)
----Nihon shihon shugi no kaigai shinshutsu.
    - 1984.
        (000235)
----Production cost differentials and
    foreign direct investment: a test of two
    models. - 1986.
        (000061)

----Protection et promotion des
    investissements. - 1985.
        (002137)
----The reconstruction of international
    monetary arrangements. - 1987.
        (001290)
----The stability of the international
    monetary system. - 1987.
        (001294)
----A theory of expropriation and deviations
    from perfect capital mobility. - 1984.
        (001571)
----Toward a theory of industrial
    development in the Third World. - 1984.
        (001331)
----Transnational corporations and uneven
    development : the internationalization
    of capital and the Third World. - 1987.
        (001270)
----Transnational information and data
    communication. - 1983.
        (000866)
----Vyvoz kapitala v 80-e gody. - 1986.
        (002697)
----The welfare impact of foreign investment
    in the presence of specific factors and
    non-traded goods. - 1987.
        (001340)

CAPITAL MOVEMENTS--AFRICA.
----Nezavisimye strany Afriki. - 1986.
        (001280)

CAPITAL MOVEMENTS--ASIA.
----The impact of foreign capital inflow on
    investment and economic growth in
    developing Asia. - 1985.
        (001048)

CAPITAL MOVEMENTS--BANGLADESH.
----Domestic saving and foreign capital
    inflow : the case of Bangladesh. - 1986.
        (001034)

CAPITAL MOVEMENTS--CANADA.
----Canada's reversal from importer to
    exporter of foreign direct investment. -
    1987.
        (000181)

CAPITAL MOVEMENTS--CARIBBEAN REGION.
----Los flujos de capital hacia América
    Latina y el Caribe, y el financiamiento
    del desarrollo, en los años venideros. -
    1985.
        (001231)

CAPITAL MOVEMENTS--CHINA.
----On the issue of utilizing foreign
    capital. - 1985.
        (002207)

CAPITAL MOVEMENTS--EASTERN EUROPE.
----Handels- und Zahlungsprobleme in
    Osteuropa. - 1983.
        (000215)

CAPITAL MOVEMENTS--ECUADOR.
----La evolución del capitalismo ecuatoriano
    en el último decenio y perspectivas. -
    1984.
        (001105)

CAPITAL MOVEMENTS--GHANA.
----The capital intensity of foreign,
    private local and state owned firms in a
    less developed country: Ghana. - 1986.
    (001018)

CAPITAL MOVEMENTS--JAPAN.
----Japan as capital exporter and the world
    economy. - 1985.
    (000384)

CAPITAL MOVEMENTS--KENYA.
----Labor, capital, and management slack in
    multinational and local firms in Kenyan
    manufacturing. - 1986.
    (001026)

CAPITAL MOVEMENTS--LATIN AMERICA.
----Las empresas transnacionales y la
    inversión extranjera directa en la
    primera mitad de los años ochenta. -
    1987.
    (000194)
----Los flujos de capital hacia América
    Latina y el Caribe, y el financiamiento
    del desarrollo, en los años venideros. -
    1985.
    (001231)
----Transnacionalización y periferia
    semindustrializada. - 1983.
    (001017)

CAPITAL MOVEMENTS--UNITED KINGDOM.
----Two arguments for the restriction of
    international capital flows. - 1986.
    (001240)

CAPITAL MOVEMENTS--UNITED STATES.
----Die Aussenexpansion des Kapitals. - 1984.
    (000037)
----Canada's reversal from importer to
    exporter of foreign direct investment. -
    1987.
    (000181)
----Capital expenditures by majority-owned
    foreign affiliates of U.S. companies,
    1986 and 1987. - 1986.
    (000479)
----Handels- und Zahlungsprobleme in
    Osteuropa. - 1983.
    (000215)
----The overseas expansion of capital. -
    1985.
    (000038)
----The role of foreign direct investment in
    U.S. capital outflows. - 1986.
    (000179)
----What's causing America's capital
    imports? - 1987.
    (000539)

CAPITAL MOVEMENTS--USSR.
----Gold, foreign capital and the
    industrialization of Russia. - 1985.
    (001184)

CAPITAL MOVEMENTS--WESTERN EUROPE.
----Handels- und Zahlungsprobleme in
    Osteuropa. - 1983.
    (000215)
----La libération des mouvements de capitaux
    et l'intégration financière de la
    Communauté. - 1987.
    (001230)

CAPITAL PRODUCTIVITY.
----Divisions over the international
    division of labour. - 1984.
    (001269)
----Excess market value, the multinational
    corporation, and Tobin's q-ratio. - 1986.
    (000050)

CAPITALISM.
----Le capitalisme mondial. - 1985.
    (000065)
----Corporations and the common good. - 1986.
    (000022)
----Corporations, classes, and capitalism. -
    1985.
    (000090)
----Internatsionalizatsiia
    monopoliticheskogo nakopleniia i
    razvivaiushchiesia strany. - 1986.
    (000082)
----Issues in business and society. - 1985.
    (001878)
----Mirovoe kapitalisticheskoe khoziaistvo i
    razvivaiushchiesia strany Vostoka. -
    1986.
    (001279)
----Nihon shihon shugi no kaigai shinshutsu.
    - 1984.
    (000235)
----Postimperialism. - 1987.
    (001232)
----Transnational monopoly capitalism. -
    1987.
    (001666)

CAPITALISM--ECUADOR.
----Capitalismo, burguesia y crisis en el
    Ecuador. - 1983.
    (001104)

CAPITALISM--GUYANA.
----Ethnicity, class, and international
    capitalist penetration in Guyana and
    Trinidad. - 1985.
    (001096)

CAPITALISM--LATIN AMERICA.
----Capitalismo neocolonial. - 1983.
    (001109)

CAPITALISM--TRINIDAD AND TOBAGO.
----Ethnicity, class, and international
    capitalist penetration in Guyana and
    Trinidad. - 1985.
    (001096)

CARGO HANDLING.
----Reference book and buyers' guide. -
    1984-   .
    (000797)

CARIBBEAN BASIN ECONOMIC RECOVERY ACT 1983
(UNITED STATES).
----The Caribbean Basin Economic Recovery
    Act and its implications for foreign
    private investment. - 1984.
    (001965)
----La presentación de la iniciativa de la
    Cuenca del Caribe al GATT. - 1985.
    (001972)

CARIBBEAN COMMUNITY.
----Can CARICOM countries replicate the
    Singapore experience. - 1987.
      (001093)
----Measures strengthening the negotiating
    capacity of Governments in their
    relations with transnational
    corporations. - 1983.
      (002461)

CARIBBEAN REGION--AGRIBUSINESS.
----Agro-industrial co-operation between the
    European Community and the ACP
    countries. - 1986.
      (002605)

CARIBBEAN REGION--ALUMINIUM INDUSTRY.
----Multinational corporations and regional
    revenue retention in a vertically
    integrated industry: bauxite/aluminium
    in the Caribbean. - 1983.
      (000582)

CARIBBEAN REGION--BAUXITE INDUSTRY.
----Multinational corporations and regional
    revenue retention in a vertically
    integrated industry: bauxite/aluminium
    in the Caribbean. - 1983.
      (000582)

CARIBBEAN REGION--CAPITAL INVESTMENTS.
----Regulación de la inversión extranjera en
    América Latina y el Caribe. - 1984.
      (002194)

CARIBBEAN REGION--CAPITAL MOVEMENTS.
----Los flujos de capital hacia América
    Latina y el Caribe, y el financiamiento
    del desarrollo, en los años venideros. -
    1985.
      (001231)

CARIBBEAN REGION--DEVELOPMENT ASSISTANCE.
----The Caribbean Basin Economic Recovery
    Act and its implications for foreign
    private investment. - 1984.
      (001965)

CARIBBEAN REGION--DEVELOPMENT FINANCE.
----Los flujos de capital hacia América
    Latina y el Caribe, y el financiamiento
    del desarrollo, en los años venideros. -
    1985.
      (001231)

CARIBBEAN REGION--ECONOMIC ASSISTANCE.
----La presentación de la iniciativa de la
    Cuenca del Caribe al GATT. - 1985.
      (001972)

CARIBBEAN REGION--ECONOMIC DEVELOPMENT.
----Can CARICOM countries replicate the
    Singapore experience. - 1987.
      (001093)

CARIBBEAN REGION--EXPORT ORIENTED INDUSTRIES.
----Can CARICOM countries replicate the
    Singapore experience. - 1987.
      (001093)

CARIBBEAN REGION--FOREIGN DIRECT INVESTMENT.
----Las empresas transnacionales y la
    inversión extranjera directa en la
    primera mitad de los años ochenta. -
    1987.
      (000194)
----Investment in ACP states. - 1987.
      (001004)

CARIBBEAN REGION--FOREIGN INVESTMENTS.
----The Caribbean Basin Economic Recovery
    Act and its implications for foreign
    private investment. - 1984.
      (001965)
----Legal framework for foreign investment
    in the Caribbean and Central America. -
    1984.
      (001964)
----Regulación de la inversión extranjera en
    América Latina y el Caribe. - 1984.
      (002194)

CARIBBEAN REGION--FREE TRADE AREAS.
----La presentación de la iniciativa de la
    Cuenca del Caribe al GATT. - 1985.
      (001972)

CARIBBEAN REGION--INDUSTRIAL CO-OPERATION.
----Agro-industrial co-operation between the
    European Community and the ACP
    countries. - 1986.
      (002605)

CARIBBEAN REGION--INDUSTRY.
----Investment in ACP states. - 1987.
      (001004)

CARIBBEAN REGION--INFORMATION SOURCES.
----Caribbean Basin business information
    starter kit. - 1984.
      (001782)

CARIBBEAN REGION--INVESTMENT INSURANCE.
----Investment in ACP states. - 1987.
      (001004)

CARIBBEAN REGION--JOINT VENTURES.
----Investment in ACP states. - 1987.
      (001004)

CARIBBEAN REGION--REGIONAL CO-OPERATION.
----The Caribbean Basin Economic Recovery
    Act and its implications for foreign
    private investment. - 1984.
      (001965)

CARIBBEAN REGION--REVENUE SHARING.
----Multinational corporations and regional
    revenue retention in a vertically
    integrated industry: bauxite/aluminium
    in the Caribbean. - 1983.
      (000582)

CARIBBEAN REGION--SCIENCE AND TECHNOLOGY
CAPABILITY.
----Microelectronics-based automation
    technologies and development - 1985.
      (000753)

CARIBBEAN REGION--TAX HAVENS.
----Tax havens in the Caribbean Basin. -
    1984.
      (001762)

CARIBBEAN REGION--TOURISM.
----Reassessing Third World tourism. - 1984.
   (000802)

CARIBBEAN REGION--TRADE AGREEMENTS.
----The Caribbean Basin Economic Recovery
   Act and its implications for foreign
   private investment. - 1984.
   (001965)
----La presentación de la iniciativa de la
   Cuenca del Caribe al GATT. - 1985.
   (001972)

CARIBBEAN REGION--TRADE INFORMATION.
----Caribbean Basin business information
   starter kit. - 1984.
   (001782)

CARIBBEAN REGION--TRADE PROMOTION.
----Caribbean Basin business information
   starter kit. - 1984.
   (001782)

CARIBBEAN REGION--TRANSNATIONAL CORPORATIONS.
----Multinational corporations and regional
   revenue retention in a vertically
   integrated industry: bauxite/aluminium
   in the Caribbean. - 1983.
   (000582)
----Le rôle des multinationales dans
   l'économie des Caraïbes. - 1984.
   (001088)
----Transnational corporations in the
   Caribbean. - 1984.
   (001118)

CARTELS.
----The aluminum multinationals and the
   bauxite cartel. - 1987.
   (000599)
----Extraterritorial effects of United
   States commercial and antitrust
   legislation. - 1983.
   (002352)
----Managing an oligopoly of would-be
   sovereigns. - 1987.
   (000623)
----Multinational corporations, OPEC,
   cartels, foreign investment, and
   technology transfer special studies,
   1982-1985. - 1987.
   (000589)
----Multinational monopolies and
   international cartels. - 1984.
   (001663)

CASH MANAGEMENT.
----International treasury management. -
   1988.
   (000440)

CENTER FOR INTERNATIONAL PRIVATE ENTERPRISE
(WASHINGTON, D.C.).
----Democratic development. - 1986.
   (001334)

CENTRAL AFRICA--TECHNOLOGY TRANSFER.
----Le transfert de technologie dans les
   industries agro-alimentaires en Afrique
   Centrale. - 1987.
   (001510)

CENTRAL AMERICA--BANANAS.
----Las transnacionales del banano en
   Centroamérica. - 1983.
   (000564)

CENTRAL AMERICA--CAPITAL INVESTMENTS.
----Capital intensity and export propensity
   in some Latin American countries. - 1987.
   (001389)

CENTRAL AMERICA--CHOICE OF TECHNOLOGY.
----Capital intensity and export propensity
   in some Latin American countries. - 1987.
   (001389)

CENTRAL AMERICA--EXPORT ORIENTED INDUSTRIES.
----Capital intensity and export propensity
   in some Latin American countries. - 1987.
   (001389)
----Industrialización y exportaciones no
   tradicionales. - 1984.
   (001316)

CENTRAL AMERICA--FOREIGN INVESTMENTS.
----Legal framework for foreign investment
   in the Caribbean and Central America. -
   1984.
   (001964)

CENTRAL AMERICA--INDUSTRIAL POLICY.
----Industrialización y exportaciones no
   tradicionales. - 1984.
   (001316)

CENTRAL AMERICA--INDUSTRIALIZATION.
----Industrialización y exportaciones no
   tradicionales. - 1984.
   (001316)

CENTRAL AMERICA--STRUCTURAL ADJUSTMENT.
----Industrialización y exportaciones no
   tradicionales. - 1984.
   (001316)

CENTRAL AMERICA--TRANSNATIONAL CORPORATIONS.
----Las transnacionales del banano en
   Centroamérica. - 1983.
   (000564)

CENTRAL BANKS.
----Annual report (Bank for International
   Settlements). - 1930-   .
   (001228)

CENTRALLY PLANNED ECONOMIES.
----Des multinationales a l'Est? (With
   English summary.). - 1984.
   (000331)
----Les entreprises à participation
   étrangère installées dans les pays
   socialistes. - 1987.
   (001183)
----The foreign investment activity of the
   Comecon countries. - 1983.
   (000355)
----Information industries in the CMEA
   countries : a foreign trade dimension. -
   1986.
   (000894)
----L'informatique dans les pays du CAEM :
   quelques aspects des politiques suivies.
   - 1986.
   (000711)

CENTRALLY PLANNED ECONOMIES (continued)
----L'investissement productif en Europe de
l'Est : gaspillage des ressources,
délais de réalisation importants, retard
technologique? - 1986.
(000126)
----Kelet : nyugati közös vállalatok néhány
elvi kérdése. - 1984.
(001180)
----Mezhdunarodnata investitsionna banka i
neinata rolia v razvitieto na
sotsialisticheskata ikonomicheska
integratsiia. - 1986.
(002153)
----Países socialistas y corporaciones
transnacionales. - 1984.
(001178)
----Production and trade in services. - 1985.
(000978)
----Socialist economic integration and the
investment cooperation of the CMEA
countries. - 1984.
(001185)
----Technology export from the socialist
countries. - 1986.
(001470)
----Transborder data flows. - 1983.
(000973)
----Transborder data flows. - 1984.
(000974)
----Trends and issues in foreign direct
investment and related flows. - 1985.
(000192)

CENTRALLY PLANNED ECONOMIES--EASTERN EUROPE.
----Equity cooperation ventures (ECV)
domiciled in the socialist countries :
trends and patterns. - 1986.
(001603)
----Pravovye formy organizatsii sovmestnykh
proizvodstv stran-chlenov SEV. - 1985.
(002157)

CENTRALLY PLANNED ECONOMIES--USSR.
----L'URSS et le Tiers Monde. - 1984.
(002040)

CENTRALLY PLANNED ECONOMIES--WESTERN EUROPE.
----Western direct investment in centrally
planned economies. - 1986.
(000159)

CENTRE FOR INDUSTRIAL DEVELOPMENT.
----Agro-industrial co-operation between the
European Community and the ACP
countries. - 1986.
(002605)

CERAMICS INDUSTRY--THAILAND.
----Technology acquisition under alternative
arrangements with transnational
corporations. - 1987.
(001512)
----Technology transfer under alternative
arrangements with transnational
corporations. - 1987.
(001513)

CHAMBERS OF COMMERCE--EUROPE.
----Directory of European industrial [and]
trade associations. - 1986-   .
(002707)

CHARCOAL--LATIN AMERICA.
----La industria siderúrgica
latinoamericana. - 1984.
(000601)

CHEMICAL INDUSTRY.
----Analyse de l'activité de 95 firmes
industrielles étrangères dans la
bio-industrie. - 1983.
(000652)
----The spatial organisation of
multinational corporations. - 1985.
(000017)

CHEMICAL INDUSTRY--BHOPAL (INDIA).
----The lessons of Bhopal. - 1985.
(001933)
----Mass disasters and multinational
liability : the Bhopal case. - 1986.
(001936)

CHEMICAL INDUSTRY--FRANCE.
----Le role des grandes entreprises
diversifiées du pétrole et de la chimie
dans la production alimentaire. - 1985.
(000699)

CHEMICAL INDUSTRY--GERMANY, FEDERAL REPUBLIC
OF.
----La recherche-développement dans la
stratégie des grandes entreprises
chimiques de l'entre-deux-guerres: Du
Pont de Nemours, Imperial Chemical
Industries, I. G. Farben. (With English
summary.). - 1984.
(000295)

CHEMICAL INDUSTRY--INDIA.
----The lessons of Bhopal. - 1985.
(001933)

CHEMICAL INDUSTRY--INDONESIA.
----Technology transfer under alternative
arrangements with transnational
corporations. - 1987.
(001513)

CHEMICAL INDUSTRY--SOUTHEAST ASIA.
----The allure of Southeast Asia's chemical
market. - 1987.
(000661)

CHEMICAL INDUSTRY--THAILAND.
----Technology transfer under alternative
arrangements with transnational
corporations. - 1987.
(001513)

CHEMICAL INDUSTRY--UNITED STATES.
----A competitive assessment of the U.S.
methanol industry. - 1985.
(000671)
----Le role des grandes entreprises
diversifiées du pétrole et de la chimie
dans la production alimentaire. - 1985.
(000699)

CHEMICALS.
----Consolidated list of products whose
consumption and/or sale have been
banned, withdrawn, severely restricted
or not approved by Governments. - 1987.
(002702)

CHEMICALS (continued)
----Second revised draft Guidelines for the
    Exchange of Information on Potentially
    Harmful Chemicals in International
    Trade. - 1986.
        (002019)

CHEMICALS--MEXICO.
----Estructura y comportamiento de la
    industria químico-farmacéutica en
    México. - 1984.
        (000737)

CHEVRON OIL COMPANY (KHARTOUM).
----Chevron, Sudan and political risk. -
    1984.
        (001858)

CHILE--CONCESSIONS.
----Einige juristische Aspekte des
    Ausverkaufs der chilenischen Wirtschaft
    an die internationalen Monopole. - 1984.
        (002161)

CHILE--COPPER.
----Chile : creative economic management. -
    1987.
        (001784)

CHILE--CREDITWORTHINESS.
----Debt equity swaps, investment, and
    creditworthiness. - 1987.
        (000259)

CHILE--DEBT MANAGEMENT.
----Debt equity swaps, investment, and
    creditworthiness. - 1987.
        (000259)

CHILE--DEVELOPMENT.
----Las empresas transnacionales en la
    economía de Chile, 1974-1980. - 1983.
        (001123)

CHILE--ECONOMIC CONDITIONS.
----Chile : creative economic management. -
    1987.
        (001784)
----Las empresas transnacionales en la
    economía de Chile, 1974-1980. - 1983.
        (001123)

CHILE--EXPORTS.
----Chile : creative economic management. -
    1987.
        (001784)

CHILE--EXTERNAL DEBT.
----Chile : creative economic management. -
    1987.
        (001784)
----Debt equity swaps, investment, and
    creditworthiness. - 1987.
        (000259)

CHILE--FOREIGN DIRECT INVESTMENT.
----Aspectos relevantes de la inversión
    extranjera en Chile. - 1984.
        (002171)
----Chile : creative economic management. -
    1987.
        (001784)

----Las empresas transnacionales y la
    inversión extranjera directa en la
    primera mitad de los años ochenta. -
    1987.
        (000194)

CHILE--FOREIGN INVESTMENTS.
----National legislation and regulations
    relating to transnational corporations.
    Volume 4. - 1986.
        (002253)

CHILE--INVESTMENTS.
----Debt equity swaps, investment, and
    creditworthiness. - 1987.
        (000259)

CHILE--IRON AND STEEL INDUSTRY.
----La industria siderúrgica
    latinoamericana. - 1984.
        (000601)

CHILE--LAWS AND REGULATIONS.
----Aspectos relevantes de la inversión
    extranjera en Chile. - 1984.
        (002171)
----National legislation and regulations
    relating to transnational corporations.
    Volume 4. - 1986.
        (002253)

CHILE--METALLURGICAL INDUSTRY.
----La industria siderúrgica
    latinoamericana. - 1984.
        (000601)

CHILE--MINING INDUSTRY.
----Einige juristische Aspekte des
    Ausverkaufs der chilenischen Wirtschaft
    an die internationalen Monopole. - 1984.
        (002161)

CHILE--TRANSNATIONAL CORPORATIONS.
----Einige juristische Aspekte des
    Ausverkaufs der chilenischen Wirtschaft
    an die internationalen Monopole. - 1984.
        (002161)
----Las empresas transnacionales en la
    economía de Chile, 1974-1980. - 1983.
        (001123)
----National legislation and regulations
    relating to transnational corporations.
    Volume 4. - 1986.
        (002253)

CHINA--AGRICULTURAL POLICY.
----Agriculture in China. - 1985.
        (000561)

CHINA--AGRICULTURAL PRODUCTION.
----Agriculture in China. - 1985.
        (000561)

CHINA--AGRICULTURAL PRODUCTS.
----Agriculture in China. - 1985.
        (000561)

CHINA--AUTOMATION.
----Microelectronics-based automation
    technologies and development. - 1985.
        (000753)

CHINA--BANKING.
----The People's Republic of China. - 1986.
    (001841)

CHINA--BANKING SYSTEMS.
----Ouverture et dynamique interne du
    capital en Chine. - 1987.
    (001064)

CHINA--BUSINESS.
----The People's Republic of China. - 1986.
    (001841)

CHINA--BUSINESS ENTERPRISES.
----China adopts law on foreign enterprises.
    - 1986.
    (002294)
----Tax aspects of doing business with the
    People's Republic of China. - 1984.
    (001713)

CHINA--CAPITAL INVESTMENTS.
----China experiments with modernisation. -
    1983.
    (002384)
----Ouverture et dynamique interne du
    capital en Chine. - 1987.
    (001064)

CHINA--CAPITAL MOVEMENTS.
----On the issue of utilizing foreign
    capital. - 1985.
    (002207)

CHINA--CLAIMS.
----United States policy regarding
    nationalization of American investments.
    - 1984.
    (002332)

CHINA--COMMERCIAL ARBITRATION.
----Dispute resolution in the People's
    Republic of China. - 1984.
    (002558)
----Mediation, conciliation, arbitration and
    litigation in the People's Republic of
    China. - 1987.
    (002565)

CHINA--COMMERCIAL LAW.
----China laws for foreign business. -
    1985-   .
    (002187)
----China's foreign economic contract law. -
    1987.
    (002297)
----Foreign economic contract law of the
    People's Republic of China. - 1987.
    (002166)
----Foreign investment law in the People's
    Republic of China. - 1987.
    (002299)
----International dispute resolution and the
    People's Republic of China. - 1984.
    (002522)
----The joint venture and related contract
    laws of mainland China and Taiwan. -
    1987.
    (002278)
----The law applicable to a transnational
    economic development contract. - 1987.
    (002164)

CHINA--COMMUNES.
----Private enterprise in China. - 1985.
    (002184)

CHINA--COMPENSATION TRADE.
----China's special economic zones. - 1983.
    (002381)

CHINA--CONCILIATION.
----Mediation, conciliation, arbitration and
    litigation in the People's Republic of
    China. - 1987.
    (002565)

CHINA--CONTRACTS.
----China's foreign economic contract law. -
    1987.
    (002297)
----Foreign economic contract law of the
    People's Republic of China. - 1987.
    (002166)
----The law applicable to a transnational
    economic development contract. - 1987.
    (002164)
----The new foreign contract law in China. -
    1986.
    (002276)
----United States-China commercial
    contracts. - 1986.
    (002439)
----The 1981 Economic Contract Law of the
    People's Republic of China. - 1986.
    (002237)

CHINA--CORPORATION TAX.
----The People's Republic of China. - 1986.
    (001841)

CHINA--CORPORATIONS.
----The China directory of industry and
    commerce and economic annual. - 1984.
    (002626)

CHINA--DECISION-MAKING.
----The China trade: making the deal/the
    China trade: making the deal work. -
    1986.
    (001845)

CHINA--DEVELOPMENT PLANNING.
----The 1981 Economic Contract Law of the
    People's Republic of China. - 1986.
    (002237)

CHINA--DIRECTORIES.
----The China directory of industry and
    commerce and economic annual. - 1984.
    (002626)

CHINA--ECONOMIC AGREEMENTS.
----The law applicable to a transnational
    economic development contract. - 1987.
    (002164)

CHINA--ECONOMIC CONDITIONS.
----The China directory of industry and
    commerce and economic annual. - 1984.
    (002626)
----The 1982-83 overinvestment crisis in
    China. - 1984.
    (000120)

CHINA--ECONOMIC CO-OPERATION.
----Investitions- und
    Kooperationsmöglichkeit "Equity joint
    venture" in der Volksrepublik China. -
    1986.
      (002199)

CHINA--ECONOMIC DEVELOPMENT.
----The role of oil in China's economic
    development, growth, and
    internationalization. - 1985.
      (000602)

CHINA--ECONOMIC FORECASTS.
----Die chinesischen Wirtschaftsreformen im
    neunten Jahr. - 1986.
      (002217)

CHINA--ECONOMIC GROWTH.
----Investitions- und
    Kooperationsmöglichkeit "Equity joint
    venture" in der Volksrepublik China. -
    1986.
      (002199)

CHINA--ECONOMIC HISTORY.
----Partnership with China. - 1986.
      (001035)

CHINA--ECONOMIC LAW.
----Like bamboo shoots after a rain :
    exploiting the Chinese law and new
    regulations on Sino-foreign joint
    ventures. - 1987.
      (002298)
----The new foreign contract law in China. -
    1986.
      (002276)
----The 1981 Economic Contract Law of the
    People's Republic of China. - 1986.
      (002237)

CHINA--ECONOMIC POLICY.
----China's modernization and transnational
    corporations. - 1984.
      (001077)
----China's open door policy. - 1984.
      (002219)
----China's open door policy and the
    prospects for FDI. - 1986.
      (001043)
----China's opening to the world. - 1986.
      (002221)
----China's reform of the economic structure
    and its open-door policy. - 1985.
      (002273)
----China's special economic zones. - 1986.
      (002366)
----Chinese economic reforms since 1978 with
    particular emphasis on the special
    economic zones. - 1987.
      (002375)
----Die chinesischen Wirtschaftsreformen im
    neunten Jahr. - 1986.
      (002217)
----Foreign economic contract law of the
    People's Republic of China. - 1987.
      (002166)
----The investment implications of China's
    offshore oil development. - 1986.
      (000612)
----Kina különleges gazdasági övezetei. -
    1987.
      (002374)

----Private enterprise in China. - 1985.
      (002184)
----Recent developments in China's special
    economic zones : problems and prognosis.
    - 1987.
      (002404)
----Shenzhen : a Chinese development zone in
    global perspective. - 1985.
      (002393)
----Special economic zones and economic
    policy in China. - 1983.
      (002394)
----Special economic zones in China's
    modernization. - 1986.
      (002385)
----Special economic zones in the PRC. -
    1986.
      (002369)

CHINA--ECONOMIC REFORM.
----On economic reforms, trade and foreign
    investment in China. - 1986.
      (001336)
----The reform of the Chinese system of
    enterprise ownership. - 1987.
      (002185)

CHINA--ECONOMIC RELATIONS.
----China's modernization and transnational
    corporations. - 1984.
      (001077)
----Collection of laws and regulations of
    the People's Republic of China
    concerning foreign economic affairs. -
    1985-   .
      (002188)
----The European Community and China. - 1986.
      (002045)
----Guide to China's foreign economic
    relations and trade. - 1983.
      (001806)
----The open policy at work. - 1985.
      (001072)
----Shenzhen : a Chinese development zone in
    global perspective. - 1985.
      (002393)
----Sino-Indian economic relations. - 1984.
      (000307)
----Transnational corporations and China's
    open door policy. - 1988.
      (001074)

CHINA--ECONOMIC STRUCTURE.
----China's reform of the economic structure
    and its open-door policy. - 1985.
      (002273)

CHINA--ECONOMIC ZONING.
----China experiments with modernisation. -
    1983.
      (002384)
----China's special economic zones. - 1984.
      (002386)
----China's special economic zones. - 1986.
      (002382)
----China's special economic zones. - 1986.
      (002366)
----The investment implications of China's
    offshore oil development. - 1986.
      (000612)
----Kina különleges gazdasági övezetei. -
    1987.
      (002374)

CHINA--ECONOMIC ZONING (continued)
----Special economic zones in China's
modernization. - 1986.
(002385)

CHINA--EMPLOYEES.
----The training component. - 1986.
(001920)

CHINA--EXCLUSIVE ECONOMIC ZONE.
----Special economic zones and economic
policy in China. - 1983.
(002394)

CHINA--EXPORT ORIENTED INDUSTRIES.
----China's special economic zones. - 1983.
(002381)

CHINA--FOOD CONSUMPTION.
----Agriculture in China. - 1985.
(000561)

CHINA--FOREIGN DIRECT INVESTMENT.
----China's open door policy. - 1984.
(002219)
----China's open door policy and the
prospects for FDI. - 1986.
(001043)
----China's special economic zones. - 1986.
(002382)
----Chung-kuo tui wai shui wu shou ts'e. -
1983.
(001704)
----Eight years of the open policy. - 1987.
(001051)
----Foreign direct investment in the
People's Republic of China. - 1988.
(000191)
----Foreign investment and trade; origins of
the modernization policy. - 1983.
(001354)
----Guide to China's foreign economic
relations and trade. - 1983.
(001806)
----Insuring investment projects. - 1988.
(002033)
----Les investissements directs des Chinois
d'outre-mer en Chine. - 1987.
(000201)
----A külföldi tokebefektetések néhány
tapasztalata Kínában. - 1987.
(001049)
----Legal aspects of joint ventures in
China. - 1986.
(002178)
----Like bamboo shoots after a rain :
exploiting the Chinese law and new
regulations on Sino-foreign joint
ventures. - 1987.
(002298)
----The new legal framework for joint
ventures in China. - 1984.
(002282)
----On economic reforms, trade and foreign
investment in China. - 1986.
(001336)
----On the issue of utilizing foreign
capital. - 1985.
(002207)
----The open policy at work. - 1985.
(001072)
----Ouverture et dynamique interne du
capital en Chine. - 1987.
(001064)

----Partnership with China. - 1986.
(001035)
----The present situation and problems of
direct investment in China. - 1986.
(000163)
----Singapore's role in China's offshore oil
venture. - 1985.
(000608)
----Special economic zones in the People's
Republic of China. - 1986.
(002361)
----Strategies for joint ventures in the
People's Republic of China. - 1987.
(001610)

CHINA--FOREIGN EXCHANGE.
----Foreign direct investment in the
People's Republic of China. - 1988.
(000191)

CHINA--FOREIGN INVESTMENTS.
----Almanac of China's foreign economic
relations and trade. - 1984-   .
(002615)
----China : new provisions to encourage
foreign investment. - 1987.
(002313)
----China laws for foreign business. -
1985-   .
(002187)
----China's opening to the world. - 1986.
(002221)
----China's utilization of foreign funds and
relevant policies. - 1984.
(002227)
----Chinese solutions to legal problems. -
1987.
(002295)
----Creating a favorable investment
environment. - 1987.
(001794)
----Dispute resolution in the People's
Republic of China. - 1984.
(002558)
----Foreign investment law in the People's
Republic of China. - 1987.
(002299)
----Foreign trade, investment and the law in
the People's Republic of China. - 1985.
(002211)
----International dispute resolution and the
People's Republic of China. - 1984.
(002522)
----An introduction to foreign investment
law in China. - 1986.
(002296)
----Investitions- und
Kooperationsmöglichkeit "Equity joint
venture" in der Volksrepublik China. -
1986.
(002199)
----The investment climate in China. - 1987.
(001810)
----The investment implications of China's
offshore oil development. - 1986.
(000612)
----Joint ventures in China. - 1986.
(002281)
----The law applicable to a transnational
economic development contract. - 1987.
(002164)

CHINA--FOREIGN INVESTMENTS (continued)
----The new foreign contract law in China. -
    1986.
        (002276)
----The People's Republic of China. - 1986.
        (001841)
----Realities confronting China's foreign
    investment policy. - 1984.
        (002292)
----Shenzhen : a Chinese development zone in
    global perspective. - 1985.
        (002393)
----The special economic zones. - 1987.
        (002379)
----Special economic zones in China's
    modernization. - 1986.
        (002385)
----The special economic zones of China. -
    1985.
        (002392)
----Taxation of foreign business and
    investment in the People's Republic of
    China. - 1987.
        (001708)
----To open wider, or to close again :
    China's foreign investment policies and
    laws. - 1984.
        (002163)
----United States policy regarding
    nationalization of American investments.
    - 1984.
        (002332)
----Les zones économiques spéciales de la
    République populaire chinoise. - 1985.
        (002383)

CHINA--FOREIGN LOANS.
----China's utilization of foreign funds and
    relevant policies. - 1984.
        (002227)

CHINA--FOREIGN TRADE.
----Agriculture in China. - 1985.
        (000561)
----Almanac of China's foreign economic
    relations and trade. - 1984-   .
        (002615)
----China special economic zones in
    perspective. - 1986.
        (002397)
----The China trade: making the deal/the
    China trade: making the deal work. -
    1986.
        (001845)
----China's foreign economic contract law. -
    1987.
        (002297)
----China's opening to the world. - 1986.
        (002221)
----China's special economic zones. - 1984.
        (002395)
----China's special economic zones. - 1986.
        (002382)
----Doing business with China. - 1974-   .
        (001792)
----Foreign investment and trade; origins of
    the modernization policy. - 1983.
        (001354)
----Foreign trade, investment and the law in
    the People's Republic of China. - 1985.
        (002211)

----Formation of contract and contract law
    through multinational joint ventures. -
    1983.
        (002435)
----Guide to China's foreign economic
    relations and trade. - 1983.
        (001806)
----On economic reforms, trade and foreign
    investment in China. - 1986.
        (001336)
----Recent changes in China's pure trade
    theory. - 1986.
        (001677)
----Shantou SEZ orientated towards export. -
    1987.
        (002377)
----Sino-Indian economic relations. - 1984.
        (000307)
----Special economic zones in the PRC. -
    1986.
        (002369)
----Trade policies in the PRC. - 1986.
        (001387)
----United States-China commercial
    contracts. - 1986.
        (002439)
----Les zones économiques spéciales de la
    République populaire chinoise. - 1985.
        (002383)

CHINA--FREE EXPORT ZONES.
----China special economic zones in
    perspective. - 1986.
        (002397)
----China's opening to the world. - 1986.
        (002221)
----China's special economic zones. - 1984.
        (002386)
----China's special economic zones. - 1984.
        (002395)
----China's special economic zones. - 1986.
        (002382)
----China's special economic zones. - 1986.
        (002366)
----Chinese economic reforms since 1978 with
    particular emphasis on the special
    economic zones. - 1987.
        (002375)
----Eight years of the open policy. - 1987.
        (001051)
----Kína különleges gazdasági övezetei. -
    1987.
        (002374)
----Recent developments in China's special
    economic zones : problems and prognosis.
    - 1987.
        (002404)
----Shantou SEZ orientated towards export. -
    1987.
        (002377)
----Shenzhen : a Chinese development zone in
    global perspective. - 1985.
        (002393)
----The special economic zones. - 1987.
        (002379)
----Special economic zones in the People's
    Republic of China. - 1986.
        (002361)
----Special economic zones in the PRC. -
    1986.
        (002369)

Subject Index - Index des matières

CHINA--FREE EXPORT ZONES (continued)
----The special economic zones of China. -
    1985.
        (002392)
----Trade policies in the PRC. - 1986.
        (001387)
----Les zones économiques spéciales de la
    République populaire chinoise. - 1985.
        (002383)

CHINA--INCOME TAX.
----A comparative analysis of the United
    States-People's Republic of China tax
    treaty. - 1986.
        (002037)
----Taxation of foreign business and
    investment in the People's Republic of
    China. - 1987.
        (001708)

CHINA--INDUSTRIAL CO-OPERATION.
----Industrial co-operation between China
    and Hong Kong. - 1983.
        (001554)

CHINA--INDUSTRIAL DEVELOPMENT.
----La politique chinoise d'ouverture. -
    1983.
        (002186)

CHINA--INDUSTRIAL PLANNING.
----Strategies for joint ventures in the
    People's Republic of China. - 1987.
        (001610)

CHINA--INDUSTRY.
----Business opportunities in China. - 1984.
        (000999)
----The China directory of industry and
    commerce and economic annual. - 1984.
        (002626)

CHINA--INFORMATION.
----The People's Republic of China. - 1986.
        (001841)

CHINA--INSURANCE COMPANIES.
----Insuring investment projects. - 1988.
        (002033)

CHINA--INSURANCE LAW.
----Insuring investment projects. - 1988.
        (002033)

CHINA--INTERNATIONAL COMMERCIAL TRANSACTIONS.
----China laws for foreign business. -
    1985-   .
        (002187)

CHINA--INVESTMENT DISPUTES.
----Dispute resolution in the People's
    Republic of China. - 1984.
        (002558)

CHINA--INVESTMENT POLICY.
----China's open door policy and the
    prospects for FDI. - 1986.
        (001043)
----China's special economic zones. - 1984.
        (002395)
----China's trade, tax and investment laws
    and regulations. - 1984.
        (002189)

----Chinese solutions to legal problems. -
    1987.
        (002295)
----Realities confronting China's foreign
    investment policy. - 1984.
        (002292)
----The 1982-83 overinvestment crisis in
    China. - 1984.
        (000120)

CHINA--JOINT VENTURES.
----Business opportunities in China. - 1984.
        (000999)
----China : new provisions to encourage
    foreign investment. - 1987.
        (002313)
----China adopts law on foreign enterprises.
    - 1986.
        (002294)
----China special economic zones in
    perspective. - 1986.
        (002397)
----China strategies. - 1986.
        (001037)
----The China trade: making the deal/the
    China trade: making the deal work. -
    1986.
        (001845)
----China's special economic zones. - 1983.
        (002381)
----China's trade, tax and investment laws
    and regulations. - 1984.
        (002189)
----Chinese solutions to legal problems. -
    1987.
        (002295)
----Chung wai ho tzu ching ying ch'i yeh fa
    chi ch'i shih shih ching yen ch'ien
    t'an. - 1983.
        (002190)
----Chung-kuo tui wai shui wu shou ts'e. -
    1983.
        (001704)
----Eight years of the open policy. - 1987.
        (001051)
----Foreign direct investment in the
    People's Republic of China. - 1988.
        (000191)
----Foreign investment law in the People's
    Republic of China. - 1987.
        (002299)
----Foreign trade, investment and the law in
    the People's Republic of China. - 1985.
        (002211)
----Formation of contract and contract law
    through multinational joint ventures. -
    1983.
        (002435)
----Guide to China's foreign economic
    relations and trade. - 1983.
        (001806)
----Investitions- und
    Kooperationsmöglichkeit "Equity joint
    venture" in der Volksrepublik China. -
    1986.
        (002199)
----The joint venture and related contract
    laws of mainland China and Taiwan. -
    1987.
        (002278)
----Joint ventures in China. - 1986.
        (002281)

-56-

CHINA--JOINT VENTURES (continued)
----Joint ventures in the People's Republic
    of China. - 1985.
      (001647)
----Joint ventures in the PRC. - 1987.
      (000478)
----Legal aspects of joint ventures in
    China. - 1986.
      (002178)
----Like bamboo shoots after a rain :
    exploiting the Chinese law and new
    regulations on Sino-foreign joint
    ventures. - 1987.
      (002298)
----The new legal framework for joint
    ventures in China. - 1984.
      (002282)
----The open policy at work. - 1985.
      (001072)
----Partnership with China. - 1986.
      (001035)
----La politique chinoise d'ouverture. -
    1983.
      (002186)
----Realities confronting China's foreign
    investment policy. - 1984.
      (002292)
----Singapore's role in China's offshore oil
    venture. - 1985.
      (000608)
----Sino-Indian economic relations. - 1984.
      (000307)
----Strategies for joint ventures in the
    People's Republic of China. - 1987.
      (001610)
----Tax aspects of doing business with the
    People's Republic of China. - 1984.
      (001713)
----Taxation of foreign business and
    investment in the People's Republic of
    China. - 1987.
      (001708)
----To open wider, or to close again :
    China's foreign investment policies and
    laws. - 1984.
      (002163)
----The training component. - 1986.
      (001920)
----Trends and issues in foreign direct
    investment and related flows. - 1985.
      (000192)

CHINA--LAW.
----China laws for foreign business. -
    1985-   .
      (002187)

CHINA--LAWS AND REGULATIONS.
----China adopts law on foreign enterprises.
    - 1986.
      (002294)
----Chung wai ho tzu ching ying ch'i yeh fa
    chi ch'i shih shih ching yen ch'ien
    t'an. - 1983.
      (002190)
----Chung-kuo tui wai shui wu shou ts'e. -
    1983.
      (001704)
----Collection of laws and regulations of
    the People's Republic of China
    concerning foreign economic affairs. -
    1985-   .
      (002188)

----Foreign direct investment in the
    People's Republic of China. - 1988.
      (000191)
----The investment climate in China. - 1987.
      (001810)
----Joint ventures in China. - 1986.
      (002281)
----Legal aspects of joint ventures in
    China. - 1986.
      (002178)
----The new legal framework for joint
    ventures in China. - 1984.
      (002282)
----Ouverture et dynamique interne du
    capital en Chine. - 1987.
      (001064)
----Private enterprise in China. - 1985.
      (002184)
----Realities confronting China's foreign
    investment policy. - 1984.
      (002292)
----Special economic zones in the People's
    Republic of China. - 1986.
      (002361)
----To open wider, or to close again :
    China's foreign investment policies and
    laws. - 1984.
      (002163)

CHINA--LICENCE AGREEMENTS.
----United States-China commercial
    contracts. - 1986.
      (002439)

CHINA--MANAGEMENT.
----China strategies. - 1986.
      (001037)
----The China trade: making the deal/the
    China trade: making the deal work. -
    1986.
      (001845)
----Strategies for joint ventures in the
    People's Republic of China. - 1987.
      (001610)

CHINA--MANAGERS.
----The training component. - 1986.
      (001920)

CHINA--MARKET ACCESS.
----Foreign direct investment in the
    People's Republic of China. - 1988.
      (000191)

CHINA--MEDIATION.
----Mediation, conciliation, arbitration and
    litigation in the People's Republic of
    China. - 1987.
      (002565)

CHINA--MICROELECTRONICS.
----Microelectronics-based automation
    technologies and development. - 1985.
      (000753)

CHINA--NATIONALIZATION.
----United States policy regarding
    nationalization of American investments.
    - 1984.
      (002332)

CHINA--NATURAL RESOURCES.
----The law applicable to a transnational
economic development contract. - 1987.
(002164)

CHINA--OFFSHORE OIL DRILLING.
----The investment implications of China's
offshore oil development. - 1986.
(000612)
----Singapore's role in China's offshore oil
venture. - 1985.
(000608)

CHINA--PATENT LAW.
----Collection of laws and regulations of
the People's Republic of China
concerning foreign economic affairs. -
1985-   .
(002188)

CHINA--PETROLEUM EXPLORATION.
----Social and economic effects of petroleum
development. - 1987.
(000633)

CHINA--PETROLEUM INDUSTRY.
----The role of oil in China's economic
development, growth, and
internationalization. - 1985.
(000602)
----Social and economic effects of petroleum
development. - 1987.
(000633)
----Some aspects of the Chinese petroleum
industry. - 1983.
(000615)

CHINA--PETROLEUM PRODUCTS.
----The role of oil in China's economic
development, growth, and
internationalization. - 1985.
(000602)

CHINA--PHARMACEUTICAL INDUSTRY.
----Joint ventures in the PRC. - 1987.
(000478)

CHINA--PRIVATE ENTERPRISES.
----China : private enterprise on the march.
- 1987.
(001054)
----Private enterprise in China. - 1985.
(002184)
----The reform of the Chinese system of
enterprise ownership. - 1987.
(002185)

CHINA--PRIVATE SECTOR.
----Die chinesischen Wirtschaftsreformen im
neunten Jahr. - 1986.
(002217)

CHINA--PUBLIC ENTERPRISES.
----The reform of the Chinese system of
enterprise ownership. - 1987.
(002185)

CHINA--REGIONAL DEVELOPMENT.
----China experiments with modernisation. -
1983.
(002384)

CHINA--RISK MANAGEMENT.
----Joint ventures in the PRC. - 1987.
(000478)

CHINA--SCIENCE AND TECHNOLOGY POLICY.
----Proceedings of the SSTCC/UNCTC/ESCAP
Asia-Pacific Training Workshop on
Regulating and Negotiating Technology
Transfer through Transnational
Corporations, 14-25 October 1985,
Fuzhou, Fujian, China. - 1986.
(001405) (002169)

CHINA--SERVICE INDUSTRIES.
----Die chinesischen Wirtschaftsreformen im
neunten Jahr. - 1986.
(002217)

CHINA--STRATEGY.
----China strategies. - 1986.
(001037)
----Strategies for joint ventures in the
People's Republic of China. - 1987.
(001610)

CHINA--TAX LAW.
----China's trade, tax and investment laws
and regulations. - 1984.
(002189)
----A comparative analysis of the United
States-People's Republic of China tax
treaty. - 1986.
(002037)
----Revenue law and practice in the People's
Republic of China. - 1983.
(002271)
----Taxation of foreign business and
investment in the People's Republic of
China. - 1987.
(001708)

CHINA--TAX SYSTEMS.
----Tax aspects of doing business with the
People's Republic of China. - 1984.
(001713)

CHINA--TAX TREATIES.
----A comparative analysis of the United
States-People's Republic of China tax
treaty. - 1986.
(002037)
----Taxation of foreign business and
investment in the People's Republic of
China. - 1987.
(001708)

CHINA--TAXATION.
----Foreign direct investment in the
People's Republic of China. - 1988.
(000191)
----Like bamboo shoots after a rain :
exploiting the Chinese law and new
regulations on Sino-foreign joint
ventures. - 1987.
(002298)
----The People's Republic of China. - 1986.
(001841)

CHINA--TECHNICAL TRAINING.
----The training component. - 1986.
(001920)

CHINA--TECHNOLOGY TRANSFER.
----China's open door policy. - 1984.
　　(002219)
----China's opening to the world. - 1986.
　　(002221)
----Foreign direct investment in the
　　People's Republic of China. - 1988.
　　(000191)
----La politique chinoise d'ouverture. -
　　1983.
　　(002186)
----Proceedings of the SSTCC/UNCTC/ESCAP
　　Asia-Pacific Training Workshop on
　　Regulating and Negotiating Technology
　　Transfer through Transnational
　　Corporations, 14-25 October 1985,
　　Fuzhou, Fujian, China. - 1986.
　　(001405) (002169)

CHINA--TRADE AGREEMENTS.
----The European Community and China. - 1986.
　　(002045)

CHINA--TRADE NEGOTIATIONS.
----China's modernization and transnational
　　corporations. - 1984.
　　(001077)

CHINA--TRADE POLICY.
----China's modernization and transnational
　　corporations. - 1984.
　　(001077)
----The People's Republic of China. - 1986.
　　(001841)
----Strategies for joint ventures in the
　　People's Republic of China. - 1987.
　　(001610)
----Trade policies in the PRC. - 1986.
　　(001387)

CHINA--TRADE PROMOTION.
----Special economic zones in the People's
　　Republic of China. - 1986.
　　(002361)

CHINA--TRADE REGULATION.
----Almanac of China's foreign economic
　　relations and trade. - 1984-　　.
　　(002615)
----China's foreign economic contract law. -
　　1987.
　　(002297)
----China's trade, tax and investment laws
　　and regulations. - 1984.
　　(002189)

CHINA--TRADE STATISTICS.
----Almanac of China's foreign economic
　　relations and trade. - 1984-　　.
　　(002615)

CHINA--TRADEMARKS.
----Collection of laws and regulations of
　　the People's Republic of China
　　concerning foreign economic affairs. -
　　1985-　　.
　　(002188)

CHINA--TRAINING PROGRAMMES.
----The training component. - 1986.
　　(001920)

CHINA--TRANSNATIONAL CORPORATIONS.
----Business opportunities in China. - 1984.
　　(000999)
----China strategies. - 1986.
　　(001037)
----China's modernization and transnational
　　corporations. - 1984.
　　(001077)
----China's trade, tax and investment laws
　　and regulations. - 1984.
　　(002189)
----Chung wai ho tzu ching ying ch'i yeh fa
　　chi ch'i shih shih ching yen ch'ien
　　t'an. - 1983.
　　(002190)
----Foreign direct investment in the
　　People's Republic of China. - 1988.
　　(000191)
----Joint ventures in the People's Republic
　　of China. - 1985.
　　(001647)
----Revenue law and practice in the People's
　　Republic of China. - 1983.
　　(002271)
----The training component. - 1986.
　　(001920)
----Transnational corporations and China's
　　open door policy. - 1988.
　　(001074)

CHINA--TREATIES.
----An introduction to foreign investment
　　law in China. - 1986.
　　(002296)

CHINA--VACCINES.
----Joint ventures in the PRC. - 1987.
　　(000478)

CHOICE OF LAW.
----The two-way mirror : international
　　arbitration as comparative procedure. -
　　1985.
　　(002540)

CHOICE OF TECHNOLOGY.
----The capital goods sector in developing
　　countries. - 1985.
　　(001651)
----Technology and employment in industry. -
　　1985.
　　(001503)
----Technology choice and change in
　　developing countries. - 1983.
　　(001505)
----Technology choice and employment
　　generation by multinational enterprises
　　in developing countries. - 1984.
　　(001646)

CHOICE OF TECHNOLOGY--BRAZIL.
----Capital intensity and export propensity
　　in some Latin American countries. - 1987.
　　(001389)

CHOICE OF TECHNOLOGY--CENTRAL AMERICA.
----Capital intensity and export propensity
　　in some Latin American countries. - 1987.
　　(001389)

CHOICE OF TECHNOLOGY--COLOMBIA.
----Capital intensity and export propensity
　　in some Latin American countries. - 1987.
　　(001389)

CHOICE OF TECHNOLOGY--MEXICO.
----Capital intensity and export propensity in some Latin American countries. - 1987.
(001389)

CHRYSLER UNITED KINGDOM LIMITED.
----Foreign divestment and international rationalisation in the motor industry. - 1985.
(000664)

CHURCH.
----Churches and the transnational corporations. - 1983.
(002586)

CIVIL LAW.
----International trade disputes and the individual : private party involvement in national and international procedures regarding unfair foreign trade practices. - 1986.
(002514)
----Trade policy as a constitutional problem : on the "domestic policy functions" of international trade rules. - 1986.
(001379)

CLAIMS--CHINA.
----United States policy regarding nationalization of American investments. - 1984.
(002332)

CLAIMS--IRAN (ISLAMIC REPUBLIC OF).
----Current developments in the law of expropriation and compensation. - 1987.
(002318)
----The expropriation issue before the Iran-United States Claims Tribunal. - 1984.
(002320)
----Iran-U.S. Claims Tribunal. - 1986.
(002335)
----Partnership claims before the Iran-United States Claims Tribunal. - 1987.
(002322)

CLAIMS--UNITED STATES.
----Current developments in the law of expropriation and compensation. - 1987.
(002318)
----The expropriation issue before the Iran-United States Claims Tribunal. - 1984.
(002320)
----Forum non conveniens and multinational corporations. - 1986.
(002568)
----Iran-U.S. Claims Tribunal. - 1986.
(002335)
----Partnership claims before the Iran-United States Claims Tribunal. - 1987.
(002322)
----Recent developments in international commercial arbitration. - 1987.
(002549)
----United States policy regarding nationalization of American investments. - 1984.
(002332)

CLASSIFICATION--CANADA.
----Canadian standard industrial classification for companies and enterprises, 1980. - 1986-   .
(002718)

CLOTHING--INDIA.
----Foreign cooperation and the marketing of manufactured exports from developing countries. - 1985.
(001377)

CLOTHING--SRI LANKA.
----Foreign cooperation and the marketing of manufactured exports from developing countries. - 1985.
(001377)

CLOTHING INDUSTRY.
----Multinational companies in the textile, garment and leather industries. - 1984.
(000722)
----Social and labour practices of multinational enterprises in the textiles, clothing and footwear industries. - 1984.
(001922)
----Textile and clothing industries. - 1983.
(000740)
----Transnational corporations in the man-made fibre, textile and clothing industries. - 1987.
(000751)

CLOTHING INDUSTRY--HUNGARY.
----The impact of cooperation with Western firms on the Hungarian clothing industry. - 1983.
(001189)

CMEA.
----Capital movements within the CMEA. - 1986.
(001256)
----CMEA direct investments in the western countries. - 1987.
(000158)
----Cooperation in investments: a factor in the intensification of production in CMEA member nations. - 1983.
(001187)
----Eastern bloc international enterprises -- still in statu nascendi. - 1985.
(000332)
----East-West joint ventures. - 1988.
(001570)
----East-West trade and CMEA indebtedness in the seventies and eighties. - 1979.
(000209)
----Un exemple d'investissement du CAEM : liste des sociétés mixtes établies dans les pays en développement. - 1987.
(000284)
----The foreign investment activity of the Comecon countries. - 1983.
(000355)
----Information industries in the CMEA countries : a foreign trade dimension. - 1986.
(000894)
----L'informatique dans les pays du CAEM : quelques aspects des politiques suivies. - 1986.
(000711)

CMEA (continued)
----International economic organizations and
    multinational corporations. - 1986.
    (002590)
----L'investissement productif en Europe de
    l'Est : gaspillage des ressources,
    délais de réalisation importants, retard
    technologique? - 1986.
    (000126)
----Joint-ventures in Eastern Europe. - 1984.
    (001173)
----Kooperacja przemyslowa Polski z krajami
    RWPG. - 1986.
    (001172)
----A magyar gépipari vállalatok
    nagyságrendje és piaci magatartásuk. -
    1984.
    (000957)
----Les mouvements de capital au sein du
    Comecon. - 1984.
    (001257)
----Multinational companies and the COMECON
    countries. - 1986.
    (001177)
----Multinationals from the Second World :
    growth of foreign investment by Soviet
    and East European enterprises. - 1987.
    (000356)
----Pravovye formy organizatsii sovmestnykh
    proizvodstv stran-chlenov SEV. - 1985.
    (002157)
----Socialist economic integration and the
    investment cooperation of the CMEA
    countries. - 1984.
    (001185)
----The Soviet Union's other tax agreements.
    - 1986.
    (002043)
----Technological cooperation and
    specialization. - 1986.
    (001500)
----Technology export from the socialist
    countries. - 1986.
    (001470)
----L'URSS et le Tiers Monde. - 1984.
    (002040)
----Zum Einfluss von Modernisierung und
    Rekonstruktion auf die internationale
    sozialistische Arbeitsteilung. - 1987.
    (001227)

CMEA--WESTERN EUROPE.
----Tapping Eastern bloc technology. - 1983.
    (001452)

COAL--LATIN AMERICA.
----La industria siderúrgica
    latinoamericana. - 1984.
    (000601)

COAL INDUSTRY.
----Le nouveau marché international du
    charbon. - 1986.
    (000637)

CODE OF CONDUCT ON TRANSNATIONAL
CORPORATIONS (DRAFT).
----Bilateral investment treaties. - 1988.
    (002054)
----Code of Conduct on Transnational
    Corporations. - 1988.
    (002018)

----Commission on Transnational Corporations
    : report on the reconvened special
    session, 20-31 January 1986. - 1986.
    (002016)
----K mezinárodne právní úprave cinnosti
    nadnárodnich spolecnosti. - 1986.
    (001960)
----Measures to strengthen the capabilities
    of developing countries in their dealing
    with transnational corporations. - 1985.
    (002612)
----The question of a reference to
    international law in the United Nations
    Code of Conduct on Transnational
    Corporations. - 1986.
    (002007)
----The question of a reference to
    international obligations in the United
    Nations Code of Conduct on Transnational
    Corporations. - 1986.
    (002020)
----Regulation of transnational
    corporations. - 1984.
    (001998)
----Transnational corporations in world
    development. - 1983.
    (000102)
----UNCTC bibliography, 1974-1987. - 1988.
    (002695)
----The United Nations Code of Conduct on
    Transnational Corporations. - 1986.
    (002014)
----Work by the United Nations Centre on
    Transnational Corporations on the Code
    of Conduct on Transnational
    Corporations, other international
    arrangements and agreements, and
    national laws and regulations relating
    to transnational corporations. - 1986.
    (002694)

COLLECTIVE BARGAINING.
----El debate sindical nacional e
    internacional. - 1984.
    (002602)
----Employee consultation and information in
    multinational corporations. - 1986.
    (002603)
----Issues in management-labour relations in
    the 1990s. - 1985.
    (001914)
----Multinational business and labour. -
    1985.
    (001896)
----The OECD guidelines for multinational
    enterprises and labour relations,
    1982-1984. - 1985.
    (001961)
----The Vredeling proposal. - 1983.
    (002604)
----The Vredeling proposal and multinational
    trade unionism. - 1983.
    (002598)

COLLUSIVE TENDERING.
----Competition, tacit collusion and free
    entry. - 1987.
    (001679)

COLOMBIA--BUSINESS ENTERPRISES.
----Directorio de empresas y ejecutivos. -
    1979-
    (002628)

COLOMBIA--CAPITAL INVESTMENTS.
----Capital intensity and export propensity
in some Latin American countries. - 1987.
(001389)

COLOMBIA--CHOICE OF TECHNOLOGY.
----Capital intensity and export propensity
in some Latin American countries. - 1987.
(001389)

COLOMBIA--COMMERCIAL ARBITRATION.
----Arbitraje-conciliación. - 1985.
(002472)

COLOMBIA--CONCILIATION.
----Arbitraje-conciliación. - 1985.
(002472)

COLOMBIA--CONTRACTS.
----Petroleum service contracts in
Argentina, Brazil and Colombia : issues
arising from their legal nature. - 1987.
(002422)

COLOMBIA--DEVELOPMENT FINANCE.
----Las empresas transnacionales en el
desarrollo colombiano. - 1986.
(001121)

COLOMBIA--DIRECTORIES.
----Directorio de empresas y ejecutivos. -
1979-   .
(002628)

COLOMBIA--EXPORT DIVERSIFICATION.
----Las empresas transnacionales en el
desarrollo colombiano. - 1986.
(001121)

COLOMBIA--EXPORT ORIENTED INDUSTRIES.
----Capital intensity and export propensity
in some Latin American countries. - 1987.
(001389)

COLOMBIA--EXPORTS.
----Las empresas transnacionales en el
desarrollo colombiano. - 1986.
(001121)

COLOMBIA--FOREIGN DIRECT INVESTMENT.
----Empresas multinacionales y Pacto andino.
- 1983.
(001102)
----Las empresas transnacionales en el
desarrollo colombiano. - 1986.
(001121)
----Las empresas transnacionales y la
inversión extranjera directa en la
primera mitad de los años ochenta. -
1987.
(000194)
----Evolución contradictoria de la industria
en Colombia. - 1984.
(001095)
----The subsidiary role of direct foreign
investment in industrialization: the
Colombian manufacturing sector. - 1985.
(001106)

COLOMBIA--FOREIGN INVESTMENTS.
----National legislation and regulations
relating to transnational corporations.
Volume 4. - 1986.
(002253)

COLOMBIA--INDUSTRIAL DEVELOPMENT.
----Las empresas transnacionales en el
desarrollo colombiano. - 1986.
(001121)

COLOMBIA--INDUSTRIAL POLICY.
----Las empresas transnacionales en el
desarrollo colombiano. - 1986.
(001121)

COLOMBIA--INDUSTRIALIZATION.
----The subsidiary role of direct foreign
investment in industrialization: the
Colombian manufacturing sector. - 1985.
(001106)

COLOMBIA--INDUSTRY.
----Evolución contradictoria de la industria
en Colombia. - 1984.
(001095)

COLOMBIA--IRON AND STEEL INDUSTRY.
----La industria siderúrgica
latinoamericana. - 1984.
(000601)

COLOMBIA--JOINT VENTURES.
----La asociación por partes de interes en
Colombia. - 1983.
(001614)
----Los contratos petroleros. - 1984.
(002454)

COLOMBIA--LAWS AND REGULATIONS.
----National legislation and regulations
relating to transnational corporations.
Volume 4. - 1986.
(002253)

COLOMBIA--MANUFACTURING.
----Las empresas transnacionales en el
desarrollo colombiano. - 1986.
(001121)

COLOMBIA--MANUFACTURING ENTERPRISES.
----The subsidiary role of direct foreign
investment in industrialization: the
Colombian manufacturing sector. - 1985.
(001106)

COLOMBIA--METALLURGICAL INDUSTRY.
----La industria siderúrgica
latinoamericana. - 1984.
(000601)

COLOMBIA--MINERAL RESOURCES.
----Las empresas transnacionales en el
desarrollo colombiano. - 1986.
(001121)

COLOMBIA--MINING LAW.
----Petroleum service contracts in
Argentina, Brazil and Colombia : issues
arising from their legal nature. - 1987.
(002422)

COLOMBIA--NATURAL RESOURCES.
----Petroleum service contracts in
Argentina, Brazil and Colombia : issues
arising from their legal nature. - 1987.
(002422)

COLOMBIA--OIL AND GAS LEASES.
----Los contratos petroleros. - 1984.
    (002454)

COLOMBIA--PETROLEUM EXPLORATION.
----Las empresas transnacionales en el
    desarrollo colombiano. - 1986.
    (001121)

COLOMBIA--PETROLEUM INDUSTRY.
----Los contratos petroleros. - 1984.
    (002454)
----Las empresas transnacionales en el
    desarrollo colombiano. - 1986.
    (001121)

COLOMBIA--PETROLEUM LAW.
----Los contratos petroleros. - 1984.
    (002454)
----Petroleum service contracts in
    Argentina, Brazil and Colombia : issues
    arising from their legal nature. - 1987.
    (002422)

COLOMBIA--PHARMACEUTICAL INDUSTRY.
----Transnational corporations in the
    pharmaceutical industry of developing
    countries. - 1984.
    (000749)

COLOMBIA--POLITICAL CONDITIONS.
----Notes from Latin America. - 1983.
    (000628)

COLOMBIA--PUBLIC ENTERPRISES.
----Directorio de empresas y ejecutivos. -
    1979-   .
    (002628)

COLOMBIA--TECHNOLOGY TRANSFER.
----Las empresas transnacionales en el
    desarrollo colombiano. - 1986.
    (001121)

COLOMBIA--TRANSNATIONAL CORPORATIONS.
----Empresas multinacionales y Pacto andino.
    - 1983.
    (001102)
----Las empresas transnacionales en el
    desarrollo colombiano. - 1986.
    (001121)
----Evolución contradictoria de la industria
    en Colombia. - 1984.
    (001095)
----National legislation and regulations
    relating to transnational corporations.
    Volume 4. - 1986.
    (002253)

COMMERCIAL ARBITRATION.
----Arbitration and renegotiation of
    international investment agreements. -
    1986.
    (002557)
----L'arbitre et le contrat. - 1984.
    (002488)
----Les institutions permanentes d'arbitrage
    devant le juge étatique (à propos d'une
    jurisprudence récente). - 1987.
    (002505)
----International investment disputes. -
    1985.
    (002524)

----Problèmes de base de l'arbitrage. -
    1987-   .
    (002531)
----The UNCITRAL model law on international
    commercial arbitration. - 1986.
    (002517)

COMMERCIAL ARBITRATION--ARAB COUNTRIES.
----Particularités et problèmes de
    l'arbitrage dans les droits des pays
    arabes. - 1986.
    (002530)

COMMERCIAL ARBITRATION--CHINA.
----Dispute resolution in the People's
    Republic of China. - 1984.
    (002558)
----Mediation, conciliation, arbitration and
    litigation in the People's Republic of
    China. - 1987.
    (002565)

COMMERCIAL ARBITRATION--COLOMBIA.
----Arbitraje-conciliación. - 1985.
    (002472)

COMMERCIAL ARBITRATION--CUBA.
----Cuba's system of international
    commercial arbitration. - 1984.
    (002490)

COMMERCIAL ARBITRATION--CZECHOSLOVAKIA.
----Czechoslovak regulations governing
    arbitration in international trade. -
    1985.
    (002518)

COMMERCIAL ARBITRATION--FRANCE.
----Arbitral adjudication. - 1984.
    (002484)
----Etude historique et comparée de
    l'arbitrage. - 1984.
    (002485)

COMMERCIAL ARBITRATION--HONG KONG.
----Arbitration in Hong Kong. - 1986.
    (002578)
----Arbitration in Hong Kong. - 1986.
    (002529)

COMMERCIAL ARBITRATION--IRAN (ISLAMIC
REPUBLIC OF).
----L'arbitrage Elf Aquitaine Iran c/
    National Iranian Oil Company. - 1984.
    (002504)

COMMERCIAL ARBITRATION--KUWAIT.
----Host countries permanent sovereignty
    over national resources and protection
    of foreign investors. - 1983.
    (002566)

COMMERCIAL ARBITRATION--LATIN AMERICA.
----International commercial arbitration in
    Latin America. - 1986.
    (002546)

COMMERCIAL ARBITRATION--LIBYAN ARAB
JAMAHIRIYA.
----The new international economic order,
    (2). - 1984.
    (001271)

COMMERCIAL ARBITRATION--PERU.
----Schiedsklauseln in Peru und Venezuela. -
      1987.
        (002570)

COMMERCIAL ARBITRATION--SAUDI ARABIA.
----Abfassen von Schiedsklauseln in
      Verträgen mit saudiarabischen Parteien.
      - 1987.
        (002548)

COMMERCIAL ARBITRATION--SPAIN.
----Major international treaties regulating
      arbitration in Spain. - 1983.
        (002489)

COMMERCIAL ARBITRATION--UNITED KINGDOM.
----Arbitral adjudication. - 1984.
        (002484)
----Commercial arbitration. - 1983.
        (002499)
----Etude historique et comparée de
      l'arbitrage. - 1984.
        (002485)

COMMERCIAL ARBITRATION--UNITED STATES.
----Arbitral adjudication. - 1984.
        (002484)
----Arbitration of private antitrust claims
      in international trade. - 1986.
        (002471)
----Etude historique et comparée de
      l'arbitrage. - 1984.
        (002485)
----Host countries permanent sovereignty
      over national resources and protection
      of foreign investors. - 1983.
        (002566)
----The new international economic order,
      (2). - 1984.
        (001271)

COMMERCIAL ARBITRATION--VENEZUELA.
----Schiedsklauseln in Peru und Venezuela. -
      1987.
        (002570)

COMMERCIAL BANKS.
----Commercial banks and the restructuring
      of cross-border debt. - 1983.
        (000250)
----Funding direct investment through
      cofinancing: the commercial banker's
      view. - 1986.
        (001265)
----The growth of transnational banking. -
      1983.
        (000991)
----Transnational banks and the external
      finance of Latin America : the
      experience of Peru. - 1983.
        (000840)
----Uncertain future. - 1984.
        (000977)

COMMERCIAL BANKS--AFRICA.
----The role of transnational banks and
      financial institutions in Africa's
      development process. - 1986.
        (000935)

COMMERCIAL BANKS--JAPAN.
----Internationalization of Japanese
      commercial banking-the recent experience
      of city banks. - 1984.
        (000855)

COMMERCIAL BANKS--LIBERIA.
----The impact of the transnational
      corporations in the banking and other
      financial institutions on the economy of
      Liberia. - 1986.
        (000873)

COMMERCIAL BANKS--PERU.
----Transnational banks and the external
      finance of Latin America : the
      experience of Peru. - 1983.
        (000840)
----Transnational banks and the external
      finance of Latin America : the
      experience of Peru. - 1985.
        (000975)

COMMERCIAL BANKS--UNITED STATES.
----U.S. and Canadian investment in South
      Africa and Namibia. - 1986.
        (001212) (002671) (002672)

COMMERCIAL LAW.
----The arbitrator's power to award punitive
      damages in international contract
      actions. - 1986.
        (002534)
----The choice of applicable law in
      international arbitration. - 1986.
        (002491)
----Competition policy and joint ventures. -
      1986.
        (001684)
----The digest of commercial laws of the
      world : forms of contracts. - 1971-   .
        (002424)
----Digest of commercial laws of the world.
      - 1966-   .
        (002200)
----International business transactions in a
      nutshell. - 1984.
        (002457)
----The international void in the law of
      multinational bankruptcies. - 1987.
        (002214)
----Der internationale Rechtsverkehr in
      Zivil- und Handelssachen. - 1984-   .
        (002225)
----Lex mercatoria et arbitrage
      international. - 1983.
        (002575)
----Maryland journal of international law
      and trade. - 1984-   .
        (002138)

COMMERCIAL LAW--AFRICA.
----International marketing to Black Africa
      and the Third World. - 1988.
        (001001)

COMMERCIAL LAW--ARGENTINA.
----Sociedades y grupos multinacionales. -
      1985.
        (000004)

COMMERCIAL LAW--AUSTRALIA.
----Extraterritorial effects of United
     States commercial and antitrust
     legislation. - 1983.
       (002352)

COMMERCIAL LAW--CHINA.
----China laws for foreign business. -
     1985-   .
       (002187)
----China's foreign economic contract law. -
     1987.
       (002297)
----Foreign economic contract law of the
     People's Republic of China. - 1987.
       (002166)
----Foreign investment law in the People's
     Republic of China. - 1987.
       (002299)
----International dispute resolution and the
     People's Republic of China. - 1984.
       (002522)
----The joint venture and related contract
     laws of mainland China and Taiwan. -
     1987.
       (002278)
----The law applicable to a transnational
     economic development contract. - 1987.
       (002164)

COMMERCIAL LAW--GULF STATES.
----Commercial law in the Gulf States : the
     Islamic legal tradition. - 1984.
       (002195)

COMMERCIAL LAW--IRAQ.
----Business laws of Iraq. - 1984-   .
       (002226)

COMMERCIAL LAW--JAPAN.
----The administrative regulation of
     technology induction contracts in Japan.
     - 1987.
       (002447)
----Antitrust aspects of U.S.-Japanese
     trade. - 1983.
       (002345)
----Doing business in Japan. - 1983.
       (001820)
----The legal framework of trade and
     investment in Japan. - 1986.
       (002241)

COMMERCIAL LAW--LATIN AMERICA.
----Latin America at a glance. - 1986.
       (001821)

COMMERCIAL LAW--OMAN.
----The commercial legal system of the
     Sultanate of Oman. - 1983.
       (002218)

COMMERCIAL LAW--SENEGAL.
----Réflexions sur les régimes fiscaux
     privilégiés du code des investissements
     au Gabon. - 1985.
       (002243)

COMMERCIAL LAW--TAIWAN (CHINA).
----The joint venture and related contract
     laws of mainland China and Taiwan. -
     1987.
       (002278)

COMMERCIAL LAW--UNITED ARAB EMIRATES.
----Business laws of the United Arab
     Emirates. - 1984-   .
       (002285)

COMMERCIAL LAW--UNITED STATES.
----Antitrust aspects of U.S.-Japanese
     trade. - 1983.
       (002345)
----Antitrust law developments (second). -
     1984.
       (002339)
----Countertrade. - 1984.
       (001371)
----Digest of commercial laws of the world.
     - 1985-   .
       (002256)
----Extraterritorial effects of United
     States commercial and antitrust
     legislation. - 1983.
       (002352)
----A manual of U.S. trade laws. - 1985.
       (002220)
----On Third World debt. - 1984.
       (000211)
----Recent developments in international
     commercial arbitration. - 1987.
       (002549)
----Reviewing the situation : what is to be
     done with the Foreign Corrupt Practices
     Act? - 1987.
       (002235)

COMMERCIAL LAW--YUGOSLAVIA.
----Doing business with Yugoslavia. - 1986.
       (001793)

COMMERCIAL LEASES.
----Cross-border leasing. - 1983.
       (000836) (001705)
----Leasing in an international context. -
     1983.
       (000929)
----Trends in international taxation. - 1985.
       (001746)

COMMODITIES.
----Revitalizing development, growth and
     international trade. - 1987.
       (001394)
----Transnational corporations and non-fuel
     primary commodities in developing
     countries. - 1987.
       (000639)
----Transnational corporations in world
     development. - 1983.
       (000102)

COMMODITIES--AUSTRALIA.
----Kompass Australia. - 1970-   .
       (002649)

COMMODITY CONTROL--UNITED STATES.
----United States regulation of
     high-technology exports. - 1986.
       (001462)

COMMODITY TRADE.
----Foreign trade by commodities. -
     1983-   .
       (001357)
----Revitalizing development, growth and
     international trade. - 1987.
       (001394)

COMMODITY TRADE (continued)
----Rola korporacji transnarodowych w
    miedzynarodowej wymianie towarów
    przemyslowych. - 1986.
        (001369)
----Transnational corporations and non-fuel
    primary commodities in developing
    countries. - 1987.
        (000639)
----The Uruguay round of multilateral trade
    talks. - 1987.
        (000983)

COMMON MARKET--WESTERN EUROPE.
----Air and maritime transport and the EEC
    competition rules : Ministère Publique
    v. Asjes, Nouvelles Frontières et al. -
    1987.
        (000794)

COMMONWEALTH SECRETARIAT.
----Developing country access to capital
    markets in transition. - 1987.
        (001609)

COMMUNES--CHINA.
----Private enterprise in China. - 1985.
        (002184)

COMMUNICATION INDUSTRY.
----International communications and
    information systems. - 1985.
        (000787)
----International policy issues in satellite
    communications. - 1985.
        (000791)
----Meeting the challenges of the world
    information economy. - 1984.
        (000853)
----Multinational union organizations in the
    white-collar, service, and
    communications industries. - 1983.
        (002600)

COMMUNICATION INDUSTRY--BRAZIL.
----La industria nacional de informática. -
    1987.
        (000818)

COMMUNICATION INDUSTRY--PACIFIC OCEAN REGION.
----Information technology and the
    developing Pacific. - 1986.
        (000703)

COMMUNICATION INDUSTRY--UNITED STATES.
----The knowledge industry 200. - 1983.
        (000884) (002646)

COMMUNICATION POLICY--LATIN AMERICA.
----Trade and foreign direct investment in
    data services. - 1986.
        (000948)

COMMUNICATION POLICY--UNITED STATES.
----Implications of deregulating satellite
    communications. - 1985.
        (002242)

COMMUNICATION TECHNOLOGY.
----Technology gaps in the international
    telecommunications industry. - 1986.
        (000795)

COMPARATIVE ADVANTAGE.
----Avantage comparatif et performance dans
    le commerce international des produits
    différenciés. - 1986.
        (001669)
----Comparative advantage and trade in
    service. - 1984.
        (000870)
----The global factory. - 1985.
        (001254)
----Les implications juridiques du principe
    de l'avantage comparatif dynamique. -
    1986.
        (001676)
----Industry in the 1980s. - 1985.
        (001341)
----The inflationary effect on the structure
    of trade. - 1986.
        (001672)
----Investissements internationaux et
    dynamique des avantages comparatifs des
    nouveaux pays industrialises. - 1984.
        (000496)
----Mezinárodní delba práce a socialistická
    ekonomická integrace. - 1987.
        (001667)
----Multinationalisation des firmes et
    avantages comparatifs des pays: une vue
    d'ensemble. (With English summary.). -
    1985.
        (001687)
----Ownership and development. - 1987.
        (001129)
----Pollution and the struggle for the world
    product. - 1988.
        (001948)
----Recent changes in China's pure trade
    theory. - 1986.
        (001677)
----Technical advance and trade advantage. -
    1983.
        (001497)
----Toward a theory of industrial
    restructuring and dynamic comparative
    advantage. - 1985.
        (000054)

COMPARATIVE ADVANTAGE--COTE D'IVOIRE.
----Comparative advantage as a development
    model. - 1985.
        (001691)

COMPARATIVE ADVANTAGES--UNITED STATES.
----The competitive position of U.S.
    manufacturing firms. - 1985.
        (000353)

COMPARATIVE ANALYSIS.
----The characteristics of joint
    ventures in developed and developing
    countries. - 1985.
        (001541)
----Comparative and multinational
    management. - 1986.
        (000439)
----Comparative international auditing
    standards. - 1985.
        (002073)
----Intra-LDCs foreign direct investment: a
    comparative analysis of Third World
    multinationals. - 1985.
        (000303)

COMPARATIVE ANALYSIS (continued)
----A magyar feldolgozó ipar koncentrációs folyamata a 70-es évtizedben, nemzetközi összehasonlításban. - 1986.
  (001181)
----New forms of investment in developing countries by US companies: a five industry comparison. - 1987.
  (000328)
----Trade policy issues and empirical analysis /edited by Robert Baldwin. - 1988.
  (001348)

COMPARATIVE ANALYSIS--AUSTRALIA.
----Foreign investment control in the mining sector. - 1983.
  (000577)

COMPARATIVE ANALYSIS--BRAZIL.
----Technological spill-overs and manpower training: a comparative analysis of multinational and national enterprises in Brazilian manufacturing. - 1986.
  (001899)

COMPARATIVE ANALYSIS--CANADA.
----Foreign investment control in the mining sector. - 1983.
  (000577)

COMPARATIVE ANALYSIS--GERMANY, FEDERAL REPUBLIC OF.
----Multinational enterprise and world competition. - 1987.
  (000018)

COMPARATIVE ANALYSIS--JAPAN.
----Multinational enterprise and world competition. - 1987.
  (000018)
----Postindustrial manufacturing. - 1986.
  (000698)
----Transfer of technology from Japan and the United States to Korean manufacturing industries: a comparative study. - 1984.
  (001461)

COMPARATIVE ANALYSIS--LATIN AMERICA.
----Evaluating differences in technological activity between transnational and domestic firms in Latin America. - 1986.
  (001431)

COMPARATIVE ANALYSIS--REPUBLIC OF KOREA.
----Transfer of technology from Japan and the United States to Korean manufacturing industries: a comparative study. - 1984.
  (001461)

COMPARATIVE ANALYSIS--SOUTHEAST ASIA.
----Comparative accounting practices in ASEAN. - 1984.
  (002072)

COMPARATIVE ANALYSIS--SWEDEN.
----Multinational enterprise and world competition. - 1987.
  (000018)

COMPARATIVE ANALYSIS--TURKEY.
----Transnational corporations and local capital: comparative conduct and performance in the Turkish pharmaceutical industry. - 1986.
  (000705)

COMPARATIVE ANALYSIS--UNITED KINGDOM.
----Comparative analysis of UK domestic and international firms. - 1984.
  (000343)
----Multinational enterprise and world competition. - 1987.
  (000018.)

COMPARATIVE ANALYSIS--UNITED STATES.
----American and Chinese managers in U.S. companies in Taiwan: a comparison. - 1985.
  (000395)
----International joint ventures. - 1985.
  (001590)
----Multinational enterprise and world competition. - 1987.
  (000018)
----Postindustrial manufacturing. - 1986.
  (000698)
----Transfer of technology from Japan and the United States to Korean manufacturing industries: a comparative study. - 1984.
  (001461)

COMPARATIVE ECONOMICS.
----Vergleichende System- und Industriestudien. - 1983.
  (001342)

COMPARATIVE LAW.
----The international lawyer. - 1966-   .
  (001983)

COMPENSATION.
----Acronyms and compensation for oil pollution damage from tankers. - 1983.
  (001937)
----Compensation for expropriation. - 1984.
  (002334)
----Current developments in the law of expropriation and compensation. - 1987.
  (002318)
----Dead in the water : international law, diplomacy, and compensation for chemical pollution at sea. - 1986.
  (001938)
----The definition of pollution damage in the 1984 Protocols to the 1969 Civil Liability Convention and the 1971 Fund Convention. - 1986.
  (001943)
----Dommages causés par les marées noires. - 1984.
  (001952)
----Eigentum, Enteignung und Entschädigung im geltenden Völkerrecht. - 1985.
  (002321)
----The international law of expropriation of foreign-owned property. - 1983.
  (002330)
----An international standard of partial compensation upon the expropriation of an alien's property. - 1987.
  (002317)

COMPENSATION (continued)
----Liability and compensation for damage in connection with the carriage of hazardous and noxious substances by sea. - 1986.
(001939)
----Liability for shipments by sea of hazardous and noxious substances. - 1985.
(001951)
----New trends in compensation for oil pollution damage. - 1985.
(001944)
----Oil pollution. - 1984.
(001942)

COMPENSATION--INDIA.
----For whom the bell tolls in the aftermath of the Bhopal tragedy. - 1987.
(001950)

COMPENSATION--IRAN (ISLAMIC REPUBLIC OF).
----The expropriation issue before the Iran-United States Claims Tribunal. - 1984.
(002320)

COMPENSATION--KUWAIT.
----State contracts and oil expropriations. - 1984.
(002577)

COMPENSATION--UNITED STATES.
----The expropriation issue before the Iran-United States Claims Tribunal. - 1984.
(002320)
----For whom the bell tolls in the aftermath of the Bhopal tragedy. - 1987.
(001950)
----Oil spill liability and compensation. - 1985.
(001940)
----State contracts and oil expropriations. - 1984.
(002577)

COMPENSATION TRADE.
----Corporate performance: America's international winners. - 1986.
(000344)
----Countertrade contracts in international business. - 1986.
(002429)
----Counter-trade: untying those blocked funds. - 1987.
(001398)
----Guide to countertrade and international barter. - 1985.
(001368)
----Should one countertrade? - 1987.
(001366)
----Threats and opportunities of global countertrade : marketing, financing and organizational implications. - 1984.
(001353)
----161 more checklists : decision making in international operations. - 1985.
(000462)

COMPENSATION TRADE--CHINA.
----China's special economic zones. - 1983.
(002381)

COMPENSATION TRADE--EASTERN EUROPE.
----101 checklists for success in East European markets. - 1984.
(001779)

COMPENSATION TRADE--UNITED STATES.
----Controlling the cost of international compensation. - 1983.
(002323)
----Countertrade. - 1984.
(001371)
----International countertrade. - 1984.
(001396)

COMPENSATORY FINANCING.
----Legal trends in international lending and investment in the developing countries. - 1984.
(000207)

COMPETITION.
----Competition in the Marxist tradition. - 1983.
(001697)
----Competition policy and deregulation. - 1986.
(001683)
----Corporation, technological gaps and growth in OECD countries. - 1987.
(001438)
----La gestion marketing dans un développemnt turbulent et hautement concurrentiel. - 1983.
(000487)
----Innovation and market structure. - 1987.
(000681)
----Internationale Wettbewerbsfähigkeit. - 1984.
(000005)
----Joint ventures : do they restrict competition? - 1986.
(001596)
----Market competition, conflict and collusion. - 1983.
(000492)
----Market competition, conflict and collusion. - 1987.
(001680)
----The military origins of industrialisation and international trade rivalry. - 1984.
(001335)
----Product diversity, economies of scale, and international trade. - 1983.
(000488)
----Strategic behaviour and industrial competition. - 1986.
(000512)
----Swiss review of international competition law. - 197?-
(002150)
----Trade and dynamic efficiency. - 1987.
(001698)
----Trade policy as a constitutional problem : on the "domestic policy functions" of international trade rules. - 1986.
(001379)

COMPETITION--CANADA.
----Industrial organization paradigms, empirical evidence, and the economic case for competition policy. - 1987.
(001670)

COMPETITION--EUROPE.
----Competitive strategies for Europe. -
  1983.
    (000463)

COMPETITION--FRANCE.
----Competing for prosperity. - 1986.
    (001338)

COMPETITION--GERMANY, FEDERAL REPUBLIC OF.
----Stärken und Schwächen der Bundesrepublik
  Deutschland in der internationalen
  Arbeitsteilung. - 1984.
    (001260)

COMPETITION--JAPAN.
----Competition in the Pacific Basin. - 1987.
    (001673)
----A competitive assessment of the U.S.
  fiber optics industry. - 1984.
    (000800)
----Competitive edge. - 1984.
    (000673)
----Employment and competitiveness in the
  European Community. - 1984.
    (001929)

COMPETITION--UNITED KINGDOM.
----Privatisation and regulation : the UK
  experience. - 1986.
    (001627)

COMPETITION--UNITED STATES.
----An assessment of U.S. competitiveness in
  high technology industries. - 1983.
    (000653)
----Balancing the national interest : U.S.
  national security export controls and
  global economic competition. - 1987.
    (001417)
----Competition and world markets. - 1983.
    (001665)
----Competition in the Pacific Basin. - 1987.
    (001673)
----A competitive assessment of the
  renewable energy equipment industry. -
  1984.
    (000775)
----A competitive assessment of the U.S.
  fiber optics industry. - 1984.
    (000800)
----A competitive assessment of the U.S.
  international construction industry. -
  1984.
    (000779)
----A competitive assessment of the U.S.
  manufacturing automation equipment
  industries. - 1984.
    (000756)
----A competitive assessment of the U.S. oil
  field equipment industry. - 1985.
    (000764)
----A competitive assessment of the U.S.
  petrochemical industry. - 1982.
    (000755)
----A competitive assessment of the U.S.
  pharmaceutical industry. - 1984.
    (000757)
----Competitive edge. - 1984.
    (000673)
----EEC competition policy. - 1986.
    (001989)

----Employment and competitiveness in the
  European Community. - 1984.
    (001929)
----La haute technologie américaine. - 1987.
    (000680)
----Manufacturing matters : the myth of the
  post-industrial economy. - 1987.
    (000669)

COMPETITION--WESTERN EUROPE.
----Air and maritime transport and the EEC
  competition rules : Ministère Publique
  v. Asjes, Nouvelles Frontières et al. -
  1987.
    (000794)
----Application des règles de concurrence du
  Traité de Rome à l'autorité publique. -
  1987.
    (002021)
----Attempt to regulate restrictive
  commercial practices in the field of air
  transportation within a transnational
  antitrust legal and institutional
  framework. - 1984.
    (000788) (001659)
----A competitive assessment of the U.S.
  fiber optics industry. - 1984.
    (000800)
----EEC competition policy. - 1986.
    (001989)
----EEC law of competition. - 1985.
    (002151)
----Employment and competitiveness in the
  European Community. - 1984.
    (001929)
----Exclusive territorial rights in patent
  licenses and Article 85 of the EEC
  Treaty. - 1987.
    (002418)
----Extraterritorial application of the
  EEC-competition law. - 1984.
    (002349)
----La licence de marque et le droit
  européen de la concurrence. - 1984.
    (001448)
----La réglementation communautaire des
  transports. - 1984.
    (001994)
----Territorial and exclusive trademark
  licensing under the EEC law of
  competition. - 1984.
    (001987)

COMPUTER APPLICATIONS.
----Microelectronics-based automation
  technologies and development. - 1985.
    (000753) (000753)
----The third industrial revolution. - 1987.
    (000966)
----Le tout-ordinateur. - 1986.
    (000743)

COMPUTER INDUSTRY.
----Foreign direct investment, the service
  sector and international banking. - 1987.
    (000972)
----The global race in microelectronics. -
  1983.
    (000684)
----Information industries in the CMEA
  countries : a foreign trade dimension. -
  1986.
    (000894)

COMPUTER INDUSTRY (continued)
----Innovation and market structure. - 1987.
    (000681)
----Microelectronics-based automation
    technologies and development. - 1985.
    (000753)
----Le tout-ordinateur. - 1986.
    (000743)

COMPUTER INDUSTRY--ARGENTINA.
----L'informatique en Argentine. - 1986.
    (000772)

COMPUTER INDUSTRY--BRAZIL.
----Brazilian informatics policy. - 1985.
    (000880)
----L'informatique brésilienne dans la
    nouvelle république. - 1986.
    (000765)
----Politische Gestaltungsspielräume von
    Schwellenländern in der
    Mikroelektronik-Industrie. - 1987.
    (000617)
----Technology and competition in the
    Brazilian computer industry. - 1983.
    (000741)

COMPUTER INDUSTRY--CANADA.
----High technology plant location
    decisions. - 1983.
    (000528)

COMPUTER INDUSTRY--EASTERN EUROPE.
----L'informatique dans les pays du CAEM :
    quelques aspects des politiques suivies.
    - 1986.
    (000711)

COMPUTER INDUSTRY--INDIA.
----Between dependency and autonomy. - 1984.
    (000691)

COMPUTER INDUSTRY--JAPAN.
----Competitive edge. - 1984.
    (000673)

COMPUTER INDUSTRY--REPUBLIC OF KOREA.
----Politische Gestaltungsspielräume von
    Schwellenländern in der
    Mikroelektronik-Industrie. - 1987.
    (000617)

COMPUTER INDUSTRY--SOUTHEAST ASIA.
----Computer vendors re-shape product
    strategy for Asian market. - 1986.
    (000689)

COMPUTER INDUSTRY--SRI LANKA.
----Microelectronics-based automation
    technologies and development. - 1985.
    (000753)

COMPUTER INDUSTRY--UNITED STATES.
----A competitive assessment of the U.S.
    flexible manufacturing systems industry.
    - 1985.
    (000763)
----A competitive assessment of the United
    States data processing services
    industry. - 1984.
    (000981)
----A competitive assessment of the United
    States disk storage industry. - 1985.
    (000672)

----A competitive assessment of the United
    States software industry. - 1984.
    (000980)
----Competitive edge. - 1984.
    (000673)
----High technology industries. - 1983-   .
    (000695)
----High technology plant location
    decisions. - 1983.
    (000528)
----National security and the semiconductor
    industry. - 1987.
    (000675)
----The top 100. - 1984.
    (000742) (002670)

COMPUTER INDUSTRY--USSR.
----Computergebruik in de Sovjetunie. - 1987.
    (000677)

COMPUTER INDUSTRY--WESTERN EUROPE.
----Information technology and economic
    recovery in Western Europe. - 1986.
    (000874)

COMPUTER INPUT OUTPUT EQUIPMENT.
----PTS company directory. - 1985-   .
    (002661)

COMPUTER SCIENCE.
----The third industrial revolution. - 1987.
    (000966)

COMPUTER SCIENCE--ARGENTINA.
----L'informatique en Argentine. - 1986.
    (000772)

COMPUTER SOFTWARE.
----Recent developments in operations and
    behaviour of transnational corporations.
    - 1987.
    (000103)

COMPUTER SOFTWARE--EASTERN EUROPE.
----L'informatique dans les pays du CAEM :
    quelques aspects des politiques suivies.
    - 1986.
    (000711)

COMPUTER SOFTWARE--UNITED STATES.
----A competitive assessment of the United
    States software industry. - 1984.
    (000980)

COMPUTER-AIDED DESIGN.
----Microelectronics-based automation
    technologies and development. - 1985.
    (000753)
----Technological trends and challenges in
    electronics. - 1983.
    (000739)

COMPUTER-AIDED DESIGN--UNITED STATES.
----A competitive assessment of the U.S.
    manufacturing automation equipment
    industries. - 1984.
    (000756)

COMPUTERS.
----Le tout-ordinateur. - 1986.
    (000743)

COMPUTERS--INDIA.
----Between dependency and autonomy. - 1984.
(000691)
----New information technology in India. -
1986.
(000651)

COMPUTERS--UNITED STATES.
----The top 100. - 1984.
(000742) (002670)

CONCESSIONS.
----The evolution of the legal relationship
between international petroleum mining
companies and host countries. - 1983.
(000647)
----Negotiation and drafting of mining
development agreements. - 1976.
(002432)
----The question of a reference to
international obligations in the United
Nations Code of Conduct on Transnational
Corporations. - 1986.
(002020)

CONCESSIONS--CHILE.
----Einige juristische Aspekte des
Ausverkaufs der chilenischen Wirtschaft
an die internationalen Monopole. - 1984.
(002161)

CONCILIATION.
----Peaceful settlement of international
trade disputes. - 1983.
(002500)
----UNCITRAL, the United Nations Commission
on International Trade Law. - 1986.
(002155)

CONCILIATION--AUSTRALIA.
----Mediation, conciliation and arbitration
: an international comparison of
Australia, Great Britain and the United
States. - 1987.
(002476)

CONCILIATION--CHINA.
----Mediation, conciliation, arbitration and
litigation in the People's Republic of
China. - 1987.
(002565)

CONCILIATION--COLOMBIA.
----Arbitraje-conciliación. - 1985.
(002472)

CONCILIATION--UNITED KINGDOM.
----Mediation, conciliation and arbitration
: an international comparison of
Australia, Great Britain and the United
States. - 1987.
(002476)

CONCILIATION--UNITED STATES.
----Mediation, conciliation and arbitration
: an international comparison of
Australia, Great Britain and the United
States. - 1987.
(002476)

CONFISCATIONS--FRANCE.
----Les nationalisations françaises face à
l'ordre juridique suisse. - 1984.
(002325)

CONFISCATIONS--SWITZERLAND.
----Les nationalisations françaises face à
l'ordre juridique suisse. - 1984.
(002325)

CONFLICT.
----Measures of manifest conflict in
international joint ventures. - 1987.
(001583)

CONGLOMERATE CORPORATIONS.
----Treuepflicht im internationalen Konzern
gegenüber Hoheitsakten im Heimatstaate
der Muttergesellschaft. - 1983.
(002343)

CONGLOMERATE CORPORATIONS--INDONESIA.
----Japanese direct investment in ASEAN. -
1983.
(000171)

CONGLOMERATE CORPORATIONS--JAPAN.
----The invisible link. - 1986.
(000992)
----Japanese direct investment in ASEAN. -
1983.
(000171)
----Japan's general trading companies. -
1984.
(000887)

CONGO--FOREIGN DIRECT INVESTMENT.
----Le transfert de technologie dans les
industries agro-alimentaires en Afrique
Centrale. - 1987.
(001510)

CONGO--MANAGEMENT CONTRACTS.
----Le transfert de technologie dans les
industries agro-alimentaires en Afrique
Centrale. - 1987.
(001510)

CONGO--STATISTICAL DATA.
----Le transfert de technologie dans les
industries agro-alimentaires en Afrique
Centrale. - 1987.
(001510)

CONGO--SUGAR INDUSTRY.
----Le transfert de technologie dans les
industries agro-alimentaires en Afrique
Centrale. - 1987.
(001510)

CONGO--TECHNICAL CO-OPERATION.
----Le transfert de technologie dans les
industries agro-alimentaires en Afrique
Centrale. - 1987.
(001510)

CONGO--TECHNOLOGY TRANSFER.
----Le transfert de technologie dans les
industries agro-alimentaires en Afrique
Centrale. - 1987.
(001510)

CONGO--TRANSNATIONAL CORPORATIONS.
----Le transfert de technologie dans les
industries agro-alimentaires en Afrique
Centrale. - 1987.
(001510)

CONSTITUTIONAL LAW.
----Trade policy as a constitutional problem
: on the "domestic policy functions" of
international trade rules. - 1986.
(001379)

CONSTITUTIONAL LAW--UNITED KINGDOM.
----Privatising nationalised industries :
constitutional issues and new legal
techniques. - 1987.
(001582)

CONSTRUCTION EQUIPMENT--UNITED STATES.
----A competitive assessment of the U.S.
construction machinery industry. - 1985.
(000761)

CONSTRUCTION INDUSTRY.
----International construction business
management. - 1985.
(000427)
----International construction contracts. -
1983.
(002445)
----International construction contracts,
(2). - 1983.
(002446)
----The multinational construction industry.
- 1987.
(000778)

CONSTRUCTION INDUSTRY--UNITED STATES.
----A competitive assessment of the U.S.
international construction industry. -
1984.
(000779)

CONSULTANTS.
----Analysis of engineering and technical
assistance consultancy contracts. - 1986.
(002449)

CONSULTANTS--ISLAMIC COUNTRIES.
----Consultancy services. - 1986.
(000831)

CONSULTANTS--LATIN AMERICA.
----The use and promotion of consultancy
joint ventures by public entities in
Latin America. - 1985.
(000834)

CONSULTANTS--MIDDLE EAST.
----An international directory of 600
consultants and contractors with
experience in the Middle East. - 1985.
(002645)

CONSULTATIONS.
----Multinational enterprises : information
and consultation concerning their
manpower plans. - 1985.
(000431)

CONSUMER EDUCATION.
----Guidelines for Consumer Protection. -
1986.
(002017)

CONSUMER GOODS--SOUTHEAST ASIA.
----Transnational corporations and the
electronics industries of ASEAN
economies. - 1987.
(000754)

CONSUMER PROTECTION.
----Consumers, transnational corporations,
and development. - 1986.
(001343)
----Guidelines for Consumer Protection. -
1986.
(002017)
----The lessons of Bhopal. - 1985.
(001933)

CONSUMERS.
----Consumer choice in the Third World. -
1983.
(000878)

CONSUMPTION.
----Industry in the 1980s. - 1985.
(001341)

CONTAINER TRANSPORT.
----International income taxation and
developing countries. - 1988.
(001759)

CONTRACT LABOUR.
----The drilling gap in non-OPEC developing
countries: the role of contractual and
fiscal arrangements. - 1985.
(002413)

CONTRACT LABOUR--REPUBLIC OF KOREA.
----Korean contractors in Saudi Arabia. -
1986.
(001139)

CONTRACT LABOUR--SAUDI ARABIA.
----Korean contractors in Saudi Arabia. -
1986.
(001139)

CONTRACTS.
----Adaptation and renegotiation of
contracts in international trade and
finance. - 1985.
(002406)
----Analysis of engineering and technical
assistance consultancy contracts. - 1986.
(002449)
----Analysis of equipment leasing contracts.
- 1984.
(002407)
----Annual survey of developments in
international trade law, 1983. - 1984.
(002136)
----Applicable law under international
transfer of technology regulations. -
1984.
(001412)
----L'arbitre et le contrat. - 1984.
(002488)
----Arrangements between joint venture
partners in developing countries. - 1987.
(002450)
----Contractual adaptation and conflict
resolution based on venture contracts
for mining projects in developing
countries. - 1985.
(002475)
----Contratos de licencia y de transferencia
de tecnología en el derecho privado. -
1980.
(002415)

CONTRACTS (continued)
----Les contrats de transfert de
technologie. - 1983.
(001468)
----Countertrade contracts in international
business. - 1986.
(002429)
----The digest of commercial laws of the
world : forms of contracts. - 1971-   .
(002424)
----Dispute resolution techniques in
international contracts involving the
sale of goods. - 1987.
(002506)
----La durée des accords de coopération et
les clauses gouvernant leur adaptation.
- 1984.
(002425)
----Encyclopedia of practical usages of
terminology for business agreements. -
1983.
(002426) (002708) (002709)

----Die Gestaltung des internationalen
Privatrechts der Schuldverträge unter
allgemeinen Leitprinzipien. - 1983.
(002025)
----Impact of the operations of
transnational corporations on
development in Kuwait. - 1987.
(001143)
----International arbitration of multi-party
contract disputes. - 1983.
(002508)
----International business negotiation and
contract. - 1982.
(002715)
----International construction contracts. -
1983.
(002445)
----International construction contracts,
(2). - 1983.
(002446)
----International equipment leasing. - 1984.
(000905) (002139)
----Kin'yu torihiki to kokusai sosho. - 1983.
(002525)
----Klauzule abritrazowe w kontraktach
handlu zagranicznego sektora
nieuspolecznionego. - 1984.
(002579)
----Le transfert de technologie dans les
industries agro-alimentaires en Afrique
Centrale. - 1987.
(001510)
----Natural gas clauses in petroleum
arrangements. - 1987.
(002452)
----Negotiating and drafting contracts in
international barter and countertrade
transactions. - 1984.
(002428)
----Les obligations "survivant au contrat"
dans les contrats internationaux. - 1984.
(002427)
----Problèmes d'assurance en matière de
contrats internationaux. - 1984.
(002412)

----Proceedings of the SSTCC/UNCTC/ESCAP
Asia-Pacific Training Workshop on
Regulating and Negotiating Technology
Transfer through Transnational
Corporations, 14-25 October 1985,
Fuzhou, Fujian, China. - 1986.
(001405) (002169)
----The question of a reference to
international obligations in the United
Nations Code of Conduct on Transnational
Corporations. - 1986.
(002020)
----Technical co-operation programme,
1976-1987 : United Nations Centre on
Transnational Corporations. - 1988.
(002611)
----Le Tiers monde dans l'arbitrage
commercial international. - 1983.
(002554)
----Transnational corporations and
contractual relations in the world
uranium industry. - 1983.
(002448)
----Transnational corporations and
technology transfer. - 1987.
(001509)
----Transnational corporations in world
development. - 1983.
(000102)
----The transnational law of international
commercial transactions. - 1982.
(002012)
----UNCITRAL, the United Nations Commission
on International Trade Law. - 1986.
(002155)

CONTRACTS--ARGENTINA.
----Petroleum service contracts in
Argentina, Brazil and Colombia : issues
arising from their legal nature. - 1987.
(002422)

CONTRACTS--BRAZIL.
----Petroleum service contracts in
Argentina, Brazil and Colombia : issues
arising from their legal nature. - 1987.
(002422)

CONTRACTS--CHINA.
----China's foreign economic contract law. -
1987.
(002297)
----Foreign economic contract law of the
People's Republic of China. - 1987.
(002166)
----The law applicable to a transnational
economic development contract. - 1987.
(002164)
----The new foreign contract law in China. -
1986.
(002276)
----United States-China commercial
contracts. - 1986.
(002439)
----The 1981 Economic Contract Law of the
People's Republic of China. - 1986.
(002237)

CONTRACTS--COLOMBIA.
----Petroleum service contracts in
Argentina, Brazil and Colombia : issues
arising from their legal nature. - 1987.
(002422)

CONTRACTS--FRANCE.
----Les caractéristiques juridiques des
    contrats internationaux de coopération
    industrielle. - 1984.
      (002438)
----Preliminary agreements in international
    contract negotiation. - 1983.
      (002465)

CONTRACTS--GULF STATES.
----Commercial law in the Gulf States : the
    Islamic legal tradition. - 1984.
      (002195)

CONTRACTS--INDONESIA.
----Formation of contract and contract law
    through multinational joint ventures. -
    1983.
      (002435)

CONTRACTS--ITALY.
----La responsabilita contrattuale degli
    appaltatori in joint venture. - 1984.
      (001594)

CONTRACTS--JAPAN.
----The administrative regulation of
    technology induction contracts in Japan.
    - 1987.
      (002447)
----Doing business in Japan. - 1983.
      (001820)
----Kokusai torihikiho. - 1984.
      (002458)

CONTRACTS--LATIN AMERICA.
----Petroleum service contracts in
    Argentina, Brazil and Colombia : issues
    arising from their legal nature. - 1987.
      (002422)

CONTRACTS--NIGERIA.
----Contractual forms in the oil industry. -
    1986.
      (002441)

CONTRACTS--REPUBLIC OF KOREA.
----Les joint ventures en Corée du Sud. -
    1986.
      (002436)

CONTRACTS--ROMANIA.
----Implications of international commercial
    agreements on the juridical regime of
    international commercial contracts. -
    1983.
      (002408)

CONTRACTS--SAUDI ARABIA.
----Service agents regulation and related
    laws affecting foreign companies in
    Saudi Arabia. - 1983.
      (002182)

CONTRACTS--SOUTH AMERICA.
----Financing implications of mineral
    development agreements. - 1986.
      (002456)

CONTRACTS--UNITED STATES.
----United States-China commercial
    contracts. - 1986.
      (002439)

CONTRACTS--USSR.
----La négociation des contrats de transfert
    de techniques avec l'Union soviétique. -
    1984.
      (002466)
----The problem of autonomy in Soviet
    international contract law. - 1983.
      (002167)

CONTRACTS--WESTERN EUROPE.
----A contract law for Europe. - 1985.
      (001991)
----EEC law of competition. - 1985.
      (002151)
----La négociation du contrat international.
    - 1983.
      (002464)

CONVENTION ESTABLISHING THE MULTILATERAL
INVESTMENT GUARANTEE AGENCY (1985).
----The Convention Establishing the
    Multilateral Investment Guarantee
    Agency. - 1987.
      (002127)
----The Multilateral Investment Guarantee
    Agency. - 1986.
      (002146)
----Zur Bedeutung der Multilateral
    Investment Guarantee Agency für den
    internationalen Ressourcentransfer. -
    1987.
      (002129)

CONVENTION ON THE RECOGNITION AND
ENFORCEMENT OF FOREIGN ARBITRAL AWARDS
(1958).
----The arbitrator's power to award punitive
    damages in international contract
    actions. - 1986.
      (002534)
----The availability of provisional relief
    in international commercial arbitration.
    - 1984.
      (002543)
----International commercial arbitration. -
    1983.
      (002538)
----Klauzule abritrazowe w kontraktach
    handlu zagranicznego sektora
    nieuspolecznionego. - 1984.
      (002579)
----Mitsubishi and the arbitrability of
    antitrust claims. - 1986.
      (002486)

CONVENTION ON THE SETTLEMENT OF INVESTMENT
DISPUTES BETWEEN STATES AND NATIONALS OF
OTHER STATES (1965).
----Arbitration with governments. - 1983.
      (002493)
----ICSID arbitration. - 1984.
      (002495)
----ICSID implementation. - 1985.
      (002574)
----ICSID's emerging jurisprudence. - 1986.
      (002562)
----The International Centre for the
    Settlement of Investment Disputes. -
    1983.
      (002542)

CO-OPERATION COUNCIL FOR THE ARAB STATES OF THE GULF.
----Economic co-operation of the Arab Gulf States. - 1986.
   (001133)
----A historical perspective of U.S.-GCC economic and financial interdependence. - 1987.
   (000143)

COORDINATING COMMITTEE ON EXPORT CONTROLS.
----Technology transfer in the Pacific Basin. - 1985.
   (001413)

CO-ORDINATION WITHIN UN SYSTEM.
----UNCITRAL, the United Nations Commission on International Trade Law. - 1986.
   (002155)

COPPER--CHILE.
----Chile : creative economic management. - 1987.
   (001784)

COPPER INDUSTRY--PERU.
----Las perspectivas de la refinación del cobre en el Peru. - 1984.
   (000580)
----Privilegios y capital transnacional. - 1985.
   (000269)

COPPER INDUSTRY--ZAMBIA.
----The mines, class power, and foreign policy in Zambia. - 1984.
   (001023)

CORPORATE ANALYSIS--GERMANY, FEDERAL REPUBLIC OF.
----New trends in internationalization: processes and theories. Diversified patterns of multinational enterprise and old and new forms of foreign involvement of the firm. - 1983.
   (000068)

CORPORATE ANALYSIS--JAPAN.
----New trends in internationalization: processes and theories. Diversified patterns of multinational enterprise and old and new forms of foreign involvement of the firm. - 1983.
   (000068)

CORPORATE ANALYSIS--UNITED STATES.
----New trends in internationalization: processes and theories. Diversified patterns of multinational enterprise and old and new forms of foreign involvement of the firm. - 1983.
   (000068)

CORPORATE CORRUPTION--UNITED STATES.
----Reviewing the situation : what is to be done with the Foreign Corrupt Practices Act? - 1987.
   (002235)

CORPORATE MERGERS.
----Advanced accounting. - 1988.
   (002089)

----Antitrust for high-technology industries: assessing research joint ventures and mergers. - 1985.
   (001621)
----An examination of multijurisdictional corporate income taxation under formula apportionment. - 1986.
   (001715)
----International mergers and acquisitions. - 1986.
   (001569)
----International mergers and acquisitions. - 1988.
   (001561)
----Kauf und Verkauf von Unternehmen; wie man 'mergers and acquisitions' erfolgreich realisiert, eine Wegleitung. - 1986.
   (001547)
----Merger control in the EEC. - 1983.
   (001634)
----Merger policies and recent trends in mergers. - 1984.
   (001611) (001618)
----Mergers. - 1983.
   (001580)
----Overseas acquisitions and mergers. - 1986.
   (001585)
----Profitability of mergers in food manufacturing. - 1986.
   (001584)
----Recent developments in operations and behaviour of transnational corporations. - 1987.
   (000103)
----Tax aspects of acquisitions and mergers. - 1983.
   (001645) (001756)
----Vertical integration and joint ventures in the aluminum industry. - 1983.
   (000636)
----The 1984 Justice Department guidelines toward horizontal mergers. - 1986.
   (001551)

CORPORATE MERGERS--ASIA.
----International law of take-overs and mergers. - 1986.
   (001572)

CORPORATE MERGERS--AUSTRALIA.
----International law of take-overs and mergers. - 1986.
   (001572)
----Private agreements for takeovers of public companies. - 1984.
   (001626)

CORPORATE MERGERS--CANADA.
----A cross sectional study of relative take-over activity. - 1983.
   (001633)
----International law of take-overs and mergers. - 1986.
   (001573)
----Private agreements for takeovers of public companies. - 1984.
   (001626)

CORPORATE MERGERS--GERMANY, FEDERAL REPUBLIC OF.
----Private agreements for takeovers of
     public companies. - 1984.
        (001626)

CORPORATE MERGERS--JAPAN.
----Recent developments in operations and
     behaviour of transnational corporations.
     - 1987.
        (000103)

CORPORATE MERGERS--LATIN AMERICA.
----International law of take-overs and
     mergers. - 1986.
        (001573)

CORPORATE MERGERS--NETHERLANDS.
----Private agreements for takeovers of
     public companies. - 1984.
        (001626)

CORPORATE MERGERS--UNITED KINGDOM.
----Corporate acquisitions and mergers. -
     1985.
        (001544)
----Private agreements for takeovers of
     public companies. - 1984.
        (001626)
----Recent developments in operations and
     behaviour of transnational corporations.
     - 1987.
        (000103)
----The United Kingdom merger boom in
     perspective. - 1987.
        (001638)

CORPORATE MERGERS--UNITED STATES.
----Acquisitions and joint ventures among
     large corporations. - 1985.
        (001653)
----The effect of conglomerate mergers on
     changes in industry concentration. -
     1986.
        (001527)
----International law of take-overs and
     mergers. - 1986.
        (001573)
----La loi anti-fusions et l'industrie
     pétrolière américaine, (2). - 1986.
        (000581)
----Oil industry mergers. - 1984.
        (001652)
----On vertical mergers. - 1986.
        (001641)
----Private agreements for takeovers of
     public companies. - 1984.
        (001626)
----Recent developments in operations and
     behaviour of transnational corporations.
     - 1987.
        (000103)

CORPORATE MERGERS--WESTERN EUROPE.
----Centralized European merger regulation.
     - 1985.
        (001625)
----Corporate acquisitions and mergers. -
     1985.
        (001544)
----European industry on the march. - 1987.
        (001155)

----Recent developments in operations and
     behaviour of transnational corporations.
     - 1987.
        (000103)

CORPORATE PLANNING.
----Autonomy and centralization in
     multinational firms. - 1984.
        (000393)
----Business strategy and the
     internationalization of business: recent
     approaches. - 1987.
        (000520)
----Cases in strategic management and
     business policy. - 1986.
        (000483)
----The competitive effects of partial
     equity interests and joint ventures. -
     1986.
        (001635)
----Multinational corporate strategy. - 1985.
        (000489)
----Multinationals and global competitive
     strategy. - 1985.
        (000510)
----On planning and forecasting the location
     of retail and service activity. - 1984.
        (000550)
----Strategic planning for international
     corporations. - 1979.
        (000461)
----The theory of vertical integration. -
     1984.
        (000015)
----161 more checklists : decision making in
     international operations. - 1985.
        (000462)
----The 1984 Justice Department guidelines
     toward horizontal mergers. - 1986.
        (001551)

CORPORATE PLANNING--ARGENTINA.
----The new Argentina. - 1984.
        (001777)

CORPORATE PLANNING--CANADA.
----Operating strategies for a Canada in
     transition. - 1984.
        (001778)

CORPORATE PLANNING--KENYA.
----Corporate strategy and employment
     relations in multinational corporations:
     some evidence from Kenya and Malaysia. -
     1983.
        (001902)

CORPORATE PLANNING--MALAYSIA.
----Corporate strategy and employment
     relations in multinational corporations:
     some evidence from Kenya and Malaysia. -
     1983.
        (001902)

CORPORATE PLANNING--MEXICO.
----Wandel der mexikanischen Politik
     gegenuber Auslandsinvestitionen? Die
     "irationale" Komponente der
     Mexikanisierungsstrategie. - 1985.
        (002338)

CORPORATE PLANNING--TAIWAN (CHINA).
----Networks of Taiwanese big business. -
    1986.
        (001063)

CORPORATION LAW.
----Merger policies and recent trends in
    mergers. - 1984.
        (001611)
----Le traitement national des entreprises
    sous contrôle étranger établies dans les
    pays de l'OCDE. - 1978.
        (002000)

CORPORATION LAW--ASIA.
----International law of take-overs and
    mergers. - 1986.
        (001572)

CORPORATION LAW--AUSTRALIA.
----International law of take-overs and
    mergers. - 1986.
        (001572)

CORPORATION LAW--BRAZIL.
----Capitais estrangeiros. - 1984.
        (002275)

CORPORATION LAW--CANADA.
----International law of take-overs and
    mergers. - 1986.
        (001573)

CORPORATION LAW--EAST ASIA.
----East Asian executive reports. -
    1979-   .
        (002203)

CORPORATION LAW--EUROPE.
----The seventh directive. - 1984.
        (002094)

CORPORATION LAW--FRANCE.
----Code des sociétés. - 1977.
        (001975)
----Répertoire des sociétés. - 1970-   .
        (002265)

CORPORATION LAW--GERMANY, FEDERAL REPUBLIC
OF.
----Abhangigkeit und Konzernzugehorigkeit
    von Gemeinschaftsunternehmen. - 1985.
        (002239)

CORPORATION LAW--JORDAN.
----Companies in Jordan and Saudi Arabia. -
    1984.
        (002643)

CORPORATION LAW--LATIN AMERICA.
----International law of take-overs and
    mergers. - 1986.
        (001573)

CORPORATION LAW--SAUDI ARABIA.
----Companies in Jordan and Saudi Arabia. -
    1984.
        (002643)

CORPORATION LAW--UNITED KINGDOM.
----Corporate acquisitions and mergers. -
    1985.
        (001544)

CORPORATION LAW--UNITED STATES.
----International law of take-overs and
    mergers. - 1986.
        (001573)
----La loi anti-fusions et l'industrie
    pétrolière américaine, (2). - 1986.
        (000581)
----United States corporations operating in
    Saudi Arabia and laws affecting
    discrimination in employment. - 1985.
        (002354)
----United States jurisdiction over foreign
    subsidiaries. - 1983.
        (002355)
----The United States, transnational
    business and the law. - 1985.
        (001982)

CORPORATION LAW--WESTERN EUROPE.
----Abhängige Unternehmen und Konzerne im
    europäischen Gemeinschaftsrecht. - 1984.
        (002133)
----Corporate acquisitions and mergers. -
    1985.
        (001544)
----The protection of corporate privacy. -
    1983.
        (002291)
----Zur Angleichung des Bilanzrechts in der
    Europäischen Gemeinschaft. - 1984.
        (002097)

CORPORATION REPORTS.
----Consolidation policies in OECD
    countries. - 1987.
        (002101)

CORPORATION TAX.
----Probleme der Gerwinnverlagerungen
    multinationaler Unternehmen :
    Konzerninterne Verrechnungspreise und
    deren wirtschaftspolitische Wirkungen. -
    1983.
        (001755)
----Tax aspects of acquisitions and mergers.
    - 1983.
        (001645) (001756)

CORPORATION TAX--CANADA.
----The corporate income tax system. - 1985.
        (001767)
----The taxation of controlled foreign
    corporations. - 1986.
        (001699)

CORPORATION TAX--CHINA.
----The People's Republic of China. - 1986.
        (001841)

CORPORATION TAX--GERMANY, FEDERAL REPUBLIC
OF.
----German transfer pricing. - 1984.
        (001748)

CORPORATION TAX--UNITED KINGDOM.
----Corporate acquisitions and mergers. -
    1985.
        (001544)

CORPORATION TAX--UNITED STATES.
----The final report of the Worldwide
Unitary Taxation Working Group :
Chairman's report and supplemental
views. - 1984.
(001763)
----Fundamentals of international taxation.
- 1985.
(001700)
----Worldwide unitary taxation : nature and
alternative solutions. - 1986.
(001766)

CORPORATION TAX--WESTERN EUROPE.
----Corporate acquisitions and mergers. -
1985.
(001544)

CORPORATIONS.
----The American-Dutch tax series. -
1983-   .
(002028)
----Corporations and the common good. - 1986.
(000022)
----Corporations, classes, and capitalism. -
1985.
(000090)
----Genetic engineering and biotechnology
firms worldwide directory. - 1981-   .
(000688) (002642)
----How to find information about companies.
- 1983.
(002714)
----List of company directories and summary
of their contents. - 1983.
(002686)
----The world's largest industrial
enterprises, 1962-1983. - 1985.
(000298)

CORPORATIONS--CANADA.
----Canadian standard industrial
classification for companies and
enterprises, 1980. - 1986-   .
(002718)

CORPORATIONS--CHINA.
----The China directory of industry and
commerce and economic annual. - 1984.
(002626)

CORPORATIONS--EUROPE.
----The seventh directive. - 1984.
(002094)

CORPORATIONS--FRANCE.
----Competing for prosperity. - 1986.
(001338)
----Répertoire des sociétés. - 1970-   .
(002265)

CORPORATIONS--GERMANY, FEDERAL REPUBLIC OF.
----Die Haftungsproblematik bei Konkurs
einer Gesellschaft innerhalb eines
transnationalen Unternehmens. - 1984.
(002233)
----Handbuch der Grossunternehmen. -
1940-   .
(002644)

CORPORATIONS--JAPAN.
----The Rising Sun in America (Part Two)
-- Japanese management in the United
States. - 1986.
(000391)
----The economic analysis of the Japanese
firm. - 1984.
(000322)
----The Rising Sun in America (Part One). -
1986.
(000392)

CORPORATIONS--PHILIPPINES.
----Factors influencing the choice of
location : local and foreign firms in
the Philippines. - 1987.
(000547)

CORPORATIONS--SOUTH AFRICA.
----McGregor's investors' handbook. -
1986-   .
(001203) (002654)

CORPORATIONS--SWEDEN.
----Sveriges största företag. - 1968-   .
(002667)

CORPORATIONS--UNITED KINGDOM.
----The prospect for direct investment by
United Kingdom companies in developing
countries. - 1985.
(000169)
----Sell's British exporters. - 1916-   .
(002663)
----The Times 1000. - 1966-   .
(002668)

CORPORATIONS--UNITED STATES.
----The Rising Sun in America (Part Two)
-- Japanese management in the United
States. - 1986.
(000391)
----America's corporate families. -
1982-   .
(002616)
----America's corporate families and
international affiliates. - 1983-   .
(002617)
----Corporate capital structures in the
United States. - 1985.
(000315)
----Directory of American firms operating in
foreign countries. - 1955-   .
(002630)
----Forbes annual directory. - 1969-   .
(002640)
----Internal accountability. - 1984.
(002055)
----Major companies of the USA. - 1986-   .
(002652)
----Mezhdunarodnyi marketing amerikanskoi
tekhnologii. - 1985.
(000494)
----The Rising Sun in America (Part One). -
1986.
(000392)
----U.S. corporate interests and the
political economy of trade policy. -
1985.
(000368)

CORPORATIONS--WESTERN EUROPE.
----Abhängige Unternehmen und Konzerne im
    europäischen Gemeinschaftsrecht. - 1984.
    (002133)

CORRUPT PRACTICES.
----Extortion and bribery in business
    transactions. - 1977.
    (001979)

CORRUPT PRACTICES--UNITED STATES.
----Reviewing the situation : what is to be
    done with the Foreign Corrupt Practices
    Act? - 1987.
    (002235)

COST BENEFIT ANALYSIS.
----Multinational ventures in the commercial
    aircraft industry. - 1985.
    (000721)
----New theories of the multinational
    enterprise: an assessment of
    internalization theory. - 1986.
    (000089)
----Social cost/benefit analysis for MNCs. -
    1983.
    (001881)
----Towards a theory of multinational
    enterprise. - 1986.
    (000032)
----Transactions cost economics and the
    multinational enterprise: an assessment.
    - 1986.
    (000448)

COST BENEFIT ANALYSIS--MALAYSIA.
----Malaysia's industrial enclaves :
    benefits and costs. - 1987.
    (002402)

COST EFFECTIVENESS.
----Licensing in international strategy. -
    1985.
    (001419)
----Transactions cost economics and the
    multinational enterprise: an assessment.
    - 1986.
    (000448)
----Transnational corporations and
    technology transfer. - 1987.
    (001509)

COST EFFECTIVENESS--AFRICA.
----Gaspillages technologiques. - 1985.
    (001435)

COSTA RICA--DEVELOPMENT ASSISTANCE.
----The private sector, the public sector,
    and donor assistance in economic
    development. - 1983.
    (000268)

COSTA RICA--ECONOMIC CONDITIONS.
----Notes from Latin America. - 1983.
    (000628)

COSTA RICA--ECONOMIC DEVELOPMENT.
----The private sector, the public sector,
    and donor assistance in economic
    development. - 1983.
    (000268)

COSTA RICA--ECONOMIC POLICY.
----The private sector, the public sector,
    and donor assistance in economic
    development. - 1983.
    (000268)

COSTA RICA--EXPORT ORIENTED INDUSTRIES.
----La industria de la maquila y la
    explotación de la fuerza de trabajo de
    la mujer. - 1984.
    (001900)

COSTA RICA--LABOUR EXPLOITATION.
----La industria de la maquila y la
    explotación de la fuerza de trabajo de
    la mujer. - 1984.
    (001900)

COSTA RICA--LAWS AND REGULATIONS.
----National legislation and regulations
    relating to transnational corporations.
    Volume 3. - 1983.
    (002252)

COSTA RICA--PHARMACEUTICAL INDUSTRY.
----Transnational corporations in the
    pharmaceutical industry of developing
    countries. - 1984.
    (000749)

COSTA RICA--PRIVATE ENTERPRISES.
----The private sector, the public sector,
    and donor assistance in economic
    development. - 1983.
    (000268)

COSTA RICA--PUBLIC SECTOR.
----The private sector, the public sector,
    and donor assistance in economic
    development. - 1983.
    (000268)

COSTA RICA--TRANSNATIONAL CORPORATIONS.
----National legislation and regulations
    relating to transnational corporations.
    Volume 3. - 1983.
    (002252)

COSTA RICA--WOMEN WORKERS.
----La industria de la maquila y la
    explotación de la fuerza de trabajo de
    la mujer. - 1984.
    (001900)

COTE D'IVOIRE--COMPARATIVE ADVANTAGE.
----Comparative advantage as a development
    model. - 1985.
    (001691)

COTE D'IVOIRE--DEVELOPMENT POLICY.
----Comparative advantage as a development
    model. - 1985.
    (001691)

COTE D'IVOIRE--ECONOMIC CONDITIONS.
----Comparative advantage as a development
    model. - 1985.
    (001691)

COTE D'IVOIRE--ECONOMIC DEVELOPMENT.
----Multinationals and maldevelopment. -
    1987.
    (000995)

COTE D'IVOIRE--ECONOMIC POLICY.
----Multinationals and maldevelopment. -
    1987.
        (000995)

COTE D'IVOIRE--EXTERNAL DEBT.
----Comparative advantage as a development
    model. - 1985.
        (001691)

COTE D'IVOIRE--FOREIGN INVESTMENTS.
----National legislation and regulations
    relating to transnational corporations.
    Volume 4. - 1986.
        (002253)

COTE D'IVOIRE--LAWS AND REGULATIONS.
----National legislation and regulations
    relating to transnational corporations.
    Volume 4. - 1986.
        (002253)

COTE D'IVOIRE--TRANSNATIONAL CORPORATIONS.
----Multinationals and maldevelopment. -
    1987.
        (000995)
----National legislation and regulations
    relating to transnational corporations.
    Volume 4. - 1986.
        (002253)

COTTAGE INDUSTRIES--SOUTHEAST ASIA.
----Small-and medium-scale industries in the
    ASEAN countries. - 1984.
        (001036)

COUNTERVAILING DUTIES.
----Negotiating and drafting contracts in
    international barter and countertrade
    transactions. - 1984.
        (002428)

COURTS.
----L'Arbitrage transnational et les
    tribunaux nationaux. - 1984.
        (002492)
----Arbitration and the courts. - 1985.
        (002532)

CREDIT.
----The intertemporal effects of
    international transfers. - 1986.
        (001262)
----Le risque-pays, son traitement dans les
    banques. - 1983.
        (001783)
----Uncertain future. - 1984.
        (000977)

CREDIT--PERU.
----Transnational banks and the external
    finance of Latin America : the
    experience of Peru. - 1985.
        (000975)

CREDIT POLICY.
----Incentives and disincentives for foreign
    direct investment in less developed
    countries. - 1984.
        (002301)

CREDIT POLICY--AFRICA.
----Nezavisimye strany Afriki. - 1986.
        (001280)

CREDIT POLICY--UNITED STATES.
----U.S. and Canadian investment in South
    Africa and Namibia. - 1986.
        (001212) (002671) (002672)

CREDITWORTHINESS.
----Current problems of economic
    integration. - 1986.
        (001312)

CREDITWORTHINESS--CHILE.
----Debt equity swaps, investment, and
    creditworthiness. - 1987.
        (000259)

CROSS-CULTURAL ANALYSIS.
----Anthropology and international business.
    - 1986.
        (001892)
----International business and cultures. -
    1987.
        (001872)
----Managing cultural differences. - 1983.
        (001871)

CROSS-CULTURAL ANALYSIS--JAPAN.
----Japan's emerging multinationals. - 1985.
        (000379)

CROSS-ORGANIZATIONAL PROGRAMME ANALYSES.
----Expropriations of foreign-owned firms in
    developing countries: a cross-national
    analysis. - 1984.
        (001552)

CUBA--ARBITRAL AWARDS.
----Cuba's system of international
    commercial arbitration. - 1984.
        (002490)

CUBA--AUTOMATION.
----Microelectronics-based automation
    technologies and development. - 1985.
        (000753)

CUBA--COMMERCIAL ARBITRATION.
----Cuba's system of international
    commercial arbitration. - 1984.
        (002490)

CUBA--SUGAR INDUSTRY.
----Microelectronics-based automation
    technologies and development. - 1985.
        (000753)

CULTURAL AND SOCIAL ANTHROPOLOGY.
----Managing cultural differences. - 1983.
        (001871)

CULTURE DIFFUSION.
----Tourism and the Third World. - 1986.
        (000896)

CURRENCY.
----International accounting and reporting
    issues, 1985 review. - 1985.
        (002116)
----The practice of currency exposure
    management. - 1983.
        (000460)

CURRENCY CONVERTIBILITY.
----Counter-trade: untying those blocked
    funds. - 1987.
    (001398)
----Empresas multinacionales, gestión de
    cambios y crisis monetarias=Multination
    businesses, change of money, management
    and monetary crisis. With English
    summary.). - 1983.
    (001292)

CURRENCY INSTABILITY.
----Correcting the world monetary scandal. -
    1986.
    (001304)
----Currency exposure management. - 1983.
    (000409)
----Defining and measuring currency
    exposure. - 1983.
    (000504)
----UNCITRAL, the United Nations Commission
    on International Trade Law. - 1986.
    (002155)
----Wisselkoersinstabiliteit en
    schuldproblematiek. - 1984.
    (001310)

CUSTOMS UNIONS.
----Effets de la mobilité internationale du
    capital sur les pays membres d'une union
    douanière. - 1987.
    (001250)

CZECHOSLOVAKIA--COMMERCIAL ARBITRATION.
----Czechoslovak regulations governing
    arbitration in international trade. -
    1985.
    (002518)

CZECHOSLOVAKIA--ECONOMIC RELATIONS.
----East-West technology transfer. - 1984.
    (001463)

CZECHOSLOVAKIA--INTERNATIONAL TRADE.
----Czechoslovak regulations governing
    arbitration in international trade. -
    1985.
    (002518)

CZECHOSLOVAKIA--JOINT VENTURES.
----East-West joint ventures. - 1988.
    (001570)

CZECHOSLOVAKIA--LAWS AND REGULATIONS.
----East-West joint ventures. - 1988.
    (001570)

CZECHOSLOVAKIA--PROFIT.
----K mereni zisku podniku. - 1987.
    (000888)

CZECHOSLOVAKIA--SERVICE INDUSTRIES.
----Nekteré otázky budoucího rozvoje
    terciárního sektoru. - 1987.
    (000909)

CZECHOSLOVAKIA--STATE TRADING ENTERPRISES.
----K mereni zisku podniku. - 1987.
    (000888)

CZECHOSLOVAKIA--STATISTICAL DATA.
----East-West joint ventures. - 1988.
    (001570)

CZECHOSLOVAKIA--TECHNOLOGY TRANSFER.
----East-West technology transfer. - 1984.
    (001463)

DAMAGES.
----Dommages causés par les marées noires. -
    1984.
    (001952)
----Measure of damages in international
    commercial arbitration. - 1987.
    (002560)

DANGEROUS GOODS.
----Liability and compensation for damage in
    connection with the carriage of
    hazardous and noxious substances by sea.
    - 1986.
    (001939)
----Liability for shipments by sea of
    hazardous and noxious substances. - 1985.
    (001951)

DATA BASE MANAGEMENT.
----The third industrial revolution. - 1987.
    (000966)

DATA BASES.
----Top 100 data processing almanac. -
    1980-   .
    (000967)
----Transborder data flows. - 1983.
    (000973)
----UNCTC bibliography, 1974-1987. - 1988.
    (002695)

DATA PROCESSING.
----UNCITRAL, the United Nations Commission
    on International Trade Law. - 1986.
    (002155)

DATA PROCESSING--LATIN AMERICA.
----Trade and foreign direct investment in
    data services. - 1986.
    (000948)

DATA PROCESSING SERVICES.
----L'informatique du Nord au Sud. - 1986.
    (000678)
----PTS company directory. - 1985-   .
    (002661)
----Top 100 data processing almanac. -
    1980-   .
    (000967)
----Trade in data services. - 1986.
    (000949)

DATA PROCESSING SERVICES--UNITED STATES.
----A competitive assessment of the United
    States data processing services
    industry. - 1984.
    (000981)

DATA STORAGE--UNITED STATES.
----A competitive assessment of the United
    States disk storage industry. - 1985.
    (000672)

DATA TRANSMISSION.
----Transborder data flows. - 1983.
    (000973)

DEBT MANAGEMENT.
----Bank lending to developing countries. -
    1985.
        (000212)
----A closed circle for the developing
    countries? : debt and financial flows. -
    1986.
        (000218)
----The debt crisis and the world economy. -
    1984.
        (000220)
----The debt problem. - 1985.
        (000249)
----Debt rescheduling from an intertemporal
    choice theoretic point of view. - 1983.
        (000214)
----International lending and debt. - 1983.
        (000208)

DEBT MANAGEMENT--ARGENTINA.
----Los bancos transnacionales y el
    endeudamiento externo en la Argentina. -
    1987.
        (000819)

DEBT MANAGEMENT--CHILE.
----Debt equity swaps, investment, and
    creditworthiness. - 1987.
        (000259)

DEBT RENEGOTIATION.
----Bank lending to developing countries. -
    1985.
        (000212)
----Internationale Verschuldung-Wege aus der
    Krise. - 1983.
        (000253)

DEBT RENEGOTIATION--ARGENTINA.
----Los bancos transnacionales y el
    endeudamiento externo en la Argentina. -
    1987.
        (000819)

DEBT RENEGOTIATION--LATIN AMERICA.
----Evaluación de los criterios ortodoxos de
    reprogramación de la deuda externa. -
    1984.
        (000225)

DEBT REORGANIZATION.
----Bank lending to developing countries. -
    1985.
        (000212)
----Commercial banks and the restructuring
    of cross-border debt. - 1983.
        (000250)
----The international debt crisis. - 1985.
        (000240)

DEBT REORGANIZATION--ARGENTINA.
----Los bancos transnacionales y el
    endeudamiento externo en la Argentina. -
    1987.
        (000819)

DEBT SERVICING.
----Bank lending to developing countries. -
    1985.
        (000212)

----Changes in the international financial
    market and implications for
    transnational banks, transnational
    corporations and developing countries. -
    1986.
        (000976)
----The importance of international monetary
    markets and the international crisis of
    indebtedness. - 1987.
        (000244)

DEBT SERVICING--LATIN AMERICA.
----Evaluación de los criterios ortodoxos de
    reprogramación de la deuda externa. -
    1984.
        (000225)
----Foreign direct investment in Latin
    America. - 1986.
        (000190)
----Transnacionalización y periferia
    semindustrializada. - 1983.
        (001017)

DEBT SERVICING--MEXICO.
----A note on the burden of the Mexican
    foreign debt. - 1986.
        (000254)

DEBT SERVICING--UNITED STATES.
----Rehearing granted : Allied Bank
    International v. Banco Agricola Credito
    de Cartago and the current international
    debt crisis. - 1984.
        (000233)

DEBTS.
----Foreign direct investment and the debt
    crisis. - 1986.
        (000246)
----Global debt. - 1986.
        (000236)
----International finance. - 1983.
        (000266)
----International financial relations as
    part of the world-system. - 1987.
        (001285)
----The intertemporal effects of
    international transfers. - 1986.
        (001262)

DECISION-MAKING.
----Decision-making in multinational
    enterprises. - 1984.
        (000410)
----Decision-making regarding restructuring
    in multinational enterprises. - 1986.
        (000411)
----Making decisions in multinational
    corporations. - 1988.
        (001827)
----Making the multinational decision. -
    1983.
        (000542)
----Multinational enterprises : information
    and consultation concerning their
    manpower plans. - 1985.
        (000431)
----161 more checklists : decision making in
    international operations. - 1985.
        (000462)

DECISION-MAKING--BELGIUM.
----Employment decision-making in
     multinational enterprises. - 1984.
       (001888)

DECISION-MAKING--CANADA.
----Operating foreign subsidiaries. - 1983.
       (000388)

DECISION-MAKING--CHINA.
----The China trade: making the deal/the
     China trade: making the deal work. -
     1986.
       (001845)

DECISION-MAKING--UNITED KINGDOM.
----Decision-making in foreign-owned
     multinational subsidiaries in the United
     Kingdom. - 1985.
       (000521)

DECISION-MAKING--UNITED STATES.
----Operating foreign subsidiaries. - 1983.
       (000388)

DECISION-MAKING--WESTERN EUROPE.
----Operating foreign subsidiaries. - 1983.
       (000388)

DECLARATIONS.
----Declaration by the governments of OECD
     member countries and decisions of the
     OECD Council on international investment
     and multinational enterprises. - 1984.
       (001999)
----Measures regarding the activities of
     transnational corporations in South
     Africa and Namibia. - 1985.
       (001220)
----Trade in services : growth and balance
     of payments implications for countries
     of Western Asia. - 1987.
       (000968)

DECREE FOR THE PROTECTION OF THE NATURAL
RESOURCES OF NAMIBIA (1974).
----Transnational corporations in South
     Africa and Namibia : United Nations
     public hearings. Volume 1, Reports of
     the Panel of Eminent Persons and of the
     Secretary-General. - 1986.
       (001216)

DEFENCE CONTRACTS--UNITED STATES.
----The nuclear weapons industry. - 1984.
       (000659)
----Stocking the arsenal. - 1985.
       (000738)

DEFICIT FINANCING.
----International capital movements and
     developing countries. - 1985.
       (001282)

DEMOCRACY.
----Democratic development. - 1986.
       (001334)

DEMOCRACY--VENEZUELA.
----Petroleum and political pacts. - 1987.
       (001816)

DEVELOPED COUNTRIES.
----The characteristics of joint
     ventures in developed and developing
     countries. - 1985.
       (001541)
----Analysis of equipment leasing contracts.
     - 1984.
       (002407)
----La fiscalité internationale des
     entreprises. - 1985.
       (001743)
----Foreign currency translation. - 1986.
       (002102)
----The international law of expropriation
     of foreign-owned property. - 1983.
       (002330)
----Investissements internationaux et
     dynamique des avantages comparatifs des
     nouveaux pays industrialises. - 1984.
       (000496)
----Safety and health practices of
     multinational enterprises. - 1984.
       (001918)
----Structural adjustment and multinational
     enterprises. - 1985.
       (000095)
----Technological trends and challenges in
     electronics. - 1983.
       (000739)

DEVELOPED COUNTRIES--EAST ASIA.
----Entrepreneurial cooperation between
     industrialized countries and the
     developing countries in East and
     South-East Asia. - 1985.
       (001649)

DEVELOPED COUNTRIES--PACIFIC OCEAN REGION.
----Regulation to deregulation. - 1985.
       (000798)

DEVELOPED COUNTRIES--SOUTHEAST ASIA.
----Entrepreneurial cooperation between
     industrialized countries and the
     developing countries in East and
     South-East Asia. - 1985.
       (001649)

DEVELOPED COUNTRIES--UNITED STATES.
----A competitive assessment of the U.S.
     construction machinery industry. - 1985.
       (000761)
----A competitive assessment of the U.S.
     semiconductor manufacturing equipment
     industry. - 1985.
       (000758)

DEVELOPED MARKET ECONOMIES.
----Current financial and monetary problems
     of the developing countries in the world
     capitalist economy. - 1987.
       (001246)
----Enjeux technologiques et relations
     internationales. - 1986.
       (001429)
----Industry in the 1980s. - 1985.
       (001341)
----Kelet : nyugati közös vállalatok néhány
     elvi kérdése. - 1984.
       (001180)
----Limits and problems of taxation. - 1984.
       (001736)

DEVELOPED MARKET ECONOMIES (continued)
----Mezhdunarodnaia kapitalisticheskaia
    torgovlia uslugami i problemy ee
    regulirovaniia. - 1987.
       (000918) (001378)
----Mezinárodní financní a kapitálové vztahy
    rozvojovych zemí. - 1985.
       (000230)
----Multinationals from the Second World :
    growth of foreign investment by Soviet
    and East European enterprises. - 1987.
       (000356)
----North-South issues in trade in services.
    - 1985.
       (000944)
----North-South technology transfer: two
    neglected problems. - 1986.
       (001437)
----The political economy of international
    technology transfer. - 1987.
       (001482)
----Production and trade in services. - 1985.
       (000978)
----The regulation and supervision of
    international lending, (2). - 1986.
       (000234)
----Report on international industrial
    competitiveness, 1984. - 1984.
       (001690)
----Salient features and trends in foreign
    direct investment. - 1983.
       (000182)
----Services and the development process. -
    1985.
       (000979)
----The Soviet Union's other tax agreements.
    - 1986.
       (002043)
----Tax aspects of acquisitions and mergers.
    - 1983.
       (001645) (001756)
----The taxation of controlled foreign
    corporations. - 1986.
       (001699)
----Transborder data flows. - 1984.
       (000974)
----Transnacionalización y periferia
    semindustrializada. - 1983.
       (001017)
----Trends and issues in foreign direct
    investment and related flows. - 1985.
       (000192)
----Triad power. - 1985.
       (001686)
----Western firms participating in the
    East-West industrial co-operation. -
    1983.
       (001175)

DEVELOPED MARKET ECONOMIES--JAPAN.
----Zur Internationalisierung der
    japanischen Wirtschaft. - 1984.
       (000117)

DEVELOPED MARKET ECONOMIES--POLAND.
----CMEA direct investments in the western
    countries. - 1987.
       (000158)

DEVELOPED MARKET ECONOMIES--WESTERN EUROPE.
----Transnatsional'nye korporatsii v
    ekonomike malykh stran Zapadnoi Evropy.
    - 1983.
       (001163)

DEVELOPING COUNTRIES.
----The characteristics of joint
    ventures in developed and developing
    countries. - 1985.
       (001541)
----The multinational corporation in the
    less developed country: the economic
    development model versus the North-South
    model. - 1985.
       (001011)
----Accounting in developing countries. -
    1986.
       (002057)
----Accounting reports and performance
    measurement of multinational enterprises
    in less developed countries. - 1987.
       (002107)
----Accounting technology transfer to less
    developed countries and the Singapore
    experience. - 1986.
       (001498)
----The aluminum multinationals and the
    bauxite cartel. - 1987.
       (000599)
----Analysis of equipment leasing contracts.
    - 1984.
       (002407)
----The applicability of GATT to
    international trade in services :
    general considerations and the interest
    of developing countries. - 1987.
       (000885)
----Appropriate financing for petroleum
    development in developing countries. -
    1984.
       (000576)
----Appropriate pharmaceutical policies in
    developing countries. - 1985.
       (000707)
----Appropriate policies towards
    multinational hotel corporations in
    developing countries. - 1983.
       (000781)
----Arrangements between joint venture
    partners in developing countries. - 1987.
       (002450)
----Asia's struggle to affirm wholeness of
    life : report of a consultation on TNC's
    in Asia. - 1985.
       (001935)
----Aspecte juridice ale investitiilor
    straine directe în tarile în curs de
    dezvoltare. - 1987.
       (002245)
----Aspects des réglementations nationales
    de certains pays en voie de
    développement concernant le régime des
    investissements étrangers directs. -
    1987.
       (002248)
----Auslandsinvestitionen deutscher
    Unternehmen in Entwicklungsländern. -
    1984.
       (000167)
----Automation and the worldwide
    restructuring of the electronics
    industry: strategic implications for
    developing countries. - 1985.
       (000683)
----Bank lending to developing countries. -
    1985.
       (000212)

DEVELOPING COUNTRIES (continued)
----Banking on crisis. - 1983.
 (000868)
----Bargaining power, ownership, and
profitability of transnational
corporations in developing countries. -
1984.
 (001007)
----Basic framework for ASEAN industrial
co-operation. - 1986.
 (002149)
----Bibliography of appropriate technology
information for developing countries. -
1983.
 (002683)
----Biznes na pomoshchi. - 1984.
 (001298)
----Breves rasgos de la crisis. - 1983.
 (001307)
----Capital allowance schemes for mining
projects in LDCs. - 1983.
 (000607)
----The capital goods sector in developing
countries. - 1985.
 (001651)
----Capital inflows to LDC's and their
impact on imports. - 1986.
 (001010)
----Changes in the international financial
market and implications for
transnational banks, transnational
corporations and developing countries. -
1986.
 (000976)
----Channels and modalities for the transfer
of technology to public enterprises in
developing countries. - 1983.
 (001522)
----Churches and the transnational
corporations. - 1983.
 (002586)
----A closed circle for the developing
countries? : debt and financial flows. -
1986.
 (000218)
----Comercio internacional,
industrialización y nuevo orden
económico internacional. - 1983.
 (001242)
----A comparative analysis of the United
States-People's Republic of China tax
treaty. - 1986.
 (002037)
----Compendium of selected studies on
international monetary and financial
issues for the developing countries. -
1987.
 (001243)
----Compensation or opportunity? - 1986.
 (001293)
----Conscience and dividends. - 1985.
 (002587)
----Consumer choice in the Third World. -
1983.
 (000878)
----Contract efficiency and natural resource
investment in developing countries. -
1984.
 (002409)
----Contractual adaptation and conflict
resolution based on venture contracts
for mining projects in developing
countries. - 1985.
 (002475)

----Les contrats de transfert de
technologie. - 1983.
 (001468)
----The contribution of foreign direct
investment to exports : an empirical
study of 23 LDCs. - 1986.
 (001376)
----Co-production: a viable consideration
for developing nations. - 1984.
 (001629)
----Corporate aid programs in twelve
less-developed countries. - 1983.
 (002609)
----Counter-trade: untying those blocked
funds. - 1987.
 (001398)
----A country risk appraisal model of
foreign asset expropriation in
developing countries. - 1987.
 (001553) (001775)
----Current financial and monetary problems
of the developing countries in the world
capitalist economy. - 1987.
 (001246)
----Current problems of economic
integration. - 1986.
 (001312)
----The debt crisis and the world economy. -
1984.
 (000220)
----The debt problem. - 1985.
 (000249)
----Debt problems. - 1986.
 (000229)
----Debt rescheduling from an intertemporal
choice theoretic point of view. - 1983.
 (000214)
----Debt-equity swaps and the heavily
indebted countries. - 1987.
 (000263)
----The determinants of direct foreign
investment in a small LDC. - 1985.
 (000556)
----Determinants of offshore production in
developing countries. - 1986.
 (000544)
----La dette du Tiers monde. - 1984.
 (000223)
----Dette du Tiers monde. - 1984.
 (000260)
----Dette du Tiers-Monde. - 1987.
 (000224)
----La deuda de los países en desarrollo a
mediados de los ochenta. - 1987.
 (000210)
----Developing countries and services in the
Uruguay Round. - 1987.
 (000886)
----Developing country access to capital
markets in transition. - 1987.
 (001609)
----Developing with foreign investment. -
1987.
 (000998)
----Développement sans croissance. - 1983.
 (000632)
----Divisions over the international
division of labour. - 1984.
 (001269)
----Does concessionary aid lead to higher
investment rates in low-income
countries? - 1987.
 (002311)

DEVELOPING COUNTRIES (continued)
----Does de-industrialisation beget
    industrialisation which begets
    re-industrialisation? Review article. -
    1985.
        (001320)
----Double dividends? - 1986.
        (000682)
----The drilling gap in non-OPEC developing
    countries: the role of contractual and
    fiscal arrangements. - 1985.
        (002413)
----Economic and political determinants of
    foreign direct investment. - 1985.
        (000551)
----Economic development, investment
    dependence, and the rise of services in
    less developed nations. - 1986.
        (000958)
----The economic impact of direct foreign
    investments on developing countries. -
    1984.
        (001311)
----Economically rational design of
    developing countries' expropriation
    policies towards foreign investment. -
    1985.
        (001599)
----Economics of change in less developed
    countries. - 1986.
        (001000)
----The economics of joint ventures in less
    developed countries. - 1984.
        (001643)
----The effects of foreign investment on
    overall and sectoral groups in Third
    World states. - 1984.
        (001332)
----Ekspansiia mezhdunarodnykh monopolii v
    razvivaiushchiesia strany Azii. - 1987.
        (001068)
----Employment and technological choice of
    multinational enterprises in developing
    countries. - 1983.
        (001909)
----Las empresas transnacionales. - 1984.
        (001013)
----Endettement international et
    multinationalisation. - 1984.
        (000248)
----Energy sector investment in LDCs. - 1986.
        (000773)
----Enjeux technologiques et relations
    internationales. - 1986.
        (001429)
----Az észak-déli technológiaátadás
    formaváltozásai. - 1985.
        (001458)
----Evaluación de los criterios ortodoxoś de
    reprogramación de la deuda externa. -
    1984.
        (000225)
----Un exemple d'investissement du CAEM :
    liste des sociétés mixtes établies dans
    les pays en développement. - 1987.
        (000284)
----Export processing zones in developing
    countries. - 1987.
        (002376)
----Export-processing zones and
    industrialization: some considerations
    from the economics of large
    organizations. - 1983.
        (002364)

----Exports of manufactures from developing
    countries : performance and prospects
    for market access. - 1984.
        (001355)
----Exports of technology by newly
    industrializing countries: an overview.
    - 1984.
        (001454)
----Exports of technology from the South. -
    1985.
        (001469)
----Expropriations of foreign-owned firms in
    developing countries: a cross-national
    analysis. - 1984.
        (001552)
----Factors influencing the flow of foreign
    investment and the relevance of a
    multilateral investment guarantee
    scheme. - 1987.
        (002144)
----Fertilizer supplies for developing
    countries : issues in the transfer and
    development of technology. - 1985.
        (001471)
----Finance and protection of investments in
    developing countries. - 1987.
        (002128)
----Financing and external debt of
    developing countries: ...survey. - 1986-
    .
        (000231)
----Fiscal incentives and direct foreign
    investment in less developed countries.
    - 1983.
        (002312)
----La fiscalité internationale des
    entreprises. - 1985.
        (001743)
----Food-processing contracts with
    developing countries. - 1985.
        (002419)
----Foreign direct investment from
    developing countries. - 1986.
        (000325)
----Foreign direct investment in developing
    countries. - 1985.
        (000137)
----Foreign investment in mining projects. -
    1983.
        (000619)
----Foreign private investors and the host
    country. - 1985.
        (001851)
----Formy transferu technologie
    mezinarodnimi monopoly a technologicka
    transformace rozvojovych zemi. - 1985.
        (001457)
----Forum on economic crisis and Third World
    countries. - 1987.
        (001251)
----Free zones in developing countries. -
    1983.
        (002390)
----Funding direct investment through
    cofinancing: the commercial banker's
    view. - 1986.
        (001265)
----A general equilibrium model of
    multinational corporations in developing
    economies. - 1986.
        (000003)
----Global debt. - 1986.
        (000236)

DEVELOPING COUNTRIES (continued)
----Government policy and private investment
    in developing countries. - 1984.
    (002177)
----Hard bargaining ahead. - 1985.
    (001361)
----Host countries permanent sovereignty
    over national resources and protection
    of foreign investors. - 1983.
    (002566)
----ICSID : an international method for
    handling foreign investment disputes in
    LDCs. - 1987.
    (002474)
----The impact of direct foreign investment
    upon developing countries : a case study
    of Yugoslavia. - 1986.
    (001174)
----Les implications juridiques du principe
    de l'avantage comparatif dynamique. -
    1986.
    (001676)
----The importance of direct investment for
    developing countries. - 1986.
    (000142)
----Improving environmental cooperation. -
    1984.
    (001955)
----Improving the investment climate in
    developing countries. - 1984.
    (002572)
----Incentives and disincentives for foreign
    direct investment in less developed
    countries. - 1984.
    (002301)
----Increasing private capital flows to
    LDCs. - 1984.
    (001297)
----Industrial cooperation in regional
    economic groupings among developing
    countries and lessons for SAARC. - 1987.
    (001009)
----Industrial free zones and
    industrialization in developing
    countries. - 1986.
    (002403)
----Industrial structure and policy in less
    developed countries. - 1984.
    (001322)
----The industrialisation of less developed
    countries. - 1983.
    (001003)
----Industry in the 1980s. - 1985.
    (001341)
----Information technology in the Third
    World. - 1983.
    (000676)
----L'informatique dans les pays en
    développement. - 1984.
    (000839)
----L'informatique du Nord au Sud. - 1986.
    (000678)
----Infratechnologies, technologies de
    pointe, investissements dans et pour les
    pays en développement. - 1985.
    (001444)
----Institutions financières publiques de
    développement. - 1986.
    (000237)
----The insurance industry in economic
    development. - 1986.
    (000987)

----International banks and financial
    markets in developing countries. - 1984.
    (000859)
----International capital flows and economic
    development. - 1985.
    (001241)
----International Colloquium on the Proposed
    New Round of Multilateral Trade
    Negotiations and Developing Countries :
    proceedings and papers. - 1986.
    (001365)
----International corporate linkages. - 1987.
    (002430)
----International debt quagmire. - 1983.
    (000262)
----International financing of investments
    in tourism. - 1983.
    (000822)
----International income taxation and
    developing countries. - 1988.
    (001759)
----The international law of expropriation
    of foreign-owned property. - 1983.
    (002330)
----International lending and debt. - 1983.
    (000208)
----International marketing planning and
    state trading organisations. - 1986.
    (000369)
----International marketing to Black Africa
    and the Third World. - 1988.
    (001001)
----International protection of direct
    foreign investments in the Third World.
    - 1987.
    (002124)
----International regulation of
    transnational corporations. - 1986.
    (001956)
----International trademark licensing
    agreements. - 1986.
    (002421)
----Internationale Direktinvestitionen,
    1950-1973. - 1975-   .
    (000156)
----Internationalization of capital and the
    semi-industrialized countries: the case
    of the motor industry. - 1985.
    (000700)
----Internatsionalizatsiia
    monopoliticheskogo nakopleniia i
    razvivaiushchiesia strany. - 1986.
    (000082)
----Intra-LDCs foreign direct investment: a
    comparative analysis of Third World
    multinationals. - 1985.
    (000303)
----Investing in developing countries. -
    1970-   .
    (001985)
----Investing in development. - 1986.
    (000149)
----Investing in free export processing
    zones. - 1984.
    (002362)
----Investir dans les zones franches
    industrielles d'exportation. - 1984.
    (002363)
----Les investissements des multinationales
    de l'automobile dans le Tiers-Monde.
    (With English summary.). - 1984.
    (000729)

DEVELOPING COUNTRIES (continued)
----Les investissements miniers
    internationaux dans les pays en
    développement. - 1986.
       (000609)
----Investitionen und Kooperationen in
    Ubersee. - 1983.
       (001567)
----The investment development cycle and
    Third World multinationals. - 1986.
       (000529)
----The investment development cycle
    revisited. - 1986.
       (000320)
----Investment penetration in manufacturing
    and extraction and external public debt
    in Third World states. - 1984.
       (001015)
----Inwestycje zagraniczne a transfer wiedzy
    technicznej do krajów rozwijajacych sie.
    - 1984.
       (001476)
----Issues in capital flows to developing
    countries. - 1987.
       (001276)
----Issues in negotiating international loan
    agreements with transnational banks. -
    1983.
       (002459)
----Joint venture partner selection. - 1988.
       (001577)
----Joint ventures and Third World maritime
    development. - 1985.
       (000799)
----Joint ventures in LDCs. - 1987.
       (000997)
----Joint ventures of public enterprises in
    Argentina with other developing
    countries. - 1984.
       (001657)
----Kisvállatok Azsia fejlodo országainak
    elektronikai iparban. - 1987.
       (000630)
----Legal trends in international lending
    and investment in the developing
    countries. - 1984.
       (000207)
----Lending without limits. - 1979.
       (000228)
----Licence agreements in developing
    countries. - 1987.
       (002437)
----Licensing of technology and intellectual
    property rights to developing countries.
    - 1983.
       (001403)
----Macroproject development in the third
    world. - 1983.
       (001327)
----Marketing in less developed countries. -
    1986.
       (000465)
----Marketing supplementary food products in
    LDCs. - 1983.
       (000665)
----Marktstrategien multinationaler
    Pharmaunternehmen und die
    Arzneimittelmarkte der Dritten Welt. -
    1986.
       (000768)
----Measures to strengthen the capabilities
    of developing countries in their dealing
    with transnational corporations. - 1985.
       (002612)

----Mezinárodni financni a kapitálové vztahy
    rozvojovych zemi. - 1985.
       (000230)
----Microelectronics-based automation
    technologies and development. - 1985.
       (000753)
----MIGA and foreign investment. - 1988.
       (002145)
----Mirovoe kapitalisticheskoe khoziaistvo i
    razvivaiushchiesia strany Vostoka. -
    1986.
       (001279)
----Modelling foreign aid, capital inflows
    and economic development. - 1987.
       (001313)
----Muködotoke-beruházások a fejlodo
    országokban. - 1986.
       (001275)
----Multilateral investment insurance and
    private investment in the Third World. -
    1984.
       (002131)
----Multilateral investment insurance and
    private investment in the Third World. -
    1987.
       (002132)
----Multinational companies and world
    development. - 1983.
       (000071)
----Multinational companies in the textile,
    garment and leather industries. - 1984.
       (000722)
----Multinational corporations : the
    political economy of foreign direct
    investment. - 1985.
       (000072)
----Multinational corporations and the Third
    World. - 1986.
       (000073)
----Multi-national corporations and Third
    World development. - 1984.
       (000074)
----Multinational corporations, environment,
    and the Third World business matters. -
    1987.
       (001012)
----Multinational enterprises of developing
    countries. - 1986.
       (000357)
----Multinational firms' global strategies,
    host country indigenisation of ownership
    and welfare. - 1983.
       (000486)
----Multinational institutions and the Third
    World. - 1985.
       (001253)
----Multinational joint ventures in
    developing countries. - 1988.
       (001543)
----Multinational managers and host
    government interactions. - 1987.
       (001857)
----Multinationale ondernemingen en de Derde
    Wereld. - 1985.
       (001002)
----Multinationals from the Second World :
    growth of foreign investment by Soviet
    and East European enterprises. - 1987.
       (000356)
----Multinationals in a changing
    environment. - 1984.
       (001769)

DEVELOPING COUNTRIES (continued)
----Multinationals of the South. - 1986.
    (000359)
----Multinationals, technology and exports.
    - 1985.
    (001456)
----Multinationals, technology, and
    industrialization. - 1986.
    (001466)
----Municipal accounting for developing
    countries. - 1984.
    (002090)
----Mutual investments and the formation of
    multinational enterprises by developing
    countries. - 1987.
    (000378)
----Les nationalisations dans quelques pays
    d'Asie de tradition britannique : Inde,
    Sri Lanca, Birmanie. - 1984.
    (002329)
----Needs of developing countries for
    information on transnational
    corporations. - 1987.
    (002721)
----Negotiating with Third World
    governments. - 1983.
    (002468)
----Negotiation and drafting of mining
    development agreements. - 1976.
    (002432)
----Neokolonializm. - 1984.
    (000996)
----New forms of international investment in
    developing countries. - 1984.
    (001615)
----New forms of international investment in
    developing countries. - 1984.
    (001619)
----New forms of international technology
    transfer by Italian enterprises to
    developing countries. - 1984.
    (001474)
----New forms of investment in developing
    countries by US companies: a five
    industry comparison. - 1987.
    (000328)
----The new multinationals. - 1983.
    (000348)
----New technologies and Third World
    development. - 1986.
    (001475)
----Nezavisimye strany Afriki. - 1986.
    (001280)
----North-South issues in trade in services.
    - 1985.
    (000944)
----North-South technology transfer: two
    neglected problems. - 1986.
    (001437)
----Les nouvelles formes d'investissement
    dans les pays on développement. - 1984.
    (001620)
----Les nouvelles formes d'investissement
    international dans les pays en
    développement. - 1984.
    (000165)
----On the choice between capital import and
    labor export. - 1983.
    (002370)
----The political economy of international
    technology transfer. - 1987.
    (001482)
----Postimperialism. - 1987.
    (001232)

----La presentación de la iniciativa de la
    Cuenca del Caribe al GATT. - 1985.
    (001972)
----Private co-financing. - 1983.
    (000257)
----Private direct investment, finance and
    development. - 1985.
    (001324)
----Private investment in developing
    countries. - 1984.
    (000114)
----The problems of developing-country debt
    and a strategy for Arab banking
    institutions. - 1983.
    (000256)
----Problems of mineral development in
    developing countries. - 1983.
    (000583)
----Production and trade in services. - 1985.
    (000978)
----Promotion of direct investment in
    developing countries. - 1986.
    (002143)
----Promotion of foreign direct investment
    to developing countries: an exercise in
    cooperation. - 1986.
    (002035)
----Promotion of foreign direct investment
    to developing countries: opening
    address. - 1986.
    (002050)
----Prospects for automotive transnationals
    in the Third World. - 1983.
    (000708)
----Public enterprise and the developing
    world. - 1984.
    (001014)
----Public enterprise in mixed economies. -
    1984.
    (001574)
----The question of a reference to
    international law in the United Nations
    Code of Conduct on Transnational
    Corporations. - 1986.
    (002007)
----Recent trends in international direct
    investment. - 1987.
    (000176)
----Recommendation on development
    cooperation and employment in developing
    countries. - 1984.
    (001911)
----Recommendation on industry and
    development cooperation. - 1984.
    (001329)
----Los regímenes de garantía a la inversión
    extranjera y su aplicabilidad en los
    países de la ALADI. - 1985.
    (002126)
----Rekindling development. - 1988.
    (001302)
----The relationship between the state and
    the multinational corporation in the
    exploitation of resources. - 1984.
    (000584)
----Research and technology for the Third
    World. - 1985.
    (001489)
----Research on Third World multinationals.
    - 1985.
    (000321)

DEVELOPING COUNTRIES (continued)

----Restricción del crédito de la banca comercial en situaciones de crisis de la deuda internacional. - 1983.
(000226)

----Restrictive business practices in international trade. - 1987.
(001661)

----Restrictive clauses in licensing agreements: the pharmaceutical industry in developing countries. - 1984.
(002420)

----The restructuring of international loans and the international debt crisis. - 1984.
(000239)

----Revitalizing development, growth and international trade. - 1987.
(001394)

----The rise of multinationals from the Third World. - 1983.
(000351)

----Le risque-pays, son traitement dans les banques. - 1983.
(001783)

----Rola korporacji transnarodowych w miedzynarodowej wymianie towarów przemysłowych. - 1986.
(001369)

----Safety and health practices of multinational enterprises. - 1984.
(001918)

----Salient features and trends in foreign direct investment. - 1983.
(000182)

----Second thoughts on MIGA. - 1986.
(002148)

----Service industries and economic development. - 1984.
(000959)

----Les services : clé du développement économique? - 1986.
(000892)

----Services and the development process. - 1985.
(000979)

----Shaping a future for foreign direct investment in the Third World. - 1988.
(002140)

----Sovereignty and natural resource taxation in developing countries. - 1987.
(001741)

----Die Stabilisierungspolitik des Internationalen Währungsfonds. - 1986.
(001234)

----The stages of developing country policy toward foreign investment. - 1985.
(002277)

----State intervention, foreign economic aid, savings and growth in LDCs. - 1985.
(001337)

----A strategy for the technological transformation of developing countries. - 1985.
(001515)

----Strukturveränderungen der internationalen Direktinvestitionen und inländischer Arbeitsmarkt. - 1983.
(001913)

----The taking of foreign property under international law. - 1984.
(002336)

----Takokuseki kigyo to chushin kogyokoku. - 1983.
(001319)

----Taxation of international tourism in developing countries. - 1986.
(000900)

----Technological inconsistencies in promoting development. - 1984.
(001516)

----Technological trends and challenges in electronics. - 1983.
(000739)

----Technology choice and change in developing countries. - 1983.
(001505)

----Technology choice and employment generation by multinational enterprises in developing countries. - 1984.
(001646)

----Technology transfer to developing countries via multinationals. - 1986.
(001467)

----Testing the bargaining hypothesis in the manufacturing sector in developing countries. - 1987.
(000706)

----Third World debt crisis threatens a collapse of world trade and financial systems. - 1987.
(000217)

----Third World mineral development in crisis: the impact of the worldwide recession on legal instruments governing Third World mineral development. - 1985.
(000649)

----Third World multinationals. - 1983.
(000383)

----Third World resource directory. - 1984.
(002719)

----Threats and opportunities of global countertrade : marketing, financing and organizational implications. - 1984.
(001353)

----Le Tiers monde dans l'arbitrage commercial international. - 1983.
(002554)

----'Tikhaia' agressiia imperializma. - 1986.
(001272)

----Tobacco and food crops production in the Third World. - 1983.
(000572)

----De toekomst van 'export-processing free zones'. - 1987.
(002398)

----Tourism and the Third World. - 1983.
(000901)

----Tourism and the Third World. - 1986.
(000896)

----Tourism as a vehicle for Third World development. - 1985.
(000906)

----Toward a theory of industrial development in the Third World. - 1984.
(001331)

----Trade in investment-related technological services. - 1986.
(000945)

----Trade in services : obstacles and opportunities. - 1987.
(000984)

----Trade in services and developing countries. - 1986.
(000952)

DEVELOPING COUNTRIES (continued)
----Transborder data flows. - 1983.
    (000973)
----Transborder data flows. - 1984.
    (000974)
----Transfer pricing problems and economic
    strategies in developing countries. -
    1983.
    (001747)
----Transferring food production technology
    to developing nations. - 1983.
    (001508)
----Transfert de technologie. - 1983.
    (001460)
----Las transnacionales en el Paraguay. -
    1985.
    (001113)
----Las transnacionales en el Paraguay. -
    1985.
    (001116)
----Transnacionalización y periferia
    semindustrializada. - 1983.
    (001017)
----Transnacionalización y periferia
    semindustrializada. - 1984-   .
    (001339)
----Transnacional'nye korporacii na rynkah
    razvivajuscihsja stran: Ogranicit.
    delovaja praktika. - 1985.
    (001662)
----Transnational [and] the Third World. -
    1983.
    (001875)
----Transnational banks and the external
    finance of Latin America : the
    experience of Peru. - 1983.
    (000840)
----Transnational corporations and
    contractual relations in the world
    uranium industry. - 1983.
    (002448)
----Transnational corporations and
    technology transfer. - 1987.
    (001509)
----Transnational corporations and
    underdevelopment. - 1985.
    (001314)
----Transnational corporations and uneven
    development : the internationalization
    of capital and the Third World. - 1987.
    (001270)
----Transnational corporations: choice of
    techniques and employment in developing
    countries. -   .
    (001882)
----Transnational corporations in peripheral
    societies. - 1983.
    (001016)
----Transnational corporations in the
    agricultural machinery and equipment
    industry. - 1983.
    (000746)
----Transnational corporations in the
    man-made fibre, textile and clothing
    industries. - 1987.
    (000751)
----Transnational corporations in the
    pharmaceutical industry of developing
    countries. - 1984.
    (000749)
----Transnational corporations in world
    development. - 1988.
    (000101)

----Transnational corporations versus the
    state. - 1985.
    (000657)
----Transnationale Konzerne der Dritten Welt
    und der Entwicklungsprozess
    unterentwickelter Lander. - 1985.
    (000334)
----Transnationals and the Third World. -
    1984.
    (001005)
----Transnationals and the Third World:
    changing perceptions. - 1984.
    (001006)
----Transnatsional'nye korporatsii na
    rynkakh razvivaiushchikhsia stran. -
    1985.
    (001660)
----Trends and issues in foreign direct
    investment and related flows. - 1985.
    (000192)
----A tripartite model of the international
    debt crisis. - 1985.
    (000238)
----The U.S. drive to bring services into
    GATT. - 1986.
    (000926)
----Uncertain future. - 1984.
    (000977)
----US monopolies and developing countries.
    - 1986.
    (001692)
----Ways out of the debt crisis. - 1984.
    (000245)
----The welfare impact of foreign investment
    in the presence of specific factors and
    non-traded goods. - 1987.
    (001340)
----Why are services cheaper in the poor
    countries? - 1984.
    (000813)
----Why freer trade in services is in the
    interest of developing countries. - 1985.
    (000850)
----Women and work in the Third World. -
    1983.
    (001893)
----Women in industry. - 1985.
    (001930)
----Women in the global factory. - 1983.
    (001898)
----Women workers in multinational
    enterprises in developing countries. -
    1985.
    (001926)
----World development report. - 1987-   .
    (001345)

DEVELOPING COUNTRIES--ASIA.
----Japanese direct foreign investment in
    Asian developing countries. - 1983.
    (000155)

DEVELOPING COUNTRIES--AUSTRIA.
----Investitionsschutzabkommen. - 1986.
    (002041)

DEVELOPING COUNTRIES--EAST ASIA.
----International trading companies for
    developing countries-Latin America. -
    1984.
    (000838)

DEVELOPING COUNTRIES--EUROPE.
----The export of hazard. - 1985.
   (001941)

DEVELOPING COUNTRIES--FRANCE.
----Les investissements français dans le
   Tiers monde. - 1984.
   (000150)
----Le processus d'acquisition technologique
   par les entreprises d'un pays
   semi-industrialise. Deux études de cas.
   (With English summary.). - 1983.
   (001407)

DEVELOPING COUNTRIES--GERMANY, FEDERAL
REPUBLIC OF.
----Direktinvestitionen in
   Entwicklungsländern. - 1983.
   (000125)
----Investitionsschutzabkommen. - 1986.
   (002041)

DEVELOPING COUNTRIES--GUYANA.
----Commercialization of technology and
   dependence in the Caribbean. - 1985.
   (001477)

DEVELOPING COUNTRIES--HONG KONG.
----Multinational corporations, technology
   and employment. - 1983.
   (001891)

DEVELOPING COUNTRIES--JAMAICA.
----Commercialization of technology and
   dependence in the Caribbean. - 1985.
   (001477)

DEVELOPING COUNTRIES--JAPAN.
----Technology transfer and
   industrialization in the developing
   countries. - 1984.
   (001430)

DEVELOPING COUNTRIES--LATIN AMERICA.
----The international debt crisis and the
   banks. - 1985.
   (000227)
----International trading companies for
   developing countries-Latin America. -
   1984.
   (000838)

DEVELOPING COUNTRIES--PACIFIC OCEAN REGION.
----Regulation to deregulation. - 1985.
   (000798)

DEVELOPING COUNTRIES--PAPUA NEW GUINEA.
----Ok Tedi : evolution of a Third World
   mining project. - 1984.
   (000293)

DEVELOPING COUNTRIES--REPUBLIC OF KOREA.
----Foreign investment as an aid in moving
   from least developed to newly
   industrializing: a study in Korea. -
   1986.
   (000186)

DEVELOPING COUNTRIES--SOUTH ASIA.
----Multinational corporations, technology
   and employment. - 1983.
   (001891)

DEVELOPING COUNTRIES--SOUTHEAST ASIA.
----Corporate policy, strategic groups and
   the performance of transnational
   corporations in less developed
   countries. - 1982.
   (001008)

DEVELOPING COUNTRIES--SWITZERLAND.
----Halbgotter, Giftkriege und Kondensmilch.
   - 1983.
   (000658)

DEVELOPING COUNTRIES--TRINIDAD AND TOBAGO.
----Commercialization of technology and
   dependence in the Caribbean. - 1985.
   (001477)

DEVELOPING COUNTRIES--TURKEY.
----Le processus d'acquisition technologique
   par les entreprises d'un pays
   semi-industrialise. Deux études de cas.
   (With English summary.). - 1983.
   (001407)

DEVELOPING COUNTRIES--UNITED KINGDOM.
----The prospect for direct investment by
   United Kingdom companies in developing
   countries. - 1985.
   (000169)

DEVELOPING COUNTRIES--UNITED STATES.
----A competitive assessment of the United
   States equipment leasing industry. -
   1985.
   (000982)
----The export of hazard. - 1985.
   (001941)
----International countertrade. - 1984.
   (001396)
----The international debt crisis. - 1985.
   (000240)
----The international debt crisis and the
   banks. - 1985.
   (000227)
----International finance and investment. -
   1985.
   (001249)
----On Third World debt. - 1984.
   (000211)
----Performance requirements for foreign
   business. - 1983.
   (002314)
----The role of private investment in Third
   World development. - 1986.
   (001328)
----Towards a new treaty framework for
   direct foreign investment. - 1985.
   (002047)
----Trade in services. - 1986.
   (000962)
----The U.S. renewal of the GSP. - 1986.
   (001996)

DEVELOPING COUNTRIES--USSR.
----L'URSS et le Tiers Monde. - 1984.
   (002040)

DEVELOPING COUNTRIES--WESTERN EUROPE.
----Trade in services. - 1986.
   (000962)

DEVELOPMENT.
----Le commerce international de la
     technologie. - 1985.
       (001445)
----Consumers, transnational corporations,
     and development. - 1986.
       (001343)
----Développement sans croissance. - 1983.
       (000632)
----Environmental aspects of the activities
     of transnational corporations. - 1985.
       (001954)
----Forum on economic crisis and Third World
     countries. - 1987.
       (001251)
----Multi-national corporations and Third
     World development. - 1984.
       (000074)
----Revitalizing development, growth and
     international trade. - 1987.
       (001394)
----Technological inconsistencies in
     promoting development. - 1984.
       (001516)
----Tourism as a vehicle for Third World
     development. - 1985.
       (000906)
----Transnational corporations and
     underdevelopment. - 1985.
       (001314)

DEVELOPMENT--CHILE.
----Las empresas transnacionales en la
     economía de Chile, 1974-1980. - 1983.
       (001123)

DEVELOPMENT--EAST ASIA.
----The role of direct foreign investment in
     developing East Asian countries. - 1985.
       (001052)

DEVELOPMENT--FRANCE.
----L'économie française et le développement
     des services : Annuaire 1985-1986. -
     1986.
       (000847)

DEVELOPMENT--GHANA.
----Technology and development :
     socio-economic implications for Ghana. -
     1987.
       (001478)

DEVELOPMENT--JAPAN.
----The role of direct foreign investment in
     developing East Asian countries. - 1985.
       (001052)

DEVELOPMENT--PARAGUAY.
----Las empresas transnacionales en la
     economía del Paraguay. - 1987.
       (001108)

DEVELOPMENT--POLAND.
----Development, social justice, and
     dependence in Poland. - 1985.
       (001188)

DEVELOPMENT--UNITED STATES.
----The role of direct foreign investment in
     developing East Asian countries. - 1985.
       (001052)

DEVELOPMENT ASSISTANCE.
----Factors influencing the flow of foreign
     investment and the relevance of a
     multilateral investment guarantee
     scheme. - 1987.
       (002144)
----Foreign direct investment, the service
     sector and international banking. - 1987.
       (000972)
----Modelling foreign aid, capital inflows
     and economic development. - 1987.
       (001313)
----Private direct investment, finance and
     development. - 1985.
       (001324)
----The private sector, the public sector,
     and donor assistance in economic
     development. - 1983.
       (000268)
----State intervention, foreign economic
     aid, savings and growth in LDCs. - 1985.
       (001337)
----Takokuseki kigyo to chushin kogyokoku. -
     1983.
       (001319)

DEVELOPMENT ASSISTANCE--AFRICA.
----Foreign powers and Africa. - 1983.
       (001031)

DEVELOPMENT ASSISTANCE--BELGIUM.
----Infratechnologies, technologies de
     pointe, investissements dans et pour les
     pays en développement. - 1985.
       (001444)

DEVELOPMENT ASSISTANCE--CAMEROON.
----The private sector, the public sector,
     and donor assistance in economic
     development. - 1983.
       (000268)

DEVELOPMENT ASSISTANCE--CARIBBEAN REGION.
----The Caribbean Basin Economic Recovery
     Act and its implications for foreign
     private investment. - 1984.
       (001965)

DEVELOPMENT ASSISTANCE--COSTA RICA.
----The private sector, the public sector,
     and donor assistance in economic
     development. - 1983.
       (000268)

DEVELOPMENT ASSISTANCE--FRANCE.
----Infratechnologies, technologies de
     pointe, investissements dans et pour les
     pays en développement. - 1985.
       (001444)

DEVELOPMENT ASSISTANCE--MALAWI.
----The private sector, the public sector,
     and donor assistance in economic
     development. - 1983.
       (000268)

DEVELOPMENT ASSISTANCE--SAUDI ARABIA.
----Impact of the operations of
     transnational corporations on
     development in Saudi Arabia. - 1987.
       (001140)

DEVELOPMENT ASSISTANCE--SWEDEN.
----Infratechnologies, technologies de
    pointe, investissements dans et pour les
    pays en développement. - 1985.
      (001444)

DEVELOPMENT ASSISTANCE--THAILAND.
----The private sector, the public sector,
    and donor assistance in economic
    development. - 1983.
      (000268)

DEVELOPMENT ASSISTANCE--UNITED STATES.
----The Caribbean Basin Economic Recovery
    Act and its implications for foreign
    private investment. - 1984.
      (001965)
----U.S. foreign assistance. - 1984.
      (000203)

DEVELOPMENT BANKS.
----Current problems of economic
    integration. - 1986.
      (001312)
----La dette du Tiers monde. - 1984.
      (000223)

DEVELOPMENT BANKS--WESTERN EUROPE.
----The European Investment Bank. - 1985.
      (002134)

DEVELOPMENT CREDITS.
----Restricción del crédito de la banca
    comercial en situaciones de crisis de la
    deuda internacional. - 1983.
      (000226)

DEVELOPMENT FINANCE.
----Appropriate financing for petroleum
    development in developing countries. -
    1984.
      (000576)
----Bilateral investment promotion
    protection and treaties : a model for
    Community promotion of mining
    investment? - 1986.
      (002052)
----The changing role of international bank
    lending in development finance. - 1985.
      (000232)
----Compendium of selected studies on
    international monetary and financial
    issues for the developing countries. -
    1987.
      (001243)
----Current problems of economic
    integration. - 1986.
      (001312)
----Developing country access to capital
    markets in transition. - 1987.
      (001609)
----International banks and financial
    markets in developing countries. - 1984.
      (000859)
----International financial relations as
    part of the world-system. - 1987.
      (001285)
----Promotion of mining and energy
    investment under the Lomé Convention. -
    1986.
      (002607)
----Revitalizing development, growth and
    international trade. - 1987.
      (001394)

DEVELOPMENT FINANCE--ASIA.
----The impact of foreign capital inflow on
    investment and economic growth in
    developing Asia. - 1985.
      (001048)

DEVELOPMENT FINANCE--CARIBBEAN REGION.
----Los flujos de capital hacia América
    Latina y el Caribe, y el financiamiento
    del desarrollo, en los años venideros. -
    1985.
      (001231)

DEVELOPMENT FINANCE--COLOMBIA.
----Las empresas transnacionales en el
    desarrollo colombiano. - 1986.
      (001121)

DEVELOPMENT FINANCE--LATIN AMERICA.
----Los flujos de capital hacia América
    Latina y el Caribe, y el financiamiento
    del desarrollo, en los años venideros. -
    1985.
      (001231)

DEVELOPMENT FINANCE INSTITUTIONS.
----Current problems of economic
    integration. - 1986.
      (001312)
----Institutions financières publiques de
    développement. - 1986.
      (000237)
----Measures to strengthen the capabilities
    of developing countries in their dealing
    with transnational corporations. - 1985.
      (002612)

DEVELOPMENT FINANCE INSTITUTIONS--AFRICA.
----The role of transnational banks and
    financial institutions in Africa's
    development process. - 1986.
      (000935)

DEVELOPMENT FINANCE INSTITUTIONS--LIBERIA.
----The impact of the transnational
    corporations in the banking and other
    financial institutions on the economy of
    Liberia. - 1986.
      (000873)

DEVELOPMENT PLANNING--CHINA.
----The 1981 Economic Contract Law of the
    People's Republic of China. - 1986.
      (002237)

DEVELOPMENT PLANS--OMAN.
----Impact of the operations of
    transnational corporations on
    development in the Sultanate of Oman. -
    1988.
      (001144)

DEVELOPMENT POLICY--CAMEROON.
----The political economy of development in
    Cameroon. - 1985.
      (001833)
----The political economy of development in
    Cameroon. - 1986.
      (001834)

DEVELOPMENT POLICY--COTE D'IVOIRE.
----Comparative advantage as a development
    model. - 1985.
      (001691)

DEVELOPMENT RESEARCH.
----The choice of a technique in analysing
    national development strategy. - 1986.
      (001323)
----Infratechnologies, technologies de
    pointe, investissements dans et pour les
    pays en développement. - 1985.
      (001444)

DEVELOPMENT RESEARCH--GERMANY, FEDERAL
REPUBLIC OF.
----La recherche-développement dans la
    stratégie des grandes entreprises
    chimiques de l'entre-deux-guerres: Du
    Pont de Nemours, Imperial Chemical
    Industries, I. G. Farben. (With English
    summary.). - 1984.
      (000295)

DEVELOPMENT STRATEGIES.
----The choice of a technique in analysing
    national development strategy. - 1986.
      (001323)
----Industrialisation et commerce du Tiers
    monde. - 1986.
      (001318)
----A strategy for the technological
    transformation of developing countries.
    - 1985.
      (001515)
----Trade policy options in the design of
    development strategies. - 1986.
      (001399)
----Transnational corporations and
    technology transfer. - 1987.
      (001509)

DICTIONARIES.
----Dictionnaire des industries. - 1986.
      (002705)
----Glossary of terms for state auditors. -
    1983.
      (002711)
----Management accounting terminology. -
    1983.
      (002092) (002717)
----Multinational enterprise. - 1987.
      (002713)

DIFFUSION OF INNOVATIONS.
----Le commerce international de la
    technologie. - 1985.
      (001445)
----The world of appropriate technology. -
    1983.
      (001447)

DIFFUSION OF INNOVATIONS--ARGENTINA.
----Exportaciones de tecnología de Brasil y
    Argentina. - 1986.
      (001491)

DIFFUSION OF INNOVATIONS--BRAZIL.
----Exportaciones de tecnología de Brasil y
    Argentina. - 1986.
      (001491)

DIRECT FOREIGN INVESTMENT--INDIA.
----Trade in investment-related
    technological studies. - 1986.
      (001386)

DIRECTORIES.
----An AEA directory of international
    electronics facilities. - 1982.
      (000650) (002613)
----Analyse de l'activité de 95 firmes
    industrielles étrangères dans la
    bio-industrie. - 1983.
      (000652)
----The blue book of Canadian business. -
    1976-   .
      (002622)
----Consultancy services. - 1986.
      (000831)
----Directory of foreign capital affiliated
    enterprises in Japan. - 198?-   .
      (002632)
----Double dividends? - 1986.
      (000682)
----E [and] MJ international directory of
    mining. - 1968-   .
      (002637)
----Financial directories of the world. -
    1982-   .
      (002685)
----Financial Times mining international
    yearbook. - 1887-   .
      (002639)
----Genetic engineering and biotechnology
    firms worldwide directory. - 1981-   .
      (000688) (002642)
----The global marketplace. - 1987.
      (000290)
----The GT guide to world equity markets. -
    1986-   .
      (002712)
----Indo-U.S. cooperation in business and
    industry, 1986. - 1986.
      (002675)
----International business travel and
    relocation directory. - 1984.
      (002710)
----An international directory of 600
    consultants and contractors with
    experience in the Middle East. - 1985.
      (002645)
----International financial reporting and
    auditing. - 1984.
      (002088)
----List of company directories and summary
    of their contents. - 1983.
      (002686)
----Neue Wachstumsmärkte in Fernost. - 1983.
      (001800)
----PTS company directory. - 1985-   .
      (002661)
----Reference book and buyers' guide. -
    1984-   .
      (000797)
----Spotlight on international business: the
    Forbes foreign rankings. - 1986.
      (002665)
----Third World resource directory. - 1984.
      (002719)
----Top 100 data processing almanac. -
    1980-   .
      (000967)
----Trade union directory. - 1971-   .
      (002720)

DIRECTORIES (continued)
----The world directory of multinational
enterprises. - 1980-   .
    (002676)
----The world's largest industrial
enterprises, 1962-1983. - 1985.
    (000298)
----Worldscope : industrial company
profiles. - 1987.
    (000299)
----Worldwide synthetic fuels and alternate
energy directory. - 1981-   .
    (002677)

DIRECTORIES--AFRICA.
----African trade unions. - 1983-   .
    (002592) (002593) (002698)

----Asia-Pacific/Africa-Middle East
petroleum directory. - 1984-   .
    (000579) (002618)
----Directory of African technology
institutions. - 1985.
    (002706)
----Owen's Worldtrade Africa business
directory. - 1986-   .
    (002657)
----Répertoire de la législation relative
aux investissements étrangers dans les
pays membres de L'OCI. - 1984.
    (002264)

DIRECTORIES--ASIA.
----Asia-Pacific/Africa-Middle East
petroleum directory. - 1984-   .
    (000579) (002618)
----Asia's 7500 largest companies. -
1985-   .
    (002619)
----Bankers handbook for Asia. - 1976-   .
    (002621)
----Major companies of the Far East. -
1983-   .
    (002651)

DIRECTORIES--AUSTRALIA.
----Kompass Australia. - 1970-   .
    (002649)

DIRECTORIES--CANADA.
----Business directory of Canadian trade
representation abroad. - 1984-   .
    (002700)
----Foreign investment in South Africa and
Namibia. - 1984.
    (001198) (002641)

DIRECTORIES--CHINA.
----The China directory of industry and
commerce and economic annual. - 1984.
    (002626)

DIRECTORIES--COLOMBIA.
----Directorio de empresas y ejecutivos. -
1979-   .
    (002628)

DIRECTORIES--EL SALVADOR.
----Directorió comercial e industrial de El
Salvador. - 1986-   .
    (002627)

DIRECTORIES--EQUATORIAL GUINEA.
----Directorio nacional de empresas y
establecimientos. - 1985-   .
    (002629)

DIRECTORIES--EUROPE.
----Directory of European industrial [and]
trade associations. - 1986-   .
    (002707)

DIRECTORIES--GERMANY, FEDERAL REPUBLIC OF.
----Handbuch der Grossunternehmen. -
1940-   .
    (002644)

DIRECTORIES--HUNGARY.
----Directory of Hungarian foreign trade
companies. - 1976-   .
    (002635)
----Hungarian Chamber of Commerce handbook.
- 1984-   .
    (001811)

DIRECTORIES--INDIA.
----All-India directory of industrial
establishments. - 1984-   .
    (002614)

DIRECTORIES--ISLAMIC COUNTRIES.
----A directory of foreign investment
legislation in O.I.C. member countries.
- 1984.
    (002201)
----Répertoire de la législation relative
aux investissements étrangers dans les
pays membres de L'OCI. - 1984.
    (002264)

DIRECTORIES--LATIN AMERICA.
----Dun's Latin America's top 25,000. -
1984-   .
    (002636)

DIRECTORIES--LUXEMBOURG.
----Répertoire des entreprises
luxembourgeoises. - 1979-   .
    (002662)

DIRECTORIES--MALAWI.
----Malawi buyers' guide. - 1983-   .
    (002653)

DIRECTORIES--MEXICO.
----1985 directory of in-bond plants
(maquiladoras) in Mexico. - 1984.
    (001132) (002678)

DIRECTORIES--MIDDLE EAST.
----Asia-Pacific/Africa-Middle East
petroleum directory. - 1984-   .
    (000579) (002618)

DIRECTORIES--NAMIBIA.
----Foreign investment in South Africa and
Namibia. - 1984.
    (001198) (002641)
----Reference book on major transnational
corporations operating in Namibia. -
1985.
    (000297) (001213) (002673)

DIRECTORIES--NEW YORK (N.Y.).
----Moody's industrial manual. - 1954-   .
    (002656)

DIRECTORIES--NORWAY.
----Kompass. - 1970-   .
    (002647)

DIRECTORIES--PACIFIC OCEAN REGION.
----Asia-Pacific/Africa-Middle East
    petroleum directory. - 1984-   .
    (000579) (002618)

DIRECTORIES--SINGAPORE.
----Leading international companies
    manufacturing and providing technical
    services in Singapore. - 1983-   .
    (002650)
----Singapore manufacturers and products
    directory. - 1977-   .
    (002664)

DIRECTORIES--SOUTH AFRICA.
----Foreign investment in South Africa and
    Namibia. - 1984.
    (001198) (002641)
----McGregor's investors' handbook. -
    1986-   .
    (001203) (002654)

DIRECTORIES--SWEDEN.
----Sveriges största företag. - 1968-   .
    (002667)

DIRECTORIES--UNITED KINGDOM.
----The bankers' almanac and year book. -
    1886-   .
    (002620)
----Britain's privately owned companies. -
    198?-   .
    (002624)
----Foreign investment in South Africa and
    Namibia. - 1984.
    (001198) (002641)
----Kompass. - 196?-   .
    (002648)
----Sell's British exporters. - 1916-   .
    (002663)
----The Times 1000. - 1966-   .
    (002668)

DIRECTORIES--UNITED STATES.
----America's corporate families. -
    1982-   .
    (002616)
----America's corporate families and
    international affiliates. - 1983-   .
    (002617)
----Bradford's directory of marketing
    research agencies and management
    consultants in the United States and the
    world. - 1966-   .
    (002623)
----Consultants and consulting organizations
    directory. - 197?-   .
    (000832)
----Directory of American firms operating in
    foreign countries. - 1955-   .
    (002630)
----Directory of business, trade and public
    policy organizations. - 1982-   .
    (002631)

----Directory of foreign firms operating in
    the United States. - 1969-   .
    (002633)
----Export trading companies. - 1984-   .
    (000851) (002638)
----Forbes annual directory. - 1969-   .
    (002640)
----Foreign investment in South Africa and
    Namibia. - 1984.
    (001198) (002641)
----The knowledge industry 200. - 1983.
    (000884) (002646)
----Krupneishie promyshlennye i torgovye
    monopolii. - 1986.
    (002658)
----Major companies of the USA. - 1986-   .
    (002652)
----Million dollar directory. - 1959-   .
    (002655)
----Moody's industrial manual. - 1954-   .
    (002656)
----The nuclear weapons industry. - 1984.
    (000659)
----Stocking the arsenal. - 1985.
    (000738)
----U.S. and Canadian investment in South
    Africa and Namibia. - 1986.
    (001212) (002671) (002672)

DIRECTORIES--USSR.
----Businessman's Moscow. - 1984-   .
    (002625)

DIRECTORIES--YUGOSLAVIA.
----Privredni adresar SFRJ. - 1965-   .
    (002660)

DISARMAMENT.
----Third World resource directory. - 1984.
    (002719)

DISPUTE SETTLEMENT.
----Arrangements between joint venture
    partners in developing countries. - 1987.
    (002450)
----Bilateral investment treaties. - 1988.
    (002054)
----Case studies in the jurisdiction of the
    International Centre for Settlement of
    Investment Disputes. - 1986.
    (002580)
----Contractual adaptation and conflict
    resolution based on venture contracts
    for mining projects in developing
    countries. - 1985.
    (002475)
----Dispute resolution techniques in
    international contracts involving the
    sale of goods. - 1987.
    (002506)
----ICSID : an international method for
    handling foreign investment disputes in
    LDCs. - 1987.
    (002474)
----Multilateral negotiations and
    third-party roles. - 1986.
    (002689)
----Les négociations : moyen principal du
    règlement pacifique des différends
    internationaux. - 1984.
    (002510)
----Négociations internationales. - 1984.
    (002463)

DISPUTE SETTLEMENT (continued)
----Negotiation journal. - 1985-   .
    (002547)
----Note sur l'extension du "système CIRDI".
    - 1984.
    (002561)
----Peaceful settlement of international
    trade disputes. - 1983.
    (002500)
----La pratique du CIRDI. - 1987.
    (002550)
----Sanctions to control party misbehavior
    in international arbitration. - 1986.
    (002537)

DISPUTE SETTLEMENT--AUSTRALIA.
----Dispute resolution in the Asia/Pacific
    region. - 1987.
    (002556)

DISPUTE SETTLEMENT--IRAN (ISLAMIC REPUBLIC
OF).
----Current developments in the law of
    expropriation and compensation. - 1987.
    (002318)
----Iran-U.S. Claims Tribunal. - 1986.
    (002335)
----Partnership claims before the
    Iran-United States Claims Tribunal. -
    1987.
    (002322)

DISPUTE SETTLEMENT--UNITED STATES.
----Current developments in the law of
    expropriation and compensation. - 1987.
    (002318)
----International antitrust law. - 1985.
    (002539)
----International commercial arbitration. -
    1985.
    (002516)
----Iran-U.S. Claims Tribunal. - 1986.
    (002335)
----Partnership claims before the
    Iran-United States Claims Tribunal. -
    1987.
    (002322)

DISPUTES.
----Alternatives to litigation. - 1983.
    (002567)
----Choosing the substantive law to apply in
    international commercial arbitration. -
    1986.
    (002477)

DISPUTES--INDIA.
----For whom the bell tolls in the aftermath
    of the Bhopal tragedy. - 1987.
    (001950)

DISPUTES--UNITED STATES.
----For whom the bell tolls in the aftermath
    of the Bhopal tragedy. - 1987.
    (001950)

DISTRIBUTION--EUROPE.
----Market share strategy in Europe. - 1985.
    (000493)

DISTRIBUTIVE AND SERVICE TRADE
STATISTICS--CANADA.
----Canada's international trade in
    services. - 1986-   .
    (000821)

DIVESTMENT.
----Foreign and domestic divestment and
    investment decisions: like or unlike? -
    1983.
    (000523)
----Foreign direct divestment theory: is it
    the reverse of FDI theory? - 1983.
    (001546)
----Theories of foreign direct investment
    and divestment: a classificatory note. -
    1985.
    (000558)

DIVESTMENT--BELGIUM.
----Recent trends in foreign direct
    investment and disinvestment in Belgium.
    - 1985.
    (000185)

DIVESTMENT--EUROPE.
----Foreign divestment and international
    rationalisation in the motor industry. -
    1985.
    (000664)

DIVESTMENT--HONG KONG.
----Exploiting Hong Kong's uncertain future.
    - 1987.
    (001862)

DIVESTMENT--NAMIBIA.
----Transnational corporations : follow-up
    to the recommendations of the Panel of
    Eminent Persons Established to Conduct
    the Public Hearings on the Activities of
    Transnational Corporations in South
    Africa and Namibia. - 1988.
    (001221)

DIVESTMENT--SOUTH AFRICA.
----Activities of transnational corporations
    in South Africa and Namibia and the
    responsibilities of home countries with
    respect to their operations in this
    area. - 1986.
    (001192)
----The costs of disinvestment. - 1986.
    (001207)
----Disinvestment and black workers
    attitudes in South Africa. - 1985.
    (001210)
----Leaving South Africa/Kellogg's
    private war against apartheid/Black
    unions. - 1985.
    (001200)
----Measures regarding the activities of
    transnational corporations in South
    Africa and Namibia. - 1985.
    (001220)
----Time to quit South Africa? - 1985.
    (001206)

DIVESTMENT--SOUTH AFRICA (continued)
----Transnational corporations : follow-up
    to the recommendations of the Panel of
    Eminent Persons Established to Conduct
    the Public Hearings on the Activities of
    Transnational Corporations in South
    Africa and Namibia. - 1988.
        (001221)

DIVESTMENT--UNITED STATES.
----The costs of disinvestment. - 1986.
        (001207)
----Disinvestment and black workers
    attitudes in South Africa. - 1985.
        (001210)
----Time to quit South Africa? - 1985.
        (001206)

DIVESTMENTS--SOUTH AFRICA.
----The crisis in South Africa: rising
    pressures on multinationals. - 1986.
        (001201)

DIVISION OF LABOUR.
----A theory of the international division
    of labour. - 1984.
        (001239)

DIVISION OF LABOUR--SPAIN.
----Hacia dónde va el empleo? - 1986.
        (001252)

DIVISION OF LABOUR--WESTERN EUROPE.
----Hacia dónde va el empleo? - 1986.
        (001252)

DOCUMENTS.
----Transnational corporations in South
    Africa and Namibia : United Nations
    public hearings. Volume 1, Reports of
    the Panel of Eminent Persons and of the
    Secretary-General. - 1986.
        (001216)

DOMESTIC ECONOMIC ASSISTANCE--CANADA.
----An automotive strategy for Canada. -
    1983.
        (000686)

DOMESTIC TRADE--AUSTRALIA.
----Multinational enterprise behaviour and
    domestic industry adjustment under
    import threat. - 1986.
        (000518)

DOMESTIC TRADE--BRAZIL.
----Technological spill-overs and manpower
    training: a comparative analysis of
    multinational and national enterprises
    in Brazilian manufacturing. - 1986.
        (001899)

DOMESTIC TRADE--CANADA.
----Concentration and foreign control in
    retail and wholesale trade in Canada,
    1979. - 1983.
        (000783)

DOMESTIC TRADE--GHANA.
----The capital intensity of foreign,
    private local and state owned firms in a
    less developed country: Ghana. - 1986.
        (001018)

DOMESTIC TRADE--LATIN AMERICA.
----Evaluating differences in technological
    activity between transnational and
    domestic firms in Latin America. - 1986.
        (001431)

DOMESTIC TRADE--UNITED KINGDOM.
----Comparative analysis of UK domestic and
    international firms. - 1984.
        (000343)

DOUBLE TAXATION.
----Cross-border transactions between
    related companies. - 1985.
        (001735)
----Die Einwirkung internationaler
    Organisationen auf das Steuerrecht. -
    1984.
        (001990)
----Die finanzielle Führung und Kontrolle
    von Auslandsgesellschaften. - 1983.
        (000447)
----La fiscalité internationale des
    entreprises. - 1985.
        (001743)
----GATT versus tax treaties? - 1987.
        (002032)
----International income taxation and
    developing countries. - 1988.
        (001759)
----Prix de transfert et entreprises
    multinationales. - 1984.
        (002099)
----A reference guide to international
    taxation. - 1987.
        (001714)
----Transfer pricing and multinational
    enterprises. - 1984.
        (001745)
----Trends in international taxation. - 1985.
        (001746)

DOUBLE TAXATION--GERMANY, FEDERAL REPUBLIC
OF.
----Gewinne verbundener Unternehmen,
    Verrechnungspreise. - 1984.
        (001749)
----Internationale Unternehmensbesteuerung.
    - 1983.
        (001727)

DOUBLE TAXATION--SWEDEN.
----Underskott vid joint venture- och annan
    verksamhet i utlandet, m.m. - 1985.
        (001760)

DOUBLE TAXATION--UNITED STATES.
----Federal taxation of international
    transactions. - 1988.
        (001730)
----The Soviet Union's other tax agreements.
    - 1986.
        (002043)
----Tax aspects of international
    transactions. - 1984.
        (001757)
----Tax treaty abuse. - 1983.
        (002046)

DOUBLE TAXATION--USSR.
----The Soviet Union's other tax agreements.
    - 1986.
        (002043)

DRIED MILK.
----The implementation process of the
International Code of Marketing of
Breastmilk Substitutes. - 1984.
(001970) (001971)

DRILLING RIGS--UNITED STATES.
----A competitive assessment of the U.S. oil
field equipment industry. - 1985.
(000764)

E.I. DU PONT DE NEMOURS (WILMINGTON, DEL.).
----La recherche-développement dans la
stratégie des grandes entreprises
chimiques de l'entre-deux-guerres: Du
Pont de Nemours, Imperial Chemical
Industries, I. G. Farben. (With English
summary.). - 1984.
(000295)

EAST AFRICAN COMMUNITY.
----Industrial cooperation in regional
economic groupings among developing
countries and lessons for SAARC. - 1987.
(001009)

EAST ASIA--CORPORATION LAW.
----East Asian executive reports. -
1979-   .
(002203)

EAST ASIA--DEVELOPED COUNTRIES.
----Entrepreneurial cooperation between
industrialized countries and the
developing countries in East and
South-East Asia. - 1985.
(001649)

EAST ASIA--DEVELOPING COUNTRIES.
----International trading companies for
developing countries-Latin America. -
1984.
(000838)

EAST ASIA--DEVELOPMENT.
----The role of direct foreign investment in
developing East Asian countries. - 1985.
(001052)

EAST ASIA--ECONOMIC CO-OPERATION.
----Entrepreneurial cooperation between
industrialized countries and the
developing countries in East and
South-East Asia. - 1985.
(001649)

EAST ASIA--FOREIGN DIRECT INVESTMENT.
----Die Direktinvestitionen der japanischen
Wirtschaft in den Schwellenländern Ost-
Südostasiens. - 1984.
(000157)
----The role of direct foreign investment in
developing East Asian countries. - 1985.
(001052)

EAST ASIA--FOREIGN INVESTMENTS.
----Entrepreneurial cooperation between
industrialized countries and the
developing countries in East and
South-East Asia. - 1985.
(001649)

EAST ASIA--INDUSTRIAL INSTITUTIONS.
----International trading companies for
developing countries-Latin America. -
1984.
(000838)

EAST ASIA--INDUSTRIAL LEGISLATION.
----East Asian executive reports. -
1979-   .
(002203)

EAST ASIA--INTERNATIONAL TRADE.
----International trading companies for
developing countries-Latin America. -
1984.
(000838)

EAST ASIA--JOINT VENTURES.
----Entrepreneurial cooperation between
industrialized countries and the
developing countries in East and
South-East Asia. - 1985.
(001649)

EAST CARIBBEAN COMMON MARKET.
----Industrial cooperation in regional
economic groupings among developing
countries and lessons for SAARC. - 1987.
(001009)

EASTERN EUROPE--AFFILIATE CORPORATIONS.
----Eastern bloc international enterprises
-- still in statu nascendi. - 1985.
(000332)

EASTERN EUROPE--AGROINDUSTRY.
----Technological cooperation and
specialization. - 1986.
(001500)

EASTERN EUROPE--BALANCE OF PAYMENTS.
----Les mécanismes de l'endettement des pays
de l'Europe de l'Est envers les
économies de marché. - 1984.
(000221)

EASTERN EUROPE--CAPITAL MOVEMENTS.
----Handels- und Zahlungsprobleme in
Osteuropa. - 1983.
(000215)

EASTERN EUROPE--CENTRALLY PLANNED ECONOMIES.
----Equity cooperation ventures (ECV)
domiciled in the socialist countries :
trends and patterns. - 1986.
(001603)
----Pravovye formy organizatsii sovmestnykh
proizvodstv stran-chlenov SEV. - 1985.
(002157)

EASTERN EUROPE--COMPENSATION TRADE.
----101 checklists for success in East
European markets. - 1984.
(001779)

EASTERN EUROPE--COMPUTER INDUSTRY.
----L'informatique dans les pays du CAEM :
quelques aspects des politiques suivies.
- 1986.
(000711)

Subject Index - Index des matières

EASTERN EUROPE--COMPUTER SOFTWARE.
----L'informatique dans les pays du CAEM :
     quelques aspects des politiques suivies.
     - 1986.
     (000711)

EASTERN EUROPE--ECONOMIC INTEGRATION.
----International economic organizations and
     multinational corporations. - 1986.
     (002590)
----Pravovye formy organizatsii sovmestnykh
     proizvodstv stran-chlenov SEV. - 1985.
     (002157)

EASTERN EUROPE--ECONOMIC POLICY.
----L'investissement productif en Europe de
     l'Est : gaspillage des ressources,
     délais de réalisation importants, retard
     technologique? - 1986.
     (000126)

EASTERN EUROPE--EXTERNAL DEBT.
----Les mécanismes de l'endettement des pays
     de l'Europe de l'Est envers les
     économies de marché. - 1984.
     (000221)

EASTERN EUROPE--FOREIGN DIRECT INVESTMENT.
----Equity cooperation ventures (ECV)
     domiciled in the socialist countries :
     trends and patterns. - 1986.
     (001603)
----Un exemple d'investissement du CAEM :
     liste des sociétés mixtes établies dans
     les pays en développement. - 1987.
     (000284)
----Joint-ventures in Eastern Europe. - 1984.
     (001173)
----Western direct investment in centrally
     planned economies. - 1986.
     (000159)

EASTERN EUROPE--FOREIGN INVESTMENTS.
----Multinationals from the Second World :
     growth of foreign investment by Soviet
     and East European enterprises. - 1987.
     (000356)
----Ownership and investment in Poland. -
     1985.
     (001595)
----101 checklists for success in East
     European markets. - 1984.
     (001779)

EASTERN EUROPE--FOREIGN TRADE.
----East-West trade, industrial co-operation
     and technology transfer. - 1984.
     (001441)
----Saisie et effets des transferts de la
     technologie incorporée dans le commerce
     est-ouest. - 1986.
     (001464)
----Technological cooperation and
     specialization. - 1986.
     (001500)

EASTERN EUROPE--IMPORT PLANNING.
----Patterns of technology imports:
     interregional comparison. - 1986.
     (001483)

EASTERN EUROPE--INDUSTRIAL CO-OPERATION.
----East-West trade, industrial co-operation
     and technology transfer. - 1984.
     (001441)
----Equity cooperation ventures (ECV)
     domiciled in the socialist countries :
     trends and patterns. - 1986.
     (001603)
----Expectations and results of
     contractual joint ventures by US and UK
     MNCs in Eastern Europe. - 1984.
     (001623)
----Technological cooperation and
     specialization. - 1986.
     (001500)
----Zum Einfluss von Modernisierung und
     Rekonstruktion auf die internationale
     sozialistische Arbeitsteilung. - 1987.
     (001227)

EASTERN EUROPE--INDUSTRIAL MANAGEMENT.
----Red multinationals or red herring : the
     activities of enterprises from socialist
     countries in the West. - 1986.
     (000371)

EASTERN EUROPE--INDUSTRIAL ORGANIZATION.
----101 checklists for success in East
     European markets. - 1984.
     (001779)

EASTERN EUROPE--INDUSTRIAL POLICY.
----L'informatique dans les pays du CAEM :
     quelques aspects des politiques suivies.
     - 1986.
     (000711)

EASTERN EUROPE--INVESTMENT POLICY.
----L'investissement productif en Europe de
     l'Est : gaspillage des ressources,
     délais de réalisation importants, retard
     technologique? - 1986.
     (000126)

EASTERN EUROPE--JOINT VENTURES.
----East-West joint ventures. - 1988.
     (001570)
----Equity cooperation ventures (ECV)
     domiciled in the socialist countries :
     trends and patterns. - 1986.
     (001603)
----Un exemple d'investissement du CAEM :
     liste des sociétés mixtes établies dans
     les pays en développement. - 1987.
     (000284)
----Expectations and results of
     contractual joint ventures by US and UK
     MNCs in Eastern Europe. - 1984.
     (001623)
----Joint-ventures in Eastern Europe. - 1984.
     (001173)
----Multinational companies and the COMECON
     countries. - 1986.
     (001177)
----Pravovye formy organizatsii sovmestnykh
     proizvodstv stran-chlenov SEV. - 1985.
     (002157)
----Trends and issues in foreign direct
     investment and related flows. - 1985.
     (000192)
----Western direct investment in centrally
     planned economies. - 1986.
     (000159)

-101-

EAST-WEST TRADE (continued)
----The international payments crisis and
the development of East-West trade. -
1977.
(000242)
----Kelet : nyugati közös vállalatok néhány
elvi kérdése. - 1984.
(001180)
----Long term contracts and East-West trade
in non-fuel minerals. - 1986.
(002444)
----Les mécanismes de l'endettement des pays
de l'Europe de l'Est envers les
économies de marché. - 1984.
(000221)
----The politics of international economic
relations. - 1985.
(001300)
----Saisie et effets des transferts de la
technologie incorporée dans le commerce
est-ouest. - 1986.
(001464)
----Technology and East-West trade. - 1983.
(001502)
----Technology transfer and East-West
relations. - 1985.
(001507)
----Transnational corporations in world
development. - 1983.
(000102)

ECONOMETRIC MODELS.
----An appraisal of different theoretical
approaches and models of foreign direct
investment and international trade. -
1987.
(000060)
----Capital intensity and export propensity
in some Latin American countries. - 1987.
(001389)
----A country risk appraisal model of
foreign asset expropriation in
developing countries. - 1987.
(001553) (001775)
----Cyclical variations in service
industries' employment in the UK. - 1987.
(000844)
----The economics of joint ventures in less
developed countries. - 1984.
(001643)
----An examination of multijurisdictional
corporate income taxation under formula
apportionment. - 1986.
(001715)
----Government policy and private investment
in developing countries. - 1984.
(002177)
----Growth patterns of the world's largest
firms, 1962-82. - 1984.
(000041)
----Limits and problems of taxation. - 1984.
(001736)
----Market competition, conflict and
collusion. - 1983.
(000492)
----Une méthode d'évaluation interne des
modèles multinationaux. - 1985.
(000056)
----Micro- and macro-economic models of
direct foreign investment: toward a
synthesis. - 1984.
(000053)

----Modelling foreign aid, capital inflows
and economic development. - 1987.
(001313)
----On the choice between capital import and
labor export. - 1983.
(002370)
----Optimum product diversity and the
incentives for entry in natural
oligopolies. - 1987.
(000485)
----Product diversity, economies of scale,
and international trade. - 1983.
(000488)
----State intervention, foreign economic
aid, savings and growth in LDCs. - 1985.
(001337)
----Subsidy to capital through tax
incentives in the ASEAN countries. -
1983.
(002300)
----Testing the bargaining hypothesis in the
manufacturing sector in developing
countries. - 1987.
(000706)
----Transnationals and the Third World:
changing perceptions. - 1984.
(001006)
----Unemployment and the formation of
duty-free zones. - 1987.
(001931)
----The welfare impact of foreign investment
in the presence of specific factors and
non-traded goods. - 1987.
(001340)

ECONOMETRIC MODELS--BELGIUM.
----Location and investment decisions by
multinational enterprises. - 1984.
(000552)

ECONOMETRIC MODELS--YUGOSLAVIA.
----Direct foreign investment in Yugoslavia.
- 1986.
(000183)

ECONOMIC AGREEMENTS.
----Arbitraje-conciliación. - 1985.
(002472)

ECONOMIC AGREEMENTS--AUSTRIA.
----Investitionsschutzabkommen. - 1986.
(002041)

ECONOMIC AGREEMENTS--CHINA.
----The law applicable to a transnational
economic development contract. - 1987.
(002164)

ECONOMIC AGREEMENTS--GERMANY, FEDERAL
REPUBLIC OF.
----Investitionsschutzabkommen. - 1986.
(002041)

ECONOMIC AGREEMENTS--UNITED STATES.
----Structuring natural resources
development agreements between foreign
governments and United States companies
to prevent transfer of rights under the
agreement should the company enter
bankruptcy. - 1984.
(002411)

ECONOMIC ANALYSIS.
----Public enterprise in mixed economies. -
1984.
(001574)

ECONOMIC ANALYSIS--EGYPT.
----Determinants of foreign direct
investment in developing countries. -
1986.
(000531)

ECONOMIC ANALYSIS--FRANCE.
----Competing for prosperity. - 1986.
(001338)

ECONOMIC ANALYSIS--JAPAN.
----The economic analysis of the
multinational enterprise: Reading versus
Japan? - 1985.
(000008)

ECONOMIC ANALYSIS--UNITED STATES.
----The external deficit. - 1987.
(000216)

ECONOMIC ANALYSIS--YUGOSLAVIA.
----An economic analysis of Yugoslav joint
ventures. - 1983.
(001563)

ECONOMIC ASSISTANCE.
----Biznes na pomoshchi. - 1984.
(001298)

ECONOMIC ASSISTANCE--CARIBBEAN REGION.
----La presentación de la iniciativa de la
Cuenca del Caribe al GATT. - 1985.
(001972)

ECONOMIC ASSISTANCE--SOUTH AFRICA.
----The roots of crisis in southern Africa.
- 1985.
(001208)

ECONOMIC ASSISTANCE--UNITED STATES.
----La presentación de la iniciativa de la
Cuenca del Caribe al GATT. - 1985.
(001972)
----The roots of crisis in southern Africa.
- 1985.
(001208)

ECONOMIC COMMUNITY OF WEST AFRICAN STATES.
----Industrial cooperation in regional
economic groupings among developing
countries and lessons for SAARC. - 1987.
(001009)

ECONOMIC CONDITIONS.
----The economic impact of direct foreign
investments on developing countries. -
1984.
(001311)
----Economics of change in less developed
countries. - 1986.
(001000)
----Forum on economic crisis and Third World
countries. - 1987.
(001251)
----State of the world. - 1984-   .
(001301)

ECONOMIC CONDITIONS--AFRICA SOUTH OF SAHARA.
----La privatisation des entreprises
publiques en Afrique au sud du Sahara,
(2). - 1986.
(001564)

ECONOMIC CONDITIONS--ARGENTINA.
----The new Argentina. - 1984.
(001777)
----Transnacionalización y política
económica en la Argentina. - 1985.
(001115)

ECONOMIC CONDITIONS--ASIA.
----Asia yearbook. - 1973-   .
(002699)

ECONOMIC CONDITIONS--BELGIUM.
----Note sur la transnationalisation de
l'économie belge. - 1985.
(000123)

ECONOMIC CONDITIONS--BURUNDI.
----Guide des investisseurs. - 1983-   .
(001805)

ECONOMIC CONDITIONS--CAMEROON.
----The political economy of development in
Cameroon. - 1986.
(001834)

ECONOMIC CONDITIONS--CHILE.
----Chile : creative economic management. -
1987.
(001784)
----Las empresas transnacionales en la
economía de Chile, 1974-1980. - 1983.
(001123)

ECONOMIC CONDITIONS--CHINA.
----The China directory of industry and
commerce and economic annual. - 1984.
(002626)
----The 1982-83 overinvestment crisis in
China. - 1984.
(000120)

ECONOMIC CONDITIONS--COSTA RICA.
----Notes from Latin America. - 1983.
(000628)

ECONOMIC CONDITIONS--COTE D'IVOIRE.
----Comparative advantage as a development
model. - 1985.
(001691)

ECONOMIC CONDITIONS--ECUADOR.
----Capitalismo, burguesia y crisis en el
Ecuador. - 1983.
(001104)
----Ecuador. - 1984.
(001831)
----Invest in Ecuador. - 1982.
(001771)
----La presencia de las empresas
transnacionales en la economía
ecuatoriana. - 1984.
(001125)

ECONOMIC CONDITIONS--FIJI.
----Fiji : client State of Australasia? -
1984.
(001046) (002358)

ECONOMIC CONDITIONS--FRANCE.
----L'économie française et le développement
   des services : Annuaire 1985-1986. -
   1986.
      (000847)

ECONOMIC CONDITIONS--HUNGARY.
----Hungarian Chamber of Commerce handbook.
   - 1984-
      (001811)

ECONOMIC CONDITIONS--INDONESIA.
----The Indonesian business. - 1986.
      (001839)

ECONOMIC CONDITIONS--LATIN AMERICA.
----Breves rasgos de la crisis. - 1983.
      (001307)
----La crisis internacional y la América
   Latina. - 1984.
      (001245)
----Inostrannye monopolii v Latinskoi
   Amerike. - 1983.
      (001103)
----Los laberintos de la crisis. - 1984.
      (001079)
----Latin America at a glance. - 1986.
      (001821)
----Mezhdunarodnye monopolii v Latinskoi
   Amerike. - 1986.
      (001128)

ECONOMIC CONDITIONS--LESOTHO.
----Lagging behind the bantustans. - 1985.
      (001223)

ECONOMIC CONDITIONS--MALAYSIA.
----Multinationals and market structure in
   an open developing economy: the case of
   Malaysia. - 1983.
      (001056)

ECONOMIC CONDITIONS--MEXICO.
----Política económica y empresas
   transnacionales en México. - 1983.
      (001127)

ECONOMIC CONDITIONS--NAMIBIA.
----Activities of transnational corporations
   in South Africa and Namibia and the
   responsibilities of home countries with
   respect to their operations in this
   area. - 1986.
      (001192)
----Transnational corporations in South
   Africa and Namibia. - 1986.
      (001217)

ECONOMIC CONDITIONS--NICARAGUA.
----Política económica y capital extranjero
   en Nicaragua. - 1984.
      (002081)

ECONOMIC CONDITIONS--PARAGUAY.
----Las empresas transnacionales en la
   economía del Paraguay. - 1987.
      (001108)

ECONOMIC CONDITIONS--PERU.
----Empresas transnacionales, estado y
   burguesía nativa. - 1983.
      (001877)

ECONOMIC CONDITIONS--PHILIPPINES.
----The Marcos regime. - 1985.
      (001070)
----The Philippines : authoritarian
   government, multinationals and ancestral
   lands. - 1983.
      (001066)

ECONOMIC CONDITIONS--POLAND.
----Development, social justice, and
   dependence in Poland. - 1985.
      (001188)
----East-West technology transfer : study of
   Poland, 1971-1980. - 1983.
      (001432)

ECONOMIC CONDITIONS--SINGAPORE.
----Multinationals and the growth of the
   Singapore economy. - 1986.
      (001062)

ECONOMIC CONDITIONS--SOUTH AFRICA.
----Activities of transnational corporations
   in South Africa and Namibia and the
   responsibilities of home countries with
   respect to their operations in this
   area. - 1986.
      (001192)
----Political change in South Africa. - 1986.
      (001205)
----South Africa : economic responses to
   international pressures. - 1985.
      (001193)
----Transnational corporations in South
   Africa and Namibia. - 1986.
      (001217)

ECONOMIC CONDITIONS--SOUTHEAST ASIA.
----Neue Wachstumsmärkte in Fernost. - 1983.
      (001800)

ECONOMIC CONDITIONS--SRI LANKA.
----Agribusiness TNCs in Sri Lanka. - 1986.
      (000560)
----Economic prospects of Sri Lanka and
   potential for foreign investment. - 1984.
      (001788)

ECONOMIC CONDITIONS--SWEDEN.
----De Svenska storforetagen. - 1985.
      (000324)

ECONOMIC CONDITIONS--UNITED KINGDOM.
----Foreign multinationals and the British
   economy. - 1988.
      (001167)

ECONOMIC CONDITIONS--YUGOSLAVIA.
----Doing business with Yugoslavia. - 1986.
      (001793)

ECONOMIC CO-OPERATION.
----Cooperation in investments: a factor in
   the intensification of production in
   CMEA member nations. - 1983.
      (001187)
----Economic interdependence between rich
   and poor nations. - 1983.
      (001268)
----Fiscal policies, current accounts and
   real exchange rates : in search of a
   logic of international policy
   coordination. - 1986.
      (001244)

ECONOMIC CO-OPERATION (continued)
----International investment. - 1983.
    (000525)
----Países socialistas y corporaciones
    transnacionales. - 1984.
    (001178)
----Revitalizing development, growth and
    international trade. - 1987.
    (001394)
----A theory of co-operation in
    international business. - 1987.
    (000011)
----Work by the United Nations Centre on
    Transnational Corporations on the Code
    of Conduct on Transnational
    Corporations, other international
    arrangements and agreements, and
    national laws and regulations relating
    to transnational corporations. - 1986.
    (002694)

ECONOMIC CO-OPERATION--AFRICA.
----Current problems of economic
    integration. - 1986.
    (001312)

ECONOMIC CO-OPERATION--ARAB COUNTRIES.
----Arab joint ventures. - 1986.
    (001137)
----Current problems of economic
    integration. - 1986.
    (001312)

ECONOMIC CO-OPERATION--ARGENTINA.
----Cooperación empresarial entre países
    semiindutrializados. - 1984.
    (000202)

ECONOMIC CO-OPERATION--ASIA.
----Current problems of economic
    integration. - 1986.
    (001312)

ECONOMIC CO-OPERATION--BRAZIL.
----Cooperación empresarial entre países
    semiindutrializados. - 1984.
    (000202)

ECONOMIC CO-OPERATION--CHINA.
----Investitions- und
    Kooperationsmöglichkeit "Equity joint
    venture" in der Volksrepublik China. -
    1986.
    (002199)

ECONOMIC CO-OPERATION--EAST ASIA.
----Entrepreneurial cooperation between
    industrialized countries and the
    developing countries in East and
    South-East Asia. - 1985.
    (001649)

ECONOMIC CO-OPERATION--GERMANY, FEDERAL
REPUBLIC OF.
----Wachstumsmarkt Südostasien. - 1984.
    (001785)

ECONOMIC CO-OPERATION--GULF STATES.
----Economic co-operation of the Arab Gulf
    States. - 1986.
    (001133)

ECONOMIC CO-OPERATION--LATIN AMERICA.
----Current problems of economic
    integration. - 1986.
    (001312)

ECONOMIC CO-OPERATION--SOUTHEAST ASIA.
----ASEAN economic co-operation. - 1985.
    (001039)
----Entrepreneurial cooperation between
    industrialized countries and the
    developing countries in East and
    South-East Asia. - 1985.
    (001649)
----Wachstumsmarkt Südostasien. - 1984.
    (001785)

ECONOMIC CO-OPERATION--WESTERN EUROPE.
----Current problems of economic
    integration. - 1986.
    (001312)
----Wachstumsmarkt Südostasien. - 1984.
    (001785)

ECONOMIC CO-OPERATION AMONG DEVELOPING
COUNTRIES.
----Current problems of economic
    integration. - 1986.
    (001312)
----Mutual investments and the formation of
    multinational enterprises by developing
    countries. - 1987.
    (000378)
----Services and the development process. -
    1985.
    (000979)

ECONOMIC CO-OPERATION AMONG DEVELOPING
COUNTRIES--SOUTHEAST ASIA.
----Aspects of ASEAN. - 1984.
    (001406)

ECONOMIC DEPENDENCE.
----Economic interdependence between rich
    and poor nations. - 1983.
    (001268)
----Internatsionalizatsiia
    monopoliticheskogo nakopleniia i
    razvivaiushchiesia strany. - 1986.
    (000082)

ECONOMIC DEPENDENCE--AUSTRALIA.
----Beyond dependence. - 1986.
    (000640)

ECONOMIC DEPENDENCE--LATIN AMERICA.
----Capitalismo neocolonial. - 1983.
    (001109)
----Disfraces del coloniaje. - 1984.
    (001114)
----Mezhdunarodnye monopolii v Latinskoi
    Amerike. - 1986.
    (001128)

ECONOMIC DEPENDENCE--UNITED STATES.
----Disfraces del coloniaje. - 1984.
    (001114)

ECONOMIC DEVELOPMENT.
----The multinational corporation in the
    less developed country: the economic
    development model versus the North-South
    model. - 1985.
    (001011)

ECONOMIC DEVELOPMENT (continued)
----The antinomies of interdependence. -
    1983.
    (001229)
----Economic development, investment
    dependence, and the rise of services in
    less developed nations. - 1986.
    (000958)
----Economics of change in less developed
    countries. - 1986.
    (001000)
----Les entreprises multinationales et les
    services. - 1985.
    (000956)
----Export processing zones: new catalysts
    for economic development. - 1983.
    (002391)
----Export-enclave economies, international
    corporations, and development. - 1985.
    (002367)
----Free zones in developing countries. -
    1983.
    (002390)
----Industrial structure and policy in less
    developed countries. - 1984.
    (001322)
----The industrialisation of less developed
    countries. - 1983.
    (001003)
----Industrie touristique et développement.
    - 1987.
    (000963)
----Inostrannyi kapital v ekonomike
    kapitalisticheskikh gosudarstv. - 1984.
    (001225)
----International capital flows and economic
    development. - 1985.
    (001241)
----International marketing planning and
    state trading organisations. - 1986.
    (000369)
----Modelling foreign aid, capital inflows
    and economic development. - 1987.
    (001313)
----Multinationals of the South. - 1986.
    (000359)
----Rekindling development. - 1988.
    (001302)
----Il ruolo del finanziamento estero nello
    sviluppo economico e la problematica
    attuale dell'indebitamento. - 1983.
    (001289)
----Service-led growth. - 1986.
    (000931)
----Les services : clé du développement
    économique? - 1986.
    (000892)
----Services and the development process. -
    1985.
    (000979)
----Transnational corporations: choice of
    techniques and employment in developing
    countries. -   .
    (001882)
----World development report. - 1987-   .
    (001345)

ECONOMIC DEVELOPMENT--AFRICA.
----The role of transnational banks and
    financial institutions in Africa's
    development process. - 1986.
    (000935)

ECONOMIC DEVELOPMENT--AFRICA SOUTH OF SAHARA.
----The differentiation process in the
    economies of black Africa. - 1984.
    (001694)

ECONOMIC DEVELOPMENT--ARGENTINA.
----Multinationals and maldevelopment. -
    1987.
    (000995)

ECONOMIC DEVELOPMENT--ASIA.
----Foreign trade and investment. - 1985.
    (001047)

ECONOMIC DEVELOPMENT--CAMEROON.
----The ICSID Klöckner v. Cameroon award. -
    1984.
    (002553)
----The private sector, the public sector,
    and donor assistance in economic
    development. - 1983.
    (000268)

ECONOMIC DEVELOPMENT--CARIBBEAN REGION.
----Can CARICOM countries replicate the
    Singapore experience. - 1987.
    (001093)

ECONOMIC DEVELOPMENT--CHINA.
----The role of oil in China's economic
    development, growth, and
    internationalization. - 1985.
    (000602)

ECONOMIC DEVELOPMENT--COSTA RICA.
----The private sector, the public sector,
    and donor assistance in economic
    development. - 1983.
    (000268)

ECONOMIC DEVELOPMENT--COTE D'IVOIRE.
----Multinationals and maldevelopment. -
    1987.
    (000995)

ECONOMIC DEVELOPMENT--GERMANY, FEDERAL
REPUBLIC OF.
----The ICSID Klöckner v. Cameroon award. -
    1984.
    (002553)

ECONOMIC DEVELOPMENT--INDIA.
----Changing perspectives on the role of
    multinationals in economic development:
    some evidence from India. - 1985.
    (001040)

ECONOMIC DEVELOPMENT--JAPAN.
----Japan's general trading companies. -
    1984.
    (000887)

ECONOMIC DEVELOPMENT--LATIN AMERICA.
----Foreign debt, direct investment, and
    economic development in the Andean Pact.
    - 1987.
    (001110)
----Transnacionalización y desarrollo
    nacional en América Latina. - 1984.
    (001117)
----Transnacionalización y periferia
    semindustrializada. - 1983.
    (001017)

ECONOMIC DEVELOPMENT--MALAWI.
----The private sector, the public sector,
  and donor assistance in economic
  development. - 1983.
    (000268)

ECONOMIC DEVELOPMENT--MALAYSIA.
----Multinationals and market structure in
  an open developing economy: the case of
  Malaysia. - 1983.
    (001056)

ECONOMIC DEVELOPMENT--PHILIPPINES.
----The Manila-Washington connection. - 1983.
    (001855)
----The Philippines under Marcos. - 1986.
    (001071)

ECONOMIC DEVELOPMENT--REPUBLIC OF KOREA.
----Multinationals and maldevelopment. -
  1987.
    (000995)

ECONOMIC DEVELOPMENT--SINGAPORE.
----Can CARICOM countries replicate the
  Singapore experience. - 1987.
    (001093)
----Multinationals and the growth of the
  Singapore economy. - 1986.
    (001062)

ECONOMIC DEVELOPMENT--SOUTHEAST ASIA.
----Small-and medium-scale industries in the
  ASEAN countries. - 1984.
    (001036)
----Vlijanie TNK na social'no-ekonomiceskoe
  razvivtie stran Jugo-Vosticnoj Azii. -
  1985.
    (001075)
----Wachstumsmarkt Südostasien. - 1984.
    (001785)

ECONOMIC DEVELOPMENT--THAILAND.
----The private sector, the public sector,
  and donor assistance in economic
  development. - 1983.
    (000268)

ECONOMIC DEVELOPMENT--UNITED STATES.
----The significance of foreign investment
  in US development 1879 to mid-1914. -
  1982.
    (001344)

ECONOMIC FORECASTS--CHINA.
----Die chinesischen Wirtschaftsreformen im
  neunten Jahr. - 1986.
    (002217)

ECONOMIC FORECASTS--LATIN AMERICA.
----Latin America at a glance. - 1986.
    (001821)

ECONOMIC GROWTH.
----Compensation or opportunity? - 1986.
    (001293)
----Corporation, technological gaps and
  growth in OECD countries. - 1987.
    (001438)
----Développement sans croissance. - 1983.
    (000632)

----The effects of foreign investment on
  overall and sectoral groups in Third
  World states. - 1984.
    (001332)
----The military origins of
  industrialisation and international
  trade rivalry. - 1984.
    (001335)
----Revitalizing development, growth and
  international trade. - 1987.
    (001394)
----Size, growth, and transnationality among
  the world's largest banks. - 1983.
    (000969)

ECONOMIC GROWTH--ASIA.
----Effects of foreign capital inflows on
  developing countries of Asia. - 1986.
    (001059)
----The impact of foreign capital inflow on
  investment and economic growth in
  developing Asia. - 1985.
    (001048)

ECONOMIC GROWTH--ASIA AND THE PACIFIC.
----Foreign direct investment and economic
  growth in the Asian and Pacific region.
  - 1987.
    (000175)
----The great continental divide : Asian and
  Latin American countries in the world
  economic crisis. - 1986.
    (001299)

ECONOMIC GROWTH--CHINA.
----Investitions- und
  Kooperationsmöglichkeit "Equity joint
  venture" in der Volksrepublik China. -
  1986.
    (002199)

ECONOMIC GROWTH--JAPAN.
----Japanese direct investment abroad. -
  1986.
    (000311)
----Le Japon : transformations
  industrielles, croissance et
  internationalisation. - 1983.
    (000319)

ECONOMIC GROWTH--LATIN AMERICA.
----The great continental divide : Asian and
  Latin American countries in the world
  economic crisis. - 1986.
    (001299)

ECONOMIC GROWTH--REPUBLIC OF KOREA.
----The South Korean success story. - 1986.
    (001050)

ECONOMIC GROWTH--TUNISIA.
----L'industrie manufacturière tunisienne et
  sa place dans l'économie nationale. -
  1985.
    (000744)

ECONOMIC HISTORY.
----Concentración global y
  transnacionalización. - 1985.
    (000100)
----Diskontinuitatenmanagement. - 1984.
    (000490)

ECONOMIC HISTORY--CHINA.
----Partnership with China. - 1986.
(001035)

ECONOMIC HISTORY--PARAGUAY.
----Las empresas transnacionales en la
economía del Paraguay. - 1987.
(001124)

ECONOMIC HISTORY--UNITED STATES.
----The emergence of a U.S. multinational
enterprise: the Goodyear Tire and Rubber
Company, 1910-1939. - 1987.
(000281)

ECONOMIC INDICATORS.
----World development report. - 1987-   .
(001345)

ECONOMIC INTEGRATION.
----Basic framework for ASEAN industrial
co-operation. - 1986.
(002149)
----Current problems of economic
integration. - 1986.
(001312)
----Mezhdunarodnata investitsionna banka i
neinata rolia v razvitieto na
sotsialisticheskata ikonomicheska
integratsiia. - 1986.
(002153)
----Socialist economic integration and the
investment cooperation of the CMEA
countries. - 1984.
(001185)
----The spatial distribution of the effects
of economic integration schemes. - 1984.
(001346)

ECONOMIC INTEGRATION--AFRICA.
----Current problems of economic
integration. - 1986.
(001312)

ECONOMIC INTEGRATION--ANDEAN REGION.
----Andean multinational enterprises: a new
approach to multinational investment in
the Andean Group. - 1983.
(000313)

ECONOMIC INTEGRATION--ARAB COUNTRIES.
----Current problems of economic
integration. - 1986.
(001312)

ECONOMIC INTEGRATION--ASIA.
----Current problems of economic
integration. - 1986.
(001312)

ECONOMIC INTEGRATION--ASIA AND THE PACIFIC.
----Japanese transnational corporations and
the economic integration of Australian
and the Asian-Pacific region. - 1983.
(000323)

ECONOMIC INTEGRATION--AUSTRALIA.
----Japanese transnational corporations and
the economic integration of Australian
and the Asian-Pacific region. - 1983.
(000323)

ECONOMIC INTEGRATION--EASTERN EUROPE.
----International economic organizations and
multinational corporations. - 1986.
(002590)
----Pravovye formy organizatsii sovmestnykh
proizvodstv stran-chlenov SEV. - 1985.
(002157)

ECONOMIC INTEGRATION--JAPAN.
----Japanese transnational corporations and
the economic integration of Australian
and the Asian-Pacific region. - 1983.
(000323)

ECONOMIC INTEGRATION--LATIN AMERICA.
----Current problems of economic
integration. - 1986.
(001312)
----The role of transnational enterprises in
Latin American economic integration
efforts. - 1983.
(001126)

ECONOMIC INTEGRATION--PORTUGAL.
----Portugal's accession to the EEC and its
impact on foreign direct investment. -
1986.
(000554)

ECONOMIC INTEGRATION--WESTERN EUROPE.
----Current problems of economic
integration. - 1986.
(001312)
----La libération des mouvements de capitaux
et l'intégration financière de la
Communauté. - 1987.
(001230)
----Multinational corporations and European
integration. - 1987.
(001325)

ECONOMIC LAW.
----The implementation of international
antitrust principles. - 1983.
(002344)

ECONOMIC LAW--CHINA.
----Like bamboo shoots after a rain :
exploiting the Chinese law and new
regulations on Sino-foreign joint
ventures. - 1987.
(002298)
----The new foreign contract law in China. -
1986.
(002276)
----The 1981 Economic Contract Law of the
People's Republic of China. - 1986.
(002237)

ECONOMIC NEGOTIATIONS.
----Arbitration and renegotiation of
international investment agreements. -
1986.
(002557)
----Measures to strengthen the capabilities
of developing countries in their dealing
with transnational corporations. - 1985.
(002612)
----Multilateral economic negotiation. -
1987.
(002470)

ECONOMIC NEGOTIATIONS (continued)
----Les négociations internationales sur les
    services ou la quadrature du cercle.
    (With English summary.). - 1986.
      (000912)
----Negotiating with Third World
    governments. - 1983.
      (002468)
----Sovereignty en garde. - 1985.
      (002469)

ECONOMIC PLANNING.
----Technology choice and employment
    generation by multinational enterprises
    in developing countries. - 1984.
      (001646)

ECONOMIC POLICY.
----Une méthode d'évaluation interne des
    modèles multinationaux. - 1985.
      (000056)
----Muködotoke-beruházások a fejlodo
    országokban. - 1986.
      (001275)
----The political economy of innovation. -
    1984.
      (001450)
----The political economy of international
    technology transfer. - 1987.
      (001482)
----Production and trade in services. - 1985.
      (000978)
----Revitalizing development, growth and
    international trade. - 1987.
      (001394)
----Les services : nouvelle donne de
    l'économie. - 1984.
      (000913)
----State of the world. - 1984-   .
      (001301)
----Takokuseki kigyo to chushin kogyokoku. -
    1983.
      (001319)
----Trends and issues in foreign direct
    investment and related flows. - 1985.
      (000192)

ECONOMIC POLICY--ALGERIA.
----Aperçu sur le statut de la société mixte
    en Algérie. - 1984.
      (002283)

ECONOMIC POLICY--ARGENTINA.
----Multinationals and maldevelopment. -
    1987.
      (000995)
----The new Argentina. - 1984.
      (001777)
----Transnacionalización y política
    económica en la Argentina. - 1985.
      (001115)

ECONOMIC POLICY--ASIA.
----Export processing zones and economic
    development in Asia. - 1987.
      (002389)

ECONOMIC POLICY--ASIA AND THE PACIFIC.
----The great continental divide : Asian and
    Latin American countries in the world
    economic crisis. - 1986.
      (001299)

----Transnational corporations and external
    financial flows of developing economies
    in Asia and the Pacific. - 1986.
      (000196)

ECONOMIC POLICY--BANGLADESH.
----Courting private foreign investment :
    the Bangladesh experience. - 1986.
      (001854)

ECONOMIC POLICY--BRAZIL.
----Business in a democratic Brazil. - 1985.
      (001776)

ECONOMIC POLICY--CAMEROON.
----The private sector, the public sector,
    and donor assistance in economic
    development. - 1983.
      (000268)

ECONOMIC POLICY--CANADA.
----Industrial organization paradigms,
    empirical evidence, and the economic
    case for competition policy. - 1987.
      (001670)

ECONOMIC POLICY--CHINA.
----China's modernization and transnational
    corporations. - 1984.
      (001077)
----China's open door policy. - 1984.
      (002219)
----China's open door policy and the
    prospects for FDI. - 1986.
      (001043)
----China's opening to the world. - 1986.
      (002221)
----China's reform of the economic structure
    and its open-door policy. - 1985.
      (002273)
----China's special economic zones. - 1986.
      (002366)
----Chinese economic reforms since 1978 with
    particular emphasis on the special
    economic zones. - 1987.
      (002375)
----Die chinesischen Wirtschaftsreformen im
    neunten Jahr. - 1986.
      (002217)
----Foreign economic contract law of the
    People's Republic of China. - 1987.
      (002166)
----The investment implications of China's
    offshore oil development. - 1986.
      (000612)
----Kína különleges gazdasági övezetei. -
    1987.
      (002374)
----Private enterprise in China. - 1985.
      (002184)
----Recent developments in China's special
    economic zones : problems and prognosis.
    - 1987.
      (002404)
----Shenzhen : a Chinese development zone in
    global perspective. - 1985.
      (002393)
----Special economic zones and economic
    policy in China. - 1983.
      (002394)
----Special economic zones in China's
    modernization. - 1986.
      (002385)

ECONOMIC POLICY--CHINA (continued)
----Special economic zones in the PRC. -
    1986.
        (002369)

ECONOMIC POLICY--COSTA RICA.
----The private sector, the public sector,
    and donor assistance in economic
    development. - 1983.
        (000268)

ECONOMIC POLICY--COTE D'IVOIRE.
----Multinationals and maldevelopment. -
    1987.
        (000995)

ECONOMIC POLICY--EASTERN EUROPE.
----L'investissement productif en Europe de
    l'Est : gaspillage des ressources,
    délais de réalisation importants, retard
    technologique? - 1986.
        (000126)

ECONOMIC POLICY--EGYPT.
----Determinants of foreign direct
    investment in developing countries. -
    1986.
        (000531)

ECONOMIC POLICY--FRANCE.
----The dilemma of denationalisation. - 1986.
        (001644)

ECONOMIC POLICY--HUNGARY.
----A hazai elektronikai ipar helyzete és
    problemái. - 1986.
        (000634)
----Hungarian foreign trade reform. - 1986.
        (002250)

ECONOMIC POLICY--JAPAN.
----The Japanese economic strategy. - 1983.
        (000366)

ECONOMIC POLICY--LATIN AMERICA.
----Foreign direct investment in Latin
    America. - 1986.
        (000190)
----The great continental divide : Asian and
    Latin American countries in the world
    economic crisis. - 1986.
        (001299)

ECONOMIC POLICY--MALAWI.
----The private sector, the public sector,
    and donor assistance in economic
    development. - 1983.
        (000268)

ECONOMIC POLICY--MALAYSIA.
----Business prospects in Malaysia, coping
    with change in a new era. - 1983.
        (001780)
----Malaysia's new economic policy: the role
    of the transnational corporations. -
    1985.
        (001060)

ECONOMIC POLICY--MEXICO.
----De la improvisación al fracaso : la
    política de inversión extranjera en
    México. - 1983.
        (001112)

ECONOMIC POLICY--NETHERLANDS.
----Recommendation on industry and
    development cooperation. - 1984.
        (001329)

ECONOMIC POLICY--PAPUA NEW GUINEA.
----Economic policies pertaining to foreign
    enterprises in PNG. - 1986.
        (002287)

ECONOMIC POLICY--REPUBLIC OF KOREA.
----Multinationals and maldevelopment. -
    1987.
        (000995)

ECONOMIC POLICY--SIBERIA (USSR).
----Investment and reindustrialization in
    the Soviet economy. - 1984.
        (001333)

ECONOMIC POLICY--SOUTH AFRICA.
----The costs of disinvestment. - 1986.
        (001207)
----Political change in South Africa. - 1986.
        (001205)

ECONOMIC POLICY--SOUTHEAST ASIA.
----Economic policies towards transnational
    corporations. - 1983.
        (002229)
----The Japanese economic strategy. - 1983.
        (000366)
----Kulturelle und wirtschaftliche
    Interdependenz der ASEAN-Staaten. - 1986.
        (001067)

ECONOMIC POLICY--SRI LANKA.
----Economic prospects of Sri Lanka and
    potential for foreign investment. - 1984.
        (001788)

ECONOMIC POLICY--THAILAND.
----The private sector, the public sector,
    and donor assistance in economic
    development. - 1983.
        (000268)

ECONOMIC POLICY--TUNISIA.
----L'industrie manufacturière tunisienne et
    sa place dans l'économie nationale. -
    1985.
        (000744)

ECONOMIC POLICY--UNITED KINGDOM.
----Assessing the consequences of overseas
    investment. - 1986.
        (001296)

ECONOMIC POLICY--UNITED STATES.
----EEC competition policy. - 1986.
        (001989)
----Manufacturing matters : the myth of the
    post-industrial economy. - 1987.
        (000669)
----The U.S. drive to bring services into
    GATT. - 1986.
        (000926)

ECONOMIC POLICY--USSR.
----Investment and reindustrialization in
    the Soviet economy. - 1984.
        (001333)

ECONOMIC POLICY--USSR (continued)
----The Soviet industrial enterprise. - 1984.
    (000330)

ECONOMIC POLICY--WESTERN EUROPE.
----EEC competition policy. - 1986.
    (001989)

ECONOMIC POLÍCY--ZAMBIA.
----The mines, class power, and foreign
    policy in Zambia. - 1984.
    (001023)

ECONOMIC RECESSION.
----Compensation or opportunity? - 1986.
    (001293)

ECONOMIC RECESSION--JAMAICA.
----La Jamaïque, ou le dilemme politique
    d'un petit pays déshérité. - 1984.
    (001819)

ECONOMIC REFORM--CHINA.
----On economic reforms, trade and foreign
    investment in China. - 1986.
    (001336)
----The reform of the Chinese system of
    enterprise ownership. - 1987.
    (002185)

ECONOMIC REFORM--HUNGARY.
----Joint ventures in Hungary. - 1987.
    (001171)

ECONOMIC REFORM--POLAND.
----L'entreprise polonaise. - 1987.
    (000305)

ECONOMIC REFORM--USSR.
----La nouvelle législation soviétique sur
    les entreprises mixtes. - 1987.
    (002181)

ECONOMIC RELATIONS.
----Biznes na pomoshchi. - 1984.
    (001298)
----Current financial and monetary problems
    of the developing countries in the world
    capitalist economy. - 1987.
    (001246)
----Exploring the global economy : emerging
    issues in trade and investment. - 1985.
    (001306)
----Los laberintos de la crisis. - 1984.
    (001079)
----Mezinárodní financní a kapitálové vztahy
    rozvojovych zemí. - 1985.   •
    (000230)
----Neokolonializm. - 1984.
    (000996)

ECONOMIC RELATIONS--AFRICA.
----Les sociétés transnationales en Afrique.
    - 1986.
    (001028)
----Toward Lomé III. - 1984.
    (002606)

ECONOMIC RELATIONS--ARAB COUNTRIES.
----The Arab world is still importing. -
    1987.
    (001134)

ECONOMIC RELATIONS--CANADA.
----The role of multinational enterprises in
    US-Canadian economic relations. - 1986.
    (001159)

ECONOMIC RELATIONS--CHINA.
----China's modernization and transnational
    corporations. - 1984.
    (001077)
----Collection of laws and regulations of
    the People's Republic of China
    concerning foreign economic affairs. -
    1985-   .
    (002188)
----The European Community and China. - 1986.
    (002045)
----Guide to China's foreign economic
    relations and trade. - 1983.
    (001806)
----The open policy at work. - 1985.
    (001072)
----Shenzhen : a Chinese development zone in
    global perspective. - 1985.
    (002393)
----Sino-Indian economic relations. - 1984.
    (000307)
----Transnational corporations and China's
    open door policy. - 1988.
    (001074)

ECONOMIC RELATIONS--CZECHOSLOVAKIA.
----East-West technology transfer. - 1984.
    (001463)

ECONOMIC RELATIONS--GERMANY, FEDERAL
REPUBLIC OF.
----Neue Wachstumsmärkte in Fernost. - 1983.
    (001800)
----Wachstumsmarkt Südostasien. - 1984.
    (001785)

ECONOMIC RELATIONS--HONG KONG.
----Shenzhen : a Chinese development zone in
    global perspective. - 1985.
    (002393)

ECONOMIC RELATIONS--HUNGARY.
----Economic associations in Hungary with
    foreign participation. - 1986.
    (001606)

ECONOMIC RELATIONS--INDIA.
----Sino-Indian economic relations. - 1984.
    (000307)

ECONOMIC RELATIONS--JAPAN.
----Competition in the Pacific Basin. - 1987.
    (001673)
----The Japanese economic strategy. - 1983.
    (000366)
----Two hungry giants. - 1983.
    (000645)

ECONOMIC RELATIONS--LATIN AMERICA.
----La crisis internacional y la América
    Latina. - 1984.
    (001245)
----Grace. - 1985.
    (000276)
----Inversiones extranjeras en América
    Latina. - 1984.
    (001098)

ECONOMIC RELATIONS--LATIN AMERICA (continued)
----Transnacionalización y desarrollo
nacional en América Latina. - 1984.
(001117)

ECONOMIC RELATIONS--PACIFIC OCEAN REGION.
----Competition in the Pacific Basin. - 1987.
(001673)

ECONOMIC RELATIONS--PERU.
----Grace. - 1985.
(000276)

ECONOMIC RELATIONS--POLAND.
----Development, social justice, and
dependence in Poland. - 1985.
(001188)
----Industrial cooperation between Poland
and the West. - 1985.
(001576)
----Kooperacja przemyslowa Polski z krajami
RWPG. - 1986.
(001172)

ECONOMIC RELATIONS--SOUTH AFRICA.
----Measures regarding the activities of
transnational corporations in South
Africa and Namibia. - 1985.
(001220)
----The political economy of U.S. policy
toward South Africa. - 1985.
(001196)
----The roots of crisis in southern Africa.
- 1985.
(001208)
----Transnational corporations in South
Africa and Namibia : United Nations
public hearings. Volume 1, Reports of
the Panel of Eminent Persons and of the
Secretary-General. - 1986.
(001216)

ECONOMIC RELATIONS--SOUTHEAST ASIA.
----The Japanese economic strategy. - 1983.
(000366)
----Neue Wachstumsmärkte in Fernost. - 1983.
(001800) (001800)
----Wachstumsmarkt Südostasien. - 1984.
(001785)

ECONOMIC RELATIONS--UNITED KINGDOM.
----Britain and the multinationals. - 1985.
(001164)

ECONOMIC RELATIONS--UNITED STATES.
----The Arab world is still importing. -
1987.
(001134)
----Die Aussenexpansion des Kapitals. - 1984.
(000037)
----Competition in the Pacific Basin. - 1987.
(001673)
----Estados Unidos y el proceso de
transnacionalización en la postguerra. -
1984.
(001235)
----Grace. - 1985.
(000276)
----The overseas expansion of capital. -
1985.
(000038)
----The political economy of U.S. policy
toward South Africa. - 1985.
(001196)

----The role of multinational enterprises in
US-Canadian economic relations. - 1986.
(001159)
----The roots of crisis in southern Africa.
- 1985.
(001208)
----Two hungry giants. - 1983.
(000645)
----The U.S. renewal of the GSP. - 1986.
(001996)

ECONOMIC RELATIONS--USSR.
----The new Soviet joint venture
regulations. - 1987.
(002202)
----L'URSS et le Tiers Monde. - 1984.
(002040)

ECONOMIC RELATIONS--WEST AFRICA.
----Tendentsii ekspansii TNK v strany
Zapadnoi Afriki v 70-kh-nachale 80-kh
godov. - 1986.
(001021)

ECONOMIC RELATIONS--WESTERN EUROPE.
----The European Community and China. - 1986.
(002045)
----Toward Lomé III. - 1984.
(002606)
----Wachstumsmarkt Südostasien. - 1984.
(001785)

ECONOMIC RELATIONS--YUGOSLAVIA.
----Doing business with Yugoslavia. - 1986.
(001793)

ECONOMIC RESEARCH--SWEDEN.
----Multinationella fortag. - 1985.
(000030)

ECONOMIC RIGHTS AND DUTIES OF STATES.
----The antinomies of interdependence. -
1983.
(001229)

ECONOMIC STATISTICS.
----Le tourisme : un phénomène économique. -
1986.
(000925)
----Transnational corporations in world
development. - 1983.
(000102)

ECONOMIC STATISTICS--ARGENTINA.
----Las empresas transnacionales en la
Argentina. - 1986.
(001122)

ECONOMIC STATISTICS--UNITED STATES.
----Selected data on foreign direct
investment in the United States,
1950-79. - 1984.
(000184)

ECONOMIC STRUCTURE.
----The primary, secondary, tertiary and
quaternary sectors of the economy. -
1987.
(000883)
----Vergleichende System- und
Industriestudien. - 1983.
(001342)

ECONOMIC STRUCTURE--AFRICA SOUTH OF SAHARA.
----The differentiation process in the
    economies of black Africa. - 1984.
    (001694)

ECONOMIC STRUCTURE--ASIA AND THE PACIFIC.
----The great continental divide : Asian and
    Latin American countries in the world
    economic crisis. - 1986.
    (001299)

ECONOMIC STRUCTURE--CHINA.
----China's reform of the economic structure
    and its open-door policy. - 1985.
    (002273)

ECONOMIC STRUCTURE--LATIN AMERICA.
----The great continental divide : Asian and
    Latin American countries in the world
    economic crisis. - 1986.
    (001299)

ECONOMIC STRUCTURE--WESTERN EUROPE.
----Die ordnungspolitische Dimension der
    EG-Technologiepolitik. - 1987.
    (001495)

ECONOMIC TRENDS.
----Revitalizing development, growth and
    international trade. - 1987.
    (001394)
----Trends and issues in foreign direct
    investment and related flows. - 1985.
    (000192)

ECONOMIC TRENDS--JAPAN.
----Trends in multinational business and
    global environments: a perspective. -
    1984.
    (000029)

ECONOMIC TRENDS--LIBERIA.
----The impact of the transnational
    corporations in the banking and other
    financial institutions on the economy of
    Liberia. - 1986.
    (000873)

ECONOMIC TRENDS--PERU.
----Transnational banks and the external
    finance of Latin America : the
    experience of Peru. - 1983.
    (000840)

ECONOMIC TRENDS--UNITED STATES.
----Trends in multinational business and
    global environments: a perspective. -
    1984.
    (000029)

ECONOMIC TRENDS--WESTERN EUROPE.
----Trends in multinational business and
    global environments: a perspective. -
    1984.
    (000029)

ECONOMIC ZONING.
----Export processing zones: new catalysts
    for economic development. - 1983.
    (002391)

ECONOMIC ZONING--CHINA.
----China experiments with modernisation. -
    1983.
    (002384)
----China's special economic zones. - 1984.
    (002386)
----China's special economic zones. - 1986.
    (002382)
----China's special economic zones. - 1986.
    (002366)
----The investment implications of China's
    offshore oil development. - 1986.
    (000612)
----Kina különleges gazdasági övezetei. -
    1987.
    (002374)
----Special economic zones in China's
    modernization. - 1986.
    (002385)

ECONOMICS.
----The economic theory of the multinational
    enterprise. - 1985.
    (000009)
----Multinational corporations and the
    political economy of power. - 1983.
    (001846)
----Les services : nouvelle donne de
    l'économie. - 1984.
    (000913)
----The theory of vertical integration. -
    1984.
    (000015)

ECUADOR--CAPITAL.
----Ecuador. - 1984.
    (001831)

ECUADOR--CAPITAL MOVEMENTS.
----La evolución del capitalismo ecuatoriano
    en el último decenio y perspectivas. -
    1984.
    (001105)

ECUADOR--CAPITALISM.
----Capitalismo, burguesia y crisis en el
    Ecuador. - 1983.
    (001104)

ECUADOR--ECONOMIC CONDITIONS.
----Capitalismo, burguesia y crisis en el
    Ecuador. - 1983.
    (001104)
----Ecuador. - 1984.
    (001831)
----Invest in Ecuador. - 1982.
    (001771)
----La presencia de las empresas
    transnacionales en la economía
    ecuatoriana. - 1984.
    (001125)

ECUADOR--FINANCIAL INSTITUTIONS.
----La presencia de las empresas
    transnacionales en la economía
    ecuatoriana. - 1984.
    (001125)

ECUADOR--FOREIGN INVESTMENTS.
----Invest in Ecuador. - 1982.
    (001771)

ECUADOR--FOREIGN INVESTMENTS (continued)
----La presencia de las empresas
transnacionales en la economía
ecuatoriana. - 1984.
(001125)

ECUADOR--INDUSTRY.
----La evolución del capitalismo ecuatoriano
en el último decenio y perspectivas. -
1984.
(001105)

ECUADOR--IRON AND STEEL INDUSTRY.
----La industria siderúrgica
latinoamericana. - 1984.
(000601)

ECUADOR--METALLURGICAL INDUSTRY.
----La industria siderúrgica
latinoamericana. - 1984.
(000601)

ECUADOR--PETROLEUM EXPLORATION.
----Risk-bearing and the choice of contract
forms for oil exploration and
development. - 1984.
(002410)

ECUADOR--PETROLEUM INDUSTRY.
----Natural gas clauses in petroleum
arrangements. - 1987.
(002452)

ECUADOR--RISK ASSESSMENT.
----Risk-bearing and the choice of contract
forms for oil exploration and
development. - 1984.
(002410)

ECUADOR--SOCIAL CONDITIONS.
----Ecuador. - 1984.
(001831)

ECUADOR--STANDARDIZED TERMS OF CONTRACT.
----Risk-bearing and the choice of contract
forms for oil exploration and
development. - 1984.
(002410)

ECUADOR--TRANSNATIONAL CORPORATIONS.
----Capitalismo, burguesia y crisis en el
Ecuador. - 1983.
(001104)
----Ecuador. - 1984.
(001831)
----La evolución del capitalismo ecuatoriano
en el último decenio y perspectivas. -
1984.
(001105)
----Natural gas clauses in petroleum
arrangements. - 1987.
(002452)
----La presencia de las empresas
transnacionales en la economía
ecuatoriana. - 1984.
(001125)
----Risk-bearing and the choice of contract
forms for oil exploration and
development. - 1984.
(002410)

ECUMENICAL MOVEMENT.
----Churches and the transnational
corporations. - 1983.
(002586)

EDUCATION.
----The third industrial revolution. - 1987.
(000966)

EDUCATION--ASIA AND THE PACIFIC.
----Proceedings : Asia and Pacific
Conference on Accounting Education for
Development, Manila, Philippines,
November 12-16, 1984. - 1985.
(002060)

EDUCATION--INDIA.
----Nation-building media and TNCs. - 1984.
(000941)

EDUCATIONAL ASSISTANCE.
----Technical co-operation programme of the
United Nations Centre on Transnational
Corporations. - 1988.
(002610)
----Technical co-operation programme,
1976-1987 : United Nations Centre on
Transnational Corporations. - 1988.
(002611)

EEC.
----L'Afrique, l'Europe et la crise. - 1986.
(001287)
----The antitrust law of the European
Community and the UNCTAD code on
restrictive business practices. - 1984.
(001992)
----Attempt to regulate restrictive
commercial practices in the field of air
transportation within a transnational
antitrust legal and institutional
framework. - 1984.
(000788) (001659)
----Centralized European merger regulation.
- 1985.
(001625)
----Commercial arbitration and the European
Economic Community. - 1985.
(002481)
----A contract law for Europe. - 1985.
(001991)
----East-West joint ventures. - 1988.
(001570)
----EEC law of competition. - 1985.
(002151)
----The European Investment Bank. - 1985.
(002134)
----Exclusive licenses as restraints of
trade under US and Common Market
antitrust law. - 1984.
(002414)
----Extraterritorial application of the
EEC-competition law. - 1984.
(002349)
----Gemeinschaftsunternehmen im EGKS- und
EWG-Kartellrecht. - 1986.
(001978)
----In the wake of windsurfing : patent
licensing in the Common Market. - 1987.
(002455)
----Merger control in the EEC. - 1983.
(001634)

Subject Index - Index des matières

EEC (continued)
----New challenges to the U.S. multinational
    corporation in the European Economic
    Community. - 1985.
       (002192)
----New technology and the new services :
    towards an innovation strategy for
    Europe. - 1986.
       (000807)
----La réglementation communautaire des
    transports. - 1984.
       (001994)
----The seventh directive. - 1984.
       (002094)
----Le societa multinazionali nel diritto
    comunitario. - 1984.
       (002011)
----Territorial and exclusive trademark
    licensing under the EEC law of
    competition. - 1984.
       (001987)
----U.S.-EEC confrontation in the
    international trade of agricultural
    products: consequences for third
    parties. - 1985.
       (001380)
----The Vredeling proposal. - 1983.
       (002604)
----The Vredeling proposal and multinational
    trade unionism. - 1983.
       (002598)

EEC--MEMBERS.
----Portugal's accession to the EEC and its
    impact on foreign direct investment. -
    1986.
       (000554)

EEC--RESOLUTIONS AND DECISIONS.
----Measures regarding the activities of
    transnational corporations in South
    Africa and Namibia. - 1985.
       (001220)

EEC CODE OF CONDUCT FOR COMPANIES WITH
SUBSIDIARIES, BRANCHES OR REPRESENTATION IN
SOUTH AFRICA (1977).
----A code for misconduct? - 1980.
       (002009)

EGYPT--ECONOMIC ANALYSIS.
----Determinants of foreign direct
    investment in developing countries. -
    1986.
       (000531)

EGYPT--ECONOMIC POLICY.
----Determinants of foreign direct
    investment in developing countries. -
    1986.
       (000531)

EGYPT--EMPLOYMENT POLICY.
----The growth of employment in services:
    Egypt, 1960-75. - 1985.
       (000858)

EGYPT--FEASIBILITY STUDIES.
----Operations of multinational corporations
    and local enterprises in Arab countries.
    - 1985.
       (001141)

EGYPT--FINANCIAL STATISTICS.
----Egypt's experience in regulating
    technology imports. - 1987.
       (001514)

EGYPT--FOREIGN DIRECT INVESTMENT.
----Determinants of foreign direct
    investment in developing countries. -
    1986.
       (000531)
----Egypt's experience in regulating
    technology imports. - 1987.
       (001514)

EGYPT--FOREIGN INVESTMENTS.
----Egypt's experience in regulating
    technology imports. - 1987.
       (001514)
----National legislation and regulations
    relating to transnational corporations.
    Volume 4. - 1986.
       (002253)

EGYPT--GOVERNMENT SPENDING POLICY.
----The South Korean success story. - 1986.
       (001050)

EGYPT--INCOME DISTRIBUTION.
----The South Korean success story. - 1986.
       (001050)

EGYPT--INDUSTRIAL RESEARCH.
----Operations of multinational corporations
    and local enterprises in Arab countries.
    - 1985.
       (001141)

EGYPT--JOINT VENTURES.
----Egypt's experience in regulating
    technology imports. - 1987.
       (001514)

EGYPT--LAWS AND REGULATIONS.
----Egypt's experience in regulating
    technology imports. - 1987.
       (001514)
----National legislation and regulations
    relating to transnational corporations.
    Volume 4. - 1986.
       (002253)

EGYPT--LEGISLATION.
----Egypt's experience in regulating
    technology imports. - 1987.
       (001514)

EGYPT--PETROLEUM INDUSTRY.
----Natural gas clauses in petroleum
    arrangements. - 1987.
       (002452)

EGYPT--PHARMACEUTICAL INDUSTRY.
----Transnational corporations in the
    pharmaceutical industry of developing
    countries. - 1984.
       (000749)

EGYPT--RESTRICTIVE BUSINESS PRACTICES.
----Egypt's experience in regulating
    technology imports. - 1987.
       (001514)

EGYPT--SERVICE INDUSTRIES.
----The growth of employment in services:
Egypt, 1960-75. - 1985.
(000858)

EGYPT--STANDARD OF LIVING.
----The South Korean success story. - 1986.
(001050)

EGYPT--STATISTICAL DATA.
----Egypt's experience in regulating
technology imports. - 1987.
(001514)

EGYPT--TECHNOLOGY TRANSFER.
----Egypt's experience in regulating
technology imports. - 1987.
(001514)

EGYPT--TRANSNATIONAL CORPORATIONS.
----Egypt's experience in regulating
technology imports. - 1987.
(001514)
----National legislation and regulations
relating to transnational corporations.
Volume 4. - 1986.
(002253)
----Natural gas clauses in petroleum
arrangements. - 1987.
(002452)
----Operations of multinational corporations
and local enterprises in Arab countries.
- 1985.
(001141)

EL SALVADOR--BUSINESS ENTERPRISES.
----Directorió comercial e industrial de El
Salvador. - 1986-   .
(002627)

EL SALVADOR--DIRECTORIES.
----Directorió comercial e industrial de El
Salvador. - 1986-   .
(002627)

EL SALVADOR--INDUSTRY.
----Directorió comercial e industrial de El
Salvador. - 1986-   .
(002627)

ELECTIONS--JAMAICA.
----La Jamaïque, ou le dilemme politique
d'un petit pays déshérité. - 1984.
(001819)

ELECTRIC POWER--UNITED STATES.
----A competitive assessment of the U.S.
electric power generating equipment
industry. - 1985.
(000762)

ELECTRIC POWER PLANTS--UNITED STATES.
----A competitive assessment of the U.S.
electric power generating equipment
industry. - 1985.
(000762)

ELECTRIC POWER RATES--GHANA.
----The price and availability of energy for
an aluminium smelter : recent
renegotiations in Ghana. - 1987.
(002467)

ELECTRONIC CIRCUITS.
----Microelectronics-based automation
technologies and development. - 1985.
(000753)

ELECTRONIC FUNDS TRANSFER.
----Aspectos jurídicos das transferências
electrônicas internacionais de fundos. -
1986.
(000805)
----UNCITRAL, the United Nations Commission
on International Trade Law. - 1986.
(002155)

ELECTRONIC FUNDS TRANSFER--LATIN AMERICA.
----Financial transfers in the MNE. - 1986.
(000416)

ELECTRONIC FUNDS TRANSFER--UNITED STATES.
----Financial transfers in the MNE. - 1986.
(000416)

ELECTRONICS INDUSTRY.
----An AEA directory of international
electronics facilities. - 1982.
(000650) (002613)
----Automation and the worldwide
restructuring of the electronics
industry: strategic implications for
developing countries. - 1985.
(000683)
----Electronic information services. - 1986.
(000837)
----Microelectronics-based automation
technologies and development. - 1985.
(000753)
----Les multinationales de l'électronique:
des stratégies différenciees. (With
English summary.). - 1984.
(000679)
----New technologies and Third World
development. - 1986.
(001475)
----Shifts in the world economy and the
restructuring of economic sectors. -
1987.
(000734)
----Technological trends and challenges in
electronics. - 1983.
(000739)
----A tecnológiatranszfer néhány sajátos
vonása az elektronikai iparban. - 1987.
(001404)
----The third industrial revolution. - 1987.
(000966)
----Transnational corporations in the
international semiconductor industry. -
1986.
(000748)

ELECTRONICS INDUSTRY--ARGENTINA.
----La industria electrónica argentina :
apertura comercial y
desindustrialización. - 1987.
(000654)
----Telecomunicaciones. - 1987.
(000792)

ELECTRONICS INDUSTRY--ASIA.
----Kisvállatok Azsia fejlodo országainak
elektronikai iparban. - 1987.
(000630)

ELECTRONICS INDUSTRY--EUROPE.
----The semiconductor business. - 1985.
   (000715)

ELECTRONICS INDUSTRY--HUNGARY.
----A hazai elektronikai ipar helyzete és
   problemái. - 1986.
   (000634)
----L'industria elettronica unghrese. - 1986.
   (000731)

ELECTRONICS INDUSTRY--INDIA.
----New information technology in India. -
   1986.
   (000651)
----Technology transfer under alternative
   arrangements with transnational
   corporations. - 1987.
   (001513)

ELECTRONICS INDUSTRY--JAPAN.
----High-tech trade. - 1986.
   (000696)
----Le Japon : transformations
   industrielles, croissance et
   internationalisation. - 1983.
   (000319)
----Postwar development of Japanese
   electronics industry. - 1986.
   (000732)
----The semiconductor business. - 1985.
   (000715)
----Transnational corporations in the
   international semiconductor industry. -
   1986.
   (000748)
----Vers la mondialisation de l'appareil
   productif japonais. - 1986.
   (000725)

ELECTRONICS INDUSTRY--MALAYSIA.
----Technology transfer under alternative
   arrangements with transnational
   corporations. - 1987.
   (001513)

ELECTRONICS INDUSTRY--MAURITIUS.
----Jobs for the girls. - 1984.
   (001901)

ELECTRONICS INDUSTRY--MEXICO.
----L'électronique dans la politique
   industrielle mexicaine. - 1986.
   (000697)

ELECTRONICS INDUSTRY--REPUBLIC OF KOREA.
----Technology transfer under alternative
   arrangements with transnational
   corporations. - 1987.
   (001513)

ELECTRONICS INDUSTRY--SCOTLAND (UNITED
KINGDOM).
----Semiconductors, Scotland and the
   international division of labour. - 1987.
   (000694)

ELECTRONICS INDUSTRY--SOUTHEAST ASIA.
----Transnational corporations and the
   electronics industries of ASEAN
   economies. - 1987.
   (000754)

ELECTRONICS INDUSTRY--TAIWAN (CHINA).
----The production characteristics of
   multinational firms and the effects of
   tax incentives: the case of Taiwan's
   electronics industry. - 1986.
   (001038) (002305)
----L'industrie électronique à Taiwan. -
   1987.
   (000668)

ELECTRONICS INDUSTRY--UNITED KINGDOM.
----Inward investment. - 1984.
   (000116)
----Microelectronics in British industry. -
   1984.
   (000723)
----Semiconductors, Scotland and the
   international division of labour. - 1987.
   (000694)

ELECTRONICS INDUSTRY--UNITED STATES.
----High-tech trade. - 1986.
   (000696)
----The semiconductor business. - 1985.
   (000715)
----Transnational corporations in the
   international semiconductor industry. -
   1986.
   (000748)

ELECTRONICS INDUSTRY--WESTERN EUROPE.
----European industrial policy for the
   electronics and information technology
   sector. - 1984.
   (000849)
----Transnational corporations in the
   international semiconductor industry. -
   1986.
   (000748)

ELITE.
----Postimperialism. - 1987.
   (001232)

EMPLOYEES--CHINA.
----The training component. - 1986.
   (001920)

EMPLOYERS' LIABILITY INSURANCE--BHOPAL
(INDIA).
----Mass disasters and multinational
   liability : the Bhopal case. - 1986.
   (001936)

EMPLOYMENT.
----L'expansion des services à productivité
   stable. - 1987.
   (001917)
----Export processing zones in developing
   countries. - 1987.
   (002376)
----Industry in the 1980s. - 1985.
   (001341)
----Microelectronics-based automation
   technologies and development. - 1985.
   (000753)
----Recommendation on development
   cooperation and employment in developing
   countries. - 1984.
   (001911)
----Les services : enjeux pour l'emploi et
   le commerce international. - 1986.
   (000960)

EMPLOYMENT (continued)
----Les services : nouvelle donne pour
     l'emploi. - 1987.
     (000961)
----Les services contre le chômage. - 1987.
     (000857)
----The services industries: employment,
     productivity, and inflation. - 1985.
     (000940)
----Technological change. - 1985.
     (001499)
----Technology and employment in industry. -
     1985.
     (001503)
----Technology choice and employment
     generation by multinational enterprises
     in developing countries. - 1984.
     (001646)
----Le tout-ordinateur. - 1986.
     (000743)
----Transnational corporations: choice of
     techniques and employment in developing
     countries. -   .
     (001882)
----Women in industry. - 1985.
     (001930)

EMPLOYMENT--FRANCE.
----Activité comparée des établissements
     industriels d'origine étrangère et des
     établissements industriels français. -
     1984.
     (001927)

EMPLOYMENT--GERMANY, FEDERAL REPUBLIC OF.
----Strukturveränderungen der
     internationalen Direktinvestitionen und
     inländischer Arbeitsmarkt. - 1983.
     (001913)

EMPLOYMENT--HONG KONG.
----Multinational corporations, technology
     and employment. - 1983.
     (001891)

EMPLOYMENT--JAPAN.
----Employment and competitiveness in the
     European Community. - 1984.
     (001929)
----Le Japon : transformations
     industrielles, croissance et
     internationalisation. - 1983.
     (000319)

EMPLOYMENT--KENYA.
----Multinational enterprises, transfer of
     managerial know-how, technology choice
     and employment effects. - 1983.
     (001436)

EMPLOYMENT--KUWAIT.
----Impact of the operations of
     transnational corporations on
     development in Kuwait. - 1987.
     (001143)

EMPLOYMENT--LATIN AMERICA.
----Las empresas transnacionales y la
     inversión extranjera directa en la
     primera mitad de los años ochenta. -
     1987.
     (000194)

EMPLOYMENT--MEXICO.
----Las maquiladoras en México. - 1984.
     (001906)

EMPLOYMENT--NAMIBIA.
----Transnational corporations in South
     Africa and Namibia : United Nations
     public hearings. Volume 1, Reports of
     the Panel of Eminent Persons and of the
     Secretary-General. - 1986.
     (001216)

EMPLOYMENT--OMAN.
----Impact of the operations of
     transnational corporations on
     development in the Sultanate of Oman. -
     1988.
     (001144)

EMPLOYMENT--REPUBLIC OF KOREA.
----An information sector perspective of
     employment expansion in the Republic of
     Korea, 1975-80. - 1987.
     (000848)

EMPLOYMENT--SOUTH AFRICA.
----Disinvestment and black workers
     attitudes in South Africa. - 1985.
     (001210)
----Transnational corporations in South
     Africa and Namibia : United Nations
     public hearings. Volume 1, Reports of
     the Panel of Eminent Persons and of the
     Secretary-General. - 1986.
     (001216)

EMPLOYMENT--SOUTH ASIA.
----Multinational corporations, technology
     and employment. - 1983.
     (001891)

EMPLOYMENT--SPAIN.
----Hacia dónde va el empleo? - 1986.
     (001252)

EMPLOYMENT--UNITED KINGDOM.
----Cyclical variations in service
     industries' employment in the UK. - 1987.
     (000844)

EMPLOYMENT--UNITED STATES.
----Croissance de l'emploi dans les
     services. - 1987.
     (000846)
----The effects of foreign direct investment
     on U.S. employment during recession and
     structural change. - 1986.
     (001908)
----Employment and competitiveness in the
     European Community. - 1984.
     (001929)

EMPLOYMENT--WESTERN EUROPE.
----Employment and competitiveness in the
     European Community. - 1984.
     (001929)
----Hacia dónde va el empleo? - 1986.
     (001252)

EMPLOYMENT DISCRIMINATION--SAUDI ARABIA.
----United States corporations operating in
Saudi Arabia and laws affecting
discrimination in employment. - 1985.
(002354)

EMPLOYMENT DISCRIMINATION--UNITED STATES.
----United States corporations operating in
Saudi Arabia and laws affecting
discrimination in employment. - 1985.
(002354)

EMPLOYMENT POLICY.
----Anthropology and international business.
- 1986.
(001892)
----Employee consultation and information in
multinational corporations. - 1986.
(002603)
----Employment in multinational banking. -
1987.
(001916)
----La empresa transnacional en el marco
laboral. - 1983.
(001910)
----Is employment policy a thing of the
past? - 1983.
(001889)
----Multinational business and labour. -
1985.
(001896)
----Multinational corporation and national
regulation: an economic audit. - 1987.
(002270)
----Multinationals are mushrooming. - 1986.
(001861)
----Multinationals square off against
Central American workers. - 1985.
(001923)
----The new expatriates. - 1988.
(001925)
----Present and desired methods of
selecting expatriate managers for
international assignments. - 1984.
(000522)
----Publicidad. - 1987.
(000937)
----Rabochii klass protiv
transnatsional'nykh korporatsii. - 1984.
(001278)
----The Vredeling proposal. - 1983.
(002604)
----The Vredeling proposal and multinational
trade unionism. - 1983.
(002598)

EMPLOYMENT POLICY--BELGIUM.
----Employment decision-making in
multinational enterprises. - 1984.
(001888)

EMPLOYMENT POLICY--BRAZIL.
----Employment effects of exports by
multinationals and of export processing
zones in Brazil. - 1987.
(001915)

EMPLOYMENT POLICY--EGYPT.
----The growth of employment in services:
Egypt, 1960-75. - 1985.
(000858)

EMPLOYMENT POLICY--GERMANY, FEDERAL REPUBLIC
OF.
----The development of employment in
multinational enterprises in the Federal
Republic of Germany. - 1985.
(001912)

EMPLOYMENT POLICY--GREECE.
----The employment impact of multinational
enterprises in Greece, Portugal and
Spain. - 1987.
(001887)

EMPLOYMENT POLICY--JAPAN.
----Key to Japan's economic strength. - 1984.
(001924)

EMPLOYMENT POLICY--KENYA.
----Corporate strategy and employment
relations in multinational corporations:
some evidence from Kenya and Malaysia. -
1983.
(001902)

EMPLOYMENT POLICY--LIBERIA.
----Multinationals and employment in a West
African sub-region. - 1984.
(001904)

EMPLOYMENT POLICY--MALAYSIA.
----Corporate strategy and employment
relations in multinational corporations:
some evidence from Kenya and Malaysia. -
1983.
(001902)

EMPLOYMENT POLICY--NIGERIA.
----Third World multinationals. - 1983.
(000361)

EMPLOYMENT POLICY--PORTUGAL.
----The employment impact of multinational
enterprises in Greece, Portugal and
Spain. - 1987.
(001887)

EMPLOYMENT POLICY--SIERRA LEONE.
----Multinationals and employment in a West
African sub-region. - 1984.
(001904)

EMPLOYMENT POLICY--SINGAPORE.
----Direct foreign investment in
manufacturing and the impact on
employment and export performance in
Singapore. - 1984.
(001932)

EMPLOYMENT POLICY--SPAIN.
----The employment impact of multinational
enterprises in Greece, Portugal and
Spain. - 1987.
(001887)

EMPLOYMENT POLICY--UNITED KINGDOM.
----A code for misconduct? - 1980.
(002009)

EMPLOYMENT POLICY--UNITED STATES.
----American multinationals and American
employment. - 1983.
(001890)

EMPLOYMENT POLICY--UNITED STATES (continued)
----International business travel and
    relocation directory. - 1984.
      (002710)
----Key to Japan's economic strength. - 1984.
      (001924)
----Staffing of management and professional
    positions at overseas subsidiaries of
    U.S. multinational enterprises. - 1983.
      (001885)

EMPRESA MULTINACIONAL ANDINA.
----Estudios jurídicos sobre la Empresa
    Multinacional Andina, E.M.A. - 1986.
      (000314)

ENERGY LEGISLATION.
----Energy law '86. - 1986.
      (002224)

ENERGY LEGISLATION--ARAB COUNTRIES.
----Arab comparative and commercial law. -
    1987.
      (002223)

ENERGY LEGISLATION--WESTERN EUROPE.
----International aspects of nuclear
    instalations licensing. - 1987.
      (002434)

ENERGY POLICY.
----World oil markets. - 1986.
      (000590)

ENERGY POLICY--UNITED STATES.
----Foreign oil and taxation. - 1983.
      (002039)

ENERGY PRICES.
----Natural gas clauses in petroleum
    arrangements. - 1987.
      (002452)
----Transnational corporations in world
    development. - 1983.
      (000102)

ENERGY RESOURCES--NAMIBIA.
----Transnational corporations in South
    Africa and Namibia : United Nations
    public hearings. Volume 1, Reports of
    the Panel of Eminent Persons and of the
    Secretary-General. - 1986.
      (001216)

ENERGY RESOURCES--SOUTH AFRICA.
----Transnational corporations in South
    Africa and Namibia : United Nations
    public hearings. Volume 3, Statements
    and submissions. - 1987.
      (001215)

ENERGY RESOURCES--UNITED STATES.
----Profiles of foreign direct investment in
    U.S. energy. - 1985-   .
      (000774)

ENERGY RESOURCES DEVELOPMENT.
----Energy law '86. - 1986.
      (002224)
----Insurance against the political risks of
    petroleum investment. - 1986.
      (001866) (002160)

----Promotion of mining and energy
    investment under the Lomé Convention. -
    1986.
      (002607)
----Transnational corporations in world
    development. - 1983.
      (000102)

ENERGY RESOURCES DEVELOPMENT--UNITED STATES.
----A competitive assessment of the
    renewable energy equipment industry. -
    1984.
      (000775)

ENGINEERING.
----Analysis of engineering and technical
    assistance consultancy contracts. - 1986.
      (002449)

ENGINEERING INDUSTRIES.
----Microelectronics-based automation
    technologies and development. - 1985.
      (000753)

ENGINEERING INDUSTRIES--HUNGARY.
----A magyar gépipari vállalatok
    nagyságrendje és piaci magatartásuk. -
    1984.
      (000957)

ENGINEERING INDUSTRIES--INDIA.
----Microelectronics-based automation
    technologies and development. - 1985.
      (000753)
----Top hundred engineering companies. -
    197?-   .
      (002669)

ENGINEERING INDUSTRIES--REPUBLIC OF KOREA.
----Microelectronics-based automation
    technologies and development. - 1985.
      (000753)

ENGINEERS--LATIN AMERICA.
----The use and promotion of consultancy
    joint ventures by public entities in
    Latin America. - 1985.
      (000834)

ENGINEERS--UNITED STATES.
----The engineers and the price system
    revisited: the future of the
    international oil corporations. - 1983.
      (000587)

ENGLISH LANGUAGE.
----Glossary of terms for state auditors. -
    1983.
      (002711)
----Management accounting terminology. -
    1983.
      (002092) (002717)

ENTREPRENEURSHIP.
----Coming of age of the service economy. -
    1986.
      (000860)

ENTREPRENEURSHIP--POLAND.
----The functioning of private enterprise in
    Poland. - 1984.
      (001168)

ENVIRONMENT.
----Environmental aspects of the activities
    of transnational corporations. - 1985.
      (001954)

ENVIRONMENTAL DEGRADATION--BHOPAL (INDIA).
----Mass disasters and multinational
    liability : the Bhopal case. - 1986.
      (001936)

ENVIRONMENTAL HEALTH--EUROPE.
----The export of hazard. - 1985.
      (001941)

ENVIRONMENTAL HEALTH--UNITED STATES.
----The export of hazard. - 1985.
      (001941)

ENVIRONMENTAL IMPACT ASSESSMENT.
----Environmental aspects of the activities
    of transnational corporations. - 1985.
      (001954)

ENVIRONMENTAL IMPACT ASSESSMENT--BHOPAL
(INDIA).
----Mass disasters and multinational
    liability : the Bhopal case. - 1986.
      (001936)

ENVIRONMENTAL LAW.
----Environmental aspects of the activities
    of transnational corporations. - 1985.
      (001954)
----Liability for shipments by sea of
    hazardous and noxious substances. - 1985.
      (001951)

ENVIRONMENTAL LAW--UNITED STATES.
----Are environmental regulations driving
    U.S. industry overseas? - 1984.
      (001947)

ENVIRONMENTAL MANAGEMENT.
----Environmental aspects of the activities
    of transnational corporations. - 1985.
      (001954)

ENVIRONMENTAL POLICY.
----Environmental aspects of the activities
    of transnational corporations. - 1985.
      (001954)
----Improving environmental cooperation. -
    1984.
      (001955)

ENVIRONMENTAL PROTECTION.
----Environmental aspects of the activities
    of transnational corporations. - 1985.
      (001954)
----Transnational corporations in world
    development. - 1983.
      (000102)
----Völkerrechtliche Haftung für das Handeln
    Privater im Bereich des internationalen
    Umweltschutzes. - 1984.
      (001945)

ENVIRONMENTALLY SOUND TECHNOLOGY.
----Technology choice and change in
    developing countries. - 1983.
      (001505)

EQUATORIAL GUINEA--BUSINESS ENTERPRISES.
----Directorio nacional de empresas y
    establecimientos. - 1985-   .
      (002629)

EQUATORIAL GUINEA--DIRECTORIES.
----Directorio nacional de empresas y
    establecimientos. - 1985-   .
      (002629)

EQUATORIAL GUINEA--INDUSTRY.
----Directorio nacional de empresas y
    establecimientos. - 1985-   .
      (002629)

EQUIPMENT AND SUPPLIES.
----International communications and
    information systems. - 1985.
      (000787)
----Reference book and buyers' guide. -
    1984-
      (000797)

ETHICS.
----A code of ethics for arbitrators in
    international commercial arbitration? -
    1985.
      (002519)

ETHNOPSYCHOLOGY.
----Going international. - 1985.
      (001786)

ETHNOPSYCHOLOGY--GUYANA.
----Ethnicity, class, and international
    capitalist penetration in Guyana and
    Trinidad. - 1985.
      (001096)

ETHNOPSYCHOLOGY--TRINIDAD AND TOBAGO.
----Etnnicity, class, and international
    capitalist penetration in Guyana and
    Trinidad. - 1985.
      (001096)

EUROCURRENCY CREDITS.
----Issues in negotiating international loan
    agreements with transnational banks. -
    1983.
      (002459)

EUROCURRENCY MARKET.
----Changes in the international financial
    market and implications for
    transnational banks, transnational
    corporations and developing countries. -
    1986.
      (000976)
----Stratégies des entreprises et marché
    international des capitaux. - 1984.
      (001273)

EURODOLLARS.
----A practitioner's guide to international
    banking and trade finance. - 1986.
      (000922)

EUROPE--ACCOUNTING.
----The seventh directive. - 1984.
      (002094)

EUROPE--ACCOUNTING AND REPORTING.
----The seventh directive. - 1984.
      (002094)

EUROPE--ADVERTISING.
----Market share strategy in Europe. - 1985.
    (000493)

EUROPE--CHAMBERS OF COMMERCE.
----Directory of European industrial [and]
    trade associations. - 1986-   .
    (002707)

EUROPE--COMPETITION.
----Competitive strategies for Europe. -
    1983.
    (000463)

EUROPE--CORPORATION LAW.
----The seventh directive. - 1984.
    (002094)

EUROPE--CORPORATIONS.
----The seventh directive. - 1984.
    (002094)

EUROPE--DEVELOPING COUNTRIES.
----The export of hazard. - 1985.
    (001941)

EUROPE--DIRECTORIES.
----Directory of European industrial [and]
    trade associations. - 1986-   .
    (002707)

EUROPE--DISTRIBUTION.
----Market share strategy in Europe. - 1985.
    (000493)

EUROPE--DIVESTMENT.
----Foreign divestment and international
    rationalisation in the motor industry. -
    1985.
    (000664)

EUROPE--ELECTRONICS INDUSTRY.
----The semiconductor business. - 1985.
    (000715)

EUROPE--ENVIRONMENTAL HEALTH.
----The export of hazard. - 1985.
    (001941)

EUROPE--EXPORTS.
----The export of hazard. - 1985.
    (001941)

EUROPE--FARMERS ASSOCIATIONS.
----Directory of European industrial [and]
    trade associations. - 1986-   .
    (002707)

EUROPE--FINANCING.
----Market share strategy in Europe. - 1985.
    (000493)

EUROPE--FOREIGN DIRECT INVESTMENT.
----Becoming a triad power: the new global
    corporation. - 1986.
    (000500)
----Direct investment by Sogo-Shosha in
    Europe. - 1983.
    (000310)
----The relationship between foreign
    ownership and technology transfer. -
    1983.
    (001422)

EUROPE--HARMFUL PRODUCTS.
----The export of hazard. - 1985.
    (001941)

EUROPE--HEALTH HAZARDS.
----The export of hazard. - 1985.
    (001941)

EUROPE--INDUSTRIAL CO-OPERATION.
----Industrial collaboration with Japan. -
    1986.
    (001648)

EUROPE--INDUSTRIAL POLICY.
----Governments and microelectronics. - 1983.
    (000648)

EUROPE--INDUSTRIAL ROBOTS.
----Robots in manufacturing. - 1983.
    (000656)

EUROPE--INDUSTRY.
----The quality of shipping services. - 1986.
    (000789)

EUROPE--INFORMATION SOURCES.
----Sources of joint venture information and
    assistance in the United States and
    Europe. - 1983.
    (001617)

EUROPE--JOINT VENTURES.
----Becoming a triad power: the new global
    corporation. - 1986.
    (000500)
----Industrial collaboration with Japan. -
    1986.
    (001648)
----Sources of joint venture information and
    assistance in the United States and
    Europe. - 1983.
    (001617)

EUROPE--MANAGEMENT.
----Direct investment by Sogo-Shosha in
    Europe. - 1983.
    (000310)

EUROPE--MARITIME TRANSPORT.
----The quality of shipping services. - 1986.
    (000789)

EUROPE--MARKET ACCESS.
----Competitive strategies for Europe. -
    1983.
    (000463)

EUROPE--MARKETING.
----Becoming a triad power: the new global
    corporation. - 1986.
    (000500)
----Market share strategy in Europe. - 1985.
    (000493)

EUROPE--MICROELECTRONICS.
----Governments and microelectronics. - 1983.
    (000648)

EUROPE--MINERAL INDUSTRY.
----Mineral industries of Europe and the
    U.S.S.R. - 1984.
    (000642)

EUROPE--MOTOR VEHICLE INDUSTRY.
----Foreign divestment and international
    rationalisation in the motor industry. -
    1985.
        (000664)

EUROPE--NATIONALIZATION.
----Nationalized companies : a threat to
    American business. - 1983.
        (002327)

EUROPE--NEW PRODUCTS.
----Market share strategy in Europe. - 1985.
        (000493)

EUROPE--PUBLIC ENTERPRISES.
----Nationalized companies : a threat to
    American business. - 1983.
        (002327)

EUROPE--ROBOTICS.
----Robots in manufacturing. - 1983.
        (000656)

EUROPE--SEMICONDUCTORS.
----The semiconductor business. - 1985.
        (000715)

EUROPE--TECHNOLOGICAL INNOVATIONS.
----European multinationals in core
    technologies. - 1988.
        (000380)

EUROPE--TECHNOLOGY TRANSFER.
----The relationship between foreign
    ownership and technology transfer. -
    1983.
        (001422)

EUROPE--TOXIC SUBSTANCES.
----The export of hazard. - 1985.
        (001941)

EUROPE--TRADE ASSOCIATIONS.
----Directory of European industrial [and]
    trade associations. - 1986-   .
        (002707)

EUROPE--TRANSNATIONAL CORPORATIONS.
----Competitive strategies for Europe. -
    1983.
        (000463)
----Les entreprises multinationales dans la
    Communauté européenne. - 1984.
        (001154)
----European multinationals in core
    technologies. - 1988.
        (000380)
----The export of hazard. - 1985.
        (001941)
----Market share strategy in Europe. - 1985.
        (000493)
----The relationship between foreign
    ownership and technology transfer. -
    1983.
        (001422)

EUROPEAN COMMUNITIES.
----Abhängige Unternehmen und Konzerne im
    europäischen Gemeinschaftsrecht. - 1984.
        (002133)

----Agro-industrial co-operation between the
    European Community and the ACP
    countries. - 1986.
        (002605)
----Air and maritime transport and the EEC
    competition rules : Ministère Publique
    v. Asjes, Nouvelles Frontières et al. -
    1987.
        (000794)
----Current problems of economic
    integration. - 1986.
        (001312)
----EC trade effects and factor mobility. -
    1983.
        (001370)
----Employment and competitiveness in the
    European Community. - 1984.
        (001929)
----Les entreprises multinationales dans la
    Communauté européenne. - 1984.
        (001154)
----The European Community and China. - 1986.
        (002045)
----European Community tariff preferences
    and foreign direct investment. - 1987.
        (002159)
----Information technology and economic
    recovery in Western Europe. - 1986.
        (000874)
----La libération des mouvements de capitaux
    et l'intégration financière de la
    Communauté. - 1987.
        (001230)
----Mélanges 2 : harmonisation fiscale,
    marché commun des services, perspectives
    budgétaires 1988, fonds structurels. -
    1987.
        (000897)
----Merger policies and recent trends in
    mergers. - 1984.
        (001611)
----Multinational corporations and European
    integration. - 1987.
        (001325)
----Die ordnungspolitische Dimension der
    EG-Technologiepolitik. - 1987.
        (001495)
----The relative distribution of United
    States direct investment : the UK/EEC
    experience. - 1987.
        (000113)
----Services and regional policy. - 1987.
        (000903)
----Le système conjoint de garantie des
    investissements CEE/ACP de la Convention
    de Lomé III. - 1987.
        (002147)
----Transnational services policy? - 1987.
        (000867)
----Wachstumsmarkt Südostasien. - 1984.
        (001785)
----Zur Angleichung des Bilanzrechts in der
    Europäischen Gemeinschaft. - 1984.
        (002097)

EUROPEAN COMMUNITIES. COMMISSION.
----Commercial arbitration and the European
    Economic Community. - 1985.
        (002481)
----The EEC patent licencing regulation :
    practical guidelines. - 1986.
        (001966)

EUROPEAN COMMUNITIES. COMMISSION (continued)
----Exclusive territorial rights in patent
      licenses and Article 85 of the EEC
      Treaty. - 1987.
        (002418)
----Transborder data flows. - 1983.
        (000973)

EUROPEAN COMMUNITIES. COURT OF JUSTICE.
----Application des règles de concurrence du
      Traité de Rome à l'autorité publique. -
      1987.
        (002021)
----Commercial arbitration and the European
      Economic Community. - 1985.
        (002481)
----The EEC patent licencing regulation :
      practical guidelines. - 1986.
        (001966)
----In the wake of windsurfing : patent
      licensing in the Common Market. - 1987.
        (002455)

EUROPEAN CONVENTION ON THE LAW APPLICABLE TO
CONTRACTUAL OBLIGATIONS (1980).
----Die Gestaltung des internationalen
      Privatrechts der Schuldverträge unter
      allgemeinen Leitprinzipien. - 1983.
        (002025)

EUROPEAN DEVELOPMENT FUND.
----Agro-industrial co-operation between the
      European Community and the ACP
      countries. - 1986.
        (002605)
----Promotion of mining and energy
      investment under the Lomé Convention. -
      1986.
        (002607)

EUROPEAN FEDERATION OF EQUIPMENT LEASING
COMPANY ASSOCIATIONS.
----Analysis of equipment leasing contracts.
      - 1984.
        (002407)

EUROPEAN INVESTMENT BANK.
----Agro-industrial co-operation between the
      European Community and the ACP
      countries. - 1986.
        (002605)
----The European Investment Bank. - 1985.
        (002134)
----Investment in ACP states. - 1987.
        (001004)
----Promotion of mining and energy
      investment under the Lomé Convention. -
      1986.
        (002607)

EUROPEAN MONETARY SYSTEM (ORGANIZATION).
----Dette du Tiers monde. - 1984.
        (000260)

EVALUATION.
----Accounting analysis of the efficiency of
      public enterprises. - 1984.
        (002114)
----The quality of shipping services. - 1986.
        (000789)

EVALUATION--UNITED STATES.
----A competitive assessment of the U.S.
      flexible manufacturing systems industry.
      - 1985.
        (000763)
----A competitive assessment of the U.S.
      methanol industry. - 1985.
        (000671)
----A competitive assessment of the United
      States disk storage industry. - 1985.
        (000672)

EVALUATIVE RESEARCH--MAURITANIA.
----Towards an evaluative study of joint
      venture projects with socio-economic
      indicators. - 1983.
        (001555)

EVIDENCE.
----Symposium : a guide to international
      civil practice. - 1984.
        (002576)

EXCESS PROFITS TAX--UNITED STATES.
----Intercorporate transfer pricing: the
      role of the functionally determined
      profit split explored. - 1985.
        (001753)

EXCLUSIVE ECONOMIC ZONE--CANADA.
----U.S. fishery negotiations with Canada
      and Mexico. - 1985.
        (002462)

EXCLUSIVE ECONOMIC ZONE--CHINA.
----Special economic zones and economic
      policy in China. - 1983.
        (002394)

EXCLUSIVE ECONOMIC ZONE--LATIN AMERICA.
----The exclusive economic zone. - 1984.
        (002368)

EXCLUSIVE ECONOMIC ZONE--MEXICO.
----U.S. fishery negotiations with Canada
      and Mexico. - 1985.
        (002462)

EXCLUSIVE ECONOMIC ZONE--UNITED STATES.
----U.S. fishery negotiations with Canada
      and Mexico. - 1985.
        (002462)

EXECUTIVE ABILITY.
----How multinational should your top
  • managers be? - 1983.
        (000436)

EXPORT ADMINISTRATION ACT 1979 (UNITED
STATES).
----Licensing impact of foreign policy
      motivated retroactive reexport
      regulations. - 1983.
        (001352)

EXPORT CREDITS--PERU.
----Transnational banks and the external
      finance of Latin America : the
      experience of Peru. - 1983.
        (000840)

EXPORT CREDITS--UNITED STATES.
----Eximbank's role in international banking
    and finance. - 1986.
      (000816)

EXPORT DIVERSIFICATION.
----Diversification strategy and choice
    of country: diversifying acquisitions
    abroad by U.S. multinationals,
    1978-1980. - 1985.
      (000536)

EXPORT DIVERSIFICATION--COLOMBIA.
----Las empresas transnacionales en el
    desarrollo colombiano. - 1986.
      (001121)

EXPORT EARNINGS--UNITED STATES.
----International business planning. - 1983.
      (002279)

EXPORT FINANCING--BRAZIL.
----O sistema brasileiro de financiamento às
    exportaçoes. - 1985.
      (001349)

EXPORT IMPORT BANK OF JAPAN.
----Japan's largest financier of
    multinationalism: the EXIM Bank. - 1986.
      (000255)

EXPORT INCENTIVES--UNITED STATES.
----The Export Trading Company Act. - 1983.
      (002206)

EXPORT MARKETING.
----Aussenwirtschaft der Unternehmung. -
    1984.
      (000064)
----Big business blunders. - 1983.
      (000507)
----Entry strategies for international
    markets. - 1987.
      (000509)
----Estructuras empresarias para el comercio
    internacional. - 1984.
      (001383)
----Finding, entering, and succeeding in a
    foreign market. - 1987.
      (000468)
----International business. - 1987.
      (000453)
----International marketing. - 1986.
      (000482)
----Leading und Lagging kurzfristig
    variierbarer gruppeninterner Geldflusse
    im Wahrungsrisikomanagement einer
    internationalen Unternehmung. - 1986.
      (000501)
----Meeting the challenges of foreign
    expansion. - 1985.
      (000035)
----Strategic international marketing. -
    1985.
      (000467)

EXPORT MARKETING--AFRICA.
----International marketing to Black Africa
    and the Third World. - 1988.
      (001001)

EXPORT MARKETING--INDIA.
----Foreign cooperation and the marketing of
    manufactured exports from developing
    countries. - 1985.
      (001377)

EXPORT MARKETING--MALAYSIA.
----Chinese business, multinationals and the
    state: manufacturing for export in
    Malaysia and Singapore. - 1983.
      (000713)

EXPORT MARKETING--SINGAPORE.
----Chinese business, multinationals and the
    state: manufacturing for export in
    Malaysia and Singapore. - 1983.
      (000713)

EXPORT MARKETING--SRI LANKA.
----Foreign cooperation and the marketing of
    manufactured exports from developing
    countries. - 1985.
      (001377)

EXPORT MARKETING--UNITED STATES.
----Export trading companies. - 1984-   .
      (000851) (002638)
----Identifying export potential in the
    service sector. - 1986.
      (000882)
----The information needs of exporters:
    theory, framework and empirical tests. -
    1986.
      (000989)

EXPORT ORIENTED INDUSTRIES.
----Investing in free export processing
    zones. - 1984.
      (002362)
----Investir dans les zones franches
    industrielles d'exportation. - 1984.
      (002363)

EXPORT ORIENTED INDUSTRIES--BRAZIL.
----Capital intensity and export propensity
    in some Latin American countries. - 1987.
      (001389)

EXPORT ORIENTED INDUSTRIES--CARIBBEAN REGION.
----Can CARICOM countries replicate the
    Singapore experience. - 1987.
      (001093)

EXPORT ORIENTED INDUSTRIES--CENTRAL AMERICA.
----Capital intensity and export propensity
    in some Latin American countries. - 1987.
      (001389)
----Industrialización y exportaciones no
    tradicionales. - 1984.
      (001316)

EXPORT ORIENTED INDUSTRIES--CHINA.
----China's special economic zones. - 1983.
      (002381)

EXPORT ORIENTED INDUSTRIES--COLOMBIA.
----Capital intensity and export propensity
    in some Latin American countries. - 1987.
      (001389)

EXPORT ORIENTED INDUSTRIES--COSTA RICA.
----La industria de la maquila y la
    explotación de la fuerza de trabajo de
    la mujer. - 1984.
      (001900)

EXPORT ORIENTED INDUSTRIES--INDIA.
----Industrial distribution of Indian
    exports and joint ventures abroad. -
    1985.
      (000316)

EXPORT ORIENTED INDUSTRIES--MEXICO.
----Capital intensity and export propensity
    in some Latin American countries. - 1987.
      (001389)
----Restructuring industry offshore. - 1983.
      (000692)

EXPORT ORIENTED INDUSTRIES--REPUBLIC OF
KOREA.
----The effectiveness of export promotion
    policies. - 1986.
      (002310)

EXPORT ORIENTED INDUSTRIES--SINGAPORE.
----Can CARICOM countries replicate the
    Singapore experience. - 1987.
      (001093)

EXPORT ORIENTED INDUSTRIES--UNITED STATES.
----Export trading companies. - 1984-   .
      (000851) (002638)
----The Export Trading Company Act. - 1983.
      (002206)
----Restructuring industry offshore. - 1983.
      (000692)

EXPORT POLICY.
----Technology and East-West trade. - 1983.
      (001502)

EXPORT POLICY--UNITED STATES.
----The Export Trading Company Act. - 1983.
      (002206)

EXPORT PROCEDURES.
----Natural gas clauses in petroleum
    arrangements. - 1987.
      (002452)

EXPORT PROMOTION.
----Transnational corporations in world
    development. - 1983.
      (000102)

EXPORT PROMOTION--BRAZIL.
----Política industrial, joint ventures e
    exportaçoes. - 1986.
      (001658)

EXPORT PROMOTION--MALAWI.
----Malawi buyers' guide. - 1983-   .
      (002653)

EXPORT PROMOTION--PHILIPPINES.
----Export promotion via industrial
    enclaves. - 1987.
      (002399)

EXPORT PROMOTION--REPUBLIC OF KOREA.
----The effectiveness of export promotion
    policies. - 1986.
      (002310)

EXPORT PROMOTION--UNITED STATES.
----Identifying export potential in the
    service sector. - 1986.
      (000882)

EXPORT RESTRICTIONS.
----Annual survey of developments in
    international trade law, 1983. - 1984.
      (002136)

EXPORT RESTRICTIONS--UNITED STATES.
----Balancing the national interest : U.S.
    national security export controls and
    global economic competition. - 1987.
      (001417)
----Licensing impact of foreign policy
    motivated retroactive reexport
    regulations. - 1983.
      (001352)
----United States regulation of
    high-technology exports. - 1986.
      (001462)

EXPORT SUBSIDIES--INDONESIA.
----The Jakarta export processing zone:
    benefits and costs. - 1983.
      (002400)

EXPORT TRADING COMPANY ACT 1982 (UNITED
STATES).
----The Export Trading Company Act. - 1983.
      (002206)

EXPORT-IMPORT BANK OF THE UNITED STATES.
----Eximbank's role in international banking
    and finance. - 1986.
      (000816)

EXPORTS.
----The contribution of foreign direct
    investment to exports : an empirical
    study of 23 LDCs. - 1986.
      (001376)
----Corporate performance: America's
    international winners. - 1986.
      (000344)
----Multinationals, technology and exports.
    - 1985.
      (001456)
----Trade in investment-related
    technological services. - 1986.
      (000945)
----Transnational corporations and
    international trade : selected issues. -
    1985.
      (001393)

EXPORTS--ARGENTINA.
----Internacionalización de empresas y
    tecnología de origen argentino. - 1985.
      (000301)

EXPORTS--CHILE.
----Chile : creative economic management. -
    1987.
      (001784)

EXPORTS--COLOMBIA.
----Las empresas transnacionales en el
    desarrollo colombiano. - 1986.
      (001121)

EXPORTS--EUROPE.
----The export of hazard. - 1985.
   (001941)

EXPORTS--JAPAN.
----Le Japon : transformations
   industrielles, croissance et
   internationalisation. - 1983.
   (000319)

EXPORTS--LATIN AMERICA.
----Banco de datos sobre inversión
   extranjera directa en América Latina y
   el Caribe : información de los países
   receptores y de organismos regionales y
   subregionales, t. 2. - 1987.
   (000193)

EXPORTS--PARAGUAY.
----Las empresas transnacionales en la
   economía del Paraguay. - 1987.
   (001124)

EXPORTS--REPUBLIC OF KOREA.
----The South Korean success story. - 1986.
   (001050)

EXPORTS--UNITED STATES.
----A competitive assessment of the U.S.
   herbicide industry. - 1985.
   (000670)
----The export of hazard. - 1985.
   (001941)
----The information needs of exporters:
   theory, framework and empirical tests. -
   1986.
   (000989)

EXPROPRIATION.
----Compensation for expropriation. - 1984.
   (002334)
----A country risk appraisal model of
   foreign asset expropriation in
   developing countries. - 1987.
   (001553) (001775)
----Current developments in the law of
   expropriation and compensation. - 1987.
   (002318)
----Economically rational design of
   developing countries' expropriation
   policies towards foreign investment. -
   1985.
   (001599)
----Eigentum, Enteignung und Entschädigung
   im geltenden Völkerrecht. - 1985.
   (002321)
----Expropriations of foreign-owned firms in
   developing countries: a cross-national
   analysis. - 1984.
   (001552)
----The international law of expropriation
   of foreign-owned property. - 1983.
   (002330)
----An international standard of partial
   compensation upon the expropriation of
   an alien's property. - 1987.
   (002317)
----Nationalization of foreign property. -
   1983.
   (002324)
----The taking of foreign property under
   international law. - 1984.
   (002336)

EXPROPRIATION--IRAN (ISLAMIC REPUBLIC OF).
----The expropriation issue before the
   Iran-United States Claims Tribunal. -
   1984.
   (002320)
----Iran-U.S. Claims Tribunal. - 1986.
   (002335)

EXPROPRIATION--KUWAIT.
----Host countries permanent sovereignty
   over national resources and protection
   of foreign investors. - 1983.
   (002566)
----State contracts and oil expropriations.
   - 1984.
   (002577)

EXPROPRIATION--MEXICO.
----Expropriation and aftermath : the
   prospects for foreign enterprise in the
   Mexico of Miguel de la Madrid. - 1983.
   (002328)

EXPROPRIATION--UNITED STATES.
----The expropriation issue before the
   Iran-United States Claims Tribunal. -
   1984.
   (002320)
----Host countries permanent sovereignty
   over national resources and protection
   of foreign investors. - 1983.
   (002566)
----Iran-U.S. Claims Tribunal. - 1986.
   (002335)
----Jurisdiction over foreign governments. -
   1986.
   (002347)

EXTERNAL DEBT.
----Bank lending to developing countries. -
   1985.
   (000212)
----Banking on crisis. - 1983.
   (000868)
----Changes in the international financial
   market and implications for
   transnational banks, transnational
   corporations and developing countries. -
   1986.
   (000976)
----A closed circle for the developing
   countries? : debt and financial flows. -
   1986.
   (000218)
----Compendium of selected studies on
   international monetary and financial
   issues for the developing countries. -
   1987.
   (001243)
----Current financial and monetary problems
   of the developing countries in the world
   capitalist economy. - 1987.
   (001246)
----The debt crisis and the world economy. -
   1984.
   (000220)
----The debt problem. - 1985.
   (000249)
----Debt problems. - 1986.
   (000229)
----Debt rescheduling from an intertemporal
   choice theoretic point of view. - 1983.
   (000214)

EXTERNAL DEBT (continued)
----Debt-equity swaps and the heavily
indebted countries. - 1987.
(000263)
----La dette du Tiers monde. - 1984.
(000223)
----Dette du Tiers monde. - 1984.
(000260)
----Dette du Tiers-Monde. - 1987.
(000224)
----La deuda de los países en desarrollo a
mediados de los ochenta. - 1987.
(000210)
----Developing country access to capital
markets in transition. - 1987.
(001609)
----East-West trade and CMEA indebtedness in
the seventies and eighties. - 1979.
(000209)
----Endettement international et
multinationalisation. - 1984.
(000248)
----Endettement international et théorie des
transferts. - 1987.
(000213)
----Financing and external debt of
developing countries: ...survey. - 1986-
.
(000231)
----Foreign direct investment, the service
sector and international banking. - 1987.
(000972)
----The importance of international monetary
markets and the international crisis of
indebtedness. - 1987.
(000244)
----The international debt crisis. - 1985.
(000240)
----International debt quagmire. - 1983.
(000262)
----International lending and debt. - 1983.
(000208)
----International lending in a fragile world
economy. - 1983.
(000241)
----Internationale Verschuldung-Wege aus der
Krise. - 1983.
(000253)
----Investment penetration in manufacturing
and extraction and external public debt
in Third World states. - 1984.
(001015)
----Lending without limits. - 1979.
(000228)
----Mezinárodní financní a kapitálové vztahy
rozvojových zemí. - 1985.
(000230)
----Multinational institutions and the Third
World. - 1985.
(001253)
----On Third World debt. - 1984.
(000211)
----The problems of developing-country debt
and a strategy for Arab banking
institutions. - 1983.
(000256)
----Promotion of direct investment in
developing countries. - 1986.
(002143)
----Rehearing granted : Allied Bank
International v. Banco Agricola Credito
de Cartago and the current international
debt crisis. - 1984.
(000233)

----Rekindling development. - 1988.
(001302)
----Restricción del crédito de la banca
comercial en situaciones de crisis de la
deuda internacional. - 1983.
(000226)
----The restructuring of international loans
and the international debt crisis. -
1984.
(000239)
----Revitalizing development, growth and
international trade. - 1987.
(001394)
----Il ruolo del finanziamento estero nello
sviluppo economico e la problematica
attuale dell'indebitamento. - 1983.
(001289)
----Shaping a future for foreign direct
investment in the Third World. - 1988.
(002140)
----Third World debt crisis threatens a
collapse of world trade and financial
systems. - 1987.
(000217)
----Transnational banking and the
international monetary crisis. - 1983.
(001303)
----A tripartite model of the international
debt crisis. - 1985.
(000238)
----Ways out of the debt crisis. - 1984.
(000245)
----Wisselkoersinstabiliteit en
schuldproblematiek. - 1984.
(001310)

EXTERNAL DEBT--ARGENTINA.
----Los bancos transnacionales y el
endeudamiento externo en la Argentina. -
1987.
(000819)

EXTERNAL DEBT--ASIA AND THE PACIFIC.
----The great continental divide : Asian and
Latin American countries in the world
economic crisis. - 1986.
(001299)

EXTERNAL DEBT--BRAZIL.
----La internacionalización financiera en
Brasil. - 1983.
(001082)

EXTERNAL DEBT--CHILE.
----Chile : creative economic management. -
1987.
(001784)
----Debt equity swaps, investment, and
creditworthiness. - 1987.
(000259)

EXTERNAL DEBT--COTE D'IVOIRE.
----Comparative advantage as a development
model. - 1985.
(001691)

EXTERNAL DEBT--EASTERN EUROPE.
----Les mécanismes de l'endettement des pays
de l'Europe de l'Est envers les
économies de marché. - 1984.
(000221)

EXTERNAL DEBT--LATIN AMERICA.
----Crisis de endeudamiento y primeras
    redefiniciones respecto al tratamiento
    del capital extranjero en América
    Latina. - 1986.
    (000247)
----La crisis internacional y la América
    Latina. - 1984.
    (001245)
----The debt crisis and bank lending to
    subsidiaries of transnational
    corporations in Latin America. - 1984.
    (000219)
----Deuda externa, inversión extranjera y
    transferencia de tecnología en América
    Latina. - 1986.
    (001080)
----Las empresas transnacionales y la
    inversión extranjera directa en la
    primera mitad de los años ochenta. -
    1987.
    (000194)
----Foreign debt, direct investment, and
    economic development in the Andean Pact.
    - 1987.
    (001110)
----Foreign direct investment in Latin
    America. - 1986.
    (000190)
----The great continental divide : Asian and
    Latin American countries in the world
    economic crisis. - 1986.
    (001299)
----The international debt crisis and the
    banks. - 1985.
    (000227)
----Private investment in Latin America. -
    1984.
    (002460)
----El proceso de revisión de los mecanismos
    financieros de la ALADI. - 1983.
    (001248)
----Reaction to economic crisis: trade and
    finance of US firms operating in Latin
    America. - 1986.
    (000333)
----Transnacionalización y desarrollo
    nacional en América Latina. - 1984.
    (001117)
----Transnacionalización y periferia
    semindustrializada. - 1983.
    (001017)

EXTERNAL DEBT--MEXICO.
----La internacionalización financiera
    mexicana. - 1983.
    (001288)
----A note on the burden of the Mexican
    foreign debt. - 1986.
    (000254)

EXTERNAL DEBT--PERU.
----Transnational banks and the external
    finance of Latin America : the
    experience of Peru. - 1983.
    (000840)
----Transnational banks and the external
    finance of Latin America : the
    experience of Peru. - 1985.
    (000975)

EXTERNAL DEBT--POLAND.
----Handels- und Zahlungsprobleme in
    Osteuropa. - 1983.
    (000215)

EXTERNAL DEBT--SOUTH AFRICA.
----South Africa : economic responses to
    international pressures. - 1985.
    (001193)

EXTERNAL DEBT--UNITED STATES.
----The external deficit. - 1987.
    (000216)
----The international debt crisis and the
    banks. - 1985.
    (000227)

EXTERNAL DEBT--VENEZUELA.
----La internacionalización financiera en
    Venezuela. - 1983.
    (001286)

EXTERNAL DEBT--ZAMBIA.
----The mines, class power, and foreign
    policy in Zambia. - 1984.
    (001023)

EXTERRITORIALITY.
----The extraterritorial application of
    national laws. - 1987.
    (002348)
----Extraterritorial jurisdiction. - 1983.
    (002350) (002688)
----Extraterritoriality: current policy of
    the United States. - 1986.
    (002341)
----International business and national
    jurisdiction. - 1988.
    (002351)
----Treuepflicht im internationalen Konzern
    gegenüber Hoheitsakten im Heimatstaate
    der Muttergesellschaft. - 1983.
    (002343)

FACTOR ANALYSIS.
----Common mistakes of joint venture
    experienced firms. - 1987.
    (001604)
----The determinants of direct foreign
    investment in a small LDC. - 1985.
    (000556)
----EC trade effects and factor mobility. -
    1983.
    (001370)
----Measures of manifest conflict in
    international joint ventures. - 1987.
    (001583)

FACTOR ANALYSIS--GREECE.
----The determinants of foreign direct
    investment in the Greek economy. - 1984.
    (000548)

FACTOR ANALYSIS--INDONESIA.
----Factor proportions and productive
    efficiency of foreign owned firms in the
    Indonesian manufacturing sector. - 1984.
    (000655)

FACTOR ANALYSIS--UNITED STATES.
----Determinants of direct foreign
    investment. - 1987.
    (000534)

Subject Index - Index des matières

FACTORIES.
----Recent developments in operations and
behaviour of transnational corporations.
- 1987.
(000103)
----Where in the world should we put that
plant? - 1983.
(000553)
----Women in the global factory. - 1983.
(001898)

FACTORIES--INDIA.
----All-India directory of industrial
establishments. - 1984-   .
(002614)

FACTORY CONSTRUCTION.
----UNCITRAL, the United Nations Commission
on International Trade Law. - 1986.
(002155)

FAO.
----Microelectronics-based automation
technologies and development. - 1985.
(000753)

FARMERS ASSOCIATIONS--EUROPE.
----Directory of European industrial [and]
trade associations. - 1986-   .
(002707)

FEASIBILITY STUDIES.
----Creating the GM-Toyota joint venture: a
case in complex negotiation. - 1987.
(001656)

FEASIBILITY STUDIES--EGYPT.
----Operations of multinational corporations
and local enterprises in Arab countries.
- 1985.
(001141)

FEASIBILITY STUDIES--KUWAIT.
----Operations of multinational corporations
and local enterprises in Arab countries.
- 1985.
(001141)

FELLOWSHIPS.
----Technical co-operation programme of the
United Nations Centre on Transnational
Corporations. - 1988.
(002610)
----Technical co-operation programme,
1976-1987 : United Nations Centre on
Transnational Corporations. - 1988.
(002611)

FERTILIZER INDUSTRY.
----Fertilizer supplies for developing
countries : issues in the transfer and
development of technology. - 1985.
(001471)

FERTILIZERS.
----Fertilizer supplies for developing
countries : issues in the transfer and
development of technology. - 1985.
(001471)

FIBRE OPTICS--JAPAN.
----A competitive assessment of the U.S.
fiber optics industry. - 1984.
(000800)

FIBRE OPTICS--UNITED STATES.
----A competitive assessment of the U.S.
fiber optics industry. - 1984.
(000800)

FIBRE OPTICS--WESTERN EUROPE.
----A competitive assessment of the U.S.
fiber optics industry. - 1984.
(000800)

FIJI--CAPITAL MARKETS.
----Financial institutions and markets in
the Southwest Pacific. - 1985.
(000854)

FIJI--ECONOMIC CONDITIONS.
----Fiji : client State of Australasia? -
1984.
(001046) (002358)

FIJI--FINANCIAL INSTITUTIONS.
----Financial institutions and markets in
the Southwest Pacific. - 1985.
(000854)

FIJI--FOREIGN DIRECT INVESTMENT.
----Fiji : client State of Australasia? -
1984.
(001046) (002358)

FIJI--SCIENCE AND TECHNOLOGY POLICY.
----Proceedings of the SSTCC/UNCTC/ESCAP
Asia-Pacific Training Workshop on
Regulating and Negotiating Technology
Transfer through Transnational
Corporations, 14-25 October 1985,
Fuzhou, Fujian, China. - 1986.
(001405) (002169)

FIJI--TECHNOLOGY TRANSFER.
----Proceedings of the SSTCC/UNCTC/ESCAP
Asia-Pacific Training Workshop on
Regulating and Negotiating Technology
Transfer through Transnational
Corporations, 14-25 October 1985,
Fuzhou, Fujian, China. - 1986.
(001405) (002169)

FIJI--TRANSNATIONAL CORPORATIONS.
----Fiji : client State of Australasia? -
1984.
(001046) (002358)

FINANCE.
----Multinational business finance. - 1983.
(000403)
----Transnational corporations and uneven
development : the internationalization
of capital and the Third World. - 1987.
(001270)

FINANCE--GERMANY, FEDERAL REPUBLIC OF.
----Die finanzielle Führung und Kontrolle
von Auslandsgesellschaften. - 1983.
(000447)

FINANCE--MEXICO.
----Doing business in Mexico. - 1984.
(001791)
----La internacionalización financiera
mexicana. - 1983.
(001288)

FINANCE--NAMIBIA.
----Transnational corporations in South
    Africa and Namibia : United Nations
    public hearings. Volume 1, Reports of
    the Panel of Eminent Persons and of the
    Secretary-General. - 1986.
        (001216)

FINANCIAL ASSISTANCE.
----Issues in capital flows to developing
    countries. - 1987.
        (001276)
----Private co-financing. - 1983.
        (000257)
----Private direct investment, finance and
    development. - 1985.
        (001324)

FINANCIAL ASSISTANCE--UNITED STATES.
----The international debt crisis. - 1985.
        (000240)

FINANCIAL FLOWS.
----A closed circle for the developing
    countries? : debt and financial flows. -
    1986.
        (000218)
----La deuda de los países en desarrollo a
    mediados de los ochenta. - 1987.
        (000210)
----Endettement international et
    multinationalisation. - 1984.
        (000248)
----Financial and fiscal aspects of
    petroleum exploitation. - 1987.
        (002451)
----Financing and external debt of
    developing countries: ...survey. - 1986-
        (000231)
----Foreign direct investment, the service
    sector and international banking. - 1987.
        (000972)
----Globalisation of financial flows and
    trends in international capital market.
    - 1986.
        (001281)
----International capital markets :
    developments and prospects. - 1986.
        (001266)
----International capital movements and
    developing countries. - 1985.
        (001282)
----International financial relations as
    part of the world-system. - 1987.
        (001285)
----Private co-financing. - 1983.
        (000257)
----Putting world trade back on a growth
    course. - 1984.
        (001358)
----Revitalizing development, growth and
    international trade. - 1987.
        (001394)
----Trends and issues in foreign direct
    investment and related flows. - 1985.
        (000192)

FINANCIAL FLOWS--ASIA.
----The impact of foreign capital inflow on
    investment and economic growth in
    developing Asia. - 1985.
        (001048)

FINANCIAL FLOWS--ASIA AND THE PACIFIC.
----Transnational corporations and external
    financial flows of developing economies
    in Asia and the Pacific. - 1986.
        (000196)

FINANCIAL FLOWS--UNITED STATES.
----International finance and investment. -
    1985.
        (001249)

FINANCIAL INSTITUTIONS.
----Financial directories of the world. -
    1982-
        (002685)
----A GATT for international banking? - 1985.
        (002130)
----La structure financière du capitalisme
    multinational. - 1983.
        (001259)

FINANCIAL INSTITUTIONS--AFRICA.
----The role of transnational banks and
    financial institutions in Africa's
    development process. - 1986.
        (000935)

FINANCIAL INSTITUTIONS--ARAB COUNTRIES.
----The development of Arab international
    banking. - 1983.
        (000803)

FINANCIAL INSTITUTIONS--ASIA.
----Bankers handbook for Asia. - 1976-
        (002621)

FINANCIAL INSTITUTIONS--AUSTRALIA.
----Financial institutions and markets in
    the Southwest Pacific. - 1985.
        (000854)

FINANCIAL INSTITUTIONS--ECUADOR.
----La presencia de las empresas
    transnacionales en la economía
    ecuatoriana. - 1984.
        (001125)

FINANCIAL INSTITUTIONS--FIJI.
----Financial institutions and markets in
    the Southwest Pacific. - 1985.
        (000854)

FINANCIAL INSTITUTIONS--JAPAN.
----The European investments of Japanese
    financial institutions. - 1986.
        (000118)

FINANCIAL INSTITUTIONS--LIBERIA.
----The impact of the transnational
    corporations in the banking and other
    financial institutions on the economy of
    Liberia. - 1986.
        (000873)

FINANCIAL INSTITUTIONS--NEW ZEALAND.
----Financial institutions and markets in
    the Southwest Pacific. - 1985.
        (000854)

FINANCIAL INSTITUTIONS--PAPUA NEW GUINEA.
----Financial institutions and markets in
    the Southwest Pacific. - 1985.
        (000854)

FINANCIAL INSTITUTIONS--UNITED STATES.
----Banking deregulation and the new
competition in financial services. -
1984.
(000833)

FINANCIAL REGULATIONS.
----Changes in the international financial
market and implications for
transnational banks, transnational
corporations and developing countries. -
1986.
(000976)
----International financial reporting and
auditing. - 1984.
(002088)

FINANCIAL REGULATIONS--BURUNDI.
----Guide des investisseurs. - 1983-   .
(001805)

FINANCIAL STATEMENTS.
----Accounting analysis of the efficiency of
public enterprises. - 1984.
(002114)
----Advanced accounting. - 1988.
(002089)
----Availability of financial statements. -
1987.
(002100)
----Coping with worldwide accounting
changes. - 1984.
(002067)
----Foreign currency translation. - 1986.
(002102)
----Harmonization of accounting standards. -
1986.
(002082)
----Information disclosure and the
multinational corporation. - 1984.
(002078)
----International accounting and reporting
issues, 1985 review. - 1985.
(002116)
----International accounting and reporting
issues, 1986 review. - 1986.
(002117)
----Managerial accounting. - 1984.
(002093)
----The relationship between taxation and
financial reporting. - 1987.
(002103)
----Le risque de change et la consolidation
des comptes de groupes multinationaux. -
1983.
(002104)
----Statements of international accounting
standards. - 1985-   .
(002112)
----Working documents. - 1986-   .
(002123)
----Worldscope : industrial company
profiles. - 1987.
(000299)

FINANCIAL STATEMENTS--GERMANY, FEDERAL
REPUBLIC OF.
----Der konsolidierte Abschluss. - 1983.
(002091)

FINANCIAL STATEMENTS--INDIA.
----Compendium of statements and standards.
- 1986.
(002074)

FINANCIAL STATEMENTS--SOUTHEAST ASIA.
----Comparative accounting practices in
ASEAN. - 1984.
(002072)

FINANCIAL STATISTICS.
----Changes in the international financial
market and implications for
transnational banks, transnational
corporations and developing countries. -
1986.
(000976)
----Foreign direct investment, the service
sector and international banking. - 1987.
(000972)
----Transnational corporations in world
development. - 1983.
(000102)
----Trends and issues in foreign direct
investment and related flows. - 1985.
(000192)

FINANCIAL STATISTICS--AFRICA.
----The role of transnational banks and
financial institutions in Africa's
development process. - 1986.
(000935)

FINANCIAL STATISTICS--ARGENTINA.
----Las empresas transnacionales en la
Argentina. - 1986.
(001122)

FINANCIAL STATISTICS--ASIA AND THE PACIFIC.
----Transnational corporations and external
financial flows of developing economies
in Asia and the Pacific. - 1986.
(000196)

FINANCIAL STATISTICS--EGYPT.
----Egypt's experience in regulating
technology imports. - 1987.
(001514)

FINANCIAL STATISTICS--INDIA.
----Top hundred engineering companies. -
197?-   .
(002669)

FINANCIAL STATISTICS--LATIN AMERICA.
----Banco de datos sobre inversión
extranjera directa en América Latina y
el Caribe : información de los países
receptores y de organismos regionales y
subregionales, t. 2. - 1987.
(000193)
----Banco de datos sobre inversión
extranjera directa en América Latina y
el Caribe, sobre la base de información
de organismos multilaterales y de
gobiernos de países de origen de la
inversión, t. 1. - 1986.
(000195)

FINANCIAL STATISTICS--LIBERIA.
----The impact of the transnational
corporations in the banking and other
financial institutions on the economy of
Liberia. - 1986.
(000873)

FINANCIAL STATISTICS--MOROCCO.
----Expérience marocaine dans
l'établissement d'entreprises
multinationales. - 1986.
(001027)

FINANCIAL STATISTICS--OMAN.
----Impact of the operations of
transnational corporations on
development in the Sultanate of Oman. -
1988.
(001144)

FINANCIAL STATISTICS--WESTERN ASIA.
----Trade in services : growth and balance
of payments implications for countries
of Western Asia. - 1987.
(000968)

FINANCING.
----International financing of investments
in tourism. - 1983.
(000822)
----Technical co-operation programme of the
United Nations Centre on Transnational
Corporations. - 1988.
(002610)

FINANCING--AFRICA.
----Nezavisimye strany Afriki. - 1986.
(001280)

FINANCING--EUROPE.
----Market share strategy in Europe. - 1985.
(000493)

FINANCING--UNITED STATES.
----Corporate capital structures in the
United States. - 1985.
(000315)

FINLAND--MANAGEMENT.
----Creating a world enterprise. - 1983.
(000398)

FINLAND--TRANSNATIONAL CORPORATIONS.
----Creating a world enterprise. - 1983.
(000398)
----Foretagens internationalisering. - 1986.
(000057)

FISCAL POLICY.
----Contract efficiency and natural resource
investment in developing countries. -
1984.
(002409)
----Fiscal incentives and direct foreign
investment in less developed countries.
- 1983.
(002312)
----Fiscal policies, current accounts and
real exchange rates : in search of a
logic of international policy
coordination. - 1986.
(001244)
----Is employment policy a thing of the
past? - 1983.
(001889)

FISCAL POLICY--LATIN AMERICA.
----El proceso de revisión de los mecanismos
financieros de la ALADI. - 1983.
(001248)

FISCAL POLICY--SENEGAL.
----Réflexions sur les régimes fiscaux
privilégiés du code des investissements
au Gabon. - 1985.
(002243)

FISCAL POLICY--WESTERN EUROPE.
----Mélanges 2 : harmonisation fiscale,
marché commun des services, perspectives
budgétaires 1988, fonds structurels. -
1987.
(000897)

FISHERIES--SOUTHEAST ASIA.
----Joint fishing ventures. - 1983.
(000570)

FISHERY EXPLOITATION--CANADA.
----U.S. fishery negotiations with Canada
and Mexico. - 1985.
(002462)

FISHERY EXPLOITATION--MEXICO.
----U.S. fishery negotiations with Canada
and Mexico. - 1985.
(002462)

FISHERY EXPLOITATION--UNITED STATES.
----U.S. fishery negotiations with Canada
and Mexico. - 1985.
(002462)

FISHERY MANAGEMENT--SOUTHEAST ASIA.
----Joint fishing ventures. - 1983.
(000570)

FISHING--NAMIBIA.
----Transnational corporations in South
Africa and Namibia : United Nations
public hearings. Volume 1, Reports of
the Panel of Eminent Persons and of the
Secretary-General. - 1986.
(001216)

FLEXIBLE MANUFACTURING SYSTEMS.
----Microelectronics-based automation
technologies and development. - 1985.
(000753)

FLEXIBLE MANUFACTURING SYSTEMS--JAPAN.
----Postindustrial manufacturing. - 1986.
(000698)

FLEXIBLE MANUFACTURING SYSTEMS--UNITED
STATES.
----A competitive assessment of the U.S.
flexible manufacturing systems industry.
- 1985.
(000763)
----Postindustrial manufacturing. - 1986.
(000698)

FOOD.
----Third World resource directory. - 1984.
(002719)

FOOD--MOROCCO.
----Marketing supplementary food products in
LDCs. - 1983.
(000665)

FOOD CONSUMPTION--CHINA.
----Agriculture in China. - 1985.
(000561)

FOOD INDUSTRY.
----Analyse de l'activité de 95 firmes
    industrielles étrangères dans la
    bio-industrie. - 1983.
    (000652)
----Industry in the 1980s. - 1985.
    (001341)
----Profitability of mergers in food
    manufacturing. - 1986.
    (001584)
----Rol'mezhdunarodnykh monopolii v
    prodovol'stvennoi sisteme. - 1985.
    (000728)
----Transnational corporations in world
    development. - 1983.
    (000102)

FOOD INDUSTRY--AFRICA.
----Agribusiness in Africa. - 1984.
    (001025)

FOOD INDUSTRY--FRANCE.
----L'internationalisation de l'agriculture
    francaise. - 1984.
    (000567)

FOOD INDUSTRY--INDONESIA.
----Technology transfer under alternative
    arrangements with transnational
    corporations. - 1987.
    (001513)

FOOD INDUSTRY--LATIN AMERICA.
----L'émpire Nestle. - 1983.
    (000283)

FOOD INDUSTRY--SWEDEN.
----De Transnationella foretagens roll i
    varldshandeln ; Gransskydd i andra
    lander. - 1984.
    (000685)

FOOD INDUSTRY--SWITZERLAND.
----L'émpire Nestle. - 1983.
    (000283)
----Halbgotter, Giftkriege und Kondensmilch.
    - 1983.
    (000658)

FOOD INDUSTRY--THAILAND.
----Technology acquisition under alternative
    arrangements with transnational
    corporations. - 1987.
    (001512)

FOOD INDUSTRY--UNITED STATES.
----Determinants of foreign direct
    investment by food and tobacco
    manufacturers. - 1983.
    (000527)
----Foreign direct investment in U.S. food
    and tobacco manufacturing and domestic
    economic performance. - 1983.
    (000170)
----Increased foreign investment in U.S.
    food industries. - 1985.
    (000714)
----Où va l'investissement direct
    international? USA/monde : le cas du
    secteur alimentaire. - 1984.
    (000666)

FOOD PROCESSING.
----Food-processing contracts with
    developing countries. - 1985.
    (002419)

FOOD PRODUCTION.
----Profitability of mergers in food
    manufacturing. - 1986.
    (001584)
----Tobacco and food crops production in the
    Third World. - 1983.
    (000572)
----Transferring food production technology
    to developing nations. - 1983.
    (001508)
----Transnational corporations in the
    agricultural machinery and equipment
    industry. - 1983.
    (000746)

FOOD PRODUCTION--FRANCE.
----Le role des grandes entreprises
    diversifiées du pétrole et de la chimie
    dans la production alimentaire. - 1985.
    (000699)

FOOD PRODUCTION--UNITED STATES.
----Le role des grandes entreprises
    diversifiées du pétrole et de la chimie
    dans la production alimentaire. - 1985.
    (000699)

FOOD SUPPLY.
----Rol'mezhdunarodnykh monopolii v
    prodovol'stvennoi sisteme. - 1985.
    (000728)

FOREIGN CORRUPT PRACTICES ACT 1977 (UNITED
STATES).
----Reviewing the situation : what is to be
    done with the Foreign Corrupt Practices
    Act? - 1987.
    (002235)

FOREIGN DIRECT INVESTMENT.
----Analyzing political risk. - 1986.
    (001850)
----An appraisal of different theoretical
    approaches and models of foreign direct
    investment and international trade. -
    1987.
    (000060)
----Appraising corporate investment policy:
    a financial center theory of foreign
    direct investment. - 1983.
    (000084)
----Aspecte juridice ale investitiilor
    straine directe in tarile in curs de
    dezvoltare. - 1987.
    (002245)
----Aspects des réglementations nationales
    de certains pays en voie de
    développement concernant le régime des
    investissements étrangers directs. -
    1987.
    (002248)
----Auditing non-U.S. operations. - 1984.
    (002113)
----Balance of payments statistics. - 1983.
    (000111)

FOREIGN DIRECT INVESTMENT (continued)

----Banco de datos sobre inversión
extranjera directa en América Latina y
el Caribe, sobre la base de información
de organismos multilaterales y de
gobiernos de países de origen de la
inversión, t. 1. - 1986.
(000195)

----Bilateral investment treaties. - 1988.
(002054)

----Choosing between direct investment and
licensing. - 1984.
(001418)

----Circuits des capitaux, balances
extérieures et flux majeurs
d'investissement.= Capital circuits,
foreign balances and major flows of
investment). - 1985.
(001308)

----Compensation or opportunity? - 1986.
(001293)

----The contribution of foreign direct
investment to exports : an empirical
study of 23 LDCs. - 1986.
(001376)

----Controls and impediments affecting
inward direct investment in OECD member
countries. - 1987.
(000122) (002193)

----The determinants of direct foreign
investment in a small LDC. - 1985.
(000556)

----Dette du Tiers-Monde. - 1987.
(000224)

----Developing with foreign investment. -
1987.
(000998)

----Direct foreign investment. - 1987.
(000178) (000549)

----Diversification strategy and choice
of country: diversifying acquisitions
abroad by U.S. multinationals,
1978-1980. - 1985.
(000536)

----Economic and political determinants of
foreign direct investment. - 1985.
(000551)

----Effets de la mobilité internationale du
capital sur les pays membres d'une union
douanière. - 1987.
(001250)

----Les entreprises à participation
étrangère installées dans les pays
socialistes. - 1987.
(001183)

----Environmental aspects of the activities
of transnational corporations. - 1985.
(001954)

----Establishing overseas operations: tax
and treasury considerations. - 1987.
(001768)

----Factors influencing the flow of foreign
investment and the relevance of a
multilateral investment guarantee
scheme. - 1987.
(002144)

----Les firmes multinationales. - 1985.
(000070)

----Fiscal incentives and direct foreign
investment in less developed countries.
- 1983.
(002312)

----Foreign direct investment with
unemployment and endogenous taxes and
tariffs. - 1987.
(000559)

----Foreign and domestic divestment and
investment decisions: like or unlike? -
1983.
(000523)

----Foreign direct divestment theory: is it
the reverse of FDI theory? - 1983.
(001546)

----Foreign direct investment and the debt
crisis. - 1986.
(000246)

----Foreign direct investment and the
multinational enterprise. - 1988.
(002696)

----Foreign direct investment as a
sequential process. - 1983.
(000052)

----Foreign direct investment in developing
countries. - 1985.
(000137)

----Foreign direct investment in the
People's Republic of China. - 1988.
(000191)

----Foreign direct investment, the service
sector and international banking. - 1987.
(000972)

----Foreign direct investment 1973-87. -
1984.
(000133)

----Foreign exchange risk and direct foreign
investment. - 1983.
(001852)

----The foreign investment activity of the
Comecon countries. - 1983.
(000355)

----Foreign investment in mining projects. -
1983.
(000619)

----Foreign investment in the present and a
new international economic order. - 1988.
(001247)

----Foreign ownership: when hosts change the
rules. - 1985.
(001798)

----Foreign policy objectives and the
extraterritorial application of law. -
1983.
(002346)

----Funding direct investment through
cofinancing: the commercial banker's
view. - 1986.
(001265)

----Governments and multinationals. - 1983.
(002267)

----Guidelines for international investment.
- 1974.
(001980)

----How to analyze foreign investment
climates. - 1983.
(001856)

----The impact of direct foreign investment
upon developing countries : a case study
of Yugoslavia. - 1986.
(001174)

----The importance of direct investment for
developing countries. - 1986.
(000142)

Subject Index - Index des matières

FOREIGN DIRECT INVESTMENT (continued)
----Incentives and disincentives for foreign
    direct investment in less developed
    countries. - 1984.
    (002301)
----The influence of Hymer's dissertation on
    the theory of foreign direct investment.
    - 1985.
    (000024)
----International business. - 1986.
    (000469)
----International business: an alternative
    view. - 1986.
    (001559)
----International business and the national
    interest. - 1986.
    (001817)
----International business, the recession
    and economic restructuring. - 1985.
    (000025)
----International capital movements. - 1984.
    (001224)
----International corporate linkages. - 1987.
    (002430)
----International financing of investments
    in tourism. - 1983.
    (000822)
----International flows of technology. -
    1986.
    (001517)
----International investment disputes. -
    1985.
    (002524)
----International protection of direct
    foreign investments in the Third World.
    - 1987.
    (002124)
----Internationale Direktinvestitionen,
    1950-1973. - 1975-   .
    (000156)
----Intra-firm service trade by the
    multinational enterprise. - 1987.
    (000902)
----Intra-industry foreign direct
    investment. - 1984.
    (001375)
----Intra-industry production as a form of
    international economic involvement. -
    1983.
    (000026)
----Intra-LDCs foreign direct investment: a
    comparative analysis of Third World
    multinationals. - 1985.
    (000303)
----Investing in developing countries. -
    1970-   .
    (001985)
----Investing in development. - 1986.
    (000149)
----Investing in free export processing
    zones. - 1984.
    (002362)
----Investir dans les zones franches
    industrielles d'exportation. - 1984.
    (002363)
----L'investissement direct et la firme
    multinationale. - 1984.
    (000140)
----Les investissements des multinationales
    de l'automobile dans le Tiers-Monde.
    (With English summary.). - 1984.
    (000729)

----Investissements directs, coopération
    internationale et firmes
    multinationales. - 1984.
    (000045)
----Investissements internationaux et
    dynamique des avantages comparatifs des
    nouveaux pays industrialises. - 1984.
    (000496)
----Investment in the United States by
    foreign government: effects of the Tax
    Reform Act of 1986. - 1987.
    (002231)
----Investment and the international
    monetary and financial environment. -
    1983.
    (001274)
----The investment development cycle and
    Third World multinationals. - 1986.
    (000529)
----The investment development cycle
    revisited. - 1986.
    (000320)
----Investment incentives and disincentives
    and the international investment
    process. - 1983.
    (002309)
----Investment penetration in manufacturing
    and extraction and external public debt
    in Third World states. - 1984.
    (001015)
----Investment-related trade distortions in
    petrochemicals. - 1983.
    (000595)
----Inwestycje zagraniczne a transfer wiedzy
    technicznej do krajów rozwijajacych sie.
    - 1984.
    (001476)
----Licensing versus direct investment: a
    model of internationalization by the
    multinational enterprise. - 1987.
    (001443)
----A mean-variance model of MNF location
    strategy. - 1985.
    (000535)
----Measures strengthening the negotiating
    capacity of Governments in their
    relations with transnational
    corporations. - 1983.
    (002461)
----Micro- and macro-economic models of
    direct foreign investment: toward a
    synthesis. - 1984.
    (000053)
----MIGA and foreign investment. - 1988.
    (002145)
----MNCs and the Iranian revolution: an
    empirical study. - 1985.
    (001772)
----The Multilateral Investment Guarantee
    Agency. - 1986.
    (002146)
----Multilateral investment insurance and
    private investment in the Third World. -
    1984.
    (002131)
----Multilateral investment insurance and
    private investment in the Third World. -
    1987.
    (002132)
----The multinational corporation in the
    1980s. - 1983.
    (000051)

FOREIGN DIRECT INVESTMENT (continued)
----Multinational corporations : the
  political economy of foreign direct
  investment. - 1985.
    (000072)
----Multinational corporations, OPEC, .
  cartels, foreign investment, and
  technology transfer special studies,
  1982-1985. - 1987.
    (000589)
----Multinational enterprise, internal
  governance, and industrial organization.
  - 1985.
    (000096)
----Multinational enterprises, economic
  structure and international
  competitiveness. - 1985.
    (000075)
----Multinational excursions. - 1984.
    (000543)
----A multinational firm. - 1986.
    (000031)
----Multinational production: effect on
  brand value. - 1986.
    (000540)
----Multinationals are mushrooming. - 1986.
    (001861)
----Multinationals as mutual invaders. -
  1985.
    (000077)
----National treatment for
  foreign-controlled enterprises. - 1985.
    (002258)
----National treatment for
  foreign-controlled enterprises. - 1985.
    (002004)
----A negotiating strategy for trade in
  services. - 1983.
    (000865)
----Neokolonializm. - 1984.
    (000996)
----New theories of the multinational
  enterprise: an assessment of
  internalization theory. - 1986.
    (000089)
----New forms of international investment in
  developing countries. - 1984.
    (001615)
----Nihon shihon shugi no kaigai shinshutsu.
  - 1984.
    (000235)
----Les nouvelles formes d'investissement
  dans les pays on développement. - 1984.
    (001620)
----Les nouvelles formes d'investissement
  international dans les pays en
  développement. - 1984.
    (000165)
----Les nouvelles formes d'investissement
  (NFI): définition, contraintes et
  perspectives. (With English summary.). -
  1985.
    (001539)
----On new trends in internationalization: a
  synthesis toward a general model. - 1985.
    (000081)
----Ownership and development. - 1987.
    (001129)
----Political dynamics of direct foreign
  investment. - 1985.
    (001853)

----Political events and the foreign direct
  investment decision: an empirical
  examination. - 1986.
    (001836)
----Pourquoi les multinationales? : une
  revue de la littérature sur les
  motivations de la croissance
  multinationale des firmes. - 1987.
    (000020)
----Private direct investment, finance and
  development. - 1985.
    (001324)
----Privatization and public enterprise. -
  1988.
    (001588)
----Proceedings of the SSTCC/UNCTC/ESCAP
  Asia-Pacific Training Workshop on
  Regulating and Negotiating Technology
  Transfer through Transnational
  Corporations, 14-25 October 1985,
  Fuzhou, Fujian, China. - 1986.
    (001405) (002169)
----Production and trade in services. - 1985.
    (000978)
----Production cost differentials and
  foreign direct investment: a test of two
  models. - 1986.
    (000061)
----Promotion of direct investment in
  developing countries. - 1986.
    (002143)
----Promotion of foreign direct investment
  to developing countries: an exercise in
  cooperation. - 1986.
    (002035)
----Promotion of foreign direct investment
  to developing countries: opening
  address. - 1986.
    (002050)
----Recent trends in international direct
  investment. - 1987.
    (000176)
----Il ruolo del finanziamento estero nello
  sviluppo economico e la problematica
  attuale dell'indebitamento. - 1983.
    (001289)
----Salient features and trends in foreign
  direct investment. - 1983.
    (000182)
----Second thoughts on MIGA. - 1986.
    (002148)
----Services and the development process. -
  1985.
    (000979)
----Shaping a future for foreign direct
  investment in the Third World. - 1988.
    (002140)
----Some evidences between foreign direct
  investments and foreign exchange rates:
  a preliminary note. - 1983.
    (000147)
----Sovereignty en garde. - 1985.
    (002469)
----Spotlight on international business: the
  Forbes foreign rankings. - 1986.
    (002665)
----Staatsmonopolistische Regulierung in der
  kapitalistischen Weltwirtschaft. - 1984.
    (001263)
----Strukturveränderungen der
  internationalen Direktinvestitionen und
  inländischer Arbeitsmarkt. - 1983.
    (001913)

FOREIGN DIRECT INVESTMENT (continued)
----Taxation of foreign income - principles
     and practice. - 1985.
       (001764)
----Testing the bargaining hypothesis in the
     manufacturing sector in developing
     countries. - 1987.
       (000706)
----Theories of foreign direct investment
     and divestment: a classificatory note. -
     1985.
       (000558)
----A theory of expropriation and deviations
     from perfect capital mobility. - 1984.
       (001571)
----The theory of international production.
     - 1985.
       (000028)
----Trade in data services. - 1986.
       (000949)
----Trade in services and the multilateral
     trade negotiations. - 1987.
       (000812)
----Trade-related investment issues. - 1983.
       (001385)
----Transnacionalización y periferia
     semindustrializada. - 1984-   .
       (001339)
----Transnational corporations and
     technology transfer. - 1987.
       (001509)
----Transnational corporations in world
     development. - 1988.
       (000101)
----Transnational corporations in world
     development. - 1983.
       (000102)
----Transnatsional'nye korporatsii na
     rynkakh razvivaiushchikhsia stran. -
     1985.
       (001660)
----Trends and issues in foreign direct
     investment and related flows. - 1985.
       (000192)
----Trends in the internationalisation of
     production. - 1986.
       (002597)
----Vneshneekonomicheskaia ekspansiia
     imperialisticheskikh stran. - 1984.
       (002680)
----The volatility of offshore investment. -
     1984.
       (001799)
----Vyvoz kapitala v 80-e gody. - 1986.
       (002697)
----The welfare effects of foreign
     enterprise. - 1986.
       (000016)
----The welfare impact of foreign investment
     in the presence of specific factors and
     non-traded goods. - 1987.
       (001340)
----Wisselkoersinstabiliteit en
     schuldproblematiek. - 1984.
       (001310)
----Wohin expandieren multinationale
     Konzerne? - 1985.
       (000063)
----The World Bank's Multilateral Investment
     Guaranty Agency. - 1987.
       (002125)
----The world's new property barons. - 1987.
       (000904)

----The 1984 review of the 1976 declaration
     and decisions. - 1984.
       (002001)

FOREIGN DIRECT INVESTMENT--AFRICA.
----Investment in ACP states. - 1987.
       (001004)

FOREIGN DIRECT INVESTMENT--ANDEAN REGION.
----The Andean foreign investment code's
     impact on multinational enterprises. -
     1983.
       (001977)
----Empresas multinacionales y Pacto andino.
     - 1983.
       (001102)
----Legislación de inversiones extranjeras y
     Pacto Andino. - 1984.
       (002234)

FOREIGN DIRECT INVESTMENT--ARGENTINA.
----Las empresas transnacionales en la
     Argentina. - 1986.
       (001122)
----Las empresas transnacionales y la
     inversión extranjera directa en la
     primera mitad de los años ochenta. -
     1987.
       (000194)

FOREIGN DIRECT INVESTMENT--ASIA.
----The allocation of Japanese direct
     foreign investment and its evolution in
     Asia. - 1985.
       (000153)
----Effects of foreign capital inflows on
     developing countries of Asia. - 1986.
       (001059)
----Foreign trade and investment. - 1985.
       (001047)
----Japanese and American direct investment
     in Asia. - 1985.
       (000154)

FOREIGN DIRECT INVESTMENT--ASIA AND THE
PACIFIC.
----Foreign direct investment and economic
     growth in the Asian and Pacific region.
     - 1987.
       (000175)
----Technology transfer under alternative
     arrangements with transnational
     corporations. - 1987.
       (001513)
----Transnational corporations and external
     financial flows of developing economies
     in Asia and the Pacific. - 1986.
       (000196)

FOREIGN DIRECT INVESTMENT--AUSTRALIA.
----Australia deregulated : new freedoms for
     multinational investment. - 1987.
       (001797)
----Australian direct investment abroad. -
     1984.
       (000108)
----Australian direct investment in New
     Zealand. - 1983.
       (000109)
----Australian direct investment in the
     ASEAN countries. - 1983.
       (000110)

FOREIGN DIRECT INVESTMENT--AUSTRALIA
(continued)
----The Australian multinational -- parent
   and subsidiary relationships. - 1986.
   (000390)
----Capital xenophobia. - 1984.
   (002228)
----Fiji : client State of Australasia? -
   1984.
   (001046) (002358)
----Foreign investment control in the mining
   sector. - 1983.
   (000577)
----Foreign investment in Australia,
   1960-1981. - 1983.
   (000141)
----Foreign investment law in Australia. -
   1985.
   (002210)
----New Zealand business. - 1985.
   (000352)
----Some aspects of Japanese manufacturing
   investment in Australia. - 1984.
   (001044)

FOREIGN DIRECT INVESTMENT--BELGIUM.
----Recent trends in foreign direct
   investment and disinvestment in Belgium.
   - 1985.
   (000185)

FOREIGN DIRECT INVESTMENT--BRAZIL.
----Las empresas transnacionales y la
   inversión extranjera directa en la
   primera mitad de los años ochenta. -
   1987.
   (000194)
----Investimentos estrangeiros no Brasil. -
   1985.
   (000177)
----New forms of overseas investment by
   developing countries : the case of
   India, Korea and Brazil. - 1986.
   (001616)
----Regulation of foreign investment in
   Brazil. - 1983.
   (002266)

FOREIGN DIRECT INVESTMENT--BRITISH COLUMBIA
(CANADA).
----Foreign investment in the American and
   Canadian West, 1870-1914. - 1986.
   (002690)

FOREIGN DIRECT INVESTMENT--BURUNDI.
----Manuel de procedures contractuelles
   susceptibles d'être mise en oeuvre par
   les contrats internationaux concernant
   la realisation de projets industriels. -
   1984.
   (002417)

FOREIGN DIRECT INVESTMENT--CAMEROON.
----L'investissement dans les pays en
   développement. - 1985.
   (000135)

FOREIGN DIRECT INVESTMENT--CANADA.
----Advising nonresidents on taking care of
   Canadian business. - 1986.
   (001789)
----Beyond borders. - 1986.
   (000280)

----Canada in the USA : foreign direct
   investment flows reversed. - 1987.
   (000180)
----Canada's reversal from importer to
   exporter of foreign direct investment. -
   1987.
   (000181)
----Foreign direct investment. - 1985.
   (001160)
----Foreign investment control in the mining
   sector. - 1983.
   (000577)
----Foreign investment in South Africa and
   Namibia. - 1984.
   (001198) (002641)
----Foreign investment law in Canada. - 1983.
   (002222)
----Operating foreign subsidiaries. - 1983.
   (000388)
----Regulation of foreign direct investment
   in Canada and the United States. - 1983.
   (002263)
----Taxation in Canada. - 1985.
   (001701)
----Taxation of income of foreign
   affiliates. - 1983.
   (001765)
----U.S. and Canadian investment in South
   Africa and Namibia. - 1986.
   (001212) (002671) (002672)

FOREIGN DIRECT INVESTMENT--CARIBBEAN REGION.
----Las empresas transnacionales y la
   inversión extranjera directa en la
   primera mitad de los años ochenta. -
   1987.
   (000194)
----Investment in ACP states. - 1987.
   (001004)

FOREIGN DIRECT INVESTMENT--CHILE.
----Aspectos relevantes de la inversión
   extranjera en Chile. - 1984.
   (002171)
----Chile : creative economic management. -
   1987.
   (001784)
----Las empresas transnacionales y la
   inversión extranjera directa en la
   primera mitad de los años ochenta. -
   1987.
   (000194)

FOREIGN DIRECT INVESTMENT--CHINA.
----China's open door policy. - 1984.
   (002219)
----China's open door policy and the
   prospects for FDI. - 1986.
   (001043)
----China's special economic zones. - 1986.
   (002382)
----Chung-kuo tui wai shui wu shou ts'e. -
   1983.
   (001704)
----Eight years of the open policy. - 1987.
   (001051)
----Foreign direct investment in the
   People's Republic of China. - 1988.
   (000191)

FOREIGN DIRECT INVESTMENT--CHINA (continued)
----Foreign investment and trade; origins of
    the modernization policy. - 1983.
      (001354)
----Guide to China's foreign economic
    relations and trade. - 1983.
      (001806)
----Insuring investment projects. - 1988.
      (002033)
----Les investissements directs des Chinois
    d'outre-mer en Chine. - 1987.
      (000201)
----A külföldi tokebefektetések néhány
    tapasztalata Kínában. - 1987.
      (001049)
----Legal aspects of joint ventures in
    China. - 1986.
      (002178)
----Like bamboo shoots after a rain :
    exploiting the Chinese law and new
    regulations on Sino-foreign joint
    ventures. - 1987.
      (002298)
----The new legal framework for joint
    ventures in China. - 1984.
      (002282)
----On economic reforms, trade and foreign
    investment in China. - 1986.
      (001336)
----On the issue of utilizing foreign
    capital. - 1985.
      (002207)
----The open policy at work. - 1985.
      (001072)
----Ouverture et dynamique interne du
    capital en Chine. - 1987.
      (001064)
----Partnership with China. - 1986.
      (001035)
----The present situation and problems of
    direct investment in China. - 1986.
      (000163)
----Singapore's role in China's offshore oil
    venture. - 1985.
      (000608)
----Special economic zones in the People's
    Republic of China. - 1986.
      (002361)
----Strategies for joint ventures in the
    People's Republic of China. - 1987.
      (001610)

FOREIGN DIRECT INVESTMENT--COLOMBIA.
----Empresas multinacionales y Pacto andino.
    - 1983.
      (001102)
----Las empresas transnacionales en el
    desarrollo colombiano. - 1986.
      (001121)
----Las empresas transnacionales y la
    inversión extranjera directa en la
    primera mitad de los años ochenta. -
    1987.
      (000194)
----Evolución contradictoria de la industria
    en Colombia. - 1984.
      (001095)
----The subsidiary role of direct foreign
    investment in industrialization: the
    Colombian manufacturing sector. - 1985.
      (001106)

FOREIGN DIRECT INVESTMENT--CONGO.
----Le transfert de technologie dans les
    industries agro-alimentaires en Afrique
    Centrale. - 1987.
      (001510)

FOREIGN DIRECT INVESTMENT--EAST ASIA.
----Die Direktinvestitionen der japanischen
    Wirtschaft in den Schwellenländern Ost-
    Südostasiens. - 1984.
      (000157)
----The role of direct foreign investment in
    developing East Asian countries. - 1985.
      (001052)

FOREIGN DIRECT INVESTMENT--EASTERN EUROPE.
----Equity cooperation ventures (ECV)
    domiciled in the socialist countries :
    trends and patterns. - 1986.
      (001603)
----Un exemple d'investissement du CAEM :
    liste des sociétés mixtes établies dans
    les pays en développement. - 1987.
      (000284)
----Joint-ventures in Eastern Europe. - 1984.
      (001173)
----Western direct investment in centrally
    planned economies. - 1986.
      (000159)

FOREIGN DIRECT INVESTMENT--EGYPT.
----Determinants of foreign direct
    investment in developing countries. -
    1986.
      (000531)
----Egypt's experience in regulating
    technology imports. - 1987.
      (001514)

FOREIGN DIRECT INVESTMENT--EUROPE.
----Becoming a triad power: the new global
    corporation. - 1986.
      (000500)
----Direct investment by Sogo-Shosha in
    Europe. - 1983.
      (000310)
----The relationship between foreign
    ownership and technology transfer. -
    1983.
      (001422)

FOREIGN DIRECT INVESTMENT--FIJI.
----Fiji : client State of Australasia? -
    1984.
      (001046) (002358)

FOREIGN DIRECT INVESTMENT--FRANCE.
----Les flux d'investissement direct entre
    la France et l'extérieur, 1965-1978. -
    1981.
      (000119)
----French multinationals. - 1984.
      (000375)
----L'impact de l'investissement étranger en
    France sur l'emploi industriel
    (1974-1983). (With English summary.). -
    1984.
      (001161)
----Investissements directs et flux
    commerciaux compléments ou substituts?
    Le cas francais 1968-1978. (With English
    summary.). - 1985.
      (000107)

FOREIGN DIRECT INVESTMENT--GERMANY, FEDERAL REPUBLIC OF.
----Auslandsinvestitionen deutscher Unternehmen in Entwicklungsländern. - 1984.
(000167)
----Direktinvestitionen in Entwicklungsländern. - 1983.
(000125)
----DM-Investitionen in Südafrika. - 1983.
(001197)
----Las empresas transnacionales y la inversión extranjera directa en la primera mitad de los años ochenta. - 1987.
(000194)
----Die finanzielle Führung und Kontrolle von Auslandsgesellschaften. - 1983.
(000447)
----International trade and foreign direct investment in West German manufacturing industries. - 1984.
(000771)
----Neue Wachstumsmärkte in Fernost. - 1983.
(001800)
----New trends in internationalization: processes and theories. Diversified patterns of multinational enterprise and old and new forms of foreign involvement of the firm. - 1983.
(000068)
----Strukturveränderungen der internationalen Direktinvestitionen und inländischer Arbeitsmarkt. - 1983.
(001913)
----Trends and issues in foreign direct investment and related flows. - 1985.
(000192)
----West Germany: expanding where the markets are. - 1987.
(000136)

FOREIGN DIRECT INVESTMENT--GHANA.
----The capital intensity of foreign, private local and state owned firms in a less developed country: Ghana. - 1986.
(001018)
----Ghana's new Investment Code. - 1985.
(002213)

FOREIGN DIRECT INVESTMENT--GREECE.
----The determinants of foreign direct investment in the Greek economy. - 1984.
(000548)
----Investment legislation in Greece, Portugal and Spain: the background to foreign investment in Mediterranean Europe. - 1983.
(002168)

FOREIGN DIRECT INVESTMENT--HONG KONG.
----Les investissements directs des Chinois d'outre-mer en Chine. - 1987.
(000201)
----Multinational corporations, technology and employment. - 1983.
(001891)
----The real threat from Asia. - 1987.
(001055)

FOREIGN DIRECT INVESTMENT--HUNGARY.
----A muködo toke becsalogatása Magyarországra : nyugati szemszögbol. - 1987.
(001608)
----Egy vegyesvállalat története az alapitástól a Kezdeti sikerekig : esettanulmány a Sancella Hungary Kft-röl. - 1987.
(001191)

FOREIGN DIRECT INVESTMENT--INDIA.
----Foreign direct investment in manufacturing from an LDC: India. - 1985.
(000317)
----Industrial distribution of Indian exports and joint ventures abroad. - 1985.
(000316)
----Multinationals from the Third World. - 1986.
(000345)
----Multinationals in Indian big business. - 1983.
(001057)
----Multinationals in Indian big business: industrial characteristics of foreign investments in a heavily regulated economy. - 1983.
(001058)
----New forms of overseas investment by developing countries : the case of India, Korea and Brazil. - 1986.
(001616)
----Pros and cons of Third World multinationals. - 1985.
(000304)
----Taxation of foreign companies. - 1984.
(001717)

FOREIGN DIRECT INVESTMENT--INDONESIA.
----Foreign investment and government policy in the Third World. - 1988.
(001790)
----Foreign investment and industrialization in Indonesia. - 1988.
(001053)
----Japanese direct investment in ASEAN. - 1983.
(000171)
----Japanese direct investment in Indonesian manufacturing. - 1984.
(000187)
----Japanese investment in Indonesia: problems and prospects. - 1986.
(000152)
----MNCs and the host country, the Indonesian case. - 1984.
(001073)

FOREIGN DIRECT INVESTMENT--IRELAND.
----Foreign investment in the Republic of Ireland. - 1987.
(000129)
----Input-output linkages and foreign direct investment in Ireland. - 1984.
(001158)
----Multinational investment strategies in the British Isles. - 1983.
(001151)

FOREIGN DIRECT INVESTMENT--ITALY.
----Existing opportunities and prospects for
    investment in Southern Italy. - 1984.
        (001830)

FOREIGN DIRECT INVESTMENT--JAMAICA.
----La Jamaïque, ou le dilemme politique
    d'un petit pays déshérité. - 1984.
        (001819)

FOREIGN DIRECT INVESTMENT--JAPAN.
----The Rising Sun in America (Part Two)
    -- Japanese management in the United
    States. - 1986.
        (000391)
----The allocation of Japanese direct
    foreign investment and its evolution in
    Asia. - 1985.
        (000153)
----America's new no. 4 automaker -- Honda.
    - 1985.
        (000294)
----Becoming a triad power: the new global
    corporation. - 1986.
        (000500)
----Direct investment by Sogo-Shosha in
    Europe. - 1983.
        (000310)
----Die Direktinvestitionen der japanischen
    Wirtschaft in den Schwellenländern Ost-
    Südostasiens. - 1984.
        (000157)
----Las empresas transnacionales y la
    inversión extranjera directa en la
    primera mitad de los años ochenta. -
    1987.
        (000194)
----The European investments of Japanese
    financial institutions. - 1986.
        (000118)
----Les investissements japonais en Asie du
    sud-est: compléments ou concurrents de
    l'industrie au Japon. (With English
    summary.). - 1985.
        (000146)
----Japanese and American direct investment
    in Asia. - 1985.
        (000154)
----Japanese direct foreign investment in
    Asian developing countries. - 1983.
        (000155)
----Japanese direct investment abroad. -
    1986.
        (000311)
----Japanese direct investment in ASEAN. -
    1983.
        (000171)
----Japanese direct investment in Indonesian
    manufacturing. - 1984.
        (000187)
----Japanese investment in Indonesia:
    problems and prospects. - 1986.
        (000152)
----Japanese investment in Thailand. - 1987.
        (000200)
----Japan's direct investment in California
    and the new protectionism. - 1984.
        (000145)
----Japon : du commerce à la finance. - 1987.
        (000374)

----New trends in internationalization:
    processes and theories. Diversified
    patterns of multinational enterprise and
    old and new forms of foreign involvement
    of the firm. - 1983.
        (000068)
----Pacific Basin financing -- Japan:
    straddling the world/both borrower and
    lender. - 1987.
        (000258)
----The process of internationalization at
    Asahi Glass Co. - 1986.
        (000360)
----The Rising Sun in America (Part One). -
    1986.
        (000392)
----The role of direct foreign investment in
    developing East Asian countries. - 1985.
        (001052)
----Some aspects of Japanese manufacturing
    investment in Australia. - 1984.
        (001044)
----Technology transfer through direct
    foreign investment. - 1985.
        (001490)
----Trends and issues in foreign direct
    investment and related flows. - 1985.
        (000192)
----Trends in Japan's direct investment
    abroad for FY 1985. - 1987.
        (000164)
----Trends in multinational business and
    global environments: a perspective. -
    1984.
        (000029)
----US and Japanese manufacturing affiliates
    in the UK. - 1985.
        (001149)
----Zur Internationalisierung der
    japanischen Wirtschaft. - 1984.
        (000117)

FOREIGN DIRECT INVESTMENT--LATIN AMERICA.
----Banco de datos sobre inversión
    extranjera directa en América Latina y
    el Caribe : información de los países
    receptores y de organismos regionales y
    subregionales, t. 2. - 1987.
        (000193)
----Banco de datos sobre inversión
    extranjera directa en América Latina y
    el Caribe, sobre la base de información
    de organismos multilaterales y de
    gobiernos de países de origen de la
    inversión, t. 1. - 1986.
        (000195)
----O capital transnacional e o estado. -
    1985.
        (002274)
----Deuda externa, inversión extranjera y
    transferencia de tecnología en América
    Latina. - 1986.
        (001080)
----Doing business in key Latin American
    markets: U.S. international executive
    perceptions. - 1983.
        (001824)
----Las empresas transnacionales y la
    inversión extranjera directa en la
    primera mitad de los años ochenta. -
    1987.
        (000194)

Subject Index - Index des matières

FOREIGN DIRECT INVESTMENT--LATIN AMERICA
(continued)
----Foreign debt, direct investment, and
     economic development in the Andean Pact.
     - 1987.
        (001110)
----Foreign direct investment in Latin
     America. - 1986.
        (000190)
----Foreign investment and technology
     transfer. - 1984.
        (000769)
----Inostrannye monopolii v Latinskoi
     Amerike. - 1983.
        (001103)
----Inversiones extranjeras en América
     Latina. - 1984.
        (001098)
----Las inversiones extranjeras y la crisis
     económica en América Latina. - 1986.
        (001309)
----Inversiones nórdicas en América Latina.
     - 1986.
        (000206)
----Latinskaia Amerika, ekspansiia
     inostrannykh monopolii. - 1984.
        (001090)
----Performance requirements: the general
     debate and a review of Latin American
     practices. - 1983.
        (002315)
----Reaction to economic crisis: trade and
     finance of US firms operating in Latin
     America. - 1986.
        (000333)
----The relationship of MNC direct
     investment to host country trade and
     trade policy: some preliminary evidence.
     - 1983.
        (001351)
----Trade and foreign direct investment in
     data services. - 1986.
        (000948)
----Transnacionalización y desarrollo
     nacional en América Latina. - 1984.
        (001117)
----Transnatsional'nye korporatsii SShA v
     Latinskoi Amerike. - 1985.
        (001087)

FOREIGN DIRECT INVESTMENT--MALAYSIA.
----Internalization in practice: early
     foreign direct investments in
     Malaysian tin mining. - 1986.
        (000597)
----Wages and work conditions, and the
     effects of foreign investment and the
     separation of ownership from management
     on them: a study of Malaysian
     manufacturing. - 1983.
        (001907)

FOREIGN DIRECT INVESTMENT--MEXICO.
----De la improvisación al fracaso : la
     política de inversión extranjera en
     México. - 1983.
        (001112)
----Doing business in Mexico. - 1984.
        (001791)
----Las empresas transnacionales y la
     inversión extranjera directa en la
     primera mitad de los años ochenta. -
     1987.
        (000194)

----Inversión extranjera directa. - 1985.
        (000138)
----Política económica y empresas
     transnacionales en México. - 1983.
        (001127)
----Wandel der mexikanischen Politik
     gegenuber Auslandsinvestitionen? Die
     "irationale" Komponente der
     Mexikanisierungsstrategie. - 1985.
        (002338)

FOREIGN DIRECT INVESTMENT--MIDDLE EAST.
----Legal consideration in doing business in
     the Middle East, Turkey and Pakistan. -
     1986.
        (002172)

FOREIGN DIRECT INVESTMENT--NAMIBIA.
----Foreign investment in South Africa and
     Namibia. - 1984.
        (001198) (002641)

FOREIGN DIRECT INVESTMENT--NEW ZEALAND.
----Australian direct investment in New
     Zealand. - 1983.
        (000109)
----Fiji : client State of Australasia? -
     1984.
        (001046) (002358)
----New Zealand business. - 1985.
        (000352)

FOREIGN DIRECT INVESTMENT--NIGERIA.
----MNC's in Nigeria. - 1983.
        (001029)
----State strategies toward Nigerian and
     foreign business. - 1983.
        (001770)

FOREIGN DIRECT INVESTMENT--NORDIC COUNTRIES.
----Industrial structure and country risks
     in a Nordic perspective. - 1984.
        (001838)
----Inversiones nórdicas en América Latina.
     - 1986.
        (000206)

FOREIGN DIRECT INVESTMENT--PACIFIC OCEAN
REGION.
----Investment in ACP states. - 1987.
        (001004)
----Transfer of industrial technology and
     foreign investment in the Pacific
     region. - 1983.
        (001440)

FOREIGN DIRECT INVESTMENT--PAKISTAN.
----Legal consideration in doing business in
     the Middle East, Turkey and Pakistan. -
     1986.
        (002172)

FOREIGN DIRECT INVESTMENT--PANAMA.
----Las empresas transnacionales y la
     inversión extranjera directa en la
     primera mitad de los años ochenta. -
     1987.
        (000194)

FOREIGN DIRECT INVESTMENT--PAPUA NEW GUINEA.
----Foreign direct investment in Papua New
    Guinea. - 1985.
      (000172)
----Foreign investment in Papua New Guinea.
    - 1986.
      (002197)

FOREIGN DIRECT INVESTMENT--PARAGUAY.
----Las empresas transnacionales en la
    economía del Paraguay. - 1987.
      (001124)
----Las transnacionales en el Paraguay. -
    1985.
      (001113)

FOREIGN DIRECT INVESTMENT--POLAND.
----CMEA direct investments in the western
    countries. - 1987.
      (000158)

FOREIGN DIRECT INVESTMENT--PORTUGAL.
----Investment legislation in Greece,
    Portugal and Spain: the background to
    foreign investment in Mediterranean
    Europe. - 1983.
      (002168)
----Portugal's accession to the EEC and its
    impact on foreign direct investment. -
    1986.
      (000554)

FOREIGN DIRECT INVESTMENT--REPUBLIC OF KOREA.
----Foreign direct investment from
    developing countries. - 1986.
      (000325)
----Foreign investment as an aid in moving
    from least developed to newly
    industrializing: a study in Korea. -
    1986.
      (000186)
----Les joint ventures en Corée du Sud. -
    1986.
      (002436)
----The Korean manufacturing multinationals.
    - 1984.
      (000342)
----New forms of overseas investment by
    developing countries : the case of
    India, Korea and Brazil. - 1986.
      (001616)
----The South Korean success story. - 1986.
      (001050)

FOREIGN DIRECT INVESTMENT--SAUDI ARABIA.
----A guide to establishing joint ventures
  • in Saudi Arabia. - 1985.
      (001807)
----Joint ventures in the Kingdom of Saudi
    Arabia. - 1985.
      (001655)
----The legal regime of foreign private
    investment in the Sudan and Saudi
    Arabia. - 1984.
      (002204)

FOREIGN DIRECT INVESTMENT--SINGAPORE.
----Direct foreign investment in
    manufacturing and the impact on
    employment and export performance in
    Singapore. - 1984.
      (001932)
----The real threat from Asia. - 1987.
      (001055)

----Singapore's role in China's offshore oil
    venture. - 1985.
      (000608)

FOREIGN DIRECT INVESTMENT--SOUTH AFRICA.
----Disinvestment and black workers
    attitudes in South Africa. - 1985.
      (001210)
----DM-Investitionen in Südafrika. - 1983.
      (001197)
----Foreign investment in South Africa and
    Namibia. - 1984.
      (001198) (002641)
----The politics of sentiment. - 1984.
      (002588)
----The roots of crisis in southern Africa.
    - 1985.
      (001208)
----U.S. and Canadian investment in South
    Africa and Namibia. - 1986.
      (001212) (002671) (002672)

FOREIGN DIRECT INVESTMENT--SOUTH ASIA.
----Multinational corporations, technology
    and employment. - 1983.
      (001891)

FOREIGN DIRECT INVESTMENT--SOUTHEAST ASIA.
----Australian direct investment in the
    ASEAN countries. - 1983.
      (000110)
----Die Direktinvestitionen der japanischen
    Wirtschaft in den Schwellenländern Ost-
    Südostasiens. - 1984.
      (000157)
----Foreign direct investment and
    industrialization in ASEAN countries. -
    1987.
      (000144)
----Foreign direct investment in ASEAN. -
    1987.
      (000139)
----Les investissements japonais en Asie du
    sud-est: compléments ou concurrents de
    l'industrie au Japon. (With English
    summary.). - 1985.
      (000146)
----Neue Wachstumsmärkte in Fernost. - 1983.
      (001800)
----Sverkhmonopolii v IUgo-Vostochnoi Azii.
    - 1983.
      (001041)
----Wachstumsmarkt Südostasien. - 1984.
      (001785)

FOREIGN DIRECT INVESTMENT--SPAIN.
----El control de las empresas
    multinacionales. - 1983.
      (002209)
----Investment legislation in Greece,
    Portugal and Spain: the background to
    foreign investment in Mediterranean
    Europe. - 1983.
      (002168)

FOREIGN DIRECT INVESTMENT--SRI LANKA.
----Economic prospects of Sri Lanka and
    potential for foreign investment. - 1984.
      (001788)

FOREIGN DIRECT INVESTMENT--SUDAN.
----Chevron, Sudan and political risk. - 1984.
    (001858)
----The legal regime of foreign private investment in the Sudan and Saudi Arabia. - 1984.
    (002204)

FOREIGN DIRECT INVESTMENT--SWEDEN.
----Sysselsattningsstrukturen i internationella foretag. - 1983.
    (001165)

FOREIGN DIRECT INVESTMENT--TAIWAN (CHINA).
----Taiwan's foreign direct investment. - 1986.
    (000121)

FOREIGN DIRECT INVESTMENT--THAILAND.
----Japanese investment in Thailand. - 1987.
    (000200)

FOREIGN DIRECT INVESTMENT--TURKEY.
----Foreign investment regulation and application forms. - 1985.
    (002198)
----Law for encouragement of foreign capital investments=Yabanci sermayeyi tesvik kanunu. - 1984.
    (002284)
----Legal consideration in doing business in the Middle East, Turkey and Pakistan. - 1986.
    (002172)
----Turkey's new open-door policy of direct foreign investment: a critical analysis of problems and prospects. - 1986.
    (002205)

FOREIGN DIRECT INVESTMENT--UNITED KINGDOM.
----Assessing the consequences of overseas investment. - 1986.
    (001296)
----The Atlantic two-way switch. - 1986.
    (000852)
----Decision-making in foreign-owned multinational subsidiaries in the United Kingdom. - 1985.
    (000521)
----Las empresas transnacionales y la inversión extranjera directa en la primera mitad de los años ochenta. - 1987.
    (000194)
----Foreign direct investment and the competitiveness of UK manufacturing industry, 1963-1979. - 1984.
    (000766)
----Foreign investment in South Africa and Namibia. - 1984.
    (001198) (002641)
----Foundations of foreign success. - 1987.
    (000421)
----Inward investment. - 1984.
    (000116)
----Multinational investment strategies in the British Isles. - 1983.
    (001151)
----Multinationals and Britain. - 1986.
    (000205)

----The prospect for direct investment by United Kingdom companies in developing countries. - 1985.
    (000169)
----The relative distribution of United States direct investment : the UK/EEC experience. - 1987.
    (000113)
----Trends and issues in foreign direct investment and related flows. - 1985.
    (000192)
----US and Japanese manufacturing affiliates in the UK. - 1985.
    (001149)

FOREIGN DIRECT INVESTMENT--UNITED STATES.
----The effect of political events on United States direct foreign investment: a pooled time-series cross-sectional analysis. - 1985.
    (001835)
----The Rising Sun in America (Part Two) -- Japanese management in the United States. - 1986.
    (000391)
----America's foreign debt. - 1987.
    (000243)
----America's new no. 4 automaker -- Honda. - 1985.
    (000294)
----Anglo in America. - 1986.
    (000292)
----Applying uniform margin requirements to foreign entities attempting to acquire U.S. corporations. - 1984.
    (002173)
----The Atlantic two-way switch. - 1986.
    (000852)
----Becoming a triad power: the new global corporation. - 1986.
    (000500)
----Canada in the USA : foreign direct investment flows reversed. - 1987.
    (000180)
----Canada's reversal from importer to exporter of foreign direct investment. - 1987.
    (000181)
----Capital expenditures by majority-owned foreign affiliates of U.S. companies, 1986 and 1987. - 1986.
    (000479)
----Determinants of direct foreign investment. - 1987.
    (000534)
----Determinants of foreign direct investment by food and tobacco manufacturers. - 1983.
    (000527)
----Direct foreign investment in the United States. - 1986.
    (000174)
----Direct investment activity of foreign firms. - 1987.
    (000541)
----Direct investment in the United States by foreign government-owned companies, 1974-81. - 1983.
    (000124)
----Disinvestment and black workers attitudes in South Africa. - 1985.
    (001210)

FOREIGN DIRECT INVESTMENT--UNITED STATES
(continued)
----Doing business in key Latin American
   markets: U.S. international executive
   perceptions. - 1983.
   (001824)
----The effects of foreign direct investment
   on U.S. employment during recession and
   structural change. - 1986.
   (001908)
----Las empresas transnacionales y la
   inversión extranjera directa en la
   primera mitad de los años ochenta. -
   1987.
   (000194)
----Federal taxation of international
   transactions. - 1988.
   (001730)
----Foreign direct investment in the U.S.
   minerals industry. - 1987.
   (000635)
----Foreign direct investment in the United
   States. - 1985.
   (000130)
----Foreign direct investment in the United
   States. - 1985-   .
   (000131)
----Foreign direct investment in the United
   States. - 1985.
   (000197)
----Foreign direct investment in the United
   States. - 1983-   .
   (000132)
----Foreign direct investment in the United
   States: old currents, 'new waves," and
   the theory of direct investment. - 1983.
   (000161)
----Foreign direct investment in the United
   States: the balance of foreign and
   domestic policy. - 1983.
   (000173)
----Foreign direct investment in U.S. food
   and tobacco manufacturing and domestic
   economic performance. - 1983.
   (000170)
----Foreign investment in South Africa and
   Namibia. - 1984.
   (001198) (002641)
----Foreign investment in the American and
   Canadian West, 1870-1914. - 1986.
   (002690)
----Foreign investment in the United States.
   - 1983.
   (000198)
----Foreign investment in the United States
   after the Tax Reform Act of 1986. - 1987.
   (002232)
----Foreign investments and financings in
   the United States. - 1983.
   (002175)
----Foreign location decisions by U.S.
   transnational firms: an empirical study.
   - 1984.
   (000537)
----Foreign manufacturing investment in the
   United States: competitive strategies
   and international location. - 1985.
   (000733)
----Foreign trade and investment. - 1987.
   (002191)

----Geoinvestment: the interdependence among
   space, market size, and political
   turmoil in attracting foreign direct
   investment. - 1984.
   (000555)
----Increased foreign investment in U.S.
   food industries. - 1985.
   (000714)
----International direct investment. - 1984.
   (000199)
----International finance and investment. -
   1985.
   (001249)
----International investment. - 1983.
   (000525)
----The international investment position of
   the United States in 1985. - 1986.
   (001295)
----International joint ventures: how
   important are they? - 1987.
   (001556)
----Japanese and American direct investment
   in Asia. - 1985.
   (000154)
----Japan's direct investment in California
   and the new protectionism. - 1984.
   (000145)
----Linkages and foreign direct investment
   in the United States. - 1984.
   (000166)
----Manual of foreign investment in the
   United States. - 1984.
   (002238)
----A muködo toke becsalogatása
   Magyarországra : nyugati szemszögbol. -
   1987.
   (001608)
----New forms of investment in developing
   countries by US companies: a five
   industry comparison. - 1987.
   (000328)
----New trends in internationalization:
   processes and theories. Diversified
   patterns of multinational enterprise and
   old and new forms of foreign involvement
   of the firm. - 1983.
   (000068)
----OPEC direct investment in the United
   States. - 1981-   .
   (000168)
----Operating foreign subsidiaries. - 1983.
   (000388)
----Où va l'investissement direct
   international? USA/monde : le cas du
   secteur alimentaire. - 1984.
   (000666)
----Profiles of foreign direct investment in
   U.S. energy. - 1985-   .
   (000774)
----Regulating the multinational enterprise.
   - 1983.
   (002006)
----Regulation of foreign direct investment
   in Canada and the United States. - 1983.
   (002263)
----The Rising Sun in America (Part One). -
   1986.
   (000392)
----The role of direct foreign investment in
   developing East Asian countries. - 1985.
   (001052)

FOREIGN DIRECT INVESTMENT--UNITED STATES
(continued)
----The role of foreign direct investment in
    U.S. capital outflows. - 1986.
      (000179)
----The roots of crisis in southern Africa.
    - 1985.
      (001208)
----Selected data on foreign direct
    investment in the United States,
    1950-79. - 1984.
      (000184)
----Tax policy and foreign direct
    investment. - 1985.
      (001721)
----Tax policy and foreign direct investment
    in the United States. - 1984.
      (001722)
----Towards a new treaty framework for
    direct foreign investment. - 1985.
      (002047)
----Transnatsional'nye korporatsii SShA v
    Latinskoi Amerike. - 1985.
      (001087)
----Trends and issues in foreign direct
    investment and related flows. - 1985.
      (000192)
----Trends in multinational business and
    global environments: a perspective. -
    1984.
      (000029)
----U.S. and Canadian investment in South
    Africa and Namibia. - 1986.
      (001212) (002671) (002672)

----U.S. direct investment abroad. -
    1981-   .
      (000188)
----U.S. direct investment abroad. -
    1985-   .
      (000189)
----The U.S. in the world economy. - 1988.
      (000128)
----US and Japanese manufacturing affiliates
    in the UK. - 1985.
      (001149)
----Venturing abroad. - 1988.
      (000376)
----The World Bank's Multilateral Investment
    Guaranty Agency. - 1987.
      (002125)

FOREIGN DIRECT INVESTMENT--VENEZUELA.
----Legislación de inversiones extranjeras y
    Pacto Andino. - 1984.
      (002234)

FOREIGN DIRECT INVESTMENT--WESTERN EUROPE.
----European Community tariff preferences
    and foreign direct investment. - 1987.
      (002159)
----The European investments of Japanese
    financial institutions. - 1986.
      (000118)
----Multinational corporations and European
    integration. - 1987.
      (001325)
----Operating foreign subsidiaries. - 1983.
      (000388)
----The relative distribution of United
    States direct investment : the UK/EEC
    experience. - 1987.
      (000113)

----Trends in multinational business and
    global environments: a perspective. -
    1984.
      (000029)
----Western direct investment in centrally
    planned economies. - 1986.
      (000159)

FOREIGN DIRECT INVESTMENT--YUGOSLAVIA.
----Direct foreign investment in Yugoslavia.
    - 1986.
      (000183)
----An economic analysis of Yugoslav joint
    ventures. - 1983.
      (001563)
----The impact of direct foreign investment
    upon developing countries : a case study
    of Yugoslavia. - 1986.
      (001174)
----Industrial co-operation and investment
    in Yugoslavia. - 1986.
      (001540)
----Joint venturing in Yugoslavia. - 1987.
      (001536)
----Oberlegungen zur jugoslawischen Joint
    Venture-Gesetzgebung. - 1986.
      (002268)
----Visi oblici privredne saradnje izmethu
    domacih organizacija udruzenog rada i
    stranih lica. - 1984.
      (001182)

FOREIGN DIRECT INVESTMENT--ZIMBABWE.
----H.J. Heinz success in Zimbabwe. - 1987.
      (000279)
----Investment by foreign companies:
    Zimbabwe. - 1987.
      (001740)

FOREIGN DIRECT INVESTMENTS.
----Muködotoke-beruházások a fejlodo
    országokban. - 1986.
      (001275)

FOREIGN DIRECT INVESTMENTS--KUWAIT.
----Impact of the operations of
    transnational corporations on
    development in Kuwait. - 1987.
      (001143)

FOREIGN DIRECT INVESTMENTS--OMAN.
----Impact of the operations of
    transnational corporations on
    development in the Sultanate of Oman. -
    1988.
      (001144)

FOREIGN EXCHANGE.
----Foreign exchange risk and direct foreign
    investment. - 1983.
      (001852)
----International money flows and currency
    crises. - 1984.
      (001261)
----International treasury management. -
    1988.
      (000440)
----Inventories and foreign currency
    translation requirements. - 1983.
      (002064)

FOREIGN EXCHANGE (continued)
----Issues in negotiating international loan
    agreements with transnational banks. -
    1983.
      (002459)
----Multinational finance. - 1986.
      (001237)
----Die Umrechnung der Jahresabschlusse
    auslandischer Konzernunternehmen und die
    Verrechnung der daraus resultierenden
    Umrechnungsdifferenzen. - 1986.
      (002095)
----Die Wahrungsumrechnung im Rahmen der
    internationalen Konzernrechnungslegung.
    - 1985.
      (002096)

FOREIGN EXCHANGE--CHINA.
----Foreign direct investment in the
    People's Republic of China. - 1988.
      (000191)

FOREIGN EXCHANGE AGREEMENTS.
----Issues in negotiating international loan
    agreements with transnational banks. -
    1983.
      (002459)
----The reconstruction of international
    monetary arrangements. - 1987.
      (001290)

FOREIGN EXCHANGE CONTROL.
----Effective control of currency risks. -
    1988.
      (000502)
----International transfer pricing
    objectives. - 1985.
      (001732)

FOREIGN EXCHANGE CONTROL--JAPAN.
----The administrative regulation of
    technology induction contracts in Japan.
    - 1987.
      (002447)

FOREIGN EXCHANGE CONTROL--MEXICO.
----Doing business in Mexico. - 1984.
      (001791)

FOREIGN EXCHANGE MARKETS.
----Research on Third World multinationals.
    - 1985.
      (000321)

FOREIGN EXCHANGE RATES.
----Les désajustements mondiaux de balances
    des paiements. - 1984.
      (001284)
----Fiscal policies, current accounts and
    real exchange rates : in search of a
    logic of international policy
    coordination. - 1986.
      (001244)
----Recent developments in international
    banking and finance. - 1987-   .
      (000928)
----The reconstruction of international
    monetary arrangements. - 1987.
      (001290)
----Some evidences between foreign direct
    investments and foreign exchange rates:
    a preliminary note. - 1983.
      (000147)

----The stability of the international
    monetary system. - 1987.
      (001294)
----Wisselkoersinstabiliteit en
    schuldproblematiek. - 1984.
      (001310)

FOREIGN INTERESTS--SAUDI ARABIA.
----Impact of the operations of
    transnational corporations on
    development in Saudi Arabia. - 1987.
      (001140)

FOREIGN INTERESTS--UNITED ARAB EMIRATES.
----Impact of operations of transnational
    corporations on development in United
    Arab Emirates. - 1987.
      (001136)

FOREIGN INTERESTS--UNITED STATES.
----Foreign government and foreign investor
    control of U.S. banks. - 1983.
      (001654)

FOREIGN INVESTMENT REVIEW REGULATIONS 1983
(CANADA).
----Foreign investment law in Canada. - 1983.
      (002222)

FOREIGN INVESTMENTS.
----L'Agence multilatérale de garantie des
    investissements. - 1987.
      (002152)
----Les années quatre-vingts : quelles
    perspectives pour l'industrie américaine
    et les investissements internationaux? -
    1983.
      (000106)
----Arbitration and renegotiation of
    international investment agreements. -
    1986.
      (002557)
----Bibliografía sobre inversiones
    extranjeras y empresas multinacionales.
    - 1986.
      (002681)
----Case studies in the jurisdiction of the
    International Centre for Settlement of
    Investment Disputes. - 1986.
      (002580)
----Codes des investissements des Etats
    A.C.P. - 1978.
      (002162)
----Controls and impediments affecting
    inward direct investment in OECD member
    countries. - 1987.
      (000122) (002193)
----The Convention Establishing the
    Multilateral Investment Guarantee
    Agency. - 1987.
      (002127)
----Declaration by the governments of OECD
    member countries and decisions of the
    OECD Council on international investment
    and multinational enterprises. - 1984.
      (001999)
----Les désajustements mondiaux de balances
    des paiements. - 1984.
      (001284)
----Le développement de la protection
    conventionnelle des investissements
    étrangers. - 1986.
      (002048)

FOREIGN INVESTMENTS (continued)
----Do performance requirements and
 investment incentives work? - 1986.
  (002306)
----Does concessionary aid lead to higher
 investment rates in low-income
 countries? - 1987.
  (002311)
----Economic development, investment
 dependence, and the rise of services in
 less developed nations. - 1986.
  (000958)
----The economic impact of direct foreign
 investments on developing countries. -
 1984.
  (001311)
----Economically rational design of
 developing countries' expropriation
 policies towards foreign investment. -
 1985.
  (001599)
----The effects of foreign investment on
 overall and sectoral groups in Third
 World states. - 1984.
  (001332)
----Az észak-déli technológiaátadás
 formaváltozásai. - 1985.
  (001458)
----Exploring the global economy : emerging
 issues in trade and investment. - 1985.
  (001306)
----Exports of technology from the South. -
 1985.
  (001469)
----Factors influencing the flow of foreign
 investment and the relevance of a
 multilateral investment guarantee
 scheme. - 1987.
  (002144)
----Finance and protection of investments in
 developing countries. - 1987.
  (002128)
----Die finanzielle Führung und Kontrolle
 von Auslandsgesellschaften. - 1983.
  (000447)
----Foreign business practices. - 1985.
  (001433)
----Foreign investment, technical efficiency
 and structural change. - 1983.
  (001085)
----Foreign private investors and the host
 country. - 1985.
  (001851)
----Global risk assessments. - 1983.
  (001803)
----Government policy and private investment
 in developing countries. - 1984.
  (002177)
----The GT guide to world equity markets. -
 1986- .
  (002712)
----ICSID : an international method for
 handling foreign investment disputes in
 LDCs. - 1987.
  (002474)
----Improving the investment climate in
 developing countries. - 1984.
  (002572)
----Infratechnologies, technologies de
 pointe, investissements dans et pour les
 pays en développement. - 1985.
  (001444)

----Institutions financières publiques de
 développement. - 1986.
  (000237)
----International income taxation and
 developing countries. - 1988.
  (001759)
----International investment and
 multinational enterprises. - 1983.
  (002308)
----International investment and
 multinational enterprises. - 1984.
  (001981)
----International law and investments. -
 1987.
  (001958)
----Investissement international et
 entreprises multinationales. - 1983.
  (000538)
----Les investissements miniers
 internationaux dans les pays en
 développement. - 1986.
  (000609)
----Investment protection agreements. - 1987.
  (002135)
----IRM directory of statistics of
 international investment and production.
 - 1987.
  (000151) (002716)
----Joint venturing abroad. - 1985.
  (001598)
----Die Konfrontationen zwischen Staaten und
 ausländischen Unternehmen. - 1983.
  (001864)
----Legal trends in international lending
 and investment in the developing
 countries. - 1984.
  (000207)
----The literature of international business
 finance. - 1984.
  (002687)
----Measures to strengthen the capabilities
 of developing countries in their dealing
 with transnational corporations. - 1985.
  (002612)
----The Multilateral Investment Guarantee
 Agency : status, mandate, concept,
 features, implications. - 1987.
  (002158)
----Multilateral investment insurance and
 private investment in the Third World. -
 1987.
  (002132)
----Die Multilaterale
 Investitions-Garantie-Agentur (MIGA). -
 1986.
  (002142)
----Multinational management. - 1984.
  (000449)
----Multinationals : change of strategy in
 the face of crisis. - 1983.
  (000495)
----Nationalisations et
 internationalisation. - 1983.
  (000497)
----Negotiation and drafting of mining
 development agreements. - 1976.
  (002432)
----New forms of international investment in
 developing countries. - 1984.
  (001615)
----New forms of international investment in
 developing countries. - 1984.
  (001619)

FOREIGN INVESTMENTS (continued)
----The OECD guidelines for multinational
enterprises. - 1986.
(002002)
----Permanent sovereignty over natural
resources in international law. - 1984.
(002141)
----The politics of international
investment. - 1983.
(000532)
----Les principes directeurs de l'OCDE à
l'intention des entreprises
multinationales. - 1986.
(002005)
----Protection et promotion des
investissements. - 1985.
(002137)
----Recent trends in international direct
investment. - 1987.
(000176)
----Les services : enjeux pour l'emploi et
le commerce international. - 1986.
(000960)
----The stages of developing country policy
toward foreign investment. - 1985.
(002277)
----State intervention, foreign economic
aid, savings and growth in LDCs. - 1985.
(001337)
----State responsibility and bilateral
investment treaties. - 1986.
(002051)
----Stratégies des entreprises et marché
international des capitaux. - 1984.
(001273)
----The taking of foreign property under
international law. - 1984.
(002336)
----Technical co-operation programme of the
United Nations Centre on Transnational
Corporations. - 1988.
(002610)
----Technical co-operation programme,
1976-1987 : United Nations Centre on
Transnational Corporations. - 1988.
(002611)
----Third World multinationals. - 1983.
(000383)
----Transnational corporations and uneven
development : the internationalization
of capital and the Third World. - 1987.
(001270)
----University of Reading discussion papers
in international investment and business
studies. - 197?-   .
(000104)
----World business reports. - 1982-   .
(001863)
----Zur Bedeutung der Multilateral
Investment Guarantee Agency für den
internationalen Ressourcentransfer. -
1987.
(002129)
----161 more checklists : decision making in
international operations. - 1985.
(000462)

FOREIGN INVESTMENTS--AFRICA.
----L'Afrique, l'Europe et la crise. - 1986.
(001287)
----Répertoire de la législation relative
aux investissements étrangers dans les
pays membres de L'OCI. - 1984.
(002264)

FOREIGN INVESTMENTS--ALGERIA.
----Aperçu sur le statut de la société mixte
en Algérie. - 1984.
(002283)

FOREIGN INVESTMENTS--ARGENTINA.
----The new Argentina. - 1984.
(001777)

FOREIGN INVESTMENTS--ASIA.
----Effects of foreign capital inflows on
developing countries of Asia. - 1986.
(001059)
----The impact of foreign capital inflow on
investment and economic growth in
developing Asia. - 1985.
(001048)
----New business strategies for developing
Asia, 1983-1990. - 1984.
(000498)
----The special economic zones of China. -
1985.
(002392)

FOREIGN INVESTMENTS--AUSTRALIA.
----Australia's foreign investment policy. -
198?-   .
(002170)
----Investment protection agreements. - 1987.
(002135)
----United States investment in Australia. -
1987.
(002180)

FOREIGN INVESTMENTS--AUSTRIA.
----Investitionsschutzabkommen. - 1986.
(002041)

FOREIGN INVESTMENTS--BANGLADESH.
----Courting private foreign investment :
the Bangladesh experience. - 1986.
(001854)
----Domestic saving and foreign capital
inflow : the case of Bangladesh. - 1986.
(001034)

FOREIGN INVESTMENTS--BOLIVIA.
----National legislation and regulations
relating to transnational corporations.
Volume 4. - 1986.
(002253)

FOREIGN INVESTMENTS--BOTSWANA.
----National legislation and regulations
relating to transnational corporations.
Volume 4. - 1986.   .
(002253)

FOREIGN INVESTMENTS--BRAZIL.
----Business in a democratic Brazil. - 1985.
(001776)
----Capitais estrangeiros. - 1984.
(002275)
----The comparative performance of foreign
and domestic firms in Brazil. - 1986.
(001130)
----La internacionalización financiera en
Brasil. - 1983.
(001082)
----Investments in Brazil. - 1981.
(002165)

FOREIGN INVESTMENTS--BRAZIL (continued)
----Mining investment in Brazil, Peru, and
     Mexico. - 1984.
       (002443)
----National legislation and regulations
     relating to transnational corporations.
     Volume 4. - 1986.
       (002253)

FOREIGN INVESTMENTS--CAMEROON.
----The political economy of development in
     Cameroon. - 1985.
       (001833)
----The political economy of development in
     Cameroon. - 1986.
       (001834)

FOREIGN INVESTMENTS--CANADA.
----Canada's Foreign Investment Review
     Agency and the direct investment process
     in Canada. - 1984.
       (002359)
----An examination of the legality of the
     use of the Foreign Investment Review Act
     by the government of Canada to control
     intra- and extraterritorial commercial
     activity by aliens. - 1984.
       (002257)
----Operating strategies for a Canada in
     transition. - 1984.
       (001778)
----U.S. and Canadian business in South
     Africa. - 1987-   .
       (001211)

FOREIGN INVESTMENTS--CARIBBEAN REGION.
----The Caribbean Basin Economic Recovery
     Act and its implications for foreign
     private investment. - 1984.
       (001965)
----Legal framework for foreign investment
     in the Caribbean and Central America. -
     1984.
       (001964)
----Regulación de la inversión extranjera en
     América Latina y el Caribe. - 1984.
       (002194)

FOREIGN INVESTMENTS--CENTRAL AMERICA.
----Legal framework for foreign investment
     in the Caribbean and Central America. -
     1984.
       (001964)

FOREIGN INVESTMENTS--CHILE.
----National legislation and regulations
     relating to transnational corporations.
     Volume 4. - 1986.
       (002253)

FOREIGN INVESTMENTS--CHINA.
----Almanac of China's foreign economic
     relations and trade. - 1984-   .
       (002615)
----China : new provisions to encourage
     foreign investment. - 1987.
       (002313)
----China laws for foreign business. -
     1985-   .
       (002187)
----China's opening to the world. - 1986.
       (002221)

----China's utilization of foreign funds and
     relevant policies. - 1984.
       (002227)
----Chinese solutions to legal problems. -
     1987.
       (002295)
----Creating a favorable investment
     environment. - 1987.
       (001794)
----Dispute resolution in the People's
     Republic of China. - 1984.
       (002558)
----Foreign investment law in the People's
     Republic of China. - 1987.
       (002299)
----Foreign trade, investment and the law in
     the People's Republic of China. - 1985.
       (002211)
----International dispute resolution and the
     People's Republic of China. - 1984.
       (002522)
----An introduction to foreign investment
     law in China. - 1986.
       (002296)
----Investitions- und
     Kooperationsmöglichkeit "Equity joint
     venture" in der Volksrepublik China. -
     1986.
       (002199)
----The investment climate in China. - 1987.
       (001810)
----The investment implications of China's
     offshore oil development. - 1986.
       (000612)
----Joint ventures in China. - 1986.
       (002281)
----The law applicable to a transnational
     economic development contract. - 1987.
       (002164)
----The new foreign contract law in China. -
     1986.
       (002276)
----The People's Republic of China. - 1986.
       (001841)
----Realities confronting China's foreign
     investment policy. - 1984.
       (002292)
----Shenzhen : a Chinese development zone in
     global perspective. - 1985.
       (002393)
----The special economic zones. - 1987.
       (002379)
----Special economic zones in China's
     modernization. - 1986.
       (002385)
----The special economic zones of China. -
     1985.
       (002392)
----Taxation of foreign business and
     investment in the People's Republic of
     China. - 1987.
       (001708)
----To open wider, or to close again :
     China's foreign investment policies and
     laws. - 1984.
       (002163)
----United States policy regarding
     nationalization of American investments.
     - 1984.
       (002332)
----Les zones économiques spéciales de la
     République populaire chinoise. - 1985.
       (002383)

FOREIGN INVESTMENTS--COLOMBIA.
----National legislation and regulations
relating to transnational corporations.
Volume 4. - 1986.
(002253)

FOREIGN INVESTMENTS--COTE D'IVOIRE.
----National legislation and regulations
relating to transnational corporations.
Volume 4. - 1986.
(002253)

FOREIGN INVESTMENTS--EAST ASIA.
----Entrepreneurial cooperation between
industrialized countries and the
developing countries in East and
South-East Asia. - 1985.
(001649)

FOREIGN INVESTMENTS--EASTERN EUROPE.
----Multinationals from the Second World :
growth of foreign investment by Soviet
and East European enterprises. - 1987.
(000356)
----Ownership and investment in Poland. -
1985.
(001595)
----101 checklists for success in East
European markets. - 1984.
(001779)

FOREIGN INVESTMENTS--ECUADOR.
----Invest in Ecuador. - 1982.
(001771)
----La presencia de las empresas
transnacionales en la economía
ecuatoriana. - 1984.
(001125)

FOREIGN INVESTMENTS--EGYPT.
----Egypt's experience in regulating
technology imports. - 1987.
(001514)
----National legislation and regulations
relating to transnational corporations.
Volume 4. - 1986.
(002253)

FOREIGN INVESTMENTS--FRANCE.
----L'Afrique, l'Europe et la crise. - 1986.
(001287)
----Les investissements français dans le
Tiers monde. - 1984.
(000150)
----Propriété et pouvoir dans l'industrie. -
1987.
(001628)

FOREIGN INVESTMENTS--GERMANY, FEDERAL
REPUBLIC OF.
----Investitionsbedingungen in der
ASEAN-region. - 1986.
(001814)
----Investitionsschutzabkommen. - 1986.
(002041)
----National legislation and regulations
relating to transnational corporations.
Volume 4. - 1986.
(002253)
----Transfert de technologie. - 1983.
(001460)

FOREIGN INVESTMENTS--INDIA.
----National legislation and regulations
relating to transnational corporations.
Volume 4. - 1986.
(002253)

FOREIGN INVESTMENTS--ISLAMIC COUNTRIES.
----A directory of foreign investment
legislation in O.I.C. member countries.
- 1984.
(002201)
----Répertoire de la législation relative
aux investissements étrangers dans les
pays membres de L'OCI. - 1984.
(002264)

FOREIGN INVESTMENTS--ISRAEL.
----National legislation and regulations
relating to transnational corporations.
Volume 4. - 1986.
(002253)

FOREIGN INVESTMENTS--ITALY.
----National legislation and regulations
relating to transnational corporations.
Volume 4. - 1986.
(002253)

FOREIGN INVESTMENTS--JAPAN.
----Les investissements européens au Japon :
les causes de la faiblesse et les
difficultés du rattrapage. - 1986.
(000105)
----Japanese investment in UK industry. -
1984.
(000127)
----Japanese overseas investment. - 1983.
(000160)
----Japan's general trading companies. -
1984.
(000887)
----The pattern of Japanese multinational
investment. - 1984.
(000327)

FOREIGN INVESTMENTS--KENYA.
----National legislation and regulations
relating to transnational corporations.
Volume 4. - 1986.
(002253)

FOREIGN INVESTMENTS--KUWAIT.
----National legislation and regulations
relating to transnational corporations.
Volume 4. - 1986.
(002253)
----State contracts and oil expropriations.
- 1984.
(002577)

FOREIGN INVESTMENTS--LATIN AMERICA.
----Crisis de endeudamiento y primeras
redefiniciones respecto al tratamiento
del capital extranjero en América
Latina. - 1986.
(000247)
----Entrada de capital extranjero, ahorro
interno e inversión en la América Latina
: una historia negativa y precautoria. -
1986.
(001101)
----La inversión estadounidense en el Grupo
Andino. - 1985.
(000112)

FOREIGN INVESTMENTS--LATIN AMERICA
(continued)
----La inversión extranjera : instrumento de
    liberación o dependencia? - 1984.
    (000148)
----Las inversiones extranjeras en América
    Latina. - 1984.
    (000162)
----Inversiones Nórdicas en América Latina.
    - 1987.
    (000115)
----Nueva división internacional del trabajo
    y reestructuración productiva en América
    Latina. - 1984.
    (001264)
----Las nuevas formas de inversión
    internacional en la agroindustria
    latinoamericana. - 1986.
    (000569)
----Private investment in Latin America. -
    1984.
    (002460)
----Régimen jurídico de las inversiones
    extranjeras en los países de la ALADI. -
    1985.
    (002262)
----Los regímenes de garantía a la inversión
    extranjera y su aplicabilidad en los
    países de la ALADI. - 1985.
    (002126)
----Regulación de la inversión extranjera en
    América Latina y el Caribe. - 1984.
    (002194)

FOREIGN INVESTMENTS--LESOTHO.
----Lagging behind the bantustans. - 1985.
    (001223)

FOREIGN INVESTMENTS--LIBERIA.
----National legislation and regulations
    relating to transnational corporations.
    Volume 4. - 1986.
    (002253)

FOREIGN INVESTMENTS--LIBYAN ARAB JAMAHIRIYA.
----National legislation and regulations
    relating to transnational corporations.
    Volume 4. - 1986.
    (002253)

FOREIGN INVESTMENTS--MALAYSIA.
----Business prospects in Malaysia, coping
    with change in a new era. - 1983.
    (001780)

FOREIGN INVESTMENTS--MEXICO.
----Foreign investment and productive
    efficiency. - 1986.
    (001084)
----The foreign investment transaction in
    Mexico. - 1985.
    (002260)
----Mining investment in Brazil, Peru, and
    Mexico. - 1984.
    (002443)
----National legislation and regulations
    relating to transnational corporations.
    Volume 4. - 1986.
    (002253)
----A note on the burden of the Mexican
    foreign debt. - 1986.
    (000254)

FOREIGN INVESTMENTS--MOROCCO.
----Expérience marocaine dans
    l'établissement d'entreprises
    multinationales. - 1986.
    (001027)
----National legislation and regulations
    relating to transnational corporations.
    Volume 4. - 1986.
    (002253)
----Le nouveau droit des investissements
    étrangers au Maroc. - 1984.
    (002269)

FOREIGN INVESTMENTS--NAMIBIA.
----Activities of transnational corporations
    in South Africa and Namibia and the
    responsibilities of home countries with
    respect to their operations in this
    area. - 1986.
    (001192)
----Transnational corporations in South
    Africa and Namibia. - 1986.
    (001217)
----Transnational corporations in South
    Africa and Namibia : United Nations
    public hearings. Volume 3, Statements
    and submissions. - 1987.
    (001215)
----U.S. and Canadian business in South
    Africa. - 1987-
    (001211)

FOREIGN INVESTMENTS--NETHERLANDS.
----Recommendation on industry and
    development cooperation. - 1984.
    (001329)

FOREIGN INVESTMENTS--NICARAGUA.
----Política económica y capital extranjero
    en Nicaragua. - 1984.
    (002081)

FOREIGN INVESTMENTS--NIGERIA.
----National legislation and regulations
    relating to transnational corporations.
    Volume 4. - 1986.
    (002253)

FOREIGN INVESTMENTS--OMAN.
----Impact of the operations of
    transnational corporations on
    development in the Sultanate of Oman. -
    1988.
    (001144)

FOREIGN INVESTMENTS--PAPUA NEW GUINEA.
----Economic policies pertaining to foreign
    enterprises in PNG. - 1986.
    (002287)

FOREIGN INVESTMENTS--PERU.
----Empresas transnacionales, estado y
    burguesia nativa. - 1983.
    (001877)
----Mining investment in Brazil, Peru, and
    Mexico. - 1984.
    (002443)
----National legislation and regulations
    relating to transnational corporations.
    Volume 4. - 1986.
    (002253)

FOREIGN INVESTMENTS--PHILIPPINES.
----Factors influencing the choice of
   location : local and foreign firms in
   the Philippines. - 1987.
   (000547)
----National legislation and regulations
   relating to transnational corporations.
   Volume 4. - 1986.
   (002253)

FOREIGN INVESTMENTS--POLAND.
----New legislation on foreign private firms
   in Poland. - 1984.
   (002244)
----Ownership and investment in Poland. -
   1985.
   (001595)

FOREIGN INVESTMENTS--PORTUGAL.
----National legislation and regulations
   relating to transnational corporations.
   Volume 4. - 1986.
   (002253)

FOREIGN INVESTMENTS--REPUBLIC OF KOREA.
----National legislation and regulations
   relating to transnational corporations.
   Volume 4. - 1986.
   (002253)
----Riding a tiger : joint ventures under
   South Korea's new Foreign Capital
   Inducement Act. - 1985.
   (002290)

FOREIGN INVESTMENTS--SAUDI ARABIA.
----National legislation and regulations
   relating to transnational corporations.
   Volume 4. - 1986.
   (002253)

FOREIGN INVESTMENTS--SOUTH AFRICA.
----Activities of transnational corporations
   in South Africa and Namibia and the
   responsibilities of home countries with
   respect to their operations in this
   area. - 1986.
   (001192)
----The costs of disinvestment. - 1986.
   (001207)
----Lagging behind the bantustans. - 1985.
   (001223)
----Political change in South Africa. - 1986.
   (001205)
----South Africa : economic responses to
   international pressures. - 1985.
   (001193)
----Transnational corporations in South
   Africa and Namibia : United Nations
   public hearings. Volume 1, Reports of
   the Panel of Eminent Persons and of the
   Secretary-General. - 1986.
   (001216)
----Transnational corporations in South
   Africa and Namibia. - 1986.
   (001217)
----Transnational corporations in South
   Africa and Namibia : United Nations
   public hearings. Volume 3, Statements
   and submissions. - 1987.
   (001215)
----Two decades of debate. - 1983.
   (001199)

----U.S. and Canadian business in South
   Africa. - 1987-   .
   (001211)
----U.S. corporate activities in South
   Africa. - 1983.
   (001222)

FOREIGN INVESTMENTS--SOUTH AMERICA.
----Financing implications of mineral
   development agreements. - 1986.
   (002456)

FOREIGN INVESTMENTS--SOUTHEAST ASIA.
----Entrepreneurial cooperation between
   industrialized countries and the
   developing countries in East and
   South-East Asia. - 1985.
   (001649)
----Investitionsbedingungen in der
   ASEAN-region. - 1986.
   (001814)

FOREIGN INVESTMENTS--SUDAN.
----National legislation and regulations
   relating to transnational corporations.
   Volume 4. - 1986.
   (002253)

FOREIGN INVESTMENTS--THAILAND.
----National legislation and regulations
   relating to transnational corporations.
   Volume 4. - 1986.
   (002253)

FOREIGN INVESTMENTS--TURKEY.
----Foreign investments in Turkey. - 1983.
   (000134)

FOREIGN INVESTMENTS--UNITED KINGDOM.
----British manufacturing investment
   overseas. - 1985.
   (000735)
----Japanese investment in UK industry. -
   1984.
   (000127)
----National legislation and regulations
   relating to transnational corporations.
   Volume 4. - 1986.
   (002253)

FOREIGN INVESTMENTS--UNITED STATES.
----Die Aussenexpansion des Kapitals. - 1984.
   (000037)
----The Caribbean Basin Economic Recovery
   Act and its implications for foreign
   private investment. - 1984.
   (001965)
----Direct investment techniques for the
   USA. - 1983.
   (001808)
----Empresas multinacionales y concentración
   de la inversión extranjera. - 1985.
   (000545)
----Estados Unidos y el proceso de
   transnacionalización en la postguerra. -
   1984.
   (001235)
----Federal regulation of certain foreign
   investment in the United States. - 1985.
   (002215)
----Foreign government and foreign investor
   control of U.S. banks. - 1983.
   (001654)

FOREIGN INVESTMENTS--UNITED STATES
(continued)
----Foreign investment in United States oil
    and gas ventures. - 1987.
      (000606)
----La inversión estadounidense en el Grupo
    Andino. - 1985.
      (000112)
----Investment climate in foreign countries.
    - 1983-   .
      (001812)
----The overseas expansion of capital. -
    1985.
      (000038)
----The Overseas Private Investment
    Corporation and international
    investment. - 1984.
      (002360)
----Political risk in the international oil
    and gas industry. - 1983.
      (001823)
----Riding a tiger : joint ventures under
    South Korea's new Foreign Capital
    Inducement Act. - 1985.
      (002290)
----The role of private investment in Third
    World development. - 1986.
      (001328)
----The significance of foreign investment
    in US development 1879 to mid-1914. -
    1982.
      (001344)
----Tax planning for foreign investors in
    the United States. - 1983.
      (001773)
----Two decades of debate. - 1983.
      (001199)
----U.S. and Canadian business in South
    Africa. - 1987-   .
      (001211)
----The U.S. bilateral investment treaty
    program. - 1985.
      (002034)
----U.S. corporate activities in South
    Africa. - 1983.
      (001222)
----U.S. federal regulation of foreign
    involvement in aviation, government
    procurement and national security. -
    1985.
      (002216)
----United States investment in Australia. -
    1987.
      (002180)
----United States policy regarding
    nationalization of American investments.
    - 1984.
      (002332)
----What's causing America's capital
    imports? - 1987.
      (000539)

FOREIGN INVESTMENTS--USSR.
----Multinationals from the Second World :
    growth of foreign investment by Soviet
    and East European enterprises. - 1987.
      (000356)

FOREIGN INVESTMENTS--VENEZUELA.
----National legislation and regulations
    relating to transnational corporations.
    Volume 4. - 1986.
      (002253)

FOREIGN INVESTMENTS--WESTERN EUROPE.
----L'Afrique, l'Europe et la crise. - 1986.
      (001287)
----Les investissements européens au Japon :
    les causes de la faiblesse et les
    difficultés du rattrapage. - 1986.
      (000105)
----Le système conjoint de garantie des
    investissements CEE/ACP de la Convention
    de Lomé III. - 1987.
      (002147)

FOREIGN INVESTMENTS--YUGOSLAVIA.
----Joint ventures in Yugoslav industry. -
    1985.
      (001535)
----National legislation and regulations
    relating to transnational corporations.
    Volume 4. - 1986.
      (002253)

FOREIGN INVESTMENTS--ZAMBIA.
----The mines, class power, and foreign
    policy in Zambia. - 1984.
      (001023)

FOREIGN LOANS.
----Bank lending to developing countries. -
    1985.
      (000212)
----International lending in a fragile world
    economy. - 1983.
      (000241)
----Issues in negotiating international loan
    agreements with transnational banks. -
    1983.
      (002459)
----Lending without limits. - 1979.
      (000228)
----The restructuring of international loans
    and the international debt crisis. -
    1984.
      (000239)
----Syndicating and rescheduling
    international financial transactions. -
    1984.
      (000261)

FOREIGN LOANS--ARGENTINA.
----Los bancos transnacionales y el
    endeudamiento externo en la Argentina. -
    1987.
      (000819)

FOREIGN LOANS--CHINA.
----China's utilization of foreign funds and
    relevant policies. - 1984.
      (002227)

FOREIGN LOANS--HONG KONG.
----Hong Kong and Singapore. - 1985.
      (000879)

FOREIGN LOANS--LATIN AMERICA.
----The international debt crisis and the
    banks. - 1985.
      (000227)
----El proceso de revisión de los mecanismos
    financieros de la ALADI. - 1983.
      (001248)

FOREIGN LOANS--PERU.
----Transnational banks and the external
    finance of Latin America : the
    experience of Peru. - 1983.
        (000840)
----Transnational banks and the external
    finance of Latin America : the
    experience of Peru. - 1985.
        (000975)

FOREIGN LOANS--SINGAPORE.
----Hong Kong and Singapore. - 1985.
        (000879)

FOREIGN LOANS--UNITED STATES.
----International bank lending. - 1983.
        (000265)
----The international debt crisis and the
    banks. - 1985.
        (000227)
----On Third World debt. - 1984.
        (000211)

FOREIGN RELATIONS--BRAZIL.
----Brazilian imports of technology from
    Sweden, 1965-1980. - 1985.
        (001408)

FOREIGN RELATIONS--JAPAN.
----Competition in the Pacific Basin. - 1987.
        (001673)

FOREIGN RELATIONS--PHILIPPINES.
----The Philippines under Marcos. - 1986.
        (001071)

FOREIGN RELATIONS--SOUTH AFRICA.
----The political economy of U.S. policy
    toward South Africa. - 1985.
        (001196)

FOREIGN RELATIONS--SWEDEN.
----Brazilian imports of technology from
    Sweden, 1965-1980. - 1985.
        (001408)

FOREIGN RELATIONS--UNITED STATES.
----Competition in the Pacific Basin. - 1987.
        (001673)
----Democratic development. - 1986.
        (001334)
----Hard bargaining ahead. - 1985.
        (001361)
----International countertrade. - 1984.
        (001396)
----The political economy of U.S. policy
    toward South Africa. - 1985.
        (001196)
----SShA, transnatsional'nye korporatsii i
    vneshniaia politika. - 1984.
        (001815)
----Third World resource directory. - 1984.
        (002719)
----U.S. foreign assistance. - 1984.
        (000203)

FOREIGN RELATIONS--ZAMBIA.
----The mines, class power, and foreign
    policy in Zambia. - 1984.
        (001023)

FOREIGN SOVEREIGN IMMUNITIES ACT 1976
(UNITED STATES).
----The extraterritorial effects of
    antitrust laws. - 1984.
        (002342)
----Jurisdiction over foreign governments. -
    1986.
        (002347)
----Jurisdiction over foreign sovereigns. -
    1983.
        (002480)
----On Third World debt. - 1984.
        (000211)
----United States law of sovereign immunity
    relating to international financial
    transactions. - 1983.
        (002353)

FOREIGN TRADE.
----Avantage comparatif et performance dans
    le commerce international des produits
    différenciés. - 1986.
        (001669)
----Divisions over the international
    division of labour. - 1984.
        (001269)
----Information industries in the CMEA
    countries : a foreign trade dimension. -
    1986.
        (000894)
----Intra-firm pricing and the multinational
    corporations. - 1986.
        (000471)
----Mezhdunarodnaia kapitalisticheskaia
    torgovlia uslugami i problemy ee
    regulirovaniia. - 1987.
        (001378)
----North-South issues in trade in services.
    - 1985.
        (000944)
----Patterns of bilateral trade flows within
    the characteristics approach to trade. -
    1986.
        (001397)
----Rola korporacji transnarodowych w
    miedzynarodowej wymianie towarów
    przemyslowych. - 1986.
        (001369)
----Technology export from the socialist
    countries. - 1986.
        (001470)

FOREIGN TRADE--ARAB COUNTRIES.
----The Arab world is still importing. -
    1987.
        (001134)

FOREIGN TRADE--ARGENTINA.
----La industria electrónica argentina :
    apertura comercial y
    desindustrialización. - 1987.
        (000654)

FOREIGN TRADE--ASIA.
----Export processing zones and economic
    development in Asia. - 1987.
        (002389)
----Foreign trade and investment. - 1985.
        (001047)

FOREIGN TRADE--BANGLADESH.
----Trade and investment possibilities in
    Bangladesh, Nepal and Sri Lanka. - 1983.
        (001840)

FOREIGN TRADE--CANADA.
----Business directory of Canadian trade
    representation abroad. - 1984-   .
    (002700)

FOREIGN TRADE--CHINA.
----Agriculture in China. - 1985.
    (000561)
----Almanac of China's foreign economic
    relations and trade. - 1984-   .
    (002615)
----China special economic zones in
    perspective. - 1986.
    (002397)
----The China trade: making the deal/the
    China trade: making the deal work. -
    1986.
    (001845)
----China's foreign economic contract law. -
    1987.
    (002297)
----China's opening to the world. - 1986.
    (002221)
----China's special economic zones. - 1984.
    (002395)
----China's special economic zones. - 1986.
    (002382)
----Doing business with China. - 1974-   .
    (001792)
----Foreign investment and trade; origins of
    the modernization policy. - 1983.
    (001354)
----Foreign trade, investment and the law in
    the People's Republic of China. - 1985.
    (002211)
----Formation of contract and contract law
    through multinational joint ventures. -
    1983.
    (002435)
----Guide to China's foreign economic
    relations and trade. - 1983.
    (001806)
----On economic reforms, trade and foreign
    investment in China. - 1986.
    (001336)
----Recent changes in China's pure trade
    theory. - 1986.
    (001677)
----Shantou SEZ orientated towards export. -
    1987.
    (002377)
----Sino-Indian economic relations. - 1984.
    (000307)
----Special economic zones in the PRC. -
    1986.
    (002369)
----Trade policies in the PRC. - 1986.
    (001387)
----United States-China commercial
    contracts. - 1986.
    (002439)
----Les zones économiques spéciales de la
    République populaire chinoise. - 1985.
    (002383)

FOREIGN TRADE--EASTERN EUROPE.
----East-West trade, industrial co-operation
    and technology transfer. - 1984.
    (001441)
----Saisie et effets des transferts de la
    technologie incorporée dans le commerce
    est-ouest. - 1986.
    (001464)

----Technological cooperation and
    specialization. - 1986.
    (001500)

FOREIGN TRADE--GERMANY, FEDERAL REPUBLIC OF.
----Der internationale Handel mit
    Dienstleistungen aus der Sicht der
    Bundesrepublik Deutschland. - 1984.
    (000877)
----Stärken und Schwächen der Bundesrepublik
    Deutschland in der internationalen
    Arbeitsteilung. - 1984.
    (001260)
----Wachstumsmarkt Südostasien. - 1984.
    (001785)

FOREIGN TRADE--HUNGARY.
----How to trade with Hungary. - 1983.
    (001826)
----Hungarian foreign trade reform. - 1986.
    (002250)

FOREIGN TRADE--INDIA.
----Role of multinationals in India's
    foreign trade. - 1987.
    (001069)
----Sino-Indian economic relations. - 1984.
    (000307)
----Trade and investment possibilities in
    Bangladesh, Nepal and Sri Lanka. - 1983.
    (001840)
----Trade in investment-related
    technological studies. - 1986.
    (001386)

FOREIGN TRADE--ISRAEL.
----U.S.-Israel free trade area. - 1986.
    (002049)

FOREIGN TRADE--JAPAN.
----The administrative regulation of
    technology induction contracts in Japan.
    - 1987.
    (002447)
----Antitrust aspects of U.S.-Japanese
    trade. - 1983.
    (002345)
----Japán multinacionális kereskedoházai és
    nyitása a világgazdaság felé. - 1986.
    (000354)
----Japan's general trading companies. -
    1984.
    (000887)
----The legal framework of trade and
    investment in Japan. - 1986.
    (002241)
----The Sogo Shosha: can it be exported
    (imported)? - 1983.
    (000338)
----Zur Internationalisierung der
    japanischen Wirtschaft. - 1984.
    (000117)

FOREIGN TRADE--KUWAIT.
----Impact of the operations of
    transnational corporations on
    development in Kuwait. - 1987.
    (001143)

FOREIGN TRADE--LATIN AMERICA.
----Las empresas transnacionales y la
    inversión extranjera directa en la
    primera mitad de los años ochenta. -
    1987.
       (000194)
----Latin America at a glance. - 1986.
       (001821)
----The relationship of MNC direct
    investment to host country trade and
    trade policy: some preliminary evidence.
    - 1983.
       (001351)
----Trade and foreign direct investment in
    data services. - 1986.
       (000948)

FOREIGN TRADE--MEXICO.
----Restructuring industry offshore. - 1983.
       (000692)

FOREIGN TRADE--MIDDLE EAST.
----International business in the Middle
    East. - 1986.
       (001135)

FOREIGN TRADE--NEPAL.
----Trade and investment possibilities in
    Bangladesh, Nepal and Sri Lanka. - 1983.
       (001840)·

FOREIGN TRADE--OMAN.
----Impact of the operations of
    transnational corporations on
    development in the Sultanate of Oman. -
    1988.
       (001144)

FOREIGN TRADE--POLAND.
----CMEA direct investments in the western
    countries. - 1987.
       (000158)

FOREIGN TRADE--REPUBLIC OF KOREA.
----The Sogo Shosha: can it be exported
    (imported)? - 1983.
       (000338)

FOREIGN TRADE--SOUTHEAST ASIA.
----Wachstumsmarkt Südostasien. - 1984.
       (001785)

FOREIGN TRADE--SRI LANKA.
----Trade and investment possibilities in
    Bangladesh, Nepal and Sri Lanka. - 1983.
       (001840)

FOREIGN TRADE--UNITED KINGDOM.
----East-West trade, industrial co-operation
    and technology transfer. - 1984.
       (001441)

FOREIGN TRADE--UNITED STATES.
----Les années quatre-vingts : quelles
    perspectives pour l'industrie américaine
    et les investissements internationaux? -
    1983.
       (000106)
----Antitrust aspects of U.S.-Japanese
    trade. - 1983.
       (002345)
----The Arab world is still importing. -
    1987.
       (001134)

----Doing business with China. - 1974-
       (001792)
----Journal of the US-USSR Trade and
    Economic Council. - 1976-
       (001179)
----Protectionist threat to trade and
    investment in services. - 1983.
       (000951)
----Restructuring industry offshore. - 1983.
       (000692)
----Trade policies in the PRC. - 1986.
       (001387)
----U.S. high technology trade and
    competitiveness. - 1985.
       (001362)
----U.S.-Israel free trade area. - 1986.
       (002049)
----United States-China commercial
    contracts. - 1986.
       (002439)

FOREIGN TRADE--USSR.
----Anderungen im sowjetischen
    Aussenwirtschaftssystem zu Beginn des
    Jahres 1987. - 1987.
       (001176)
----Foreign trade with the USSR. - 1987.
       (001774)
----Journal of the US-USSR Trade and
    Economic Council. - 1976-
       (001179)
----La négociation des contrats de transfert
    de techniques avec l'Union soviétique. -
    1984.
       (002466)
----The new Soviet joint venture
    regulations. - 1987.
       (002202)
----The problem of autonomy in Soviet
    international contract law. - 1983.
       (002167)
----La réforme du commerce extérieur
    soviétique. - 1987.
       (002261)
----The Soviet position on international
    arbitration. - 1986.
       (002571)

FOREIGN TRADE--WESTERN EUROPE.
----Saisie et effets des transferts de la
    technologie incorporée dans le commerce
    est-ouest. - 1986.
       (001464)
----Wachstumsmarkt Südostasien. - 1984.
       (001785)

FOREIGN TRADE--YUGOSLAVIA.
----Doing business with Yugoslavia. - 1986.
       (001793)

FORESTRY INDUSTRY--PAPUA NEW GUINEA.
----Reconciling ethical behaviour. - 1986.
       (001719)

FRANCE--AGROINDUSTRY.
----L'internationalisation de l'agriculture
    francaise. - 1984.
       (000567)

FRANCE--AUTOMOBILE INDUSTRY.
----Labour, production and the state :
    decentralization of the French
    automobile industry. - 1987.
       (000724)

FRANCE--BANKS.
----Nationalisation of the banks in France.
     - 1983.
     (001568)
----Die Nationalisierungen in Frankreich
     1981/82. - 1983.
     (002337)

FRANCE--BUSINESS ENTERPRISES.
----Ces patrons qui gagnent. - 1986.
     (001146)

FRANCE--CHEMICAL INDUSTRY.
----Le role des grandes entreprises
     diversifiées du pétrole et de la chimie
     dans la production alimentaire. - 1985.
     (000699)

FRANCE--COMMERCIAL ARBITRATION.
----Arbitral adjudication. - 1984.
     (002484)
----Etude historique et comparée de
     l'arbitrage. - 1984.
     (002485)

FRANCE--COMPETITION.
----Competing for prosperity. - 1986.
     (001338)

FRANCE--CONFISCATIONS.
----Les nationalisations françaises face à
     l'ordre juridique suisse. - 1984.
     (002325)

FRANCE--CONTRACTS.
----Les caractéristiques juridiques des
     contrats internationaux de coopération
     industrielle. - 1984.
     (002438)
----Preliminary agreements in international
     contract negotiation. - 1983.
     (002465)

FRANCE--CORPORATION LAW.
----Code des sociétés. - 1977.
     (001975)
----Répertoire des sociétés. - 1970-   .
     (002265)

FRANCE--CORPORATIONS.
----Competing for prosperity. - 1986.
     (001338)
----Répertoire des sociétés. - 1970-   .
     (002265)

FRANCE--DEVELOPING COUNTRIES.
----Les investissements français dans le
     Tiers monde. - 1984.
     (000150)
----Le processus d'acquisition technologique
     par les entreprises d'un pays
     semi-industrialise. Deux études de cas.
     (With English summary.). - 1983.
     (001407)

FRANCE--DEVELOPMENT.
----L'économie française et le développement
     des services : Annuaire 1985-1986. -
     1986.
     (000847)

FRANCE--DEVELOPMENT ASSISTANCE.
----Infratechnologies, technologies de
     pointe, investissements dans et pour les
     pays en développement. - 1985.
     (001444)

FRANCE--ECONOMIC ANALYSIS.
----Competing for prosperity. - 1986.
     (001338)

FRANCE--ECONOMIC CONDITIONS.
----L'économie française et le développement
     des services : Annuaire 1985-1986. -
     1986.
     (000847)

FRANCE--ECONOMIC POLICY.
----The dilemma of denationalisation. - 1986.
     (001644)

FRANCE--EMPLOYMENT.
----Activité comparée des établissements
     industriels d'origine étrangère et des
     établissements industriels français. -
     1984.
     (001927)

FRANCE--FOOD INDUSTRY.
----L'internationalisation de l'agriculture
     francaise. - 1984.
     (000567)

FRANCE--FOOD PRODUCTION.
----Le role des grandes entreprises
     diversifiées du pétrole et de la chimie
     dans la production alimentaire. - 1985.
     (000699)

FRANCE--FOREIGN DIRECT INVESTMENT.
----Les flux d'investissement direct entre
     la France et l'extérieur, 1965-1978. -
     1981.
     (000119)
----French multinationals. - 1984.
     (000375)
----L'impact de l'investissement étranger en
     France sur l'emploi industriel
     (1974-1983). (With English summary.). -
     1984.
     (001161)
----Investissements directs et flux
     commerciaux compléments ou substituts?
     Le cas francais 1968-1978. (With English
     summary.). - 1985.
     (000107)

FRANCE--FOREIGN INVESTMENTS.
----L'Afrique, l'Europe et la crise. - 1986.
     (001287)
----Les investissements français dans le
     Tiers monde. - 1984.
     (000150)
----Propriété et pouvoir dans l'industrie. -
     1987.
     (001628)

FRANCE--HISTORY.
----Ces patrons qui gagnent. - 1986.
     (001146)

FRANCE--INDUSTRIAL CO-OPERATION.
----Les caractéristiques juridiques des
     contrats internationaux de coopération
     industrielle. - 1984.
       (002438)
----La specialisation internationale de la
     France dans les échanges de services.
     (With English summary.). - 1986.
       (000907)

FRANCE--INDUSTRIAL ENTERPRISES.
----Activité comparée des établissements
     industriels d'origine étrangère et des
     établissements industriels français. -
     1984.
       (001927)
----Die Nationalisierungen in Frankreich
     1981/82. - 1983.
       (002337)
----Le processus d'acquisition technologique
     par les entreprises d'un pays
     semi-industrialise. Deux études de cas.
     (With English summary.). - 1983.
       (001407)

FRANCE--INDUSTRIAL EQUIPMENT LEASES.
----Analysis of equipment leasing contracts.
     - 1984.
       (002407)

FRANCE--INDUSTRIAL LOCATION.
----Labour, production and the state :
     decentralization of the French
     automobile industry. - 1987.
       (000724)

FRANCE--INDUSTRIAL POLICY.
----Competing for prosperity. - 1986.
       (001338)
----Nationalisations et développement
     régional. - 1983.
       (001550)

FRANCE--INDUSTRIAL WORKERS.
----L'impact de l'investissement étranger en
     France sur l'emploi industriel
     (1974-1983). (With English summary.). -
     1984.
       (001161)

FRANCE--INDUSTRY.
----Propriété et pouvoir dans l'industrie. -
     1987.
       (001628)

FRANCE--INTRA-INDUSTRY TRADE.
----La specialisation internationale de la
     France dans les échanges de services.
     (With English summary.). - 1986.
       (000907)

FRANCE--INVESTMENT TAX CREDIT.
----International income taxation and
     developing countries. - 1988.
       (001759)

FRANCE--INVESTMENTS.
----Les flux d'investissement direct entre
     la France et l'extérieur, 1965-1978. -
     1981.
       (000119)

FRANCE--LAWS AND REGULATIONS.
----Fraude fiscale internationale et
     repression. - 1986.
       (001742)
----International income taxation and
     developing countries. - 1988.
       (001759)
----National legislation and regulations
     relating to transnational corporations.
     Volume 3. - 1983.
       (002252)

FRANCE--MANAGEMENT.
----Ces patrons qui gagnent. - 1986.
       (001146)
----Propriété et pouvoir dans l'industrie. -
     1987.
       (001628)

FRANCE--NATIONALIZATION.
----La contribution des nationalisations
     françaises de 1982 au droit
     international des nationalisations. -
     1985.
       (002319)
----Nationalisation of the banks in France.
     - 1983.
       (001568)
----Nationalisations et développement
     régional. - 1983.
       (001550)
----Les nationalisations françaises face à
     l'ordre juridique suisse. - 1984.
       (002325)
----Nationalisations, un bilan en
     demi-teinte. - 1983.
       (001579)
----Die Nationalisierungen in Frankreich
     1981/82. - 1983.
       (002337)

FRANCE--NEGOTIATION.
----Preliminary agreements in international
     contract negotiation. - 1983.
       (002465)

FRANCE--PETROCHEMICAL INDUSTRY.
----Le role des grandes entreprises
     diversifiées du pétrole et de la chimie
     dans la production alimentaire. - 1985.
       (000699)

FRANCE--PRICES.
----La formation du prix dans les
     transactions internationales. - 1985.
       (001712)

FRANCE--PRIVATE ENTERPRISES.
----The dilemma of denationalisation. - 1986.
       (001644)

FRANCE--PRIVATE SECTOR.
----Propriété et pouvoir dans l'industrie. -
     1987.
       (001628)

FRANCE--PRODUCTION PLANNING.
----Labour, production and the state :
     decentralization of the French
     automobile industry. - 1987.
       (000724)

FRANCE--PUBLIC FINANCE.
----Nationalisations, un bilan en
    demi-teinte. - 1983.
       (001579)

FRANCE--PUBLIC LAW.
----Die Nationalisierungen in Frankreich
    1981/82. - 1983.
       (002337)

FRANCE--PUBLIC SECTOR.
----Nationalisations, un bilan en
    demi-teinte. - 1983.
       (001579)
----Die Nationalisierungen in Frankreich
    1981/82. - 1983.
       (002337)
----Propriété et pouvoir dans l'industrie. -
    1987.
       (001628)

FRANCE--RECOGNITION (INTERNATIONAL LAW).
----Les nationalisations françaises face à
    l'ordre juridique suisse. - 1984.
       (002325)

FRANCE--REGIONAL DEVELOPMENT.
----Activité comparée des établissements
    industriels d'origine étrangère et des
    établissements industriels français. -
    1984.
       (001927)
----Nationalisations et développement
    régional. - 1983.
       (001550)

FRANCE--SERVICE INDUSTRIES.
----L'économie française et le développement
    des services : Annuaire 1985-1986. -
    1986.
       (000847)
----La specialisation internationale de la
    France dans les échanges de services.
    (With English summary.). - 1986.
       (000907)

FRANCE--TAX EVASION.
----Fraude fiscale internationale et
    repression. - 1986.
       (001742)

FRANCE--TAX INCENTIVES.
----International income taxation and
    developing countries. - 1988.
       (001759)

FRANCE--TAX SYSTEMS.
----Les tendances récentes des conventions
    fiscales. - 1985.
       (002053)

FRANCE--TAX TREATIES.
----Les tendances récentes des conventions
    fiscales. - 1985.
       (002053)

FRANCE--TAXATION.
----Fraude fiscale internationale et
    repression. - 1986.
       (001742)
----International income taxation and
    developing countries. - 1988.
       (001759)

FRANCE--TECHNOLOGY TRANSFER.
----Le processus d'acquisition technologique
    par les entreprises d'un pays
    semi-industrialise. Deux études de cas.
    (With English summary.). - 1983.
       (001407)

FRANCE--TRANSFER PRICING.
----La formation du prix dans les
    transactions internationales. - 1985.
       (001712)
----Fraude fiscale internationale et
    repression. - 1986.
       (001742)

FRANCE--TRANSNATIONAL CORPORATIONS.
----Activité comparée des établissements
    industriels d'origine étrangère et des
    établissements industriels français. -
    1984.
       (001927)
----Ces patrons qui gagnent. - 1986.
       (001146)
----Les firmes multinationales francaises et
    la hiérarchisation des nations. (With
    English summary.). - 1985.
       (000358)
----Fraude fiscale internationale et
    repression. - 1986.
       (001742)
----French multinationals. - 1984.
       (000375)
----Gestion financière internationale des
    entreprises. - 1984.
       (000437)
----L'internationalisation de l'agriculture
    francaise. - 1984.
       (000567)
----National legislation and regulations
    relating to transnational corporations.
    Volume 3. - 1983.
       (002252)
----Nationalisations et
    internationalisation. - 1983.
       (000497)
----Le role des grandes entreprises
    diversifiées du pétrole et de la chimie
    dans la production alimentaire. - 1985.
       (000699)

FRANCHISES.
----Licence agreements in developing
    countries. - 1987.
       (002437)

FRANCHISES--GERMANY, FEDERAL REPUBLIC OF.
----Trademark and related rights in
    franchise agreements in Germany. - 1983.
       (001523)

FRANCHISES--UNITED STATES.
----Trademark and related rights in
    franchise agreements in Germany. - 1983.
       (001523)

FREE EXPORT ZONES.
----The economic and social effects of
    multinational enterprises in export
    processing zones. - 1988.
       (002371)
----Export processing zones. - 1983.
       (002372)

FREE EXPORT ZONES (continued)
----Export processing zones in developing
countries. - 1987.
(002376)
----Export processing zones: new catalysts
for economic development. - 1983.
(002391)
----Export-processing zones and
industrialization: some considerations
from the economics of large
organizations. - 1983.
(002364)
----Free zones in developing countries. -
1983.
(002390)
----Industrial free zones and
industrialization in developing
countries. - 1986.
(002403)
----Investing in free export processing
zones. - 1984.
(002362)
----Investir dans les zones franches
industrielles d'exportation. - 1984.
(002363)
----On the choice between capital import and
labor export. - 1983.
(002370)
----De toekomst van 'export-processing free
zones'. - 1987.
(002398)
----Transnational corporations in world
development. - 1983.
(000102)
----Unemployment and the formation of
duty-free zones. - 1987.
(001931)
----Les zones franches dans le monde. - 1987.
(002378)

FREE EXPORT ZONES--ASIA.
----Economic and social impacts of export
processing zones in Asia. - 1983.
(002387)
----Export processing zones and economic
development in Asia. - 1987.
(002389)
----The special economic zones of China. -
1985.
(002392)
----TWARO (ITGLWF-ARO) Asian Seminar on Free
Trade Zones, Tokyo, 6th-13th March 1983.
- 1983.
(002396)
----Wages, hours and working conditions in
Asian free trade zones. - 1984.
(001897)

FREE EXPORT ZONES--BRAZIL.
----Employment effects of exports by
multinationals and of export processing
zones in Brazil. - 1987.
(001915)

FREE EXPORT ZONES--CHINA.
----China special economic zones in
perspective. - 1986.
(002397)
----China's opening to the world. - 1986.
(002221)
----China's special economic zones. - 1984.
(002386)
----China's special economic zones. - 1984.
(002395)

----China's special economic zones. - 1986.
(002382)
----China's special economic zones. - 1986.
(002366)
----Chinese economic reforms since 1978 with
particular emphasis on the special
economic zones. - 1987.
(002375)
----Eight years of the open policy. - 1987.
(001051)
----Kina különleges gazdasági övezetei. -
1987.
(002374)
----Recent developments in China's special
economic zones : problems and prognosis.
- 1987.
(002404)
----Shantou SEZ orientated towards export. -
1987.
(002377)
----Shenzhen : a Chinese development zone in
global perspective. - 1985.
(002393)
----The special economic zones. - 1987.
(002379)
----Special economic zones in the People's
Republic of China. - 1986.
(002361)
----Special economic zones in the PRC. -
1986.
(002369)
----The special economic zones of China. -
1985.
(002392)
----Trade policies in the PRC. - 1986.
(001387)
----Les zones économiques spéciales de la
République populaire chinoise. - 1985.
(002383)

FREE EXPORT ZONES--GHANA.
----Employment and multinational enterprises
in export processing zones. - 1984.
(001886)

FREE EXPORT ZONES--INDONESIA.
----The Jakarta export processing zone:
benefits and costs. - 1983.
(002400)

FREE EXPORT ZONES--LIBERIA.
----Employment and multinational enterprises
in export processing zones. - 1984.
(001886)

FREE EXPORT ZONES--MALAYSIA.
----Malaysia's industrial enclaves :
benefits and costs. - 1987.
(002402)

FREE EXPORT ZONES--MAURITIUS.
----Aspects of labour law and relations in
selected export processing zones. - 1984.
(001895)

**FREE EXPORT ZONES--MEXICAN-AMERICAN BORDER
REGION.**
----Mexican border and free zone areas:
implications for development. - 1983.
(002380)

FREE EXPORT ZONES--PAKISTAN.
----Aspects of labour law and relations in
     selected export processing zones. - 1984.
     (001895)

FREE EXPORT ZONES--PHILIPPINES.
----Aspects of labour law and relations in
     selected export processing zones. - 1984.
     (001895)
----The Bataan export processing zone. -
     1982.
     (002365)
----Export channels in the Philippines. -
     1987.
     (002373)
----Export promotion via industrial
     enclaves. - 1987.
     (002399)

FREE EXPORT ZONES--REPUBLIC OF KOREA.
----Korea's Masan free export zone. - 1984.
     (002401)

FREE EXPORT ZONES--SINGAPORE.
----Export processing and industrialisation.
     - 1982.
     (002405)

FREE EXPORT ZONES--SRI LANKA.
----Aspects of labour law and relations in
     selected export processing zones. - 1984.
     (001895)
----The Katunayake investment promotion
     zone. - 1982.
     (002388)

FREE EXPORT ZONES--UNITED STATES.
----Political and policy dimensions of
     foreign trade zones. - 1985.
     (001356)

FREE TRADE.
----Introduction to the OECD codes of
     liberalisation. - 1987.
     (001984)
----Power and protectionism. - 1983.
     (001865)
----Putting world trade back on a growth
     course. - 1984.
     (001358)

FREE TRADE--CANADA.
----The legal markets of international
     trade. - 1987.
     (002038)
----Multinationals and free trade: the
     implications of a US-Canadian
     agreement. - 1986.
     (002029)

FREE TRADE--UNITED STATES.
----The legal markets of international
     trade. - 1987.
     (002038)
----Multinationals and free trade: the
     implications of a US-Canadian
     agreement. - 1986.
     (002029)

FREE TRADE--WESTERN EUROPE.
----Perspektiven für eine engere
     Zusammenarbeit zwischen der Europäischen
     Gemeinschaft und den
     EFTA-Mitgliedstaaten. - 1985.
     (001962)

FREE TRADE AREAS--ASIA.
----Export processing zones and economic
     development in Asia. - 1987.
     (002389)
----TWARO (ITGLWF-ARO) Asian Seminar on Free
     Trade Zones, Tokyo, 6th-13th March 1983.
     - 1983.
     (002396)

FREE TRADE AREAS--CARIBBEAN REGION.
----La presentación de la iniciativa de la
     Cuenca del Caribe al GATT. - 1985.
     (001972)

FREE TRADE AREAS--ISRAEL.
----U.S.-Israel free trade area. - 1986.
     (002049)

FREE TRADE AREAS--UNITED STATES.
----La presentación de la iniciativa de la
     Cuenca del Caribe al GATT. - 1985.
     (001972)
----U.S.-Israel free trade area. - 1986.
     (002049)

FRENCH LANGUAGE.
----Dictionnaire des industries. - 1986.
     (002705)

GABON--PETROLEUM INDUSTRY.
----Les conventions dans la fiscalité
     pétrolière gabonaise. - 1987.
     (002030)

GABON--PETROLEUM LAW.
----Les conventions dans la fiscalité
     pétrolière gabonaise. - 1987.
     (002030)

GABON--TREATIES.
----Les conventions dans la fiscalité
     pétrolière gabonaise. - 1987.
     (002030)

GAME THEORY.
----Cooperation in the liberalization of
     international trade. - 1987.
     (001400)

GATT.
----All traded services are embodied in
     materials or people. - 1987.
     (000869)
----The applicability of GATT to
     international trade in services :
     general considerations and the interest
     of developing countries. - 1987.
     (000885)
----The Caribbean Basin Economic Recovery
     Act and its implications for foreign
     private investment. - 1984.
     (001965)
----The competence of GATT. - 1987.
     (001382)
----Cooperation in the liberalization of
     international trade. - 1987.
     (001400)

GATT (continued)
----The future of services : basic issues
    for the long-term goals of the new GATT
    round. - 1987.
       (000862)
----The GATT and multilateral treaty making.
    - 1983.
       (001995)
----GATT and recent international trade
    problems. - 1987.
       (001986)
----GATT surveillance of industrial
    policies. - 1986.
       (001350)
----Intellectual property rights,
    investment, and trade in services in the
    Uruguay round. - 1987.
       (000817)
----International Colloquium on the Proposed
    New Round of Multilateral Trade
    Negotiations and Developing Countries :
    proceedings and papers. - 1986.
       (001365)
----International services-trade issues and
    the GATT. - 1983.
       (000830)
----International trade disputes and the
    individual : private party involvement
    in national and international procedures
    regarding unfair foreign trade
    practices. - 1986.
       (002514)
----Issues and data needs for GATT
    negotiations on services. - 1987.
       (000964)
----Legal problems in expanding the scope of
    GATT to include trade in services. -
    1983.
       (000864)
----Meeting the challenges of the world
    information economy. - 1984.
       (000853)
----Les négociations internationales sur les
    services ou la quadrature du cercle. -
    1986.
       (000911)
----Protectionism and structural adjustment.
    - 1986.
       (001689)
----Protectionist threat to trade and
    investment in services. - 1983.
       (000951)
----Putting services on the table : the new
    GATT round. - 1987.
       (000932)
----Putting world trade back on a growth
    course. - 1984.
       (001358)
----Revitalizing development, growth and
    international trade. - 1987.
       (001394)
----The scope, limits and function of the
    GATT legal system. - 1985.
       (002008)
----Services and the development process. -
    1985.
       (000979)
----A szolgáltatások a nemzetközi gazdasági
    kapcsolatokban. - 1986.
       (000895)
----Trade in services. - 1984.
       (000955)

----Trade in services : obstacles and
    opportunities. - 1987.
       (000984)
----Trade in services. - 1986.
       (000962)
----Trade in services and developing
    countries. - 1986.
       (000952)
----Trade liberalization and the global
    service economy. - 1985.
       (000811)
----Trade policy as a constitutional problem
    : on the "domestic policy functions" of
    international trade rules. - 1986..
       (001379)
----Trade trouble-shooting. - 1986.
       (001967)
----Transnational services policy? - 1987.
       (000867)
----The U.S. drive to bring services into
    GATT. - 1986.
       (000926)
----World-traded services : the challenge
    for the eighties. - 1984.
       (000889)

GATT. MINISTERIAL MEETING (1986 : PUNTA DEL
ESTE, URUGUAY).
----Developing countries and services in the
    Uruguay Round. - 1987.
       (000886)
----Intellectual property rights,
    investment, and trade in services in the
    Uruguay round. - 1987.
       (000817)
----Punta del Este and after. - 1987.
       (000927)
----Putting services on the table : the new
    GATT round. - 1987.
       (000932)
----Services and the GATT. - 1987.
       (000954)
----The Uruguay Round and the international
    trading system. - 1987.
       (001976)
----The Uruguay round of multilateral trade
    talks. - 1987.
       (000983)

GENERAL AGREEMENT ON TARIFFS AND TRADE
(1947).
----The competence of GATT. - 1987.
       (001382)
----Estados Unidos, América Latina y el
    debate internacional sobre el comercio
    de servicios. - 1986.
       (000934)
----La formation du prix dans les
    transactions internationales. - 1985.
       (001712)
----The fourth multifibre arrangement and
    the new legal regime for international
    trade in textiles. - 1987.
       (001401)
----GATT versus tax treaties? - 1987.
       (002032)
----La internacionalización de los
    servicios. - 1986.
       (000923)
----The legal markets of international
    trade. - 1987.
       (002038)

GENERAL AGREEMENT ON TARIFFS AND TRADE
(1947) (continued)
----La presentación de la iniciativa de la
    Cuenca del Caribe al GATT. - 1985.
        (001972)
----Punta del Este and after. - 1987.
        (000927)
----Putting services on the table : the new
    GATT round. - 1987.
        (000932)
----Restrictive business practices in
    international trade. - 1987.
        (001661)
----The scope, limits and function of the
    GATT legal system. - 1985.
        (002008)
----The Uruguay round of multilateral trade
    talks. - 1987.
        (000983)

GENERAL MOTORS CORPORATION.
----Creating the GM-Toyota joint venture: a
    case in complex negotiation. - 1987.
        (001656)

GENERALE BISCUIT (ATHIS-MONS, FRANCE).
----Importance et implantations comparées
    des quatre plus grands biscuitiers
    mondiaux, Nabisco Brands, United
    Biscuits, Générale Biscuit, Bahlsen. -
    1984.
        (000273)

GENERALIZED SYSTEM OF PREFERENCES--UNITED
STATES.
----The U.S. renewal of the GSP. - 1986.
        (001996)

GENETIC ENGINEERING.
----Economic aspects of biotechnology. -
    1986.
        (000693)
----Genetic engineering and biotechnology
    firms worldwide directory. - 1981-   .
        (000688) (002642)

GERMAN DEMOCRATIC REPUBLIC--AUTOMATION.
----Microelectronics-based automation
    technologies and development. - 1985.
        (000753)

GERMAN DEMOCRATIC REPUBLIC--INDUSTRIAL
CO-OPERATION.
----Zum Einfluss von Modernisierung und
    Rekonstruktion auf die internationale
    sozialistische Arbeitsteilung. - 1987.
        (001227)

GERMAN DEMOCRATIC REPUBLIC--INDUSTRIAL
MARKETING.
----Die Anwendung der Mikrorechentechnik :
    wichtige Voraussetzung für eine
    reaktionsfähige und effektive
    Absatzwirtschaft. - 1987.
        (000908)

GERMAN DEMOCRATIC REPUBLIC--MANAGEMENT
INFORMATION SYSTEMS.
----Die Anwendung der Mikrorechentechnik :
    wichtige Voraussetzung für eine
    reaktionsfähige und effektive
    Absatzwirtschaft. - 1987.
        (000908)

GERMAN DEMOCRATIC REPUBLIC--MICROCOMPUTERS.
----Die Anwendung der Mikrorechentechnik :
    wichtige Voraussetzung für eine
    reaktionsfähige und effektive
    Absatzwirtschaft. - 1987.
        (000908)

GERMAN DEMOCRATIC REPUBLIC--NEW TECHNOLOGIES.
----Zum Einfluss von Modernisierung und
    Rekonstruktion auf die internationale
    sozialistische Arbeitsteilung. - 1987.
        (001227)

GERMANY--MANAGEMENT.
----External and internal functioning of
    American, German, and Japanese
    multinational corporations:
    decisionmaking and policy issues. - 1983.
        (000432)

GERMANY--TRANSNATIONAL CORPORATIONS.
----External and internal functioning of
    American, German, and Japanese
    multinational corporations:
    decisionmaking and policy issues. - 1983.
        (000432)

GERMANY, FEDERAL REPUBLIC OF--ACCOUNTING.
----Die finanzielle Führung und Kontrolle
    von Auslandsgesellschaften. - 1983.
        (000447)

GERMANY, FEDERAL REPUBLIC OF--ACCOUNTING AND
REPORTING.
----Der konsolidierte Abschluss. - 1983.
        (002091)

GERMANY, FEDERAL REPUBLIC OF--AFFILIATE
CORPORATIONS.
----Gewinne verbundener Unternehmen,
    Verrechnungspreise. - 1984.
        (001749)
----Die Steuerung ausländischer
    Tochtergesellschaften. - 1983.
        (000400)

GERMANY, FEDERAL REPUBLIC OF--ANTITRUST LAW.
----Fakultatives Kollisonsrecht im
    internationalen Wettbewerbsrecht? - 1984.
        (002247)

GERMANY, FEDERAL REPUBLIC OF--BALANCE OF
PAYMENTS.
----Technological balance of payments and
    international competitiveness. - 1983.
        (001442)

GERMANY, FEDERAL REPUBLIC OF--BANKRUPTCY.
----Die Haftungsproblematik bei Konkurs
    einer Gesellschaft innerhalb eines
    transnationalen Unternehmens. - 1984.
        (002233)

GERMANY, FEDERAL REPUBLIC OF--BUSINESS
ENTERPRISES.
----Handbuch der Grossunternehmen. -
    1940-   .
        (002644)

GERMANY, FEDERAL REPUBLIC OF--CHEMICAL
INDUSTRY.
----La recherche-développement dans la
stratégie des grandes entreprises
chimiques de l'entre-deux-guerres: Du
Pont de Nemours, Imperial Chemical
Industries, I. G. Farben. (With English
summary.). - 1984.
(000295)

GERMANY, FEDERAL REPUBLIC OF--COMPARATIVE
ANALYSIS.
----Multinational enterprise and world
competition. - 1987.
(000018)

GERMANY, FEDERAL REPUBLIC OF--COMPETITION.
----Stärken und Schwächen der Bundesrepublik
Deutschland in der internationalen
Arbeitsteilung. - 1984.
(001260)

GERMANY, FEDERAL REPUBLIC OF--CORPORATE
ANALYSIS.
----New trends in internationalization:
processes and theories. Diversified
patterns of multinational enterprise and
old and new forms of foreign involvement
of the firm. - 1983.
(000068)

GERMANY, FEDERAL REPUBLIC OF--CORPORATE
MERGERS.
----Private agreements for takeovers of
public companies. - 1984.
(001626)

GERMANY, FEDERAL REPUBLIC OF--CORPORATION
LAW.
----Abhangigkeit und Konzernzugehorigkeit
von Gemeinschaftsunternehmen. - 1985.
(002239)

GERMANY, FEDERAL REPUBLIC OF--CORPORATION
TAX.
----German transfer pricing. - 1984.
(001748)

GERMANY, FEDERAL REPUBLIC OF--CORPORATIONS.
----Die Haftungsproblematik bei Konkurs
einer Gesellschaft innerhalb eines
transnationalen Unternehmens. - 1984.
(002233)
----Handbuch der Grossunternehmen. -
1940-
(002644)

GERMANY, FEDERAL REPUBLIC OF--DEVELOPING
COUNTRIES.
----Direktinvestitionen in
Entwicklungsländern. - 1983.
(000125)
----Investitionsschutzabkommen. - 1986.
(002041)

GERMANY, FEDERAL REPUBLIC OF--DEVELOPMENT
RESEARCH.
----La recherche-développement dans la
stratégie des grandes entreprises
chimiques de l'entre-deux-guerres: Du
Pont de Nemours, Imperial Chemical
Industries, I. G. Farben. (With English
summary.). - 1984.
(000295)

GERMANY, FEDERAL REPUBLIC OF--DIRECTORIES.
----Handbuch der Grossunternehmen. -
1940-
(002644)

GERMANY, FEDERAL REPUBLIC OF--DOUBLE
TAXATION.
----Gewinne verbundener Unternehmen,
Verrechnungspreise. - 1984.
(001749)
----Internationale Unternehmensbesteuerung.
- 1983.
(001727)

GERMANY, FEDERAL REPUBLIC OF--ECONOMIC
AGREEMENTS.
----Investitionsschutzabkommen. - 1986.
(002041)

GERMANY, FEDERAL REPUBLIC OF--ECONOMIC
CO-OPERATION.
----Wachstumsmarkt Südostasien. - 1984.
(001785)

GERMANY, FEDERAL REPUBLIC OF--ECONOMIC
DEVELOPMENT.
----The ICSID Klöckner v. Cameroon award. -
1984.
(002553)

GERMANY, FEDERAL REPUBLIC OF--ECONOMIC
RELATIONS.
----Neue Wachstumsmärkte in Fernost. - 1983.
(001800)
----Wachstumsmarkt Südostasien. - 1984.
(001785)

GERMANY, FEDERAL REPUBLIC OF--EMPLOYMENT.
----Strukturveränderungen der
internationalen Direktinvestitionen und
inländischer Arbeitsmarkt. - 1983.
(001913)

GERMANY, FEDERAL REPUBLIC OF--EMPLOYMENT
POLICY.
----The development of employment in
multinational enterprises in the Federal
Republic of Germany. - 1985.
(001912)

GERMANY, FEDERAL REPUBLIC OF--FINANCE.
----Die finanzielle Führung und Kontrolle
von Auslandsgesellschaften. - 1983.
(000447)

GERMANY, FEDERAL REPUBLIC OF--FINANCIAL
STATEMENTS.
----Der konsolidierte Abschluss. - 1983.
(002091)

GERMANY, FEDERAL REPUBLIC OF--FOREIGN DIRECT
INVESTMENT.
----Auslandsinvestitionen deutscher
Unternehmen in Entwicklungsländern. -
1984.
(000167)
----Direktinvestitionen in
Entwicklungsländern. - 1983.
(000125)
----DM-Investitionen in Südafrika. - 1983.
(001197)

Subject Index - Index des matières

GERMANY, FEDERAL REPUBLIC OF--FOREIGN DIRECT
INVESTMENT (continued)
----Las empresas transnacionales y la
inversión extranjera directa en la
primera mitad de los años ochenta. -
1987.
(000194)
----Die finanzielle Führung und Kontrolle
von Auslandsgesellschaften. - 1983.
(000447)
----International trade and foreign direct
investment in West German manufacturing
industries. - 1984.
(000771)
----Neue Wachstumsmärkte in Fernost. - 1983.
(001800)
----New trends in internationalization:
processes and theories. Diversified
patterns of multinational enterprise and
old and new forms of foreign involvement
of the firm. - 1983.
(000068)
----Strukturveränderungen der
internationalen Direktinvestitionen und
inländischer Arbeitsmarkt. - 1983.
(001913)
----Trends and issues in foreign direct
investment and related flows. - 1985.
(000192)
----West Germany: expanding where the
markets are. - 1987.
(000136)

GERMANY, FEDERAL REPUBLIC OF--FOREIGN
INVESTMENTS.
----Investitionsbedingungen in der
ASEAN-region. - 1986.
(001814)
----Investitionsschutzabkommen. - 1986.
(002041)
----National legislation and regulations
relating to transnational corporations.
Volume 4. - 1986.
(002253)
----Transfert de technologie. - 1983.
(001460)

GERMANY, FEDERAL REPUBLIC OF--FOREIGN TRADE.
----Der internationale Handel mit
Dienstleistungen aus der Sicht der
Bundesrepublik Deutschland. - 1984.
(000877)
----Stärken und Schwächen der Bundesrepublik
Deutschland in der internationalen
Arbeitsteilung. - 1984.
(001260)
----Wachstumsmarkt Südostasien. - 1984.
(001785)

GERMANY, FEDERAL REPUBLIC OF--FRANCHISES.
----Trademark and related rights in
franchise agreements in Germany. - 1983.
(001523)

GERMANY, FEDERAL REPUBLIC OF--INDUSTRIAL
EQUIPMENT LEASES.
----Analysis of equipment leasing contracts.
- 1984.
(002407)

GERMANY, FEDERAL REPUBLIC OF--INDUSTRIAL
ORGANIZATION.
----Industry structure and performance. -
1985.
(000442)

GERMANY, FEDERAL REPUBLIC OF--INDUSTRIAL
SECTOR.
----Industry structure and performance. -
1985.
(000442)

GERMANY, FEDERAL REPUBLIC OF--INDUSTRY.
----Entry by diversified firms into German
industries. - 1986.
(001162)

GERMANY, FEDERAL REPUBLIC OF--INTERNATIONAL
COMPETITION.
----Multinational enterprise and world
competition. - 1987.
(000018)

GERMANY, FEDERAL REPUBLIC OF--INTERNATIONAL
ECONOMIC RELATIONS.
----Politik als Investitionsmotor? - 1985.
(001131)

GERMANY, FEDERAL REPUBLIC OF--INVESTMENT
DISPUTES.
----The ICSID Klöckner v. Cameroon award. -
1984.
(002553)

GERMANY, FEDERAL REPUBLIC OF--INVESTMENT
POLICY.
----Investitionsbedingungen in der
ASEAN-region. - 1986.
(001814)

GERMANY, FEDERAL REPUBLIC OF--INVESTMENT TAX
CREDIT.
----International income taxation and
developing countries. - 1988.
(001759)

GERMANY, FEDERAL REPUBLIC OF--JOINT VENTURES.
----Abhangigkeit und Konzernzugehorigkeit
von Gemeinschaftsunternehmen. - 1985.
(002239)
----Die Steuerung auslandischer
Tochtergesellschaften. - 1983.
(000400)

GERMANY, FEDERAL REPUBLIC OF--LABOUR SUPPLY.
----The development of employment in
multinational enterprises in the Federal
Republic of Germany. - 1985.
(001912)

GERMANY, FEDERAL REPUBLIC OF--LAW.
----German transfer pricing. - 1984.
(001748)

GERMANY, FEDERAL REPUBLIC OF--LAWS AND
REGULATIONS.
----International income taxation and
developing countries. - 1988.
(001759)
----Konzerntransferpreise im internationalen
Steuerrecht. - 1986.
(001710)

GERMANY, FEDERAL REPUBLIC OF--LAWS AND
REGULATIONS (continued)
----National legislation and regulations
   relating to transnational corporations.
   Volume 4. - 1986.
      (002253)
----Probleme der Gewinn- und
   Verlustrealisierung. - 1986.
      (001703)
----Steuerhinterziehung im internationalen
   Wirtschaftsverkehr. - 1984.
      (001706)

GERMANY, FEDERAL REPUBLIC OF--LIABILITY.
----Die Haftungsproblematik bei Konkurs
   einer Gesellschaft innerhalb eines
   transnationalen Unternehmens. - 1984.
      (002233)

GERMANY, FEDERAL REPUBLIC OF--MANAGEMENT.
----Die Steuerung auslandischer
   Tochtergesellschaften. - 1983.
      (000400)

GERMANY, FEDERAL REPUBLIC OF--MANUFACTURING
ENTERPRISES.
----International trade and foreign direct
   investment in West German manufacturing
   industries. - 1984.
      (000771)

GERMANY, FEDERAL REPUBLIC OF--MATHEMATICAL
MODELS.
----Entry by diversified firms into German
   industries. - 1986.
      (001162)

GERMANY, FEDERAL REPUBLIC OF--NEW PRODUCTS.
----Entry by diversified firms into German
   industries. - 1986.
      (001162)

GERMANY, FEDERAL REPUBLIC OF--PRIVATE
INTERNATIONAL LAW.
----Fakultatives Kollisonsrecht im
   internationalen Wettbewerbsrecht? - 1984.
      (002247)

GERMANY, FEDERAL REPUBLIC OF--PRODUCTION
DIVERSIFICATION.
----Entry by diversified firms into German
   industries. - 1986.
      (001162)

GERMANY, FEDERAL REPUBLIC OF--PRODUCTION
(ECONOMIC THEORY).
----Stärken und Schwächen der Bundesrepublik
   Deutschland in der internationalen
   Arbeitsteilung. - 1984.
      (001260)

GERMANY, FEDERAL REPUBLIC OF--PUBLIC
ENTERPRISES.
----Private agreements for takeovers of
   public companies. - 1984.
      (001626)

GERMANY, FEDERAL REPUBLIC OF--RESTRICTIVE
BUSINESS PRACTICES.
----Fakultatives Kollisonsrecht im
   internationalen Wettbewerbsrecht? - 1984.
      (002247)

GERMANY, FEDERAL REPUBLIC OF--SERVICE
INDUSTRIES.
----Der internationale Handel mit
   Dienstleistungen aus der Sicht der
   Bundesrepublik Deutschland. - 1984.
      (000877)

GERMANY, FEDERAL REPUBLIC OF--STATISTICAL
DATA.
----DM-Investitionen in Südafrika. - 1983.
      (001197)

GERMANY, FEDERAL REPUBLIC OF--SUPPLY AND
DEMAND.
----Stärken und Schwächen der Bundesrepublik
   Deutschland in der internationalen
   Arbeitsteilung. - 1984.
      (001260)

GERMANY, FEDERAL REPUBLIC OF--TAX AVOIDANCE.
----Steuerplanung internationaler
   Unternehmungen. - 1986.
      (001733)

GERMANY, FEDERAL REPUBLIC OF--TAX EVASION.
----Steuerhinterziehung im internationalen
   Wirtschaftsverkehr. - 1984.
      (001706)

GERMANY, FEDERAL REPUBLIC OF--TAX INCENTIVES.
----International income taxation and
   developing countries. - 1988.
      (001759)

GERMANY, FEDERAL REPUBLIC OF--TAX LAW.
----Internationale Unternehmensbesteuerung.
   - 1983.
      (001727)

GERMANY, FEDERAL REPUBLIC OF--TAXATION.
----Die finanzielle Führung und Kontrolle
   von Auslandsgesellschaften. - 1983.
      (000447)
----Gewinne verbundener Unternehmen,
   Verrechnungspreise. - 1984.
      (001749)
----International income taxation and
   developing countries. - 1988.
      (001759)
----Konzerntransferpreise im internationalen
   Steuerrecht. - 1986.
      (001710)
----Probleme der Gewinn- und
   Verlustrealisierung. - 1986.
      (001703)
----Steuerhinterziehung im internationalen
   Wirtschaftsverkehr. - 1984.
      (001706)
----Steuerplanung internationaler
   Unternehmungen. - 1986.
      (001733)

GERMANY, FEDERAL REPUBLIC OF--TECHNICAL
CO-OPERATION.
----Transfert de technologie. - 1983.
      (001460)

GERMANY, FEDERAL REPUBLIC OF--TECHNOLOGY
TRANSFER.
----Der internationale Handel mit
Dienstleistungen aus der Sicht der
Bundesrepublik Deutschland. - 1984.
(000877)
----Technological balance of payments and
international competitiveness. - 1983.
(001442)
----Transfert de technologie. - 1983.
(001460)

GERMANY, FEDERAL REPUBLIC OF--TRADE
AGREEMENTS.
----Trademark and related rights in
franchise agreements in Germany. - 1983.
(001523)

GERMANY, FEDERAL REPUBLIC OF--TRADEMARKS.
----Trademark and related rights in
franchise agreements in Germany. - 1983.
(001523)

GERMANY, FEDERAL REPUBLIC OF--TRANSFER
PRICING.
----German transfer pricing. - 1984.
(001748)
----Konzerntransferpreise im internationalen
Steuerrecht. - 1986.
(001710)
----Verrechnungspreise fur Sachleistungen im
internationalen Konzern. - 1984.
(001720)

GERMANY, FEDERAL REPUBLIC OF--TRANSNATIONAL
CORPORATIONS.
----The development of employment in
multinational enterprises in the Federal
Republic of Germany. - 1985.
(001912)
----DM-Investitionen in Südafrika. - 1983.
(001197)
----Die finanzielle Führung und Kontrolle
von Auslandsgesellschaften. - 1983.
(000447)
----German transfer pricing. - 1984.
(001748)
----Gewinne verbundener Unternehmen,
Verrechnungspreise. - 1984.
(001749)
----Die Haftungsproblematik bei Konkurs
einer Gesellschaft innerhalb eines
transnationalen Unternehmens. - 1984.
(002233)
----Internationale Unternehmensbesteuerung.
- 1983.
(001727)
----Der konsolidierte Abschluss. - 1983.
(002091)
----Konzerntransferpreise im internationalen
Steuerrecht. - 1986.
(001710)
----Multinational enterprise and world
competition. - 1987.
(000018)
----Multinationale Konzerne in der
Bundesrepublik Deutschland. - 1985.
(001157)
----National legislation and regulations
relating to transnational corporations.
Volume 4. - 1986.
(002253)

----New trends in internationalization:
processes and theories. Diversified
patterns of multinational enterprise and
old and new forms of foreign involvement
of the firm. - 1983.
(000068)
----Politik als Investitionsmotor? - 1985.
(001131)
----Probleme der Gewinn- und
Verlustrealisierung. - 1986.
(001703)
----La recherche-développement dans la
stratégie des grandes entreprises
chimiques de l'entre-deux-guerres: Du
Pont de Nemours, Imperial Chemical
Industries, I. G. Farben. (With English
summary.). - 1984.
(000295)
----Steuerhinterziehung im internationalen
Wirtschaftsverkehr. - 1984.
(001706)
----Steuerplanung internationaler
Unternehmungen. - 1986.
(001733)
----Die Steuerung auslandischer
Tochtergesellschaften. - 1983.
(000400)
----Verrechnungspreise fur Sachleistungen im
internationalen Konzern. - 1984.
(001720)
----West Germany: expanding where the
markets are. - 1987.
(000136)

GERMANY, FEDERAL REPUBLIC OF.
----Taxation of foreign income - principles
and practice. - 1985.
(001764)

GHANA--ALUMINIUM INDUSTRY.
----The price and availability of energy for
an aluminium smelter : recent
renegotiations in Ghana. - 1987.
(002467)

GHANA--APPROPRIATE TECHNOLOGY.
----Technology and development :
socio-economic implications for Ghana. -
1987.
(001478)

GHANA--CAPITAL MOVEMENTS.
----The capital intensity of foreign,
private local and state owned firms in a
less developed country: Ghana. - 1986.
(001018)

GHANA--DEVELOPMENT.
----Technology and development :
socio-economic implications for Ghana. -
1987.
(001478)

GHANA--DOMESTIC TRADE.
----The capital intensity of foreign,
private local and state owned firms in a
less developed country: Ghana. - 1986.
(001018)

GHANA--ELECTRIC POWER RATES.
----The price and availability of energy for
an aluminium smelter : recent
renegotiations in Ghana. - 1987.
(002467)

GHANA--FOREIGN DIRECT INVESTMENT.
----The capital intensity of foreign,
    private local and state owned firms in a
    less developed country: Ghana. - 1986.
      (001018)
----Ghana's new Investment Code. - 1985.
      (002213)

GHANA--FREE EXPORT ZONES.
----Employment and multinational enterprises
    in export processing zones. - 1984.
      (001886)

GHANA--INVESTMENT POLICY.
----Ghana's new Investment Code. - 1985.
      (002213)

GHANA--LABOUR SUPPLY.
----Employment and multinational enterprises
    in export processing zones. - 1984.
      (001886)

GHANA--LAWS AND REGULATIONS.
----National legislation and regulations
    relating to transnational corporations.
    Volume 3. - 1983.
      (002252)

GHANA--LEGISLATION.
----Ghana's new Investment Code. - 1985.
      (002213)

GHANA--PROFIT.
----The profits of foreign firms in a less
    developed country: Ghana. - 1986.
      (001019)

GHANA--PUBLIC ENTERPRISES.
----The capital intensity of foreign,
    private local and state owned firms in a
    less developed country: Ghana. - 1986.
      (001018)

GHANA--SUPPLY AND DEMAND.
----The price and availability of energy for
    an aluminium smelter : recent
    renegotiations in Ghana. - 1987.
      (002467)

GHANA--TRANSNATIONAL CORPORATIONS.
----The capital intensity of foreign,
    private local and state owned firms in a
    less developed country: Ghana. - 1986.
      (001018)
----Employment and multinational enterprises
    in export processing zones. - 1984.
      (001886)
----National legislation and regulations
    relating to transnational corporations.
    Volume 3. - 1983.
      (002252)
----The price and availability of energy for
    an aluminium smelter : recent
    renegotiations in Ghana. - 1987.
      (002467)
----The profits of foreign firms in a less
    developed country: Ghana. - 1986.
      (001019)

GLASS INDUSTRY--JAPAN.
----The process of internationalization at
    Asahi Glass Co. - 1986.
      (000360)

GLOSSARIES.
----Glossary of terms for state auditors. -
    1983.
      (002711)

GOLD--USSR.
----Gold, foreign capital and the
    industrialization of Russia. - 1985.
      (001184)

GOODS.
----Goods and services in OECD countries. -
    1987.
      (000814)

GOODS--REPUBLIC OF KOREA.
----An information sector perspective of
    employment expansion in the Republic of
    Korea, 1975-80. - 1987.
      (000848)

GOODYEAR TIRE AND RUBBER CO.
----The emergence of a U.S. multinational
    enterprise: the Goodyear Tire and Rubber
    Company, 1910-1939. - 1987.
      (000281)

GOVE PENINSULA (AUSTRALIA)--ALUMINA.
----The history and contractual arrangements
    of the Gove bauxite/alumina project in
    the Northern Territory of Australia. -
    1985.
      (000596)

GOVE PENINSULA (AUSTRALIA)--BAUXITE.
----The history and contractual arrangements
    of the Gove bauxite/alumina project in
    the Northern Territory of Australia. -
    1985.
      (000596)

GOVE PENINSULA (AUSTRALIA)--MINING.
----The history and contractual arrangements
    of the Gove bauxite/alumina project in
    the Northern Territory of Australia. -
    1985.
      (000596)

GOVE PENINSULA (AUSTRALIA)--TRANSNATIONAL
CORPORATIONS.
----The history and contractual arrangements
    of the Gove bauxite/alumina project in
    the Northern Territory of Australia. -
    1985.
      (000596)

GOVERNMENT FINANCIAL INSTITUTIONS.
----Institutions financières publiques de
    développement. - 1986.
      (000237)

GOVERNMENT INFORMATION--UNITED STATES.
----Inside Washington. - 1988.
      (002703)
----Washington's best kept secrets. - 1983.
      (002704)

GOVERNMENT LENDING--JAPAN.
----The nature and tools of Japan's
    industrial policy. - 1986.
      (000557)

GOVERNMENT MONOPOLIES--LATIN AMERICA.
----Government control over public
    enterprises in Latin America. - 1983.
      (002179)

GOVERNMENT PURCHASING.
----The effects of taxation price control
    and government contracts in oligopoly
    and monopolistic competition. - 1987.
      (001693)

GOVERNMENT SPENDING POLICY--EGYPT.
----The South Korean success story. - 1986.
      (001050)

GRAINS--ARGENTINA.
----Empresas transnacionales en la industria
    de alimentos. - 1983.
      (000573)

GREECE--EMPLOYMENT POLICY.
----The employment impact of multinational
    enterprises in Greece, Portugal and
    Spain. - 1987.
      (001887)

GREECE--FACTOR ANALYSIS.
----The determinants of foreign direct
    investment in the Greek economy. - 1984.
      (000548)

GREECE--FOREIGN DIRECT INVESTMENT.
----The determinants of foreign direct
    investment in the Greek economy. - 1984.
      (000548)
----Investment legislation in Greece,
    Portugal and Spain: the background to
    foreign investment in Mediterranean
    Europe. - 1983.
      (002168)

GREECE--INDUSTRIAL DEVELOPMENT.
----Licensing and industrial development. -
    1986.
      (001449)

GREECE--INTERNATIONAL BANKING.
----Foreign banks in Greece. - 1985.
      (000919)

GREECE--LEGISLATION.
----Investment legislation in Greece,
    Portugal and Spain: the background to
    foreign investment in Mediterranean
    Europe. - 1983.
      (002168)

GREECE--LICENCE AGREEMENTS.
----Licensing and industrial development. -
    1986.
      (001449)

GREECE--LICENCES.
----Licensing and industrial development. -
    1986.
      (001449)

GREECE--PATENTS.
----Licensing and industrial development. -
    1986.
      (001449)

GREECE--TECHNOLOGY TRANSFER.
----Licensing and industrial development. -
    1986.
      (001449)

GREECE--TRADEMARK LICENCES.
----Licensing and industrial development. -
    1986.
      (001449)

GREECE--TRANSNATIONAL CORPORATIONS.
----The employment impact of multinational
    enterprises in Greece, Portugal and
    Spain. - 1987.
      (001887)

GROSS DOMESTIC PRODUCT.
----Private investment in developing
    countries. - 1984.
      (000114)

GROSS DOMESTIC PRODUCT--KUWAIT.
----Impact of the operations of
    transnational corporations on
    development in Kuwait. - 1987.
      (001143)

GROSS DOMESTIC PRODUCT--UNITED KINGDOM.
----Cyclical variations in service
    industries' employment in the UK. - 1987.
      (000844)

GROSS NATIONAL PRODUCT.
----Economic and political determinants of
    foreign direct investment. - 1985.
      (000551)

GROSS NATIONAL PRODUCT--KUWAIT.
----Impact of the operations of
    transnational corporations on
    development in Kuwait. - 1987.
      (001143)

GROUP OF TEN.
----Los bancos transnacionales y el
    endeudamiento externo en la Argentina. -
    1987.
      (000819)

GRUPO ANDINO.
----Measures strengthening the negotiating
    capacity of Governments in their
    relations with transnational
    corporations. - 1983.
      (002461)

GUANCHIAS LTDA. (HONDURAS).
----Guanchias Limitada. - 1985.
      (001094)

GUARANTEE AGREEMENTS.
----Current problems of economic
    integration. - 1986.
      (001312)

GUIDELINES.
----Guidelines for Consumer Protection. -
    1986.
      (002017)

GUIDELINES (continued)
----International co-operation in tax
   matters : guidelines for international
   co-operation against the evasion and
   avoidance of taxes (with special
   reference to taxes on income, profits,
   capital and capital gains). - 1984.
      (001724)
----Natural gas clauses in petroleum
   arrangements. - 1987.
      (002452)
----The OECD guidelines for multinational
   enterprises and labour relations,
   1982-1984. - 1985.
      (001961)
----Second revised draft Guidelines for the
   Exchange of Information on Potentially
   Harmful Chemicals in International
   Trade. - 1986.
      (002019)
----Transnational corporations in world
   development. - 1983.
      (000102)

GUIDELINES--ANDEAN REGION.
----The Andean foreign investment code's
   impact on multinational enterprises. -
   1983.
      (001977)

GUIDELINES FOR CONSUMER PROTECTION (1985).
----Guidelines for Consumer Protection. -
   1986.
      (002017)

GUIDELINES FOR THE EXCHANGE OF INFORMATION
ON POTENTIALLY HARMFUL CHEMICALS IN
INTERNATIONAL TRADE (DRAFT).
----Second revised draft Guidelines for the
   Exchange of Information on Potentially
   Harmful Chemicals in International
   Trade. - 1986.
      (002019)

GUINEA--BAUXITE.
----Les enjeux de la bauxite. - 1983.
      (000585)

GULF STATES--BANKING.
----A historical perspective of U.S.-GCC
   economic and financial interdependence.
   - 1987.
      (000143)

GULF STATES--COMMERCIAL LAW.
----Commercial law in the Gulf States : the
   Islamic legal tradition. - 1984.
      (002195)

GULF STATES--CONTRACTS.
----Commercial law in the Gulf States : the
   Islamic legal tradition. - 1984.
      (002195)

GULF STATES--ECONOMIC CO-OPERATION.
----Economic co-operation of the Arab Gulf
   States. - 1986.
      (001133)

GULF STATES--INTERDEPENDENCE.
----A historical perspective of U.S.-GCC
   economic and financial interdependence.
   - 1987.
      (000143)

GULF STATES--INVESTMENTS.
----A historical perspective of U.S.-GCC
   economic and financial interdependence.
   - 1987.
      (000143)

GULF STATES--ISLAMIC LAW.
----Commercial law in the Gulf States : the
   Islamic legal tradition. - 1984.
      (002195)

GULF STATES--JOINT VENTURES.
----Economic co-operation of the Arab Gulf
   States. - 1986.
      (001133)
----A historical perspective of U.S.-GCC
   economic and financial interdependence.
   - 1987.
      (000143)

GULF STATES--PETROLEUM RESERVES.
----A historical perspective of U.S.-GCC
   economic and financial interdependence.
   - 1987.
      (000143)

GULF STATES--REGIONAL CO-OPERATION.
----Economic co-operation of the Arab Gulf
   States. - 1986.
      (001133)

GUYANA--ALUMINIUM INDUSTRY.
----The American take-over. - 1983.
      (000287)

GUYANA--CAPITALISM.
----Ethnicity, class, and international
   capitalist penetration in Guyana and
   Trinidad. - 1985.
      (001096)

GUYANA--DEVELOPING COUNTRIES.
----Commercialization of technology and
   dependence in the Caribbean. - 1985.
      (001477)

GUYANA--ETHNOPSYCHOLOGY.
----Ethnicity, class, and international
   capitalist penetration in Guyana and
   Trinidad. - 1985.
      (001096)

GUYANA--INDUSTRIAL DEVELOPMENT.
----The American take-over. - 1983.
      (000287)

GUYANA--INDUSTRIAL PLANNING.
----Commercialization of technology and
   dependence in the Caribbean. - 1985.
      (001477)

GUYANA--LAWS AND REGULATIONS.
----National legislation and regulations
   relating to transnational corporations.
   Volume 3. - 1983.
      (002252)

GUYANA--SOCIAL CLASSES.
----Ethnicity, class, and international
   capitalist penetration in Guyana and
   Trinidad. - 1985.
      (001096)

GUYANA--TECHNICAL CO-OPERATION.
----Commercialization of technology and
dependence in the Caribbean. - 1985.
(001477)

GUYANA--TECHNOLOGY TRANSFER.
----Commercialization of technology and
dependence in the Caribbean. - 1985.
(001477)

GUYANA--TRANSNATIONAL CORPORATIONS.
----Ethnicity, class, and international
capitalist penetration in Guyana and
Trinidad. - 1985.
(001096)
----National legislation and regulations
relating to transnational corporations.
Volume 3. - 1983.
(002252)

HARD FIBRES--UNITED STATES.
----A competitive assessment of selected
reinforced composite fibers. - 1985.
(000644)

HARMFUL PRODUCTS.
----Consolidated list of products whose
consumption and/or sale have been
banned, withdrawn, severely restricted
or not approved by Governments. - 1987.
(002702)
----Second revised draft Guidelines for the
Exchange of Information on Potentially
Harmful Chemicals in International
Trade. - 1986.
(002019)

HARMFUL PRODUCTS--EUROPE.
----The export of hazard. - 1985.
(001941)

HARMFUL PRODUCTS--UNITED STATES.
----The export of hazard. - 1985.
(001941)

HEALTH HAZARDS.
----Smoke ring : the politics of tobacco. -
1984.
(000571)

HEALTH HAZARDS--EUROPE.
----The export of hazard. - 1985.
(001941)

HEALTH HAZARDS--UNITED STATES.
----The export of hazard. - 1985.
(001941)

HEARINGS.
----Transnational corporations in South
Africa and Namibia : United Nations
public hearings. Volume 1, Reports of
the Panel of Eminent Persons and of the
Secretary-General. - 1986.
(001216)
----Transnational corporations in South
Africa and Namibia : United Nations
Public Hearings. Volume 4, Policy
instruments and statements. - 1987.
(001218)

HEGEMONISM.
----Cooperation in the liberalization of
international trade. - 1987.
(001400)
----The TNCs and the policy of hegemonism. -
1987.
(000093)

HERBICIDES--UNITED STATES.
----A competitive assessment of the U.S.
herbicide industry. - 1985.
(000670)

HISTORY.
----International business in the nineteenth
century. - 1987.
(000046)
----Multinational enterprise in historical
perspective. - 1986.
(000098)

HISTORY--FRANCE.
----Ces patrons qui gagnent. - 1986.
(001146)

HISTORY--UNITED KINGDOM.
----British multinationals. - 1986.
(000337)

HOLDING COMPANIES--SOUTH AFRICA.
----Foreign investment in South Africa and
Namibia. - 1984.
(001198) (002641)
----McGregor's investors' handbook. -
1986- .
(001203) (002654)

HOLDING COMPANIES--UNITED STATES.
----Foreign investment in South Africa and
Namibia. - 1984.
(001198) (002641)
----U.S. and Canadian investment in South
Africa and Namibia. - 1986.
(001212) (002671) (002672)

HONDA MOTOR COMPANY(JAPAN)--JAPAN.
----America's new no. 4 automaker -- Honda.
- 1985.
(000294)

HONDA MOTOR COMPANY(JAPAN)--UNITED STATES.
----America's new no. 4 automaker -- Honda.
- 1985.
(000294)

HONDURAS--AGRARIAN REFORM.
----Guanchias Limitada. - 1985.
(001094)

HONDURAS--AGRICULTURAL CO-OPERATIVES.
----Guanchias Limitada. - 1985.
(001094)

HONDURAS--AGRICULTURAL DEVELOPMENT.
----Guanchias Limitada. - 1985.
(001094)

HONDURAS--TRANSNATIONAL CORPORATIONS.
----Guanchias Limitada. - 1985.
(001094)

HONG KONG--ARBITRATION RULES.
----Arbitration in Hong Kong. - 1986.
   (002578)

HONG KONG--BANKING LAW.
----A survey of banking laws and policies in
   Hong Kong and Singapore. - 1986.
   (001829)

HONG KONG--CAPITAL MARKETS.
----Hong Kong and Singapore. - 1985.
   (000879)

HONG KONG--COMMERCIAL ARBITRATION.
----Arbitration in Hong Kong. - 1986.
   (002578)
----Arbitration in Hong Kong. - 1986.
   (002529)

HONG KONG--DEVELOPING COUNTRIES.
----Multinational corporations, technology
   and employment. - 1983.
   (001891)

HONG KONG--DIVESTMENT.
----Exploiting Hong Kong's uncertain future.
   - 1987.
   (001862)

HONG KONG--ECONOMIC RELATIONS.
----Shenzhen : a Chinese development zone in
   global perspective. - 1985.
   (002393)

HONG KONG--EMPLOYMENT.
----Multinational corporations, technology
   and employment. - 1983.
   (001891)

HONG KONG--FOREIGN DIRECT INVESTMENT.
----Les investissements directs des Chinois
   d'outre-mer en Chine. - 1987.
   (000201)
----Multinational corporations, technology
   and employment. - 1983.
   (001891)
----The real threat from Asia. - 1987.
   (001055)

HONG KONG--FOREIGN LOANS.
----Hong Kong and Singapore. - 1985.
   (000879)

HONG KONG--INDUSTRIAL CO-OPERATION.
----Industrial co-operation between China
   and Hong Kong. - 1983.
   (001554)

HONG KONG--INDUSTRIALIZATION.
----Exports of technology by newly
   industrializing countries: Hong Kong. -
   1984.
   (001414)

HONG KONG--INTERNATIONAL ARBITRATION.
----Arbitration in Hong Kong. - 1986.
   (002529)

HONG KONG--LAWS AND REGULATIONS.
----Arbitration in Hong Kong. - 1986.
   (002529)

HONG KONG--MANUFACTURING ENTERPRISES.
----Multinational corporations and
   technology diffusion in Hong Kong
   manufacturing. - 1983.
   (001415)

HONG KONG--RELOCATION OF INDUSTRY.
----Exploiting Hong Kong's uncertain future.
   - 1987.
   (001862)

HONG KONG--TAX LAW.
----A survey of banking laws and policies in
   Hong Kong and Singapore. - 1986.
   (001829)

HONG KONG--TECHNOLOGY TRANSFER.
----Exports of technology by newly
   industrializing countries: Hong Kong. -
   1984.
   (001414)
----Multinational corporations and
   technology diffusion in Hong Kong
   manufacturing. - 1983.
   (001415)
----Multinational corporations, technology
   and employment. - 1983.
   (001891)

HONG KONG--TRANSNATIONAL CORPORATIONS.
----Multinational corporations and
   technology diffusion in Hong Kong
   manufacturing. - 1983.
   (001415)
----Multinational corporations, technology
   and employment. - 1983.
   (001891)
----Multinationals from Hong Kong. - 1983.
   (000312)
----Singapore multinationals. - 1985.
   (000365)

HONG KONG--UNCERTAINTY.
----Exploiting Hong Kong's uncertain future.
   - 1987.
   (001862)

HONG KONG INTERNATIONAL ARBITRATION CENTRE.
----Arbitration in Hong Kong. - 1986.
   (002529)

HOST COUNTRY RELATIONS.
----Analyzing political risk. - 1986.
   (001850)
----Bargaining power, ownership, and
   profitability of transnational
   corporations in developing countries. -
   1984.
   (001007)
----Foreign ownership: when hosts change the
   rules. - 1985.
   (001798)
----Host countries and the R [and] D of
   multinationals. - 1987.
   (001479)
----How MNCs cope with host government
   intervention. - 1983.
   (001795)
----International business and the national
   interest. - 1986.
   (001817)

HOST COUNTRY RELATIONS (continued)
----International financial center
preeminence in MNC and nation-state
interaction. - 1983.
(001291)
----Making decisions in multinational
corporations. - 1988.
(001827)
----Managing the multinational subsidiary. -
1986.
(000405)
----MNCs and the Iranian revolution: an
empirical study. - 1985.
(001772)
----Multinational corporation and national
regulation: an economic audit. - 1987.
(002270)
----Multinational enterprise and host
country policy: opportunities for mutual
benefit. - 1986.
(001828)
----Multinational firms' global strategies,
host country indigenisation of ownership
and welfare. - 1983.
(000486)
----Multinational managers and host
government interactions. - 1987.
(001857)
----National ownership requirements and
transfer pricing. - 1986.
(001711)
----Negotiating with Third World
governments. - 1983.
(002468)
----The new multinationals: synthesis and
conclusions. -
(000349)
----The new multinationals: the theoretical
background. - 1983.
(000350)
----On new trends in internationalization: a
synthesis toward a general model. - 1985.
(000081)
----Political events and the foreign direct
investment decision: an empirical
examination. - 1986.
(001836)
----Present and desired methods of
selecting expatriate managers for
international assignments. - 1984.
(000522)
----Production cost differentials and
foreign direct investment: a test of two
models. - 1986.
(000061)
----Quando l'impresa diventa multinazionale:
il problema del controllo. - 1983.
(001607)
----State enterprise-multinational
corporation joint ventures: how well do
they meet both partners' needs? - 1983.
(001632)
----Tax holidays as signals. - 1986.
(002303)
----Transfer pricing provisions, rulings and
case law: Thailand. - 1986.
(001723)

HOST COUNTRY RELATIONS--AUSTRALIA.
----MNCs and the Australian government: some
emerging policy issues. - 1983.
(002289)

HOST COUNTRY RELATIONS--CANADA.
----Performance of the multinational drug
industry in home and host countries: a
Canadian case study. - 1983.
(000690)

HOST COUNTRY RELATIONS--INDIA.
----Multinationals in Indian big business:
industrial characteristics of foreign
investments in a heavily regulated
economy. - 1983.
(001058)

HOST COUNTRY RELATIONS--INDONESIA.
----MNCs and the host country, the
Indonesian case. - 1984.
(001073)
----The politics of oil in Indonesia. - 1986.
(001818)

HOST COUNTRY RELATIONS--JAPAN.
----Doing business in Japan. - 1986.
(001809)

HOST COUNTRY RELATIONS--LATIN AMERICA.
----O capital transnacional e o estado. -
1985.
(002274)
----The relationship of MNC direct
investment to host country trade and
trade policy: some preliminary evidence.
- 1983.
(001351)

HOST COUNTRY RELATIONS--NIGERIA.
----Multinationals, the state, and control
of the Nigerian economy. - 1987.
(001022)
----State strategies toward Nigerian and
foreign business. - 1983.
(001770)

HOST COUNTRY RELATIONS--TURKEY.
----Transnational corporations and local
capital: comparative conduct and
performance in the Turkish
pharmaceutical industry. - 1986.
(000705)

HOST COUNTRY RELATIONS--UNITED STATES.
----The effect of political events on
United States direct foreign
investment: a pooled time-series
cross-sectional analysis. - 1985.
(001835)

HOST COUNTRY RELATIONS--WESTERN EUROPE.
----International industries, multinational
companies, and host government control:
a framework. - 1983.
(001796)

HOTEL INDUSTRY.
----Appropriate policies towards
multinational hotel corporations in
developing countries. - 1983
(000781)

HOTEL INDUSTRY--AUSTRALIA.
----Characteristics of major industries
supplying tourist services in Australia.
- 1983.
(000824)

HOTEL INDUSTRY--KENYA.
----The role of transnational corporations in hotel and tourism industry in selected PTA member countries. - 1986.
(000782) (000936)

HOTEL INDUSTRY--MAURITIUS.
----The role of transnational corporations in hotel and tourism industry in selected PTA member countries. - 1986.
(000782) (000936)

HOTEL INDUSTRY--ZIMBABWE.
----The role of transnational corporations in hotel and tourism industry in selected PTA member countries. - 1986.
(000782) (000936)

HOURS OF WORK--ASIA.
----Wages, hours and working conditions in Asian free trade zones. - 1984.
(001897)

HUMAN RESOURCES.
----Analysis of engineering and technical assistance consultancy contracts. - 1986.
(002449)
----Human resource management in multinational cooperative ventures. - 1986.
(000426)
----Human resources management in international joint ventures: directions for research. - 1987.
(001921)
----Transnational corporations: choice of techniques and employment in developing countries. -   .
(001882)

HUMAN RESOURCES--ASIA AND THE PACIFIC.
----Technology transfer under alternative arrangements with transnational corporations. - 1987.
(001513)

HUMAN RIGHTS.
----Multinationales et droits de l'homme. - 1984.
(001876)
----Third World resource directory. - 1984.
(002719)

HUNGARY--BUSINESS ENTERPRISES.
----Hungarian Chamber of Commerce handbook. - 1984-   .
(001811)
----Hungarian foreign trade reform. - 1986.
(002250)

HUNGARY--CLOTHING INDUSTRY.
----The impact of cooperation with Western firms on the Hungarian clothing industry. - 1983.
(001189)

HUNGARY--DIRECTORIES.
----Directory of Hungarian foreign trade companies. - 1976-   .
(002635)
----Hungarian Chamber of Commerce handbook. - 1984-   .
(001811)

HUNGARY--ECONOMIC CONDITIONS.
----Hungarian Chamber of Commerce handbook. - 1984-   .
(001811)

HUNGARY--ECONOMIC POLICY.
----A hazai elektronikai ipar helyzete és problemái. - 1986.
(000634)
----Hungarian foreign trade reform. - 1986.
(002250)

HUNGARY--ECONOMIC REFORM.
----Joint ventures in Hungary. - 1987.
(001171)

HUNGARY--ECONOMIC RELATIONS.
----Economic associations in Hungary with foreign participation. - 1986.
(001606)

HUNGARY--ELECTRONICS INDUSTRY.
----A hazai elektronikai ipar helyzete és problemái. - 1986.
(000634)
----L'industria elettronica unghrese. - 1986.
(000731)

HUNGARY--ENGINEERING INDUSTRIES.
----A magyar gépipari vállalatok nagyságrendje és piaci magatartásuk. - 1984.
(000957)

HUNGARY--FOREIGN DIRECT INVESTMENT.
----A muködo toke becsalogatása Magyarországra : nyugati szemszögbol. - 1987.
(001608)
----Egy vegyesvállalat története az alapítástól a Kezdeti sikerekig : esettanulmány a Sancella Hungary Kft-röl. - 1987.
(001191)

HUNGARY--FOREIGN TRADE.
----How to trade with Hungary. - 1983.
(001826)
----Hungarian foreign trade reform. - 1986.
(002250)

HUNGARY--INDUSTRIAL CONCENTRATION.
----A magyar feldolgozó ipar koncentrációs folyamata a 70-es évtizedben, nemzetközi összehasonlításban. - 1986.
(001181)

HUNGARY--INDUSTRIAL CO-OPERATION.
----A magyar gépipari vállalatok nagyságrendje és piaci magatartásuk. - 1984.
(000957)

HUNGARY--INDUSTRY.
----Hungarian Chamber of Commerce handbook. - 1984-   .
(001811)

HUNGARY--INTERNATIONAL CO-OPERATION.
----The impact of cooperation with Western firms on the Hungarian clothing industry. - 1983.
(001189)

HUNGARY--JOINT VENTURES.
----East-West joint ventures. - 1988.
    (001570)
----Economic associations in Hungary with
    foreign participation. - 1986.
    (001606)
----Les expériences et possibilités récentes
    concernant les sociétés mixtes de
    Hongrie. - 1987.
    (001169)
----Gemischte Unternehmen in Ungarn. - 1987.
    (001170)
----Joint ventures in Hungary. - 1987.
    (001171)
----A muködo toke becsalogatása
    Magyarországra : nyugati szemszögbol. -
    1987.
    (001608)
----Up-to-date rules of joint ventures in
    Hungary. - 1986.
    (001537)
----Utmutato kulfoldi reszvetellel mukodo
    gazdasagi tarsulas alapitasahoz es
    mukodtetesehez. - 1984.
    (001186)
----Egy vegyesvállalat története az
    alapitástól a Kezdeti sikerekig :
    esettanulmány a Sancella Hungary
    Kft-röl. - 1987.
    (001191)
----Vegyesvallalatok mukodesi feltetelei
    Magyarorszagon. - 1986.
    (002280)

HUNGARY--LAWS AND REGULATIONS.
----East-West joint ventures. - 1988.
    (001570)
----Up-to-date rules of joint ventures in
    Hungary. - 1986.
    (001537)

HUNGARY--LEGISLATION.
----Vegyesvallalatok mukodesi feltetelei
    Magyarorszagon. - 1986.
    (002280)

HUNGARY--MANUFACTURING ENTERPRISES.
----A magyar feldolgozó ipar koncentrációs
    folyamata a 70-es évtizedben, nemzetközi
    összehasonlításban. - 1986.
    (001181)

HUNGARY--MARKETING.
----A magyar gépipari vállalatok
    nagyságrendje és piaci magatartásuk. -
    1984.
    (000957)

HUNGARY--STATE TRADING ENTERPRISES.
----Enterprise organization of East European
    socialist countries. - 1987.
    (000441)

HUNGARY--STATISTICAL DATA.
----East-West joint ventures. - 1988.
    (001570)

HUNGARY--TRADE ASSOCIATIONS.
----Economic associations in Hungary with
    foreign participation. - 1986.
    (001606)

HUNGARY--TRANSNATIONAL CORPORATIONS.
----Directory of Hungarian foreign trade
    companies. - 1976-   .
    (002635)
----The impact of cooperation with Western
    firms on the Hungarian clothing
    industry. - 1983.
    (001189)
----A muködo toke becsalogatása
    Magyarországra : nyugati szemszögbol. -
    1987.
    (001608)

HYDRAULIC MACHINERY--UNITED STATES.
----A competitive assessment of the U.S.
    water resources equipment industry. -
    1985.
    (000776)

I.G. FARBEN (FIRM).
----La recherche-développement dans la
    stratégie des grandes entreprises
    chimiques de l'entre-deux-guerres: Du
    Pont de Nemours, Imperial Chemical
    Industries, I. G. Farben. (With English
    summary.). - 1984.
    (000295)

IBM.
----The global IBM. - 1987.
    (000288)

IBRD.
----L'Agence multilatérale de garantie des
    investissements. - 1987.
    (002152)
----Current problems of economic
    integration. - 1986.
    (001312)
----Do performance requirements and
    investment incentives work? - 1986.
    (002306)
----Global debt. - 1986.
    (000236)
----Legal trends in international lending
    and investment in the developing
    countries. - 1984.
    (000207)
----The Multilateral Investment Guarantee
    Agency. - 1986.
    (002146)
----La pratique du CIRDI. - 1987.
    (002550)
----Private co-financing. - 1983.
    (000257)
----Shaping a future for foreign direct
    investment in the Third World. - 1988.
    (002140)
----State intervention, foreign economic
    aid, savings and growth in LDCs. - 1985.
    (001337)
----Trade in investment-related
    technological services. - 1986.
    (000945)
----Uncertain future. - 1984.
    (000977)
----The World Bank's Multilateral Investment
    Guaranty Agency. - 1987.
    (002125)

ICFTU PROGRAMME OF ACTION IN SUPPORT OF THE
INDEPENDENT BLACK TRADE UNION MOVEMENT IN
SOUTH AFRICA (1980).
----Trade unions against apartheid. - 1984.
    (002601)

ILO.
----Aspects of labour law and relations in
    selected export processing zones. - 1984.
    (001895)
----International codes and guidelines for
    multinational enterprises. - 1983.
    (002023)
----Microelectronics-based automation
    technologies and development. - 1985.
    (000753)

IMF.
----Appropriate financing for petroleum
    development in developing countries. -
    1984.
    (000576)
----Los bancos transnacionales y el
    endeudamiento externo en la Argentina. -
    1987.
    (000819)
----Breves rasgos de la crisis. - 1983.
    (001307)
----Foreign direct investment and economic
    growth in the Asian and Pacific region.
    - 1987.
    (000175)
----Global debt. - 1986.
    (000236)
----International bank lending. - 1983.
    (000265)
----The international debt crisis. - 1985.
    (000240)
----The international debt crisis and the
    banks. - 1985.
    (000227)
----International debt quagmire. - 1983.
    (000262)
----International finance and investment. -
    1985.
    (001249)
----International lending and debt. - 1983.
    (000208)
----International money flows and currency
    crises. - 1984.
    (001261)
----Legal trends in international lending
    and investment in the developing
    countries. - 1984.
    (000207)
----A longer view of debt. - 1983.
    (000251)
----On Third World debt. - 1984.
    (000211)
----Opportunities and constraints in
    international lending. - 1983.
    (000267)
----The problems of developing-country debt
    and a strategy for Arab banking
    institutions. - 1983.
    (000256)
----Rehearing granted : Allied Bank
    International v. Banco Agricola Credito
    de Cartago and the current international
    debt crisis. - 1984.
    (000233)
----Revitalizing development, growth and
    international trade. - 1987.
    (001394)

----Die Stabilisierungspolitik des
    Internationalen Währungsfonds. - 1986.
    (001234)
----Uncertain future. - 1984.
    (000977)
----Ways out of the debt crisis. - 1984.
    (000245)

IMO.
----Dead in the water : international law,
    diplomacy, and compensation for chemical
    pollution at sea. - 1986.
    (001938)
----The definition of pollution damage in
    the 1984 Protocols to the 1969 Civil
    Liability Convention and the 1971 Fund
    Convention. - 1986.
    (001943)
----Liability and compensation for damage in
    connection with the carriage of
    hazardous and noxious substances by sea.
    - 1986.
    (001939)
----Liability for shipments by sea of
    hazardous and noxious substances. - 1985.
    (001951)
----New trends in compensation for oil
    pollution damage. - 1985.
    (001944)

IMPERIAL CHEMICAL INDUSTRIES (LONDON).
----La recherche-développement dans la
    stratégie des grandes entreprises
    chimiques de l'entre-deux-guerres: Du
    Pont de Nemours, Imperial Chemical
    Industries, I. G. Farben. (With English
    summary.). - 1984.
    (000295)
----The spatial organisation of
    multinational corporations. - 1985.
    (000017)

IMPORT CHARGES AND SUBCHARGES--BRAZIL.
----Market imperfections and import pricing
    behavior by multinational enterprises. -
    1986.
    (001681)

IMPORT PLANNING.
----Technology importation policies in
    developing countries: some implications
    of recent theoretical and empirical
    evidence. - 1983.
    (001420)

IMPORT PLANNING--EASTERN EUROPE.
----Patterns of technology imports:
    interregional comparison. - 1986.
    (001483)

IMPORT PLANNING--LATIN AMERICA.
----Patterns of technology imports:
    interregional comparison. - 1986.
    (001483)

IMPORT RESTRICTIONS.
----Transnational corporations and
    technology transfer. - 1987.
    (001509)

IMPORT RESTRICTIONS--AUSTRALIA.
----Multinational enterprise behaviour and
    domestic industry adjustment under
    import threat. - 1986.
    (000518)

IMPORT RESTRICTIONS--POLAND.
----Import licencji a zmiany w systemie
    gospodarki. - 1984.
    (002440)

IMPORT SUBSTITUTION.
----Transnational corporations in world
    development. - 1983.
    (000102)

IMPORTS.
----Capital inflows to LDC's and their
    impact on imports. - 1986.
    (001010)
----Transnational corporations and
    international trade : selected issues. -
    1985.
    (001393)

IMPORTS--ARAB COUNTRIES.
----The Arab world is still importing. -
    1987.
    (001134)

IMPORTS--ARGENTINA.
----La industria electrónica argentina :
    apertura comercial y
    desindustrialización. - 1987.
    (000654)

IMPORTS--JAPAN.
----Automotive parts industry and the U.S.
    aftermarket for Japanese cars and light
    trucks. - 1985.
    (000759)

IMPORTS--LATIN AMERICA.
----Banco de datos sobre inversión
    extranjera directa en América Latina y
    el Caribe : información de los países
    receptores y de organismos regionales y
    subregionales, t. 2. - 1987.
    (000193)

IMPORTS--UNITED STATES.
----Automotive parts industry and the U.S.
    aftermarket for Japanese cars and light
    trucks. - 1985.
    (000759)
----Transnational corporations and
    international trade : selected issues. -
    1985.
    (001393)

INCOME.
----Private investment in developing
    countries. - 1984.
    (000114)

INCOME DISTRIBUTION--EGYPT.
----The South Korean success story. - 1986.
    (001050)

INCOME DISTRIBUTION--REPUBLIC OF KOREA.
----The South Korean success story. - 1986.
    (001050)

INCOME TAX.
----An examination of multijurisdictional
    corporate income taxation under formula
    apportionment. - 1986.
    (001715)
----Financial and fiscal aspects of
    petroleum exploitation. - 1987.
    (002451)
----International co-operation in tax
    matters : guidelines for international
    co-operation against the evasion and
    avoidance of taxes (with special
    reference to taxes on income, profits,
    capital and capital gains). - 1984.
    (001724)
----International income taxation and
    developing countries. - 1988.
    (001759)
----International tax and business service.
    - 1984-   .
    (001725)
----The relationship between taxation and
    financial reporting. - 1987.
    (002103)
----Trends in international taxation. - 1985.
    (001746)

INCOME TAX--CHINA.
----A comparative analysis of the United
    States-People's Republic of China tax
    treaty. - 1986.
    (002037)
----Taxation of foreign business and
    investment in the People's Republic of
    China. - 1987.
    (001708)

INCOME TAX--UNITED STATES.
----A comparative analysis of the United
    States-People's Republic of China tax
    treaty. - 1986.
    (002037)
----Introduction to United States
    international taxation. - 1981.
    (001738)

INDEXES.
----Business International index. -
    1983-   .
    (002684)
----List of company directories and summary
    of their contents. - 1983.
    (002686)

INDIA--ACCOUNTING.
----Compendium of statements and standards.
    - 1986.
    (002074)

INDIA--AUDITING.
----Compendium of statements and standards.
    - 1986.
    (002074)

INDIA--AUTOMOBILE INDUSTRY.
----Technology transfer under alternative
    arrangements with transnational
    corporations. - 1987.
    (001513)

INDIA--BIG BUSINESS.
----Multinationals in Indian big business:
  industrial characteristics of foreign
  investments in a heavily regulated
  economy. - 1983.
    (001058)

INDIA--BOOK INDUSTRY.
----Nation-building media and TNCs. - 1984.
    (000941)

INDIA--CHEMICAL INDUSTRY.
----The lessons of Bhopal. - 1985.
    (001933)

INDIA--CLOTHING.
----Foreign cooperation and the marketing of
  manufactured exports from developing
  countries. - 1985.
    (001377)

INDIA--COMPENSATION.
----For whom the bell tolls in the aftermath
  of the Bhopal tragedy. - 1987.
    (001950)

INDIA--COMPUTER INDUSTRY.
----Between dependency and autonomy. - 1984.
    (000691)

INDIA--COMPUTERS.
----Between dependency and autonomy. - 1984.
    (000691)
----New information technology in India. -
  1986.
    (000651)

INDIA--DIRECT FOREIGN INVESTMENT.
----Trade in investment-related
  technological studies. - 1986.
    (001386)

INDIA--DIRECTORIES.
----All-India directory of industrial
  establishments. - 1984-   .
    (002614)

INDIA--DISPUTES.
----For whom the bell tolls in the aftermath
  of the Bhopal tragedy. - 1987.
    (001950)

INDIA--ECONOMIC DEVELOPMENT.
----Changing perspectives on the role of
  multinationals in economic development:
  some evidence from India. - 1985.
    (001040)

INDIA--ECONOMIC RELATIONS.
----Sino-Indian economic relations. - 1984.
    (000307)

INDIA--EDUCATION.
----Nation-building media and TNCs. - 1984.
    (000941)

INDIA--ELECTRONICS INDUSTRY.
----New information technology in India. -
  1986.
    (000651)
----Technology transfer under alternative
  arrangements with transnational
  corporations. - 1987.
    (001513)

INDIA--ENGINEERING INDUSTRIES.
----Microelectronics-based automation
  technologies and development. - 1985.
    (000753)
----Top hundred engineering companies. -
  197?-   .
    (002669)

INDIA--EXPORT MARKETING.
----Foreign cooperation and the marketing of
  manufactured exports from developing
  countries. - 1985.
    (001377)

INDIA--EXPORT ORIENTED INDUSTRIES.
----Industrial distribution of Indian
  exports and joint ventures abroad. -
  1985.
    (000316)

INDIA--FACTORIES.
----All-India directory of industrial
  establishments. - 1984-   .
    (002614)

INDIA--FINANCIAL STATEMENTS.
----Compendium of statements and standards.
  - 1986.
    (002074)

INDIA--FINANCIAL STATISTICS.
----Top hundred engineering companies. -
  197?-   .
    (002669)

INDIA--FOREIGN DIRECT INVESTMENT.
----Foreign direct investment in
  manufacturing from an LDC: India. - 1985.
    (000317)
----Industrial distribution of Indian
  exports and joint ventures abroad. -
  1985.
    (000316)
----Multinationals from the Third World. -
  1986.
    (000345)
----Multinationals in Indian big business. -
  1983.
    (001057)
----Multinationals in Indian big business:
  industrial characteristics of foreign
  investments in a heavily regulated
  economy. - 1983.
    (001058)
----New forms of overseas investment by
  developing countries : the case of
  India, Korea and Brazil. - 1986.
    (001616)
----Pros and cons of Third World
  multinationals. - 1985.
    (000304)
----Taxation of foreign companies. - 1984.
    (001717)

INDIA--FOREIGN INVESTMENTS.
----National legislation and regulations
  relating to transnational corporations.
  Volume 4. - 1986.
    (002253)

INDIA--FOREIGN TRADE.
----Role of multinationals in India's
    foreign trade. - 1987.
      (001069)
----Sino-Indian economic relations. - 1984.
      (000307)
----Trade and investment possibilities in
    Bangladesh, Nepal and Sri Lanka. - 1983.
      (001840)
----Trade in investment-related
    technological studies. - 1986.
      (001386)

INDIA--HOST COUNTRY RELATIONS.
----Multinationals in Indian big business:
    industrial characteristics of foreign
    investments in a heavily regulated
    economy. - 1983.
      (001058)

INDIA--INDUSTRIAL ACCIDENTS.
----The Bhopal case : controlling
    ultrahazardous industrial activities
    undertaken by foreign investors. - 1987.
      (001949)
----For whom the bell tolls in the aftermath
    of the Bhopal tragedy. - 1987.
      (001950)
----The lessons of Bhopal. - 1985.
      (001933)

INDIA--INDUSTRIAL CO-OPERATION.
----Indo-U.S. cooperation in business and
    industry, 1986. - 1986.
      (002675)

INDIA--INDUSTRIAL ENTERPRISES.
----All-India directory of industrial
    establishments. - 1984-   .
      (002614)
----Licensing industrial technology to
    developing countries : the operations of
    Swedish firms in India. - 1986.
      (002442)

INDIA--INDUSTRIAL RESEARCH.
----Trade in investment-related
    technological studies. - 1986.
      (001386)

INDIA--INDUSTRIAL STATISTICS.
----Technology transfer under alternative
    arrangements with transnational
    corporations. - 1987.
      (001513)

INDIA--INDUSTRIAL TECHNOLOGY.
----Licensing industrial technology to
    developing countries : the operations of
    Swedish firms in India. - 1986.
      (002442)

INDIA--INDUSTRIALIZATION.
----Exports of technology by newly
    industrializing countries: India. - 1984.
      (001455)

INDIA--INFORMATION TECHNOLOGY.
----New information technology in India. -
    1986.
      (000651)

INDIA--INVESTMENT POLICY.
----Joint ventures abroad. - 1983.
      (001592)
----Joint ventures abroad. - 1984.
      (001528)
----Multinationals in Indian big business:
    industrial characteristics of foreign
    investments in a heavily regulated
    economy. - 1983.
      (001058)

INDIA--JOINT VENTURES.
----Indo-U.S. cooperation in business and
    industry, 1986. - 1986.
      (002675)
----Industrial distribution of Indian
    exports and joint ventures abroad. -
    1985.
      (000316)
----Joint ventures abroad. - 1983.
      (001592)
----Joint ventures abroad. - 1984.
      (001528)
----New forms of overseas investment by
    developing countries : the case of
    India, Korea and Brazil. - 1986.
      (001616)
----Sino-Indian economic relations. - 1984.
      (000307)

INDIA--LAWS AND REGULATIONS.
----National legislation and regulations
    relating to transnational corporations.
    Volume 4. - 1986.
      (002253)
----Regulations in vain? - 1986.
      (002240)

INDIA--LIABILITY.
----The Bhopal case : controlling
    ultrahazardous industrial activities
    undertaken by foreign investors. - 1987.
      (001949)

INDIA--LICENCE AGREEMENTS.
----Licensing industrial technology to
    developing countries : the operations of
    Swedish firms in India. - 1986.
      (002442)

INDIA--MACHINE TOOL INDUSTRY.
----Industrial strategy and technological
    dynamism in machine tool manufacture. -
    1983.
      (000716)

INDIA--MAN-MADE DISASTERS.
----For whom the bell tolls in the aftermath
    of the Bhopal tragedy. - 1987.
      (001950)

INDIA--MANUFACTURES.
----Foreign cooperation and the marketing of
    manufactured exports from developing
    countries. - 1985.
      (001377)

INDIA--MANUFACTURING.
----Multinationals in Indian big business. -
    1983.
      (001057)

INDIA--MANUFACTURING ENTERPRISES.
----The determinants of manufacturing
ownership in less developed countries. -
1986.
(000712)
----Foreign direct investment in
manufacturing from an LDC: India. - 1985.
(000317)

INDIA--MASS MEDIA.
----Nation-building media and TNCs. - 1984.
(000941)

INDIA--METALWORKING INDUSTRY.
----Technology transfer under alternative
arrangements with transnational
corporations. - 1987.
(001513)

INDIA--NATIONALIZATION.
----Les nationalisations dans quelques pays
d'Asie de tradition britannique : Inde,
Sri Lanca, Birmanie. - 1984.
(002329)

INDIA--NEW TECHNOLOGIES.
----New information technology in India. -
1986.
(000651)

INDIA--PETROCHEMICAL INDUSTRY.
----Transnational corporations and
technology transfer. - 1984.
(000704)

INDIA--PETROLEUM EXPLORATION.
----Social and economic effects of petroleum
development. - 1987.
(000633)

INDIA--PETROLEUM INDUSTRY.
----Oil and other multinationals in India. -
1986.
(001065)
----Social and economic effects of petroleum
development. - 1987.
(000633)

INDIA--PHARMACEUTICAL INDUSTRY.
----Business strategies of multinational
corporations in India. - 1983.
(000484)
----Multinational corporations and Indian
drug industry. - 1985.
(000736)
----Multinationals and Indian pharmaceutical
industry. - 1984.
(000727)
----Transnational corporations in the
pharmaceutical industry of developing
countries. - 1984.
(000749)

INDIA--PRIVATE ENTERPRISES.
----The determinants of manufacturing
ownership in less developed countries. -
1986.
(000712)

INDIA--PUBLIC ENTERPRISES.
----The determinants of manufacturing
ownership in less developed countries. -
1986.
(000712)

INDIA--PUBLISHING.
----Nation-building media and TNCs. - 1984.
(000941)

INDIA--SCIENCE AND TECHNOLOGY POLICY.
----Proceedings of the SSTCC/UNCTC/ESCAP
Asia-Pacific Training Workshop on
Regulating and Negotiating Technology
Transfer through Transnational
Corporations, 14-25 October 1985,
Fuzhou, Fujian, China. - 1986.
(001405) (002169)

INDIA--STANDARDS.
----Compendium of statements and standards.
- 1986.
(002074)

INDIA--STATISTICAL DATA.
----Technology transfer under alternative
arrangements with transnational
corporations. - 1987.
(001513)

INDIA--TAX AUDITING.
----India: measures against tax avoidance by
multinationals. - 1986.
(001716)

INDIA--TAX AVOIDANCE.
----India: measures against tax avoidance by
multinationals. - 1986.
(001716)

INDIA--TAXATION.
----Taxation of foreign companies. - 1984.
(001717)

INDIA--TECHNICAL CO-OPERATION.
----Technology transfer under alternative
arrangements with transnational
corporations. - 1987.
(001513)

INDIA--TECHNOLOGICAL INNOVATIONS.
----Trade in investment-related
technological studies. - 1986.
(001386)

INDIA--TECHNOLOGY TRANSFER.
----Exports of technology by newly
industrializing countries: India. - 1984.
(001455)
----Proceedings of the SSTCC/UNCTC/ESCAP
Asia-Pacific Training Workshop on
Regulating and Negotiating Technology
Transfer through Transnational
Corporations, 14-25 October 1985,
Fuzhou, Fujian, China. - 1986.
(001405) (002169)
----Technology transfer under alternative
arrangements with transnational
corporations. - 1987.
(001513)
----Transnational corporations and
technology transfer. - 1984.
(000704)

INDIA--TOXIC SUBSTANCES.
----The Bhopal case : controlling
ultrahazardous industrial activities
undertaken by foreign investors. - 1987.
(001949)

INDIA--TRANSNATIONAL CORPORATIONS.
----Between dependency and autonomy. - 1984.
 (000691)
----The Bhopal case : controlling
 ultrahazardous industrial activities
 undertaken by foreign investors. - 1987.
 (001949)
----Business strategies of multinational
 corporations in India. - 1983.
 (000484)
----Changing perspectives on the role of
 multinationals in economic development:
 some evidence from India. - 1985.
 (001040)
----The determinants of manufacturing
 ownership in less developed countries. -
 1986.
 (000712)
----India: measures against tax avoidance by
 multinationals. - 1986.
 (001716)
----Indo-U.S. cooperation in business and
 industry, 1986. - 1986.
 (002675)
----The lessons of Bhopal. - 1985.
 (001933)
----Multinational corporations and Indian
 drug industry. - 1985.
 (000736)
----Multinationals and Indian pharmaceutical
 industry. - 1984.
 (000727)
----Multinationals from India. - 1983.
 (000347)
----Multinationals from the Third World. -
 1986.
 (000345)
----Multinationals in Indian big business. -
 1983.
 (001057)
----Multinationals in Indian big business:
 industrial characteristics of foreign
 investments in a heavily regulated
 economy. - 1983.
 (001058)
----Multinationals, technology and exports.
 - 1985.
 (001456)
----National legislation and regulations
 relating to transnational corporations.
 Volume 4. - 1986.
 (002253)
----Nation-building media and TNCs. - 1984.
 (000941)
----New forms of overseas investment by
 developing countries : the case of
 India, Korea and Brazil. - 1986. .
 (001616)
----Oil and other multinationals in India. -
 1986.
 (001065)
----Pros and cons of Third World
 multinationals. - 1985.
 (000304)
----Regulations in vain? - 1986.
 (002240)
----Role of multinationals in India's
 foreign trade. - 1987.
 (001069)
----Technology transfer under alternative
 arrangements with transnational
 corporations. - 1987.
 (001513)

----Third World multinationals: the
 characteristics of Indian firms
 investing abroad. - 1986.
 (000346)
----Transnational corporations and
 technology transfer. - 1984.
 (000704)

INDIGENOUS POPULATIONS--NORTH AMERICA.
----Indigenous resource rights and mining
 companies in North America and
 Australia. - 1986.
 (000616)

INDIGENOUS POPULATIONS--PHILIPPINES.
----The Philippines : authoritarian
 government, multinationals and ancestral
 lands. - 1983.
 (001066)

INDONESIA--BUSINESS.
----The Indonesian business. - 1986.
 (001839)

INDONESIA--CHEMICAL INDUSTRY.
----Technology transfer under alternative
 arrangements with transnational
 corporations. - 1987.
 (001513)

INDONESIA--CONGLOMERATE CORPORATIONS.
----Japanese direct investment in ASEAN. -
 1983.
 (000171)

INDONESIA--CONTRACTS.
----Formation of contract and contract law
 through multinational joint ventures. -
 1983.
 (002435)

INDONESIA--ECONOMIC CONDITIONS.
----The Indonesian business. - 1986.
 (001839)

INDONESIA--EXPORT SUBSIDIES.
----The Jakarta export processing zone:
 benefits and costs. - 1983.
 (002400)

INDONESIA--FACTOR ANALYSIS.
.----Factor proportions and productive
 efficiency of foreign owned firms in the
 Indonesian manufacturing sector. - 1984.
 (000655)

INDONESIA--FOOD INDUSTRY.
----Technology transfer under alternative
 arrangements with transnational
 corporations. - 1987.
 (001513)

INDONESIA--FOREIGN DIRECT INVESTMENT.
----Foreign investment and government policy
 in the Third World. - 1988.
 (001790)
----Foreign investment and industrialization
 in Indonesia. - 1988.
 (001053)
----Japanese direct investment in ASEAN. -
 1983.
 (000171)

INDONESIA--FOREIGN DIRECT INVESTMENT
(continued)
----Japanese direct investment in Indonesian
    manufacturing. - 1984.
    (000187)
----Japanese investment in Indonesia:
    problems and prospects. - 1986.
    (000152)
----MNCs and the host country, the
    Indonesian case. - 1984.
    (001073)

INDONESIA--FREE EXPORT ZONES.
----The Jakarta export processing zone:
    benefits and costs. - 1983.
    (002400)

INDONESIA--HOST COUNTRY RELATIONS.
----MNCs and the host country, the
    Indonesian case. - 1984.
    (001073)
----The politics of oil in Indonesia. - 1986.
    (001818)

INDONESIA--INDUSTRIAL POLICY.
----The politics of oil in Indonesia. - 1986.
    (001818)

INDONESIA--INDUSTRIAL PRODUCTION.
----Multinational corporations and host
    country technology. - 1984.
    (001493)

INDONESIA--INDUSTRIAL PROMOTION.
----The Indonesian business. - 1986.
    (001839)

INDONESIA--INDUSTRIAL STATISTICS.
----Technology transfer under alternative
    arrangements with transnational
    corporations. - 1987.
    (001513)

INDONESIA--INDUSTRIALIZATION.
----Foreign investment and industrialization
    in Indonesia. - 1988.
    (001053)

INDONESIA--INVESTMENT POLICY.
----Foreign investment and government policy
    in the Third World. - 1988.
    (001790)

INDONESIA--JOINT VENTURES.
----Japanese direct investment in ASEAN. -
    1983.
    (000171)

INDONESIA--LAWS AND REGULATIONS.
----MNCs and the host country, the
    Indonesian case. - 1984.
    (001073)
----National legislation and regulations
    relating to transnational corporations.
    Volume 3. - 1983.
    (002252)

INDONESIA--MANUFACTURING ENTERPRISES.
----Factor proportions and productive
    efficiency of foreign owned firms in the
    Indonesian manufacturing sector. - 1984.
    (000655)

----Japanese direct investment in Indonesian
    manufacturing. - 1984.
    (000187)

INDONESIA--NATURAL GAS INDUSTRY.
----The Indonesian petroleum industry. -
    1986.
    (000614)

INDONESIA--PETROLEUM INDUSTRY.
----The Indonesian petroleum industry. -
    1986.
    (000614)
----The politics of oil in Indonesia. - 1986.
    (001818)

INDONESIA--PHARMACEUTICAL INDUSTRY.
----Technology transfer under alternative
    arrangements with transnational
    corporations. - 1987.
    (001513)

INDONESIA--PRODUCTIVITY.
----Factor proportions and productive
    efficiency of foreign owned firms in the
    Indonesian manufacturing sector. - 1984.
    (000655)

INDONESIA--RISK ASSESSMENT.
----How multinationals analyze political
    risk. - 1983.
    (001849)

INDONESIA--SCIENCE AND TECHNOLOGY POLICY.
----Proceedings of the SSTCC/UNCTC/ESCAP
    Asia-Pacific Training Workshop on
    Regulating and Negotiating Technology
    Transfer through Transnational
    Corporations, 14-25 October 1985,
    Fuzhou, Fujian, China. - 1986.
    (001405) (002169)

INDONESIA--STATISTICAL DATA.
----Technology transfer under alternative
    arrangements with transnational
    corporations. - 1987.
    (001513)

INDONESIA--STOCK MARKETS.
----Foreign investment and government policy
    in the Third World. - 1988.
    (001790)

INDONESIA--STOCKS.
----Foreign investment and government policy
    in the Third World. - 1988.
    (001790)

INDONESIA--TECHNOLOGY TRANSFER.
----Multinational corporations and host
    country technology. - 1984.
    (001493)
----Proceedings of the SSTCC/UNCTC/ESCAP
    Asia-Pacific Training Workshop on
    Regulating and Negotiating Technology
    Transfer through Transnational
    Corporations, 14-25 October 1985,
    Fuzhou, Fujian, China. - 1986.
    (001405) (002169)

Subject Index - Index des matières

INDONESIA--TECHNOLOGY TRANSFER (continued)
----Technology transfer under alternative
    arrangements with transnational
    corporations. - 1987.
      (001513)

INDONESIA--TRADE FINANCING.
----The Jakarta export processing zone:
    benefits and costs. - 1983.
      (002400)

INDONESIA--TRANSNATIONAL CORPORATIONS.
----Factor proportions and productive
    efficiency of foreign owned firms in the
    Indonesian manufacturing sector. - 1984.
      (000655)
----How multinationals analyze political
    risk. - 1983.
      (001849)
----Indigenization policies and structural
    cooptation by multinational
    corporations. - 1985.
      (002331)
----Japanese direct investment in ASEAN. -
    1983.
      (000171)
----MNCs and the host country, the
    Indonesian case. - 1984.
      (001073)
----Multinational corporations and host
    country technology. - 1984.
      (001493)
----National legislation and regulations
    relating to transnational corporations.
    Volume 3. - 1983.
      (002252)
----The politics of oil in Indonesia. - 1986.
      (001818)
----Technology transfer under alternative
    arrangements with transnational
    corporations. - 1987.
      (001513)

INDUSTRIAL ACCIDENTS--BHOPAL (INDIA).
----For whom the bell tolls in the aftermath
    of the Bhopal tragedy. - 1987.
      (001950)
----The lessons of Bhopal. - 1985.
      (001933)
----Mass disasters and multinational
    liability : the Bhopal case. - 1986.
      (001936)

INDUSTRIAL ACCIDENTS--INDIA.
----The Bhopal case : controlling
    ultrahazardous industrial activities
    undertaken by foreign investors. - 1987.
      (001949)
----For whom the bell tolls in the aftermath
    of the Bhopal tragedy. - 1987.
      (001950)
----The lessons of Bhopal. - 1985.
      (001933)

INDUSTRIAL ACCIDENTS--UNITED STATES.
----The Bhopal case : controlling
    ultrahazardous industrial activities
    undertaken by foreign investors. - 1987.
      (001949)

INDUSTRIAL ADMINISTRATION--JAPAN.
----The nature and tools of Japan's
    industrial policy. - 1986.
      (000557)

INDUSTRIAL APPLICATIONS--UNITED STATES.
----A competitive assessment of selected
    reinforced composite fibers. - 1985.
      (000644)

INDUSTRIAL ARBITRATION--AUSTRALIA.
----Mediation, conciliation and arbitration
    : an international comparison of
    Australia, Great Britain and the United
    States. - 1987.
      (002476)

INDUSTRIAL ARBITRATION--UNITED KINGDOM.
----Mediation, conciliation and arbitration
    : an international comparison of
    Australia, Great Britain and the United
    States. - 1987.
      (002476)

INDUSTRIAL ARBITRATION--UNITED STATES.
----Mediation, conciliation and arbitration
    : an international comparison of
    Australia, Great Britain and the United
    States. - 1987.
      (002476)

INDUSTRIAL CAPACITY.
----The capital goods sector in developing
    countries. - 1985.
      (001651)

INDUSTRIAL CAPACITY--THAILAND.
----Technology acquisition under alternative
    arrangements with transnational
    corporations. - 1987.
      (001512)

INDUSTRIAL CONCENTRATION.
----Sovremennyi kontsern,
    politekonomicheskii aspekt. - 1983.
      (001668)
----The spatial distribution of the effects
    of economic integration schemes. - 1984.
      (001346)

INDUSTRIAL CONCENTRATION--HUNGARY.
----A magyar feldolgozó ipar koncentrációs
    folyamata a 70-es évtizedben, nemzetközi
    összehasonlításban. - 1986.
      (001181)

INDUSTRIAL CONCENTRATION--LATIN AMERICA.
----Las empresas transnacionales y la
    inversión extranjera directa en la
    primera mitad de los años ochenta. -
    1987.
      (000194)

INDUSTRIAL CONSULTING--UNITED STATES.
----Consultants and consulting organizations
    directory. - 197?-   .
      (000832)

INDUSTRIAL CO-OPERATION.
----Co-production: a viable consideration
    for developing nations. - 1984.
      (001629)
----East-West joint ventures. - 1988.
      (001570)

INDUSTRIAL CO-OPERATION (continued)
----Fertilizer supplies for developing
    countries : issues in the transfer and
    development of technology. - 1985.
    (001471)
----Food-processing contracts with
    developing countries. - 1985.
    (002419)
----The global factory. - 1985.
    (001254)
----Industrialisation et commerce du Tiers
    monde. - 1986.
    (001318)
----Investitionen und Kooperationen in
    Ubersee. - 1983.
    (001567)
----Joint ventures and global strategies. -
    1984.
    (001586)
----Kelet : nyugati közös vállalatok néhány
    elvi kérdése. - 1984.
    (001180)
----New forms of international investment in
    developing countries. - 1984.
    (001615)
----Recent developments in operations and
    behaviour of transnational corporations.
    - 1987.
    (000103)
----State enterprise-multinational
    corporation joint ventures: how well do
    they meet both partners' needs? - 1983.
    (001632)
----Threats and opportunities of global
    countertrade : marketing, financing and
    organizational implications. - 1984.
    (001353)
----UNCTC bibliography, 1974-1987. - 1988.
    (002695)
----The 1984 Justice Department guidelines
    toward horizontal mergers. - 1986.
    (001551)

INDUSTRIAL CO-OPERATION--AFRICA.
----Agro-industrial co-operation between the
    European Community and the ACP
    countries. - 1986.
    (002605)
----Current problems of economic
    integration. - 1986.
    (001312)

INDUSTRIAL CO-OPERATION--ARAB COUNTRIES.
----Current problems of economic
    integration. - 1986.
    (001312)

INDUSTRIAL CO-OPERATION--ARGENTINA.
----La cooperación empresarial
    argentino-brasileña. - 1983.
    (001097)
----Joint venture y sociedad. - 1984.
    (001602)

INDUSTRIAL CO-OPERATION--ASIA.
----Current problems of economic
    integration. - 1986.
    (001312)
----Joint ventures in Asien. - 1983.
    (001597)

INDUSTRIAL CO-OPERATION--BRAZIL.
----La cooperación empresarial
    argentino-brasileña. - 1983.
    (001097)

INDUSTRIAL CO-OPERATION--CAMEROON.
----Agro-industrial co-operation between the
    European Community and the ACP
    countries. - 1986.
    (002605)

INDUSTRIAL CO-OPERATION--CARIBBEAN REGION.
----Agro-industrial co-operation between the
    European Community and the ACP
    countries. - 1986.
    (002605)

INDUSTRIAL CO-OPERATION--CHINA.
----Industrial co-operation between China
    and Hong Kong. - 1983.
    (001554)

INDUSTRIAL CO-OPERATION--EASTERN EUROPE.
----East-West trade, industrial co-operation
    and technology transfer. - 1984.
    (001441)
----Equity cooperation ventures (ECV)
    domiciled in the socialist countries :
    trends and patterns. - 1986.
    (001603)
----Expectations and results of
    contractual joint ventures by US and UK
    MNCs in Eastern Europe. - 1984.
    (001623)
----Technological cooperation and
    specialization. - 1986.
    (001500)
----Zum Einfluss von Modernisierung und
    Rekonstruktion auf die internationale
    sozialistische Arbeitsteilung. - 1987.
    (001227)

INDUSTRIAL CO-OPERATION--EUROPE.
----Industrial collaboration with Japan. -
    1986.
    (001648)

INDUSTRIAL CO-OPERATION--FRANCE.
----Les caractéristiques juridiques des
    contrats internationaux de coopération
    industrielle. - 1984.
    (002438)
----La specialisation internationale de la
    France dans les échanges de services.
    (With English summary.). - 1986.
    (000907)

INDUSTRIAL CO-OPERATION--GERMAN DEMOCRATIC
REPUBLIC.
----Zum Einfluss von Modernisierung und
    Rekonstruktion auf die internationale
    sozialistische Arbeitsteilung. - 1987.
    (001227)

INDUSTRIAL CO-OPERATION--HONG KONG.
----Industrial co-operation between China
    and Hong Kong. - 1983.
    (001554)

INDUSTRIAL CO-OPERATION--HUNGARY.
----A magyar gépipari vállalatok
    nagyságrendje és piaci magatartásuk. -
    1984.
      (000957)

INDUSTRIAL CO-OPERATION--INDIA.
----Indo-U.S. cooperation in business and
    industry, 1986. - 1986.
      (002675)

INDUSTRIAL CO-OPERATION--JAPAN.
----The Asianization of British industry. -
    1983.
      (000204)
----Industrial collaboration with Japan. -
    1986.
      (001648)
----New patterns in the formation of US/
    Japanese cooperative ventures: the role
    of technology. - 1987.
      (001622)
----Planning a joint venture for the
    Japanese market. - 1987.
      (000508)

INDUSTRIAL CO-OPERATION--LATIN AMERICA.
----Current problems of economic
    integration. - 1986.
      (001312)

INDUSTRIAL CO-OPERATION--NETHERLANDS.
----Recommendation on industry and
    development cooperation. - 1984.
      (001329)

INDUSTRIAL CO-OPERATION--PACIFIC OCEAN
REGION.
----Agro-industrial co-operation between the
    European Community and the ACP
    countries. - 1986.
      (002605)
----Technology transfer in the Pacific
    Basin. - 1985.
      (001413)

INDUSTRIAL CO-OPERATION--POLAND.
----Industrial cooperation between Poland
    and the West. - 1985.
      (001576)
----Kooperacja przemyslowa Polski z krajami
    RWPG. - 1986.
      (001172)
----The regulation of technology transfer in
    Poland. - 1983.
      (001416)
----Western firms participating in the
    East-West industrial co-operation. -
    1983.
      (001175)

INDUSTRIAL CO-OPERATION--RWANDA.
----Agro-industrial co-operation between the
    European Community and the ACP
    countries. - 1986.
      (002605)

INDUSTRIAL CO-OPERATION--SOUTH ASIA.
----Industrial cooperation in regional
    economic groupings among developing
    countries and lessons for SAARC. - 1987.
      (001009)

INDUSTRIAL CO-OPERATION--SOUTHEAST ASIA.
----ASEAN economic co-operation. - 1985.
      (001039)
----Basic framework for ASEAN industrial
    co-operation. - 1986.
      (002149)

INDUSTRIAL CO-OPERATION--UNITED KINGDOM.
----The Asianization of British industry. -
    1983.
      (000204)
----East-West trade, industrial co-operation
    and technology transfer. - 1984.
      (001441)
----Expectations and results of
    contractual joint ventures by US and UK
    MNCs in Eastern Europe. - 1984.
      (001623)

INDUSTRIAL CO-OPERATION--UNITED STATES.
----American enterprise in foreign markets.
    - 1984.
      (000526)
----Controlling the cost of international
    compensation. - 1983.
      (002323)
----Expectations and results of
    contractual joint ventures by US and UK
    MNCs in Eastern Europe. - 1984.
      (001623)
----Indo-U.S. cooperation in business and
    industry, 1986. - 1986.
      (002675)
----Industrial collaboration with Japan. -
    1986.
      (001648)
----International Harvester in Russia: the
    Washington-St. Petersburg connection? -
    1983.
      (000272)
----Joint venture y sociedad. - 1984.
      (001602)
----New patterns in the formation of US/
    Japanese cooperative ventures: the role
    of technology. - 1987.
      (001622)
----Planning a joint venture for the
    Japanese market. - 1987.
      (000508)

INDUSTRIAL CO-OPERATION--USSR.
----American enterprise in foreign markets.
    - 1984.
      (000526)
----International Harvester in Russia: the
    Washington-St. Petersburg connection? -
    1983.
      (000272)

INDUSTRIAL CO-OPERATION--WESTERN EUROPE.
----Agro-industrial co-operation between the
    European Community and the ACP
    countries. - 1986.
      (002605)
----Industrialization and the ACPs. - 1984.
      (002608)

INDUSTRIAL CO-OPERATION--YUGOSLAVIA.
----Industrial co-operation and investment
    in Yugoslavia. - 1986.
      (001540)

INDUSTRIAL COSTS.
----Multinationals, transaction costs and
    choice of institutional form. - 1986.
    (000078)

INDUSTRIAL COSTS--UNITED STATES.
----Industrial renaissance : producing a
    competitive future for America. - 1983.
    (000300)

INDUSTRIAL DESIGN--UNITED STATES.
----Design patents. - 1983.
    (001425)

INDUSTRIAL DEVELOPMENT.
----The capital goods sector in developing
    countries. - 1985.
    (001651)
----Economics of change in less developed
    countries. - 1986.
    (001000)
----Fertilizer supplies for developing
    countries : issues in the transfer and
    development of technology. - 1985.
    (001471)
----Global shift. - 1987.
    (001315)
----Industry in the 1980s. - 1985.
    (001341)
----Investing in free export processing
    zones. - 1984.
    (002362)
----Investir dans les zones franches
    industrielles d'exportation. - 1984.
    (002363)
----Strategic investments and the
    development of multinationals. - 1987.
    (000044)
----A strategy for the technological
    transformation of developing countries.
    - 1985.
    (001515)
----Toward a theory of industrial
    development in the Third World. - 1984.
    (001331)
----Transnacionalización y periferia
    semindustrializada. - 1984-   .
    (001339)

INDUSTRIAL DEVELOPMENT--AFRICA SOUTH OF
SAHARA.
----The differentiation process in the
    economies of black Africa. - 1984.
    (001694)

INDUSTRIAL DEVELOPMENT--AUSTRALIA.
----The public interest IR & D program. -
    1985.
    (001485)

INDUSTRIAL DEVELOPMENT--BURUNDI.
----Guide des investisseurs. - 1983-   .
    (001805)

INDUSTRIAL DEVELOPMENT--CHINA.
----La politique chinoise d'ouverture. -
    1983.
    (002186)

INDUSTRIAL DEVELOPMENT--COLOMBIA.
----Las empresas transnacionales en el
    desarrollo colombiano. - 1986.
    (001121)

INDUSTRIAL DEVELOPMENT--GREECE.
----Licensing and industrial development. -
    1986.
    (001449)

INDUSTRIAL DEVELOPMENT--GUYANA.
----The American take-over. - 1983.
    (000287)

INDUSTRIAL DEVELOPMENT--JAPAN.
----Le Japon : transformations
    industrielles, croissance et
    internationalisation. - 1983.
    (000319)

INDUSTRIAL DEVELOPMENT--LATIN AMERICA.
----Nueva división internacional del trabajo
    y reestructuración productiva en América
    Latina. - 1984.
    (001264)
----Transnational corporations and
    industrial transformation in Latin
    America. - 1984.
    (001099)

INDUSTRIAL DEVELOPMENT--LESOTHO.
----Lagging behind the bantustans. - 1985.
    (001223)

INDUSTRIAL DEVELOPMENT--SAUDI ARABIA.
----Petroleum based development and the
    private sector. - 1985.
    (001138)

INDUSTRIAL DEVELOPMENT--SURINAME.
----The American take-over. - 1983.
    (000287)

INDUSTRIAL DEVELOPMENT--ZAIRE.
----Les sociétés transnationales en Afrique.
    - 1986.
    (001028)

INDUSTRIAL EFFICIENCY.
----Contract efficiency and natural resource
    investment in developing countries. -
    1984.
    (002409)
----Foreign investment, technical efficiency
    and structural change. - 1983.
    (001085)
----Report on international industrial
    competitiveness, 1984. - 1984.
    (001690)
----Trade and dynamic efficiency. - 1987.
    (001698)

INDUSTRIAL EFFICIENCY--MEXICO.
----Foreign investment and productive
    efficiency. - 1986.
    (001084)

INDUSTRIAL ENTERPRISES--FRANCE.
----Activité comparée des établissements
    industriels d'origine étrangère et des
    établissements industriels français. -
    1984.
    (001927)
----Die Nationalisierungen in Frankreich
    1981/82. - 1983.
    (002337)

INDUSTRIAL ENTERPRISES--FRANCE (continued)
----Le processus d'acquisition technologique
   par les entreprises d'un pays
   semi-industrialise. Deux études de cas.
   (With English summary.). - 1983.
      (001407)

INDUSTRIAL ENTERPRISES--INDIA.
----All-India directory of industrial
   establishments. - 1984-   .
      (002614)
----Licensing industrial technology to
 _ developing countries : the operations of
   Swedish firms in India. - 1986.
      (002442)

INDUSTRIAL ENTERPRISES--ITALY.
----New forms of international technology
   transfer by Italian enterprises to
   developing countries. - 1984.
      (001474)

INDUSTRIAL ENTERPRISES--LATIN AMERICA.
----Profits, progress and poverty. - 1985.
      (001111)

INDUSTRIAL ENTERPRISES--SWEDEN.
----Licensing industrial technology to
   developing countries : the operations of
   Swedish firms in India. - 1986.
      (002442)

INDUSTRIAL ENTERPRISES--TURKEY.
----Le processus d'acquisition technologique
   par les entreprises d'un pays
   semi-industrialise. Deux études de cas.
   (With English summary.). - 1983.
      (001407)

INDUSTRIAL ENTERPRISES--UNITED KINGDOM.
 ----The United Kingdom merger boom in
   perspective. - 1987.
      (001638)

INDUSTRIAL ENTERPRISES--USSR.
----The Soviet industrial enterprise. - 1984.
      (000330)

INDUSTRIAL ENTERPRISES--WESTERN EUROPE.
----European industry on the march. - 1987.
      (001155)

INDUSTRIAL EQUIPMENT LEASES.
----Analysis of equipment leasing contracts.
   - 1984.
      (002407)
----International equipment leasing. - 1984.
      (000905) (002139)
----Trends in international taxation. - 1985.
      (001746)

INDUSTRIAL EQUIPMENT LEASES--BRAZIL.
----Analysis of equipment leasing contracts.
   - 1984.
      (002407)

INDUSTRIAL EQUIPMENT LEASES--FRANCE.
----Analysis of equipment leasing contracts.
   - 1984.
      (002407)

INDUSTRIAL EQUIPMENT LEASES--GERMANY,
FEDERAL REPUBLIC OF.
----Analysis of equipment leasing contracts.
   - 1984.
      (002407)

INDUSTRIAL EQUIPMENT LEASES--JAPAN.
----Analysis of equipment leasing contracts.
   - 1984.
      (002407)

INDUSTRIAL EQUIPMENT LEASES--REPUBLIC OF
KOREA.
----Analysis of equipment leasing contracts.
   - 1984.
      (002407)

INDUSTRIAL EQUIPMENT LEASES--THAILAND.
----Analysis of equipment leasing contracts.
   - 1984.
      (002407)

INDUSTRIAL EQUIPMENT LEASES--UNITED KINGDOM.
----Analysis of equipment leasing contracts.
   - 1984.
      (002407)

INDUSTRIAL EQUIPMENT LEASES--UNITED STATES.
----Analysis of equipment leasing contracts.
   - 1984.
      (002407)
----A competitive assessment of the United
   States equipment leasing industry. -
   1985.
      (000982)

INDUSTRIAL FINANCING.
----Japan's largest financier of
   multinationalism: the EXIM Bank. - 1986.
      (000255)
----Profitability of mergers in food
   manufacturing. - 1986.
      (001584)
----The role of multilateral development
   finance institutions in promoting and
   financing joint ventures. - 1986.
      (000252)

INDUSTRIAL FINANCING--UNITED STATES.
----The funding of high technology ventures.
   - 1983.
      (000412)

INDUSTRIAL FORECASTS.
----U.S. industrial outlook. - 1960-   .
      (000750) (000971)

INDUSTRIAL INSTITUTIONS--EAST ASIA.
----International trading companies for
   developing countries-Latin America. -
   1984.
      (000838)

INDUSTRIAL INSTITUTIONS--LATIN AMERICA.
----International trading companies for
   developing countries-Latin America. -
   1984.
      (000838)

INDUSTRIAL LEGISLATION.
----National legislation and regulations
relating to transnational corporations.
Volume 2. - 1983.
(002251)

INDUSTRIAL LEGISLATION--EAST ASIA.
----East Asian executive reports. -
1979-   .
(002203)

INDUSTRIAL LEGISLATION--MOROCCO.
----Le nouveau droit des investissements
étrangers au Maroc. - 1984.
(002269)

INDUSTRIAL LOCATION.
----Diversification strategy and choice
of country: diversifying acquisitions
abroad by U.S. multinationals,
1978-1980. - 1985.
(000536)
----Environment of international business. -
1985.
(000055)
----Establishing overseas operations: tax
and treasury considerations. - 1987.
(001768)
----Industrial change in advanced economies.
- 1987.
(001317)
----Intra-industry production as a form of
international economic involvement. -
1983.
(000026)
----The location choice of offices of
international companies. - 1987.
(000530)
----Making the multinational decision. -
1983.
(000542)
----A mean-variance model of MNF location
strategy. - 1985.
(000535)
----On planning and forecasting the location
of retail and service activity. - 1984.
(000550)
----Towards a theory of multinational
enterprise. - 1986.
(000032)
----Where in the world should we put that
plant? - 1983.
(000553)

INDUSTRIAL LOCATION--AUSTRALIA.
----The geography of Australian corporate
power. - 1984.
(001166)

INDUSTRIAL LOCATION--CANADA.
----High technology plant location
decisions. - 1983.
(000528)

INDUSTRIAL LOCATION--FRANCE.
----Labour, production and the state :
decentralization of the French
automobile industry. - 1987.
(000724)

INDUSTRIAL LOCATION--NIGERIA.
----The politics of industrial location in
Nigeria. - 1985.
(001837)

INDUSTRIAL LOCATION--PHILIPPINES.
----Factors influencing the choice of
location : local and foreign firms in
the Philippines. - 1987.
(000547)

INDUSTRIAL LOCATION--UNITED STATES.
----Are environmental regulations driving
U.S. industry overseas? - 1984.
(001947)
----Foreign location decisions by U.S.
transnational firms: an empirical study.
- 1984.
(000537)
----Foreign manufacturing investment in the
United States: competitive strategies
and international location. - 1985.
(000733)
----High technology plant location
decisions. - 1983.
(000528)
----The international location of
manufacturing investments: recent
behaviour of foreign-owned corporations
in the United States. - 1983.
(001156)

INDUSTRIAL MANAGEMENT.
----Cases in strategic management and
business policy. - 1986.
(000483)
----Industriebetriebslehre in Wissenschaft
und Praxis. - 1985.
(000404)
----The spatial organisation of
multinational corporations. - 1985.
(000017)
----La structure financière du capitalisme
multinational. - 1983.
(001259)

INDUSTRIAL MANAGEMENT--BRAZIL.
----Como enfrentar as multinacionais. - 1983.
(001092)

INDUSTRIAL MANAGEMENT--EASTERN EUROPE.
----Red multinationals or red herring : the
activities of enterprises from socialist
countries in the West. - 1986.
(000371)

INDUSTRIAL MANAGEMENT--JAPAN.
----Developing new leadership in a
multinational environment. - 1985.
(000444)
----The economic analysis of the Japanese
firm. - 1984.
(000322)

INDUSTRIAL MANAGEMENT--MIDDLE EAST.
----International business in the Middle
East. - 1986.
(001135)

INDUSTRIAL MANAGEMENT--UNITED STATES.
----The competitive challenge. - 1987.
(000513)

INDUSTRIAL MARKETING.
----Natural gas clauses in petroleum
arrangements. - 1987.
(002452)

INDUSTRIAL MARKETING (continued)
----Strategic behaviour and industrial
    competition. - 1986.
      (000512)
----Strategic international marketing. -
    1985.
      (000467)

INDUSTRIAL MARKETING--GERMAN DEMOCRATIC
REPUBLIC.
----Die Anwendung der Mikrorechentechnik :
    wichtige Voraussetzung für eine
    reaktionsfähige und effektive
    Absatzwirtschaft. - 1987.
      (000908)

INDUSTRIAL ORGANIZATION.
----Collapse and survival. - 1983.
      (000459)
----Market competition, conflict and
    collusion. - 1983.
      (000492)
----Profitability of mergers in food
    manufacturing. - 1986.
      (001584)
----Strategic behaviour and industrial
    competition. - 1986.
      (000512)
----Toward a theory of industrial
    restructuring and dynamic comparative
    advantage. - 1985.
      (000054)
----Trade and dynamic efficiency. - 1987.
      (001698)
----The 1984 Justice Department guidelines
    toward horizontal mergers. - 1986.
      (001551)

INDUSTRIAL ORGANIZATION--CANADA.
----Industrial organization paradigms,
    empirical evidence, and the economic
    case for competition policy. - 1987.
      (001670)

INDUSTRIAL ORGANIZATION--EASTERN EUROPE.
----101 checklists for success in East
    European markets. - 1984.
      (001779)

INDUSTRIAL ORGANIZATION--GERMANY, FEDERAL
REPUBLIC OF.
----Industry structure and performance. -
    1985.
      (000442)

INDUSTRIAL ORGANIZATION--JAPAN.
----The economic analysis of the Japanese
    firm. - 1984.
      (000322)

INDUSTRIAL ORGANIZATION--NORDIC COUNTRIES.
----Industrial structure and country risks
    in a Nordic perspective. - 1984.
      (001838)

INDUSTRIAL ORGANIZATION--UNITED KINGDOM.
----Privatisation and regulation : the UK
    experience. - 1986.
      (001627)

INDUSTRIAL ORGANIZATION--UNITED STATES.
----The effect of conglomerate mergers on
    changes in industry concentration. -
    1986.
      (001527)
----Global competition. - 1985-   .
      (001696)
----On vertical mergers. - 1986.
      (001641)

INDUSTRIAL PLANNING.
----The capital goods sector in developing
    countries. - 1985.
      (001651)
----Entry strategies for international
    markets. - 1987.
      (000509)
----Joint ventures and global strategies. -
    1984.
      (001586)
----Multinational firms' global strategies,
    host country indigenisation of ownership
    and welfare. - 1983.
      (000486)
----Strategic investments and the
    development of multinationals. - 1987.
      (000044)
----Strategic management in multinational
    companies. - 1986.
      (000472)
----Strategic management of multinational
    corporations. - 1985.
      (000519)
----Strategies for structuring joint
    ventures: a negotiations planning
    paradigm. - 1984.
      (001560)
----Strategies for joint venture success. -
    1983.
      (001600)

INDUSTRIAL PLANNING--CHINA.
----Strategies for joint ventures in the
    People's Republic of China. - 1987.
      (001610)

INDUSTRIAL PLANNING--GUYANA.
----Commercialization of technology and
    dependence in the Caribbean. - 1985.
      (001477)

INDUSTRIAL PLANNING--JAMAICA.
----Commercialization of technology and
    dependence in the Caribbean. - 1985.
      (001477)

INDUSTRIAL PLANNING--MEXICO.
----Alliance for production. - 1984.
      (002316)

INDUSTRIAL PLANNING--TRINIDAD AND TOBAGO.
----Commercialization of technology and
    dependence in the Caribbean. - 1985.
      (001477)

INDUSTRIAL PLANNING--UNITED KINGDOM.
----Multinational enterprises and industrial
    restructuring in the UK. - 1985.
      (001148)

INDUSTRIAL PLANNING--UNITED STATES.
----The competitive challenge. - 1987.
      (000513)

INDUSTRIAL PLANNING--UNITED STATES
(continued)
----International business planning. - 1983.
   (002279)

INDUSTRIAL PLANNING--USSR.
----Vers une réforme de la planification des
   services en URSS? - 1985.
   (000845)

INDUSTRIAL POLICY.
----Appropriate pharmaceutical policies in
   developing countries. - 1985.
   (000707)
----The capital goods sector in developing
   countries. - 1985.
   (001651)
----Collapse and survival. - 1983.
   (000459)
----GATT surveillance of industrial
   policies. - 1986.
   (001350)
----Global shift. - 1987.
   (001315)
----Governments and multinationals. - 1983.
   (001804)
----Industrial policies. - 1984.
   (001233)
----Industrial structure and policy in less
   developed countries. - 1984.
   (001322)
----International dimensions of business
   policy and strategy. - 1986.
   (000477)
----Managing the service economy. - 1985.
   (000899)
----Multinational enterprises [and]
   government intervention. - 1985.
   (001844)
----Protectionism and structural adjustment.
   - 1986.
   (001689)
----Technical co-operation programme,
   1976-1987 : United Nations Centre on
   Transnational Corporations. - 1988.
   (002611)
----Textile and clothing industries. - 1983.
   (000740)

INDUSTRIAL POLICY--ARGENTINA.
----La estructura de los mercados y la
   desindustrialización en la Argentina
   1976-1981. - 1983.
   (001321)

INDUSTRIAL POLICY--BRAZIL.
----Política industrial, joint ventures e
   exportaçoes. - 1986.
   (001658)

INDUSTRIAL POLICY--BURUNDI.
----Guide des investisseurs. - 1983-   .
   (001805)

INDUSTRIAL POLICY--CANADA.
----Transnational corporations and the
   state. - 1985.
   (001860)

INDUSTRIAL POLICY--CENTRAL AMERICA.
----Industrialización y exportaciones no
   tradicionales. - 1984.
   (001316)

INDUSTRIAL POLICY--COLOMBIA.
----Las empresas transnacionales en el
   desarrollo colombiano. - 1986.
   (001121)

INDUSTRIAL POLICY--EASTERN EUROPE.
----L'informatique dans les pays du CAEM :
   quelques aspects des politiques suivies.
   - 1986.
   (000711)

INDUSTRIAL POLICY--EUROPE.
----Governments and microelectronics. - 1983.
   (000648)

INDUSTRIAL POLICY--FRANCE.
----Competing for prosperity. - 1986.
   (001338)
----Nationalisations et développement
   régional. - 1983.
   (001550)

INDUSTRIAL POLICY--INDONESIA.
----The politics of oil in Indonesia. - 1986.
   (001818)

INDUSTRIAL POLICY--JAPAN.
----High-tech trade. - 1986.
   (000696)
----The nature and tools of Japan's
   industrial policy. - 1986.
   (000557)

INDUSTRIAL POLICY--LATIN AMERICA.
----Government control over public
   enterprises in Latin America. - 1983.
   (002179)

INDUSTRIAL POLICY--MEXICO.
----L'électronique dans la politique
   industrielle mexicaine. - 1986.
   (000697)

INDUSTRIAL POLICY--PERU.
----Política económica y empresas
   transnacionales en el Perú, 1968-1975. -
   1983.
   (001107)

INDUSTRIAL POLICY--PHILIPPINES.
----Transnational corporations and the
   state. - 1985.
   (001860)

INDUSTRIAL POLICY--REPUBLIC OF KOREA.
----Transnational corporations and the
   state. - 1985.
   (001860)

INDUSTRIAL POLICY--SIBERIA (USSR).
----Investment and reindustrialization in
   the Soviet economy. - 1984.
   (001333)

INDUSTRIAL POLICY--SINGAPORE.
----Export processing and industrialisation.
   - 1982.
   (002405)

INDUSTRIAL POLICY--UNITED KINGDOM.
----Transnational corporations and the
    state. - 1985.
      (001860)

INDUSTRIAL POLICY--UNITED STATES.
----A competitive assessment of the U.S. oil
    field equipment industry. - 1985.
      (000764)
----Global competition. - 1985-   .
      (001696)
----High-tech trade. - 1986.
      (000696)

INDUSTRIAL POLICY--USSR.
----Investment and reindustrialization in
    the Soviet economy. - 1984.
      (001333)

INDUSTRIAL POLICY--WESTERN EUROPE.
----European industrial policy for the
    electronics and information technology
    sector. - 1984.
      (000849)

INDUSTRIAL POLLUTION--ASIA.
----Asia's struggle to affirm wholeness of
    life : report of a consultation on TNC's
    in Asia. - 1985.
      (001935)

INDUSTRIAL PRODUCTION.
----Divisions over the international
    division of labour. - 1984.
      (001269)
----Global shift. - 1987.
      (001315)
----Transnational corporations in the
    man-made fibre, textile and clothing
    industries. - 1987.
      (000751)

INDUSTRIAL PRODUCTION--ARGENTINA.
----Las empresas transnacionales en la
    Argentina. - 1986.
      (001122)

INDUSTRIAL PRODUCTION--INDONESIA.
----Multinational corporations and host
    country technology. - 1984.
      (001493)

INDUSTRIAL PROMOTION--INDONESIA.
----The Indonesian business. - 1986.
      (001839)

INDUSTRIAL PROMOTION--ITALY.
----L'impresa pubblica italiana e la
    dimensione internazionale. - 1983.
      (001145)

INDUSTRIAL PROMOTION--SOUTHEAST ASIA.
----Computer vendors re-shape product
    strategy for Asian market. - 1986.
      (000689)

INDUSTRIAL PROMOTION--UNITED STATES.
----Inside Washington. - 1988.
      (002703)

INDUSTRIAL PROPERTY.
----Multinationales et propriété
    industrielle. - 1986.
      (001409)

----Multinationals and industrial property.
    - 1988.
      (001410)

INDUSTRIAL REDEPLOYMENT.
----Microelectronics-based automation
    technologies and development. - 1985.
      (000753)
----Transnational corporations in world
    development. - 1983.
      (000102)

INDUSTRIAL RELATIONS.
----Mergers. - 1983.
      (001580)

INDUSTRIAL RELATIONS--MIDDLE EAST.
----Major causes of joint-venture failures
    in the Middle East: the case of Iran. -
    1983.
      (001640)

INDUSTRIAL RESEARCH.
----Innovation and market structure. - 1987.
      (000681)

INDUSTRIAL RESEARCH--AUSTRALIA.
----The public interest IR & D program. -
    1985.
      (001485)

INDUSTRIAL RESEARCH--CANADA.
----Multinationals and technology transfer.
    - 1983.
      (001636)

INDUSTRIAL RESEARCH--EGYPT.
----Operations of multinational corporations
    and local enterprises in Arab countries.
    - 1985.
      (001141)

INDUSTRIAL RESEARCH--INDIA.
----Trade in investment-related
    technological studies. - 1986.
      (001386)

INDUSTRIAL RESEARCH--KUWAIT.
----Operations of multinational corporations
    and local enterprises in Arab countries.
    - 1985.
      (001141)

INDUSTRIAL RESEARCH--UNITED STATES.
----High technology industries. - 1983-   .
      (000695)
----Multinationals and technology transfer.
    - 1983.
      (001636)

INDUSTRIAL ROBOTS.
----Microelectronics-based automation
    technologies and development. - 1985.
      (000753)
----The third industrial revolution. - 1987.
      (000966)
----Le tout-ordinateur. - 1986.
      (000743)

INDUSTRIAL ROBOTS--EUROPE.
----Robots in manufacturing. - 1983.
      (000656)

INDUSTRIAL ROBOTS--JAPAN.
----Robots in manufacturing. - 1983.
    (000656)

INDUSTRIAL ROBOTS--UNITED STATES.
----A competitive assessment of the U.S.
    manufacturing automation equipment
    industries. - 1984.
    (000756)
----Competitive position of U.S. producers
    of robotics in domestic and world
    markets. - 1983.
    (000674)
----Robots in manufacturing. - 1983.
    (000656)

INDUSTRIAL SECTOR.
----The capital goods sector in developing
    countries. - 1985.
    (001651)
----The primary, secondary, tertiary and
    quaternary sectors of the economy. -
    1987.
    (000883)

INDUSTRIAL SECTOR--BELGIUM.
----La structure professionnelle des
    secteurs secondaire et tertiaire. - 1987.
    (000823)

INDUSTRIAL SECTOR--GERMANY, FEDERAL REPUBLIC
OF.
----Industry structure and performance. -
    1985.
    (000442)

INDUSTRIAL SECTOR--MOROCCO.
----Expérience marocaine dans
    l'établissement d'entreprises
    multinationales. - 1986.
    (001027)

INDUSTRIAL SECTOR--UNITED STATES.
----Diversification : the European versus
    the US experience. - 1987.
    (000491)
----Manufacturing matters : the myth of the
    post-industrial economy. - 1987.
    (000669)

INDUSTRIAL SECTOR--WESTERN EUROPE.
----Diversification : the European versus
    the US experience. - 1987.
    (000491)

INDUSTRIAL STATISTICS.
----The capital goods sector in developing
    countries. - 1985.
    (001651)
----Industry in the 1980s. - 1985.
    (001341)
----Où va l'investissement direct
    international? USA/monde : le cas du
    secteur alimentaire. - 1984.
    (000666)
----Transnational corporations in the
    man-made fibre, textile and clothing
    industries. - 1987.
    (000751)

INDUSTRIAL STATISTICS--ARGENTINA.
----Las empresas transnacionales en la
    Argentina. - 1986.
    (001122)

INDUSTRIAL STATISTICS--INDIA.
----Technology transfer under alternative
    arrangements with transnational
    corporations. - 1987.
    (001513)

INDUSTRIAL STATISTICS--INDONESIA.
----Technology transfer under alternative
    arrangements with transnational
    corporations. - 1987.
    (001513)

INDUSTRIAL STATISTICS--MALAYSIA.
----Technology transfer under alternative
    arrangements with transnational
    corporations. - 1987.
    (001513)

INDUSTRIAL STATISTICS--MOROCCO.
----Expérience marocaine dans
    l'établissement d'entreprises
    multinationales. - 1986.
    (001027)

INDUSTRIAL STATISTICS--REPUBLIC OF KOREA.
----Technology transfer under alternative
    arrangements with transnational
    corporations. - 1987.
    (001513)

INDUSTRIAL STATISTICS--SOUTHEAST ASIA.
----Transnational corporations and the
    electronics industries of ASEAN
    economies. - 1987.
    (000754)

INDUSTRIAL STATISTICS--THAILAND.
----Technology transfer under alternative
    arrangements with transnational
    corporations. - 1987.
    (001513)

INDUSTRIAL SUBCONTRACTING.
----Bedolgozók és bedolgoztatók. - 1986.
    (000710)
----Technology, marketing and
    industrialisation. - 1983.
    (001506)
----Vertical corporate linkages. - 1986.
    (000709)

INDUSTRIAL SUBCONTRACTING--MEXICO.
----Las maquiladoras en México. - 1984.
    (001906)
----1985 directory of in-bond plants
    (maquiladoras) in Mexico. - 1984.
    (001132) (002678)

INDUSTRIAL SURVEYS.
----Industry in the 1980s. - 1985.
    (001341)
----Report on international industrial
    competitiveness, 1984. - 1984.
    (001690)

INDUSTRIAL TECHNOLOGY.
----A decision theoretic model of
    innovation, technology transfer, and
    trade. - 1987.
    (001446)
----Exports of technology from the South. -
    1985.
    (001469)

INDUSTRIAL TECHNOLOGY (continued)
----Industry in the 1980s. - 1985.
   (001341)
----Multinationals, governments and
   international technology transfer. -
   198?.
   (001472)
----Wettlauf um die Zukunft :
   Technologiepolitik im internationalen
   Vergleich. - 1987.
   (001453)

INDUSTRIAL TECHNOLOGY--ARGENTINA.
----Exportaciones de tecnología de Brasil y
   Argentina. - 1986.
   (001491)

INDUSTRIAL TECHNOLOGY--BRAZIL.
----Exportaciones de tecnología de Brasil y
   Argentina. - 1986.
   (001491)

INDUSTRIAL TECHNOLOGY--INDIA.
----Licensing industrial technology to
   developing countries : the operations of
   Swedish firms in India. - 1986.
   (002442)

INDUSTRIAL TECHNOLOGY--JAPAN.
----A high technology gap? - 1987.
   (001439)

INDUSTRIAL TECHNOLOGY--SWEDEN.
----Licensing industrial technology to
   developing countries : the operations of
   Swedish firms in India. - 1986.
   (002442)

INDUSTRIAL TECHNOLOGY--UNITED STATES.
----The funding of high technology ventures.
   - 1983.
   (000412)
----A high technology gap? - 1987.
   (001439)
----High technology industries. - 1983-   .
   (000695)

INDUSTRIAL TECHNOLOGY--WESTERN EUROPE.
----A high technology gap? - 1987.
   (001439)

INDUSTRIAL WORKERS--FRANCE.
----L'impact de l'investissement étranger en
   France sur l'emploi industriel
   (1974-1983). (With English summary.). -
   1984.
   (001161)

INDUSTRIALIZATION.
----The capital goods sector in developing
   countries. - 1985.
   (001651)
----Concentración global y
   transnacionalización. - 1985.
   (000100)
----Does de-industrialisation beget
   industrialisation which begets
   re-industrialisation? Review article. -
   1985.
   (001320)

----Export-processing zones and
   industrialization: some considerations
   from the economics of large
   organizations. - 1983.
   (002364)
----Exports of technology by newly
   industrializing countries: an overview.
   - 1984.
   (001454)
----Industrial change in advanced economies.
   - 1987.
   (001317)
----Industrial free zones and
   industrialization in developing
   countries. - 1986.
   (002403)
----Industrialisation et commerce du Tiers
   monde. - 1986.
   (001318)
----The industrialisation of less developed
   countries. - 1983.
   (001003)
----Multinationals, technology, and
   industrialization. - 1986.
   (001466)
----Pollution and the struggle for the world
   product. - 1988.
   (001948)

INDUSTRIALIZATION--AFRICA SOUTH OF SAHARA.
----Industrialization and the ACPs. - 1984.
   (002608)

INDUSTRIALIZATION--ARGENTINA.
----Exports of technology by newly
   industrializing countries: Argentina. -
   1984.
   (001494)

INDUSTRIALIZATION--BRAZIL.
----Exports of technology by newly
   industrializing countries: Brazil. -
   1984.
   (001492)

INDUSTRIALIZATION--CENTRAL AMERICA.
----Industrialización y exportaciones no
   tradicionales. - 1984.
   (001316)

INDUSTRIALIZATION--COLOMBIA.
----The subsidiary role of direct foreign
   investment in industrialization: the
   Colombian manufacturing sector. - 1985.
   (001106)

INDUSTRIALIZATION--HONG KONG.
----Exports of technology by newly
   industrializing countries: Hong Kong. -
   1984.
   (001414)

INDUSTRIALIZATION--INDIA.
----Exports of technology by newly
   industrializing countries: India. - 1984.
   (001455)

INDUSTRIALIZATION--INDONESIA.
----Foreign investment and industrialization
   in Indonesia. - 1988.
   (001053)

INDUSTRIALIZATION--IRELAND.
----The problem of late industrialisation
     and the experience of the Republic of
     Ireland. - 1985.
       (001330)

INDUSTRIALIZATION--JAPAN.
----Technology transfer and
     industrialization in the developing
     countries. - 1984.
       (001430)

INDUSTRIALIZATION--MEXICO.
----Exports of technology by newly
     industrializing countries: Mexico. -
     1984.
       (001423)
----Industrialización, capital extranjero y
     transferencia de tecnología. - 1986.
       (001524)

INDUSTRIALIZATION--QATAR.
----Petro-industrialization in Qatar. - 1985.
       (000600)

INDUSTRIALIZATION--REPUBLIC OF KOREA.
----Exports of technology by newly
     industrializing countries: Republic of
     Korea. - 1984.
       (001521)
----Foreign investment as an aid in moving
     from least developed to newly
     industrializing: a study in Korea. -
     1986.
       (000186)

INDUSTRIALIZATION--SOUTHEAST ASIA.
----Foreign direct investment and
     industrialization in ASEAN countries. -
     1987.
       (000144)

INDUSTRIALIZATION--TAIWAN (CHINA).
----Exports of technology by newly
     industrializing countries: Taiwan. -
     1984.
       (001402)

INDUSTRIALIZATION--USSR.
----Gold, foreign capital and the
     industrialization of Russia. - 1985.
       (001184)

INDUSTRY.
----Dictionnaire des industries. - 1986.
       (002705)
----Environmental aspects of the activities
     of transnational corporations. - 1985.
       (001954)
----Financial directories of the world. -
     1982-   .
       (002685)
----Global shift. - 1987.
       (001315)
----Industrial structure and policy in less
     developed countries. - 1984.
       (001322)
----Issues in business and society. - 1985.
       (001878)
----Mezhdunarodnyi chastnyi biznes i
     gosudarstvo. - 1985.
       (001832)
----Postimperialism. - 1987.
       (001232)

----Report on international industrial
     competitiveness, 1984. - 1984.
       (001690)
----The role of vertical integration in the
     shipping industry. - 1985.
       (000790)
----Technological change. - 1985.
       (001499)
----Technology and employment in industry. -
     1985.
       (001503)
----Transnational retailing. - 1988.
       (000780)
----Transnatsional'nye korporatsii v sisteme
     gosudarstvenno-monopolisticheskogo
     regulirovaniia ekonomiki. - 1985.
       (002679)
----Vergleichende System- und
     Industriestudien. - 1983.
       (001342)
----Women in industry. - 1985.
       (001930)
----Worldscope : industrial company
     profiles. - 1987.
       (000299)

INDUSTRY--AFRICA.
----Investment in ACP states. - 1987.
       (001004)
----Owen's Worldtrade Africa business
     directory. - 1986-   .
       (002657)

INDUSTRY--ARGENTINA.
----La estructura de los mercados y la
     desindustrialización en la Argentina
     1976-1981. - 1983.
       (001321)
----The new Argentina. - 1984.
       (001777)

INDUSTRY--ASIA.
----Major companies of the Far East. -
     1983-   .
       (002651)

INDUSTRY--AUSTRALIA.
----Australia deregulated : new freedoms for
     multinational investment. - 1987.
       (001797)
----Kompass Australia. - 1970-   .
       (002649)

INDUSTRY--CANADA.
----Canadian standard industrial
     classification for companies and
   • enterprises, 1980. - 1986-   .
       (002718)

INDUSTRY--CARIBBEAN REGION.
----Investment in ACP states. - 1987.
       (001004)

INDUSTRY--CHINA.
----Business opportunities in China. - 1984.
       (000999)
----The China directory of industry and
     commerce and economic annual. - 1984.
       (002626)

INDUSTRY--COLOMBIA.
----Evolución contradictoria de la industria
     en Colombia. - 1984.
       (001095)

INDUSTRY--ECUADOR.
----La evolución del capitalismo ecuatoriano
    en el último decenio y perspectivas. -
    1984.
      (001105)

INDUSTRY--EL SALVADOR.
----Directorió comercial e industrial de El
    Salvador. - 1986- .
      (002627)

INDUSTRY--EQUATORIAL GUINEA.
----Directorio nacional de empresas y
    establecimientos. - 1985-   .
      (002629)

INDUSTRY--EUROPE.
----The quality of shipping services. - 1986.
      (000789)

INDUSTRY--FRANCE.
----Propriété et pouvoir dans l'industrie. -
    1987.
      (001628)

INDUSTRY--GERMANY, FEDERAL REPUBLIC OF.
----Entry by diversified firms into German
    industries. - 1986.
      (001162)

INDUSTRY--HUNGARY.
----Hungarian Chamber of Commerce handbook.
    - 1984-   .
      (001811)

INDUSTRY--JAPAN.
----A competitive assessment of the U.S.
    fiber optics industry. - 1984.
      (000800)
----Les investissements japonais en Asie du
    sud-est: compléments ou concurrents de
    l'industrie au Japon. (With English
    summary.). - 1985.
      (000146)
----The Sogo Shosha: can it be exported
    (imported)? - 1983.
      (000338)

INDUSTRY--KEDAH (MALAYSIA).
----Transnational corporations in Kedah,
    West Malaysia. - 1985.
      (001061)

INDUSTRY--MALAWI.
----Malawi buyers' guide. - 1983-   .
      (002653)

INDUSTRY--MALAYSIA.
----Transnational corporations in Kedah,
    West Malaysia. - 1985.
      (001061)

INDUSTRY--NETHERLANDS.
----Verdiende lonen van werknemers in
    nijverheid en dienstensector ontleend
    aan het halfjaarlijks loononderzoek. -
    1985.
      (001928)

INDUSTRY--NORWAY.
----Kompass. - 1970-   .
      (002647)

INDUSTRY--PACIFIC OCEAN REGION.
----Investment in ACP states. - 1987.
      (001004)

INDUSTRY--REPUBLIC OF KOREA.
----The Sogo Shosha: can it be exported
    (imported)? - 1983.
      (000338)

INDUSTRY--SIBERIA (USSR).
----Investment and reindustrialization in
    the Soviet economy. - 1984.
      (001333)

INDUSTRY--SOUTHEAST ASIA.
----Les investissements japonais en Asie du
    sud-est: compléments ou concurrents de
    l'industrie au Japon. (With English
    summary.). - 1985.
      (000146)

INDUSTRY--SWEDEN.
----Sveriges största företag. - 1968-   .
      (002667)
----Sysselsattningsstrukturen i
    internationella foretag. - 1983.
      (001165)

INDUSTRY--UNITED KINGDOM.
----Kompass. - 196?-   .
      (002648)
----Microelectronics in British industry. -
    1984.
      (000723)
----The Times 1000. - 1966-   .
      (002668)

INDUSTRY--UNITED STATES.
----Les années quatre-vingts : quelles
    perspectives pour l'industrie américaine
    et les investissements internationaux? -
    1983.
      (000106)
----A competitive assessment of the U.S.
    ball and roller bearings industry. -
    1985.
      (000760)
----A competitive assessment of the U.S.
    construction machinery industry. - 1985.
      (000761)
----A competitive assessment of the U.S.
    fiber optics industry. - 1984.
      (000800)
----A competitive assessment of the U.S.
    herbicide industry. - 1985.
      (000670)
----A competitive assessment of the U.S.
    water resources equipment industry. -
    1985.
      (000776)
----A competitive assessment of the United
    States equipment leasing industry. -
    1985.
      (000982)
----Million dollar directory. - 1959-   .
      (002655)

INDUSTRY--USSR.
----Investment and reindustrialization in
    the Soviet economy. - 1984.
      (001333)
----The Soviet industrial enterprise. - 1984.
      (000330)

INDUSTRY--WESTERN EUROPE.
----A competitive assessment of the U.S.
    fiber optics industry. - 1984.
    (000800)

INDUSTRY--YUGOSLAVIA.
----Privredni adresar SFRJ. - 1965-   .
    (002660)

INFANT FEEDING.
----The implementation process of the
    International Code of Marketing of
    Breastmilk Substitutes. - 1984.
    (001970) (001971)

INFLATION.
----Inflation accounting. - 1975.
    (002156)
----The inflationary effect on the structure
    of trade. - 1986.
    (001672)
----Is employment policy a thing of the
    past? - 1983.
    (001889)
----The services industries: employment,
    productivity, and inflation. - 1985.
    (000940)

INFORMATION--CHINA.
----The People's Republic of China. - 1986.
    (001841)

INFORMATION--REPUBLIC OF KOREA.
----An information sector perspective of
    employment expansion in the Republic of
    Korea, 1975-80. - 1987.
    (000848)

INFORMATION DISSEMINATION.
----UNCITRAL, the United Nations Commission
    on International Trade Law. - 1986.
    (002155)

INFORMATION EXCHANGE.
----Exchange of information under the OECD
    and US model tax treaties. - 1983.
    (002042)
----International co-operation in tax
    matters : guidelines for international
    co-operation against the evasion and
    avoidance of taxes (with special
    reference to taxes on income, profits,
    capital and capital gains). - 1984.
    (001724)
----Measures to strengthen the capabilities
    of developing countries in their dealing
    with transnational corporations. - 1985.
    (002612)
----Safety and health practices of
    multinational enterprises. - 1984.
    (001918)
----Second revised draft Guidelines for the
    Exchange of Information on Potentially
    Harmful Chemicals in International
    Trade. - 1986.
    (002019)

INFORMATION MANAGEMENT.
----Strategic planning for information
    resource management. - 1983.
    (000443)

INFORMATION NEEDS.
----Needs of developing countries for
    information on transnational
    corporations. - 1987.
    (002721)

INFORMATION NETWORKS.
----Transborder data flows. - 1983.
    (000973)

INFORMATION POLICY.
----L'informatique dans les pays en
    développement. - 1984.
    (000839)

INFORMATION POLICY--BRAZIL.
----Brazilian informatics policy. - 1985.
    (000880)

INFORMATION POLICY--POLAND.
----Transborder data flows and Poland :
    Polish case study. - 1984.
    (000920)

INFORMATION POLICY--WESTERN EUROPE.
----Information technology and economic
    recovery in Western Europe. - 1986.
    (000874)

INFORMATION SERVICES.
----Electronic information services. - 1986.
    (000837)
----International transactions in services.
    - 1986.
    (000946)
----Meeting the challenges of the world
    information economy. - 1984.
    (000853)
----Technical co-operation programme of the
    United Nations Centre on Transnational
    Corporations. - 1988.
    (002610)
----Technical co-operation programme,
    1976-1987 : United Nations Centre on
    Transnational Corporations. - 1988.
    (002611)
----Transborder data flows. - 1983.
    (000973)

INFORMATION SOURCES.
----Business information sources. - 1985.
    (002701)
----How to find information about companies.
    - 1983.
    (002714)
----Third World resource directory. - 1984.
    (002719)
----UNCTC bibliography, 1974-1987. - 1988.
    (002695)

INFORMATION SOURCES--CARIBBEAN REGION.
----Caribbean Basin business information
    starter kit. - 1984.
    (001782)

INFORMATION SOURCES--EUROPE.
----Sources of joint venture information and
    assistance in the United States and
    Europe. - 1983.
    (001617)

INFORMATION SOURCES--SAUDI ARABIA.
----A guide to establishing joint ventures
    in Saudi Arabia. - 1985.
        (001807)

INFORMATION SOURCES--UNITED STATES.
----Caribbean Basin business information
    starter kit. - 1984.
        (001782)
----Inside Washington. - 1988.
        (002703)
----Sources of joint venture information and
    assistance in the United States and
    Europe. - 1983.
        (001617)

INFORMATION SYSTEMS.
----International accounting and reporting
    issues : 1984 review. - 1985.
        (002115)
----International communications and
    information systems. - 1985.
        (000787)
----Measures to strengthen the capabilities
    of developing countries in their dealing
    with transnational corporations. - 1985.
        (002612)
----Technical co-operation programme of the
    United Nations Centre on Transnational
    Corporations. - 1988.
        (002610)
----UNCTC bibliography, 1974-1987. - 1988.
        (002695)

INFORMATION SYSTEMS--USSR.
----Computergebruik in de Sovjetunie. - 1987.
        (000677)

INFORMATION TECHNOLOGY.
----Electronic information services. - 1986.
        (000837)
----Information technology and
    competitiveness in the service industry.
    - 1987.
        (000891)
----Information technology in the Third
    World. - 1983.
        (000676)
----L'informatique du Nord au Sud. - 1986.
        (000678)
----Recent developments in operations and
    behaviour of transnational corporations.
    - 1987.
        (000103)
----Shifts in the world economy and the
    restructuring of economic sectors. -
    1987.
        (000734)
----The third industrial revolution. - 1987.
        (000966)
----Towards a theory of innovation in
    services. - 1986.
        (000808)
----Trade in services : growth and balance
    of payments implications for countries
    of Western Asia. - 1987.
        (000968)

INFORMATION TECHNOLOGY--BRAZIL.
----Brazilian informatics policy. - 1985.
        (000880)
----La industria nacional de informática. -
    1987.
        (000818)

INFORMATION TECHNOLOGY--INDIA.
----New information technology in India. -
    1986.
        (000651)

INFORMATION TECHNOLOGY--LATIN AMERICA.
----Trade and foreign direct investment in
    data services. - 1986.
        (000948)

INFORMATION TECHNOLOGY--PACIFIC OCEAN REGION.
----Information technology and the
    developing Pacific. - 1986.
        (000703)

INFORMATION TECHNOLOGY--POLAND.
----Transborder data flows and Poland :
    Polish case study. - 1984.
        (000920)

INFORMATION TECHNOLOGY--UNITED STATES.
----A competitive assessment of the United
    States data processing services
    industry. - 1984.
        (000981)
----A competitive assessment of the United
    States disk storage industry. - 1985.
        (000672)

INFORMATION TECHNOLOGY--WESTERN EUROPE.
----European industrial policy for the
    electronics and information technology
    sector. - 1984.
        (000849)
----Information technology and economic
    recovery in Western Europe. - 1986.
        (000874)
----New technology and the new services :
    towards an innovation strategy for
    Europe. - 1986.
        (000807)
----Société d'information et Europe des
    services : quelles infrastructures? -
    1987.
        (000893)

INFORMATION TRANSFER.
----Enjeux technologiques et relations
    internationales. - 1986.
        (001429)
----Trade in data services. - 1986.
        (000949)

INFORMATION TRANSFER--UNITED STATES.
----New challenges to the U.S. multinational
    corporation in the European Economic
    Community. - 1985.
        (002192)

INFORMATION TRANSFER--WESTERN EUROPE.
----New challenges to the U.S. multinational
    corporation in the European Economic
    Community. - 1985.
        (002192)

INJUNCTIONS.
----How international arbitration can always
    prevail over litigation. - 1987.
        (002497)

INNOVATIONS.
----The political economy of innovation. -
    1984.
        (001450)
----I rischi di una crescita incontrollata
    dell'innovazione finanziaria nel mondo.
    - 1986.
        (000835)
----The third industrial revolution. - 1987.
        (000966)

INPUT OUTPUT ANALYSIS.
----The primary, secondary, tertiary and
    quaternary sectors of the economy. -
    1987.
        (000883)

INPUT OUTPUT ANALYSIS--IRELAND.
----Input-output linkages and foreign direct
    investment in Ireland. - 1984.
        (001158)

INSTITUTION BUILDING.
----Measures to strengthen the capabilities
    of developing countries in their dealing
    with transnational corporations. - 1985.
        (002612)

INSURANCE.
----Analysis of engineering and technical
    assistance consultancy contracts. - 1986.
        (002449)
----Analysis of equipment leasing contracts.
    - 1984.
        (002407)
----Grundzuge der internationalen
    Unternehmenspolitik des
    Versicherungsunternehmens. - 1983.
        (000930)
----The insurance industry in economic
    development. - 1986.
        (000987)
----Market competition, conflict and
    collusion. - 1987.
        (001680)
----Multilateral investment insurance and
    private investment in the Third World. -
    1987.
        (002132)
----Multinational corporations. - 1986.
        (000058)
----Problèmes d'assurance en matière de
    contrats internationaux. - 1984.
        (002412)
----Services and the development process. -
    1985.
        (000979)

INSURANCE COMPANIES--AFRICA.
----The role of transnational banks and
    financial institutions in Africa's
    development process. - 1986.
        (000935)

INSURANCE COMPANIES--CHINA.
----Insuring investment projects. - 1988.
        (002033)

INSURANCE COMPANIES--LIBERIA.
----The impact of the transnational
    corporations in the banking and other
    financial institutions on the economy of
    Liberia. - 1986.
        (000873)

INSURANCE COMPANIES--TURKEY.
----Turkish banking and finance : the
    markets mature. - 1986.
        (000970)

INSURANCE LAW--AFRICA.
----The role of transnational banks and
    financial institutions in Africa's
    development process. - 1986.
        (000935)

INSURANCE LAW--CHINA.
----Insuring investment projects. - 1988.
        (002033)

INTELLECTUAL PROPERTY.
----Intellectual property rights,
    investment, and trade in services in the
    Uruguay round. - 1987.
        (000817)
----International flows of technology. -
    1986.
        (001517)
----Licensing of technology and intellectual
    property rights to developing countries.
    - 1983.
        (001403)

INTELSAT.
----Implications of deregulating satellite
    communications. - 1985.
        (002242)
----International policy issues in satellite
    communications. - 1985.
        (000791)

INTER-AMERICAN CONVENTION ON INTERNATIONAL
COMMERCIAL ARBITRATION (1975).
----International commercial arbitration. -
    1983.
        (002538)

INTER-AMERICAN DEVELOPMENT BANK.
----Current problems of economic
    integration. - 1986.
        (001312)
----On Third World debt. - 1984.
        (000211)

INTERDEPENDENCE.
----The antinomies of interdependence. -
    1983.
        (001229)
----Economic interdependence between rich
    and poor nations. - 1983.
        (001268)
----The effects of markets on public
    enterprise conduct ; and vice versa. -
    1983.
        (001675)
----Industry in the 1980s. - 1985.
        (001341)
----The organisation of international
    economic interdependence. - 1984.
        (000027)

INTERDEPENDENCE--GULF STATES.
----A historical perspective of U.S.-GCC
    economic and financial interdependence.
    - 1987.
        (000143)

INTERDEPENDENCE--UNITED STATES.
----A historical perspective of U.S.-GCC
    economic and financial interdependence.
    - 1987.
    (000143)

INTEREST RATES.
----International debt quagmire. - 1983.
    (000262)

INTERGOVERNMENTAL INFORMATICS PROGRAMME.
----The third industrial revolution. - 1987.
    (000966)

INTERGOVERNMENTAL ORGANIZATIONS.
----L'Agence multilatérale de garantie des
    investissements. - 1987.
    (002152)
----International accounting and reporting
    issues, 1985 review. - 1985.
    (002116)
----Measures regarding the activities of
    transnational corporations in South
    Africa and Namibia. - 1985.
    (001220)
----Mezhdunarodnaia kapitalisticheskaia
    torgovlia uslugami i problemy ee
    regulirovaniia. - 1987.
    (001378)
----La pratique du CIRDI. - 1987.
    (002550)

INTERNATIONAL ACCOUNTING STANDARDS COMMITTEE.
----International accounting standards. -
    1986.
    (002087)

INTERNATIONAL AND MUNICIPAL LAW--TURKEY.
----La nouvelle loi turque sur le droit
    international privé et la procédure
    internationale et le principe de la
    reciprocité dans l'arbitrage. - 1983.
    (002533)

INTERNATIONAL ARBITRATION.
----Arbitral adjudication. - 1984.
    (002484)
----ICSID arbitration. - 1984.
    (002495)
----ICSID implementation. - 1985.
    (002574)
----The ICSID Klöckner v. Cameroon award. -
    1984.
    (002553)
----Journal of international arbitration. -
    1984-   .
    (002528)
----Problèmes de base de l'arbitrage. -
    1987-   .
    (002531)

INTERNATIONAL ARBITRATION--HONG KONG.
----Arbitration in Hong Kong. - 1986.
    (002529)

INTERNATIONAL BANKING.
----American banks in the international
    interbank market. - 1983.
    (000829)
----Annual report (Bank for International
    Settlements). - 1930-   .
    (001228)

----Bank lending to developing countries. -
    1985.
    (000212)
----Banking on crisis. - 1983.
    (000868)
----Les banques multinationales. - 1983.
    (000938)
----Changes in the international financial
    market and implications for
    transnational banks, transnational
    corporations and developing countries. -
    1986.
    (000976)
----The changing role of international bank
    lending in development finance. - 1985.
    (000232)
----Commercial banks and the restructuring
    of cross-border debt. - 1983.
    (000250)
----Employment in multinational banking. -
    1987.
    (001916)
----Evaluación de los criterios ortodoxos de
    reprogramación de la deuda externa. -
    1984.
    (000225)
----Eximbank's role in international banking
    and finance. - 1986.
    (000816)
----Finanz- und bankwirtschaftliche Probleme
    bei internationaler
    Unternehmenstatigkeit. - 1985.
    (001277)
----A GATT for international banking? - 1985.
    (002130)
----Global debt. - 1986.
    (000236)
----The growth of international bank
    lending, 1972-1982: concepts,
    measurement and causes. - 1983.
    (000222)
----The growth of transnational banking. -
    1983.
    (000991)
----Hong Kong and Singapore. - 1985.
    (000879)
----The importance of international monetary
    markets and the international crisis of
    indebtedness. - 1987.
    (000244)
----International bank lending. - 1983.
    (000265)
----International bank lending. - 1984.
    (000988)
----International banks and financial
    markets in developing countries. - 1984.
    (000859)
----The international debt crisis. - 1985.
    (000240)
----The international debt crisis and the
    banks. - 1985.
    (000227)
----International debt quagmire. - 1983.
    (000262)
----International finance. - 1983.
    (000266)
----International lending and debt. - 1983.
    (000208)
----International lending in a fragile world
    economy. - 1983.
    (000241)
----International trade in services. - 1984.
    (000876)

INTERNATIONAL BANKING (continued)
----Issues in negotiating international loan
    agreements with transnational banks. -
    1983.
      (002459)
----Japanese offshore banking. - 1984.
      (000933)
----Multinational institutions and the Third
    World. - 1985.
      (001253)
----Multinationale Bankenverflechtungen. -
    1983.
      (001549)
----Opportunities and constraints in
    international lending. - 1983.
      (000267)
----A practitioner's guide to international
    banking and trade finance. - 1986.
      (000922)
----Recent developments in international
    banking and finance. - 1987-   .
      (000928)
----The regulation and supervision of
    international lending, (2). - 1986.
      (000234)
----Rehearing granted : Allied Bank
    International v. Banco Agricola Credito
    de Cartago and the current international
    debt crisis. - 1984.
      (000233)
----Restricción del crédito de la banca
    comercial en situaciones de crisis de la
    deuda internacional. - 1983.
      (000226)
----The restructuring of international loans
    and the international debt crisis. -
    1984.
      (000239)
----I rischi di una crescita incontrollata
    dell'innovazione finanziaria nel mondo.
    - 1986.
      (000835)
----Le risque-pays, son traitement dans les
    banques. - 1983.
      (001783)
----Size, growth, and transnationality among
    the world's largest banks. - 1983.
      (000969)
----Syndicating and rescheduling
    international financial transactions. -
    1984.
      (000261)
----Tax havens and offshore finance. - 1983.
      (001729)
----Transnational banking and the
    international monetary crisis. - 1983.
      (001303)
----Transnational banks and the external
    finance of Latin America : the
    experience of Peru. - 1983.
      (000840)
----Transnational banks and the external
    finance of Latin America : the
    experience of Peru. - 1985.
      (000975)
----Ways out of the debt crisis. - 1984.
      (000245)
----Les zones franches dans le monde. - 1987.
      (002378)

INTERNATIONAL BANKING--ARAB COUNTRIES.
----The development of Arab international
    banking. - 1983.
      (000803)

----The problems of developing-country debt
    and a strategy for Arab banking
    institutions. - 1983.
      (000256)

INTERNATIONAL BANKING--GREECE.
----Foreign banks in Greece. - 1985.
      (000919)

INTERNATIONAL BANKING--JAPAN.
----Internationalization of Japanese
    commercial banking-the recent experience
    of city banks. - 1984.
      (000855)

INTERNATIONAL BANKING--REPUBLIC OF KOREA.
----About the establishment of an offshore
    financial center in Seoul. - 1986.
      (000827)

INTERNATIONAL BANKING--UNITED STATES.
----Foreign bank offices in the U.S. since
    the International Banking Act of 1978. -
    1986.
      (000872)
----Foreign ownership of U.S. banks: trends
    and effects. - 1983.
      (001591)
----A longer view of debt. - 1983.
      (000251)
----A practitioner's guide to international
    banking and trade finance. - 1986.
      (000922)

INTERNATIONAL BANKING--VENEZUELA.
----La internacionalización financiera en
    Venezuela. - 1983.
      (001286)

INTERNATIONAL BANKING ACT 1978 (UNITED
STATES).
----Foreign bank offices in the U.S. since
    the International Banking Act of 1978. -
    1986.
      (000872)

INTERNATIONAL CENTRE FOR SETTLEMENT OF
INVESTMENT DISPUTES.
----Arbitration clauses in international
    loans. - 1987.
      (002569)
----Arbitration with governments. - 1983.
      (002493)
----Case studies in the jurisdiction of the
    International Centre for Settlement of
    Investment Disputes. - 1986.
      (002580)
----Le CIRDI et l'immunité des états. - 1983.
      (002494)
----Enforcement of arbitral awards issued by
    the Additional Facility of the
    International Centre of Settlement of
    Investment Disputes (ICSID). - 1985.
      (002536)
----ICSID : an international method for
    handling foreign investment disputes in
    LDCs. - 1987.
      (002474)
----ICSID arbitration. - 1984.
      (002495)
----ICSID implementation. - 1985.
      (002574)

INTERNATIONAL CENTRE FOR SETTLEMENT OF
INVESTMENT DISPUTES (continued)
----The ICSID Klöckner v. Cameroon award. -
     1984.
     (002553)
----ICSID's emerging jurisprudence. - 1986.
     (002562)
----Improving the investment climate in
     developing countries. - 1984.
     (002572)
----The International Centre for the
     Settlement of Investment Disputes. -
     1983.
     (002542)
----International investment disputes. -
     1985.
     (002524)
----International protection of direct
     foreign investments in the Third World.
     - 1987.
     (002124)
----International trade disputes and the
     individual : private party involvement
     in national and international procedures
     regarding unfair foreign trade
     practices. - 1986.
     (002514)
----Note sur l'extension du "système CIRDI".
     - 1984.
     (002561)
----La pratique du CIRDI. - 1987.
     (002550)
----Probleme der Zuständigkeit des
     International Centre for Settlement of
     Investment Disputes (ICSID). - 1986.
     (002544)
----Promotion of direct investment in
     developing countries. - 1986.
     (002143)
----Quelques observations sur la rédaction
     des clauses d'arbitrage CIRDI. - 1987.
     (002509)
----The role of ICSID and the projected
     Multilateral Investment Guarantee Agency
     (MIGA). - 1986.
     (002585)
----Selecting an arbitral forum. - 1984.
     (002478)

INTERNATIONAL CHAMBER OF COMMERCE.
----Drafting the international arbitration
     clause. - 1986.
     (002581)
----Les institutions permanentes d'arbitrage
     devant le juge étatique (à propos d'une
     jurisprudence récente). - 1987.
     (002505)
----International arbitration of multi-party
     contract disputes. - 1983.
     (002508)
----Selecting an arbitral forum. - 1984.
     (002478)
----The status of the UNCITRAL Model Law on
     International Commercial Arbitration
     vis-à-vis the ICC, LCIA and UNCITRAL
     arbitration rules. - 1986.
     (002583)

INTERNATIONAL CHAMBER OF COMMERCE. COURT OF
ARBITRATION.
----L'arbitrage commercial dans les
     relations Est-Ouest. - 1984.
     (002526)

INTERNATIONAL CODE OF CONDUCT ON THE
TRANSFER OF TECHNOLOGY (DRAFT).
----Licence agreements in developing
     countries. - 1987.
     (002437)

INTERNATIONAL CODE OF MARKETING OF
BREASTMILK SUBSTITUTES (1981).
----The implementation process of the
     International Code of Marketing of
     Breastmilk Substitutes. - 1984.
     (001970) (001971)

INTERNATIONAL COMMERCIAL ARBITRATION.
----L'accès des tribunaux arbitraux à
     l'entraide judiciaire internationale. -
     1984.
     (002483)
----Alternatives to litigation. - 1983.
     (002567)
----L'arbitrage commercial dans les
     relations Est-Ouest. - 1984.
     (002526)
----L'Arbitrage transnational et les
     tribunaux nationaux. - 1984.
     (002492)
----Arbitraje-conciliación. - 1985.
     (002472)
----Arbitration and the courts. - 1985.
     (002532)
----Arbitration clauses in international
     loans. - 1987.
     (002569)
----Arbitration of private antitrust claims
     in international trade. - 1986.
     (002471)
----Arbitration with governments. - 1983.
     (002493)
----The arbitrator's power to award punitive
     damages in international contract
     actions. - 1986.
     (002534)
----The availability of provisional relief
     in international commercial arbitration.
     - 1984.
     (002543)
----Bilateral investment treaties. - 1988.
     (002054)
----The choice of applicable law in
     international arbitration. - 1986.
     (002491)
----Choosing the substantive law to apply in
     international commercial arbitration. -
     1986.
     (002477)
----Le CIRDI et l'immunité des états. - 1983.
     (002494)
----A code of ethics for arbitrators in
     international commercial arbitration? -
     1985.
     (002519)
----La conciliation, nouvelle méthode de
     règlement des différends. - 1985.
     (002512)
----The conduct of the arbitration. - 1985.
     (002584)
----Contractual adaptation and conflict
     resolution based on venture contracts
     for mining projects in developing
     countries. - 1985.
     (002475)

INTERNATIONAL COMMERCIAL ARBITRATION
(continued)
----Cuba's system of international
    commercial arbitration. - 1984.
    (002490)
----Delocalisation of international
    commercial arbitration. - 1983.
    (002552)
----Les développements nouveaux concernant
    la reconnaissance et l'exécution des
    sentences arbitrales étrangères en
    Yougoslavie. - 1983.
    (002582)
----Dispute resolution in the Asia/Pacific
    region. - 1987.
    (002556)
----Dispute resolution in the People's
    Republic of China. - 1984.
    (002558)
----Drafting the international arbitration
    clause. - 1986.
    (002581)
----Droit international et contrats d'états.
    - 1983.
    (002482)
----Enforcement of arbitral awards issued by
    the Additional Facility of the
    International Centre of Settlement of
    Investment Disputes (ICSID). - 1985.
    (002536)
----Etude historique et comparée de
    l'arbitrage. - 1984.
    (002485)
----The future of international commercial
    arbitration. - 1987.
    (002573)
----How international arbitration can always
    prevail over litigation. - 1987.
    (002497)
----ICSID's emerging jurisprudence. - 1986.
    (002562)
----Les institutions permanentes d'arbitrage
    devant le juge étatique (à propos d'une
    jurisprudence récente). - 1987.
    (002505)
----International ad hoc arbitration. - 1987.
    (002473)
----International arbitration of multi-party
    contract disputes. - 1983.
    (002508)
----International commercial arbitration. -
    1974-   .
    (002523)
----International commercial arbitration : a
    comparative analysis of the United
    States system and the UNCITRAL model
    law. - 1986.
    (002487)
----International commercial arbitration. -
    1985.
    (002516)
----International commercial arbitration. -
    1984.
    (002498)
----International commercial arbitration. -
    1983.
    (002520)
----International commercial arbitration. -
    1983.
    (002511)
----International commercial arbitration in
    Latin America. - 1986.
    (002546)
----International commercial arbitrations. -
    1984.
    (002521)
----International construction contracts. -
    1983.
    (002445)
----International dispute resolution and the
    People's Republic of China. - 1984.
    (002522)
----International trade disputes and the
    individual : private party involvement
    in national and international procedures
    regarding unfair foreign trade
    practices. - 1986.
    (002514)
----Introductory note on the UNCITRAL Model
    Law on International Commercial
    Arbitration. - 1985.
    (002513)
----Journal of international arbitration. -
    1984-   .
    (002528)
----The jurisdiction of an international
    commercial arbitrator. - 1986.
    (002563)
----Klauzule abritrazowe w kontraktach
    handlu zagranicznego sektora
    nieuspolecznionego. - 1984.
    (002579)
----The lex loci arbitri and international
    commercial arbitration. - 1983.
    (002551)
----Lex mercatoria et arbitrage
    international. - 1983.
    (002575)
----La loi-type de la C.N.U.D.C.I. sur
    l'arbitrage commercial international. -
    1986.
    (002527)
----Measure of damages in international
    commercial arbitration. - 1987.
    (002560)
----Mitsubishi and the arbitrability of
    antitrust claims. - 1986.
    (002486)
----Mitsubishi v. Soler and its impact on
    international commercial arbitration. -
    1985.
    (002507)
----A model law on international commercial
    arbitration? - 1984.
    (002479)
----The nature and extent of an arbitrator's
    powers in international commercial
    arbitration. - 1987.
    (002559)
----New approaches to the resolution of
    international commercial disputes. -
    1983.
    (002555)
----Note sur l'extension du "système CIRDI".
    - 1984.
    (002561)
----La nouvelle loi turque sur le droit
    international privé et la procédure
    internationale et le principe de la
    reciprocité dans l'arbitrage. - 1983.
    (002533)
----L'ordre public et le droit applicable au
    fond du litige dans l'arbitrage
    international. - 1986.
    (002496)

INTERNATIONAL COMMERCIAL ARBITRATION
(continued)
----Particularités et problèmes de
l'arbitrage dans les droits des pays
arabes. - 1986.
(002530)
----Problèmes de base de l'arbitrage. -
1987-   .
(002531)
----Quelques observations sur la rédaction
des clauses d'arbitrage CIRDI. - 1987.
(002509)
----Recent developments in international
commercial arbitration. - 1987.
(002549)
----La reconnaissance et l'exécution des
sentences arbitrales étrangères. - 1985.
(002564)
----Sanctions to control party misbehavior
in international arbitration. - 1986.
(002537)
----Selecting an arbitral forum. - 1984.
(002478)
----The Soviet position on international
arbitration. - 1986.
(002571)
----The status of the UNCITRAL Model Law on
International Commercial Arbitration
vis-à-vis the ICC, LCIA and UNCITRAL
arbitration rules. - 1986.
(002583)
----Symposium : a guide to international
civil practice. - 1984.
(002576)
----Le Tiers monde dans l'arbitrage
commercial international. - 1983.
(002554)
----The two-way mirror : international
arbitration as comparative procedure. -
1985.
(002540)
----Uloga arbitraze u stvaranju medunarodnog
privrednog prava. - 1986.
(002501)
----UNCITRAL and international commercial
dispute settlement/ Carl August
Fleischhauer. - 1983.
(002502)
----UNCITRAL Model Law on International
Commercial Arbitration. - 1986.
(002503)
----The UNCITRAL model law on international
commercial arbitration. - 1986.
(002541)
----UNCITRAL, the United Nations Commission
on International Trade Law. - 1986.
(002155)

INTERNATIONAL COMMERCIAL
ARBITRATION--AMERICAS.
----Les conventions interaméricaines sur
l'arbitrage commercial et la Commission
interaméricaine d'arbitrage commercial.
- 1983.
(002535)

INTERNATIONAL COMMERCIAL ARBITRATION--LATIN
AMERICA.
----International commercial arbitration. -
1983.
(002538)

INTERNATIONAL COMMERCIAL ARBITRATION--SWEDEN.
----Das anzuwendende Recht beim
internationalen Schiedsverfahren in
Schweden. - 1986.
(002515)

INTERNATIONAL COMMERCIAL ARBITRATION--UNITED
STATES.
----International antitrust law. - 1985.
(002539)
----International commercial arbitration. -
1983.
(002538)
----Jurisdiction over foreign sovereigns. -
1983.
(002480)

INTERNATIONAL COMMERCIAL
ARBITRATION--WESTERN EUROPE.
----Commercial arbitration and the European
Economic Community. - 1985.
(002481)

INTERNATIONAL COMMERCIAL TRANSACTIONS.
----Adaptation and renegotiation of
contracts in international trade and
finance. - 1985.
(002406)
----Arrangements between joint venture
partners in developing countries. - 1987.
(002450)
----Cross-border leasing. - 1983.
(000836) (001705)
----Extortion and bribery in business
transactions. - 1977.
(001979)
----Foreign business practices. - 1985.
(001433)
----International technology transactions
and the theory of the firm. - 1984. .
(001424)
----Mitsubishi and the arbitrability of
antitrust claims. - 1986.
(002486)
----Negotiating issues in international
services transactions. - 1983.
(000841)
----The role of transborder data flows in
the international services debate. -
1987.
(000947)
----Trade in services : growth and balance
of payments implications for countries
of Western Asia. - 1987.
(000968)
----Transnational corporations and
technology transfer. - 1987.
(001509)

INTERNATIONAL COMMERCIAL TRANSACTIONS--CHINA.
----China laws for foreign business. -
1985-   .
(002187)

INTERNATIONAL COMMERCIAL TRANSACTIONS--LATIN
AMERICA.
----Estados Unidos, América Latina y el
debate internacional sobre el comercio
de servicios. - 1986.
(000934)

INTERNATIONAL COMMERCIAL TRANSACTIONS--LATIN
AMERICA (continued)
----La internacionalización de los
    servicios. - 1986.
    (000923)
----Los servicios en las transacciones
    internacionales de América Latina. -
    1986.
    (000820)

INTERNATIONAL COMMERCIAL
TRANSACTIONS--UNITED STATES.
----Estados Unidos, América Latina y el
    debate internacional sobre el comercio
    de servicios. - 1986.
    (000934)
----Foreign direct investment in the United
    States. - 1985.
    (000130)
----Fundamentals of international taxation.
    - 1985.
    (001700)

INTERNATIONAL COMPETITION.
----Automotive parts industry and the U.S.
    aftermarket for Japanese cars and light
    trucks. - 1985.
    (000759)
----Blind intersection? policy and the
    automobile industry. - 1987.
    (000660)
----Collapse and survival. - 1983.
    (000459)
----Competing for prosperity. - 1986.
    (001338)
----Competition in global industries. - 1986.
    (001688)
----Competition policy and joint ventures. -
    1986.
    (001684)
----A competitive assessment of selected
    reinforced composite fibers. - 1985.
    (000644)
----A competitive assessment of the U.S.
    ball and roller bearings industry. -
    1985.
    (000760)
----A competitive assessment of the U.S.
    construction machinery industry. - 1985.
    (000761)
----A competitive assessment of the U.S.
    electric power generating equipment
    industry. - 1985.
    (000762)
----A competitive assessment of the U.S.
    flexible manufacturing systems industry.
    - 1985.
    (000763)
----A competitive assessment of the U.S.
    herbicide industry. - 1985.
    (000670)
----A competitive assessment of the U.S.
    semiconductor manufacturing equipment
    industry. - 1985.
    (000758)
----A competitive assessment of the U.S.
    water resources equipment industry. -
    1985.
    (000776)
----A competitive assessment of the United
    States data processing services
    industry. - 1984.
    (000981)

----A competitive assessment of the United
    States equipment leasing industry. -
    1985.
    (000982)
----A competitive assessment of the United
    States software industry. - 1984.
    (000980)
----The competitive effects of partial
    equity interests and joint ventures. -
    1986.
    (001635)
----Foreign direct investment and the
    competitiveness of UK manufacturing
    industry, 1963-1979. - 1984.
    (000766)
----A global comeback. - 1987.
    (000275)
----Global competition. - 1985-   .
    (001696)
----Industrial renaissance : producing a
    competitive future for America. - 1983.
    (000300)
----Information technology and
    competitiveness in the service industry.
    - 1987.
    (000891)
----International trade in services :
    securities. - 1987.
    (000915)
----Joint ventures and global strategies. -
    1984.
    (001586)
----Multinational enterprises, economic
    structure and international
    competitiveness. - 1985.
    (000075)
----Nationalisations et
    internationalisation. - 1983.
    (000497)
----Pricing and sourcing strategies in a
    multinational oligopoly. - 1983.
    (000466)
----Report on international industrial
    competitiveness, 1984. - 1984.
    (001690)
----Strategic management of multinational
    corporations. - 1985.
    (000519)
----Swiss review of international
    competition law. - 197?-   .
    (002150)
----Technology and competition in the
    Brazilian computer industry. - 1983.
    (000741)
----Triad power. - 1985.
    (001686)
----Two hungry giants. - 1983.
    (000645)
----U.S. high technology trade and
    competitiveness. - 1985.
    (001362)
----The U.S. in the world economy. - 1988.
    (000128)
----Wielkie przedsiebiorstwa transnarodowe a
    ograniczanie konkurencji w wysoko
    rozwiniętych krajach kapitalistycznych.
    - 1983.
    (001153)

INTERNATIONAL COMPETITION--CANADA.
----Trade among multinationals. - 1987.
    (001678)

INTERNATIONAL COMPETITION--GERMANY, FEDERAL
REPUBLIC OF.
----Multinational enterprise and world
    competition. - 1987.
        (000018)

INTERNATIONAL COMPETITION--JAPAN.
----Multinational enterprise and world
    competition. - 1987.
        (000018)

INTERNATIONAL COMPETITION--SWEDEN.
----Multinational enterprise and world
    competition. - 1987.
        (000018)

INTERNATIONAL COMPETITION--SWITZERLAND.
----Global structural change and
    international competition among
    industrial firms: the case of
    Switzerland. - 1985.
        (000308)

INTERNATIONAL COMPETITION--UNITED KINGDOM.
----Multinational enterprise and world
    competition. - 1987.
        (000018)
----Multinationals and Britain. - 1986.
        (000205)

INTERNATIONAL COMPETITION--UNITED STATES.
----Alliance politics and economics. - 1987.
        (000719)
----The competitive challenge. - 1987.
        (000513)
----The competitive position of U.S.
    manufacturing firms. - 1985.
        (000353)
----International collaborative ventures in
    U.S. manufacturing. - 1988.
        (000720)
----Multinational enterprise and world
    competition. - 1987.
        (000018)

INTERNATIONAL CONFERENCE ON LIABILITY AND
COMPENSATION FOR DAMAGE IN CONNEXION WITH
THE CARRIAGE OF CERTAIN SUBSTANCES BY SEA
(1984 : LONDON).
----The definition of pollution damage in
    the 1984 Protocols to the 1969 Civil
    Liability Convention and the 1971 Fund
    Convention. - 1986.
        (001943)
----Liability and compensation for damage in
    connection with the carriage of
    hazardous and noxious substances by sea.
    - 1986.
        (001939)
----New trends in compensation for oil
    pollution damage. - 1985.
        (001944)

INTERNATIONAL CONVENTION ON CIVIL LIABILITY
FOR OIL POLLUTION DAMAGE (1969).
----Dommages causés par les marées noires. -
    1984.
        (001952)
----Oil spill liability and compensation. -
    1985.
        (001940)

INTERNATIONAL CONVENTION ON CIVIL LIABILITY
FOR OIL POLLUTION DAMAGE (1969). PROTOCOLS,
ETC., 1984 MAY 24.
----The definition of pollution damage in
    the 1984 Protocols to the 1969 Civil
    Liability Convention and the 1971 Fund
    Convention. - 1986.
        (001943)
----Oil spill liability and compensation. -
    1985.
        (001940)

INTERNATIONAL CONVENTION ON THE
ESTABLISHMENT OF AN INTERNATIONAL FUND FOR
COMPENSATION FOR OIL POLLUTION DAMAGE (1971).
----Dommages causés par les marées noires. -
    1984.
        (001952)
----Oil spill liability and compensation. -
    1985.
        (001940)

INTERNATIONAL CONVENTION ON THE
ESTABLISHMENT OF AN INTERNATIONAL FUND FOR
COMPENSATION FOR OIL POLLUTION DAMAGE
(1971). PROTOCOLS, ETC., 1984 MAY 25.
----The definition of pollution damage in
    the 1984 Protocols to the 1969 Civil
    Liability Convention and the 1971 Fund
    Convention. - 1986.
        (001943)

INTERNATIONAL CO-OPERATION.
----Anthropology and international business.
    - 1986.
        (001892)
----Cooperate to compete globally. - 1986.
        (001624)
----Cooperation in investments: a factor in
    the intensification of production in
    CMEA member nations. - 1983.
        (001187)
----Dispersion of risk through multinational
    teamwork. - 1987.
        (001558)
----La durée des accords de coopération et
    les clauses gouvernant leur adaptation.
    - 1984.
        (002425)
----Environmental aspects of the activities
    of transnational corporations. - 1985.
        (001954)
----Foreign investment and the restructuring
    of technology. - 1987.
        (000702)
----Guidelines for Consumer Protection. -
    1986.
        (002017)
----Human resource management in
    multinational cooperative ventures. -
    1986.
        (000426)
----Improving environmental cooperation. -
    1984.
        (001955)
----L'informatique dans les pays en
    développement. - 1984.
        (000839)

Subject Index - Index des matières

INTERNATIONAL CO-OPERATION (continued)
----International co-operation in tax
matters : guidelines for international
co-operation against the evasion and
avoidance of taxes (with special
reference to taxes on income, profits,
capital and capital gains). - 1984.
(001724)
----Leasing in an international context. -
1983.
(000929)
----Mergers. - 1983.
(001580)
----Services and the development process. -
1985.
(000979)

INTERNATIONAL CO-OPERATION--HUNGARY.
----The impact of cooperation with Western
firms on the Hungarian clothing
industry. - 1983.
(001189)

INTERNATIONAL CO-OPERATION--MIDDLE EAST.
----Internationale Produktionskooperation im
Vorderen Orient. - 1983.
(001142)

INTERNATIONAL CO-OPERATION--UNITED STATES.
----Alliance politics and economics. - 1987.
(000719)

INTERNATIONAL CO-OPERATION--WESTERN EUROPE.
----International aspects of nuclear
instalations licensing. - 1987.
(002434)

INTERNATIONAL COURTS.
----L'arbitrage commercial dans les
relations Est-Ouest. - 1984.
(002526)
----Les institutions permanentes d'arbitrage
devant le juge étatique (à propos d'une
jurisprudence récente). - 1987.
(002505)

INTERNATIONAL DEVELOPMENT ASSOCIATION.
----Current problems of economic
integration. - 1986.
(001312)
----A longer view of debt. - 1983.
(000251)

INTERNATIONAL DEVELOPMENT STRATEGY FOR THE
THIRD UNITED NATIONS DEVELOPMENT DECADE
(1980).
----A strategy for the technological
transformation of developing countries.
- 1985.
(001515)

INTERNATIONAL DIVISION OF LABOUR.
----The antinomies of interdependence. -
1983.
(001229)
----Collapse and survival. - 1983.
(000459)
----La dette du Tiers monde. - 1984.
(000223)
----Divisions over the international
division of labour. - 1984.
(001269)

----The eclectic paradigm of international
production. - 1985.
(000023)
----Foreign investment and the restructuring
of technology. - 1987.
(000702)
----The global factory. - 1985.
(001254)
----L'internazionalizzazione dell'industria.
- 1984.
(000080)
----Is there a service economy? The changing
capitalist division of labor. - 1985.
(000986)
----Labour, production and the state :
decentralization of the French
automobile industry. - 1987.
(000724)
----Mezinárodní delba práce a socialistická
ekonomická integrace. - 1987.
(001667)
----Mirovoe kapitalisticheskoe khoziaistvo i
razvivaiushchiesia strany Vostoka. -
1986.
(001279)
----Multinational business and labour. -
1985.
(001896)
----Multinationals and world trade. - 1986.
(001238)
----North-South issues in trade in services.
- 1985.
(000944)
----Semiconductors, Scotland and the
international division of labour. - 1987.
(000694)
----Stärken und Schwächen der Bundesrepublik
Deutschland in der internationalen
Arbeitsteilung. - 1984.
(001260)
----Techno-economic aspects of the
international division of labour in the
automotive industry. - 1983.
(000752)
----A theory of the international division
of labour. - 1984.
(001239)
----Transnational corporations in world
development. - 1983.
(000102)
----Trends in international taxation. - 1985.
(001746)

INTERNATIONAL DIVISION OF LABOUR--LATIN
AMERICA.
----Nueva división internacional del trabajo
y reestructuración productiva en América
Latina. - 1984.
(001264)

INTERNATIONAL ECONOMIC LAW.
----La contribution des nationalisations
françaises de 1982 au droit
international des nationalisations. -
1985.
(002319)
----Current issues in international trade. -
1985.
(001359)
----Die Multilaterale
Investitions-Garantie-Agentur (MIGA). -
1986.
(002142)

INTERNATIONAL ECONOMIC LAW (continued)
----Nationalization of foreign property. -
1983.
(002324)
----Protection et promotion des
investissements. - 1985.
(002137)
----Uloga arbitraze u stvaranju medunarodnog
privrednog prava. - 1986.
(002501)

INTERNATIONAL ECONOMIC RELATIONS.
----Les années quatre-vingts : quelles
perspectives pour l'industrie américaine
et les investissements internationaux? -
1983.
(000106)
----The antinomies of interdependence. -
1983.
(001229)
----Antitrust and direct regulation of
international transfer of technology
transactions. - 1984.
(001411)
----Le capitalisme mondial. - 1985.
(000065)
----A closed circle for the developing
countries? : debt and financial flows. -
1986.
(000218)
----Collapse and survival. - 1983.
(000459)
----Collection of laws and regulations of
the People's Republic of China
concerning foreign economic affairs. -
1985- .
(002188)
----Current issues in international trade. -
1985.
(001359)
----A decision theoretic model of
innovation, technology transfer, and
trade. - 1987.
(001446)
----The economic environment of
international business. - 1986.
(001305)
----Economic interdependence between rich
and poor nations. - 1983.
(001268)
----Emerging standards of international
trade and investment. - 1983.
(001973)
----Environment of international business. -
1985.
(000055)
----The extraterritorial application of
national laws. - 1987.
(002348)
----Foreign policy objectives and the
extraterritorial application of law. -
1983.
(002346)
----Géopolitique des ressources minières. -
1983.
(000593)
----Global debt. - 1986.
(000236)
----Industrial policies. - 1984.
(001233)
----International business. - 1986.
(000469)
----International business. - 1985.
(000002)

----International business. - 1987.
(000453)
----International business and technological
innovation. - 1983.
(001486)
----International regulation of
transnational corporations. - 1986.
(001956)
----International trade and investment. -
1984.
(001384)
----Internationale Wirtschafts- und
Finanzpolitik in der Herausforderung der
achtziger Jahre [Added Entry Conference
Name]?Internationale
Management-Gesprache; (14th. - 1984.
(000419)
----L'internazionalizzazione dell'industria.
- 1984.
(000080)
----Introduction to business. - 1987.
(000066)
----Manager in the international economy. -
1986.
(000451)
----Mirovoe kapitalisticheskoe khoziaistvo i
razvivaiushchiesia strany Vostoka. -
1986.
(001279)
----Multinational corporations and the
political economy of power. - 1983.
(001846)
----Multinational institutions and the Third
World. - 1985.
(001253)
----Multinationals and the restructuring of
the world economy. - 1986.
(000076)
----Multinationals of the South. - 1986.
(000359)
----Nationalisations et
internationalisation. - 1983.
(000497)
----The new international economic order,
(2). - 1984.
(001271)
----The organisation of international
economic interdependence. - 1984.
(000027)
----The overseas expansion of capital. -
1985.
(000038)
----The politics of international economic
relations. - 1985.
(001300)
----Red multinationals or red herring : the
activities of enterprises from socialist
countries in the West. - 1986.
(000371)
----Rekindling development. - 1988.
(001302)
----Revitalizing development, growth and
international trade. - 1987.
(001394)
----Les sociétés multinationales. - 1985.
(000021)
----Staatsmonopolistische Regulierung in der
kapitalistischen Weltwirtschaft. - 1984.
(001263)
----Strategic management of multinational
corporations. - 1985.
(000519)

INTERNATIONAL ECONOMIC RELATIONS (continued)
----'Tikhaia' agressiia imperializma. - 1986.
   (001272)
----Trade [and] structural change. - 1984.
   (001391)
----Transnational corporations in world
   development. - 1988.
   (000101)
----Transnational oil. - 1986.
   (000618)

INTERNATIONAL ECONOMIC RELATIONS--AFRICA
SOUTH OF SAHARA.
----Uoll-strit protiv Afriki. - 1985.
   (001030)

INTERNATIONAL ECONOMIC RELATIONS--GERMANY,
FEDERAL REPUBLIC OF.
----Politik als Investitionsmotor? - 1985.
   (001131)

INTERNATIONAL ECONOMIC RELATIONS--LATIN
AMERICA.
----Politik als Investitionsmotor? - 1985.
   (001131)

INTERNATIONAL ECONOMIC RELATIONS--UNITED
STATES.
----The U.S. in the world economy. - 1988.
   (000128)
----Uoll-strit protiv Afriki. - 1985.
   (001030)

INTERNATIONAL FINANCE.
----Adaptation and renegotiation of
   contracts in international trade and
   finance. - 1985.
   (002406)
----Compendium of selected studies on
   international monetary and financial
   issues for the developing countries. -
   1987.
   (001243)
----Endettement international et
   multinationalisation. - 1984.
   (000248)
----Foreign direct investment in Latin
   America. - 1986.
   (000190)
----Gestion et stratégie financières
   internationales. - 1985.
   (000422)
----Handbook of international financial
   management. - 1984.
   (000446)
----International banks and financial
   markets in developing countries. - 1984.
   (000859)
----International business. - 1987.
   (000453)
----International business finance. - 1983.
   (000049)
----International corporate finance. - 1986.
   (000091)
----International finance. - 1983.
   (000425)
----International finance and investment. -
   1985.
   (001249)
----International financial intermediation.
   - 1987.
   (001236)

----International financial management. -
   1983.
   (001283)
----International financial management. -
   1985.
   (000424)
----International financial management. -
   1986.
   (000418)
----International financial management. -
   1984.
   (000438)
----International financial management: the
   overall investment and financing plan. -
   1983.
   (000401)
----International financial markets and
   capital movements. - 1985.
   (001267)
----International financial relations as
   part of the world-system. - 1987.
   (001285)
----International financial reporting. -
   1984.
   (002079)
----International financing of investments
   in tourism. - 1983.
   (000822)
----International lending in a fragile world
   economy. - 1983.
   (000241)
----International money flows and currency
   crises. - 1984.
   (001261)
----The international payments crisis and
   the development of East-West trade. -
   1977.
   (000242)
----International trade and investment. -
   1984.
   (001384)
----Investment and the international
   monetary and financial environment. -
   1983.
   (001274)
----Japan's largest financier of
   multinationalism: the EXIM Bank. - 1986.
   (000255)
----Kin'yu torihiki to kokusai sosho. - 1983.
   (002525)
----Legal trends in international lending
   and investment in the developing
   countries. - 1984.
   (000207)
----The literature of international business
   finance. - 1984.
   (002687)
----Managing international risk. - 1983.
   (000480)
----Multinational finance. - 1986.
   (001237)
----New forms of international investment in
   developing countries. - 1984.
   (001615)
----On Third World debt. - 1984.
   (000211)
----Praxis des internationalen
   Finanzmanagement. - 1985.
   (000435)
----Précis de gestion financière
   internationale. - 1986.
   (001255)

INTERNATIONAL FINANCE (continued)
----Principles of international accounting.
    - 1986.
      (002077)
----Recent developments in international
    banking and finance. - 1987-   .
      (000928)
----Recent trends in international direct
    investment. - 1987.
      (000176)
----The reconstruction of international
    monetary arrangements. - 1987.
      (001290)
----Research in international business and
    finance. - 1979-   .
      (000085)
----Staatsmonopolistische Regulierung in der
    kapitalistischen Weltwirtschaft. - 1984.
      (001263)
----Die Stabilisierungspolitik des
    Internationalen Währungsfonds. - 1986.
      (001234)
----The stability of the international
    monetary system. - 1987.
      (001294)
----Stratégies des entreprises et marché
    international des capitaux. - 1984.
      (001273)
----Syndicating and rescheduling
    international financial transactions. -
    1984.
      (000261)
----Uncertain future. - 1984.
      (000977)
----United States law of sovereign immunity
    relating to international financial
    transactions. - 1983.
      (002353)
----The use of international finance
    subsidiaries in the Netherlands
    Antilles. - 1983.
      (000871)

INTERNATIONAL FINANCE CORPORATION.
----Analysis of equipment leasing contracts.
    - 1984.
      (002407)
----Promotion of direct investment in
    developing countries. - 1986.
      (002143)

INTERNATIONAL FINANCIAL INSTITUTIONS.
----Les banques multinationales. - 1983.
      (000938)
----Current problems of economic
    integration. - 1986.
      (001312)
----The debt crisis and the world economy. -
    1984.
      (000220)
----International financial center
    preeminence in MNC and nation-state
    interaction. - 1983.
      (001291)
----The Multilateral Investment Guarantee
    Agency : status, mandate, concept,
    features, implications. - 1987.
      (002158)
----The Multilateral Investment Guarantee
    Agency. - 1986.
      (002146)
----Opportunities and constraints in
    international lending. - 1983.
      (000267)

----A practitioner's guide to international
    banking and trade finance. - 1986.
      (000922)
----The role of multilateral development
    finance institutions in promoting and
    financing joint ventures. - 1986.
      (000252)
----Trasferimento internazionale di risorse
    per lo sviluppo: il ruolo delle
    istituzioni multilaterali. - 1984.
      (001997)
----Zur Bedeutung der Multilateral
    Investment Guarantee Agency für den
    internationalen Ressourcentransfer. -
    1987.
      (002129)

INTERNATIONAL FINANCIAL INSTITUTIONS--UNITED
STATES.
----A longer view of debt. - 1983.
      (000251)

INTERNATIONAL HARVESTER.
----American enterprise in foreign markets.
    - 1984.
      (000526)
----International Harvester in Russia: the
    Washington-St. Petersburg connection? -
    1983.
      (000272)

INTERNATIONAL INSTITUTE FOR THE UNIFICATION
OF PRIVATE LAW.
----Analysis of equipment leasing contracts.
    - 1984.
      (002407)
----A contract law for Europe. - 1985.
      (001991)
----International equipment leasing. - 1984.
      (000905) (002139)

INTERNATIONAL INSTRUMENTS.
----The definition of pollution damage in
    the 1984 Protocols to the 1969 Civil
    Liability Convention and the 1971 Fund
    Convention. - 1986.
      (001943)
----Third World mineral development in
    crisis: the impact of the worldwide
    recession on legal instruments governing
    Third World mineral development. - 1985.
      (000649)
----Transnational corporations in world
    development. - 1988.
      (000101)
----UNCTC bibliography, 1974-1987. - 1988.
      (002695)

INTERNATIONAL INVESTMENT BANK.
----Mezhdunarodnata investitsionna banka i
    neinata rolia v razvitieto na
    sotsialisticheskata ikonomicheska
    integratsiia. - 1986.
      (002153)

INTERNATIONAL JURISDICTION.
----Application des règles de concurrence du
    Traité de Rome à l'autorité publique. -
    1987.
      (002021)

INTERNATIONAL JURISDICTION (continued)
----Choosing the substantive law to apply in
    international commercial arbitration. -
    1986.
    (002477)
----Extraterritorial application of the
    EEC-competition law. - 1984.
    (002349)
----Les négociations : moyen principal du
    règlement pacifique des différends
    internationaux. - 1984.
    (002510)

INTERNATIONAL LABOUR ACTIVITIES.
----El debate sindical nacional e
    internacional. - 1984.
    (002602)
----International labour affairs. - 1987.
    (002595)
----Labor confronts the transnationals. -
    1984.
    (002594)
----Multinational union organizations in the
    white-collar, service, and
    communications industries. - 1983.
    (002600)
----Les sociétés multinationales. - 1985.
    (000021)
----Transnational labor relations. - 1985.
    (001905)

INTERNATIONAL LABOUR LEGISLATION.
----La empresa transnacional en el marco
    laboral. - 1983.
    (001910)
----La regolamentazione internazionale dei
    rapporti di lavoro con imprese
    multinazionali. - 1986.
    (001919)
----Social clauses and international trade.
    - 1983.
    (001360)

INTERNATIONAL LABOUR STANDARDS.
----Social clauses and international trade.
    - 1983.
    (001360)

INTERNATIONAL LAW.
----L'arbitrage Elf Aquitaine Iran c/
    National Iranian Oil Company. - 1984.
    (002504)
----Compensation for expropriation. - 1984.
    (002334)
----Le développement de la protection
    conventionnelle des investissements
    étrangers. - 1986.
    (002048)
----Eigentum, Enteignung und Entschädigung
    im geltenden Völkerrecht. - 1985.
    (002321)
----The expropriation issue before the
    Iran-United States Claims Tribunal. -
    1984.
    (002320)
----Implications of international commercial
    agreements on the juridical regime of
    international commercial contracts. -
    1983.
    (002408)
----International law and investments. -
    1987.
    (001958)

----The international law of expropriation
    of foreign-owned property. - 1983.
    (002330)
----The international lawyer. - 1966-
    (001983)
----An international standard of partial
    compensation upon the expropriation of
    an alien's property. - 1987.
    (002317)
----Les investissements miniers
    internationaux dans les pays en
    développement. - 1986.
    (000609)
----Maryland journal of international law
    and trade. - 1984-
    (002138)
----Merger control in the EEC. - 1983.
    (001634)
----New trends in compensation for oil
    pollution damage. - 1985.
    (001944)
----Permanent sovereignty over natural
    resources in international law. - 1984.
    (002141)
----The question of a reference to
    international law in the United Nations
    Code of Conduct on Transnational
    Corporations. - 1986.
    (002007)
----The question of a reference to
    international obligations in the United
    Nations Code of Conduct on Transnational
    Corporations. - 1986.
    (002020)
----Regulation of transnational
    corporations. - 1984.
    (001998)
----Swiss review of international
    competition law. - 197?-
    (002150)
----The taking of foreign property under
    international law. - 1984.
    (002336)
----Unitary taxation and general
    international law. - 1987.
    (002044)
----United States jurisdiction over foreign
    subsidiaries. - 1983.
    (002355)

INTERNATIONAL LAW--SAUDI ARABIA.
----Service agents regulation and related
    laws affecting foreign companies in
    Saudi Arabia. - 1983.
    (002182)

INTERNATIONAL LIQUIDITY.
----International bank lending. - 1983.
    (000265)

INTERNATIONAL MONETARY SITUATION.
----Compendium of selected studies on
    international monetary and financial
    issues for the developing countries. -
    1987.
    (001243)
----Correcting the world monetary scandal. -
    1986.
    (001304)
----Currency exposure management. - 1983.
    (000409)

INTERNATIONAL MONETARY SITUATION (continued)
----Current financial and monetary problems
    of the developing countries in the world
    capitalist economy. - 1987.
    (001246)
----Defining and measuring currency
    exposure. - 1983.
    (000504)
----Empresas multinacionales, gestión de
    cambios y crisis monetarias=Multination
    businesses, change of money, management
    and monetary crisis. With English
    summary.). - 1983.
    (001292)
----The external deficit. - 1987.
    (000216)
----International money flows and currency
    crises. - 1984.
    (001261)
----The practice of currency exposure
    management. - 1983.
    (000460)
----Die Stabilisierungspolitik des
    Internationalen Währungsfonds. - 1986.
    (001234)
----The stability of the international
    monetary system. - 1987.
    (001294)
----Transnational banking and the
    international monetary crisis. - 1983.
    (001303)
----Uncertain future. - 1984.
    (000977)

INTERNATIONAL MONETARY SYSTEM.
----Les banques multinationales. - 1983.
    (000938)
----Compendium of selected studies on
    international monetary and financial
    issues for the developing countries. -
    1987.
    (001243)
----Correcting the world monetary scandal. -
    1986.
    (001304)
----Dette du Tiers-Monde. - 1987.
    (000224)
----Investment and the international
    monetary and financial environment. -
    1983.
    (001274)
----The politics of international economic
    relations. - 1985.
    (001300)
----The reconstruction of international
    monetary arrangements. - 1987.
    (001290)
----The stability of the international
    monetary system. - 1987.
    (001294)
----Third World debt crisis threatens a
    collapse of world trade and financial
    systems. - 1987.
    (000217)

INTERNATIONAL NICKEL CO.
----International movements and crises in
    resource oriented companies: the case of
    INCO in the nickel sector. - 1985.
    (000271)

INTERNATIONAL OBLIGATIONS.
----The question of a reference to
    international obligations in the United
    Nations Code of Conduct on Transnational
    Corporations. - 1986.
    (002020)

INTERNATIONAL OIL POLLUTION COMPENSATION
FUND.
----The definition of pollution damage in
    the 1984 Protocols to the 1969 Civil
    Liability Convention and the 1971 Fund
    Convention. - 1986.
    (001943)

INTERNATIONAL ORGANIZATIONS.
----Die Einwirkung internationaler
    Organisationen auf das Steuerrecht. -
    1984.
    (001990)
----ICSID : an international method for
    handling foreign investment disputes in
    LDCs. - 1987.
    (002474)
----The International Centre for the
    Settlement of Investment Disputes. -
    1983.
    (002542)
----Managing international public affairs. -
    1985.
    (000428)
----Multinational union organizations in the
    white-collar, service, and
    communications industries. - 1983.
    (002600)

INTERNATIONAL PAYMENTS.
----Aspectos jurídicos das transferências
    electrónicas internacionais de fundos. -
    1986.
    (000805)
----A practitioner's guide to international
    banking and trade finance. - 1986.
    (000922)

INTERNATIONAL RELATIONS.
----Enjeux technologiques et relations
    internationales. - 1986.
    (001429)
----International dynamics of technology. -
    1983.
    (001488)
----Multinational corporations and global
    welfare: an extension of Kojima and
    Ozawa. - 1985.
    (000036)
----Multinational corporations and the
    nations. - 1983.
    (000006)
----Technology and international relations.
    - 1987.
    (001504)

INTERNATIONAL SALE OF GOODS.
----Dispute resolution techniques in
    international contracts involving the
    sale of goods. - 1987.
    (002506)
----EEC law of competition. - 1985.
    (002151)
----The transnational law of international
    commercial transactions. - 1982.
    (002012)

INTERNATIONAL SALE OF GOODS (continued)
----UNCITRAL, the United Nations Commission
on International Trade Law. - 1986.
(002155)

INTERNATIONAL SALE OF GOODS--WESTERN EUROPE.
----Territorial and exclusive trademark
licensing under the EEC law of
competition. - 1984.
(001987)

INTERNATIONAL SUBCONTRACTING.
----New forms of international investment in
developing countries. - 1984.
(001619)

INTERNATIONAL TRADE.
----. - 1984.
(000810)
----All traded services are embodied in
materials or people. - 1987.
(000869)
----An appraisal of different theoretical
approaches and models of foreign direct
investment and international trade. -
1987.
(000060)
----Areas for further research on
intra-industry trade. - 1983.
(000099)
----Les associations d'entreprises (joint
ventures) dans le commerce
international. - 1986.
(001538)
----Business International index. -
1983-   .
(002684)
----The capital goods sector in developing
countries. - 1985.
(001651)
----Comercio internacional,
industrialización y nuevo orden
económico internacional. - 1983.
(001242)
----Competition and trade policies. - 1984.
(001664)
----Competition and world markets. - 1983.
(001665)
----Cooperation in the liberalization of
international trade. - 1987.
(001400)
----A decision theoretic model of
innovation, technology transfer, and
trade. - 1987.
(001446)
----EC trade effects and factor mobility. -
1983.
(001370)
----Economics of change in less developed
countries. - 1986.
(001000)
----Excess market value, the multinational
corporation, and Tobin's q-ratio. - 1986.
(000050)
----Export-enclave economies, international
corporations, and development. - 1985.
(002367)
----Extraterritoriality: current policy of
the United States. - 1986.
(002341)
----Foreign trade by commodities. -
1983-   .
(001357)

----The fourth multifibre arrangement and
the new legal regime for international
trade in textiles. - 1987.
(001401)
----GATT versus tax treaties? - 1987.
(002032)
----A global comeback. - 1987.
(000275)
----The growth of transnational banking. -
1983.
(000991)
----Historical statistics of foreign trade.
Ser. A. - 1982-   .
(001364)
----The implementation of international
antitrust principles. - 1983.
(002344)
----Industrialisation et commerce du Tiers
monde. - 1986.
(001318)
----Industry in the 1980s. - 1985.
(001341)
----Intellectual property rights,
investment, and trade in services in the
Uruguay round. - 1987.
(000817)
----Internacionalización de empresas y
tecnología de origen argentino. - 1985.
(000301)
----International business. - 1984.
(000069)
----International business. - 1987.
(000453)
----International business and cultures. -
1987.
(001872)
----International business and multinational
enterprises. - 1983.
(000087)
----International business and technological
innovation. - 1983.
(001486)
----International business in the nineteenth
century. - 1987.
(000046)
----International business reference
sources. - 1983.
(002691)
----International communications and
information systems. - 1985.
(000787)
----International orientation of exporters:
some North-South trade implications. -
1983.
(001374)
----International services-trade issues and
the GATT. - 1983.
(000830)
----International trade and foreign direct
investment in West German manufacturing
industries. - 1984.
(000771)
----International trade and investment. -
1984.
(001384)
----International trade in business
services. - 1988.
(000910)
----International trade in services :
securities. - 1987.
(000915)

INTERNATIONAL TRADE (continued)
----International trademark licensing
    agreements. - 1986.
        (002421)
----The international uranium market. - 1984.
        (000626)
----Intra-firm service trade by the
    multinational enterprise. - 1987.
        (000902)
----Intra-industry foreign direct
    investment. - 1984.
        (001375)
----Intra-industry production as a form of
    international economic involvement. -
    1983.
        (000026)
----Introduction to business. - 1987.
        (000066)
----Introduction to the OECD codes of
    liberalisation. - 1987.
        (001984)
----Legal problems in expanding the scope of
    GATT to include trade in services. -
    1983.
        (000864)
----Meeting the challenges of the world
    information economy. - 1984.
        (000853)
----The military origins of
    industrialisation and international
    trade rivalry. - 1984.
        (001335)
----Monthly statistics of foreign trade.
    Ser. A. - 1983-   .
        (001373)
----Multinational corporations in world
    trade. - 1983.
        (001390)
----A multinational firm. - 1986.
        (000031)
----Multinational firms, international
    trade, and international
    telecommunications. - 1984.
        (000786)
----Multinationals and marketplace magic in
    the 1980s. - 1983.
        (001682)
----Multinationals and world trade. - 1986.
        (001238)
----Les négociations internationales sur les
    services ou la quadrature du cercle. -
    1986.
        (000911)
----New theories of the multinational
    enterprise: an assessment of
    internalization theory. - 1986.
        (000089)
----New theories of international business:
    some unresolved issues. - 1983.
        (000010)
----The pharmaceutical industry. - 1985.
        (000726)
----Problèmes d'assurance en matière de
    contrats internationaux. - 1984.
        (002412)
----Product diversity, economies of scale,
    and international trade. - 1983.
        (000488)
----Production and trade in services. - 1985.
        (000978)
----Protectionism and structural adjustment.
    - 1986.
        (001689)

----Punta del Este and after. - 1987.
        (000927)
----Putting services on the table : the new
    GATT round. - 1987.
        (000932)
----Putting world trade back on a growth
    course. - 1984.
        (001358)
----Restrictive business practices in
    international trade. - 1987.
        (001661)
----Revitalizing development, growth and
    international trade. - 1987.
        (001394)
----Second revised draft Guidelines for the
    Exchange of Information on Potentially
    Harmful Chemicals in International
    Trade. - 1986.
        (002019)
----Les services : clé du développement
    économique? - 1986.
        (000892)
----Les services : enjeux pour l'emploi et
    le commerce international. - 1986.
        (000960)
----Services and the development process. -
    1985.
        (000979)
----Social clauses and international trade.
    - 1983.
        (001360)
----A szolgáltatások a nemzetközi gazdasági
    kapcsolatokban. - 1986.
        (000895)
----Technical advance and trade advantage. -
    1983.
        (001497)
----Third World debt crisis threatens a
    collapse of world trade and financial
    systems. - 1987.
        (000217)
----Threats and opportunities of global
    countertrade : marketing, financing and
    organizational implications. - 1984.
        (001353)
----Trade and dynamic efficiency. - 1987.
        (001698)
----Trade [and] structural change. - 1984.
        (001391)
----Trade in data services. - 1986.
        (000949)
----Trade in services : growth and balance
    of payments implications for countries
    of Western Asia. - 1987.
        (000968)
----Trade in services. - 1984.
        (000955)
----Trade in services and developing
    countries. - 1986.
        (000952)
----Trade liberalization and the global
    service economy. - 1985.
        (000811)
----Trade trouble-shooting. - 1986.
        (001967)
----Trade-related investment issues. - 1983.
        (001385)
----Transnational business problems. - 1986.
        (000516)
----Transnational corporations and
    international trade : selected issues. -
    1985.
        (001393)

INTERNATIONAL TRADE (continued)
----Transnational corporations in the
     agricultural machinery and equipment
     industry. - 1983.
        (000746)
----Transnational corporations in the
     international semiconductor industry. -
     1986.
        (000748)
----Transnational corporations in the
     man-made fibre, textile and clothing
     industries. - 1987.
        (000751)
----Transnational corporations in the
     pharmaceutical industry of developing
     countries. - 1984.
        (000749)
----The Uruguay Round and the international
     trading system. - 1987.
        (001976)
----The welfare impact of foreign investment
     in the presence of specific factors and
     non-traded goods. - 1987.
        (001340)
----Why freer trade in services is in the
     interest of developing countries. - 1985.
        (000850)
----The world's new property barons. - 1987.
        (000904)
----World-traded services : the challenge
     for the eighties. - 1984.
        (000889)

INTERNATIONAL TRADE--BRAZIL.
----Dos estudios sobre empresas
     transnacionales en Brasil. - 1983.
        (001120)

INTERNATIONAL TRADE--CANADA.
----The strategic management of
     multinationals and world product
     mandating. - 1986.
        (000511)

INTERNATIONAL TRADE--CZECHOSLOVAKIA.
----Czechoslovak regulations governing
     arbitration in international trade. -
     1985.
        (002518)

INTERNATIONAL TRADE--EAST ASIA.
----International trading companies for
     developing countries-Latin America. -
     1984.
        (000838)

INTERNATIONAL TRADE--JAPAN.
----Action programs by Japan's major
     manufacturers. - 1986.
        (000456)
----A transactions cost approach to
     international trading structures: the
     case of the Japanese general trading
     companies. - 1983.
        (000372)

INTERNATIONAL TRADE--LATIN AMERICA.
----International trading companies for
     developing countries-Latin America. -
     1984.
        (000838)
----The transnational corporations and Latin
     America's international trade. - 1985.
        (001100)

INTERNATIONAL TRADE--UNITED STATES.
----International trade in services: its
     composition, importance and links to
     merchandise trade. - 1987.
        (000890)
----U.S.-EEC confrontation in the
     international trade of agricultural
     products: consequences for third
     parties. - 1985.
        (001380)
----Washington's best kept secrets. - 1983.
        (002704)

INTERNATIONAL TRADE LAW.
----Annual survey of developments in
     international trade law, 1983. - 1984.
        (002136)
----Arbitraje-conciliación. - 1985.
        (002472)
----Current issues in international trade. -
     1985.
        (001359)
----Formation of contract and contract law
     through multinational joint ventures. -
     1983.
        (002435)
----GATT and recent international trade
     problems. - 1987.
        (001986)
----Guide to countertrade and international
     barter. - 1985.
        (001368)
----International ad hoc arbitration. - 1987.
        (002473)
----International codes and multinational
     business. - 1985.
        (001988)
----International equipment leasing. - 1984.
        (000905) (002139)
----International trade disputes and the
     individual : private party involvement
     in national and international procedures
     regarding unfair foreign trade
     practices. - 1986.
        (002514)
----The legal markets of international
     trade. - 1987.
        (002038)
----A manual of U.S. trade laws. - 1985.
        (002220)
----Peaceful settlement of international
     trade disputes. - 1983.
        (002500)
----Protectionism and structural adjustment.
     - 1986.
        (001689)
----Trade policy as a constitutional problem
     : on the "domestic policy functions" of
     international trade rules. - 1986.
        (001379)
----The transnational law of international
     commercial transactions. - 1982.
        (002012)
----UNCITRAL, the United Nations Commission
     on International Trade Law. - 1986.
        (002155)

INTERNATIONALISM.
----Managing cultural differences. - 1983.
        (001871)

INTERNATIONALISM--LATIN AMERICA.
----Transnational corporations and
    industrial transformation in Latin
    America. - 1984.
      (001099)

INTERPERSONAL RELATIONS--MIDDLE EAST.
----Major causes of joint-venture failures
    in the Middle East: the case of Iran. -
    1983.
      (001640)

INTRAFIRM TRADE.
----Transnational corporations in world
  . development. - 1983.
      (000102)

INTRA-INDUSTRY TRADE.
----Areas for further research on
    intra-industry trade. - 1983.
      (000099)
----Avantage comparatif et performance dans
    le commerce international des produits
    différenciés. - 1986.
      (001669)
----Intra-industry foreign direct
    investment. - 1984.
      (001375)
----Intra-industry production as a form of
  . international economic involvement. -
    1983.
      (000026)
----Profits, tariffs, and intra-industry
    trade. - 1985.
      (001347)

INTRA-INDUSTRY TRADE--CANADA.
----Le commerce interregional des services:
    le role des relations intra-firme et des
    facteurs organisationnels. - 1983.
      (000921)
----Trade among multinationals. - 1987.
      (001678)

INTRA-INDUSTRY TRADE--FRANCE.
----La specialisation internationale de la
    France dans les échanges de services.
    (With English summary.). - 1986.
      (000907)

INTRA-INDUSTRY TRADE--UNITED STATES.
----Intra-firm trade and U.S. protectionism:
    thoughts based on a small survey. - 1986.
      (001367)

INTRA-INDUSTRY TRADE--WESTERN EUROPE.
----Multinational corporations and European
    integration. - 1987.
      (001325)

INTRAREGIONAL TRADE--POLAND.
----Intra-industry trade in Poland's foreign
    trade in 1950-1984 : empirical results
    and policy implications. - 1986.
      (001372)

INTRAREGIONAL TRADE--SOUTHEAST ASIA.
----Legal development and the promotion of
    intra-ASEAN trade and investment. - 1986.
      (002307)

INVENTIONS.
----World technology. - 1975-   .
      (001525)

INVENTORIES.
----Inventories and foreign currency
    translation requirements. - 1983.
      (002064)

INVESTMENT AGREEMENTS.
----Bilateral investment treaties. - 1988.
      (002054)
----Le transfert de technologie dans les
    industries agro-alimentaires en Afrique
    Centrale. - 1987.
      (001510)
----Natural gas clauses in petroleum
    arrangements. - 1987.
      (002452)
----Transnational corporations in world
    development. - 1983.
      (000102)

INVESTMENT ANALYSIS.
----How to analyze foreign investment
    climates. - 1983.
      (001856)

INVESTMENT ANALYSIS--LATIN AMERICA.
----Latin American investment climate. -
    198?-   .
      (001822)

INVESTMENT BANKING.
----L'Agence multilatérale de garantie des
    investissements. - 1987.
      (002152)
----Current problems of economic
    integration. - 1986.
      (001312)
----International trade in services. - 1984.
      (000876)
----Mezhdunarodnata investitsionna banka i
    neinata rolia v razvitieto na
    sotsialisticheskata ikonomicheska
    integratsiia. - 1986.
      (002153)
----The Multilateral Investment Guarantee
    Agency. - 1986.
      (002146)

INVESTMENT BANKING--WESTERN EUROPE.
----The European Investment Bank. - 1985.
      (002134)

INVESTMENT DISPUTES.
----Bilateral investment treaties. - 1988.
      (002054)
----Case studies in the jurisdiction of the
    International Centre for Settlement of
    Investment Disputes. - 1986.
      (002580)
----Le CIRDI et l'immunité des états. - 1983.
      (002494)
----The Convention Establishing the
    Multilateral Investment Guarantee
    Agency. - 1987.
      (002127)
----Finance and protection of investments in
    developing countries. - 1987.
      (002128)
----ICSID : an international method for
    handling foreign investment disputes in
    LDCs. - 1987.
      (002474)
----ICSID arbitration. - 1984.
      (002495)

INVESTMENT DISPUTES (continued)
----ICSID implementation. - 1985.
  (002574)
----ICSID's emerging jurisprudence. - 1986.
  (002562)
----Improving the investment climate in
developing countries. - 1984.
  (002572)
----The International Centre for the
Settlement of Investment Disputes. -
1983.
  (002542)
----International investment disputes. -
1985.
  (002524)
----International protection of direct
foreign investments in the Third World.
- 1987.
  (002124)
----La pratique du CIRDI. - 1987.
  (002550)
----Probleme der Zuständigkeit des
International Centre for Settlement of
Investment Disputes (ICSID). - 1986.
  (002544)
----Quelques observations sur la rédaction
des clauses d'arbitrage CIRDI. - 1987.
  (002509)

INVESTMENT DISPUTES--CAMEROON.
----The ICSID Klöckner v. Cameroon award. -
1984.
  (002553)

INVESTMENT DISPUTES--CHINA.
----Dispute resolution in the People's
Republic of China. - 1984.
  (002558)

INVESTMENT DISPUTES--GERMANY, FEDERAL
REPUBLIC OF.
----The ICSID Klöckner v. Cameroon award. -
1984.
  (002553)

INVESTMENT FOLLOW-UP.
----The investment development cycle
revisited. - 1986.
  (000320)

INVESTMENT FOLLOW-UP--ITALY.
----Existing opportunities and prospects for
investment in Southern Italy. - 1984.
  (001830)

INVESTMENT INSURANCE.
----Aspects des réglementations nationales
de certains pays en voie de
développement concernant le régime des
investissements étrangers directs. -
1987.
  (002248)
----Factors influencing the flow of foreign
investment and the relevance of a
multilateral investment guarantee
scheme. - 1987.
  (002144)
----Finance and protection of investments in
developing countries. - 1987.
  (002128)
----Insurance against the political risks of
petroleum investment. - 1986.
  (001866) (002160)

----Investment protection treaties: recent
trends and prospects. - 1986.
  (002031)
----MIGA and foreign investment. - 1988.
  (002145)
----The Multilateral Investment Guarantee
Agency : status, mandate, concept,
features, implications. - 1987.
  (002158)
----Multilateral investment insurance and
private investment in the Third World. -
1984.
  (002131)
----Multilateral investment insurance and
private investment in the Third World. -
1987.
  (002132)
----Die Multilaterale
Investitions-Garantie-Agentur (MIGA). -
1986.
  (002142)
----Promotion of direct investment in
developing countries. - 1986.
  (002143)
----Protection et promotion des
investissements. - 1985.
  (002137)
----Second thoughts on MIGA. - 1986.
  (002148)
----The World Bank's Multilateral Investment
Guaranty Agency. - 1987.
  (002125)
----Zur Bedeutung der Multilateral
Investment Guarantee Agency für den
internationalen Ressourcentransfer. -
1987.
  (002129)

INVESTMENT INSURANCE--AFRICA.
----Investment in ACP states. - 1987.
  (001004)

INVESTMENT INSURANCE--CARIBBEAN REGION.
----Investment in ACP states. - 1987.
  (001004)

INVESTMENT INSURANCE--LATIN AMERICA.
----Los regímenes de garantía a la inversión
extranjera y su aplicabilidad en los
países de la ALADI. - 1985.
  (002126)

INVESTMENT INSURANCE--MOROCCO.
----Le nouveau droit des investissements
étrangers au Maroc. - 1984.
  (002269)

INVESTMENT INSURANCE--PACIFIC OCEAN REGION.
----Investment in ACP states. - 1987.
  (001004)

INVESTMENT INSURANCE--UNITED STATES.
----The World Bank's Multilateral Investment
Guaranty Agency. - 1987.
  (002125)

INVESTMENT INSURANCE--WESTERN EUROPE.
----Le système conjoint de garantie des
investissements CEE/ACP de la Convention
de Lomé III. - 1987.
  (002147)

INVESTMENT POLICY.
----Analyzing political risk. - 1986.
(001850)
----Appraising corporate investment policy:
a financial center theory of foreign
direct investment. - 1983.
(000084)
----Aspects des réglementations nationales
de certains pays en voie de
développement concernant le régime des
investissements étrangers directs. -
1987.
(002248)
----Controls and impediments affecting
inward direct investment in OECD member
countries. - 1987.
(000122) (002193)
----Developing with foreign investment. -
1987.
(000998)
----Do performance requirements and
investment incentives work? - 1986.
(002306)
----Eliminating barriers to international
trade and investment in services. - 1986.
(000809)
----Foreign and domestic divestment and
investment decisions: like or unlike? -
1983.
(000523)
----Foreign direct investment as a
sequential process. - 1983.
(000052)
----Foreign private investors and the host
country. - 1985.
(001851)
----Governments and multinationals. - 1983.
(002267)
----International dimensions of business
policy and strategy. - 1986.
(000477)
----International financial management: the
overall investment and financing plan. -
1983.
(000401)
----International investment and
multinational enterprises. - 1983.
(002308)
----Investissement international et
entreprises multinationales. - 1983.
(000538)
----Investment protection agreements. - 1987.
(002135)
----Multinational corporations. - 1986.
(000058)
----Multinational corporations and
discriminatory investment controls. -
1983.
(002249)
----Multinational enterprise and host
country policy: opportunities for mutual
benefit. - 1986.
(001828)
----Mutual investments and the formation of
multinational enterprises by developing
countries. - 1987.
(000378)
----New forms of international investment in
developing countries. - 1984.
(001619)
----The new multinationals: synthesis and
conclusions. -   .
(000349)

----The new multinationals: the theoretical
background. - 1983.
(000350)
----The OECD Declaration on International
Investment and Multinational
Enterprises. -   .
(001993)
----Private investment in developing
countries. - 1984.
(000114)
----Production and trade in services. - 1985.
(000978)
----Quando l'impresa diventa multinazionale:
il problema del controllo. - 1983.
(001607)
----Socialist economic integration and the
investment cooperation of the CMEA
countries. - 1984.
(001185)
----The stages of developing country policy
toward foreign investment. - 1985.
(002277)
----Strategic investments and the
development of multinationals. - 1987.
(000044)
----Transnational corporations in world
development. - 1983.
(000102)

INVESTMENT POLICY--ANDEAN REGION.
----The Andean foreign investment code's
impact on multinational enterprises. -
1983.
(001977)

INVESTMENT POLICY--AUSTRALIA.
----Australia deregulated : new freedoms for
multinational investment. - 1987.
(001797)
----Australia's foreign investment policy. -
198?-   .
(002170)
----Capital xenophobia. - 1984.
(002228)
----Foreign investment control in the mining
sector. - 1983.
(000577)
----Foreign investment in Australia,
1960-1981. - 1983.
(000141)
----MNCs and the Australian government: some
emerging policy issues. - 1983.
(002289)
----New Zealand business. - 1985.
(000352)
----United States investment in Australia. -
1987.
(002180)

INVESTMENT POLICY--BANGLADESH.
----Trade and investment possibilities in
Bangladesh, Nepal and Sri Lanka. - 1983.
(001840)

INVESTMENT POLICY--CAMEROON.
----The political economy of development in
Cameroon. - 1986.
(001834)

INVESTMENT POLICY--CANADA.
----Foreign investment control in the mining
sector. - 1983.
(000577)

INVESTMENT POLICY--CHINA.
----China's open door policy and the
    prospects for FDI. - 1986.
    (001043)
----China's special economic zones. - 1984.
    (002395)
----China's trade, tax and investment laws
    and regulations. - 1984.
    (002189)
----Chinese solutions to legal problems. -
    1987.
    (002295)
----Realities confronting China's foreign
    investment policy. - 1984.
    (002292)
----The 1982-83 overinvestment crisis in
    China. - 1984.
    (000120)

INVESTMENT POLICY--EASTERN EUROPE.
----L'investissement productif en Europe de
    l'Est : gaspillage des ressources,
    délais de réalisation importants, retard
    technologique? - 1986.
    (000126)

INVESTMENT POLICY--GERMANY, FEDERAL REPUBLIC
OF.
----Investitionsbedingungen in der
    ASEAN-region. - 1986.
    (001814)

INVESTMENT POLICY--GHANA.
----Ghana's new Investment Code. - 1985.
    (002213)

INVESTMENT POLICY--INDIA.
----Joint ventures abroad. - 1983.
    (001592)
----Joint ventures abroad. - 1984.
    (001528)
----Multinationals in Indian big business:
    industrial characteristics of foreign
    investments in a heavily regulated
    economy. - 1983.
    (001058)

INVESTMENT POLICY--INDONESIA.
----Foreign investment and government policy
    in the Third World. - 1988.
    (001790)

INVESTMENT POLICY--JAPAN.
----The legal framework of trade and
    investment in Japan. - 1986.
    (002241)

INVESTMENT POLICY--LATIN AMERICA.
----O capital transnacional e o estado. -
    1985.
    (002274)
----Las empresas transnacionales y la
    inversión extranjera directa en la
    primera mitad de los años ochenta. -
    1987.
    (000194)
----Foreign direct investment in Latin
    America. - 1986.
    (000190)
----Performance requirements: the general
    debate and a review of Latin American
    practices. - 1983.
    (002315)

INVESTMENT POLICY--MEXICO.
----The foreign investment transaction in
    Mexico. - 1985.
    (002260)

INVESTMENT POLICY--NEPAL.
----Trade and investment possibilities in
    Bangladesh, Nepal and Sri Lanka. - 1983.
    (001840)

INVESTMENT POLICY--NEW ZEALAND.
----New Zealand business. - 1985.
    (000352)

INVESTMENT POLICY--NIGERIA.
----Multinationals, the state, and control
    of the Nigerian economy. - 1987.
    (001022)
----State strategies toward Nigerian and
    foreign business. - 1983.
    (001770)

INVESTMENT POLICY--PAPUA NEW GUINEA.
----Foreign investment in Papua New Guinea.
    - 1986.
    (002197)

INVESTMENT POLICY--PHILIPPINES.
----Telecommunications and investment
    decisions in the Philippines. - 1984.
    (000533)

INVESTMENT POLICY--SAUDI ARABIA.
----Investment and joint-venture experiences
    in Saudi Arabia. - 1985.
    (001526)

INVESTMENT POLICY--SENEGAL.
----Réflexions sur les régimes fiscaux
    privilégiés du code des investissements
    au Gabon. - 1985.
    (002243)

INVESTMENT POLICY--SOUTHEAST ASIA.
----Investitionsbedingungen in der
    ASEAN-region. - 1986.
    (001814)

INVESTMENT POLICY--SRI LANKA.
----Trade and investment possibilities in
    Bangladesh, Nepal and Sri Lanka. - 1983.
    (001840)

INVESTMENT POLICY--TUNISIA.
----L'industrie manufacturière tunisienne et
    sa place dans l'économie nationale. -
    1985.
    (000744)
----Tunisie : l'Agence de promotion des
    investissements. - 1987.
    (002357)

INVESTMENT POLICY--UNITED ARAB EMIRATES.
----The UAE and the joint-venture
    opportunity. - 1985.
    (001530)

INVESTMENT POLICY--UNITED KINGDOM.
----Foreign multinationals and the British
    economy. - 1988.
    (001167)
----Inward investment. - 1984.
    (000116)

INVESTMENT POLICY--UNITED KINGDOM (continued)
----Multinationals and Britain. - 1986.
(000205)
----Two arguments for the restriction of
international capital flows. - 1986.
(001240)

INVESTMENT POLICY--UNITED STATES.
----Foreign direct investment in the United
States: the balance of foreign and
domestic policy. - 1983.
(000173)
----The international investment position of
the United States in 1985. - 1986.
(001295)

INVESTMENT POLICY--ZAIRE.
----Protection, distortions and investment
incentives in Zaire. - 1986.
(002272)

INVESTMENT PROMOTION.
----Bilateral investment promotion
protection and treaties : a model for
Community promotion of mining
investment? - 1986.
(002052)
----Current problems of economic
integration. - 1986.
(001312)
----Foreign private investors and the host
country. - 1985.
(001851)
----Investment incentives and disincentives
and the international investment
process. - 1983.
(002309)
----Investment incentives as tariff
substitutes: a comprehensive measure of
protection. - 1985.
(002302)
----Promotion of mining and energy
investment under the Lomé Convention. -
1986.
(002607)
----The role of multilateral development
finance institutions in promoting and
financing joint ventures. - 1986.
(000252)
----Transnational corporations in world
development. - 1983.
(000102)

INVESTMENT PROMOTION--AUSTRALIA.
----The effectiveness of investment
incentives. - 1985.
(002304)

INVESTMENT PROMOTION--LATIN AMERICA.
----Las empresas transnacionales y la
inversión extranjera directa en la
primera mitad de los años ochenta. -
1987.
(000194)
----La inversión estadounidense en el Grupo
Andino. - 1985.
(000112)

INVESTMENT PROMOTION--SOUTHEAST ASIA.
----Legal development and the promotion of
intra-ASEAN trade and investment. - 1986.
(002307)

INVESTMENT PROMOTION--SRI LANKA.
----The Katunayake investment promotion
zone. - 1982.
(002388)

INVESTMENT PROMOTION--TUNISIA.
----Tunisie : l'Agence de promotion des
investissements. - 1987.
(002357)

INVESTMENT PROMOTION--UNITED STATES.
----La inversión estadounidense en el Grupo
Andino. - 1985.
(000112)

INVESTMENT PROMOTION--WESTERN EUROPE.
----Industrialization and the ACPs. - 1984.
(002608)

INVESTMENT RETURNS.
----Probleme der Gerwinnverlagerungen
multinationaler Unternehmen :
Konzerninterne Verrechnungspreise und
deren wirtschaftspolitische Wirkungen. -
1983.
(001755)
----Transnational corporations and non-fuel
primary commodities in developing
countries. - 1987.
(000639)

INVESTMENT TAX CREDIT.
----Investment incentives as tariff
substitutes: a comprehensive measure of
protection. - 1985.
(002302)

INVESTMENT TAX CREDIT--CANADA.
----International income taxation and
developing countries. - 1988.
(001759)

INVESTMENT TAX CREDIT--FRANCE.
----International income taxation and
developing countries. - 1988.
(001759)

INVESTMENT TAX CREDIT--GERMANY, FEDERAL
REPUBLIC OF.
----International income taxation and
developing countries. - 1988.
(001759)

INVESTMENT TAX CREDIT--JAPAN.
----International income taxation and
developing countries. - 1988.
(001759)

INVESTMENT TAX CREDIT--MEXICO.
----Alliance for production. - 1984.
(002316)

INVESTMENT TAX CREDIT--SOUTHEAST ASIA.
----Subsidy to capital through tax
incentives in the ASEAN countries. -
1983.
(002300)

INVESTMENT TAX CREDIT--UNITED KINGDOM.
----International income taxation and
developing countries. - 1988.
(001759)

INVESTMENT TAX CREDIT--UNITED STATES.
----International business planning. - 1983.
   (002279)
----International income taxation and
   developing countries. - 1988.
   (001759)

INVESTMENT TRUSTS--SOUTH AFRICA.
----McGregor's investors' handbook. -
   1986-
   (001203) (002654)

INVESTMENT TRUSTS--UNITED STATES.
----Realty joint ventures, 1986. - 1986.
   (000881)

INVESTMENTS.
----Cooperation in investments: a factor in
   the intensification of production in
   CMEA member nations. - 1983.
   (001187)
----Empirical studies of investment
   behaviour. - 1985.
   (000524)
----Intellectual property rights,
   investment, and trade in services in the
   Uruguay round. - 1987.
   (000817)
----International accounting and reporting
   issues, 1986 review. - 1986.
   (002117)
----International trade in services :
   securities. - 1987.
   (000915)
----Investment protection treaties: recent
   trends and prospects. - 1986.
   (002031)
----Multilateral investment insurance and
   private investment in the Third World. -
   1987.
   (002132)
----Recent trends in international direct
   investment. - 1987.
   (000176)

INVESTMENTS--ASIA.
----The impact of foreign capital inflow on
   investment and economic growth in
   developing Asia. - 1985.
   (001048)

INVESTMENTS--AUSTRALIA.
----The effectiveness of investment
   incentives. - 1985.
   (002304)

INVESTMENTS--CHILE.
----Debt equity swaps, investment, and
   creditworthiness. - 1987.
   (000259)

INVESTMENTS--FRANCE.
----Les flux d'investissement direct entre
   la France et l'extérieur, 1965-1978. -
   1981.
   (000119)

INVESTMENTS--GULF STATES.
----A historical perspective of U.S.-GCC
   economic and financial interdependence.
   - 1987.
   (000143)

INVESTMENTS--JAPAN.
----What trade war? - 1987.
   (000481)

INVESTMENTS--LATIN AMERICA.
----Latin American investment climate. -
   198?-   .
   (001822)

INVESTMENTS--POLAND.
----Import licencji a zmiany w systemie
   gospodarki. - 1984.
   (002440)

INVESTMENTS--TAIWAN (CHINA).
----Taiwan's foreign direct investment. -
   1986.
   (000121)

INVESTMENTS--UNITED STATES.
----A historical perspective of U.S.-GCC
   economic and financial interdependence.
   - 1987.
   (000143)
----What trade war? - 1987.
   (000481)

INVISIBLES.
----Production and trade in services. - 1985.
   (000978)

IRAN.
----MNCs and the Iranian revolution: an
   empirical study. - 1985.
   (001772)

IRAN (ISLAMIC REPUBLIC OF)--CLAIMS.
----Current developments in the law of
   expropriation and compensation. - 1987.
   (002318)
----The expropriation issue before the
   Iran-United States Claims Tribunal. -
   1984.
   (002320)
----Iran-U.S. Claims Tribunal. - 1986.
   (002335)
----Partnership claims before the
   Iran-United States Claims Tribunal. -
   1987.
   (002322)

IRAN (ISLAMIC REPUBLIC OF)--COMMERCIAL
ARBITRATION.
----L'arbitrage Elf Aquitaine Iran c/
   National Iranian Oil Company. - 1984.
   (002504)

IRAN (ISLAMIC REPUBLIC OF)--COMPENSATION.
----The expropriation issue before the
   Iran-United States Claims Tribunal. -
   1984.
   (002320)

IRAN (ISLAMIC REPUBLIC OF)--DISPUTE
SETTLEMENT.
----Current developments in the law of
   expropriation and compensation. - 1987.
   (002318)
----Iran-U.S. Claims Tribunal. - 1986.
   (002335)
----Partnership claims before the
   Iran-United States Claims Tribunal. -
   1987.
   (002322)

IRAN (ISLAMIC REPUBLIC OF)--EXPROPRIATION.
----The expropriation issue before the
    Iran-United States Claims Tribunal. -
    1984.
        (002320)
----Iran-U.S. Claims Tribunal. - 1986.
        (002335)

IRAN (ISLAMIC REPUBLIC OF)--PETROLEUM
INDUSTRY.
----The oil companies and the Arab world. -
    1984.
        (000613)

IRAN (ISLAMIC REPUBLIC OF)--TRANSNATIONAL
CORPORATIONS.
----The oil companies and the Arab world. -
    1984.
        (000613)

IRAN-UNITED STATES CLAIMS TRIBUNAL (HAGUE).
----Current developments in the law of
    expropriation and compensation. - 1987.
        (002318)
----The expropriation issue before the
    Iran-United States Claims Tribunal. -
    1984.
        (002320)
----Iran-U.S. Claims Tribunal. - 1986.
        (002335)
----Partnership claims before the
    Iran-United States Claims Tribunal. -
    1987.
        (002322)

IRAQ--COMMERCIAL LAW.
----Business laws of Iraq. - 1984-   .
        (002226)

IRAQ--LAWS AND REGULATIONS.
----National legislation and regulations
    relating to transnational corporations.
    Volume 3. - 1983.
        (002252)

IRAQ--TRANSNATIONAL CORPORATIONS.
----National legislation and regulations
    relating to transnational corporations.
    Volume 3. - 1983.
        (002252)

IRELAND--FOREIGN DIRECT INVESTMENT.
----Foreign investment in the Republic of
    Ireland. - 1987.
        (000129)
----Input-output linkages and foreign direct
    investment in Ireland. - 1984.
        (001158)
----Multinational investment strategies in
    the British Isles. - 1983.
        (001151)

IRELAND--INDUSTRIALIZATION.
----The problem of late industrialisation
    and the experience of the Republic of
    Ireland. - 1985.
        (001330)

IRELAND--INPUT OUTPUT ANALYSIS.
----Input-output linkages and foreign direct
    investment in Ireland. - 1984.
        (001158)

IRELAND--STATISTICAL DATA.
----Foreign investment in the Republic of
    Ireland. - 1987.
        (000129)

IRELAND--STRATEGY.
----Multinational investment strategies in
    the British Isles. - 1983.
        (001151)

IRELAND--TRANSNATIONAL CORPORATIONS.
----Foreign investment in the Republic of
    Ireland. - 1987.
        (000129)
----Multinational investment strategies in
    the British Isles. - 1983.
        (001151)

IRON--LATIN AMERICA.
----La industria siderúrgica
    latinoamericana. - 1984.
        (000601)

IRON AND STEEL INDUSTRY--ARGENTINA.
----La industria siderúrgica
    latinoamericana. - 1984.
        (000601)

IRON AND STEEL INDUSTRY--BOLIVIA.
----La industria siderúrgica
    latinoamericana. - 1984.
        (000601)

IRON AND STEEL INDUSTRY--BRAZIL.
----La industria siderúrgica
    latinoamericana. - 1984.
        (000601)

IRON AND STEEL INDUSTRY--CHILE.
----La industria siderúrgica
    latinoamericana. - 1984.
        (000601)

IRON AND STEEL INDUSTRY--COLOMBIA.
----La industria siderúrgica
    latinoamericana. - 1984.
        (000601)

IRON AND STEEL INDUSTRY--ECUADOR.
----La industria siderúrgica
    latinoamericana. - 1984.
        (000601)

IRON AND STEEL INDUSTRY--LATIN AMERICA.
----La industria siderúrgica
    latinoamericana. - 1984.
        (000601)

IRON AND STEEL INDUSTRY--MEXICO.
----La industria siderúrgica
    latinoamericana. - 1984.
        (000601)

IRON AND STEEL INDUSTRY--PARAGUAY.
----La industria siderúrgica
    latinoamericana. - 1984.
        (000601)

IRON AND STEEL INDUSTRY--PERU.
----La industria siderúrgica
    latinoamericana. - 1984.
        (000601)

IRON AND STEEL INDUSTRY--VENEZUELA.
----La industria siderúrgica
   latinoamericana. - 1984.
   (000601)

ISLAMIC COUNTRIES--CONSULTANTS.
----Consultancy services. - 1986.
   (000831)

ISLAMIC COUNTRIES--DIRECTORIES.
----A directory of foreign investment
   legislation in O.I.C. member countries.
   - 1984.
   (002201)
----Répertoire de la législation relative
   aux investissements étrangers dans les
   pays membres de L'OCI. - 1984.
   (002264)

ISLAMIC COUNTRIES--FOREIGN INVESTMENTS.
----A directory of foreign investment
   legislation in O.I.C. member countries.
   - 1984.
   (002201)
----Répertoire de la législation relative
   aux investissements étrangers dans les
   pays membres de L'OCI. - 1984.
   (002264)

ISLAMIC COUNTRIES--LEGISLATION.
----A directory of foreign investment
   legislation in O.I.C. member countries.
   - 1984.
   (002201)
----Répertoire de la législation relative
   aux investissements étrangers dans les
   pays membres de L'OCI. - 1984.
   (002264)

ISLAMIC LAW--GULF STATES.
----Commercial law in the Gulf States : the
   Islamic legal tradition. - 1984.
   (002195)

ISLAMIC LAW--SAUDI ARABIA.
----United States corporations operating in
   Saudi Arabia and laws affecting
   discrimination in employment. - 1985.
   (002354)

ISRAEL--FOREIGN INVESTMENTS.
----National legislation and regulations
   relating to transnational corporations.
   Volume 4. - 1986.
   (002253)

ISRAEL--FOREIGN TRADE.
----U.S.-Israel free trade area. - 1986.
   (002049)

ISRAEL--FREE TRADE AREAS.
----U.S.-Israel free trade area. - 1986.
   (002049)

ISRAEL--LAWS AND REGULATIONS.
----National legislation and regulations
   relating to transnational corporations.
   Volume 4. - 1986.
   (002253)

ISRAEL--MODEL CONTRACTS.
----Controlling standard contracts. - 1985.
   (002423)

ISRAEL--STANDARDIZED TERMS OF CONTRACT.
----Controlling standard contracts. - 1985.
   (002423)

ISRAEL--TRADE AGREEMENTS.
----U.S.-Israel free trade area. - 1986.
   (002049)

ISRAEL--TRANSNATIONAL CORPORATIONS.
----National legislation and regulations
   relating to transnational corporations.
   Volume 4. - 1986.
   (002253)

ISTITUTO PER LA RICOSTRUZIONE INDUSTRIALE
(ITALY).
----L'impresa pubblica italiana e la
   dimensione internazionale. - 1983.
   (001145)

ITALY--CONTRACTS.
----La responsabilita contrattuale degli
   appaltatori in joint venture. - 1984.
   (001594)

ITALY--FOREIGN DIRECT INVESTMENT.
----Existing opportunities and prospects for
   investment in Southern Italy. - 1984.
   (001830)

ITALY--FOREIGN INVESTMENTS.
----National legislation and regulations
   relating to transnational corporations.
   Volume 4. - 1986.
   (002253)

ITALY--INDUSTRIAL ENTERPRISES.
----New forms of international technology
   transfer by Italian enterprises to
   developing countries. - 1984.
   (001474)

ITALY--INDUSTRIAL PROMOTION.
----L'impresa pubblica italiana e la
   dimensione internazionale. - 1983.
   (001145)

ITALY--INVESTMENT FOLLOW-UP.
----Existing opportunities and prospects for
   investment in Southern Italy. - 1984.
   (001830)

ITALY--JOINT VENTURES.
----Le associazioni temporanee di imprese. -
   1983.
   (001562)
----New forms of international technology
   transfer by Italian enterprises to
   developing countries. - 1984.
   (001474)
----La responsabilita contrattuale degli
   appaltatori in joint venture. - 1984.
   (001594)

ITALY--LAWS AND REGULATIONS.
----National legislation and regulations
   relating to transnational corporations.
   Volume 4. - 1986.
   (002253)

ITALY--LIABILITY.
----La responsabilita contrattuale degli
   appaltatori in joint venture. - 1984.
   (001594)

ITALY--PUBLIC ENTERPRISES.
----L'impresa pubblica italiana e la
    dimensione internazionale. - 1983.
    (001145)

ITALY--TECHNOLOGICAL INNOVATIONS.
----Cambiamento tecnologico e impresa
    multinazionale. - 1984.
    (000784)

ITALY--TECHNOLOGY TRANSFER.
----New forms of international technology
 _ transfer by Italian enterprises to
    developing countries. - 1984.
    (001474)

ITALY--TELECOMMUNICATION INDUSTRY.
----Cambiamento tecnologico e impresa
    multinazionale. - 1984.
    (000784)

ITALY--TRADE PROMOTION.
----L'impresa pubblica italiana e la
    dimensione internazionale. - 1983.
    (001145)

ITALY--TRANSNATIONAL CORPORATIONS.
----Cambiamento tecnologico e impresa
    multinazionale. - 1984.
    (000784)
----L'impresa pubblica italiana e la
    dimensione internazionale. - 1983.
    (001145)
----Italian multinationals. - 1986.
    (000336)
----Le multinazionali italiane. - 1985.
    (000302)
----National legislation and regulations
    relating to transnational corporations.
    Volume 4. - 1986.
    (002253)

ITU.
----Meeting the challenges of the world
    information economy. - 1984.
    (000853)

JAMAICA--DEVELOPING COUNTRIES.
----Commercialization of technology and
    dependence in the Caribbean. - 1985.
    (001477)

JAMAICA--ECONOMIC RECESSION.
----La Jamaïque, ou le dilemme politique
    d'un petit pays déshérité. - 1984.
    (001819)

JAMAICA--ELECTIONS.
----La Jamaïque, ou le dilemme politique
    d'un petit pays déshérité. - 1984.
    (001819)

JAMAICA--FOREIGN DIRECT INVESTMENT.
----La Jamaïque, ou le dilemme politique
    d'un petit pays déshérité. - 1984.
    (001819)

JAMAICA--INDUSTRIAL PLANNING.
----Commercialization of technology and
    dependence in the Caribbean. - 1985.
    (001477)

JAMAICA--POLITICAL CONDITIONS.
----La Jamaïque, ou le dilemme politique
    d'un petit pays déshérité. - 1984.
    (001819)

JAMAICA--TECHNICAL CO-OPERATION.
----Commercialization of technology and
    dependence in the Caribbean. - 1985.
    (001477)

JAMAICA--TECHNOLOGY TRANSFER.
----Commercialization of technology and
    dependence in the Caribbean. - 1985.
    (001477)

JAMAICA--UNEMPLOYMENT.
----La Jamaïque, ou le dilemme politique
    d'un petit pays déshérité. - 1984.
    (001819)

JAPAN--AFFILIATE CORPORATIONS.
----Directory of foreign capital affiliated
    enterprises in Japan. - 198?-   .
    (002632)
----US and Japanese manufacturing affiliates
    in the UK. - 1985.
    (001149)

JAPAN--ANTIDUMPING DUTIES.
----Antitrust aspects of U.S.-Japanese
    trade. - 1983.
    (002345)

JAPAN--ANTITRUST LAW.
----Antitrust aspects of U.S.-Japanese
    trade. - 1983.
    (002345)

JAPAN--AUTOMATION.
----Microelectronics-based automation
    technologies and development. - 1985.
    (000753)
----Postindustrial manufacturing. - 1986.
    (000698)

JAPAN--AUTOMOBILE INDUSTRY.
----America's new no. 4 automaker -- Honda.
    - 1985.
    (000294)
----Automotive parts industry and the U.S.
    aftermarket for Japanese cars and light
    trucks. - 1985.
    (000759)
----The Japanese automobile industry. - 1985.
    (000278)

JAPAN--BALANCE OF PAYMENTS.
----Japan as capital exporter and the world
    economy. - 1985.
    (000384)
----Japon : du commerce à la finance. - 1987.
    (000374)

JAPAN--BANKING.
----Japanese offshore banking. - 1984.
    (000933)

JAPAN--BIOTECHNOLOGY.
----Commercial biotechnology. - 1984.
    (000643)

JAPAN--BUSINESS ENTERPRISES.
----The economic analysis of the Japanese
    firm. - 1984.
        (000322)

JAPAN--CAPITAL MARKETS.
----The European investments of Japanese
    financial institutions. - 1986.
        (000118)
----Japan as capital exporter and the world
    economy. - 1985.
        (000384)

JAPAN--CAPITAL MOVEMENTS.
----Japan as capital exporter and the world
    economy. - 1985.
        (000384)

JAPAN--COMMERCIAL BANKS.
----Internationalization of Japanese
    commercial banking-the recent experience
    of city banks. - 1984.
        (000855)

JAPAN--COMMERCIAL LAW.
----The administrative regulation of
    technology induction contracts in Japan.
    - 1987.
        (002447)
----Antitrust aspects of U.S.-Japanese
    trade. - 1983.
        (002345)
----Doing business in Japan. - 1983.
        (001820)
----The legal framework of trade and
    investment in Japan. - 1986.
        (002241)

JAPAN--COMPARATIVE ANALYSIS.
----Multinational enterprise and world
    competition. - 1987.
        (000018)
----Postindustrial manufacturing. - 1986.
        (000698)
----Transfer of technology from Japan and
    the United States to Korean
    manufacturing industries: a comparative
    study. - 1984.
        (001461)

JAPAN--COMPETITION.
----Competition in the Pacific Basin. - 1987.
        (001673)
----A competitive assessment of the U.S.
    fiber optics industry. - 1984.
        (000800)
----Competitive edge. - 1984.
        (000673)
----Employment and competitiveness in the
    European Community. - 1984.
        (001929)

JAPAN--COMPUTER INDUSTRY.
----Competitive edge. - 1984.
        (000673)

JAPAN--CONGLOMERATE CORPORATIONS.
----The invisible link. - 1986.
        (000992)
----Japanese direct investment in ASEAN. -
    1983.
        (000171)

----Japan's general trading companies. -
    1984.
        (000887)

JAPAN--CONTRACTS.
----The administrative regulation of
    technology induction contracts in Japan.
    - 1987.
        (002447)
----Doing business in Japan. - 1983.
        (001820)
----Kokusai torihikiho. - 1984.
        (002458)

JAPAN--CORPORATE ANALYSIS.
----New trends in internationalization:
    processes and theories. Diversified
    patterns of multinational enterprise and
    old and new forms of foreign involvement
    of the firm. - 1983.
        (000068)

JAPAN--CORPORATE MERGERS.
----Recent developments in operations and
    behaviour of transnational corporations.
    - 1987.
        (000103)

JAPAN--CORPORATIONS.
----The Rising Sun in America (Part Two)
    -- Japanese management in the United
    States. - 1986.
        (000391)
----The economic analysis of the Japanese
    firm. - 1984.
        (000322)
----The Rising Sun in America (Part One). -
    1986.
        (000392)

JAPAN--CROSS-CULTURAL ANALYSIS.
----Japan's emerging multinationals. - 1985.
        (000379)

JAPAN--DEVELOPED MARKET ECONOMIES.
----Zur Internationalisierung der
    japanischen Wirtschaft. - 1984.
        (000117)

JAPAN--DEVELOPING COUNTRIES.
----Technology transfer and
    industrialization in the developing
    countries. - 1984.
        (001430)

JAPAN--DEVELOPMENT.
----The role of direct foreign investment in
    developing East Asian countries. - 1985.
        (001052)

JAPAN--ECONOMIC ANALYSIS.
----The economic analysis of the
    multinational enterprise: Reading versus
    Japan? - 1985.
        (000008)

JAPAN--ECONOMIC DEVELOPMENT.
----Japan's general trading companies. -
    1984.
        (000887)

JAPAN--ECONOMIC GROWTH.
----Japanese direct investment abroad. -
    1986.
    (000311)
----Le Japon : transformations
    industrielles, croissance et
    internationalisation. - 1983.
    (000319)

JAPAN--ECONOMIC INTEGRATION.
----Japanese transnational corporations and
    the economic integration of Australian
    and the Asian-Pacific region. - 1983.
    (000323)

JAPAN--ECONOMIC POLICY.
----The Japanese economic strategy. - 1983.
    (000366)

JAPAN--ECONOMIC RELATIONS.
----Competition in the Pacific Basin. - 1987.
    (001673)
----The Japanese economic strategy. - 1983.
    (000366)
----Two hungry giants. - 1983.
    (000645)

JAPAN--ECONOMIC TRENDS.
----Trends in multinational business and
    global environments: a perspective. -
    1984.
    (000029)

JAPAN--ELECTRONICS INDUSTRY.
----High-tech trade. - 1986.
    (000696)
----Le Japon : transformations
    industrielles, croissance et
    internationalisation. - 1983.
    (000319)
----Postwar development of Japanese
    electronics industry. - 1986.
    (000732)
----The semiconductor business. - 1985.
    (000715)
----Transnational corporations in the
    international semiconductor industry. -
    1986.
    (000748)
----Vers la mondialisation de l'appareil
    productif japonais. - 1986.
    (000725)

JAPAN--EMPLOYMENT.
----Employment and competitiveness in the
    European Community. - 1984.
    (001929)
----Le Japon : transformations
    industrielles, croissance et
    internationalisation. - 1983.
    (000319)

JAPAN--EMPLOYMENT POLICY.
----Key to Japan's economic strength. - 1984.
    (001924)

JAPAN--EXPORTS.
----Le Japon : transformations
    industrielles, croissance et
    internationalisation. - 1983.
    (000319)

JAPAN--FIBRE OPTICS.
----A competitive assessment of the U.S.
    fiber optics industry. - 1984.
    (000800)

JAPAN--FINANCIAL INSTITUTIONS.
----The European investments of Japanese
    financial institutions. - 1986.
    (000118)

JAPAN--FLEXIBLE MANUFACTURING SYSTEMS.
----Postindustrial manufacturing. - 1986.
    (000698)

JAPAN--FOREIGN DIRECT INVESTMENT.
----The Rising Sun in America (Part Two)
    -- Japanese management in the United
    States. - 1986.
    (000391)
----The allocation of Japanese direct
    foreign investment and its evolution in
    Asia. - 1985.
    (000153)
----America's new no. 4 automaker -- Honda.
    - 1985.
    (000294)
----Becoming a triad power: the new global
    corporation. - 1986.
    (000500)
----Direct investment by Sogo-Shosha in
    Europe. - 1983.
    (000310)
----Die Direktinvestitionen der japanischen
    Wirtschaft in den Schwellenländern Ost-
    Südostasiens. - 1984.
    (000157)
----Las empresas transnacionales y la
    inversión extranjera directa en la
    primera mitad de los años ochenta. -
    1987.
    (000194)
----The European investments of Japanese
    financial institutions. - 1986.
    (000118)
----Les investissements japonais en Asie du
    sud-est: compléments ou concurrents de
    l'industrie au Japon. (With English
    summary.). - 1985.
    (000146)
----Japanese and American direct investment
    in Asia. - 1985.
    (000154)
----Japanese direct foreign investment in
    Asian developing countries. - 1983.
    (000155)
----Japanese direct investment abroad. -
    1986.
    (000311)
----Japanese direct investment in ASEAN. -
    1983.
    (000171)
----Japanese direct investment in Indonesian
    manufacturing. - 1984.
    (000187)
----Japanese investment in Indonesia:
    problems and prospects. - 1986.
    (000152)
----Japanese investment in Thailand. - 1987.
    (000200)
----Japan's direct investment in California
    and the new protectionism. - 1984.
    (000145)
----Japon : du commerce à la finance. - 1987.
    (000374)

JAPAN--FOREIGN DIRECT INVESTMENT (continued)
----New trends in internationalization:
     processes and theories. Diversified
     patterns of multinational enterprise and
     old and new forms of foreign involvement
     of the firm. - 1983.
       (000068)
----Pacific Basin financing -- Japan:
     straddling the world/both borrower and
     lender. - 1987.
       (000258)
----The process of internationalization at
     Asahi Glass Co. - 1986.
       (000360)
----The Rising Sun in America (Part One). -
     1986.
       (000392)
----The role of direct foreign investment in
     developing East Asian countries. - 1985.
       (001052)
----Some aspects of Japanese manufacturing
     investment in Australia. - 1984.
       (001044)
----Technology transfer through direct
     foreign investment. - 1985.
       (001490)
----Trends and issues in foreign direct
     investment and related flows. - 1985.
       (000192)
----Trends in Japan's direct investment
     abroad for FY 1985. - 1987.
       (000164)
----Trends in multinational business and
     global environments: a perspective. -
     1984.
       (000029)
----US and Japanese manufacturing affiliates
     in the UK. - 1985.
       (001149)
----Zur Internationalisierung der
     japanischen Wirtschaft. - 1984.
       (000117)

JAPAN--FOREIGN EXCHANGE CONTROL.
----The administrative regulation of
     technology induction contracts in Japan.
     - 1987.
       (002447)

JAPAN--FOREIGN INVESTMENTS.
----Les investissements européens au Japon :
     les causes de la faiblesse et les
     difficultés du rattrapage. - 1986.
       (000105)
----Japanese investment in UK industry. -
     1984.
       (000127)
----Japanese overseas investment. - 1983.
       (000160)
----Japan's general trading companies. -
     1984.
       (000887)
----The pattern of Japanese multinational
     investment. - 1984.
       (000327)

JAPAN--FOREIGN RELATIONS.
----Competition in the Pacific Basin. - 1987.
       (001673)

JAPAN--FOREIGN TRADE.
----The administrative regulation of
     technology induction contracts in Japan.
     - 1987.
       (002447)
----Antitrust aspects of U.S.-Japanese
     trade. - 1983.
       (002345)
----Japán multinacionális kereskedoházai és
     nyitása a világgazdaság felé. - 1986.
       (000354)
----Japan's general trading companies. -
     1984.
       (000887)
----The legal framework of trade and
     investment in Japan. - 1986.
       (002241)
----The Sogo Shosha: can it be exported
     (imported)? - 1983.
       (000338)
----Zur Internationalisierung der
     japanischen Wirtschaft. - 1984.
       (000117)

JAPAN--GLASS INDUSTRY.
----The process of internationalization at
     Asahi Glass Co. - 1986.
       (000360)

JAPAN--GOVERNMENT LENDING.
----The nature and tools of Japan's
     industrial policy. - 1986.
       (000557)

JAPAN--HONDA MOTOR COMPANY(JAPAN).
----America's new no. 4 automaker -- Honda.
     - 1985.
       (000294)

JAPAN--HOST COUNTRY RELATIONS.
----Doing business in Japan. - 1986.
       (001809)

JAPAN--IMPORTS.
----Automotive parts industry and the U.S.
     aftermarket for Japanese cars and light
     trucks. - 1985.
       (000759)

JAPAN--INDUSTRIAL ADMINISTRATION.
----The nature and tools of Japan's
     industrial policy. - 1986.
       (000557)

JAPAN--INDUSTRIAL CO-OPERATION.
----The Asianization of British industry. -
     1983.
       (000204)
----Industrial collaboration with Japan. -
     1986.
       (001648)
----New patterns in the formation of US/
     Japanese cooperative ventures: the role
     of technology. - 1987.
       (001622)
----Planning a joint venture for the
     Japanese market. - 1987.
       (000508)

JAPAN--INDUSTRIAL DEVELOPMENT.
----Le Japon : transformations
    industrielles, croissance et
    internationalisation. - 1983.
      (000319)

JAPAN--INDUSTRIAL EQUIPMENT LEASES.
----Analysis of equipment leasing contracts.
    - 1984.
      (002407)

JAPAN--INDUSTRIAL MANAGEMENT.
----Developing new leadership in a
    multinational environment. - 1985.
      (000444)
----The economic analysis of the Japanese
    firm. - 1984.
      (000322)

JAPAN--INDUSTRIAL ORGANIZATION.
----The economic analysis of the Japanese
    firm. - 1984.
      (000322)

JAPAN--INDUSTRIAL POLICY.
----High-tech trade. - 1986.
      (000696)
----The nature and tools of Japan's
    industrial policy. - 1986.
      (000557)

JAPAN--INDUSTRIAL ROBOTS.
----Robots in manufacturing. - 1983.
      (000656)

JAPAN--INDUSTRIAL TECHNOLOGY.
----A high technology gap? - 1987.
      (001439)

JAPAN--INDUSTRIALIZATION.
----Technology transfer and
    industrialization in the developing
    countries. - 1984.
      (001430)

JAPAN--INDUSTRY.
----A competitive assessment of the U.S.
    fiber optics industry. - 1984.
      (000800)
----Les investissements japonais en Asie du
    sud-est: compléments ou concurrents de
    l'industrie au Japon. (With English
    summary.). - 1985.
      (000146)
----The Sogo Shosha: can it be exported
    (imported)? - 1983.
      (000338).

JAPAN--INTERNATIONAL BANKING.
----Internationalization of Japanese
    commercial banking-the recent experience
    of city banks. - 1984.
      (000855)

JAPAN--INTERNATIONAL COMPETITION.
----Multinational enterprise and world
    competition. - 1987.
      (000018)

JAPAN--INTERNATIONAL TRADE.
----Action programs by Japan's major
    manufacturers. - 1986.
      (000456)

----A transactions cost approach to
    international trading structures: the
    case of the Japanese general trading
    companies. - 1983.
      (000372)

JAPAN--INVESTMENT POLICY.
----The legal framework of trade and
    investment in Japan. - 1986.
      (002241)

JAPAN--INVESTMENT TAX CREDIT.
----International income taxation and
    developing countries. - 1988.
      (001759)

JAPAN--INVESTMENTS.
----What trade war? - 1987.
      (000481)

JAPAN--JOINT VENTURES.
----The Asianization of British industry. -
    1983.
      (000204)
----Becoming a triad power: the new global
    corporation. - 1986.
      (000500)
----Doing business in Japan. - 1986.
      (001809)
----Industrial collaboration with Japan. -
    1986.
      (001648)
----International corporate linkages. - 1987.
      (002430)
----Japanese direct investment in ASEAN. -
    1983.
      (000171)
----New patterns in the formation of US/
    Japanese cooperative ventures: the role
    of technology. - 1987.
      (001622)
----Planning a joint venture for the
    Japanese market. - 1987.
      (000508)
----What trade war? - 1987.
      (000481)

JAPAN--LABOUR MARKET.
----Employment and competitiveness in the
    European Community. - 1984.
      (001929)

JAPAN--LABOUR RELATIONS.
----Technology strategy and industrial
    relations: case studies of Japanese
    multinationals in the United States. -
    1983.
      (002599)

JAPAN--LAW.
----Doing business in Japan. - 1983.
      (001820)

JAPAN--LAWS AND REGULATIONS.
----International income taxation and
    developing countries. - 1988.
      (001759)
----Kokusai kankei no horitsu sodan. - 1983.
      (002293)

JAPAN--LICENCES.
----The administrative regulation of
technology induction contracts in Japan.
- 1987.
(002447)

JAPAN--MACHINE TOOL INDUSTRY.
----Industrial strategy and technological
dynamism in machine tool manufacture. -
1983.
(000716)

JAPAN--MACHINE TOOLS.
----Microelectronics-based automation
technologies and development. - 1985.
(000753)

JAPAN--MANAGEMENT.
----The Rising Sun in America (Part Two)
-- Japanese management in the United
States. - 1986.
(000391)
----Direct investment by Sogo-Shosha in
Europe. - 1983.
(000310)
----External and internal functioning of
American, German, and Japanese
multinational corporations:
decisionmaking and policy issues. - 1983.
(000432)·
----Internationalization at the top. - 1987.
(000454)
----The invisible link. - 1986.
(000992)
----The Rising Sun in America (Part One). -
1986.
(000392)
----A transactions cost approach to
international trading structures: the
case of the Japanese general trading
companies. - 1983.
(000372)

JAPAN--MANAGERS.
----Internationalization at the top. - 1987.
(000454)

JAPAN--MANUFACTURING.
----Some aspects of Japanese manufacturing
investment in Australia. - 1984.
(001044)

JAPAN--MANUFACTURING ENTERPRISES.
----Action programs by Japan's major
manufacturers. - 1986.
(000456)
----Japanese direct investment in Indonesian
manufacturing. - 1984.
(000187)
----Japanese investment in UK industry. -
1984.
(000127)
----Transfer of technology from Japan and
the United States to Korean
manufacturing industries: a comparative
study. - 1984.
(001461)
----Trends in Japan's manufacturing
investment in the United States. - 1987.
(000767)
----US and Japanese manufacturing affiliates
in the UK. - 1985.
(001149)

JAPAN--MARKET RESEARCH.
----Planning a joint venture for the
Japanese market. - 1987.
(000508)

JAPAN--MARKETING.
----Becoming a triad power: the new global
corporation. - 1986.
(000500)

JAPAN--MONETARY POLICY.
----Japan as capital exporter and the world
economy. - 1985. ·
(000384)
----Japanese offshore banking. - 1984.
(000933)

JAPAN--MONOPOLIES.
----The invisible link. - 1986.
(000992)

JAPAN--MOTOR VEHICLE EQUIPMENT.
----Automotive parts industry and the U.S.
aftermarket for Japanese cars and light
trucks. - 1985.
(000759)

JAPAN--MOTOR VEHICLE INDUSTRY.
----Automotive parts industry and the U.S.
aftermarket for Japanese cars and light
trucks. - 1985.
(000759)

JAPAN--NEW TECHNOLOGIES.
----A high technology gap? - 1987.
(001439)

JAPAN--PERSONNEL MANAGEMENT.
----Japanese multinationals in the United
States. - 1986.
(000341)
----Japan's emerging multinationals. - 1985.
(000379)
----Key to Japan's economic strength. - 1984.
(001924)
----Personalpolitik fur multinationale
Unternehmen. - 1985.
(000417) (001903)

JAPAN--PRIVATE ENTERPRISES.
----The Japanese economic strategy. - 1983.
(000366)
----Privatisierung in Japan. - 1987.
(001601)

JAPAN--PRIVATE INTERNATIONAL LAW.
----Kokusai torihikiho. - 1984.
(002458)

JAPAN--PRODUCTION CONTROL.
----Vers la mondialisation de l'appareil
productif japonais. - 1986.
(000725)

JAPAN--PROTECTIONISM.
----Japan's direct investment in California
and the new protectionism. - 1984.
(000145)

JAPAN--PUBLIC ENTERPRISES.
----Privatisierung in Japan. - 1987.
(001601)

JAPAN--RESEARCH AND DEVELOPMENT.
----High-tech trade. - 1986.
     (000696)

JAPAN--ROBOTICS.
----Robots in manufacturing. - 1983.
     (000656)

JAPAN--SCIENCE AND TECHNOLOGY POLICY.
----Technology strategy and industrial
     relations: case studies of Japanese
     multinationals in the United States. -
     1983.
     (002599)

JAPAN--SEMICONDUCTORS.
----Competitive edge. - 1984.
     (000673)
----High-tech trade. - 1986.
     (000696)
----The semiconductor business. - 1985.
     (000715)

JAPAN--SMALL ENTERPRISES.
----Microelectronics-based automation
     technologies and development. - 1985.
     (000753)

JAPAN--TAX AVOIDANCE.
----International tax evasion and avoidance
     in Japan. - 1984.
     (001726)

JAPAN--TAX EVASION.
----International tax evasion and avoidance
     in Japan. - 1984.
     (001726)

JAPAN--TAX INCENTIVES.
----International income taxation and
     developing countries. - 1988.
     (001759)
----The nature and tools of Japan's
     industrial policy. - 1986.
     (000557)

JAPAN--TAXATION.
----International income taxation and
     developing countries. - 1988.
     (001759)

JAPAN--TECHNICAL CO-OPERATION.
----Technology transfer through direct
     foreign investment. - 1985.
     (001490)

JAPAN--TECHNOLOGICAL INNOVATIONS.
----A high technology gap? - 1987.
     (001439)

JAPAN--TECHNOLOGICAL TRENDS.
----Trends in multinational business and
     global environments: a perspective. -
     1984.
     (000029)

JAPAN--TECHNOLOGY.
----A high technology gap? - 1987.
     (001439)

JAPAN--TECHNOLOGY TRANSFER.
----The administrative regulation of
     technology induction contracts in Japan.
     - 1987.
     (002447)
----A high technology gap? - 1987.
     (001439)
----Technology transfer and
     industrialization in the developing
     countries. - 1984.
     (001430)
----Technology transfer through direct
     foreign investment. - 1985.
     (001490)
----The transfer of organizational culture
     overseas: an approach to control in the
     multinational corporation. - 1983.
     (000420)
----Transfer of technology from Japan and
     the United States to Korean
     manufacturing industries: a comparative
     study. - 1984.
     (001461)

JAPAN--TEXTILE INDUSTRY.
----Technology transfer and
     industrialization in the developing
     countries. - 1984.
     (001430)

JAPAN--TRADE EXPANSION.
----Japanese direct investment abroad. -
     1986.
     (000311)

JAPAN--TRADE LIBERALIZATION.
----High-tech trade. - 1986.
     (000696)

JAPAN--TRADE POLICY.
----Doing business in Japan. - 1986.
     (001809)
----High-tech trade. - 1986.
     (000696)
----A transactions cost approach to
     international trading structures: the
     case of the Japanese general trading
     companies. - 1983.
     (000372)

JAPAN--TRADE REGULATION.
----The legal framework of trade and
     investment in Japan. - 1986.
     (002241)

JAPAN--TRADE STRUCTURE.
----The invisible link. - 1986.
     (000992)
----Japan's general trading companies. -
     1984.
     (000887)

JAPAN--TRANSNATIONAL BANKS.
----Foreign direct investment, the service
     sector and international banking. - 1987.
     (000972)

JAPAN--TRANSNATIONAL CORPORATIONS.
----Action programs by Japan's major
     manufacturers. - 1986.
     (000456)
----Developing new leadership in a
     multinational environment. - 1985.
     (000444)

JAPAN--TRANSNATIONAL CORPORATIONS (continued)
----Directory of foreign capital affiliated
    enterprises in Japan. - 198?-   .
      (002632)
----Doing business in Japan. - 1986.
      (001809)
----The economic analysis of the
    multinational enterprise: Reading versus
    Japan? - 1985.
      (000008)
----External and internal functioning of
    American, German, and Japanese
    multinational corporations:
    decisionmaking and policy issues. - 1983.
      (000432)
----Indigenization policies and structural
    cooptation by multinational
    corporations. - 1985.
      (002331)
----International tax evasion and avoidance
    in Japan. - 1984.
      (001726)
----Internationalization at the top. - 1987.
      (000454)
----Japanese direct investment in ASEAN. -
    1983.
      (000171)
----Japanese multinationals in the United
    States. - 1986.
      (000341)
----Japanese transnational corporations and
    the economic integration of Australian
    and the Asian-Pacific region. - 1983.
      (000323)
----Japan's emerging multinationals. - 1985.
      (000379)
----Key to Japan's economic strength. - 1984.
      (001924)
----Kokusai kankei no horitsu sodan. - 1983.
      (002293)
----Kokusai torihikiho. - 1984.
      (002458)
----Multinational enterprise and world
    competition. - 1987.
      (000018)
----New trends in internationalization:
    processes and theories. Diversified
    patterns of multinational enterprise and
    old and new forms of foreign involvement
    of the firm. - 1983.
      (000068)
----Pacific Basin financing -- Japan:
    straddling the world/both borrower and
    lender. - 1987.
      (000258)
----The pattern of Japanese multinational
    investment. - 1984.
      (000327)
----Personalpolitik fur multinationale
    Unternehmen. - 1985.
      (000417) (001903)
----Recent developments in operations and
    behaviour of transnational corporations.
    - 1987.
      (000103)
----Takokuseki kigyoron. - 1983.
      (000339)
----Technology strategy and industrial
    relations: case studies of Japanese
    multinationals in the United States. -
    1983.
      (002599)

----The threat of Japanese multinationals. -
    1983.
      (000329)
----Togoteki takokuseki kigyoron. - 1983.
      (000364)
----A transactions cost approach to
    international trading structures: the
    case of the Japanese general trading
    companies. - 1983.
      (000372)
----The transfer of organizational culture
    overseas: an approach to control in the
    multinational corporation. - 1983.
      (000420)
----Transnational corporations in the
    international semiconductor industry. -
    1986.
      (000748)
----Trends in Japan's manufacturing
    investment in the United States. - 1987.
      (000767)
----Trends in multinational business and
    global environments: a perspective. -
    1984.
      (000029)

JOINT VENTURES.
----The characteristics of joint
    ventures in developed and developing
    countries. - 1985.
      (001541)
----Antitrust for high-technology
    industries: assessing research joint
    ventures and mergers. - 1985.
      (001621)
----Arrangements between joint venture
    partners in developing countries. - 1987.
      (002450)
----Les associations d'entreprises (joint
    ventures) dans le commerce
    international. - 1986.
      (001538)
----Common mistakes of joint venture
    experienced firms. - 1987.
      (001604)
----Competition policy and joint ventures. -
    1986.
      (001684)
----The competitive effects of partial
    equity interests and joint ventures. -
    1986.
      (001635)
----Contractual adaptation and conflict
    resolution based on venture contracts
    for mining projects in developing
    countries. - 1985.
      (002475)
----Cooperate to compete globally. - 1986.
      (001624)
----Cooperative strategies in international
    business. - 1988.
      (001557)
----Co-production: a viable consideration
    for developing nations. - 1984.
      (001629)
----Creating the GM-Toyota joint venture: a
    case in complex negotiation. - 1987.
      (001656)
----Current problems of economic
    integration. - 1986.
      (001312)

JOINT VENTURES (continued)
----Dispersion of risk through multinational
    teamwork. - 1987.
    (001558)
----East-West joint ventures. - 1988.
    (001570)
----The economics of joint ventures in less
    developed countries. - 1984.
    (001643)
----Les entreprises à participation
    étrangère installées dans les pays
    socialistes. - 1987.
    (001183)
----Equity joint ventures and the theory of
    the multinational enterprise. - 987 .
    (001542)
----Food-processing contracts with
    developing countries. - 1985.
    (002419)
----Foreign business practices. - 1985.
    (001433)
----Gemeinschaftsunternehmen im EGKS- und
    EWG-Kartellrecht. - 1986.
    (001978)
----Human resource management in
    multinational cooperative ventures. -
    1986.
    (000426)
----Human resources management in
    international joint ventures: directions
    for research. - 1987.
    (001921)
----International business: an alternative
    view. - 1986.
    (001559)
----International corporate linkages. - 1987.
    (002430)
----International joint ventures:
    implications for organisation
    development. - 1987.
    (001639)
----International technology joint ventures.
    - 1985.
    (001593)
----Les investissements miniers
    internationaux dans les pays en
    développement. - 1986.
    (000609)
----Investitionen und Kooperationen in
    Ubersee. - 1983.
    (001567)
----Joint venture instability: is it a
    problem? - 1987.
    (001581)
----Joint ventures : do they restrict
    competition? - 1986.
    (001596)
----Joint ventures and global strategies. -
    1984.
    (001586)
----Joint ventures and Third World maritime
    development. - 1985.
    (000799)
----Joint ventures in LDCs. - 1987.
    (000997)
----Joint venturing abroad. - 1985.
    (001598)
----Kelet : nyugati közös vállalatok néhány
    elvi kérdése. - 1984.
    (001180)
----Lehetosegek es kenyszerpalyak a szellemi
    termekek letrehozasaban es nemzetkozi
    kereskedelmeben. - 1984.
    (001465)

----Measures of manifest conflict in
    international joint ventures. - 1987.
    (001583)
----MNCs and the Iranian revolution: an
    empirical study. - 1985.
    (001772)
----Multinational joint ventures in
    developing countries. - 1988.
    (001543)
----Multinational ventures in the commercial
    aircraft industry. - 1985.
    (000721)
----Multinationale Bankenverflechtungen. -
    1983.
    (001549)
----New forms of international investment in
    developing countries. - 1984.
    (001619)
----Les nouvelles formes d'investissement
    dans les pays on développement. - 1984.
    (001620)
----Les nouvelles formes d'investissement
    international dans les pays en
    développement. - 1984.
    (000165)
----Overseas acquisitions and mergers. -
    1986.
    (001585)
----Partnership claims before the
    Iran-United States Claims Tribunal. -
    1987.
    (002322)
----Public enterprise and the developing
    world. - 1984.
    (001014)
----The role of multilateral development
    finance institutions in promoting and
    financing joint ventures. - 1986.
    (000252)
----Selecting a foreign partner for
    technology transfer. - 1984.
    (001459)
----State enterprise-multinational
    corporation joint ventures: how well do
    they meet both partners' needs? - 1983.
    (001632)
----Strategies for structuring joint
    ventures: a negotiations planning
    paradigm. - 1984.
    (001560)
----Strategies for joint venture success. -
    1983.
    (001600)
----Transnational corporations in world
    development. - 1983.
    (000102)
----Triad power. - 1985.
    (001686)
----UNCTC bibliography, 1974-1987. - 1988.
    (002695)
----Vertical integration and joint ventures
    in the aluminum industry. - 1983.
    (000636)

JOINT VENTURES--AFRICA.
----Investment in ACP states. - 1987.
    (001004)

JOINT VENTURES--ARAB COUNTRIES.
----Arab comparative and commercial law. -
    1987.
    (002223)

JOINT VENTURES--ARAB COUNTRIES (continued)
----Arab joint ventures. - 1986.
   (001137)
----The Arab world is still importing. -
   1987.
   (001134)

JOINT VENTURES--ARGENTINA.
----Joint venture y sociedad. - 1984.
   (001602)
----Joint ventures of public enterprises in
   Argentina with other developing
   countries. - 1984.
   (001657)

JOINT VENTURES--ASIA.
----Joint ventures in Asien. - 1983.
   (001597)
----New business strategies for developing
   Asia, 1983-1990. - 1984.
   (000498)

JOINT VENTURES--AUSTRALIA.
----The mineral and petroleum joint venture
   in Australia. - 1986.
   (000588)

JOINT VENTURES--BRAZIL.
----New forms of overseas investment by
   developing countries : the case of
   India, Korea and Brazil. - 1986.
   (001616)
----Politica industrial, joint ventures e
   exportaçoes. - 1986.
   (001658)

JOINT VENTURES--BULGARIA.
----East-West joint ventures. - 1988.
   (001570)

JOINT VENTURES--BURUNDI.
----Manuel de procedures contractuelles
   susceptibles d'être mise en oeuvre par
   les contrats internationaux concernant
   la realisation de projets industriels. -
   1984.
   (002417)

JOINT VENTURES--CANADA.
----Public and private returns from joint
   venture research: an example from
   agriculture. - 1986.
   (001650)

JOINT VENTURES--CARIBBEAN REGION.
----Investment in ACP states. - 1987.
   (001004)

JOINT VENTURES--CHINA.
----Business opportunities in China. - 1984.
   (000999)
----China : new provisions to encourage
   foreign investment. - 1987.
   (002313)
----China adopts law on foreign enterprises.
   - 1986.
   (002294)
----China special economic zones in
   perspective. - 1986.
   (002397)
----China strategies. - 1986.
   (001037)

----The China trade: making the deal/the
   China trade: making the deal work. -
   1986.
   (001845)
----China's special economic zones. - 1983.
   (002381)
----China's trade, tax and investment laws
   and regulations. - 1984.
   (002189)
----Chinese solutions to legal problems. -
   1987.
   (002295)
----Chung wai ho tzu ching ying ch'i yeh fa
   chi ch'i shih shih ching yen ch'ien
   t'an. - 1983.
   (002190)
----Chung-kuo tui wai shui wu shou ts'e. -
   1983.
   (001704)
----Eight years of the open policy. - 1987.
   (001051)
----Foreign direct investment in the
   People's Republic of China. - 1988.
   (000191)
----Foreign investment law in the People's
   Republic of China. - 1987.
   (002299)
----Foreign trade, investment and the law in
   the People's Republic of China. - 1985.
   (002211)
----Formation of contract and contract law
   through multinational joint ventures. -
   1983.
   (002435)
----Guide to China's foreign economic
   relations and trade. - 1983.
   (001806)
----Investitions- und
   Kooperationsmöglichkeit "Equity joint
   venture" in der Volksrepublik China. -
   1986.
   (002199)
----The joint venture and related contract
   laws of mainland China and Taiwan. -
   1987.
   (002278)
----Joint ventures in China. - 1986.
   (002281)
----Joint ventures in the People's Republic
   of China. - 1985.
   (001647)
----Joint ventures in the PRC. - 1987.
   (000478)
----Legal aspects of joint ventures in
   China. - 1986.
   (002178)
----Like bamboo shoots after a rain :
   exploiting the Chinese law and new
   regulations on Sino-foreign joint
   ventures. - 1987.
   (002298)
----The new legal framework for joint
   ventures in China. - 1984.
   (002282)
----The open policy at work. - 1985.
   (001072)
----Partnership with China. - 1986.
   (001035)
----La politique chinoise d'ouverture. -
   1983.
   (002186)

JOINT VENTURES--CHINA (continued)
----Realities confronting China's foreign
    investment policy. - 1984.
      (002292)
----Singapore's role in China's offshore oil
    venture. - 1985.
      (000608)
----Sino-Indian economic relations. - 1984.
      (000307)
----Strategies for joint ventures in the
    People's Republic of China. - 1987.
      (001610)
----Tax aspects of doing business with the
    People's Republic of China. - 1984.
      (001713)
----Taxation of foreign business and
    investment in the People's Republic of
    China. - 1987.
      (001708)
----To open wider, or to close again :
    China's foreign investment policies and
    laws. - 1984.
      (002163)
----The training component. - 1986.
      (001920)
----Trends and issues in foreign direct
    investment and related flows. - 1985.
      (000192)

JOINT VENTURES--COLOMBIA.
----La asociación por partes de interes en
    Colombia. - 1983.
      (001614)
----Los contratos petroleros. - 1984.
      (002454)

JOINT VENTURES--CZECHOSLOVAKIA.
----East-West joint ventures. - 1988.
      (001570)

JOINT VENTURES--EAST ASIA.
----Entrepreneurial cooperation between
    industrialized countries and the
    developing countries in East and
    South-East Asia. - 1985.
      (001649)

JOINT VENTURES--EASTERN EUROPE.
----East-West joint ventures. - 1988.
      (001570)
----Equity cooperation ventures (ECV)
    domiciled in the socialist countries :
    trends and patterns. - 1986.
      (001603)
----Un exemple d'investissement du CAEM :
    liste des sociétés mixtes établies dans
    les pays en développement. - 1987.
      (000284)
----Expectations and results of
    contractual joint ventures by US and UK
    MNCs in Eastern Europe. - 1984.
      (001623)
----Joint-ventures in Eastern Europe. - 1984.
      (001173)
----Multinational companies and the COMECON
    countries. - 1986.
      (001177)
----Pravovye formy organizatsii sovmestnykh
    proizvodstv stran-chlenov SEV. - 1985.
      (002157)
----Trends and issues in foreign direct
    investment and related flows. - 1985.
      (000192)

----Western direct investment in centrally
    planned economies. - 1986.
      (000159)
----101 checklists for success in East
    European markets. - 1984.
      (001779)

JOINT VENTURES--EGYPT.
----Egypt's experience in regulating
    technology imports. - 1987.
      (001514)

JOINT VENTURES--EUROPE.
----Becoming a triad power: the new global
    corporation. - 1986.
      (000500)
----Industrial collaboration with Japan. -
    1986.
      (001648)
----Sources of joint venture information and
    assistance in the United States and
    Europe. - 1983.
      (001617)

JOINT VENTURES--GERMANY, FEDERAL REPUBLIC OF.
----Abhangigkeit und Konzernzugehorigkeit
    von Gemeinschaftsunternehmen. - 1985.
      (002239)
----Die Steuerung auslandischer
    Tochtergesellschaften. - 1983.
      (000400)

JOINT VENTURES--GULF STATES.
----Economic co-operation of the Arab Gulf
    States. - 1986.
      (001133)
----A historical perspective of U.S.-GCC
    economic and financial interdependence.
    - 1987.
      (000143)

JOINT VENTURES--HUNGARY.
----East-West joint ventures. - 1988.
      (001570)
----Economic associations in Hungary with
    foreign participation. - 1986.
      (001606)
----Les expériences et possibilités récentes
    concernant les sociétés mixtes de
    Hongrie. - 1987.
      (001169)
----Gemischte Unternehmen in Ungarn. - 1987.
      (001170)
----Joint ventures in Hungary. - 1987.
      (001171)
----A muködo toke becsalogatása
    Magyarországra : nyugati szemszögbol. -
    1987.
      (001608)
----Up-to-date rules of joint ventures in
    Hungary. - 1986.
      (001537)
----Utmutato kulfoldi reszvetellel mukodo
    gazdasagi tarsulas alapitasahoz es
    mukodtetesehez. - 1984.
      (001186)
----Egy vegyesvállalat története az
    alapítástól a Kezdeti sikerekig :
    esettanulmány a Sancella Hungary
    Kft-röl. - 1987.
      (001191)

JOINT VENTURES--HUNGARY (continued)
----Vegyesvallalatok mukodesi feltetelei
    Magyarorszagon. - 1986.
      (002280)

JOINT VENTURES--INDIA.
----Indo-U.S. cooperation in business and
    industry, 1986. - 1986.
      (002675)
----Industrial distribution of Indian
    exports and joint ventures abroad. -
    1985.
      (000316)
----Joint ventures abroad. - 1983.
      (001592)
----Joint ventures abroad. - 1984.
      (001528)
----New forms of overseas investment by
    developing countries : the case of
    India, Korea and Brazil. - 1986.
      (001616)
----Sino-Indian economic relations. - 1984.
      (000307)

JOINT VENTURES--INDONESIA.
----Japanese direct investment in ASEAN. -
    1983.
      (000171)

JOINT VENTURES--ITALY.
----Le associazioni temporanee di imprese. -
    1983.
      (001562)
----New forms of international technology
    transfer by Italian enterprises to
    developing countries. - 1984.
      (001474)
----La responsabilita contrattuale degli
    appaltatori in joint venture. - 1984.
      (001594)

JOINT VENTURES--JAPAN.
----The Asianization of British industry. -
    1983.
      (000204)
----Becoming a triad power: the new global
    corporation. - 1986.
      (000500)
----Doing business in Japan. - 1986.
      (001809)
----Industrial collaboration with Japan. -
    1986.
      (001648)
----International corporate linkages. - 1987.
      (002430)
----Japanese direct investment in ASEAN. -
    1983.
      (000171)
----New patterns in the formation of US/
    Japanese cooperative ventures: the role
    of technology. - 1987.
      (001622)
----Planning a joint venture for the
    Japanese market. - 1987.
      (000508)
----What trade war? - 1987.
      (000481)

JOINT VENTURES--JORDAN.
----Companies in Jordan and Saudi Arabia. -
    1984.
      (002643)

JOINT VENTURES--LATIN AMERICA.
----Measures strengthening the negotiating
    capacity of Governments in their
    relations with transnational
    corporations. - 1983.
      (002461)
----The use and promotion of consultancy
    joint ventures by public entities in
    Latin America. - 1985.
      (000834)

JOINT VENTURES--MAURITANIA.
----Towards an evaluative study of joint
    venture projects with socio-economic
    indicators. - 1983.
      (001555)

JOINT VENTURES--MEXICO.
----The foreign investment transaction in
    Mexico. - 1985.
      (002260)
----Joint ventures in Mexico. - 1984.
      (001631)

JOINT VENTURES--MIDDLE EAST.
----Internationale Produktionskooperation im
    Vorderen Orient. - 1983.
      (001142)
----Major causes of joint-venture failures
    in the Middle East: the case of Iran. -
    1983.
      (001640)

JOINT VENTURES--NIGERIA.
----Contractual forms in the oil industry. -
    1986.
      (002441)

JOINT VENTURES--PACIFIC OCEAN REGION.
----Investment in ACP states. - 1987.
      (001004)

JOINT VENTURES--POLAND.
----East-West joint ventures. - 1988.
      (001570)
----Industrial cooperation between Poland
    and the West. - 1985.
      (001576)
----Neue joint-venture-Gesetzgebung in
    Polen. - 1986.
      (002174)

JOINT VENTURES--REPUBLIC OF KOREA.
----Les joint ventures en Corée du Sud. -
    1986.
      (002436)
----Korean contractors in Saudi Arabia. -
    1986.
      (001139)
----New forms of overseas investment by
    developing countries : the case of
    India, Korea and Brazil. - 1986.
      (001616)
----Riding a tiger : joint ventures under
    South Korea's new Foreign Capital
    Inducement Act. - 1985.
      (002290)

JOINT VENTURES--ROMANIA.
----East-West joint ventures. - 1988.
      (001570)

JOINT VENTURES--SAUDI ARABIA.
----Companies in Jordan and Saudi Arabia. -
    1984.
      (002643)
----A guide to establishing joint ventures
    in Saudi Arabia. - 1985.
      (001807)
----Investment and joint-venture experiences
    in Saudi Arabia. - 1985.
      (001526)
----Joint ventures in the Kingdom of Saudi
    Arabia. - 1985.
      (001655)
----Korean contractors in Saudi Arabia. -
    1986.
      (001139)
----Service agents regulation and related
    laws affecting foreign companies in
    Saudi Arabia. - 1983.
      (002182)

JOINT VENTURES--SINGAPORE.
----Singapore's role in China's offshore oil
    venture. - 1985.
      (000608)

JOINT VENTURES--SOUTH ASIA.
----Industrial cooperation in regional
    economic groupings among developing
    countries and lessons for SAARC. - 1987.
      (001009)

JOINT VENTURES--SOUTHEAST ASIA.
----Entrepreneurial cooperation between
    industrialized countries and the
    developing countries in East and
    South-East Asia. - 1985.
      (001649)
----Joint fishing ventures. - 1983.
      (000570)
----Taming troubled waters. - 1986.
      (002453)

JOINT VENTURES--SWEDEN.
----Underskott vid joint venture- och annan
    verksamhet i utlandet, m.m. - 1985.
      (001760)

JOINT VENTURES--TAIWAN (CHINA).
----The joint venture and related contract
    laws of mainland China and Taiwan. -
    1987.
      (002278)

JOINT VENTURES--TUNISIA.
----Tunisie : l'Agence de promotion des
    investissements. - 1987.
      (002357)

JOINT VENTURES--UNITED ARAB EMIRATES.
----The UAE and the joint-venture
    opportunity. - 1985.
      (001530)

JOINT VENTURES--UNITED KINGDOM.
----The Asianization of British industry. -
    1983.
      (000204)
----Expectations and results of
    contractual joint ventures by US and UK
    MNCs in Eastern Europe. - 1984.
      (001623)
----Joint ventures. - 1983.
      (001589)

JOINT VENTURES--UNITED STATES.
----Acquisitions and joint ventures among
    large corporations. - 1985.
      (001653)
----Alliance politics and economics. - 1987.
      (000719)
----Antitrust policy and joint research and
    development ventures. - 1984.
      (002356)
----The Arab world is still importing. -
    1987.
      (001134)
----Becoming a triad power: the new global
    corporation. - 1986.
      (000500)
----Cooperative research and development. -
    1984.
      (001630)
----East-West joint ventures. - 1988.
      (001570)
----Evidence on joint venture formation for
    offshore oil lease sales. - 1983.
      (000592)
----Expectations and results of
    contractual joint ventures by US and UK
    MNCs in Eastern Europe. - 1984.
      (001623)
----Foreign investment in United States oil
    and gas ventures. - 1987.
      (000606)
----The funding of high technology ventures.
    - 1983.
      (000412)
----A historical perspective of U.S.-GCC
    economic and financial interdependence.
    - 1987.
      (000143)
----The impact of joint ventures on bidding
    for offshore oil. - 1983.
      (000604)
----Indo-U.S. cooperation in business and
    industry, 1986. - 1986.
      (002675)
----Industrial collaboration with Japan. -
    1986.
      (001648)
----International collaborative ventures in
    U.S. manufacturing. - 1988.
      (000720)
----International corporate linkages. - 1987.
      (002430)
----International joint ventures. - 1985.
      (001590)
----International joint ventures. - 1986.
      (001566)
----International joint ventures: how
    important are they? - 1987.
      (001556)
----Joint research and development
    legislation. - 1987.
      (002286)
----Joint venture partner selection. - 1988.
      (001577)
----Joint venture y sociedad. - 1984.
      (001602)
----Joint ventures. - 1987.
      (001613)
----Joint ventures. - 1985.
      (001605)
----Joint ventures and offshore oil lease
    sales. - 1985.
      (001578)

JOINT VENTURES--UNITED STATES (continued)
----Managing for joint venture success. -
    1986.
        (001587)
----A muködo toke becsalogatása
    Magyarországra : nyugati szemszögbol. -
    1987.
        (001608)
----The new attractions of corporate joint
    ventures. - 1985.
        (001612)
----New patterns in the formation of US/
    Japanese cooperative ventures: the role
    of technology. - 1987.
        (001622)
----Oil industry mergers. - 1984.
        (001652)
----Planning a joint venture for the
    Japanese market. - 1987.
        (000508)
----Quantifying the competitive effects of
    production joint ventures. - 1986.
        (001548)
----Realty joint ventures, 1986. - 1986.
        (000881)
----Riding a tiger : joint ventures under
    South Korea's new Foreign Capital
    Inducement Act. - 1985.
        (002290)
----Sources of joint venture information and
    assistance in the United States and
    Europe. - 1983.
        (001617)
----Die Steuerung auslandischer
    Tochtergesellschaften. - 1983.
        (000400)
----Venturing abroad. - 1988.
        (000376)
----Vertical integration and joint ventures
    in the aluminum industry. - 1983.
        (001642)
----What trade war? - 1987.
        (000481)

JOINT VENTURES--URUGUAY.
----La transformación de sociedad irregular
    en sociedad regular. - 1984.
        (001545)

JOINT VENTURES--USSR.
----Anderungen im sowjetischen
    Aussenwirtschaftssystem zu Beginn des
    Jahres 1987. - 1987.
        (001176)
----East-West joint ventures. - 1988.
        (001570)
----Foreign trade with the USSR. - 1987.
        (001774)
----The new Soviet joint venture
    regulations. - 1987.
        (002202)
----La nouvelle législation soviétique sur
    les entreprises mixtes. - 1987.
        (002181)
----La réforme du commerce extérieur
    soviétique. - 1987.
        (002261)
----USSR, tendensen tot decentralisatie. -
    1987.
        (001190)

JOINT VENTURES--WESTERN ASIA.
----Trade in services : growth and balance
    of payments implications for countries
    of Western Asia. - 1987.
        (000968)

JOINT VENTURES--WESTERN EUROPE.
----East-West joint ventures. - 1988.
        (001570)
----European industry on the march. - 1987.
        (001155)
----Western direct investment in centrally
    planned economies. - 1986.
        (000159)

JOINT VENTURES--YUGOSLAVIA.
----Direct foreign investment in Yugoslavia.
    - 1986.
        (000183)
----An economic analysis of Yugoslav joint
    ventures. - 1983.
        (001563)
----Industrial co-operation and investment
    in Yugoslavia. - 1986.
        (001540)
----Joint ventures in Yugoslav industry. -
    1985.
        (001535)
----Joint ventures in Yugoslavia: comment/
    reply. - 1984.
        (001533)
----Joint ventures in Yugoslavia:
    opportunities and constraints. - 1985.
        (001534)
----Joint venturing in Yugoslavia. - 1987.
        (001536)
----Überlegungen zur jugoslawischen Joint
    Venture-Gesetzgebung. - 1986.
        (002268)
----Visi oblici privredne saradnje izmethu
    domacih organizacija udruzenog rada i
    stranih lica. - 1984.
        (001182)

JOINT VENTURES--ZIMBABWE.
----H.J. Heinz success in Zimbabwe. - 1987.
        (000279)

JORDAN--CORPORATION LAW.
----Companies in Jordan and Saudi Arabia. -
    1984.
        (002643)

JORDAN--JOINT VENTURES.
----Companies in Jordan and Saudi Arabia. -
    1984.
        (002643)

JUDICIAL ASSISTANCE.
----L'accès des tribunaux arbitraux à
    l'entraide judiciaire internationale. -
    1984.
        (002483)
----International co-operation in tax
    matters : guidelines for international
    co-operation against the evasion and
    avoidance of taxes (with special
    reference to taxes on income, profits,
    capital and capital gains). - 1984.
        (001724)

JURISDICTION.
----ICSID's emerging jurisprudence. - 1986.
    (002562)
----International income taxation and
    developing countries. - 1988.
    (001759)
----The jurisdiction of an international
    commercial arbitrator. - 1986.
    (002563)

JURISDICTION--UNITED STATES.
----Jurisdiction over foreign governments. -
    1986.
    (002347)
----United States jurisdiction over foreign
    subsidiaries. - 1983.
    (002355)

JURISPRUDENCE--WESTERN EUROPE.
----La licence de marque et le droit
    européen de la concurrence. - 1984.
    (001448)

KEDAH (MALAYSIA)--INDUSTRY.
----Transnational corporations in Kedah,
    West Malaysia. - 1985.
    (001061)

KEDAH (MALAYSIA)--TRANSNATIONAL CORPORATIONS.
----Transnational corporations in Kedah,
    West Malaysia. - 1985.
    (001061)

KENYA--AIR TRANSPORT.
----The role of transnational corporations
    in hotel and tourism industry in
    selected PTA member countries. - 1986.
    (000782) (000936)

KENYA--CAPITAL MOVEMENTS.
----Labor, capital, and management slack in
    multinational and local firms in Kenyan
    manufacturing. - 1986.
    (001026)

KENYA--CORPORATE PLANNING.
----Corporate strategy and employment
    relations in multinational corporations:
    some evidence from Kenya and Malaysia. -
    1983.
    (001902)

KENYA--EMPLOYMENT.
----Multinational enterprises, transfer of
    managerial know-how, technology choice
    and employment effects. - 1983.
    (001436)

KENYA--EMPLOYMENT POLICY.
----Corporate strategy and employment
    relations in multinational corporations:
    some evidence from Kenya and Malaysia. -
    1983.
    (001902)

KENYA--FOREIGN INVESTMENTS.
----National legislation and regulations
    relating to transnational corporations.
    Volume 4. - 1986.
    (002253)

KENYA--HOTEL INDUSTRY.
----The role of transnational corporations
    in hotel and tourism industry in
    selected PTA member countries. - 1986.
    (000782) (000936)

KENYA--LABOUR MOBILITY.
----Labor, capital, and management slack in
    multinational and local firms in Kenyan
    manufacturing. - 1986.
    (001026)

KENYA--LAWS AND REGULATIONS.
----National legislation and regulations
    relating to transnational corporations.
    Volume 4. - 1986.
    (002253)

KENYA--MANAGEMENT DEVELOPMENT.
----Labor, capital, and management slack in
    multinational and local firms in Kenyan
    manufacturing. - 1986.
    (001026)

KENYA--PHARMACEUTICAL INDUSTRY.
----Transnational corporations in the
    pharmaceutical industry of developing
    countries. - 1984.
    (000749)

KENYA--STATISTICAL DATA.
----The role of transnational corporations
    in hotel and tourism industry in
    selected PTA member countries. - 1986.
    (000782) (000936)

KENYA--TECHNOLOGY TRANSFER.
----Multinational enterprises, transfer of
    managerial know-how, technology choice
    and employment effects. - 1983.
    (001436)

KENYA--TOURISM DEVELOPMENT.
----The role of transnational corporations
    in hotel and tourism industry in
    selected PTA member countries. - 1986.
    (000782) (000936)

KENYA--TOURISM STATISTICS.
----The role of transnational corporations
    in hotel and tourism industry in
    selected PTA member countries. - 1986.
    (000782) (000936)

KENYA--TRANSNATIONAL CORPORATIONS.
----Corporate strategy and employment
    relations in multinational corporations:
    some evidence from Kenya and Malaysia. -
    1983.
    (001902)
----Labor, capital, and management slack in
    multinational and local firms in Kenyan
    manufacturing. - 1986.
    (001026)
----Multinational enterprises, transfer of
    managerial know-how, technology choice
    and employment effects. - 1983.
    (001436)
----National legislation and regulations
    relating to transnational corporations.
    Volume 4. - 1986.
    (002253)

KENYA--TRANSNATIONAL CORPORATIONS (continued)
----The role of transnational corporations
    in hotel and tourism industry in
    selected PTA member countries. - 1986.
    (000782) (000936)

KNOW-HOW.
----International flows of technology. -
    1986.
    (001517)

KOMPANIIA ZINGER.
----American enterprise in foreign markets.
    - 1984.
    (000526)

KUWAIT--ARBITRATION.
----State contracts and oil expropriations.
    - 1984.
    (002577)

KUWAIT--BALANCE OF PAYMENTS.
----Impact of the operations of
    transnational corporations on
    development in Kuwait. - 1987.
    (001143)

KUWAIT--BUSINESS ENTERPRISES.
----Impact of the operations of
    transnational corporations on
    development in Kuwait. - 1987.
    (001143)

KUWAIT--COMMERCIAL ARBITRATION.
----Host countries permanent sovereignty
    over national resources and protection
    of foreign investors. - 1983.
    (002566)

KUWAIT--COMPENSATION.
----State contracts and oil expropriations.
    - 1984.
    (002577)

KUWAIT--EMPLOYMENT.
----Impact of the operations of
    transnational corporations on
    development in Kuwait. - 1987.
    (001143)

KUWAIT--EXPROPRIATION.
----Host countries permanent sovereignty
    over national resources and protection
    of foreign investors. - 1983.
    (002566)
----State contracts and oil expropriations.
    - 1984.
    (002577)

KUWAIT--FEASIBILITY STUDIES.
----Operations of multinational corporations
    and local enterprises in Arab countries.
    - 1985.
    (001141)

KUWAIT--FOREIGN DIRECT INVESTMENTS.
----Impact of the operations of
    transnational corporations on
    development in Kuwait. - 1987.
    (001143)

KUWAIT--FOREIGN INVESTMENTS.
----National legislation and regulations
    relating to transnational corporations.
    Volume 4. - 1986.
    (002253)
----State contracts and oil expropriations.
    - 1984.
    (002577)

KUWAIT--FOREIGN TRADE.
----Impact of the operations of
    transnational corporations on
    development in Kuwait. - 1987.
    (001143)

KUWAIT--GROSS DOMESTIC PRODUCT.
----Impact of the operations of
    transnational corporations on
    development in Kuwait. - 1987.
    (001143)

KUWAIT--GROSS NATIONAL PRODUCT.
----Impact of the operations of
    transnational corporations on
    development in Kuwait. - 1987.
    (001143)

KUWAIT--INDUSTRIAL RESEARCH.
----Operations of multinational corporations
    and local enterprises in Arab countries.
    - 1985.
    (001141)

KUWAIT--LAWS AND REGULATIONS.
----Impact of the operations of
    transnational corporations on
    development in Kuwait. - 1987.
    (001143)
----National legislation and regulations
    relating to transnational corporations.
    Volume 4. - 1986.
    (002253)

KUWAIT--OIL AND GAS LEASES.
----Droit international et contrats d'états.
    - 1983.
    (002482)

KUWAIT--PETROLEUM INDUSTRY.
----Impact of the operations of
    transnational corporations on
    development in Kuwait. - 1987.
    (001143)
----State contracts and oil expropriations.
    - 1984.
    (002577)

KUWAIT--PRICES.
----Impact of the operations of
    transnational corporations on
    development in Kuwait. - 1987.
    (001143)

KUWAIT--PUBLIC ENTERPRISES.
----Impact of the operations of
    transnational corporations on
    development in Kuwait. - 1987.
    (001143)

KUWAIT--STATISTICAL DATA.
----Impact of the operations of
transnational corporations on
development in Kuwait. - 1987.
(001143)

KUWAIT--TAX REVENUES.
----Impact of the operations of
transnational corporations on
development in Kuwait. - 1987.
(001143)

KUWAIT--TECHNOLOGY TRANSFER.
----Impact of the operations of
transnational corporations on
development in Kuwait. - 1987.
(001143)

KUWAIT--TRANSNATIONAL CORPORATIONS.
----Impact of the operations of
transnational corporations on
development in Kuwait. - 1987.
(001143)
----National legislation and regulations
relating to transnational corporations.
Volume 4. - 1986.
(002253)
----Operations of multinational corporations
and local enterprises in Arab countries.
- 1985.
(001141)

LABOUR.
----Transnatsional'nye korporatsii i
rabochii klass. - 1987.
(001953)

LABOUR COSTS.
----Why are services cheaper in the poor
countries? - 1984.
(000813)

LABOUR DISPUTES--AUSTRALIA.
----Mediation, conciliation and arbitration
: an international comparison of
Australia, Great Britain and the United
States. - 1987.
(002476)

LABOUR DISPUTES--UNITED KINGDOM.
----Mediation, conciliation and arbitration
: an international comparison of
Australia, Great Britain and the United
States. - 1987.
(002476)

LABOUR DISPUTES--UNITED STATES.
----Mediation, conciliation and arbitration
: an international comparison of
Australia, Great Britain and the United
States. - 1987.
(002476)

LABOUR EXPLOITATION--COSTA RICA.
----La industria de la maquila y la
explotación de la fuerza de trabajo de
la mujer. - 1984.
(001900)

LABOUR LAW.
----Transnatsional'nye korporatsii i
burzhuaznoe trudovoe pravo. - 1985.
(001946) (002230)

LABOUR LAW--MAURITIUS.
----Aspects of labour law and relations in
selected export processing zones. - 1984.
(001895)

LABOUR LAW--PAKISTAN.
----Aspects of labour law and relations in
selected export processing zones. - 1984.
(001895)

LABOUR LAW--PHILIPPINES.
----Aspects of labour law and relations in
selected export processing zones. - 1984.
(001895)

LABOUR LAW--SRI LANKA.
----Aspects of labour law and relations in
selected export processing zones. - 1984.
(001895)

LABOUR LEGISLATIONS--OMAN.
----Impact of the operations of
transnational corporations on
development in the Sultanate of Oman. -
1988.
(001144)

LABOUR MARKET.
----Les services : nouvelle donne pour
l'emploi. - 1987.
(000961)

LABOUR MARKET--JAPAN.
----Employment and competitiveness in the
European Community. - 1984.
(001929)

LABOUR MARKET--UNITED STATES.
----Employment and competitiveness in the
European Community. - 1984.
(001929)

LABOUR MARKET--WESTERN EUROPE.
----Employment and competitiveness in the
European Community. - 1984.
(001929)

LABOUR MOBILITY--KENYA.
----Labor, capital, and management slack in
multinational and local firms in Kenyan
manufacturing. - 1986.
(001026)

LABOUR POLICY.
----Social and labour practices of
multinational enterprises in the
textiles, clothing and footwear
industries. - 1984.
(001922)

LABOUR PRODUCTIVITY.
----L'expansion des services à productivité
stable. - 1987.
(001917)
----Foreign investment, technical efficiency
and structural change. - 1983.
(001085)

LABOUR PRODUCTIVITY--UNITED STATES.
----Industrial renaissance : producing a
competitive future for America. - 1983.
(000300)

LABOUR RELATIONS.
----Corporation, technological gaps and
    growth in OECD countries. - 1987.
    (001438)
----Export processing zones. - 1983.
    (002372)
----Issues in management-labour relations in
    the 1990s. - 1985.
    (001914)
----Multinational enterprises and the OECD
    industrial relations guidelines. - 1983.
    (001963)
----Multinationales et droits de l'homme. -
    1984.
    (001876)
----The OECD guidelines for multinational
    enterprises and labour relations,
    1982-1984. - 1985.
    (001961)
----Les sociétés multinationales. - 1985.
    (000021)
----Technological change. - 1985.
    (001499)
----Trends in the internationalisation of
    production. - 1986.
    (002597)
----Tripartite Declaration of Principles
    Concerning Multinational Enterprises and
    Social Policy. - 1977.
    (002013)

LABOUR RELATIONS--JAPAN.
----Technology strategy and industrial
    relations: case studies of Japanese
    multinationals in the United States. -
    1983.
    (002599)

LABOUR RELATIONS--MAURITIUS.
----Aspects of labour law and relations in
    selected export processing zones. - 1984.
    (001895)

LABOUR RELATIONS--NETHERLANDS.
----Michelin : een zwart profiel : over
    werken in een bandenfabriek in Den
    Bosch. - 1984.
    (000289)

LABOUR RELATIONS--PAKISTAN.
----Aspects of labour law and relations in
    selected export processing zones.. - 1984.
    (001895)

LABOUR RELATIONS--PHILIPPINES.
----Aspects of labour law and relations in
    selected export processing zones. - 1984.
    (001895)

LABOUR RELATIONS--SOUTH AFRICA.
----Business in the shadow of apartheid :
    U.S. firms in South Africa. - 1985.
    (001194)
----Transnational corporations in South
    Africa and Namibia : United Nations
    public hearings. Volume 3, Statements
    and submissions. - 1987.
    (001215)

LABOUR RELATIONS--SRI LANKA.
----Aspects of labour law and relations in
    selected export processing zones. - 1984.
    (001895)

LABOUR RELATIONS--UNITED STATES.
----Technology strategy and industrial
    relations: case studies of Japanese
    multinationals in the United States. -
    1983.
    (002599)

LABOUR SUPPLY.
----Employment and technological choice of
    multinational enterprises in developing
    countries. - 1983.
    (001909)
----Las empresas transnacionales. - 1984.
    (001013)
----Multinational corporations. - 1986.
    (000058)
----Multinationals square off against
    Central American workers. - 1985.
    (001923)
----Rabochii klass protiv
    transnatsional'nykh korporatsii. - 1984.
    (001278)
----Recommendation on development
    cooperation and employment in developing
    countries. - 1984.
    (001911)

LABOUR SUPPLY--BRAZIL.
----Technological spill-overs and manpower
    training: a comparative analysis of
    multinational and national enterprises
    in Brazilian manufacturing. - 1986.
    (001899)

LABOUR SUPPLY--GERMANY, FEDERAL REPUBLIC OF.
----The development of employment in
    multinational enterprises in the Federal
    Republic of Germany. - 1985.
    (001912)

LABOUR SUPPLY--GHANA.
----Employment and multinational enterprises
    in export processing zones. - 1984.
    (001886)

LABOUR SUPPLY--LIBERIA.
----Employment and multinational enterprises
    in export processing zones. - 1984.
    (001886)
----Multinationals and employment in a West
    African sub-region. - 1984.
    (001904)

LABOUR SUPPLY--NIGERIA.
----Third World multinationals. - 1983.
    (000361)

LABOUR SUPPLY--SIERRA LEONE.
----Multinationals and employment in a West
    African sub-region. - 1984.
    (001904)

LABOUR SUPPLY--SOUTH AFRICA.
----U.S. firms and black labor in South
    Africa: creating a structure for change.
    - 1986.
    (001195)

LABOUR SUPPLY--SWEDEN.
----Sysselsattningsstrukturen i
    internationella foretag. - 1983.
    (001165)

LABOUR SUPPLY--UNITED STATES.
----American multinationals and American
    employment. - 1983.
        (001890)
----U.S. firms and black labor in South
    Africa: creating a structure for change.
    - 1986.
        (001195)

LAND RIGHTS--AUSTRALIA.
----Indigenous resource rights and mining
    companies in North America and
    Australia. - 1986.
        (000616)

LAND RIGHTS--NORTH AMERICA.
----Indigenous resource rights and mining
    companies in North America and
    Australia. - 1986.
        (000616)

LAND TENURE--AUSTRALIA.
----Aborigines and mining companies in
    Northern Australia. - 1983.
        (001874)

LATIN AMERICA--AFFILIATE CORPORATIONS.
----The debt crisis and bank lending to
    subsidiaries of transnational
    corporations in Latin America. - 1984.
        (000219)

LATIN AMERICA--AGRIBUSINESS.
----Agricultura y alimentos en América
    Latina. - 1985.
        (000562)
----Transnacionalizacion y desarrollo
    agropecuario en America Latina. - 1984.
        (000574)

LATIN AMERICA--AGROINDUSTRY.
----Las nuevas formas de inversión
    internacional en la agroindustria
    latinoamericana. - 1986.
        (000569)

LATIN AMERICA--ALLOYS.
----La industria siderúrgica
    latinoamericana. - 1984.
        (000601)

LATIN AMERICA--ARBITRAL AWARDS.
----International commercial arbitration. -
    1983.
        (002538)
----International commercial arbitration in
    Latin America. - 1986.
        (002546)

LATIN AMERICA--AUTOMOBILE INDUSTRY.
----Transnational corporations and the Latin
    American automobile industry. - 1987.
        (000701)

LATIN AMERICA--BALANCE OF PAYMENTS.
----Banco de datos sobre inversión
    extranjera directa en América Latina y
    el Caribe : información de los países
    receptores y de organismos regionales y
    subregionales, t. 2. - 1987.
        (000193)

----Las empresas transnacionales y la
    inversión extranjera directa en la
    primera mitad de los años ochenta. -
    1987.
        (000194)

LATIN AMERICA--BANK LOANS.
----The debt crisis and bank lending to
    subsidiaries of transnational
    corporations in Latin America. - 1984.
        (000219)
----Foreign direct investment in Latin
    America. - 1986.
        (000190)

LATIN AMERICA--BIBLIOGRAPHIES.
----Transnational corporations and
    industrial transformation in Latin
    America. - 1984.
        (001099)

LATIN AMERICA--BIG BUSINESS.
----Small nations, giant firms. - 1987.
        (001091)

LATIN AMERICA--BUSINESS ENTERPRISES.
----Dun's Latin America's top 25,000. -
    1984-   .
        (002636)

LATIN AMERICA--CAPITAL INVESTMENTS.
----Regulación de la inversión extranjera en
    América Latina y el Caribe. - 1984.
        (002194)

LATIN AMERICA--CAPITAL MOVEMENTS.
----Las empresas transnacionales y la
    inversión extranjera directa en la
    primera mitad de los años ochenta. -
    1987.
        (000194)
----Los flujos de capital hacia América
    Latina y el Caribe, y el financiamiento
    del desarrollo, en los años venideros. -
    1985.
        (001231)
----Transnacionalización y periferia
    semindustrializada. - 1983.
        (001017)

LATIN AMERICA--CAPITALISM.
----Capitalismo neocolonial. - 1983.
        (001109)

LATIN AMERICA--CHARCOAL.
----La industria siderúrgica
    latinoamericana. - 1984.
        (000601)

LATIN AMERICA--COAL.
----La industria siderúrgica
    latinoamericana. - 1984.
        (000601)

LATIN AMERICA--COMMERCIAL ARBITRATION.
----International commercial arbitration in
    Latin America. - 1986.
        (002546)

LATIN AMERICA--COMMERCIAL LAW.
----Latin America at a glance. - 1986.
        (001821)

LATIN AMERICA--COMMUNICATION POLICY.
----Trade and foreign direct investment in
data services. - 1986.
(000948)

LATIN AMERICA--COMPARATIVE ANALYSIS.
----Evaluating differences in technological
activity between transnational and
domestic firms in Latin America. - 1986.
(001431)

LATIN AMERICA--CONSULTANTS.
----The use and promotion of consultancy
joint ventures by public entities in
Latin America. - 1985.
(000834)

LATIN AMERICA--CONTRACTS.
----Petroleum service contracts in
Argentina, Brazil and Colombia : issues
arising from their legal nature. - 1987.
(002422)

LATIN AMERICA--CORPORATE MERGERS.
----International law of take-overs and
mergers. - 1986.
(001573)

LATIN AMERICA--CORPORATION LAW.
----International law of take-overs and
mergers. - 1986.
(001573)

LATIN AMERICA--DATA PROCESSING.
----Trade and foreign direct investment in
data services. - 1986.
(000948)

LATIN AMERICA--DEBT RENEGOTIATION.
----Evaluación de los criterios ortodoxos de
reprogramación de la deuda externa. -
1984.
(000225)

LATIN AMERICA--DEBT SERVICING.
----Evaluación de los criterios ortodoxos de
reprogramación de la deuda externa. -
1984.
(000225)
----Foreign direct investment in Latin
America. - 1986.
(000190)
----Transnacionalización y periferia
semindustrializada. - 1983.
(001017)

LATIN AMERICA--DEVELOPING COUNTRIES.
----The international debt crisis and the
banks. - 1985.
(000227)
----International trading companies for
developing countries-Latin America. -
1984.
(000838)

LATIN AMERICA--DEVELOPMENT FINANCE.
----Los flujos de capital hacia América
Latina y el Caribe, y el financiamiento
del desarrollo, en los años venideros. -
1985.
(001231)

LATIN AMERICA--DIRECTORIES.
----Dun's Latin America's top 25,000. -
1984-   .
(002636)

LATIN AMERICA--DOMESTIC TRADE.
----Evaluating differences in technological
activity between transnational and
domestic firms in Latin America. - 1986.
(001431)

LATIN AMERICA--ECONOMIC CONDITIONS.
----Breves rasgos de la crisis. - 1983.
(001307)
----La crisis internacional y la América
Latina. - 1984.
(001245)
----Inostrannye monopolii v Latinskoi
Amerike. - 1983.
(001103)
----Los laberintos de la crisis. - 1984.
(001079)
----Latin America at a glance. - 1986.
(001821)
----Mezhdunarodnye monopolii v Latinskoi
Amerike. - 1986.
(001128)

LATIN AMERICA--ECONOMIC CO-OPERATION.
----Current problems of economic
integration. - 1986.
(001312)

LATIN AMERICA--ECONOMIC DEPENDENCE.
----Capitalismo neocolonial. - 1983.
(001109)
----Disfraces del coloniaje. - 1984.
(001114)
----Mezhdunarodnye monopolii v Latinskoi
Amerike. - 1986.
(001128)

LATIN AMERICA--ECONOMIC DEVELOPMENT.
----Foreign debt, direct investment, and
economic development in the Andean Pact.
- 1987.
(001110)
----Transnacionalización y desarrollo
nacional en América Latina. - 1984.
(001117)
----Transnacionalización y periferia
semindustrializada. - 1983.
(001017)

LATIN AMERICA--ECONOMIC FORECASTS.
----Latin America at a glance. - 1986.
(001821)

LATIN AMERICA--ECONOMIC GROWTH.
----The great continental divide : Asian and
Latin American countries in the world
economic crisis. - 1986.
(001299)

LATIN AMERICA--ECONOMIC INTEGRATION.
----Current problems of economic
integration. - 1986.
(001312)
----The role of transnational enterprises in
Latin American economic integration
efforts. - 1983.
(001126)

LATIN AMERICA--ECONOMIC POLICY.
----Foreign direct investment in Latin
   America. - 1986.
      (000190)
----The great continental divide : Asian and
   Latin American countries in the world
   economic crisis. - 1986.
      (001299)

LATIN AMERICA--ECONOMIC RELATIONS.
----La crisis internacional y la América
   Latina. - 1984.
      (001245)
----Grace. - 1985.
      (000276)
----Inversiones extranjeras en América
   Latina. - 1984.
      (001098)
----Transnacionalización y desarrollo
   nacional en América Latina. - 1984.
      (001117)

LATIN AMERICA--ECONOMIC STRUCTURE.
----The great continental divide : Asian and
   Latin American countries in the world
   economic crisis. - 1986.
      (001299)

LATIN AMERICA--ELECTRONIC FUNDS TRANSFER.
----Financial transfers in the MNE. - 1986.
      (000416)

LATIN AMERICA--EMPLOYMENT.
----Las empresas transnacionales y la
   inversión extranjera directa en la
   primera mitad de los años ochenta. -
   1987.
      (000194)

LATIN AMERICA--ENGINEERS.
----The use and promotion of consultancy
   joint ventures by public entities in
   Latin America. - 1985.
      (000834)

LATIN AMERICA--EXCLUSIVE ECONOMIC ZONE.
----The exclusive economic zone. - 1984.
      (002368)

LATIN AMERICA--EXPORTS.
----Banco de datos sobre inversión
   extranjera directa en América Latina y
   el Caribe : información de los países
   receptores y de organismos regionales y
   subregionales, t. 2. - 1987.
      (000193)

LATIN AMERICA--EXTERNAL DEBT.
----Crisis de endeudamiento y primeras
   redefiniciones respecto al tratamiento
   del capital extranjero en América
   Latina. - 1986.
      (000247)
----La crisis internacional y la América
   Latina. - 1984.
      (001245)
----The debt crisis and bank lending to
   subsidiaries of transnational
   corporations in Latin America. - 1984.
      (000219)
----Deuda externa, inversión extranjera y
   transferencia de tecnología en América
   Latina. - 1986.
      (001080)

----Las empresas transnacionales y la
   inversión extranjera directa en la
   primera mitad de los años ochenta. -
   1987.
      (000194)
----Foreign debt, direct investment, and
   economic development in the Andean Pact.
   - 1987.
      (001110)
----Foreign direct investment in Latin
   America. - 1986.
      (000190)
----The great continental divide : Asian and
   Latin American countries in the world
   economic crisis. - 1986.
      (001299)
----The international debt crisis and the
   banks. - 1985.
      (000227)
----Private investment in Latin America. -
   1984.
      (002460)
----El proceso de revisión de los mecanismos
   financieros de la ALADI. - 1983.
      (001248)
----Reaction to economic crisis: trade and
   finance of US firms operating in Latin
   America. - 1986.
      (000333)
----Transnacionalización y desarrollo
   nacional en América Latina. - 1984.
      (001117)
----Transnacionalización y periferia
   semindustrializada. - 1983.
      (001017)

LATIN AMERICA--FINANCIAL STATISTICS.
----Banco de datos sobre inversión
   extranjera directa en América Latina y
   el Caribe : información de los países
   receptores y de organismos regionales y
   subregionales, t. 2. - 1987.
      (000193)
----Banco de datos sobre inversión
   extranjera directa en América Latina y
   el Caribe, sobre la base de información
   de organismos multilaterales y de
   gobiernos de países de origen de la
   inversión, t. 1. - 1986.
      (000195)

LATIN AMERICA--FISCAL POLICY.
----El proceso de revisión de los mecanismos
   financieros de la ALADI. - 1983.
      (001248)

LATIN AMERICA--FOOD INDUSTRY.
----L'émpire Nestle. - 1983.
      (000283)

LATIN AMERICA--FOREIGN DIRECT INVESTMENT.
----Banco de datos sobre inversión
   extranjera directa en América Latina y
   el Caribe : información de los países
   receptores y de organismos regionales y
   subregionales, t. 2. - 1987.
      (000193)
----Banco de datos sobre inversión
   extranjera directa en América Latina y
   el Caribe, sobre la base de información
   de organismos multilaterales y de
   gobiernos de países de origen de la
   inversión, t. 1. - 1986.
      (000195)

LATIN AMERICA--FOREIGN DIRECT INVESTMENT
(continued)
----O capital transnacional e o estado. -
1985.
(002274)
----Deuda externa, inversión extranjera y
transferencia de tecnología en América
Latina. - 1986.
(001080)
----Doing business in key Latin American
markets: U.S. international executive
perceptions. - 1983.
(001824)
----Las empresas transnacionales y la
inversión extranjera directa en la
primera mitad de los años ochenta. -
1987.
(000194)
----Foreign debt, direct investment, and
economic development in the Andean Pact.
- 1987.
(001110)
----Foreign direct investment in Latin
America. - 1986.
(000190)
----Foreign investment and technology
transfer. - 1984.
(000769)
----Inostrannye monopolii v Latinskoi
Amerike. - 1983.
(001103)
----Inversiones extranjeras en América
Latina. - 1984.
(001098)
----Las inversiones extranjeras y la crisis
económica en América Latina. - 1986.
(001309)
----Inversiones nórdicas en América Latina.
- 1986.
(000206)
----Latinskaia Amerika, ekspansiia
inostrannykh monopolii. - 1984.
(001090)
----Performance requirements: the general
debate and a review of Latin American
practices. - 1983.
(002315)
----Reaction to economic crisis: trade and
finance of US firms operating in Latin
America. - 1986.
(000333)
----The relationship of MNC direct
investment to host country trade and
trade policy: some preliminary evidence.
- 1983.
(001351)
----Trade and foreign direct investment in
data services. - 1986.
(000948)
----Transnacionalización y desarrollo
nacional en América Latina. - 1984.
(001117)
----Transnatsional'nye korporatsii SShA v
Latinskoi Amerike. - 1985.
(001087)

LATIN AMERICA--FOREIGN INVESTMENTS.
----Crisis de endeudamiento y primeras
redefiniciones respecto al tratamiento
del capital extranjero en América
Latina. - 1986.
(000247)

----Entrada de capital extranjero, ahorro
interno e inversión en la América Latina
: una historia negativa y precautoria. -
1986.
(001101)
----La inversión estadounidense en el Grupo
Andino. - 1985.
(000112)
----La inversión extranjera : instrumento de
liberación o dependencia? - 1984.
(000148)
----Las inversiones extranjeras en América
Latina. - 1984.
(000162)
----Inversiones Nórdicas en América Latina.
- 1987.
(000115)
----Nueva división internacional del trabajo
y reestructuración productiva en América
Latina. - 1984.
(001264)
----Las nuevas formas de inversión
internacional en la agroindustria
latinoamericana. - 1986.
(000569)
----Private investment in Latin America. -
1984.
(002460)
----Régimen jurídico de las inversiones
extranjeras en los países de la ALADI. -
1985.
(002262)
----Los regímenes de garantía a la inversión
extranjera y su aplicabilidad en los
países de la ALADI. - 1985.
(002126)
----Regulación de la inversión extranjera en
América Latina y el Caribe. - 1984.
(002194)

LATIN AMERICA--FOREIGN LOANS.
----The international debt crisis and the
banks. - 1985.
(000227)
----El proceso de revisión de los mecanismos
financieros de la ALADI. - 1983.
(001248)

LATIN AMERICA--FOREIGN TRADE.
----Las empresas transnacionales y la
inversión extranjera directa en la
primera mitad de los años ochenta. -
1987.
(000194)
----Latin America at a glance. - 1986.
(001821)
----The relationship of MNC direct
investment to host country trade and
trade policy: some preliminary evidence.
- 1983.
(001351)
----Trade and foreign direct investment in
data services. - 1986.
(000948)

LATIN AMERICA--GOVERNMENT MONOPOLIES.
----Government control over public
enterprises in Latin America. - 1983.
(002179)

LATIN AMERICA--HOST COUNTRY RELATIONS.
----O capital transnacional e o estado. -
    1985.
        (002274)
----The relationship of MNC direct
    investment to host country trade and
    trade policy: some preliminary evidence.
    - 1983.
        (001351)

LATIN AMERICA--IMPORT PLANNING.
----Patterns of technology imports:
    interregional comparison. - 1986.
        (001483)

LATIN AMERICA--IMPORTS.
----Banco de datos sobre inversión
    extranjera directa en América Latina y
    el Caribe : información de los países
    receptores y de organismos regionales y
    subregionales, t. 2. - 1987.
        (000193)

LATIN AMERICA--INDUSTRIAL CONCENTRATION.
----Las empresas transnacionales y la
    inversión extranjera directa en la
    primera mitad de los años ochenta. -
    1987.
        (000194)

LATIN AMERICA--INDUSTRIAL CO-OPERATION.
----Current problems of economic
    integration. - 1986.
        (001312)

LATIN AMERICA--INDUSTRIAL DEVELOPMENT.
----Nueva división internacional del trabajo
    y reestructuración productiva en América
    Latina. - 1984.
        (001264)
----Transnational corporations and
    industrial transformation in Latin
    America. - 1984.
        (001099)

LATIN AMERICA--INDUSTRIAL ENTERPRISES.
----Profits, progress and poverty. - 1985.
        (001111)

LATIN AMERICA--INDUSTRIAL INSTITUTIONS.
----International trading companies for
    developing countries-Latin America. -
    1984.
        (000838)

LATIN AMERICA--INDUSTRIAL POLICY.
----Government control over public
    enterprises in Latin America. - 1983.
        (002179)

LATIN AMERICA--INFORMATION TECHNOLOGY.
----Trade and foreign direct investment in
    data services. - 1986.
        (000948)

LATIN AMERICA--INTERNATIONAL COMMERCIAL
ARBITRATION.
----International commercial arbitration. -
    1983.
        (002538)

LATIN AMERICA--INTERNATIONAL COMMERCIAL
TRANSACTIONS.
----Estados Unidos, América Latina y el
    debate internacional sobre el comercio
    de servicios. - 1986.
        (000934)
----La internacionalización de los
    servicios. - 1986.
        (000923)
----Los servicios en las transacciones
    internacionales de América Latina. -
    1986.
        (000820)

LATIN AMERICA--INTERNATIONAL DIVISION OF
LABOUR.
----Nueva división internacional del trabajo
    y reestructuración productiva en América
    Latina. - 1984.
        (001264)

LATIN AMERICA--INTERNATIONAL ECONOMIC
RELATIONS.
----Politik als Investitionsmotor? - 1985.
        (001131)

LATIN AMERICA--INTERNATIONAL TRADE.
----International trading companies for
    developing countries-Latin America. -
    1984.
        (000838)
----The transnational corporations and Latin
    America's international trade. - 1985.
        (001100)

LATIN AMERICA--INTERNATIONALISM.
----Transnational corporations and
    industrial transformation in Latin
    America. - 1984.
        (001099)

LATIN AMERICA--INVESTMENT ANALYSIS.
----Latin American investment climate. -
    198?-
        (001822)

LATIN AMERICA--INVESTMENT INSURANCE.
----Los regímenes de garantía a la inversión
    extranjera y su aplicabilidad en los
    países de la ALADI. - 1985.
        (002126)

LATIN AMERICA--INVESTMENT POLICY.
----O capital transnacional e o estado. -
    1985.
        (002274)
----Las empresas transnacionales y la
    inversión extranjera directa en la
    primera mitad de los años ochenta. -
    1987.
        (000194)
----Foreign direct investment in Latin
    America. - 1986.
        (000190)
----Performance requirements: the general
    debate and a review of Latin American
    practices. - 1983.
        (002315)

LATIN AMERICA--INVESTMENT PROMOTION.
----Las empresas transnacionales y la
    inversión extranjera directa en la
    primera mitad de los años ochenta. -
    1987.
      (000194)
----La inversión estadounidense en el Grupo
    Andino. - 1985.
      (000112)

LATIN AMERICA--INVESTMENTS.
----Latin American investment climate. -
    198?- .
      (001822)

LATIN AMERICA--IRON.
----La industria siderúrgica
    latinoamericana. - 1984.
      (000601)

LATIN AMERICA--IRON AND STEEL INDUSTRY.
----La industria siderúrgica
    latinoamericana. - 1984.
      (000601)

LATIN AMERICA--JOINT VENTURES.
----Measures strengthening the negotiating
    capacity of Governments in their
    relations with transnational
    corporations. - 1983.
      (002461)
----The use and promotion of consultancy
    joint ventures by public entities in
    Latin America. - 1985.
      (000834)

LATIN AMERICA--LAW OF THE SEA.
----The exclusive economic zone. - 1984.
      (002368)

LATIN AMERICA--LEGISLATION.
----Régimen jurídico de las inversiones
    extranjeras en los países de la ALADI. -
    1985.
      (002262)

LATIN AMERICA--MANAGEMENT.
----Doing business in key Latin American
    markets: U.S. international executive
    perceptions. - 1983.
      (001824)

LATIN AMERICA--MANUFACTURING.
----Banco de datos sobre inversión
    extranjera directa en América Latina y
    el Caribe : información de los países
    receptores y de organismos regionales y
    subregionales, t. 2. - 1987.
      (000193)
----Las empresas transnacionales y la
    inversión extranjera directa en la
    primera mitad de los años ochenta. -
    1987.
      (000194)

LATIN AMERICA--MARKETING.
----Latin America at a glance. - 1986.
      (001821)

LATIN AMERICA--METALLURGICAL INDUSTRY.
----La industria siderúrgica
    latinoamericana. - 1984.
      (000601)

LATIN AMERICA--METALLURGY.
----La industria siderúrgica
    latinoamericana. - 1984.
      (000601)

LATIN AMERICA--MINERAL RESOURCES DEVELOPMENT.
----The role of the public sector and
    transnational corporations in the mining
    development of Latin America. - 1986.
      (000605)

LATIN AMERICA--MINING INDUSTRY.
----The role of the public sector and
    transnational corporations in the mining
    development of Latin America. - 1986.
      (000605)

LATIN AMERICA--MINING LAW.
----Petroleum service contracts in
    Argentina, Brazil and Colombia : issues
    arising from their legal nature. - 1987.
      (002422)

LATIN AMERICA--MULTINATIONAL INDUSTRIAL
PROJECTS.
----Current problems of economic
    integration. - 1986.
      (001312)

LATIN AMERICA--NATURAL GAS.
----La industria siderúrgica
    latinoamericana. - 1984.
      (000601)

LATIN AMERICA--NATURAL RESOURCES.
----Petroleum service contracts in
    Argentina, Brazil and Colombia : issues
    arising from their legal nature. - 1987.
      (002422)

LATIN AMERICA--OLIGOPOLIES.
----Profits, progress and poverty. - 1985.
      (001111)

LATIN AMERICA--PERFORMANCE STANDARDS.
----Performance requirements: the general
    debate and a review of Latin American
    practices. - 1983.
      (002315)

LATIN AMERICA--PETROCHEMICAL INDUSTRY.
----North-South technology transfer. - 1984.
      (001421)

LATIN AMERICA--PETROLEUM INDUSTRY.
----Notes from Latin America. - 1983.
      (000628)

LATIN AMERICA--PETROLEUM LAW.
----Petroleum service contracts in
    Argentina, Brazil and Colombia : issues
    arising from their legal nature. - 1987.
      (002422)

LATIN AMERICA--PHARMACEUTICAL INDUSTRY.
----La industria farmacéutica y las
    transnacionales. - 1985.
      (000667)

LATIN AMERICA--PROTECTIONISM.
----Transnacionalización y periferia
    semindustrializada. - 1983.
      (001017)

LATIN AMERICA--PUBLIC ENTERPRISES.
----Government control over public
     enterprises in Latin America. - 1983.
     (002179)
----The use and promotion of consultancy
     joint ventures by public entities in
     Latin America. - 1985.
     (000834)

LATIN AMERICA--PUBLIC SECTOR.
----The role of the public sector and
     transnational corporations in the mining
     development of Latin America. - 1986.
     (000605)

LATIN AMERICA--REGIONAL CO-OPERATION.
----Current problems of economic
     integration. - 1986.
     (001312)
----Measures strengthening the negotiating
     capacity of Governments in their
     relations with transnational
     corporations. - 1983.
     (002461)
----El proceso de revisión de los mecanismos
     financieros de la ALADI. - 1983.
     (001248)

LATIN AMERICA--REGIONAL DEVELOPMENT.
----Multinational corporations and regional
     development. - 1983.
     (001326)

LATIN AMERICA--REGIONAL DEVELOPMENT BANKS.
----Current problems of economic
     integration. - 1986.
     (001312)

LATIN AMERICA--RISK ASSESSMENT.
----Yanqui come back! - 1986.
     (001825)

LATIN AMERICA--SAVINGS.
----Entrada de capital extranjero, ahorro
     interno e inversión en la América Latina
     : una historia negativa y precautoria. -
     1986.
     (001101)

LATIN AMERICA--SERVICE INDUSTRIES.
----Las empresas transnacionales y la
     inversión extranjera directa en la
     primera mitad de los años ochenta. -
     1987.
     (000194)
----Estados Unidos, América Latina y el
     debate internacional sobre el comercio
     de servicios. - 1986.
     (000934)
----La internacionalización de los
     servicios. - 1986.
     (000923)
----Los servicios en las transacciones
     internacionales de América Latina. -
     1986.
     (000820)

LATIN AMERICA--SMALL STATES.
----Small nations, giant firms. - 1987.
     (001091)

LATIN AMERICA--STATISTICAL DATA.
----Banco de datos sobre inversión
     extranjera directa en América Latina y
     el Caribe : información de los países
     receptores y de organismos regionales y
     subregionales, t. 2. - 1987.
     (000193)
----Banco de datos sobre inversión
     extranjera directa en América Latina y
     el Caribe, sobre la base de información
     de organismos multilaterales y de
     gobiernos de países de origen de la
     inversión, t. 1. - 1986.
     (000195)
----Las empresas transnacionales y la
     inversión extranjera directa en la
     primera mitad de los años ochenta. -
     1987.
     (000194)
----Measures strengthening the negotiating
     capacity of Governments in their
     relations with transnational
     corporations. - 1983.
     (002461)
----The role of the public sector and
     transnational corporations in the mining
     development of Latin America. - 1986.
     (000605)

LATIN AMERICA--TECHNOLOGICAL INNOVATIONS.
----Evaluating differences in technological
     activity between transnational and
     domestic firms in Latin America. - 1986.
     (001431)

LATIN AMERICA--TECHNOLOGY TRANSFER.
----Deuda externa, inversión extranjera y
     transferencia de tecnología en América
     Latina. - 1986.
     (001080)
----Foreign investment and technology
     transfer. - 1984.
     (000769)
----La industria siderúrgica
     latinoamericana. - 1984.
     (000601)
----Measures strengthening the negotiating
     capacity of Governments in their
     relations with transnational
     corporations. - 1983.
     (002461)
----North-South technology transfer. - 1984.
     (001421)

LATIN AMERICA--TECHNOLOGYTRANSFER.
----Patterns of technology imports:
     interregional comparison. - 1986.
     (001483)

LATIN AMERICA--TIRE INDUSTRY.
----Foreign investment and technology
     transfer. - 1984.
     (000769)

LATIN AMERICA--TRADE POLICY.
----Patterns of technology imports:
     interregional comparison. - 1986.
     (001483)
----The relationship of MNC direct
     investment to host country trade and
     trade policy: some preliminary evidence.
     - 1983.
     (001351)

LATIN AMERICA--TRANSNATIONAL CORPORATIONS.
----Agricultura y alimentos en América
    Latina. - 1985.
        (000562)
----Banco de datos sobre inversión
    extranjera directa en América Latina y
    el Caribe : información de los países
    receptores y de organismos regionales y
    subregionales, t. 2. - 1987.
        (000193)
----Banco de datos sobre inversión
    extranjera directa en América Latina y
    el Caribe, sobre la base de información
    de organismos multilaterales y de
    gobiernos de países de origen de la
    inversión, t. 1. - 1986.
        (000195)
----Breves rasgos de la crisis. - 1983.
        (001307)
----O capital transnacional e o estado. -
    1985.
        (002274)
----Capitalismo neocolonial. - 1983.
        (001109)
----La crisis internacional y la América
    Latina. - 1984.
        (001245)
----Deuda externa, inversión extranjera y
    transferencia de tecnología en América
    Latina. - 1986.
        (001080)
----Disfraces del coloniaje. - 1984.
        (001114)
----Doing business in key Latin American
    markets: U.S. international executive
    perceptions. - 1983.
        (001824)
----L'émpire Nestle. - 1983.
        (000283)
----Las empresas transnacionales y la
    inversión extranjera directa en la
    primera mitad de los años ochenta. -
    1987.
        (000194)
----Evaluating differences in technological
    activity between transnational and
    domestic firms in Latin America. - 1986.
        (001431)
----Financial transfers in the MNE. - 1986.
        (000416)
----Grace. - 1985.
        (000276)
----La industria farmacéutica y las
    transnacionales. - 1985.
        (000667)
----Inostrannye monopolii v Latinskoi
    Amerike. - 1983.
        (001103)
----International law of take-overs and
    mergers. - 1986.
        (001573)
----Latinskaia Amerika, ekspansiia
    inostrannykh monopolii. - 1984.
        (001090)
----Latinskaja Amerika. - 1984.
        (001089)
----Measures strengthening the negotiating
    capacity of Governments in their
    relations with transnational
    corporations. - 1983.
        (002461)
----Mezhdunarodnye monopolii v Latinskoi
    Amerike. - 1986.
        (001128)

----Patterns of technology imports:
    interregional comparison. - 1986.
        (001483)
----Politik als Investitionsmotor? - 1985.
        (001131)
----Profits, progress and poverty. - 1985.
        (001111)
----Regulation of transnational
    corporations. - 1984.
        (001998)
----The role of the public sector and
    transnational corporations in the mining
    development of Latin America. - 1986.
        (000605)
----The role of transnational enterprises in
    Latin American economic integration
    efforts. - 1983.
        (001126)
----Small nations, giant firms. - 1987.
        (001091)
----Transnacionalizacion y desarrollo
    agropecuario en America Latina. - 1984.
        (000574)
----Transnacionalización y desarrollo
    nacional en América Latina. - 1984.
        (001117)
----Transnacional'nye korporacii SSA v
    Latinskoj Amerike/edited by N.G. Zajcev.
    - 1985.
        (000326)
----Transnational corporations and
    industrial transformation in Latin
    America. - 1984.
        (001099)
----The transnational corporations and Latin
    America's international trade. - 1985.
        (001100)
----Transnational corporations and the Latin
    American automobile industry. - 1987.
        (000701)
----Transnatsional'nye korporatsii SShA v
    Latinskoi Amerike. - 1985.
        (001087)
----Yanqui come back! - 1986.
        (001825)

LATIN AMERICAN ECONOMIC SYSTEM.
----Measures strengthening the negotiating
    capacity of Governments in their
    relations with transnational
    corporations. - 1983.
        (002461)

LAW.
----Oil [and] gas : law and taxation review.
    - 1983-   .
        (002259)

LAW--CHINA.
----China laws for foreign business. -
    1985-   .
        (002187)

LAW--GERMANY, FEDERAL REPUBLIC OF.
----German transfer pricing. - 1984.
        (001748)

LAW--JAPAN.
----Doing business in Japan. - 1983.
        (001820)

LAW--UNITED STATES.
----Accounting and law in a nutshell. - 1984.
        (002208)

LAW--WESTERN EUROPE.
----Extraterritorial application of the
EEC-competition law. - 1984.
(002349)

LAW OF THE SEA--LATIN AMERICA.
----The exclusive economic zone. - 1984.
(002368)

LAW REPORTS AND DIGESTS.
----The digest of commercial laws of the
world : forms of contracts. - 1971-   .
(002424)
----Digest of commercial laws of the world.
- 1985-   .
(002256)
----Digest of commercial laws of the world.
- 1966-   .
(002200)

LAWS AND LEGISLATION--YUGOSLAVIA.
----Visi oblici privredne saradnje izmethu
domacih organizacija udruzenog rada i
stranih lica. - 1984.
(001182)

LAWS AND REGULATIONS.
----Arbitration and renegotiation of
international investment agreements. -
1986.
(002557)
----Chinese economic reforms since 1978 with
particular emphasis on the special
economic zones. - 1987.
(002375)
----Codes des investissements des Etats
A.C.P. - 1978.
(002162)
----Las empresas transnacionales en el
desarrollo colombiano. - 1986.
(001121)
----Environmental aspects of the activities
of transnational corporations. - 1985.
(001954)
----Extraterritorial jurisdiction. - 1983.
(002350) (002688)
----Die extraterritoriale Anwendung
nationalen Wettbewerbsrechts unter
besonderer Berucksichtigung
landerubergreifender Fusionen. - 1986.
(002340)
----Foreign direct investment and the
multinational enterprise. - 1988.
(002696)
----Foreign investment in the present and a
new international economic order. - 1988.
(001247)
----Le imprese internazionali. - 1983.
(000062)
----International accounting and reporting
issues, 1985 review. - 1985.
(002116)
----International business and national
jurisdiction. - 1988.
(002351)
----International business transactions in a
nutshell. - 1984.
(002457)
----International regulation of
transnational corporations. - 1986.
(001956)
----Legal control of the multinational
enterprise. - 1983.
(002024)

----Medicine advertising regulation and
self-regulation in 54 countries. - 1985.
(000815)
----MIGA and foreign investment. - 1988.
(002145)
----Multinational corporation and national
regulation: an economic audit. - 1987.
(002270)
----Multinational corporations and
discriminatory investment controls. -
1983.
(002249)
----National legislation and regulations
relating to transnational corporations.
Volume 2. - 1983.
(002251)
----National legislation and regulations
relating to transnational corporations.
Volume 5. - 1986.
(002254)
----National legislation and regulations
relating to transnational corporations.
Volume 6. - 1988.
(002255)
----National treatment for
foreign-controlled enterprises. - 1985.
(002258)
----National treatment for
foreign-controlled enterprises. - 1985.
(002004)
----Proceedings of the SSTCC/UNCTC/ESCAP
Asia-Pacific Training Workshop on
Regulating and Negotiating Technology
Transfer through Transnational
Corporations, 14-25 October 1985,
Fuzhou, Fujian, China. - 1986.
(001405) (002169)
----Le régime fiscal des societés étrangeres
en droit comparé. - 1985.
(001752)
----Regulating international business
through codes of conduct. - 1980.
(002022)
----Le societa multinazionali nel diritto
comunitario. - 1984.
(002011)
----Tax treatment of cost-contribution
arrangements. - 1988.
(001737)
----Technical co-operation programme,
1976-1987 : United Nations Centre on
Transnational Corporations. - 1988.
(002611)
----Transfer pricing provisions, rulings and
case law: Thailand. - 1986.
(001723)
----Transnational corporations in world
development. - 1988.
(000101)
----Transnational corporations in world
development. - 1983.
(000102)
----UNCTC bibliography, 1974-1987. - 1988.
(002695)
----Work by the United Nations Centre on
Transnational Corporations on the Code
of Conduct on Transnational
Corporations, other international
arrangements and agreements, and
national laws and regulations relating
to transnational corporations. - 1986.
(002694)

LAWS AND REGULATIONS--ALGERIA.
----National legislation and regulations
    relating to transnational corporations.
    Volume 3. - 1983.
    (002252)

LAWS AND REGULATIONS--ANDEAN REGION.
----La empresa multinacional andina. - 1983.
    (002246)
----Legislación de inversiones extranjeras y
    Pacto Andino. - 1984.
    (002234)

LAWS AND REGULATIONS--AUSTRALIA.
----Foreign investment law in Australia. -
    1985.
    (002210)
----National legislation and regulations
    relating to transnational corporations.
    Volume 3. - 1983.
    (002252)
----New Zealand business. - 1985.
    (000352)
----United States investment in Australia. -
    1987.
    (002180)

LAWS AND REGULATIONS--BOLIVIA.
----National legislation and regulations
    relating to transnational corporations.
    Volume 4. - 1986.
    (002253)

LAWS AND REGULATIONS--BOTSWANA.
----National legislation and regulations
    relating to transnational corporations.
    Volume 4. - 1986.
    (002253)

LAWS AND REGULATIONS--BRAZIL.
----O codigo de conduta das empresas
    transnacionais. - 1984.
    (001968)
----Multinacionais. - 1984.
    (002183)
----National legislation and regulations
    relating to transnational corporations.
    Volume 4. - 1986.
    (002253)
----Regulation of foreign investment in
    Brazil. - 1983.
    (002266)

LAWS AND REGULATIONS--BULGARIA.
----East-West joint ventures. - 1988.
    (001570)

LAWS AND REGULATIONS--BURUNDI.
----Manuel de procedures contractuelles
    susceptibles d'être mise en oeuvre par
    les contrats internationaux concernant
    la realisation de projets industriels. -
    1984.
    (002417)

LAWS AND REGULATIONS--CANADA.
----An examination of the legality of the
    use of the Foreign Investment Review Act
    by the government of Canada to control
    intra- and extraterritorial commercial
    activity by aliens. - 1984.
    (002257)

----Foreign investment law in Canada. - 1983.
    (002222)
----International income taxation and
    developing countries. - 1988.
    (001759)
----National legislation and regulations
    relating to transnational corporations.
    Volume 3. - 1983.
    (002252)
----Regulation of foreign direct investment
    in Canada and the United States. - 1983.
    (002263)
----Taxation in Canada. - 1985.
    (001701)
----Taxation of income of foreign
    affiliates. - 1983.
    (001765)

LAWS AND REGULATIONS--CHILE.
----Aspectos relevantes de la inversión
    extranjera en Chile. - 1984.
    (002171)
----National legislation and regulations
    relating to transnational corporations.
    Volume 4. - 1986.
    (002253)

LAWS AND REGULATIONS--CHINA.
----China adopts law on foreign enterprises.
    - 1986.
    (002294)
----Chung wai ho tzu ching ying ch'i yeh fa
    chi ch'i shih shih ching yen ch'ien
    t'an. - 1983.
    (002190)
----Chung-kuo tui wai shui wu shou ts'e. -
    1983.
    (001704)
----Collection of laws and regulations of
    the People's Republic of China
    concerning foreign economic affairs. -
    1985-   .
    (002188)
----Foreign direct investment in the
    People's Republic of China. - 1988.
    (000191)
----The investment climate in China. - 1987.
    (001810)
----Joint ventures in China. - 1986.
    (002281)
----Legal aspects of joint ventures in
    China. - 1986.
    (002178)
----The new legal framework for joint
    ventures in China. - 1984.
    (002282)
----Ouverture et dynamique interne du
    capital en Chine. - 1987.
    (001064)
----Private enterprise in China. - 1985.
    (002184)
----Realities confronting China's foreign
    investment policy. - 1984.
    (002292)
----Special economic zones in the People's
    Republic of China. - 1986.
    (002361)
----To open wider, or to close again :
    China's foreign investment policies and
    laws. - 1984.
    (002163)

LAWS AND REGULATIONS--COLOMBIA.
----National legislation and regulations
  relating to transnational corporations.
  Volume 4. - 1986.
    (002253)

LAWS AND REGULATIONS--COSTA RICA.
----National legislation and regulations
  relating to transnational corporations.
  Volume 3. - 1983.
    (002252)

LAWS AND REGULATIONS--COTE D'IVOIRE.
----National legislation and regulations
  relating to transnational corporations.
  Volume 4. - 1986.
    (002253)

LAWS AND REGULATIONS--CZECHOSLOVAKIA.
----East-West joint ventures. - 1988.
    (001570)

LAWS AND REGULATIONS--EASTERN EUROPE.
----East-West joint ventures. - 1988.
    (001570)
----Ownership and investment in Poland. -
  1985.
    (001595)

LAWS AND REGULATIONS--EGYPT.
----Egypt's experience in regulating
  technology imports. - 1987.
    (001514)
----National legislation and regulations
  relating to transnational corporations.
  Volume 4. - 1986.
    (002253)

LAWS AND REGULATIONS--FRANCE.
----Fraude fiscale internationale et
  repression. - 1986.
    (001742)
----International income taxation and
  developing countries. - 1988.
    (001759)
----National legislation and regulations
  relating to transnational corporations.
  Volume 3. - 1983.
    (002252)

LAWS AND REGULATIONS--GERMANY, FEDERAL
REPUBLIC OF.
----International income taxation and
  developing countries. - 1988.
    (001759)
----Konzerntransferpreise im internationalen
  Steuerrecht. - 1986.
    (001710)
----National legislation and regulations
  relating to transnational corporations.
  Volume 4. - 1986.
    (002253)
----Probleme der Gewinn- und
  Verlustrealisierung. - 1986.
    (001703)
----Steuerhinterziehung im internationalen
  Wirtschaftsverkehr. - 1984.
    (001706)

LAWS AND REGULATIONS--GHANA.
----National legislation and regulations
  relating to transnational corporations.
  Volume 3. - 1983.
    (002252)

LAWS AND REGULATIONS--GUYANA.
----National legislation and regulations
  relating to transnational corporations.
  Volume 3. - 1983.
    (002252)

LAWS AND REGULATIONS--HONG KONG.
----Arbitration in Hong Kong. - 1986.
    (002529)

LAWS AND REGULATIONS--HUNGARY.
----East-West joint ventures. - 1988.
    (001570)
----Up-to-date rules of joint ventures in
  Hungary. - 1986.
    (001537)

LAWS AND REGULATIONS--INDIA.
----National legislation and regulations
  relating to transnational corporations.
  Volume 4. - 1986.
    (002253)
----Regulations in vain? - 1986.
    (002240)

LAWS AND REGULATIONS--INDONESIA.
----MNCs and the host country, the
  Indonesian case. - 1984.
    (001073)
----National legislation and regulations
  relating to transnational corporations.
  Volume 3. - 1983.
    (002252)

LAWS AND REGULATIONS--IRAQ.
----National legislation and regulations
  relating to transnational corporations.
  Volume 3. - 1983.
    (002252)

LAWS AND REGULATIONS--ISRAEL.
----National legislation and regulations
  relating to transnational corporations.
  Volume 4. - 1986.
    (002253)

LAWS AND REGULATIONS--ITALY.
----National legislation and regulations
  relating to transnational corporations.
  Volume 4. - 1986.
    (002253)

LAWS AND REGULATIONS--JAPAN.
----International income taxation and
  developing countries. - 1988.
    (001759)
----Kokusai kankei no horitsu sodan. - 1983.
    (002293)

LAWS AND REGULATIONS--KENYA.
----National legislation and regulations
  relating to transnational corporations.
  Volume 4. - 1986.
    (002253)

LAWS AND REGULATIONS--KUWAIT.
----Impact of the operations of
  transnational corporations on
  development in Kuwait. - 1987.
    (001143)

LAWS AND REGULATIONS--KUWAIT (continued)
----National legislation and regulations
relating to transnational corporations.
Volume 4. - 1986.
(002253)

LAWS AND REGULATIONS--LIBERIA.
----National legislation and regulations
relating to transnational corporations.
Volume 4. - 1986.
(002253)

LAWS AND REGULATIONS--LIBYAN ARAB JAMAHIRIYA.
----National legislation and regulations
relating to transnational corporations.
Volume 4. - 1986.
(002253)

LAWS AND REGULATIONS--MEXICO.
----Doing business in Mexico. - 1984.
(001791)
----The foreign investment transaction in
Mexico. - 1985.
(002260)
----National legislation and regulations
relating to transnational corporations.
Volume 4. - 1986.
(002253)

LAWS AND REGULATIONS--MIDDLE EAST.
----Legal implications of marketing in the
Middle East. - 1985.
(002196)

LAWS AND REGULATIONS--MOROCCO.
----National legislation and regulations
relating to transnational corporations.
Volume 4. - 1986.
(002253)

LAWS AND REGULATIONS--NEW ZEALAND.
----New Zealand business. - 1985.
(000352)

LAWS AND REGULATIONS--NIGERIA.
----National legislation and regulations
relating to transnational corporations.
Volume 4. - 1986.
(002253)

LAWS AND REGULATIONS--OMAN.
----Impact of the operations of
transnational corporations on
development in the Sultanate of Oman. -
1988.
(001144)

LAWS AND REGULATIONS--PAKISTAN.
----National legislation and regulations
relating to transnational corporations.
Volume 3. - 1983.
(002252)

LAWS AND REGULATIONS--PANAMA.
----National legislation and regulations
relating to transnational corporations.
Volume 3. - 1983.
(002252)

LAWS AND REGULATIONS--PAPUA NEW GUINEA.
----National legislation and regulations
relating to transnational corporations.
Volume 3. - 1983.
(002252)

LAWS AND REGULATIONS--PERU.
----National legislation and regulations
relating to transnational corporations.
Volume 4. - 1986.
(002253)

LAWS AND REGULATIONS--PHILIPPINES.
----National legislation and regulations
relating to transnational corporations.
Volume 4. - 1986.
(002253)

LAWS AND REGULATIONS--POLAND.
----East-West joint ventures. - 1988.
(001570)
----New legislation on foreign private firms
in Poland. - 1984.
(002244)
----Ownership and investment in Poland. -
1985.
(001595)

LAWS AND REGULATIONS--PORTUGAL.
----National legislation and regulations
relating to transnational corporations.
Volume 4. - 1986.
(002253)

LAWS AND REGULATIONS--REPUBLIC OF KOREA.
----National legislation and regulations
relating to transnational corporations.
Volume 4. - 1986.
(002253)

LAWS AND REGULATIONS--ROMANIA.
----East-West joint ventures. - 1988.
(001570)
----National legislation and regulations
relating to transnational corporations.
Volume 3. - 1983.
(002252)

LAWS AND REGULATIONS--SAUDI ARABIA.
----Joint ventures in the Kingdom of Saudi
Arabia. - 1985.
(001655)
----National legislation and regulations
relating to transnational corporations.
Volume 4. - 1986.
(002253)

LAWS AND REGULATIONS--SINGAPORE.
----National legislation and regulations
relating to transnational corporations.
Volume 3. - 1983.
(002252)

LAWS AND REGULATIONS--SPAIN.
----El control de las empresas
multinacionales. - 1983.
(002209)

LAWS AND REGULATIONS--SUDAN.
----National legislation and regulations
relating to transnational corporations.
Volume 4. - 1986.
(002253)

LAWS AND REGULATIONS--THAILAND.
----National legislation and regulations
    relating to transnational corporations.
    Volume 4. - 1986.
        (002253)

LAWS AND REGULATIONS--TRINIDAD AND TOBAGO.
----National legislation and regulations
    relating to transnational corporations.
    Volume 3. - 1983.
        (002252)

LAWS AND REGULATIONS--TUNISIA.
----National legislation and regulations
    relating to transnational corporations.
    Volume 3. - 1983.
        (002252)

LAWS AND REGULATIONS--TURKEY.
----Foreign investment regulation and
    application forms. - 1985.
        (002198)
----Law for encouragement of foreign capital
    investments=Yabanci sermayeyi tesvik
    kanunu. - 1984.
        (002284)
----National legislation and regulations
    relating to transnational corporations.
    Volume 3. - 1983.
        (002252)

LAWS AND REGULATIONS--UNITED KINGDOM.
----International income taxation and
    developing countries. - 1988.
        (001759)
----National legislation and regulations
    relating to transnational corporations.
    Volume 4. - 1986.
        (002253)

LAWS AND REGULATIONS--UNITED REPUBLIC OF
TANZANIA.
----National legislation and regulations
    relating to transnational corporations.
    Volume 3. - 1983.
        (002252)

LAWS AND REGULATIONS--UNITED STATES.
----A competitive assessment of the U.S.
    herbicide industry. - 1985.
        (000670)
----East-West joint ventures. - 1988.
        (001570)
----Federal regulation of certain foreign
    investment in the United States. - 1985.
        (002215)
----Foreign investments and financings in
    the United States. - 1983.
        (002175)
----Foreign trade and investment. - 1987.
        (002191)
----International business planning. - 1983.
        (002279)
----International income taxation and
    developing countries. - 1988.
        (001759)
----International joint ventures. - 1986.
        (001566)
----Manual of foreign investment in the
    United States. - 1984.
        (002238)

----New challenges to the U.S. multinational
    corporation in the European Economic
    Community. - 1985.
        (002192)
----Oil industry mergers. - 1984.
        (001652)
----Oil spill liability and compensation. -
    1985.
        (001940)
----Regulation of foreign direct investment
    in Canada and the United States. - 1983.
        (002263)
----Tax aspects of international
    transactions. - 1984.
        (001757)
----U.S. federal regulation of foreign
    involvement in aviation, government
    procurement and national security. -
    1985.
        (002216)

LAWS AND REGULATIONS--USSR.
----East-West joint ventures. - 1988.
        (001570)

LAWS AND REGULATIONS--VENEZUELA.
----Legislación de inversiones extranjeras y
    Pacto Andino. - 1984.
        (002234)
----National legislation and regulations
    relating to transnational corporations.
    Volume 4. - 1986.
        (002253)

LAWS AND REGULATIONS--WESTERN EUROPE.
----East-West joint ventures. - 1988.
        (001570)
----New challenges to the U.S. multinational
    corporation in the European Economic
    Community. - 1985.
        (002192)

LAWS AND REGULATIONS--YUGOSLAVIA.
----An economic analysis of Yugoslav joint
    ventures. - 1983.
        (001563)
----National legislation and regulations
    relating to transnational corporations.
    Volume 4. - 1986.
        (002253)
----Überlegungen zur jugoslawischen Joint
    Venture-Gesetzgebung. - 1986.
        (002268)

LAWS AND REGULATIONS--ZAIRE.
----National legislation and regulations
    relating to transnational corporations.
    Volume 3. - 1983.
        (002252)

LAWS AND REGULATIONS--ZAMBIA.
----National legislation and regulations
    relating to transnational corporations.
    Volume 3. - 1983.
        (002252)

LEAST DEVELOPED COUNTRIES.
----The industrialisation of less developed
    countries. - 1983.
        (001003)
----Industry in the 1980s. - 1985.
        (001341)
----International finance. - 1983.
        (000266)

LEAST DEVELOPED COUNTRIES (continued)
----Investing in development. - 1986.
  (000149)
----Revitalizing development, growth and
  international trade. - 1987.
  (001394)
----Technology, marketing and
  industrialisation. - 1983.
  (001506)

LEATHER INDUSTRY.
----Multinational companies in the textile,
  garment and leather industries. - 1984.
  (000722)

LEGAL ETHICS.
----Transnational legal practice and
  professional ideology. - 1985.
  (002212)

LEGAL REMEDIES--UNITED STATES.
----The availability of provisional relief
  in international commercial arbitration.
  - 1984.
  (002543)

LEGISLATION--AFRICA.
----Répertoire de la législation relative
  aux investissements étrangers dans les
  pays membres de L'OCI. - 1984.
  (002264)

LEGISLATION--EGYPT.
----Egypt's experience in regulating
  technology imports. - 1987.
  (001514)

LEGISLATION--GHANA.
----Ghana's new Investment Code. - 1985.
  (002213)

LEGISLATION--GREECE.
----Investment legislation in Greece,
  Portugal and Spain: the background to
  foreign investment in Mediterranean
  Europe. - 1983.
  (002168)

LEGISLATION--HUNGARY.
----Vegyesvallalatok mukodesi feltetelei
  Magyarorszagon. - 1986.
  (002280)

LEGISLATION--ISLAMIC COUNTRIES.
----A directory of foreign investment
  legislation in O.I.C. member countries.
  - 1984.
  (002201)
----Répertoire de la législation relative
  aux investissements étrangers dans les
  pays membres de L'OCI. - 1984.
  (002264)

LEGISLATION--LATIN AMERICA.
----Régimen jurídico de las inversiones
  extranjeras en los países de la ALADI. -
  1985.
  (002262)

LEGISLATION--POLAND.
----Neue joint-venture-Gesetzgebung in
  Polen. - 1986.
  (002174)

LEGISLATION--PORTUGAL.
----Investment legislation in Greece,
  Portugal and Spain: the background to
  foreign investment in Mediterranean
  Europe. - 1983.
  (002168)

LEGISLATION--SOUTH AMERICA.
----Financing implications of mineral
  development agreements. - 1986.
  (002456)

LEGISLATION--SPAIN.
----Investment legislation in Greece,
  Portugal and Spain: the background to
  foreign investment in Mediterranean
  Europe. - 1983.
  (002168)

LEGISLATION--UNITED STATES.
----United States law of sovereign immunity
  relating to international financial
  transactions. - 1983.
  (002353)

LEGISLATION--USSR.
----La nouvelle législation soviétique sur
  les entreprises mixtes. - 1987.
  (002181)

LEGISLATIVE HEARINGS--UNITED STATES.
----Foreign government and foreign investor
  control of U.S. banks. - 1983.
  (001654)

LESOTHO--ECONOMIC CONDITIONS.
----Lagging behind the bantustans. - 1985.
  (001223)

LESOTHO--FOREIGN INVESTMENTS.
----Lagging behind the bantustans. - 1985.
  (001223)

LESOTHO--INDUSTRIAL DEVELOPMENT.
----Lagging behind the bantustans. - 1985.
  (001223)

LESOTHO NATIONAL DEVELOPMENT CORPORATION.
----Lagging behind the bantustans. - 1985.
  (001223)

LIABILITY.
----UNCITRAL, the United Nations Commission
  on International Trade Law. - 1986.
  (002155)
----Völkerrechtliche Haftung für das Handeln
  Privater im Bereich des internationalen
  Umweltschutzes. - 1984.
  (001945)

LIABILITY--GERMANY, FEDERAL REPUBLIC OF.
----Die Haftungsproblematik bei Konkurs
  einer Gesellschaft innerhalb eines
  transnationalen Unternehmens. - 1984.
  (002233)

LIABILITY--INDIA.
----The Bhopal case : controlling
  ultrahazardous industrial activities
  undertaken by foreign investors. - 1987.
  (001949)

LIABILITY--ITALY.
----La responsabilita contrattuale degli
   appaltatori in joint venture. - 1984.
      (001594)

LIABILITY--UNITED STATES.
----The Bhopal case : controlling
   ultrahazardous industrial activities
   undertaken by foreign investors. - 1987.
      (001949)

LIABILITY FOR MARINE ACCIDENTS.
----The definition of pollution damage in
   the 1984 Protocols to the 1969 Civil
   Liability Convention and the 1971 Fund
   Convention. - 1986.
      (001943)
----Liability and compensation for damage in
   connection with the carriage of
   hazardous and noxious substances by sea.
   - 1986.
      (001939)
----Liability for shipments by sea of
   hazardous and noxious substances. - 1985.
      (001951)
----New trends in compensation for oil
   pollution damage. - 1985.
      (001944)
----Oil pollution. - 1984.
      (001942)

LIABILITY FOR MARINE ACCIDENTS--UNITED
STATES.
----Oil spill liability and compensation. -
   1985.
      (001940)

LIABILITY INSURANCE--BHOPAL (INDIA).
----Mass disasters and multinational
   liability : the Bhopal case. - 1986.
      (001936)

LIBERIA--BANKS.
----The impact of the transnational
   corporations in the banking and other
   financial institutions on the economy of
   Liberia. - 1986.
      (000873)

LIBERIA--COMMERCIAL BANKS.
----The impact of the transnational
   corporations in the banking and other
   financial institutions on the economy of
   Liberia. - 1986.
      (000873)

LIBERIA--DEVELOPMENT FINANCE INSTITUTIONS.
----The impact of the transnational
   corporations in the banking and other
   financial institutions on the economy of
   Liberia. - 1986.
      (000873)

LIBERIA--ECONOMIC TRENDS.
----The impact of the transnational
   corporations in the banking and other
   financial institutions on the economy of
   Liberia. - 1986.
      (000873)

LIBERIA--EMPLOYMENT POLICY.
----Multinationals and employment in a West
   African sub-region. - 1984.
      (001904)

LIBERIA--FINANCIAL INSTITUTIONS.
----The impact of the transnational
   corporations in the banking and other
   financial institutions on the economy of
   Liberia. - 1986.
      (000873)

LIBERIA--FINANCIAL STATISTICS.
----The impact of the transnational
   corporations in the banking and other
   financial institutions on the economy of
   Liberia. - 1986.
      (000873)

LIBERIA--FOREIGN INVESTMENTS.
----National legislation and regulations
   relating to transnational corporations.
   Volume 4. - 1986.
      (002253)

LIBERIA--FREE EXPORT ZONES.
----Employment and multinational enterprises
   in export processing zones. - 1984.
      (001886)

LIBERIA--INSURANCE COMPANIES.
----The impact of the transnational
   corporations in the banking and other
   financial institutions on the economy of
   Liberia. - 1986.
      (000873)

LIBERIA--LABOUR SUPPLY.
----Employment and multinational enterprises
   in export processing zones. - 1984.
      (001886)
----Multinationals and employment in a West
   African sub-region. - 1984.
      (001904)

LIBERIA--LAWS AND REGULATIONS.
----National legislation and regulations
   relating to transnational corporations.
   Volume 4. - 1986.
      (002253)

LIBERIA--STATISTICAL DATA.
----The impact of the transnational
   corporations in the banking and other
   financial institutions on the economy of
   Liberia. - 1986.
      (000873)

LIBERIA--TRANSNATIONAL CORPORATIONS.
----Employment and multinational enterprises
   in export processing zones. - 1984.
      (001886)
----The impact of the transnational
   corporations in the banking and other
   financial institutions on the economy of
   Liberia. - 1986.
      (000873)
----Multinationals and employment in a West
   African sub-region. - 1984.
      (001904)
----National legislation and regulations
   relating to transnational corporations.
   Volume 4. - 1986.
      (002253)

LIBYAN ARAB JAMAHIRIYA--COMMERCIAL
ARBITRATION:
----The new international economic order,
    (2). - 1984.
        (001271)

LIBYAN ARAB JAMAHIRIYA--FOREIGN INVESTMENTS.
----National legislation and regulations
    relating to transnational corporations.
    Volume 4. - 1986.
        (002253)

LIBYAN ARAB JAMAHIRIYA--LAWS AND REGULATIONS.
----National legislation and regulations
    relating to transnational corporations.
    Volume 4. - 1986.
        (002253)

LIBYAN ARAB JAMAHIRIYA--TRANSNATIONAL
CORPORATIONS.
----National legislation and regulations
    relating to transnational corporations.
    Volume 4. - 1986.
        (002253)

LICENCE AGREEMENT--ASIA AND THE PACIFIC.
----Technology transfer under alternative
    arrangements with transnational
    corporations. - 1987.
        (001513)

LICENCE AGREEMENTS.
----Analysis of engineering and technical
    assistance consultancy contracts. - 1986.
        (002449)
----Applicable law under international
    transfer of technology regulations. -
    1984.
        (001412)
----Arrangements between joint venture
    partners in developing countries. - 1987.
        (002450)
----The capital goods sector in developing
    countries. - 1985.
        (001651)
----Choosing between direct investment and
    licensing. - 1984.
        (001418)
----Contratos de licencia y de transferencia
    de tecnología en el derecho privado. -
    1980.
        (002415)
----Food-processing contracts with
    developing countries. - 1985.
        (002419)
----International trademark licensing
    agreements. - 1986.
        (002421)
----Les techniques de negociation en matière
    de transfert de technologie. - 1987.
        (001511)
----Licence agreements in developing
    countries. - 1987.
        (002437)
----Licensing in international strategy. -
    1985.
        (001419)
----Les nouvelles formes d'investissement
    dans les pays on développement. - 1984.
        (001620)
----Les nouvelles formes d'investissement
    international dans les pays en
    développement. - 1984.
        (000165)

----Proceedings of the SSTCC/UNCTC/ESCAP
    Asia-Pacific Training Workshop on
    Regulating and Negotiating Technology
    Transfer through Transnational
    Corporations, 14-25 October 1985,
    Fuzhou, Fujian, China. - 1986.
        (001405) (002169)
----Restrictive clauses in licensing
    agreements: the pharmaceutical industry
    in developing countries. - 1984.
        (002420)
----The transnational law of international
    commercial transactions. - 1982.
        (002012)

LICENCE AGREEMENTS--CHINA.
----United States-China commercial
    contracts. - 1986.
        (002439)

LICENCE AGREEMENTS--GREECE.
----Licensing and industrial development. -
    1986.
        (001449)

LICENCE AGREEMENTS--INDIA.
----Licensing industrial technology to
    developing countries : the operations of
    Swedish firms in India. - 1986.
        (002442)

LICENCE AGREEMENTS--POLAND.
----Import licencji a zmiany w systemie
    gospodarki. - 1984.
        (002440)
----The regulation of technology transfer in
    Poland. - 1983.
        (001416)

LICENCE AGREEMENTS--SWEDEN.
----Licensing industrial technology to
    developing countries : the operations of
    Swedish firms in India. - 1986.
        (002442)

LICENCE AGREEMENTS--UNITED STATES.
----Coping with foreign-law impediments to
    the export licensing of United States
    technology. - 1986.
        (001473)
----Licensing impact of foreign policy
    motivated retroactive reexport
    regulations. - 1983.
        (001352)
----United States regulation of
    high-technology exports. - 1986.
        (001462)
----United States-China commercial
    contracts. - 1986.
        (002439)

LICENCE AGREEMENTS--WESTERN EUROPE.
----The EEC patent licencing regulation :
    practical guidelines. - 1986.
        (001966)

LICENCES.
----Foreign business practices. - 1985.
        (001433)
----Licence agreements in developing
    countries. - 1987.
        (002437)

LICENCES (continued)
----Licensing of technology and intellectual
property rights to developing countries.
- 1983.
(001403)
----Market competition, conflict and
collusion. - 1987.
(001680)

LICENCES--CANADA.
----Comparative licensing aspects of
Canadian and United Kingdom petroleum
law. - 1986.
(002176)

LICENCES--GREECE.
----Licensing and industrial development. -
1986.
(001449)

LICENCES--JAPAN.
----The administrative regulation of
technology induction contracts in Japan.
- 1987.
(002447)

LICENCES--UNITED KINGDOM.
----Comparative licensing aspects of
Canadian and United Kingdom petroleum
law. - 1986.
(002176)

LICENCES--UNITED STATES.
----Exclusive licenses as restraints of
trade under US and Common Market
antitrust law. - 1984.
(002414)
----Reverse technology flows. - 1985.
(001451)

LICENCES--USSR.
----Reverse technology flows. - 1985.
(001451)

LICENCES--WESTERN EUROPE.
----Exclusive licenses as restraints of
trade under US and Common Market
antitrust law. - 1984.
(002414)
----Exclusive territorial rights in patent
licenses and Article 85 of the EEC
Treaty. - 1987.
(002418)
----In the wake of windsurfing : patent
licensing in the Common Market. - 1987.
(002455)
----International aspects of nuclear
instalations licensing. - 1987.
(002434)

LICENSE AGREEMENTS.
----Corporate performance: America's
international winners. - 1986.
(000344)
----International technology joint ventures.
- 1985.
(001593)
----Lehetosegek es kenyszerpalyak a szellemi
termekek letrehozasaban es nemzetkozi
kereskedelmeben. - 1984.
(001465)

----Licensing strategy and policy for
internationalization and technology
transfer. - 1983.
(001519)
----Licensing versus direct investment: a
model of internationalization by the
multinational enterprise. - 1987.
(001443)
----Selecting a foreign partner for
technology transfer. - 1984.
(001459)
----The technology transfer process in
foreign licensing arrangements. - 1983.
(001520)
----Transnational corporations in world
development. - 1983.
(000102)

LICENSES.
----The technology transfer process in
foreign licensing arrangements. - 1983.
(001520)

LIGHT INDUSTRY--SOUTHEAST ASIA.
----Corporate policy, strategic groups and
the performance of transnational
corporations in less developed
countries. - 1982.
(001008)

LIQUIDATED DAMAGES.
----UNCITRAL, the United Nations Commission
on International Trade Law. - 1986.
(002155)

LOANS.
----Arbitration clauses in international
loans. - 1987.
(002569)
----Current problems of economic
integration. - 1986.
(001312)
----International bank lending. - 1984.
(000988)
----Legal trends in international lending
and investment in the developing
countries. - 1984.
(000207)
----Opportunities and constraints in
international lending. - 1983.
(000267)
----A practitioner's guide to international
banking and trade finance. - 1986.
(000922)
----The regulation and supervision of
international lending, (2). - 1986.
(000234)

LOANS--MEXICO.
----La internacionalización financiera
mexicana. - 1983.
(001288)

LOANS--UNITED STATES.
----Eximbank's role in international banking
and finance. - 1986.
(000816)

LOCAL FINANCE.
----Municipal accounting for developing
countries. - 1984.
(002090)

LUXEMBOURG--BUSINESS ENTERPRISES.
----Répertoire des entreprises
      luxembourgeoises. - 1979-   .
         (002662)

LUXEMBOURG--DIRECTORIES.
----Répertoire des entreprises
      luxembourgeoises. - 1979-   .
         (002662)

MACHINE TOOL INDUSTRY--INDIA.
----Industrial strategy and technological
      dynamism in machine tool manufacture. -
      1983.
         (000716)

MACHINE TOOL INDUSTRY--JAPAN.
----Industrial strategy and technological
      dynamism in machine tool manufacture. -
      1983.
         (000716)

MACHINE TOOL INDUSTRY--UNITED STATES.
----A competitive assessment of the U.S.
      flexible manufacturing systems industry.
      - 1985.
         (000763)
----A competitive assessment of the U.S.
      manufacturing automation equipment
      industries. - 1984.
         (000756)

MACHINE TOOLS.
----Microelectronics-based automation
      technologies and development. - 1985.
         (000753)

MACHINE TOOLS--JAPAN.
----Microelectronics-based automation
      technologies and development. - 1985.
         (000753)

MACHINERY--UNITED STATES.
----A competitive assessment of the U.S.
      semiconductor manufacturing equipment
      industry. - 1985.
         (000758)

MACHINERY INDUSTRY.
----Transnational corporations in the
      agricultural machinery and equipment
      industry. - 1983.
         (000746)

MACHINERY INDUSTRY--CANADA.
----An automotive strategy for Canada. -
      1983.
         (000686)

MACHINERY INDUSTRY--UNITED STATES.
----A competitive assessment of the U.S.
      construction machinery industry. - 1985.
         (000761)
----A competitive assessment of the U.S.
      electric power generating equipment
      industry. - 1985.
         (000762)

MACROECONOMICS.
----Public enterprise in mixed economies. -
      1984.
         (001574)

MAGNETIC DISKS--UNITED STATES.
----A competitive assessment of the United
      States disk storage industry. - 1985.
         (000672)

MAGYAR KERESKEDELMI KAMARA--ACTIVITIES.
----Hungarian Chamber of Commerce handbook.
      - 1984-   .
         (001811)

MALAWI--BUSINESS ENTERPRISES.
----Malawi buyers' guide. - 1983-   .
         (002653)

MALAWI--DEVELOPMENT ASSISTANCE.
----The private sector, the public sector,
      and donor assistance in economic
      development. - 1983.
         (000268)

MALAWI--DIRECTORIES.
----Malawi buyers' guide. - 1983-   .
         (002653)

MALAWI--ECONOMIC DEVELOPMENT.
----The private sector, the public sector,
      and donor assistance in economic
      development. - 1983.
         (000268)

MALAWI--ECONOMIC POLICY.
----The private sector, the public sector,
      and donor assistance in economic
      development. - 1983.
         (000268)

MALAWI--EXPORT PROMOTION.
----Malawi buyers' guide. - 1983-   .
         (002653)

MALAWI--INDUSTRY.
----Malawi buyers' guide. - 1983-   .
         (002653)

MALAWI--PRIVATE ENTERPRISES.
----The private sector, the public sector,
      and donor assistance in economic
      development. - 1983.
         (000268)

MALAWI--PUBLIC SECTOR.
----The private sector, the public sector,
      and donor assistance in economic
      development. - 1983.
         (000268)

MALAYSIA--CORPORATE PLANNING.
----Corporate strategy and employment
      relations in multinational corporations:
      some evidence from Kenya and Malaysia. -
      1983.
         (001902)

MALAYSIA--COST BENEFIT ANALYSIS.
----Malaysia's industrial enclaves :
      benefits and costs. - 1987.
         (002402)

MALAYSIA--ECONOMIC CONDITIONS.
----Multinationals and market structure in
      an open developing economy: the case of
      Malaysia. - 1983.
         (001056)

MALAYSIA--ECONOMIC DEVELOPMENT.
----Multinationals and market structure in
an open developing economy: the case of
Malaysia. - 1983.
(001056)

MALAYSIA--ECONOMIC POLICY.
----Business prospects in Malaysia, coping
with change in a new era. - 1983.
(001780)
----Malaysia's new economic policy: the role
of the transnational corporations. -
1985.
(001060)

MALAYSIA--ELECTRONICS INDUSTRY.
----Technology transfer under alternative
arrangements with transnational
corporations. - 1987.
(001513)

MALAYSIA--EMPLOYMENT POLICY.
----Corporate strategy and employment
relations in multinational corporations:
some evidence from Kenya and Malaysia. -
1983.
(001902)

MALAYSIA--EXPORT MARKETING.
----Chinese business, multinationals and the
state: manufacturing for export in
Malaysia and Singapore. - 1983.
(000713)

MALAYSIA--FOREIGN DIRECT INVESTMENT.
----Internalization in practice: early
foreign direct investments in
Malaysian tin mining. - 1986.
(000597)
----Wages and work conditions, and the
effects of foreign investment and the
separation of ownership from management
on them: a study of Malaysian
manufacturing. - 1983.
(001907)

MALAYSIA--FOREIGN INVESTMENTS.
----Business prospects in Malaysia, coping
with change in a new era. - 1983.
(001780)

MALAYSIA--FREE EXPORT ZONES.
----Malaysia's industrial enclaves :
benefits and costs. - 1987.
(002402)

MALAYSIA--INDUSTRIAL STATISTICS.
----Technology transfer under alternative
arrangements with transnational
corporations. - 1987.
(001513)

MALAYSIA--INDUSTRY.
----Transnational corporations in Kedah,
West Malaysia. - 1985.
(001061)

MALAYSIA--MANAGEMENT.
----Wages and work conditions, and the
effects of foreign investment and the
separation of ownership from management
on them: a study of Malaysian
manufacturing. - 1983.
(001907)

MALAYSIA--MANUFACTURING ENTERPRISES.
----Chinese business, multinationals and the
state: manufacturing for export in
Malaysia and Singapore. - 1983.
(000713)
----Wages and work conditions, and the
effects of foreign investment and the
separation of ownership from management
on them: a study of Malaysian
manufacturing. - 1983.
(001907)

MALAYSIA--MARKET POTENTIAL.
----Multinationals and market structure in
an open developing economy: the case of
Malaysia. - 1983.
(001056)

MALAYSIA--METALWORKING INDUSTRY.
----Technology transfer under alternative
arrangements with transnational
corporations. - 1987.
(001513)

MALAYSIA--PETROLEUM EXPLORATION.
----Social and economic effects of petroleum
development. - 1987.
(000633)

MALAYSIA--PETROLEUM INDUSTRY.
----Social and economic effects of petroleum
development. - 1987.
(000633)

MALAYSIA--PHARMACEUTICAL INDUSTRY.
----Transnational corporations in the
pharmaceutical industry of developing
countries. - 1984.
(000749)

MALAYSIA--STATISTICAL DATA.
----Technology transfer under alternative
arrangements with transnational
corporations. - 1987.
(001513)

MALAYSIA--TEXTILE INDUSTRY.
----Technology transfer under alternative
arrangements with transnational
corporations. - 1987.
(001513)

MALAYSIA--TIN INDUSTRY.
----Internalization in practice: early
foreign direct investments in
Malaysian tin mining. - 1986.
(000597)

MALAYSIA--TRADE REGULATION.
----Business prospects in Malaysia, coping
with change in a new era. - 1983.
(001780)

MALAYSIA--TRANSNATIONAL CORPORATIONS.
----Business prospects in Malaysia, coping
with change in a new era. - 1983.
(001780)
----Chinese business, multinationals and the
state: manufacturing for export in
Malaysia and Singapore. - 1983.
(000713)

MALAYSIA--TRANSNATIONAL CORPORATIONS
(continued)
----Corporate strategy and employment
    relations in multinational corporations:
    some evidence from Kenya and Malaysia. -
    1983.
        (001902)
----Malaysia's new economic policy: the role
    of the transnational corporations. -
    1985.
        (001060)
----Multinationals and market structure in
    an open developing economy: the case of
    Malaysia. - 1983.
        (001056)
----Technology transfer under alternative
    arrangements with transnational
    corporations. - 1987.
        (001513)
----Transnational corporations in Kedah,
    West Malaysia. - 1985.
        (001061)
----Wages and work conditions, and the
    effects of foreign investment and the
    separation of ownership from management
    on them: a study of Malaysian
    manufacturing. - 1983.
        (001907)

MALAYSIA--WAGES.
----Wages and work conditions, and the
    effects of foreign investment and the
    separation of ownership from management
    on them: a study of Malaysian
    manufacturing. - 1983.
        (001907)

MALAYSIA--WORKING CONDITIONS.
----Wages and work conditions, and the
    effects of foreign investment and the
    separation of ownership from management
    on them: a study of Malaysian
    manufacturing. - 1983.
        (001907)

MANAGEMENT.
----Arrangements between joint venture
    partners in developing countries. - 1987.
        (002450)
----Aussenwirtschaft der Unternehmung. -
    1984.
        (000064)
----Autonomy and centralization in
    multinational firms. - 1984.
        (000393)
----Business information sources. - 1985.
        (002701)
----Can you standardize multinational
    marketing? - 1983.
        (000464)
----Case studies in international business.
    - 1988.
        (000415)
----Common mistakes of joint venture
    experienced firms. - 1987.
        (001604)
----Comparative and multinational
    management. - 1986.
        (000439)
----Diskontinuitatenmanagement. - 1984.
        (000490)
----The economic environment of
    international business. - 1986.
        (001305)

----Empresas multinacionales, gestión de
    cambios y crisis monetarias=Multination
    businesses, change of money, management
    and monetary crisis. With English
    summary.). - 1983.
        (001292)
----Finding, entering, and succeeding in a
    foreign market. - 1987.
        (000468)
----Foreign direct investment as a
    sequential process. - 1983.
        (000052)
----Fundamentals of international business
    management. - 1986.
        (000414)
----Gestion internationale de l'entreprise.
    - 1984.
        (000389)
----The global IBM. - 1987.
        (000288)
----Going international. - 1985.
        (001786)
----Handbook of international management. -
    1988.
        (000452)
----How MNCs cope with host government
    intervention. - 1983.
        (001795)
----How multinational should your top
    managers be? - 1983.
        (000436)
----Le imprese internazionali. - 1983.
        (000062)
----Indigenization policies and structural
    cooptation by multinational
    corporations. - 1985.
        (002331)
----International business. - 1985.
        (000002)
----International business. - 1984.
        (000069)
----International business and multinational
    enterprises. - 1983.
        (000087)
----International business classics. - 1988.
        (000001)
----International business, environment and
    management. - 1985.
        (000423)
----International business knowledge. - 1987.
        (000402)
----International construction business
    management. - 1985.
        (000427)
----International dimensions of business
    policy and strategy. - 1986.
        (000477)
----International dimensions of financial
    management. - 1988.
        (000407)
----International finance. - 1983.
        (000425)
----International financial management. -
    1983.
        (001283)
----International financial management. -
    1985.
        (000424)
----International financial management. -
    1986.
        (000418)

MANAGEMENT (continued)
----International financial management. -
1984.
   (000438)
----International financial management: the
overall investment and financing plan. -
1983.
   (000401)
----International management. - 1987.
   (000433)
----International marketing. - 1986.
   (000482)
----International political risk management.
- 1984.
   (001802)
----Internationale Wirtschafts- und
Finanzpolitik in der Herausforderung der
achtziger Jahre [Added Entry Conference
Name]?Internationale
Management-Gesprache; (14th. - 1984.
   (000419)
----Internationales Konzernmarketing. - 1986.
   (000515)
----Internationalization of business. - 1984.
   (000086)
----Introduction to business. - 1987.
   (000066)
----Issues management and the multinational
enterprise. - 1987.
   (000434)
----Management. - 1987.
   (000430)
----Management accounting terminology. -
1983.
   (002092) (002717)
----Management international. - 1985.
   (000450)
----Management of international production.
- 1983.
   (000455)
----Manager in the international economy. -
1986.
   (000451)
----Manager international. - 1985.
   (000429)
----A managerial procedure for political
risk forecasting. - 1986.
   (001847)
----Managing cultural differences. - 1983.
   (001871)
----Managing international public affairs. -
1985.
   (000428)
----Managing the multinational subsidiary. -
1986.
   (000405)
----Managing the service economy. - 1985.
   (000899)
----Meeting the challenges of foreign
expansion. - 1985.
   (000035)
----Multinational corporate strategy. - 1985.
   (000489)
----Multinational corporations, environment,
and the Third World business matters. -
1987.
   (001012)
----The multinational enterprise in
transition. - 1986.
   (000040)
----Multinational financial management. -
1986.
   (000445)

----Multinational management. - 1984.
   (000449)
----Multinational managers and host
government interactions. - 1987.
   (001857)
----The multinational mission. - 1987.
   (000083)
----The new multinationals: synthesis and
conclusions. -   .
   (000349)
----The new multinationals: the theoretical
background. - 1983.
   (000350)
----The practice of currency exposure
management. - 1983.
   (000460)
----Seminar on Managing State Trading
Organisations. - 1986.
   (000370)
----Sozio-politische Strategien
multinationaler Unternehmungen. - 1985.
   (000387)
----Strategic management in multinational
companies. - 1986.
   (000472)
----Strategic management of multinational
corporations. - 1985.
   (000519)
----Strategies for joint venture success. -
1983.
   (001600)
----Taxation of intercorporate transfer
pricing: a management responsibility:
U.S.A. - 1986.
   (001754)
----Technological and organisational factors
in the theory of the multinational
enterprise. - 1983.
   (000097)
----Towards a theory of multinational
enterprise. - 1986.
   (000032)
----Vertical corporate linkages. - 1986.
   (000709)
----Zielbildung und strategisches Zielsystem
der internationalen Unternehmung. - 1984.
   (000474)
----161 more checklists : decision making in
international operations. - 1985.
   (000462)

MANAGEMENT--ASIA.
----Critical issues for business in Asia. -
1984.
   (001787)

MANAGEMENT--BRAZIL.
----Multinacionais. - 1984.
   (002183)

MANAGEMENT--CANADA.
----A cross sectional study of relative
take-over activity. - 1983.
   (001633)
----Entry, exit, and the theory of the
multinational corporation. - 1983.
   (000092)
----The strategic management of
multinationals and world product
mandating. - 1986.
   (000511)

MANAGEMENT--CHINA.
----China strategies. - 1986.
    (001037)
----The China trade: making the deal/the
    China trade: making the deal work. -
    1986.
    (001845)
----Strategies for joint ventures in the
    People's Republic of China. - 1987.
    (001610)

MANAGEMENT--EASTERN EUROPE.
----International economic organizations and
    multinational corporations. - 1986.
    (002590)

MANAGEMENT--EUROPE.
----Direct investment by Sogo-Shosha in
    Europe. - 1983.
    (000310)

MANAGEMENT--FINLAND.
----Creating a world enterprise. - 1983.
    (000398)

MANAGEMENT--FRANCE.
----Ces patrons qui gagnent. - 1986.
    (001146)
----Propriété et pouvoir dans l'industrie. -
    1987.
    (001628)

MANAGEMENT--GERMANY.
----External and internal functioning of
    American, German, and Japanese
    multinational corporations:
    decisionmaking and policy issues. - 1983.
    (000432)

MANAGEMENT--GERMANY, FEDERAL REPUBLIC OF.
----Die Steuerung auslandischer
    Tochtergesellschaften. - 1983.
    (000400)

MANAGEMENT--JAPAN.
----The Rising Sun in America (Part Two)
    -- Japanese management in the United
    States. - 1986.
    (000391)
----Direct investment by Sogo-Shosha in
    Europe. - 1983.
    (000310)
----External and internal functioning of
    American, German, and Japanese
    multinational corporations:
    decisionmaking and policy issues. - 1983.
    (000432)
----Internationalization at the top. - 1987.
    (000454)
----The invisible link. - 1986.
    (000992)
----The Rising Sun in America (Part One). -
    1986.
    (000392)
----A transactions cost approach to
    international trading structures: the
    case of the Japanese general trading
    companies. - 1983.
    (000372)

MANAGEMENT--LATIN AMERICA.
----Doing business in key Latin American
    markets: U.S. international executive
    perceptions. - 1983.
    (001824)

MANAGEMENT--MALAYSIA.
----Wages and work conditions, and the
    effects of foreign investment and the
    separation of ownership from management
    on them: a study of Malaysian
    manufacturing. - 1983.
    (001907)

MANAGEMENT--MEXICO.
----Joint ventures in Mexico. - 1984.
    (001631)

MANAGEMENT--PAPUA NEW GUINEA.
----Foreign investment in Papua New Guinea.
    - 1986.
    (002197)

MANAGEMENT--SINGAPORE.
----Multinational business and national
    development. - 1983.
    (000397)

MANAGEMENT--SOUTHEAST ASIA.
----Corporate policy, strategic groups and
    the performance of transnational
    corporations in less developed
    countries. - 1982.
    (001008)

MANAGEMENT--SWITZERLAND.
----Das Bally-Lehrstuck. - 1985.
    (000286)

MANAGEMENT--UNITED KINGDOM.
----British multinationals. - 1986.
    (000337)
----Decision-making in foreign-owned
    multinational subsidiaries in the United
    Kingdom. - 1985.
    (000521)
----Foundations of foreign success. - 1987.
    (000421)

MANAGEMENT--UNITED STATES.
----The Rising Sun in America (Part Two)
    -- Japanese management in the United
    States. - 1986.
    (000391)
----Doing business in key Latin American
    markets: U.S. international executive
    perceptions. - 1983.
    (001824)
----External and internal functioning of
    American, German, and Japanese
    multinational corporations:
    decisionmaking and policy issues. - 1983.
    (000432)
----Joint ventures. - 1987.
    (001613)
----Managing. - 1984.
    (000408)
----Managing effectively in the world
    marketplace. - 1983.
    (000399)
----Managing for joint venture success. -
    1986.
    (001587)

MANAGEMENT--UNITED STATES (continued)
----The new attractions of corporate joint
ventures. - 1985.
(001612)
----Performance requirements for foreign
business. - 1983.
(002314)
----Quantifying the competitive effects of
production joint ventures. - 1986.
(001548)
----The Rising Sun in America (Part One). -
1986.
(000392)
----Staffing of management and professional
positions at overseas subsidiaries of
U.S. multinational enterprises. - 1983.
(001885)
----Die Steuerung auslandischer
Tochtergesellschaften. - 1983.
(000400)
----U.S. multinational companies: operations
in 1984. - 1986.
(000309)
----U.S. multinational corporations: a
lesson in the failure of success. - 1983.
(000306)

MANAGEMENT--USSR.
----Creating a world enterprise. - 1983.
(000398)

MANAGEMENT CONSULTANTS--UNITED STATES.
----Bradford's directory of marketing
research agencies and management
consultants in the United States and the
world. - 1966-   .
(002623)
----Consultants and consulting organizations
directory. - 197?-   .
(000832)

MANAGEMENT CONSULTING.
----[Planning and execution of R&D]. - 1987.
(001481)

MANAGEMENT CONTRACTS.
----The competitive effects of partial
equity interests and joint ventures. -
1986.
(001635)
----Le transfert de technologie dans les
industries agro-alimentaires en Afrique
Centrale. - 1987.
(001510)
----Transnational corporations in world
development. - 1983.
(000102)

MANAGEMENT CONTRACTS--CONGO.
----Le transfert de technologie dans les
industries agro-alimentaires en Afrique
Centrale. - 1987.
(001510)

MANAGEMENT DEVELOPMENT.
----The making of a global manager/
managing in an age of velocity/global
partnering: making a good match. - 1987.
(000394)
----Methods and techniques of training
public enterprise managers. - 1983.
(001884)

MANAGEMENT DEVELOPMENT--KENYA.
----Labor, capital, and management slack in
multinational and local firms in Kenyan
manufacturing. - 1986.
(001026)

MANAGEMENT DEVELOPMENT--UNITED STATES.
----American and Chinese managers in U.S.
companies in Taiwan: a comparison. -
1985.
(000395)

MANAGEMENT INFORMATION SYSTEMS--GERMAN
DEMOCRATIC REPUBLIC.
----Die Anwendung der Mikrorechentechnik :
wichtige Voraussetzung für eine
reaktionsfähige und effektive
Absatzwirtschaft. - 1987.
(000908)

MANAGEMENT INFORMATIONS SYSTEMS.
----Strategic planning for information
resource management. - 1983.
(000443)

MANAGERIAL ECONOMICS.
----Managerial accounting and analysis in
multinational enterprises. - 1986.
(002084)
----Managerial finance. - 1985.
(000413)

MANAGERS.
----The making of a global manager/
managing in an age of velocity/global
partnering: making a good match. - 1987.
(000394)
----How multinational should your top
managers be? - 1983.
(000436)
----A managerial procedure for political
risk forecasting. - 1986.
(001847)
----Methods and techniques of training
public enterprise managers. - 1983.
(001884)
----Present and desired methods of
selecting expatriate managers for
international assignments. - 1984.
(000522)
----The world-class executive. - 1985.
(000396)

MANAGERS--CANADA.
----The blue book of Canadian business. -
1976-   .
(002622)

MANAGERS--CHINA.
----The training component. - 1986.
(001920)

MANAGERS--JAPAN.
----Internationalization at the top. - 1987.
(000454)

MANAGERS--UNITED STATES.
----American and Chinese managers in U.S.
companies in Taiwan: a comparison. -
1985.
(000395)
----Internal accountability. - 1984.
(002055)

MANDATES--CANADA.
----The strategic management of
    multinationals and world product
    mandating. - 1986.
    (000511)

MAN-MADE DISASTERS--BHOPAL (INDIA).
----Asia's struggle to affirm wholeness of
    life : report of a consultation on TNC's
    in Asia. - 1985.
    (001935)
----For whom the bell tolls in the aftermath
    of the Bhopal tragedy. - 1987.
    (001950)

MAN-MADE DISASTERS--INDIA.
----For whom the bell tolls in the aftermath
    of the Bhopal tragedy. - 1987.
    (001950)

MANO RIVER UNION.
----Industrial cooperation in regional
    economic groupings among developing
    countries and lessons for SAARC. - 1987.
    (001009)

MANPOWER NEEDS--BRAZIL.
----Technological spill-overs and manpower
    training: a comparative analysis of
    multinational and national enterprises
    in Brazilian manufacturing. - 1986.
    (001899)

MANPOWER NEEDS--SOUTH AFRICA.
----Political change in South Africa. - 1986.
    (001205)

MANPOWER PLANNING.
----Multinational enterprises : information
    and consultation concerning their
    manpower plans. - 1985.
    (000431)

MANUFACTURES.
----Exports of manufactures from developing
    countries : performance and prospects
    for market access. - 1984.
    (001355)
----U.S. high technology trade and
    competitiveness. - 1985.
    (001362)

MANUFACTURES--ARGENTINA.
----Internacionalización de empresas y
    tecnología de origen argentino. - 1985.
    (000301)

MANUFACTURES--INDIA.
----Foreign cooperation and the marketing of
    manufactured exports from developing
    countries. - 1985.
    (001377)

MANUFACTURES--SINGAPORE.
----Singapore manufacturers and products
    directory. - 1977-   .
    (002664)

MANUFACTURES--SRI LANKA.
----Foreign cooperation and the marketing of
    manufactured exports from developing
    countries. - 1985.
    (001377)

MANUFACTURES--TUNISIA.
----L'industrie manufacturière tunisienne et
    sa place dans l'économie nationale. -
    1985.
    (000744)

MANUFACTURES--UNITED STATES.
----U.S. high technology trade and
    competitiveness. - 1985.
    (001362)

MANUFACTURING.
----The capital goods sector in developing
    countries. - 1985.
    (001651)
----Empirical studies of investment
    behaviour. - 1985.
    (000524)
----Industry in the 1980s. - 1985.
    (001341)
----Microelectronics-based automation
    technologies and development. - 1985.
    (000753)
----The military origins of
    industrialisation and international
    trade rivalry. - 1984.
    (001335)
----Technology and employment in industry. -
    1985.
    (001503)
----The third industrial revolution. - 1987.
    (000966)
----Transnational corporations in the
    pharmaceutical industry of developing
    countries. - 1984.
    (000749)
----Transnational corporations in world
    development. - 1983.
    (000102)
----Trends and issues in foreign direct
    investment and related flows. - 1985.
    (000192)
----UNCTC bibliography, 1974-1987. - 1988.
    (002695)

MANUFACTURING--ARGENTINA.
----Las empresas transnacionales en la
    Argentina. - 1986.
    (001122)

MANUFACTURING--AUSTRALIA.
----Some aspects of Japanese manufacturing
    investment in Australia. - 1984.
    (001044)

MANUFACTURING--COLOMBIA.
----Las empresas transnacionales en el
    desarrollo colombiano. - 1986.
    (001121)

MANUFACTURING--INDIA.
----Multinationals in Indian big business. -
    1983.
    (001057)

MANUFACTURING--JAPAN.
----Some aspects of Japanese manufacturing
    investment in Australia. - 1984.
    (001044)

MANUFACTURING--LATIN AMERICA.
----Banco de datos sobre inversión
extranjera directa en América Latina y
el Caribe : información de los países
receptores y de organismos regionales y
subregionales, t. 2. - 1987.
(000193)
----Las empresas transnacionales y la
inversión extranjera directa en la
primera mitad de los años ochenta. -
1987.
(000194)

MANUFACTURING--MEXICO.
----Foreign investment and productive
efficiency. - 1986.
(001084)

MANUFACTURING--NAMIBIA.
----Transnational corporations in South
Africa and Namibia : United Nations
public hearings. Volume 1, Reports of
the Panel of Eminent Persons and of the
Secretary-General. - 1986.
(001216)

MANUFACTURING--PARAGUAY.
----Las empresas transnacionales en la
economía del Paraguay. - 1987.
(001124)

MANUFACTURING--UNITED KINGDOM.
----British manufacturing investment
overseas. - 1985.
(000735)
----The relative distribution of United
States direct investment : the UK/EEC
experience. - 1987.
(000113)

MANUFACTURING--UNITED STATES.
----A competitive assessment of the U.S.
manufacturing automation equipment
industries. - 1984.
(000756)
----A competitive assessment of the U.S.
semiconductor manufacturing equipment
industry. - 1985.
(000758)
----Manufacturing matters : the myth of the
post-industrial economy. - 1987.
(000669)
----Political and policy dimensions of
foreign trade zones. - 1985.
(001356)

MANUFACTURING--WESTERN EUROPE.
----The relative distribution of United
States direct investment : the UK/EEC
experience. - 1987.
(000113)

MANUFACTURING ENTERPRICES--REPUBLIC OF KOREA.
----The Korean manufacturing multinationals.
- 1984.
(000342)

MANUFACTURING ENTERPRISES.
----Investment penetration in manufacturing
and extraction and external public debt
in Third World states. - 1984.
(001015)

----Multinationals are mushrooming. - 1986.
(001861)
----Ownership and development. - 1987.
(001129)
----Political events and the foreign direct
investment decision: an empirical
examination. - 1986.
(001836)
----Technology, marketing and
industrialisation. - 1983.
(001506)
----Testing the bargaining hypothesis in the
manufacturing sector in developing
countries. - 1987.
(000706)
----Transnational corporations and
technology transfer. - 1987.
(001509)

MANUFACTURING ENTERPRISES--ARGENTINA.
----Internacionalización de empresas y
tecnología de origen argentino. - 1985.
(000301)

MANUFACTURING ENTERPRISES--BRAZIL.
----The comparative performance of foreign
and domestic firms in Brazil. - 1986.
(001130)
----The determinants of manufacturing
ownership in less developed countries. -
1986.
(000712)
----Technological spill-overs and manpower
training: a comparative analysis of
multinational and national enterprises
in Brazilian manufacturing. - 1986.
(001899)

MANUFACTURING ENTERPRISES--COLOMBIA.
----The subsidiary role of direct foreign
investment in industrialization: the
Colombian manufacturing sector. - 1985.
(001106)

MANUFACTURING ENTERPRISES--GERMANY, FEDERAL
REPUBLIC OF.
----International trade and foreign direct
investment in West German manufacturing
industries. - 1984.
(000771)

MANUFACTURING ENTERPRISES--HONG KONG.
----Multinational corporations and
technology diffusion in Hong Kong
manufacturing. - 1983.
(001415)

MANUFACTURING ENTERPRISES--HUNGARY.
----A magyar feldolgozó ipar koncentrációs
folyamata a 70-es évtizedben, nemzetközi
összehasonlításban. - 1986.
(001181)

MANUFACTURING ENTERPRISES--INDIA.
----The determinants of manufacturing
ownership in less developed countries. -
1986.
(000712)
----Foreign direct investment in
manufacturing from an LDC: India. - 1985.
(000317)

MANUFACTURING ENTERPRISES--INDONESIA.
----Factor proportions and productive
      efficiency of foreign owned firms in the
      Indonesian manufacturing sector. - 1984.
      (000655)
----Japanese direct investment in Indonesian
      manufacturing. - 1984.
      (000187)

MANUFACTURING ENTERPRISES--JAPAN.
----Action programs by Japan's major
      manufacturers. - 1986.
      (000456)
----Japanese direct investment in Indonesian
      manufacturing. - 1984.
      (000187)
----Japanese investment in UK industry. -
      1984.
      (000127)
----Transfer of technology from Japan and
      the United States to Korean
      manufacturing industries: a comparative
      study. - 1984.
      (001461)
----Trends in Japan's manufacturing
      investment in the United States. - 1987.
      (000767)
----US and Japanese manufacturing affiliates
      in the UK. - 1985.
      (001149)

MANUFACTURING ENTERPRISES--MALAYSIA.
----Chinese business, multinationals and the
      state: manufacturing for export in
      Malaysia and Singapore. - 1983.
      (000713)
----Wages and work conditions, and the
      effects of foreign investment and the
      separation of ownership from management
      on them: a study of Malaysian
      manufacturing. - 1983.
      (001907)

MANUFACTURING ENTERPRISES--MEXICO.
----The determinants of manufacturing
      ownership in less developed countries. -
      1986.
      (000712)
----Foreign investment, technical efficiency
      and structural change. - 1983.
      (001085)
----1985 directory of in-bond plants
      (maquiladoras) in Mexico. - 1984.
      (001132) (002678)

MANUFACTURING ENTERPRISES--REPUBLIC OF KOREA.
----The determinants of manufacturing
      ownership in less developed countries. -
      1986.
      (000712)
----Transfer of technology from Japan and
      the United States to Korean
      manufacturing industries: a comparative
      study. - 1984.
      (001461)

MANUFACTURING ENTERPRISES--SINGAPORE.
----Chinese business, multinationals and the
      state: manufacturing for export in
      Malaysia and Singapore. - 1983.
      (000713)

----Direct foreign investment in
      manufacturing and the impact on
      employment and export performance in
      Singapore. - 1984.
      (001932)
----Leading international companies
      manufacturing and providing technical
      services in Singapore. - 1983-   .
      (002650)
----Singapore manufacturers and products
      directory. - 1977-   .
      (002664)

MANUFACTURING ENTERPRISES--SOUTH AFRICA.
----The determinants of manufacturing
      ownership in less developed countries. -
      1986.
      (000712)

MANUFACTURING ENTERPRISES--SOUTHEAST ASIA.
----Corporate policy, strategic groups and
      the performance of transnational
      corporations in less developed
      countries. - 1982.
      (001008)

MANUFACTURING ENTERPRISES--TUNISIA.
----L'industrie manufacturière tunisienne et
      sa place dans l'économie nationale. -
      1985.
      (000744)

MANUFACTURING ENTERPRISES--UNITED KINGDOM.
----A comparison of embodied technical
      change in services and manufacturing
      industry. - 1986.
      (000806)
----Foreign direct investment and the
      competitiveness of UK manufacturing
      industry, 1963-1979. - 1984.
      (000766)
----Japanese investment in UK industry. -
      1984.
      (000127)
----Kompass. - 196?-   .
      (002648)
----Sell's British exporters. - 1916-   .
      (002663)
----US and Japanese manufacturing affiliates
      in the UK. - 1985.
      (001149)

MANUFACTURING ENTERPRISES--UNITED STATES.
----The effect of political events on
      United States direct foreign
      investment: a pooled time-series
    • cross-sectional analysis. - 1985.
      (001835)
----The competitive position of U.S.
      manufacturing firms. - 1985.
      (000353)
----Directory of foreign manufacturers in
      the United States. - 1975-   .
      (002634)
----Foreign manufacturing investment in the
      United States: competitive strategies
      and international location. - 1985.
      (000733)
----International collaborative ventures in
      U.S. manufacturing. - 1988.
      (000720)

MANUFACTURING ENTERPRISES--UNITED STATES
(continued)
----The international location of
manufacturing investments: recent
behaviour of foreign-owned corporations
in the United States. - 1983.
(001156)
----Transfer of technology from Japan and
the United States to Korean
manufacturing industries: a comparative
study. - 1984.
(001461)
----Trends in Japan's manufacturing
investment in the United States. - 1987.
(000767)
----US and Japanese manufacturing affiliates
in the UK. - 1985.
(001149)

MARINE POLLUTION.
----Dead in the water : international law,
diplomacy, and compensation for chemical
pollution at sea. - 1986.
(001938)
----Dommages causés par les marées noires. -
1984.
(001952)

MARINE RESOURCES POLICY.
----Taming troubled waters. - 1986.
(002453)

MARITIME CLAIMS.
----Taming troubled waters. - 1986.
(002453)

MARITIME LAW.
----New trends in compensation for oil
pollution damage. - 1985.
(001944)

MARITIME TRANSPORT.
----International income taxation and
developing countries. - 1988.
(001759)
----Joint ventures and Third World maritime
development. - 1985.
(000799)
----Liability and compensation for damage in
connection with the carriage of
hazardous and noxious substances by sea.
- 1986.
(001939)
----Liability for shipments by sea of
hazardous and noxious substances. - 1985.
(001951)
----Multinational ownership of shipping
activities. - 1985.
(000793)
----The role of vertical integration in the
shipping industry. - 1985.
(000790)
----Services and the development process. -
1985.
(000979)
----UNCITRAL, the United Nations Commission
on International Trade Law. - 1986.
(002155)

MARITIME TRANSPORT--EUROPE.
----The quality of shipping services. - 1986.
(000789)

MARITIME TRANSPORT--WESTERN EUROPE.
----Air and maritime transport and the EEC
competition rules : Ministère Publique
v. Asjes, Nouvelles Frontières et al. -
1987.
(000794)

MARKET ACCESS.
----Developing country access to capital
markets in transition. - 1987.
(001609)
----Exports of manufactures from developing
countries : performance and prospects
for market access. - 1984.
(001355)
----The firm and the market. - 1987.
(000013)
----The multinationals in the world oil
market: the 1970s and the 1980s. - 1983.
(000575)
----Pricing and sourcing strategies in a
multinational oligopoly. - 1983.
(000466)
----Profitability of mergers in food
manufacturing. - 1986.
(001584)
----The 1984 Justice Department guidelines
toward horizontal mergers. - 1986.
(001551)

MARKET ACCESS--CHINA.
----Foreign direct investment in the
People's Republic of China. - 1988.
(000191)

MARKET ACCESS--EUROPE.
----Competitive strategies for Europe. -
1983.
(000463)

MARKET ACCESS--REPUBLIC OF KOREA.
----Korean contractors in Saudi Arabia. -
1986.
(001139)

MARKET ACCESS--SAUDI ARABIA.
----Korean contractors in Saudi Arabia. -
1986.
(001139)

MARKET ACCESS--SOUTHEAST ASIA.
----Computer vendors re-shape product
strategy for Asian market. - 1986.
(000689)

MARKET ACCESS--UNITED STATES.
----The effect of conglomerate mergers on
changes in industry concentration. -
1986.
(001527)
----On vertical mergers. - 1986.
(001641)

MARKET DISRUPTION--BRAZIL.
----Market imperfections and import pricing
behavior by multinational enterprises. -
1986.
(001681)

MARKET POTENTIAL.
----Electronic information services. - 1986.
(000837)

MARKET POTENTIAL (continued)
----Excess market value, the multinational
    corporation, and Tobin's q-ratio. - 1986.
    (000050)
----Multinationals and marketplace magic in
    the 1980s. - 1983.
    (001682)
----Natural gas clauses in petroleum
    arrangements. - 1987.
    (002452)

MARKET POTENTIAL--MALAYSIA.
----Multinationals and market structure in
    an open developing economy: the case of
    Malaysia. - 1983.
    (001056)

MARKET POTENTIAL--MEXICO.
----Multinationals and market structure in
    Mexico. - 1986.
    (001086)

MARKET POTENTIAL--SOUTHEAST ASIA.
----The allure of Southeast Asia's chemical
    market. - 1987.
    (000661)

MARKET POTENTIAL--UNITED STATES.
----Geoinvestment: the interdependence among
    space, market size, and political
    turmoil in attracting foreign direct
    investment. - 1984.
    (000555)

MARKET RESEARCH.
----International corporate diversification,
    market valuation, and size-adjusted
    evidence. - 1984.
    (000475)
----World business reports. - 1982-   .
    (001863)

MARKET RESEARCH--JAPAN.
----Planning a joint venture for the
    Japanese market. - 1987.
    (000508)

MARKET RESEARCH--UNITED STATES.
----Bradford's directory of marketing
    research agencies and management
    consultants in the United States and the
    world. - 1966-   .
    (002623)
----Planning a joint venture for the
    Japanese market. - 1987.
    (000508)

MARKETING.
----Can you standardize multinational
    marketing? - 1983.
    (000464)
----La gestion marketing dans un
    développemnt turbulent et hautement
    concurrentiel. - 1983.
    (000487)
----A global comeback. - 1987.
    (000275)
----The implementation process of the
    International Code of Marketing of
    Breastmilk Substitutes. - 1984.
    (001970) (001971)
----International marketing planning and
    state trading organisations. - 1986.
    (000369)

----Making the multinational decision. -
    1983.
    (000542)
----Market competition, conflict and
    collusion. - 1983.
    (000492)
----Marketing in less developed countries. -
    1986.
    (000465)
----Multinational management. - 1984.
    (000449)
----Multinational risk assessment and
    management. - 1987.
    (000514)
----The political economy of innovation. -
    1984.
    (001450)
----Problems that plague multinational
    marketers. - 1983.
    (000517)
----Should one countertrade? - 1987.
    (001366)
----Standardisation of marketing strategy by
    multinationals. - 1987.
    (000506)
----Technology, marketing and
    industrialisation. - 1983.
    (001506)
----Threats and opportunities of global
    countertrade : marketing, financing and
    organizational implications. - 1984.
    (001353)
----Transnational corporations in the
    pharmaceutical industry of developing
    countries. - 1984.
    (000749)
----Transnatsional'nye korporatsii na
    rynkakh razvivaiushchikhsia stran. -
    1985.
    (001660)
----161 more checklists : decision making in
    international operations. - 1985.
    (000462)

MARKETING--ASIA.
----New business strategies for developing
    Asia, 1983-1990. - 1984.
    (000498)

MARKETING--EASTERN EUROPE.
----Eastern bloc international enterprises
    -- still in statu nascendi. - 1985.
    (000332)
----101 checklists for success in East
    European markets. - 1984.
    (001779)

MARKETING--EUROPE.
----Becoming a triad power: the new global
    corporation. - 1986.
    (000500)
----Market share strategy in Europe. - 1985.
    (000493)

MARKETING--HUNGARY.
----A magyar gépipari vállalatok
    nagyságrendje és piaci magatartásuk. -
    1984.
    (000957)

MARKETING--JAPAN.
----Becoming a triad power: the new global
corporation. - 1986.
(000500)

MARKETING--LATIN AMERICA.
----Latin America at a glance. - 1986.
(001821)

MARKETING--MIDDLE EAST.
----International business in the Middle
East. - 1986.
(001135)
----Legal implications of marketing in the
Middle East. - 1985.
(002196)

MARKETING--MOROCCO.
----Marketing supplementary food products in
LDCs. - 1983.
(000665)

MARKETING--UNITED STATES.
----Becoming a triad power: the new global
corporation. - 1986.
(000500)
----Mezhdunarodnyi marketing amerikanskoi
tekhnologii. - 1985.
(000494)
----Profiles of foreign direct investment in
U.S. energy. - 1985-   .
(000774)

MARKETS.
----The effects of markets on public
enterprise conduct ; and vice versa. -
1983.
(001675)
----The globalization of markets. - 1983.
(000059)

MARXIAN ECONOMICS.
----Competition in the Marxist tradition. -
1983.
(001697)

MASS MEDIA--INDIA.
----Nation-building media and TNCs. - 1984.
(000941)

MASS MEDIA--UNITED STATES.
----The knowledge industry 200. - 1983.
(000884) (002646)

MATHEMATICAL ANALYSIS.
----The welfare effects of foreign
enterprise. - 1986.
(000016)

MATHEMATICAL MODELS.
----A decision theoretic model of
innovation, technology transfer, and
trade. - 1987.
(001446)
----Determinants of multinational banks. -
1986.
(000825)
----Economic development, investment
dependence, and the rise of services in
less developed nations. - 1986.
(000958)
----Empirical studies of investment
behaviour. - 1985.
(000524)

----The intertemporal effects of
international transfers. - 1986.
(001262)
----A mean-variance model of MNF location
strategy. - 1985.
(000535)
----Patterns of bilateral trade flows within
the characteristics approach to trade. -
1986.
(001397)
----Sovereignty and natural resource
taxation in developing countries. - 1987.
(001741)
----A theory of the international division
of labour. - 1984.
(001239)

MATHEMATICAL MODELS--GERMANY, FEDERAL
REPUBLIC OF.
----Entry by diversified firms into German
industries. - 1986.
(001162)

MATRICES.
----Organizing to implement strategies of
diversity and globalization: the role of
matrix designs. - 1986.
(000476)

MAURITANIA--EVALUATIVE RESEARCH.
----Towards an evaluative study of joint
venture projects with socio-economic
indicators. - 1983.
(001555)

MAURITANIA--JOINT VENTURES.
----Towards an evaluative study of joint
venture projects with socio-economic
indicators. - 1983.
(001555)

MAURITANIA--SOCIO-ECONOMIC INDICATORS.
----Towards an evaluative study of joint
venture projects with socio-economic
indicators. - 1983.
(001555)

MAURITIUS--AIR TRANSPORT.
----The role of transnational corporations
in hotel and tourism industry in
selected PTA member countries. - 1986.
(000782) (000936)

MAURITIUS--ELECTRONICS INDUSTRY.
----Jobs for the girls. - 1984.
(001901)

MAURITIUS--FREE EXPORT ZONES.
----Aspects of labour law and relations in
selected export processing zones. - 1984.
(001895)

MAURITIUS--HOTEL INDUSTRY.
----The role of transnational corporations
in hotel and tourism industry in
selected PTA member countries. - 1986.
(000782) (000936)

MAURITIUS--LABOUR LAW.
----Aspects of labour law and relations in
selected export processing zones. - 1984.
(001895)

MAURITIUS--LABOUR RELATIONS.
----Aspects of labour law and relations in
    selected export processing zones. - 1984.
    (001895)

MAURITIUS--STATISTICAL DATA.
----The role of transnational corporations
    in hotel and tourism industry in
    selected PTA member countries. - 1986.
    (000782) (000936)

MAURITIUS--TEXTILE INDUSTRY.
----Jobs for the girls. - 1984.
    (001901)

MAURITIUS--TOURISM DEVELOPMENT.
----The role of transnational corporations
    in hotel and tourism industry in
    selected PTA member countries. - 1986.
    (000782) (000936)

MAURITIUS--TOURISM STATISTICS.
----The role of transnational corporations
    in hotel and tourism industry in
    selected PTA member countries. - 1986.
    (000782) (000936)

MAURITIUS--TRANSNATIONAL CORPORATIONS.
----The role of transnational corporations
    in hotel and tourism industry in
    selected PTA member countries. - 1986.
    (000782) (000936)

MAURITIUS--WOMEN WORKERS.
----Jobs for the girls. - 1984.
    (001901)

MAURITIUS--YOUNG WORKERS.
----Jobs for the girls. - 1984.
    (001901)

MEAT INDUSTRY--ARGENTINA.
----Empresas transnacionales en la industria
    de alimentos. - 1983.
    (000573)

MEAT INDUSTRY--BRAZIL.
----Empresas transnacionales y ganadería de
    carnes en Brasil. - 1983.
    (000568)

MEDIATION.
----Multilateral negotiation and mediation.
    - 1985.
    (002545)

MEDIATION--AUSTRALIA.
----Mediation, conciliation and arbitration
    : an international comparison of
    Australia, Great Britain and the United
    States. - 1987.
    (002476)

MEDIATION--CHINA.
----Mediation, conciliation, arbitration and
    litigation in the People's Republic of
    China. - 1987.
    (002565)

MEDIATION--UNITED KINGDOM.
----Mediation, conciliation and arbitration
    : an international comparison of
    Australia, Great Britain and the United
    States. - 1987.
    (002476)

MEDIATION--UNITED STATES.
----Mediation, conciliation and arbitration
    : an international comparison of
    Australia, Great Britain and the United
    States. - 1987.
    (002476)

MEDICINE.
----Medicine advertising regulation and
    self-regulation in 54 countries. - 1985.
    (000815)

MEETING OF GOVERNMENTAL EXPERTS ON THE
TRANSFER, APPLICATION AND DEVELOPMENT OF
TECHNOLOGY IN THE CAPITAL GOODS AND
INDUSTRIAL MACHINERY SECTOR (1982 :
GENEVA)--RECOMMENDATIONS.
----The capital goods sector in developing
    countries. - 1985.
    (001651)

MEETING OF SECRETARIATS OF ECONOMIC
CO-OPERATION AND INTEGRATION GROUPINGS OF
DEVELOPING COUNTRIES AND MULTILATERAL
DEVELOPMENT FINANCE INSTITUTIONS TO EXAMINE
THE PROBLEMS OF PROMOTING AND FINANCING
INTEGRATION PROJECTS (1984 :
GENEVA)--RECOMMENDATIONS.
----Current problems of economic
    integration. - 1986.
    (001312)

MEETING OF SECRETARIATS OF ECONOMIC
CO-OPERATION AND INTEGRATION GROUPINGS OF
DEVELOPING COUNTRIES AND MULTILATERAL
DEVELOPMENT FINANCE INSTITUTIONS TO EXAMINE
THE PROBLEMS OF PROMOTING AND FINANCING
INTEGRATION PROJECTS (1984 : GENEVA)--WORK
ORGANIZATION.
----Current problems of economic
    integration. - 1986.
    (001312)

MERCADO COMUN CENTROAMERICANO.
----Industrial cooperation in regional
    economic groupings among developing
    countries and lessons for SAARC. - 1987.
    (001009)
----Measures strengthening the negotiating
    capacity of Governments in their
    relations with transnational
    corporations. - 1983.
    (002461)

MERCADO COM?U1N CENTROAM?E1RICANO.
----The role of transnational enterprises in
    Latin American economic integration
    efforts. - 1983.
    (001126)

METALLURGICAL INDUSTRY--ARGENTINA.
----La industria siderúrgica
    latinoamericana. - 1984.
    (000601)

METALLURGICAL INDUSTRY--BOLIVIA.
----La industria siderúrgica
    latinoamericana. - 1984.
       (000601)

METALLURGICAL INDUSTRY--BRAZIL.
----La industria siderúrgica
    latinoamericana. - 1984.
       (000601)

METALLURGICAL INDUSTRY--CHILE.
----La industria siderúrgica
    latinoamericana. - 1984.
       (000601)

METALLURGICAL INDUSTRY--COLOMBIA.
----La industria siderúrgica
    latinoamericana. - 1984.
       (000601)

METALLURGICAL INDUSTRY--ECUADOR.
----La industria siderúrgica
    latinoamericana. - 1984.
       (000601)

METALLURGICAL INDUSTRY--LATIN AMERICA.
----La industria siderúrgica
    latinoamericana. - 1984.
       (000601)

METALLURGICAL INDUSTRY--MEXICO.
----La industria siderúrgica
    latinoamericana. - 1984.
       (000601)

METALLURGICAL INDUSTRY--PARAGUAY.
----La industria siderúrgica
    latinoamericana. - 1984.
       (000601)

METALLURGICAL INDUSTRY--PERU.
----La industria siderúrgica
    latinoamericana. - 1984.
       (000601)

METALLURGICAL INDUSTRY--VENEZUELA.
----La industria siderúrgica
    latinoamericana. - 1984.
       (000601)

METALLURGY--LATIN AMERICA.
----La industria siderúrgica
    latinoamericana. - 1984.
       (000601)

METALWORKING INDUSTRY--INDIA.
----Technology transfer under alternative
    arrangements with transnational
    corporations. - 1987.
       (001513)

METALWORKING INDUSTRY--MALAYSIA.
----Technology transfer under alternative
    arrangements with transnational
    corporations. - 1987.
       (001513)

MEXICAN-AMERICAN BORDER REGION--FREE EXPORT
ZONES.
----Mexican border and free zone areas:
    implications for development. - 1983.
       (002380)

MEXICO--ASSEMBLY-LINE WORK.
----Restructuring industry offshore. - 1983.
       (000692)

MEXICO--AUTOMOBILE INDUSTRY.
----Transnational corporations versus the
    state. - 1985.
       (000657)

MEXICO--BANKING.
----La internacionalización financiera
    mexicana. - 1983.
       (001288)

MEXICO--BANKING SYSTEMS.
----Doing business in Mexico. - 1984.
       (001791)

MEXICO--BANKS.
----Expropriation and aftermath : the
    prospects for foreign enterprise in the
    Mexico of Miguel de la Madrid. - 1983.
       (002328)
----La nacionalización de la banca. - 1983.
       (001529)

MEXICO--BUSINESS ENTERPRISES.
----Inversión extranjera directa. - 1985.
       (000138)

MEXICO--CAPITAL INVESTMENTS.
----Capital intensity and export propensity
    in some Latin American countries. - 1987.
       (001389)
----Industrialización, capital extranjero y
    transferencia de tecnología. - 1986.
       (001524)

MEXICO--CHEMICALS.
----Estructura y comportamiento de la
    industria químico-farmacéutica en
    México. - 1984.
       (000737)

MEXICO--CHOICE OF TECHNOLOGY.
----Capital intensity and export propensity
    in some Latin American countries. - 1987.
       (001389)

MEXICO--CORPORATE PLANNING.
----Wandel der mexikanischen Politik
    gegenuber Auslandsinvestitionen? Die
    "irationale" Komponente der
    Mexikanisierungsstrategie. - 1985.
       (002338)

MEXICO--DEBT SERVICING.
----A note on the burden of the Mexican
    foreign debt. - 1986.
       (000254)

MEXICO--DIRECTORIES.
----1985 directory of in-bond plants
    (maquiladoras) in Mexico. - 1984.
       (001132) (002678)

MEXICO--ECONOMIC CONDITIONS.
----Política económica y empresas
    transnacionales en México. - 1983.
       (001127)

MEXICO--ECONOMIC POLICY.
----De la improvisación al fracaso : la
     política de inversión extranjera en
     México. - 1983.
       (001112)

MEXICO--ELECTRONICS INDUSTRY.
----L'électronique dans la politique
     industrielle mexicaine. - 1986.
       (000697)

MEXICO--EMPLOYMENT.
----Las maquiladoras en México. - 1984.
       (001906)

MEXICO--EXCLUSIVE ECONOMIC ZONE.
----U.S. fishery negotiations with Canada
     and Mexico. - 1985.
       (002462)

MEXICO--EXPORT ORIENTED INDUSTRIES.
----Capital intensity and export propensity
     in some Latin American countries. - 1987.
       (001389)
----Restructuring industry offshore. - 1983.
       (000692)

MEXICO--EXPROPRIATION.
----Expropriation and aftermath : the
     prospects for foreign enterprise in the
     Mexico of Miguel de la Madrid. - 1983.
       (002328)

MEXICO--EXTERNAL DEBT.
----La internacionalización financiera
     mexicana. - 1983.
       (001288)
----A note on the burden of the Mexican
     foreign debt. - 1986.
       (000254)

MEXICO--FINANCE.
----Doing business in Mexico. - 1984.
       (001791)
----La internacionalización financiera
     mexicana. - 1983.
       (001288)

MEXICO--FISHERY EXPLOITATION.
----U.S. fishery negotiations with Canada
     and Mexico. - 1985.
       (002462)

MEXICO--FOREIGN DIRECT INVESTMENT.
----De la improvisación al fracaso : la
     política de inversión extranjera en
     México. - 1983.
       (001112)
----Doing business in Mexico. - 1984.
       (001791)
----Las empresas transnacionales y la
     inversión extranjera directa en la
     primera mitad de los años ochenta. -
     1987.
       (000194)
----Inversión extranjera directa. - 1985.
       (000138)
----Política económica y empresas
     transnacionales en México. - 1983.
       (001127)

----Wandel der mexikanischen Politik
     gegenuber Auslandsinvestitionen? Die
     "irationale" Komponente der
     Mexikanisierungsstrategie. - 1985.
       (002338)

MEXICO--FOREIGN EXCHANGE CONTROL.
----Doing business in Mexico. - 1984.
       (001791)

MEXICO--FOREIGN INVESTMENTS.
----Foreign investment and productive
     efficiency. - 1986.
       (001084)
----The foreign investment transaction in
     Mexico. - 1985.
       (002260)
----Mining investment in Brazil, Peru, and
     Mexico. - 1984.
       (002443)
----National legislation and regulations
     relating to transnational corporations.
     Volume 4. - 1986.
       (002253)
----A note on the burden of the Mexican
     foreign debt. - 1986.
       (000254)

MEXICO--FOREIGN TRADE.
----Restructuring industry offshore. - 1983.
       (000692)

MEXICO--INDUSTRIAL EFFICIENCY.
----Foreign investment and productive
     efficiency. - 1986.
       (001084)

MEXICO--INDUSTRIAL PLANNING.
----Alliance for production. - 1984.
       (002316)

MEXICO--INDUSTRIAL POLICY.
----L'électronique dans la politique
     industrielle mexicaine. - 1986.
       (000697)

MEXICO--INDUSTRIAL SUBCONTRACTING.
----Las maquiladoras en México. - 1984.
       (001906)
----1985 directory of in-bond plants
     (maquiladoras) in Mexico. - 1984.
       (001132) (002678)

MEXICO--INDUSTRIALIZATION.
----Exports of technology by newly
     industrializing countries: Mexico. -
     1984.
       (001423)
----Industrialización, capital extranjero y
     transferencia de tecnología. - 1986.
       (001524)

MEXICO--INVESTMENT POLICY.
----The foreign investment transaction in
     Mexico. - 1985.
       (002260)

MEXICO--INVESTMENT TAX CREDIT.
----Alliance for production. - 1984.
       (002316)

MEXICO--IRON AND STEEL INDUSTRY.
----La industria siderúrgica
    latinoamericana. - 1984.
        (000601)

MEXICO--JOINT VENTURES.
----The foreign investment transaction in
    Mexico. - 1985.
        (002260)
----Joint ventures in Mexico. - 1984.
        (001631)

MEXICO--LAWS AND REGULATIONS.
----Doing business in Mexico. - 1984.
        (001791)
----The foreign investment transaction in
    Mexico. - 1985.
        (002260)
----National legislation and regulations
    relating to transnational corporations.
    Volume 4. - 1986.
        (002253)

MEXICO--LOANS.
----La internacionalización financiera
    mexicana. - 1983.
        (001288)

MEXICO--MANAGEMENT.
----Joint ventures in Mexico. - 1984.
        (001631)

MEXICO--MANUFACTURING.
----Foreign investment and productive
    efficiency. - 1986.
        (001084)

MEXICO--MANUFACTURING ENTERPRISES.
----The determinants of manufacturing
    ownership in less developed countries. -
    1986.
        (000712)
----Foreign investment, technical efficiency
    and structural change. - 1983.
        (001085)
----1985 directory of in-bond plants
    (maquiladoras) in Mexico. - 1984.
        (001132) (002678)

MEXICO--MARKET POTENTIAL.
----Multinationals and market structure in
    Mexico. - 1986.
        (001086)

MEXICO--METALLURGICAL INDUSTRY.
----La industria siderúrgica
    latinoamericana. - 1984.
        (000601)

MEXICO--MINING INDUSTRY.
----Mining investment in Brazil, Peru, and
    Mexico. - 1984.
        (002443)

MEXICO--MINING LAW.
----Mining investment in Brazil, Peru, and
    Mexico. - 1984.
        (002443)

MEXICO--MIXED ENTERPRISES.
----Las empresas transnacionales y la
    inversión extranjera directa en la
    primera mitad de los años ochenta. -
    1987.
        (000194)

MEXICO--MONETARY SYSTEMS.
----La internacionalización financiera
    mexicana. - 1983.
        (001288)

MEXICO--MONOPOLIES.
----La nacionalización de la banca. - 1983.
        (001529)

MEXICO--NATIONALIZATION.
----La nacionalización de la banca. - 1983.
        (001529)

MEXICO--NEGOTIATION.
----U.S. fishery negotiations with Canada
    and Mexico. - 1985.
        (002462)

MEXICO--PHARMACEUTICAL INDUSTRY.
----Estructura y comportamiento de la
    industria químico-farmacéutica en
    México. - 1984.
        (000737)
----Médicaments pour tous en l'an 2000? -
    1983.
        (000662)
----Research and development in
    pharmaceuticals: Mexico. - 1983.
        (000770)
----Las transnacionales de la salud. - 1983.
        (000745)
----Transnational corporations in the
    pharmaceutical industry of developing
    countries. - 1984.
        (000749)

MEXICO--PHARMACEUTICALS.
----Médicaments pour tous en l'an 2000? -
    1983.
        (000662)

MEXICO--PRIVATE ENTERPRISES.
----The determinants of manufacturing
    ownership in less developed countries. -
    1986.
        (000712)

MEXICO--PUBLIC ENTERPRISES.
----The determinants of manufacturing
    ownership in less developed countries. -
    1986.
        (000712)
----The role of public enterprises in the
    advancement of women in Mexico. - 1983.
        (001894)

MEXICO--RESEARCH AND DEVELOPMENT.
----Research and development in
    pharmaceuticals: Mexico. - 1983.
        (000770)

MEXICO--STATISTICAL DATA.
----Estructura y comportamiento de la
    industria químico-farmacéutica en
    México. - 1984.
        (000737)

MEXICO--STRATEGY.
----Wandel der mexikanischen Politik
gegenuber Auslandsinvestitionen? Die
"irationale" Komponente der
Mexikanisierungsstrategie. - 1985.
(002338)

MEXICO--TAX INCENTIVES.
----Alliance for production. - 1984.
(002316)

MEXICO--TECHNOLOGY TRANSFER.
----Exports of technology by newly
industrializing countries: Mexico. -
1984.
(001423)
----Industrialización, capital extranjero y
transferencia de tecnología. - 1986.
(001524)

MEXICO--TRANSNATIONAL CORPORATIONS.
----El comportamiento de las empresas
nacionales y estranjeras en México. -
1986.
(001083)
----De la improvisación al fracaso : la
política de inversión extranjera en
México. - 1983.
(001112)
----The determinants of manufacturing
ownership in less developed countries. -
1986.
(000712)
----Estructura y comportamiento de la
industria quimico-farmacéutica en
México. - 1984.
(000737)
----Foreign investment, technical efficiency
and structural change. - 1983.
(001085)
----Inversión extranjera directa. - 1985.
(000138)
----Las maquiladoras en México. - 1984.
(001906)
----Médicaments pour tous en l'an 2000? -
1983.
(000662)
----Multinationals and market structure in
Mexico. - 1986.
(001086)
----La nacionalización de la banca. - 1983.
(001529)
----National legislation and regulations
relating to transnational corporations.
Volume 4. - 1986.
(002253)
----Política económica y empresas
transnacionales en México. - 1983.
(001127)
----Research and development in
pharmaceuticals: Mexico. - 1983.
(000770)
----Las transnacionales de la salud. - 1983.
(000745)
----Transnational corporations versus the
state. - 1985.
(000657)
----Wandel der mexikanischen Politik
gegenuber Auslandsinvestitionen? Die
"irationale" Komponente der
Mexikanisierungsstrategie. - 1985.
(002338)

----1985 directory of in-bond plants
(maquiladoras) in Mexico. - 1984.
(001132) (002678)

MEXICO--WOMEN.
----Las maquiladoras en México. - 1984.
(001906)

MEXICO--WOMEN'S ADVANCEMENT.
----The role of public enterprises in the
advancement of women in Mexico. - 1983.
(001894)

MEXICO--WOMEN'S STATUS.
----The role of public enterprises in the
advancement of women in Mexico. - 1983.
(001894)

MEZHDUNARODNYI TSENTR NAUCHOI I
TEKHNICHESKOI INFORMATSII.
----Technological cooperation and
specialization. - 1986.
(001500)

MICHELIN ET CIE (CLERMONT-FERRAND, FRANCE).
----Michelin : een zwart profiel : over
werken in een bandenfabriek in Den
Bosch. - 1984.
(000289)

MICROCOMPUTERS--GERMAN DEMOCRATIC REPUBLIC.
----Die Anwendung der Mikrorechentechnik :
wichtige Voraussetzung für eine
reaktionsfähige und effektive
Absatzwirtschaft. - 1987.
(000908)

MICROELECTRONICS.
----The global race in microelectronics. -
1983.
(000684)
----Microelectronics-based automation
technologies and development. - 1985.
(000753)

MICROELECTRONICS--BRAZIL.
----Microelectronics-based automation
technologies and development. - 1985.
(000753)
----Politische Gestaltungsspielräume von
Schwellenländern in der
Mikroelektronik-Industrie. - 1987.
(000617)

MICROELECTRONICS--CHINA.
----Microelectronics-based automation
technologies and development. - 1985.
(000753)

MICROELECTRONICS--EUROPE.
----Governments and microelectronics. - 1983.
(000648)

MICROELECTRONICS--REPUBLIC OF KOREA.
----Politische Gestaltungsspielräume von
Schwellenländern in der
Mikroelektronik-Industrie. - 1987.
(000617)

MICROELECTRONICS--UNITED KINGDOM.
----Microelectronics in British industry. -
1984.
(000723)

MICROELECTRONICS--UNITED STATES.
----Microelectronics. - 1981-   .
    (000718)

MIDDLE CLASSES.
----International business in the nineteenth
    century. - 1987.
    (000046)

MIDDLE EAST--ACCOUNTING AND REPORTING.
----The recent accounting and economic
    developments in the Middle East. - 1985.
    (002109)

MIDDLE EAST--BUSINESS.
----International business in the Middle
    East. - 1986.
    (001135)

MIDDLE EAST--CONSULTANTS.
----An international directory of 600
    consultants and contractors with
    experience in the Middle East. - 1985.
    (002645)

MIDDLE EAST--DIRECTORIES.
----Asia-Pacific/Africa-Middle East
    petroleum directory. - 1984-   .
    (000579) (002618)

MIDDLE EAST--FOREIGN DIRECT INVESTMENT.
----Legal consideration in doing business in
    the Middle East, Turkey and Pakistan. -
    1986.
    (002172)

MIDDLE EAST--FOREIGN TRADE.
----International business in the Middle
    East. - 1986.
    (001135)

MIDDLE EAST--INDUSTRIAL MANAGEMENT.
----International business in the Middle
    East. - 1986.
    (001135)

MIDDLE EAST--INDUSTRIAL RELATIONS.
----Major causes of joint-venture failures
    in the Middle East: the case of Iran. -
    1983.
    (001640)

MIDDLE EAST--INTERNATIONAL CO-OPERATION.
----Internationale Produktionskooperation im
    Vorderen Orient. - 1983.
    (001142)

MIDDLE EAST--INTERPERSONAL RELATIONS.
----Major causes of joint-venture failures
    in the Middle East: the case of Iran. -
    1983.
    (001640)

MIDDLE EAST--JOINT VENTURES.
----Internationale Produktionskooperation im
    Vorderen Orient. - 1983.
    (001142)
----Major causes of joint-venture failures
    in the Middle East: the case of Iran. -
    1983.
    (001640)

MIDDLE EAST--LAWS AND REGULATIONS.
----Legal implications of marketing in the
    Middle East. - 1985.
    (002196)

MIDDLE EAST--MARKETING.
----International business in the Middle
    East. - 1986.
    (001135)
----Legal implications of marketing in the
    Middle East. - 1985.
    (002196)

MIDDLE EAST--PETROLEUM INDUSTRY.
----Asia-Pacific/Africa-Middle East
    petroleum directory. - 1984-   .
    (000579) (002618)

MIDDLE EAST--PUBLIC CONTRACTS.
----An introduction to contract procedures
    in the Near East and North Africa. -
    1978-   .
    (002433)

MIDDLE EAST--REGRESSION ANALYSIS.
----Major causes of joint-venture failures
    in the Middle East: the case of Iran. -
    1983.
    (001640)

MIDDLE EAST--TRANSNATIONAL CORPORATIONS.
----International business in the Middle
    East. - 1986.
    (001135)
----An international directory of 600
    consultants and contractors with
    experience in the Middle East. - 1985.
    (002645)
----Internationale Produktionskooperation im
    Vorderen Orient. - 1983.
    (001142)

MIGRANT WORKERS--NAMIBIA.
----Transnational corporations in South
    Africa and Namibia : United Nations
    public hearings. Volume 1, Reports of
    the Panel of Eminent Persons and of the
    Secretary-General. - 1986.
    (001216)
----Transnational corporations in South
    Africa and Namibia. - 1986.
    (001217)

MIGRANT WORKERS--SOUTH AFRICA.
----Transnational corporations in South
    Africa and Namibia : United Nations
    public hearings. Volume 1, Reports of
    the Panel of Eminent Persons and of the
    Secretary-General. - 1986.
    (001216)
----Transnational corporations in South
    Africa and Namibia. - 1986.
    (001217)

MILITARISM.
----Transnational corporations and
    militarism. - 1985.
    (000663)

MILITARY ASSISTANCE--UNITED STATES.
----U.S. foreign assistance. - 1984.
    (000203)

MILITARY EXPENDITURES--UNITED STATES.
----National security and the semiconductor
industry. - 1987.
(000675)

MILITARY GOVERNMENT--PERU.
----The Peruvian military government and the
international corporations. - 1983.
(001801)
----Política económica y empresas
transnacionales en el Perú, 1968-1975. -
1983.
(001107)

MILITARY OCCUPATION--NAMIBIA.
----Transnational corporations in South
Africa and Namibia : United Nations
public hearings. Volume 1, Reports of
the Panel of Eminent Persons and of the
Secretary-General. - 1986.
(001216)

MILITARY OCCUPATION--SOUTH AFRICA.
----Transnational corporations in South
Africa and Namibia : United Nations
public hearings. Volume 1, Reports of
the Panel of Eminent Persons and of the
Secretary-General. - 1986.
(001216)

MILITARY POLICY.
----The military origins of
industrialisation and international
trade rivalry. - 1984.
(001335)

MILITARY RELATIONS--SOUTH AFRICA.
----Measures regarding the activities of
transnational corporations in South
Africa and Namibia. - 1985.
(001220)
----Transnational corporations in South
Africa and Namibia : United Nations
public hearings. Volume 1, Reports of
the Panel of Eminent Persons and of the
Secretary-General. - 1986.
(001216)
----Transnational corporations in South
Africa and Namibia : United Nations
public hearings. Volume 3, Statements
and submissions. - 1987.
(001215)

MILITARY SCIENCE--SOUTH AFRICA.
----Activities of transnational corporations
in South Africa and Namibia and the
responsibilities of home countries with
respect to their operations in this
area. - 1986.
(001192)

MINERAL INDUSTRY.
----E [and] MJ international directory of
mining. - 1968-   .
(002637)
----Financial Times mining international
yearbook. - 1887-   .
(002639)
----Foreign investment in mining projects. -
1983.
(000619)
----Géopolitique des ressources minières. -
1983.
(000593)

----Minerals yearbook. - 1933-   .
(000621)
----Problems of mineral development in
developing countries. - 1983.
(000583)
----Third World mineral development in
crisis: the impact of the worldwide
recession on legal instruments governing
Third World mineral development. - 1985.
(000649)
----Trends and issues in foreign direct
investment and related flows. - 1985.
(000192)

MINERAL INDUSTRY--AFRICA.
----Mineral industries of Africa. -
1976-   .
(000620)

MINERAL INDUSTRY--AUSTRALIA.
----Beyond dependence. - 1986.
(000640)
----Foreign investment control in the mining
sector. - 1983.
(000577)
----The mineral and petroleum joint venture
in Australia. - 1986.
(000588)
----Mineral industries of Australia, Canada,
and Oceania. - 1985.
(000603)

MINERAL INDUSTRY--CANADA.
----Foreign investment control in the mining
sector. - 1983.
(000577)
----Mineral industries of Australia, Canada,
and Oceania. - 1985.
(000603)

MINERAL INDUSTRY--EUROPE.
----Mineral industries of Europe and the
U.S.S.R. - 1984.
(000642)

MINERAL INDUSTRY--OCEANIA.
----Mineral industries of Australia, Canada,
and Oceania. - 1985.
(000603)

MINERAL INDUSTRY--UNITED STATES.
----Foreign direct investment in the U.S.
minerals industry. - 1987.
(000635)
----Political risk in the international oil
and gas industry. - 1983.
(001823)

MINERAL INDUSTRY--USSR.
----Mineral industries of Europe and the
U.S.S.R. - 1984.
(000642)

MINERAL RESOURCES.
----The relationship between the state and
the multinational corporation in the
exploitation of resources. - 1984.
(000584)
----Transnational corporations in world
development. - 1983.
(000102)

MINERAL RESOURCES--AUSTRALIA.
----Indigenous resource rights and mining
    companies in North America and
    Australia. - 1986.
        (000616)

MINERAL RESOURCES--COLOMBIA.
----Las empresas transnacionales en el
    desarrollo colombiano. - 1986.
        (001121)

MINERAL RESOURCES--NAMIBIA.
----Transnational corporations in South
    Africa and Namibia. - 1986.
        (001217)

MINERAL RESOURCES--NORTH AMERICA.
----Indigenous resource rights and mining
    companies in North America and
    Australia. - 1986.
        (000616)

MINERAL RESOURCES--SOUTH AFRICA.
----Transnational corporations in South
    Africa and Namibia. - 1986.
        (001217)

MINERAL RESOURCES DEVELOPMENT.
----Negotiation and drafting of mining
    development agreements. - 1976.
        (002432)

MINERAL RESOURCES DEVELOPMENT--LATIN AMERICA.
----The role of the public sector and
    transnational corporations in the mining
    development of Latin America. - 1986.
        (000605)

MINERAL RESOURCES DEVELOPMENT--PAPUA NEW
GUINEA.
----Ok Tedi : evolution of a Third World
    mining project. - 1984.
        (000293)

MINERAL RESOURCES DEVELOPMENT--SOUTH AMERICA.
----Financing implications of mineral
    development agreements. - 1986.
        (002456)

MINERALS.
----Long term contracts and East-West trade
    in non-fuel minerals. - 1986.
        (002444)

MINING.
----Bilateral investment promotion
    protection and treaties : a model for
    Community promotion of mining
    investment? - 1986.
        (002052)
----Capital allowance schemes for mining
    projects in LDCs. - 1983.
        (000607)
----Foreign investment in mining projects. -
    1983.
        (000619)
----Promotion of mining and energy
    investment under the Lomé Convention. -
    1986.
        (002607)
----Technical co-operation programme,
    1976-1987 : United Nations Centre on
    Transnational Corporations. - 1988.
        (002611)

MINING--GOVE PENINSULA (AUSTRALIA).
----The history and contractual arrangements
    of the Gove bauxite/alumina project in
    the Northern Territory of Australia. -
    1985.
        (000596)

MINING--NAMIBIA.
----Mines and independence. - 1983.
        (001204)

MINING--NORTHERN TERRITORY (AUSTRALIA).
----The history and contractual arrangements
    of the Gove bauxite/alumina project in
    the Northern Territory of Australia. -
    1985.
        (000596)

MINING--PAPUA NEW GUINEA.
----Ok Tedi : evolution of a Third World
    mining project. - 1984.
        (000293)

MINING--ZAMBIA.
----Mining legislation and mineral
    development in Zambia. - 1986.
        (000625)

MINING ENGINEERING.
----E [and] MJ international directory of
    mining. - 1968-   .
        (002637)

MINING INDUSTRY.
----Contractual adaptation and conflict
    resolution based on venture contracts
    for mining projects in developing
    countries. - 1985.
        (002475)
----E [and] MJ international directory of
    mining. - 1968-   .
        (002637)
----Financial Times mining international
    yearbook. - 1887-   .
        (002639)
----Negotiation and drafting of mining
    development agreements. - 1976.
        (002432)
----Transnational corporations in world
    development. - 1983.
        (000102)
----UNCTC bibliography, 1974-1987. - 1988.
        (002695)

MINING INDUSTRY--AUSTRALIA.
----Aborigines and mining companies in
    Northern Australia. - 1983.
        (001874)
----Beyond dependence. - 1986.
        (000640)
----Indigenous resource rights and mining
    companies in North America and
    Australia. - 1986.
        (000616)

MINING INDUSTRY--BRAZIL.
----Mining investment in Brazil, Peru, and
    Mexico. - 1984.
        (002443)

MINING INDUSTRY--CHILE.
----Einige juristische Aspekte des
    Ausverkaufs der chilenischen Wirtschaft
    an die internationalen Monopole. - 1984.
    (002161)

MINING INDUSTRY--LATIN AMERICA.
----The role of the public sector and
    transnational corporations in the mining
    development of Latin America. - 1986.
    (000605)

MINING INDUSTRY--MEXICO.
----Mining investment in Brazil, Peru, and
    Mexico. - 1984.
    (002443)

MINING INDUSTRY--NAMIBIA.
----Transnational corporations in South
    Africa and Namibia : United Nations
    public hearings. Volume 1, Reports of
    the Panel of Eminent Persons and of the
    Secretary-General. - 1986.
    (001216)

MINING INDUSTRY--NORTH AMERICA.
----Indigenous resource rights and mining
    companies in North America and
    Australia. - 1986.
    (000616)

MINING INDUSTRY--PERU.
----Mining investment in Brazil, Peru, and
    Mexico. - 1984.
    (002443)
----Política económica y empresas
    transnacionales en el Perú, 1968-1975. -
    1983.
    (001107)

MINING INDUSTRY--ZAIRE.
----Les sociétés transnationales en Afrique.
    - 1986.
    (001028)

MINING LAW.
----The evolution of the legal relationship
    between international petroleum mining
    companies and host countries. - 1983.
    (000647)

MINING LAW--ARGENTINA.
----Petroleum service contracts in
    Argentina, Brazil and Colombia : issues
    arising from their legal nature. - 1987.
    (002422)

MINING LAW--BRAZIL.
----Mining investment in Brazil, Peru, and
    Mexico. - 1984.
    (002443)
----Petroleum service contracts in
    Argentina, Brazil and Colombia : issues
    arising from their legal nature. - 1987.
    (002422)

MINING LAW--COLOMBIA.
----Petroleum service contracts in
    Argentina, Brazil and Colombia : issues
    arising from their legal nature. - 1987.
    (002422)

MINING LAW--LATIN AMERICA.
----Petroleum service contracts in
    Argentina, Brazil and Colombia : issues
    arising from their legal nature. - 1987.
    (002422)

MINING LAW--MEXICO.
----Mining investment in Brazil, Peru, and
    Mexico. - 1984.
    (002443)

MINING LAW--PERU.
----Mining investment in Brazil, Peru, and
    Mexico. - 1984.
    (002443)

MINING LAW--ZAMBIA.
----Mining legislation and mineral
    development in Zambia. - 1986.
    (000625)

MINISTERIAL DECLARATION ON THE URUGUAY ROUND
(1986).
----Intellectual property rights,
    investment, and trade in services in the
    Uruguay round. - 1987.
    (000817)
----Trade in services : growth and balance
    of payments implications for countries
    of Western Asia. - 1987.
    (000968)
----The Uruguay Round and the international
    trading system. - 1987.
    (001976)

MIXED ENTERPRISES--BRAZIL.
----Las empresas transnacionales y la
    inversión extranjera directa en la
    primera mitad de los años ochenta. -
    1987.
    (000194)

MIXED ENTERPRISES--MEXICO.
----Las empresas transnacionales y la
    inversión extranjera directa en la
    primera mitad de los años ochenta. -
    1987.
    (000194)

MODEL CONTRACTS.
----Joint venturing abroad. - 1985.
    (001598)

MODEL CONTRACTS--ISRAEL.
----Controlling standard contracts. - 1985.
    (002423)

MODEL DOUBLE TAXATION CONVENTION ON INCOME
AND CAPITAL (1977).
----A comparative analysis of the United
    States-People's Republic of China tax
    treaty. - 1986.
    (002037)
----International bank lending. - 1984.
    (000988)
----The Soviet Union's other tax agreements.
    - 1986.
    (002043)

MODEL LAW ON INTERNATIONAL COMMERCIAL
ARBITRATION (1985).
----International commercial arbitration : a
comparative analysis of the United
States system and the UNCITRAL model
law. - 1986.
(002487)
----Introductory note on the UNCITRAL Model
Law on International Commercial
Arbitration. - 1985.
(002513)
----The status of the UNCITRAL Model Law on
International Commercial Arbitration
vis-à-vis the ICC, LCIA and UNCITRAL
arbitration rules. - 1986.
(002583)
----UNCITRAL Model Law on International
Commercial Arbitration. - 1986.
(002503)
----The UNCITRAL model law on international
commercial arbitration. - 1986.
(002517)
----The UNCITRAL model law on international
commercial arbitration. - 1986.
(002541)

MODEL LAWS.
----The status of the UNCITRAL Model Law on
International Commercial Arbitration
vis-à-vis the ICC, LCIA and UNCITRAL
arbitration rules. - 1986.
(002583)
----The UNCITRAL model law on international
commercial arbitration. - 1986.
(002517)
----The UNCITRAL model law on international
commercial arbitration. - 1986.
(002541)

MODEL LAWS--UNITED STATES.
----Tax treaty abuse. - 1983.
(002046)

MONETARY POLICY.
----Annual report (Bank for International
Settlements). - 1930-   .
(001228)
----Currency exposure management. - 1983.
(000409)
----Defining and measuring currency
exposure. - 1983.
(000504)
----The stability of the international
monetary system. - 1987.
(001294)

MONETARY POLICY--AFRICA.
----Nezavisimye strany Afriki. - 1986.
(001280)

MONETARY POLICY--JAPAN.
----Japan as capital exporter and the world
economy. - 1985.
(000384)
----Japanese offshore banking. - 1984.
(000933)

MONETARY SYSTEMS--BRAZIL.
----La internacionalización financiera en
Brasil. - 1983.
(001082)

MONETARY SYSTEMS--MEXICO.
----La internacionalización financiera
mexicana. - 1983.
(001288)

MONEY.
----Money, multinationals, and sovereigns. -
1983.
(001226)

MONOPOLIES.
----Competition in the Marxist tradition. -
1983.
(001697)
----The effects of taxation price control
and government contracts in oligopoly
and monopolistic competition. - 1987.
(001693)
----Innovation und internationale Monopole.
- 1983.
(001671)
----Internatsionalizatsiia
monopoliticheskogo nakopleniia i
razvivaiushchiesia strany. - 1986.
(000082)
----Merger policies and recent trends in
mergers. - 1984.
(001618)
----Multinational monopolies and
international cartels. - 1984.
(001663)
----Rol' mezhdunarodnykh monopolii v mirovoi
ekonomike. - 1983.
(000047)
----Rol'mezhdunarodnykh monopolii v
prodovol'stvennoi sisteme. - 1985.
(000728)
----Sovremennyi kontsern,
politekonomicheskii aspekt. - 1983.
(001668)
----Transnational corporations and uneven
development : the internationalization
of capital and the Third World. - 1987.
(001270)
----Transnational monopoly capitalism. -
1987.
(001666)
----Transnatsional'nye korporatsii i
burzhuaznoe trudovoe pravo. - 1985.
(001946) (002230)
----The 1984 Justice Department guidelines
toward horizontal mergers. - 1986.
(001551)

MONOPOLIES--JAPAN.
----The invisible link. - 1986.
(000992).

MONOPOLIES--MEXICO.
----La nacionalización de la banca. - 1983.
(001529)

MONOPOLIES--UNITED STATES.
----US monopolies and developing countries.
- 1986.
(001692)

MOROCCO--FINANCIAL STATISTICS.
----Expérience marocaine dans
l'établissement d'entreprises
multinationales. - 1986.
(001027)

MOROCCO--FOOD.
----Marketing supplementary food products in
      LDCs. - 1983.
      (000665)

MOROCCO--FOREIGN INVESTMENTS.
----Expérience marocaine dans
      l'établissement d'entreprises
      multinationales. - 1986.
      (001027)
----National legislation and regulations
      relating to transnational corporations.
      Volume 4. - 1986.
      (002253)
----Le nouveau droit des investissements
      étrangers au Maroc. - 1984.
      (002269)

MOROCCO--INDUSTRIAL LEGISLATION.
----Le nouveau droit des investissements
      étrangers au Maroc. - 1984.
      (002269)

MOROCCO--INDUSTRIAL SECTOR.
----Expérience marocaine dans
      l'établissement d'entreprises
      multinationales. - 1986.
      (001027)

MOROCCO--INDUSTRIAL STATISTICS.
----Expérience marocaine dans
      l'établissement d'entreprises
      multinationales. - 1986.
      (001027)

MOROCCO--INVESTMENT INSURANCE.
----Le nouveau droit des investissements
      étrangers au Maroc. - 1984.
      (002269)

MOROCCO--LAWS AND REGULATIONS.
----National legislation and regulations
      relating to transnational corporations.
      Volume 4. - 1986.
      (002253)

MOROCCO--MARKETING.
----Marketing supplementary food products in
      LDCs. - 1983.
      (000665)

MOROCCO--STATISTICAL DATA.
----Expérience marocaine dans
      l'établissement d'entreprises
      multinationales. - 1986.
      (001027)

MOROCCO--TRANSNATIONAL CORPORATIONS.
----Expérience marocaine dans
      l'établissement d'entreprises
      multinationales. - 1986.
      (001027)
----National legislation and regulations
      relating to transnational corporations.
      Volume 4. - 1986.
      (002253)

MOST FAVOURED NATION CLAUSE.
----Bilateral investment treaties. - 1988.
      (002054)
----UNCITRAL, the United Nations Commission
      on International Trade Law. - 1986.
      (002155)

MOTOR VEHICLE EQUIPMENT--JAPAN.
----Automotive parts industry and the U.S.
      aftermarket for Japanese cars and light
      trucks. - 1985.
      (000759)

MOTOR VEHICLE EQUIPMENT--UNITED STATES.
----Automotive parts industry and the U.S.
      aftermarket for Japanese cars and light
      trucks. - 1985.
      (000759)

MOTOR VEHICLE INDUSTRY.
----Internationalization of capital and the
      semi-industrialized countries: the case
      of the motor industry. - 1985.
      (000700)

MOTOR VEHICLE INDUSTRY--CANADA.
----An automotive strategy for Canada. -
      1983.
      (000686)

MOTOR VEHICLE INDUSTRY--EUROPE.
----Foreign divestment and international
      rationalisation in the motor industry. -
      1985.
      (000664)

MOTOR VEHICLE INDUSTRY--JAPAN.
----Automotive parts industry and the U.S.
      aftermarket for Japanese cars and light
      trucks. - 1985.
      (000759)

MOTOR VEHICLE INDUSTRY--UNITED STATES.
----Automotive parts industry and the U.S.
      aftermarket for Japanese cars and light
      trucks. - 1985.
      (000759)

MULTILATERAL INVESTMENT GUARANTEE AGENCY.
----L'Agence multilatérale de garantie des
      investissements. - 1987.
      (002152)
----The Convention Establishing the
      Multilateral Investment Guarantee
      Agency. - 1987.
      (002127)
----Factors influencing the flow of foreign
      investment and the relevance of a
      multilateral investment guarantee
      scheme. - 1987.
      (002144)
----Insurance against the political risks of
      petroleum investment. - 1986.
      (001866) (002160)
----Investment in ACP states. - 1987.
      (001004)
----MIGA and foreign investment. - 1988.
      (002145)
----Die Multilaterale
      Investitions-Garantie-Agentur (MIGA). -
      1986.
      (002142)
----Promotion of direct investment in
      developing countries. - 1986.
      (002143)
----The role of ICSID and the projected
      Multilateral Investment Guarantee Agency
      (MIGA). - 1986.
      (002585)

MULTILATERAL INVESTMENT GUARANTEE AGENCY
(continued)
----The role of multilateral development
finance institutions in promoting and
financing joint ventures. - 1986.
(000252)
----Second thoughts on MIGA. - 1986.
(002148)
----Shaping a future for foreign direct
investment in the Third World. - 1988.
(002140)
----The World Bank's Multilateral Investment
Guaranty Agency. - 1987.
(002125)
----Zur Bedeutung der Multilateral
Investment Guarantee Agency für den
internationalen Ressourcentransfer. -
1987.
(002129)

MULTILATERAL INVESTMENT GUARANTEE
AGENCY--ORGANIZATIONAL STRUCTURE.
----The Multilateral Investment Guarantee
Agency : status, mandate, concept,
features, implications. - 1987.
(002158)
----The Multilateral Investment Guarantee
Agency. - 1986.
(002146)

MULTILATERAL TRADE NEGOTIATIONS.
----The applicability of GATT to
international trade in services :
general considerations and the interest
of developing countries. - 1987.
(000885)
----The competence of GATT. - 1987.
(001382)
----The GATT and multilateral treaty making.
- 1983.
(001995)
----GATT and recent international trade
problems. - 1987.
(001986)
----GATT surveillance of industrial
policies. - 1986.
(001350)
----Intellectual property rights,
investment, and trade in services in the
Uruguay round. - 1987.
(000817)
----International Colloquium on the Proposed
New Round of Multilateral Trade
Negotiations and Developing Countries :
proceedings and papers. - 1986.
(001365) (001365)
----Issues and data needs for GATT
negotiations on services. - 1987.
(000964)
----Multilateral economic negotiation. -
1987.
(002470)
----Les négociations internationales sur les
services ou la quadrature du cercle. -
1986.
(000911)
----Punta del Este and after. - 1987.
(000927)
----Putting services on the table : the new
GATT round. - 1987.
(000932)
----Services and the GATT. - 1987.
(000954)

----Trade in services : growth and balance
of payments implications for countries
of Western Asia. - 1987.
(000968)
----Trade in services. - 1984.
(000955)
----Trade in services : obstacles and
opportunities. - 1987.
(000984)
----Trade in services and developing
countries. - 1986.
(000952)
----Trade trouble-shooting. - 1986.
(001967)
----Transnational services policy? - 1987.
(000867)
----The U.S. drive to bring services into
GATT. - 1986.
(000926)
----The Uruguay Round and the international
trading system. - 1987.
(001976)
----The Uruguay round of multilateral trade
talks. - 1987.
(000983)

MULTILATERAL TRADE NEGOTIATIONS--UNITED
STATES.
----Intellectual property rights,
investment, and trade in services in the
Uruguay round. - 1987.
(000817)

MULTILATERAL TRADE NEGOTIONS.
----Trade in services and the multilateral
trade negotiations. - 1987.
(000812)

MULTINATIONAL INDUSTRIAL PROJECTS.
----Current problems of economic
integration. - 1986.
(001312)
----Macroproject development in the third
world. - 1983.
(001327)

MULTINATIONAL INDUSTRIAL PROJECTS--AFRICA.
----Current problems of economic
integration. - 1986.
(001312)

MULTINATIONAL INDUSTRIAL PROJECTS--ARAB
COUNTRIES.
----Current problems of economic
integration. - 1986.
(001312)

MULTINATIONAL INDUSTRIAL PROJECTS--ASIA.
----Current problems of economic
integration. - 1986.
(001312)

MULTINATIONAL INDUSTRIAL PROJECTS--BHOPAL
(INDIA).
----Mass disasters and multinational
liability : the Bhopal case. - 1986.
(001936)

MULTINATIONAL INDUSTRIAL PROJECTS--BURUNDI.
----Manuel de procedures contractuelles
    susceptibles d'être mise en oeuvre par
    les contrats internationaux concernant
    la realisation de projets industriels. -
    1984.
      (002417)

MULTINATIONAL INDUSTRIAL PROJECTS--LATIN
AMERICA.
----Current problems of economic
    integration. - 1986.
      (001312)

MULTINATIONAL MARKETING ENTERPRISES.
----Japán multinacionális kereskedoházai és
    nyitása a világgazdaság felé. - 1986.
      (000354)
----Le nouveau marché international du
    charbon. - 1986.
      (000637)

MULTINATIONAL MARKETING ENTERPRISES--BRAZIL.
----Market imperfections and import pricing
    behavior by multinational enterprises. -
    1986.
      (001681)

MULTINATIONAL OIL LIMITED.
----Multinational Oil Limited: issues in
    transfer pricing and foreign ownership.
    - 1985.
      (001750)

MULTINATIONAL PUBLIC CORPORATIONS.
----Multinational enterprises of developing
    countries. - 1986.
      (000357)

NABISCO BRANDS (NEW YORK).
----Importance et implantations comparées
    des quatre plus grands biscuitiers
    mondiaux, Nabisco Brands, United
    Biscuits, Générale Biscuit, Bahlsen. -
    1984.
      (000273)

NAMIBIA--AGRICULTURE.
----Transnational corporations in South
    Africa and Namibia : United Nations
    public hearings. Volume 1, Reports of
    the Panel of Eminent Persons and of the
    Secretary-General. - 1986.
      (001216)

NAMIBIA--BANKING.
----Transnational corporations in South
    Africa and Namibia. - 1986.
      (001217)

NAMIBIA--DIRECTORIES.
----Foreign investment in South Africa and
    Namibia. - 1984.
      (001198) (002641)
----Reference book on major transnational
    corporations operating in Namibia. -
    1985.
      (000297) (001213) (002673)

NAMIBIA--DIVESTMENT.
----Transnational corporations : follow-up
    to the recommendations of the Panel of
    Eminent Persons Established to Conduct
    the Public Hearings on the Activities of
    Transnational Corporations in South
    Africa and Namibia. - 1988.
      (001221)

NAMIBIA--ECONOMIC CONDITIONS.
----Activities of transnational corporations
    in South Africa and Namibia and the
    responsibilities of home countries with
    respect to their operations in this
    area. - 1986.
      (001192)
----Transnational corporations in South
    Africa and Namibia. - 1986.
      (001217)

NAMIBIA--EMPLOYMENT.
----Transnational corporations in South
    Africa and Namibia : United Nations
    public hearings. Volume 1, Reports of
    the Panel of Eminent Persons and of the
    Secretary-General. - 1986.
      (001216)

NAMIBIA--ENERGY RESOURCES.
----Transnational corporations in South
    Africa and Namibia : United Nations
    public hearings. Volume 1, Reports of
    the Panel of Eminent Persons and of the
    Secretary-General. - 1986.
      (001216)

NAMIBIA--FINANCE.
----Transnational corporations in South
    Africa and Namibia : United Nations
    public hearings. Volume 1, Reports of
    the Panel of Eminent Persons and of the
    Secretary-General. - 1986.
      (001216)

NAMIBIA--FISHING.
----Transnational corporations in South
    Africa and Namibia : United Nations
    public hearings. Volume 1, Reports of
    the Panel of Eminent Persons and of the
    Secretary-General. - 1986.
      (001216)

NAMIBIA--FOREIGN DIRECT INVESTMENT.
----Foreign investment in South Africa and
    Namibia. - 1984.
      (001198) (002641)

NAMIBIA--FOREIGN INVESTMENTS.
----Activities of transnational corporations
    in South Africa and Namibia and the
    responsibilities of home countries with
    respect to their operations in this
    area. - 1986.
      (001192)
----Transnational corporations in South
    Africa and Namibia. - 1986.
      (001217)
----Transnational corporations in South
    Africa and Namibia : United Nations
    public hearings. Volume 3, Statements
    and submissions. - 1987.
      (001215)

NAMIBIA--URANIUM.
----Transnational corporations in South
    Africa and Namibia : United Nations
    public hearings. Volume 3, Statements
    and submissions. - 1987.
        (001215)

NAMIBIA--WORKING CONDITIONS.
----Transnational corporations in South
    Africa and Namibia : United Nations
    public hearings. Volume 1, Reports of
    the Panel of Eminent Persons and of the
    Secretary-General. - 1986.
        (001216)

NAMIBIA QUESTION.
----Measures regarding the activities of
    transnational corporations in South
    Africa and Namibia. - 1985.
        (001220)
----Reference book on major transnational
    corporations operating in Namibia. -
    1985.
        (002674)

NATIONAL CHARACTERISTICS.
----Going international. - 1985.
        (001786)
----International business and cultures. -
    1987.
        (001872)

NATIONAL SECURITY--UNITED STATES.
----Balancing the national interest : U.S.
    national security export controls and
    global economic competition. - 1987.
        (001417)
----National security and the semiconductor
    industry. - 1987.
        (000675)

NATIONALIZATION.
----Le développement de la protection
    conventionnelle des investissements
    étrangers. - 1986.
        (002048)
----Diffusion as an explanation of oil
    nationalization or the domino effect
    rides again. - 1985.
        (002326)
----National ownership requirements and
    transfer pricing. - 1986.
        (001711)
----Nationalised oil corporations and the
    changing world industry. - 1983.
        (002333)
----The taking of foreign property under
    international law. - 1984.
        (002336)
----A theory of expropriation and deviations
    from perfect capital mobility. - 1984.
        (001571)

NATIONALIZATION--BURMA.
----Les nationalisations dans quelques pays
    d'Asie de tradition britannique : Inde,
    Sri Lanca, Birmanie. - 1984.
        (002329)

NATIONALIZATION--CHINA.
----United States policy regarding
    nationalization of American investments.
    - 1984.
        (002332)

NATIONALIZATION--EUROPE.
----Nationalized companies : a threat to
    American business. - 1983.
        (002327)

NATIONALIZATION--FRANCE.
----La contribution des nationalisations
    françaises de 1982 au droit
    international des nationalisations. -
    1985.
        (002319)
----Nationalisation of the banks in France.
    - 1983.
        (001568)
----Nationalisations et développement
    régional. - 1983.
        (001550)
----Les nationalisations françaises face à
    l'ordre juridique suisse. - 1984.
        (002325)
----Nationalisations, un bilan en
    demi-teinte. - 1983.
        (001579)
----Die Nationalisierungen in Frankreich
    1981/82. - 1983.
        (002337)

NATIONALIZATION--INDIA.
----Les nationalisations dans quelques pays
    d'Asie de tradition britannique : Inde,
    Sri Lanca, Birmanie. - 1984.
        (002329)

NATIONALIZATION--MEXICO.
----La nacionalización de la banca. - 1983.
        (001529)

NATIONALIZATION--SRI LANKA.
----Les nationalisations dans quelques pays
    d'Asie de tradition britannique : Inde,
    Sri Lanca, Birmanie. - 1984.
        (002329)

NATIONALIZATION--SWITZERLAND.
----Les nationalisations françaises face à
    l'ordre juridique suisse. - 1984.
        (002325)

NATIONALIZATION--UNITED KINGDOM.
----Privatising nationalised industries :
    constitutional issues and new legal
    techniques. - 1987.
        (001582)

NATIONALIZATION--VENEZUELA.
----The nationalization of the Venezuelan
    oil industry. - 1983.
        (000586)
----Petroleos de Venezuela. - 1983.
        (000646)

NATO.
----Zloveshchii molokh. - 1987.
        (000385) (000994)

NATURAL GAS.
----Natural gas clauses in petroleum
    arrangements. - 1987.
        (002452)
----Oil [and] gas : law and taxation review.
    - 1983-   .
        (002259)

NATURAL GAS--LATIN AMERICA.
----La industria siderúrgica
latinoamericana. - 1984.
(000601)

NATURAL GAS INDUSTRY.
----Natural gas clauses in petroleum
arrangements. - 1987.
(002452)

NATURAL GAS INDUSTRY--ASIA AND THE PACIFIC.
----Natural gas clauses in petroleum
arrangements. - 1987.
(002452)

NATURAL GAS INDUSTRY--INDONESIA.
----The Indonesian petroleum industry. -
1986.
(000614)

NATURAL GAS INDUSTRY--UNITED STATES.
----Evidence on joint venture formation for
offshore oil lease sales. - 1983.
(000592)
----Political risk in the international oil
and gas industry. - 1983.
(001823)

NATURAL RESOURCES.
----Arbitration and renegotiation of
international investment agreements. -
1986.
(002557)
----Environmental aspects of the activities
of transnational corporations. - 1985.
(001954)
----Host countries permanent sovereignty
over national resources and protection
of foreign investors. - 1983.
(002566)
----Permanent sovereignty over natural
resources in international law. - 1984.
(002141)
----Sovereignty and natural resource
taxation in developing countries. - 1987.
(001741)
----Technical co-operation programme,
1976-1987 : United Nations Centre on
Transnational Corporations. - 1988.
(002611)

NATURAL RESOURCES--ARGENTINA.
----Petroleum service contracts in
Argentina, Brazil and Colombia : issues
arising from their legal nature. - 1987.
(002422)

NATURAL RESOURCES--BRAZIL.
----Petroleum service contracts in
Argentina, Brazil and Colombia : issues
arising from their legal nature. - 1987.
(002422)

NATURAL RESOURCES--CHINA.
----The law applicable to a transnational
economic development contract. - 1987.
(002164)

NATURAL RESOURCES--COLOMBIA.
----Petroleum service contracts in
Argentina, Brazil and Colombia : issues
arising from their legal nature. - 1987.
(002422)

NATURAL RESOURCES--LATIN AMERICA.
----Petroleum service contracts in
Argentina, Brazil and Colombia : issues
arising from their legal nature. - 1987.
(002422)

NATURAL RESOURCES--NAMIBIA.
----Reference book on major transnational
corporations operating in Namibia. -
1985.
(002674)
----Transnational corporations in South
Africa and Namibia : United Nations
public hearings. Volume 1, Reports of
the Panel of Eminent Persons and of the
Secretary-General. - 1986.
(001216)
----Transnational corporations in South
Africa and Namibia : United Nations
public hearings. Volume 3, Statements
and submissions. - 1987.
(001215)

NATURAL RESOURCES DEVELOPMENT.
----Contract efficiency and natural resource
investment in developing countries. -
1984.
(002409)

NATURAL RESOURCES DEVELOPMENT--UNITED STATES.
----Structuring natural resources
development agreements between foreign
governments and United States companies
to prevent transfer of rights under the
agreement should the company enter
bankruptcy. - 1984.
(002411)

NATURAL RESOURCES POLICY.
----Improving environmental cooperation. -
1984.
(001955)

NEGOTIABLE INSTRUMENTS.
----Les techniques de negociation en matière
de transfert de technologie. - 1987.
(001511)
----UNCITRAL, the United Nations Commission
on International Trade Law. - 1986.
(002155)

NEGOTIATION.
----Encyclopedia of practical usages of
terminology for business agreements. -
1983.
(002426) (002708) (002709)

----International business negotiation and
contract. - 1982.
(002715)
----Issues in negotiating international loan
agreements with transnational banks. -
1983.
(002459)
----Multilateral economic negotiation. -
1987.
(002470)
----Multilateral negotiation and mediation.
- 1985.
(002545)
----Multilateral negotiations and
third-party roles. - 1986.
(002689)

NEGOTIATION (continued)
----Les négociations : moyen principal du
    règlement pacifique des différends
    internationaux. - 1984.
      (002510)
----Négociations internationales. - 1984.
      (002463)
----Negotiation and drafting of mining
    development agreements. - 1976.
      (002432)
----Negotiation journal. - 1985-   .
      (002547)
----Proceedings of the SSTCC/UNCTC/ESCAP
    Asia-Pacific Training Workshop on
    Regulating and Negotiating Technology
    Transfer through Transnational
    Corporations, 14-25 October 1985,
    Fuzhou, Fujian, China. - 1986.
      (001405) (002169)
----Sociedades y grupos multinacionales. -
    1985.
      (000004)
----Strategies for structuring joint
    ventures: a negotiations planning
    paradigm. - 1984.
      (001560)
----Technical co-operation programme,
    1976-1987 : United Nations Centre on
    Transnational Corporations. - 1988.
      (002611)

NEGOTIATION--CANADA.
----U.S. fishery negotiations with Canada
    and Mexico. - 1985.
      (002462)

NEGOTIATION--FRANCE.
----Preliminary agreements in international
    contract negotiation. - 1983.
      (002465)

NEGOTIATION--MEXICO.
----U.S. fishery negotiations with Canada
    and Mexico. - 1985.
      (002462)

NEGOTIATION--UNITED STATES.
----U.S. fishery negotiations with Canada
    and Mexico. - 1985.
      (002462)

NEGOTIATION--WESTERN EUROPE.
----La négociation du contrat international.
    - 1983.
      (002464)

NEPAL--FOREIGN TRADE.
----Trade and investment possibilities in
    Bangladesh, Nepal and Sri Lanka. - 1983.
      (001840)

NEPAL--INVESTMENT POLICY.
----Trade and investment possibilities in
    Bangladesh, Nepal and Sri Lanka. - 1983.
      (001840)

NEPAL--TRADE POLICY.
----Trade and investment possibilities in
    Bangladesh, Nepal and Sri Lanka. - 1983.
      (001840)

NESTLE COMPANY.
----L'émpire Nestle. - 1983.
      (000283)

NESTL?E1 S.A.
----The world according to Nestlé. - 1987.
      (000291)

NETHERLANDS--BUSINESS ENTERPRISES.
----Statistiek van het ondernemingen- en
    vestigingenbestand. - 1983-   .
      (002666)

NETHERLANDS--CORPORATE MERGERS.
----Private agreements for takeovers of
    public companies. - 1984.
      (001626)

NETHERLANDS--ECONOMIC POLICY.
----Recommendation on industry and
    development cooperation. - 1984.
      (001329)

NETHERLANDS--FOREIGN INVESTMENTS.
----Recommendation on industry and
    development cooperation. - 1984.
      (001329)

NETHERLANDS--INDUSTRIAL CO-OPERATION.
----Recommendation on industry and
    development cooperation. - 1984.
      (001329)

NETHERLANDS--INDUSTRY.
----Verdiende lonen van werknemers in
    nijverheid en dienstensector ontleend
    aan het halfjaarlijks loononderzoek. -
    1985.
      (001928)

NETHERLANDS--LABOUR RELATIONS.
----Michelin : een zwart profiel : over
    werken in een bandenfabriek in Den
    Bosch. - 1984.
      (000289)

NETHERLANDS--PETROLEUM INDUSTRY.
----Oil industry restructuring in the
    Netherlands and its European context. -
    1987.
      (000629)

NETHERLANDS--PETROLEUM REFINERIES.
----Oil industry restructuring in the
    Netherlands and its European context. -
    1987.
      (000629)

NETHERLANDS--PUBLIC ENTERPRISES.
----Private agreements for takeovers of
    public companies. - 1984.
      (001626)

NETHERLANDS--SERVICE INDUSTRIES.
----Verdiende lonen van werknemers in
    nijverheid en dienstensector ontleend
    aan het halfjaarlijks loononderzoek. -
    1985.
      (001928)

NETHERLANDS--STATISTICAL DATA.
----Statistiek van het ondernemingen- en
    vestigingenbestand. - 1983-   .
      (002666)

NETHERLANDS--STATISTICAL DATA (continued)
----Verdiende lonen van werknemers in
    nijverheid en dienstensector ontleend
    aan het halfjaarlijks loononderzoek. -
    1985.
        (001928)

NETHERLANDS--TAX TREATIES.
----The American-Dutch tax series. -
    1983-   .
        (002028)

NETHERLANDS--TAXATION.
----The American-Dutch tax series. -
    1983-   .
        (002028)

NETHERLANDS--TECHNOLOGY TRANSFER.
----Technology transfer: the approach of a
    Dutch multinational. - 1986.
        (001484)

NETHERLANDS--TIRE INDUSTRY.
----Michelin : een zwart profiel : over
    werken in een bandenfabriek in Den
    Bosch. - 1984.
        (000289)

NETHERLANDS--TRANSNATIONAL CORPORATIONS.
----Michelin : een zwart profiel : over
    werken in een bandenfabriek in Den
    Bosch. - 1984.
        (000289)
----Technology transfer: the approach of a
    Dutch multinational. - 1986.
        (001484)

NETHERLANDS--WAGES.
----Verdiende lonen van werknemers in
    nijverheid en dienstensector ontleend
    aan het halfjaarlijks loononderzoek. -
    1985.
        (001928)

NETHERLANDS ANTILLES--TAX HAVENS.
----The American-Dutch tax series. -
    1983-   .
        (002028)
----Tax evasion through the Netherlands
    Antilles and other tax haven countries.
    - 1983.
        (001761)
----The use of international finance
    subsidiaries in the Netherlands
    Antilles. - 1983.
        (000871)

NEW INTERNATIONAL ECONOMIC ORDER.
----Comercio internacional,
    industrialización y nuevo orden
    económico internacional. - 1983.
        (001242)
----The economic aspects of a new
    international information-communication
    order. - 1984.
        (000917)
----Foreign investment in the present and a
    new international economic order. - 1988.
        (001247)
----Les investissements miniers
    internationaux dans les pays en
    développement. - 1986.
        (000609)

----Los laberintos de la crisis. - 1984.
        (001079)
----Mirovoe kapitalisticheskoe khoziaistvo i
    razvivaiushchiesia strany Vostoka. -
    1986.
        (001279)
----The new international economic order,
    (2). - 1984.
        (001271)
----Permanent sovereignty over natural
    resources in international law. - 1984.
        (002141)
----The politics of international economic
    relations. - 1985.
        (001300)
----Regulation of transnational
    corporations. - 1984.
        (001998)
----Rola korporacji transnarodowych w
    miedzynarodowej wymianie towarów
    przemyslowych. - 1986.
        (001369)
----UNCITRAL, the United Nations Commission
    on International Trade Law. - 1986.
        (002155)

NEW PRODUCTS.
----Consumer choice in the Third World. -
    1983.
        (000878)

NEW PRODUCTS--EUROPE.
----Market share strategy in Europe. - 1985.
        (000493)

NEW PRODUCTS--GERMANY, FEDERAL REPUBLIC OF.
----Entry by diversified firms into German
    industries. - 1986.
        (001162)

NEW TECHNOLOGIES.
----The changing role of multinational
    enterprises in the international
    creation, transfer and diffusion of
    technology. - 1987.
        (001426)
----New technologies and Third World
    development. - 1986.
        (001475)
----Recent developments in operations and
    behaviour of transnational corporations.
    - 1987.
        (000103)
----Technology choice and change in
    developing countries. - 1983.
        (001505)
----U.S. high technology trade and
    competitiveness. - 1985.
        (001362)

NEW TECHNOLOGIES--EASTERN EUROPE.
----Zum Einfluss von Modernisierung und
    Rekonstruktion auf die internationale
    sozialistische Arbeitsteilung. - 1987.
        (001227)

NEW TECHNOLOGIES--GERMAN DEMOCRATIC REPUBLIC.
----Zum Einfluss von Modernisierung und
    Rekonstruktion auf die internationale
    sozialistische Arbeitsteilung. - 1987.
        (001227)

NEW TECHNOLOGIES--INDIA.
----New information technology in India. -
1986.
(000651)

NEW TECHNOLOGIES--JAPAN.
----A high technology gap? - 1987.
(001439)

NEW TECHNOLOGIES--UNITED STATES.
----An assessment of U.S. competitiveness in
high technology industries. - 1983.
(000653)
----Balancing the national interest : U.S.
national security export controls and
global economic competition. - 1987.
(001417)
----La haute technologie américaine. - 1987.
(000680)
----A high technology gap? - 1987.
(001439)
----U.S. high technology trade and
competitiveness. - 1985.
(001362)

NEW TECHNOLOGIES--WESTERN EUROPE.
----A high technology gap? - 1987.
(001439)

NEW WORLD INFORMATION AND COMMUNICATION
ORDER.
----The economic aspects of a new
international information-communication
order. - 1984.
(000917)
----Los laberintos de la crisis. - 1984.
(001079)
----Transnational information and data
communication. - 1983.
(000866)

NEW YORK (N.Y.)--DIRECTORIES.
----Moody's industrial manual. - 1954-   .
(002656)

NEW YORK (N.Y.)--SECURITIES.
----Moody's industrial manual. - 1954-   .
(002656)

NEW YORK (N.Y.)--STOCK COMPANIES.
----Moody's industrial manual. - 1954-   .
(002656)

NEW YORK (N.Y.)--STOCK MARKETS.
----Moody's industrial manual. - 1954-   .
(002656)

NEW ZEALAND--CAPITAL MARKETS.
----Financial institutions and markets in
the Southwest Pacific. - 1985.
(000854)

NEW ZEALAND--FINANCIAL INSTITUTIONS.
----Financial institutions and markets in
the Southwest Pacific. - 1985.
(000854)

NEW ZEALAND--FOREIGN DIRECT INVESTMENT.
----Australian direct investment in New
Zealand. - 1983.
(000109)
----Fiji : client State of Australasia? -
1984.
(001046) (002358)

----New Zealand business. - 1985.
(000352)

NEW ZEALAND--INVESTMENT POLICY.
----New Zealand business. - 1985.
(000352)

NEW ZEALAND--LAWS AND REGULATIONS.
----New Zealand business. - 1985.
(000352)

NEW ZEALAND--STATISTICAL DATA.
----Australian direct investment in New
Zealand. - 1983.
(000109)

NEW ZEALAND--TAXATION.
----New Zealand business. - 1985.
(000352)

NEW ZEALAND--TRADE UNIONS.
----Trade union directory. - 1971-   .
(002720)

NEW ZEALAND--TRANSNATIONAL CORPORATIONS.
----Fiji : client State of Australasia? -
1984.
(001046) (002358)

NICARAGUA--ECONOMIC CONDITIONS.
----Política económica y capital extranjero
en Nicaragua. - 1984.
(002081)

NICARAGUA--FOREIGN INVESTMENTS.
----Política económica y capital extranjero
en Nicaragua. - 1984.
(002081)

NICARAGUA--POLITICAL CONDITIONS.
----Política económica y capital extranjero
en Nicaragua. - 1984.
(002081)

NICKEL INDUSTRY.
----International movements and crises in
resource oriented companies: the case of
INCO in the nickel sector. - 1985.
(000271)

NIGERIA--AUTOMOBILE INDUSTRY.
----Vertical corporate linkages. - 1986.
(000709)

NIGERIA--CONTRACTS.
----Contractual forms in the oil industry. -
1986.
(002441)

NIGERIA--EMPLOYMENT POLICY.
----Third World multinationals. - 1983.
(000361)

NIGERIA--FOREIGN DIRECT INVESTMENT.
----MNC's in Nigeria. - 1983.
(001029)
----State strategies toward Nigerian and
foreign business. - 1983.
(001770)

NIGERIA--FOREIGN INVESTMENTS.
----National legislation and regulations
   relating to transnational corporations.
   Volume 4. - 1986.
      (002253)

NIGERIA--HOST COUNTRY RELATIONS.
----Multinationals, the state, and control
   of the Nigerian economy. - 1987.
      (001022)
----State strategies toward Nigerian and
   foreign business. - 1983.
      (001770)

NIGERIA--INDUSTRIAL LOCATION.
----The politics of industrial location in
   Nigeria. - 1985.
      (001837)

NIGERIA--INVESTMENT POLICY.
----Multinationals, the state, and control
   of the Nigerian economy. - 1987.
      (001022)
----State strategies toward Nigerian and
   foreign business. - 1983.
      (001770)

NIGERIA--JOINT VENTURES.
----Contractual forms in the oil industry. -
   1986.
      (002441)

NIGERIA--LABOUR SUPPLY.
----Third World multinationals. - 1983.
      (000361)

NIGERIA--LAWS AND REGULATIONS.
----National legislation and regulations
   relating to transnational corporations.
   Volume 4. - 1986.
      (002253)

NIGERIA--PETROLEUM EXPLORATION.
----Contractual forms in the oil industry. -
   1986.
      (002441)

NIGERIA--PETROLEUM INDUSTRY.
----Contractual forms in the oil industry. -
   1986.
      (002441)

NIGERIA--TECHNOLOGY TRANSFER.
----Third World multinationals. - 1983.
      (000361)

NIGERIA--TRANSNATIONAL CORPORATIONS.
----MNC's in Nigeria. - 1983.
      (001029)
----Multinationals, the state, and control
   of the Nigerian economy. - 1987.
      (001022)
----National legislation and regulations
   relating to transnational corporations.
   Volume 4. - 1986.
      (002253)
----Third World multinationals. - 1983.
      (000361)

NISSAN JIDOSHA KABUSHIKI KAISHA.
----The Japanese automobile industry. - 1985.
      (000278)

NONCITIZENS--UNITED STATES.
----Introduction to United States
   international taxation. - 1981.
      (001738)

NONCONVENTIONAL ENERGY SOURCES.
----Worldwide synthetic fuels and alternate
   energy directory. - 1981-   .
      (002677)

NONCONVENTIONAL ENERGY SOURCES--UNITED
STATES.
----A competitive assessment of the
   renewable energy equipment industry. -
   1984.
      (000775)

NONGOVERNMENTAL ORGANIZATIONS.
----International accounting and reporting
   issues, 1985 review. - 1985.
      (002116)
----Measures regarding the activities of
   transnational corporations in South
   Africa and Namibia. - 1985.
      (001220)

NONPROFIT CORPORATIONS.
----Advanced accounting. - 1988.
      (002089)

NORDIC COUNTRIES--FOREIGN DIRECT INVESTMENT.
----Industrial structure and country risks
   in a Nordic perspective. - 1984.
      (001838)
----Inversiones nórdicas en América Latina.
   - 1986.
      (000206)

NORDIC COUNTRIES--INDUSTRIAL ORGANIZATION.
----Industrial structure and country risks
   in a Nordic perspective. - 1984.
      (001838)

NORDIC COUNTRIES--PRODUCTION DIVERSIFICATION.
----Industrial structure and country risks
   in a Nordic perspective. - 1984.
      (001838)

NORDIC COUNTRIES--RISK ASSESSMENT.
----Industrial structure and country risks
   in a Nordic perspective. - 1984.
      (001838)

NORTH AFRICA--PUBLIC CONTRACTS.
----An introduction to contract procedures
   in the Near East and North Africa. -
   1978-   .
      (002433)

NORTH AMERICA--INDIGENOUS POPULATIONS.
----Indigenous resource rights and mining
   companies in North America and
   Australia. - 1986.
      (000616)

NORTH AMERICA--LAND RIGHTS.
----Indigenous resource rights and mining
   companies in North America and
   Australia. - 1986.
      (000616)

NORTH AMERICA--MINERAL RESOURCES.
----Indigenous resource rights and mining
    companies in North America and
    Australia. - 1986.
      (000616)

NORTH AMERICA--MINING INDUSTRY.
----Indigenous resource rights and mining
    companies in North America and
    Australia. - 1986.
      (000616)

NORTH AMERICA--TRANSNATIONAL CORPORATIONS.
----Indigenous resource rights and mining
    companies in North America and
    Australia. - 1986.
      (000616)

NORTH SOUTH DIALOGUE.
----L'Agence multilatérale de garantie des
    investissements. - 1987.
      (002152)
----La crisis internacional y la América
    Latina. - 1984.
      (001245)
----Dette du Tiers monde. - 1984.
      (000260)
----Az északi-déli technológiaátadás
    formaváltozásai. - 1985.
      (001458)
----Muködotoke-beruházások a fejlodo
    országokban. - 1986.
      (001275)
----Nationalization of foreign property. -
    1983.
      (002324)
----The politics of international economic
    relations. - 1985.
      (001300)
----Toward Lomé III. - 1984.
      (002606)
----The U.S. renewal of the GSP. - 1986.
      (001996)

NORTHERN TERRITORY (AUSTRALIA)--ALUMINA.
----The history and contractual arrangements
    of the Gove bauxite/alumina project in
    the Northern Territory of Australia. -
    1985.
      (000596)

NORTHERN TERRITORY (AUSTRALIA)--BAUXITE.
----The history and contractual arrangements
    of the Gove bauxite/alumina project in
    the Northern Territory of Australia. -
    1985.
      (000596)

NORTHERN TERRITORY (AUSTRALIA)--MINING.
----The history and contractual arrangements
    of the Gove bauxite/alumina project in
    the Northern Territory of Australia. -
    1985.
      (000596)

NORTHERN TERRITORY
(AUSTRALIA)--TRANSNATIONAL CORPORATIONS.
----The history and contractual arrangements
    of the Gove bauxite/alumina project in
    the Northern Territory of Australia. -
    1985.
      (000596)

NORWAY--BUSINESS ENTERPRISES.
----Kompass. - 1970-   .
      (002647)

NORWAY--DIRECTORIES.
----Kompass. - 1970-   .
      (002647)

NORWAY--INDUSTRY.
----Kompass. - 1970-   .
      (002647)

NUCLEAR ENERGY--SOUTH AFRICA.
----Transnational corporations in South
    Africa and Namibia : United Nations
    public hearings. Volume 3, Statements
    and submissions. - 1987.
      (001215)

NUCLEAR FACILITIES--WESTERN EUROPE.
----International aspects of nuclear
    instalations licensing. - 1987.
      (002434)

NUCLEAR TECHNOLOGY--SOUTH AFRICA.
----Measures regarding the activities of
    transnational corporations in South
    Africa and Namibia. - 1985.
      (001220)
----Transnational corporations in South
    Africa and Namibia : United Nations
    public hearings. Volume 1, Reports of
    the Panel of Eminent Persons and of the
    Secretary-General. - 1986.
      (001216)

NUCLEAR WEAPONS--SOUTH AFRICA.
----Transnational corporations in South
    Africa and Namibia : United Nations
    public hearings. Volume 3, Statements
    and submissions. - 1987.
      (001215)

NUCLEAR WEAPONS--UNITED STATES.
----The nuclear weapons industry. - 1984.
      (000659)

NUMERICAL CONTROL--UNITED STATES.
----A competitive assessment of the U.S.
    flexible manufacturing systems industry.
    - 1985.
      (000763)

OAU--RESOLUTIONS AND DECISIONS.
----Measures regarding the activities of
    transnational corporations in South
    Africa and Namibia. - 1985.
      (001220)

OBLIGATIONS.
----Les obligations "survivant au contrat"
    dans les contrats internationaux. - 1984.
      (002427)

OCCUPATIONAL HEALTH.
----Environmental aspects of the activities
    of transnational corporations. - 1985.
      (001954)
----Safety and health practices of
    multinational enterprises. - 1984.
      (001918)

OCCUPATIONAL QUALIFICATIONS.
----Les services : nouvelle donne pour
     l'emploi. - 1987.
        (000961)

OCCUPATIONAL SAFETY.
----Environmental aspects of the activities
     of transnational corporations. - 1985.
        (001954)
----Safety and health practices of
     multinational enterprises. - 1984.
        (001918)

OCEANIA--MINERAL INDUSTRY.
----Mineral industries of Australia, Canada,
     and Oceania. - 1985.
        (000603)

OECD.
----Availability of financial statements. -
     1987.
        (002100)
----Competition and trade policies. - 1984.
        (001664)
----Consolidation policies in OECD
     countries. - 1987.
        (002101)
----Controls and impediments affecting
     inward direct investment in OECD member
     countries. - 1987.
        (000122) (002193)
----Corporation, technological gaps and
     growth in OECD countries. - 1987.
        (001438)
----Disclosure of information by
     multinational enterprises. - 1983.
        (002075)
----East-West technology transfer. - 1984.
        (001463)
----Elements of a conceptual framework for
     trade in services. - 1987.
        (000914)
----Employment and competitiveness in the
     European Community. - 1984.
        (001929)
----Exchange of information under the OECD
     and US model tax treaties. - 1983.
        (002042)
----GATT surveillance of industrial
     policies. - 1986.
        (001350)
----Goods and services in OECD countries. -
     1987.
        (000814)
----Harmonization of accounting standards. -
     1986.
        (002082)
----International comparisons of tax levels.
     - 1987.
        (001739)
----International investment and
     multinational enterprises. - 1983.
        (002308)
----International investment and
     multinational enterprises. - 1984.
        (001981)
----International trade in services. - 1984.
        (000876)
----International trade in services :
     securities. - 1987.
        (000915)
----Introduction to the OECD codes of
     liberalisation. - 1987.
        (001984)

----Investissement international et
     entreprises multinationales. - 1983.
        (000538)
----Investment incentives and disincentives
     and the international investment
     process. - 1983.
        (002309)
----Meeting the challenges of the world
     information economy. - 1984.
        (000853)
----Merger policies and recent trends in
     mergers. - 1984.
        (001611)
----The OECD guidelines for multinational
     enterprises. - 1986.
        (002002)
----The OECD guidelines for multinational
     enterprises and labour relations,
     1982-1984. - 1985.
        (001961)
----Les principes directeurs de l'OCDE à
     l'intention des entreprises
     multinationales. - 1986.
        (002005)
----Protectionist threat to trade and
     investment in services. - 1983.
        (000951)
----Recent trends in international direct
     investment. - 1987.
        (000176)
----The relationship between taxation and
     financial reporting. - 1987.
        (002103)
----Services and the development process. -
     1985.
        (000979)
----The Soviet Union's other tax agreements.
     - 1986.
        (002043)
----Structural adjustment and multinational
     enterprises. - 1985.
        (000095)
----Textile and clothing industries. - 1983.
        (000740)
----Trade in services. - 1984.
        (000955)
----Trade liberalization and the global
     service economy. - 1985.
        (000811)
----Transnational services policy? - 1987.
        (000867)
----Trends in international taxation. - 1985.
        (001746)
----Working documents. - 1986-   .
        (002123)

OECD. COMMITTEE ON INTERNATIONAL INVESTMENT
AND MULTINATIONAL ENTERPRISES.
----Multinational enterprises and the OECD
     industrial relations guidelines. - 1983.
        (001963)

OECD. COUNCIL--RESOLUTIONS AND DECISIONS.
----Declaration by the governments of OECD
     member countries and decisions of the
     OECD Council on international investment
     and multinational enterprises. - 1984.
        (001999)

OECD. DEVELOPMENT ASSISTANCE COMMITTEE.
----Foreign direct investment and economic
     growth in the Asian and Pacific region.
     - 1987.
        (000175)

OECD DECLARATION ON INTERNATIONAL INVESTMENT
AND MULTINATIONAL ENTERPRISES (1976).
----International investment and
    multinational enterprises. - 1984.
    (001981)
----The OECD Declaration on International
    Investment and Multinational
    Enterprises. -   .
    (001993)

OECD GUIDELINES FOR MULTINATIONAL
ENTERPRISES (1976).
----Clarification of the accounting terms in
    the OECD Guidelines. - 1983.
    (002071)
----Disclosure of information by
    multinational enterprises. - 1983.
    (002075)
----Multinational enterprises and the OECD
    industrial relations guidelines. - 1983.
    (001963)
----OECD Guidelines for Multinational Firms
    remain relevant after ten years. - 1986.
    (002003)
----The 1984 revision of the OECD Guidelines
    for Multinational Enterprises. - 1985.
    (002010)

OFFSHORE OIL DRILLING.
----The drilling gap in non-OPEC developing
    countries: the role of contractual and
    fiscal arrangements. - 1985.
    (002413)

OFFSHORE OIL DRILLING--CHINA.
----The investment implications of China's
    offshore oil development. - 1986.
    (000612)
----Singapore's role in China's offshore oil
    venture. - 1985.
    (000608)

OFFSHORE OIL DRILLING--SINGAPORE.
----Singapore's role in China's offshore oil
    venture. - 1985.
    (000608)

OFFSHORE OIL FIELDS--UNITED STATES.
----The impact of joint ventures on bidding
    for offshore oil. - 1983.
    (000604)

OFFSHORE STRUCTURES--UNITED STATES.
----A competitive assessment of the U.S. oil
    field equipment industry. - 1985.
    (000764)

OIL AND GAS LEASES--CANADA.
----Comparative licensing aspects of
    Canadian and United Kingdom petroleum
    law. - 1986.
    (002176)

OIL AND GAS LEASES--COLOMBIA.
----Los contratos petroleros. - 1984.
    (002454)

OIL AND GAS LEASES--KUWAIT.
----Droit international et contrats d'états.
    - 1983.
    (002482)

OIL AND GAS LEASES--UNITED KINGDOM.
----Comparative licensing aspects of
    Canadian and United Kingdom petroleum
    law. - 1986.
    (002176)

OIL AND GAS LEASES--UNITED STATES.
----Evidence on joint venture formation for
    offshore oil lease sales. - 1983.
    (000592)
----Foreign investment in United States oil
    and gas ventures. - 1987.
    (000606)
----The impact of joint ventures on bidding
    for offshore oil. - 1983.
    (000604)
----Joint ventures and offshore oil lease
    sales. - 1985.
    (001578)

OIL EMBARGO--SOUTH AFRICA.
----Activities of transnational corporations
    in South Africa and Namibia and the
    responsibilities of home countries with
    respect to their operations in this
    area. - 1986.
    (001192)
----Measures regarding the activities of
    transnational corporations in South
    Africa and Namibia. - 1985.
    (001220)
----Transnational corporations in South
    Africa and Namibia : United Nations
    public hearings. Volume 1, Reports of
    the Panel of Eminent Persons and of the
    Secretary-General. - 1986.
    (001216)
----Transnational corporations in South
    Africa and Namibia. - 1986.
    (001217)
----Transnational corporations in South
    Africa and Namibia : United Nations
    public hearings. Volume 3, Statements
    and submissions. - 1987.
    (001215)

OIL INDUSTRIES--VENEZUELA.
----Petroleum and political pacts. - 1987.
    (001816)

OIL POLLUTION.
----Acronyms and compensation for oil
    pollution damage from tankers. - 1983.
    (001937)
----Dead in the water : international law,
    diplomacy, and compensation for chemical
    pollution at sea. - 1986.
    (001938)
----The definition of pollution damage in
    the 1984 Protocols to the 1969 Civil
    Liability Convention and the 1971 Fund
    Convention. - 1986.
    (001943)
----New trends in compensation for oil
    pollution damage. - 1985.
    (001944)

OIL SPILLAGES.
----Dommages causés par les marées noires. -
    1984.
    (001952)
----Oil pollution. - 1984.
    (001942)

OIL SPILLAGES--UNITED STATES.
----Oil spill liability and compensation. -
     1985.
        (001940)

OIL WELL DRILLING--UNITED STATES.
----A competitive assessment of the U.S. oil
     field equipment industry. - 1985.
        (000764)

OLIGOPOLIES.
----Competition, tacit collusion and free
     entry. - 1987.
        (001679)
----The effects of taxation price control
     and government contracts in oligopoly
     and monopolistic competition. - 1987.
        (001693)
----Market competition, conflict and
     collusion. - 1987.
        (001680)
----Optimum product diversity and the
     incentives for entry in natural
     oligopolies. - 1987.
        (000485)

OLIGOPOLIES--LATIN AMERICA.
----Profits, progress and poverty. - 1985.
        (001111)

OMAN--BALANCE OF PAYMENTS.
----Impact of the operations of
     transnational corporations on
     development in the Sultanate of Oman. -
     1988.
        (001144)

OMAN--BANKING.
----Impact of the operations of
     transnational corporations on
     development in the Sultanate of Oman. -
     1988.
        (001144)

OMAN--BUSINESS.
----The commercial legal system of the
     Sultanate of Oman. - 1983.
        (002218)

OMAN--COMMERCIAL LAW.
----The commercial legal system of the
     Sultanate of Oman. - 1983.
        (002218)

OMAN--DEVELOPMENT PLANS.
----Impact of the operations of
     transnational corporations on
     development in the Sultanate of Oman. -
     1988.
        (001144)

OMAN--EMPLOYMENT.
----Impact of the operations of
     transnational corporations on
     development in the Sultanate of Oman. -
     1988.
        (001144)

OMAN--FINANCIAL STATISTICS.
----Impact of the operations of
     transnational corporations on
     development in the Sultanate of Oman. -
     1988.
        (001144)

OMAN--FOREIGN DIRECT INVESTMENTS.
----Impact of the operations of
     transnational corporations on
     development in the Sultanate of Oman. -
     1988.
        (001144)

OMAN--FOREIGN INVESTMENTS.
----Impact of the operations of
     transnational corporations on
     development in the Sultanate of Oman. -
     1988.
        (001144)

OMAN--FOREIGN TRADE.
----Impact of the operations of
     transnational corporations on
     development in the Sultanate of Oman. -
     1988.
        (001144)

OMAN--LABOUR LEGISLATIONS.
----Impact of the operations of
     transnational corporations on
     development in the Sultanate of Oman. -
     1988.
        (001144)

OMAN--LAWS AND REGULATIONS.
----Impact of the operations of
     transnational corporations on
     development in the Sultanate of Oman. -
     1988.
        (001144)

OMAN--STATISTICAL DATA.
----Impact of the operations of
     transnational corporations on
     development in the Sultanate of Oman. -
     1988.
        (001144)

OMAN--TECHNOLOGY TRANSFER.
----Impact of the operations of
     transnational corporations on
     development in the Sultanate of Oman. -
     1988.
        (001144)

OMAN--TRANSNATIONAL CORPORATIONS.
----Impact of the operations of
     transnational corporations on
     development in the Sultanate of Oman. -
     1988.
        (001144)

ON-LINE DATA PROCESSING.
----PTS company directory. - 1985-
        (002661)
----Transborder data flows. - 1983.
        (000973)

ON-LINE SEARCHING.
----Transborder data flows. - 1983.
        (000973)

OPEC.
----Managing an oligopoly of would-be
     sovereigns. - 1987.
        (000623)

OPEC (continued)
----Multinational corporations, OPEC,
     cartels, foreign investment, and
     technology transfer special studies,
     1982-1985. - 1987.
     (000589)
----Ölmärkte im Umbruch. - 1986.
     (000631)
----OPEC direct investment in the United
     States. - 1981-   .
     (000168)
----Private investment in Latin America. -
     1984.
     (002460)
----The problems of developing-country debt
     and a strategy for Arab banking
     institutions. - 1983.
     (000256)

OPERATIONAL ACTIVITIES.
----International business. - 1986.
     (000469)

OPTICAL DISKS--UNITED STATES.
----A competitive assessment of the United
     States disk storage industry. - 1985.
     (000672)

ORGANIZATION OF THE ISLAMIC CONFERENCE.
----Consultancy services. - 1986.
     (000831)

ORGANIZATIONAL CHANGE.
----The diffusion of an organizational
     innovation: international data
     telecommunications and multinational
     industrial firms. - 1985.
     (000785)
----Indigenization policies and structural
     cooptation by multinational
     corporations. - 1985.
     (002331)
----Toward a theory of industrial
     restructuring and dynamic comparative
     advantage. - 1985.
     (000054)

P.S.A. PEUGEOT-CITROEN (PARIS).
----Foreign divestment and international
     rationalisation in the motor industry. -
     1985.
     (000664)

PACIFIC OCEAN REGION--AGRIBUSINESS.
----Agro-industrial co-operation between the
     European Community and the ACP
     countries. - 1986.
     (002605)

PACIFIC OCEAN REGION--ARMS INDUSTRY.
----Technology transfer in the Pacific
     Basin. - 1985.
     (001413)

PACIFIC OCEAN REGION--COMMUNICATION INDUSTRY.
----Information technology and the
     developing Pacific. - 1986.
     (000703)

PACIFIC OCEAN REGION--DEVELOPED COUNTRIES.
----Regulation to deregulation. - 1985.
     (000798)

PACIFIC OCEAN REGION--DEVELOPING COUNTRIES.
----Regulation to deregulation. - 1985.
     (000798)

PACIFIC OCEAN REGION--DIRECTORIES.
----Asia-Pacific/Africa-Middle East
     petroleum directory. - 1984-   .
     (000579) (002618)

PACIFIC OCEAN REGION--ECONOMIC RELATIONS.
----Competition in the Pacific Basin. - 1987.
     (001673)

PACIFIC OCEAN REGION--FOREIGN DIRECT
INVESTMENT.
----Investment in ACP states. - 1987.
     (001004)
----Transfer of industrial technology and
     foreign investment in the Pacific
     region. - 1983.
     (001440)

PACIFIC OCEAN REGION--INDUSTRIAL
CO-OPERATION.
----Agro-industrial co-operation between the
     European Community and the ACP
     countries. - 1986.
     (002605)
----Technology transfer in the Pacific
     Basin. - 1985.
     (001413)

PACIFIC OCEAN REGION--INDUSTRY.
----Investment in ACP states. - 1987.
     (001004)

PACIFIC OCEAN REGION--INFORMATION TECHNOLOGY.
----Information technology and the
     developing Pacific. - 1986.
     (000703)

PACIFIC OCEAN REGION--INVESTMENT INSURANCE.
----Investment in ACP states. - 1987.
     (001004)

PACIFIC OCEAN REGION--JOINT VENTURES.
----Investment in ACP states. - 1987.
     (001004)

PACIFIC OCEAN REGION--PETROLEUM INDUSTRY.
----Asia-Pacific/Africa-Middle East
     petroleum directory. - 1984-   .
     (000579) (002618)

PACIFIC OCEAN REGION--PRIVATE ENTERPRISES.
----Regulation to deregulation. - 1985.
     (000798)

PACIFIC OCEAN REGION--SATELLITE
COMMUNICATION.
----Regulation to deregulation. - 1985.
     (000798)

PACIFIC OCEAN REGION--TECHNOLOGY TRANSFER.
----Technology transfer in the Pacific
     Basin. - 1985.
     (001413)
----Transfer of industrial technology and
     foreign investment in the Pacific
     region. - 1983.
     (001440)

PACIFIC OCEAN REGION--TELECOMMUNICATION
INDUSTRY.
----Regulation to deregulation. - 1985.
    (000798)

PAKISTAN--FOREIGN DIRECT INVESTMENT.
----Legal consideration in doing business in
    the Middle East, Turkey and Pakistan. -
    1986.
    (002172)

PAKISTAN--FREE EXPORT ZONES.
----Aspects of labour law and relations in
    selected export processing zones. - 1984.
    (001895)

PAKISTAN--LABOUR LAW.
----Aspects of labour law and relations in
    selected export processing zones. - 1984.
    (001895)

PAKISTAN--LABOUR RELATIONS.
----Aspects of labour law and relations in
    selected export processing zones. - 1984.
    (001895)

PAKISTAN--LAWS AND REGULATIONS.
----National legislation and regulations
    relating to transnational corporations.
    Volume 3. - 1983.
    (002252)

PAKISTAN--PETROLEUM INDUSTRY.
----Natural gas clauses in petroleum
    arrangements. - 1987.
    (002452)

PAKISTAN--SCIENCE AND TECHNOLOGY POLICY.
----Proceedings of the SSTCC/UNCTC/ESCAP
    Asia-Pacific Training Workshop on
    Regulating and Negotiating Technology
    Transfer through Transnational
    Corporations, 14-25 October 1985,
    Fuzhou, Fujian, China. - 1986.
    (001405) (002169)

PAKISTAN--TECHNOLOGY TRANSFER.
----Proceedings of the SSTCC/UNCTC/ESCAP
    Asia-Pacific Training Workshop on
    Regulating and Negotiating Technology
    Transfer through Transnational
    Corporations, 14-25 October 1985,
    Fuzhou, Fujian, China. - 1986.
    (001405) (002169)

PAKISTAN--TRANSNATIONAL CORPORATIONS.
----National legislation and regulations
    relating to transnational corporations.
    Volume 3. - 1983.
    (002252)
----Natural gas clauses in petroleum
    arrangements. - 1987.
    (002452)

PANAMA--FOREIGN DIRECT INVESTMENT.
----Las empresas transnacionales y la
    inversión extranjera directa en la
    primera mitad de los años ochenta. -
    1987.
    (000194)

PANAMA--LAWS AND REGULATIONS.
----National legislation and regulations
    relating to transnational corporations.
    Volume 3. - 1983.
    (002252)

PANAMA--TRANSNATIONAL CORPORATIONS.
----National legislation and regulations
    relating to transnational corporations.
    Volume 3. - 1983.
    (002252)

PAPUA NEW GUINEA--BUSINESS ETHICS.
----Economic policies pertaining to foreign
    enterprises in PNG. - 1986.
    (002287)
----Reconciling ethical behaviour. - 1986.
    (001719)

PAPUA NEW GUINEA--CAPITAL MARKETS.
----Financial institutions and markets in
    the Southwest Pacific. - 1985.
    (000854)

PAPUA NEW GUINEA--DEVELOPING COUNTRIES.
----Ok Tedi : evolution of a Third World
    mining project. - 1984.
    (000293)

PAPUA NEW GUINEA--ECONOMIC POLICY.
----Economic policies pertaining to foreign
    enterprises in PNG. - 1986.
    (002287)

PAPUA NEW GUINEA--FINANCIAL INSTITUTIONS.
----Financial institutions and markets in
    the Southwest Pacific. - 1985.
    (000854)

PAPUA NEW GUINEA--FOREIGN DIRECT INVESTMENT.
----Foreign direct investment in Papua New
    Guinea. - 1985.
    (000172)
----Foreign investment in Papua New Guinea.
    - 1986.
    (002197)

PAPUA NEW GUINEA--FOREIGN INVESTMENTS.
----Economic policies pertaining to foreign
    enterprises in PNG. - 1986.
    (002287)

PAPUA NEW GUINEA--FORESTRY INDUSTRY.
----Reconciling ethical behaviour. - 1986.
    (001719)

PAPUA NEW GUINEA--INVESTMENT POLICY.
----Foreign investment in Papua New Guinea.
    - 1986.
    (002197)

PAPUA NEW GUINEA--LAWS AND REGULATIONS.
----National legislation and regulations
    relating to transnational corporations.
    Volume 3. - 1983.
    (002252)

PAPUA NEW GUINEA--MANAGEMENT.
----Foreign investment in Papua New Guinea.
    - 1986.
    (002197)

PAPUA NEW GUINEA--MINERAL RESOURCES
DEVELOPMENT.
----Ok Tedi : evolution of a Third World
    mining project. - 1984.
      (000293)

PAPUA NEW GUINEA--MINING.
----Ok Tedi : evolution of a Third World
    mining project. - 1984.
      (000293)

PAPUA NEW GUINEA--TRANSFER PRICING.
----Reconciling ethical behaviour. - 1986.
      (001719)

PAPUA NEW GUINEA--TRANSNATIONAL CORPORATIONS.
----National legislation and regulations
    relating to transnational corporations.
    Volume 3. - 1983.
      (002252)

PARAGUAY--AGRICULTURAL PRODUCTS.
----Las empresas transnacionales en la
    economía del Paraguay. - 1987.
      (001124)

PARAGUAY--DEVELOPMENT.
----Las empresas transnacionales en la
    economía del Paraguay. - 1987.
      (001108)

PARAGUAY--ECONOMIC CONDITIONS.
----Las empresas transnacionales en la
    economía del Paraguay. - 1987.
      (001108)

PARAGUAY--ECONOMIC HISTORY.
----Las empresas transnacionales en la
    economía del Paraguay. - 1987.
      (001124)

PARAGUAY--EXPORTS.
----Las empresas transnacionales en la
    economía del Paraguay. - 1987.
      (001124)

PARAGUAY--FOREIGN DIRECT INVESTMENT.
----Las empresas transnacionales en la
    economía del Paraguay. - 1987.
      (001124)
----Las transnacionales en el Paraguay. -
    1985.
      (001113)

PARAGUAY--IRON AND STEEL INDUSTRY.
----La industria siderúrgica
    latinoamericana. - 1984.
      (000601)

PARAGUAY--MANUFACTURING.
----Las empresas transnacionales en la
    economía del Paraguay. - 1987.
      (001124)

PARAGUAY--METALLURGICAL INDUSTRY.
----La industria siderúrgica
    latinoamericana. - 1984.
      (000601)

PARAGUAY--TRANSNATIONAL BANKS.
----Las empresas transnacionales en la
    economía del Paraguay. - 1987.
      (001124)

PARAGUAY--TRANSNATIONAL CORPORATIONS.
----Las empresas transnacionales en la
    economía del Paraguay. - 1987.
      (001108) (001124)
----Las transnacionales en el Paraguay. -
    1985.
      (001113)
----Las transnacionales en el Paraguay. -
    1985.
      (001116)

PARTNERSHIP.
----The making of a global manager/
    managing in an age of velocity/global
    partnering: making a good match. - 1987.
      (000394)
----Arrangements between joint venture
    partners in developing countries. - 1987.
      (002450)
----Distribution of benefits from regional
    trade liberalisation among country
    partners in the presence of
    transnational corporations. - 1983.
      (001392)
----International business: an alternative
    view. - 1986.
      (001559)
----Macroproject development in the third
    world. - 1983.
      (001327)
----Multinationale Bankenverflechtungen. -
    1983.
      (001549)
----Notes on partnerships in the services
    sector. - 1985.
      (000916)
----Partnership claims before the
    Iran-United States Claims Tribunal. -
    1987.
      (002322)
----Selecting a foreign partner for
    technology transfer. - 1984.
      (001459)

PARTNERSHIP--UNITED STATES.
----International joint ventures. - 1985.
      (001590)

PASSENGER TRANSPORT--AUSTRALIA.
----Characteristics of major industries
    supplying tourist services in Australia.
    - 1983.
      (000824)

PATENT LAW.
----Multinationals and industrial property.
    - 1988.
      (001410)

PATENT LAW--CHINA.
----Collection of laws and regulations of
    the People's Republic of China
    concerning foreign economic affairs. -
    1985-   .
      (002188)

PATENT LAW--WESTERN EUROPE.
----The EEC patent licencing regulation :
    practical guidelines. - 1986.
      (001966)
----Exclusive territorial rights in patent
    licenses and Article 85 of the EEC
    Treaty. - 1987.
      (002418)

PATENTS.
----International flows of technology. -
    1986.
        (001517)
----Licence agreements in developing
    countries. - 1987.
        (002437)
----Licensing of technology and intellectual
    property rights to developing countries.
    - 1983.
        (001403)
----Multinationales et propriété
    industrielle. - 1986.
        (001409)
----World technology. - 1975-   .
        (001525)

PATENTS--GREECE.
----Licensing and industrial development. -
    1986.
        (001449)

PATENTS--UNITED STATES.
----Design patents. - 1983.
        (001425)
----Microelectronics. - 1981-   .
        (000718)

PATENTS--WESTERN EUROPE.
----In the wake of windsurfing : patent
    licensing in the Common Market. - 1987.
        (002455)
----La licence de marque et le droit
    européen de la concurrence. - 1984.
        (001448)

PAYMENTS ARRANGEMENTS.
----Analysis of engineering and technical
    assistance consultancy contracts. - 1986.
        (002449)

PERFORMANCE ANALYSIS--UNITED STATES.
----Examining performance of U.S.
    multinationals in foreign markets. -
    1983.
        (000318)

PERFORMANCE APPRAISAL.
----Accounting reports and performance
    measurement of multinational enterprises
    in less developed countries. - 1987.
        (002107)
----Corporate performance: America's
    international winners. - 1986.
        (000344)
----Joint ventures in LDCs. - 1987.
        (000997)
----Une méthode d'évaluation interne des
    modèles multinationaux. - 1985.
        (000056)

PERFORMANCE APPRAISAL--TURKEY.
----Transnational corporations and local
    capital: comparative conduct and
    performance in the Turkish
    pharmaceutical industry. - 1986.
        (000705)

PERFORMANCE APPRAISAL--UNITED KINGDOM.
----British multinationals. - 1986.
        (000337)

PERFORMANCE APPRAISAL--UNITED STATES.
----Foreign direct investment in U.S. food
    and tobacco manufacturing and domestic
    economic performance. - 1983.
        (000170)
----Internal accountability. - 1984.
        (002055)

PERFORMANCE APPRAISAL--YUGOSLAVIA.
----Joint ventures in Yugoslavia: comment/
    reply. - 1984.
        (001533)

PERFORMANCE STANDARDS--LATIN AMERICA.
----Performance requirements: the general
    debate and a review of Latin American
    practices. - 1983.
        (002315)

PERIODICALS.
----The international accounting and tax
    researches' publication guide. - 1982.
        (002066)

PERMANENT SOVEREIGNTY.
----Host countries permanent sovereignty
    over national resources and protection
    of foreign investors. - 1983.
        (002566)
----Permanent sovereignty over natural
    resources in international law. - 1984.
        (002141)

PERSONAL DATA FILES--UNITED STATES.
----New challenges to the U.S. multinational
    corporation in the European Economic
    Community. - 1985.
        (002192)

PERSONAL DATA FILES--WESTERN EUROPE.
----New challenges to the U.S. multinational
    corporation in the European Economic
    Community. - 1985.
        (002192)

PERSONNEL MANAGEMENT.
----Anthropology and international business.
    - 1986.
        (001892)
----Human resources management in
    international joint ventures: directions
    for research. - 1987.
        (001921)
----International joint ventures:
    implications for organisation
    development. - 1987.
        (001639)
----The new expatriates. - 1988.
        (001925)

PERSONNEL MANAGEMENT--BELGIUM.
----Employment decision-making in
    multinational enterprises. - 1984.
        (001888)

PERSONNEL MANAGEMENT--JAPAN.
----Japanese multinationals in the United
    States. - 1986.
        (000341)
----Japan's emerging multinationals. - 1985.
        (000379)
----Key to Japan's economic strength. - 1984.
        (001924)

PERSONNEL MANAGEMENT--JAPAN (continued)
----Personalpolitik fur multinationale
    Unternehmen. - 1985.
        (000417) (001903)

PERSONNEL MANAGEMENT--SWITZERLAND.
----Personalpolitik fur multinationale
    Unternehmen. - 1985.
        (000417) (001903)

PERSONNEL MANAGEMENT--UNITED STATES.
----International business travel and
    relocation directory. - 1984.
        (002710)
----Japanese multinationals in the United
    States. - 1986.
        (000341)
----Key to Japan's economic strength. - 1984.
        (001924)
----Personalpolitik fur multinationale
    Unternehmen. - 1985.
        (000417) (001903)

PERSONNEL RESEARCH.
----Human resources management in
    international joint ventures: directions
    for research. - 1987.
        (001921)

PERU--AGROINDUSTRY.
----Agroindustria y transnacionales en el
    Perú. - 1983.
        (000565)

PERU--BALANCE OF PAYMENTS.
----Transnational banks and the external
    finance of Latin America : the
    experience of Peru. - 1983.
        (000840)
----Transnational banks and the external
    finance of Latin America : the
    experience of Peru. - 1985.
        (000975)

PERU--BANK LOANS.
----Transnational banks and the external
    finance of Latin America : the
    experience of Peru. - 1983.
        (000840)
----Transnational banks and the external
    finance of Latin America : the
    experience of Peru. - 1985.
        (000975)

PERU--BANKING.
----Transnational banks and the external
    finance of Latin America : the
    experience of Peru. - 1985.
        (000975)

PERU--COMMERCIAL ARBITRATION.
----Schiedsklauseln in Peru und Venezuela. -
    1987.
        (002570)

PERU--COMMERCIAL BANKS.
----Transnational banks and the external
    finance of Latin America : the
    experience of Peru. - 1983.
        (000840)
----Transnational banks and the external
    finance of Latin America : the
    experience of Peru. - 1985.
        (000975)

PERU--COPPER INDUSTRY.
----Las perspectivas de la refinación del
    cobre en el Peru. - 1984.
        (000580)
----Privilegios y capital transnacional. -
    1985.
        (000269)

PERU--CREDIT.
----Transnational banks and the external
    finance of Latin America : the
    experience of Peru. - 1985.
        (000975)

PERU--ECONOMIC CONDITIONS.
----Empresas transnacionales, estado y
    burguesia nativa. - 1983.
        (001877)

PERU--ECONOMIC RELATIONS.
----Grace. - 1985.
        (000276)

PERU--ECONOMIC TRENDS.
----Transnational banks and the external
    finance of Latin America : the
    experience of Peru. - 1983.
        (000840)

PERU--EXPORT CREDITS.
----Transnational banks and the external
    finance of Latin America : the
    experience of Peru. - 1983.
        (000840)

PERU--EXTERNAL DEBT.
----Transnational banks and the external
    finance of Latin America : the
    experience of Peru. - 1983.
        (000840)
----Transnational banks and the external
    finance of Latin America : the
    experience of Peru. - 1985.
        (000975)

PERU--FOREIGN INVESTMENTS.
----Empresas transnacionales, estado y
    burguesia nativa. - 1983.
        (001877)
----Mining investment in Brazil, Peru, and
    Mexico. - 1984.
        (002443)
----National legislation and regulations
    relating to transnational corporations.
    Volume 4. - 1986.
        (002253)

PERU--FOREIGN LOANS.
----Transnational banks and the external
    finance of Latin America : the
    experience of Peru. - 1983.
        (000840)
----Transnational banks and the external
    finance of Latin America : the
    experience of Peru. - 1985.
        (000975)

PERU--INDUSTRIAL POLICY.
----Política económica y empresas
    transnacionales en el Perú, 1968-1975. -
    1983.
        (001107)

PERU--IRON AND STEEL INDUSTRY.
----La industria siderúrgica
latinoamericana. - 1984.
(000601)

PERU--LAWS AND REGULATIONS.
----National legislation and regulations
relating to transnational corporations.
Volume 4. - 1986.
(002253)

PERU--METALLURGICAL INDUSTRY.
----La industria siderúrgica
latinoamericana. - 1984.
(000601)

PERU--MILITARY GOVERNMENT.
----The Peruvian military government and the
international corporations. - 1983.
(001801)
----Política económica y empresas
transnacionales en el Perú, 1968-1975. -
1983.
(001107)

PERU--MINING INDUSTRY.
----Mining investment in Brazil, Peru, and
Mexico. - 1984.
(002443)
----Política económica y empresas
transnacionales en el Perú, 1968-1975. -
1983.
(001107)

PERU--MINING LAW.
----Mining investment in Brazil, Peru, and
Mexico. - 1984.
(002443)

PERU--PETROLEUM EXPLORATION.
----Social and economic effects of petroleum
development. - 1987.
(000633)

PERU--PETROLEUM INDUSTRY.
----Política económica y empresas
transnacionales en el Perú, 1968-1975. -
1983.
(001107)
----Social and economic effects of petroleum
development. - 1987.
(000633)

PERU--PUBLIC SECTOR.
----Transnational banks and the external
finance of Latin America : the
experience of Peru. - 1983.
(000840)

PERU--RISK MANAGEMENT.
----The Peruvian military government and the
international corporations. - 1983.
(001801)

PERU--TRANSNATIONAL BANKS.
----Transnational banks and the external
finance of Latin America : the
experience of Peru. - 1983.
(000840)

PERU--TRANSNATIONAL CORPORATIONS.
----Agroindustria y transnacionales en el
Perú. - 1983.
(000565)

----Empresas transnacionales, estado y
burguesia nativa. - 1983.
(001877)
----Grace. - 1985.
(000276)
----National legislation and regulations
relating to transnational corporations.
Volume 4. - 1986.
(002253)
----Las perspectivas de la refinación del
cobre en el Peru. - 1984.
(000580)
----The Peruvian military government and the
international corporations. - 1983.
(001801)
----Política económica y empresas
transnacionales en el Perú, 1968-1975. -
1983.
(001107)
----Privilegios y capital transnacional. -
1985.
(000269)

PETROCHEMICAL INDUSTRY.
----Investment-related trade distortions in
petrochemicals. - 1983.
(000595)

PETROCHEMICAL INDUSTRY--FRANCE.
----Le role des grandes entreprises
diversifiées du pétrole et de la chimie
dans la production alimentaire. - 1985.
(000699)

PETROCHEMICAL INDUSTRY--INDIA.
----Transnational corporations and
technology transfer. - 1984.
(000704)

PETROCHEMICAL INDUSTRY--LATIN AMERICA.
----North-South technology transfer. - 1984.
(001421)

PETROCHEMICAL INDUSTRY--UNITED STATES.
----A competitive assessment of the U.S.
petrochemical industry. - 1982.
(000755)
----Le role des grandes entreprises
diversifiées du pétrole et de la chimie
dans la production alimentaire. - 1985.
(000699)

PETROLEO BRASILEIRO, S.A.
----PETROBRAS : eines der grössten
Industrieunternehmen der
kapitalistischen Welt. - 1984.
(000282)
----Petroleum development in Brazil. - 1987.
(000638)

PETROLEUM.
----Las empresas transnacionales en el
desarrollo colombiano. - 1986.
(001121)
----Oil [and] gas : law and taxation review.
- 1983- .
(002259)
----Technical co-operation programme,
1976-1987 : United Nations Centre on
Transnational Corporations. - 1988.
(002611)

PETROLEUM ENGINEERING--UNITED STATES.
----A competitive assessment of the U.S. oil
field equipment industry. - 1985.
(000764)

PETROLEUM EXPLORATION.
----Financial and fiscal aspects of
petroleum exploitation. - 1987.
(002451)
----Insurance against the political risks of
petroleum investment. - 1986.
(001866) (002160)
----International petroleum exploration
[and] exploitation agreements. - 1986.
(002431).
----Transnational corporations in world
development. - 1983.
(000102)

PETROLEUM EXPLORATION--BRAZIL.
----Social and economic effects of petroleum
development. - 1987.
(000633)

PETROLEUM EXPLORATION--CHINA.
----Social and economic effects of petroleum
development. - 1987.
(000633)

PETROLEUM EXPLORATION--COLOMBIA.
----Las empresas transnacionales en el
desarrollo colombiano. - 1986.
(001121)

PETROLEUM EXPLORATION--ECUADOR.
----Risk-bearing and the choice of contract
forms for oil exploration and
development. - 1984.
(002410)

PETROLEUM EXPLORATION--INDIA.
----Social and economic effects of petroleum
development. - 1987.
(000633)

PETROLEUM EXPLORATION--MALAYSIA.
----Social and economic effects of petroleum
development. - 1987.
(000633)

PETROLEUM EXPLORATION--NIGERIA.
----Contractual forms in the oil industry. -
1986.
(002441)

PETROLEUM EXPLORATION--PERU.
----Social and economic effects of petroleum
development. - 1987.
(000633)

PETROLEUM EXPLORATION--THAILAND.
----Social and economic effects of petroleum
development. - 1987.
(000633)

PETROLEUM EXPORTING COUNTRIES.
----Développement sans croissance. - 1983.
(000632)
----The international oil industry in the
1980s. - 1984.
(000622)
----Managing an oligopoly of would-be
sovereigns. - 1987.
(000623)

PETROLEUM IMPORTING DEVELOPING COUNTRIES.
----International capital movements and
developing countries. - 1985.
(001282)
----The petroleum industry in oil-importing
developing countries. - 1983.
(000591)

PETROLEUM IMPORTS.
----Foreign oil and taxation. - 1983.
(002039)

PETROLEUM INDUSTRY.
----Annual oil market report. - 1984-   .
(000578)
----Appropriate financing for petroleum
development in developing countries. -
1984.
(000576)
----Coanda flaring for pollution control. -
1986.
(001934)
----Développement sans croissance. - 1983.
(000632)
----Diffusion as an explanation of oil
nationalization or the domino effect
rides again. - 1985.
(002326)
----The evolution of the legal relationship
between international petroleum mining
companies and host countries. - 1983.
(000647)
----Financial and fiscal aspects of
petroleum exploitation. - 1987.
(002451)
----The international oil industry in the
1980s. - 1984.
(000622)
----Managing an oligopoly of would-be
sovereigns. - 1987.
(000623)
----Multinational corporations and the
political economy of power. - 1983.
(001846)
----Multinational corporations, OPEC,
cartels, foreign investment, and
technology transfer special studies,
1982-1985. - 1987.
(000589)
----The multinationals in the world oil
market: the 1970s and the 1980s. - 1983.
(000575)
----Nationalised oil corporations and the
changing world industry. - 1983.
(002333)
----Oil companies in the international
system. - 1983.
(000641)
----Ölmärkte im Umbruch. - 1986.
(000631)
----The petroleum industry in oil-importing
developing countries. - 1983.
(000591)
----Transnational corporations in world
development. - 1983.
(000102)
----Transnational oil. - 1986.
(000618)
----Trends and issues in foreign direct
investment and related flows. - 1985.
(000192)
----World oil markets. - 1986.
(000590)

PETROLEUM INDUSTRY--AFRICA.
----Asia-Pacific/Africa-Middle East
    petroleum directory. - 1984-   .
      (000579) (002618)

PETROLEUM INDUSTRY--ARAB COUNTRIES.
----The oil companies and the Arab world. -
    1984.
      (000613)

PETROLEUM INDUSTRY--ASIA.
----Asia-Pacific/Africa-Middle East
    petroleum directory. - 1984-   .
      (000579) (002618)

PETROLEUM INDUSTRY--AUSTRALIA.
----The mineral and petroleum joint venture
    in Australia. - 1986.
      (000588)

PETROLEUM INDUSTRY--BOLIVIA.
----Transnacionales y nación. - 1986.
      (000594)

PETROLEUM INDUSTRY--BRAZIL.
----Natural gas clauses in petroleum
    arrangements. - 1987.
      (002452)
----PETROBRAS : eines der grössten
    Industrieunternehmen der
    kapitalistischen Welt. - 1984.
      (000282)
----Petroleum development in Brazil. - 1987.
      (000638)
----Social and economic effects of petroleum
    development. - 1987.
      (000633)

PETROLEUM INDUSTRY--CANADA.
----Multinational Oil Limited: issues in
    transfer pricing and foreign ownership.
    - 1985.
      (001750)
----La multinationalisation des pétrolières
    canadiennes. - 1984.
      (000627)

PETROLEUM INDUSTRY--CHINA.
----The role of oil in China's economic
    development, growth, and
    internationalization. - 1985.
      (000602)
----Social and economic effects of petroleum
    development. - 1987.
      (000633)
----Some aspects of the Chinese petroleum
    industry. - 1983.
      (000615)

PETROLEUM INDUSTRY--COLOMBIA.
----Los contratos petroleros. - 1984.
      (002454)
----Las empresas transnacionales en el
    desarrollo colombiano. - 1986.
      (001121)

PETROLEUM INDUSTRY--ECUADOR.
----Natural gas clauses in petroleum
    arrangements. - 1987.
      (002452)

PETROLEUM INDUSTRY--EGYPT.
----Natural gas clauses in petroleum
    arrangements. - 1987.
      (002452)

PETROLEUM INDUSTRY--GABON.
----Les conventions dans la fiscalité
    pétrolière gabonaise. - 1987.
      (002030)

PETROLEUM INDUSTRY--INDIA.
----Oil and other multinationals in India. -
    1986.
      (001065)
----Social and economic effects of petroleum
    development. - 1987.
      (000633)

PETROLEUM INDUSTRY--INDONESIA.
----The Indonesian petroleum industry. -
    1986.
      (000614)
----The politics of oil in Indonesia. - 1986.
      (001818)

PETROLEUM INDUSTRY--IRAN (ISLAMIC REPUBLIC
OF).
----The oil companies and the Arab world. -
    1984.
      (000613)

PETROLEUM INDUSTRY--KUWAIT.
----Impact of the operations of
    transnational corporations on
    development in Kuwait. - 1987.
      (001143)
----State contracts and oil expropriations.
    - 1984.
      (002577)

PETROLEUM INDUSTRY--LATIN AMERICA.
----Notes from Latin America. - 1983.
      (000628)

PETROLEUM INDUSTRY--MALAYSIA.
----Social and economic effects of petroleum
    development. - 1987.
      (000633)

PETROLEUM INDUSTRY--MIDDLE EAST.
----Asia-Pacific/Africa-Middle East
    petroleum directory. - 1984-   .
      (000579) (002618)

PETROLEUM INDUSTRY--NETHERLANDS.
----Oil industry restructuring in the
    Netherlands and its European context. -
    1987.
      (000629)

PETROLEUM INDUSTRY--NIGERIA.
----Contractual forms in the oil industry. -
    1986.
      (002441)

PETROLEUM INDUSTRY--PACIFIC OCEAN REGION.
----Asia-Pacific/Africa-Middle East
    petroleum directory. - 1984-   .
      (000579) (002618)

PETROLEUM INDUSTRY--PAKISTAN.
----Natural gas clauses in petroleum
    arrangements. - 1987.
      (002452)

PETROLEUM INDUSTRY--PERU.
----Política económica y empresas
    transnacionales en el Perú, 1968-1975. -
    1983.
        (001107)
----Social and economic effects of petroleum
    development. - 1987.
        (000633)

PETROLEUM INDUSTRY--QATAR.
----Petro-industrialization in Qatar. - 1985.
        (000600)

PETROLEUM INDUSTRY--THAILAND.
----Social and economic effects of petroleum
    development. - 1987.
        (000633)

PETROLEUM INDUSTRY--TRINIDAD AND TOBAGO.
----The petroleum industry in Trinidad, West
    Indies, 1857-1983. - 1985.
        (000624)

PETROLEUM INDUSTRY--UNITED KINGDOM.
----A golden adventure. - 1985.
        (000270)

PETROLEUM INDUSTRY--UNITED STATES.
----A competitive assessment of the U.S. oil
    field equipment industry. - 1985.
        (000764)
----Empirical models of political risks in
    U.S. oil production operations in
    Venezuela. - 1984.
        (001813)
----The engineers and the price system
    revisited: the future of the
    international oil corporations. - 1983.
        (000587)
----Evidence on joint venture formation for
    offshore oil lease sales. - 1983.
        (000592)
----Joint ventures and offshore oil lease
    sales. - 1985.
        (001578)
----La loi anti-fusions et l'industrie
    pétrolière américaine, (2). - 1986.
        (000581)
----Oil industry mergers. - 1984.
        (001652)
----Political risk in the international oil
    and gas industry. - 1983.
        (001823)

PETROLEUM INDUSTRY--VENEZUELA.
----Empirical models of political risks in
    U.S. oil production operations in
    Venezuela. - 1984.
        (001813)
----The nationalization of the Venezuelan
    oil industry. - 1983.
        (000586)
----Petroleos de Venezuela. - 1983.
        (000646)

PETROLEUM INDUSTRY--WESTERN EUROPE.
----Oil industry restructuring in the
    Netherlands and its European context. -
    1987.
        (000629)

PETROLEUM LAW.
----The evolution of the legal relationship
    between international petroleum mining
    companies and host countries. - 1983.
        (000647)

PETROLEUM LAW--ARGENTINA.
----Petroleum service contracts in
    Argentina, Brazil and Colombia : issues
    arising from their legal nature. - 1987.
        (002422)

PETROLEUM LAW--BRAZIL.
----Petroleum service contracts in
    Argentina, Brazil and Colombia : issues
    arising from their legal nature. - 1987.
        (002422)

PETROLEUM LAW--CANADA.
----Comparative licensing aspects of
    Canadian and United Kingdom petroleum
    law. - 1986.
        (002176)

PETROLEUM LAW--COLOMBIA.
----Los contratos petroleros. - 1984.
        (002454)
----Petroleum service contracts in
    Argentina, Brazil and Colombia : issues
    arising from their legal nature. - 1987.
        (002422)

PETROLEUM LAW--GABON.
----Les conventions dans la fiscalité
    pétrolière gabonaise. - 1987.
        (002030)

PETROLEUM LAW--LATIN AMERICA.
----Petroleum service contracts in
    Argentina, Brazil and Colombia : issues
    arising from their legal nature. - 1987.
        (002422)

PETROLEUM LAW--UNITED KINGDOM.
----Comparative licensing aspects of
    Canadian and United Kingdom petroleum
    law. - 1986.
        (002176)

PETROLEUM POLICY--BRAZIL.
----Petroleum development in Brazil. - 1987.
        (000638)

PETROLEUM POLICY--SAUDI ARABIA.
----Petroleum based development and the
    private sector. - 1985.
        (001138)

PETROLEUM POLICY--VENEZUELA.
----Petroleum and political pacts. - 1987.
        (001816)

PETROLEUM PRICES.
----Appropriate financing for petroleum
    development in developing countries. -
    1984.
        (000576)
----The international oil industry in the
    1980s. - 1984.
        (000622)
----Olmärkte im Umbruch. - 1986.
        (000631)

PETROLEUM PRICES (continued)
----Private investment in Latin America. -
    1984.
    (002460)
----World oil markets. - 1986.
    (000590)

PETROLEUM PRICES--UNITED STATES.
----The engineers and the price system
    revisited: the future of the
    international oil corporations. - 1983.
    (000587)

PETROLEUM PRODUCTS--CHINA.
----The role of oil in China's economic
    development, growth, and
    internationalization. - 1985.
    (000602)

PETROLEUM REFINERIES--NETHERLANDS.
----Oil industry restructuring in the
    Netherlands and its European context. -
    1987.
    (000629)

PETROLEUM REFINERIES--WESTERN EUROPE.
----Oil industry restructuring in the
    Netherlands and its European context. -
    1987.
    (000629)

PETROLEUM RESERVES.
----International petroleum exploration
    [and] exploitation agreements. - 1986.
    (002431)
----Olmärkte im Umbruch. - 1986.
    (000631)
----The relationship between the state and
    the multinational corporation in the
    exploitation of resources. - 1984.
    (000584)
----Taming troubled waters. - 1986.
    (002453)
----Transnational oil. - 1986.
    (000618)

PETROLEUM RESERVES--GULF STATES.
----A historical perspective of U.S.-GCC
    economic and financial interdependence.
    - 1987.
    (000143)

PETROLEUM REVENUES.
----Financial and fiscal aspects of
    petroleum exploitation. - 1987.
    (002451)

PHARMACEUTICAL INDUSTRY.
----Appropriate pharmaceutical policies in
    developing countries. - 1985.
    (000707)
----Marktstrategien multinationaler
    Pharmaunternehmen und die
    Arzneimittelmarkte der Dritten Welt. -
    1986.
    (000768)
----Les multinationales de la pharmacie. -
    1985.
    (000730)
----The pharmaceutical industry. - 1985.
    (000726)

----Restrictive clauses in licensing
    agreements: the pharmaceutical industry
    in developing countries. - 1984.
    (002420)
----Transnational corporations in the
    pharmaceutical industry of developing
    countries. - 1984.
    (000749)
----Vergleichende System- und
    Industriestudien. - 1983.
    (001342)
----The wrong kind of medicine? - 1984.
    (000717)

PHARMACEUTICAL INDUSTRY--ARGENTINA.
----Transnational corporations in the
    pharmaceutical industry of developing
    countries. - 1984.
    (000749)

PHARMACEUTICAL INDUSTRY--BRAZIL.
----Transnational corporations in the
    pharmaceutical industry of developing
    countries. - 1984.
    (000749)

PHARMACEUTICAL INDUSTRY--CANADA.
----Performance of the multinational drug
    industry in home and host countries: a
    Canadian case study. - 1983.
    (000690)

PHARMACEUTICAL INDUSTRY--CHINA.
----Joint ventures in the PRC. - 1987.
    (000478)

PHARMACEUTICAL INDUSTRY--COLOMBIA.
----Transnational corporations in the
    pharmaceutical industry of developing
    countries. - 1984.
    (000749)

PHARMACEUTICAL INDUSTRY--COSTA RICA.
----Transnational corporations in the
    pharmaceutical industry of developing
    countries. - 1984.
    (000749)

PHARMACEUTICAL INDUSTRY--EGYPT.
----Transnational corporations in the
    pharmaceutical industry of developing
    countries. - 1984.
    (000749)

PHARMACEUTICAL INDUSTRY--INDIA.
----Business strategies of multinational
    corporations in India. - 1983.
    (000484)
----Multinational corporations and Indian
    drug industry. - 1985.
    (000736)
----Multinationals and Indian pharmaceutical
    industry. - 1984.
    (000727)
----Transnational corporations in the
    pharmaceutical industry of developing
    countries. - 1984.
    (000749)

PHARMACEUTICAL INDUSTRY--INDONESIA.
----Technology transfer under alternative
    arrangements with transnational
    corporations. - 1987.
      (001513)

PHARMACEUTICAL INDUSTRY--KENYA.
----Transnational corporations in the
    pharmaceutical industry of developing
    countries. - 1984.
      (000749)

PHARMACEUTICAL INDUSTRY--LATIN AMERICA.
----La industria farmacéutica y las
    transnacionales. - 1985.
      (000667)

PHARMACEUTICAL INDUSTRY--MALAYSIA.
----Transnational corporations in the
    pharmaceutical industry of developing
    countries. - 1984.
      (000749)

PHARMACEUTICAL INDUSTRY--MEXICO.
----Estructura y comportamiento de la
    industria químico-farmacéutica en
    México. - 1984.
      (000737)
----Médicaments pour tous en l'an 2000? -
    1983.
      (000662)
----Research and development in
    pharmaceuticals: Mexico. - 1983.
      (000770)
----Las transnacionales de la salud. - 1983.
      (000745)
----Transnational corporations in the
    pharmaceutical industry of developing
    countries. - 1984.
      (000749)

PHARMACEUTICAL INDUSTRY--REPUBLIC OF KOREA.
----Technology transfer under alternative
    arrangements with transnational
    corporations. - 1987.
      (001513)
----Transnational corporations in the
    pharmaceutical industry of developing
    countries. - 1984.
      (000749)

PHARMACEUTICAL INDUSTRY--SIERRA LEONE.
----Transnational corporations in the
    pharmaceutical industry of developing
    countries. - 1984.
      (000749)

PHARMACEUTICAL INDUSTRY--SWITZERLAND.
----Médicaments pour tous en l'an 2000? -
    1983.
      (000662)

PHARMACEUTICAL INDUSTRY--THAILAND.
----Transnational corporations in the
    pharmaceutical industry of developing
    countries. - 1984.
      (000749)

PHARMACEUTICAL INDUSTRY--TURKEY.
----Transnational corporations and local
    capital: comparative conduct and
    performance in the Turkish
    pharmaceutical industry. - 1986.
      (000705)

PHARMACEUTICAL INDUSTRY--UNITED KINGDOM.
----From national to multinational
    enterprise. - 1983.
      (000277)
----Inward investment. - 1984.
      (000116)

PHARMACEUTICAL INDUSTRY--UNITED STATES.
----A competitive assessment of the U.S.
    pharmaceutical industry. - 1984.
      (000757)

PHARMACEUTICAL INDUSTRY--URUGUAY.
----La industria farmacéutica y las
    transnacionales. - 1985.
      (000667)

PHARMACEUTICALS.
----Consolidated list of products whose
    consumption and/or sale have been
    banned, withdrawn, severely restricted
    or not approved by Governments. - 1987.
      (002702)
----Transnational corporations in the
    pharmaceutical industry of developing
    countries. - 1984.
      (000749)
----The wrong kind of medicine? - 1984.
      (000717)

PHARMACEUTICALS--MEXICO.
----Médicaments pour tous en l'an 2000? -
    1983.
      (000662)

PHARMACEUTICALS--SWITZERLAND.
----Médicaments pour tous en l'an 2000? -
    1983.
      (000662)

PHILIPPINES--CORPORATIONS.
----Factors influencing the choice of
    location : local and foreign firms in
    the Philippines. - 1987.
      (000547)

PHILIPPINES--ECONOMIC CONDITIONS.
----The Marcos regime. - 1985.
      (001070)
----The Philippines : authoritarian
    government, multinationals and ancestral
    lands. - 1983.
      (001066)

PHILIPPINES--ECONOMIC DEVELOPMENT.
----The Manila-Washington connection. - 1983.
      (001855)
----The Philippines under Marcos. - 1986.
      (001071)

PHILIPPINES--EXPORT PROMOTION.
----Export promotion via industrial
    enclaves. - 1987.
      (002399)

PHILIPPINES--FOREIGN INVESTMENTS.
----Factors influencing the choice of
    location : local and foreign firms in
    the Philippines. - 1987.
      (000547)

PHILIPPINES--FOREIGN INVESTMENTS (continued)
----National legislation and regulations
    relating to transnational corporations.
    Volume 4. - 1986.
        (002253)

PHILIPPINES--FOREIGN RELATIONS.
----The Philippines under Marcos. - 1986.
        (001071)

PHILIPPINES--FREE EXPORT ZONES.
----Aspects of labour law and relations in
    selected export processing zones. - 1984.
        (001895)
----The Bataan export processing zone. -
    1982.
        (002365)
----Export channels in the Philippines. -
    1987.
        (002373)
----Export promotion via industrial
    enclaves. - 1987.
        (002399)

PHILIPPINES--INDIGENOUS POPULATIONS.
----The Philippines : authoritarian
    government, multinationals and ancestral
    lands. - 1983.
        (001066)

PHILIPPINES--INDUSTRIAL LOCATION.
----Factors influencing the choice of
    location : local and foreign firms in
    the Philippines. - 1987.
        (000547)

PHILIPPINES--INDUSTRIAL POLICY.
----Transnational corporations and the
    state. - 1985.
        (001860)

PHILIPPINES--INVESTMENT POLICY.
----Telecommunications and investment
    decisions in the Philippines. - 1984.
        (000533)

PHILIPPINES--LABOUR LAW.
----Aspects of labour law and relations in
    selected export processing zones. - 1984.
        (001895)

PHILIPPINES--LABOUR RELATIONS.
----Aspects of labour law and relations in
    selected export processing zones. - 1984.
        (001895)

PHILIPPINES--LAWS AND REGULATIONS.
----National legislation and regulations
    relating to transnational corporations.
    Volume 4. - 1986.
        (002253)

PHILIPPINES--POLITICAL CONDITIONS.
----The Philippines : authoritarian
    government, multinationals and ancestral
    lands. - 1983.
        (001066)
----The Philippines under Marcos. - 1986.
        (001071)

PHILIPPINES--SCIENCE AND TECHNOLOGY POLICY.
----Proceedings of the SSTCC/UNCTC/ESCAP
    Asia-Pacific Training Workshop on
    Regulating and Negotiating Technology
    Transfer through Transnational
    Corporations, 14-25 October 1985,
    Fuzhou, Fujian, China. - 1986.
        (001405) (002169)

PHILIPPINES--TECHNOLOGY TRANSFER.
----Proceedings of the SSTCC/UNCTC/ESCAP
    Asia-Pacific Training Workshop on
    Regulating and Negotiating Technology
    Transfer through Transnational
    Corporations, 14-25 October 1985,
    Fuzhou, Fujian, China. - 1986.
        (001405) (002169)

PHILIPPINES--TELECOMMUNICATION.
----Telecommunications and investment
    decisions in the Philippines. - 1984.
        (000533)

PHILIPPINES--TRANSNATIONAL CORPORATIONS.
----The Manila-Washington connection. - 1983.
        (001855)
----The Marcos regime. - 1985.
        (001070)
----National legislation and regulations
    relating to transnational corporations.
    Volume 4. - 1986.
        (002253)
----The Philippines : authoritarian
    government, multinationals and ancestral
    lands. - 1983.
        (001066)
----The Philippines under Marcos. - 1986.
        (001071)
----Transnational corporations and the
    state. - 1985.
        (001860)

PHILIPS GLOEILAMPENFABRIEKEN (NATHERLANDS).
----Technology transfer: the approach of a
    Dutch multinational. - 1986.
        (001484)

PHOSPHATES.
----Fertilizer supplies for developing
    countries : issues in the transfer and
    development of technology. - 1985.
        (001471)

POLAND--DEVELOPED MARKET ECONOMIES.
----CMEA direct investments in the western
    countries. - 1987.   •
        (000158)

POLAND--DEVELOPMENT.
----Development, social justice, and
    dependence in Poland. - 1985.
        (001188)

POLAND--ECONOMIC CONDITIONS.
----Development, social justice, and
    dependence in Poland. - 1985.
        (001188)
----East-West technology transfer : study of
    Poland, 1971-1980. - 1983.
        (001432)

POLAND--ECONOMIC REFORM.
----L'entreprise polonaise. - 1987.
    (000305)

POLAND--ECONOMIC RELATIONS.
----Development, social justice, and
    dependence in Poland. - 1985.
    (001188)
----Industrial cooperation between Poland
    and the West. - 1985.
    (001576)
----Kooperacja przemyslowa Polski z krajami
    RWPG. - 1986.
    (001172)

POLAND--ENTREPRENEURSHIP.
----The functioning of private enterprise in
    Poland. - 1984.
    (001168)

POLAND--EXTERNAL DEBT.
----Handels- und Zahlungsprobleme in
    Osteuropa. - 1983.
    (000215)

POLAND--FOREIGN DIRECT INVESTMENT.
----CMEA direct investments in the western
    countries. - 1987.
    (000158)

POLAND--FOREIGN INVESTMENTS.
----New legislation on foreign private firms
    in Poland. - 1984.
    (002244)
----Ownership and investment in Poland. -
    1985.
    (001595)

POLAND--FOREIGN TRADE.
----CMEA direct investments in the western
    countries. - 1987.
    (000158)

POLAND--IMPORT RESTRICTIONS.
----Import licencji a zmiany w systemie
    gospodarki. - 1984.
    (002440)

POLAND--INDUSTRIAL CO-OPERATION.
----Industrial cooperation between Poland
    and the West. - 1985.
    (001576)
----Kooperacja przemyslowa Polski z krajami
    RWPG. - 1986.
    (001172)
----The regulation of technology transfer in
    Poland. - 1983.
    (001416)
----Western firms participating in the
    East-West industrial co-operation. -
    1983.
    (001175)

POLAND--INFORMATION POLICY.
----Transborder data flows and Poland :
    Polish case study. - 1984.
    (000920)

POLAND--INFORMATION TECHNOLOGY.
----Transborder data flows and Poland :
    Polish case study. - 1984.
    (000920)

POLAND--INTRAREGIONAL TRADE.
----Intra-industry trade in Poland's foreign
    trade in 1950-1984 : empirical results
    and policy implications. - 1986.
    (001372)

POLAND--INVESTMENTS.
----Import licencji a zmiany w systemie
    gospodarki. - 1984.
    (002440)

POLAND--JOINT VENTURES.
----East-West joint ventures. - 1988.
    (001570)
----Industrial cooperation between Poland
    and the West. - 1985.
    (001576)
----Neue joint-venture-Gesetzgebung in
    Polen. - 1986.
    (002174)

POLAND--LAWS AND REGULATIONS.
----East-West joint ventures. - 1988.
    (001570)
----New legislation on foreign private firms
    in Poland. - 1984.
    (002244)
----Ownership and investment in Poland. -
    1985.
    (001595)

POLAND--LEGISLATION.
----Neue joint-venture-Gesetzgebung in
    Polen. - 1986.
    (002174)

POLAND--LICENCE AGREEMENTS.
----Import licencji a zmiany w systemie
    gospodarki. - 1984.
    (002440)
----The regulation of technology transfer in
    Poland. - 1983.
    (001416)

POLAND--PRIVATE ENTERPRISES.
----The functioning of private enterprise in
    Poland. - 1984.
    (001168)

POLAND--RESEARCH AND DEVELOPMENT.
----Transborder data flows and Poland :
    Polish case study. - 1984.
    (000920)

POLAND--SERVICE INDUSTRIES.
----Provision of services in Poland. - 1987.
    (000856)

POLAND--SOCIAL CONDITIONS.
----Development, social justice, and
    dependence in Poland. - 1985.
    (001188)

POLAND--SOCIAL JUSTICE.
----Development, social justice, and
    dependence in Poland. - 1985.
    (001188)

POLAND--STATE TRADING ENTERPRISES.
----Enterprise organization of East European
    socialist countries. - 1987.
    (000441)
----L'entreprise polonaise. - 1987.
    (000305)

POLAND--STATISTICAL DATA.
----East-West joint ventures. - 1988.
     (001570)
----East-West technology transfer : study of
     Poland, 1971-1980. - 1983.
     (001432)

POLAND--TECHNOLOGY TRANSFER.
----East-West technology transfer : study of
     Poland, 1971-1980. - 1983.
     (001432)
----The regulation of technology transfer in
     Poland. - 1983.
     (001416)

POLAND--TELECOMMUNICATION.
----Transborder data flows and Poland :
     Polish case study. - 1984.
     (000920)

POLAND--TRADE POLICY.
----Intra-industry trade in Poland's foreign
     trade in 1950-1984 : empirical results
     and policy implications. - 1986.
     (001372)

POLAND--TRADE STATISTICS.
----Intra-industry trade in Poland's foreign
     trade in 1950-1984 : empirical results
     and policy implications. - 1986.
     (001372)

POLAND--TRANSNATIONAL CORPORATIONS.
----Industrial cooperation between Poland
     and the West. - 1985.
     (001576)

POLITICAL CONDITIONS.
----Global risk assessments. - 1983.
     (001803)
----Multinational risk assessment and
     management. - 1987.
     (000514)
----Political risk analysis. - 1985.
     (001859)
----Political risks in international
     business. - 1985.
     (001843)

POLITICAL CONDITIONS--ARGENTINA.
----The new Argentina. - 1984.
     (001777)
----Transnacionalización y política
     económica en la Argentina. - 1985.
     (001115)

POLITICAL CONDITIONS--ASIA.
----Asia yearbook. - 1973-   .
     (002699)

POLITICAL CONDITIONS--BRAZIL.
----Business in a democratic Brazil. - 1985.
     (001776)

POLITICAL CONDITIONS--COLOMBIA.
----Notes from Latin America. - 1983.
     (000628)

POLITICAL CONDITIONS--JAMAICA.
----La Jamaïque, ou le dilemme politique
     d'un petit pays déshérité. - 1984.
     (001819)

POLITICAL CONDITIONS--NICARAGUA.
----Política económica y capital extranjero
     en Nicaragua. - 1984.
     (002081)

POLITICAL CONDITIONS--PHILIPPINES.
----The Philippines : authoritarian
     government, multinationals and ancestral
     lands. - 1983.
     (001066)
----The Philippines under Marcos. - 1986.
     (001071)

POLITICAL CONDITIONS--SOUTH AFRICA.
----Political change in South Africa. - 1986.
     (001205)

POLITICAL CONDITIONS--SOUTHEAST ASIA.
----Neue Wachstumsmärkte in Fernost. - 1983.
     (001800)

POLITICAL CONDITIONS--SUDAN.
----Chevron, Sudan and political risk. -
     1984.
     (001858)

POLITICAL CONDITIONS--VENEZUELA.
----Petroleum and political pacts. - 1987.
     (001816)

POLITICAL POWER.
----Multinational corporations and the
     political economy of power. - 1983.
     (001846)

POLLUTION.
----Pollution and the struggle for the world
     product. - 1988.
     (001948)

POLLUTION CONTROL.
----Coanda flaring for pollution control. -
     1986.
     (001934)
----Environmental aspects of the activities
     of transnational corporations. - 1985.
     (001954)

POPULATION GROWTH--UNITED STATES.
----What's causing America's capital
     imports? - 1987.
     (000539)

PORTUGAL--ECONOMIC INTEGRATION.
----Portugal's accession to the EEC and its
     impact on foreign direct investment. -
     1986.
     (000554)

PORTUGAL--EMPLOYMENT POLICY.
----The employment impact of multinational
     enterprises in Greece, Portugal and
     Spain. - 1987.
     (001887)

PORTUGAL--FOREIGN DIRECT INVESTMENT.
----Investment legislation in Greece,
     Portugal and Spain: the background to
     foreign investment in Mediterranean
     Europe. - 1983.
     (002168)

PORTUGAL--FOREIGN DIRECT INVESTMENT
(continued)
----Portugal's accession to the EEC and its
     impact on foreign direct investment. -
     1986.
        (000554)

PORTUGAL--FOREIGN INVESTMENTS.
----National legislation and regulations
     relating to transnational corporations.
     Volume 4. - 1986.
        (002253)

PORTUGAL--LAWS AND REGULATIONS.
----National legislation and regulations
     relating to transnational corporations.
     Volume 4. - 1986.
        (002253)

PORTUGAL--LEGISLATION.
----Investment legislation in Greece,
     Portugal and Spain: the background to
     foreign investment in Mediterranean
     Europe. - 1983.
        (002168)

PORTUGAL--TRANSNATIONAL CORPORATIONS.
----The employment impact of multinational
     enterprises in Greece, Portugal and
     Spain. - 1987.
        (001887)
----National legislation and regulations
     relating to transnational corporations.
     Volume 4. - 1986.
        (002253)

POTASH.
----Fertilizer supplies for developing
     countries : issues in the transfer and
     development of technology. - 1985.
        (001471)

POWER INDUSTRY.
----Energy sector investment in LDCs. - 1986.
        (000773)

PREFERENTIAL AGREEMENTS.
----The theory of preferential trading
     arrangements. - 1986.
        (001381)

PRICE CONTROLS.
----The effects of taxation price control
     and government contracts in oligopoly
     and monopolistic competition. - 1987.
        (001693)

PRICE STABILIZATION.
----Pricing and sourcing strategies in a
     multinational oligopoly. - 1983.
        (000466)

PRICES.
----La gestion marketing dans un
     développemnt turbulent et hautement
     concurrentiel. - 1983.
        (000487)
----Market competition, conflict and
     collusion. - 1987.
        (001680)
----Transnational corporations in the
     pharmaceutical industry of developing
     countries. - 1984.
        (000749)

PRICES--FRANCE.
----La formation du prix dans les
     transactions internationales. - 1985.
        (001712)

PRICES--KUWAIT.
----Impact of the operations of
     transnational corporations on
     development in Kuwait. - 1987.
        (001143)

PRICES--UNITED STATES.
----La formation du prix dans les
     transactions internationales. - 1985.
        (001712)

PRICES--WESTERN EUROPE.
----La formation du prix dans les
     transactions internationales. - 1985.
        (001712)

PRIMARY SECTOR.
----The primary, secondary, tertiary and
     quaternary sectors of the economy. -
     1987.
        (000883)

PRIVACY LAW--UNITED STATES.
----New challenges to the U.S. multinational
     corporation in the European Economic
     Community. - 1985.
        (002192)

PRIVACY LAW--WESTERN EUROPE.
----New challenges to the U.S. multinational
     corporation in the European Economic
     Community. - 1985.
        (002192)

PRIVATE ENTERPRISES.
----Dénationalisations : les leçons de
     l'étranger. - 1986.
        (001565)
----Financial reporting by private
     companies. - 1983.
        (002056)
----Free zones in developing countries. -
     1983.
        (002390)
----Measures to strengthen the capabilities
     of developing countries in their dealing
     with transnational corporations. - 1985.
        (002612)
----Privatization and public enterprise. -
     1988.
        (001588)
----Völkerrechtliche Haftung für das Handeln
     Privater im Bereich des internationalen
     Umweltschutzes. - 1984.
        (001945)

PRIVATE ENTERPRISES--AFRICA.
----Limite des alternatives capitalistes
     d'état ou privées à la crise agricole
     africaine. - 1985.
        (001575)

PRIVATE ENTERPRISES--AFRICA SOUTH OF SAHARA.
----La privatisation des entreprises
    publiques en Afrique au sud du Sahara,
    (2). - 1986.
        (001564)

PRIVATE ENTERPRISES--ASIA.
----Private enterprise wins in Asia. - 1985.
        (001078)

PRIVATE ENTERPRISES--BRAZIL.
----The determinants of manufacturing
    ownership in less developed countries. -
    1986.
        (000712)

PRIVATE ENTERPRISES--CAMEROON.
----The private sector, the public sector,
    and donor assistance in economic
    development. - 1983.
        (000268)

PRIVATE ENTERPRISES--CANADA.
----Public and private returns from joint
    venture research: an example from
    agriculture. - 1986.
        (001650)

PRIVATE ENTERPRISES--CHINA.
----China : private enterprise on the march.
    - 1987.
        (001054)
----Private enterprise in China. - 1985.
        (002184)
----The reform of the Chinese system of
    enterprise ownership. - 1987.
        (002185)

PRIVATE ENTERPRISES--COSTA RICA.
----The private sector, the public sector,
    and donor assistance in economic
    development. - 1983.
        (000268)

PRIVATE ENTERPRISES--FRANCE.
----The dilemma of denationalisation. - 1986.
        (001644)

PRIVATE ENTERPRISES--INDIA.
----The determinants of manufacturing
    ownership in less developed countries. -
    1986.
        (000712)

PRIVATE ENTERPRISES--JAPAN.
----The Japanese economic strategy. - 1983.
        (000366)
----Privatisierung in Japan. - 1987.
        (001601)

PRIVATE ENTERPRISES--MALAWI.
----The private sector, the public sector,
    and donor assistance in economic
    development. - 1983.
        (000268)

PRIVATE ENTERPRISES--MEXICO.
----The determinants of manufacturing
    ownership in less developed countries. -
    1986.
        (000712)

PRIVATE ENTERPRISES--PACIFIC OCEAN REGION.
----Regulation to deregulation. - 1985.
        (000798)

PRIVATE ENTERPRISES--POLAND.
----The functioning of private enterprise in
    Poland. - 1984.
        (001168)

PRIVATE ENTERPRISES--REPUBLIC OF KOREA.
----The determinants of manufacturing
    ownership in less developed countries. -
    1986.
        (000712)

PRIVATE ENTERPRISES--SAUDI ARABIA.
----Petroleum based development and the
    private sector. - 1985.
        (001138)

PRIVATE ENTERPRISES--SOUTH AFRICA.
----The determinants of manufacturing
    ownership in less developed countries. -
    1986.
        (000712)

PRIVATE ENTERPRISES--SOUTHEAST ASIA.
----The Japanese economic strategy. - 1983.
        (000366)

PRIVATE ENTERPRISES--THAILAND.
----The private sector, the public sector,
    and donor assistance in economic
    development. - 1983.
        (000268)

PRIVATE ENTERPRISES--UNITED KINGDOM.
----Britain's privately owned companies. -
    198?-   .
        (002624)
----Privatisation and regulation : the UK
    experience. - 1986.
        (001627)

PRIVATE ENTERPRISES--UNITED STATES.
----Implications of deregulating satellite
    communications. - 1985.
        (002242)

PRIVATE INTERNATIONAL LAW.
----Anti-trust and restrictive business
    practices. - 1983-   .
        (001957)
----Contratos de licencia y de transferencia
    de tecnología en el derecho privado. -
    1980.
        (002415)
----The extraterritorial application of
    national laws. - 1987.
        (002348)
----Extraterritorial jurisdiction. - 1983.
        (002350) (002688)
----Die Gestaltung des internationalen
    Privatrechts der Schuldverträge unter
    allgemeinen Leitprinzipien. - 1983.
        (002025)
----Die Haftungsproblematik bei Konkurs
    einer Gesellschaft innerhalb eines
    transnationalen Unternehmens. - 1984.
        (002233)
----International business and national
    jurisdiction. - 1988.
        (002351)

PRIVATE INTERNATIONAL LAW (continued)
----International equipment leasing. - 1984.
  (000905) (002139)
----Kin'yu torihiki to kokusai sosho. - 1983.
  (002525)
----L'ordre public et le droit applicable au
  fond du litige dans l'arbitrage
  international. - 1986.
  (002496)
----Private international law as a means to
  control the multinational enterprise. -
  1986.
  (002154)

PRIVATE INTERNATIONAL LAW--GERMANY, FEDERAL
REPUBLIC OF.
----Fakultatives Kollisonsrecht im
  internationalen Wettbewerbsrecht? - 1984.
  (002247)

PRIVATE INTERNATIONAL LAW--JAPAN.
----Kokusai torihikiho. - 1984.
  (002458)

PRIVATE INTERNATIONAL LAW--SWEDEN.
----Das anzuwendende Recht beim
  internationalen Schiedsverfahren in
  Schweden. - 1986.
  (002515)

PRIVATE SECTOR.
----Los bancos transnacionales y el
  endeudamiento externo en la Argentina. -
  1987.
  (000819)
----Dénationalisations : les leçons de
  l'étranger. - 1986.
  (001565)
----The private sector and rural
  development: can agribusiness help the
  small farmer? - 1985.
  (000566)
----Transnational corporations in world
  development. - 1983.
  (000102)

PRIVATE SECTOR--CHINA.
----Die chinesischen Wirtschaftsreformen im
  neunten Jahr. - 1986.
  (002217)

PRIVATE SECTOR--FRANCE.
----Propriété et pouvoir dans l'industrie. -
  1987.
  (001628)

PRIVATE SECTOR--UNITED KINGDOM.
----Britain's privately owned companies. -
  198?-
  (002624)
----Privatising nationalised industries :
  constitutional issues and new legal
  techniques. - 1987.
  (001582)

PROCTOR AND GAMBLE COMPANY (CINCINNATI,OHIO).
----A global comeback. - 1987.
  (000275)

PRODUCT DEVELOPMENT.
----La notion de produit-système et la
  décomposition internationale des
  processus productifs dans l'industrie
  automobile. (With English summary.). -
  1984.
  (000687)

PRODUCT SAFETY.
----Guidelines for Consumer Protection. -
  1986.
  (002017)

PRODUCTION CONTROL--EASTERN EUROPE.
----Multinationals from the Second World :
  growth of foreign investment by Soviet
  and East European enterprises. - 1987.
  (000356)

PRODUCTION CONTROL--JAPAN.
----Vers la mondialisation de l'appareil
  productif japonais. - 1986.
  (000725)

PRODUCTION CONTROL--USSR.
----Multinationals from the Second World :
  growth of foreign investment by Soviet
  and East European enterprises. - 1987.
  (000356)

PRODUCTION COSTS.
----Production cost differentials and
  foreign direct investment: a test of two
  models. - 1986.
  (000061)
----Why are services cheaper in the poor
  countries? - 1984.
  (000813)

PRODUCTION DIVERSIFICATION.
----Industrial diversification amongst the
  world's leading multinational
  enterprises. - 1983.
  (000546)
----International corporate diversification,
  market valuation, and size-adjusted
  evidence. - 1984.
  (000475)
----Mergers. - 1983.
  (001580)
----Optimum product diversity and the
  incentives for entry in natural
  oligopolies. - 1987.
  (000485)
----Organizing to implement strategies of
  diversity and globalization: the role of
  matrix designs. - 1986.
  (000476)
----Production flexibility as a motive for
  multinationality. - 1987.
  (000470)
----Research intensity, international
  production and US-based multinationals.
  - 1983.
  (000367)

PRODUCTION DIVERSIFICATION--GERMANY, FEDERAL
REPUBLIC OF.
----Entry by diversified firms into German
  industries. - 1986.
  (001162)

PRODUCTION DIVERSIFICATION--NORDIC COUNTRIES.
----Industrial structure and country risks
   in a Nordic perspective. - 1984.
      (001838)

PRODUCTION DIVERSIFICATION--UNITED STATES.
----Diversification : the European versus
   the US experience. - 1987.
      (000491)

PRODUCTION DIVERSIFICATION--WESTERN EUROPE.
----Diversification : the European versus
   the US experience. - 1987.
      (000491)

PRODUCTION (ECONOMIC THEORY).
----Strategic behaviour and industrial
   competition. - 1986.
      (000512)

PRODUCTION (ECONOMIC THEORY)--GERMANY,
FEDERAL REPUBLIC OF.
----Stärken und Schwächen der Bundesrepublik
   Deutschland in der internationalen
   Arbeitsteilung. - 1984.
      (001260)

PRODUCTION (ECONOMIC THEORY)--UNITED STATES.
----Quantifying the competitive effects of
   production joint ventures. - 1986.
      (001548)

PRODUCTION PLANNING.
----Management of international production.
   - 1983.
      (000455)
----Production flexibility as a motive for
   multinationality. - 1987.
      (000470)
----The theory of international production.
   - 1985.
      (000028)

PRODUCTION PLANNING--FRANCE.
----Labour, production and the state :
   decentralization of the French
   automobile industry. - 1987.
      (000724)

PRODUCTION SPECIALIZATION.
----The eclectic paradigm of international
   production. - 1985.
      (000023)
----The global factory. - 1985.
      (001254)

PRODUCTIVITY.
----Industry in the 1980s. - 1985.
      (001341)
----Managing the service economy. - 1985.
      (000899)
----La productivité dans les services. -
   1985.
      (000924)
----The services industries: employment,
   productivity, and inflation. - 1985.
      (000940)

PRODUCTIVITY--EASTERN EUROPE.
----L'investissement productif en Europe de
   l'Est : gaspillage des ressources,
   délais de réalisation importants, retard
   technologique? - 1986.
      (000126)

PRODUCTIVITY--INDONESIA.
----Factor proportions and productive
   efficiency of foreign owned firms in the
   Indonesian manufacturing sector. - 1984.
      (000655)

PRODUCTIVITY--TAIWAN (CHINA).
----The production characteristics of
   multinational firms and the effects of
   tax incentives: the case of Taiwan's
   electronics industry. - 1986.
      (001038) (002305)

PRODUCTIVITY STATISTICS--UNITED KINGDOM.
----A comparison of embodied technical
   change in services and manufacturing
   industry. - 1986.
      (000806)

PROFESSIONAL EDUCATION.
----International accounting and reporting
   issues, 1985 review. - 1985.
      (002116)

PROFESSIONAL WORKERS--BELGIUM.
----La structure professionnelle des
   secteurs secondaire et tertiaire. - 1987.
      (000823)

PROFIT.
----Probleme der Gerwinnverlagerungen
   multinationaler Unternehmen :
   Konzerninterne Verrechnungspreise und
   deren wirtschaftspolitische Wirkungen. -
   1983.
      (001755)
----Profits, tariffs, and intra-industry
   trade. - 1985.
      (001347)

PROFIT--CZECHOSLOVAKIA.
----K mereni zisku podniku. - 1987.
      (000888)

PROFIT--GHANA.
----The profits of foreign firms in a less
   developed country: Ghana. - 1986.
      (001019)

PROFIT--YUGOSLAVIA.
----Joint ventures in Yugoslavia: comment/
   reply. - 1984.
      (001533)

PROGRAMA CENTROAMERICANO DE DESARROLLO DE
LAS CIENCIAS SOCIALES (SAN JOSE).
----Las transnacionales del banano en
   Centroamérica. - 1983.
      (000564)

PROGRAMME EVALUATION.
----Technical co-operation programme,
   1976-1987 : United Nations Centre on
   Transnational Corporations. - 1988.
      (002611)

PROGRAMME EVALUATION--AUSTRALIA.
----The public interest IR & D program. -
   1985.
      (001485)

PROGRAMME IMPLEMENTATION.
----Measures regarding the activities of
    transnational corporations in South
    Africa and Namibia. - 1985.
    (001220)

PROJECT EVALUATION.
----[Planning and execution of R&D]. - 1987.
    (001481)
----Technical co-operation programme,
    1976-1987 : United Nations Centre on
    Transnational Corporations. - 1988.
    (002611)

PROJECT EVALUATION AND REVIEW TECHNIQUE.
----The choice of a technique in analysing
    national development strategy. - 1986.
    (001323)

PROJECT FINANCE.
----Current problems of economic
    integration. - 1986.
    (001312)

PROJECT IMPLEMENTATION.
----Current problems of economic
    integration. - 1986.
    (001312)

PROJECT MANAGEMENT.
----Environmental aspects of the activities
    of transnational corporations. - 1985.
    (001954)

PROPERTY.
----Eigentum, Enteignung und Entschädigung
    im geltenden Völkerrecht. - 1985.
    (002321)
----The taking of foreign property under
    international law. - 1984.
    (002336)

PROPERTY RIGHTS.
----The question of a reference to
    international obligations in the United
    Nations Code of Conduct on Transnational
    Corporations. - 1986.
    (002020)

PROPERTY RIGHTS--UNITED STATES.
----Jurisdiction over foreign governments. -
    1986.
    (002347)

PROTECTIONISM.
----Exports of manufactures from developing
    countries : performance and prospects
    for market access. - 1984.
    (001355)
----Industrialisation et commerce du Tiers
    monde. - 1986.
    (001318)
----International Colloquium on the Proposed
    New Round of Multilateral Trade
    Negotiations and Developing Countries :
    proceedings and papers. - 1986.
    (001365)
----Multinational firms and the theory of
    effective protection. - 1983.
    (001674)
----Power and protectionism. - 1983.
    (001865)

----Protectionism and structural adjustment.
    - 1986.
    (001689)
----Protectionist tendencies in
    international trade in services. - 1986.
    (000953)
----Putting world trade back on a growth
    course. - 1984.
    (001358)
----Revitalizing development, growth and
    international trade. - 1987.
    (001394)
----Trade [and] structural change. - 1984.
    (001391)
----US corporate interests and the political
    economy of trade policy. - 1984.
    (000505)

PROTECTIONISM--JAPAN.
----Japan's direct investment in California
    and the new protectionism. - 1984.
    (000145)

PROTECTIONISM--LATIN AMERICA.
----Transnacionalización y periferia
    semindustrializada. - 1983.
    (001017)

PROTECTIONISM--UNITED STATES.
----Intra-firm trade and U.S. protectionism:
    thoughts based on a small survey. - 1986.
    (001367)
----Japan's direct investment in California
    and the new protectionism. - 1984.
    (000145)
----Protectionist threat to trade and
    investment in services. - 1983.
    (000951)

PROTECTIONISM--ZAIRE.
----Protection, distortions and investment
    incentives in Zaïre. - 1986.
    (002272)

PUBLIC CONTRACTS--MIDDLE EAST.
----An introduction to contract procedures
    in the Near East and North Africa. -
    1978-   .
    (002433)

PUBLIC CONTRACTS--NORTH AFRICA.
----An introduction to contract procedures
    in the Near East and North Africa. -
    1978-   .
    (002433)

PUBLIC DEBT--UNITED STATES.
----America's foreign debt. - 1987.
    (000243)

PUBLIC ENTERPRISES.
----Accounting analysis of the efficiency of
    public enterprises. - 1984.
    (002114)
----Channels and modalities for the transfer
    of technology to public enterprises in
    developing countries. - 1983.
    (001522)
----Dénationalisations : les leçons de
    l'étranger. - 1986.
    (001565)

PUBLIC ENTERPRISES (continued)
----The effects of markets on public
enterprise conduct ; and vice versa. -
1983.
(001675)
----Measures to strengthen the capabilities
of developing countries in their dealing
with transnational corporations. - 1985.
(002612)
----Methods and techniques of training
public enterprise managers. - 1983.
(001884)
----Mezhdunarodnyi chastnyi biznes i
gosudarstvo. - 1985.
(001832)
----Les multinationales publiques. - 1985.
(001531)
----Multinationals, governments and
international technology transfer. -
198?.
(001472)
----Privatization and public enterprise. -
1988.
(001588)
----Public enterprise and the developing
world. - 1984.
(001014)
----Public enterprise in mixed economies. -
1984.
(001574)
----State-owned multinationals. - 1987.
(001532)
----Transnational corporations in world
development. - 1983.
(000102)

PUBLIC ENTERPRISES--AFRICA.
----Limite des alternatives capitalistes
d'état ou privées à la crise agricole
africaine. - 1985.
(001575)

PUBLIC ENTERPRISES--AFRICA SOUTH OF SAHARA.
----La privatisation des entreprises
publiques en Afrique au sud du Sahara,
(2). - 1986.
(001564)

PUBLIC ENTERPRISES--ARGENTINA.
----Las empresas públicas en la Argentina. -
1984.
(001119)
----Joint ventures of public enterprises in
Argentina with other developing
countries. - 1984.
(001657)

PUBLIC ENTERPRISES--AUSTRALIA.
----Private agreements for takeovers of
public companies. - 1984.
(001626)

PUBLIC ENTERPRISES--BRAZIL.
----The determinants of manufacturing
ownership in less developed countries. -
1986.
(000712)
----PETROBRAS : eines der grössten
Industrieunternehmen der
kapitalistischen Welt. - 1984.
(000282)

PUBLIC ENTERPRISES--CANADA.
----Private agreements for takeovers of
public companies. - 1984.
(001626)
----Public and private returns from joint
venture research: an example from
agriculture. - 1986.
(001650)

PUBLIC ENTERPRISES--CHINA.
----The reform of the Chinese system of
enterprise ownership. - 1987.
(002185)

PUBLIC ENTERPRISES--COLOMBIA.
----Directorio de empresas y ejecutivos. -
1979-   .
(002628)

PUBLIC ENTERPRISES--EUROPE.
----Nationalized companies : a threat to
American business. - 1983.
(002327)

PUBLIC ENTERPRISES--GERMANY, FEDERAL
REPUBLIC OF.
----Private agreements for takeovers of
public companies. - 1984.
(001626)

PUBLIC ENTERPRISES--GHANA.
----The capital intensity of foreign,
private local and state owned firms in a
less developed country: Ghana. - 1986.
(001018)

PUBLIC ENTERPRISES--INDIA.
----The determinants of manufacturing
ownership in less developed countries. -
1986.
(000712)

PUBLIC ENTERPRISES--ITALY.
----L'impresa pubblica italiana e la
dimensione internazionale. - 1983.
(001145)

PUBLIC ENTERPRISES--JAPAN.
----Privatisierung in Japan. - 1987.
(001601)

PUBLIC ENTERPRISES--KUWAIT.
----Impact of the operations of
transnational corporations on
development in Kuwait. - 1987.
(001143)

PUBLIC ENTERPRISES--LATIN AMERICA.
----Government control over public
enterprises in Latin America. - 1983.
(002179)
----The use and promotion of consultancy
joint ventures by public entities in
Latin America. - 1985.
(000834)

PUBLIC ENTERPRISES--MEXICO.
----The determinants of manufacturing
ownership in less developed countries. -
1986.
(000712)

PUBLIC ENTERPRISES--MEXICO (continued)
----The role of public enterprises in the
advancement of women in Mexico. - 1983.
(001894)

PUBLIC ENTERPRISES--NETHERLANDS.
----Private agreements for takeovers of
public companies. - 1984.
(001626)

PUBLIC ENTERPRISES--REPUBLIC OF KOREA.
----The determinants of manufacturing
ownership in less developed countries. -
1986.
(000712)

PUBLIC ENTERPRISES--SOUTH AFRICA.
----The determinants of manufacturing
ownership in less developed countries. -
1986.
(000712)

PUBLIC ENTERPRISES--TUNISIA.
----Responsabilités des entreprises
publiques dans l'amélioration de la
condition de la femme. - 1983.
(001883)

PUBLIC ENTERPRISES--UNITED KINGDOM.
----Private agreements for takeovers of
public companies. - 1984.
(001626)
----Privatisation and regulation : the UK
experience. - 1986.
(001627)

PUBLIC ENTERPRISES--UNITED STATES.
----Private agreements for takeovers of
public companies. - 1984.
(001626)

PUBLIC FINANCE.
----The relationship between taxation and
financial reporting. - 1987.
(002103)

PUBLIC FINANCE--FRANCE.
----Nationalisations, un bilan en
demi-teinte. - 1983.
(001579)

PUBLIC HEARINGS ON THE ACTIVITIES OF
TRANSNATIONAL CORPORATIONS IN SOUTH AFRICA
AND NAMIBIA (1985 : NEW YORK)--PARTICIPANTS.
----Transnational corporations in South
Africa and Namibia. - 1986.
(001217)

PUBLIC INFORMATION.
----Availability of financial statements. -
1987.
(002100)

PUBLIC LAW--FRANCE.
----Die Nationalisierungen in Frankreich
1981/82. - 1983.
(002337)

PUBLIC OPINION--SOUTH AFRICA.
----Disinvestment and black workers
attitudes in South Africa. - 1985.
(001210)

PUBLIC SECTOR.
----Los bancos transnacionales y el
endeudamiento externo en la Argentina. -
1987.
(000819)
----Dénationalisation : les leçons de
l'étranger. - 1986.
(001565)
----Industrial structure and policy in less
developed countries. - 1984.
(001322)

PUBLIC SECTOR--ARGENTINA.
----Las empresas públicas en la Argentina. -
1984.
(001119)

PUBLIC SECTOR--CAMEROON.
----The private sector, the public sector,
and donor assistance in economic
development. - 1983.
(000268)

PUBLIC SECTOR--COSTA RICA.
----The private sector, the public sector,
and donor assistance in economic
development. - 1983.
(000268)

PUBLIC SECTOR--FRANCE.
----Nationalisations, un bilan en
demi-teinte. - 1983.
(001579)
----Die Nationalisierungen in Frankreich
1981/82. - 1983.
(002337)
----Propriété et pouvoir dans l'industrie. -
1987.
(001628)

PUBLIC SECTOR--LATIN AMERICA.
----The role of the public sector and
transnational corporations in the mining
development of Latin America. - 1986.
(000605)

PUBLIC SECTOR--MALAWI.
----The private sector, the public sector,
and donor assistance in economic
development. - 1983.
(000268)

PUBLIC SECTOR--PERU.
----Transnational banks and the external
finance of Latin America : the
experience of Peru. - 1983.
(000840)

PUBLIC SECTOR--THAILAND.
----The private sector, the public sector,
and donor assistance in economic
development. - 1983.
(000268)

PUBLIC SECTOR--UNITED KINGDOM.
----Privatising nationalised industries :
constitutional issues and new legal
techniques. - 1987.
(001582)

PUBLIC SECTOR--WESTERN EUROPE.
----Services and regional policy. - 1987.
(000903)

PUBLIC SERVICES--UNITED STATES.
----Directory of business, trade and public
    policy organizations. - 1982-   .
    (002631)

PUBLICATIONS.
----Sales publications of the United Nations
    Centre on Transnational Corporations,
    1973-1987. - 1987.
    (002693)

PUBLISHING--INDIA.
----Nation-building media and TNCs. - 1984.
    (000941)

PULP AND PAPER INDUSTRY--THAILAND.
----Technology acquisition under alternative
    arrangements with transnational
    corporations. - 1987.
    (001512)
----Technology transfer under alternative
    arrangements with transnational
    corporations. - 1987.
    (001513)

PURCHASING.
----Should one countertrade? - 1987.
    (001366)

QATAR--CAPITAL INVESTMENTS.
----Petro-industrialization in Qatar. - 1985.
    (000600)

QATAR--INDUSTRIALIZATION.
----Petro-industrialization in Qatar. - 1985.
    (000600)

QATAR--PETROLEUM INDUSTRY.
----Petro-industrialization in Qatar. - 1985.
    (000600)

QUALITY CONTROL.
----Guidelines for Consumer Protection. -
    1986.
    (002017)

QUESTIONNAIRES.
----International accounting and reporting
    issues : 1984 review. - 1985.
    (002115)
----International accounting and reporting
    issues, 1986 review. - 1986.
    (002117)
----Natural gas clauses in petroleum
    arrangements. - 1987.
    (002452)
----Trade in services : growth and balance
    of payments implications for countries
    of Western Asia. - 1987.
    (000968)

R. J. REYNOLDS INDUSTRIES.
----The RJR story. - 1983.
    (000296)

RACE RELATIONS--SOUTH AFRICA.
----Business in the shadow of apartheid :
    U.S. firms in South Africa. - 1985.
    (001194)
----The politics of sentiment. - 1984.
    (002588)

RAW MATERIALS.
----Two hungry giants. - 1983.
    (000645)

REAL ESTATE BUSINESS.
----The world's new property barons. - 1987.
    (000904)

REAL ESTATE BUSINESS--UNITED STATES.
----Realty joint ventures, 1986. - 1986.
    (000881)

REAL PROPERTY.
----Cross-border leasing. - 1983.
    (000836) (001705)
----International income taxation and
    developing countries. - 1988.
    (001759)

REAL RESOURCES TRANSFER.
----Trasferimento internazionale di risorse
    per lo sviluppo: il ruolo delle
    istituzioni multilaterali. - 1984.
    (001997)

RECIPROCITY.
----Patterns of bilateral trade flows within
    the characteristics approach to trade. -
    1986.
    (001397)

RECOGNITION (INTERNATIONAL LAW).
----La reconnaissance et l'exécution des
    sentences arbitrales étrangères. - 1985.
    (002564)

RECOGNITION (INTERNATIONAL LAW)--FRANCE.
----Les nationalisations françaises face à
    l'ordre juridique suisse. - 1984.
    (002325)

RECOGNITION (INTERNATIONAL LAW)--SWITZERLAND.
----Les nationalisations françaises face à
    l'ordre juridique suisse. - 1984.
    (002325)

REFERENCE MATERIALS.
----International business reference
    sources. - 1983.
    (002691)
----Reference book on major transnational
    corporations operating in Namibia. -
    1985.
    (002674)

REFRACTORY MATERIALS--THAILAND.
----Technology transfer under alternative
    arrangements with transnational
    corporations. - 1987.
    (001513)

REGIONAL CO-OPERATION.
----Promotion of foreign direct investment
    to developing countries: an exercise in
    cooperation. - 1986.
    (002035)

REGIONAL CO-OPERATION--AFRICA.
----Current problems of economic
    integration. - 1986.
    (001312)

REGIONAL CO-OPERATION--ARAB COUNTRIES.
----Current problems of economic
    integration. - 1986.
    (001312)

REGIONAL CO-OPERATION--ASIA.
----Current problems of economic
    integration. - 1986.
    (001312)

REGIONAL CO-OPERATION--CARIBBEAN REGION.
----The Caribbean Basin Economic Recovery
    Act and its implications for foreign
    private investment. - 1984.
    (001965)

REGIONAL CO-OPERATION--GULF STATES.
----Economic co-operation of the Arab Gulf
    States. - 1986.
    (001133)

REGIONAL CO-OPERATION--LATIN AMERICA.
----Current problems of economic
    integration. - 1986.
    (001312)
----Measures strengthening the negotiating
    capacity of Governments in their
    relations with transnational
    corporations. - 1983.
    (002461)
----El proceso de revisión de los mecanismos
    financieros de la ALADI. - 1983.
    (001248)

REGIONAL CO-OPERATION--SOUTH ASIA.
----Industrial cooperation in regional
    economic groupings among developing
    countries and lessons for SAARC. - 1987.
    (001009)

REGIONAL CO-OPERATION FOR DEVELOPMENT.
----Industrial cooperation in regional
    economic groupings among developing
    countries and lessons for SAARC. - 1987.
    (001009)

REGIONAL DEVELOPMENT.
----Multinational corporations and regional
    development. - 1983.
    (001326)

REGIONAL DEVELOPMENT--CANADA.
----Multinational corporations and regional
    development. - 1983.
    (001326)

REGIONAL DEVELOPMENT--CHINA.
----China experiments with modernisation. -
    1983.
    (002384)

REGIONAL DEVELOPMENT--FRANCE.
----Activité comparée des établissements
    industriels d'origine étrangère et des
    établissements industriels français. -
    1984.
    (001927)
----Nationalisations et développement
    régional. - 1983.
    (001550)

REGIONAL DEVELOPMENT--LATIN AMERICA.
----Multinational corporations and regional
    development. - 1983.
    (001326)

REGIONAL DEVELOPMENT BANKS.
----Current financial and monetary problems
    of the developing countries in the world
    capitalist economy. - 1987.
    (001246)

REGIONAL DEVELOPMENT BANKS--AFRICA.
----Current problems of economic
    integration. - 1986.
    (001312)

REGIONAL DEVELOPMENT BANKS--ARAB COUNTRIES.
----Current problems of economic
    integration. - 1986.
    (001312)

REGIONAL DEVELOPMENT BANKS--ASIA.
----Current problems of economic
    integration. - 1986.
    (001312)

REGIONAL DEVELOPMENT BANKS--LATIN AMERICA.
----Current problems of economic
    integration. - 1986.
    (001312)

REGIONAL ORGANIZATIONS.
----Multilateral negotiation and mediation.
    - 1985.
    (002545)

REGIONAL PROGRAMMES.
----Technical co-operation programme of the
    United Nations Centre on Transnational
    Corporations. - 1988.
    (002610)

REGRESSION ANALYSIS.
----Common mistakes of joint venture
    experienced firms. - 1987.
    (001604)
----Multinational production: effect on
    brand value. - 1986.
    (000540)
----Political events and the foreign direct
    investment decision: an empirical
    examination. - 1986.
    (001836)

REGRESSION ANALYSIS--MIDDLE EAST.
----Major causes of joint-venture failures
    in the Middle East: the case of Iran. -
    1983.
    (001640)

REGRESSION ANALYSIS--UNITED STATES.
----U.S. multinational corporations: a
    lesson in the failure of success. - 1983.
    (000306)

REINSURANCE.
----The multinational reinsurance market. -
    1984.
    (000990)

RELATED PARTY TRANSACTIONS.
----Transnational corporations in world
    development. - 1983.
    (000102)

RELOCATION OF INDUSTRY.
----Environmental aspects of the activities
    of transnational corporations. - 1985.
      (001954)

RELOCATION OF INDUSTRY--AUSTRALIA.
----The geography of Australian corporate
    power. - 1984.
      (001166)

RELOCATION OF INDUSTRY--HONG KONG.
----Exploiting Hong Kong's uncertain future.
    - 1987.
      (001862)

RELOCATION OF INDUSTRY--UNITED STATES.
----Are environmental regulations driving
    U.S. industry overseas? - 1984.
      (001947)
----International business travel and
    relocation directory. - 1984.
      (002710)

REMOTE SENSING.
----Transborder data flows. - 1984.
      (000974)

RENEWABLE RESOURCES.
----Research and technology for the Third
    World. - 1985.
      (001489)

RENEWABLE RESOURCES--UNITED STATES.
----A competitive assessment of the
    renewable energy equipment industry. -
    1984.
      (000775)

REPORTING PROCEDURES.
----Financial reporting by private
    companies. - 1983.
      (002056)

REPUBLIC OF KOREA--AUTOMOBILE INDUSTRY.
----Technology transfer under alternative
    arrangements with transnational
    corporations. - 1987.
      (001513)

REPUBLIC OF KOREA--CAPITAL MARKETS.
----Riding a tiger : joint ventures under
    South Korea's new Foreign Capital
    Inducement Act. - 1985.
      (002290)

REPUBLIC OF KOREA--COMPARATIVE ANALYSIS.
----Transfer of technology from Japan and
    the United States to Korean
    manufacturing industries: a comparative
    study. - 1984.
      (001461)

REPUBLIC OF KOREA--COMPUTER INDUSTRY.
----Politische Gestaltungsspielräume von
    Schwellenländern in der
    Mikroelektronik-Industrie. - 1987.
      (000617)

REPUBLIC OF KOREA--CONTRACT LABOUR.
----Korean contractors in Saudi Arabia. -
    1986.
      (001139)

REPUBLIC OF KOREA--CONTRACTS.
----Les joint ventures en Corée du Sud. -
    1986.
      (002436)

REPUBLIC OF KOREA--DEVELOPING COUNTRIES.
----Foreign investment as an aid in moving
    from least developed to newly
    industrializing: a study in Korea. -
    1986.
      (000186)

REPUBLIC OF KOREA--ECONOMIC DEVELOPMENT.
----Multinationals and maldevelopment. -
    1987.
      (000995)

REPUBLIC OF KOREA--ECONOMIC GROWTH.
----The South Korean success story. - 1986.
      (001050)

REPUBLIC OF KOREA--ECONOMIC POLICY.
----Multinationals and maldevelopment. -
    1987.
      (000995)

REPUBLIC OF KOREA--ELECTRONICS INDUSTRY.
----Technology transfer under alternative
    arrangements with transnational
    corporations. - 1987.
      (001513)

REPUBLIC OF KOREA--EMPLOYMENT.
----An information sector perspective of
    employment expansion in the Republic of
    Korea, 1975-80. - 1987.
      (000848)

REPUBLIC OF KOREA--ENGINEERING INDUSTRIES.
----Microelectronics-based automation
    technologies and development. - 1985.
      (000753)

REPUBLIC OF KOREA--EXPORT ORIENTED
INDUSTRIES.
----The effectiveness of export promotion
    policies. - 1986.
      (002310)

REPUBLIC OF KOREA--EXPORT PROMOTION.
----The effectiveness of export promotion
    policies. - 1986.
      (002310)

REPUBLIC OF KOREA--EXPORTS.
----The South Korean success story. - 1986.
      (001050)

REPUBLIC OF KOREA--FOREIGN DIRECT INVESTMENT.
----Foreign direct investment from
    developing countries. - 1986.
      (000325)
----Foreign investment as an aid in moving
    from least developed to newly
    industrializing: a study in Korea. -
    1986.
      (000186)
----Les joint ventures en Corée du Sud. -
    1986.
      (002436)
----The Korean manufacturing multinationals.
    - 1984.
      (000342)

REPUBLIC OF KOREA--FOREIGN DIRECT INVESTMENT
(continued)
----New forms of overseas investment by
     developing countries : the case of
     India, Korea and Brazil. - 1986.
        (001616)
----The South Korean success story. - 1986.
        (001050)

REPUBLIC OF KOREA--FOREIGN INVESTMENTS.
----National legislation and regulations
     relating to transnational corporations.
     Volume 4. - 1986.
        (002253)
----Riding a tiger : joint ventures under
     South Korea's new Foreign Capital
     Inducement Act. - 1985.
        (002290)

REPUBLIC OF KOREA--FOREIGN TRADE.
----The Sogo Shosha: can it be exported
     (imported)? - 1983.
        (000338)

REPUBLIC OF KOREA--FREE EXPORT ZONES.
----Korea's Masan free export zone. - 1984.
        (002401)

REPUBLIC OF KOREA--GOODS.
----An information sector perspective of
     employment expansion in the Republic of
     Korea, 1975-80. - 1987.
        (000848)

REPUBLIC OF KOREA--INCOME DISTRIBUTION.
----The South Korean success story. - 1986.
        (001050)

REPUBLIC OF KOREA--INDUSTRIAL EQUIPMENT
LEASES.
----Analysis of equipment leasing contracts.
     - 1984.
        (002407)

REPUBLIC OF KOREA--INDUSTRIAL POLICY.
----Transnational corporations and the
     state. - 1985.
        (001860)

REPUBLIC OF KOREA--INDUSTRIAL STATISTICS.
----Technology transfer under alternative
     arrangements with transnational
     corporations. - 1987.
        (001513)

REPUBLIC OF KOREA--INDUSTRIALIZATION.
----Exports of technology by newly
     industrializing countries: Republic of
     Korea. - 1984.
        (001521)
----Foreign investment as an aid in moving
     from least developed to newly
     industrializing: a study in Korea. -
     1986.
        (000186)

REPUBLIC OF KOREA--INDUSTRY.
----The Sogo Shosha: can it be exported
     (imported)? - 1983.
        (000338)

REPUBLIC OF KOREA--INFORMATION.
----An information sector perspective of
     employment expansion in the Republic of
     Korea, 1975-80. - 1987.
        (000848)

REPUBLIC OF KOREA--INTERNATIONAL BANKING.
----About the establishment of an offshore
     financial center in Seoul. - 1986.
        (000827)

REPUBLIC OF KOREA--JOINT VENTURES.
----Les joint ventures en Corée du Sud. -
     1986.
        (002436)
----Korean contractors in Saudi Arabia. -
     1986.
        (001139)
----New forms of overseas investment by
     developing countries : the case of
     India, Korea and Brazil. - 1986.
        (001616)
----Riding a tiger : joint ventures under
     South Korea's new Foreign Capital
     Inducement Act. - 1985.
        (002290)

REPUBLIC OF KOREA--LAWS AND REGULATIONS.
----National legislation and regulations
     relating to transnational corporations.
     Volume 4. - 1986.
        (002253)

REPUBLIC OF KOREA--MANUFACTURING ENTERPRICES.
----The Korean manufacturing multinationals.
     - 1984.
        (000342)

REPUBLIC OF KOREA--MANUFACTURING ENTERPRISES.
----The determinants of manufacturing
     ownership in less developed countries. -
     1986.
        (000712)
----Transfer of technology from Japan and
     the United States to Korean
     manufacturing industries: a comparative
     study. - 1984.
        (001461)

REPUBLIC OF KOREA--MARKET ACCESS.
----Korean contractors in Saudi Arabia. -
     1986.
        (001139)

REPUBLIC OF KOREA--MICROELECTRONICS.
----Politische Gestaltungsspielräume von
     Schwellenländern in der
     Mikroelektronik-Industrie. - 1987.
        (000617)

REPUBLIC OF KOREA--PHARMACEUTICAL INDUSTRY.
----Technology transfer under alternative
     arrangements with transnational
     corporations. - 1987.
        (001513)
----Transnational corporations in the
     pharmaceutical industry of developing
     countries. - 1984.
        (000749)

REPUBLIC OF KOREA--PRIVATE ENTERPRISES.
----The determinants of manufacturing
    ownership in less developed countries. -
    1986.
        (000712)

REPUBLIC OF KOREA--PUBLIC ENTERPRISES.
----The determinants of manufacturing
    ownership in less developed countries. -
    1986.
        (000712)

REPUBLIC OF KOREA--RULES AND REGULATIONS.
-----Les joint ventures en Corée du Sud. -
    1986.
        (002436)

REPUBLIC OF KOREA--SCIENCE AND TECHNOLOGY
POLICY.
----Proceedings of the SSTCC/UNCTC/ESCAP
    Asia-Pacific Training Workshop on
    Regulating and Negotiating Technology
    Transfer through Transnational
    Corporations, 14-25 October 1985,
    Fuzhou, Fujian, China. - 1986.
        (001405) (002169)

REPUBLIC OF KOREA--SERVICE INDUSTRIES.
----An information sector perspective of
    employment expansion in the Republic of
    Korea, 1975-80. - 1987.
        (000848)

REPUBLIC OF KOREA--STATISTICAL DATA.
----Technology transfer under alternative
    arrangements with transnational
    corporations. - 1987.
        (001513)

REPUBLIC OF KOREA--TAX HAVENS.
----About the establishment of an offshore
    financial center in Seoul. - 1986.
        (000827)

REPUBLIC OF KOREA--TECHNOLOGY TRANSFER.
----Exports of technology by newly
    industrializing countries: Republic of
    Korea. - 1984.
        (001521)
----Les joint ventures en Corée du Sud. -
    1986.
        (002436)
----Politische Gestaltungsspielräume von
    Schwellenländern in der
    Mikroelektronik-Industrie. - 1987.
        (000617)
----Proceedings of the SSTCC/UNCTC/ESCAP
    Asia-Pacific Training Workshop on
    Regulating and Negotiating Technology
    Transfer through Transnational
    Corporations, 14-25 October 1985,
    Fuzhou, Fujian, China. - 1986.
        (001405) (002169)
----Transfer of technology from Japan and
    the United States to Korean
    manufacturing industries: a comparative
    study. - 1984.
        (001461)

REPUBLIC OF KOREA--TEXTILE INDUSTRY.
----Technology transfer under alternative
    arrangements with transnational
    corporations. - 1987.
        (001513)

REPUBLIC OF KOREA--TRANSNATIONAL
CORPORATIONS.
----The determinants of manufacturing
    ownership in less developed countries. -
    1986.
        (000712)
----The Korean manufacturing multinationals.
    - 1984.
        (000342)
----Multinationals and maldevelopment. -
    1987.
        (000995)
----National legislation and regulations
    relating to transnational corporations.
    Volume 4. - 1986.
        (002253)
----New forms of overseas investment by
    developing countries : the case of
    India, Korea and Brazil. - 1986.
        (001616)
----Technology transfer under alternative
    arrangements with transnational
    corporations. - 1987.
        (001513)
----Transnational corporations and the
    state. - 1985.
        (001860)

RESEARCH.
----Measures to strengthen the capabilities
    of developing countries in their dealing
    with transnational corporations. - 1985.
        (002612)
----Occasional paper (University of Sydney.
    Transnational Corporations Research
    Project). - 1978-   .
        (000079)
----Research intensity, international
    production and US-based multinationals.
    - 1983.
        (000367)
----Research on Third World multinationals.
    - 1985.
        (000321)

RESEARCH AND DEVELOPMENT.
----The capital goods sector in developing
    countries. - 1985.
        (001651)
----A decision theoretic model of
    innovation, technology transfer, and
    trade. - 1987.
        (001446)
----Decision-making in multinational
    enterprises. - 1984.
        (000410)
----Environmental aspects of the activities
    of transnational corporations. - 1985.
        (001954)
----Host countries and the R [and] D of
    multinationals. - 1987.
        (001479)
----International accounting and reporting
    issues, 1985 review. - 1985.
        (002116)
----International flows of technology. -
    1986.
        (001517)
----The internationalisation of research and
    development by leading enterprises. -
    1986.
        (001480)

RESEARCH AND DEVELOPMENT (continued)
----Les multinationales de la pharmacie. -
     1985.
        (000730)
----[Planning and execution of R&D]. - 1987.
        (001481)
----Shifts in the world economy and the
     restructuring of economic sectors. -
     1987.
        (000734)
----Technical advance and trade advantage. -
     1983.
        (001497)
----Technology and international relations.
     - 1987.
        (001504)

RESEARCH AND DEVELOPMENT--JAPAN.
----High-tech trade. - 1986.
        (000696)

RESEARCH AND DEVELOPMENT--MEXICO.
----Research and development in
     pharmaceuticals: Mexico. - 1983.
        (000770)

RESEARCH AND DEVELOPMENT--POLAND.
----Transborder data flows and Poland :
     Polish case study. - 1984.
        (000920)

RESEARCH AND DEVELOPMENT--UNITED STATES.
----La haute technologie américaine. - 1987.
        (000680)
----High-tech trade. - 1986.
        (000696)

RESEARCH AND DEVELOPMENT CONTRACTS.
----Alternative contractual arrangements for
     technology transfer. - 1986.
        (002416)

RESEARCH AND DEVELOPMENT CONTRACTS--BURUNDI.
----Manuel de procedures contractuelles
     susceptibles d'être mise en oeuvre par
     les contrats internationaux concernant
     la realisation de projets industriels. -
     1984.
        (002417)

RESEARCH AND DEVELOPMENT CONTRACTS--UNITED
STATES.
----Antitrust policy and joint research and
     development ventures. - 1984.
        (002356)
----Cooperative research and development. -
     1984.
        (001630)
----Joint research and development
     legislation. - 1987.
        (002286)

RESOURCES EXPLORATION.
----Taming troubled waters. - 1986.
        (002453)

RESOURCES MOBILIZATION.
----Current problems of economic
     integration. - 1986.
        (001312)
----On the theory of an exhaustible resource
     extractive multinational firm. - 1986.
        (000610)

----Revitalizing development, growth and
     international trade. - 1987.
        (001394)

RESTRICTIVE BUSINESS PRACTICE.
----Wielkie przedsiebiorstwa transnarodowe a
     ograniczanie konkurencji w wysoko
     rozwinietych krajach kapitalistycznych.
     - 1983.
        (001153)

RESTRICTIVE BUSINESS PRACTICES.
----Anti-trust and restrictive business
     practices. - 1983-   .
        (001957)
----Competition and trade policies. - 1984.
        (001664)
----Developing countries and services in the
     Uruguay Round. - 1987.
        (000886)
----Die extraterritoriale Anwendung
     nationalen Wettbewerbsrechts unter
     besonderer Berucksichtigung
     landerubergreifender Fusionen. - 1986.
        (002340)
----Gemeinschaftsunternehmen im EGKS- und
     EWG-Kartellrecht. - 1986.
        (001978)
----Restrictive business practices in
     international trade. - 1987.
        (001661)
----Services and the development process. -
     1985.
        (000979)
----Set of multilaterally agreed equitable
     principles and rules for the control of
     restrictive business practices. - 1981.
        (001695) (002015)
----Transnacional'nye korporacii na rynkah
     razvivajuscihsja stran: Ogranicit.
     delovaja praktika. - 1985.
        (001662)

RESTRICTIVE BUSINESS PRACTICES--EGYPT.
----Egypt's experience in regulating
     technology imports. - 1987.
        (001514)

RESTRICTIVE BUSINESS PRACTICES--GERMANY,
FEDERAL REPUBLIC OF.
----Fakultatives Kollisonsrecht im
     internationalen Wettbewerbsrecht? - 1984.
        (002247)

RESTRICTIVE BUSINESS PRACTICES--UNITED
STATES.
----Antitrust law developments (second). -
     1984.
        (002339)
----The extraterritorial effects of
     antitrust laws. - 1984.
        (002342)

RESTRICTIVE BUSINESS PRACTICES--WESTERN
EUROPE.
----The antitrust law of the European
     Community and the UNCTAD code on
     restrictive business practices. - 1984.
        (001992)
----EEC law of competition. - 1985.
        (002151)

RETAIL TRADE.
----On planning and forecasting the location
    of retail and service activity. - 1984.
        (000550)
----Transnational retailing. - 1988.
        (000780)

REVENUE SHARING--CARIBBEAN REGION.
----Multinational corporations and regional
    revenue retention in a vertically
    integrated industry: bauxite/aluminium
    in the Caribbean. - 1983.
        (000582)

RIGHT TO PRIVACY.
----International co-operation in tax
    matters : guidelines for international
    co-operation against the evasion and
    avoidance of taxes (with special
    reference to taxes on income, profits,
    capital and capital gains). - 1984.
        (001724)

RISK.
----Foreign ownership: when hosts change the
    rules. - 1985.
        (001798)

RISK ASSESSMENT.
----Analyzing political risk. - 1986.
        (001850)
----A country risk appraisal model of
    foreign asset expropriation in
    developing countries. - 1987.
        (001553) (001775)
----Foreign exchange risk and direct foreign
    investment. - 1983.
        (001852)
----Global risk assessments. - 1983.
        (001803)
----Insurance against the political risks of
    petroleum investment. - 1986.
        (001866) (002160)
----A managerial procedure for political
    risk forecasting. - 1986.
        (001847)
----Political risk analysis. - 1985.
        (001859)
----Political risk assessment. - 1985.
        (001842) (002659)
----Political risks in international
    business. - 1985.
        (001843)
----The volatility of offshore investment. -
    1984.
        (001799)
----161 more checklists : decision making in
    international operations. - 1985.
        (000462)

RISK ASSESSMENT--ASIA.
----Critical issues for business in Asia. -
    1984.
        (001787)
----New business strategies for developing
    Asia, 1983-1990. - 1984.
        (000498)

RISK ASSESSMENT--BRAZIL.
----Business in a democratic Brazil. - 1985.
        (001776)

RISK ASSESSMENT--ECUADOR.
----Risk-bearing and the choice of contract
    forms for oil exploration and
    development. - 1984.
        (002410)

RISK ASSESSMENT--INDONESIA.
----How multinationals analyze political
    risk. - 1983.
        (001849)

RISK ASSESSMENT--LATIN AMERICA.
----Yanqui come back! - 1986.
        (001825)

RISK ASSESSMENT--NORDIC COUNTRIES.
----Industrial structure and country risks
    in a Nordic perspective. - 1984.
        (001838)

RISK ASSESSMENT--SUDAN.
----Chevron, Sudan and political risk. -
    1984.
        (001858)

RISK ASSESSMENT--UNITED STATES.
----Political risk in the international oil
    and gas industry. - 1983.
        (001823)

RISK MANAGEMENT.
----American banks in the international
    interbank market. - 1983.
        (000829)
----Chevron, Sudan and political risk. -
    1984.
        (001858)
----Coming of age of the service economy. -
    1986.
        (000860)
----A global comeback. - 1987.
        (000275)
----Global risk assessments. - 1983.
        (001803)
----International political risk management.
    - 1984.
        (001802)
----International risk management. - 1983.
        (000499)
----Leading und Lagging kurzfristig
    variierbarer gruppeninterner Geldflusse
    im Wahrungsrisikomanagement einer
    internationalen Unternehmung. - 1986.
        (000501)
----The lessons of Bhopal. - 1985.
        (001933)
----Managing international risk. - 1983.
        (000480)
----Multinational accounting. - 1986.
        (002105)
----Multinational risk assessment and
    management. - 1987.
        (000514)
----Multinational ventures in the commercial
    aircraft industry. - 1985.
        (000721)
----Political risk analysis. - 1985.
        (001859)
----Political risk assessment. - 1985.
        (001842) (002659)
----Political risks in international
    business. - 1985.
        (001843)

RISK MANAGEMENT--CHINA.
----Joint ventures in the PRC. - 1987.
(000478)

RISK MANAGEMENT--PERU.
----The Peruvian military government and the
international corporations. - 1983.
(001801)

RISK MANAGEMENT--UNITED STATES.
----Empirical models of political risks in
U.S. oil production operations in
Venezuela. - 1984.
(001813)

RISK MANAGEMENT--VENEZUELA.
----Empirical models of political risks in
U.S. oil production operations in
Venezuela. - 1984.
(001813)

ROBOTICS.
----Le tout-ordinateur. - 1986.
(000743)

ROBOTICS--EUROPE.
----Robots in manufacturing. - 1983.
(000656)

ROBOTICS--JAPAN.
----Robots in manufacturing. - 1983.
(000656)

ROBOTICS--UNITED STATES.
----A competitive assessment of the U.S.
flexible manufacturing systems industry.
- 1985.
(000763)
----A competitive assessment of the U.S.
manufacturing automation equipment
industries. - 1984.
(000756)
----Competitive position of U.S. producers
of robotics in domestic and world
markets. - 1983.
(000674)
----High technology industries. - 1983-   .
(000695)
----Robots in manufacturing. - 1983.
(000656)

ROLLER BEARINGS--UNITED STATES.
----A competitive assessment of the U.S.
ball and roller bearings industry. -
1985.
(000760)

ROMANIA--CONTRACTS.
----Implications of international commercial
agreements on the juridical regime of
international commercial contracts. -
1983.
(002408)

ROMANIA--JOINT VENTURES.
----East-West joint ventures. - 1988.
(001570)

ROMANIA--LAWS AND REGULATIONS.
----East-West joint ventures. - 1988.
(001570)

----National legislation and regulations
relating to transnational corporations.
Volume 3. - 1983.
(002252)

ROMANIA--STATISTICAL DATA.
----East-West joint ventures. - 1988.
(001570)

ROMANIA--TRADE AGREEMENTS.
----Implications of international commercial
agreements on the juridical regime of
international commercial contracts. -
1983.
(002408)

ROMANIA--TRANSNATIONAL CORPORATIONS.
----National legislation and regulations
relating to transnational corporations.
Volume 3. - 1983.
(002252)

ROUND-TABLE ON FOREIGN DIRECT INVESTMENT
(1987 : BEIJING)--WORK ORGANIZATION.
----Foreign direct investment in the
People's Republic of China. - 1988.
(000191)

ROYALTIES.
----Financial and fiscal aspects of
petroleum exploitation. - 1987.
(002451)

RUBBER INDUSTRY--UNITED STATES.
----The emergence of a U.S. multinational
enterprise: the Goodyear Tire and Rubber
Company, 1910-1939. - 1987.
(000281)

RULES AND REGULATIONS.
----Air and maritime transport and the EEC
competition rules : Ministère Publique
v. Asjes, Nouvelles Frontières et al. -
1987.
(000794)
----International financial reporting and
auditing. - 1984.
(002088)
----The regulation and supervision of
international lending, (2). - 1986.
(000234)

RULES AND REGULATIONS--REPUBLIC OF KOREA.
----Les joint ventures en Corée du Sud. -
1986.
(002436)

RULES AND REGULATIONS--UNITED KINGDOM.
----Privatisation and regulation : the UK
experience. - 1986.
(001627)

RULES AND REGULATIONS--UNITED STATES.
----Regulating the multinational enterprise.
- 1983.
(002006)

RULES AND REGULATIONS--WESTERN EUROPE.
----Centralized European merger regulation.
- 1985.
(001625)

RURAL DEVELOPMENT.
----The private sector and rural
     development: can agribusiness help the
     small farmer? - 1985.
        (000566)

RWANDA--AGRIBUSINESS.
----Agro-industrial co-operation between the
     European Community and the ACP
     countries. - 1986.
        (002605)

RWANDA--INDUSTRIAL CO-OPERATION.
----Agro-industrial co-operation between the
     European Community and the ACP
     countries. - 1986.
        (002605)

SANCTIONS--SOUTH AFRICA.
----Activities of transnational corporations
     in South Africa and Namibia and the
     responsibilities of home countries with
     respect to their operations in this
     area. - 1986.
        (001192)
----Economic effects of a trade and
     investment boycott against South Africa.
     - 1984.
        (001202)
----South Africa : economic responses to
     international pressures. - 1985.
        (001193)
----Transnational corporations in South
     Africa and Namibia : United Nations
     public hearings. Volume 1, Reports of
     the Panel of Eminent Persons and of the
     Secretary-General. - 1986.
        (001216)
----Transnational corporations in South
     Africa and Namibia. - 1986.
        (001217)
----Transnational corporations in South
     Africa and Namibia : United Nations
     public hearings. Volume 3, Statements
     and submissions. - 1987.
        (001215)
----Transnational corporations in South
     Africa and Namibia : United Nations
     Public Hearings. Volume 4, Policy
     instruments and statements. - 1987.
        (001218)

SATELLITE COMMUNICATION.
----International policy issues in satellite
     communications. - 1985.
        (000791)

SATELLITE COMMUNICATION--PACIFIC OCEAN
REGION.
----Regulation to deregulation. - 1985.
        (000798)

SATELLITE COMMUNICATION--UNITED STATES.
----Implications of deregulating satellite
     communications. - 1985.
        (002242)

SAUDI ARABIA--BUSINESS ENTERPRISES.
----Impact of the operations of
     transnational corporations on
     development in Saudi Arabia. - 1987.
        (001140)

SAUDI ARABIA--COMMERCIAL ARBITRATION.
----Abfassen von Schiedsklauseln in
     Verträgen mit saudiarabischen Parteien.
     - 1987.
        (002548)

SAUDI ARABIA--CONTRACT LABOUR.
----Korean contractors in Saudi Arabia. -
     1986.
        (001139)

SAUDI ARABIA--CONTRACTS.
----Service agents regulation and related
     laws affecting foreign companies in
     Saudi Arabia. - 1983.
        (002182)

SAUDI ARABIA--CORPORATION LAW.
----Companies in Jordan and Saudi Arabia. -
     1984.
        (002643)

SAUDI ARABIA--DEVELOPMENT ASSISTANCE.
----Impact of the operations of
     transnational corporations on
     development in Saudi Arabia. - 1987.
        (001140)

SAUDI ARABIA--EMPLOYMENT DISCRIMINATION.
----United States corporations operating in
     Saudi Arabia and laws affecting
     discrimination in employment. - 1985.
        (002354)

SAUDI ARABIA--FOREIGN DIRECT INVESTMENT.
----A guide to establishing joint ventures
     in Saudi Arabia. - 1985.
        (001807)
----Joint ventures in the Kingdom of Saudi
     Arabia. - 1985.
        (001655)
----The legal regime of foreign private
     investment in the Sudan and Saudi
     Arabia. - 1984.
        (002204)

SAUDI ARABIA--FOREIGN INTERESTS.
----Impact of the operations of
     transnational corporations on
     development in Saudi Arabia. - 1987.
        (001140)

SAUDI ARABIA--FOREIGN INVESTMENTS.
----National legislation and regulations
     relating to transnational corporations.
     Volume 4. - 1986.
        (002253)

SAUDI ARABIA--INDUSTRIAL DEVELOPMENT.
----Petroleum based development and the
     private sector. - 1985.
        (001138)

SAUDI ARABIA--INFORMATION SOURCES.
----A guide to establishing joint ventures
     in Saudi Arabia. - 1985.
        (001807)

SAUDI ARABIA--INTERNATIONAL LAW.
----Service agents regulation and related
     laws affecting foreign companies in
     Saudi Arabia. - 1983.
        (002182)

SAUDI ARABIA--INVESTMENT POLICY.
----Investment and joint-venture experiences
    in Saudi Arabia. - 1985.
        (001526)

SAUDI ARABIA--ISLAMIC LAW.
----United States corporations operating in
    Saudi Arabia and laws affecting
    discrimination in employment. - 1985.
        (002354)

SAUDI ARABIA--JOINT VENTURES.
----Companies in Jordan and Saudi Arabia. -
    1984.
        (002643)
----A guide to establishing joint ventures
    in Saudi Arabia. - 1985.
        (001807)
----Investment and joint-venture experiences
    in Saudi Arabia. - 1985.
        (001526)
----Joint ventures in the Kingdom of Saudi
    Arabia. - 1985.
        (001655)
----Korean contractors in Saudi Arabia. -
    1986.
        (001139)
----Service agents regulation and related
    laws affecting foreign companies in
    Saudi Arabia. - 1983.
        (002182)

SAUDI ARABIA--LAWS AND REGULATIONS.
----Joint ventures in the Kingdom of Saudi
    Arabia. - 1985.
        (001655)
----National legislation and regulations
    relating to transnational corporations.
    Volume 4. - 1986.
        (002253)

SAUDI ARABIA--MARKET ACCESS.
----Korean contractors in Saudi Arabia. -
    1986.
        (001139)

SAUDI ARABIA--PETROLEUM POLICY.
----Petroleum based development and the
    private sector. - 1985.
        (001138)

SAUDI ARABIA--PRIVATE ENTERPRISES.
----Petroleum based development and the
    private sector. - 1985.
        (001138)

SAUDI ARABIA--TRANSNATIONAL CORPORATIONS.
----Impact of the operations of
    transnational corporations on
    development in Saudi Arabia. - 1987.
        (001140)
----National legislation and regulations
    relating to transnational corporations.
    Volume 4. - 1986.
        (002253)
----United States corporations operating in
    Saudi Arabia and laws affecting
    discrimination in employment. - 1985.
        (002354)

SAVINGS.
----Does concessionary aid lead to higher
    investment rates in low-income
    countries? - 1987.
        (002311)
----State intervention, foreign economic
    aid, savings and growth in LDCs. - 1985.
        (001337)

SAVINGS--ASIA.
----Effects of foreign capital inflows on
    developing countries of Asia. - 1986.
        (001059)

SAVINGS--BANGLADESH.
----Domestic saving and foreign capital
    inflow : the case of Bangladesh. - 1986.
        (001034)

SAVINGS--LATIN AMERICA.
----Entrada de capital extranjero, ahorro
    interno e inversión en la América Latina
    : una historia negativa y precautoria. -
    1986.
        (001101)

SAVINGS--UNITED STATES.
----What's causing America's capital
    imports? - 1987.
        (000539)

SCIENCE AND TECHNOLOGY.
----Technology and international relations.
    - 1987.
        (001504)

SCIENCE AND TECHNOLOGY CAPABILITY.
----Microelectronics-based automation
    technologies and development. - 1985.
        (000753)

SCIENCE AND TECHNOLOGY CAPABILITY--CARIBBEAN
REGION.
----Microelectronics-based automation
    technologies and development. - 1985.
        (000753)

SCIENCE AND TECHNOLOGY CAPABILITY--UNITED
REPUBLIC OF TANZANIA.
----Microelectronics-based automation
    technologies and development. - 1985.
        (000753)

SCIENCE AND TECHNOLOGY OBJECTIVES.
----A strategy for the technological
    transformation of developing countries.
    - 1985.
        (001515)

SCIENCE AND TECHNOLOGY PLANNING.
----A strategy for the technological
    transformation of developing countries.
    - 1985.
        (001515)

SCIENCE AND TECHNOLOGY POLICY.
----The political economy of international
    technology transfer. - 1987.
        (001482)

SCIENCE AND TECHNOLOGY POLICY (continued)
----Proceedings of the SSTCC/UNCTC/ESCAP
   Asia-Pacific Training Workshop on
   Regulating and Negotiating Technology
   Transfer through Transnational
   Corporations, 14-25 October 1985,
   Fuzhou, Fujian, China. - 1986.
   (001405) (002169)
----Technology : management and acquisition.
   - 1984-
   (001501)
----Technology and employment in industry. -
   1985.
   (001503)
----Technology importation policies in
   developing countries: some implications
   of recent theoretical and empirical
   evidence. - 1983.
   (001420)

SCIENCE AND TECHNOLOGY POLICY--CHINA.
----Proceedings of the SSTCC/UNCTC/ESCAP
   Asia-Pacific Training Workshop on
   Regulating and Negotiating Technology
   Transfer through Transnational
   Corporations, 14-25 October 1985,
   Fuzhou, Fujian, China. - 1986.
   (001405) (002169)

SCIENCE AND TECHNOLOGY POLICY--FIJI.
----Proceedings of the SSTCC/UNCTC/ESCAP
   Asia-Pacific Training Workshop on
   Regulating and Negotiating Technology
   Transfer through Transnational
   Corporations, 14-25 October 1985,
   Fuzhou, Fujian, China. - 1986.
   (001405) (002169)

SCIENCE AND TECHNOLOGY POLICY--INDIA.
----Proceedings of the SSTCC/UNCTC/ESCAP
   Asia-Pacific Training Workshop on
   Regulating and Negotiating Technology
   Transfer through Transnational
   Corporations, 14-25 October 1985,
   Fuzhou, Fujian, China. - 1986.
   (001405) (002169)

SCIENCE AND TECHNOLOGY POLICY--INDONESIA.
----Proceedings of the SSTCC/UNCTC/ESCAP
   Asia-Pacific Training Workshop on
   Regulating and Negotiating Technology
   Transfer through Transnational
   Corporations, 14-25 October 1985,
   Fuzhou, Fujian, China. - 1986.
   (001405) (002169)

SCIENCE AND TECHNOLOGY POLICY--JAPAN.   .
----Technology strategy and industrial
   relations: case studies of Japanese
   multinationals in the United States. -
   1983.
   (002599)

SCIENCE AND TECHNOLOGY POLICY--PAKISTAN.
----Proceedings of the SSTCC/UNCTC/ESCAP
   Asia-Pacific Training Workshop on
   Regulating and Negotiating Technology
   Transfer through Transnational
   Corporations, 14-25 October 1985,
   Fuzhou, Fujian, China. - 1986.
   (001405) (002169)

SCIENCE AND TECHNOLOGY POLICY--PHILIPPINES.
----Proceedings of the SSTCC/UNCTC/ESCAP
   Asia-Pacific Training Workshop on
   Regulating and Negotiating Technology
   Transfer through Transnational
   Corporations, 14-25 October 1985,
   Fuzhou, Fujian, China. - 1986.
   (001405) (002169)

SCIENCE AND TECHNOLOGY POLICY--REPUBLIC OF
KOREA.
----Proceedings of the SSTCC/UNCTC/ESCAP
   Asia-Pacific Training Workshop on
   Regulating and Negotiating Technology
   Transfer through Transnational
   Corporations, 14-25 October 1985,
   Fuzhou, Fujian, China. - 1986.
   (001405) (002169)

SCIENCE AND TECHNOLOGY POLICY--SRI LANKA.
----Proceedings of the SSTCC/UNCTC/ESCAP
   Asia-Pacific Training Workshop on
   Regulating and Negotiating Technology
   Transfer through Transnational
   Corporations, 14-25 October 1985,
   Fuzhou, Fujian, China. - 1986.
   (001405) (002169)

SCIENCE AND TECHNOLOGY POLICY--THAILAND.
----Proceedings of the SSTCC/UNCTC/ESCAP
   Asia-Pacific Training Workshop on
   Regulating and Negotiating Technology
   Transfer through Transnational
   Corporations, 14-25 October 1985,
   Fuzhou, Fujian, China. - 1986.
   (001405) (002169)

SCIENCE AND TECHNOLOGY POLICY--UNITED STATES.
----Technology strategy and industrial
   relations: case studies of Japanese
   multinationals in the United States. -
   1983.
   (002599)

SCIENCE AND TECHNOLOGY POLICY--WESTERN
EUROPE.
----Die ordnungspolitische Dimension der
   EG-Technologiepolitik. - 1987.
   (001495)

SCOTLAND (UNITED KINGDOM)--ELECTRONICS
INDUSTRY.
----Semiconductors, Scotland and the
   international division of labour. - 1987.
   (000694)

SCOTLAND (UNITED KINGDOM)--SEMICONDUCTORS.
----Semiconductors, Scotland and the
   international division of labour. - 1987.
   (000694)

SECURITIES.
----International trade in services :
   securities. - 1987.
   (000915)

SECURITIES--NEW YORK (N.Y.).
----Moody's industrial manual. - 1954-   .
   (002656)

SECURITIES--UNITED STATES.
----Applying uniform margin requirements to
    foreign entities attempting to acquire
    U.S. corporations. - 1984.
    (002173)
----Moody's industrial manual. - 1954-   .
    (002656)

SECURITIES EXCHANGE ACT 1934 (UNITED STATES).
----Applying uniform margin requirements to
    foreign entities attempting to acquire
    U.S. corporations. - 1984.
    (002173)

SECURITY INTERESTS IN GOODS.
----UNCITRAL, the United Nations Commission
    on International Trade Law. - 1986.
    (002155)

SEMICONDUCTORS.
----Innovation and market structure. - 1987.
    (000681)
----Shifts in the world economy and the
    restructuring of economic sectors. -
    1987.
    (000734)
----Transnational corporations in the
    international semiconductor industry. -
    1986.
    (000748)

SEMICONDUCTORS--EUROPE.
----The semiconductor business. - 1985.
    (000715)

SEMICONDUCTORS--JAPAN.
----Competitive edge. - 1984.
    (000673)
----High-tech trade. - 1986.
    (000696)
----The semiconductor business. - 1985.
    (000715)

SEMICONDUCTORS--SCOTLAND (UNITED KINGDOM).
----Semiconductors, Scotland and the
    international division of labour. - 1987.
    (000694)

SEMICONDUCTORS--SOUTHEAST ASIA.
----Transnational corporations and the
    electronics industries of ASEAN
    economies. - 1987.
    (000754)

SEMICONDUCTORS--UNITED KINGDOM.
----Semiconductors, Scotland and the
    international division of labour. - 1987.
    (000694)

SEMICONDUCTORS--UNITED STATES.
----A competitive assessment of the U.S.
    semiconductor manufacturing equipment
    industry. - 1985.
    (000758)
----Competitive edge. - 1984.
    (000673)
----The global factory. - 1985.
    (001254)
----High technology industries. - 1983-   .
    (000695)
----High-tech trade. - 1986.
    (000696)

----National security and the semiconductor
    industry. - 1987.
    (000675)
----The semiconductor business. - 1985.
    (000715)

SEMINAR ON MANAGING STATE TRADING
ORGANIZATIONS (1986 : GENEVA).
----Seminar on Managing State Trading
    Organisations. - 1986.
    (000370)

SENEGAL--COMMERCIAL LAW.
----Réflexions sur les régimes fiscaux
    privilégiés du code des investissements
    au Gabon. - 1985.
    (002243)

SENEGAL--FISCAL POLICY.
----Réflexions sur les régimes fiscaux
    privilégiés du code des investissements
    au Gabon. - 1985.
    (002243)

SENEGAL--INVESTMENT POLICY.
----Réflexions sur les régimes fiscaux
    privilégiés du code des investissements
    au Gabon. - 1985.
    (002243)

SERVICE INDUSTRIES.
----All traded services are embodied in
    materials or people. - 1987.
    (000869)
----The applicability of GATT to
    international trade in services :
    general considerations and the interest
    of developing countries. - 1987.
    (000885)
----Coming of age of the service economy. -
    1986.
    (000860)
----Comparative advantage and trade in
    service. - 1984.
    (000870)
----Continuing the international debate on
    services. - 1985.
    (000863)
----Developing countries and services in the
    Uruguay Round. - 1987.
    (000886)
----Developing productive activities for the
    wealth of nations in the service
    economy. - 1986.
    (000861)
----Economic development, investment
    dependence, and the rise of services in
    less developed nations. - 1986.
    (000958)
----Elements of a conceptual framework for
    trade in services. - 1987.
    (000914)
----Eliminating barriers to international
    trade and investment in services. - 1986.
    (000809)
----Les entreprises multinationales et les
    services. - 1985.
    (000956)
----L'expansion des services à productivité
    stable. - 1987.
    (001917)
----Foreign direct investment, the service
    sector and international banking. - 1987.
    (000972)

SERVICE INDUSTRIES (continued)
----Forum on economic crisis and Third World
    countries. - 1987.
      (001251)
----The future of services : basic issues
    for the long-term goals of the new GATT
    round. - 1987.
      (000862)
----Goods and services in OECD countries. -
    1987.
      (000814)
----Information technology and
    competitiveness in the service industry.
    - 1987.
      (000891)
----Intellectual property rights,
    investment, and trade in services in the
    Uruguay round. - 1987.
      (000817)
----International Colloquium on the Proposed
    New Round of Multilateral Trade
    Negotiations and Developing Countries :
    proceedings and papers. - 1986.
      (001365) (001365)
----International services-trade issues and
    the GATT. - 1983.
      (000830)
----International trade in business
    services. - 1988.
      (000910)
----Intra-firm service trade by the
    multinational enterprise. - 1987.
      (000902)
----Issues and data needs for GATT
    negotiations on services. - 1987.
      (000964)
----Legal problems in expanding the scope of
    GATT to include trade in services. -
    1983.
      (000864)
----Makroekonomické hypotézy o rozvoji
    sluzeb. - 1987.
      (000842)
----Managing the service economy. - 1985.
      (000899)
----Metodologické prístupy k vymezeni sféry
    sluzeb. - 1987.
      (000843)
----Mezhdunarodnaia kapitalisticheskaia
    torgovlia uslugami i problemy ee
    regulirovaniia. - 1987.
      (000918) (001378)
----Multinational union organizations in the
    white-collar, service, and
    communications industries. - 1983.
      (002600)
----Multinationals and trade in services. -
    1987.
      (000939)
----Les négociations internationales sur les
    services ou la quadrature du cercle. -
    1986.
      (000911)
----Les négociations internationales sur les
    services ou la quadrature du cercle.
    (With English summary.). - 1986.
      (000912)
----Negotiating international rules for
    trade in services. - 1985.
      (000898)
----Negotiating issues in international
    services transactions. - 1983.
      (000841)

----A negotiating strategy for trade in
    services. - 1983.
      (000865)
----North-South issues in trade in services.
    - 1985.
      (000944)
----Notes on partnerships in the services
    sector. - 1985.
      (000916)
----On planning and forecasting the location
    of retail and service activity. - 1984.
      (000550)
----The primary, secondary, tertiary and
    quaternary sectors of the economy. -
    1987.
      (000883)
----Production and trade in services. - 1985.
      (000978)
----La productivité dans les services. -
    1985.
      (000924)
----Protectionist tendencies in
    international trade in services. - 1986.
      (000953)
----Punta del Este and after. - 1987.
      (000927)
----Putting services on the table : the new
    GATT round. - 1987.
      (000932)
----Recent developments in operations and
    behaviour of transnational corporations.
    - 1987.
      (000103)
----Revitalizing development, growth and
    international trade. - 1987.
      (001394)
----The role of transborder data flows in
    the international services debate. -
    1987.
      (000947)
----Service industries and economic
    development. - 1984.
      (000959)
----Service-led growth. - 1986.
      (000931)
----Les services : clé du développement
    économique? - 1986.
      (000892)
----Les services : enjeux pour l'emploi et
    le commerce international. - 1986.
      (000960)
----Les services : nouvelle donne de
    l'économie. - 1984.
      (000913)
----Les services : nouvelle donne pour
    l'emploi. - 1987.
      (000961)
----Services and the development process. -
    1985.
      (000979)
----Services and the GATT. - 1987.
      (000954)
----Les services contre le chômage. - 1987.
      (000857)
----The services industries: employment,
    productivity, and inflation. - 1985.
      (000940)
----A szolgáltatások a nemzetközi gazdasági
    kapcsolatokban. - 1986.
      (000895)

SERVICE INDUSTRIES (continued)
----Technical co-operation programme,
1976-1987 : United Nations Centre on
Transnational Corporations. - 1988.
(002611)
----Tourism as a vehicle for Third World
development. - 1985.
(000906)
----Towards a theory of innovation in
services. - 1986.
(000808)
----Trade in data services. - 1986.
(000949)
----Trade in investment-related
technological services. - 1986.
(000945)
----Trade in services : growth and balance
of payments implications for countries
of Western Asia. - 1987.
(000968)
----Trade in services. - 1984.
(000955)
----Trade in services : the theory and trade
policy. - 1987.
(000943)
----Trade in services and developing
countries. - 1986.
(000952)
----Trade in services and the multilateral
trade negotiations. - 1987.
(000812)
----Trade liberalization and the global
service economy. - 1985.
(000811)
----Transnational corporations and services.
- 1984.
(000828)
----Transnational corporations in world
development. - 1988.
(000101)
----Transnational services policy? - 1987.
(000867)
----Trends and issues in foreign direct
investment and related flows. - 1985.
(000192)
----The U.S. drive to bring services into
GATT. - 1986.
(000926)
----UNCTC bibliography, 1974-1987. - 1988.
(002695)
----The Uruguay round of multilateral trade
talks. - 1987.
(000983)
----The welfare impact of foreign investment
in the presence of specific factors and
non-traded goods. - 1987.
(001340)
----Why freer trade in services is in the
interest of developing countries. - 1985.
(000850)

SERVICE INDUSTRIES--BELGIUM.
----La structure professionnelle des
secteurs secondaire et tertiaire. - 1987.
(000823)

SERVICE INDUSTRIES--CANADA.
----Canada's international trade in
services. - 1986-   .
(000821)
----Le commerce interregional des services:
le role des relations intra-firme et des
facteurs organisationnels. - 1983.
(000921)

----The service sector: engine of growth? -
1985.
(000965)

SERVICE INDUSTRIES--CHINA.
----Die chinesischen Wirtschaftsreformen im
neunten Jahr. - 1986.
(002217)

SERVICE INDUSTRIES--CZECHOSLOVAKIA.
----Nekteré otázky budouciho rozvoje
terciárniho sektoru. - 1987.
(000909)

SERVICE INDUSTRIES--EASTERN EUROPE.
----Multinationals from the Second World :
growth of foreign investment by Soviet
and East European enterprises. - 1987.
(000356)

SERVICE INDUSTRIES--EGYPT.
----The growth of employment in services:
Egypt, 1960-75. - 1985.
(000858)

SERVICE INDUSTRIES--FRANCE.
----L'économie française et le développement
des services : Annuaire 1985-1986. -
1986.
(000847)
----La specialisation internationale de la
France dans les échanges de services.
(With English summary.). - 1986.
(000907)

SERVICE INDUSTRIES--GERMANY, FEDERAL
REPUBLIC OF.
----Der internationale Handel mit
Dienstleistungen aus der Sicht der
Bundesrepublik Deutschland. - 1984.
(000877)

SERVICE INDUSTRIES--LATIN AMERICA.
----Las empresas transnacionales y la
inversión extranjera directa en la
primera mitad de los años ochenta. -
1987.
(000194)
----Estados Unidos, América Latina y el
debate internacional sobre el comercio
de servicios. - 1986.
(000934)
----La internacionalización de los
servicios. - 1986.
(000923)
----Los servicios en las transacciones
internacionales de América Latina. -
1986.
(000820)

SERVICE INDUSTRIES--NETHERLANDS.
----Verdiende lonen van werknemers in
nijverheid en dienstensector ontleend
aan het halfjaarlijks loononderzoek. -
1985.
(001928)

SERVICE INDUSTRIES--POLAND.
----Provision of services in Poland. - 1987.
(000856)

SERVICE INDUSTRIES--REPUBLIC OF KOREA.
----An information sector perspective of
   employment expansion in the Republic of
   Korea, 1975-80. - 1987.
      (000848)

SERVICE INDUSTRIES--SPAIN.
----Hacia dónde va el empleo? - 1986.
      (001252)

SERVICE INDUSTRIES--UNITED KINGDOM.
----A comparison of embodied technical
   change in services and manufacturing
   industry. - 1986.
      (000806)
----Cyclical variations in service
   industries' employment in the UK. - 1987.
      (000844)

SERVICE INDUSTRIES--UNITED STATES.
----A competitive assessment of the United
   States data processing services
   industry. - 1984.
      (000981)
----Croissance de l'emploi dans les
   services. - 1987.
      (000846)
----Estados Unidos, América Latina y el
   debate internacional sobre el comercio
   de servicios. - 1986.
      (000934)
----Identifying export potential in the
   service sector. - 1986.
      (000882)
----International trade in services: its
   composition, importance and links to
   merchandise trade. - 1987.
      (000890)
----Protectionist threat to trade and
   investment in services. - 1983.
      (000951)
----Trade in services : obstacles and
   opportunities. - 1987.
      (000984)
----Trade in services. - 1986.
      (000962)

SERVICE INDUSTRIES--USSR.
----Multinationals from the Second World :
   growth of foreign investment by Soviet
   and East European enterprises. - 1987.
      (000356)
----Vers une réforme de la planification des
   services en URSS? - 1985.
      (000845)

SERVICE INDUSTRIES--WESTERN ASIA.
----Trade in services : growth and balance
   of payments implications for countries
   of Western Asia. - 1987.
      (000968)

SERVICE INDUSTRIES--WESTERN EUROPE.
----Hacia dónde va el empleo? - 1986.
      (001252)
----Mélanges 2 : harmonisation fiscale,
   marché commun des services, perspectives
   budgétaires 1988, fonds structurels. -
   1987.
      (000897)
----New technology and the new services :
   towards an innovation strategy for
   Europe. - 1986.
      (000807)

----Services and regional policy. - 1987.
      (000903)
----Société d'information et Europe des
   services : quelles infrastructures? -
   1987.
      (000893)
----Trade in services. - 1986.
      (000962)

SERVICE INDUSTRIES WORKERS.
----Is there a service economy? The changing
   capitalist division of labor. - 1985.
      (000986)
----Why are services cheaper in the poor
   countries? - 1984.
      (000813)

SHERMAN ANTITRUST ACT 1890 (UNITED STATES).
----The extraterritorial effects of
   antitrust laws. - 1984.
      (002342)

SHIPOWNERS.
----Dommages causés par les marées noires. -
   1984.
      (001952)

SHOE INDUSTRY.
----Social and labour practices of
   multinational enterprises in the
   textiles, clothing and footwear
   industries. - 1984.
      (001922)

SHOE INDUSTRY--CANADA.
----Beyond borders. - 1986.
      (000280)

SHOE INDUSTRY--SWITZERLAND.
----Das Bally-Lehrstuck. - 1985.
      (000286)

SIBERIA (USSR)--CAPITAL INVESTMENTS.
----Investment and reindustrialization in
   the Soviet economy. - 1984.
      (001333)

SIBERIA (USSR)--ECONOMIC POLICY.
----Investment and reindustrialization in
   the Soviet economy. - 1984.
      (001333)

SIBERIA (USSR)--INDUSTRIAL POLICY.
----Investment and reindustrialization in
   the Soviet economy. - 1984.
      (001333)

SIBERIA (USSR)--INDUSTRY.
----Investment and reindustrialization in
   the Soviet economy. - 1984.
      (001333)

SIERRA LEONE--EMPLOYMENT POLICY.
----Multinationals and employment in a West
   African sub-region. - 1984.
      (001904)

SIERRA LEONE--LABOUR SUPPLY.
----Multinationals and employment in a West
   African sub-region. - 1984.
      (001904)

SIERRA LEONE--PHARMACEUTICAL INDUSTRY.
----Transnational corporations in the
  pharmaceutical industry of developing
  countries. - 1984.
    (000749)

SIERRA LEONE--TRANSNATIONAL CORPORATIONS.
----Multinationals and employment in a West
  African sub-region. - 1984.
    (001904)

SILICON.
----Microelectronics-based automation
  technologies and development. - 1985.
    (000753)

SINGAPORE--ACCOUNTING.
----Accounting technology transfer to less
  developed countries and the Singapore
  experience. - 1986.
    (001498)

SINGAPORE--BANKING LAW.
----A survey of banking laws and policies in
  Hong Kong and Singapore. - 1986.
    (001829)

SINGAPORE--CAPITAL MARKETS.
----Hong Kong and Singapore. - 1985.
    (000879)

SINGAPORE--DIRECTORIES.
----Leading international companies
  manufacturing and providing technical
  services in Singapore. - 1983-   .
    (002650)
----Singapore manufacturers and products
  directory. - 1977-   .
    (002664)

SINGAPORE--ECONOMIC CONDITIONS.
----Multinationals and the growth of the
  Singapore economy. - 1986.
    (001062)

SINGAPORE--ECONOMIC DEVELOPMENT.
----Can CARICOM countries replicate the
  Singapore experience. - 1987.
    (001093)
----Multinationals and the growth of the
  Singapore economy. - 1986.
    (001062)

SINGAPORE--EMPLOYMENT POLICY.
----Direct foreign investment in
  manufacturing and the impact on
  employment and export performance in
  Singapore. - 1984.
    (001932)

SINGAPORE--EXPORT MARKETING.
----Chinese business, multinationals and the
  state: manufacturing for export in
  Malaysia and Singapore. - 1983.
    (000713)

SINGAPORE--EXPORT ORIENTED INDUSTRIES.
----Can CARICOM countries replicate the
  Singapore experience. - 1987.
    (001093)

SINGAPORE--FOREIGN DIRECT INVESTMENT.
----Direct foreign investment in
  manufacturing and the impact on
  employment and export performance in
  Singapore. - 1984.
    (001932)
----The real threat from Asia. - 1987.
    (001055)
----Singapore's role in China's offshore oil
  venture. - 1985.
    (000608)

SINGAPORE--FOREIGN LOANS.
----Hong Kong and Singapore. - 1985.
    (000879)

SINGAPORE--FREE EXPORT ZONES.
----Export processing and industrialisation.
  - 1982.
    (002405)

SINGAPORE--INDUSTRIAL POLICY.
----Export processing and industrialisation.
  - 1982.
    (002405)

SINGAPORE--JOINT VENTURES.
----Singapore's role in China's offshore oil
  venture. - 1985.
    (000608)

SINGAPORE--LAWS AND REGULATIONS.
----National legislation and regulations
  relating to transnational corporations.
  Volume 3. - 1983.
    (002252)

SINGAPORE--MANAGEMENT.
----Multinational business and national
  development. - 1983.
    (000397)

SINGAPORE--MANUFACTURES.
----Singapore manufacturers and products
  directory. - 1977-   .
    (002664)

SINGAPORE--MANUFACTURING ENTERPRISES.
----Chinese business, multinationals and the
  state: manufacturing for export in
  Malaysia and Singapore. - 1983.
    (000713)
----Direct foreign investment in
  manufacturing and the impact on
  employment and export performance in
  Singapore. - 1984.
    (001932)
----Leading international companies
  manufacturing and providing technical
  services in Singapore. - 1983-   .
    (002650)
----Singapore manufacturers and products
  directory. - 1977-   .
    (002664)

SINGAPORE--OFFSHORE OIL DRILLING.
----Singapore's role in China's offshore oil
  venture. - 1985.
    (000608)

SINGAPORE--STATISTICAL DATA.
----Multinationals and the growth of the
  Singapore economy. - 1986.
    (001062)

SINGAPORE--TAX LAW.
----A survey of banking laws and policies in
    Hong Kong and Singapore. - 1986.
        (001829)

SINGAPORE--TECHNOLOGY TRANSFER.
----Accounting technology transfer to less
    developed countries and the Singapore
    experience. - 1986.
        (001498)

SINGAPORE--TRANSNATIONAL CORPORATIONS.
----Chinese business, multinationals and the
    state: manufacturing for export in
    Malaysia and Singapore. - 1983.
        (000713)
----Leading international companies
    manufacturing and providing technical
    services in Singapore. - 1983-   .
        (002650)
----Multinational business and national
    development. - 1983.
        (000397)
----Multinationals and the growth of the
    Singapore economy. - 1986.
        (001062)
----National legislation and regulations
    relating to transnational corporations.
    Volume 3. - 1983.
        (002252)
----Singapore multinationals. - 1985.
        (000365)

SIZE OF ENTERPRISE.
----Size, growth, and transnationality among
    the world's largest banks. - 1983.
        (000969)

SMALL ENTERPRISES.
----Establishing overseas operations: tax
    and treasury considerations. - 1987.
        (001768)

SMALL ENTERPRISES--JAPAN.
----Microelectronics-based automation
    technologies and development. - 1985.
        (000753)

SMALL ENTERPRISES--SOUTHEAST ASIA.
----Small-and medium-scale industries in the
    ASEAN countries. - 1984.
        (001036)

SMALL ENTERPRISES--UNITED STATES.
----Directory of business, trade and public
    policy organizations. - 1982-   .
        (002631)

SMALL SCALE INDUSTRY--SOUTHEAST ASIA.
----Small-and medium-scale industries in the
    ASEAN countries. - 1984.
        (001036)

SMALL STATES--LATIN AMERICA.
----Small nations, giant firms. - 1987.
        (001091)

SMOKING.
----Smoke ring : the politics of tobacco. -
    1984.
        (000571)

SOCIAL ASPECT.
----Multinational corporations and global
    welfare: an extension of Kojima and
    Ozawa. - 1985.
        (000036)

SOCIAL CLASSES.
----Corporations, classes, and capitalism. -
    1985.
        (000090)

SOCIAL CLASSES--GUYANA.
----Ethnicity, class, and international
    capitalist penetration in Guyana and
    Trinidad. - 1985.
        (001096)

SOCIAL CLASSES--TRINIDAD AND TOBAGO.
----Ethnicity, class, and international
    capitalist penetration in Guyana and
    Trinidad. - 1985.
        (001096)

SOCIAL CONDITIONS--ECUADOR.
----Ecuador. - 1984.
        (001831)

SOCIAL CONDITIONS--POLAND.
----Development, social justice, and
    dependence in Poland. - 1985.
        (001188)

SOCIAL CONFLICT.
----How multinationals can manage social
    conflict. - 1983.
        (001869)

SOCIAL DEVELOPMENT--SOUTHEAST ASIA.
----Vlijanie TNK na social'no-ekonomiceskoe
    razvivtie stran Jugo-Vosticnoj Azii. -
    1985.
        (001075)

SOCIAL INTERACTION.
----How multinationals can manage social
    conflict. - 1983.
        (001869)

SOCIAL JUSTICE--POLAND.
----Development, social justice, and
    dependence in Poland. - 1985.
        (001188)

SOCIAL POLICY.
----Multinational enterprises : information
    and consultation concerning their
    manpower plans. - 1985.
        (000431)
----Social and labour practices of
    multinational enterprises in the
    textiles, clothing and footwear
    industries. - 1984.
        (001922)
----Tripartite Declaration of Principles
    Concerning Multinational Enterprises and
    Social Policy. - 1977.
        (002013)

SOCIAL PROBLEMS.
----A transnacionalizacao da America Latina
    e a missao das igrejas. - 1983.
        (002591)

SOCIETE SUCRIERE DE HAUTE-VOLTA.
----Une enclave industrielle : la Société
sucrière de Haute-Volta. - 1984.
(001032)

SOCIO-ECONOMIC INDICATORS--MAURITANIA.
----Towards an evaluative study of joint
venture projects with socio-economic
indicators. - 1983.
(001555)

SODIUM GLUTAMATE.
----Technology acquisition under alternative
arrangements with transnational
corporations. - 1987.
(001512)

SOUND RECORDINGS--UNITED KINGDOM.
----The Gramophone Company: an
Anglo-American multinational, 1898-1931.
- 1985.
(000285)

SOUND RECORDINGS--UNITED STATES.
----The Gramophone Company: an
Anglo-American multinational, 1898-1931.
- 1985.
(000285)

SOUTH AFRICA--ANTI-APARTHEID MOVEMENTS.
----Trade unions against apartheid. - 1984.
(002601)

SOUTH AFRICA--APARTHEID.
----Leaving South Africa/Kellogg's
private war against apartheid/Black
unions. - 1985.
(001200)

SOUTH AFRICA--ARMAMENTS.
----Transnational corporations in South
Africa and Namibia : United Nations
public hearings. Volume 1, Reports of
the Panel of Eminent Persons and of the
Secretary-General. - 1986.
(001216)

SOUTH AFRICA--ARMS EMBARGO.
----Activities of transnational corporations
in South Africa and Namibia and the
responsibilities of home countries with
respect to their operations in this
area. - 1986.
(001192)
----Transnational corporations in South
Africa and Namibia : United Nations
public hearings. Volume 1, Reports of
the Panel of Eminent Persons and of the
Secretary-General. - 1986.
(001216)
----Transnational corporations in South
Africa and Namibia. - 1986.
(001217)

SOUTH AFRICA--BANK LOANS.
----Activities of transnational corporations
in South Africa and Namibia and the
responsibilities of home countries with
respect to their operations in this
area. - 1986.
(001192)
----Foreign investment in South Africa and
Namibia. - 1984.
(001198) (002641)

----U.S. and Canadian investment in South
Africa and Namibia. - 1986.
(001212) (002671) (002672)

SOUTH AFRICA--BANKING.
----Transnational corporations in South
Africa and Namibia. - 1986.
(001217)

SOUTH AFRICA--BLACKS.
----Business in the shadow of apartheid :
U.S. firms in South Africa. - 1985.
(001194)
----A code for misconduct? - 1980.
(002009)
----Disinvestment and black workers
attitudes in South Africa. - 1985.
(001210)
----Leaving South Africa/Kellogg's
private war against apartheid/Black
unions. - 1985.
(001200)
----Political change in South Africa. - 1986.
(001205)
----Trade unions against apartheid. - 1984.
(002601)
----U.S. firms and black labor in South
Africa: creating a structure for change.
- 1986.
(001195)

SOUTH AFRICA--BUSINESS ETHICS.
----The politics of sentiment. - 1984.
(002588)
----South Africa: the churches vs. the
corporations. - 1983.
(002589)

SOUTH AFRICA--CORPORATIONS.
----McGregor's investors' handbook. -
1986-   .
(001203) (002654)

SOUTH AFRICA--DIRECTORIES.
----Foreign investment in South Africa and
Namibia. - 1984.
(001198) (002641)
----McGregor's investors' handbook. -
1986-   .
(001203) (002654)

SOUTH AFRICA--DIVESTMENT.
----Activities of transnational corporations
in South Africa and Namibia and the
responsibilities of home countries with
respect to their operations in this
area. - 1986.
(001192)
----The costs of disinvestment. - 1986.
(001207)
----Disinvestment and black workers
attitudes in South Africa. - 1985.
(001210)
----Leaving South Africa/Kellogg's
private war against apartheid/Black
unions. - 1985.
(001200)
----Measures regarding the activities of
transnational corporations in South
Africa and Namibia. - 1985.
(001220)
----Time to quit South Africa? - 1985.
(001206)

SOUTH AFRICA--FOREIGN RELATIONS.
----The political economy of U.S. policy
    toward South Africa. - 1985.
      (001196)

SOUTH AFRICA--HOLDING COMPANIES.
----Foreign investment in South Africa and
    Namibia. - 1984.
      (001198) (002641)
----McGregor's investors' handbook. -
    1986- .
      (001203) (002654)

SOUTH AFRICA--INVESTMENT TRUSTS.
----McGregor's investors' handbook. -
    1986- .
      (001203) (002654)

SOUTH AFRICA--LABOUR RELATIONS.
----Business in the shadow of apartheid :
    U.S. firms in South Africa. - 1985.
      (001194)
----Transnational corporations in South
    Africa and Namibia : United Nations
    public hearings. Volume 3, Statements
    and submissions. - 1987.
      (001215)

SOUTH AFRICA--LABOUR SUPPLY.
----U.S. firms and black labor in South
    Africa: creating a structure for change.
    - 1986.
      (001195)

SOUTH AFRICA--MANPOWER NEEDS.
----Political change in South Africa. - 1986.
      (001205)

SOUTH AFRICA--MANUFACTURING ENTERPRISES.
----The determinants of manufacturing
    ownership in less developed countries. -
    1986.
      (000712)

SOUTH AFRICA--MIGRANT WORKERS.
----Transnational corporations in South
    Africa and Namibia : United Nations
    public hearings. Volume 1, Reports of
    the Panel of Eminent Persons and of the
    Secretary-General. - 1986.
      (001216)
----Transnational corporations in South
    Africa and Namibia. - 1986.
      (001217)

SOUTH AFRICA--MILITARY OCCUPATION.
----Transnational corporations in South
    Africa and Namibia : United Nations
    public hearings. Volume 1, Reports of
    the Panel of Eminent Persons and of the
    Secretary-General. - 1986.
      (001216)

SOUTH AFRICA--MILITARY RELATIONS.
----Measures regarding the activities of
    transnational corporations in South
    Africa and Namibia. - 1985.
      (001220)
----Transnational corporations in South
    Africa and Namibia : United Nations
    public hearings. Volume 1, Reports of
    the Panel of Eminent Persons and of the
    Secretary-General. - 1986.
      (001216)

----Transnational corporations in South
    Africa and Namibia : United Nations
    public hearings. Volume 3, Statements
    and submissions. - 1987.
      (001215)

SOUTH AFRICA--MILITARY SCIENCE.
----Activities of transnational corporations
    in South Africa and Namibia and the
    responsibilities of home countries with
    respect to their operations in this
    area. - 1986.
      (001192)

SOUTH AFRICA--MINERAL RESOURCES.
----Transnational corporations in South
    Africa and Namibia. - 1986.
      (001217)

SOUTH AFRICA--NUCLEAR ENERGY.
----Transnational corporations in South
    Africa and Namibia : United Nations
    public hearings. Volume 3, Statements
    and submissions. - 1987.
      (001215)

SOUTH AFRICA--NUCLEAR TECHNOLOGY.
----Measures regarding the activities of
    transnational corporations in South
    Africa and Namibia. - 1985.
      (001220)
----Transnational corporations in South
    Africa and Namibia : United Nations
    public hearings. Volume 1, Reports of
    the Panel of Eminent Persons and of the
    Secretary-General. - 1986.
      (001216)

SOUTH AFRICA--NUCLEAR WEAPONS.
----Transnational corporations in South
    Africa and Namibia : United Nations
    public hearings. Volume 3, Statements
    and submissions. - 1987.
      (001215)

SOUTH AFRICA--OIL EMBARGO.
----Activities of transnational corporations
    in South Africa and Namibia and the
    responsibilities of home countries with
    respect to their operations in this
    area. - 1986.
      (001192)
----Measures regarding the activities of
    transnational corporations in South
    Africa and Namibia. - 1985.
      (001220)
----Transnational corporations in South
    Africa and Namibia : United Nations
    public hearings. Volume 1, Reports of
    the Panel of Eminent Persons and of the
    Secretary-General. - 1986.
      (001216)
----Transnational corporations in South
    Africa and Namibia. - 1986.
      (001217)
----Transnational corporations in South
    Africa and Namibia : United Nations
    public hearings. Volume 3, Statements
    and submissions. - 1987.
      (001215)

SOUTH AFRICA--POLITICAL CONDITIONS.
----Political change in South Africa. - 1986.
      (001205)

SOUTH AFRICA--TRANSNATIONAL CORPORATIONS
(continued)
----The role of multinational corporations
    in South Africa. - 1980.
    (001209)
----The roots of crisis in southern Africa.
    - 1985.
    (001208)
----South Africa: the churches vs. the
    corporations. - 1983.
    (002589)
----Transnational corporations : follow-up
    to the recommendations of the Panel of
    Eminent Persons Established to Conduct
    the Public Hearings on the Activities of
    Transnational Corporations in South
    Africa and Namibia. - 1988.
    (001221)
----Transnational corporations in South
    Africa and Namibia : United Nations
    public hearings. Volume 1, Reports of
    the Panel of Eminent Persons and of the
    Secretary-General. - 1986.
    (001216)
----Transnational corporations in South
    Africa and Namibia. - 1986.
    (001217)
----Transnational corporations in South
    Africa and Namibia : United Nations
    public hearings. Volume 3, Statements
    and submissions. - 1987.
    (001215)
----Transnational corporations in South
    Africa and Namibia : United Nations
    Public Hearings. Volume 4, Policy
    instruments and statements. - 1987.
    (001218)
----U.S. and Canadian business in South
    Africa. - 1987-   .
    (001211)
----U.S. and Canadian investment in South
    Africa and Namibia. - 1986.
    (001212) (002671) (002672)

----U.S. corporate activities in South
    Africa. - 1983.
    (001222)
----U.S. firms and black labor in South
    Africa: creating a structure for change.
    - 1986.
    (001195)
----UNCTC bibliography, 1974-1987. - 1988.
    (002695)

SOUTH AFRICA--TROOP WITHDRAWAL.
----Transnational corporations in South
    Africa and Namibia : United Nations
    public hearings. Volume 1, Reports of
    the Panel of Eminent Persons and of the
    Secretary-General. - 1986.
    (001216)

SOUTH AFRICA--WAGE POLICY.
----A code for misconduct? - 1980.
    (002009)

SOUTH AFRICA--WORKING CONDITIONS.
----Transnational corporations in South
    Africa and Namibia : United Nations
    public hearings. Volume 1, Reports of
    the Panel of Eminent Persons and of the
    Secretary-General. - 1986.
    (001216)

SOUTH AMERICA--CONTRACTS.
----Financing implications of mineral
    development agreements. - 1986.
    (002456)

SOUTH AMERICA--FOREIGN INVESTMENTS.
----Financing implications of mineral
    development agreements. - 1986.
    (002456)

SOUTH AMERICA--LEGISLATION.
----Financing implications of mineral
    development agreements. - 1986.
    (002456)

SOUTH AMERICA--MINERAL RESOURCES DEVELOPMENT.
----Financing implications of mineral
    development agreements. - 1986.
    (002456)

SOUTH ASIA--DEVELOPING COUNTRIES.
----Multinational corporations, technology
    and employment. - 1983.
    (001891)

SOUTH ASIA--EMPLOYMENT.
----Multinational corporations, technology
    and employment. - 1983.
    (001891)

SOUTH ASIA--FOREIGN DIRECT INVESTMENT.
----Multinational corporations, technology
    and employment. - 1983.
    (001891)

SOUTH ASIA--INDUSTRIAL CO-OPERATION.
----Industrial cooperation in regional
    economic groupings among developing
    countries and lessons for SAARC. - 1987.
    (001009)

SOUTH ASIA--JOINT VENTURES.
----Industrial cooperation in regional
    economic groupings among developing
    countries and lessons for SAARC. - 1987.
    (001009)

SOUTH ASIA--REGIONAL CO-OPERATION.
----Industrial cooperation in regional
    economic groupings among developing
    countries and lessons for SAARC. - 1987.
    (001009)

SOUTH ASIA--TECHNOLOGY TRANSFER.
----Multinational corporations, technology
    and employment. - 1983.
    (001891)

SOUTH ASIA--TRANSNATIONAL CORPORATIONS.
----Multinational corporations, technology
    and employment. - 1983.
    (001891)

SOUTH ASIAN ASSOCIATION FOR REGIONAL
CO-OPERATION.
----Industrial cooperation in regional
    economic groupings among developing
    countries and lessons for SAARC. - 1987.
    (001009)

SOUTH PACIFIC OCEAN REGION--TRANSNATIONAL
CORPORATIONS.
----Multinational enterprises in the
developing South Pacific region. - 1986.
(001045)

SOUTHEAST ASIA--ACCOUNTING AND REPORTING.
----Comparative accounting practices in
ASEAN. - 1984.
(002072)

SOUTHEAST ASIA--CHEMICAL INDUSTRY.
----The allure of Southeast Asia's chemical
market. - 1987.
(000661)

SOUTHEAST ASIA--COMPARATIVE ANALYSIS.
----Comparative accounting practices in
ASEAN. - 1984.
(002072)

SOUTHEAST ASIA--COMPUTER INDUSTRY.
----Computer vendors re-shape product
strategy for Asian market. - 1986.
(000689)

SOUTHEAST ASIA--CONSUMER GOODS.
----Transnational corporations and the
electronics industries of ASEAN
economies. - 1987.
(000754)

SOUTHEAST ASIA--COTTAGE INDUSTRIES.
----Small-and medium-scale industries in the
ASEAN countries. - 1984.
(001036)

SOUTHEAST ASIA--DEVELOPED COUNTRIES.
----Entrepreneurial cooperation between
industrialized countries and the
developing countries in East and
South-East Asia. - 1985.
(001649)

SOUTHEAST ASIA--DEVELOPING COUNTRIES.
----Corporate policy, strategic groups and
the performance of transnational
corporations in less developed
countries. - 1982.
(001008)

SOUTHEAST ASIA--ECONOMIC CONDITIONS.
----Neue Wachstumsmärkte in Fernost. - 1983.
(001800)

SOUTHEAST ASIA--ECONOMIC CO-OPERATION.
----ASEAN economic co-operation. - 1985.
(001039)
----Entrepreneurial cooperation between
industrialized countries and the
developing countries in East and
South-East Asia. - 1985.
(001649)
----Wachstumsmarkt Südostasien. - 1984.
(001785)

SOUTHEAST ASIA--ECONOMIC CO-OPERATION AMONG
DEVELOPING COUNTRIES.
----Aspects of ASEAN. - 1984.
(001406)

SOUTHEAST ASIA--ECONOMIC DEVELOPMENT.
----Small-and medium-scale industries in the
ASEAN countries. - 1984.
(001036)
----Vlijanie TNK na social'no-ekonomiceskoe
razvivtie stran Jugo-Vosticnoj Azii. -
1985.
(001075)
----Wachstumsmarkt Südostasien. - 1984.
(001785)

SOUTHEAST ASIA--ECONOMIC POLICY.
----Economic policies towards transnational
corporations. - 1983.
(002229)
----The Japanese economic strategy. - 1983.
(000366)
----Kulturelle und wirtschaftliche
Interdependenz der ASEAN-Staaten. - 1986.
(001067)

SOUTHEAST ASIA--ECONOMIC RELATIONS.
----The Japanese economic strategy. - 1983.
(000366)
----Neue Wachstumsmärkte in Fernost. - 1983.
(001800) (001800)
----Wachstumsmarkt Südostasien. - 1984.
(001785)

SOUTHEAST ASIA--ELECTRONICS INDUSTRY.
----Transnational corporations and the
electronics industries of ASEAN
economies. - 1987.
(000754)

SOUTHEAST ASIA--FINANCIAL STATEMENTS.
----Comparative accounting practices in
ASEAN. - 1984.
(002072)

SOUTHEAST ASIA--FISHERIES.
----Joint fishing ventures. - 1983.
(000570)

SOUTHEAST ASIA--FISHERY MANAGEMENT.
----Joint fishing ventures. - 1983.
(000570)

SOUTHEAST ASIA--FOREIGN DIRECT INVESTMENT.
----Australian direct investment in the
ASEAN countries. - 1983.
(000110)
----Die Direktinvestitionen der japanischen
Wirtschaft in den Schwellenländern Ost-
Südostasiens. - 1984.
(000157)
----Foreign direct investment and
industrialization in ASEAN countries. -
1987.
(000144)
----Foreign direct investment in ASEAN. -
1987.
(000139)
----Les investissements japonais en Asie du
sud-est: compléments ou concurrents de
l'industrie au Japon. (With English
summary.). - 1985.
(000146)
----Neue Wachstumsmärkte in Fernost. - 1983.
(001800)
----Sverkhmonopolii v IUgo-Vostochnoi Azii.
- 1983.
(001041)

SOUTHEAST ASIA--FOREIGN DIRECT INVESTMENT
(continued)
----Wachstumsmarkt Südostasien. - 1984.
(001785)

SOUTHEAST ASIA--FOREIGN INVESTMENTS.
----Entrepreneurial cooperation between
industrialized countries and the
developing countries in East and
South-East Asia. - 1985.
(001649)
----Investitionsbedingungen in der
ASEAN-region. - 1986.
(001814)

SOUTHEAST ASIA--FOREIGN TRADE.
----Wachstumsmarkt Südostasien. - 1984.
(001785)

SOUTHEAST ASIA--INDUSTRIAL CO-OPERATION.
----ASEAN economic co-operation. - 1985.
(001039)
----Basic framework for ASEAN industrial
co-operation. - 1986.
(002149)

SOUTHEAST ASIA--INDUSTRIAL PROMOTION.
----Computer vendors re-shape product
strategy for Asian market. - 1986.
(000689)

SOUTHEAST ASIA--INDUSTRIAL STATISTICS.
----Transnational corporations and the
electronics industries of ASEAN
economies. - 1987.
(000754)

SOUTHEAST ASIA--INDUSTRIALIZATION.
----Foreign direct investment and
industrialization in ASEAN countries. -
1987.
(000144)

SOUTHEAST ASIA--INDUSTRY.
----Les investissements japonais en Asie du
sud-est: compléments ou concurrents de
l'industrie au Japon. (With English
summary.). - 1985.
(000146)

SOUTHEAST ASIA--INTRAREGIONAL TRADE.
----Legal development and the promotion of
intra-ASEAN trade and investment. - 1986.
(002307)

SOUTHEAST ASIA--INVESTMENT POLICY.
----Investitionsbedingungen in der
ASEAN-region. - 1986.
(001814)

SOUTHEAST ASIA--INVESTMENT PROMOTION.
----Legal development and the promotion of
intra-ASEAN trade and investment. - 1986.
(002307)

SOUTHEAST ASIA--INVESTMENT TAX CREDIT.
----Subsidy to capital through tax
incentives in the ASEAN countries. -
1983.
(002300)

SOUTHEAST ASIA--JOINT VENTURES.
----Entrepreneurial cooperation between
industrialized countries and the
developing countries in East and
South-East Asia. - 1985.
(001649)
----Joint fishing ventures. - 1983.
(000570)
----Taming troubled waters. - 1986.
(002453)

SOUTHEAST ASIA--LIGHT INDUSTRY.
----Corporate policy, strategic groups and
the performance of transnational
corporations in less developed
countries. - 1982.
(001008)

SOUTHEAST ASIA--MANAGEMENT.
----Corporate policy, strategic groups and
the performance of transnational
corporations in less developed
countries. - 1982.
(001008)

SOUTHEAST ASIA--MANUFACTURING ENTERPRISES.
----Corporate policy, strategic groups and
the performance of transnational
corporations in less developed
countries. - 1982.
(001008)

SOUTHEAST ASIA--MARKET ACCESS.
----Computer vendors re-shape product
strategy for Asian market. - 1986.
(000689)

SOUTHEAST ASIA--MARKET POTENTIAL.
----The allure of Southeast Asia's chemical
market. - 1987.
(000661)

SOUTHEAST ASIA--POLITICAL CONDITIONS.
----Neue Wachstumsmärkte in Fernost. - 1983.
(001800)

SOUTHEAST ASIA--PRIVATE ENTERPRISES.
----The Japanese economic strategy. - 1983.
(000366)

SOUTHEAST ASIA--SEMICONDUCTORS.
----Transnational corporations and the
electronics industries of ASEAN
economies. - 1987.
(000754)

SOUTHEAST ASIA--SMALL ENTERPRISES.
----Small-and medium-scale industries in the
ASEAN countries. - 1984.
(001036)

SOUTHEAST ASIA--SMALL SCALE INDUSTRY.
----Small-and medium-scale industries in the
ASEAN countries. - 1984.
(001036)

SOUTHEAST ASIA--SOCIAL DEVELOPMENT.
----Vlijanie TNK na social'no-ekonomiceskoe
razvivtie stran Jugo-Vosticnoj Azii. -
1985.
(001075)

SOUTHEAST ASIA--STATISTICAL DATA.
----Australian direct investment in the
ASEAN countries. - 1983.
(000110)
----Transnational corporations and the
electronics industries of ASEAN
economies. - 1987.
(000754)

SOUTHEAST ASIA--TAX INCENTIVES.
----Subsidy to capital through tax
incentives in the ASEAN countries. -
1983.
(002300)

SOUTHEAST ASIA--TECHNOLOGICAL INNOVATIONS.
----Transnational corporations and the
electronics industries of ASEAN
economies. - 1987.
(000754)

SOUTHEAST ASIA--TECHNOLOGY TRANSFER.
----Aspects of ASEAN. - 1984.
(001406)

SOUTHEAST ASIA--TRADE LIBERALIZATION.
----ASEAN economic co-operation. - 1985.
(001039)

SOUTHEAST ASIA--TRADE PROMOTION.
----Legal development and the promotion of
intra-ASEAN trade and investment. - 1986.
(002307)

SOUTHEAST ASIA--TRANSNATIONAL CORPORATIONS.
----Aspects of ASEAN. - 1984.
(001406)
----Computer vendors re-shape product
strategy for Asian market. - 1986.
(000689)
----Corporate policy, strategic groups and
the performance of transnational
corporations in less developed
countries. - 1982.
(001008)
----Economic policies towards transnational
corporations. - 1983.
(002229)
----Singapore multinationals. - 1985.
(000365)
----The social and cultural impact of the
activities of transnational corporations
in Southeast Asia. - 1982.
(001880)
----Sverkhmonopolii v IUgo-Vostochnoi Azii.
- 1983.
(001041)
----Transnational corporations and the
electronics industries of ASEAN
economies. - 1987.
(000754)
----Vlijanie TNK na social'no-ekonomiceskoe
razvivtie stran Jugo-Vosticnoj Azii. -
1985.
(001075)

SOUTHERN PERU COPPER CORPORATION.
----Privilegios y capital transnacional. -
1985.
(000269)

SOVEREIGNTY.
----Money, multinationals, and sovereigns. -
1983.
(001226)

SPAIN--COMMERCIAL ARBITRATION.
----Major international treaties regulating
arbitration in Spain. - 1983.
(002489)

SPAIN--DIVISION OF LABOUR.
----Hacia dónde va el empleo? - 1986.
(001252)

SPAIN--EMPLOYMENT.
----Hacia dónde va el empleo? - 1986.
(001252)

SPAIN--EMPLOYMENT POLICY.
----The employment impact of multinational
enterprises in Greece, Portugal and
Spain. - 1987.
(001887)

SPAIN--FOREIGN DIRECT INVESTMENT.
----El control de las empresas
multinacionales. - 1983.
(002209)
----Investment legislation in Greece,
Portugal and Spain: the background to
foreign investment in Mediterranean
Europe. - 1983.
(002168)

SPAIN--LAWS AND REGULATIONS.
----El control de las empresas
multinacionales. - 1983.
(002209)

SPAIN--LEGISLATION.
----Investment legislation in Greece,
Portugal and Spain: the background to
foreign investment in Mediterranean
Europe. - 1983.
(002168)

SPAIN--SERVICE INDUSTRIES.
----Hacia dónde va el empleo? - 1986.
(001252)

SPAIN--TECHNOLOGY TRANSFER.
----El control de las empresas
multinacionales. - 1983.
(002209)

SPAIN--TRANSNATIONAL CORPORATIONS.
----El control de las empresas
multinacionales. - 1983.
(002209)
----The employment impact of multinational
enterprises in Greece, Portugal and
Spain. - 1987.
(001887)
----Les multinacionals a Catalunya. - 1984.
(001147)

SPAIN--TREATIES.
----Major international treaties regulating
arbitration in Spain. - 1983.
(002489)

SPECIAL DRAWING RIGHTS.
----Ways out of the debt crisis. - 1984.
(000245)

SRI LANKA--AGRIBUSINESS.
----Agribusiness TNCs in Sri Lanka. - 1986.
    (000560)

SRI LANKA--CLOTHING.
----Foreign cooperation and the marketing of
    manufactured exports from developing
    countries. - 1985.
    (001377)

SRI LANKA--COMPUTER INDUSTRY.
----Microelectronics-based automation
    technologies and development. - 1985.
    (000753)

SRI LANKA--ECONOMIC CONDITIONS.
----Agribusiness TNCs in Sri Lanka. - 1986.
    (000560)
----Economic prospects of Sri Lanka and
    potential for foreign investment. - 1984.
    (001788)

SRI LANKA--ECONOMIC POLICY.
----Economic prospects of Sri Lanka and
    potential for foreign investment. - 1984.
    (001788)

SRI LANKA--EXPORT MARKETING.
----Foreign cooperation and the marketing of
    manufactured exports from developing
    countries. - 1985.
    (001377)

SRI LANKA--FOREIGN DIRECT INVESTMENT.
----Economic prospects of Sri Lanka and
    potential for foreign investment. - 1984.
    (001788)

SRI LANKA--FOREIGN TRADE.
----Trade and investment possibilities in
    Bangladesh, Nepal and Sri Lanka. - 1983.
    (001840)

SRI LANKA--FREE EXPORT ZONES.
----Aspects of labour law and relations in
    selected export processing zones. - 1984.
    (001895)
----The Katunayake investment promotion
    zone. - 1982.
    (002388)

SRI LANKA--INVESTMENT POLICY.
----Trade and investment possibilities in
    Bangladesh, Nepal and Sri Lanka. - 1983.
    (001840)

SRI LANKA--INVESTMENT PROMOTION.
----The Katunayake investment promotion
    zone. - 1982.
    (002388)

SRI LANKA--LABOUR LAW.
----Aspects of labour law and relations in
    selected export processing zones. - 1984.
    (001895)

SRI LANKA--LABOUR RELATIONS.
----Aspects of labour law and relations in
    selected export processing zones. - 1984.
    (001895)

SRI LANKA--MANUFACTURES.
----Foreign cooperation and the marketing of
    manufactured exports from developing
    countries. - 1985.
    (001377)

SRI LANKA--NATIONALIZATION.
----Les nationalisations dans quelques pays
    d'Asie de tradition britannique : Inde,
    Sri Lanca, Birmanie. - 1984.
    (002329)

SRI LANKA--SCIENCE AND TECHNOLOGY POLICY.
----Proceedings of the SSTCC/UNCTC/ESCAP
    Asia-Pacific Training Workshop on
    Regulating and Negotiating Technology
    Transfer through Transnational
    Corporations, 14-25 October 1985,
    Fuzhou, Fujian, China. - 1986.
    (001405) (002169)

SRI LANKA--TECHNOLOGY TRANSFER.
----Proceedings of the SSTCC/UNCTC/ESCAP
    Asia-Pacific Training Workshop on
    Regulating and Negotiating Technology
    Transfer through Transnational
    Corporations, 14-25 October 1985,
    Fuzhou, Fujian, China. - 1986.
    (001405) (002169)

SRI LANKA--TOURISM.
----Perceptions of socio-economic and
    cultural impact of tourism in Sri Lanka.
    - 1987.
    (001867)

SRI LANKA--TRADE POLICY.
----Trade and investment possibilities in
    Bangladesh, Nepal and Sri Lanka. - 1983.
    (001840)

SRI LANKA--TRANSNATIONAL CORPORATIONS.
----Agribusiness TNCs in Sri Lanka. - 1986.
    (000560)

STAFFING.
----Environmental aspects of the activities
    of transnational corporations. - 1985.
    (001954)

STAGFLATION.
----La gestion marketing dans un
    développemnt turbulent et hautement
    concurrentiel. - 1983.
    (000487)

STANDARD OF LIVING--EGYPT.
----The South Korean success story. - 1986.
    (001050)

STANDARDIZATION.
----Can you standardize multinational
    marketing? - 1983.
    (000464)
----Harmonization of accounting standards. -
    1986.
    (002082)
----Standardisation of marketing strategy by
    multinationals. - 1987.
    (000506)

STANDARDIZED TERMS OF CONTRACT--ECUADOR.
----Risk-bearing and the choice of contract
    forms for oil exploration and
    development. - 1984.
        (002410)

STANDARDIZED TERMS OF CONTRACT--ISRAEL.
----Controlling standard contracts. - 1985.
        (002423)

STANDARDS.
----Accounting in developing countries. -
    1986.
        (002057)
----Comparative international auditing
    standards. - 1985.
        (002073)
----International accounting and reporting
    issues : 1984 review. - 1985.
        (002115)
----International accounting and reporting
    issues, 1986 review. - 1986.
        (002117)
----International accounting and
    transnational decisions. - 1983.
        (002086)
----International accounting standards. -
    1986.
        (002087)
----International standards of accounting
    and reporting. - 1984.
        (002119)
----The recent accounting and economic
    developments in the Middle East. - 1985.
        (002109)
----Statements of international accounting
    standards. - 1985-   .
        (002112)

STANDARDS--CANADA.
----Canadian standard industrial
    classification for companies and
    enterprises, 1980. - 1986-   .
        (002718)

STANDARDS--INDIA.
----Compendium of statements and standards.
    - 1986.
        (002074)

STANDARDS OF CONDUCT.
----Emerging standards of international
    trade and investment. - 1983.
        (001973)

STATE IMMUNITIES.
----Le CIRDI et l'immunité des états. - 1983.
        (002494)
----Drafting the international arbitration
    clause. - 1986.
        (002581)
----On Third World debt. - 1984.
        (000211)

STATE IMMUNITIES--UNITED STATES.
----The extraterritorial effects of
    antitrust laws. - 1984.
        (002342)
----Jurisdiction over foreign governments. -
    1986.
        (002347)
----Jurisdiction over foreign sovereigns. -
    1983.
        (002480)

----United States law of sovereign immunity
    relating to international financial
    transactions. - 1983.
        (002353)

STATE PROPERTY.
----Divisions over the international
    division of labour. - 1984.
        (001269)

STATE RESPONSIBILITY.
----State responsibility and bilateral
    investment treaties. - 1986.
        (002051)

STATE TRADING ENTERPRISES.
----Exploring the global economy : emerging
    issues in trade and investment. - 1985.
        (001306)
----International marketing planning and
    state trading organisations. - 1986.
        (000369)
----Seminar on Managing State Trading
    Organisations. - 1986.
        (000370)

STATE TRADING ENTERPRISES--CZECHOSLOVAKIA.
----K mereni zisku podniku. - 1987.
        (000888)

STATE TRADING ENTERPRISES--HUNGARY.
----Enterprise organization of East European
    socialist countries. - 1987.
        (000441)

STATE TRADING ENTERPRISES--POLAND.
----Enterprise organization of East European
    socialist countries. - 1987.
        (000441)
----L'entreprise polonaise. - 1987.
        (000305)

STATE TRADING ENTERPRISES--USSR.
----La réforme du commerce extérieur
    soviétique. - 1987.
        (002261)

STATE TRADING ENTERPRISES--YUGOSLAVIA.
----Enterprise organization of East European
    socialist countries. - 1987.
        (000441)

STATISTICAL DATA.
----Annual oil market report. - 1984-   .
        (000578)
----Arrangements between joint venture
    partners in developing countries. - 1987.
        (002450)
----Bilateral investment treaties. - 1988.
        (002054)
----The capital goods sector in developing
    countries. - 1985.
        (001651)
----Les cent premiers groupes
    agro-industriels mondiaux. - 1983.
        (000563)
----Changes in the international financial
    market and implications for
    transnational banks, transnational
    corporations and developing countries. -
    1986.
        (000976)

STATISTICAL DATA (continued)

----Compendium of selected studies on
international monetary and financial
issues for the developing countries. -
1987.
(001243)

----A competitive assessment of the U.S. oil
field equipment industry. - 1985.
(000764)

----A competitive assessment of the U.S.
pharmaceutical industry. - 1984.
(000757)

----Competitive position of U.S. producers
of robotics in domestic and world
markets. - 1983.
(000674)

----Corporate aid programs in twelve
less-developed countries. - 1983.
(002609)

----The debt crisis and the world economy. -
1984.
(000220)

----Les enjeux de la bauxite. - 1983.
(000585)

----Environmental aspects of the activities
of transnational corporations. - 1985.
(001954)

----Fertilizer supplies for developing
countries : issues in the transfer and
development of technology. - 1985.
(001471)

----Foreign direct investment in Latin
America. - 1986.
(000190)

----Foreign direct investment, the service
sector and international banking. - 1987.
(000972)

----Industry in the 1980s. - 1985.
(001341)

----International accounting and reporting
issues : 1984 review. - 1985.
(002115)

----Internationale Direktinvestitionen,
1950-1973. - 1975-   .
(000156)

----IRM directory of statistics of
international investment and production.
- 1987.
(000151) (002716)

----Japanese overseas investment. - 1983.
(000160)

----Latin America at a glance. - 1986.
(001821)

----Merger policies and recent trends in
mergers. - 1984.
(001611)

----New forms of international investment in
developing countries. - 1984.
(001615)

----New forms of overseas investment by
developing countries : the case of
India, Korea and Brazil. - 1986.
(001616)

----Les nouvelles formes d'investissement
international dans les pays en
développement. - 1984.
(000165)

----Proceedings of the SSTCC/UNCTC/ESCAP
Asia-Pacific Training Workshop on
Regulating and Negotiating Technology
Transfer through Transnational
Corporations, 14-25 October 1985,
Fuzhou, Fujian, China. - 1986.
(001405) (002169)

----Production and trade in services. - 1985.
(000978)

----Public enterprise in mixed economies. -
1984.
(001574)

----Reference book on major transnational
corporations operating in Namibia. -
1985.
(002674)

----Revitalizing development, growth and
international trade. - 1987.
(001394)

----Salient features and trends in foreign
direct investment. - 1983.
(000182)

----The semiconductor business. - 1985.
(000715)

----Structural adjustment and multinational
enterprises. - 1985.
(000095)

----Technical co-operation programme of the
United Nations Centre on Transnational
Corporations. - 1988.
(002610)

----Technical co-operation programme,
1976-1987 : United Nations Centre on
Transnational Corporations. - 1988.
(002611)

----Trade and foreign direct investment in
data services. - 1986.
(000948)

----Transborder data flows. - 1983.
(000973)

----Transborder data flows. - 1984.
(000974)

----Transnacionalización y periferia
semindustrializada. - 1983.
(001017)

----Transnational banks and the external
finance of Latin America : the
experience of Peru. - 1983.
(000840)

----Transnational corporations and
international trade : selected issues. -
1985.
(001393)

----Transnational corporations and non-fuel
primary commodities in developing
countries. - 1987.
(000639)

----Transnational corporations and services.
- 1984.
(000828)

----Transnational corporations and
technology transfer. - 1987.
(001509)

----Transnational corporations in the
man-made fibre, textile and clothing
industries. - 1987.
(000751)

----Transnational corporations in the
pharmaceutical industry of developing
countries. - 1984.
(000749)

----Transnational corporations in world
development. - 1983.
(000102)

----Trends and issues in foreign direct
investment and related flows. - 1985.
(000192)

STATISTICAL DATA (continued)
----TWARO (ITGLWF-ARO) Asian Seminar on Free
    Trade Zones, Tokyo, 6th-13th March 1983.
    - 1983.
       (002396)
----Who audits the world. - 1983.
       (002061)
----The world's largest industrial
    enterprises, 1962-1983. - 1985.
       (000298)

STATISTICAL DATA--AFRICA.
----The role of transnational banks and
    financial institutions in Africa's
    development process. - 1986.
       (000935)

STATISTICAL DATA--ARGENTINA.
----Las empresas transnacionales en la
    Argentina. - 1986.
       (001122)

STATISTICAL DATA--ASIA AND THE PACIFIC.
----Transnational corporations and external
    financial flows of developing economies
    in Asia and the Pacific. - 1986.
       (000196)

STATISTICAL DATA--AUSTRALIA.
----Australian direct investment in New
    Zealand. - 1983.
       (000109)
----Australian direct investment in the
    ASEAN countries. - 1983.
       (000110)
----Characteristics of major industries
    supplying tourist services in Australia.
    - 1983.
       (000824)

STATISTICAL DATA--BRAZIL.
----Brazilian imports of technology from
    Sweden, 1965-1980. - 1985.
       (001408)
----O sistema brasileiro de financiamento às
    exportaçoes. - 1985.
       (001349)

STATISTICAL DATA--BULGARIA.
----East-West joint ventures. - 1988.
       (001570)

STATISTICAL DATA--CANADA.
----Concentration and foreign control in
    retail and wholesale trade in Canada,
    1979. - 1983.
       (000783)

STATISTICAL DATA--CONGO.
----Le transfert de technologie dans les
    industries agro-alimentaires en Afrique
    Centrale. - 1987.
       (001510)

STATISTICAL DATA--CZECHOSLOVAKIA.
----East-West joint ventures. - 1988.
       (001570)

STATISTICAL DATA--EASTERN EUROPE.
----East-West joint ventures. - 1988.
       (001570)

STATISTICAL DATA--EGYPT.
----Egypt's experience in regulating
    technology imports. - 1987.
       (001514)

STATISTICAL DATA--GERMANY, FEDERAL REPUBLIC
OF.
----DM-Investitionen in Südafrika. - 1983.
       (001197)

STATISTICAL DATA--HUNGARY.
----East-West joint ventures. - 1988.
       (001570)

STATISTICAL DATA--INDIA.
----Technology transfer under alternative
    arrangements with transnational
    corporations. - 1987.
       (001513)

STATISTICAL DATA--INDONESIA.
----Technology transfer under alternative
    arrangements with transnational
    corporations. - 1987.
       (001513)

STATISTICAL DATA--IRELAND.
----Foreign investment in the Republic of
    Ireland. - 1987.
       (000129)

STATISTICAL DATA--KENYA.
----The role of transnational corporations
    in hotel and tourism industry in
    selected PTA member countries. - 1986.
       (000782) (000936)

STATISTICAL DATA--KUWAIT.
----Impact of the operations of
    transnational corporations on
    development in Kuwait. - 1987.
       (001143)

STATISTICAL DATA--LATIN AMERICA.
----Banco de datos sobre inversión
    extranjera directa en América Latina y
    el Caribe : información de los países
    receptores y de organismos regionales y
    subregionales, t. 2. - 1987.
       (000193)
----Banco de datos sobre inversión
    extranjera directa en América Latina y
    el Caribe, sobre la base de información
    de organismos multilaterales y de
    gobiernos de países de origen de la
    inversión, t. 1. - 1986.
       (000195)
----Las empresas transnacionales y la
    inversión extranjera directa en la
    primera mitad de los años ochenta. -
    1987.
       (000194)
----Measures strengthening the negotiating
    capacity of Governments in their
    relations with transnational
    corporations. - 1983.
       (002461)
----The role of the public sector and
    transnational corporations in the mining
    development of Latin America. - 1986.
       (000605)

STATISTICAL DATA--LIBERIA.
----The impact of the transnational
corporations in the banking and other
financial institutions on the economy of
Liberia. - 1986.
(000873)

STATISTICAL DATA--MALAYSIA.
----Technology transfer under alternative
arrangements with transnational
corporations. - 1987.
(001513)

STATISTICAL DATA--MAURITIUS.
----The role of transnational corporations
in hotel and tourism industry in
selected PTA member countries. - 1986.
(000782) (000936)

STATISTICAL DATA--MEXICO.
----Estructura y comportamiento de la
industria químico-farmacéutica en
México. - 1984.
(000737)

STATISTICAL DATA--MOROCCO.
----Expérience marocaine dans
l'établissement d'entreprises
multinationales. - 1986.
(001027)

STATISTICAL DATA--NAMIBIA.
----Mines and independence. - 1983.
(001204)

STATISTICAL DATA--NETHERLANDS.
----Statistiek van het ondernemingen- en
vestigingenbestand. - 1983-   .
(002666)
----Verdiende lonen van werknemers in
nijverheid en dienstensector ontleend
aan het halfjaarlijks loononderzoek. -
1985.
(001928)

STATISTICAL DATA--NEW ZEALAND.
----Australian direct investment in New
Zealand. - 1983.
(000109)

STATISTICAL DATA--OMAN.
----Impact of the operations of
transnational corporations on
development in the Sultanate of Oman. -
1988.
(001144)

STATISTICAL DATA--POLAND.
----East-West joint ventures. - 1988.
(001570)
----East-West technology transfer : study of
Poland, 1971-1980. - 1983.
(001432)

STATISTICAL DATA--REPUBLIC OF KOREA.
----Technology transfer under alternative
arrangements with transnational
corporations. - 1987.
(001513)

STATISTICAL DATA--ROMANIA.
----East-West joint ventures. - 1988.
(001570)

STATISTICAL DATA--SINGAPORE.
----Multinationals and the growth of the
Singapore economy. - 1986.
(001062)

STATISTICAL DATA--SOUTH AFRICA.
----DM-Investitionen in Südafrika. - 1983.
(001197)

STATISTICAL DATA--SOUTHEAST ASIA.
----Australian direct investment in the
ASEAN countries. - 1983.
(000110)
----Transnational corporations and the
electronics industries of ASEAN
economies. - 1987.
(000754)

STATISTICAL DATA--SWEDEN.
----Brazilian imports of technology from
Sweden, 1965-1980. - 1985.
(001408)

STATISTICAL DATA--THAILAND.
----Technology transfer under alternative
arrangements with transnational
corporations. - 1987.
(001513)

STATISTICAL DATA--TRINIDAD AND TOBAGO.
----The petroleum industry in Trinidad, West
Indies, 1857-1983. - 1985.
(000624)

STATISTICAL DATA--UNITED KINGDOM.
----Inward investment. - 1984.
(000116)
----Microelectronics in British industry. -
1984.
(000723)

STATISTICAL DATA--UNITED STATES.
----A competitive assessment of the U.S.
ball and roller bearings industry. -
1985.
(000760)
----A competitive assessment of the U.S.
flexible manufacturing systems industry.
- 1985.
(000763)
----A competitive assessment of the U.S.
herbicide industry. - 1985.
(000670)
----A competitive assessment of the U.S.
international construction industry. -
1984.
(000779)
----A competitive assessment of the U.S.
manufacturing automation equipment
industries. - 1984.
(000756)
----Direct investment in the United States
by foreign government-owned companies,
1974-81. - 1983.
(000124)
----East-West joint ventures. - 1988.
(001570)
----Foreign direct investment in the United
States. - 1985.
(000130)
----Foreign direct investment in the United
States. - 1985-   .
(000131)

STATISTICAL DATA--UNITED STATES (continued)
----Tax havens in the Caribbean Basin. -
    1984.
      (001762)
----Transnational corporations and
    international trade : selected issues. -
    1985.
      (001393)

STATISTICAL DATA--USSR.
----East-West joint ventures. - 1988.
      (001570)

STATISTICAL DATA--WESTERN ASIA.
----Trade in services : growth and balance
    of payments implications for countries
    of Western Asia. - 1987.
      (000968)

STATISTICAL DATA--WESTERN EUROPE.
----East-West joint ventures. - 1988.
      (001570)

STATISTICAL DATA--ZIMBABWE.
----The role of transnational corporations
    in hotel and tourism industry in
    selected PTA member countries. - 1986.
      (000782) (000936)

STATISTICS.
----Balance of payments statistics. - 1983.
      (000111)
----Historical statistics of foreign trade.
    Ser. A. - 1982-   .
      (001364)
----Minerals yearbook. - 1933-   .
      (000621)
----Monthly statistics of foreign trade.
    Ser. A. - 1983-   .
      (001373)
----Sovremennye transnatsional'nye
    korporatsii. - 1983.
      (000007)

STOCK COMPANIES--NEW YORK (N.Y.).
----Moody's industrial manual. - 1954-   .
      (002656)

STOCK COMPANIES--UNITED STATES.
----Moody's industrial manual. - 1954-   .
      (002656)

STOCK MARKETS.
----The GT guide to world equity markets. -
    1986-   .
      (002712)
----Recent developments in international
    banking and finance. - 1987-   .
      (000928)

STOCK MARKETS--INDONESIA.
----Foreign investment and government policy
    in the Third World. - 1988.
      (001790)

STOCK MARKETS--NEW YORK (N.Y.).
----Moody's industrial manual. - 1954-   .
      (002656)

STOCK MARKETS--UNITED STATES.
----Moody's industrial manual. - 1954-   .
      (002656)

STOCKHOLDERS--UNITED KINGDOM.
----Corporate acquisitions and mergers. -
    1985.
      (001544)

STOCKHOLDERS--WESTERN EUROPE.
----Corporate acquisitions and mergers. -
    1985.
      (001544)

STOCKS--INDONESIA.
----Foreign investment and government policy
    in the Third World. - 1988.
      (001790)

STRATEGY.
----Business strategy and the
    internationalization of business: recent
    approaches. - 1987.
      (000520)
----Cases in strategic management and
    business policy. - 1986.
      (000483)
----Diskontinuitatenmanagement. - 1984.
      (000490)
----Dispersion of risk through multinational
    teamwork. - 1987.
      (001558)
----Entry strategies for international
    markets. - 1987.
      (000509)
----A internacional capitalista. - 1986.
      (000473)
----International dimensions of business
    policy and strategy. - 1986.
      (000477)
----Joint ventures and global strategies. -
    1984.
      (001586)
----Strategic investments and the
    development of multinationals. - 1987.
      (000044)
----Strategic management in multinational
    companies. - 1986.
      (000472)
----Strategies for structuring joint
    ventures: a negotiations planning
    paradigm. - 1984.
      (001560)

STRATEGY--CHINA.
----China strategies. - 1986.
      (001037)
----Strategies for joint ventures in the
    People's Republic of China. - 1987.
      (001610)

STRATEGY--IRELAND.
----Multinational investment strategies in
    the British Isles. - 1983.
      (001151)

STRATEGY--MEXICO.
----Wandel der mexikanischen Politik
    gegenuber Auslandsinvestitionen? Die
    "irationale" Komponente der
    Mexikanisierungsstrategie. - 1985.
      (002338)

STRATEGY--UNITED KINGDOM.
----Multinational investment strategies in
    the British Isles. - 1983.
      (001151)

STRUCTURAL ADJUSTMENT.
----Industry in the 1980s. - 1985.
    (001341)
----International income taxation and
    developing countries. - 1988.
    (001759)
----Multinational firms and the theory of
    effective protection. - 1983.
    (001674)
----On new trends in internationalization: a
    synthesis toward a general model. - 1985.
    (000081)
----Revitalizing development, growth and
    international trade. - 1987.
    (001394)
----Structural adjustment and multinational
    enterprises. - 1985.
    (000095)

STRUCTURAL ADJUSTMENT--CENTRAL AMERICA.
----Industrialización y exportaciones no
    tradicionales. - 1984.
    (001316)

STRUCTURAL ADJUSTMENT--SOUTH AFRICA.
----U.S. firms and black labor in South
    Africa: creating a structure for change.
    - 1986.
    (001195)

STRUCTURAL ADJUSTMENT--SWITZERLAND.
----Global structural change and
    international competition among
    industrial firms: the case of
    Switzerland. - 1985.
    (000308)

STRUCTURAL ADJUSTMENT--UNITED KINGDOM.
----Multinational enterprises and industrial
    restructuring in the UK. - 1985.
    (001148)

STRUCTURAL ADJUSTMENT--UNITED STATES.
----The effects of foreign direct investment
    on U.S. employment during recession and
    structural change. - 1986.
    (001908)
----U.S. firms and black labor in South
    Africa: creating a structure for change.
    - 1986.
    (001195)

SUBSIDIARY BODIES--CANADA.
----Operating foreign subsidiaries. - 1983.
    (000388)

SUBSIDIARY BODIES--UNITED STATES.
----Operating foreign subsidiaries. - 1983.
    (000388)

SUBSIDIARY BODIES--WESTERN EUROPE.
----Operating foreign subsidiaries. - 1983.
    (000388)

SUBSIDIES--ZAIRE.
----Protection, distortions and investment
    incentives in Zaïre. - 1986.
    (002272)

SUBSTANTIAL NEW PROGRAMME OF ACTION FOR THE
1980S FOR THE LEAST DEVELOPED COUNTRIES
(1981).
----Revitalizing development, growth and
    international trade. - 1987.
    (001394)

SUDAN--FOREIGN DIRECT INVESTMENT.
----Chevron, Sudan and political risk. -
    1984.
    (001858)
----The legal regime of foreign private
    investment in the Sudan and Saudi
    Arabia. - 1984.
    (002204)

SUDAN--FOREIGN INVESTMENTS.
----National legislation and regulations
    relating to transnational corporations.
    Volume 4. - 1986.
    (002253)

SUDAN--LAWS AND REGULATIONS.
----National legislation and regulations
    relating to transnational corporations.
    Volume 4. - 1986.
    (002253)

SUDAN--POLITICAL CONDITIONS.
----Chevron, Sudan and political risk. -
    1984.
    (001858)

SUDAN--RISK ASSESSMENT.
----Chevron, Sudan and political risk. -
    1984.
    (001858)

SUDAN--TRANSNATIONAL CORPORATIONS.
----Chevron, Sudan and political risk. -
    1984.
    (001858)
----National legislation and regulations
    relating to transnational corporations.
    Volume 4. - 1986.
    (002253)

SUGAR INDUSTRY--BURKINA FASO.
----Une enclave industrielle : la Société
    sucrière de Haute-Volta. - 1984.
    (001032)

SUGAR INDUSTRY--CONGO.
----Le transfert de technologie dans les
    industries agro-alimentaires en Afrique
    Centrale. - 1987.
    (001510)

SUGAR INDUSTRY--CUBA.
----Microelectronics-based automation
    technologies and development. - 1985.
    (000753)

SUGAR TRADE INDUSTRY--UNITED KINGDOM.
----Tate and Lyle, geant du sucre. - 1983.
    (000274)

SUPPLY AND DEMAND.
----Fertilizer supplies for developing
    countries : issues in the transfer and
    development of technology. - 1985.
    (001471)

SUPPLY AND DEMAND--GERMANY, FEDERAL REPUBLIC
OF.
----Stärken und Schwächen der Bundesrepublik
   Deutschland in der internationalen
   Arbeitsteilung. - 1984.
   (001260)

SUPPLY AND DEMAND--GHANA.
----The price and availability of energy for
   an aluminium smelter : recent
   renegotiations in Ghana. - 1987.
   (002467)

SUPPORT COSTS.
----Multinationals, transaction costs and
   choice of institutional form. - 1986.
   (000078)

SURINAME--ALUMINIUM INDUSTRY.
----The American take-over. - 1983.
   (000287)

SURINAME--INDUSTRIAL DEVELOPMENT.
----The American take-over. - 1983.
   (000287)

SWEDEN--AFFILIATE CORPORATIONS.
----Underskott vid joint venture- och annan
   verksamhet i utlandet, m.m. - 1985.
   (001760)

SWEDEN--ARBITRAL AWARDS.
----Das anzuwendende Recht beim
   internationalen Schiedsverfahren in
   Schweden. - 1986.
   (002515)

SWEDEN--AUTOMATION.
----Microelectronics-based automation
   technologies and development. - 1985.
   (000753)

SWEDEN--BIG BUSINESS.
----De Svenska storforetagen. - 1985.
   (000324)

SWEDEN--BUSINESS ENTERPRISES.
----Sveriges största företag. - 1968-   .
   (002667)

SWEDEN--COMPARATIVE ANALYSIS.
----Multinational enterprise and world
   competition. - 1987.
   (000018)

SWEDEN--CORPORATIONS.
----Sveriges största företag. - 1968-   .
   (002667)

SWEDEN--DEVELOPMENT ASSISTANCE.
----Infratechnologies, technologies de
   pointe, investissements dans et pour les
   pays en développement. - 1985.
   (001444)

SWEDEN--DIRECTORIES.
----Sveriges största företag. - 1968-   .
   (002667)

SWEDEN--DOUBLE TAXATION.
----Underskott vid joint venture- och annan
   verksamhet i utlandet, m.m. - 1985.
   (001760)

SWEDEN--ECONOMIC CONDITIONS.
----De Svenska storforetagen. - 1985.
   (000324)

SWEDEN--ECONOMIC RESEARCH.
----Multinationella fortag. - 1985.
   (000030)

SWEDEN--FOOD INDUSTRY.
----De Transnationella foretagens roll i
   varldshandeln ; Gransskydd i andra
   lander. - 1984.
   (000685)

SWEDEN--FOREIGN DIRECT INVESTMENT.
----Sysselsattningsstrukturen i
   internationella foretag. - 1983.
   (001165)

SWEDEN--FOREIGN RELATIONS.
----Brazilian imports of technology from
   Sweden, 1965-1980. - 1985.
   (001408)

SWEDEN--INDUSTRIAL ENTERPRISES.
----Licensing industrial technology to
   developing countries : the operations of
   Swedish firms in India. - 1986.
   (002442)

SWEDEN--INDUSTRIAL TECHNOLOGY.
----Licensing industrial technology to
   developing countries : the operations of
   Swedish firms in India. - 1986.
   (002442)

SWEDEN--INDUSTRY.
----Sveriges största företag. - 1968-   .
   (002667)
----Sysselsattningsstrukturen i
   internationella foretag. - 1983.
   (001165)

SWEDEN--INTERNATIONAL COMMERCIAL ARBITRATION.
----Das anzuwendende Recht beim
   internationalen Schiedsverfahren in
   Schweden. - 1986.
   (002515)

SWEDEN--INTERNATIONAL COMPETITION.
----Multinational enterprise and world
   competition. - 1987.
   (000018)

SWEDEN--JOINT VENTURES.
----Underskott vid joint venture- och annan
   verksamhet i utlandet, m.m. - 1985.
   (001760)

SWEDEN--LABOUR SUPPLY.
----Sysselsattningsstrukturen i
   internationella foretag. - 1983.
   (001165)

SWEDEN--LICENCE AGREEMENTS.
----Licensing industrial technology to
   developing countries : the operations of
   Swedish firms in India. - 1986.
   (002442)

SWEDEN--PRIVATE INTERNATIONAL LAW.
----Das anzuwendende Recht beim
    internationalen Schiedsverfahren in
    Schweden. - 1986.
       (002515)

SWEDEN--STATISTICAL DATA.
----Brazilian imports of technology from
    Sweden, 1965-1980. - 1985.
       (001408)

SWEDEN--TAXATION.
----Underskott vid joint venture- och annan
    verksamhet i utlandet, m.m. - 1985.
       (001760)
----Utlandsagda dotterbolag i Sverige. -
    1984.
       (001728)

SWEDEN--TECHNOLOGY TRANSFER.
----Brazilian imports of technology from
    Sweden, 1965-1980. - 1985.
       (001408)

SWEDEN--TRANSNATIONAL CORPORATIONS.
----Multinational enterprise and world
    competition. - 1987.
       (000018)
----Multinationals. - 1986.
       (000335)
----Multinationella fortag. - 1985.
       (000030)
----De Svenska storforetagen. - 1985.
       (000324)
----Sverige i imperialismens nat. - 1986.
       (001150)
----Sysselsattningsstrukturen i
    internationella foretag. - 1983.
       (001165)
----De Transnationella foretagens roll i
    varldshandeln ; Gransskydd i andra
    lander. - 1984.
       (000685)
----Utlandsagda dotterbolag i Sverige. -
    1984.
       (001728)

SWITZERLAND--CONFISCATIONS.
----Les nationalisations françaises face à
    l'ordre juridique suisse. - 1984.
       (002325)

SWITZERLAND--DEVELOPING COUNTRIES.
----Halbgotter, Giftkriege und Kondensmilch.
    - 1983.
       (000658)

SWITZERLAND--FOOD INDUSTRY.
----L'émpire Nestle. - 1983.
       (000283)
----Halbgotter, Giftkriege und Kondensmilch.
    - 1983.
       (000658)

SWITZERLAND--INTERNATIONAL COMPETITION.
----Global structural change and
    international competition among
    industrial firms: the case of
    Switzerland. - 1985.
       (000308)

SWITZERLAND--MANAGEMENT.
----Das Bally-Lehrstuck. - 1985.
       (000286)

SWITZERLAND--NATIONALIZATION.
----Les nationalisations françaises face à
    l'ordre juridique suisse. - 1984.
       (002325)

SWITZERLAND--PERSONNEL MANAGEMENT.
----Personalpolitik fur multinationale
    Unternehmen. - 1985.
       (000417) (001903)

SWITZERLAND--PHARMACEUTICAL INDUSTRY.
----Médicaments pour tous en l'an 2000? -
    1983.
       (000662)

SWITZERLAND--PHARMACEUTICALS.
----Médicaments pour tous en l'an 2000? -
    1983.
       (000662)

SWITZERLAND--RECOGNITION (INTERNATIONAL LAW).
----Les nationalisations françaises face à
    l'ordre juridique suisse. - 1984.
       (002325)

SWITZERLAND--SHOE INDUSTRY.
----Das Bally-Lehrstuck. - 1985.
       (000286)

SWITZERLAND--STRUCTURAL ADJUSTMENT.
----Global structural change and
    international competition among
    industrial firms: the case of
    Switzerland. - 1985.
       (000308)

SWITZERLAND--TAX AVOIDANCE.
----Konzernstruktur und Steuerplanung. -
    1984.
       (001758)

SWITZERLAND--TAXATION.
----Konzernstruktur und Steuerplanung. -
    1984.
       (001758)

SWITZERLAND--TRANSNATIONAL CORPORATIONS.
----Das Bally-Lehrstuck. - 1985.
       (000286)
----L'émpire Nestle. - 1983.
       (000283)
----Global structural change and
    international competition among
    industrial firms: the case of
    Switzerland. - 1985.
       (000308)
----Halbgotter, Giftkriege und Kondensmilch.
    - 1983.
       (000658)
----Konzernstruktur und Steuerplanung. -
    1984.
       (001758)
----Médicaments pour tous en l'an 2000? -
    1983.
       (000662)
----Personalpolitik fur multinationale
    Unternehmen. - 1985.
       (000417) (001903)

SYNTHETIC DETERGENTS.
----A global comeback. - 1987.
       (000275)

SYNTHETIC FIBRES.
----Transnational corporations in the
man-made fibre, textile and clothing
industries. - 1987.
(000751)

SYNTHETIC FIBRES--UNITED STATES.
----A competitive assessment of selected
reinforced composite fibers. - 1985.
(000644)

SYNTHETIC FUELS.
----Worldwide synthetic fuels and alternate
energy directory. - 1981-   .
(002677)

TAIWAN (CHINA)--BIG BUSINESS.
----Networks of Taiwanese big business. -
1986.
(001063)

TAIWAN (CHINA)--BUSINESS ENTERPRISES.
----Networks of Taiwanese big business. -
1986.
(001063)

TAIWAN (CHINA)--COMMERCIAL LAW.
----The joint venture and related contract
laws of mainland China and Taiwan. -
1987.
(002278)

TAIWAN (CHINA)--CORPORATE PLANNING.
----Networks of Taiwanese big business. -
1986.
(001063)

TAIWAN (CHINA)--ELECTRONICS INDUSTRY.
----The production characteristics of
multinational firms and the effects of
tax incentives: the case of Taiwan's
electronics industry. - 1986.
(001038) (002305)
----L'industrie électronique à Taiwan. -
1987.
(000668)

TAIWAN (CHINA)--FOREIGN DIRECT INVESTMENT.
----Taiwan's foreign direct investment. -
1986.
(000121)

TAIWAN (CHINA)--INDUSTRIALIZATION.
----Exports of technology by newly
industrializing countries: Taiwan. -
1984.
(001402)

TAIWAN (CHINA)--INVESTMENTS.
----Taiwan's foreign direct investment. -
1986.
(000121)

TAIWAN (CHINA)--JOINT VENTURES.
----The joint venture and related contract
laws of mainland China and Taiwan. -
1987.
(002278)

TAIWAN (CHINA)--PRODUCTIVITY.
----The production characteristics of
multinational firms and the effects of
tax incentives: the case of Taiwan's
electronics industry. - 1986.
(001038) (002305)

TAIWAN (CHINA)--TAX INCENTIVES.
----The production characteristics of
multinational firms and the effects of
tax incentives: the case of Taiwan's
electronics industry. - 1986.
(001038) (002305)

TAIWAN (CHINA)--TECHNOLOGY TRANSFER.
----Exports of technology by newly
industrializing countries: Taiwan. -
1984.
(001402)

TAIWAN (CHINA)--TRANSNATIONAL CORPORATIONS.
----The production characteristics of
multinational firms and the effects of
tax incentives: the case of Taiwan's
electronics industry. - 1986.
(001038) (002305)

TAIWAN(CHINA)--UNITED STATES.
----American and Chinese managers in U.S.
companies in Taiwan: a comparison. -
1985.
(000395)

TANKER SAFETY.
----Acronyms and compensation for oil
pollution damage from tankers. - 1983.
(001937)

TARIFF PREFERENCES--WESTERN EUROPE.
----European Community tariff preferences
and foreign direct investment. - 1987.
(002159)

TARIFFS.
----Foreign direct investment with
unemployment and endogenous taxes and
tariffs. - 1987.
(000559)
----Profits, tariffs, and intra-industry
trade. - 1985.
(001347)

TARIFFS--WESTERN EUROPE.
----La réglementation communautaire des
transports. - 1984.
(001994)

TATE & LYLE, LTD.
----Tate and Lyle, géant du sucre. - 1983.
(000274)

TAX ADMINISTRATION.
----International co-operation in tax
matters : guidelines for international
co-operation against the evasion and
avoidance of taxes (with special
reference to taxes on income, profits,
capital and capital gains). - 1984.
(001724)

TAX AUDITING--INDIA.
----India: measures against tax avoidance by
multinationals. - 1986.
(001716)

TAX AVOIDANCE.
----La fiscalité internationale des
    entreprises. - 1985.
      (001743)
----International co-operation in tax
    matters : guidelines for international
    co-operation against the evasion and
    avoidance of taxes (with special
    reference to taxes on income, profits,
    capital and capital gains). - 1984.
      (001724)
----International income taxation and
    developing countries. - 1988.
      (001759)
----A reference guide to international
    taxation. - 1987.
      (001714)
----Tax havens and their uses. - 1985.
      (001707)
----Tax holidays as signals. - 1986.
      (002303)

TAX AVOIDANCE--GERMANY, FEDERAL REPUBLIC OF.
----Steuerplanung internationaler
    Unternehmungen. - 1986.
      (001733)

TAX AVOIDANCE--INDIA.
----India: measures against tax avoidance by
    multinationals. - 1986.
      (001716)

TAX AVOIDANCE--JAPAN.
----International tax evasion and avoidance
    in Japan. - 1984.
      (001726)

TAX AVOIDANCE--SWITZERLAND.
----Konzernstruktur und Steuerplanung. -
    1984.
      (001758)

TAX AVOIDANCE--UNITED STATES.
----Tax evasion through the Netherlands
    Antilles and other tax haven countries.
    - 1983.
      (001761)
----Tax havens in the Caribbean Basin. -
    1984.
      (001762)
----Tax planning for foreign investors in
    the United States. - 1983.
      (001773)
----The use of international finance
    subsidiaries in the Netherlands
    Antilles. - 1983.
      (000871)

TAX EVASION.
----Foreign direct investment with
    unemployment and endogenous taxes and
    tariffs. - 1987.
      (000559)
----International co-operation in tax
    matters : guidelines for international
    co-operation against the evasion and
    avoidance of taxes (with special
    reference to taxes on income, profits,
    capital and capital gains). - 1984.
      (001724)
----International income taxation and
    developing countries. - 1988.
      (001759)

TAX EVASION--FRANCE.
----Fraude fiscale internationale et
    repression. - 1986.
      (001742)

TAX EVASION--GERMANY, FEDERAL REPUBLIC OF.
----Steuerhinterziehung im internationalen
    Wirtschaftsverkehr. - 1984.
      (001706)

TAX EVASION--JAPAN.
----International tax evasion and avoidance
    in Japan. - 1984.
      (001726)

TAX EVASION--UNITED STATES.
----Exchange of information under the OECD
    and US model tax treaties. - 1983.
      (002042)
----Tax evasion through the Netherlands
    Antilles and other tax haven countries.
    - 1983.
      (001761)
----Tax havens in the Caribbean Basin. -
    1984.
      (001762)

TAX HAVENS.
----International co-operation in tax
    matters : guidelines for international
    co-operation against the evasion and
    avoidance of taxes (with special
    reference to taxes on income, profits,
    capital and capital gains). - 1984.
      (001724)
----International income taxation and
    developing countries. - 1988.
      (001759)
----A reference guide to international
    taxation. - 1987.
      (001714)
----Tax havens and offshore finance. - 1983.
      (001729)
----Tax havens and their uses. - 1985.
      (001707)
----Tax holidays as signals. - 1986.
      (002303)

TAX HAVENS--CARIBBEAN REGION.
----Tax havens in the Caribbean Basin. -
    1984.
      (001762)

TAX HAVENS--NETHERLANDS ANTILLES.
----The American-Dutch tax series. -
    1983-   .
      (002028)
----Tax evasion through the Netherlands
    Antilles and other tax haven countries.
    - 1983.
      (001761)
----The use of international finance
    subsidiaries in the Netherlands
    Antilles. - 1983.
      (000871)

TAX HAVENS--REPUBLIC OF KOREA.
----About the establishment of an offshore
    financial center in Seoul. - 1986.
      (000827)

TAX INCENTIVES.
----Investment incentives as tariff
    substitutes: a comprehensive measure of
    protection. - 1985.
        (002302)

TAX INCENTIVES--AUSTRALIA.
----The effectiveness of investment
    incentives. - 1985.
        (002304)

TAX INCENTIVES--CANADA.
----International income taxation and
    developing countries. - 1988.
        (001759)

TAX INCENTIVES--FRANCE.
----International income taxation and
    developing countries. - 1988.
        (001759)

TAX INCENTIVES--GERMANY, FEDERAL REPUBLIC OF.
----International income taxation and
    developing countries. - 1988.
        (001759)

TAX INCENTIVES--JAPAN.
----International income taxation and
    developing countries. - 1988.
        (001759)
----The nature and tools of Japan's
    industrial policy. - 1986.
        (000557)

TAX INCENTIVES--MEXICO.
----Alliance for production. - 1984.
        (002316)

TAX INCENTIVES--SOUTHEAST ASIA.
----Subsidy to capital through tax
    incentives in the ASEAN countries. -
    1983.
        (002300)

TAX INCENTIVES--TAIWAN (CHINA).
----The production characteristics of
    multinational firms and the effects of
    tax incentives: the case of Taiwan's
    electronics industry. - 1986.
        (001038) (002305)

TAX INCENTIVES--UNITED KINGDOM.
----International income taxation and
    developing countries. - 1988.
        (001759)

TAX INCENTIVES--UNITED STATES.
----International income taxation and
    developing countries. - 1988.
        (001759)

TAX LAW.
----Cross-border transactions between
    related companies. - 1985.
        (001735)
----La fiscalité internationale des
    entreprises. - 1985.
        (001743)
----GATT versus tax treaties? - 1987.
        (002032)
----A reference guide to international
    taxation. - 1987.
        (001714)

----The taxation of controlled foreign
    corporations. - 1986.
        (001699)

TAX LAW--BRAZIL.
----Investimentos estrangeiros no Brasil. -
    1985.
        (000177)

TAX LAW--CHINA.
----China's trade, tax and investment laws
    and regulations. - 1984.
        (002189)
----A comparative analysis of the United
    States-People's Republic of China tax
    treaty. - 1986.
        (002037)
----Revenue law and practice in the People's
    Republic of China. - 1983.
        (002271)
----Taxation of foreign business and
    investment in the People's Republic of
    China. - 1987.
        (001708)

TAX LAW--GERMANY, FEDERAL REPUBLIC OF.
----Internationale Unternehmensbesteuerung.
    - 1983.
        (001727)

TAX LAW--HONG KONG.
----A survey of banking laws and policies in
    Hong Kong and Singapore. - 1986.
        (001829)

TAX LAW--SINGAPORE.
----A survey of banking laws and policies in
    Hong Kong and Singapore. - 1986.
        (001829)

TAX LAW--UNITED STATES.
----A comparative analysis of the United
    States-People's Republic of China tax
    treaty. - 1986.
        (002037)
----Exchange of information under the OECD
    and US model tax treaties. - 1983.
        (002042)
----Foreign investment in the United States
    after the Tax Reform Act of 1986. - 1987.
        (002232)
----Fundamentals of international taxation.
    - 1985.
        (001700)
----International business planning. - 1983.
        (002279)
----Tax policy and foreign direct investment
    in the United States. - 1984.
        (001722)
----The use of international finance
    subsidiaries in the Netherlands
    Antilles. - 1983.
        (000871)

TAX REFORM ACT 1986 (UNITED STATES).
----Foreign investment in the United States
    after the Tax Reform Act of 1986. - 1987.
        (002232)
----Investment in the United States by
    foreign government: effects of the Tax
    Reform Act of 1986. - 1987.
        (002231)

TAX RESEARCH.
----The international accounting and tax
    researches' publication guide. - 1982.
    (002066)

TAX RETURNS.
----Transnational corporations and non-fuel
    primary commodities in developing
    countries. - 1987.
    (000639)

TAX REVENUES.
----International comparisons of tax levels.
    - 1987.
    (001739)

TAX REVENUES--CANADA.
----Transfer pricing issues: a critical
    discussion of the Revenue Draft
    Information Circular. - 1984.
    (001702)

TAX REVENUES--KUWAIT.
----Impact of the operations of
    transnational corporations on
    development in Kuwait. - 1987.
    (001143)

TAX SYSTEMS.
----International tax and business service.
    - 1984-   .
    (001725)

TAX SYSTEMS--CANADA.
----The corporate income tax system. - 1985.
    (001767)

TAX SYSTEMS--CHINA.
----Tax aspects of doing business with the
    People's Republic of China. - 1984.
    (001713)

TAX SYSTEMS--FRANCE.
----Les tendances récentes des conventions
    fiscales. - 1985.
    (002053)

TAX SYSTEMS--UNITED STATES.
----Les tendances récentes des conventions
    fiscales. - 1985.
    (002053)

TAX TREATIES.
----International bank lending. - 1984.
    (000988)
----International co-operation in tax
    matters : guidelines for international
    co-operation against the evasion and
    avoidance of taxes (with special
    reference to taxes on income, profits,
    capital and capital gains). - 1984.
    (001724)
----International income taxation and
    developing countries. - 1988.
    (001759)
----International tax developments. - 1983.
    (002036)

TAX TREATIES--CANADA.
----Advising nonresidents on taking care of
    Canadian business. - 1986.
    (001789)

TAX TREATIES--CHINA.
----A comparative analysis of the United
    States-People's Republic of China tax
    treaty. - 1986.
    (002037)
----Taxation of foreign business and
    investment in the People's Republic of
    China. - 1987.
    (001708)

TAX TREATIES--FRANCE.
----Les tendances récentes des conventions
    fiscales. - 1985.
    (002053)

TAX TREATIES--NETHERLANDS.
----The American-Dutch tax series. -
    1983-   .
    (002028)

TAX TREATIES--UNITED STATES.
----The American-Dutch tax series. -
    1983-   .
    (002028)
----A comparative analysis of the United
    States-People's Republic of China tax
    treaty. - 1986.
    (002037)
----Exchange of information under the OECD
    and US model tax treaties. - 1983.
    (002042)
----The Soviet Union's other tax agreements.
    - 1986.
    (002043)
----Tax treaty abuse. - 1983.
    (002046)
----Les tendances récentes des conventions
    fiscales. - 1985.
    (002053)

TAX TREATIES--USSR.
----The Soviet Union's other tax agreements.
    - 1986.
    (002043)

TAXATION.
----Comparative advantage and trade in
    service. - 1984.
    (000870)
----Cross-border leasing. - 1983.
    (000836) (001705)
----Cross-border transactions between
    related companies. - 1985.
    (001735)
----The drilling gap in non-OPEC developing
    countries: the role of contractual and
    fiscal arrangements. - 1985.
    (002413)
----Die Einwirkung internationaler
    Organisationen auf das Steuerrecht. -
    1984.
    (001990)
----Establishing overseas operations: tax
    and treasury considerations. - 1987.
    (001768)
----La fiscalité internationale des
    entreprises. - 1985.
    (001743)
----Foreign oil and taxation. - 1983.
    (002039)
----GATT versus tax treaties? - 1987.
    (002032)

Subject Index - Index des matières

TAXATION (continued)
----International comparisons of tax levels.
- 1987.
(001739)
----International co-operation in tax
matters : guidelines for international
co-operation against the evasion and
avoidance of taxes (with special
reference to taxes on income, profits,
capital and capital gains). - 1984.
(001724)
----International income taxation and
developing countries. - 1988.
(001759)
----International tax and business service.
- 1984-   .
(001725)
----International tax developments. - 1983.
(002036)
----Investment in the United States by
foreign government: effects of the Tax
Reform Act of 1986. - 1987.
(002231)
----Limits and problems of taxation. - 1984.
(001736)
----Making the multinational decision. -
1983.
(000542)
----Multinational corporations. - 1986.
(000058)
----Multinationals are mushrooming. - 1986.
(001861)
----Oil [and] gas : law and taxation review.
- 1983-   .
(002259)
----Prix de transfert et entreprises
multinationales. - 1984.
(002099)
----Le régime fiscal des sociétés étrangeres
en droit comparé. - 1985.
(001752)
----The relationship between taxation and
.   financial reporting. - 1987.
(002103)
----Sovereignty and natural resource
taxation in developing countries. - 1987.
(001741)
----Die Steuerung auslandischer
Tochtergesellschaften. - 1985.
(001731)
----Tax aspects of acquisitions and mergers.
- 1983.
(001645) (001756)
----Tax treatment of cost-contribution
arrangements. - 1988.
(001737)
----Taxation of foreign income - principles
and practice. - 1985.
(001764)
----Taxation of intercorporate transfer
pricing: a management responsibility:
U.S.A. - 1986.
(001754)
----Taxation of international tourism in
developing countries. - 1986.
(000900)
----Le traitement national des entreprises
sous contrôle étranger établies dans les
pays de l'OCDE. - 1978.
(002000)
----Transfer pricing and multinational
enterprises. - 1984.
(001745)

----Transfer pricing provisions, rulings and
case law: Thailand. - 1986.
(001723)
----Transnational corporations in world
development. - 1983.
(000102)
----Unitary taxation and general
international law. - 1987.
(002044)
----World business reports. - 1982-   .
(001863)

TAXATION--AUSTRALIA.
----New Zealand business. - 1985.
(000352)

TAXATION--CANADA.
----Advising nonresidents on taking care of
Canadian business. - 1986.
(001789)
----Draft guidelines on international
transfer pricing: Canada. - 1986.
(001734)
----International income taxation and
developing countries. - 1988.
(001759)
----Multinational Oil Limited: issues in
transfer pricing and foreign ownership.
- 1985.
(001750)
----Taxation in Canada. - 1985.
(001701)
----The taxation of controlled foreign
corporations. - 1986.
(001699)
----Taxation of income of foreign
affiliates. - 1983.
(001765)

TAXATION--CHINA.
----Foreign direct investment in the
People's Republic of China. - 1988.
(000191)
----Like bamboo shoots after a rain :
exploiting the Chinese law and new
regulations on Sino-foreign joint
ventures. - 1987.
(002298)
----The People's Republic of China. - 1986.
(001841)

TAXATION--FRANCE.
----Fraude fiscale internationale et
repression. - 1986.
(001742)
----International income taxation and
developing countries. - 1988.
(001759)

TAXATION--GERMANY, FEDERAL REPUBLIC OF.
----Die finanzielle Führung und Kontrolle
von Auslandsgesellschaften. - 1983.
(000447)
----Gewinne verbundener Unternehmen,
Verrechnungspreise. - 1984.
(001749)
----International income taxation and
developing countries. - 1988.
(001759)
----Konzerntransferpreise im internationalen
Steuerrecht. - 1986.
(001710)

TAXATION--GERMANY, FEDERAL REPUBLIC OF
(continued)
----Probleme der Gewinn- und
    Verlustrealisierung. - 1986.
    (001703)
----Steuerhinterziehung im internationalen
    Wirtschaftsverkehr. - 1984.
    (001706)
----Steuerplanung internationaler
    Unternehmungen. - 1986.
    (001733)

TAXATION--INDIA.
----Taxation of foreign companies. - 1984.
    (001717)

TAXATION--JAPAN.
----International income taxation and
    developing countries. - 1988.
    (001759)

TAXATION--NETHERLANDS.
----The American-Dutch tax series. -
    1983-   .
    (002028)

TAXATION--NEW ZEALAND.
----New Zealand business. - 1985.
    (000352)

TAXATION--SWEDEN.
----Underskott vid joint venture- och annan
    verksamhet i utlandet, m.m. - 1985.
    (001760)
----Utlandsagda dotterbolag i Sverige. -
    1984.
    (001728)

TAXATION--SWITZERLAND.
----Konzernstruktur und Steuerplanung. -
    1984.
    (001758)

TAXATION--UNITED KINGDOM.
----Allied Dunbar tax guide. - 1985-   .
    (002027)
----International income taxation and
    developing countries. - 1988.
    (001759)

TAXATION--UNITED STATES.
----The American-Dutch tax series. -
    1983-   .
    (002028)
----Federal taxation of international
    transactions. - 1988.
    (001730)
----The final report of the Worldwide
    Unitary Taxation Working Group :
    Chairman's report and supplemental
    views. - 1984.
    (001763)
----Foreign investment in the United States
    after the Tax Reform Act of 1986. - 1987.
    (002232)
----Fundamentals of international taxation.
    - 1985.
    (001700)
----International income taxation and
    developing countries. - 1988.
    (001759)
----Joint ventures. - 1987.
    (001613)

----Tax aspects of international
    transactions. - 1984.
    (001757)
----Tax planning for foreign investors in
    the United States. - 1983.
    (001773)
----Tax policy and foreign direct
    investment. - 1985.
    (001721)
----Worldwide unitary tax. - 1986.
    (001718)

TAXATION--ZIMBABWE.
----Investment by foreign companies:
    Zimbabwe. - 1987.
    (001740)

TECHNICAL CO-OPERATION.
----Analysis of engineering and technical
    assistance consultancy contracts. - 1986.
    (002449)
----Enjeux technologiques et relations
    internationales. - 1986.
    (001429)
----Measures to strengthen the capabilities
    of developing countries in their dealing
    with transnational corporations. - 1985.
    (002612)
----Recent developments in operations and
    behaviour of transnational corporations.
    - 1987.
    (000103)
----Technical co-operation programme of the
    United Nations Centre on Transnational
    Corporations. - 1988.
    (002610)
----Technical co-operation programme,
    1976-1987 : United Nations Centre on
    Transnational Corporations. - 1988.
    (002611)
----UNCTC bibliography, 1974-1987. - 1988.
    (002695)

TECHNICAL CO-OPERATION--CONGO.
----Le transfert de technologie dans les
    industries agro-alimentaires en Afrique
    Centrale. - 1987.
    (001510)

TECHNICAL CO-OPERATION--EASTERN EUROPE.
----Technological cooperation and
    specialization. - 1986.
    (001500)

TECHNICAL CO-OPERATION--GERMANY, FEDERAL
REPUBLIC OF.
----Transfert de technologie. - 1983.
    (001460)

TECHNICAL CO-OPERATION--GUYANA.
----Commercialization of technology and
    dependence in the Caribbean. - 1985.
    (001477)

TECHNICAL CO-OPERATION--INDIA.
----Technology transfer under alternative
    arrangements with transnational
    corporations. - 1987.
    (001513)

Subject Index - Index des matières

TECHNICAL CO-OPERATION--JAMAICA.
----Commercialization of technology and
     dependence in the Caribbean. - 1985.
     (001477)

TECHNICAL CO-OPERATION--JAPAN.
----Technology transfer through direct
     foreign investment. - 1985.
     (001490)

TECHNICAL CO-OPERATION--SOUTH AFRICA.
----Activities of transnational corporations
     in South Africa and Namibia and the
     responsibilities of home countries with
     respect to their operations in this
     area. - 1986.
     (001192)

TECHNICAL CO-OPERATION--TRINIDAD AND TOBAGO.
----Commercialization of technology and
     dependence in the Caribbean. - 1985.
     (001477)

TECHNICAL CO-OPERATION AMONG DEVELOPING
COUNTRIES.
----A strategy for the technological
     transformation of developing countries.
     - 1985.
     (001515)

TECHNICAL TRAINING.
----Analysis of engineering and technical
     assistance consultancy contracts. - 1986.
     (002449)
----International accounting and reporting
     issues, 1985 review. - 1985.
     (002116)
----Transborder data flows. - 1983.
     (000973)

TECHNICAL TRAINING--CHINA.
----The training component. - 1986.
     (001920)

TECHNOLOGICAL CHANGE.
----Corporation, technological gaps and
     growth in OECD countries. - 1987.
     (001438)
----Industrial change in advanced economies.
     - 1987.
     (001317)
----International dynamics of technology. -
     1983.
     (001488)
----Microelectronics-based automation
     technologies and development. - 1985.
     (000753)
----The political economy of international
     technology transfer. - 1987.
     (001482)
----A strategy for the technological
     transformation of developing countries.
     - 1985.
     (001515)
----Technical advance and trade advantage. -
     1983.
     (001497)
----Technological change. - 1985.
     (001499)
----Transnational corporations in the
     man-made fibre, textile and clothing
     industries. - 1987.
     (000751)

TECHNOLOGICAL CHANGE--ARGENTINA.
----Telecomunicaciones. - 1987.
     (000792)

TECHNOLOGICAL CHANGE--UNITED KINGDOM.
----A comparison of embodied technical
     change in services and manufacturing
     industry. - 1986.
     (000806)

TECHNOLOGICAL INNOVATIONS.
----Changes in the international financial
     market and implications for
     transnational banks, transnational
     corporations and developing countries. -
     1986.
     (000976)
----A decision theoretic model of
     innovation, technology transfer, and
     trade. - 1987.
     (001446)
----Formy transferu technologie
     mezinarodnimi monopoly a technologicka
     transformace rozvojovych zemi. - 1985.
     (001457)
----The global race in microelectronics. -
     1983.
     (000684)
----Industrial change in advanced economies.
     - 1987.
     (001317)
----L'informatique dans les pays en
     développement. - 1984.
     (000839)
----Innovation and market structure. - 1987.
     (000681)
----Innovation und internationale Monopole.
     - 1983.
     (001671)
----International business and technological
     innovation. - 1983.
     (001486)
----Lehetosegek es kenyszerpalyak a szellemi
     termekek letrehozasaban es nemzetkozi
     kereskedelmeben. - 1984.
     (001465)
----New technologies and Third World
     development. - 1986.
     (001475)
----The pharmaceutical industry. - 1985.
     (000726)
----Strategic behaviour and industrial
     competition. - 1986.
     (000512)
----Technical advance and trade advantage. -
     1983.
     (001497)
----Technology : management and acquisition.
     - 1984-
     (001501)
----Technology and international relations.
     - 1987.
     (001504)
----Technology, marketing and
     industrialisation. - 1983.
     (001506)
----Towards a theory of innovation in
     services. - 1986.
     (000808)
----Trade and dynamic efficiency. - 1987.
     (001698)

-358-

TECHNOLOGICAL INNOVATIONS (continued)
----Wettlauf um die Zukunft :
    Technologiepolitik im internationalen
    Vergleich. - 1987.
        (001453)
----The world of appropriate technology. -
    1983.
        (001447)

TECHNOLOGICAL INNOVATIONS--ARGENTINA.
----Internacionalización de empresas y
    tecnología de origen argentino. - 1985.
        (000301)

TECHNOLOGICAL INNOVATIONS--EUROPE.
----European multinationals in core
    technologies. - 1988.
        (000380)

TECHNOLOGICAL INNOVATIONS--INDIA.
----Trade in investment-related
    technological studies. - 1986.
        (001386)

TECHNOLOGICAL INNOVATIONS--ITALY.
----Cambiamento tecnologico e impresa
    multinazionale. - 1984.
        (000784)

TECHNOLOGICAL INNOVATIONS--JAPAN.
----A high technology gap? - 1987.
        (001439)

TECHNOLOGICAL INNOVATIONS--LATIN AMERICA.
----Evaluating differences in technological
    activity between transnational and
    domestic firms in Latin America. - 1986.
        (001431)

TECHNOLOGICAL INNOVATIONS--SOUTHEAST ASIA.
----Transnational corporations and the
    electronics industries of ASEAN
    economies. - 1987.
        (000754)

TECHNOLOGICAL INNOVATIONS--UNITED KINGDOM.
----A comparison of embodied technical
    change in services and manufacturing
    industry. - 1986.
        (000806)
----Microelectronics in British industry. -
    1984.
        (000723)

TECHNOLOGICAL INNOVATIONS--UNITED STATES.
----The competitive challenge. - 1987.
        (000513)
----Design patents. - 1983.
        (001425)
----Diversification : the European versus
    the US experience. - 1987.
        (000491)
----A high technology gap? - 1987.
        (001439)
----Industrial renaissance : producing a
    competitive future for America. - 1983.
        (000300)
----Reverse technology flows. - 1985.
        (001451)

TECHNOLOGICAL INNOVATIONS--USSR.
----Reverse technology flows. - 1985.
        (001451)

TECHNOLOGICAL INNOVATIONS--WESTERN EUROPE.
----Diversification : the European versus
    the US experience. - 1987.
        (000491)
----A high technology gap? - 1987.
        (001439)
----New technology and the new services :
    towards an innovation strategy for
    Europe. - 1986.
        (000807)

TECHNOLOGICAL TRENDS.
----Fertilizer supplies for developing
    countries : issues in the transfer and
    development of technology. - 1985.
        (001471)
----Microelectronics-based automation
    technologies and development. - 1985.
        (000753)
----Multinationals, governments and
    international technology transfer. -
    198?.
        (001472)
----Technological and organisational factors
    in the theory of the multinational
    enterprise. - 1983.
        (000097)
----Technological trends and challenges in
    electronics. - 1983.
        (000739)

TECHNOLOGICAL TRENDS--JAPAN.
----Trends in multinational business and
    global environments: a perspective. -
    1984.
        (000029)

TECHNOLOGICAL TRENDS--UNITED STATES.
----Trends in multinational business and
    global environments: a perspective. -
    1984.
        (000029)

TECHNOLOGICAL TRENDS--WESTERN EUROPE.
----Trends in multinational business and
    global environments: a perspective. -
    1984.
        (000029)

TECHNOLOGY.
----Antitrust for high-technology
    industries: assessing research joint
    ventures and mergers. - 1985.
        (001621)
----The capital goods sector in developing
    countries. - 1985.
        (001651)
----Enjeux technologiques et relations
    internationales. - 1986.
        (001429)
----International technology joint ventures.
    - 1985.
        (001593)
----Microelectronics-based automation
    technologies and development. - 1985.
        (000753)
----Multinationals, technology, and
    industrialization. - 1986.
        (001466)
----A strategy for the technological
    transformation of developing countries.
    - 1985.
        (001515)

TECHNOLOGY (continued)
----Technology : management and acquisition.
- 1984- .
(001501)
----World technology. - 1975-
(001525)

TECHNOLOGY--AFRICA.
----Directory of African technology
institutions. - 1985.
(002706)

TECHNOLOGY--JAPAN.
----A high technology gap? - 1987.
(001439)

TECHNOLOGY--UNITED STATES.
----A high technology gap? - 1987.
(001439)

TECHNOLOGY--WESTERN EUROPE.
----A high technology gap? - 1987.
(001439)

TECHNOLOGY ASSESSMENT.
----International technology transactions
and the theory of the firm. - 1984.
(001424)

TECHNOLOGY ASSESSMENT--UNITED STATES.
----Commercial biotechnology. - 1984.
(000643)

TECHNOLOGY TRANSFER.
----Alternative contractual arrangements for
technology transfer. - 1986.
(002416)
----Analysis of engineering and technical
assistance consultancy contracts. - 1986.
(002449)
----Antitrust and direct regulation of
international transfer of technology
transactions. - 1984.
(001411)
----Applicable law under international
transfer of technology regulations. -
1984.
(001412)
----Appropriate or underdeveloped
technology? - 1982.
(001428)
----Bibliography of appropriate technology
information for developing countries. -
1983.
(002683)
----The capital goods sector in developing
countries. - 1985.
(001651)
----The changing role of multinational
enterprises in the international
creation, transfer and diffusion of
technology. - 1987.
(001426)
----Channels and modalities for the transfer
of technology to public enterprises in
developing countries. - 1983.
(001522)
----Choosing between direct investment and
licensing. - 1984.
(001418)
----Le commerce international de la
technologie. - 1985.
(001445)

----Contratos de licencia y de transferencia
de tecnología en el derecho privado. -
1980.
(002415)
----Les contrats de transfert de
technologie. - 1983.
(001468)
----Co-production: a viable consideration
for developing nations. - 1984.
(001629)
----A decision theoretic model of
innovation, technology transfer, and
trade. - 1987.
(001446)
----Enjeux technologiques et relations
internationales. - 1986.
(001429)
----Environmental aspects of the activities
of transnational corporations. - 1985.
(001954)
----Az észak-déli technológiaátadás
formaváltozásai. - 1985.
(001458)
----Exports of technology by newly
industrializing countries: an overview.
- 1984.
(001454)
----Exports of technology from the South. -
1985.
(001469)
----Fertilizer supplies for developing
countries : issues in the transfer and
development of technology. - 1985.
(001471)
----Formy transferu technologie
mezinarodnimi monopoly a technologicka
transformace rozvojovych zemi. - 1985.
(001457)
----A general equilibrium model of
multinational corporations in developing
economies. - 1986.
(000003)
----The industrialisation of less developed
countries. - 1983.
(001003)
----International accounting and reporting
issues, 1986 review. - 1986.
(002117)
----International business and global
technology. - 1983.
(001434)
----International dynamics of technology. -
1983.
(001488)
----International flows of technology. -
1986.
(001517)
----International technology transfer. -
1985.
(001487)
----Inwestycje zagraniczne a transfer wiedzy
technicznej do krajów rozwijajacych sie.
- 1984.
(001476)
----Lehetosegek es kenyszerpalyak a szellemi
termekek letrehozasaban es nemzetkozi
kereskedelmeben. - 1984.
(001465)
----Licence agreements in developing
countries. - 1987.
(002437)

TECHNOLOGY TRANSFER (continued)
----Licensing in international strategy. -
1985.
  (001419)
----Licensing of technology and intellectual
property rights to developing countries.
- 1983.
  (001403)
----Licensing strategy and policy for
internationalization and technology
transfer. - 1983.
  (001519)
----Market power of the firm and
international transfer of technology. -
1982.
  (001427)
----Microelectronics-based automation
technologies and development. - 1985.
  (000753)
----Multinational corporations, OPEC,
cartels, foreign investment, and
technology transfer special studies,
1982-1985. - 1987.
  (000589)
----Multinationals, governments and
international technology transfer. -
198?.
  (001472)
----Multinationals, technology and exports.
- 1985.
  (001456)
----New technologies and Third World
development. - 1986.
  (001475)
----North-South technology transfer: two
neglected problems. - 1986.
  (001437)
----The political economy of international
technology transfer. - 1987.
  (001482)
----Proceedings of the SSTCC/UNCTC/ESCAP
Asia-Pacific Training Workshop on
Regulating and Negotiating Technology
Transfer through Transnational
Corporations, 14-25 October 1985,
Fuzhou, Fujian, China. - 1986.
  (001405) (002169)
----Research and technology for the Third
World. - 1985.
  (001489)
----The role of transnationals in technology
transfer.. - 1987.
  (001518)
----Selecting a foreign partner for
technology transfer. - 1984.
  (001459)
---,-Service industries and economic
development. - 1984.
  (000959)
----Services and the development process. -
1985.
  (000979)
----A strategy for the technological
transformation of developing countries.
- 1985.
  (001515)
----Technology : management and acquisition.
- 1984-   .
  (001501)
----Technology and East-West trade. - 1983.
  (001502)
----Technology and international relations.
- 1987.
  (001504)

----Technology crossing borders. - 1984.
  (001496)
----Technology export from the socialist
countries. - 1986.
  (001470)
----Technology importation policies in
developing countries: some implications
of recent theoretical and empirical
evidence. - 1983.
  (001420)
----Technology, marketing and
industrialisation. - 1983.
  (001506)
----Technology transfer and East-West
relations. - 1985.
  (001507)
----The technology transfer process in
foreign licensing arrangements. - 1983.
  (001520)
----Technology transfer to developing
countries via multinationals. - 1986.
  (001467)
----A tecnológiatranszfer néhány sajátos
vonása az elektronikai iparban. - 1987.
  (001404)
----Transferring food production technology
to developing nations. - 1983.
  (001508)
----Transnational corporations and
technology transfer. - 1987.
  (001509)
----Transnational corporations in world
development. - 1983.
  (000102) (000102)
----Transnationals and the Third World. -
1984.
  (001005)
----Trasferimento internazionale di risorse
per lo sviluppo: il ruolo delle
istituzioni multilaterali. - 1984.
  (001997)
----UNCTC bibliography, 1974-1987. - 1988.
  (002695)
----Wettlauf um die Zukunft :
Technologiepolitik im internationalen
Vergleich. - 1987.
  (001453)

TECHNOLOGY TRANSFER--AFRICA.
----Gaspillages technologiques. - 1985.
  (001435)
----Les techniques de negociation en matière
de transfert de technologie. - 1987.
  (001511)

TECHNOLOGY TRANSFER--ARGENTINA.
----La cooperación empresarial
argentino-brasileña. - 1983.
  (001097)
----Exportaciones de tecnología de Brasil y
Argentina. - 1986.
  (001491)
----Exports of technology by newly
industrializing countries: Argentina. -
1984.
  (001494)

TECHNOLOGY TRANSFER--ASIA AND THE PACIFIC.
----Technology transfer under alternative
arrangements with transnational
corporations. - 1987.
  (001513)

TECHNOLOGY TRANSFER--BRAZIL.
----Brazilian imports of technology from
Sweden, 1965-1980. - 1985.
(001408)
----La cooperación empresarial
argentino-brasileña. - 1983.
(001097)
----Exportaciones de tecnología de Brasil y
Argentina. - 1986.
(001491)
----Exports of technology by newly
industrializing countries: Brazil. -
1984.
(001492)
----Politische Gestaltungsspielräume von
Schwellenländern in der
Mikroelektronik-Industrie. - 1987.
(000617)
----Technological spill-overs and manpower
training: a comparative analysis of
multinational and national enterprises
in Brazilian manufacturing. - 1986.
(001899)
----Technology and competition in the
Brazilian computer industry. - 1983.
(000741)

TECHNOLOGY TRANSFER--CANADA.
----Canada's reversal from importer to
exporter of foreign direct investment. -
1987.
(000181)
----Multinationals and technology transfer.
- 1983.
(001636)

TECHNOLOGY TRANSFER--CENTRAL AFRICA.
----Le transfert de technologie dans les
industries agro-alimentaires en Afrique
Centrale. - 1987.
(001510)

TECHNOLOGY TRANSFER--CHINA.
----China's open door policy. - 1984.
(002219)
----China's opening to the world. - 1986.
(002221)
----Foreign direct investment in the
People's Republic of China. - 1988.
(000191)
----La politique chinoise d'ouverture. -
1983.
(002186)
----Proceedings of the SSTCC/UNCTC/ESCAP
Asia-Pacific Training Workshop on
Regulating and Negotiating Technology
Transfer through Transnational
Corporations, 14-25 October 1985,
Fuzhou, Fujian, China. - 1986.
(001405) (002169)

TECHNOLOGY TRANSFER--COLOMBIA.
----Las empresas transnacionales en el
desarrollo colombiano. - 1986.
(001121)

TECHNOLOGY TRANSFER--CONGO.
----Le transfert de technologie dans les
industries agro-alimentaires en Afrique
Centrale. - 1987.
(001510)

TECHNOLOGY TRANSFER--CZECHOSLOVAKIA.
----East-West technology transfer. - 1984.
(001463)

TECHNOLOGY TRANSFER--EASTERN EUROPE.
----East-West trade, industrial co-operation
and technology transfer. - 1984.
(001441)
----Expectations and results of
contractual joint ventures by US and UK
MNCs in Eastern Europe. - 1984.
(001623)
----Saisie et effets des transferts de la
technologie incorporée dans le commerce
est-ouest. - 1986.
(001464)
----101 checklists for success in East
European markets. - 1984.
(001779)

TECHNOLOGY TRANSFER--EGYPT.
----Egypt's experience in regulating
technology imports. - 1987.
(001514)

TECHNOLOGY TRANSFER--EUROPE.
----The relationship between foreign
ownership and technology transfer. -
1983.
(001422)

TECHNOLOGY TRANSFER--FIJI.
----Proceedings of the SSTCC/UNCTC/ESCAP
Asia-Pacific Training Workshop on
Regulating and Negotiating Technology
Transfer through Transnational
Corporations, 14-25 October 1985,
Fuzhou, Fujian, China. - 1986.
(001405) (002169)

TECHNOLOGY TRANSFER--FRANCE.
----Le processus d'acquisition technologique
par les entreprises d'un pays
semi-industrialise. Deux études de cas.
(With English summary.). - 1983.
(001407)

TECHNOLOGY TRANSFER--GERMANY, FEDERAL
REPUBLIC OF.
----Der internationale Handel mit
Dienstleistungen aus der Sicht der
Bundesrepublik Deutschland. - 1984.
(000877)
----Technological balance of payments and
international competitiveness. - 1983.
(001442)
----Transfert de technologie. - 1983.
(001460)

TECHNOLOGY TRANSFER--GREECE.
----Licensing and industrial development. -
1986.
(001449)

TECHNOLOGY TRANSFER--GUYANA.
----Commercialization of technology and
dependence in the Caribbean. - 1985.
(001477)

TECHNOLOGY TRANSFER--HONG KONG.
----Exports of technology by newly
industrializing countries: Hong Kong. -
1984.
(001414)

TECHNOLOGY TRANSFER--HONG KONG (continued)
----Multinational corporations and
    technology diffusion in Hong Kong
    manufacturing. - 1983.
      (001415)
----Multinational corporations, technology
    and employment. - 1983.
      (001891)

TECHNOLOGY TRANSFER--INDIA.
----Exports of technology by newly
    industrializing countries: India. - 1984.
      (001455)
----Proceedings of the SSTCC/UNCTC/ESCAP
    Asia-Pacific Training Workshop on
    Regulating and Negotiating Technology
    Transfer through Transnational
    Corporations, 14-25 October 1985,
    Fuzhou, Fujian, China. - 1986.
      (001405) (002169)
----Technology transfer under alternative
    arrangements with transnational
    corporations. - 1987.
      (001513)
----Transnational corporations and
    technology transfer. - 1984.
      (000704)

TECHNOLOGY TRANSFER--INDONESIA.
----Multinational corporations and host
    country technology. - 1984.
      (001493)
----Proceedings of the SSTCC/UNCTC/ESCAP
    Asia-Pacific Training Workshop on
    Regulating and Negotiating Technology
    Transfer through Transnational
    Corporations, 14-25 October 1985,
    Fuzhou, Fujian, China. - 1986.
      (001405) (002169)
----Technology transfer under alternative
    arrangements with transnational
    corporations. - 1987.
      (001513)

TECHNOLOGY TRANSFER--ITALY.
----New forms of international technology
    transfer by Italian enterprises to
    developing countries. - 1984.
      (001474)

TECHNOLOGY TRANSFER--JAMAICA.
----Commercialization of technology and
    dependence in the Caribbean. - 1985.
      (001477)

TECHNOLOGY TRANSFER--JAPAN.
----The administrative regulation of
    technology induction contracts in Japan.
    - 1987.
      (002447)
----A high technology gap? - 1987.
      (001439)
----Technology transfer and
    industrialization in the developing
    countries. - 1984.
      (001430)
----Technology transfer through direct
    foreign investment. - 1985.
      (001490)
----The transfer of organizational culture
    overseas: an approach to control in the
    multinational corporation. - 1983.
      (000420)

----Transfer of technology from Japan and
    the United States to Korean
    manufacturing industries: a comparative
    study. - 1984.
      (001461)

TECHNOLOGY TRANSFER--KENYA.
----Multinational enterprises, transfer of
    managerial know-how, technology choice
    and employment effects. - 1983.
      (001436)

TECHNOLOGY TRANSFER--KUWAIT.
----Impact of the operations of
    transnational corporations on
    development in Kuwait. - 1987.
      (001143)

TECHNOLOGY TRANSFER--LATIN AMERICA.
----Deuda externa, inversión extranjera y
    transferencia de tecnología en América
    Latina. - 1986.
      (001080)
----Foreign investment and technology
    transfer. - 1984.
      (000769)
----La industria siderúrgica
    latinoamericana. - 1984.
      (000601)
----Measures strengthening the negotiating
    capacity of Governments in their
    relations with transnational
    corporations. - 1983.
      (002461)
----North-South technology transfer. - 1984.
      (001421)

TECHNOLOGY TRANSFER--MEXICO.
----Exports of technology by newly
    industrializing countries: Mexico. -
    1984.
      (001423)
----Industrialización, capital extranjero y
    transferencia de tecnología. - 1986.
      (001524)

TECHNOLOGY TRANSFER--NETHERLANDS.
----Technology transfer: the approach of a
    Dutch multinational. - 1986.
      (001484)

TECHNOLOGY TRANSFER--NIGERIA.
----Third World multinationals. - 1983.
      (000361)

TECHNOLOGY TRANSFER--OMAN.
----Impact of the operations of
    transnational corporations on
    development in the Sultanate of Oman. -
    1988.
      (001144)

TECHNOLOGY TRANSFER--PACIFIC OCEAN REGION.
----Technology transfer in the Pacific
    Basin. - 1985.
      (001413)
----Transfer of industrial technology and
    foreign investment in the Pacific
    region. - 1983.
      (001440)

TECHNOLOGY TRANSFER--UNITED STATES
(continued)
----International collaborative ventures in
    U.S. manufacturing. - 1988.
      (000720)
----Mezhdunarodnyi marketing amerikanskoi
    tekhnologii. - 1985.
      (000494)
----Multinationals and technology transfer.
    - 1983.
      (001636)
----Reverse technology flows. - 1985.
      (001451)
----The transfer of organizational culture
    overseas: an approach to control in the
    multinational corporation. - 1983.
      (000420)
----Transfer of technology from Japan and
    the United States to Korean
    manufacturing industries: a comparative
    study. - 1984.
      (001461)
----United States regulation of
    high-technology exports. - 1986.
      (001462)

TECHNOLOGY TRANSFER--USSR.
----La négociation des contrats de transfert
    de techniques avec l'Union soviétique. -
    1984.
      (002466)
----Reverse technology flows. - 1985.
      (001451)

TECHNOLOGY TRANSFER--WESTERN EUROPE.
----A high technology gap? - 1987.
      (001439)
----Saisie et effets des transferts de la
    technologie incorporée dans le commerce
    est-ouest. - 1986.
      (001464)
----Tapping Eastern bloc technology. - 1983.
      (001452)

TECHNOLOGY TRANSFER--YUGOSLAVIA.
----Visi oblici privredne saradnje izmethu
    domacih organizacija udruzenog rada i
    stranih lica. - 1984.
      (001182)

TECHNOLOGYTRANSFER--EASTERN EUROPE.
----Patterns of technology imports:
    interregional comparison. - 1986.
      (001483)

TECHNOLOGYTRANSFER--LATIN AMERICA.
----Patterns of technology imports:
    interregional comparison. - 1986.
      (001483)

TELECOMMUNICATION.
----Le tout-ordinateur. - 1986.
      (000743)
----Transborder data flows. - 1983.
      (000973)

TELECOMMUNICATION--PHILIPPINES.
----Telecommunications and investment
    decisions in the Philippines. - 1984.
      (000533)

TELECOMMUNICATION--POLAND.
----Transborder data flows and Poland :
    Polish case study. - 1984.
      (000920)

TELECOMMUNICATION--WESTERN EUROPE.
----Information technology and economic
    recovery in Western Europe. - 1986.
      (000874)

TELECOMMUNICATION AGREEMENTS.
----International transactions in services.
    - 1986.
      (000946)

TELECOMMUNICATION INDUSTRY.
----The diffusion of an organizational
    innovation: international data
    telecommunications and multinational
    industrial firms. - 1985.
      (000785)
----Electronic information services. - 1986.
      (000837)
----Information industries in the CMEA
    countries : a foreign trade dimension. -
    1986.
      (000894)
----Multinational firms, international
    trade, and international
    telecommunications. - 1984.
      (000786)
----Technology gaps in the international
    telecommunications industry. - 1986.
      (000795)
----Transnational services policy? - 1987.
      (000867)

TELECOMMUNICATION INDUSTRY--ARGENTINA.
----Telecomunicaciones. - 1987.
      (000792)

TELECOMMUNICATION INDUSTRY--EASTERN EUROPE.
----L'informatique dans les pays du CAEM :
    quelques aspects des politiques suivies.
    - 1986.
      (000711)

TELECOMMUNICATION INDUSTRY--ITALY.
----Cambiamento tecnologico e impresa
    multinazionale. - 1984.
      (000784)

TELECOMMUNICATION INDUSTRY--PACIFIC OCEAN
REGION.
----Regulation to deregulation. - 1985.
      (000798)

TELECOMMUNICATION INDUSTRY--UNITED STATES.
----High technology industries. - 1983-   .
      (000695)
----Implications of deregulating satellite
    communications. - 1985.
      (002242)

TENDERING.
----Financial and fiscal aspects of
    petroleum exploitation. - 1987.
      (002451)

TERMINOLOGY.
----Disclosure of information by
    multinational enterprises. - 1983.
        (002075)
----Encyclopedia of practical usages of
    terminology for business agreements. -
    1983.
        (002426) (002708) (002709)

----International business negotiation and
    contract. - 1982.
        (002715)
----Management accounting terminology. -
    1983.
        (002092) (002717)
----Multinational enterprise. - 1987.
        (002713)

TERMS AND PHRASES.
----Glossary of terms for state auditors. -
    1983.
        (002711)

TERRITORIAL JURISDICTION.
----Extraterritoriality: current policy of
    the United States. - 1986.
        (002341)
----International business and national
    jurisdiction. - 1988.
        (002351)

TEXTILE INDUSTRY.
----International Colloquium on the Proposed
    New Round of Multilateral Trade
    Negotiations and Developing Countries :
    proceedings and papers. - 1986.
        (001365) (001365)
----Multinational companies in the textile,
    garment and leather industries. - 1984.
        (000722)
----Social and labour practices of
    multinational enterprises in the
    textiles, clothing and footwear
    industries. - 1984.
        (001922)
----Textile and clothing industries. - 1983.
        (000740)
----Transnational corporations in the
    man-made fibre, textile and clothing
    industries. - 1987.
        (000751)

TEXTILE INDUSTRY--JAPAN.
----Technology transfer and
    industrialization in the developing
    countries. - 1984.
        (001430)

TEXTILE INDUSTRY--MALAYSIA.
----Technology transfer under alternative
    arrangements with transnational
    corporations. - 1987.
        (001513)

TEXTILE INDUSTRY--MAURITIUS.
----Jobs for the girls. - 1984.
        (001901)

TEXTILE INDUSTRY--REPUBLIC OF KOREA.
----Technology transfer under alternative
    arrangements with transnational
    corporations. - 1987.
        (001513)

TEXTILES.
----The fourth multifibre arrangement and
    the new legal regime for international
    trade in textiles. - 1987.
        (001401)

THAILAND--AUTOMOBILE INDUSTRY.
----Technology acquisition under alternative
    arrangements with transnational
    corporations. - 1987.
        (001512)
----Technology transfer under alternative
    arrangements with transnational
    corporations. - 1987.
        (001513)

THAILAND--CERAMICS INDUSTRY.
----Technology acquisition under alternative
    arrangements with transnational
    corporations. - 1987.
        (001512)
----Technology transfer under alternative
    arrangements with transnational
    corporations. - 1987.
        (001513)

THAILAND--CHEMICAL INDUSTRY.
----Technology transfer under alternative
    arrangements with transnational
    corporations. - 1987.
        (001513)

THAILAND--DEVELOPMENT ASSISTANCE.
----The private sector, the public sector,
    and donor assistance in economic
    development. - 1983.
        (000268)

THAILAND--ECONOMIC DEVELOPMENT.
----The private sector, the public sector,
    and donor assistance in economic
    development. - 1983.
        (000268)

THAILAND--ECONOMIC POLICY.
----The private sector, the public sector,
    and donor assistance in economic
    development. - 1983.
        (000268)

THAILAND--FOOD INDUSTRY.
----Technology acquisition under alternative
    arrangements with transnational
    corporations. - 1987.
        (001512)

THAILAND--FOREIGN DIRECT INVESTMENT.
----Japanese investment in Thailand. - 1987.
        (000200)

THAILAND--FOREIGN INVESTMENTS.
----National legislation and regulations
    relating to transnational corporations.
    Volume 4. - 1986.
        (002253)

THAILAND--INDUSTRIAL CAPACITY.
----Technology acquisition under alternative
    arrangements with transnational
    corporations. - 1987.
        (001512)

THAILAND--INDUSTRIAL EQUIPMENT LEASES.
----Analysis of equipment leasing contracts.
    - 1984.
        (002407)

THAILAND--INDUSTRIAL STATISTICS.
----Technology transfer under alternative
    arrangements with transnational
    corporations. - 1987.
        (001513)

THAILAND--LAWS AND REGULATIONS.
----National legislation and regulations
    relating to transnational corporations.
    Volume 4. - 1986.
        (002253)

THAILAND--PETROLEUM EXPLORATION.
----Social and economic effects of petroleum
    development. - 1987.
        (000633)

THAILAND--PETROLEUM INDUSTRY.
----Social and economic effects of petroleum
    development. - 1987.
        (000633)

THAILAND--PHARMACEUTICAL INDUSTRY.
----Transnational corporations in the
    pharmaceutical industry of developing
    countries. - 1984.
        (000749)

THAILAND--PRIVATE ENTERPRISES.
----The private sector. the public sector,
    and donor assistance in economic
    development. - 1983.
        (000268)

THAILAND--PUBLIC SECTOR.
----The private sector, the public sector,
    and donor assistance in economic
    development. - 1983.
        (000268)

THAILAND--PULP AND PAPER INDUSTRY.
----Technology acquisition under alternative
    arrangements with transnational
    corporations. - 1987.
        (001512)
----Technology transfer under alternative
    arrangements with transnational
    corporations. - 1987.
        (001513)

THAILAND--REFRACTORY MATERIALS.
----Technology transfer under alternative
    arrangements with transnational
    corporations. - 1987.
        (001513)

THAILAND--SCIENCE AND TECHNOLOGY POLICY.
----Proceedings of the SSTCC/UNCTC/ESCAP
    Asia-Pacific Training Workshop on
    Regulating and Negotiating Technology
    Transfer through Transnational
    Corporations, 14-25 October 1985,
    Fuzhou, Fujian, China. - 1986.
        (001405) (002169)

THAILAND--STATISTICAL DATA.
----Technology transfer under alternative
    arrangements with transnational
    corporations. - 1987.
        (001513)

THAILAND--TECHNOLOGY TRANSFER.
----Proceedings of the SSTCC/UNCTC/ESCAP
    Asia-Pacific Training Workshop on
    Regulating and Negotiating Technology
    Transfer through Transnational
    Corporations, 14-25 October 1985,
    Fuzhou, Fujian, China. - 1986.
        (001405) (002169)
----Technology acquisition under alternative
    arrangements with transnational
    corporations. - 1987.
        (001512)

THAILAND--TOURISM.
----Tourism. - 1986.
        (000985)

THAILAND--TOURISM STATISTICS.
----Tourism. - 1986.
        (000985)

THAILAND--TRANSNATIONAL CORPORATIONS.
----National legislation and regulations
    relating to transnational corporations.
    Volume 4. - 1986.
        (002253)
----Proceedings of the Conference on the
    Role of Multi-national Corporations in
    Thailand, July 7-9, 1984. - 1986.
        (001042)
----Technology acquisition under alternative
    arrangements with transnational
    corporations. - 1987.
        (001512)
----Technology transfer under alternative
    arrangements with transnational
    corporations. - 1987.
        (001513)

THE GRAMOPHONE CO.
----The Gramophone Company: an
    Anglo-American multinational, 1898-1931.
    - 1985.
        (000285)

TIN INDUSTRY--MALAYSIA.
----Internalization in practice: early
    foreign direct investments in
    Malaysian tin mining. - 1986.
        (000597)

TIRE INDUSTRY--LATIN AMERICA.
----Foreign investment and technology
    transfer. - 1984.
        (000769)

TIRE INDUSTRY--NETHERLANDS.
----Michelin : een zwart profiel : over
    werken in een bandenfabriek in Den
    Bosch. - 1984.
        (000289)

TOBACCO INDUSTRY.
----Smoke ring : the politics of tobacco. -
    1984.
        (000571)

TOBACCO INDUSTRY (continued)
----Tobacco and food crops production in the
    Third World. - 1983.
        (000572)

TOBACCO INDUSTRY--UNITED STATES.
----Determinants of foreign direct
    investment by food and tobacco
    manufacturers. - 1983.
        (000527)
----Foreign direct investment in U.S. food
    and tobacco manufacturing and domestic
    economic performance. - 1983.
        (000170)

TOKYO ROUND (1973-1979 : TOKYO AND GENEVA).
----The GATT and multilateral treaty making.
    - 1983.
        (001995)

TOP ECHELON STAFF.
----How multinational should your top
    managers be? - 1983.
        (000436)
----The world-class executive. - 1985.
        (000396)

TOP ECHELON STAFF--UNITED STATES.
----Staffing of management and professional
    positions at overseas subsidiaries of
    U.S. multinational enterprises. - 1983.
        (001885)

TOURISM.
----Im Interesse der Gäste wie der
    Gastgeber. - 1987.
        (000796)
----Industrie touristique et développement.
    - 1987.
        (000963)
----International financing of investments
    in tourism. - 1983.
        (000822)
----International tourism reports. -
    1986-   .
        (000875)
----Taxation of international tourism in
    developing countries. - 1986.
        (000900)
----Tourism : transnational corporations and
    cultural identities. - 1985.
        (000804)
----Tourism and the Third World. - 1983.
        (000901)
----Tourism and the Third World. - 1986.
        (000896)
----Tourism as a vehicle for Third World
    development. - 1985.
        (000906)
----Le tourisme : un phénomène économique. -
    1986.
        (000925)
----Vergleichende System- und
    Industriestudien. - 1983.
        (001342)

TOURISM--AUSTRALIA.
----Characteristics of major industries
    supplying tourist services in Australia.
    - 1983.
        (000824)

TOURISM--BARBADOS.
----Reassessing Third World tourism. - 1984.
        (000802)

TOURISM--CANADA.
----Business directory of Canadian trade
    representation abroad. - 1984-   .
        (002700)

TOURISM--CARIBBEAN REGION.
----Reassessing Third World tourism. - 1984.
        (000802)

TOURISM--SRI LANKA.
----Perceptions of socio-economic and
    cultural impact of tourism in Sri Lanka.
    - 1987.
        (001867)

TOURISM--THAILAND.
----Tourism. - 1986.
        (000985)

TOURISM DEVELOPMENT.
----International financing of investments
    in tourism. - 1983.
        (000822)
----Le tourisme : un phénomène économique. -
    1986.
        (000925)

TOURISM DEVELOPMENT--KENYA.
----The role of transnational corporations
    in hotel and tourism industry in
    selected PTA member countries. - 1986.
        (000782) (000936)

TOURISM DEVELOPMENT--MAURITIUS.
----The role of transnational corporations
    in hotel and tourism industry in
    selected PTA member countries. - 1986.
        (000782) (000936)

TOURISM DEVELOPMENT--ZIMBABWE.
----The role of transnational corporations
    in hotel and tourism industry in
    selected PTA member countries. - 1986.
        (000782) (000936)

TOURISM STATISTICS.
----International tourism reports. -
    1986-   .
        (000875)
----Le tourisme : un phénomène économique. -
    1986.
        (000925)

TOURISM STATISTICS--KENYA.
----The role of transnational corporations
    in hotel and tourism industry in
    selected PTA member countries. - 1986.
        (000782) (000936)

TOURISM STATISTICS--MAURITIUS.
----The role of transnational corporations
    in hotel and tourism industry in
    selected PTA member countries. - 1986.
        (000782) (000936)

TOURISM STATISTICS--THAILAND.
----Tourism. - 1986.
        (000985)

TOURISM STATISTICS--ZIMBABWE.
----The role of transnational corporations in hotel and tourism industry in selected PTA member countries. - 1986.
(000782) (000936)

TOXIC SUBSTANCES.
----Consolidated list of products whose consumption and/or sale have been banned, withdrawn, severely restricted or not approved by Governments. - 1987.
(002702)
----Dead in the water : international law, diplomacy, and compensation for chemical pollution at sea. - 1986.
(001938)
----The lessons of Bhopal. - 1985.
(001933)
----Second revised draft Guidelines for the Exchange of Information on Potentially Harmful Chemicals in International Trade. - 1986.
(002019)

TOXIC SUBSTANCES--EUROPE.
----The export of hazard. - 1985.
(001941)

TOXIC SUBSTANCES--INDIA.
----The Bhopal case : controlling ultrahazardous industrial activities undertaken by foreign investors. - 1987.
(001949)

TOXIC SUBSTANCES--UNITED STATES.
----The Bhopal case : controlling ultrahazardous industrial activities undertaken by foreign investors. - 1987.
(001949)
----The export of hazard. - 1985.
(001941)

TOYOTA JIDOSHA KOGYO KABUSHIKI KAISHA.
----The Japanese automobile industry. - 1985.
(000278)

TOYOTA MOTOR CORPORATION.
----Creating the GM-Toyota joint venture: a case in complex negotiation. - 1987.
(001656)

TRADE AGREEMENTS.
----The competence of GATT. - 1987.
(001382)
----Cooperation in the liberalization of international trade. - 1987.
(001400)
----Food-processing contracts with developing countries. - 1985.
(002419)
----The fourth multifibre arrangement and the new legal regime for international trade in textiles. - 1987.
(001401)
----The GATT and multilateral treaty making. - 1983.
(001995)
----GATT and recent international trade problems. - 1987.
(001986)
----GATT surveillance of industrial policies. - 1986.
(001350)

----Der internationale Rechtsverkehr in Zivil- und Handelssachen. - 1984-   .
(002225)
----Investment protection treaties: recent trends and prospects. - 1986.
(002031)
----Long term contracts and East-West trade in non-fuel minerals. - 1986.
(002444)
----Negotiating and drafting contracts in international barter and countertrade transactions. - 1984.
(002428)
----Protectionism and structural adjustment. - 1986.
(001689)
----The scope, limits and function of the GATT legal system. - 1985.
(002008)
----Services and the development process. - 1985.
(000979)
----The theory of preferential trading arrangements. - 1986.
(001381)
----Trade policy as a constitutional problem : on the "domestic policy functions" of international trade rules. - 1986.
(001379)
----Trade trouble-shooting. - 1986.
(001967)
----The Uruguay Round and the international trading system. - 1987.
(001976)

TRADE AGREEMENTS--AFRICA.
----Toward Lomé III. - 1984.
(002606)

TRADE AGREEMENTS--CANADA.
----Multinationals and free trade: the implications of a US-Canadian agreement. - 1986.
(002029)

TRADE AGREEMENTS--CARIBBEAN REGION.
----The Caribbean Basin Economic Recovery Act and its implications for foreign private investment. - 1984.
(001965)
----La presentación de la iniciativa de la Cuenca del Caribe al GATT. - 1985.
(001972)

TRADE AGREEMENTS--CHINA.
----The European Community and China. - 1986.
(002045)

TRADE AGREEMENTS--GERMANY, FEDERAL REPUBLIC OF.
----Trademark and related rights in franchise agreements in Germany. - 1983.
(001523)

TRADE AGREEMENTS--ISRAEL.
----U.S.-Israel free trade area. - 1986.
(002049)

TRADE AGREEMENTS--ROMANIA.
----Implications of international commercial agreements on the juridical regime of international commercial contracts. - 1983.
(002408)

TRADE AGREEMENTS--UNITED STATES.
----The Caribbean Basin Economic Recovery
    Act and its implications for foreign
    private investment. - 1984.
        (001965)
----Multinationals and free trade: the
    implications of a US-Canadian
    agreement. - 1986.
        (002029)
----La presentación de la iniciativa de la
    Cuenca del Caribe al GATT. - 1985.
        (001972)
----Trademark and related rights in
    franchise agreements in Germany. - 1983.
        (001523)
----The U.S. renewal of the GSP. - 1986.
        (001996)
----U.S.-Israel free trade area. - 1986.
        (002049)

TRADE AGREEMENTS--USSR.
----L'URSS et le Tiers Monde. - 1984.
        (002040)

TRADE AGREEMENTS--WESTERN EUROPE.
----The European Community and China. - 1986.
        (002045)
----Perspektiven für eine engere
    Zusammenarbeit zwischen der Europäischen
    Gemeinschaft und den
    EFTA-Mitgliedstaaten. - 1985.
        (001962)
----Toward Lomé III. - 1984.
        (002606)

TRADE AMONG DEVELOPING COUNTRIES.
----Trade in investment-related
    technological services. - 1986.
        (000945)

TRADE AND ECONOMIC CO-OPERATION AGREEMENT
BETWEEN THE EUROPEAN ECONOMIC COMMUNITY AND
THE PEOPLE'S REPUBLIC OF CHINA (1985).
----The European Community and China. - 1986.
        (002045)

TRADE ASSOCIATIONS--EUROPE.
----Directory of European industrial [and]
    trade associations. - 1986-   .
        (002707)

TRADE ASSOCIATIONS--HUNGARY.
----Economic associations in Hungary with
    foreign participation. - 1986.
        (001606)

TRADE ASSOCIATIONS--UNITED STATES.
----Directory of business, trade and public
    policy organizations. - 1982-   .
        (002631)

TRADE BOYCOTTS.
----Peaceful settlement of international
    trade disputes. - 1983.
        (002500)

TRADE BOYCOTTS--SOUTH AFRICA.
----Economic effects of a trade and
    investment boycott against South Africa.
    - 1984.
        (001202)

TRADE DISPUTES.
----The competence of GATT. - 1987.
        (001382)
----International trade disputes and the
    individual : private party involvement
    in national and international procedures
    regarding unfair foreign trade
    practices. - 1986.
        (002514)
----The military origins of
    industrialisation and international
    trade rivalry. - 1984.
        (001335)
----The status of the UNCITRAL Model Law on
    International Commercial Arbitration
    vis-à-vis the ICC, LCIA and UNCITRAL
    arbitration rules. - 1986.
        (002583)
----The two-way mirror : international
    arbitration as comparative procedure. -
    1985.
        (002540)

TRADE DISPUTES--UNITED STATES.
----Mitsubishi and the arbitrability of
    antitrust claims. - 1986.
        (002486)
----Mitsubishi v. Soler and its impact on
    international commercial arbitration. -
    1985.
        (002507)

TRADE EXPANSION--JAPAN.
----Japanese direct investment abroad. -
    1986.
        (000311)

TRADE FINANCING.
----A practitioner's guide to international
    banking and trade finance. - 1986.
        (000922)

TRADE FINANCING--INDONESIA.
----The Jakarta export processing zone:
    benefits and costs. - 1983.
        (002400)

TRADE INFORMATION--CARIBBEAN REGION.
----Caribbean Basin business information
    starter kit. - 1984.
        (001782)

TRADE INFORMATION--UNITED STATES.
----Caribbean Basin business information
    starter kit. - 1984.
        (001782)

TRADE LIBERALIZATION.
----The applicability of GATT to
    international trade in services :
    general considerations and the interest
    of developing countries. - 1987.
        (000885)
----Cooperation in the liberalization of
    international trade. - 1987.
        (001400)
----Distribution of benefits from regional
    trade liberalisation among country
    partners in the presence of
    transnational corporations. - 1983.
        (001392)
----Elements of a conceptual framework for
    trade in services. - 1987.
        (000914)

TRADE LIBERALIZATION (continued)
----International trade in services :
   securities. - 1987.
      (000915)
----Introduction to the OECD codes of
   liberalisation. - 1987.
      (001984)
----Les négociations internationales sur les
   services ou la quadrature du cercle. -
   1986.
      (000911)
----The scope, limits and function of the
   GATT legal system. - 1985.
      (002008)
----Trade in services and developing
   countries. - 1986.
      (000952)
----Trade liberalization and the global
   service economy. - 1985.
      (000811)
----Transnational services policy? - 1987.
      (000867)
----The U.S. drive to bring services into
   GATT. - 1986.
      (000926)
----Why freer trade in services is in the
   interest of developing countries. - 1985.
      (000850)

TRADE LIBERALIZATION--JAPAN.
----High-tech trade. - 1986.
      (000696)

TRADE LIBERALIZATION--SOUTHEAST ASIA.
----ASEAN economic co-operation. - 1985.
      (001039)

TRADE LIBERALIZATION--UNITED STATES.
----High-tech trade. - 1986.
      (000696)
----Trade in services : obstacles and
   opportunities. - 1987.
      (000984)

TRADE LIBERALIZATION--YUGOSLAVIA.
----Joint venturing in Yugoslavia. - 1987.
      (001536)

TRADE NEGOTIATIONS.
----The fourth multifibre arrangement and
   the new legal regime for international
   trade in textiles. - 1987.
      (001401)
----Les négociations internationales sur les
   services ou la quadrature du cercle.
   (With English summary.). - 1986.
      (000912)
----A negotiating strategy for trade in
   services. - 1983.
      (000865)
----Negotiating with Third World
   governments. - 1983.
      (002468)
----World-traded services : the challenge
   for the eighties. - 1984.
      (000889)

TRADE NEGOTIATIONS--CHINA.
----China's modernization and transnational
   corporations. - 1984.
      (001077)

TRADE NEGOTIATIONS--UNITED STATES.
----Trade in services. - 1986.
      (000962)

TRADE NEGOTIATIONS--WESTERN ASIA.
----Trade in services : growth and balance
   of payments implications for countries
   of Western Asia. - 1987.
      (000968)

TRADE NEGOTIATIONS--WESTERN EUROPE.
----Trade in services. - 1986.
      (000962)

TRADE POLICY.
----Burzhuaznoe gosudarstvo i
   vneshneekonomicheskie sviazi. - 1986.
      (002236)
----Competition and trade policies. - 1984.
      (001664)
----Continuing the international debate on
   services. - 1985.
      (000863)
----Current issues in international trade. -
   1985.
      (001359)
----Elements of a conceptual framework for
   trade in services. - 1987.
      (000914)
----Eliminating barriers to international
   trade and investment in services. - 1986.
      (000809)
----GATT surveillance of industrial
   policies. - 1986.
      (001350)
----International orientation of exporters:
   some North-South trade implications. -
   1983.
      (001374)
----International trade disputes and the
   individual : private party involvement
   in national and international procedures
   regarding unfair foreign trade
   practices. - 1986.
      (002514)
----Licensing versus direct investment: a
   model of internationalization by the
   multinational enterprise. - 1987.
      (001443)
----Multinational monopolies and
   international cartels. - 1984.
      (001663)
----On the choice between capital import and
   labor export. - 1983.
      (002370)
----Power and protectionism. - 1983.
      (001865)
----Protectionism and structural adjustment.
   - 1986.
      (001689)
----The scope, limits and function of the
   GATT legal system. - 1985.
      (002008)
----Services and the development process. -
   1985.
      (000979)
----Should one countertrade? - 1987.
      (001366)
----Trade in services : the theory and trade
   policy. - 1987.
      (000943)

TRADE POLICY (continued)
----Trade policy as a constitutional problem : on the "domestic policy functions" of international trade rules. - 1986. (001379)
----Trade policy issues and empirical analysis /edited by Robert Baldwin. - 1988. (001348)
----Trade policy options in the design of development strategies. - 1986. (001399)
----Trade-related investment issues. - 1983. (001385)
----U.S. corporate interests and the political economy of trade policy. - 1985. (000368)

TRADE POLICY--BANGLADESH.
----Trade and investment possibilities in Bangladesh, Nepal and Sri Lanka. - 1983. (001840)

TRADE POLICY--CANADA.
----Trade among multinationals. - 1987. (001678)

TRADE POLICY--CHINA.
----China's modernization and transnational corporations. - 1984. (001077)
----The People's Republic of China. - 1986. (001841)
----Strategies for joint ventures in the People's Republic of China. - 1987. (001610)
----Trade policies in the PRC. - 1986. (001387)

TRADE POLICY--EASTERN EUROPE.
----Patterns of technology imports: interregional comparison. - 1986. (001483)

TRADE POLICY--JAPAN.
----Doing business in Japan. - 1986. (001809)
----High-tech trade. - 1986. (000696)
----A transactions cost approach to international trading structures: the case of the Japanese general trading companies. - 1983. (000372)

TRADE POLICY--LATIN AMERICA.
----Patterns of technology imports: interregional comparison. - 1986. (001483)
----The relationship of MNC direct investment to host country trade and trade policy: some preliminary evidence. - 1983. (001351)

TRADE POLICY--NEPAL.
----Trade and investment possibilities in Bangladesh, Nepal and Sri Lanka. - 1983. (001840)

TRADE POLICY--POLAND.
----Intra-industry trade in Poland's foreign trade in 1950-1984 : empirical results and policy implications. - 1986. (001372)

TRADE POLICY--SRI LANKA.
----Trade and investment possibilities in Bangladesh, Nepal and Sri Lanka. - 1983. (001840)

TRADE POLICY--UNITED STATES.
----Blind intersection? policy and the automobile industry. - 1987. (000660)
----Countertrade. - 1984. (001371)
----Hard bargaining ahead. - 1985. (001361)
----High-tech trade. - 1986. (000696)
----International countertrade. - 1984. (001396)
----Manufacturing matters : the myth of the post-industrial economy. - 1987. (000669)
----Political and policy dimensions of foreign trade zones. - 1985. (001356)
----Trade in services. - 1986. (000962)
----Transnational corporations and international trade : selected issues. - 1985. (001393)
----US corporate interests and the political economy of trade policy. - 1984. (000505)

TRADE POLICY--USSR.
----Foreign trade with the USSR. - 1987. (001774)
----La réforme du commerce extérieur soviétique. - 1987. (002261)
----USSR, tendensen tot decentralisatie. - 1987. (001190)

TRADE POLICY--WESTERN EUROPE.
----Trade in services. - 1986. (000962)

TRADE POLICY--ZAIRE.
----Protection, distortions and investment incentives in Zaire. - 1986. (002272)

TRADE PREFERENCES.
----International Colloquium on the Proposed New Round of Multilateral Trade Negotiations and Developing Countries : proceedings and papers. - 1986. (001365) (001365)
----The theory of preferential trading arrangements. - 1986. (001381)

TRADE PROMOTION.
----Estructuras empresarias para el comercio internacional. - 1984. (001383)

TRADE PROMOTION (continued)
----Introduction to the OECD codes of
liberalisation. - 1987.
(001984)

TRADE PROMOTION--CARIBBEAN REGION.
----Caribbean Basin business information
starter kit. - 1984.
(001782)

TRADE PROMOTION--CHINA.
----Special economic zones in the People's
Republic of China. - 1986.
(002361)

TRADE PROMOTION--ITALY.
----L'impresa pubblica italiana e la
dimensione internazionale. - 1983.
(001145)

TRADE PROMOTION--SOUTHEAST ASIA.
----Legal development and the promotion of
intra-ASEAN trade and investment. - 1986.
(002307)

TRADE PROMOTION--UNITED STATES.
----Caribbean Basin business information
starter kit. - 1984.
(001782)

TRADE REGULATION.
----Burzhuaznoe gosudarstvo i
vneshneekonomicheskie sviazi. - 1986.
(002236)
----Competition policy and deregulation. -
1986.
(001683)
----Eliminating barriers to international
trade and investment in services. - 1986.
(000809)
----The extraterritorial application of
national laws. - 1987.
(002348)
----Extraterritorial jurisdiction. - 1983.
(002350) (002688)
----International business and national
jurisdiction. - 1988.
(002351)
----International business transactions in a
nutshell. - 1984.
(002457)
----International codes and multinational
business. - 1985.
(001988)
----Maryland journal of international law
and trade. - 1984-   .
(002138)
----Negotiating international rules for
trade in services. - 1985.
(000898)
----Power and protectionism. - 1983.
(001865)
----Putting services on the table : the new
GATT round. - 1987.
(000932)
----Regulating international business
through codes of conduct. - 1980.
(002022)
----Services and the development process. -
1985.
(000979)
----Social clauses and international trade.
- 1983.
(001360)

----Transnational business problems. - 1986.
(000516)
----The transnational law of international
commercial transactions. - 1982.
(002012)

TRADE REGULATION--CHINA.
----Almanac of China's foreign economic
relations and trade. - 1984-   .
(002615)
----China's foreign economic contract law. -
1987.
(002297)
----China's trade, tax and investment laws
and regulations. - 1984.
(002189)

TRADE REGULATION--JAPAN.
----The legal framework of trade and
investment in Japan. - 1986.
(002241)

TRADE REGULATION--MALAYSIA.
----Business prospects in Malaysia, coping
with change in a new era. - 1983.
(001780)

TRADE REGULATION--UNITED STATES.
----Exclusive licenses as restraints of
trade under US and Common Market
antitrust law. - 1984.
(002414)
----Foreign trade and investment. - 1987.
(002191)
----International business planning. - 1983.
(002279)
----Licensing impact of foreign policy
motivated retroactive reexport
regulations. - 1983.
(001352)
----Regulating the multinational enterprise.
- 1983.
(002006)

TRADE REGULATION--USSR.
----Anderungen im sowjetischen
Aussenwirtschaftssystem zu Beginn des
Jahres 1987. - 1987.
(001176)
----The new Soviet joint venture
regulations. - 1987.
(002202)

TRADE REGULATION--WESTERN EUROPE.
----Exclusive licenses as restraints of
trade under US and Common Market
antitrust law. - 1984.
(002414)

TRADE RESTRICTIONS.
----Legal problems in expanding the scope of
GATT to include trade in services. -
1983.
(000864)
----Protectionism and structural adjustment.
- 1986.
(001689)
----Protectionist tendencies in
international trade in services. - 1986.
(000953)
----A szolgáltatások a nemzetközi gazdasági
kapcsolatokban. - 1986.
(000895)

TRADE RESTRICTIONS (continued)
----Trade in services. - 1984.
    (000955)
----World-traded services : the challenge
    for the eighties. - 1984.
    (000889)

TRADE RESTRICTIONS--CANADA.
----Transfer pricing policies under tariff
    barriers. - 1983.
    (001709)

TRADE RESTRICTIONS--UNITED STATES.
----Transnational corporations and
    international trade : selected issues. -
    1985.
    (001393)
----United States jurisdiction over foreign
    subsidiaries. - 1983.
    (002355)

TRADE STATISTICS.
----The capital goods sector in developing
    countries. - 1985.
    (001651)
----Foreign trade by commodities. -
    1983-   .
    (001357)
----Transnational corporations and
    international trade : selected issues. -
    1985.
    (001393)
----Transnational corporations in the
    man-made fibre, textile and clothing
    industries. - 1987.
    (000751)

TRADE STATISTICS--CHINA.
----Almanac of China's foreign economic
    relations and trade. - 1984-   .
    (002615)

TRADE STATISTICS--POLAND.
----Intra-industry trade in Poland's foreign
    trade in 1950-1984 : empirical results
    and policy implications. - 1986.
    (001372)

TRADE STATISTICS--UNITED STATES.
----Transnational corporations and
    international trade : selected issues. -
    1985.
    (001393)

TRADE STRUCTURE.
----Areas for further research on
    intra-industry trade. - 1983.
    (000099)
----The inflationary effect on the structure
    of trade. - 1986.
    (001672)
----Multinational corporations and trade
    structure. - 1985.
    (001363)
----Putting world trade back on a growth
    course. - 1984.
    (001358)
----Trade [and] structural change. - 1984.
    (001391)
----Vergleichende System- und
    Industriestudien. - 1983.
    (001342)

TRADE STRUCTURE--JAPAN.
----The invisible link. - 1986.
    (000992)
----Japan's general trading companies. -
    1984.
    (000887)

TRADE STRUCTURE--UNITED STATES.
----International countertrade. - 1984.
    (001396)

TRADE UNIONS.
----El debate sindical nacional e
    internacional. - 1984.
    (002602)
----Export processing zones. - 1983.
    (002372)
----International labour affairs. - 1987.
    (002595)
----Labor confronts the transnationals. -
    1984.
    (002594)
----Multinational union organizations in the
    white-collar, service, and
    communications industries. - 1983.
    (002600)
----Transnational labor relations. - 1985.
    (001905)
----Transnatsional'nye korporatsii i
    rabochii klass. - 1987.
    (001953)
----The Vredeling proposal and multinational
    trade unionism. - 1983.
    (002598)

TRADE UNIONS--AFRICA.
----African trade unions. - 1983-   .
    (002592) (002593) (002698)

TRADE UNIONS--BRAZIL.
----Brazil, the new militancy. - 1984.
    (002596)

TRADE UNIONS--NAMIBIA.
----Transnational corporations in South
    Africa and Namibia : United Nations
    public hearings. Volume 1, Reports of
    the Panel of Eminent Persons and of the
    Secretary-General. - 1986.
    (001216)
----Transnational corporations in South
    Africa and Namibia. - 1986.
    (001217)

TRADE UNIONS--NEW ZEALAND.
----Trade union directory. - 1971-   .
    (002720)

TRADE UNIONS--SOUTH AFRICA.
----Trade unions against apartheid. - 1984.
    (002601)
----Transnational corporations in South
    Africa and Namibia : United Nations
    public hearings. Volume 1, Reports of
    the Panel of Eminent Persons and of the
    Secretary-General. - 1986.
    (001216)
----Transnational corporations in South
    Africa and Namibia. - 1986.
    (001217)

TRADE UNIONS--SOUTH AFRICA (continued)
----Transnational corporations in South
    Africa and Namibia : United Nations
    public hearings. Volume 3, Statements
    and submissions. - 1987.
       (001215)

TRADEMARK LICENCES.
----International trademark licensing
    agreements. - 1986.
       (002421)

TRADEMARK LICENCES--GREECE.
----Licensing and industrial development. -
    1986.
       (001449)

TRADEMARK LICENCES--WESTERN EUROPE.
----Territorial and exclusive trademark
    licensing under the EEC law of
    competition. - 1984.
       (001987)

TRADEMARKS.
----Licence agreements in developing
    countries. - 1987.
       (002437)

TRADEMARKS--CHINA.
----Collection of laws and regulations of
    the People's Republic of China
    concerning foreign economic affairs. -
    1985-   .
       (002188)

TRADEMARKS--GERMANY, FEDERAL REPUBLIC OF.
----Trademark and related rights in
    franchise agreements in Germany. - 1983.
       (001523)

TRADEMARKS--UNITED STATES.
----Trademark and related rights in
    franchise agreements in Germany. - 1983.
       (001523)

TRADEMARKS--WESTERN EUROPE.
----La licence de marque et le droit
    européen de la concurrence. - 1984.
       (001448)

TRAINING AND RESEARCH INSTITUTIONS--AFRICA.
----Directory of African technology
    institutions. - 1985.
       (002706)

TRAINING PROGRAMMES.
----Technical co-operation programme of the
    United Nations Centre on Transnational
    Corporations. - 1988.
       (002610)
----Technical co-operation programme,
    1976-1987 : United Nations Centre on
    Transnational Corporations. - 1988.
       (002611)
----UNCITRAL, the United Nations Commission
    on International Trade Law. - 1986.
       (002155)

TRAINING PROGRAMMES--CHINA.
----The training component. - 1986.
       (001920)

TRANSFER PRICING.
----Arrangements between joint venture
    partners in developing countries. - 1987.
       (002450)
----International accounting and reporting
    issues : 1984 review. - 1985.
       (002115)
----International co-operation in tax
    matters : guidelines for international
    co-operation against the evasion and
    avoidance of taxes (with special
    reference to taxes on income, profits,
    capital and capital gains). - 1984.
       (001724)
----International income taxation and
    developing countries. - 1988.
       (001759)
----International transfer pricing
    objectives. - 1985.
       (001732)
----Intra-firm pricing and the multinational
    corporations. - 1986.
       (000471)
----Multinationals and transfer pricing. -
    1985.
       (001751)
----National ownership requirements and
    transfer pricing. - 1986.
       (001711)
----Prix de transfert et entreprises
    multinationales. - 1979.
       (001744)
----Prix de transfert et entreprises
    multinationales. - 1984.
       (002099)
----Tax treatment of cost-contribution
    arrangements. - 1988.
       (001737)
----Taxation of intercorporate transfer
    pricing: a management responsibility:
    U.S.A. - 1986.
       (001754)
----Technical co-operation programme,
    1976-1987 : United Nations Centre on
    Transnational Corporations. - 1988.
       (002611)
----Transfer pricing and multinational
    enterprises. - 1984.
       (001745)
----Transfer pricing problems and economic
    strategies in developing countries. -
    1983.
       (001747)
----Transfer pricing provisions, rulings and
    case law: Thailand. - 1986.
       (001723)
----Transnational corporations and
    international trade : selected issues. -
    1985.
       (001393)

TRANSFER PRICING--CANADA.
----Draft guidelines on international
    transfer pricing: Canada. - 1986.
       (001734)
----Multinational Oil Limited: issues in
    transfer pricing and foreign ownership.
    - 1985.
       (001750)
----Transfer pricing issues: a critical
    discussion of the Revenue Draft
    Information Circular. - 1984.
       (001702)

TRANSFER PRICING--CANADA (continued)
----Transfer pricing policies under tariff
    barriers. - 1983.
        (001709)

TRANSFER PRICING--FRANCE.
----La formation du prix dans les
    transactions internationales. - 1985.
        (001712)
----Fraude fiscale internationale et
    repression. - 1986.
        (001742)

TRANSFER PRICING--GERMANY, FEDERAL REPUBLIC
OF.
----German transfer pricing. - 1984.
        (001748)
----Konzerntransferpreise im internationalen
    Steuerrecht. - 1986.
        (001710)
----Verrechnungspreise fur Sachleistungen im
    internationalen Konzern. - 1984.
        (001720)

TRANSFER PRICING--PAPUA NEW GUINEA.
----Reconciling ethical behaviour. - 1986.
        (001719)

TRANSFER PRICING--UNITED STATES.
----La formation du prix dans les
    transactions internationales. - 1985.
        (001712)
----Intercorporate transfer pricing: the
    role of the functionally determined
    profit split explored. - 1985.
        (001753)

TRANSFER PRICING--WESTERN EUROPE.
----La formation du prix dans les
    transactions internationales. - 1985.
        (001712)

TRANSNATIONAL BANKS.
----Changes in the international financial
    market and implications for
    transnational banks, transnational
    corporations and developing countries. -
    1986.
        (000976)
----Employment in multinational banking. -
    1987.
        (001916)
----Foreign direct investment, the service
    sector and international banking. - 1987.
        (000972)
----Issues in negotiating international loan
    agreements with transnational banks. -
    1983.
        (002459)
----Latinskaja Amerika. - 1984.
        (001089)
----Multinational banks: their identities
    and determinants. - 1985.
        (000826)
----Recent developments in operations and
    behaviour of transnational corporations.
    - 1987.
        (000103)
----Transnational banks and the external
    finance of Latin America : the
    experience of Peru. - 1985.
        (000975)

----Transnational corporations in world
    development. - 1983.
        (000102)

TRANSNATIONAL BANKS--AFRICA.
----The role of transnational banks and
    financial institutions in Africa's
    development process. - 1986.
        (000935)

TRANSNATIONAL BANKS--ARGENTINA.
----Los bancos transnacionales y el
    endeudamiento externo en la Argentina. -
    1987.
        (000819)

TRANSNATIONAL BANKS--JAPAN.
----Foreign direct investment, the service
    sector and international banking. - 1987.
        (000972)

TRANSNATIONAL BANKS--PARAGUAY.
----Las empresas transnacionales en la
    economía del Paraguay. - 1987.
        (001124)

TRANSNATIONAL BANKS--PERU.
----Transnational banks and the external
    finance of Latin America : the
    experience of Peru. - 1983.
        (000840)

TRANSNATIONAL CORPORATIONS.
----. - 1984.
        (000810)
----The characteristics of joint
    ventures in developed and developing
    countries. - 1985.
        (001541)
----The multinational corporation in the
    less developed country: the economic
    development model versus the North-South
    model. - 1985.
        (001011)
----Accounting and reporting policies and
    practices of transnational corporations.
    - 1983.
        (002120)
----Accounting reports and performance
    measurement of multinational enterprises
    in less developed countries. - 1987.
        (002107)
----Alternative contractual arrangements for
    technology transfer. - 1986.
        (002416)
----The aluminum multinationals and the
    bauxite cartel. - 1987.
        (000599)
----Anthropology and international business.
    - 1986.
        (001892)
----Appropriate measures to give effect to
    the work of the Group. - 1986.
        (002121)
----Appropriate or underdeveloped
    technology? - 1982.
        (001428)
----Appropriate pharmaceutical policies in
    developing countries. - 1985.
        (000707)

TRANSNATIONAL CORPORATIONS (continued)
----Appropriate policies towards
multinational hotel corporations in
developing countries. - 1983.
(000781)
----Arrangements between joint venture
partners in developing countries. - 1987.
(002450)
----Assessing industry concentration: the
case of aluminum. - 1984.
(000611)
----Les associations d'entreprises (joint
ventures) dans le commerce
international. - 1986.
(001538)
----Auditing non-U.S. operations. - 1984.
(002113)
----Aussenwirtschaft der Unternehmung. -
1984.
(000064)
----Automation and the worldwide
restructuring of the electronics
industry: strategic implications for
developing countries. - 1985.
(000683)
----Autonomy and centralization in
multinational firms. - 1984.
(000393)
----Bargaining power, ownership, and
profitability of transnational
corporations in developing countries. -
1984.
(001007)
----Bibliografía sobre inversiones
extranjeras y empresas multinacionales.
- 1986.
(002681)
----Big business blunders. - 1983.
(000507)
----Bilateral investment treaties. - 1988.
(002054)
----Biznes na pomoshchi. - 1984.
(001298)
----Brazilian informatics policy. - 1985.
(000880)
----Burzhuaznoe gosudarstvo i
vneshneekonomicheskie sviazi. - 1986.
(002236)
----Business strategy and the
internationalization of business: recent
approaches. - 1987.
(000520)
----Can you standardize multinational
marketing? - 1983.
(000464)
----Capital intensity and export propensity
in some Latin American countries. - 1987.
(001389)
----Le capitalisme mondial. - 1985.
(000065)
----Case studies in international business.
- 1988.
(000415)
----Cases in strategic management and
business policy. - 1986.
(000483)
----Changes in the international financial
market and implications for
transnational banks, transnational
corporations and developing countries. -
1986.
(000976)

----The changing form of multinational
enterprise expansion in the twentieth
century. - 1986.
(000012)
----The changing role of multinational
enterprises in the international
creation, transfer and diffusion of
technology. - 1987.
(001426)
----Churches and the transnational
corporations. - 1983.
(002586)
----Clarification of the accounting terms in
the OECD Guidelines. - 1983.
(002071)
----Code of Conduct on Transnational
Corporations. - 1988.
(002018)
----Codes of conduct of multinationals. -
1984.
(001974)
----Collapse and survival. - 1983.
(000459)
----Comercio internacional,
industrialización y nuevo orden
económico internacional. - 1983.
(001242)
----Commission on Transnational Corporations
: report on the reconvened special
session, 20-31 January 1986. - 1986.
(002016)
----Comparative and multinational
management. - 1986.
(000439)
----Competition in global industries. - 1986.
(001688)
----Concentración global y
transnacionalización. - 1985.
(000100)
----Conscience and dividends. - 1985.
(002587)
----Consumers, transnational corporations,
and development. - 1986.
(001343)
----Continuing the international debate on
services. - 1985.
(000863)
----Cooperate to compete globally. - 1986.
(001624)
----Cooperative strategies in international
business. - 1988.
(001557)
----Coping with worldwide accounting
changes. - 1984.
(002067)
----Co-production: a viable consideration
for developing nations. - 1984.
(001629)
----Corporate aid programs in twelve
less-developed countries. - 1983.
(002609)
----Corporate performance: America's
international winners. - 1986.
(000344)
----Corporations and the common good. - 1986.
(000022)
----Corporations, classes, and capitalism. -
1985.
(000090)
----Counter-trade: untying those blocked
funds. - 1987.
(001398)

TRANSNATIONAL CORPORATIONS (continued)
----A country risk appraisal model of
    foreign asset expropriation in
    developing countries. - 1987.
      (001553) (001775)
----Creating the GM-Toyota joint venture: a
    case in complex negotiation. - 1987.
      (001656)
----Cross-border transactions between
    related companies. - 1985.
      (001735)
----The cultural environment of
    international business. - 1985.
      (001879)
----Current financial and monetary problems
    of the developing countries in the world
    capitalist economy. - 1987.
      (001246)
----El debate sindical nacional e
    internacional. - 1984.
      (002602)
----Decision-making in multinational
    enterprises. - 1984.
      (000410)
----Decision-making regarding restructuring
    in multinational enterprises. - 1986.
      (000411)
----Declaration by the governments of OECD
    member countries and decisions of the
    OECD Council on international investment
    and multinational enterprises. - 1984.
      (001999)
----Des multinationales a l'Est? (With
    English summary.). - 1984.
      (000331)
----Determinants of multinational banks. -
    1986.
      (000825)
----Determinants of offshore production in
    developing countries. - 1986.
      (000544)
----Dette du Tiers-Monde. - 1987.
      (000224)
----Diffusion as an explanation of oil
    nationalization or the domino effect
    rides again. - 1985.
      (002326)
----The diffusion of an organizational
    innovation: international data
    telecommunications and multinational
    industrial firms. - 1985.
      (000785)
----Disclosure of information by
    multinational enterprises. - 1983.
      (002075)
----Diskontinuitatenmanagement. - 1984.
      (000490)
----Distribution of benefits from regional
    trade liberalisation among country
    partners in the presence of
    transnational corporations. - 1983.
      (001392)
----Diversification strategy and choice
    of country: diversifying acquisitions
    abroad by U.S. multinationals,
    1978-1980. - 1985.
      (000536)
----Does de-industrialisation beget
    industrialisation which begets
    re-industrialisation? Review article. -
    1985.
      (001320)

----The economic and social effects of
    multinational enterprises in export
    processing zones. - 1988.
      (002371)
----The economic environment of
    international business. - 1986.
      (001305)
----The economic theory of the multinational
    enterprise. - 1985.
      (000009)
----Economics of change in less developed
    countries. - 1986.
      (001000)
----The economics of joint ventures in less
    developed countries. - 1984.
      (001643)
----Effective control of currency risks. -
    1988.
      (000502)
----Effets de la mobilité internationale du
    capital sur les pays membres d'une union
    douanière. - 1987.
      (001250)
----Eliminating barriers to international
    trade and investment in services. - 1986.
      (000809)
----Emerging standards of international
    trade and investment. - 1983.
      (001973)
----Employee consultation and information in
    multinational corporations. - 1986.
      (002603)
----Employment and technological choice of
    multinational enterprises in developing
    countries. - 1983.
      (001909)
----La empresa transnacional en el marco
    laboral. - 1983.
      (001910)
----Empresas multinacionales, gestión de
    cambios y crisis monetarias=Multination
    businesses, change of money, management
    and monetary crisis. With English
    summary.). - 1983.
      (001292)
----Las empresas transnacionales. - 1984.
      (001013)
----Encyclopedia of practical usages of
    terminology for business agreements. -
    1983.
      (002426) (002708) (002709)

----Endettement international et
    multinationalisation. - 1984.
      (000248)
----Les enjeux de la bauxite. - 1983.
      (000585)
----Les entreprises multinationales et les
    services. - 1985.
      (000956)
----Environment of international business. -
    1985.
      (000055)
----Environmental aspects of the activities
    of transnational corporations. - 1985.
      (001954)
----Equity joint ventures and the theory of
    the multinational enterprise. - 987 .
      (001542)
----Ethics and the multinational enterprise.
    - 1986.
      (001873)

TRANSNATIONAL CORPORATIONS (continued)
----European Community tariff preferences
and foreign direct investment. - 1987.
(002159)
----An examination of multijurisdictional
corporate income taxation under formula
apportionment. - 1986.
(001715)
----Excess market value, the multinational
corporation, and Tobin's q-ratio. - 1986.
(000050)
----Export processing zones. - 1983.
(002372)
----Export-enclave economies, international
corporations, and development. - 1985.
(002367)
----Expropriations of foreign-owned firms in
developing countries: a cross-national
analysis. - 1984.
(001552)
----The extraterritorial application of
national laws. - 1987.
(002348)
----Extraterritorial jurisdiction. - 1983.
(002350) (002688)
----Die extraterritoriale Anwendung
nationalen Wettbewerbsrechts unter
besonderer Berucksichtigung
landerubergreifender Fusionen. - 1986.
(002340)
----Extraterritoriality: current policy of
the United States. - 1986.
(002341)
----Financial and fiscal aspects of
petroleum exploitation. - 1987.
(002451)
----Financial management for the
multinational firm. - 1987.
(000386)
----The financial structure of multinational
capitalism. - 1986.
(001258)
----Finanz- und bankwirtschaftliche Probleme
bei internationaler
Unternehmenstatigkeit. - 1985.
(001277)
----Die finanzielle Fuhrung und Kontrolle
von Auslandsgesellschaften. - 1983.
(000264)
----Finding, entering, and succeeding in a
foreign market. - 1987.
(000468)
----The firm and the market. - 1987.
(000013)
----Les firmes multinationales. - 1985.
(000070)
----Foreign direct investment with
unemployment and endogenous taxes and
tariffs. - 1987.
(000559)
----Foreign direct investment and the
multinational enterprise. - 1988.
(002696)
----Foreign direct investment in the
People's Republic of China. - 1988.
(000191)
----Foreign direct investment, the service
sector and international banking. - 1987.
(000972)
----Foreign direct investment 1973-87. -
1984.
(000133)
----Foreign investment and the restructuring
of technology. - 1987.
(000702)
----Foreign ownership: when hosts change the
rules. - 1985.
(001798)
----Formy transferu technologie
mezinarodnimi monopoly a technologicka
transformace rozvojovych zemi. - 1985.
(001457)
----Frontiers of international accounting. -
1985.
(002069)
----Fundamentals of international business
management. - 1986.
(000414)
----Gedragscodes voor multinationale
ondernemingen. - 1986.
(001969)
----A general equilibrium model of
multinational corporations in developing
economies. - 1986.
(000003)
----General theories of the multinational
enterprise. - 1984.
(000014)
----Géopolitique des ressources minières. -
1983.
(000593)
----Gestion et stratégie financières
internationales. - 1985.
(000422)
----Gestion internationale de l'entreprise.
- 1984.
(000389)
----The global factory. - 1985.
(001254)
----The global IBM. - 1987.
(000288)
----The global marketplace. - 1987.
(000290)
----Global risk assessments. - 1983.
(001803)
----Global shift. - 1987.
(001315)
----The globalization of markets. - 1983.
(000059)
----Going international. - 1985.
(001786)
----Governments and multinationals. - 1983.
(002267)
----Governments and multinationals. - 1983.
(001804)
----The growth of international business. -
1983.
(000039)
----Grundzuge der internationalen
Unternehmenspolitik des
Versicherungsunternehmens. - 1983.
(000930)
----Handbook of international financial
management. - 1984.
(000446)
----Handbook of international management. -
1988.
(000452)
----Host countries and the R [and] D of
multinationals. - 1987.
(001479)
----How MNCs cope with host government
intervention. - 1983.
(001795)

TRANSNATIONAL CORPORATIONS (continued)
----How multinational should your top
managers be? - 1983.
(000436)
----How multinationals can manage social
conflict. - 1983.
(001869)
----Human resource management in
multinational cooperative ventures. -
1986.
(000426)
----Human resources management in
international joint ventures: directions
for research. - 1987.
(001921)
----The implementation of international
antitrust principles. - 1983.
(002344)
----Importance et implantations comparées
des quatre plus grands biscuitiers
mondiaux, Nabisco Brands, United
Biscuits, Générale Biscuit, Bahlsen. -
1984.
(000273)
----Le imprese internazionali. - 1983.
(000062)
----Improving environmental cooperation. -
1984.
(001955)
----Incentives and disincentives for foreign
direct investment in less developed
countries. - 1984.
(002301)
----Industrial change in advanced economies.
- 1987.
(001317)
----Industrial diversification amongst the
world's leading multinational
enterprises. - 1983.
(000546)
----Industrial free zones and
industrialization in developing
countries. - 1986.
(002403)
----Industrial policies. - 1984.
(001233)
----Industrial structure and policy in less
developed countries. - 1984.
(001322)
----The industrialisation of less developed
countries. - 1983.
(001003)
----Industriebetriebslehre in Wissenschaft
und Praxis. - 1985.
(000404)
----The influence of Hymer's dissertation on
the theory of foreign direct investment.
- 1985.
(000024)
----Information disclosure and the
multinational corporation. - 1984.
(002078)
----L'informatique du Nord au Sud. - 1986.
(000678)
----Innovation und internationale Monopole.
- 1983.
(001671)
----Inostrannyi kapital v ekonomike
kapitalisticheskikh gosudarstv. - 1984.
(001225)
----A internacional capitalista. - 1986.
(000473)
----International accounting. - 1983.
(002106)

----International accounting. - 1985.
(002111)
----International accounting. - 1985.
(002062)
----International accounting. - 1984.
(002070)
----International accounting. - 1984.
(002083) (002085)
----International accounting and
multinational enterprises. - 1985.
(002058)
----International accounting and reporting.
- 1985.
(002076)
----International accounting and reporting
issues : 1984 review. - 1985.
(002115)
----International accounting and reporting
issues, 1985 review. - 1985.
(002116)
----International accounting and reporting
issues, 1986 review. - 1986.
(002117)
----International accounting and
transnational decisions. - 1983.
(002086)
----International accounting standards and
transnational corporations. - 1986.
(002108)
----International business. - 1986.
(000469)
----International business. - 1985.
(000088)
----International business. - 1985.
(000002)
----International business. - 1984.
(000069)
----International business. - 1987.
(000453)
----International business: an alternative
view. - 1986.
(001559)
----International business and cultures. -
1987.
(001872)
----International business and global
technology. - 1983.
(001434)
----International business and multinational
enterprises. - 1983.
(000087)
----International business and national
jurisdiction. - 1988.
(002351)
----International business and the national
interest. - 1986.   .
(001817)
----International business classics. - 1988.
(000001)
----International business, environment and
management. - 1985.
(000423)
----International business finance. - 1983.
(000049)
----International business in the nineteenth
century. - 1987.
(000046)
----International business knowledge. - 1987.
(000402)
----International business negotiation and
contract. - 1982.
(002715)

TRANSNATIONAL CORPORATIONS (continued)
----International business reference
    sources. - 1983.
       (002691)
----International business, the recession
    and economic restructuring. - 1985.
       (000025)
----International business transactions in a
    nutshell. - 1984.
       (002457)
----International codes and guidelines for
    multinational enterprises. - 1983.
       (002023)
----International codes and multinational
    business. - 1985.
       (001988)
----International construction business
    management. - 1985.
       (000427)
----International corporate diversification,
    market valuation, and size-adjusted
    evidence. - 1984.
       (000475)
----International corporate finance. - 1986.
       (000091)
----International dimensions of accounting.
    - 1984.
       (002059)
----International dimensions of business
    policy and strategy. - 1986.
       (000477)
----International dimensions of financial
    management. - 1988.
       (000407)
----International finance. - 1983.
       (000425)
----International financial center
    preeminence in MNC and nation-state
    interaction. - 1983.
       (001291)
----International financial intermediation.
    - 1987.
       (001236)
----International financial management. -
    1983.
       (001283)
----International financial management. -
    1985.
       (000424)
----International financial management. -
    1986.
       (000418)
----International financial management. -
    1984.
       (000438)
----International financial management: the
    overall investment and financing plan. -
    1983.
       (000401)
----International financial reporting. -
    1984.
       (002079)
----International income taxation and
    developing countries. - 1988.
       (001759)
----International investment and
    multinational enterprises. - 1984.
       (001981)
----International investment disputes. -
    1985.
       (002524)

----International joint ventures:
    implications for organisation
    development. - 1987.
       (001639)
----International labour affairs. - 1987.
       (002595)
----International management. - 1987.
       (000433)
----International marketing. - 1986.
       (000482)
----International mergers and acquisitions.
    - 1986.
       (001569)
----International mergers and acquisitions.
    - 1988.
       (001561)
----International movements and crises in
    resource oriented companies: the case of
    INCO in the nickel sector. - 1985.
       (000271)
----International political risk management.
    - 1984.
       (001802)
----International regulation of
    transnational corporations. - 1986.
       (001956)
----International risk management. - 1983.
       (000499)
----International services-trade issues and
    the GATT. - 1983.
       (000830)
----International standards of accounting
    and reporting. - 1984.
       (002119)
----International technology joint ventures.
    - 1985.
       (001593)
----International technology transactions
    and the theory of the firm. - 1984.
       (001424)
----International technology transfer. -
    1985.
       (001487)
----International trade and investment. -
    1984.
       (001384)
----International trade in business
    services. - 1988.
       (000910)
----International transactions in services.
    - 1986.
       (000946)
----International transfer pricing
    objectives. - 1985.
       (001732)
----International treasury management. -
    1988.
       (000440)
----Internationale Wirtschafts- und
    Finanzpolitik in der Herausforderung der
    achtziger Jahre [Added Entry Conference
    Name]?Internationale
    Management-Gesprache; (14th. - 1984.
       (000419)
----Internationales Konzernmarketing. - 1986.
       (000515)
----The internationalisation of research and
    development by leading enterprises. -
    1986.
       (001480)
----Internationalization of business. - 1984.
       (000086)

TRANSNATIONAL CORPORATIONS (continued)
----Internationalization of capital and the
  semi-industrialized countries: the case
  of the motor industry. - 1985.
    (000700)
----Internatsionalizatsiia
  monopoliticheskogo nakopleniia i
  razvivaiushchiesia strany. - 1986.
    (000082)
----L'internazionalizzazione dell'industria.
  - 1984.
    (000080)
----Intra-firm pricing and the multinational
  corporations. - 1986.
    (000471)
----Intra-firm service trade by the
  multinational enterprise. - 1987.
    (000902)
----Intra-industry production as a form of
  international economic involvement. -
  1983.
    (000026)
----Introduction to business. - 1987.
    (000066)
----An introduction to the multinationals. -
  1984.
    (000033)
----Inventories and foreign currency
  translation requirements. - 1983.
    (002064)
----Investing in development. - 1986.
    (000149)
----L'investissement direct et la firme
  multinationale. - 1984.
    (000140)
----Investissements directs, coopération
  internationale et firmes
  multinationales. - 1984.
    (000045)
----Investitionen und Kooperationen in
  Ubersee. - 1983.
    (001567)
----The investment development cycle and
  Third World multinationals. - 1986.
    (000529)
----Investment incentives and disincentives
  and the international investment
  process. - 1983.
    (002309)
----IRM directory of statistics of
  international investment and production.
  - 1987.
    (000151) (002716)
----Is there a service economy? The changing
  capitalist division of labor. - 1985.
    (000986)
----Issues in business and society. - 1985.
    (001878)
----Issues in international accounting. -
  1986.
    (002098)
----Issues management and the multinational
  enterprise. - 1987.
    (000434)
----Japanese investment in UK industry. -
  1984.
    (000127)
----Japan's largest financier of
  multinationalism: the EXIM Bank. - 1986.
    (000255)
----K mezinárodne právní úpravé cinnosti
  nadnárodních spolecnosti. - 1986.
    (001960)

----Kin'yu torihiki to kokusai sosho. - 1983.
    (002525)
----Kodeksy dzialalnosci przedsiebiorstw
  transnarodowych. - 1987.
    (002026)
----Die Konfrontationen zwischen Staaten und
  ausländischen Unternehmen. - 1983.
    (001864)
----Kreditnyi mekhanizm transnatsional'nykh
  korporatsii. - 1986.
    (000067)
----Los laberintos de la crisis. - 1984.
    (001079)
----Labor confronts the transnationals. -
  1984.
    (002594)
----Leading und Lagging kurzfristig
  variierbarer gruppeninterner Geldflusse
  im Wahrungsrisikomanagement einer
  internationalen Unternehmung. - 1986.
    (000501)
----Leasing in an international context. -
  1983.
    (000929)
----Legal control of the multinational
  enterprise. - 1983.
    (002024)
----Licensing strategy and policy for
  internationalization and technology
  transfer. - 1983.
    (001519)
----Licensing versus direct investment: a
  model of internationalization by the
  multinational enterprise. - 1987.
    (001443)
----The literature of international business
  finance. - 1984.
    (002687)
----The location choice of offices of
  international companies. - 1987.
    (000530)
----Macroproject development in the third
  world. - 1983.
    (001327)
----Making decisions in multinational
  corporations. - 1988.
    (001827)
----Making the multinational decision. -
  1983.
    (000542)
----Management. - 1987.
    (000430)
----Management international. - 1985.
    (000450)
----Management of international production.
  - 1983.
    (000455)
----Manager in the international economy. -
  1986.
    (000451)
----Manager international. - 1985.
    (000429)
----Managerial accounting and analysis in
  multinational enterprises. - 1986.
    (002084)
----Managerial finance. - 1985.
    (000413)
----A managerial procedure for political
  risk forecasting. - 1986.
    (001847)
----Managing cultural differences. - 1983.
    (001871)

TRANSNATIONAL CORPORATIONS (continued)
----Managing international public affairs. -
    1985.
      (000428)
----Managing international risk. - 1983.
      (000480)
----Managing the multinational subsidiary. -
    1986.
      (000405)
----Market power of the firm and
    international transfer of technology. -
    1982.
      (001427)
----Marktstrategien multinationaler
    Pharmaunternehmen und die
    Arzneimittelmarkte der Dritten Welt. -
    1986.
      (000768)
----A mean-variance model of MNF location
    strategy. - 1985.
      (000535)
----Measures of manifest conflict in
    international joint ventures. - 1987.
      (001583)
----Measures to strengthen the capabilities
    of developing countries in their dealing
    with transnational corporations. - 1985.
      (002612)
----Meeting the challenges of foreign
    expansion. - 1985.
      (000035)
----Merger policies and recent trends in
    mergers. - 1984.
      (001618)
----Mergers. - 1983.
      (001580)
----Une méthode d'évaluation interne des
    modèles multinationaux. - 1985.
      (000056)
----Mezhdunarodnye kontserny. - 1985.
      (001868)
----Mezhdunarodnyi chastnyi biznes i
    gosudarstvo. - 1985.
      (001832)
----Mezhdunarodnyi voenno-promyshlennyi
    biznes. - 1985.
      (000993)
----The military origins of
    industrialisation and international
    trade rivalry. - 1984.
      (001335)
----Mirovoe kapitalisticheskoe khoziaistvo i
    razvivaiushchiesia strany Vostoka. -
    1986.
      (001279)
----MNCs and the Iranian revolution: an
    empirical study. - 1985.
      (001772)
----MNE disclosure alternatives and their
    consequences. - 1984.
      (002065)
----Money, multinationals, and sovereigns. -
    1983.
      (001226)
----Multinational accounting. - 1986.
      (002105)
----The multinational bank. - 1987.
      (000950)
----Multinational business and labour. -
    1985.
      (001896)
----Multinational business finance. - 1983.
      (000403)

----Multinational companies and world
    development. - 1983.
      (000071)
----Multinational companies in the textile,
    garment and leather industries. - 1984.
      (000722)
----The multinational construction industry.
    - 1987.
      (000778)
----Multinational corporate strategy. - 1985.
      (000489)
----Multinational corporation and national
    regulation: an economic audit. - 1987.
      (002270)
----The multinational corporation in the
    1980s. - 1983.
      (000051)
----Multinational corporations. - 1986.
      (000058)
----Multinational corporations : the
    political economy of foreign direct
    investment. - 1985.
      (000072)
----Multinational corporations and
    discriminatory investment controls. -
    1983.
      (002249)
----Multinational corporations and European
    integration. - 1987.
      (001325)
----Multinational corporations and global
    welfare: an extension of Kojima and
    Ozawa. - 1985.
      (000036)
----Multinational corporations and regional
    development. - 1983.
      (001326)
----Multinational corporations and the
    nations. - 1983.
      (000006)
----Multinational corporations and the
    political economy of power. - 1983.
      (001846)
----Multinational corporations and the Third
    World. - 1986.
      (000073)
----Multi-national corporations and Third
    World development. - 1984.
      (000074)
----Multinational corporations and trade
    structure. - 1985.
      (001363)
----Multinational corporations, environment,
    and the Third World business matters. -
    1987.
      (001012)
----Multinational corporations in world
    trade. - 1983.
      (001390)
----Multinational corporations, OPEC,
    cartels, foreign investment, and
    technology transfer special studies,
    1982-1985. - 1987.
      (000589)
----Multinational enterprise. - 1987.
      (002713)
----Multinational enterprise and host
    country policy: opportunities for mutual
    benefit. - 1986.
      (001828)
----Multinational enterprise in historical
    perspective. - 1986.
      (000098)

TRANSNATIONAL CORPORATIONS (continued)
----The multinational enterprise in
    transition. - 1986.
      (000040)
----Multinational enterprise, internal
    governance, and industrial organization.
    - 1985.
      (000096)
----Multinational enterprises : information
    and consultation concerning their
    manpower plans. - 1985.
      (000431)
----Multinational enterprises [and]
    government intervention. - 1985.
      (001844)
----Multinational enterprises and the OECD
    industrial relations guidelines. - 1983.
      (001963)
----Multinational enterprises, economic
    structure and international
    competitiveness. - 1985.
      (000075)
----Multinational enterprises of developing
    countries. - 1986.
      (000357)
----Multinational excursions. - 1984.
      (000543)
----Multinational finance. - 1986.
      (001237)
----Multinational financial management. -
    1986.
      (000445)
----A multinational firm. - 1986.
      (000031)
----Multinational firms and the theory of
    effective protection. - 1983.
      (001674)
----Multinational firms' global strategies,
    host country indigenisation of ownership
    and welfare. - 1983.
      (000486)
----Multinational firms, international
    trade, and international
    telecommunications. - 1984.
      (000786)
----Multinational joint ventures in
    developing countries. - 1988.
      (001543)
----Multinational management. - 1984.
      (000449)
----Multinational managers and host
    government interactions. - 1987.
      (001857)
----The multinational mission. - 1987.
      (000083)
----Multinational monopolies and
    international cartels. - 1984.
      (001663)
----Multinational ownership of shipping
    activities. - 1985.
      (000793)
----The multinational reinsurance market. -
    1984.
      (000990)
----Multinational risk assessment and
    management. - 1987.
      (000514)
----Multinational ventures in the commercial
    aircraft industry. - 1985.
      (000721)
----Multinationale ondernemingen en de Derde
    Wereld. - 1985.
      (001002)

----Das Multinationale Unternehmen im
    sozialen Umfeld. - 1983.
      (001870)
----Multinationale Unternehmen und
    Mitbestimmung. - 1986.
      (000406)
----Les multinationales de la pharmacie. -
    1985.
      (000730)
----Les multinationales de l'électronique:
    des stratégies différenciees. (With
    English summary.). - 1984.
      (000679)
----Les multinationales en mutation. - 1983.
      (000019)
----Multinationales et droits de l'homme. -
    1984.
      (001876)
----Multinationales et propriété
    industrielle. - 1986.
      (001409)
----Les multinationales publiques. - 1985.
      (001531)
----Multinationalisation des firmes et
    avantages comparatifs des pays: une vue
    d'ensemble. (With English summary.). -
    1985.
      (001687)
----Multinationals : change of strategy in
    the face of crisis. - 1983.
      (000495)
----Multinationals ; company performance and
    global trends. - 1983.
      (000094)
----Multinationals and global competitive
    strategy. - 1985.
      (000510)
----Multinationals and industrial property.
    - 1988.
      (001410)
----Multinationals and marketplace magic in
    the 1980s. - 1983.
      (001682)
----Multinationals and political control. -
    1983.
      (001848)
----Multinationals and the restructuring of
    the world economy. - 1986.
      (000076)
----Multinationals and trade in services. -
    1987.
      (000939)
----Multinationals and transfer pricing. -
    1985.
      (001751)
----Multinationals and world trade. - 1986.
      (001238)
----Multinationals are mushrooming. - 1986.
      (001861)
----Multinationals as mutual invaders. -
    1985.
      (000077)
----Multinationals, governments and
    international technology transfer. -
    198?.
      (001472)
----Multinationals in a changing
    environment. - 1984.
      (001769)
----Multinationals in the world of nations.
    - 1983.
      (000034)

TRANSNATIONAL CORPORATIONS (continued)
----The multinationals in the world oil
    market: the 1970s and the 1980s. - 1983.
      (000575)
----Multinationals of the South. - 1986.
      (000359)
----Multinationals square off against
    Central American workers. - 1985.
      (001923)
----Multinationals, technology and exports.
    - 1985.
      (001456)
----Multinationals, technology, and
    industrialization. - 1986.
      (001466)
----Multinationals, transaction costs and
    choice of institutional form. - 1986.
      (000078)
----Multinationals--theory and history. -
    1986.
      (000043)
----Mutual investments and the formation of
    multinational enterprises by developing
    countries. - 1987.
      (000378)
----National legislation and regulations
    relating to transnational corporations.
    Volume 2. - 1983.
      (002251)
----National legislation and regulations
    relating to transnational corporations.
    Volume 5. - 1986.
      (002254)
----National legislation and regulations
    relating to transnational corporations.
    Volume 6. - 1988.
      (002255)
----National ownership requirements and
    transfer pricing. - 1986.
      (001711)
----National treatment for
    foreign-controlled enterprises. - 1985.
      (002258)
----National treatment for
    foreign-controlled enterprises. - 1985.
      (002004)
----Natural gas clauses in petroleum
    arrangements. - 1987.
      (002452)
----Needs of developing countries for
    information on transnational
    corporations. - 1987.
      (002721)
----Les négociations internationales sur les
    services ou la quadrature du cercle.
    (With English summary.). - 1986.
      (000912)
----Negotiating international rules for
    trade in services. - 1985.
      (000898)
----Negotiating issues in international
    services transactions. - 1983.
      (000841)
----Negotiating with Third World
    governments. - 1983.
      (002468)
----Neokolonializm. - 1984.
      (000996)
----New theories of the multinational
    enterprise: an assessment of
    internalization theory. - 1986.
      (000089)

----The new environment in international
    accounting. - 1988.
      (002063)
----The new expatriates. - 1988.
      (001925)
----New forms of international investment in
    developing countries. - 1984.
      (001615)
----The new multinationals. - 1983.
      (000348)
----The new multinationals: synthesis and
    conclusions. -   .
      (000349)
----The new multinationals: the theoretical
    background. - 1983.
      (000350)
----New theories of international business:
    some unresolved issues. - 1983.
      (000010)
----Nihon shihon shugi no kaigai shinshutsu.
    - 1984.
      (000235)
----North-South technology transfer: two
    neglected problems. - 1986.
      (001437)
----La notion de produit-système et la
    décomposition internationale des
    processus productifs dans l'industrie
    automobile. (With English summary.). -
    1984.
      (000687)
----Le nouveau marché international du
    charbon. - 1986.
      (000637)
----Occasional paper (University of Sydney.
    Transnational Corporations Research
    Project). - 1978-   .
      (000079)
----The OECD Declaration on International
    Investment and Multinational
    Enterprises. -   .
      (001993)
----The OECD guidelines for multinational
    enterprises. - 1986.
      (002002)
----The OECD guidelines for multinational
    enterprises and labour relations,
    1982-1984. - 1985.
      (001961)
----OECD Guidelines for Multinational Firms
    remain relevant after ten years. - 1986.
      (002003)
----Oil companies in the international
    system. - 1983.
      (000641)
----On the theory of an exhaustible resource
    extractive multinational firm. - 1986.
      (000610)
----Organizing to implement strategies of
    diversity and globalization: the role of
    matrix designs. - 1986.
      (000476)
----Osobennosti ekspansii
    transnatsional'nykh korporatsii v
    sovremennykh usloviiakh. - 1984.
      (000048)
----Overseas acquisitions and mergers. -
    1986.
      (001585)
----Ownership and development. - 1987.
      (001129)

TRANSNATIONAL CORPORATIONS (continued)

----Países socialistas y corporaciones transnacionales. - 1984.
(001178)

----Planungs- und Kontrollrechnung im internationalen Konzern. - 1984.
(002068)

----Political risk analysis. - 1985.
(001859)

----Political risk assessment. - 1985.
(001842) (002659)

----Political risks in international business. - 1985.
(001843)

----The politics of international economic relations. - 1985.
(001300)

----Pollution and the struggle for the world product. - 1988.
(001948)

----Postimperialism. - 1987.
(001232)

----Pourquoi les multinationales? : une revue de la littérature sur les motivations de la croissance multinationale des firmes. - 1987.
(000020)

----Praxis des internationalen Finanzmanagement. - 1985.
(000435)

----Précis de gestion financière internationale. - 1986.
(001255)

----Present and desired methods of selecting expatriate managers for international assignments. - 1984.
(000522)

----Les principes directeurs de l'OCDE à l'intention des entreprises multinationales. - 1986.
(002005)

----Principles of international accounting. - 1986.
(002077)

----Private international law as a means to control the multinational enterprise. - 1986.
(002154)

----Prix de transfert et entreprises multinationales. - 1979.
(001744)

----Prix de transfert et entreprises multinationales. - 1984.
(002099)

----Probleme der Gerwinnverlagerungen multinationaler Unternehmen : Konzerninterne Verrechnungspreise und deren wirtschaftspolitische Wirkungen. - 1983.
(001755)

----Problems of mineral development in developing countries. - 1983.
(000583)

----Problems that plague multinational marketers. - 1983.
(000517)

----Proceedings of the SSTCC/UNCTC/ESCAP Asia-Pacific Training Workshop on Regulating and Negotiating Technology Transfer through Transnational Corporations, 14-25 October 1985, Fuzhou, Fujian, China. - 1986.
(001405) (002169)

----Production cost differentials and foreign direct investment: a test of two models. - 1986.
(000061)

----Production flexibility as a motive for multinationality. - 1987.
(000470)

----Promotion of direct investment in developing countries. - 1986.
(002143)

----Prospects for automotive transnationals in the Third World. - 1983.
(000708)

----Publicidad. - 1987.
(000937)

----Quando l'impresa diventa multinazionale: il problema del controllo. - 1983.
(001607)

----The question of a reference to international law in the United Nations Code of Conduct on Transnational Corporations. - 1986.
(002007)

----The question of a reference to international obligations in the United Nations Code of Conduct on Transnational Corporations. - 1986.
(002020)

----Rabochii klass protiv transnatsional'nykh korporatsii. - 1984.
(001278)

----Recent developments in operations and behaviour of transnational corporations. - 1987.
(000103)

----Recent trends in international direct investment. - 1987.
(000176)

----A reference guide to international taxation. - 1987.
(001714)

----Le régime fiscal des sociétés étrangeres en droit comparé. - 1985.
(001752)

----La regolamentazione internazionale dei rapporti di lavoro con imprese multinazionali. - 1986.
(001919)

----Regulating international business through codes of conduct. - 1980.
(002022)

----Rekindling development. - 1988.
(001302)

----The relationship between the state and the multinational corporation in the exploitation of resources. - 1984.
(000584)

----Research in international business and finance. - 1979- .
(000085)

----Research on Third World multinationals. - 1985.
(000321)

----Restrictive clauses in licensing agreements: the pharmaceutical industry in developing countries. - 1984.
(002420)

----The rise of multinationals from the Third World. - 1983.
(000351)

TRANSNATIONAL CORPORATIONS (continued)
----Le risque de change et la consolidation
des comptes de groupes multinationaux. -
1983.
(002104)
----Rol' mezhdunarodnykh monopolii v mirovoi
ekonomike. - 1983.
(000047)
----Rola korporacji transnarodowych w
miedzynarodowej wymianie towarów
przemyslowych. - 1986.
(001369)
----The role of transnationals in technology
transfer. - 1987.
(001518)
----Rol'mezhdunarodnykh monopolii v
prodovol'stvennoi sisteme. - 1985.
(000728)
----Safety and health practices of
multinational enterprises. - 1984.
(001918)
----Sales publications of the United Nations
Centre on Transnational Corporations,
1973-1987. - 1987.
(002693)
----Selecting a foreign partner for
technology transfer. - 1984.
(001459)
----Services and the development process. -
1985.
(000979)
----Shifts in the world economy and the
restructuring of economic sectors. -
1987.
(000734)
----So you want to do business overseas? Or
ready, fire, aim. - 1988.
(001781)
----Social and labour practices of
multinational enterprises in the
textiles, clothing and footwear
industries. - 1984.
(001922)
----Social cost/benefit analysis for MNCs. -
1983.
(001881)
----Sociedades y grupos multinacionales. -
1985.
(000004)
----Le societa multinazionali nel diritto
comunitario. - 1984.
(002011)
----Les sociétés multinationales. - 1985.
(000021)
----Sovremennye transnatsional'nye
korporatsii. - 1983.
(000007)
----Sovremennyi kontsern,
politekonomicheskii aspekt. - 1983.
(001668)
----Sozio-politische Strategien
multinationaler Unternehmungen. - 1985.
(000387)
----The spatial organisation of
multinational corporations. - 1985.
(000017)
----Spotlight on international business: the
Forbes foreign rankings. - 1986.
(002665)
----Staatsmonopolistische Regulierung in der
kapitalistischen Weltwirtschaft. - 1984.
(001263)

----Standardisation of marketing strategy by
multinationals. - 1987.
(000506)
----State enterprise-multinational
corporation joint ventures: how well do
they meet both partners' needs? - 1983.
(001632)
----State-owned multinationals. - 1987.
(001532)
----Die Steuerung auslandischer
Tochtergesellschaften. - 1985.
(001731)
----Strategic international marketing. -
1985.
(000467)
----Strategic investment, multinational
corporations and trade policy. - 1987.
(001388)
----Strategic investments and the
development of multinationals. - 1987.
(000044)
----Strategic management in multinational
companies. - 1986.
(000472)
----Strategic management of multinational
corporations. - 1985.
(000519)
----Strategic planning for information
resource management. - 1983.
(000443)
----Strategic planning for international
corporations. - 1979.
(000461)
----La stratégie des multinationales. - 1985.
(000457)
----Stratégies des entreprises et marché
international des capitaux. - 1984.
(001273)
----Strategies for joint venture success. -
1983.
(001600)
----The strategy of transnational
corporations. - 1983.
(000458)
----Structural adjustment and multinational
enterprises. - 1985.
(000095)
----La structure financière du capitalisme
multinational. - 1983.
(001259)
----Takokuseki kigyo to chushin kogyokoku. -
1983.
(001319)
----Tax holidays as signals. - 1986.
(002303)
----Tax treatment of cost-contribution
arrangements. - 1988.
(001737)
----Taxation of intercorporate transfer
pricing: a management responsibility:
U.S.A. - 1986.
(001754)
----Technical co-operation programme of the
United Nations Centre on Transnational
Corporations. - 1988.
(002610)
----Technical co-operation programme,
1976-1987 : United Nations Centre on
Transnational Corporations. - 1988.
(002611)

TRANSNATIONAL CORPORATIONS (continued)
----Techno-economic aspects of the
    international division of labour in the
    automotive industry. - 1983.
      (000752)
----Technological and organisational factors
    in the theory of the multinational
    enterprise. - 1983.
      (000097)
----Technology choice and employment
    generation by multinational enterprises
    in developing countries. - 1984.
      (001646)
----Technology importation policies in
    developing countries: some implications
    of recent theoretical and empirical
    evidence. - 1983.
      (001420)
----Technology transfer to developing
    countries via multinationals. - 1986.
      (001467)
----Testing the bargaining hypothesis in the
    manufacturing sector in developing
    countries. - 1987.
      (000706)
----Theories of foreign direct investment
    and divestment: a classificatory note. -
    1985.
      (000558)
----A theory of co-operation in
    international business. - 1987.
      (000011)
----A theory of multinational enterprise. -
    1985.
      (000042)
----Third World mineral development in
    crisis: the impact of the worldwide
    recession on legal instruments governing
    Third World mineral development. - 1985.
      (000649)
----Third World multinationals. - 1983.
      (000383)
----Third World resource directory. - 1984.
      (002719)
----The threat of Japanese multinationals. -
    1983.
      (000329)
----Threats and opportunities of global
    countertrade : marketing, financing and
    organizational implications. - 1984.
      (001353)
----'Tikhaia' agressiia imperializma. - 1986.
      (001272)
----The TNCs and the policy of hegemonism. -
    1987.
      (000093)
----Tourism : transnational corporations and
    cultural identities. - 1985.
      (000804)
----Towards a theory of multinational
    enterprise. - 1986.
      (000032)
----Trade [and] structural change. - 1984.
      (001391)
----Trade in services : growth and balance
    of payments implications for countries
    of Western Asia. - 1987.
      (000968)
----Trade in services and the multilateral
    trade negotiations. - 1987.
      (000812)

----Trade policy issues and empirical
    analysis /edited by Robert Baldwin. -
    1988.
      (001348)
----Trade-related investment issues. - 1983.
      (001385)
----Le traitement national des entreprises
    sous contrôle étranger établies dans les
    pays de l'OCDE. - 1978.
      (002000)
----Transactions cost economics and the
    multinational enterprise: an assessment.
    - 1986.
      (000448)
----Transborder data flows. - 1983.
      (000973)
----Transborder data flows. - 1984.
      (000974)
----Transfer pricing and multinational
    enterprises. - 1984.
      (001745)
----Transfer pricing problems and economic
    strategies in developing countries. -
    1983.
      (001747)
----Las transnacionales en el Paraguay. -
    1985.
      (001116)
----A transnacionalizacao da America Latina
    e a missao das igrejas. - 1983.
      (002591)
----Transnacionalización y periferia
    semindustrializada. - 1984-   .
      (001339)
----Transnacional'nye korporacii na rynkah
    razvivajuscihsja stran: Ogranicit.
    delovaja praktika. - 1985.
      (001662)
----Transnational [and] the Third World. -
    1983.
      (001875)
----Transnational business problems. - 1986.
      (000516)
----Transnational corporations and
    contractual relations in the world
    uranium industry. - 1983.
      (002448)
----Transnational corporations and
    international trade : selected issues. -
    1985.
      (001393)
----Transnational corporations and
    militarism. - 1985.
      (000663)
----Transnational corporations and non-fuel
    primary commodities in developing
    countries. - 1987.
      (000639)
----Transnational corporations and services.
    - 1984.
      (000828)
----Transnational corporations and
    technology transfer. - 1987.
      (001509)
----Transnational corporations and
    underdevelopment. - 1985.
      (001314)
----Transnational corporations and uneven
    development : the internationalization
    of capital and the Third World. - 1987.
      (001270)

TRANSNATIONAL CORPORATIONS (continued)
----Transnational corporations: choice of
    techniques and employment in developing
    countries. -   .
        (001882)
----Transnational corporations in the
    agricultural machinery and equipment
    industry. - 1983.
        (000746) .
----Transnational corporations in the
    international auto industry. - 1983.
        (000747)
----Transnational corporations in the
    international semiconductor industry. -
    1986.
        (000748)
----Transnational corporations in the
    man-made fibre, textile and clothing
    industries. - 1987.
        (000751)
----Transnational corporations in the
    pharmaceutical industry of developing
    countries. - 1984.
        (000749)
----Transnational corporations in world
    development. - 1988.
        (000101)
----Transnational corporations in world
    development. - 1983.
        (000102)
----Transnational data flow constraints: a
    new challenge for multinational
    corporations. - 1984.
        (000942)
----Transnational labor relations. - 1985.
        (001905)
----Transnational legal practice and
    professional ideology. - 1985.
        (002212)
----Transnational monopoly capitalism. -
    1987.
        (001666)
----The transnational politics of the
    aluminum multinationals. - 1984.
        (000598)
----Transnational retailing. - 1988.
        (000780)
----Transnationale Konzerne der Dritten Welt
    und der Entwicklungsprozess
    unterentwickelter Lander. - 1985.
        (000334)
----Transnationals and the Third World. -
    1984.
        (001005)
----Transnationals and the Third World:
    changing perceptions. - 1984.
        (001006)
----Transnatsional'nye korporatsii i
    burzhuaznoe trudovoe pravo. - 1985.
        (001946) (002230)
----Transnatsional'nye korporatsii i
    rabochii klass. - 1987.
        (001953)
----Transnatsional'nye korporatsii na
    rynkakh razvivaiushchikhsia stran. -
    1985.
        (001660)
----Transnatsional'nye korporatsii v sisteme
    gosudarstvenno-monopolisticheskogo
    regulirovaniia ekonomiki. - 1985.
        (002679)

----Trasferimento internazionale di risorse
    per lo sviluppo: il ruolo delle
    istituzioni multilaterali. - 1984.
        (001997)
----Trends and issues in foreign direct
    investment and related flows. - 1985.
        (000192)
----Trends in the internationalisation of
    production. - 1986.
        (002597)
----Treuepflicht im internationalen Konzern
    gegenüber Hoheitsakten im Heimatstaate
    der Muttergesellschaft. - 1983.
        (002343)
----Triad power. - 1985.
        (001686)
----Tripartite Declaration of Principles
    Concerning Multinational Enterprises and
    Social Policy. - 1977.
        (002013)
----A tripartite model of the international
    debt crisis. - 1985.
        (000238)
----The U.S. drive to bring services into
    GATT. - 1986.
        (000926)
----Die Umrechnung der Jahresabschlusse
    auslandischer Konzernunternehmen und die
    Verrechnung der daraus resultierenden
    Umrechnungsdifferenzen. - 1986.
        (002095)
----UNCITRAL, the United Nations Commission
    on International Trade Law. - 1986.
        (002155)
----UNCTC bibliography, 1974-1987. - 1988.
        (002695)
----The United Nations Code of Conduct on
    Transnational Corporations. - 1986.
        (002014)
----The United States, transnational
    business and the law. - 1985.
        (001982)
----University of Reading discussion papers
    in international investment and business
    studies. - 197?-   .
        (000104)
----Verrechnungspreispolitik in
    internationalen Unternehmungen. - 1985.
        (002692)
----Vneshneekonomicheskaia ekspansiia
    imperialisticheskikh stran. - 1984.
        (002680)
----The Vredeling proposal. - 1983.
        (002604)
----The Vredeling proposal and multinational
    trade unionism. - 1983.
        (002598)
----Die Wahrungsumrechnung im Rahmen der
    internationalen Konzernrechnungslegung.
    - 1985.
        (002096)
----The welfare effects of foreign
    enterprise. - 1986.
        (000016)
----Where in the world should we put that
    plant? - 1983.
        (000553)
----Who audits the world. - 1983.
        (002061)
----Why are services cheaper in the poor
    countries? - 1984.
        (000813)

TRANSNATIONAL CORPORATIONS (continued)
----Wielkie przedsiebiorstwa transnarodowe a
    ograniczanie konkurencji w wysoko
    rozwinietych krajach kapitalistycznych.
    - 1983.
    (001153)
----Wohin expandieren multinationale
    Konzerne? - 1985.
    (000063)
----Women in the global factory. - 1983.
    (001898)
----Women workers in multinational
    enterprises in developing countries. -
    1985.
    (001926)
----Work by the United Nations Centre on
    Transnational Corporations on the Code
    of Conduct on Transnational
    Corporations, other international
    arrangements and agreements, and
    national laws and regulations relating
    to transnational corporations. - 1986.
    (002694)
----The world according to Nestlé. - 1987.
    (000291)
----The world directory of multinational
    enterprises. - 1980-   .
    (002676)
----The world-class executive. - 1985.
    (000396)
----The world's new property barons. - 1987.
    (000904)
----Zielbildung und strategisches Zielsystem
    der internationalen Unternehmung. - 1984.
    (000474)
----Zloveshchii molokh. - 1987.
    (000385) (000994)
----161 more checklists : decision making in
    international operations. - 1985.
    (000462)
----The 1984 review of the 1976 declaration
    and decisions. - 1984.
    (002001)

TRANSNATIONAL CORPORATIONS--AFRICA.
----Agribusiness in Africa. - 1984.
    (001025)
----Les finances des multinationales en
    Afrique. - 1983.
    (001024)
----Foreign powers and Africa. - 1983.
    (001031)
----International marketing to Black Africa
    and the Third World. - 1988.
    (001001)
----Les techniques de negociation en matière
    de transfert de technologie. - 1987.
    (001511)
----The political economy of regulation. -
    1985.
    (001959)
----Les sociétés transnationales en Afrique.
    - 1986.
    (001028)
----The transnational focus. - 1982-   .
    (001033)

TRANSNATIONAL CORPORATIONS--AFRICA SOUTH OF
SAHARA.
----Transnatsional'nye korporatsii v
    Tropicheskoi Afrike. - 1986.
    (001020)
----Uoll-strit protiv Afriki. - 1985.
    (001030)

TRANSNATIONAL CORPORATIONS--ALGERIA.
----National legislation and regulations
    relating to transnational corporations.
    Volume 3. - 1983.
    (002252)

TRANSNATIONAL CORPORATIONS--ANDEAN REGION.
----The Andean foreign investment code's
    impact on multinational enterprises. -
    1983.
    (001977)
----Andean multinational enterprises: a new
    approach to multinational investment in
    the Andean Group. - 1983.
    (000313)
----La empresa multinacional andina. - 1983.
    (002246)
----Empresas multinacionales y Pacto andino.
    - 1983.
    (001102)
----Estudios jurídicos sobre la Empresa
    Multinacional Andina, E.M.A. - 1986.
    (000314)

TRANSNATIONAL CORPORATIONS--ARAB COUNTRIES.
----The oil companies and the Arab world. -
    1984.
    (000613)

TRANSNATIONAL CORPORATIONS--ARGENTINA.
----Las empresas transnacionales en la
    Argentina. - 1986.
    (001122)
----Empresas transnacionales en la industria
    de alimentos. - 1983.
    (000573)
----Multinationals and maldevelopment. -
    1987.
    (000995)
----Multinationals from Argentina. - 1983.
    (000340)
----Transnacionalización y política
    económica en la Argentina. - 1985.
    (001115)
----Transnational corporations in Argentina,
    1976-1983. - 1986.
    (001081)

TRANSNATIONAL CORPORATIONS--ASIA.
----Asia's struggle to affirm wholeness of
    life : report of a consultation on TNC's
    in Asia. - 1985.
    (001935)
----Critical issues for business in Asia. -
    1984.
    (001787)
----Ekspansiia mezhdunarodnykh monopolii v
    razvivaiushchiesia strany Azii. - 1987.
    (001068)
----International law of take-overs and
    mergers. - 1986.
    (001572)
----Joint ventures in Asien. - 1983.
    (001597)
----Madison Avenue in Asia. - 1984.
    (000801)
----New business strategies for developing
    Asia, 1983-1990. - 1984.
    (000498)

TRANSNATIONAL CORPORATIONS--ASIA AND THE
PACIFIC.
----Asia-Pacific TNC review. - 1984-   .
    (001076)
----Japanese transnational corporations and
    the economic integration of Australian
    and the Asian-Pacific region. - 1983.
    (000323)
----Natural gas clauses in petroleum
    arrangements. - 1987.
    (002452)
----Technology transfer under alternative
    arrangements with transnational
    corporations. - 1987.
    (001513)
----Transnational corporations and external
    financial flows of developing economies
    in Asia and the Pacific. - 1986.
    (000196)

TRANSNATIONAL CORPORATIONS--AUSTRALIA.
----Aborigines and mining companies in
    Northern Australia. - 1983.
    (001874)
----Australia deregulated : new freedoms for
    multinational investment. - 1987.
    (001797)
----The Australian multinational -- parent
    and subsidiary relationships. - 1986.
    (000390)
----Beyond dependence. - 1986.
    (000640)
----Fiji : client State of Australasia? -
    1984.
    (001046) (002358)
----Foreign investment in Australia,
    1960-1981. - 1983.
    (000141)
----The geography of Australian corporate
    power. - 1984.
    (001166)
----Indigenous resource rights and mining
    companies in North America and
    Australia. - 1986.
    (000616)
----International law of take-overs and
    mergers. - 1986.
    (001572)
----Japanese transnational corporations and
    the economic integration of Australian
    and the Asian-Pacific region. - 1983.
    (000323)
----MNCs and the Australian government: some
    emerging policy issues. - 1983.
    (002289)
----Multinational enterprise behaviour and
    domestic industry adjustment under
    import threat. - 1986.
    (000518)
----National legislation and regulations
    relating to transnational corporations.
    Volume 3. - 1983.
    (002252)

TRANSNATIONAL CORPORATIONS--BELGIUM.
----Employment decision-making in
    multinational enterprises. - 1984.
    (001888)
----European headquarters of American
    multinational enterprises in Brussels
    and Belgium. - 1984.
    (000381)

----Location and investment decisions by
    multinational enterprises. - 1984.
    (000552)
----Note sur la transnationalisation de
    l'économie belge. - 1985.
    (000123)

TRANSNATIONAL CORPORATIONS--BHOPAL (INDIA).
----The lessons of Bhopal. - 1985.
    (001933)

TRANSNATIONAL CORPORATIONS--BOLIVIA.
----National legislation and regulations
    relating to transnational corporations.
    Volume 4. - 1986.
    (002253)
----Transnacionales y nación. - 1986.
    (000594)

TRANSNATIONAL CORPORATIONS--BOTSWANA.
----National legislation and regulations
    relating to transnational corporations.
    Volume 4. - 1986.
    (002253)

TRANSNATIONAL CORPORATIONS--BRAZIL.
----Business in a democratic Brazil. - 1985.
    (001776)
----Capitais estrangeiros. - 1984.
    (002275)
----O codigo de conduta das empresas
    transnacionais. - 1984.
    (001968)
----Como enfrentar as multinacionais. - 1983.
    (001092)
----The comparative performance of foreign
    and domestic firms in Brazil. - 1986.
    (001130)
----The determinants of manufacturing
    ownership in less developed countries. -
    1986.
    (000712)
----Dos estudios sobre empresas
    transnacionales en Brasil. - 1983.
    (001120)
----Employment effects of exports by
    multinationals and of export processing
    zones in Brazil. - 1987.
    (001915)
----Empresas transnacionales y ganadería de
    carnes en Brasil. - 1983.
    (000568)
----Multinacionais. - 1984.
    (002183)
----Multinationals from Brazil. - 1983.
    (000382)
----National legislation and regulations
    relating to transnational corporations.
    Volume 4. - 1986.
    (002253)
----Natural gas clauses in petroleum
    arrangements. - 1987.
    (002452)
----New forms of overseas investment by
    developing countries : the case of
    India, Korea and Brazil. - 1986.
    (001616)
----Technological spill-overs and manpower
    training: a comparative analysis of
    multinational and national enterprises
    in Brazilian manufacturing. - 1986.
    (001899)

TRANSNATIONAL CORPORATIONS--CHINA (continued)
----China's modernization and transnational
    corporations. - 1984.
      (001077)
----China's trade, tax and investment laws
    and regulations. - 1984.
      (002189)
----Chung wai ho tzu ching ying ch'i yeh fa
    chi ch'i shih shih ching yen ch'ien
    t'an. - 1983.
      (002190)
----Foreign direct investment in the
    People's Republic of China. - 1988.
      (000191)
----Joint ventures in the People's Republic
    of China. - 1985.
      (001647)
----Revenue law and practice in the People's
    Republic of China. - 1983.
      (002271)
----The training component. - 1986.
      (001920)
----Transnational corporations and China's
    open door policy. - 1988.
      (001074)

TRANSNATIONAL CORPORATIONS--COLOMBIA.
----Empresas multinacionales y Pacto andino.
    - 1983.
      (001102)
----Las empresas transnacionales en el
    desarrollo colombiano. - 1986.
      (001121)
----Evolución contradictoria de la industria
    en Colombia. - 1984.
      (001095)
----National legislation and regulations
    relating to transnational corporations.
    Volume 4. - 1986.
      (002253)

TRANSNATIONAL CORPORATIONS--CONGO.
----Le transfert de technologie dans les
    industries agro-alimentaires en Afrique
    Centrale. - 1987.
      (001510)

TRANSNATIONAL CORPORATIONS--COSTA RICA.
----National legislation and regulations
    relating to transnational corporations.
    Volume 3. - 1983.
      (002252)

TRANSNATIONAL CORPORATIONS--COTE D'IVOIRE.
----Multinationals and maldevelopment. -
    1987.
      (000995)
----National legislation and regulations
    relating to transnational corporations.
    Volume 4. - 1986.
      (002253)

TRANSNATIONAL CORPORATIONS--EASTERN EUROPE.
----Eastern bloc international enterprises
    -- still in statu nascendi. - 1985.
      (000332)
----International economic organizations and
    multinational corporations. - 1986.
      (002590)
----Multinational companies and the COMECON
    countries. - 1986.
      (001177)

----Multinationals from the Second World :
    growth of foreign investment by Soviet
    and East European enterprises. - 1987.
      (000356)
----Patterns of technology imports:
    interregional comparison. - 1986.
      (001483)
----Red multinationals or red herring : the
    activities of enterprises from socialist
    countries in the West. - 1986.
      (000371)
----101 checklists for success in East
    European markets. - 1984.
      (001779)

TRANSNATIONAL CORPORATIONS--ECUADOR.
----Capitalismo, burguesia y crisis en el
    Ecuador. - 1983.
      (001104)
----Ecuador. - 1984.
      (001831)
----La evolución del capitalismo ecuatoriano
    en el último decenio y perspectivas. -
    1984.
      (001105)
----Natural gas clauses in petroleum
    arrangements. - 1987.
      (002452)
----La presencia de las empresas
    transnacionales en la economía
    ecuatoriana. - 1984.
      (001125)
----Risk-bearing and the choice of contract
    forms for oil exploration and
    development. - 1984.
      (002410)

TRANSNATIONAL CORPORATIONS--EGYPT.
----Egypt's experience in regulating
    technology imports. - 1987.
      (001514)
----National legislation and regulations
    relating to transnational corporations.
    Volume 4. - 1986.
      (002253)
----Natural gas clauses in petroleum
    arrangements. - 1987.
      (002452)
----Operations of multinational corporations
    and local enterprises in Arab countries.
    - 1985.
      (001141)

TRANSNATIONAL CORPORATIONS--EUROPE.
----Competitive strategies for Europe. -
    1983.
      (000463)
----Les entreprises multinationales dans la
    Communauté européenne. - 1984.
      (001154)
----European multinationals in core
    technologies. - 1988.
      (000380)
----The export of hazard. - 1985.
      (001941)
----Market share strategy in Europe. - 1985.
      (000493)
----The relationship between foreign
    ownership and technology transfer. -
    1983.
      (001422)

TRANSNATIONAL CORPORATIONS--JAPAN (continued)
----Technology strategy and industrial
relations: case studies of Japanese
multinationals in the United States. -
1983.
(002599)
----The threat of Japanese multinationals. -
1983.
(000329)
----Togoteki takokuseki kigyoron. - 1983.
(000364)
----A transactions cost approach to
international trading structures: the
case of the Japanese general trading
companies. - 1983.
(000372)
----The transfer of organizational culture
overseas: an approach to control in the
multinational corporation. - 1983.
(000420)
----Transnational corporations in the
international semiconductor industry. -
1986.
(000748)
----Trends in Japan's manufacturing
investment in the United States. - 1987.
(000767)
----Trends in multinational business and
global environments: a perspective. -
1984.
(000029)

TRANSNATIONAL CORPORATIONS--KEDAH (MALAYSIA).
----Transnational corporations in Kedah,
West Malaysia. - 1985.
(001061)

TRANSNATIONAL CORPORATIONS--KENYA.
----Corporate strategy and employment
relations in multinational corporations:
some evidence from Kenya and Malaysia. -
1983.
(001902)
----Labor, capital, and management slack in
multinational and local firms in Kenyan
manufacturing. - 1986.
(001026)
----Multinational enterprises, transfer of
managerial know-how, technology choice
and employment effects. - 1983.
(001436)
----National legislation and regulations
relating to transnational corporations.
Volume 4. - 1986.
(002253)
----The role of transnational corporations
in hotel and tourism industry in
selected PTA member countries. - 1986.
(000782) (000936)

TRANSNATIONAL CORPORATIONS--KUWAIT.
----Impact of the operations of
transnational corporations on
development in Kuwait. - 1987.
(001143)
----National legislation and regulations
relating to transnational corporations.
Volume 4. - 1986.
(002253)
----Operations of multinational corporations
and local enterprises in Arab countries.
- 1985.
(001141)

TRANSNATIONAL CORPORATIONS--LATIN AMERICA.
----Agricultura y alimentos en América
Latina. - 1985.
(000562)
----Banco de datos sobre inversión
extranjera directa en América Latina y
el Caribe : información de los países
receptores y de organismos regionales y
subregionales, t. 2. - 1987.
(000193)
----Banco de datos sobre inversión
extranjera directa en América Latina y
el Caribe, sobre la base de información
de organismos multilaterales y de
gobiernos de países de origen de la
inversión, t. 1. - 1986.
(000195)
----Breves rasgos de la crisis. - 1983.
(001307)
----O capital transnacional e o estado. -
1985.
(002274)
----Capitalismo neocolonial. - 1983.
(001109)
----La crisis internacional y la América
Latina. - 1984.
(001245)
----Deuda externa, inversión extranjera y
transferencia de tecnología en América
Latina. - 1986.
(001080)
----Disfraces del coloniaje. - 1984.
(001114)
----Doing business in key Latin American
markets: U.S. international executive
perceptions. - 1983.
(001824)
----L'émpire Nestle. - 1983.
(000283)
----Las empresas transnacionales y la
inversión extranjera directa en la
primera mitad de los años ochenta. -
1987.
(000194)
----Evaluating differences in technological
activity between transnational and
domestic firms in Latin America. - 1986.
(001431)
----Financial transfers in the MNE. - 1986.
(000416)
----Grace. - 1985.
(000276)
----La industria farmacéutica y las
transnacionales. - 1985.
(000667)
----Inostrannye monopolii v Latinskoi
Amerike. - 1983.
(001103)
----International law of take-overs and
mergers. - 1986.
(001573)
----Latinskaia Amerika, ekspansiia
inostrannykh monopolii. - 1984.
(001090)
----Latinskaja Amerika. - 1984.
(001089)
----Measures strengthening the negotiating
capacity of Governments in their
relations with transnational
corporations. - 1983.
(002461)

TRANSNATIONAL CORPORATIONS--LATIN AMERICA
(continued)
----Mezhdunarodnye monopolii v Latinskoi
    Amerike. - 1986.
      (001128)
----Patterns of technology imports:
    interregional comparison. - 1986.
      (001483)
----Politik als Investitionsmotor? - 1985.
      (001131)
----Profits, progress and poverty. - 1985.
      (001111)
----Regulation of transnational
    corporations. - 1984.
      (001998)
----The role of the public sector and
    transnational corporations in the mining
    development of Latin America. - 1986.
      (000605)
----The role of transnational enterprises in
    Latin American economic integration
    efforts. - 1983.
      (001126)
----Small nations, giant firms. - 1987.
      (001091)
----Transnacionalizacion y desarrollo
    agropecuario en America Latina. - 1984.
      (000574)
----Transnacionalización y desarrollo
    nacional en América Latina. - 1984.
      (001117)
----Transnacional'nye korporacii SSA v
    Latinskoj Amerike/edited by N.G. Zajcev.
    - 1985.
      (000326)
----Transnational corporations and
    industrial transformation in Latin
    America. - 1984.
      (001099)
----The transnational corporations and Latin
    America's international trade. - 1985.
      (001100)
----Transnational corporations and the Latin
    American automobile industry. - 1987.
      (000701)
----Transnatsional'nye korporatsii SShA v
    Latinskoi Amerike. - 1985.
      (001087)
----Yanqui come back! - 1986.
      (001825)

TRANSNATIONAL CORPORATIONS--LIBERIA.
----Employment and multinational enterprises
    in export processing zones. - 1984.
      (001886)
----The impact of the transnational
    corporations in the banking and other
    financial institutions on the economy of
    Liberia. - 1986.
      (000873)
----Multinationals and employment in a West
    African sub-region. - 1984.
      (001904)
----National legislation and regulations
    relating to transnational corporations.
    Volume 4. - 1986.
      (002253)

TRANSNATIONAL CORPORATIONS--LIBYAN ARAB
JAMAHIRIYA.
----National legislation and regulations
    relating to transnational corporations.
    Volume 4. - 1986.
      (002253)

TRANSNATIONAL CORPORATIONS--MALAYSIA.
----Business prospects in Malaysia, coping
    with change in a new era. - 1983.
      (001780)
----Chinese business, multinationals and the
    state: manufacturing for export in
    Malaysia and Singapore. - 1983.
      (000713)
----Corporate strategy and employment
    relations in multinational corporations:
    some evidence from Kenya and Malaysia. -
    1983.
      (001902)
----Malaysia's new economic policy: the role
    of the transnational corporations. -
    1985.
      (001060)
----Multinationals and market structure in
    an open developing economy: the case of
    Malaysia. - 1983.
      (001056)
----Technology transfer under alternative
    arrangements with transnational
    corporations. - 1987.
      (001513)
----Transnational corporations in Kedah,
    West Malaysia. - 1985.
      (001061)
----Wages and work conditions, and the
    effects of foreign investment and the
    separation of ownership from management
    on them: a study of Malaysian
    manufacturing. - 1983.
      (001907)

TRANSNATIONAL CORPORATIONS--MAURITIUS.
----The role of transnational corporations
    in hotel and tourism industry in
    selected PTA member countries. - 1986.
      (000782) (000936)

TRANSNATIONAL CORPORATIONS--MEXICO.
----El comportamiento de las empresas
    nacionales y estranjeras en México. -
    1986.
      (001083)
----De la improvisación al fracaso : la
    política de inversión extranjera en
    México. - 1983.
      (001112)
----The determinants of manufacturing
    ownership in less developed countries. -
    1986.
      (000712)
----Estructura y comportamiento de la
    industria químico-farmacéutica en
    México. - 1984.
      (000737)
----Foreign investment, technical efficiency
    and structural change. - 1983.
      (001085)
----Inversión extranjera directa. - 1985.
      (000138)
----Las maquiladoras en México. - 1984.
      (001906)
----Médicaments pour tous en l'an 2000? -
    1983.
      (000662)
----Multinationals and market structure in
    Mexico. - 1986.
      (001086)

TRANSNATIONAL CORPORATIONS--MEXICO
(continued)
----La nacionalización de la banca. - 1983.
   (001529)
----National legislation and regulations
   relating to transnational corporations.
   Volume 4. - 1986.
   (002253)
----Política económica y empresas
   transnacionales en México. - 1983.
   (001127)
----Research and development in
   pharmaceuticals: Mexico. - 1983.
   (000770)
----Las transnacionales de la salud. - 1983.
   (000745)
----Transnational corporations versus the
   state. - 1985.
   (000657)
----Wandel der mexikanischen Politik
   gegenuber Auslandsinvestitionen? Die
   "irationale" Komponente der
   Mexikanisierungsstrategie. - 1985.
   (002338)
----1985 directory of in-bond plants
   (maquiladoras) in Mexico. - 1984.
   (001132) (002678)

TRANSNATIONAL CORPORATIONS--MIDDLE EAST.
----International business in the Middle
   East. - 1986.
   (001135)
----An international directory of 600
   consultants and contractors with
   experience in the Middle East. - 1985.
   (002645)
----Internationale Produktionskooperation im
   Vorderen Orient. - 1983.
   (001142)

TRANSNATIONAL CORPORATIONS--MOROCCO.
----Expérience marocaine dans
   l'établissement d'entreprises
   multinationales. - 1986.
   (001027)
----National legislation and regulations
   relating to transnational corporations.
   Volume 4. - 1986.
   (002253)

TRANSNATIONAL CORPORATIONS--NAMIBIA.
----Activities of transnational corporations
   in South Africa and Namibia and the
   responsibilities of home countries with
   respect to their operations in this
   area. - 1986.
   (001192)
----Foreign investment in South Africa and
   Namibia. - 1984.
   (001198) (002641)
----International focus on transnational
   corporations in South Africa and
   Namibia. - 1985.
   (001214)
----Measures regarding the activities of
   transnational corporations in South
   Africa and Namibia. - 1985.
   (001219) (001220)
----Reference book on major transnational
   corporations operating in Namibia. -
   1985.
   (000297) (001213) (002673) (002674)

----Transnational corporations : follow-up
   to the recommendations of the Panel of
   Eminent Persons Established to Conduct
   the Public Hearings on the Activities of
   Transnational Corporations in South
   Africa and Namibia. - 1988.
   (001221)
----Transnational corporations in South
   Africa and Namibia : United Nations
   public hearings. Volume 1, Reports of
   the Panel of Eminent Persons and of the
   Secretary-General. - 1986.
   (001216)
----Transnational corporations in South
   Africa and Namibia. - 1986.
   (001217)
----Transnational corporations in South
   Africa and Namibia : United Nations
   public hearings. Volume 3, Statements
   and submissions. - 1987.
   (001215)
----Transnational corporations in South
   Africa and Namibia : United Nations
   Public Hearings. Volume 4, Policy
   instruments and statements. - 1987.
   (001218)
----U.S. and Canadian business in South
   Africa. - 1987-   .
   (001211)
----UNCTC bibliography, 1974-1987. - 1988.
   (002695)

TRANSNATIONAL CORPORATIONS--NETHERLANDS.
----Michelin : een zwart profiel : over
   werken in een bandenfabriek in Den
   Bosch. - 1984.
   (000289)
----Technology transfer: the approach of a
   Dutch multinational. - 1986.
   (001484)

TRANSNATIONAL CORPORATIONS--NEW ZEALAND.
----Fiji : client State of Australasia? -
   1984.
   (001046) (002358)

TRANSNATIONAL CORPORATIONS--NIGERIA.
----MNC's in Nigeria. - 1983.
   (001029)
----Multinationals, the state, and control
   of the Nigerian economy. - 1987.
   (001022)
----National legislation and regulations
   relating to transnational corporations.
   Volume 4. - 1986.
   (002253)
----Third World multinationals. - 1983.
   (000361)

TRANSNATIONAL CORPORATIONS--NORTH AMERICA.
----Indigenous resource rights and mining
   companies in North America and
   Australia. - 1986.
   (000616)

TRANSNATIONAL CORPORATIONS--NORTHERN
TERRITORY (AUSTRALIA).
----The history and contractual arrangements
   of the Gove bauxite/alumina project in
   the Northern Territory of Australia. -
   1985.
   (000596)

TRANSNATIONAL CORPORATIONS--OMAN.
----Impact of the operations of
    transnational corporations on
    development in the Sultanate of Oman. -
    1988.
      (001144)

TRANSNATIONAL CORPORATIONS--PAKISTAN.
----National legislation and regulations
    relating to transnational corporations.
    Volume 3. - 1983.
      (002252)
----Natural gas clauses in petroleum
    arrangements. - 1987.
      (002452)

TRANSNATIONAL CORPORATIONS--PANAMA.
----National legislation and regulations
    relating to transnational corporations.
    Volume 3. - 1983.
      (002252)

TRANSNATIONAL CORPORATIONS--PAPUA NEW GUINEA.
----National legislation and regulations
    relating to transnational corporations.
    Volume 3. - 1983.
      (002252)

TRANSNATIONAL CORPORATIONS--PARAGUAY.
----Las empresas transnacionales en la
    economía del Paraguay. - 1987.
      (001108) (001124)
----Las transnacionales en el Paraguay. -
    1985.
      (001113)
----Las transnacionales en el Paraguay. -
    1985.
      (001116)

TRANSNATIONAL CORPORATIONS--PERU.
----Agroindustria y transnacionales en el
    Perú. - 1983.
      (000565)
----Empresas transnacionales, estado y
    burguesía nativa. - 1983.
      (001877)
----Grace. - 1985.
      (000276)
----National legislation and regulations
    relating to transnational corporations.
    Volume 4. - 1986.
      (002253)
----Las perspectivas de la refinación del
    cobre en el Peru. - 1984.
      (000580)
----The Peruvian military government and the
    international corporations. - 1983. ·
      (001801)
----Política económica y empresas
    transnacionales en el Perú, 1968-1975. -
    1983.
      (001107)
----Privilegios y capital transnacional. -
    1985.
      (000269)

TRANSNATIONAL CORPORATIONS--PHILIPPINES.
----The Manila-Washington connection. - 1983.
      (001855)
----The Marcos regime. - 1985.
      (001070)

----National legislation and regulations
    relating to transnational corporations.
    Volume 4. - 1986.
      (002253)
----The Philippines : authoritarian
    government, multinationals and ancestral
    lands. - 1983.
      (001066)
----The Philippines under Marcos. - 1986.
      (001071)
----Transnational corporations and the
    state. - 1985.
      (001860)

TRANSNATIONAL CORPORATIONS--POLAND.
----Industrial cooperation between Poland
    and the West. - 1985.
      (001576)

TRANSNATIONAL CORPORATIONS--PORTUGAL.
----The employment impact of multinational
    enterprises in Greece, Portugal and
    Spain. - 1987.
      (001887)
----National legislation and regulations
    relating to transnational corporations.
    Volume 4. - 1986.
      (002253)

TRANSNATIONAL CORPORATIONS--REPUBLIC OF
KOREA.
----The determinants of manufacturing
    ownership in less developed countries. -
    1986.
      (000712)
----The Korean manufacturing multinationals.
    - 1984.
      (000342)
----Multinationals and maldevelopment. -
    1987.
      (000995)
----National legislation and regulations
    relating to transnational corporations.
    Volume 4. - 1986.
      (002253)
----New forms of overseas investment by
    developing countries : the case of
    India, Korea and Brazil. - 1986.
      (001616)
----Technology transfer under alternative
    arrangements with transnational
    corporations. - 1987.
      (001513)
----Transnational corporations and the
    state. - 1985.
      (001860)

TRANSNATIONAL CORPORATIONS--ROMANIA.
----National legislation and regulations
    relating to transnational corporations.
    Volume 3. - 1983.
      (002252)

TRANSNATIONAL CORPORATIONS--SAUDI ARABIA.
----Impact of the operations of
    transnational corporations on
    development in Saudi Arabia. - 1987.
      (001140)
----National legislation and regulations
    relating to transnational corporations.
    Volume 4. - 1986.
      (002253)

TRANSNATIONAL CORPORATIONS--SAUDI ARABIA
(continued)
----United States corporations operating in
Saudi Arabia and laws affecting
discrimination in employment. - 1985.
(002354)

TRANSNATIONAL CORPORATIONS--SIERRA LEONE.
----Multinationals and employment in a West
African sub-region. - 1984.
(001904)

TRANSNATIONAL CORPORATIONS--SINGAPORE.
----Chinese business, multinationals and the
state: manufacturing for export in
Malaysia and Singapore. - 1983.
(000713)
----Leading international companies
manufacturing and providing technical
services in Singapore. - 1983-   .
(002650)
----Multinational business and national
development. - 1983.
(000397)
----Multinationals and the growth of the
Singapore economy. - 1986.
(001062)
----National legislation and regulations
relating to transnational corporations.
Volume 3. - 1983.
(002252)
----Singapore multinationals. - 1985.
(000365)

TRANSNATIONAL CORPORATIONS--SOUTH AFRICA.
----Activities of transnational corporations
in South Africa and Namibia and the
responsibilities of home countries with
respect to their operations in this
area. - 1986.
(001192)
----Business in the shadow of apartheid :
U.S. firms in South Africa. - 1985.
(001194)
----The crisis in South Africa: rising
pressures on multinationals. - 1986.
(001201)
----The determinants of manufacturing
ownership in less developed countries. -
1986.
(000712)
----DM-Investitionen in Südafrika. - 1983.
(001197)
----Foreign investment in South Africa and
Namibia. - 1984.
(001198) (002641)
----International focus on transnational
corporations in South Africa and
Namibia. - 1985.
(001214)
----Leaving South Africa/Kellogg's
private war against apartheid/Black
unions. - 1985.
(001200)
----Measures regarding the activities of
transnational corporations in South
Africa and Namibia. - 1985.
(001219) (001220)
----The political economy of U.S. policy
toward South Africa. - 1985.
(001196)

----Reference book on major transnational
corporations operating in Namibia. -
1985.
(002674)
----The role of multinational corporations
in South Africa. - 1980.
(001209)
----The roots of crisis in southern Africa.
- 1985.
(001208)
----South Africa: the churches vs. the
corporations. - 1983.
(002589)
----Transnational corporations : follow-up
to the recommendations of the Panel of
Eminent Persons Established to Conduct
the Public Hearings on the Activities of
Transnational Corporations in South
Africa and Namibia. - 1988.
(001221)
----Transnational corporations in South
Africa and Namibia : United Nations
public hearings. Volume 1, Reports of
the Panel of Eminent Persons and of the
Secretary-General. - 1986.
(001216)
----Transnational corporations in South
Africa and Namibia. - 1986.
(001217)
----Transnational corporations in South
Africa and Namibia : United Nations
public hearings. Volume 3, Statements
and submissions. - 1987.
(001215)
----Transnational corporations in South
Africa and Namibia : United Nations
Public Hearings. Volume 4, Policy
instruments and statements. - 1987.
(001218)
----U.S. and Canadian business in South
Africa. - 1987-   .
(001211)
----U.S. and Canadian investment in South
Africa and Namibia. - 1986.
(001212) (002671) (002672)

----U.S. corporate activities in South
Africa. - 1983.
(001222)
----U.S. firms and black labor in South
Africa: creating a structure for change.
- 1986.
(001195)
----UNCTC bibliography, 1974-1987. - 1988.
(002695)

TRANSNATIONAL CORPORATIONS--SOUTH ASIA.
----Multinational corporations, technology
and employment. - 1983.
(001891)

TRANSNATIONAL CORPORATIONS--SOUTH PACIFIC
OCEAN REGION.
----Multinational enterprises in the
developing South Pacific region. - 1986.
(001045)

TRANSNATIONAL CORPORATIONS--SOUTHEAST ASIA.
----Aspects of ASEAN. - 1984.
(001406)

TRANSNATIONAL CORPORATIONS--SOUTHEAST ASIA
(continued)
----Computer vendors re-shape product
    strategy for Asian market. - 1986.
      (000689)
----Corporate policy, strategic groups and
    the performance of transnational
    corporations in less developed
    countries. - 1982.
      (001008)
----Economic policies towards transnational
    corporations. - 1983.
      (002229)
----Singapore multinationals. - 1985.
      (000365)
----The social and cultural impact of the
    activities of transnational corporations
    in Southeast Asia. - 1982.
      (001880)
----Sverkhmonopolii v IUgo-Vostochnoi Azii.
    - 1983.
      (001041)
----Transnational corporations and the
    electronics industries of ASEAN
    economies. - 1987.
      (000754)
----Vlijanie TNK na social'no-ekonomiceskoe
    razvivtie stran Jugo-Vosticnoj Azii. -
    1985.
      (001075)

TRANSNATIONAL CORPORATIONS--SPAIN.
----El control de las empresas
    multinacionales. - 1983.
      (002209)
----The employment impact of multinational
    enterprises in Greece, Portugal and
    Spain. - 1987.
      (001887)
----Les multinacionals a Catalunya. - 1984.
      (001147)

TRANSNATIONAL CORPORATIONS--SRI LANKA.
----Agribusiness TNCs in Sri Lanka. - 1986.
      (000560)

TRANSNATIONAL CORPORATIONS--SUDAN.
----Chevron, Sudan and political risk. -
    1984.
      (001858)
----National legislation and regulations
    relating to transnational corporations.
    Volume 4. - 1986.
      (002253)

TRANSNATIONAL CORPORATIONS--SWEDEN.
----Multinational enterprise and world
    competition. - 1987.
      (000018)
----Multinationals. - 1986.
      (000335)
----Multinationella fortag. - 1985.
      (000030)
----De Svenska storforetagen. - 1985.
      (000324)
----Sverige i imperialismens nat. - 1986.
      (001150)
----Sysselsattningsstrukturen i
    internationella foretag. - 1983.
      (001165)
----De Transnationella foretagens roll i
    varldshandeln ; Gransskydd i andra
    lander. - 1984.
      (000685)

----Utlandsagda dotterbolag i Sverige. -
    1984.
      (001728)

TRANSNATIONAL CORPORATIONS--SWITZERLAND.
----Das Bally-Lehrstuck. - 1985.
      (000286)
----L'émpire Nestle. - 1983.
      (000283)
----Global structural change and
    international competition among
    industrial firms: the case of
    Switzerland. - 1985.
      (000308)
----Halbgotter, Giftkriege und Kondensmilch.
    - 1983.
      (000658)
----Konzernstruktur und Steuerplanung. -
    1984.
      (001758)
----Médicaments pour tous en l'an 2000? -
    1983.
      (000662)
----Personalpolitik fur multinationale
    Unternehmen. - 1985.
      (000417) (001903)

TRANSNATIONAL CORPORATIONS--TAIWAN (CHINA).
----The production characteristics of
    multinational firms and the effects of
    tax incentives: the case of Taiwan's
    electronics industry. - 1986.
      (001038) (002305)

TRANSNATIONAL CORPORATIONS--THAILAND.
----National legislation and regulations
    relating to transnational corporations.
    Volume 4. - 1986.
      (002253)
----Proceedings of the Conference on the
    Role of Multi-national Corporations in
    Thailand, July 7-9, 1984. - 1986.
      (001042)
----Technology acquisition under alternative
    arrangements with transnational
    corporations. - 1987.
      (001512)
----Technology transfer under alternative
    arrangements with transnational
    corporations. - 1987.
      (001513)

TRANSNATIONAL CORPORATIONS--TRINIDAD AND
TOBAGO.
----Ethnicity, class, and international
    capitalist penetration in Guyana and
    Trinidad. - 1985.
      (001096)
----National legislation and regulations
    relating to transnational corporations.
    Volume 3. - 1983.
      (002252)

TRANSNATIONAL CORPORATIONS--TUNISIA.
----National legislation and regulations
    relating to transnational corporations.
    Volume 3. - 1983.
      (002252)

TRANSNATIONAL CORPORATIONS--TURKEY.
----National legislation and regulations
relating to transnational corporations.
Volume 3. - 1983.
(002252)
----Transnational corporations and local
capital: comparative conduct and
performance in the Turkish
pharmaceutical industry. - 1986.
(000705)

TRANSNATIONAL CORPORATIONS--UNITED ARAB
EMIRATES.
----Impact of operations of transnational
corporations on development in United
Arab Emirates. - 1987.
(001136)

TRANSNATIONAL CORPORATIONS--UNITED KINGDOM.
----Accounting for overseas operations. -
1986.
(002122)
----The Atlantic two-way switch. - 1986.
(000852)
----Britain and the multinationals. - 1985.
(001164)
----British multinationals. - 1986.
(000337)
----Comparative analysis of UK domestic and
international firms. - 1984.
(000343)
----Corporate acquisitions and mergers. -
1985.
(001544)
----Decision-making in foreign-owned
multinational subsidiaries in the United
Kingdom. - 1985.
(000521)
----Foreign investment in South Africa and
Namibia. - 1984.
(001198) (002641)
----Foreign multinationals and the British
economy. - 1988.
(001167)
----From national to multinational
enterprise. - 1983.
(000277)
----A golden adventure. - 1985.
(000270)
----The Gramophone Company: an
Anglo-American multinational, 1898-1931.
- 1985.
(000285)
----International segment disclosures by
U.S. and U.K. multinational enterprises:
a descriptive study. - 1984.
(002080)
----Multinational enterprise and world
competition. - 1987.
(000018)
----Multinational enterprises and industrial
restructuring in the UK. - 1985.
(001148)
----Multinational investment strategies in
the British Isles. - 1983.
(001151)
----Multinationals and Britain. - 1986.
(000205)
----National legislation and regulations
relating to transnational corporations.
Volume 4. - 1986.
(002253)

----Recent developments in operations and
behaviour of transnational corporations.
- 1987.
(000103)
----Tate and Lyle, geant du sucre. - 1983.
(000274)
----Transnational corporations and the
state. - 1985.
(001860)

TRANSNATIONAL CORPORATIONS--UNITED REPUBLIC
OF TANZANIA.
----National legislation and regulations
relating to transnational corporations.
Volume 3. - 1983.
(002252)

TRANSNATIONAL CORPORATIONS--UNITED STATES.
----American enterprise in foreign markets.
- 1984.
(000526)
----American multinationals and American
employment. - 1983.
(001890)
----America's corporate families and
international affiliates. - 1983-   .
(002617)
----Are environmental regulations driving
U.S. industry overseas? - 1984.
(001947)
----The Atlantic two-way switch. - 1986.
(000852)
----The Bhopal case : controlling
ultrahazardous industrial activities
undertaken by foreign investors. - 1987.
(001949)
----Business in the shadow of apartheid :
U.S. firms in South Africa. - 1985.
(001194)
----Canada in the USA : foreign direct
investment flows reversed. - 1987.
(000180)
----The competitive position of U.S.
manufacturing firms. - 1985.
(000353)
----Le contrôle gouvernemental des
entreprises multinationales. - 1985.
(002288)
----Direct foreign investment in the United
States. - 1986.
(000174)
----Direct investment activity of foreign
firms. - 1987.
(000541)
----Directory of foreign firms operating in
the United States. - 1969-   .
(002633)
----Directory of foreign manufacturers in
the United States. - 1975-   .
(002634)
----Disfraces del coloniaje. - 1984.
(001114)
----Diversification : the European versus
the US experience. - 1987.
(000491)
----Doing business in key Latin American
markets: U.S. international executive
perceptions. - 1983.
(001824)
----The emergence of a U.S. multinational
enterprise: the Goodyear Tire and Rubber
Company, 1910-1939. - 1987.
(000281)

TRANSNATIONAL CORPORATIONS--UNITED STATES
(continued)
----Empresas multinacionales y concentración
  de la inversión extranjera. - 1985.
    (000545)
----The engineers and the price system
  revisited: the future of the
  international oil corporations. - 1983.
    (000587)
----European headquarters of American
  multinational enterprises in Brussels
  and Belgium. - 1984.
    (000381)
----Examining performance of U.S.
  multinationals in foreign markets. -
  1983.
    (000318)
----The export of hazard. - 1985.
    (001941)
----External and internal functioning of
  American, German, and Japanese
  multinational corporations:
  decisionmaking and policy issues. - 1983.
    (000432)
----Federal taxation of international
  transactions. - 1988.
    (001730)
----The final report of the Worldwide
  Unitary Taxation Working Group :
  Chairman's report and supplemental
  views. - 1984.
    (001763)
----Financial transfers in the MNE. - 1986.
    (000416)
----Foreign investment in South Africa and
  Namibia. - 1984.
    (001198) (002641)
----Foreign location decisions by U.S.
  transnational firms: an empirical study.
  - 1984.
    (000537)
----Foreign manufacturing investment in the
  United States: competitive strategies
  and international location. - 1985.
    (000733)
----Foreign ownership of U.S. banks: trends
  and effects. - 1983.
    (001591)
----Forum non conveniens and multinational
  corporations. - 1986.
    (002568)
----Fundamentals of international taxation.
  - 1985.
    (001700)
----Grace. - 1985.
    (000276)
----The Gramophone Company: an
  Anglo-American multinational, 1898-1931.
  - 1985.
    (000285)
----High technology plant location
  decisions. - 1983.
    (000528)
----Indigenization policies and structural
  cooptation by multinational
  corporations. - 1985.
    (002331)
----Indo-U.S. cooperation in business and
  industry, 1986. - 1986.
    (002675)
----The information needs of exporters:
  theory, framework and empirical tests. -
  1986.
    (000989)

----Inside Washington. - 1988.
    (002703)
----Internal accountability. - 1984.
    (002055)
----International business travel and
  relocation directory. - 1984.
    (002710)
----International collaborative ventures in
  U.S. manufacturing. - 1988.
    (000720)
----International Harvester in Russia: the
  Washington-St. Petersburg connection? -
  1983.
    (000272)
----International joint ventures. - 1985.
    (001590)
----International joint ventures. - 1986.
    (001566)
----International joint ventures: how
  important are they? - 1987.
    (001556)
----International law of take-overs and
  mergers. - 1986.
    (001573)
----The international location of
  manufacturing investments: recent
  behaviour of foreign-owned corporations
  in the United States. - 1983.
    (001156)
----International segment disclosures by
  U.S. and U.K. multinational enterprises:
  a descriptive study. - 1984.
    (002080)
----International trade in services: its
  composition, importance and links to
  merchandise trade. - 1987.
    (000890)
----Introduction to United States
  international taxation. - 1981.
    (001738)
----Japanese multinationals in the United
  States. - 1986.
    (000341)
----Key to Japan's economic strength. - 1984.
    (001924)
----Krupneishie promyshlennye i torgovye
  monopolii. - 1986.
    (002658)
----Madison Avenue in Asia. - 1984.
    (000801)
----Managing. - 1984.
    (000408)
----Managing effectively in the world
  marketplace. - 1983.
    (000399)
----The Manila-Washington connection. - 1983.
    (001855)
----A muködo toke becsalogatása
  Magyarországra : nyugati szemszögbol. -
  1987.
    (001608)
----Multinational enterprise and world
  competition. - 1987.
    (000018)
----La multinationalisation des firmes
  européennes aux Etats-Unis: une approche
  dynamique. - 1984.
    (001152)
----Multinationals and free trade: the
  implications of a US-Canadian
  agreement. - 1986.
    (002029)

TRANSNATIONAL CORPORATIONS--UNITED STATES
(continued)
----Multinationals and technology transfer.
   - 1983.
      (001636)
----New challenges to the U.S. multinational
   corporation in the European Economic
   Community. - 1985.
      (002192)
----New trends in internationalization:
   processes and theories. Diversified
   patterns of multinational enterprise and
   old and new forms of foreign involvement
   of the firm. - 1983.
      (000068)
----Operating foreign subsidiaries. - 1983.
      (000388)
----The Overseas Private Investment
   Corporation and international
   investment. - 1984.
      (002360)
----Performance requirements for foreign
   business. - 1983.
      (002314)
----Personalpolitik fur multinationale
   Unternehmen. - 1985.
      (000417) (001903)
----The political economy of U.S. policy
   toward South Africa. - 1985.
      (001196)
----Political risk in the international oil
   and gas industry. - 1983.
      (001823)
----Recent developments in operations and
   behaviour of transnational corporations.
   - 1987.
      (000103)
----Reference book on major transnational
   corporations operating in Namibia. -
   1985.
      (002674)
----Regulating the multinational enterprise.
   - 1983.
      (002006)
----Research intensity, international
   production and US-based multinationals.
   - 1983.
      (000367)
----The RJR story. - 1983.
      (000296)
----Le role des grandes entreprises
   diversifiées du pétrole et de la chimie
   dans la production alimentaire. - 1985.
      (000699)
----The role of multinational enterprises in
   US-Canadian economic relations. - 1986.
      (001159)
----The roots of crisis in southern Africa.
   - 1985.
      (001208)
----South Africa: the churches vs. the
   corporations. - 1983.
      (002589)
----SShA, transnatsional'nye korporatsii i
   vneshniaia politika. - 1984.
      (001815)
----Staffing of management and professional
   positions at overseas subsidiaries of
   U.S. multinational enterprises. - 1983.
      (001885)
----Die Steuerung auslandischer
   Tochtergesellschaften. - 1983.
      (000400)

----Structuring natural resources
   development agreements between foreign
   governments and United States companies
   to prevent transfer of rights under the
   agreement should the company enter
   bankruptcy. - 1984.
      (002411)
----Tax aspects of international
   transactions. - 1984.
      (001757)
----Tax policy and foreign direct
   investment. - 1985.
      (001721)
----Technology strategy and industrial
   relations: case studies of Japanese
   multinationals in the United States. -
   1983.
      (002599)
----Towards a new treaty framework for
   direct foreign investment. - 1985.
      (002047)
----The transfer of organizational culture
   overseas: an approach to control in the
   multinational corporation. - 1983.
      (000420)
----Transnacional'nye korporacii SSA v
   Latinskoj Amerike/edited by N.G. Zajcev.
   - 1985.
      (000326)
----Transnational corporations and
   international trade : selected issues. -
   1985.
      (001393)
----Transnational corporations in the
   international semiconductor industry. -
   1986.
      (000748)
----Transnatsional'nye korporatsii SShA v
   Latinskoi Amerike. - 1985.
      (001087)
----Trends in Japan's manufacturing
   investment in the United States. - 1987.
      (000767)
----Trends in multinational business and
   global environments: a perspective. -
   1984.
      (000029)
----U.S. and Canadian business in South
   Africa. - 1987-   .
      (001211)
----U.S. and Canadian investment in South
   Africa and Namibia. - 1986.
      (001212) (002671) (002672)

----U.S. corporate activities in South
   Africa. - 1983.
      (001222)
----U.S. firms and black labor in South
   Africa: creating a structure for change.
   - 1986.
      (001195)
----U.S. multinational companies. - 1983.
      (001395)
----U.S. multinational companies: operations
   in 1984. - 1986.
      (000309)
----U.S. multinational corporations: a
   lesson in the failure of success. - 1983.
      (000306)
----U.S. TNCs in an era of global challenge.
   - 1984.
      (000377)

TRANSNATIONAL CORPORATIONS--UNITED STATES
(continued)
----United States corporations operating in
    Saudi Arabia and laws affecting
    discrimination in employment. - 1985.
      (002354)
----Uoll-strit protiv Afriki. - 1985.
      (001030)
----US corporate interests and the political
    economy of trade policy. - 1984.
      (000505)
----US monopolies and developing countries.
    - 1986.
      (001692)
----Venturing abroad. - 1988.
      (000376)
----Washington's best kept secrets. - 1983.
      (002704)
----Worldwide unitary tax. - 1986.
      (001718)
----Worldwide unitary taxation : nature and
    alternative solutions. - 1986.
      (001766)

TRANSNATIONAL CORPORATIONS--URUGUAY.
----La industria farmacéutica y las
    transnacionales. - 1985.
      (000667)

TRANSNATIONAL CORPORATIONS--USSR.
----American enterprise in foreign markets.
    - 1984.
      (000526)
----Businessman's Moscow. - 1984-   .
      (002625)
----Creating a world enterprise. - 1983.
      (000398)
----Foreign trade with the USSR. - 1987.
      (001774)
----Gold, foreign capital and the
    industrialization of Russia. - 1985.
      (001184)
----International Harvester in Russia: the
    Washington-St. Petersburg connection? -
    1983.
      (000272)
----Multinationals from the Second World :
    growth of foreign investment by Soviet
    and East European enterprises. - 1987.
      (000356)
----USSR, tendensen tot decentralisatie. -
    1987.
      (001190)
----Vers une réforme de la planification des
    services en URSS? - 1985.
      (000845)

TRANSNATIONAL CORPORATIONS--VENEZUELA.
----National legislation and regulations
    relating to transnational corporations.
    Volume 4. - 1986.
      (002253)

TRANSNATIONAL CORPORATIONS--WEST AFRICA.
----Tendentsii ekspansii TNK v strany
    Zapadnoi Afriki v 70-kh-nachale 80-kh
    godov. - 1986.
      (001021)

TRANSNATIONAL CORPORATIONS--WESTERN EUROPE.
----Corporate acquisitions and mergers. -
    1985.
      (001544)

----Diversification : the European versus
    the US experience. - 1987.
      (000491)
----International industries, multinational
    companies, and host government control:
    a framework. - 1983.
      (001796)
----La multinationalisation des firmes
    européennes aux Etats-Unis: une approche
    dynamique. - 1984.
      (001152)
----New challenges to the U.S. multinational
    corporation in the European Economic
    Community. - 1985.
      (002192)
----Operating foreign subsidiaries. - 1983.
      (000388)
----Recent developments in operations and
    behaviour of transnational corporations.
    - 1987.
      (000103)
----Reference book on major transnational
    corporations operating in Namibia. -
    1985.
      (002674)
----Tapping Eastern bloc technology. - 1983.
      (001452)
----Transnational corporations in the
    international semiconductor industry. -
    1986.
      (000748)
----Transnatsional'nye korporatsii v
    ekonomike malykh stran Zapadnoi Evropy.
    - 1983.
      (001163)
----Trends in multinational business and
    global environments: a perspective. -
    1984.
      (000029)

TRANSNATIONAL CORPORATIONS--YUGOSLAVIA.
----Direct foreign investment in Yugoslavia.
    - 1986.
      (000183)
----Joint ventures in Yugoslav industry. -
    1985.
      (001535)
----Joint ventures in Yugoslavia: comment/
    reply. - 1984.
      (001533)
----Joint ventures in Yugoslavia:
    opportunities and constraints. - 1985.
      (001534)
----National legislation and regulations
    relating to transnational corporations.
    Volume 4. - 1986.
      (002253)

TRANSNATIONAL CORPORATIONS--ZAIRE.
----National legislation and regulations
    relating to transnational corporations.
    Volume 3. - 1983.
      (002252)

TRANSNATIONAL CORPORATIONS--ZAMBIA.
----National legislation and regulations
    relating to transnational corporations.
    Volume 3. - 1983.
      (002252)

TRANSNATIONAL CORPORATIONS--ZIMBABWE.
----Investment by foreign companies:
    Zimbabwe. - 1987.
    (001740)
----The role of transnational corporations
    in hotel and tourism industry in
    selected PTA member countries. - 1986.
    (000782) (000936)

TRANSNATIONAL DATA FLOW.
----Foreign direct investment, the service
    sector and international banking. - 1987.
    (000972)
----International transactions in services.
    - 1986.
    (000946)
----Meeting the challenges of the world
    information economy. - 1984.
    (000853)
----The role of transborder data flows in
    the international services debate. -
    1987.
    (000947)
----Trade in data services. - 1986.
    (000949)
----Transborder data flows. - 1983.
    (000973)
----Transborder data flows. - 1984.
    (000974)
----Transborder data flows and Poland :
    Polish case study. - 1984.
    (000920)
----Transnational information and data
    communication. - 1983.
    (000866)
----UNCTC bibliography, 1974-1987. - 1988.
    (002695)

TRANSNATIONAL DATA FLOW--WESTERN EUROPE.
----The protection of corporate privacy. -
    1983.
    (002291)

TRANSNATIONAL DATA FLOWS.
----Transnational data flow constraints: a
    new challenge for multinational
    corporations. - 1984.
    (000942)

TRANSPORT.
----UNCITRAL, the United Nations Commission
    on International Trade Law. - 1986.
    (002155)

TRANSPORT--WESTERN EUROPE.
----La réglementation communautaire des
    transports. - 1984.
    (001994)

TRANSPORT DOCUMENTS.
----UNCITRAL, the United Nations Commission
    on International Trade Law. - 1986.
    (002155)

TRAVEL.
----International business and cultures. -
    1987.
    (001872)

TRAVEL AGENTS--AUSTRALIA.
----Characteristics of major industries
    supplying tourist services in Australia.
    - 1983.
    (000824)

TREATIES.
----Annual survey of developments in
    international trade law, 1983. - 1984.
    (002136)
----Bilateral investment promotion
    protection and treaties : a model for
    Community promotion of mining
    investment? - 1986.
    (002052)
----The Convention Establishing the
    Multilateral Investment Guarantee
    Agency. - 1987.
    (002127)
----Dead in the water : international law,
    diplomacy, and compensation for chemical
    pollution at sea. - 1986.
    (001938)
----International petroleum exploration
    [and] exploitation agreements. - 1986.
    (002431)
----International trademark licensing
    agreements. - 1986.
    (002421)
----The international void in the law of
    multinational bankruptcies. - 1987.
    (002214)
----Introductory note on the UNCITRAL Model
    Law on International Commercial
    Arbitration. - 1985.
    (002513)
----Investment protection agreements. - 1987.
    (002135)
----Investment protection treaties: recent
    trends and prospects. - 1986.
    (002031)
----Issues in negotiating international loan
    agreements with transnational banks. -
    1983.
    (002459)
----Klauzule abritrazowe w kontraktach
    handlu zagranicznego sektora
    nieuspolecznionego. - 1984.
    (002579)
----Liability and compensation for damage in
    connection with the carriage of
    hazardous and noxious substances by sea.
    - 1986.
    (001939)
----Liability for shipments by sea of
    hazardous and noxious substances. - 1985.
    (001951)
----Promotion of mining and energy
    investment under the Lomé Convention. -
    1986.
    (002607)
----State responsibility and bilateral
    investment treaties. - 1986.
    (002051)
----UNCITRAL, the United Nations Commission
    on International Trade Law. - 1986.
    (002155)

TREATIES--AMERICAS.
----Les conventions interaméricaines sur
    l'arbitrage commercial et la Commission
    interaméricaine d'arbitrage commercial.
    - 1983.
    (002535)

TREATIES--CHINA.
----An introduction to foreign investment
    law in China. - 1986.
    (002296)

TREATIES--GABON.
----Les conventions dans la fiscalité
    pétrolière gabonaise. - 1987.
    (002030)

TREATIES--SPAIN.
----Major international treaties regulating
    arbitration in Spain. - 1983.
    (002489)

TREATIES--UNITED STATES.
----Oil spill liability and compensation. -
    1985.
    (001940)
----Towards a new treaty framework for
    direct foreign investment. - 1985.
    (002047)
----The U.S. bilateral investment treaty
    program. - 1985.
    (002034)
----Worldwide unitary tax. - 1986.
    (001718)

TREATIES--WESTERN EUROPE.
----Commercial arbitration and the European
    Economic Community. - 1985.
    (002481)
----International aspects of nuclear
    instalations licensing. - 1987.
    (002434)
----Le système conjoint de garantie des
    investissements CEE/ACP de la Convention
    de Lomé III. - 1987.
    (002147)

TREATY ESTABLISHING THE EUROPEAN ECONOMIC
COMMUNITY (1957).
----Application des règles de concurrence du
    Traité de Rome à l'autorité publique. -
    1987.
    (002021)
----EEC competition policy. - 1986.
    (001989)
----EEC law of competition. - 1985.
    (002151)
----Extraterritorial application of the
    EEC-competition law. - 1984.
    (002349)

TRINIDAD AND TOBAGO--CAPITALISM.
----Ethnicity, class, and international
    capitalist penetration in Guyana and
    Trinidad. - 1985.
    (001096)

TRINIDAD AND TOBAGO--DEVELOPING COUNTRIES.
----Commercialization of technology and
    dependence in the Caribbean. - 1985.
    (001477)

TRINIDAD AND TOBAGO--ETHNOPSYCHOLOGY.
----Ethnicity, class, and international
    capitalist penetration in Guyana and
    Trinidad. - 1985.
    (001096)

TRINIDAD AND TOBAGO--INDUSTRIAL PLANNING.
----Commercialization of technology and
    dependence in the Caribbean. - 1985.
    (001477)

TRINIDAD AND TOBAGO--LAWS AND REGULATIONS.
----National legislation and regulations
    relating to transnational corporations.
    Volume 3. - 1983.
    (002252)

TRINIDAD AND TOBAGO--PETROLEUM INDUSTRY.
----The petroleum industry in Trinidad, West
    Indies, 1857-1983. - 1985.
    (000624)

TRINIDAD AND TOBAGO--SOCIAL CLASSES.
----Ethnicity, class, and international
    capitalist penetration in Guyana and
    Trinidad. - 1985.
    (001096)

TRINIDAD AND TOBAGO--STATISTICAL DATA.
----The petroleum industry in Trinidad, West
    Indies, 1857-1983. - 1985.
    (000624)

TRINIDAD AND TOBAGO--TECHNICAL CO-OPERATION.
----Commercialization of technology and
    dependence in the Caribbean. - 1985.
    (001477)

TRINIDAD AND TOBAGO--TECHNOLOGY TRANSFER.
----Commercialization of technology and
    dependence in the Caribbean. - 1985.
    (001477)

TRINIDAD AND TOBAGO--TRANSNATIONAL
CORPORATIONS.
----Ethnicity, class, and international
    capitalist penetration in Guyana and
    Trinidad. - 1985.
    (001096)
----National legislation and regulations
    relating to transnational corporations.
    Volume 3. - 1983.
    (002252)

TROOP WITHDRAWAL--NAMIBIA.
----Transnational corporations in South
    Africa and Namibia : United Nations
    public hearings. Volume 1, Reports of
    the Panel of Eminent Persons and of the
    Secretary-General. - 1986.
    (001216)

TROOP WITHDRAWAL--SOUTH AFRICA.
----Transnational corporations in South
    Africa and Namibia : United Nations
    public hearings. Volume 1, Reports of
    the Panel of Eminent Persons and of the
    Secretary-General. - 1986.
    (001216)

TRUST FUNDS.
----Measures to strengthen the capabilities
    of developing countries in their dealing
    with transnational corporations. - 1985.
    (002612)

TUNISIA--ECONOMIC GROWTH.
----L'industrie manufacturière tunisienne et
    sa place dans l'économie nationale. -
    1985.
    (000744)

TUNISIA--ECONOMIC POLICY.
----L'industrie manufacturière tunisienne et
    sa place dans l'économie nationale. -
    1985.
       (000744)

TUNISIA--INVESTMENT POLICY.
----L'industrie manufacturière tunisienne et
    sa place dans l'économie nationale. -
    1985.
       (000744)
----Tunisie : l'Agence de promotion des
    investissements. - 1987.
       (002357)

TUNISIA--INVESTMENT PROMOTION.
----Tunisie : l'Agence de promotion des
    investissements. - 1987.
       (002357)

TUNISIA--JOINT VENTURES.
----Tunisie : l'Agence de promotion des
    investissements. - 1987.
       (002357)

TUNISIA--LAWS AND REGULATIONS.
----National legislation and regulations
    relating to transnational corporations.
    Volume 3. - 1983.
       (002252)

TUNISIA--MANUFACTURES.
----L'industrie manufacturière tunisienne et
    sa place dans l'économie nationale. -
    1985.
       (000744)

TUNISIA--MANUFACTURING ENTERPRISES.
----L'industrie manufacturière tunisienne et
    sa place dans l'économie nationale. -
    1985.
       (000744)

TUNISIA--PUBLIC ENTERPRISES.
----Responsabilités des entreprises
    publiques dans l'amélioration de la
    condition de la femme. - 1983.
       (001883)

TUNISIA--TRANSNATIONAL CORPORATIONS.
----National legislation and regulations
    relating to transnational corporations.
    Volume 3. - 1983.
       (002252)

TUNISIA--WOMEN'S ADVANCEMENT.
----Responsabilités des entreprises
    publiques dans l'amélioration de la
    condition de la femme. - 1983.
       (001883)

TUNISIA--WOMEN'S STATUS.
----Responsabilités des entreprises
    publiques dans l'amélioration de la
    condition de la femme. - 1983.
       (001883)

TURKEY--BANKS.
----Turkish banking and finance : the
    markets mature. - 1986.
       (000970)

TURKEY--CAPITAL MARKETS.
----Turkish banking and finance : the
    markets mature. - 1986.
       (000970)

TURKEY--COMPARATIVE ANALYSIS.
----Transnational corporations and local
    capital: comparative conduct and
    performance in the Turkish
    pharmaceutical industry. - 1986.
       (000705)

TURKEY--DEVELOPING COUNTRIES.
----Le processus d'acquisition technologique
    par les entreprises d'un pays
    semi-industrialise. Deux études de cas.
    (With English summary.). - 1983.
       (001407)

TURKEY--FOREIGN DIRECT INVESTMENT.
----Foreign investment regulation and
    application forms. - 1985.
       (002198)
----Law for encouragement of foreign capital
    investments=Yabanci sermayeyi tesvik
    kanunu. - 1984.
       (002284)
----Legal consideration in doing business in
    the Middle East, Turkey and Pakistan. -
    1986.
       (002172)
----Turkey's new open-door policy of direct
    foreign investment: a critical analysis
    of problems and prospects. - 1986.
       (002205)

TURKEY--FOREIGN INVESTMENTS.
----Foreign investments in Turkey. - 1983.
       (000134)

TURKEY--HOST COUNTRY RELATIONS.
----Transnational corporations and local
    capital: comparative conduct and
    performance in the Turkish
    pharmaceutical industry. - 1986.
       (000705)

TURKEY--INDUSTRIAL ENTERPRISES.
----Le processus d'acquisition technologique
    par les entreprises d'un pays
    semi-industrialise. Deux études de cas.
    (With English summary.). - 1983.
       (001407)

TURKEY--INSURANCE COMPANIES.
----Turkish banking and finance : the
    markets mature. - 1986.
       (000970)

TURKEY--INTERNATIONAL AND MUNICIPAL LAW.
----La nouvelle loi turque sur le droit
    international privé et la procédure
    internationale et le principe de la
    reciprocité dans l'arbitrage. - 1983.
       (002533)

TURKEY--LAWS AND REGULATIONS.
----Foreign investment regulation and
    application forms. - 1985.
       (002198)
----Law for encouragement of foreign capital
    investments=Yabanci sermayeyi tesvik
    kanunu. - 1984.
       (002284)

TURKEY--LAWS AND REGULATIONS (continued)
----National legislation and regulations
relating to transnational corporations.
Volume 3. - 1983.
(002252)

TURKEY--PERFORMANCE APPRAISAL.
----Transnational corporations and local
capital: comparative conduct and
performance in the Turkish
pharmaceutical industry. - 1986.
(000705)

TURKEY--PHARMACEUTICAL INDUSTRY.
----Transnational corporations and local
capital: comparative conduct and
performance in the Turkish
pharmaceutical industry. - 1986.
(000705)

TURKEY--TECHNOLOGY TRANSFER.
----Le processus d'acquisition technologique
par les entreprises d'un pays
semi-industrialise. Deux études de cas.
(With English summary.). - 1983.
(001407)

TURKEY--TRANSNATIONAL CORPORATIONS.
----National legislation and regulations
relating to transnational corporations.
Volume 3. - 1983.
(002252)
----Transnational corporations and local
capital: comparative conduct and
performance in the Turkish
pharmaceutical industry. - 1986.
(000705)

TURNKEY CONTRACTS.
----Transnational corporations in world
development. - 1983.
(000102) (000102)

U.S. OVERSEAS PRIVATE INVESTMENT CORPORATION.
----The Overseas Private Investment
Corporation and international
investment. - 1984.
(002360)
----The role of private investment in Third
World development. - 1986.
(001328)
----The World Bank's Multilateral Investment
Guaranty Agency. - 1987.
(002125)

ULTRAMAR PLC (LONDON).
----A golden adventure. - 1985.
(000270)

UN.
----International codes and guidelines for
multinational enterprises. - 1983.
(002023)
----K mezinárodne právní úprave cinnosti
nadnárodních spolecností. - 1986.
(001960)
----Multilateral negotiation and mediation.
- 1985.
(002545)
----The taking of foreign property under
international law. - 1984.
(002336)

----Transnational corporations in South
Africa and Namibia : United Nations
public hearings. Volume 1, Reports of
the Panel of Eminent Persons and of the
Secretary-General. - 1986.
(001216)
----Transnational corporations in the
pharmaceutical industry of developing
countries. - 1984.
(000749)

UN. CHARTER OF ECONOMIC RIGHTS AND DUTIES
OF STATES (1974).
----Deuda externa, inversión extranjera y
transferencia de tecnología en América
Latina. - 1986.
(001080)

UN--RESOLUTIONS AND DECISIONS.
----Activities of transnational corporations
in South Africa and Namibia and the
responsibilities of home countries with
respect to their operations in this
area. - 1986.
(001192)
----Measures regarding the activities of
transnational corporations in South
Africa and Namibia. - 1985.
(001220)

UN. CENTRE FOR SCIENCE AND TECHNOLOGY FOR
DEVELOPMENT.
----Microelectronics-based automation
technologies and development. - 1985.
(000753)

UN. COMMISSION ON TRANSNATIONAL CORPORATIONS.
----UNCTC bibliography, 1974-1987. - 1988.
(002695)

UN. COMMISSION ON TRANSNATIONAL CORPORATIONS
(SPECIAL SESS., 4TH PT. : 1986 : NEW
YORK)--WORK ORGANIZATION.
----Commission on Transnational Corporations
: report on the reconvened special
session, 20-31 January 1986. - 1986.
(002016)

UN. GROUP OF EXPERTS ON TAX TREATIES BETWEEN
DEVELOPED AND DEVELOPING COUNTRIES.
----Exchange of information under the OECD
and US model tax treaties. - 1983.
(002042)

UN. INTERGOVERNMENTAL WORKING GROUP OF
EXPERTS ON INTERNATIONAL STANDARDS OF
ACCOUNTING AND REPORTING--WORK PROGRAMME.
----International accounting and reporting
issues : 1984 review. - 1985.
(002115)
----International accounting and reporting
issues, 1986 review. - 1986.
(002117)

UN. INTERGOVERNMENTAL WORKING GROUP OF
EXPERTS ON INTERNATIONAL STANDARDS OF
ACCOUNTING AND REPORTING (2ND SESS. : 1984 :
NEW YORK)--WORK ORGANIZATION.
----International accounting and reporting
issues : 1984 review. - 1985.
(002115)

UN. INTERGOVERNMENTAL WORKING GROUP OF
EXPERTS ON INTERNATIONAL STANDARDS OF
ACCOUNTING AND REPORTING (3RD SESS. : 1985 :
NEW YORK).
----International accounting and reporting
    issues, 1985 review. - 1985.
      (002116)

UN. INTERGOVERNMENTAL WORKING GROUP OF
EXPERTS ON INTERNATIONAL STANDARDS OF
ACCOUNTING AND REPORTING (3RD SESS. : 1985 :
NEW YORK)--AGENDA.
----International accounting and reporting
    issues : 1984 review. - 1985.
      (002115)

UN. INTERGOVERNMENTAL WORKING GROUP OF
EXPERTS ON INTERNATIONAL STANDARDS OF
ACCOUNTING AND REPORTING (4TH SESS. : 1986 :
NEW YORK).
----International accounting and reporting
    issues, 1986 review. - 1986.
      (002117)

UN. PANEL OF EMINENT PERSONS ESTABLISHED TO
CONDUCT THE PUBLIC HEARINGS ON THE
ACTIVITIES OF TRANSNATIONAL CORPORATIONS IN
SOUTH AFRICA AND NAMIBIA--MEMBERS.
----Transnational corporations in South
    Africa and Namibia. - 1986.
      (001217)

UN. PANEL OF EMINENT PERSONS ESTABLISHED TO
CONDUCT THE PUBLIC HEARINGS ON THE
ACTIVITIES OF TRANSNATIONAL CORPORATIONS IN
SOUTH AFRICA AND NAMIBIA--RECOMMENDATIONS.
----Transnational corporations in South
    Africa and Namibia : United Nations
    public hearings. Volume 1, Reports of
    the Panel of Eminent Persons and of the
    Secretary-General. - 1986.
      (001216)

UN. PANEL OF EMINENT PERSONS ESTABLISHED TO
CONDUCT THE PUBLIC HEARINGS ON THE
ACTIVITIES OF TRANSNATIONAL CORPORATIONS IN
SOUTH AFRICA AND NAMIBIA--TERMS OF REFERENCE.
----Transnational corporations in South
    Africa and Namibia : United Nations
    public hearings. Volume 1, Reports of
    the Panel of Eminent Persons and of the
    Secretary-General. - 1986.
      (001216)
----Transnational corporations in South
    Africa and Namibia. - 1986.
      (001217)

UN. PANEL OF EMINENT PERSONS ESTABLISHED TO
CONDUCT THE PUBLIC HEARINGS ON THE
ACTIVITIES OF TRANSNATIONAL CORPORATIONS IN
SOUTH AFRICA AND NAMIBIA--WORK ORGANIZATION.
----Transnational corporations in South
    Africa and Namibia : United Nations
    public hearings. Volume 1, Reports of
    the Panel of Eminent Persons and of the
    Secretary-General. - 1986.
      (001216)

UN CENTRE ON TRANSNATIONAL CORPORATIONS.
----International accounting and reporting
    issues : 1984 review. - 1985.
      (002115)

----Measures to strengthen the capabilities
    of developing countries in their dealing
    with transnational corporations. - 1985.
      (002612)
----Sales publications of the United Nations
    Centre on Transnational Corporations,
    1973-1987. - 1987.
      (002693)
----Technical co-operation programme of the
    United Nations Centre on Transnational
    Corporations. - 1988.
      (002610)
----UNCTC bibliography, 1974-1987. - 1988.
      (002695)

UN CENTRE ON TRANSNATIONAL
CORPORATIONS--ACTIVITIES (1976-1987).
----Technical co-operation programme,
    1976-1987 : United Nations Centre on
    Transnational Corporations. - 1988.
      (002611)

UN CENTRE ON TRANSNATIONAL
CORPORATIONS--TERMS OF REFERENCE.
----Technical co-operation programme,
    1976-1987 : United Nations Centre on
    Transnational Corporations. - 1988.
      (002611)

UN COMMISSION ON INTERNATIONAL TRADE LAW.
----Arbitral adjudication. - 1984.
      (002484)
----Arbitration and the courts. - 1985.
      (002532)
----The availability of provisional relief
    in international commercial arbitration.
    - 1984.
      (002543)
----Drafting the international arbitration
    clause. - 1986.
      (002581)
----International arbitration of multi-party
    contract disputes. - 1983.
      (002508)
----International commercial arbitration : a
    comparative analysis of the United
    States system and the UNCITRAL model
    law. - 1986.
      (002487)
----International commercial arbitration. -
    1983.
      (002520)
----International commercial arbitration. -
    1983.
      (002511)
----International commercial arbitrations. -
    1984.
      (002521)
----La loi-type de la C.N.U.D.C.I. sur
    l'arbitrage commercial international. -
    1986.
      (002527)
----A model law on international commercial
    arbitration? - 1984.
      (002479)
----Peaceful settlement of international
    trade disputes. - 1983.
      (002500)
----Selecting an arbitral forum. - 1984.
      (002478)
----The Soviet position on international
    arbitration. - 1986.
      (002571)

UN COMMISSION ON INTERNATIONAL TRADE LAW
(continued)
----The status of the UNCITRAL Model Law on
International Commercial Arbitration
vis-à-vis the ICC, LCIA and UNCITRAL
arbitration rules. - 1986.
(002583)
----Symposium : a guide to international
civil practice. - 1984.
(002576)
----UNCITRAL and international commercial
dispute settlement/ Carl August
Fleischhauer. - 1983.
(002502)
----UNCITRAL Model Law on International
Commercial Arbitration. - 1986.
(002503)
----The UNCITRAL model law on international
commercial arbitration. - 1986.
(002517)
----The UNCITRAL model law on international
commercial arbitration. - 1986.
(002541)
----UNCITRAL, the United Nations Commission
on International Trade Law. - 1986.
(002155)

UN COMMISSION ON INTERNATIONAL TRADE
LAW--TERMS OF REFERENCE.
----UNCITRAL, the United Nations Commission
on International Trade Law. - 1986.
(002155)

UN COMMISSION ON INTERNATIONAL TRADE
LAW--WORK PROGRAMME.
----UNCITRAL, the United Nations Commission
on International Trade Law. - 1986.
(002155)

UN FINANCING SYSTEM FOR SCIENCE AND
TECHNOLOGY FOR DEVELOPMENT.
----Microelectronics-based automation
technologies and development. - 1985.
(000753)

UN MODEL DOUBLE TAXATION CONVENTION BETWEEN
DEVELOPED AND DEVELOPING COUNTRIES (1980).
----A comparative analysis of the United
States-People's Republic of China tax
treaty. - 1986.
(002037)
----International bank lending. - 1984.
(000988)

UN TRUST FUND FOR THE CENTRE ON
TRANSNATIONAL CORPORATIONS--BUDGET
CONTRIBUTIONS (1977-1988).
----Technical co-operation programme,
1976-1987 : United Nations Centre on
Transnational Corporations. - 1988.
(002611)

UN UNIVERSITY.
----Microelectronics-based automation
technologies and development. - 1985.
(000753)

UNCERTAINTY.
----Diffusion as an explanation of oil
nationalization or the domino effect
rides again. - 1985.
(002326)

UNCERTAINTY--HONG KONG.
----Exploiting Hong Kong's uncertain future.
- 1987.
(001862)

UNCITRAL ARBITRATION RULES.
----Recent developments in international
commercial arbitration. - 1987.
(002549)
----Sanctions to control party misbehavior
in international arbitration. - 1986.
(002537)
----The Soviet position on international
arbitration. - 1986.
(002571)
----The status of the UNCITRAL Model Law on
International Commercial Arbitration
vis-à-vis the ICC, LCIA and UNCITRAL
arbitration rules. - 1986.
(002583)

UNCTAD.
----L'Agence multilatérale de garantie des
investissements. - 1987.
(002152)
----The antitrust law of the European
Community and the UNCTAD code on
restrictive business practices. - 1984.
(001992)
----International codes and guidelines for
multinational enterprises. - 1983.
(002023)
----International trademark licensing
agreements. - 1986.
(002421)
----Mezhdunarodnaia kapitalisticheskaia
torgovlia uslugami i problemy ee
regulirovaniia. - 1987.
(000918)
----Revitalizing development, growth and
international trade. - 1987.
(001394)
----Services and the development process. -
1985.
(000979)
----Transnational corporations in the
pharmaceutical industry of developing
countries. - 1984.
(000749)
----The U.S. renewal of the GSP. - 1986.
(001996)
----The Uruguay Round and the international
trading system. - 1987.
(001976)
----Why freer trade in services is in the
interest of developing countries. - 1985.
(000850)

UNCTAD. INTEGRATED PROGRAMME FOR COMMODITIES.
----Revitalizing development, growth and
international trade. - 1987.
(001394)

UNDP.
----Transnational corporations in the
pharmaceutical industry of developing
countries. - 1984.
(000749)

UNEMPLOYMENT.
----Foreign direct investment with
unemployment and endogenous taxes and
tariffs. - 1987.
(000559)
----Les services contre le chômage. - 1987.
(000857)
----Unemployment and the formation of
duty-free zones. - 1987.
(001931)

UNEMPLOYMENT--JAMAICA.
----La Jamaïque, ou le dilemme politique
d'un petit pays déshérité. - 1984.
(001819)

UNESCO.
----Microelectronics-based automation
technologies and development. - 1985.
(000753)
----The third industrial revolution. - 1987.
(000966)

UNFAIR COMPETITION.
----Competition and trade policies. - 1984.
(001664)
----International trade disputes and the
individual : private party involvement
in national and international procedures
regarding unfair foreign trade
practices. - 1986.
(002514)

UNIDO.
----Analysis of equipment leasing contracts.
- 1984.
(002407)
----Microelectronics-based automation
technologies and development. - 1985.
(000753)
----Transnational corporations in the
pharmaceutical industry of developing
countries. - 1984.
(000749)

UNIFORM LAWS--WESTERN EUROPE.
----A contract law for Europe. - 1985.
(001991)

UNION DOUANIERE ET ECONOMIQUE DE L'AFRIQUE
CENTRALE.
----Industrial cooperation in regional
economic groupings among developing
countries and lessons for SAARC. - 1987.
(001009)

UNITED ARAB EMIRATES--BUSINESS ENTERPRISES.
----Impact of operations of transnational
corporations on development in United
Arab Emirates. - 1987.
(001136)

UNITED ARAB EMIRATES--COMMERCIAL LAW.
----Business laws of the United Arab
Emirates. - 1984-   .
(002285)

UNITED ARAB EMIRATES--FOREIGN INTERESTS.
----Impact of operations of transnational
corporations on development in United
Arab Emirates. - 1987.
(001136)

UNITED ARAB EMIRATES--INVESTMENT POLICY.
----The UAE and the joint-venture
opportunity. - 1985.
(001530)

UNITED ARAB EMIRATES--JOINT VENTURES.
----The UAE and the joint-venture
opportunity. - 1985.
(001530)

UNITED ARAB EMIRATES--TRANSNATIONAL
CORPORATIONS.
----Impact of operations of transnational
corporations on development in United
Arab Emirates. - 1987.
(001136)

UNITED BISCUITS (ISLEWORTH, MIDDLESEX).
----Importance et implantations comparées
des quatre plus grands biscuitiers
mondiaux, Nabisco Brands, United
Biscuits, Générale Biscuit, Bahlsen. -
1984.
(000273)

UNITED KINGDOM--ACCOUNTING AND REPORTING.
----Accounting for overseas operations. -
1986.
(002122)
----Inflation accounting. - 1975.
(002156)
----International segment disclosures by
U.S. and U.K. multinational enterprises:
a descriptive study. - 1984.
(002080)

UNITED KINGDOM--AFFILIATE CORPORATIONS.
----Decision-making in foreign-owned
multinational subsidiaries in the United
Kingdom. - 1985.
(000521)
----Foundations of foreign success. - 1987.
(000421)
----US and Japanese manufacturing affiliates
in the UK. - 1985.
(001149)

UNITED KINGDOM--ANTITRUST LAW.
----Corporate acquisitions and mergers. -
1985.
(001544)

UNITED KINGDOM--BALANCE OF PAYMENTS.
----Assessing the consequences of overseas
investment. - 1986.
(001296)

UNITED KINGDOM--BANKING.
----Tax havens and offshore finance. - 1983.
(001729)

UNITED KINGDOM--BANKS.
----The bankers' almanac and year book. -
1886-   .
(002620)

UNITED KINGDOM--BUSINESS ENTERPRISES.
----A code for misconduct? - 1980.
(002009)
----Kompass. - 196?-   .
(002648)
----Sell's British exporters. - 1916-   .
(002663)

UNITED KINGDOM--BUSINESS ENTERPRISES
(continued)
----The United Kingdom merger boom in
    perspective. - 1987.
        (001638)

UNITED KINGDOM--CAPITAL MOVEMENTS.
----Two arguments for the restriction of
    international capital flows. - 1986.
        (001240)

UNITED KINGDOM--COMMERCIAL ARBITRATION.
----Arbitral adjudication. - 1984.
        (002484)
----Commercial arbitration. - 1983.
        (002499)
----Etude historique et comparée de
    l'arbitrage. - 1984.
        (002485)

UNITED KINGDOM--COMPARATIVE ANALYSIS.
----Comparative analysis of UK domestic and
    international firms. - 1984.
        (000343)
----Multinational enterprise and world
    competition. - 1987.
        (000018)

UNITED KINGDOM--COMPETITION.
----Privatisation and regulation : the UK
    experience. - 1986.
        (001627)

UNITED KINGDOM--CONCILIATION.
----Mediation, conciliation and arbitration
    : an international comparison of
    Australia, Great Britain and the United
    States. - 1987.
        (002476)

UNITED KINGDOM--CONSTITUTIONAL LAW.
----Privatising nationalised industries :
    constitutional issues and new legal
    techniques. - 1987.
        (001582)

UNITED KINGDOM--CORPORATE MERGERS.
----Corporate acquisitions and mergers. -
    1985.
        (001544)
----Private agreements for takeovers of
    public companies. - 1984.
        (001626)
----Recent developments in operations and
    behaviour of transnational corporations.
    - 1987.
        (000103)
----The United Kingdom merger boom in
    perspective. - 1987.
        (001638)

UNITED KINGDOM--CORPORATION LAW.
----Corporate acquisitions and mergers. -
    1985.
        (001544)

UNITED KINGDOM--CORPORATION TAX.
----Corporate acquisitions and mergers. -
    1985.
        (001544)

UNITED KINGDOM--CORPORATIONS.
----The prospect for direct investment by
    United Kingdom companies in developing
    countries. - 1985.
        (000169)
----Sell's British exporters. - 1916-   .
        (002663)
----The Times 1000. - 1966-   .
        (002668)

UNITED KINGDOM--DECISION-MAKING.
----Decision-making in foreign-owned
    multinational subsidiaries in the United
    Kingdom. - 1985.
        (000521)

UNITED KINGDOM--DEVELOPING COUNTRIES.
----The prospect for direct investment by
    United Kingdom companies in developing
    countries. - 1985.
        (000169)

UNITED KINGDOM--DIRECTORIES.
----The bankers' almanac and year book. -
    1886-   .
        (002620)
----Britain's privately owned companies. -
    198?-   .
        (002624)
----Foreign investment in South Africa and
    Namibia. - 1984.
        (001198) (002641)
----Kompass. - 196?-   .
        (002648)
----Sell's British exporters. - 1916-   .
        (002663)
----The Times 1000. - 1966-   .
        (002668)

UNITED KINGDOM--DOMESTIC TRADE.
----Comparative analysis of UK domestic and
    international firms. - 1984.
        (000343)

UNITED KINGDOM--ECONOMIC CONDITIONS.
----Foreign multinationals and the British
    economy. - 1988.
        (001167)

UNITED KINGDOM--ECONOMIC POLICY.
----Assessing the consequences of overseas
    investment. - 1986.
        (001296)

UNITED KINGDOM--ECONOMIC RELATIONS.
----Britain and the multinationals. - 1985.
        (001164)

UNITED KINGDOM--ELECTRONICS INDUSTRY.
----Inward investment. - 1984.
        (000116)
----Microelectronics in British industry. -
    1984.
        (000723)
----Semiconductors, Scotland and the
    international division of labour. - 1987.
        (000694)

UNITED KINGDOM--EMPLOYMENT.
----Cyclical variations in service
    industries' employment in the UK. - 1987.
        (000844)

UNITED KINGDOM--EMPLOYMENT POLICY.
----A code for misconduct? - 1980.
(002009)

UNITED KINGDOM--FOREIGN DIRECT INVESTMENT.
----Assessing the consequences of overseas
investment. - 1986.
(001296)
----The Atlantic two-way switch. - 1986.
(000852)
----Decision-making in foreign-owned
multinational subsidiaries in the United
Kingdom. - 1985.
(000521)
----Las empresas transnacionales y la
inversión extranjera directa en la
primera mitad de los años ochenta. -
1987.
(000194)
----Foreign direct investment and the
competitiveness of UK manufacturing
industry, 1963-1979. - 1984.
(000766)
----Foreign investment in South Africa and
Namibia. - 1984.
(001198) (002641)
----Foundations of foreign success. - 1987.
(000421)
----Inward investment. - 1984.
(000116)
----Multinational investment strategies in
the British Isles. - 1983.
(001151)
----Multinationals and Britain. - 1986.
(000205)
----The prospect for direct investment by
United Kingdom companies in developing
countries. - 1985.
(000169)
----The relative distribution of United
States direct investment : the UK/EEC
experience. - 1987.
(000113)
----Trends and issues in foreign direct
investment and related flows. - 1985.
(000192)
----US and Japanese manufacturing affiliates
in the UK. - 1985.
(001149)

UNITED KINGDOM--FOREIGN INVESTMENTS.
----British manufacturing investment
overseas. - 1985.
(000735)
----Japanese investment in UK industry. -
1984.
(000127)
----National legislation and regulations
relating to transnational corporations.
Volume 4. - 1986.
(002253)

UNITED KINGDOM--FOREIGN TRADE.
----East-West trade, industrial co-operation
and technology transfer. - 1984.
(001441)

UNITED KINGDOM--GROSS DOMESTIC PRODUCT.
----Cyclical variations in service
industries' employment in the UK. - 1987.
(000844)

UNITED KINGDOM--HISTORY.
----British multinationals. - 1986.
(000337)

UNITED KINGDOM--INDUSTRIAL ARBITRATION.
----Mediation, conciliation and arbitration
: an international comparison of
Australia, Great Britain and the United
States. - 1987.
(002476)

UNITED KINGDOM--INDUSTRIAL CO-OPERATION.
----The Asianization of British industry. -
1983.
(000204)
----East-West trade, industrial co-operation
and technology transfer. - 1984.
(001441)
----Expectations and results of
contractual joint ventures by US and UK
MNCs in Eastern Europe. - 1984.
(001623)

UNITED KINGDOM--INDUSTRIAL ENTERPRISES.
----The United Kingdom merger boom in
perspective. - 1987.
(001638)

UNITED KINGDOM--INDUSTRIAL EQUIPMENT LEASES.
----Analysis of equipment leasing contracts.
- 1984.
(002407)

UNITED KINGDOM--INDUSTRIAL ORGANIZATION.
----Privatisation and regulation : the UK
experience. - 1986.
(001627)

UNITED KINGDOM--INDUSTRIAL PLANNING.
----Multinational enterprises and industrial
restructuring in the UK. - 1985.
(001148)

UNITED KINGDOM--INDUSTRIAL POLICY.
----Transnational corporations and the
state. - 1985.
(001860)

UNITED KINGDOM--INDUSTRY.
----Kompass. - 196?-   .
(002648)
----Microelectronics in British industry. -
1984.
(000723)
----The Times 1000. - 1966-   .
(002668)

UNITED KINGDOM--INTERNATIONAL COMPETITION.
----Multinational enterprise and world
competition. - 1987.
(000018)
----Multinationals and Britain. - 1986.
(000205)

UNITED KINGDOM--INVESTMENT POLICY.
----Foreign multinationals and the British
economy. - 1988.
(001167)
----Inward investment. - 1984.
(000116)
----Multinationals and Britain. - 1986.
(000205)

UNITED KINGDOM--INVESTMENT POLICY (continued)
----Two arguments for the restriction of
     international capital flows. - 1986.
     (001240)

UNITED KINGDOM--INVESTMENT TAX CREDIT.
----International income taxation and
     developing countries. - 1988.
     (001759)

UNITED KINGDOM--JOINT VENTURES.
----The Asianization of British industry. -
     1983.
     (000204)
----Expectations and results of
     contractual joint ventures by US and UK
     MNCs in Eastern Europe. - 1984.
     (001623)
----Joint ventures. - 1983.
     (001589)

UNITED KINGDOM--LABOUR DISPUTES.
----Mediation, conciliation and arbitration
     : an international comparison of
     Australia, Great Britain and the United
     States. - 1987.
     (002476)

UNITED KINGDOM--LAWS AND REGULATIONS.
----International income taxation and
     developing countries. - 1988.
     (001759)
----National legislation and regulations
     relating to transnational corporations.
     Volume 4. - 1986.
     (002253)

UNITED KINGDOM--LICENCES.
----Comparative licensing aspects of
     Canadian and United Kingdom petroleum
     law. - 1986.
     (002176)

UNITED KINGDOM--MANAGEMENT.
----British multinationals. - 1986.
     (000337)
----Decision-making in foreign-owned
     multinational subsidiaries in the United
     Kingdom. - 1985.
     (000521)
----Foundations of foreign success. - 1987.
     (000421)

UNITED KINGDOM--MANUFACTURING.
----British manufacturing investment
     overseas. - 1985.
     (000735)
----The relative distribution of United
     States direct investment : the UK/EEC
     experience. - 1987.
     (000113)

UNITED KINGDOM--MANUFACTURING ENTERPRISES.
----A comparison of embodied technical
     change in services and manufacturing
     industry. - 1986.
     (000806)
----Foreign direct investment and the
     competitiveness of UK manufacturing
     industry, 1963-1979. - 1984.
     (000766)
----Japanese investment in UK industry. -
     1984.
     (000127)

----Kompass. - 196?-   .
     (002648)
----Sell's British exporters. - 1916-   .
     (002663)
----US and Japanese manufacturing affiliates
     in the UK. - 1985.
     (001149)

UNITED KINGDOM--MEDIATION.
----Mediation, conciliation and arbitration
     : an international comparison of
     Australia, Great Britain and the United
     States. - 1987.
     (002476)

UNITED KINGDOM--MICROELECTRONICS.
----Microelectronics in British industry. -
     1984.
     (000723)

UNITED KINGDOM--NATIONALIZATION.
----Privatising nationalised industries :
     constitutional issues and new legal
     techniques. - 1987.
     (001582)

UNITED KINGDOM--OIL AND GAS LEASES.
----Comparative licensing aspects of
     Canadian and United Kingdom petroleum
     law. - 1986.
     (002176)

UNITED KINGDOM--PERFORMANCE APPRAISAL.
----British multinationals. - 1986.
     (000337)

UNITED KINGDOM--PETROLEUM INDUSTRY.
----A golden adventure. - 1985.
     (000270)

UNITED KINGDOM--PETROLEUM LAW.
----Comparative licensing aspects of
     Canadian and United Kingdom petroleum
     law. - 1986.
     (002176)

UNITED KINGDOM--PHARMACEUTICAL INDUSTRY.
----From national to multinational
     enterprise. - 1983.
     (000277)
----Inward investment. - 1984.
     (000116)

UNITED KINGDOM--PRIVATE ENTERPRISES.
----Britain's privately owned companies. -
     198?-   .
     (002624)
----Privatisation and regulation : the UK
     experience. - 1986.
     (001627)

UNITED KINGDOM--PRIVATE SECTOR.
----Britain's privately owned companies. -
     198?-   .
     (002624)
----Privatising nationalised industries :
     constitutional issues and new legal
     techniques. - 1987.
     (001582)

UNITED KINGDOM--PRODUCTIVITY STATISTICS.
----A comparison of embodied technical
    change in services and manufacturing
    industry. - 1986.
        (000806)

UNITED KINGDOM--PUBLIC ENTERPRISES.
----Private agreements for takeovers of
    public companies. - 1984.
        (001626)
----Privatisation and regulation : the UK
    experience. - 1986.
        (001627)

UNITED KINGDOM--PUBLIC SECTOR.
----Privatising nationalised industries :
    constitutional issues and new legal
    techniques. - 1987.
        (001582)

UNITED KINGDOM--RULES AND REGULATIONS.
----Privatisation and regulation : the UK
    experience. - 1986.
        (001627)

UNITED KINGDOM--SEMICONDUCTORS.
----Semiconductors, Scotland and the
    international division of labour. - 1987.
        (000694)

UNITED KINGDOM--SERVICE INDUSTRIES.
----A comparison of embodied technical
    change in services and manufacturing
    industry. - 1986.
        (000806)
----Cyclical variations in service
    industries' employment in the UK. - 1987.
        (000844)

UNITED KINGDOM--SOUND RECORDINGS.
----The Gramophone Company: an
    Anglo-American multinational, 1898-1931.
    - 1985.
        (000285)

UNITED KINGDOM--STATISTICAL DATA.
----Inward investment. - 1984.
        (000116)
----Microelectronics in British industry. -
    1984.
        (000723)

UNITED KINGDOM--STOCKHOLDERS.
----Corporate acquisitions and mergers. -
    1985.
        (001544)

UNITED KINGDOM--STRATEGY.
----Multinational investment strategies in
    the British Isles. - 1983.
        (001151)

UNITED KINGDOM--STRUCTURAL ADJUSTMENT.
----Multinational enterprises and industrial
    restructuring in the UK. - 1985.
        (001148)

UNITED KINGDOM--SUGAR TRADE INDUSTRY.
----Tate and Lyle, geant du sucre. - 1983.
        (000274)

UNITED KINGDOM--TAX INCENTIVES.
----International income taxation and
    developing countries. - 1988.
        (001759)

UNITED KINGDOM--TAXATION.
----Allied Dunbar tax guide. - 1985-   .
        (002027)
----International income taxation and
    developing countries. - 1988.
        (001759)

UNITED KINGDOM--TECHNOLOGICAL CHANGE.
----A comparison of embodied technical
    change in services and manufacturing
    industry. - 1986.
        (000806)

UNITED KINGDOM--TECHNOLOGICAL INNOVATIONS.
----A comparison of embodied technical
    change in services and manufacturing
    industry. - 1986.
        (000806)
----Microelectronics in British industry. -
    1984.
        (000723)

UNITED KINGDOM--TECHNOLOGY TRANSFER.
----East-West trade, industrial co-operation
    and technology transfer. - 1984.
        (001441)
----Expectations and results of
    contractual joint ventures by US and UK
    MNCs in Eastern Europe. - 1984.
        (001623)

UNITED KINGDOM--TRANSNATIONAL CORPORATIONS.
----Accounting for overseas operations. -
    1986.
        (002122)
----The Atlantic two-way switch. - 1986.
        (000852)
----Britain and the multinationals. - 1985.
        (001164)
----British multinationals. - 1986.
        (000337)
----Comparative analysis of UK domestic and
    international firms. - 1984.
        (000343)
----Corporate acquisitions and mergers. -
    1985.
        (001544)
----Decision-making in foreign-owned
    multinational subsidiaries in the United
    Kingdom. - 1985.
        (000521)
----Foreign investment in South Africa and
    Namibia. - 1984.
        (001198) (002641)
----Foreign multinationals and the British
    economy. - 1988.
        (001167)
----From national to multinational
    enterprise. - 1983.
        (000277)
----A golden adventure. - 1985.
        (000270)
----The Gramophone Company: an
    Anglo-American multinational, 1898-1931.
    - 1985.
        (000285)

Subject Index - Index des matières

UNITED KINGDOM--TRANSNATIONAL CORPORATIONS
(continued)
----International segment disclosures by
    U.S. and U.K. multinational enterprises:
    a descriptive study. - 1984.
        (002080)
----Multinational enterprise and world
    competition. - 1987.
        (000018)
----Multinational enterprises and industrial
    restructuring in the UK. - 1985.
        (001148)
----Multinational investment strategies in
    the British Isles. - 1983.
        (001151)
----Multinationals and Britain. - 1986.
        (000205)
----National legislation and regulations
    relating to transnational corporations.
    Volume 4. - 1986.
        (002253)
----Recent developments in operations and
    behaviour of transnational corporations.
    - 1987.
        (000103)
----Tate and Lyle, geant du sucre. - 1983.
        (000274)
----Transnational corporations and the
    state. - 1985.
        (001860)

UNITED REPUBLIC OF TANZANIA--LAWS AND
REGULATIONS.
----National legislation and regulations
    relating to transnational corporations.
    Volume 3. - 1983.
        (002252)

UNITED REPUBLIC OF TANZANIA--SCIENCE AND
TECHNOLOGY CAPABILITY.
----Microelectronics-based automation
    technologies and development. - 1985.
        (000753)

UNITED REPUBLIC OF TANZANIA--TRANSNATIONAL
CORPORATIONS.
----National legislation and regulations
    relating to transnational corporations.
    Volume 3. - 1983.
        (002252)

UNITED STATES--ACCOUNTING.
----Accounting and law in a nutshell. - 1984.
        (002208)

UNITED STATES--ACCOUNTING AND REPORTING.
----Internal accountability. - 1984.
        (002055)
----International segment disclosures by
    U.S. and U.K. multinational enterprises:
    a descriptive study. - 1984.
        (002080)
----Joint ventures. - 1987.
        (001613)

UNITED STATES--ADVERTISING AGENCIES.
----Madison Avenue in Asia. - 1984.
        (000801)

UNITED STATES--AFFILIATE CORPORATIONS.
----Capital expenditures by majority-owned
    foreign affiliates of U.S. companies,
    1986 and 1987. - 1986.
        (000479)

----Foreign direct investment in the United
    States. - 1985.
        (000197)
----Die Steuerung auslandischer
    Tochtergesellschaften. - 1983.
        (000400)
----US and Japanese manufacturing affiliates
    in the UK. - 1985.
        (001149)

UNITED STATES--AGRIBUSINESS.
----U.S.-EEC confrontation in the
    international trade of agricultural
    products: consequences for third
    parties. - 1985.
        (001380)

UNITED STATES--AIRCRAFT INDUSTRY.
----Alliance politics and economics. - 1987.
        (000719)

UNITED STATES--ALCOHOL FUELS.
----A competitive assessment of the U.S.
    methanol industry. - 1985.
        (000671)

UNITED STATES--ALUMINIUM INDUSTRY.
----The RJR story. - 1983.
        (000296)
----Vertical integration and joint ventures
    in the aluminum industry. - 1983.
        (001642)

UNITED STATES--ANGLO AMERICAN CORPORATION
(MARSHALLTOWN,SOUTH AFTRICA).
----Anglo in America. - 1986.
        (000292)

UNITED STATES--ANTIDUMPING DUTIES.
----Antitrust aspects of U.S.-Japanese
    trade. - 1983.
        (002345)
----Competition and world markets. - 1983.
        (001665)

UNITED STATES--ANTITRUST LAW.
----Antitrust aspects of U.S.-Japanese
    trade. - 1983.
        (002345)
----Antitrust law developments (second). -
    1984.
        (002339)
----Antitrust policy and joint research and
    development ventures. - 1984.
        (002356)
----Arbitration of private antitrust claims
    in international trade. - 1986.
        (002471)
----Competition and world markets. - 1983.
        (001665)
----Cooperative research and development. -
    1984.
        (001630)
----Exclusive licenses as restraints of
    trade under US and Common Market
    antitrust law. - 1984.
        (002414)
----The extraterritorial effects of
    antitrust laws. - 1984.
        (002342)

-418-

UNITED STATES--ANTITRUST LAW (continued)
----Extraterritorial effects of United
    States commercial and antitrust
    legislation. - 1983.
      (002352)
----International antitrust law. - 1985.
      (002539)
----Joint research and development
    legislation. - 1987.
      (002286)
----Mitsubishi and the arbitrability of
    antitrust claims. - 1986.
      (002486)

UNITED STATES--ARBITRAL AWARDS.
----Enforcement of arbitral awards issued by
    the Additional Facility of the
    International Centre of Settlement of
    Investment Disputes (ICSID). - 1985.
      (002536)
----International commercial arbitration : a
    comparative analysis of the United
    States system and the UNCITRAL model
    law. - 1986.
      (002487)
----International commercial arbitration. -
    1983.
      (002538)
----Jurisdiction over foreign sovereigns. -
    1983.
      (002480)

UNITED STATES--ARBITRATION.
----State contracts and oil expropriations.
    - 1984.
      (002577)

UNITED STATES--ARBITRATION RULES.
----International commercial arbitration : a
    comparative analysis of the United
    States system and the UNCITRAL model
    law. - 1986.
      (002487)

UNITED STATES--ARMAMENTS.
----The nuclear weapons industry. - 1984.
      (000659)

UNITED STATES--ARMS INDUSTRY.
----Stocking the arsenal. - 1985.
      (000738)

UNITED STATES--ASSEMBLY-LINE WORK.
----Restructuring industry offshore. - 1983.
      (000692)

UNITED STATES--AUTOMATION.
----A competitive assessment of the U.S.
    manufacturing automation equipment
    industries. - 1984.
      (000756)
----Postindustrial manufacturing. - 1986.
      (000698)

UNITED STATES--AUTOMOBILE INDUSTRY.
----America's new no. 4 automaker -- Honda.
    - 1985.
      (000294)
----Automotive parts industry and the U.S.
    aftermarket for Japanese cars and light
    trucks. - 1985.
      (000759)

----Blind intersection? policy and the
    automobile industry. - 1987.
      (000660)
----Industrial renaissance : producing a
    competitive future for America. - 1983.
      (000300)
----Oil industry mergers. - 1984.
      (001652)

UNITED STATES--BALANCE OF PAYMENTS.
----The external deficit. - 1987.
      (000216)

UNITED STATES--BALANCE OF TRADE.
----International countertrade. - 1984.
      (001396)

UNITED STATES--BALL BEARINGS.
----A competitive assessment of the U.S.
    ball and roller bearings industry. -
    1985.
      (000760)

UNITED STATES--BANK LOANS.
----Foreign investment in South Africa and
    Namibia. - 1984.
      (001198) (002641)
----Rehearing granted : Allied Bank
    International v. Banco Agricola Credito
    de Cartago and the current international
    debt crisis. - 1984.
      (000233)

UNITED STATES--BANKING.
----Banking deregulation and the new
    competition in financial services. -
    1984.
      (000833)
----A historical perspective of U.S.-GCC
    economic and financial interdependence.
    - 1987.
      (000143)

UNITED STATES--BANKING LAW.
----Banking deregulation and the new
    competition in financial services. -
    1984.
      (000833)

UNITED STATES--BANKRUPTCY.
----Structuring natural resources
    development agreements between foreign
    governments and United States companies
    to prevent transfer of rights under the
    agreement should the company enter
    bankruptcy. - 1984.
      (002411)

UNITED STATES--BANKS.
----American banks in the international
    interbank market. - 1983.
      (000829)
----Foreign government and foreign investor
    control of U.S. banks. - 1983.
      (001654)
----Foreign ownership of U.S. banks: trends
    and effects. - 1983.
      (001591)

UNITED STATES--BIBLIOGRAPHIES.
----Fundamentals of international taxation.
    - 1985.
      (001700)

UNITED STATES--BILATERAL TRADE AGREEMENTS.
----The legal markets of international
    trade. - 1987.
       (002038)

UNITED STATES--BIOTECHNOLOGY.
----Commercial biotechnology. - 1984.
       (000643)
----Double dividends? - 1986.
       (000682)

UNITED STATES--BLACKS.
----U.S. firms and black labor in South
    Africa: creating a structure for change.
    - 1986.
       (001195)

UNITED STATES--BUDGET DEFICITS.
----What's causing America's capital
    imports? - 1987.
       (000539)

UNITED STATES--BUSINESS ENTERPRISE BRANCHES.
----Operating foreign subsidiaries. - 1983.
       (000388)

UNITED STATES--BUSINESS ENTERPRISES.
----Democratic development. - 1986.
       (001334)
----Directory of American firms operating in
    foreign countries. - 1955-   .
       (002630)
----Forbes annual directory. - 1969-   .
       (002640)
----Foreign direct investment in the United
    States. - 1985-   .
       (000131)
----The knowledge industry 200. - 1983.
       (000884) (002646)
----Major companies of the USA. - 1986-   .
       (002652)
----Million dollar directory. - 1959-   .
       (002655)
----Performance requirements for foreign
    business. - 1983.
       (002314)
----United States jurisdiction over foreign
    subsidiaries. - 1983.
       (002355)
----US corporate interests and the political
    economy of trade policy. - 1984.
       (000505)

UNITED STATES--BUSINESS ETHICS.
----South Africa: the churches vs. the
    corporations. - 1983.
       (002589)

UNITED STATES--CAPITAL FORMATION.
----Corporate capital structures in the
    United States. - 1985.
       (000315)

UNITED STATES--CAPITAL INVESTMENTS.
----Applying uniform margin requirements to
    foreign entities attempting to acquire
    U.S. corporations. - 1984.
       (002173)

UNITED STATES--CAPITAL MARKETS.
----Die Aussenexpansion des Kapitals. - 1984.
       (000037)

UNITED STATES--CAPITAL MOVEMENTS.
----Die Aussenexpansion des Kapitals. - 1984.
       (000037)
----Canada's reversal from importer to
    exporter of foreign direct investment. -
    1987.
       (000181)
----Capital expenditures by majority-owned
    foreign affiliates of U.S. companies,
    1986 and 1987. - 1986.
       (000479)
----Handels- und Zahlungsprobleme in
    Osteuropa. - 1983.
       (000215)
----The overseas expansion of capital. -
    1985.
       (000038)
----The role of foreign direct investment in
    U.S. capital outflows. - 1986.
       (000179)
----What's causing America's capital
    imports? - 1987.
       (000539)

UNITED STATES--CHEMICAL INDUSTRY.
----A competitive assessment of the U.S.
    methanol industry. - 1985.
       (000671)
----Le role des grandes entreprises
    diversifiées du pétrole et de la chimie
    dans la production alimentaire. - 1985.
       (000699)

UNITED STATES--CLAIMS.
----Current developments in the law of
    expropriation and compensation. - 1987.
       (002318)
----The expropriation issue before the
    Iran-United States Claims Tribunal. -
    1984.
       (002320)
----Forum non conveniens and multinational
    corporations. - 1986.
       (002568)
----Iran-U.S. Claims Tribunal. - 1986.
       (002335)
----Partnership claims before the
    Iran-United States Claims Tribunal. -
    1987.
       (002322)
----Recent developments in international
    commercial arbitration. - 1987.
       (002549)
----United States policy regarding
    nationalization of American investments.
    - 1984.
       (002332)

UNITED STATES--COMMERCIAL ARBITRATION.
----Arbitral adjudication. - 1984.
       (002484)
----Arbitration of private antitrust claims
    in international trade. - 1986.
       (002471)
----Etude historique et comparée de
    l'arbitrage. - 1984.
       (002485)
----Host countries permanent sovereignty
    over national resources and protection
    of foreign investors. - 1983.
       (002566)
----The new international economic order,
    (2). - 1984.
       (001271)

UNITED STATES--COMMERCIAL BANKS.
----U.S. and Canadian investment in South
   Africa and Namibia. - 1986.
      (001212) (002671) (002672)

UNITED STATES--COMMERCIAL LAW.
----Antitrust aspects of U.S.-Japanese
   trade. - 1983.
      (002345)
----Antitrust law developments (second). -
   1984.
      (002339)
----Countertrade. - 1984.
      (001371)
----Digest of commercial laws of the world.
   - 1985-   .
      (002256)
----Extraterritorial effects of United
   States commercial and antitrust
   legislation. - 1983.
      (002352)
----A manual of U.S. trade laws. - 1985.
      (002220)
----On Third World debt. - 1984.
      (000211)
----Recent developments in international
   commercial arbitration. - 1987.
      (002549)
----Reviewing the situation : what is to be
   done with the Foreign Corrupt Practices
   Act? - 1987.
      (002235)

UNITED STATES--COMMODITY CONTROL.
----United States regulation of
   high-technology exports. - 1986.
      (001462)

UNITED STATES--COMMUNICATION INDUSTRY.
----The knowledge industry 200. - 1983.
      (000884) (002646)

UNITED STATES--COMMUNICATION POLICY.
----Implications of deregulating satellite
   communications. - 1985.
      (002242)

UNITED STATES--COMPARATIVE ADVANTAGES.
----The competitive position of U.S.
   manufacturing firms. - 1985.
      (000353)

UNITED STATES--COMPARATIVE ANALYSIS.
----American and Chinese managers in U.S.
   companies in Taiwan: a comparison. -
   1985.
      (000395)
----International joint ventures. - 1985.
      (001590)
----Multinational enterprise and world
   competition. - 1987.
      (000018)
----Postindustrial manufacturing. - 1986.
      (000698)
----Transfer of technology from Japan and
   the United States to Korean
   manufacturing industries: a comparative
   study. - 1984.
      (001461)

UNITED STATES--COMPENSATION.
----The expropriation issue before the
   Iran-United States Claims Tribunal. -
   1984.
      (002320)
----For whom the bell tolls in the aftermath
   of the Bhopal tragedy. - 1987.
      (001950)
----Oil spill liability and compensation. -
   1985.
      (001940)
----State contracts and oil expropriations.
   - 1984.
      (002577)

UNITED STATES--COMPENSATION TRADE.
----Controlling the cost of international
   compensation. - 1983.
      (002323)
----Countertrade. - 1984.
      (001371)
----International countertrade. - 1984.
      (001396)

UNITED STATES--COMPETITION.
----An assessment of U.S. competitiveness in
   high technology industries. - 1983.
      (000653)
----Balancing the national interest : U.S.
   national security export controls and
   global economic competition. - 1987.
      (001417)
----Competition and world markets. - 1983.
      (001665)
----Competition in the Pacific Basin. - 1987.
      (001673)
----A competitive assessment of the
   renewable energy equipment industry. -
   1984.
      (000775)
----A competitive assessment of the U.S.
   fiber optics industry. - 1984.
      (000800)
----A competitive assessment of the U.S.
   international construction industry. -
   1984.
      (000779)
----A competitive assessment of the U.S.
   manufacturing automation equipment
   industries. - 1984.
      (000756)
----A competitive assessment of the U.S. oil
   field equipment industry. - 1985.
      (000764)
----A competitive assessment of the U.S.
   petrochemical industry. - 1982.
      (000755)
----A competitive assessment of the U.S.
   pharmaceutical industry. - 1984.
      (000757)
----Competitive edge. - 1984.
      (000673)
----EEC competition policy. - 1986.
      (001989)
----Employment and competitiveness in the
   European Community. - 1984.
      (001929)
----La haute technologie américaine. - 1987.
      (000680)
----Manufacturing matters : the myth of the
   post-industrial economy. - 1987.
      (000669)

UNITED STATES--COMPUTER INDUSTRY.
----A competitive assessment of the U.S.
    flexible manufacturing systems industry.
    - 1985.
    (000763)
----A competitive assessment of the United
    States data processing services
    industry. - 1984.
    (000981)
----A competitive assessment of the United
    States disk storage industry. - 1985.
    (000672)
----A competitive assessment of the United
    States software industry. - 1984.
    (000980)
----Competitive edge. - 1984.
    (000673)
----High technology industries. - 1983-
    (000695)
----High technology plant location
    decisions. - 1983.
    (000528)
----National security and the semiconductor
    industry. - 1987.
    (000675)
----The top 100. - 1984.
    (000742) (002670)

UNITED STATES--COMPUTER SOFTWARE.
----A competitive assessment of the United
    States software industry. - 1984.
    (000980)

UNITED STATES--COMPUTER-AIDED DESIGN.
----A competitive assessment of the U.S.
    manufacturing automation equipment
    industries. - 1984.
    (000756)

UNITED STATES--COMPUTERS.
----The top 100. - 1984.
    (000742) (002670)

UNITED STATES--CONCILIATION.
----Mediation, conciliation and arbitration
    : an international comparison of
    Australia, Great Britain and the United
    States. - 1987.
    (002476)

UNITED STATES--CONSTRUCTION EQUIPMENT.
----A competitive assessment of the U.S.
    construction machinery industry. - 1985.
    (000761)

UNITED STATES--CONSTRUCTION INDUSTRY.
----A competitive assessment of the U.S.
    international construction industry. -
    1984.
    (000779)

UNITED STATES--CONTRACTS.
----United States-China commercial
    contracts. - 1986.
    (002439)

UNITED STATES--CORPORATE ANALYSIS.
----New trends in internationalization:
    processes and theories. Diversified
    patterns of multinational enterprise and
    old and new forms of foreign involvement
    of the firm. - 1983.
    (000068)

UNITED STATES--CORPORATE CORRUPTION.
----Reviewing the situation : what is to be
    done with the Foreign Corrupt Practices
    Act? - 1987.
    (002235)

UNITED STATES--CORPORATE MERGERS.
----Acquisitions and joint ventures among
    large corporations. - 1985.
    (001653)
----The effect of conglomerate mergers on
    changes in industry concentration. -
    1986.
    (001527)
----International law of take-overs and
    mergers. - 1986.
    (001573)
----La loi anti-fusions et l'industrie
    pétrolière américaine, (2). - 1986.
    (000581)
----Oil industry mergers. - 1984.
    (001652)
----On vertical mergers. - 1986.
    (001641)
----Private agreements for takeovers of
    public companies. - 1984.
    (001626)
----Recent developments in operations and
    behaviour of transnational corporations.
    - 1987.
    (000103)

UNITED STATES--CORPORATION LAW.
----International law of take-overs and
    mergers. - 1986.
    (001573)
----La loi anti-fusions et l'industrie
    pétrolière américaine, (2). - 1986.
    (000581)
----United States corporations operating in
    Saudi Arabia and laws affecting
    discrimination in employment. - 1985.
    (002354)
----United States jurisdiction over foreign
    subsidiaries. - 1983.
    (002355)
----The United States, transnational
    business and the law. - 1985.
    (001982)

UNITED STATES--CORPORATION TAX.
----The final report of the Worldwide
    Unitary Taxation Working Group :
    Chairman's report and supplemental
    views. - 1984.
    (001763)
----Fundamentals of international taxation.
    - 1985.
    (001700)
----Worldwide unitary taxation : nature and
    alternative solutions. - 1986.
    (001766)

UNITED STATES--CORPORATIONS.
----The Rising Sun in America (Part Two)
    -- Japanese management in the United
    States. - 1986.
    (000391)
----America's corporate families. -
    1982-
    (002616)
----America's corporate families and
    international affiliates. - 1983-
    (002617)

UNITED STATES--CORPORATIONS (continued)
----Corporate capital structures in the
     United States. - 1985.
       (000315)
----Directory of American firms operating in
     foreign countries. - 1955-   .
       (002630)
----Forbes annual directory. - 1969-   .
       (002640)
----Internal accountability. - 1984.
       (002055)
----Major companies of the USA. - 1986-   .
       (002652)
----Mezhdunarodnyi marketing amerikanskoi
     tekhnologii. - 1985.
       (000494)
----The Rising Sun in America (Part One). -
     1986.
       (000392)
----U.S. corporate interests and the
     political economy of trade policy. -
     1985.
       (000368)

UNITED STATES--CORRUPT PRACTICES.
----Reviewing the situation : what is to be
     done with the Foreign Corrupt Practices
     Act? - 1987.
       (002235)

UNITED STATES--CREDIT POLICY.
----U.S. and Canadian investment in South
     Africa and Namibia. - 1986.
       (001212) (002671) (002672)

UNITED STATES--DATA PROCESSING SERVICES.
----A competitive assessment of the United
     States data processing services
     industry. - 1984.
       (000981)

UNITED STATES--DATA STORAGE.
----A competitive assessment of the United
     States disk storage industry. - 1985.
       (000672)

UNITED STATES--DEBT SERVICING.
----Rehearing granted : Allied Bank
     International v. Banco Agricola Credito
     de Cartago and the current international
     debt crisis. - 1984.
       (000233)

UNITED STATES--DECISION-MAKING.
----Operating foreign subsidiaries. - 1983.
       (000388)

UNITED STATES--DEFENCE CONTRACTS.
----The nuclear weapons industry. - 1984.
       (000659)
----Stocking the arsenal. - 1985.
       (000738)

UNITED STATES--DEVELOPED COUNTRIES.
----A competitive assessment of the U.S.
     construction machinery industry. - 1985.
       (000761)
----A competitive assessment of the U.S.
     semiconductor manufacturing equipment
     industry. - 1985.
       (000758)

UNITED STATES--DEVELOPING COUNTRIES.
----A competitive assessment of the United
     States equipment leasing industry. -
     1985.
       (000982)
----The export of hazard. - 1985.
       (001941)
----International countertrade. - 1984.
       (001396)
----The international debt crisis. - 1985.
       (000240)
----The international debt crisis and the
     banks. - 1985.
       (000227)
----International finance and investment. -
     1985.
       (001249)
----On Third World debt. - 1984.
       (000211)
----Performance requirements for foreign
     business. - 1983.
       (002314)
----The role of private investment in Third
     World development. - 1986.
       (001328)
----Towards a new treaty framework for
     direct foreign investment. - 1985.
       (002047)
----Trade in services. - 1986.
       (000962)
----The U.S. renewal of the GSP. - 1986.
       (001996)

UNITED STATES--DEVELOPMENT.
----The role of direct foreign investment in
     developing East Asian countries. - 1985.
       (001052)

UNITED STATES--DEVELOPMENT ASSISTANCE.
----The Caribbean Basin Economic Recovery
     Act and its implications for foreign
     private investment. - 1984.
       (001965)
----U.S. foreign assistance. - 1984.
       (000203)

UNITED STATES--DIRECTORIES.
----America's corporate families. -
     1982-   .
       (002616)
----America's corporate families and
     international affiliates. - 1983-   .
       (002617)
----Bradford's directory of marketing
     research agencies and management
     consultants in the United States and the
     world. - 1966-   .
       (002623)
----Consultants and consulting organizations
     directory. - 197?-   .
       (000832)
----Directory of American firms operating in
     foreign countries. - 1955-   .
       (002630)
----Directory of business, trade and public
     policy organizations. - 1982-   .
       (002631)
----Directory of foreign firms operating in
     the United States. - 1969-   .
       (002633)
----Export trading companies. - 1984-   .
       (000851) (002638)

UNITED STATES--DIRECTORIES (continued)
----Forbes annual directory. - 1969-   .
    (002640)
----Foreign investment in South Africa and
    Namibia. - 1984.
    (001198) (002641)
----The knowledge industry 200. - 1983.
    (000884) (002646)
----Krupneishie promyshlennye i torgovye
    monopolii. - 1986.
    (002658)
----Major companies of the USA. - 1986-   .
    (002652)
----Million dollar directory. - 1959-   .
    (002655)
----Moody's industrial manual. - 1954-   .
    (002656)
----The nuclear weapons industry. - 1984.
    (000659)
----Stocking the arsenal. - 1985.
    (000738)
----U.S. and Canadian investment in South
    Africa and Namibia. - 1986.
    (001212) (002671) (002672)

UNITED STATES--DISPUTE SETTLEMENT.
----Current developments in the law of
    expropriation and compensation. - 1987.
    (002318)
----International antitrust law. - 1985.
    (002539)
----International commercial arbitration. -
    1985.
    (002516)
----Iran-U.S. Claims Tribunal. - 1986.
    (002335)
----Partnership claims before the
    Iran-United States Claims Tribunal. -
    1987.
    (002322)

UNITED STATES--DISPUTES.
----For whom the bell tolls in the aftermath
    of the Bhopal tragedy. - 1987.
    (001950)

UNITED STATES--DIVESTMENT.
----The costs of disinvestment. - 1986.
    (001207)
----Disinvestment and black workers
    attitudes in South Africa. - 1985.
    (001210)
----Time to quit South Africa? - 1985.
    (001206)

UNITED STATES--DOUBLE TAXATION.
----Federal taxation of international
    transactions. - 1988.
    (001730)
----The Soviet Union's other tax agreements.
    - 1986.
    (002043)
----Tax aspects of international
    transactions. - 1984.
    (001757)
----Tax treaty abuse. - 1983.
    (002046)

UNITED STATES--DRILLING RIGS.
----A competitive assessment of the U.S. oil
    field equipment industry. - 1985.
    (000764)

UNITED STATES--ECONOMIC AGREEMENTS.
----Structuring natural resources
    development agreements between foreign
    governments and United States companies
    to prevent transfer of rights under the
    agreement should the company enter
    bankruptcy. - 1984.
    (002411)

UNITED STATES--ECONOMIC ANALYSIS.
----The external deficit. - 1987.
    (000216)

UNITED STATES--ECONOMIC ASSISTANCE.
----La presentación de la iniciativa de la
    Cuenca del Caribe al GATT. - 1985.
    (001972)
----The roots of crisis in southern Africa.
    - 1985.
    (001208)

UNITED STATES--ECONOMIC DEPENDENCE.
----Disfraces del coloniaje. - 1984.
    (001114)

UNITED STATES--ECONOMIC DEVELOPMENT.
----The significance of foreign investment
    in US development 1879 to mid-1914. -
    1982.
    (001344)

UNITED STATES--ECONOMIC HISTORY.
----The emergence of a U.S. multinational
    enterprise: the Goodyear Tire and Rubber
    Company, 1910-1939. - 1987.
    (000281)

UNITED STATES--ECONOMIC POLICY.
----EEC competition policy. - 1986.
    (001989)
----Manufacturing matters : the myth of the
    post-industrial economy. - 1987.
    (000669)
----The U.S. drive to bring services into
    GATT. - 1986.
    (000926)

UNITED STATES--ECONOMIC RELATIONS.
----The Arab world is still importing. -
    1987.
    (001134)
----Die Aussenexpansion des Kapitals. - 1984.
    (000037)
----Competition in the Pacific Basin. - 1987.
    (001673)
----Estados Unidos y el proceso de
    transnacionalización en la postguerra. -
    1984.
    (001235)
----Grace. - 1985.
    (000276)
----The overseas expansion of capital. -
    1985.
    (000038)
----The political economy of U.S. policy
    toward South Africa. - 1985.
    (001196)
----The role of multinational enterprises in
    US-Canadian economic relations. - 1986.
    (001159)
----The roots of crisis in southern Africa.
    - 1985.
    (001208)

UNITED STATES--ECONOMIC RELATIONS (continued)
----Two hungry giants. - 1983.
    (000645)
----The U.S. renewal of the GSP. - 1986.
    (001996)

UNITED STATES--ECONOMIC STATISTICS.
----Selected data on foreign direct
    investment in the United States,
    1950-79. - 1984.
    (000184)

UNITED STATES--ECONOMIC TRENDS.
----Trends in multinational business and
    global environments: a perspective. -
    1984.
    (000029)

UNITED STATES--ELECTRIC POWER.
----A competitive assessment of the U.S.
    electric power generating equipment
    industry. - 1985.
    (000762)

UNITED STATES--ELECTRIC POWER PLANTS.
----A competitive assessment of the U.S.
    electric power generating equipment
    industry. - 1985.
    (000762)

UNITED STATES--ELECTRONIC FUNDS TRANSFER.
----Financial transfers in the MNE. - 1986.
    (000416)

UNITED STATES--ELECTRONICS INDUSTRY.
----High-tech trade. - 1986.
    (000696)
----The semiconductor business. - 1985.
    (000715)
----Transnational corporations in the
    international semiconductor industry. -
    1986.
    (000748)

UNITED STATES--EMPLOYMENT.
----Croissance de l'emploi dans les
    services. - 1987.
    (000846)
----The effects of foreign direct investment
    on U.S. employment during recession and
    structural change. - 1986.
    (001908)
----Employment and competitiveness in the
    European Community. - 1984.
    (001929)

UNITED STATES--EMPLOYMENT DISCRIMINATION.
----United States corporations operating in
    Saudi Arabia and laws affecting
    discrimination in employment. - 1985.
    (002354)

UNITED STATES--EMPLOYMENT POLICY.
----American multinationals and American
    employment. - 1983.
    (001890)
----International business travel and
    relocation directory. - 1984.
    (002710)
----Key to Japan's economic strength. - 1984.
    (001924)

----Staffing of management and professional
    positions at overseas subsidiaries of
    U.S. multinational enterprises. - 1983.
    (001885)

UNITED STATES--ENERGY POLICY.
----Foreign oil and taxation. - 1983.
    (002039)

UNITED STATES--ENERGY RESOURCES.
----Profiles of foreign direct investment in
    U.S. energy. - 1985-   .
    (000774)

UNITED STATES--ENERGY RESOURCES DEVELOPMENT.
----A competitive assessment of the
    renewable energy equipment industry. -
    1984.
    (000775)

UNITED STATES--ENGINEERS.
----The engineers and the price system
    revisited: the future of the
    international oil corporations. - 1983.
    (000587)

UNITED STATES--ENVIRONMENTAL HEALTH.
----The export of hazard. - 1985.
    (001941)

UNITED STATES--ENVIRONMENTAL LAW.
----Are environmental regulations driving
    U.S. industry overseas? - 1984.
    (001947)

UNITED STATES--EVALUATION.
----A competitive assessment of the U.S.
    flexible manufacturing systems industry.
    - 1985.
    (000763)
----A competitive assessment of the U.S.
    methanol industry. - 1985.
    (000671)
----A competitive assessment of the United
    States disk storage industry. - 1985.
    (000672)

UNITED STATES--EXCESS PROFITS TAX.
----Intercorporate transfer pricing: the
    role of the functionally determined
    profit split explored. - 1985.
    (001753)

UNITED STATES--EXCLUSIVE ECONOMIC ZONE.
----U.S. fishery negotiations with Canada
    and Mexico. - 1985.
    (002462)

UNITED STATES--EXPORT CREDITS.
----Eximbank's role in international banking
    and finance. - 1986.
    (000816)

UNITED STATES--EXPORT EARNINGS.
----International business planning. - 1983.
    (002279)

UNITED STATES--EXPORT INCENTIVES.
----The Export Trading Company Act. - 1983.
    (002206)

UNITED STATES--EXPORT MARKETING.
----Export trading companies. - 1984-   .
     (000851) (002638)
----Identifying export potential in the
     service sector. - 1986.
     (000882)
----The information needs of exporters:
     theory, framework and empirical tests. -
     1986.
     (000989)

UNITED STATES--EXPORT ORIENTED INDUSTRIES.
----Export trading companies. - 1984-   .
     (000851) (002638)
----The Export Trading Company Act. - 1983.
     (002206)
----Restructuring industry offshore. - 1983.
     (000692)

UNITED STATES--EXPORT POLICY.
----The Export Trading Company Act. - 1983.
     (002206)

UNITED STATES--EXPORT PROMOTION.
----Identifying export potential in the
     service sector. - 1986.
     (000882)

UNITED STATES--EXPORT RESTRICTIONS.
----Balancing the national interest : U.S.
     national security export controls and
     global economic competition. - 1987.
     (001417)
----Licensing impact of foreign policy
     motivated retroactive reexport
     regulations. - 1983.
     (001352)
----United States regulation of
     high-technology exports. - 1986.
     (001462)

UNITED STATES--EXPORTS.
----A competitive assessment of the U.S.
     herbicide industry. - 1985.
     (000670)
----The export of hazard. - 1985.
     (001941)
----The information needs of exporters: -
     theory, framework and empirical tests. -
     1986.
     (000989)

UNITED STATES--EXPROPRIATION.
----The expropriation issue before the
     Iran-United States Claims Tribunal. -
     1984.
     (002320)
----Host countries permanent sovereignty
     over national resources and protection
     of foreign investors. - 1983.
     (002566)
----Iran-U.S. Claims Tribunal. - 1986.
     (002335)
----Jurisdiction over foreign governments. -
     1986.
     (002347)

UNITED STATES--EXTERNAL DEBT.
----The external deficit. - 1987.
     (000216)
----The international debt crisis and the
     banks. - 1985.
     (000227)

UNITED STATES--FACTOR ANALYSIS.
----Determinants of direct foreign
     investment. - 1987.
     (000534)

UNITED STATES--FIBRE OPTICS.
----A competitive assessment of the U.S.
     fiber optics industry. - 1984.
     (000800)

UNITED STATES--FINANCIAL ASSISTANCE.
----The international debt crisis. - 1985.
     (000240)

UNITED STATES--FINANCIAL FLOWS.
----International finance and investment. -
     1985.
     (001249)

UNITED STATES--FINANCIAL INSTITUTIONS.
----Banking deregulation and the new
     competition in financial services. -
     1984.
     (000833)

UNITED STATES--FINANCING.
----Corporate capital structures in the
     United States. - 1985.
     (000315)

UNITED STATES--FISHERY EXPLOITATION.
----U.S. fishery negotiations with Canada
     and Mexico. - 1985.
     (002462)

UNITED STATES--FLEXIBLE MANUFACTURING
SYSTEMS.
----A competitive assessment of the U.S.
     flexible manufacturing systems industry.
     - 1985.
     (000763)
----Postindustrial manufacturing. - 1986.
     (000698)

UNITED STATES--FOOD INDUSTRY.
----Determinants of foreign direct
     investment by food and tobacco
     manufacturers. - 1983.
     (000527)
----Foreign direct investment in U.S. food
     and tobacco manufacturing and domestic
     economic performance. - 1983.
     (000170)
----Increased foreign investment in U.S.
     food industries. - 1985.
     (000714)
----Où va l'investissement direct
     international? USA/monde : le cas du
     secteur alimentaire. - 1984.
     (000666)

UNITED STATES--FOOD PRODUCTION.
----Le role des grandes entreprises
     diversifiées du pétrole et de la chimie
     dans la production alimentaire. - 1985.
     (000699)

UNITED STATES--FOREIGN DIRECT INVESTMENT.
----The effect of political events on
     United States direct foreign
     investment: a pooled time-series
     cross-sectional analysis. - 1985.
     (001835)

Subject Index - Index des matières

UNITED STATES--FOREIGN DIRECT INVESTMENT
(continued)
----Japanese and American direct investment
in Asia. - 1985.
(000154)
----Japan's direct investment in California
and the new protectionism. - 1984.
(000145)
----Linkages and foreign direct investment
in the United States. - 1984.
(000166)
----Manual of foreign investment in the
United States. - 1984.
(002238)
----A muködo toke becsalogatása
Magyarországra : nyugati szemszögbol. -
1987.
(001608)
----New forms of investment in developing
countries by US companies: a five
industry comparison. - 1987.
(000328)
----New trends in internationalization:
processes and theories. Diversified
patterns of multinational enterprise and
old and new forms of foreign involvement
of the firm. - 1983.
(000068)
----OPEC direct investment in the United
States. - 1981-   .
(000168)
----Operating foreign subsidiaries. - 1983.
(000388)
----Où va l'investissement direct
international? USA/monde : le cas du
secteur alimentaire. - 1984.
(000666)
----Profiles of foreign direct investment in
U.S. energy. - 1985-   .
(000774)
----Regulating the multinational enterprise.
- 1983.
(002006)
----Regulation of foreign direct investment
in Canada and the United States. - 1983.
(002263)
----The Rising Sun in America (Part One). -
1986.
(000392)
----The role of direct foreign investment in
developing East Asian countries. - 1985.
(001052)
----The role of foreign direct investment in
U.S. capital outflows. - 1986.
(000179)
----The roots of crisis in southern Africa.
- 1985.
(001208)
----Selected data on foreign direct
investment in the United States,
1950-79. - 1984.
(000184)
----Tax policy and foreign direct
investment. - 1985.
(001721)
----Tax policy and foreign direct investment
in the United States. - 1984.
(001722)
----Towards a new treaty framework for
direct foreign investment. - 1985.
(002047)
----Transnatsional'nye korporatsii SShA v
Latinskoi Amerike. - 1985.
(001087)

----Trends and issues in foreign direct
investment and related flows. - 1985.
(000192)
----Trends in multinational business and
global environments: a perspective. -
1984.
(000029)
----U.S. and Canadian investment in South
Africa and Namibia. - 1986.
(001212) (002671) (002672)

----U.S. direct investment abroad. -
1981-   .
(000188)
----U.S. direct investment abroad. -
1985-   .
(000189)
----The U.S. in the world economy. - 1988.
(000128)
----US and Japanese manufacturing affiliates
in the UK. - 1985.
(001149)
----Venturing abroad. - 1988.
(000376)
----The World Bank's Multilateral Investment
Guaranty Agency. - 1987.
(002125)

UNITED STATES--FOREIGN INTERESTS.
----Foreign government and foreign investor
control of U.S. banks. - 1983.
(001654)

UNITED STATES--FOREIGN INVESTMENTS.
----Die Aussenexpansion des Kapitals. - 1984.
(000037)
----The Caribbean Basin Economic Recovery
Act and its implications for foreign
private investment. - 1984.
(001965)
----Direct investment techniques for the
USA. - 1983.
(001808)
----Empresas multinacionales y concentración
de la inversión extranjera. - 1985.
(000545)
----Estados Unidos y el proceso de
transnacionalización en la postguerra. -
1984.
(001235)
----Federal regulation of certain foreign
investment in the United States. - 1985.
(002215)
----Foreign government and foreign investor
control of U.S. banks. - 1983.
(001654)
----Foreign investment in United States oil
and gas ventures. - 1987.
(000606)
----La inversión estadounidense en el Grupo
Andino. - 1985.
(000112)
----Investment climate in foreign countries.
- 1983-   .
(001812)
----The overseas expansion of capital. -
1985.
(000038)
----The Overseas Private Investment
Corporation and international
investment. - 1984.
(002360)

UNITED STATES--FOREIGN INVESTMENTS
(continued)
----Political risk in the international oil
    and gas industry. - 1983.
        (001823)
----Riding a tiger : joint ventures under
    South Korea's new Foreign Capital
    Inducement Act. - 1985.
        (002290)
----The role of private investment in Third
    World development. - 1986.
        (001328)
----The significance of foreign investment
    in US development 1879 to mid-1914. -
    1982.
        (001344)
----Tax planning for foreign investors in
    the United States. - 1983.
        (001773)
----Two decades of debate. - 1983.
        (001199)
----U.S. and Canadian business in South
    Africa. - 1987-   .
        (001211)
----The U.S. bilateral investment treaty
    program. - 1985.
        (002034)
----U.S. corporate activities in South
    Africa. - 1983.
        (001222)
----U.S. federal regulation of foreign
    involvement in aviation, government
    procurement and national security. -
    1985.
        (002216)
----United States investment in Australia. -
    1987.
        (002180)
----United States policy regarding
    nationalization of American investments.
    - 1984.
        (002332)
----What's causing America's capital
    imports? - 1987.
        (000539)

UNITED STATES--FOREIGN LOANS.
----International bank lending. - 1983.
        (000265)
----The international debt crisis and the
    banks. - 1985.
        (000227)
----On Third World debt. - 1984.
        (000211)

UNITED STATES--FOREIGN RELATIONS.
----Competition in the Pacific Basin. - 1987.
        (001673)
----Democratic development. - 1986.
        (001334)
----Hard bargaining ahead. - 1985.
        (001361)
----International countertrade. - 1984.
        (001396)
----The political economy of U.S. policy
    toward South Africa. - 1985.
        (001196)
----SShA, transnatsional'nye korporatsii i
    vneshniaia politika. - 1984.
        (001815)
----Third World resource directory. - 1984.
        (002719)
----U.S. foreign assistance. - 1984.
        (000203)

UNITED STATES--FOREIGN TRADE.
----Les années quatre-vingts : quelles
    perspectives pour l'industrie américaine
    et les investissements internationaux? -
    1983.
        (000106)
----Antitrust aspects of U.S.-Japanese
    trade. - 1983.
        (002345)
----The Arab world is still importing. -
    1987.
        (001134)
----Doing business with China. - 1974-   .
        (001792)
----Journal of the US-USSR Trade and
    Economic Council. - 1976-   .
        (001179)
----Protectionist threat to trade and
    investment in services. - 1983.
        (000951)
----Restructuring industry offshore. - 1983.
        (000692)
----Trade policies in the PRC. - 1986.
        (001387)
----U.S. high technology trade and
    competitiveness. - 1985.
        (001362)
----U.S.-Israel free trade area. - 1986.
        (002049)
----United States-China commercial
    contracts. - 1986.
        (002439)

UNITED STATES--FRANCHISES.
----Trademark and related rights in
    franchise agreements in Germany. - 1983.
        (001523)

UNITED STATES--FREE EXPORT ZONES.
----Political and policy dimensions of
    foreign trade zones. - 1985.
        (001356)

UNITED STATES--FREE TRADE.
----The legal markets of international
    trade. - 1987.
        (002038)
----Multinationals and free trade: the
    implications of a US-Canadian
    agreement. - 1986.
        (002029)

UNITED STATES--FREE TRADE AREAS.
----La presentación de la iniciativa de la
    Cuenca del Caribe al GATT. - 1985.
        (001972)
----U.S.-Israel free trade area. - 1986.
        (002049)

UNITED STATES--GENERALIZED SYSTEM OF
PREFERENCES.
----The U.S. renewal of the GSP. - 1986.
        (001996)

UNITED STATES--GOVERNMENT INFORMATION.
----Inside Washington. - 1988.
        (002703)
----Washington's best kept secrets. - 1983.
        (002704)

UNITED STATES--HARD FIBRES.
----A competitive assessment of selected
reinforced composite fibers. - 1985.
(000644)

UNITED STATES--HARMFUL PRODUCTS.
----The export of hazard. - 1985.
(001941)

UNITED STATES--HEALTH HAZARDS.
----The export of hazard. - 1985.
(001941)

UNITED STATES--HERBICIDES.
----A competitive assessment of the U.S.
herbicide industry. - 1985.
(000670)

UNITED STATES--HOLDING COMPANIES.
----Foreign investment in South Africa and
Namibia. - 1984.
(001198) (002641)
----U.S. and Canadian investment in South
Africa and Namibia. - 1986.
(001212) (002671) (002672)

UNITED STATES--HONDA MOTOR COMPANY(JAPAN).
----America's new no. 4 automaker -- Honda.
- 1985.
(000294)

UNITED STATES--HOST COUNTRY RELATIONS.
----The effect of political events on
United States direct foreign
investment: a pooled time-series
cross-sectional analysis. - 1985.
(001835)

UNITED STATES--HYDRAULIC MACHINERY.
----A competitive assessment of the U.S.
water resources equipment industry. -
1985.
(000776)

UNITED STATES--IMPORTS.
----Automotive parts industry and the U.S.
aftermarket for Japanese cars and light
trucks. - 1985.
(000759)
----Transnational corporations and
international trade : selected issues. -
1985.
(001393)

UNITED STATES--INCOME TAX.
----A comparative analysis of the United
States-People's Republic of China tax
treaty. - 1986.
(002037)
----Introduction to United States
international taxation. - 1981.
(001738)

UNITED STATES--INDUSTRIAL ACCIDENTS.
----The Bhopal case : controlling
ultrahazardous industrial activities
undertaken by foreign investors. - 1987.
(001949)

UNITED STATES--INDUSTRIAL APPLICATIONS.
----A competitive assessment of selected
reinforced composite fibers. - 1985.
(000644)

UNITED STATES--INDUSTRIAL ARBITRATION.
----Mediation, conciliation and arbitration
: an international comparison of
Australia, Great Britain and the United
States. - 1987.
(002476)

UNITED STATES--INDUSTRIAL CONSULTING.
----Consultants and consulting organizations
directory. - 197?-   .
(000832)

UNITED STATES--INDUSTRIAL CO-OPERATION.
----American enterprise in foreign markets.
- 1984.
(000526)
----Controlling the cost of international
compensation. - 1983.
(002323)
----Expectations and results of
contractual joint ventures by US and UK
MNCs in Eastern Europe. - 1984.
(001623)
----Indo-U.S. cooperation in business and
industry, 1986. - 1986.
(002675)
----Industrial collaboration with Japan. -
1986.
(001648)
----International Harvester in Russia: the
Washington-St. Petersburg connection? -
1983.
(000272)
----Joint venture y sociedad. - 1984.
(001602)
----New patterns in the formation of US/
Japanese cooperative ventures: the role
of technology. - 1987.
(001622)
----Planning a joint venture for the
Japanese market. - 1987.
(000508)

UNITED STATES--INDUSTRIAL COSTS.
----Industrial renaissance : producing a
competitive future for America. - 1983.
(000300)

UNITED STATES--INDUSTRIAL DESIGN.
----Design patents. - 1983.
(001425)

UNITED STATES--INDUSTRIAL EQUIPMENT LEASES.
----Analysis of equipment leasing contracts.
- 1984.
(002407)
----A competitive assessment of the United
States equipment leasing industry. -
1985.
(000982)

UNITED STATES--INDUSTRIAL FINANCING.
----The funding of high technology ventures.
- 1983.
(000412)

UNITED STATES--INDUSTRIAL LOCATION.
----Are environmental regulations driving
U.S. industry overseas? - 1984.
(001947)

UNITED STATES--INDUSTRIAL LOCATION
(continued)
----Foreign location decisions by U.S.
    transnational firms: an empirical study.
    - 1984.
      (000537)
----Foreign manufacturing investment in the
    United States: competitive strategies
    and international location. - 1985.
      (000733)
----High technology plant location
    decisions. - 1983.
      (000528)
----The international location of
    manufacturing investments: recent
    behaviour of foreign-owned corporations
    in the United States. - 1983.
      (001156)

UNITED STATES--INDUSTRIAL MANAGEMENT.
----The competitive challenge. - 1987.
      (000513)

UNITED STATES--INDUSTRIAL ORGANIZATION.
----The effect of conglomerate mergers on
    changes in industry concentration. -
    1986.
      (001527)
----Global competition. - 1985-   . .
      (001696)
----On vertical mergers. - 1986.
      (001641)

UNITED STATES--INDUSTRIAL PLANNING.
----The competitive challenge. - 1987.
      (000513)
----International business planning. - 1983.
      (002279)

UNITED STATES--INDUSTRIAL POLICY.
----A competitive assessment of the U.S. oil
    field equipment industry. - 1985.
      (000764)
----Global competition. - 1985-   .
      (001696)
----High-tech trade. - 1986.
      (000696)

UNITED STATES--INDUSTRIAL PROMOTION.
----Inside Washington. - 1988.
      (002703)

UNITED STATES--INDUSTRIAL RESEARCH.
----High technology industries. - 1983-   .
      (000695)
----Multinationals and technology transfer.
    - 1983.
      (001636)

UNITED STATES--INDUSTRIAL ROBOTS.
----A competitive assessment of the U.S.
    manufacturing automation equipment
    industries. - 1984.
      (000756)
----Competitive position of U.S. producers
    of robotics in domestic and world
    markets. - 1983.
      (000674)
----Robots in manufacturing. - 1983.
      (000656)

UNITED STATES--INDUSTRIAL SECTOR.
----Diversification : the European versus
    the US experience. - 1987.
      (000491)
----Manufacturing matters : the myth of the
    post-industrial economy. - 1987.
      (000669)

UNITED STATES--INDUSTRIAL TECHNOLOGY.
----The funding of high technology ventures.
    - 1983.
      (000412)
----A high technology gap? - 1987.
      (001439)
----High technology industries. - 1983-   .
      (000695)

UNITED STATES--INDUSTRY.
----Les années quatre-vingts : quelles
    perspectives pour l'industrie américaine
    et les investissements internationaux? -
    1983.
      (000106)
----A competitive assessment of the U.S.
    ball and roller bearings industry. -
    1985.
      (000760)
----A competitive assessment of the U.S.
    construction machinery industry. - 1985.
      (000761)
----A competitive assessment of the U.S.
    fiber optics industry. - 1984.
      (000800)
----A competitive assessment of the U.S.
    herbicide industry. - 1985.   ·
      (000670)
----A competitive assessment of the U.S.
    water resources equipment industry. -
    1985.
      (000776)
----A competitive assessment of the United
    States equipment leasing industry. -
    1985.
      (000982)
----Million dollar directory. - 1959-   .
      (002655)

UNITED STATES--INFORMATION SOURCES.
----Caribbean Basin business information
    starter kit. - 1984.
      (001782)
----Inside Washington. - 1988.
      (002703)
----Sources of joint venture information and
    assistance in the United States and
    Europe. - 1983.
      (001617)

UNITED STATES--INFORMATION TECHNOLOGY.
----A competitive assessment of the United
    States data processing services
    industry. - 1984.
      (000981)
----A competitive assessment of the United
    States disk storage industry. - 1985.
      (000672)

UNITED STATES--INFORMATION TRANSFER.
----New challenges to the U.S. multinational
    corporation in the European Economic
    Community. - 1985.
      (002192)

UNITED STATES--INTERDEPENDENCE.
----A historical perspective of U.S.-GCC
    economic and financial interdependence.
    - 1987.
      (000143)

UNITED STATES--INTERNATIONAL BANKING.
----Foreign bank offices in the U.S. since
    the International Banking Act of 1978. -
    1986.
      (000872)
----Foreign ownership of U.S. banks: trends
    and effects. - 1983.
      (001591)
----A longer view of debt. - 1983.
      (000251)
----A practitioner's guide to international
    banking and trade finance. - 1986.
      (000922)

UNITED STATES--INTERNATIONAL COMMERCIAL
ARBITRATION.
----International antitrust law. - 1985.
      (002539)
----International commercial arbitration. -
    1983.
      (002538)
----Jurisdiction over foreign sovereigns. -
    1983.
      (002480)

UNITED STATES--INTERNATIONAL COMMERCIAL
TRANSACTIONS.
----Estados Unidos, América Latina y el
    debate internacional sobre el comercio
    de servicios. - 1986.
      (000934)
----Foreign direct investment in the United
    States. - 1985.
      (000130)
----Fundamentals of international taxation.
    - 1985.
      (001700)

UNITED STATES--INTERNATIONAL COMPETITION.
----Alliance politics and economics. - 1987.
      (000719)
----The competitive challenge. - 1987.
      (000513)
----The competitive position of U.S.
    manufacturing firms. - 1985.
      (000353)
----International collaborative ventures in
    U.S. manufacturing. - 1988.
      (000720)
----Multinational enterprise and world
    competition. - 1987.
      (000018)

UNITED STATES--INTERNATIONAL CO-OPERATION.
----Alliance politics and economics. - 1987.
      (000719)

UNITED STATES--INTERNATIONAL ECONOMIC
RELATIONS.
----The U.S. in the world economy. - 1988.
      (000128)
----Uoll-strit protiv Afriki. - 1985.
      (001030)

UNITED STATES--INTERNATIONAL FINANCIAL
INSTITUTIONS.
----A longer view of debt. - 1983.
      (000251)

UNITED STATES--INTERNATIONAL TRADE.
----International trade in services: its
    composition, importance and links to
    merchandise trade. - 1987.
      (000890)
----U.S.-EEC confrontation in the
    international trade of agricultural
    products: consequences for third
    parties. - 1985.
      (001380)
----Washington's best kept secrets. - 1983.
      (002704)

UNITED STATES--INTRA-INDUSTRY TRADE.
----Intra-firm trade and U.S. protectionism:
    thoughts based on a small survey. - 1986.
      (001367)

UNITED STATES--INVESTMENT INSURANCE.
----The World Bank's Multilateral Investment
    Guaranty Agency. - 1987.
      (002125)

UNITED STATES--INVESTMENT POLICY.
----Foreign direct investment in the United
    States: the balance of foreign and
    domestic policy. - 1983.
      (000173)
----The international investment position of
    the United States in 1985. - 1986.
      (001295)

UNITED STATES--INVESTMENT PROMOTION.
----La inversión estadounidense en el Grupo
    Andino. - 1985.
      (000112)

UNITED STATES--INVESTMENT TAX CREDIT.
----International business planning. - 1983.
      (002279)
----International income taxation and
    developing countries. - 1988.
      (001759)

UNITED STATES--INVESTMENT TRUSTS.
----Realty joint ventures, 1986. - 1986.
      (000881)

UNITED STATES--INVESTMENTS.
----A historical perspective of U.S.-GCC
    economic and financial interdependence.
    - 1987.
      (000143)
----What trade war? - 1987.
      (000481)

UNITED STATES--JOINT VENTURES.
----Acquisitions and joint ventures among
    large corporations. - 1985.
      (001653)
----Alliance politics and economics. - 1987.
      (000719)
----Antitrust policy and joint research and
    development ventures. - 1984.
      (002356)
----The Arab world is still importing. -
    1987.
      (001134)
----Becoming a triad power: the new global
    corporation. - 1986.
      (000500)

UNITED STATES--JOINT VENTURES (continued)
----Cooperative research and development. -
    1984.
    (001630)
----East-West joint ventures. - 1988.
    (001570)
----Evidence on joint venture formation for
    offshore oil lease sales. - 1983.
    (000592)
----Expectations and results of
    contractual joint ventures by US and UK
    MNCs in Eastern Europe. - 1984.
    (001623)
----Foreign investment in United States oil
    and gas ventures. - 1987.
    (000606)
----The funding of high technology ventures.
    - 1983.
    (000412)
----A historical perspective of U.S.-GCC
    economic and financial interdependence.
    - 1987.
    (000143)
----The impact of joint ventures on bidding
    for offshore oil. - 1983.
    (000604)
----Indo-U.S. cooperation in business and
    industry, 1986. - 1986.
    (002675)
----Industrial collaboration with Japan. -
    1986.
    (001648)
----International collaborative ventures in
    U.S. manufacturing. - 1988.
    (000720)
----International corporate linkages. - 1987.
    (002430)
----International joint ventures. - 1985.
    (001590)
----International joint ventures. - 1986.
    (001566)
----International joint ventures: how
    important are they? - 1987.
    (001556)
----Joint research and development
    legislation. - 1987.
    (002286)
----Joint venture partner selection. - 1988.
    (001577)
----Joint venture y sociedad. - 1984.
    (001602)
----Joint ventures. - 1987.
    (001613)
----Joint ventures. - 1985.
    (001605)
----Joint ventures and offshore oil lease
    sales. - 1985.
    (001578)
----Managing for joint venture success. -
    1986.
    (001587)
----A muködo toke becsalogatása
    Magyarországra : nyugati szemszögbol. -
    1987.
    (001608)
----The new attractions of corporate joint
    ventures. - 1985.
    (001612)
----New patterns in the formation of US/
    Japanese cooperative ventures: the role
    of technology. - 1987.
    (001622)
----Oil industry mergers. - 1984.
    (001652)

----Planning a joint venture for the
    Japanese market. - 1987.
    (000508)
----Quantifying the competitive effects of
    production joint ventures. - 1986.
    (001548)
----Realty joint ventures, 1986. - 1986.
    (000881)
----Riding a tiger : joint ventures under
    South Korea's new Foreign Capital
    Inducement Act. - 1985.
    (002290)
----Sources of joint venture information and
    assistance in the United States and
    Europe. - 1983.
    (001617)
----Die Steuerung ausländischer
    Tochtergesellschaften. - 1983.
    (000400)
----Venturing abroad. - 1988.
    (000376)
----Vertical integration and joint ventures
    in the aluminum industry. - 1983.
    (001642)
----What trade war? - 1987.
    (000481)

UNITED STATES--JURISDICTION.
----Jurisdiction over foreign governments. -
    1986.
    (002347)
----United States jurisdiction over foreign
    subsidiaries. - 1983.
    (002355)

UNITED STATES--LABOUR DISPUTES.
----Mediation, conciliation and arbitration
    : an international comparison of
    Australia, Great Britain and the United
    States. - 1987.
    (002476)

UNITED STATES--LABOUR MARKET.
----Employment and competitiveness in the
    European Community. - 1984.
    (001929)

UNITED STATES--LABOUR PRODUCTIVITY.
----Industrial renaissance : producing a
    competitive future for America. - 1983.
    (000300)

UNITED STATES--LABOUR RELATIONS.
----Technology strategy and industrial
    relations: case studies of Japanese
    multinationals in the United States. -
    1983.
    (002599)

UNITED STATES--LABOUR SUPPLY.
----American multinationals and American
    employment. - 1983.
    (001890)
----U.S. firms and black labor in South
    Africa: creating a structure for change.
    - 1986.
    (001195)

UNITED STATES--LAW.
----Accounting and law in a nutshell. - 1984.
    (002208)

UNITED STATES--LAWS AND REGULATIONS.
----A competitive assessment of the U.S.
     herbicide industry. - 1985.
        (000670)
----East-West joint ventures. - 1988.
        (001570)
----Federal regulation of certain foreign
     investment in the United States. - 1985.
        (002215)
----Foreign investments and financings in
     the United States. - 1983.
        (002175)
----Foreign trade and investment. - 1987.
        (002191)
----International business planning. - 1983.
        (002279)
----International income taxation and
     developing countries. - 1988.
        (001759)
----International joint ventures. - 1986.
        (001566)
----Manual of foreign investment in the
     United States. - 1984.
        (002238)
----New challenges to the U.S. multinational
     corporation in the European Economic
     Community. - 1985.
        (002192)
----Oil industry mergers. - 1984.
        (001652)
----Oil spill liability and compensation. -
     1985.
        (001940)
----Regulation of foreign direct investment
     in Canada and the United States. - 1983.
        (002263)
----Tax aspects of international
     transactions. - 1984.
        (001757)
----U.S. federal regulation of foreign
     involvement in aviation, government
     procurement and national security. -
     1985.
        (002216)

UNITED STATES--LEGAL REMEDIES.
----The availability of provisional relief
     in international commercial arbitration.
     - 1984.
        (002543)

UNITED STATES--LEGISLATION.
----United States law of sovereign immunity
     relating to international financial
     transactions. - 1983.
        (002353)

UNITED STATES--LEGISLATIVE HEARINGS.
----Foreign government and foreign investor
     control of U.S. banks. - 1983.
        (001654)

UNITED STATES--LIABILITY.
----The Bhopal case : controlling
     ultrahazardous industrial activities
     undertaken by foreign investors. - 1987.
        (001949)

UNITED STATES--LIABILITY FOR MARINE
ACCIDENTS.
----Oil spill liability and compensation. -
     1985.
        (001940)

UNITED STATES--LICENCE AGREEMENTS.
----Coping with foreign-law impediments to
     the export licensing of United States
     technology. - 1986.
        (001473)
----Licensing impact of foreign policy
     motivated retroactive reexport
     regulations. - 1983.
        (001352)
----United States regulation of
     high-technology exports. - 1986.
        (001462)
----United States-China commercial
     contracts. - 1986.
        (002439)

UNITED STATES--LICENCES.
----Exclusive licenses as restraints of
     trade under US and Common Market
     antitrust law. - 1984.
        (002414)
----Reverse technology flows. - 1985.
        (001451)

UNITED STATES--LOANS.
----Eximbank's role in international banking
     and finance. - 1986.
        (000816)

UNITED STATES--MACHINE TOOL INDUSTRY.
----A competitive assessment of the U.S.
     flexible manufacturing systems industry.
     - 1985.
        (000763)
----A competitive assessment of the U.S.
     manufacturing automation equipment
     industries. - 1984.
        (000756)

UNITED STATES--MACHINERY.
----A competitive assessment of the U.S.
     semiconductor manufacturing equipment
     industry. - 1985.
        (000758)

UNITED STATES--MACHINERY INDUSTRY.
----A competitive assessment of the U.S.
     construction machinery industry. - 1985.
        (000761)
----A competitive assessment of the U.S.
     electric power generating equipment
     industry. - 1985.
        (000762)

UNITED STATES--MAGNETIC DISKS.
----A competitive assessment of the United
     States disk storage industry. - 1985.
        (000672)

UNITED STATES--MANAGEMENT.
----The Rising Sun in America (Part Two)
     -- Japanese management in the United
     States. - 1986.
        (000391)
----Doing business in key Latin American
     markets: U.S. international executive
     perceptions. - 1983.
        (001824)
----External and internal functioning of
     American, German, and Japanese
     multinational corporations:
     decisionmaking and policy issues. - 1983.
        (000432)

UNITED STATES--MANAGEMENT (continued)
----Joint ventures. - 1987.
    (001613)
----Managing. - 1984.
    (000408)
----Managing effectively in the world
    marketplace. - 1983.
    (000399)
----Managing for joint venture success. -
    1986.
    (001587)
----The new attractions of corporate joint
    ventures. - 1985.
    (001612)
----Performance requirements for foreign
    business. - 1983.
    (002314)
----Quantifying the competitive effects of
    production joint ventures. - 1986.
    (001548)
----The Rising Sun in America (Part One). -
    1986.
    (000392)
----Staffing of management and professional
    positions at overseas subsidiaries of
    U.S. multinational enterprises. - 1983.
    (001885)
----Die Steuerung auslandischer
    Tochtergesellschaften. - 1983.
    (000400) '
----U.S. multinational companies: operations
    in 1984. - 1986.
    (000309)
----U.S. multinational corporations: a
    lesson in the failure of success. - 1983.
    (000306)

UNITED STATES--MANAGEMENT CONSULTANTS.
----Bradford's directory of marketing
    research agencies and management
    consultants in the United States and the
    world. - 1966-   .
    (002623)
----Consultants and consulting organizations
    directory. - 197?-   .
    (000832)

UNITED STATES--MANAGEMENT DEVELOPMENT.
----American and Chinese managers in U.S.
    companies in Taiwan: a comparison. -
    1985.
    (000395)

UNITED STATES--MANAGERS.
----American and Chinese managers in U.S.
    companies in Taiwan: a comparison. -
    1985.
    (000395)
----Internal accountability. - 1984.
    (002055)

UNITED STATES--MANUFACTURES.
----U.S. high technology trade and
    competitiveness. - 1985.
    (001362)

UNITED STATES--MANUFACTURING.
----A competitive assessment of the U.S.
    manufacturing automation equipment
    industries. - 1984.
    (000756)

----A competitive assessment of the U.S.
    semiconductor manufacturing equipment
    industry. - 1985.
    (000758)
----Manufacturing matters : the myth of the
    post-industrial economy. - 1987.
    (000669)
----Political and policy dimensions of
    foreign trade zones. - 1985.
    (001356)

UNITED STATES--MANUFACTURING ENTERPRISES.
----The effect of political events on
    United States direct foreign
    investment: a pooled time-series
    cross-sectional analysis. - 1985.
    (001835)
----The competitive position of U.S.
    manufacturing firms. - 1985.
    (000353)
----Directory of foreign manufacturers in
    the United States. - 1975-   .
    (002634)
----Foreign manufacturing investment in the
    United States: competitive strategies
    and international location. - 1985.
    (000733)
----International collaborative ventures in
    U.S. manufacturing. - 1988.
    (000720)
----The international location of
    manufacturing investments: recent
    behaviour of foreign-owned corporations
    in the United States. - 1983.
    (001156)
----Transfer of technology from Japan and
    the United States to Korean
    manufacturing industries: a comparative
    study. - 1984.
    (001461)
----Trends in Japan's manufacturing
    investment in the United States. - 1987.
    (000767)
----US and Japanese manufacturing affiliates
    in the UK. - 1985.
    (001149)

UNITED STATES--MARKET ACCESS.
----The effect of conglomerate mergers on
    changes in industry concentration. -
    1986.
    (001527)
----On vertical mergers. - 1986.
    (001641)

UNITED STATES--MARKET POTENTIAL.
----Geoinvestment: the interdependence among
    space, market size, and political
    turmoil in attracting foreign direct
    investment. - 1984.
    (000555)

UNITED STATES--MARKET RESEARCH.
----Bradford's directory of marketing
    research agencies and management
    consultants in the United States and the
    world. - 1966-   .
    (002623)
----Planning a joint venture for the
    Japanese market. - 1987.
    (000508)

UNITED STATES--MARKETING.
----Becoming a triad power: the new global
    corporation. - 1986.
    (000500)
----Mezhdunarodnyi marketing amerikanskoi
    tekhnologii. - 1985.
    (000494)
----Profiles of foreign direct investment in
    U.S. energy. - 1985-   .
    (000774)

UNITED STATES--MASS MEDIA.
----The knowledge industry 200. - 1983.
    (000884) (002646)

UNITED STATES--MEDIATION.
----Mediation, conciliation and arbitration
    : an international comparison of
    Australia, Great Britain and the United
    States. - 1987.
    (002476)

UNITED STATES--MICROELECTRONICS.
----Microelectronics. - 1981-   .
    (000718)

UNITED STATES--MILITARY ASSISTANCE.
----U.S. foreign assistance. - 1984.
    (000203)

UNITED STATES--MILITARY EXPENDITURES.
----National security and the semiconductor
    industry. - 1987.
    (000675)

UNITED STATES--MINERAL INDUSTRY.
----Foreign direct investment in the U.S.
    minerals industry. - 1987.
    (000635)
----Political risk in the international oil
    and gas industry. - 1983.
    (001823)

UNITED STATES--MODEL LAWS.
----Tax treaty abuse. - 1983.
    (002046)

UNITED STATES--MONOPOLIES.
----US monopolies and developing countries.
    - 1986.
    (001692)

UNITED STATES--MOTOR VEHICLE EQUIPMENT.
----Automotive parts industry and the U.S.
    aftermarket for Japanese cars and light
    trucks. - 1985.
    (000759)

UNITED STATES--MOTOR VEHICLE INDUSTRY.
----Automotive parts industry and the U.S.
    aftermarket for Japanese cars and light
    trucks. - 1985.
    (000759)

UNITED STATES--MULTILATERAL TRADE
NEGOTIATIONS.
----Intellectual property rights,
    investment, and trade in services in the
    Uruguay round. - 1987.
    (000817)

UNITED STATES--NATIONAL SECURITY.
----Balancing the national interest : U.S.
    national security export controls and
    global economic competition. - 1987.
    (001417)
----National security and the semiconductor
    industry. - 1987.
    (000675)

UNITED STATES--NATURAL GAS INDUSTRY.
----Evidence on joint venture formation for
    offshore oil lease sales. - 1983.
    (000592)
----Political risk in the international oil
    and gas industry. - 1983.
    (001823)

UNITED STATES--NATURAL RESOURCES DEVELOPMENT.
----Structuring natural resources
    development agreements between foreign
    governments and United States companies
    to prevent transfer of rights under the
    agreement should the company enter
    bankruptcy. - 1984.
    (002411)

UNITED STATES--NEGOTIATION.
----U.S. fishery negotiations with Canada
    and Mexico. - 1985.
    (002462)

UNITED STATES--NEW TECHNOLOGIES.
----An assessment of U.S. competitiveness in
    high technology industries. - 1983.
    (000653)
----Balancing the national interest : U.S.
    national security export controls and
    global economic competition. - 1987.
    (001417)
----La haute technologie américaine. - 1987.
    (000680)
----A high technology gap? - 1987.
    (001439)
----U.S. high technology trade and
    competitiveness. - 1985.
    (001362)

UNITED STATES--NONCITIZENS.
----Introduction to United States
    international taxation. - 1981.
    (001738)

UNITED STATES--NONCONVENTIONAL ENERGY
SOURCES.
----A competitive assessment of the
    renewable energy equipment industry. -
    1984.
    (000775)

UNITED STATES--NUCLEAR WEAPONS.
----The nuclear weapons industry. - 1984.
    (000659)

UNITED STATES--NUMERICAL CONTROL.
----A competitive assessment of the U.S.
    flexible manufacturing systems industry.
    - 1985.
    (000763)

UNITED STATES--OFFSHORE OIL FIELDS.
----The impact of joint ventures on bidding
    for offshore oil. - 1983.
    (000604)

UNITED STATES--OFFSHORE STRUCTURES.
----A competitive assessment of the U.S. oil
    field equipment industry. - 1985.
    (000764)

UNITED STATES--OIL AND GAS LEASES.
----Evidence on joint venture formation for
    offshore oil lease sales. - 1983.
    (000592)
----Foreign investment in United States oil
    and gas ventures. - 1987.
    (000606)
----The impact of joint ventures on bidding
    for offshore oil. - 1983.
    (000604)
----Joint ventures and offshore oil lease
    sales. - 1985.
    (001578)

UNITED STATES--OIL SPILLAGES.
----Oil spill liability and compensation. -
    1985.
    (001940)

UNITED STATES--OIL WELL DRILLING.
----A competitive assessment of the U.S. oil
    field equipment industry. - 1985.
    (000764)

UNITED STATES--OPTICAL DISKS.
----A competitive assessment of the United
    States disk storage industry. - 1985.
    (000672)

UNITED STATES--PARTNERSHIP.
----International joint ventures. - 1985.
    (001590)

UNITED STATES--PATENTS.
----Design patents. - 1983.
    (001425)
----Microelectronics. - 1981-   .
    (000718)

UNITED STATES--PERFORMANCE ANALYSIS.
----Examining performance of U.S.
    multinationals in foreign markets. -
    1983.
    (000318)

UNITED STATES--PERFORMANCE APPRAISAL.
----Foreign direct investment in U.S. food
    and tobacco manufacturing and domestic
    economic performance. - 1983.
    (000170)
----Internal accountability. - 1984.
    (002055)

UNITED STATES--PERSONAL DATA FILES.
----New challenges to the U.S. multinational
    corporation in the European Economic
    Community. - 1985.
    (002192)

UNITED STATES--PERSONNEL MANAGEMENT.
----International business travel and
    relocation directory. - 1984.
    (002710)
----Japanese multinationals in the United
    States. - 1986.
    (000341)
----Key to Japan's economic strength. - 1984.
    (001924)

----Personalpolitik fur multinationale
    Unternehmen. - 1985.
    (000417) (001903)

UNITED STATES--PETROCHEMICAL INDUSTRY.
----A competitive assessment of the U.S.
    petrochemical industry. - 1982.
    (000755)
----Le role des grandes entreprises
    diversifiées du pétrole et de la chimie
    dans la production alimentaire. - 1985.
    (000699)

UNITED STATES--PETROLEUM ENGINEERING.
----A competitive assessment of the U.S. oil
    field equipment industry. - 1985.
    (000764)

UNITED STATES--PETROLEUM INDUSTRY.
----A competitive assessment of the U.S. oil
    field equipment industry. - 1985.
    (000764)
----Empirical models of political risks in
    U.S. oil production operations in
    Venezuela. - 1984.
    (001813)
----The engineers and the price system
    revisited: the future of the
    international oil corporations. - 1983.
    (000587)
----Evidence on joint venture formation for
    offshore oil lease sales. - 1983.
    (000592)
----Joint ventures and offshore oil lease
    sales. - 1985.
    (001578)
----La loi anti-fusions et l'industrie
    pétrolière américaine, (2). - 1986.
    (000581)
----Oil industry mergers. - 1984.
    (001652)
----Political risk in the international oil
    and gas industry. - 1983.
    (001823)

UNITED STATES--PETROLEUM PRICES.
----The engineers and the price system
    revisited: the future of the
    international oil corporations. - 1983.
    (000587)

UNITED STATES--PHARMACEUTICAL INDUSTRY.
----A competitive assessment of the U.S.
    pharmaceutical industry. - 1984.
    (000757)

UNITED STATES--POPULATION GROWTH.
----What's causing America's capital
    imports? - 1987.
    (000539)

UNITED STATES--PRICES.
----La formation du prix dans les
    transactions internationales. - 1985.
    (001712)

UNITED STATES--PRIVACY LAW.
----New challenges to the U.S. multinational
    corporation in the European Economic
    Community. - 1985.
    (002192)

UNITED STATES--PRIVATE ENTERPRISES.
----Implications of deregulating satellite
communications. - 1985.
(002242)

UNITED STATES--PRODUCTION DIVERSIFICATION.
----Diversification : the European versus
the US experience. - 1987.
(000491)

UNITED STATES--PRODUCTION (ECONOMIC THEORY).
----Quantifying the competitive effects of
production joint ventures. - 1986.
(001548)

UNITED STATES--PROPERTY RIGHTS.
----Jurisdiction over foreign governments. -
1986.
(002347)

UNITED STATES--PROTECTIONISM.
----Intra-firm trade and U.S. protectionism:
thoughts based on a small survey. - 1986.
(001367)
----Japan's direct investment in California
and the new protectionism. - 1984.
(000145)
----Protectionist threat to trade and
investment in services. - 1983.
(000951)

UNITED STATES--PUBLIC DEBT.
----America's foreign debt. - 1987.
(000243)

UNITED STATES--PUBLIC ENTERPRISES.
----Private agreements for takeovers of
public companies. - 1984.
(001626)

UNITED STATES--PUBLIC SERVICES.
----Directory of business, trade and public
policy organizations. - 1982-   .
(002631)

UNITED STATES--REAL ESTATE BUSINESS.
----Realty joint ventures, 1986. - 1986.
(000881)

UNITED STATES--REGRESSION ANALYSIS.
----U.S. multinational corporations: a
lesson in the failure of success. - 1983.
(000306)

UNITED STATES--RELOCATION OF INDUSTRY.
----Are environmental regulations driving
U.S. industry overseas? - 1984.
(001947)
----International business travel and
relocation directory. - 1984.
(002710)

UNITED STATES--RENEWABLE RESOURCES.
----A competitive assessment of the
renewable energy equipment industry. -
1984.
(000775)

UNITED STATES--RESEARCH AND DEVELOPMENT.
----La haute technologie américaine. - 1987.
(000680)
----High-tech trade. - 1986.
(000696)

UNITED STATES--RESEARCH AND DEVELOPMENT
CONTRACTS.
----Antitrust policy and joint research and
development ventures. - 1984.
(002356)
----Cooperative research and development. -
1984.
(001630)
----Joint research and development
legislation. - 1987.
(002286)

UNITED STATES--RESTRICTIVE BUSINESS
PRACTICES.
----Antitrust law developments (second). -
1984.
(002339)
----The extraterritorial effects of
antitrust laws. - 1984.
(002342)

UNITED STATES--RISK ASSESSMENT.
----Political risk in the international oil
and gas industry. - 1983.
(001823)

UNITED STATES--RISK MANAGEMENT.
----Empirical models of political risks in
U.S. oil production operations in
Venezuela. - 1984.
(001813)

UNITED STATES--ROBOTICS.
----A competitive assessment of the U.S.
flexible manufacturing systems industry.
- 1985.
(000763)
----A competitive assessment of the U.S.
manufacturing automation equipment
industries. - 1984.
(000756)
----Competitive position of U.S. producers
of robotics in domestic and world
markets. - 1983.
(000674)
----High technology industries. - 1983-   .
(000695)
----Robots in manufacturing. - 1983.
(000656)

UNITED STATES--ROLLER BEARINGS.
----A competitive assessment of the U.S.
ball and roller bearings industry. -
1985.
(000760)

UNITED STATES--RUBBER INDUSTRY.
----The emergence of a U.S. multinational
enterprise: the Goodyear Tire and Rubber
Company, 1910-1939. - 1987.
(000281)

UNITED STATES--RULES AND REGULATIONS.
----Regulating the multinational enterprise.
- 1983.
(002006)

UNITED STATES--SATELLITE COMMUNICATION.
----Implications of deregulating satellite
communications. - 1985.
(002242)

UNITED STATES--SAVINGS.
----What's causing America's capital
    imports? - 1987.
       (000539)

UNITED STATES--SCIENCE AND TECHNOLOGY POLICY.
----Technology strategy and industrial
    relations: case studies of Japanese
    multinationals in the United States. -
    1983.
       (002599)

UNITED STATES--SECURITIES.
----Applying uniform margin requirements to
    foreign entities attempting to acquire
    U.S. corporations. - 1984.
       (002173)
----Moody's industrial manual. - 1954-   .
       (002656)

UNITED STATES--SEMICONDUCTORS.
----A competitive assessment of the U.S.
    semiconductor manufacturing equipment
    industry. - 1985.
       (000758)
----Competitive edge. - 1984.
       (000673)
----The global factory. - 1985.
       (001254)
----High technology industries. - 1983-   .
       (000695)
----High-tech trade. - 1986.
       (000696)
----National security and the semiconductor
    industry. - 1987.
       (000675)
----The semiconductor business. - 1985.
       (000715)

UNITED STATES--SERVICE INDUSTRIES.
----A competitive assessment of the United
    States data processing services
    industry. - 1984.
       (000981)
----Croissance de l'emploi dans les
    services. - 1987.
       (000846)
----Estados Unidos, América Latina y el
    debate internacional sobre el comercio
    de servicios. - 1986.
       (000934)
----Identifying export potential in the
    service sector. - 1986.
       (000882)
----International trade in services: its
    composition, importance and links to
    merchandise trade. - 1987.
       (000890)
----Protectionist threat to trade and
    investment in services. - 1983.
       (000951)
----Trade in services : obstacles and
    opportunities. - 1987.
       (000984)
----Trade in services. - 1986.
       (000962)

UNITED STATES--SMALL ENTERPRISES.
----Directory of business, trade and public
    policy organizations. - 1982-   .
       (002631)

UNITED STATES--SOUND RECORDINGS.
----The Gramophone Company: an
    Anglo-American multinational, 1898-1931.
    - 1985.
       (000285)

UNITED STATES--STATE IMMUNITIES.
----The extraterritorial effects of
    antitrust laws. - 1984.
       (002342)
----Jurisdiction over foreign governments. -
    1986.
       (002347)
----Jurisdiction over foreign sovereigns. -
    1983.
       (002480)
----United States law of sovereign immunity
    relating to international financial
    transactions. - 1983.
       (002353)

UNITED STATES--STATISTICAL DATA.
----A competitive assessment of the U.S.
    ball and roller bearings industry. -
    1985.
       (000760)
----A competitive assessment of the U.S.
    flexible manufacturing systems industry.
    - 1985.
       (000763)
----A competitive assessment of the U.S.
    herbicide industry. - 1985.
       (000670)
----A competitive assessment of the U.S.
    international construction industry. -
    1984.
       (000779)
----A competitive assessment of the U.S.
    manufacturing automation equipment
    industries. - 1984.
       (000756)
----Direct investment in the United States
    by foreign government-owned companies,
    1974-81. - 1983.
       (000124)
----East-West joint ventures. - 1988.
       (001570)
----Foreign direct investment in the United
    States. - 1985.
       (000130)
----Foreign direct investment in the United
    States. - 1985-   .
       (000131)
----Tax havens in the Caribbean Basin. -
    1984.
       (001762)
----Transnational corporations and
    international trade : selected issues. -
    1985.
       (001393)

UNITED STATES--STOCK COMPANIES.
----Moody's industrial manual. - 1954-   .
       (002656)

UNITED STATES--STOCK MARKETS.
----Moody's industrial manual. - 1954-   .
       (002656)

UNITED STATES--STRUCTURAL ADJUSTMENT.
----The effects of foreign direct investment
    on U.S. employment during recession and
    structural change. - 1986.
       (001908)

UNITED STATES--STRUCTURAL ADJUSTMENT
(continued)
----U.S. firms and black labor in South
    Africa: creating a structure for change.
    - 1986.
        (001195)

UNITED STATES--SUBSIDIARY BODIES.
----Operating foreign subsidiaries. - 1983.
        (000388)

UNITED STATES--SYNTHETIC FIBRES.
----A competitive assessment of selected
    reinforced composite fibers. - 1985.
        (000644)

UNITED STATES--TAIWAN(CHINA).
----American and Chinese managers in U.S.
    companies in Taiwan: a comparison. -
    1985.
        (000395)

UNITED STATES--TAX AVOIDANCE.
----Tax evasion through the Netherlands
    Antilles and other tax haven countries.
    - 1983.
        (001761)
----Tax havens in the Caribbean Basin. -
    1984.
        (001762)
----Tax planning for foreign investors in
    the United States. - 1983.
        (001773)
----The use of international finance
    subsidiaries in the Netherlands
    Antilles. - 1983.
        (000871)

UNITED STATES--TAX EVASION.
----Exchange of information under the OECD
    and US model tax treaties. - 1983.
        (002042)
----Tax evasion through the Netherlands
    Antilles and other tax haven countries.
    - 1983.
        (001761)
----Tax havens in the Caribbean Basin. -
    1984.
        (001762)

UNITED STATES--TAX INCENTIVES.
----International income taxation and
    developing countries. - 1988.
        (001759)

UNITED STATES--TAX LAW.
----A comparative analysis of the United
    States-People's Republic of China tax
    treaty. - 1986.
        (002037)
----Exchange of information under the OECD
    and US model tax treaties. - 1983.
        (002042)
----Foreign investment in the United States
    after the Tax Reform Act of 1986. - 1987.
        (002232)
----Fundamentals of international taxation.
    - 1985.
        (001700)
----International business planning. - 1983.
        (002279)
----Tax policy and foreign direct investment
    in the United States. - 1984.
        (001722)

----The use of international finance
    subsidiaries in the Netherlands
    Antilles. - 1983.
        (000871)

UNITED STATES--TAX SYSTEMS.
----Les tendances récentes des conventions
    fiscales. - 1985.
        (002053)

UNITED STATES--TAX TREATIES.
----The American-Dutch tax series. -
    1983- .
        (002028)
----A comparative analysis of the United
    States-People's Republic of China tax
    treaty. - 1986.
        (002037)
----Exchange of information under the OECD
    and US model tax treaties. - 1983.
        (002042)
----The Soviet Union's other tax agreements.
    - 1986.
        (002043)
----Tax treaty abuse. - 1983.
        (002046)
----Les tendances récentes des conventions
    fiscales. - 1985.
        (002053)

UNITED STATES--TAXATION.
----The American-Dutch tax series. -
    1983- .
        (002028)
----Federal taxation of international
    transactions. - 1988.
        (001730)
----The final report of the Worldwide
    Unitary Taxation Working Group :
    Chairman's report and supplemental
    views. - 1984.
        (001763)
----Foreign investment in the United States
    after the Tax Reform Act of 1986. - 1987.
        (002232)
----Fundamentals of international taxation.
    - 1985.
        (001700)
----International income taxation and
    developing countries. - 1988.
        (001759)
----Joint ventures. - 1987.
        (001613)
----Tax aspects of international
    transactions. - 1984.
        (001757)
----Tax planning for foreign investors in
    the United States. - 1983.
        (001773)
----Tax policy and foreign direct
    investment. - 1985.
        (001721)
----Worldwide unitary tax. - 1986.
        (001718)

UNITED STATES--TECHNOLOGICAL INNOVATIONS.
----The competitive challenge. - 1987.
        (000513)
----Design patents. - 1983.
        (001425)

UNITED STATES--TECHNOLOGICAL INNOVATIONS
(continued)
----Diversification : the European versus
    the US experience. - 1987.
      (000491)
----A high technology gap? - 1987.
      (001439)
----Industrial renaissance : producing a
    competitive future for America. - 1983.
      (000300)
----Reverse technology flows. - 1985.
      (001451)

UNITED STATES--TECHNOLOGICAL TRENDS.
----Trends in multinational business and
    global environments: a perspective. -
    1984.
      (000029)

UNITED STATES--TECHNOLOGY.
----A high technology gap? - 1987.
      (001439)

UNITED STATES--TECHNOLOGY ASSESSMENT.
----Commercial biotechnology. - 1984.
      (000643)

UNITED STATES--TECHNOLOGY TRANSFER.
----Balancing the national interest : U.S.
    national security export controls and
    global economic competition. - 1987.
      (001417)
----Canada's reversal from importer to
    exporter of foreign direct investment. -
    1987.
      (000181)
----Coping with foreign-law impediments to
    the export licensing of United States
    technology. - 1986.
      (001473)
----Expectations and results of
    contractual joint ventures by US and UK
    MNCs in Eastern Europe. - 1984.
      (001623)
----A high technology gap? - 1987.
      (001439)
----International collaborative ventures in
    U.S. manufacturing. - 1988.
      (000720)
----Mezhdunarodnyi marketing amerikanskoi
    tekhnologii. - 1985.
      (000494)
----Multinationals and technology transfer.
    - 1983.
      (001636)
----Reverse technology flows. - 1985.
      (001451)
----The transfer of organizational culture
    overseas: an approach to control in the
    multinational corporation. - 1983.
      (000420)
----Transfer of technology from Japan and
    the United States to Korean
    manufacturing industries: a comparative
    study. - 1984.
      (001461)
----United States regulation of
    high-technology exports. - 1986.
      (001462)

UNITED STATES--TELECOMMUNICATION INDUSTRY.
----High technology industries. - 1983-   .
      (000695)

----Implications of deregulating satellite
    communications. - 1985.
      (002242)

UNITED STATES--TOBACCO INDUSTRY.
----Determinants of foreign direct
    investment by food and tobacco
    manufacturers. - 1983.
      (000527)
----Foreign direct investment in U.S. food
    and tobacco manufacturing and domestic
    economic performance. - 1983.
      (000170)

UNITED STATES--TOP ECHELON STAFF.
----Staffing of management and professional
    positions at overseas subsidiaries of
    U.S. multinational enterprises. - 1983.
      (001885)

UNITED STATES--TOXIC SUBSTANCES.
----The Bhopal case : controlling
    ultrahazardous industrial activities
    undertaken by foreign investors. - 1987.
      (001949)
----The export of hazard. - 1985.
      (001941)

UNITED STATES--TRADE AGREEMENTS.
----The Caribbean Basin Economic Recovery
    Act and its implications for foreign
    private investment. - 1984.
      (001965)
----Multinationals and free trade: the
    implications of a US-Canadian
    agreement. - 1986.
      (002029)
----La presentación de la iniciativa de la
    Cuenca del Caribe al GATT. - 1985.
      (001972)
----Trademark and related rights in
    franchise agreements in Germany. - 1983.
      (001523)
----The U.S. renewal of the GSP. - 1986.
      (001996)
----U.S.-Israel free trade area. - 1986.
      (002049)

UNITED STATES--TRADE ASSOCIATIONS.
----Directory of business, trade and public
    policy organizations. - 1982-   .
      (002631)

UNITED STATES--TRADE DISPUTES.
----Mitsubishi and the arbitrability of
    antitrust claims. - 1986.
      (002486)
----Mitsubishi v. Soler and its impact on
    international commercial arbitration. -
    1985.
      (002507)

UNITED STATES--TRADE INFORMATION.
----Caribbean Basin business information
    starter kit. - 1984.
      (001782)

UNITED STATES--TRADE LIBERALIZATION.
----High-tech trade. - 1986.
      (000696)

UNITED STATES--TRADE LIBERALIZATION
(continued)
----Trade in services : obstacles and
    opportunities. - 1987.
        (000984)

UNITED STATES--TRADE NEGOTIATIONS.
----Trade in services. - 1986.
        (000962)

UNITED STATES--TRADE POLICY.
----Blind intersection? policy and the
    automobile industry. - 1987.
        (000660)
----Countertrade. - 1984.
        (001371)
----Hard bargaining ahead. - 1985.
        (001361)
----High-tech trade. - 1986.
        (000696)
----International countertrade. - 1984.
        (001396)
----Manufacturing matters : the myth of the
    post-industrial economy. - 1987.
        (000669)
----Political and policy dimensions of
    foreign trade zones. - 1985.
        (001356)
----Trade in services. - 1986.
        (000962)
----Transnational corporations and
    international trade : selected issues. -
    1985.
        (001393)
----US corporate interests and the political
    economy of trade policy. - 1984.
        (000505)

UNITED STATES--TRADE PROMOTION.
----Caribbean Basin business information
    starter kit. - 1984.
        (001782)

UNITED STATES--TRADE REGULATION.
----Exclusive licenses as restraints of
    trade under US and Common Market
    antitrust law. - 1984.
        (002414)
----Foreign trade and investment. - 1987.
        (002191)
----International business planning. - 1983.
        (002279)
----Licensing impact of foreign policy
    motivated retroactive reexport
    regulations. - 1983.
        (001352)
----Regulating the multinational enterprise.
    - 1983.
        (002006)

UNITED STATES--TRADE RESTRICTIONS.
----Transnational corporations and
    international trade : selected issues. -
    1985.
        (001393)
----United States jurisdiction over foreign
    subsidiaries. - 1983.
        (002355)

UNITED STATES--TRADE STATISTICS.
----Transnational corporations and
    international trade : selected issues. -
    1985.
        (001393)

UNITED STATES--TRADE STRUCTURE.
----International countertrade. - 1984.
        (001396)

UNITED STATES--TRADEMARKS.
----Trademark and related rights in
    franchise agreements in Germany. - 1983.
        (001523)

UNITED STATES--TRANSFER PRICING.
----La formation du prix dans les
    transactions internationales. - 1985.
        (001712)
----Intercorporate transfer pricing: the
    role of the functionally determined
    profit split explored. - 1985.
        (001753)

UNITED STATES--TRANSNATIONAL CORPORATIONS.
----American enterprise in foreign markets.
    - 1984.
        (000526)
----American multinationals and American
    employment. - 1983.
        (001890)
----America's corporate families and
    international affiliates. - 1983-   .
        (002617)
----Are environmental regulations driving
    U.S. industry overseas? - 1984.
        (001947)
----The Atlantic two-way switch. - 1986.
        (000852)
----The Bhopal case : controlling
    ultrahazardous industrial activities
    undertaken by foreign investors. - 1987.
        (001949)
----Business in the shadow of apartheid :
    U.S. firms in South Africa. - 1985.
        (001194)
----Canada in the USA : foreign direct
    investment flows reversed. - 1987.
        (000180)
----The competitive position of U.S.
    manufacturing firms. - 1985.
        (000353)
----Le contrôle gouvernemental des
    entreprises multinationales. - 1985.
        (002288)
----Direct foreign investment in the United
    States. - 1986.
        (000174)
----Direct investment activity of foreign
    firms. - 1987.
        (000541)
----Directory of foreign firms operating in
    the United States. - 1969-   .
        (002633)
----Directory of foreign manufacturers in
    the United States. - 1975-   .
        (002634)
----Disfraces del coloniaje. - 1984.
        (001114)
----Diversification : the European versus
    the US experience. - 1987.
        (000491)
----Doing business in key Latin American
    markets: U.S. international executive
    perceptions. - 1983.
        (001824)

UNITED STATES--TRANSNATIONAL CORPORATIONS
(continued)
----U.S. TNCs in an era of global challenge.
   - 1984.
   (000377)
----United States corporations operating in
   Saudi Arabia and laws affecting
   discrimination in employment. - 1985.
   (002354)
----Uoll-strit protiv Afriki. - 1985.
   (001030)
----US corporate interests and the political
   economy of trade policy. - 1984.
   (000505)
----US monopolies and developing countries.
   - 1986.
   (001692)
----Venturing abroad. - 1988.
   (000376)
----Washington's best kept secrets. - 1983.
   (002704)
----Worldwide unitary tax. - 1986.
   (001718)
----Worldwide unitary taxation : nature and
   alternative solutions. - 1986.
   (001766)

UNITED STATES--TREATIES.
----Oil spill liability and compensation. -
   1985.
   (001940)
----Towards a new treaty framework for
   direct foreign investment. - 1985.
   (002047)
----The U.S. bilateral investment treaty
   program. - 1985.
   (002034)
----Worldwide unitary tax. - 1986.
   (001718)

UNITED STATES--URANIUM INDUSTRY.
----Extraterritorial effects of United
   States commercial and antitrust
   legislation. - 1983.
   (002352)

UNITED STATES--WAGE INCENTIVES.
----Performance requirements for foreign
   business. - 1983.
   (002314)

UNITED STATES--WATER RESOURCES.
----A competitive assessment of the U.S.
   water resources equipment industry. -
   1985.
   (000776)

UNITED STATES. DEPARTMENT OF DEFENSE.
----National security and the semiconductor
   industry. - 1987.
   (000675)

UNITED STATES. SUPREME COURT.
----Mitsubishi and the arbitrability of
   antitrust claims. - 1986.
   (002486)
----Mitsubishi v. Soler and its impact on
   international commercial arbitration. -
   1985.
   (002507)

UNITED STATES INTERNATIONAL TRADE COMMISSION.
----Antitrust aspects of U.S.-Japanese
   trade. - 1983.
   (002345)

UNITED STATES OF AMERICA.
----Banco de datos sobre inversión
   extranjera directa en América Latina y
   el Caribe, sobre la base de información
   de organismos multilaterales y de
   gobiernos de países de origen de la
   inversión, t. 1. - 1986.
   (000195)

URANIUM--NAMIBIA.
----Transnational corporations in South
   Africa and Namibia : United Nations
   public hearings. Volume 3, Statements
   and submissions. - 1987.
   (001215)

URANIUM INDUSTRY.
----The international uranium market. - 1984.
   (000626)
----Transnational corporations and
   contractual relations in the world
   uranium industry. - 1983.
   (002448)

URANIUM INDUSTRY--AUSTRALIA.
----Extraterritorial effects of United
   States commercial and antitrust
   legislation. - 1983.
   (002352)

URANIUM INDUSTRY--UNITED STATES.
----Extraterritorial effects of United
   States commercial and antitrust
   legislation. - 1983.
   (002352)

URUGUAY--BUSINESS ENTERPRISES.
----La transformación de sociedad irregular
   en sociedad regular. - 1984.
   (001545)

URUGUAY--JOINT VENTURES.
----La transformación de sociedad irregular
   en sociedad regular. - 1984.
   (001545)

URUGUAY--PHARMACEUTICAL INDUSTRY.
----La industria farmacéutica y las
   transnacionales. - 1985.
   (000667)

URUGUAY--TRANSNATIONAL CORPORATIONS.
----La industria farmacéutica y las
   transnacionales. - 1985.
   (000667)

URUGUAY ROUND (1987-   : GENEVA).
----Revitalizing development, growth and
   international trade. - 1987.
   (001394)

USSR--ARBITRATION RULES.
----The Soviet position on international
   arbitration. - 1986.
   (002571)

USSR--BUSINESS ENTERPRISES.
----Businessman's Moscow. - 1984-   .
    (002625)
----La nouvelle législation soviétique sur
    les entreprises mixtes. - 1987.
    (002181)

USSR--CAPITAL INVESTMENTS.
----Investment and reindustrialization in
    the Soviet economy. - 1984.
    (001333)

USSR--CAPITAL MOVEMENTS.
----Gold, foreign capital and the
    industrialization of Russia. - 1985.
    (001184)

USSR--CENTRALLY PLANNED ECONOMIES.
----L'URSS et le Tiers Monde. - 1984.
    (002040)

USSR--COMPUTER INDUSTRY.
----Computergebruik in de Sovjetunie. - 1987.
    (000677)

USSR--CONTRACTS.
----La négociation des contrats de transfert
    de techniques avec l'Union soviétique. -
    1984.
    (002466)
----The problem of autonomy in Soviet
    international contract law. - 1983.
    (002167)

USSR--DEVELOPING COUNTRIES.
----L'URSS et le Tiers Monde. - 1984.
    (002040)

USSR--DIRECTORIES.
----Businessman's Moscow. - 1984-   .
    (002625)

USSR--DOUBLE TAXATION.
----The Soviet Union's other tax agreements.
    - 1986.
    (002043)

USSR--ECONOMIC POLICY.
----Investment and reindustrialization in
    the Soviet economy. - 1984.
    (001333)
----The Soviet industrial enterprise. - 1984.
    (000330)

USSR--ECONOMIC REFORM.
----La nouvelle législation soviétique sur
    les entreprises mixtes. - 1987.
    (002181)

USSR--ECONOMIC RELATIONS.
----The new Soviet joint venture
    regulations. - 1987.
    (002202)
----L'URSS et le Tiers Monde. - 1984.
    (002040)

USSR--FOREIGN INVESTMENTS.
----Multinationals from the Second World :
    growth of foreign investment by Soviet
    and East European enterprises. - 1987.
    (000356)

USSR--FOREIGN TRADE.
----Anderungen im sowjetischen
    Aussenwirtschaftssystem zu Beginn des
    Jahres 1987. - 1987.
    (001176)
----Foreign trade with the USSR. - 1987.
    (001774)
----Journal of the US-USSR Trade and
    Economic Council. - 1976-   .
    (001179)
----La négociation des contrats de transfert
    de techniques avec l'Union soviétique. -
    1984.
    (002466)
----The new Soviet joint venture
    regulations. - 1987.
    (002202)
----The problem of autonomy in Soviet
    international contract law. - 1983.
    (002167)
----La réforme du commerce extérieur
    soviétique. - 1987.
    (002261)
----The Soviet position on international
    arbitration. - 1986.
    (002571)

USSR--GOLD.
----Gold, foreign capital and the
    industrialization of Russia. - 1985.
    (001184)

USSR--INDUSTRIAL CO-OPERATION.
----American enterprise in foreign markets.
    - 1984.
    (000526)
----International Harvester in Russia: the
    Washington-St. Petersburg connection? -
    1983.
    (000272)

USSR--INDUSTRIAL ENTERPRISES.
----The Soviet industrial enterprise. - 1984.
    (000330)

USSR--INDUSTRIAL PLANNING.
----Vers une réforme de la planification des
    services en URSS? - 1985.
    (000845)

USSR--INDUSTRIAL POLICY.
----Investment and reindustrialization in
    the Soviet economy. - 1984.
    (001333)

USSR--INDUSTRIALIZATION.
----Gold, foreign capital and the
    industrialization of Russia. - 1985.
    (001184)

USSR--INDUSTRY.
----Investment and reindustrialization in
    the Soviet economy. - 1984.
    (001333)
----The Soviet industrial enterprise. - 1984.
    (000330)

USSR--INFORMATION SYSTEMS.
----Computergebruik in de Sovjetunie. - 1987.
    (000677)

USSR--JOINT VENTURES.
----Anderungen im sowjetischen
    Aussenwirtschaftssystem zu Beginn des
    Jahres 1987. - 1987.
        (001176)
----East-West joint ventures. - 1988.
        (001570)
----Foreign trade with the USSR. - 1987.
        (001774)
----The new Soviet joint venture
    regulations. - 1987.
        (002202)
----La nouvelle législation soviétique sur
    les entreprises mixtes. - 1987.
        (002181) .
----La réforme du commerce extérieur
    soviétique. - 1987.
        (002261)
----USSR, tendensen tot decentralisatie. -
    1987.
        (001190)

USSR--LAWS AND REGULATIONS.
----East-West joint ventures. - 1988.
        (001570)

USSR--LEGISLATION.
----La nouvelle législation soviétique sur
    les entreprises mixtes. - 1987.
        (002181) .

USSR--LICENCES.
----Reverse technology flows. - 1985.
        (001451)

USSR--MANAGEMENT.
----Creating a world enterprise. - 1983.
        (000398)

USSR--MINERAL INDUSTRY.
----Mineral industries of Europe and the
    U.S.S.R. - 1984.
        (000642)

USSR--PRODUCTION CONTROL.
----Multinationals from the Second World :
    growth of foreign investment by Soviet
    and East European enterprises. - 1987.
        (000356)

USSR--SERVICE INDUSTRIES.
----Multinationals from the Second World :
    growth of foreign investment by Soviet
    and East European enterprises. - 1987.
        (000356)
----Vers une réforme de la planification des
    services en URSS? - 1985.
        (000845)

USSR--STATE TRADING ENTERPRISES.
----La réforme du commerce extérieur
    soviétique. - 1987.
        (002261)

USSR--STATISTICAL DATA.
----East-West joint ventures. - 1988.
        (001570)

USSR--TAX TREATIES.
----The Soviet Union's other tax agreements.
    - 1986.
        (002043)

USSR--TECHNOLOGICAL INNOVATIONS.
----Reverse technology flows. - 1985.
        (001451)

USSR--TECHNOLOGY TRANSFER.
----La négociation des contrats de transfert
    de techniques avec l'Union soviétique. -
    1984.
        (002466)
----Reverse technology flows. - 1985.
        (001451)

USSR--TRADE AGREEMENTS. .
----L'URSS et le Tiers Monde. - 1984.
        (002040)

USSR--TRADE POLICY.
----Foreign trade with the USSR. - 1987.
        (001774)
----La réforme du commerce extérieur
    soviétique. - 1987.
        (002261)
----USSR, tendensen tot decentralisatie. -
    1987.
        (001190)

USSR--TRADE REGULATION.
----Anderungen im sowjetischen
    Aussenwirtschaftssystem zu Beginn des
    Jahres 1987. - 1987.
        (001176)
----The new Soviet joint venture
    regulations. - 1987.
        (002202)

USSR--TRANSNATIONAL CORPORATIONS.
----American enterprise in foreign markets.
    - 1984.
        (000526)
----Businessman's Moscow. - 1984-   .
        (002625)
----Creating a world enterprise. - 1983.
        (000398)
----Foreign trade with the USSR. - 1987.
        (001774)
----Gold, foreign capital and the
    industrialization of Russia. - 1985.
        (001184)
----International Harvester in Russia: the
    Washington-St. Petersburg connection? -
    1983.
        (000272)
----Multinationals from the Second World :
    growth of foreign investment by Soviet
    and East European enterprises. - 1987.
        (000356)
----USSR, tendensen tot decentralisatie. -
    1987.
        (001190)
----Vers une réforme de la planification des
    services en URSS? - 1985.
        (000845)

USSR. VNESHNETORGOVAYA ARBITRAZHNAYA
KOMISSIYA.
----The Soviet position on international
    arbitration. - 1986.
        (002571)

VACCINES--CHINA.
----Joint ventures in the PRC. - 1987.
        (000478)

VALUE ADDED TAX.
----International accounting and reporting
    issues : 1984 review. - 1985.
     (002115)

VENEZUELA--COMMERCIAL ARBITRATION.
----Schiedsklauseln in Peru und Venezuela. -
    1987.
     (002570)

VENEZUELA--DEMOCRACY.
----Petroleum and political pacts. - 1987.
     (001816)

VENEZUELA--EXTERNAL DEBT.
----La internacionalización financiera en
    Venezuela. - 1983.
     (001286)

VENEZUELA--FOREIGN DIRECT INVESTMENT.
----Legislación de inversiones extranjeras y
    Pacto Andino. - 1984.
     (002234)

VENEZUELA--FOREIGN INVESTMENTS.
----National legislation and regulations
    relating to transnational corporations.
    Volume 4. - 1986.
     (002253)

VENEZUELA--INTERNATIONAL BANKING.
----La internacionalización financiera en
    Venezuela. - 1983.
     (001286)

VENEZUELA--IRON AND STEEL INDUSTRY.
----La industria siderúrgica
    latinoamericana. - 1984.
     (000601)

VENEZUELA--LAWS AND REGULATIONS.
----Legislación de inversiones extranjeras y
    Pacto Andino. - 1984.
     (002234)
----National legislation and regulations
    relating to transnational corporations.
    Volume 4. - 1986.
     (002253)

VENEZUELA--METALLURGICAL INDUSTRY.
----La industria siderúrgica
    latinoamericana. - 1984.
     (000601)

VENEZUELA--NATIONALIZATION.
----The nationalization of the Venezuelan
    oil industry. - 1983.
     (000586)
----Petroleos de Venezuela. - 1983.
     (000646)

VENEZUELA--OIL INDUSTRIES.
----Petroleum and political pacts. - 1987.
     (001816)

VENEZUELA--PETROLEUM INDUSTRY.
----Empirical models of political risks in
    U.S. oil production operations in
    Venezuela. - 1984.
     (001813)
----The nationalization of the Venezuelan
    oil industry. - 1983.
     (000586)

----Petroleos de Venezuela. - 1983.
     (000646)

VENEZUELA--PETROLEUM POLICY.
----Petroleum and political pacts. - 1987.
     (001816)

VENEZUELA--POLITICAL CONDITIONS.
----Petroleum and political pacts. - 1987.
     (001816)

VENEZUELA--RISK MANAGEMENT.
----Empirical models of political risks in
    U.S. oil production operations in
    Venezuela. - 1984.
     (001813)

VENEZUELA--TRANSNATIONAL CORPORATIONS.
----National legislation and regulations
    relating to transnational corporations.
    Volume 4. - 1986.
     (002253)

VOLTA RIVER AUTHORITY (GHANA).
----The price and availability of energy for
    an aluminium smelter : recent
    renegotiations in Ghana. - 1987.
     (002467)

W. R. GRACE & CO.
----Grace. - 1985.
     (000276)

WAGE INCENTIVES.
----Contract efficiency and natural resource
    investment in developing countries. -
    1984.
     (002409)

WAGE INCENTIVES--UNITED STATES.
----Performance requirements for foreign
    business. - 1983.
     (002314)

WAGE POLICY--SOUTH AFRICA.
----A code for misconduct? - 1980.
     (002009)

WAGE PRICE POLICY.
----Verrechnungspreispolitik in
    internationalen Unternehmungen. - 1985.
     (002692)

WAGE SURVEYS--ASIA.
----Wages, hours and working conditions in
    Asian free trade zones. - 1984.
     (001897)

WAGES--MALAYSIA.
----Wages and work conditions, and the
    effects of foreign investment and the
    separation of ownership from management
    on them: a study of Malaysian
    manufacturing. - 1983.
     (001907)

WAGES--NETHERLANDS.
----Verdiende lonen van werknemers in
    nijverheid en dienstensector ontleend
    aan het halfjaarlijks loononderzoek. -
    1985.
     (001928)

WASTE DISPOSAL.
----Environmental aspects of the activities
   of transnational corporations. - 1985.
      (001954)

WATER RESOURCES--UNITED STATES.
----A competitive assessment of the U.S.
   water resources equipment industry. -
   1985.
      (000776)

WELFARE ECONOMICS.
----Consumer choice in the Third World. -
   1983.
      (000878)

WEST AFRICA--ECONOMIC RELATIONS.
----Tendentsii ekspansii TNK v strany
   Zapadnoi Afriki v 70-kh-nachale 80-kh
   godov. - 1986.
      (001021)

WEST AFRICA--TRANSNATIONAL CORPORATIONS.
----Tendentsii ekspansii TNK v strany
   Zapadnoi Afriki v 70-kh-nachale 80-kh
   godov. - 1986.
      (001021)

WESTER EUROPE.
----Multinationals--theory and history. -
   1986.
      (000043)

WESTERN ASIA--BALANCE OF PAYMENTS.
----Trade in services : growth and balance
   of payments implications for countries
   of Western Asia. - 1987.
      (000968)

WESTERN ASIA--FINANCIAL STATISTICS.
----Trade in services : growth and balance
   of payments implications for countries
   of Western Asia. - 1987.
      (000968)

WESTERN ASIA--JOINT VENTURES.
----Trade in services : growth and balance
   of payments implications for countries
   of Western Asia. - 1987.
      (000968)

WESTERN ASIA--SERVICE INDUSTRIES.
----Trade in services : growth and balance
   of payments implications for countries
   of Western Asia. - 1987.
      (000968)

WESTERN ASIA--STATISTICAL DATA.
----Trade in services : growth and balance
   of payments implications for countries
   of Western Asia. - 1987.
      (000968)

WESTERN ASIA--TRADE NEGOTIATIONS.
----Trade in services : growth and balance
   of payments implications for countries
   of Western Asia. - 1987.
      (000968)

WESTERN EUROPE--ACCOUNTING.
----Zur Angleichung des Bilanzrechts in der
   Europäischen Gemeinschaft. - 1984.
      (002097)

WESTERN EUROPE--ACCOUNTING AND REPORTING.
----The recent accounting and economic
   developments in Western Europe. - 1985.
      (002110)

WESTERN EUROPE--AGRIBUSINESS.
----Agro-industrial co-operation between the
   European Community and the ACP
   countries. - 1986.
      (002605)

WESTERN EUROPE--AIR TRANSPORT.
----Air and maritime transport and the EEC
   competition rules : Ministère Publique
   v. Asjes, Nouvelles Frontières et al. -
   1987.
      (000794)
----Attempt to regulate restrictive
   commercial practices in the field of air
   transportation within a transnational
   antitrust legal and institutional
   framework. - 1984.
      (000788) (001659)

WESTERN EUROPE--ANTITRUST LAW.
----The antitrust law of the European
   Community and the UNCTAD code on
   restrictive business practices. - 1984.
      (001992)
----Attempt to regulate restrictive
   commercial practices in the field of air
   transportation within a transnational
   antitrust legal and institutional
   framework. - 1984.
      (000788) (001659)
----Corporate acquisitions and mergers. -
   1985.
      (001544)
----The EEC patent licencing regulation :
   practical guidelines. - 1986.
      (001966)
----Exclusive licenses as restraints of
   trade under US and Common Market
   antitrust law. - 1984.
      (002414)

WESTERN EUROPE--ARBITRAL AWARDS.
----Commercial arbitration and the European
   Economic Community. - 1985.
      (002481)

WESTERN EUROPE--AUDITING.
----The recent accounting and economic
   developments in Western Europe. - 1985.
      (002110)

WESTERN EUROPE--BIOTECHNOLOGY.
----Commercial biotechnology. - 1984.
      (000643)

WESTERN EUROPE--BUDGETARY POLICY.
----Mélanges 2 : harmonisation fiscale,
   marché commun des services, perspectives
   budgétaires 1988, fonds structurels. -
   1987.
      (000897)

WESTERN EUROPE--BUSINESS ENTERPRISE BRANCHES.
----Operating foreign subsidiaries. - 1983.
      (000388)

WESTERN EUROPE--BUSINESS ENTERPRISES.
----Abhängige Unternehmen und Konzerne im
europäischen Gemeinschaftsrecht. - 1984.
(002133)

WESTERN EUROPE--CAPITAL MOVEMENTS.
----Handels- und Zahlungsprobleme in
Osteuropa. - 1983.
(000215)
----La libération des mouvements de capitaux
et l'intégration financière de la
Communauté. - 1987.
(001230)

WESTERN EUROPE--CENTRALLY PLANNED ECONOMIES.
----Western direct investment in centrally
planned economies. - 1986.
(000159)

WESTERN EUROPE--CMEA.
----Tapping Eastern bloc technology. - 1983.
(001452)

WESTERN EUROPE--COMMON MARKET.
----Air and maritime transport and the EEC
competition rules : Ministère Publique
v. Asjes, Nouvelles Frontières et al. -
1987.
(000794)

WESTERN EUROPE--COMPETITION.
----Air and maritime transport and the EEC
competition rules : Ministère Publique
v. Asjes, Nouvelles Frontières et al. -
1987.
(000794)
----Application des règles de concurrence du
Traité de Rome à l'autorité publique. -
1987.
(002021)
----Attempt to regulate restrictive
commercial practices in the field of air
transportation within a transnational
antitrust legal and institutional
framework. - 1984.
(000788) (001659)
----A competitive assessment of the U.S.
fiber optics industry. - 1984.
(000800)
----EEC competition policy. - 1986.
(001989)
----EEC law of competition. - 1985.
(002151)
----Employment and competitiveness in the
European Community. - 1984.
(001929)
----Exclusive territorial rights in patent
licenses and Article 85 of the EEC
Treaty. - 1987.
(002418)
----Extraterritorial application of the
EEC-competition law. - 1984.
(002349)
----La licence de marque et le droit
européen de la concurrence. - 1984.
(001448)
----La réglementation communautaire des
transports. - 1984.
(001994)
----Territorial and exclusive trademark
licensing under the EEC law of
competition. - 1984.
(001987)

WESTERN EUROPE--COMPUTER INDUSTRY.
----Information technology and economic
recovery in Western Europe. - 1986.
(000874)

WESTERN EUROPE--CONTRACTS.
----A contract law for Europe. - 1985.
(001991)
----EEC law of competition. - 1985.
(002151)
----La négociation du contrat international.
- 1983.
(002464)

WESTERN EUROPE--CORPORATE MERGERS.
----Centralized European merger regulation.
- 1985.
(001625)
----Corporate acquisitions and mergers. -
1985.
(001544)
----European industry on the march. - 1987.
(001155)
----Recent developments in operations and
behaviour of transnational corporations.
- 1987.
(000103)

WESTERN EUROPE--CORPORATION LAW.
----Abhängige Unternehmen und Konzerne im
europäischen Gemeinschaftsrecht. - 1984.
(002133)
----Corporate acquisitions and mergers. -
1985.
(001544)
----The protection of corporate privacy. -
1983.
(002291)
----Zur Angleichung des Bilanzrechts in der
Europäischen Gemeinschaft. - 1984.
(002097)

WESTERN EUROPE--CORPORATION TAX.
----Corporate acquisitions and mergers. -
1985.
(001544)

WESTERN EUROPE--CORPORATIONS.
----Abhängige Unternehmen und Konzerne im
europäischen Gemeinschaftsrecht. - 1984.
(002133)

WESTERN EUROPE--DECISION-MAKING.
----Operating foreign subsidiaries. - 1983.
(000388)

WESTERN EUROPE--DEVELOPED MARKET ECONOMIES.
----Transnatsional'nye korporatsii v
ekonomike malykh stran Zapadnoi Evropy.
- 1983.
(001163)

WESTERN EUROPE--DEVELOPING COUNTRIES.
----Trade in services. - 1986.
(000962)

WESTERN EUROPE--DEVELOPMENT BANKS.
----The European Investment Bank. - 1985.
(002134)

WESTERN EUROPE--DIVISION OF LABOUR.
----Hacia dónde va el empleo? - 1986.
(001252)

WESTERN EUROPE--ECONOMIC CO-OPERATION.
----Current problems of economic
   integration. - 1986.
      (001312)
----Wachstumsmarkt Südostasien. - 1984.
      (001785)

WESTERN EUROPE--ECONOMIC INTEGRATION.
----Current problems of economic
   integration. - 1986.
      (001312)
----La libération des mouvements de capitaux
   et l'intégration financière de la
   Communauté. - 1987.
      (001230)
----Multinational corporations and European
   integration. - 1987.
      (001325)

WESTERN EUROPE--ECONOMIC POLICY.
----EEC competition policy. - 1986.
      (001989)

WESTERN EUROPE--ECONOMIC RELATIONS.
----The European Community and China. - 1986.
      (002045)
----Toward Lomé III. - 1984.
      (002606)
----Wachstumsmarkt Südostasien. - 1984.
      (001785)

WESTERN EUROPE--ECONOMIC STRUCTURE.
----Die ordnungspolitische Dimension der
   EG-Technologiepolitik. - 1987.
      (001495)

WESTERN EUROPE--ECONOMIC TRENDS.
----Trends in multinational business and
   global environments: a perspective. -
   1984.
      (000029)

WESTERN EUROPE--ELECTRONICS INDUSTRY.
----European industrial policy for the
   electronics and information technology
   sector. - 1984.
      (000849)
----Transnational corporations in the
   international semiconductor industry. -
   1986.
      (000748)

WESTERN EUROPE--EMPLOYMENT.
----Employment and competitiveness in the
   European Community. - 1984.
      (001929)
----Hacia dónde va el empleo? - 1986.
      (001252)

WESTERN EUROPE--ENERGY LEGISLATION.
----International aspects of nuclear
   instalations licensing. - 1987.
      (002434)

WESTERN EUROPE--FIBRE OPTICS.
----A competitive assessment of the U.S.
   fiber optics industry. - 1984.
      (000800)

WESTERN EUROPE--FISCAL POLICY.
----Mélanges 2 : harmonisation fiscale,
   marché commun des services, perspectives
   budgétaires 1988, fonds structurels. -
   1987.
      (000897)

WESTERN EUROPE--FOREIGN DIRECT INVESTMENT.
----European Community tariff preferences
   and foreign direct investment. - 1987.
      (002159)
----The European investments of Japanese
   financial institutions. - 1986.
      (000118)
----Multinational corporations and European
   integration. - 1987.
      (001325)
----Operating foreign subsidiaries. - 1983.
      (000388)
----The relative distribution of United
   States direct investment : the UK/EEC
   experience. - 1987.
      (000113)
----Trends in multinational business and
   global environments: a perspective. -
   1984.
      (000029)
----Western direct investment in centrally
   planned economies. - 1986.
      (000159)

WESTERN EUROPE--FOREIGN INVESTMENTS.
----L'Afrique, l'Europe et la crise. - 1986.
      (001287)
----Les investissements européens au Japon :
   les causes de la faiblesse et les
   difficultés du rattrapage. - 1986.
      (000105)
----Le système conjoint de garantie des
   investissements CEE/ACP de la Convention
   de Lomé III. - 1987.
      (002147)

WESTERN EUROPE--FOREIGN TRADE.
----Saisie et effets des transferts de la
   technologie incorporée dans le commerce
   est-ouest. - 1986.
      (001464)
----Wachstumsmarkt Südostasien. - 1984.
      (001785)

WESTERN EUROPE--FREE TRADE.
----Perspektiven für eine engere
   Zusammenarbeit zwischen der Europäischen
   Gemeinschaft und den
   EFTA-Mitgliedstaaten. - 1985.
      (001962)

WESTERN EUROPE--HOST COUNTRY RELATIONS.
----International industries, multinational
   companies, and host government control:
   a framework. - 1983.
      (001796)

WESTERN EUROPE--INDUSTRIAL CO-OPERATION.
----Agro-industrial co-operation between the
   European Community and the ACP
   countries. - 1986.
      (002605)
----Industrialization and the ACPs. - 1984.
      (002608)

WESTERN EUROPE--INDUSTRIAL ENTERPRISES.
----European industry on the march. - 1987.
    (001155)

WESTERN EUROPE--INDUSTRIAL POLICY.
----European industrial policy for the
    electronics and information technology
    sector. - 1984.
    (000849)

WESTERN EUROPE--INDUSTRIAL SECTOR.
----Diversification : the European versus
    the US experience. - 1987.
    (000491)

WESTERN EUROPE--INDUSTRIAL TECHNOLOGY.
----A high technology gap? - 1987.
    (001439)

WESTERN EUROPE--INDUSTRY.
----A competitive assessment of the U.S.
    fiber optics industry. - 1984.
    (000800)

WESTERN EUROPE--INFORMATION POLICY.
----Information technology and economic
    recovery in Western Europe. - 1986.
    (000874)

WESTERN EUROPE--INFORMATION TECHNOLOGY.
----European industrial policy for the
    electronics and information technology
    sector. - 1984.
    (000849)
----Information technology and economic
    recovery in Western Europe. - 1986.
    (000874)
----New technology and the new services :
    towards an innovation strategy for
    Europe. - 1986.
    (000807)
----Société d'information et Europe des
    services : quelles infrastructures? -
    1987.
    (000893)

WESTERN EUROPE--INFORMATION TRANSFER.
----New challenges to the U.S. multinational
    corporation in the European Economic
    Community. - 1985.
    (002192)

WESTERN EUROPE--INTERNATIONAL COMMERCIAL
ARBITRATION.
----Commercial arbitration and the European
    Economic Community. - 1985.
    (002481)

WESTERN EUROPE--INTERNATIONAL CO-OPERATION.
----International aspects of nuclear
    instalations licensing. - 1987.
    (002434)

WESTERN EUROPE--INTERNATIONAL SALE OF GOODS.
----Territorial and exclusive trademark
    licensing under the EEC law of
    competition. - 1984.
    (001987)

WESTERN EUROPE--INTRA-INDUSTRY TRADE.
----Multinational corporations and European
    integration. - 1987.
    (001325)

WESTERN EUROPE--INVESTMENT BANKING.
----The European Investment Bank. - 1985.
    (002134)

WESTERN EUROPE--INVESTMENT INSURANCE.
----Le système conjoint de garantie des
    investissements CEE/ACP de la Convention
    de Lomé III. - 1987.
    (002147)

WESTERN EUROPE--INVESTMENT PROMOTION.
----Industrialization and the ACPs. - 1984.
    (002608)

WESTERN EUROPE--JOINT VENTURES.
----East-West joint ventures. - 1988.
    (001570)
----European industry on the march. - 1987.
    (001155)
----Western direct investment in centrally
    planned economies. - 1986.
    (000159)

WESTERN EUROPE--JURISPRUDENCE.
----La licence de marque et le droit
    européen de la concurrence. - 1984.
    (001448)

WESTERN EUROPE--LABOUR MARKET.
----Employment and competitiveness in the
    European Community. - 1984.
    (001929)

WESTERN EUROPE--LAW.
----Extraterritorial application of the
    EEC-competition law. - 1984.
    (002349)

WESTERN EUROPE--LAWS AND REGULATIONS.
----East-West joint ventures. - 1988.
    (001570)
----New challenges to the U.S. multinational
    corporation in the European Economic
    Community. - 1985.
    (002192)

WESTERN EUROPE--LICENCE AGREEMENTS.
----The EEC patent licencing regulation :
    practical guidelines. - 1986.
    (001966)

WESTERN EUROPE--LICENCES.
----Exclusive licenses as restraints of
    trade under US and Common Market
    antitrust law. - 1984.
    (002414)
----Exclusive territorial rights in patent
    licenses and Article 85 of the EEC
    Treaty. - 1987.
    (002418)
----In the wake of windsurfing : patent
    licensing in the Common Market. - 1987.
    (002455)
----International aspects of nuclear
    instalations licensing. - 1987.
    (002434)

WESTERN EUROPE--MANUFACTURING.
----The relative distribution of United
    States direct investment : the UK/EEC
    experience. - 1987.
    (000113)

WESTERN EUROPE--MARITIME TRANSPORT.
----Air and maritime transport and the EEC
    competition rules : Ministère Publique
    v. Asjes, Nouvelles Frontières et al. -
    1987.
    (000794)

WESTERN EUROPE--NEGOTIATION.
----La négociation du contrat international.
    - 1983.
    (002464)

WESTERN EUROPE--NEW TECHNOLOGIES.
----A high technology gap? - 1987.
    (001439)

WESTERN EUROPE--NUCLEAR FACILITIES.
----International aspects of nuclear
    instalations licensing. - 1987.
    (002434)

WESTERN EUROPE--PATENT LAW.
----The EEC patent licencing regulation :
    practical guidelines. - 1986.
    (001966)
----Exclusive territorial rights in patent
    licenses and Article 85 of the EEC
    Treaty. - 1987.
    (002418)

WESTERN EUROPE--PATENTS.
----In the wake of windsurfing : patent
    licensing in the Common Market. - 1987.
    (002455)
----La licence de marque et le droit
    européen de la concurrence. - 1984.
    (001448)

WESTERN EUROPE--PERSONAL DATA FILES.
----New challenges to the U.S. multinational
    corporation in the European Economic
    Community. - 1985.
    (002192)

WESTERN EUROPE--PETROLEUM INDUSTRY.
----Oil industry restructuring in the
    Netherlands and its European context. -
    1987.
    (000629)

WESTERN EUROPE--PETROLEUM REFINERIES.
----Oil industry restructuring in the
    Netherlands and its European context. -
    1987.
    (000629)

WESTERN EUROPE--PRICES.
----La formation du prix dans les
    transactions internationales. - 1985.
    (001712)

WESTERN EUROPE--PRIVACY LAW.
----New challenges to the U.S. multinational
    corporation in the European Economic
    Community. - 1985.
    (002192)

WESTERN EUROPE--PRODUCTION DIVERSIFICATION.
----Diversification : the European versus
    the US experience. - 1987.
    (000491)

WESTERN EUROPE--PUBLIC SECTOR.
----Services and regional policy. - 1987.
    (000903)

WESTERN EUROPE--RESTRICTIVE BUSINESS
PRACTICES.
----The antitrust law of the European
    Community and the UNCTAD code on
    restrictive business practices. - 1984.
    (001992)
----EEC law of competition. - 1985.
    (002151)

WESTERN EUROPE--RULES AND REGULATIONS.
----Centralized European merger regulation.
    - 1985.
    (001625)

WESTERN EUROPE--SCIENCE AND TECHNOLOGY
POLICY.
----Die ordnungspolitische Dimension der
    EG-Technologiepolitik. - 1987.
    (001495)

WESTERN EUROPE--SERVICE INDUSTRIES.
----Hacia dónde va el empleo? - 1986.
    (001252)
----Mélanges 2 : harmonisation fiscale,
    marché commun des services, perspectives
    budgétaires 1988, fonds structurels. -
    1987.
    (000897)
----New technology and the new services :
    towards an innovation strategy for
    Europe. - 1986.
    (000807)
----Services and regional policy. - 1987.
    (000903)
----Société d'information et Europe des
    services : quelles infrastructures? -
    1987.
    (000893)
----Trade in services. - 1986.
    (000962)

WESTERN EUROPE--STATISTICAL DATA.
----East-West joint ventures. - 1988.
    (001570)

WESTERN EUROPE--STOCKHOLDERS.
----Corporate acquisitions and mergers. -
    1985.
    (001544)

WESTERN EUROPE--SUBSIDIARY BODIES.
----Operating foreign subsidiaries. - 1983.
    (000388)

WESTERN EUROPE--TARIFF PREFERENCES.
----European Community tariff preferences
    and foreign direct investment. - 1987.
    (002159)

WESTERN EUROPE--TARIFFS.
----La réglementation communautaire des
    transports. - 1984.
    (001994)

WESTERN EUROPE--TECHNOLOGICAL INNOVATIONS.
----Diversification : the European versus
    the US experience. - 1987.
    (000491)
----A high technology gap? - 1987.
    (001439)

WESTERN EUROPE--TECHNOLOGICAL INNOVATIONS
(continued)
----New technology and the new services :
    towards an innovation strategy for
    Europe. - 1986.
    (000807)

WESTERN EUROPE--TECHNOLOGICAL TRENDS.
----Trends in multinational business and
    global environments: a perspective. -
    1984.
    (000029)

WESTERN EUROPE--TECHNOLOGY.
----A high technology gap? - 1987.
    (001439)

WESTERN EUROPE--TECHNOLOGY TRANSFER.
----A high technology gap? - 1987.
    (001439)
----Saisie et effets des transferts de la
    technologie incorporée dans le commerce
    est-ouest. - 1986.
    (001464)
----Tapping Eastern bloc technology. - 1983.
    (001452)

WESTERN EUROPE--TELECOMMUNICATION.
----Information technology and economic
    recovery in Western Europe. - 1986.
    (000874)

WESTERN EUROPE--TRADE AGREEMENTS.
----The European Community and China. - 1986.
    (002045)
----Perspektiven für eine engere
    Zusammenarbeit zwischen der Europäischen
    Gemeinschaft und den
    EFTA-Mitgliedstaaten. - 1985.
    (001962)
----Toward Lomé III. - 1984.
    (002606)

WESTERN EUROPE--TRADE NEGÓTIATIONS.
----Trade in services. - 1986.
    (000962)

WESTERN EUROPE--TRADE POLICY.
----Trade in services. - 1986.
    (000962)

WESTERN EUROPE--TRADE REGULATION.
----Exclusive licenses as restraints of
    trade under US and Common Market
    antitrust law. - 1984.
    (002414)

WESTERN EUROPE--TRADEMARK LICENCES.
----Territorial and exclusive trademark
    licensing under the EEC law of
    competition. - 1984.
    (001987)

WESTERN EUROPE--TRADEMARKS.
----La licence de marque et le droit
    européen de la concurrence. - 1984.
    (001448)

WESTERN EUROPE--TRANSFER PRICING.
----La formation du prix dans les
    transactions internationales. - 1985.
    (001712)

WESTERN EUROPE--TRANSNATIONAL CORPORATIONS.
----Corporate acquisitions and mergers. -
    1985.
    (001544)
----Diversification : the European versus
    the US experience. - 1987.
    (000491)
----International industries, multinational
    companies, and host government control:
    a framework. - 1983.
    (001796)
----La multinationalisation des firmes
    européennes aux Etats-Unis: une approche
    dynamique. - 1984.
    (001152)
----New challenges to the U.S. multinational
    corporation in the European Economic
    Community. - 1985.
    (002192)
----Operating foreign subsidiaries. - 1983.
    (000388)
----Recent developments in operations and
    behaviour of transnational corporations.
    - 1987.
    (000103)
----Reference book on major transnational
    corporations operating in Namibia. -
    1985.
    (002674)
----Tapping Eastern bloc technology. - 1983.
    (001452)
----Transnational corporations in the
    international semiconductor industry. -
    1986.
    (000748)
----Transnatsional'nye korporatsii v
    ekonomike malykh stran Zapadnoi Evropy.
    - 1983.
    (001163)
----Trends in multinational business and
    global environments: a perspective. -
    1984.
    (000029)

WESTERN EUROPE--TRANSNATIONAL DATA FLOW.
----The protection of corporate privacy. -
    1983.
    (002291)

WESTERN EUROPE--TRANSPORT.
----La réglementation communautaire des
    transports. - 1984.
    (001994)

WESTERN EUROPE--TREATIES.
----Commercial arbitration and the European
    Economic Community. - 1985.
    (002481)
----International aspects of nuclear
    instalations licensing. - 1987.
    (002434)
----Le système conjoint de garantie des
    investissements CEE/ACP de la Convention
    de Lomé III. - 1987.
    (002147)

WESTERN EUROPE--UNIFORM LAWS.
----A contract law for Europe. - 1985.
    (001991)

WHO.
----The implementation process of the
International Code of Marketing of
Breastmilk Substitutes. - 1984.
(001970) (001971)
----Microelectronics-based automation
technologies and development. - 1985.
(000753)
----Transnational corporations in the
pharmaceutical industry of developing
countries. - 1984.
(000749)

WITHHOLDING TAX.
----International bank lending. - 1984.
(000988)
----International income taxation and
developing countries. - 1988.
(001759)

WOMEN.
----Third World resource directory. - 1984.
(002719)
----Women in industry. - 1985.
(001930)

WOMEN--MEXICO.
----Las maquiladoras en México. - 1984.
(001906)

WOMEN IN DEVELOPMENT.
----Women and work in the Third World. -
1983.
(001893)

WOMEN WORKERS.
----Women and work in the Third World. -
1983.
(001893)
----Women in industry. - 1985.
(001930)
----Women in the global factory. - 1983.
(001898)
----Women workers in multinational
enterprises in developing countries. -
1985.
(001926)

WOMEN WORKERS--COSTA RICA.
----La industria de la maquila y la
explotación de la fuerza de trabajo de
la mujer. - 1984.
(001900)

WOMEN WORKERS--MAURITIUS.
----Jobs for the girls. - 1984.
(001901)

WOMEN'S ADVANCEMENT--MEXICO.
----The role of public enterprises in the
advancement of women in Mexico. - 1983.
(001894)

WOMEN'S ADVANCEMENT--TUNISIA.
----Responsabilités des entreprises
publiques dans l'amélioration de la
condition de la femme. - 1983.
(001883)

WOMEN'S STATUS.
----Bibliographic guide to studies on the
status of women. - 1983.
(002682)

WOMEN'S STATUS--MEXICO.
----The role of public enterprises in the
advancement of women in Mexico. - 1983.
(001894)

WOMEN'S STATUS--TUNISIA.
----Responsabilités des entreprises
publiques dans l'amélioration de la
condition de la femme. - 1983.
(001883)

WORKERS' PARTICIPATION IN MANAGEMENT.
----Multinationale Unternehmen und
Mitbestimmung. - 1986.
(000406)
----The Vredeling proposal. - 1983.
(002604)

WORKING CONDITIONS.
----Women in industry. - 1985.
(001930)

WORKING CONDITIONS--ASIA.
----TWARO (ITGLWF-ARO) Asian Seminar on Free
Trade Zones, Tokyo, 6th-13th March 1983.
- 1983.
(002396)
----Wages, hours and working conditions in
Asian free trade zones. - 1984.
(001897)

WORKING CONDITIONS--MALAYSIA.
----Wages and work conditions, and the
effects of foreign investment and the
separation of ownership from management
on them: a study of Malaysian
manufacturing. - 1983.
(001907)

WORKING CONDITIONS--NAMIBIA.
----Transnational corporations in South
Africa and Namibia : United Nations
public hearings. Volume 1, Reports of
the Panel of Eminent Persons and of the
Secretary-General. - 1986.
(001216)

WORKING CONDITIONS--SOUTH AFRICA.
----Transnational corporations in South
Africa and Namibia : United Nations
public hearings. Volume 1, Reports of
the Panel of Eminent Persons and of the
Secretary-General. - 1986.
(001216)

WORLD POLITICS.
----Géopolitique des ressources minières. -
1983.
(000593)
----Multinational corporations and global
welfare: an extension of Kojima and
Ozawa. - 1985.
(000036)
----Oil companies in the international
system. - 1983.
(000641)
----The politics of international economic
relations. - 1985.
(001300)

WORLD TOURISM ORGANIZATION.
----Im Interesse der Gäste wie der
Gastgeber. - 1987.
(000796)

YOUNG WORKERS--MAURITIUS.
----Jobs for the girls. - 1984.
   (001901)

YUGOSLAVIA--ARBITRAL AWARDS.
----Les développements nouveaux concernant
   la reconnaissance et l'exécution des
   sentences arbitrales étrangères en
   Yougoslavie. - 1983.
   (002582)

YUGOSLAVIA--BUSINESS ENTERPRISES.
----Doing business with Yugoslavia. - 1986.
   (001793)
----Privredni adresar SFRJ. - 1965-   .
   (002660)

YUGOSLAVIA--COMMERCIAL LAW.
----Doing business with Yugoslavia. - 1986.
   (001793)

YUGOSLAVIA--DIRECTORIES.
----Privredni adresar SFRJ. - 1965-   .
   (002660)

YUGOSLAVIA--ECONOMETRIC MODELS.
----Direct foreign investment in Yugoslavia.
   - 1986.
   (000183)

YUGOSLAVIA--ECONOMIC ANALYSIS.
----An economic analysis of Yugoslav joint
   ventures. - 1983.
   (001563)

YUGOSLAVIA--ECONOMIC CONDITIONS.
----Doing business with Yugoslavia. - 1986.
   (001793)

YUGOSLAVIA--ECONOMIC RELATIONS.
----Doing business with Yugoslavia. - 1986.
   (001793)

YUGOSLAVIA--FOREIGN DIRECT INVESTMENT.
----Direct foreign investment in Yugoslavia.
   - 1986.
   (000183)
----An economic analysis of Yugoslav joint
   ventures. - 1983.
   (001563)
----The impact of direct foreign investment
   upon developing countries : a case study
   of Yugoslavia. - 1986.
   (001174)
----Industrial co-operation and investment
   in Yugoslavia. - 1986.
   (001540)
----Joint venturing in Yugoslavia. - 1987.
   (001536)
----Überlegungen zur jugoslawischen Joint
   Venture-Gesetzgebung. - 1986.
   (002268)
----Visi oblici privredne saradnje izmethu
   domacih organizacija udruzenog rada i
   stranih lica. - 1984.
   (001182)

YUGOSLAVIA--FOREIGN INVESTMENTS.
----Joint ventures in Yugoslav industry. -
   1985.
   (001535)

----National legislation and regulations
   relating to transnational corporations.
   Volume 4. - 1986.
   (002253)

YUGOSLAVIA--FOREIGN TRADE.
----Doing business with Yugoslavia. - 1986.
   (001793)

YUGOSLAVIA--INDUSTRIAL CO-OPERATION.
----Industrial co-operation and investment
   in Yugoslavia. - 1986.
   (001540)

YUGOSLAVIA--INDUSTRY.
----Privredni adresar SFRJ. - 1965-   .
   (002660)

YUGOSLAVIA--JOINT VENTURES.
----Direct foreign investment in Yugoslavia.
   - 1986.
   (000183)
----An economic analysis of Yugoslav joint
   ventures. - 1983.
   (001563)
----Industrial co-operation and investment
   in Yugoslavia. - 1986.
   (001540)
----Joint ventures in Yugoslav industry. -
   1985.
   (001535)
----Joint ventures in Yugoslavia: comment/
   reply. - 1984.
   (001533)
----Joint ventures in Yugoslavia:
   opportunities and constraints. - 1985.
   (001534)
----Joint venturing in Yugoslavia. - 1987.
   (001536)
----Überlegungen zur jugoslawischen Joint
   Venture-Gesetzgebung. - 1986.
   (002268)
----Visi oblici privredne saradnje izmethu
   domacih organizacija udruzenog rada i
   stranih lica. - 1984.
   (001182)

YUGOSLAVIA--LAWS AND LEGISLATION.
----Visi oblici privredne saradnje izmethu
   domacih organizacija udruzenog rada i
   stranih lica. - 1984.
   (001182)

YUGOSLAVIA--LAWS AND REGULATIONS.
----An economic analysis of Yugoslav joint
   ventures. - 1983.
   (001563)
----National legislation and regulations
   relating to transnational corporations.
   Volume 4. - 1986.
   (002253)
----Überlegungen zur jugoslawischen Joint
   Venture-Gesetzgebung. - 1986.
   (002268)

YUGOSLAVIA--PERFORMANCE APPRAISAL.
----Joint ventures in Yugoslavia comment/
   reply. - 1984.
   (001533)

YUGOSLAVIA--PROFIT.
----Joint ventures in Yugoslavia: comment/
   reply. - 1984.
   (001533)

YUGOSLAVIA--STATE TRADING ENTERPRISES.
----Enterprise organization of East European
    socialist countries. - 1987.
    (000441)

YUGOSLAVIA--TECHNOLOGY TRANSFER.
----Visi oblici privredne saradnje izmethu
    domacih organizacija udruzenog rada i
    stranih lica. - 1984.
    (001182)

YUGOSLAVIA--TRADE LIBERALIZATION.
----Joint venturing in Yugoslavia. - 1987.
    (001536)

YUGOSLAVIA--TRANSNATIONAL CORPORATIONS.
----Direct foreign investment in Yugoslavia.
    - 1986.
    (000183)
----Joint ventures in Yugoslav industry. -
    1985.
    (001535)
----Joint ventures in Yugoslavia: comment/
    reply. - 1984.
    (001533)
----Joint ventures in Yugoslavia:
    opportunities and constraints. - 1985.
    (001534)
----National legislation and regulations
    relating to transnational corporations.
    Volume 4. - 1986.
    (002253)

ZAIRE--INDUSTRIAL DEVELOPMENT.
----Les sociétés transnationales en Afrique.
    - 1986.
    (001028)

ZAIRE--INVESTMENT POLICY.
----Protection, distortions and investment
    incentives in Zaire. - 1986.
    (002272)

ZAIRE--LAWS AND REGULATIONS.
----National legislation and regulations
    relating to transnational corporations.
    Volume 3. - 1983.
    (002252)

ZAIRE--MINING INDUSTRY.
----Les sociétés transnationales en Afrique.
    - 1986.
    (001028)

ZAIRE--PROTECTIONISM.
----Protection, distortions and investment
    incentives in Zaire. - 1986.
    (002272)

ZAIRE--SUBSIDIES.
----Protection, distortions and investment
    incentives in Zaire. - 1986.
    (002272)

ZAIRE--TRADE POLICY.
----Protection, distortions and investment
    incentives in Zaire. - 1986.
    (002272)

ZAIRE--TRANSNATIONAL CORPORATIONS.
----National legislation and regulations
    relating to transnational corporations.
    Volume 3. - 1983.
    (002252)

ZAMBIA--COPPER INDUSTRY.
----The mines, class power, and foreign
    policy in Zambia. - 1984.
    (001023)

ZAMBIA--ECONOMIC POLICY.
----The mines, class power, and foreign
    policy in Zambia. - 1984.
    (001023)

ZAMBIA--EXTERNAL DEBT.
----The mines, class power, and foreign
    policy in Zambia. - 1984.
    (001023)

ZAMBIA--FOREIGN INVESTMENTS.
----The mines, class power, and foreign
    policy in Zambia. - 1984.
    (001023)

ZAMBIA--FOREIGN RELATIONS.
----The mines, class power, and foreign
    policy in Zambia. - 1984.
    (001023)

ZAMBIA--LAWS AND REGULATIONS.
----National legislation and regulations
    relating to transnational corporations.
    Volume 3. - 1983.
    (002252)

ZAMBIA--MINING.
----Mining legislation and mineral
    development in Zambia. - 1986.
    (000625)

ZAMBIA--MINING LAW.
----Mining legislation and mineral
    development in Zambia. - 1986.
    (000625)

ZAMBIA--TRANSNATIONAL CORPORATIONS.
----National legislation and regulations
    relating to transnational corporations.
    Volume 3. - 1983.
    (002252)

ZIMBABWE--AIR TRANSPORT.
----The role of transnational corporations
    in hotel and tourism industry in
    selected PTA member countries. - 1986.
    (000782) (000936)

ZIMBABWE--FOREIGN DIRECT INVESTMENT.
----H.J. Heinz success in Zimbabwe. - 1987.
    (000279)
----Investment by foreign companies:
    Zimbabwe. - 1987.
    (001740)

ZIMBABWE--HOTEL INDUSTRY.
----The role of transnational corporations
    in hotel and tourism industry in
    selected PTA member countries. - 1986.
    (000782) (000936)

ZIMBABWE--JOINT VENTURES.
----H.J. Heinz success in Zimbabwe. - 1987.
    (000279)

SELECTED LIST OF PUBLICATIONS OF THE
UNITED NATIONS CENTRE ON TRANSNATIONAL CORPORATIONS

A. Individual studies

Transnational Corporations in World Development: Trends and Issues. (Forthcoming)

Joint Ventures as a Form of International Economic Co-operation: Background
Documents of the High-level Seminar Organized by the United Nations Centre on
Transnational Corporations in Co-operation with the USSR State Foreign Economic
Commission and the USSR State Committee on Science and Technology, 10 March 1988,
Moscow. (Forthcoming)

International Income Taxation and Developing Countries. 108p.
Sales No. E.88.II.A.6. $13.50.

Transnational Corporations in Biotechnology. 136p. Sales No. E.88.II.A.4. $17.00.

Foreign Direct Investment in the People's Republic of China: Report of the
Round-table Organized by the United Nations Centre on Transnational Corporations in
Co-operation with the Ministry of Foreign Economic Relations and Trade, People's
Republic of China, Beijing, 25 and 26 May 1987. 115p. Sales No. E.88.II.A.3.
$15.50.

Bilateral Investment Treaties. 194p. Sales No. E.88.II.A.1. $20.00.

UNCTC Bibliography, 1974-1987. 83p. Sales No. 87.II.A.23. $12.00.

Licence Agreements in Developing Countries. 108p. Sales No. E.87.II.A.21. $13.50.

Consolidated List of Products Whose Consumption and/or Sale Have Been Banned,
Withdrawn, Severely Restricted or Not Approved by Governments, Second Issue (UNCTC
in collaboration with FAO, WHO, ILO and other relevant intergovernmental
organizations). 655p. Sales No. E.87.IV.1. $60.00.

Transnational Corporations and Non-fuel Primary Commodities in Developing
Countries. 89p. Sales No. E.87.II.A.17. $10.00.

Transnational Corporations in the Man-made Fibre, Textile and Clothing Industries.
154p. Sales No. E.87.II.A.11. $19.00.

Transnational Corporations and Technology Transfer: Effects and Policy Issues.
77p. Sales No. E.87.II.A.4. $11.00.

Analysis of Engineering and Technical Consultancy Contracts.
517p. Sales No. E.86.II.A.4. $45.00.

Transnational Corporations in the International Semiconductor Industry. 471p.
Sales No. E.86.II.A.1. $41.00.

Trends and Issues in Foreign Direct Investment and Related Flows.
96p. Sales No. E.85.II.A.15. $11.00.

Environmental Aspects of the Activities of Transnational Corporations:
A Survey. 114p. Sales No. E.85.II.A.11. $12.50.

Transnational Corporations and International Trade: Selected Issues.
93p. Sales No. E.85.II.A.4. $11.00.

B. Serial publications

UNCTC Current Studies, Series A

No. 1   Patrick Robinson, The Question of a Reference to International Law in
         the United Nations Code of Conduct on Transnational Corporations.
         22p. Sales No. E.86.II.A.5. $4.00.
No. 2   Detlev Vagts, The Question of a Reference to International Obligations
         in the United Nations Code of Conduct on Transnational Corporations: A
         Different View. 17p. Sales No. E.86.II.A.11. $4.00.
No. 3   Foreign Direct Investment in Latin America: Recent Trends, Prospects
         and Policy Issues. 28p. Sales No. E.86.II.A.14. $5.00.
No. 4   The United Nations Code of Conduct on Transnational Corporations.
         80p. Sales No. E.86.II.A.15. $9.50.
No. 5   Transnational Corporations and the Electronics Industries of ASEAN
         Economies. 55p. Sales No. E.87.II.A.13. $7.50.
No. 6   Technology Acquisition under Alternative Arrangements with
         Transnational Corporations: Selected Industrial Case Studies in
         Thailand. 55p. Sales No. E.87.II.A.14. $7.50.
No. 7   Foreign Direct Investment, the Service Sector and International
         Banking. 71p. Sales No. E.87.II.A.15. $9.00.

UNCTC Advisory Studies, Series B

No. 1   Natural Gas Clauses in Petroleum Arrangements.
         54p. Sales No. E.87.II.A.3. $8.00.
No. 2   Arrangements Between Joint Venture Partners in Developing Countries.
         43p. Sales No. E.87.II.A.5. $6.00.
No. 3   Financial and Fiscal Aspects of Petroleum Exploitation.
         43p. Sales No. E.87.II.A.10. $6.00.

International Accounting and Reporting Issues:

1984 Review. 122p. Sales No. E.85.II.A.2. $13.50.
1985 Review. 141p. Sales No. E.85.II.A.13. $15.00.
1986 Review. 158p. Sales No. E.86.II.A.16. $15.00.
1987 Review. 148p. (Forthcoming)

National Legislation and Regulations Relating to Transnational Corporations:

Vol. I. (part one)	302p.	Sales No. E.78.II.A.3.	$16.00.
Vol. I. (part two - supplement)	114p.	Sales No. E.80.II.A.5.	$ 9.00.
Vol. II.	338p.	Sales No. E.83.II.A.7.	$33.00
Vol. III.	345p.	Sales No. E.83.II.A.15.	$33.00.
Vol. IV.	241p.	Sales No. E.85.II.A.14.	$23.00.
Vol. V.	246p.	Sales No. E.86.II.A.3.	$23.00.
Vol. VI.	322p.	Sales No. E.87.II.A.6.	$45.00.
Vol. VII. (Forthcoming)			

Transnational Corporations in South Africa and Namibia: United Nations Public Hearings:

Vol. I.   Reports of the Panel of Eminent Persons and of the Secretary-General. 242p. Sales No. E.86.II.A.6. $65

Vol. II. * Verbatim Records. 300p. Sales No. E.86.II.A.7.

Vol. III.   Statements and Submissions. 518p. Sales No. E.86.II.A.8. $54.

Vol. IV. * Policy Instruments and Statements. 444p. Sales No. E.86.II.A.9.

Four-volume set - $200

*May not be purchased separately.

The CTC Reporter. Published twice a year. Individual issues $9.00. Annual subscription, which includes two issues and the report of the annual meetings of the Commission on Transnational Corporations - $20.00.

- -

United Nations publications may be obtained from bookstores and distributors throughout the world. Please consult your bookstore or write to:

United Nations Publications:

Room DC2-0853		Sales Section
Sales Section	or	United Nations Office at Geneva
United Nations Secretariat		Palais des Nations
New York, N.Y. 10017		CH-1211 Geneva 10
U.S.A.		Switzerland

All prices are quoted in United States dollars.

For further information on the work of the Centre, please address inquiries to:

Room DC2-1312
United Nations Centre on Transnational Corporations
United Nations
New York, N.Y. 10017
U.S.A.

Telex: UNCTNC 661062   Telephone: (212) 963-3176

QUESTIONNAIRE

<u>Transnational Corporations: A Selective Bibliography, 1983-1987</u> /
<u>Les Sociétés Transnationales: Bibliographie Sélective, 1983-1987</u> (ST/CTC/76)

    In order to improve the quality and relevance of the work of the United
Nations Centre on Transnational Corporations (UNCTC), it would be useful to
receive the views of readers on this and other similar publications. It would
therefore be greatly appreciated if you could complete the following
questionnaire and return it to:

Readership Survey
Centre on Transnational Corporations
United Nations, Room DC2-1212
New York, N.Y. 10017, USA

1.   Name and address
    of respondent
    (optional)
    _____
    _____
    _____
    _____
    _____

2.   Which of the following best describes your area of work?

Government	[ ]	Public enterprise	[ ]
Private enterprise	[ ]	Academic or research institution	[ ]
International organization	[ ]	Media	[ ]
Non-profit organization	[ ]	Other (specify)	_____

3.   In which country do you work? _____

4.   What is your assessment of the contents of this volume?

Excellent	[ ]	Adequate	[ ]
Good	[ ]	Poor	[ ]

5. How useful is this volume to your work?

    Very useful |☐| Of some use |☐| Irrelevant |☐|

6. Please indicate three things you like best about this publication:

    _____
    _____
    _____

7. Please indicate three things you like least about this volume:

    _____
    _____
    _____

8. If you have read more than the present UNCTC publications, what is your
    overall assessment of them?

    Consistently   Usually good,
    good |☐| but with some
                                          exceptions |☐|

    Generally
    mediocre |☐| Poor |☐|

9. On the average, how useful are these publications to you in your work?

    Very useful |☐| Of some use |☐| Irrelevant |☐|

10. Are you a regular recipient of The CTC Reporter,
    the Centre's semi-annual publication which
    reports on the Centre's and related work?   Yes |☐| No |☐|

    If not, please check here if you would like
    to receive a sample copy sent to the name and |☐|
    address you have given above.